745

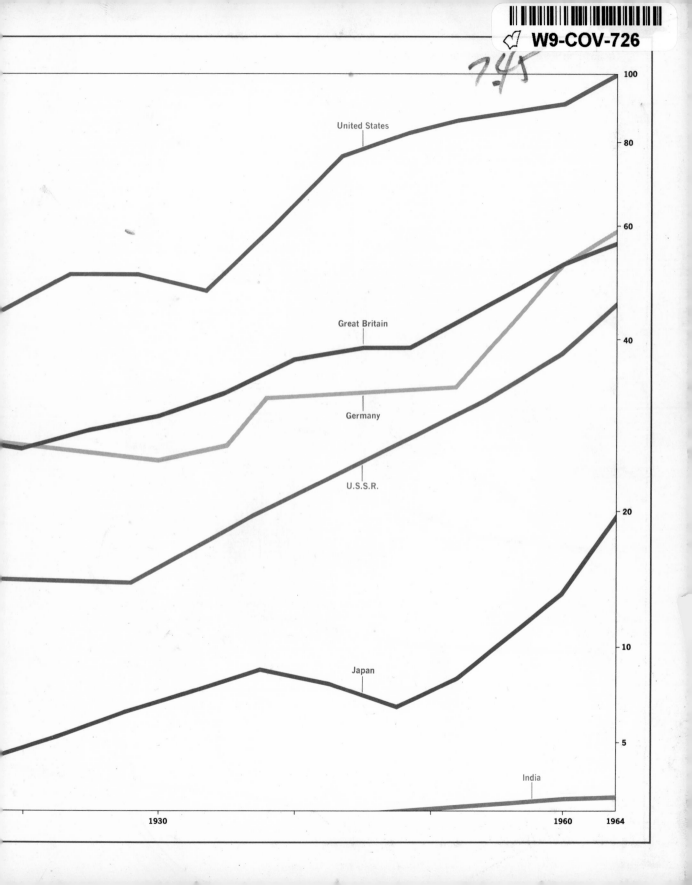

United States

Great Britain

Germany

U.S.S.R.

Japan

India

100	
80	
60	
40	
20	
10	
5	

1930

1960

1964

ECONOMICS
AN INTRODUCTORY ANALYSIS

ECONOMICS

AN INTRODUCTORY ANALYSIS

Seventh Edition

Paul A. Samuelson
Institute Professor
Massachusetts Institute of Technology

McGRAW-HILL BOOK COMPANY
New York   St. Louis   San Francisco   Toronto   London   Sydney

ECONOMICS: An Introductory Analysis

Library of Congress Catalog Card Number 67-15434

54556

1 2 3 4 5 6 7 8 9 0 BK 7 4 3 2 1 0 6 9 8 7

Preface

This is an introduction to economics. It is written for a half-year or full-year beginning course, and for students who may or may not go on to further study of economics. This seventh edition is a thorough revision of earlier editions.

Economics is an important subject. Experience shows it can also be an exciting one. University surveys show that a well-designed economics course usually scores near the top in enrollment popularity. Many autobiographies reveal the strong impact of the study of political economy. In a recent questionnaire of businessmen, asking which courses they would most like future leaders in public affairs and commerce to take, the response was surprisingly unanimous in favor of economics—in contrast to more immediately practical subjects.

A RIGOROUS INTRODUCTION   When I sat down to write the first edition of this book, I set myself a quixotically ambitious goal—to bring into the elementary textbook the most important issues facing a modern nation. Though I knew they would be exciting to the student, I could not be sure that the analytical tools needed to handle these vital problems could be presented to beginners in a one- or two-semester course. But I had before me the example of some great introductory treatises in other subjects—*The Principles of Psychology* by William James, *Differential and Integral Calculus* by Richard Courant (and, in the present age, *Lectures on Physics* by the Nobel Laureate Richard Feynman).

Written by profound scholars, these classics have given generations of students, of the most diverse backgrounds, an enviable introduction. "Why," I thought, "should not economics, which lends itself so well to a comprehensive formulation, seek to have a similar treatment that is at the same time rigorous and readable?" In any case, their motto has been my motto:

■ Nothing unnecessarily hard, but nothing essential omitted as being beyond the grasp of the serious student; and above all, nothing that later must be unlearned as wrong.

The reception of the book has been successful beyond my fondest hopes. It has been widely used, universally translated, and flatteringly imitated. Economics teachers —here and abroad, in junior colleges and great universities—were apparently ripe for a text that applied the analytical tools of *modern* economics in a readable way to the vital economic problems of our times.

Writing a beginning textbook is hard work. But its rewards have been tremendous —and I do not mean simply pecuniary rewards. Contact with millions of minds of a whole generation is an experience like no other that a scholar will ever meet. And writing out what we economists know about economics has been an exciting venture. I can only hope that some of this excitement will rub off on the reader.

REVISIONS IN THIS NEW EDITION   The major thrust of my rewriting is in microeconomics. But in view of the fact that economics is a fast-moving subject, complete updating of the facts and of the selection of topics is mandatory. Scarcely a page is left unchanged. The problems of 1970 are not those of 1960, or even of 1965. "Structural unemployment and poverty programs," "incomes policy," "fiscal drag and the full-employment surplus," "negative income tax," "exchange rates fluctuating in a widened range and adjusted according to a 'sliding peg' "—these are concepts now being argued in Washington and Paris: tomorrow they will be in the *New York Times* and the *London Economist;* yesterday, they were not available to be included in my sixth edition. Fortunately, the economies of large-scale book production makes it feasible to put into the reader's hands completely up-to-date and revised editions.

What is peculiarly new to this seventh edition is the rewriting and rearranging of microeconomic theory. A new chapter—Chapter 24—devoted exclusively to the different categories of cost, has been added. Classroom experience shows that this greatly simplifies the preceding discussions of supply under perfect competition; and it equips the student for the subsequent analysis of imperfect competition, an analysis now expanded and rearranged. Now monopoly is given a chapter to itself, Chapter 25. Now the kinked demand curve of oligopoly receives a full and leisurely treatment. Now Chamberlinian differentiation of product is linked to underlying trends of cost. And now the tools of analysis are put to work in the rewritten survey of antitrust programs and problems. (What helps pedagogically for microeconomics helps too for macroeconomics. Chapter 12, which gives the nucleus of modern income determination, has now been split into two distinct chapters: after the basic saving-investment and consumption-plus-investment tools are mastered, the reader can more easily handle the multiplier and fiscal policy.)

Chapter 1 is rewritten to include a discussion of the methodology of science. It introduces the modern approach, borrowed from the "more exact" natural sciences, that insists on the irreducibly subjective element of our perception of facts depending upon the theoretive system *through* which we look at those facts. The probability nature, normal and otherwise, of our facts is also stressed.

At the same time that this seventh edition has been an arduous one for me, it has been personally a most gratifying one. The "new economics" that people are currently talking about—and which connoisseurs know is not all that new or different—represents in a sense a vindication of the macroeconomics approach my generation has been trying to develop and teach. "Nature imitates art." The world is catching up at long last with the scholar's workshop. All the greater is the challenge to new innovation.

TO THE READER   No effort is spared to help you understand—and enjoy—economics. Each chapter is carefully planned. Each has a comprehensive summary. Color has been planned, behind the scenes, for optimal learning. Key definitions and concepts are indented in brown for emphasis and new concepts in figures and tables usually appear in green to alert the reader. Figures and tables are arranged to tell their own story. More difficult material has been placed in appendixes and footnotes. (Do not be put off by this: Experience has proved that this gives the more intensive courses meat to bite into, without inconveniencing those who work within the severest time limitations.

At the same time, the top-notch student should be warned: Don't be mislead by this book's simple style; it is interlaced with material that can challenge the acutest mind.)

An economics text is not like a novel or detective story, hammock-reading for a drowsy day. The first time you read a chapter, turn its pages for perspective. Then read it quickly for the general idea, not pausing over difficulties. In final re-readings, you can underline, utilizing the end-of-chapter discussion questions and check-list of key concepts. Get involved. (You may want to use Robinson's *Study Guide* referred to on the next page to help deepen review and test your understanding.)

Most important of all has been the choice of topics—they include some of the burning issues you will live with all your lives. Many readers have written to the author, saying that they enjoyed the exposition, or saying that—save for this page or that—the book merits commendation. Praise is always sweet to the ears of an author, and I am no exception. But I must confess that the highest praise of all is when a student, whatever he thinks of the book at the time, determines to keep it in his library as a reference work on economics. When the election of 1984 rolls around, and the issues of the protective tariff and public debt are being seriously debated, all the hours that the artists and editors and I have spent in making the pages as informative and authentic as possible will seem to me well spent if somewhere a voter turns to the old book from which he first learned economics for a rereasoning of the economic principle involved. That is this author's Walter Mitty dream of glory!

TO THE INSTRUCTOR   Almost half the classes using this book are one-semester courses. I append to the Table of Contents a suggested one-semester outline. And in the newly revised *Instructor's Manual* suggestions are given for flexible adaptation.

Forty per cent of the teachers using this book prefer to teach microeconomics before macroeconomics. A good case can be made for either ordering, and experimental programs show each to have advantages. This text has been carefully designed for either program. The instructor who wishes to deal first with microeconomics can skip from Part One to Part Three, knowing that the exposition and cross references have been tailored with his needs in mind. Because college courses in economics are taught both by large-lecture and small-section methods, I have used my MIT classroom as a laboratory, one year trying out lecturing to a large group and another year confining my class to 25 students. A good text must be prepared with both needs in mind.

I have not hesitated to segregate some of the material into appendixes. Often this involves slightly more difficult topics, which briefer courses can easily dispense with. Sometimes, as in the case of the discussion of the stock market in Chapter 4's Appendix or the presentation of cases in supply and demand in Chapter 20's Appendix, the material is not more difficult, but is such as can be conveniently skipped. Occasionally a teacher has written me questioning the advisability of this use of the appendixes. My answer is a pragmatic one based on experimentation: because courses differ in their time span and emphasis, it is incumbent upon an author to give signals on which sections are organically necessary and which are dispensable. For example, in this edition I have added a brief treatment of Leontief's input-output. The fact that it is put at the end of Chapter 37's Appendix will not inconvenience the reader eager for a terse account of this important subject; but this arrangement will be deemed a blessing by those instructors who lack the time for such a topic.

To go with this seventh edition a completely revised *Study Guide* has been prepared by Romney Robinson. Both as assigned by the instructor and as bought independently by students for self-study, the *Study Guide* has proved to be a great success. In this edition Professor Robinson has responded to the suggestion of teachers by placing answers to all the objective-type questions in the *Guide* itself where they will be of maximum benefit to the reader.

Readings in Economics has been thoroughly revised to go with this new seventh edition. Now it is keyed chapter by chapter to the main text. The great names of the past—Smith, Marshall, Ricardo, Marx—share the limelight with leading economists of the present—Galbraith, Tobin, Solow, Friedman, Triffin, Hayek, Kindleberger, Burns—in spirited debate over contemporary issues. Never before has there been so generous a supply to choose from; and we—my co-authors, John R. Coleman, and Felicity Skidmore, and I—have found the only hard part of our task that of confining ourselves to eighty-eight selections. McGraw-Hill and I have prepared film strips and experimental visual teaching aids that teachers may wish to learn about from the publisher.

ACKNOWLEDGMENTS   Again I am a hopeless bankrupt when it comes to indebtedness. Hundreds of students and scores of economics teachers have written, raising questions and giving me the benefit of unsparing criticisms. My MIT colleagues have helped in innumerable ways, including subjecting our students to multivarious experimental drafts. From other colleges I must thank for particular chapter-by-chapter commentary and suggestions William G. Bowen (Princeton), Arthur M. Okun (Yale), Robert Summers (Pennsylvania), Janet L. Weston (Illinois), Edward Coen (Minnesota), Malcolm D. Gutter (Foothill College), Sidney Herman (Northeastern), Paul T. Heyne (Southern Methodist), Philip L. Howell (Tulsa), William B. Johnson (San Jose State College), W. A. McCleary (Williams College), Hans C. Palmer (Pomona College), Newby Schweitzer (San Francisco State College), Wallace F. Smith (Berkeley), Marc R. Tool (Sacramento State College). To graduate students William H. Branson, George de Menil, and Ray C. Fair go my sincere thanks for their arduous labors in trying to assist a fussy and perfectionist author. My secretary, Norma Wasser, has been a jewel beyond price; and I owe thanks for typing assistance to Gretchen Brown, Inez J. Crandall (jewel emeritus), Susan Swanson, Carolyn Washburne, and Anthea Wilkinson. Mary Barnett provided unusually able editing. Matt Roberts prepared all of the drawings. My publisher's house rules prevent me from acknowledging by name the editor who supervised every detail of what was inevitably a mammoth task; but no one can stop me from feeling grateful to her. Felicity Skidmore, now of the Institute for Poverty at the University of Wisconsin, deserves the major credit for insisting that no deadline of time stand in the way of making this the best revision the author is capable of; for her creative judgment and unselfish help I again owe infinite thanks.

A textbook should be dedicated to one's children—of whom I have my share—but they will forgive me for naming my longest-time collaborator, Marion.

PAUL A. SAMUELSON

Contents

Part 3 The Composition and Pricing of National Output

Part 6   Current Economic Problems

Suggested Outline for a One-semester Course

*For inclusion in courses with macroeconomic emphasis.

†For inclusion in courses with microeconomic emphasis.

†† For inclusion in courses with policy emphasis.

For courses with institutional emphasis Chapters 6 to 9, dealing with income distribution, labor, and government finance, could be included.

Part 1 Basic Economic Concepts and National Income

1 Introduction

THE IDEAS OF ECONOMISTS AND POLITICAL PHILOSOPHERS, BOTH WHEN THEY ARE RIGHT AND WHEN THEY ARE WRONG, ARE MORE POWERFUL THAN IS COMMONLY UNDERSTOOD. INDEED THE WORLD IS RULED BY LITTLE ELSE. PRACTICAL MEN, WHO BELIEVE THEMSELVES TO BE QUITE EXEMPT FROM ANY INTELLECTUAL INFLUENCES, ARE USUALLY THE SLAVES OF SOME DEFUNCT ECONOMIST. MADMEN IN AUTHORITY, WHO HEAR VOICES IN THE AIR, ARE DISTILLING THEIR FRENZY FROM SOME ACADEMIC SCRIBBLER OF A FEW YEARS BACK....SOON OR LATE, IT IS IDEAS, NOT VESTED INTERESTS, WHICH ARE DANGEROUS FOR GOOD OR EVIL. J. M. KEYNES (1936)

Half a century ago, when the Harvard Business School was founded, President A. Lawrence Lowell described business as "the oldest of the arts, the newest of the professions." Almost the same words can be used to describe economics—the oldest of the arts, the newest of the sciences.

As a scholarly discipline, economics is not yet two centuries old. Adam Smith wrote his path-breaking book *The Wealth of Nations* in 1776, a year notable for the Declaration of Independence. And the nearness of timing is no coincidence: political freedom from the tyranny of monarchy was perhaps related to the emancipation of free-market pricing from the interfering hand of state regulation.

Adam Smith, of course, represented only a beginning. In more than a century and a half that elapsed from the publication of *The Wealth of Nations* to the publication of John Maynard Keynes' *General Theory of Employment, Interest and Money* (1936), economics—or political economy, as it used to be called—went through many stages of development. Thus, at almost the halfway point, there appeared the massive critique of capitalism by Karl Marx: *Das Kapital* (1867, followed by two posthumous volumes). A billion people, one-third of the world's population, blindly regard *Das Kapital* as economic gospel. And yet, without the disciplined study of economic science, how can anyone form a reasoned opinion about the merits or lack of merits in the classical, traditional economics?

■ FOR WHOM THE BELL TOLLS

Few study economics merely to form an opinion on the merits in the grand debates concerning historic capitalism, the modern mixed economy, or the collectivist economic systems of the East. One studies economics to answer many and diverse questions. Here are some of the more common ones.

1

POVERTY, DEVELOPMENT, AND AFFLUENCE   America is a prosperous nation. We grow more prosperous each year, and our present affluence is an outgrowth of the lower standard of productivity prevailing in past generations. In recent years all over the world, men have become preoccupied with economic development.

How can preindustrial economies, teeming with masses of people and poorly endowed with natural resources, break through the vicious circle of poverty and backwardness? How can policies be formulated and programs be promulgated that will speed the pace of *economic growth and development?*

Look at the front flyleaf: Contrast the Western world's affluence with the poverty of India, whose growth curve barely shows on the chart; and note the success story of Japan within its century of contact with the modern world.

Undoubtedly this new interest in development and growth has made economics an exciting and vital subject in the capitals of the world, and on Main Street as well as Wall Street.

PERSONAL STAKE IN ECONOMICS   An even more immediate reason for studying economics is that it deals with many of the matters that will concern each of us most:

What kinds of jobs are available? What do they pay? How much in goods will a dollar of wages buy now, and how much in a time of galloping inflation? What are the chances that a time will come when a man will not be able to get work? Are the black days of the depressed 1930s likely to return? Will automation and scientific discovery make man obsolete? How can one make a killing in the stock market?

ECONOMICS FOR THE CITIZEN   Beyond personal family matters, economics also deals with political decisions each citizen must face. Here are a dozen vital problems:

Will the government add to my taxes to help unemployed miners, or are there other things it can do to help mitigate the problem of unemployment? Should I vote to build a new school and road now, or vote to put this aside until business slackens and cement prices come down and jobs are needed? Should I vote to keep married women out of public employment, so there will be more jobs for men? What about antitrust legislation that purports to fight monopolies? If you are a humanitarian, deeply concerned to improve the lot of the poor, the disadvantaged Negro, and the aged, will legislating a good, stiff, high minimum wage serve to help or hinder the good cause for which you fight?

What consequences will follow if the federal budget is not balanced in every year? Is it true, as Moscow used to claim, that American prosperity is dependent on cold-war military expenditures? If "peace breaks out," are we in for a recession? Can the government wash its hands of the matter, knowing that we can rely on the spontaneous forces of private markets to convert the swords of war into the ploughshares of peace?

ECONOMICS AND NATIONAL INTEREST   As Adam Smith said, security is even more important for a nation than opulence. Survival itself can depend on economics.

Can a modern nation afford expensive military expenditures? Is it true, as ex-President Hoover once warned, that "inflation is worse than Stalin?"

Perhaps most important of all in the minds of people in the more advanced Western civilizations and in the underdeveloped regions of the world are these questions: Two decades from now, will the Soviet Union have overtaken the United States as the most affluent society in the world? Or as the most powerful military power? What is happening to the gap between these different types of economic systems? Uncommitted people all over the world are watching this peaceful competition, deliberating over which economic system to embrace.

An introduction can serve as a preview. The last diagram of this book (Fig. 40-1) is reproduced here as Fig. 1-1. It shows in one graphic picture the economic growth prospects for the Soviet Union and the United States. As we shall see, the economist does not have the clairvoyance of the astronomer, who can tell you exactly where all the planets will be in the year 2,000 A.D. The economist must give the calculated prudent odds.

ECONOMICS FOR THE LEADER Charles Darwin, the immortal discoverer of evolution through natural selection, was a modest man. He once said that he had always envied people who could use mathematics, feeling that they possessed an extra sense. A number of statesmen and leaders have expressed a similar regret—that they never acquired a grasp of basic economics, and that those with such training are to be envied for the advantage.

> Thus, Winston Churchill was a great man—a leader without peer, an orator, a gifted writer, and a shrewd judge of the Hitlerian threat while most around him slept. Yet all his life, Churchill was a babe in the woods when it came to economics. In 1925, as Chancellor of the Exchequer, he put England back on the gold standard at the pre-1914 parity of $4.87 for the British pound. (Chapter 33 will explain what this means.) Experts at the time warned against such folly, and history has recorded that England has never quite recovered from her stagnation of the late 1920s.
>
> Or take the case of Albert Einstein. A greater scientist never lived, nor a sweeter, more gentle personality. Yet Einstein's writings reveal a charmingly naïve understanding of the economic world that might shame a schoolchild.

The head of state must be constantly making vital decisions that involve economics. But of course he need not himself be a professional student of economics; he need only be an intelligent "consumer" of the (often conflicting) economic information being given him. Still, it is of interest that only the law has provided more national

Economic graphs throw light on future growth prospects:

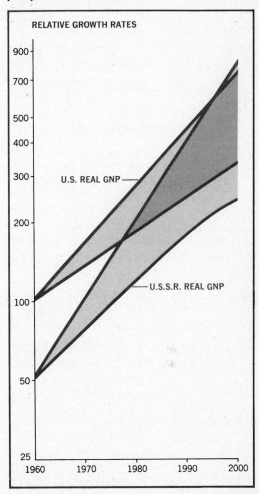

FIG. 1-1. The art of judgment, as well as scientific analysis, is involved in determining reasonable projections of growth rates free of either wishful or paranoid thinking. Not only are Americans and Russians concerned with the outcome of this economic sweepstakes, but so are Asians and Africans interested in choosing that form of economic organization which will move them most rapidly along the road of development. (Source: Fig. 40-1.)

leaders than has economics. Prime Minister Harold Wilson of the United Kingdom began
his career as an economist. Former Chancellor Erhard of West Germany, a more conservative figure, began as a professor of economics. President Woodrow Wilson took his
Ph.D. degree in political economy at Johns Hopkins. In the middle 1960s, professionally
trained economists were prime ministers or party leaders in most of Scandinavia. Even
Dictator Salazar of Portugal came from a university chair in economics.

Every national issue mentioned requires economic understanding to make any
progress in answering it. A person who has never made a systematic study of economics
is handicapped in even thinking about them; he is like a deaf man trying to appreciate
a symphony: give him a hearing aid, and he may still lack talent, but at least he has a
fighting chance of sensing what music really is.

■ LIGHT AND FRUIT

Of course most students do not expect to specialize in economics. Most will study it for
only a term or two, and this book is intended to give an overview of the whole subject.
As in the case of the man who wrote that he had "never gotten over learning long
division," your view of the world can never be quite the same after even one semester
of economics. Not only is economics at once an art and a science, economics as a subject can combine the attractive features of both the humanities and the sciences. Sir
Charles Snow, scientist and novelist, has called for an end to the separation of "the
two cultures."

Economics is part of both cultures. For two centuries, educated men have found
in it the human interest of life itself, while at the same time economic principles display
some of the logical beauty of Euclid's geometry. To appreciate the charms of quantum
physics, sophisticated mathematical techniques must first be mastered; but to sense the
aesthetic structure of economic analysis requires only a feeling for logic and a capacity
for wonderment that such mental constructs really do have a life-and-death significance
for billions of men all over the world. Of course, mere beauty is not enough. One studies
economics for the light it sheds; any pleasure along the way is an incidental bonus.

■ WHAT ECONOMICS IS

Beginners used to want a short definition of economics; and in response to this demand,
there was no shortage of supply. Here are a few such definitions:

1. Economics is the study of those activities which, with or without money,
involve exchange transactions among people.

2. Economics is the study of how men choose to use scarce or limited productive
resources (land, labor, capital goods such as machinery, technical knowledge) to produce
various commodities (such as wheat, beef, overcoats; concerts, roads, bombers, yachts)
and distribute them to various members of society for their consumption.

3. Economics is the study of men in their ordinary business of life, earning and
enjoying a living.

4. Economics is the study of how mankind goes about the business of organizing its consumption and production activities.

5. Economics is the study of wealth.

The list is a good one. Yet a scholar can extend it many times over. It is always hard to compress into a few lines an exact description of a subject, one that will differentiate its boundaries from those of other disciplines and convey to the beginner all the things it is. Economics certainly does involve all the elements stressed in these various definitions—and all those implied in the larger list that could be compiled.

Economists today agree on a general definition something like the following:

■ Economics is the study of how men and society *choose*, with or without the use of money, to employ *scarce* productive resources, which could have alternative uses, to produce various commodities over time and distribute them for consumption, now and in the future, among various people and groups in society.

■ ONE AMONG MANY

Economics borders on other important academic disciplines. *Sociology, political science, psychology,* and *anthropology* are all social sciences whose studies overlap those of economics. Here is just one example.

In impoverished India cows are sacred animals and, numbering millions, are allowed to walk through the streets foraging for food. While a naïve economist might regard these herds as a prime source for protein supplements to an already inadequate diet, the more profound scholar will take the psychology of custom into account when analyzing Indian economic development.

Economics also draws heavily on the study of *history*. Was it a coincidence that prices rose for centuries in Spain and Europe after Columbus discovered America with all its gold? Why did the age of the steamship and railroad help the Iowa farmer, hurt the farmers of Vermont and Oxfordshire, and help the slum dwellers of London? To the interpretation of recorded history, *analytical* tools must be brought for the reason that facts will never "tell their own story"; yet this need for theorizing does not deny the old Chinese proverb, "One peek is worth a thousand finesses." Facts count.

Among the numerous other subjects relating to economics, the study of *statistics* is of special importance. Governments and businesses issue vast amounts of numerical information. Most of what we know about the actual shapes of the various curves to be seen in turning over the pages of this book has to come from a careful statistical analysis of recorded information. The mathematical methods of probability and statistics find many of their most important applications in the realm of economics.

Although every introductory textbook must contain geometrical diagrams, knowledge of *mathematics* itself is needed only for the higher reaches of economic theory. Logical reasoning is the key to success in the mastery of basic economic principles, and shrewd weighing of empirical evidence is the key to success in mastery of economic applications.

■ ECONOMIC DESCRIPTION AND ANALYSIS

It is the first task of modern economic science to describe, to analyze, to explain, and to correlate the behavior of production, unemployment, prices, and similar phenomena. If they are to be significant, descriptions must be more than a series of disconnected narratives. They must be fitted into a systematic pattern, and this is what is meant by true analysis.

Because of the complexity of human and social behavior, we cannot hope to attain the precision of a few of the physical sciences. We cannot perform the controlled experiments of the chemist or biologist. Like the astronomer, we must be content largely to "observe." But economic events and statistical data observed are, alas, not so well behaved and orderly as the paths of heavenly satellites. Fortunately, our answers need not be accurate to several decimal places; on the contrary, if the right general *direction* of cause and effect can be determined, we shall have made a tremendous step forward.

A good example to show the importance of analysis is the problem of economic growth in advanced nations and economic development in poor nations. Treatment of these issues in Part Six will demonstrate that the mere facts have to be supplemented by all the analytical tools of the previous five parts if one is to master this vital subject.

■ ECONOMIC POLICY

This exposition brings us to the important problem of economic policy. Ultimately, understanding should aid in control and improvement. How can the vagaries of the business cycle be diminished? How can economic progress and efficiency be furthered? How can adequate standards of living be made more widely available?

At every point of our analysis we shall seek to shed light on these policy problems. To succeed in this, we must all try to cultivate an objective and detached ability to see things as they *are,* regardless of our likes or dislikes. The fact must be faced that economic issues are close to everybody emotionally. Blood pressures rise and voices become shrill whenever deep-seated beliefs and prejudices are involved, and some of these prejudices are thinly veiled rationalizations of special economic interests.

We know that a doctor passionately interested in stamping out disease must first train himself to observe things as they are. His bacteriology cannot be different from that of a mad scientist out to destroy mankind by plague. Wishful thinking is bad thinking and leads to little wish fulfillment. "Where it is a duty to worship the sun, the laws of heat will be poorly understood."

In the same way, there is only one valid reality in a given economic situation, however hard it may be to recognize and isolate it. There is not one theory of economics for Republicans and one for Democrats, one for workers and one for employers. On the basic economic principles concerning prices and employment, most economists are in fairly close agreement.

This statement does not mean that economists always agree in the *policy* field. Economist A may be for full employment at any cost. Economist B may not consider it of primary importance. Basic questions concerning right and wrong goals to be pursued cannot be settled by science as such. They belong in the realm of ethics and "value judgments." The citizenry must ultimately decide such issues. What the expert can do is point out the feasible alternatives and the true costs that may be involved in the different decisions.

■ METHODOLOGY OF ECONOMICS: BRIEF PREVIEW

No one can understand a complicated subject such as chemistry without long and careful study. This is an advantage and a disadvantage. The man on the street or behind a newspaper desk cannot possibly consider himself a final authority on such a subject—which is all to the good. On the other hand, the new student of chemistry must become familiar with all the basic concepts for the first time, which takes a good deal of effort.

From childhood days on, everyone knows something about economics. This acquaintance is both helpful and deceptive: helpful, because much knowledge can be taken for granted; deceptive, because it is natural and human to accept superficially plausible views. A little knowledge may be dangerous. On close examination common sense may prove to be really nonsense.

A union leader who has successfully negotiated several labor contracts may feel that he is an expert on the economics of wages. A businessman who has "met a payroll" may feel that his views on price control are final. A banker who can balance his books may conclude that he knows all there is to know about the creation of money. Each individual naturally tends to judge an economic event by its immediate effect upon himself. A worker thrown out of employment in the buggy industry cannot be expected to reflect that new jobs may have been created in the automobile industry; but we must be prepared to investigate whether this is so.

In an introductory survey, the economist is interested in the workings of the economy *as a whole* rather than in the viewpoint of any one group. Social and national policies rather than individual policy are his goals. Too often, "everybody's business is nobody's business." It is just as well, therefore, to reiterate at the beginning that an elementary course in economics does not pretend to teach one how to run a business or bank, how to spend money wisely, or how to get rich quick from the stock market. But it is to be hoped that general economics will provide a useful background for many such activities.

Certainly, the economist must know a good deal about how businessmen, consumers, and investors behave and think. This does not mean that those individuals must use the same language and methods in approaching their decisions as economists find useful in describing their behavior—any more than the planets need know that they are following the elliptical paths traced by the astronomer. Just as many of us have been "speaking prose" all our lives without knowing it, so too would many businessmen be surprised to learn that their behavior is capable of systematic economic analysis. This lack of awareness is not necessarily to be deprecated. It does not help a baseball pitcher to know the laws of aerodynamics; and if we become self-conscious about how to button our shirts, we may find it harder to do.

THEORY VERSUS PRACTICE   The economic world is extremely complicated. As we noted, it is usually not possible to make economic observations under the controlled experimental conditions characteristic of scientific laboratories. A physiologist who wishes to determine the effects of penicillin on pneumonia may be able to "hold other things equal" by using two test groups that differ only in the fact that they do and do not get penicillin injections. The economist is less fortunately situated. If he wishes to determine the effect of a gasoline tax on fuel consumption, he may be vexed by the fact that, in the same year when the tax was imposed, pipelines were first introduced. Nevertheless, he must try—if only mentally—to isolate the effects of the tax, "other things being equal." Otherwise, he will understand the economic effects neither of taxation nor of transportation improvements, nor of both together.

The difficulty of analyzing causes when controlled experimentation is impossible is well illustrated by the confusion of the savage medicine man who thinks that both witchcraft and a little arsenic are necessary to kill his enemy, or that only after he has put on a green robe in spring will the trees do the same.[1] As a result of this limitation and many others, our quantitative economic knowledge is far from complete. This does not mean that we do not have great amounts of accurate statistical knowledge available. We do. Reams of census data, market information, and financial statistics have been collected by governments, trade associations, and business concerns.

Even if we had more and better data, it would still be necessary—as in every science—to *simplify,* to *abstract* from the infinite mass of detail. No mind can comprehend a bundle of unrelated facts. All analysis involves abstraction. It is always necessary to *idealize,* to omit detail, to set up simple hypotheses and patterns by which the facts can be related, to set up the right questions before going out to look at the world as it is. Every theory, whether in the physical or biological or social sciences, distorts reality in that it oversimplifies. But if it is good theory, what is omitted is outweighed by the beam of illumination and understanding that is thrown over the diverse empirical data.

Properly understood, therefore, theory and observation, deduction and induction, cannot be in conflict. The test of a theory's validity is its usefulness in illuminating observed reality. Its logical elegance and finespun beauty are irrelevant. Consequently, when a student says, "That's all right in theory but not in practice," he really means, "That's not all right in the relevant theory," or else he is talking nonsense.

THE TYRANNY OF WORDS   Particularly in the social sciences, we must watch out for the "tyranny of words." The world is complicated enough without introducing further confusions and ambiguities because (1) two different names are unknowingly being used for the same thing or (2) the same one word is being applied to two quite different phenomena.

Jones may call Robinson a liar for holding that the cause of depression is oversaving, saying, "Underconsumption is really the cause." Schwartz may enter the argument, asserting, "You are both wrong. The real trouble is underinvestment." They may

[1] In logic we call this the *Post hoc, ergo propter hoc* fallacy (After this, therefore necessarily because of this).

go on arguing; but if they really stopped to analyze their language, they might find that there were no differences in their opinions about the facts and that only a verbal confusion was involved.

Similarly, words may be treacherous because we do not react in a neutral manner to them. Thus a man who approves of a government program to speed growth will call it a program of "sensible planning," while an unsympathetic opponent will describe the same activity as "totalitarian bureaucratic regimentation." Who can object to the former, and who could condone the latter? Yet they refer to the same thing. One does not have to be an expert in *semantics*—the study of language and its meaning—to realize that scientific discussion requires us to avoid such emotional terminology wherever possible.

SOCIAL VERSUS PHYSICAL SCIENCE? Some distortions of thinking that result from emotion and prejudice are so blatant as to be clearly recognizable. But at a deeper level, one can ask:

> Since economics deals with man and not with inanimate objects, and since the scientist is himself necessarily a man, can there be any hope of an *objective* science of economics? Can the methods of the physical sciences—observation and quantitative measurements, mathematical model building—ever work in the study of human affairs?

No simple answer can be given to this profound question. In a sense, precisely because we are ourselves men, we have an advantage over the natural scientist. He cannot usefully say, "Suppose I were an H_2O molecule; what might I do in such a situation?" The social scientist often, knowingly or unknowingly, employs such introspective acts of empathy.

Still a problem remains. Perhaps most experienced scholars would sum it up something like this:

> Slavish imitation of the physical sciences is a mistake in the study of humans and society. Yet there is no substitute for patient attendance to the empirical facts of life, and no substitute for systematic reasoning about them. As in the case of modern biology, great advances have resulted from mathematical scientific methods, despite the earlier warnings against imitating the physical sciences. Let experience tell the final story.

EXACTITUDE AND SUBJECTIVITY But note this important point. Even in the so-called exact physical sciences, how we *perceive* the observed facts depends on the theoretical spectacles we wear. The light that hits a newborn baby's eyes forms no pattern: the baby sees but it does not perceive. Modern historians of science have learned the same lesson from gestalt psychology: post-Newtonians perceived the "same facts" differently from pre-Newtonians. To a degree we are all prisoners of our theoretical preconceptions. It is not so much discordant fact that kills off an old false theory as the final emergence of a new theory.

Just as Galileo, Newton, and Einstein revolutionized perceptions in physics, so did Smith, Marshall, Keynes—indeed all the names that appear on the family tree of economics shown on the back flyleaf of this book—transform economic understand-

Facts tell different story to scientists wearing different theoretical spectacles:

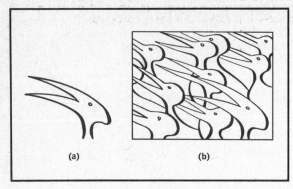

(a)   (b)

FIG. 1-2. If you look at wage problems through the spectacles of Marxian economics, you may think you see exploitation of workers by capitalists. If you look at problems of depression unemployment through pre-Keynesian glasses, you may think little of it is due to forces that government tax and expenditure policies can change. In (a) is this a picture of a leftward-looking bird? Or is it a rightward-looking antelope (or rabbit)? In the presence of (b)'s field of birds, most people think it a bird. But next to the footnote's field of antelopes, most will see it as an antelope. [Source: N. R. Hanson, *Patterns of Discovery* (Cambridge University Press, London, 1961).]

ing. Figure 1-2, taken from a philosophic study of physics, illustrates the irreducible subjective element in *any* science. Does the picture show a bird looking to the left? Or an antelope (or rabbit) looking to the right? It is not an optical illusion to say it is one rather than the other. Each is admissible.[2]

A distinguished historian of science has made the same point as the bird-antelope diagram in speaking of fundamental revolutions in science: he regards them as a process that involves "handling the same bundle of data as before, but placing them in a new system of relations with one another by giving them a different framework."[3] We do not have to be students of physics or gestalt psychology to realize how literally these words apply to the contrasts between new and old economics, or between free-world and iron-curtain economics.

So it is with many scientific facts and theories. When you adopt a new systematic model of economic principles, you comprehend reality in a new and different way.

PROBABILITY OF ERRORS: NORMAL OR NOT   There is another important difference between an exact science like physics and a less exact science like economics. Our laws may hold only "on the average," with considerable dispersion of exceptions around that average. Figure 1-3 gives a preview of a vital statistical relationship whereby con-

[2]Contrast your gestalt perception of Fig. 1-2's image with its appearance when placed next to this field of antelopes. The bird-antelope ambiguity cannot be dismissed as an optical "illusion": it is unlike the accompanying two lines, which are really the same length even though most people wrongly infer the lower line to be the longer. What Fig. 1-2 portrays is an objectively reproducible shape that looks subjectively different depending on the context in which it appears. But once we see the forelegs of the beast, we are right to perceive it as an antelope.

[3]Herbert Butterfield, *The Origins of Modern Science, 1300–1800* (London, 1949), p. 7, as quoted in Thomas S. Kuhn, *The Structure of Scientific Revolutions* (University of Chicago Press, Chicago, 1962), p. 85.

sumption spending by families can be related to the dollar incomes people have. Note that the observation points do not fall exactly on the line, as they might in chemistry or astronomy. Still, we do see a pattern that is stable in a probability sense—the same sense in which a life-insurance company can *count on* a stable proportion of deaths in a sample of 100,000 policy holders of a given age (even though any one man's living or dying cannot be foretold). And note a further important point, the chance deviations around the expected values will form an especially simple frequency pattern called the "normal curve of error." The normal curve is symmetric and bell-shaped; this is because small errors appear predictably more often than large errors—just as with gambling dice, human genetics, or surveying measurements.[4]

In economics, "normality" may not always prevail. Figure 1-4 here reproduces a later diagram, Fig. 6-5, page 115 depicting how abnormally spread out people's incomes are in comparison with the allegedly "normal" distribution

Economic laws are probability laws, not exact relationships:

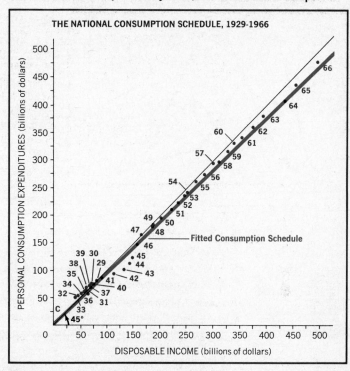

FIG. 1-3. Observed points of consumption spending fail to fall exactly on the line. But clustering of the data around the line does confirm the regularity of the relationship between dollar income and spending. (Source: Fig. 11-5, which shows that 94 per cent of income spent on consumption and 6 per cent going to saving is about par for the course.)

of their abilities (IQ's, verbal or mathematical aptitudes, etc.). The green curve of distribution of incomes is asymmetric: unlike the symmetric normal curve, it has a long tail skewed to the right. This reflects the fact that while there are a few multimillionaires with incomes equal to hundreds of times the average income, no one can be that many dollars below the average. Such asymmetric super-extended distributions, alas, appear often in economics. One says "alas" because such abnormal probability laws do not lead to the same *precision of average behavior* that the natural sciences can often count on.

[4]Gambling houses in Nevada and Monte Carlo know very well from experience that repeated coin tossing (or dice throwing) will generate a sequence with the following two properties: (a) If we write down 1 for heads and 0 for tails, a random series of tossing will give sequences—such as 0, 1, 0, 1, 1, 0, 1, 0, 0, 0, 1, 0—which eventually average out close to $\frac{1}{2}$ by the famous "law of large numbers." (b) For a long enough sequence of random tosses of a symmetric coin, the fraction of heads appearing will approach a normal-error dispersion around the expected value of $\frac{1}{2}$. This "central limit law" (of approach to a normal distribution) enabled mathematicians like de Moivre, Laplace, and Gauss to predict with great accuracy how often deviations will tend to occur, the expected size of the absolute errors halving when the sequence quadruples in length. Economic distributions, like that of income, may have tails too dispersed to be subject to this normal distribution.

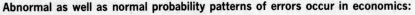

Abnormal as well as normal probability patterns of errors occur in economics:

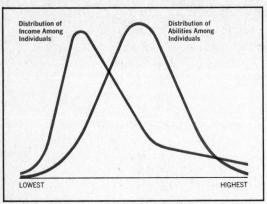

Distribution of
Income Among
Individuals

Distribution of
Abilities Among
Individuals

LOWEST   HIGHEST

FIG. 1-4. Although behavior on the average is predictable in economics, there are exceptions and deviations around the average. The brown curve depicts the well-behaved case in which the deviations follow the symmetric bell-shaped "normal curve of error." The green curve of abnormal error, which is skewed off to the right, has relatively more extreme deviations than does the normal curve. Where this occurs in the social sciences, we cannot guarantee laws of average behavior with quite so much accuracy. (Source: Fig. 6-5, where normal distribution of abilities is contrasted with asymmetric distribution of dollar incomes and great spread among them.)

■ *Summary on economic methodology.* Any social science is subject to emotional biases and semantic disputes over the proper meaning of words. Like all sciences, economics reads different meanings and patterns into the facts depending upon the theoretical eyeglasses through which it looks at the world. Although its laws of observable behavior are not exact—like the swing of a pendulum or the orbit of a planet—economics can find probability patterns around which observations cluster. Many, but unfortunately not all, of the observed data follow a well-behaved "normal curve." Abnormal distributions occur which (1) are asymmetric or skewed and (2) have super-extended tails that reflect frequent occurrence of extreme deviation from average behavior.

Despite the approximative character of economic laws, it is a field blessed with many important regularities and valid principles.

■ THE WHOLE AND THE PART: THE "FALLACY OF COMPOSITION"

A good final warning in economics is this: things are often not what they seem. The following true statements provide examples:

1. If all farmers work hard and nature cooperates in producing a bumper crop, total farm income may *fall,* and probably will.

2. *One* man may solve his own unemployment problem by great ingenuity in hunting a job or by a willingness to work for less; but *all* cannot necessarily solve their problems in this way.

3. Higher prices *for one industry* may benefit its firms; but if the prices of *everything* bought and sold increased in the same proportion, no one would be better off.

4. It may pay the United States to reduce tariffs charged on goods imported, even if *other* countries refuse to do likewise.

5. It may pay a firm to take on some business at much *less than full costs.*

6. *Attempts* of individuals to save more in depression *may lessen the total* of the community's savings.

7. What is prudent behavior for an *individual* may at times be folly for a *nation.*

Let us emphasize: Each of the above statements is true; but each is outwardly paradoxical. In the course of this book, the seeming paradoxes will be resolved. There are no magic formulas or hidden tricks. It is typical of economics that anything which is really correct must seem perfectly reasonable once the argument is carefully developed.

At this point it is just as well to note that many of the above paradoxes hinge upon a single confusion or fallacy, called by logicians the "fallacy of composition." In books on logic, this is defined as follows:

■ **Fallacy of composition:** a fallacy in which what is true of a part is, on that account alone, alleged to be also true of the whole.

Very definitely, in the field of economics, it turns out that what seems to be true for individuals is not always true for society as a whole; and conversely, what seems to be true for all may be quite false for any one individual. For everybody to stand on tiptoe to watch a parade does no good, even though a single person may gain a better view in so doing. Countless similar examples can be given in the field of economics. You might amuse yourself by checking over the previous seven examples to see which are probably related to the fallacy of composition. Or better still, try your luck at finding new examples.

We have come to the end of our introductory survey. Perhaps the best answer to the question, Why study economics, is the famous one given by Lord Keynes at the beginning of this chapter.

SUMMARY

1 ■

Economics, both a science and an art, is studied for a variety of reasons: to understand problems facing the citizen and family; to help governments in both underdeveloped and advanced nations promote vigorous growth, while avoiding depression and inflation; to analyze fascinating patterns of social behavior.

2 ■

Among many definitions, the leading one today defines economics thus: How do we choose to use scarce productive sources, with alternative uses, to meet prescribed ends—what goods to produce, how, and for whom, now or later.

3 ■

Overlapping with other social or behavioral sciences—psychology, sociology, history—economics uses the deductive methods of logic and geometry, and inductive methods of statistical and empirical inference. Because it cannot employ controlled experiments of the physicist, it raises basic problems of methodology: subjective elements of introspection and value judgment; semantic issues of ambiguous and emotional meanings; probability laws of large numbers, both of normal-error-distribution and abnormally skewed type.

QUESTIONS FOR DISCUSSION

1. Would a major depression like that of the 1930s, or a peacetime inflation, affect you (*a*) seriously, (*b*) moderately, or (*c*) not at all?

2. Discuss the emotional content of the following words: regimentation, planning, usury, monopolist, gambling, speculation, American way of life, free enterprise, cartels, thrift, hoarding.

3. Give examples of the fallacy of composition and of the *post hoc, ergo propter hoc* fallacy. Is the latter involved in the debate over cigarettes and longevity?

4. Can you fit into the brief definition of economics many of this chapter's problems?

5. In Fig. 1-3, is income the cause and consumption the effect? Or vice versa? To answer this, economic study is needed. Similarly, does the fact that smoking and cancer are related prove that smoking causes cancer? Other biological findings determine cause and effect?

6. "Facts by themselves are dumb; before they will tell us anything we have to arrange them, and the arrangement is a theory." Elucidate.

7. Review your understanding of the following concepts:

economics as distinct from other
   disciplines
analysis and policy
practice and theory
wishful thinking, semantics
exactitude and probability

subjectivity and theorizing
tyranny of words
controlled experiment
fallacy of composition
post hoc fallacy
definition of economics

■ A PREVIEW

Here in Part One we deal with the fundamental tools needed to analyze the basic facts and institutions of modern economic life, culminating this survey in the unifying concept of national income.

In Part Two we analyze the causes of prosperity and depression: how the processes of saving and investment interact to determine the level of prices, income, and employment; and how public monetary and fiscal policies can stabilize business activity at a healthy level of progressive growth.

Part Three is concerned with the forces of competition and monopoly, which act through supply and demand to help determine the composition of the national income, in terms of both goods and services to be produced and their prices. (Unlike Part Two's "macroeconomics," this is "microeconomics.")

Part Four treats distribution of income: wages, rent, interest, and profits.

Part Five discusses international trade in both its monetary and real aspects.

The last chapter of Part Five and all of Part Six deal with some of our most vital current economic problems: exciting problems such as the development of backward countries; challenging problems such as promotion of economic growth and control of inflation; sobering comparisons of alternative economic systems and competing philosophies.

2 Central Problems of Every Economic Society

TO GET LAND'S FRUIT IN QUANTITY
TAKES JOLTS OF LABOR EVER MORE,
HENCE FOOD WILL GROW LIKE ONE, TWO, THREE . . .
WHILE NUMBERS GROW LIKE ONE, TWO, FOUR . . .
Song of Malthus: A Ballad on Diminishing Returns ANONYMOUS

At the foundations of any community there will always be found a few universal economic conditions. Certain background problems are as crucial today as they were in the days of Homer and Caesar, and they will continue to be relevant in the brave new world of the future.

In Section A of this chapter we shall see that every society must meet a certain trio of *basic problems of economic organization*. Section B will show that technological knowledge, together with limited amounts of land, labor, and capital, defines the available choices between goods and services open to a community and that these *production possibilities* are subject to change and to the law of diminishing returns. Section C develops the point that the basis of any economy is its *population, or human element*.

We shall leave to Chapter 3 those important special economic features characteristic of our own mixed economy—our system of private and public enterprise.

A. PROBLEMS OF ECONOMIC ORGANIZATION

Any society, whether it consists of a totally collectivized communistic state, a tribe of South Sea Islanders, a capitalistic industrial nation, a Swiss Family Robinson, a Robinson Crusoe—or, one might almost add, a colony of bees—must somehow confront three fundamental and interdependent economic problems.

1. WHAT commodities shall be produced and in what quantities? That is, how much and which of alternative goods and services shall be produced? Food or clothing? Much food and little clothing, or vice versa? Bread and butter today, or bread and grape plantings today with bread, butter, and jam next year?

2. How shall goods be produced? That is, by whom and with what resources and in what technological manner are they to be produced? Who hunts, who fishes? Electricity from steam or from waterfall or from atoms?

3. FOR WHOM shall goods be produced? That is, who is to enjoy and get the benefit of the goods and services provided? Or, to put the same thing in another way, how is the total of national product to be *distributed*[1] among different individuals and families? A few rich and many poor? Or most people in modest comfort?

These three questions are fundamental and common to all economies, but different economic systems try to solve them differently. In a primitive civilization, custom may rule every facet of behavior. WHAT, HOW, and FOR WHOM may be decided by reference to traditional ways of doing things. To members of another culture, the practices followed may seem bizarre and unreasonable; the members of the tribe or clan may themselves be so familiar with existing practices as to be surprised, and perhaps offended, if asked the reason for their behavior. Thus, the Kwakiutl Indians consider it desirable not to accumulate wealth but to give it away in the *potlatch*—a roisterous celebration. This deviation from acquisitive behavior will not surprise anthropologists; from their studies they know that what is correct behavior in one culture is often the greatest crime in another.

In the bee colony, all such problems, even those involving an extraordinarily elaborate cooperative division of labor, are solved automatically by means of so-called "biological instincts."

At the other extreme we can imagine an omnipotent benevolent or malevolent dictator who by arbitrary decree and fiat decides WHAT, HOW, and FOR WHOM. Or we might imagine economic organization by decree, but with decrees drawn up by democratic vote or by selected legislative authorities.

> ■ As Chapter 3 develops at length, the WHAT, HOW, and FOR WHOM questions in a so-called "capitalist free enterprise economy" are determined primarily[2] by a system of prices (of markets, of profits and losses).

■ THE LAW OF SCARCITY

WHAT to produce, HOW, and FOR WHOM would not be problems if resources were unlimited: if an infinite amount of every good could be produced, or if human wants were fully satisfied, it would not then matter if too much of any particular good were produced. Nor would it then matter if labor and materials were combined unwisely.

---

[1] WARNING: Usually when an economist is talking about "distribution," he means the distribution of incomes—the principles which determine labor's wage, land's rent, capital's interest, and the whole FOR WHOM process. The man on the street usually means, by distribution, wholesaling and retailing—how goods once produced get into the hands of the consumer. Try to avoid this last usage, which can cause confusion.

[2] There has never been a 100 per cent purely automatic enterprise system. Even in our capitalistic system, the government has an important role in modifying the workings of the price system. This is what is meant by the saying that we live in a "mixed economy."

Since everyone could have as much as he pleased, it would not matter how goods and incomes were distributed among different individuals and families.

There would then be no *economic goods,* i.e., no goods that are relatively scarce; and there would hardly be any need for a study of economics or "economizing." All goods would be *free goods,* like air.

In the world as it is, even children learn in growing up that "both" is not an admissible answer to a choice of "which one." Compared with backward nations or previous centuries, modern industrial societies seem very wealthy indeed. But higher production levels seem to bring in their train higher consumption standards. People feel that they want and "need" steam heat, indoor plumbing, refrigerators, education, movies, radios, television, books, autos, travel, music, chic clothes, and so forth. The biological scientist may tell them that they can be well nourished on a thin porridge for a few cents a day,[3] but that possibility leaves them as cold as the information that the chemicals in their bodies are worth only a couple of dollars. Anyone who has kept a family budget knows that the necessities of life—the absolute musts—have little to do with the minimum *physiological* needs of food, clothing, and shelter.

In *The Affluent Society,* Harvard's Galbraith[4] has eloquently pointed out that Americans today have for the most part gone beyond the level of physiological necessity; that often the consumer flits from one purchase to another in response to pressures of fashion and advertising. Without challenging Galbraith's thesis that the time has come to spend more on public needs and less on private needs, one may properly point out that our total product would have to become many times higher than its present level if everyone were to become able to live at the level of a moderately well-off doctor, lawyer, professor, or advertising man—to say nothing of the really well-to-do.

Whether or not people would be genuinely happier spending twice as much as now, observation suggests that folks in the suburbs now act as if they want more income to spend: they take on extra work; they resist tax increases; they end up saving much the same fraction of their incomes as in 1900; and middle-class mothers seem to work harder than their mothers did. Even if the national income were divided up equally between every man, woman, and child—and it clearly cannot be—there would be only about $60 per week to go around.

■ Therefore, while it recognizes the important germ of truth in the notion that America has become an affluent society, economics must still contend with scarcity as a basic fact of life.

[3] A study suggests that modern standards of adult nutrition could be bought in 1967 for less than $100 per year. But what a diet this implies: kidneys, cabbage, buckwheat flour, and not much else! George J. Stigler, "The Cost of Subsistence," *Journal of Farm Economics,* May, 1945, pp. 303–314. This paper achieved fame as a forerunner of an important mathematical technique of economics and national defense called "linear programming." Victor E. Smith of Michigan State University in the same journal (May, 1959, pp. 272–283) reported that a family of three could get a "palatable diet" for about 50 cents per person per day, perhaps 55 cents in 1967.
[4] John Kenneth Galbraith, *The Affluent Society* (Houghton Mifflin, Boston, 1958).

B. THE TECHNOLOGICAL CHOICES OPEN TO ANY SOCIETY

■ SOCIETY'S PRODUCTION-POSSIBILITY CURVE

We have discussed the basic economic fact that *limitation* of the total resources capable of producing different commodities necessitates a choice between relatively scarce commodities. This can be illustrated quantitatively by simple arithmetic examples and geometrical diagrams. Diagrams and graphs are indispensable visual aids in many aspects of economics. A little care at the beginning in understanding them will be rewarded manyfold later on.

Consider an economy with only so many people, only so much technical knowledge, only so many factories and tools, and only so much land, water power, and natural resources. In deciding WHAT shall be produced and How, the economy must really decide just how these resources are to be allocated among the thousands of different possible commodities. How much land should go into wheat cultivation? Or into

Full employment of scarce resources means society must choose between more guns or more butter:

POSSI-BILITIES	BUTTER, MILLIONS OF POUNDS	GUNS, THOU-SANDS
A	0	15
B	1	14
C	2	12
D	3	9
E	4	5
F	5	0

TABLE 2-1. ALTERNATIVE POSSIBILITIES IN THE PRODUCTION OF BUTTER AND GUNS. Economic resources can be shifted from butter production to gun production, in effect enabling us to transform butter into guns.

1st, This can be shown pictorially:

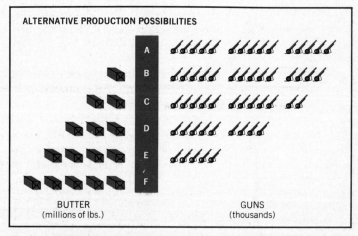

FIG. 2-1. The cost of getting extra guns can be reckoned as the extra butter we are forced to sacrifice.

pasturage? How many factories are to produce hairpins? How much skilled labor should go into machine shops?

These problems are complicated even to discuss, much less solve. Therefore we must simplify. So let us assume that only two economic goods (or classes of economic goods) are to be produced. For dramatic purposes, we can choose the pair guns and butter. These two commodities are commonly used to illustrate the problem of choosing between civilian and war goods, but the same analysis applies to any choice of goods. Thus the more resources the government uses to build public roads, the less will be left to produce private houses; the more the public chooses to consume of food, the less it can consume of clothing; the more society decides to consume today, the less can be its production of machines and capital goods to turn out more consumption goods for the next year or decade.

But let us stick to the example of guns and butter. Now, suppose that *all* resources are thrown into the production of civilian goods (butter). There will still be a *maximum* amount of butter that can be produced per year. (The exact amount depends upon the quantitative and qualitative resources of the economy in question and the technological efficiency with which they are used.) Suppose 5 million pounds of butter is the maximum amount that can be produced with the existing technology and resources.

At the other extreme, imagine that 100 per cent of society's resources had been devoted instead to the production of guns. Only some maximum number of guns could then be produced: 15 thousand guns of a certain description can perhaps be produced if we are really willing to produce no butter.

These are two extreme possibilities; in between there are still others. If we are willing to give up *some* butter, we can have *some* guns; if we are willing to give up

2d, Or it can be shown graphically by plotting the points on a grid:

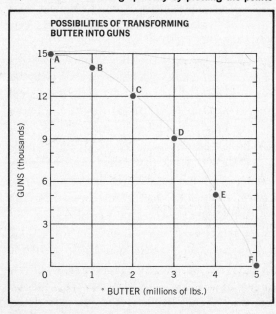

FIG. 2-2. Each marked point is a careful plot of each gun-and-butter numerical combination from Table 2-1. (Guess where the point midway between *B* and *C* might approximately fall. Read off its guns-butter numbers, and pencil them into Table 2-1 at about the right place.)

still more butter, we can have still more guns. A schedule of a number of possibilities is given in Table 2-1, *F* being the extreme where all butter and no guns are produced, and *A* being the opposite extreme where all resources go into guns. In between, at *E*, *D*, *C*, and *B*, butter is being given up increasingly in return for more guns. Butter is "transformed" into guns, not physically, but by diverting resources from one use to the other.

Table 2-1 can also be represented diagrammatically by Fig. 2-1, which should be self-explanatory.

It is even more illuminating to represent this same production-possibility or production-transformation schedule by measuring butter along the horizontal axis and guns along the vertical, as in Fig. 2-2.

The reader should now be able to go directly from the numerical table to the final diagram: for *F*, by counting over 5 butter units to the right and going up 0 gun units; for *E*, by going 4 butter units to the right and going up 5 gun units; and finally, for *A*, by going over 0 butter units and up 15 gun units.

We may fill in all intermediate positions, even those involving fractions of a million pounds or fractions of a thousand guns, as in the so-called "production-possibility curve" shown in Fig. 2-3 on the next page.

The curve that we now have represents this fundamental fact:

■ *A full-employment economy must always in producing one good be giving up something of another.* This assumes, of course, that at least some resources can be transferred from one good to another; e.g., steel is used for guns and also for butter via farm machinery.

Substitution is the law of life in a full-employment economy. The *production-possibility curve*, or *frontier*, depicts society's menu of choices.

But what if there had been widespread unemployment of resources: idle men, idle land, and idle factories? We have already warned that our economic laws may then be quite different. This is one such instance.

With unemployment, we are not on the production-possibility frontier at all, but somewhere *inside* it, say, at *U* in Fig. 2-3, producing only 2 million pounds of butter and 6 thousand guns. If resources are idle, by putting them to work we can have more butter *and* more guns. We can move from *U* to *D* or *E* and thereby get more butter and more guns.

This throws important light on the different experience in World War II of three countries: the United States, Germany, and Russia. After 1940, how was the United States able to become the "arsenal of democracy" and to enjoy civilian living standards higher than ever before? Largely by taking up the slack of unemployment. On the other hand, Hitler's war effort began in 1933, long before any formal declaration. It stemmed from a period of unemployment acute enough to win him the votes to get into power peacefully. Almost all the extra output made possible by utilizing previously unemployed workers and plants was siphoned into German war goods rather than into higher civilian consumption. Still a third case is that of the Soviet Union. The Russians had little unemployment before the war and were already on their rather low production-

Or we can picture production possibilities by drawing a smooth curve:

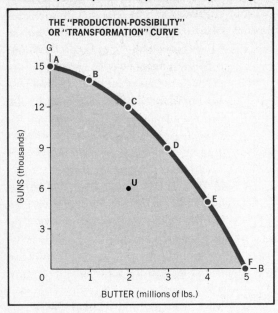

THE "PRODUCTION-POSSIBILITY"
OR "TRANSFORMATION" CURVE

FIG. 2-3. This shows how society can choose to substitute guns for butter, assuming a given state of technology and a given total of resources. Any point *inside* the curve, such as *U*, indicates that resources are not being fully employed in the best-known way. (Source: Table 2-1. A smooth curve has been passed through the points of the previous chart.)

possibility curve. They had no choice but to substitute war goods for civilian goods—with consequent privation.

■ SOME USES OF THE PRODUCTION-POSSIBILITY CONCEPT

This concept, represented as a simple curve, can help introduce many of the most basic concepts in economics. For example, Fig. 2-3 illustrates the basic definition of economics given in Chapter 1, namely, the problem of *choosing* among *scarce* or limited resources ("means" capable of *alternative* uses), in order to achieve best *goals* ("ends"). Land, labor, and capital can be used to produce guns or butter along the frontier curve in Fig. 2-3. Where does the society choose to end up? Southeastward in the diagram, with much of civilian goods? Or northwestward, with much of defense goods? Economics is a *quantitative* subject: choice is not a qualitative matter of "either-or," but rather of how many of each good and just where we draw the line of final decision.

The production-possibility frontier also permits us to give a rigorous definition of scarcity.

■ *Definition:* "Economic scarcity" refers to the basic fact of life that there exists only a finite amount of human and nonhuman resources, which the best technical knowledge is capable of using to produce only a *limited* maximum amount of each and every good, as shown by the *p-p frontier.* And thus far, nowhere on the globe is the supply of goods so plentiful or the tastes of the populace so limited that every person can have more than enough of everything he might fancy.

The production-possibility schedule can also help make clear the three basic problems of economic life: WHAT, HOW, and FOR WHOM.

Production-possibility curves illustrate many economic cases:

1st, Choice between luxuries and necessities:

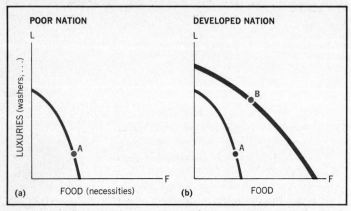

FIG. 2-4(a). Before development, the nation is so poor it must devote almost all its resources to food, enjoying few comforts.

FIG. 2-4(b). After development, it goes from *A* to *B*, expanding its food consumption very little compared with its increased consumption of nonnecessities.

2d, Choice between public and private goods:

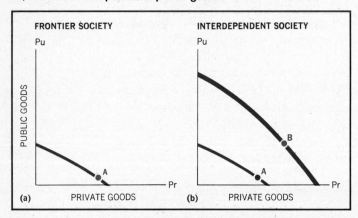

FIG. 2-5(a). The economy is poor and dispersed as in Daniel Boone's frontier days: the proportion of resources going to government is low.

FIG. 2-5(b). The economy is more prosperous and chooses to spend more of its higher income on governmental services (roads, defense, research, education); in dense urban life, it has no choice but to spend on traffic lights, police, and city planning.

WHAT goods are produced and consumed can be depicted by the point which we choose on the *p-p frontier*.

How goods are to be produced involves an efficient choice of methods and proper assignment of different amounts and kinds of limited resources to the various industries. What would happen if the men well fitted for machine-tooling of guns ended up on the farms? We would be *inside* the *p-p frontier*, not on it. Or what if government regulations made the land most suitable for corn be used for wheat production, and the land most suitable for wheat be used for corn? We would end up with less of both corn and wheat, inside the *production-possibility frontier* on a diagram whose axes were labeled *C* and *W*. Being inside the frontier is a crime of *economic* inefficiency; but it need not involve any *engineering* inefficiency, since, on the wrongly allocated land, production might still be following the latest methods known to science.[5]

FOR WHOM goods are to be produced cannot be discerned from the *p-p* diagram alone. Sometimes, though, you can make a guess from it: if you find a society on its *p-p frontier* with many yachts and few compact cars, you are justified in suspecting that it enjoys considerable inequality of income and wealth among persons.

[5] More difficult is the notion that the economy should often prefer scientifically less efficient methods over methods that are allegedly technically more efficient. EXAMPLE: Physics texts teach that converting heat to motion at 2000°F is intrinsically more efficient than converting it at 1200°. Yet if metals that can stand the higher temperature are scarce and dear, it is *economically* better for the engineer and businessman to use the thermodynamically less efficient method!

■ PICTURES IN AN EXHIBITION

The graphs of Figs. 2-4 to 2-8 are largely self-explanatory. They show that the production-possibility curve can illustrate many familiar, but basic, economic processes. Later chapters will deal with each of these in depth, and it is necessary here only to comprehend the common-sense ideas involved.

Figure 2-4 illustrates how a society consumes much food when it is poor but shifts toward comforts and luxuries as it develops—a topic to be met in Chapter 11.

Figure 2-5 illustrates how the electorate must choose between private goods bought at a price and public goods paid for largely by taxes, a topic to be met in Chapter 8.

Figure 2-6 illustrates how an economy chooses between current consumption goods and capital goods (machines, etc.), which makes possible more of *both* goods in the future. Much of Parts Two, Four, and Six will deal with this basic investment problem.

Figure 2-7 shows how economy B, blessed by scientific and engineering discoveries might surpass A which was undergoing more thrift and investing for the future, but with less progressive technology. Growth discussions, in Part Six, will develop this theme.

Finally, turn over now to, Fig. 2-8 which prepares us for the next topic, the law of diminishing returns.

■ THE LAW OF DIMINISHING RETURNS

Figure 2-8 introduces us to a famous technological economic relationship, the so-called "law of diminishing returns."

3d, Choice between more consumption today and capital goods to enhance tomorrow's possibilities:

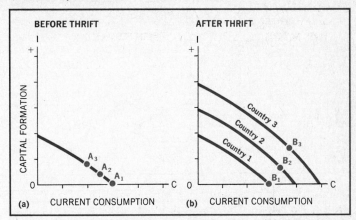

FIG. 2-6(a). Three countries start out even, but Country 1 does no saving for the future at A_1 (merely replacing used-up machines). Country 2 abstains modestly from consumption at A_2. Country 3, by democratic vote or private sacrifice, is at A_3, investing much in new machines and sacrificing much of current consumption.
FIG. 2-6(b). In the next years, Country 3 has forged ahead of Country 2, which has moved ahead of nonprogressing Country 1. Possessing more machines for labor to work with, Country 3 now can have more of *both* goods than can Country 2. Country 1 remains where it started.

4th, Case where technical advance outstrips thrift alone:

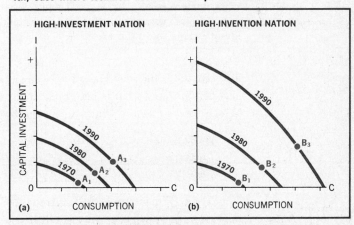

FIG. 2-7(a). Country A, on the left, is thrifty and advances by accumulating capital goods.
FIG. 2-7(b). Country B advances even more from 1970 to 1980 because it spends more on science and technical research. From 1980 to 1990 it grows faster still by using both methods: technical progress *and* much capital formation.

5th, How output on fixed land will not keep pace with population:

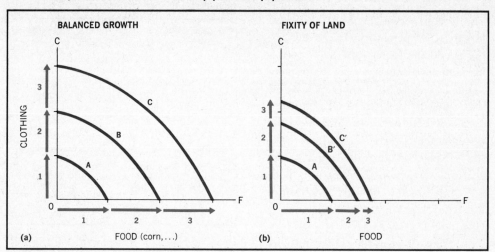

FIG. 2-8(a). We begin initially at the lower curve A. But population now doubles and is able to spread over double the previous land, leaving each county and state in the same land-labor balance as before. Hence the new curve B permits exactly twice the scale of food and clothing production.

      Finally, let labor and land both rise again by the same extra amount as between A and B. We end up at C, gaining fully as much of extra products as we did before from the same balanced additions of labor and land. Note that the arrows 1, 2, and 3 on each axis show no diminishing length.

FIG. 2-8(b). We begin at the same A curve as in Fig. 2-8(a). But now land is held constant while population doubles. Each laborer has less land to work with than under balanced growth. Hence, the B' curve is below the B curve of Fig. 2-8(a).

      Finally, add another equal increment of labor, still holding land constant. The new extra product is even lower, as shown by the diminishing lengths of the arrows 1, 2, and 3, which depict extra output. We shall understand the reasons for all this after the "law of diminishing returns" has been mastered.

This law states the relation, *not* between two goods (such as guns and butter), but rather between an input of production (such as labor) and the resulting output of a good it helps produce (such as butter or, in the traditional examples, corn).

    ■ More specifically, the law of diminishing returns refers to the amount of *extra output* that we get when we successively add equal *extra* units of a *varying input* to a *fixed* amount of some *other input*. (Note the emphasized words.)

Here is an example to illustrate the law of diminishing returns. We make the following controlled experiment: Given a fixed amount of land, say, 100 acres, we shall first add no labor at all. We note that there is then no corn output, and so we record zero output in Table 2-2.

      Now we make a second related experiment. We add 1 extra unit of labor to the same fixed amount of land. How much output do we now get? Pure reason cannot tell us: we must look to the facts of the experiment. When we do this we observe, let us say, that we now have produced positive output of corn exactly equal to 2,000 units (bushels or whatever units you choose to measure corn in). We now summarize the result of this second experiment: Adding 1 extra unit of labor to 100 of fixed land gives us extra output of 2,000 units.

To observe the law of diminishing returns, we must make a third controlled experiment. We still hold land fixed. Once more we vary the labor input and make sure to add again exactly the same extra unit of labor as before; i.e., we now go from 1 unit of labor to 2 units of labor. We breathlessly await the outcome of the experiment in terms of extra corn produced. Shall we now have a total of 4,000 units of corn, which would again represent exactly 2,000 extra units of output produced by the extra unit of the varying labor? Or shall we find *diminishing* returns, with the new extra unit of input adding less than the 2,000 extra units of output which was previously added?

If the law of diminishing returns does in fact hold, our experiment can have but one result: the second extra labor unit will add less extra output than did the first. Adding a third extra unit of labor will, if diminishing returns holds, result in still lower extra output. And so forth. Table 2-2 gives numerical values to illustrate exactly what diminishing returns means.

The law of diminishing returns is an important, often-observed, economic and technical regularity; but it is not universally valid. Often it will hold only *after* you have added a considerable number of equal doses of the varying factor. Beyond that point, we say the law of diminishing returns has set in. (Before such a point the varying factors might be yielding increasing extra returns, since until then we might find that adding extra varying inputs to a fixed input leads to increasing rather than diminishing extra outputs; but ultimately decreasing returns can be expected to prevail.)

Why is the law of diminishing returns plausible? Frequently we feel that by adding land and labor together—no input being fixed and all being varied in the same

Diminishing returns is a fundamental law of economics and technology:

MAN-YEARS OF LABOR	TOTAL PRODUCT, BUSHELS	EXTRA OUTPUT ADDED BY ADDITIONAL UNIT OF LABOR
0	0	
		2,000
1	2,000	
		1,000
2	3,000	
		500
3	3,500	
		——
4	3,800	
		100
5	3,900	

TABLE 2-2. RETURNS OF CORN WHEN EQUAL UNITS OF LABOR ARE ADDED TO FIXED LAND. Law of diminishing returns refers to successively lower extra outputs gained from adding equal increments of a variable input to a constant amount of a fixed input. (Pencil in the extra output of the fourth laborer.)

proportion so that the whole *scale* of operations is getting larger—then output should also increase proportionately and extra outputs need not diminish. For why should the extra outputs diminish if each of the inputs always has as much of the other inputs to work with?

In short, *balanced* scale changes may often be expected to leave inputs and outputs in the same ratios.

On the other hand, when we do hold one input or group of inputs constant and vary the remaining inputs, we see that the varying inputs have *less and less of the fixed inputs to work with.* Consequently, we are not too surprised that such extra varying inputs begin to add less and less extra product. In effect, the fixed factor of production (land) is decreasing in proportion to the variable input (labor). As we crowd the land more and more, we may still get some extra corn by intensive cultivation of the soil; but the amount of extra corn per unit of extra labor will become less and less. We shall see in Part Four that the real wage paid to workers depends upon the extra output a last man adds for his employer. Diminishing returns reveals that living standards in crowded China or India are low because of this basic technical truth, and not merely because land happens to be owned by the state or by private landlords.

In conclusion, we may summarize as follows:

■ *The law of diminishing returns:* An increase in some inputs relative to other fixed inputs will, in a given state of technology, cause total output to increase; *but after a point the extra output resulting from the same additions of extra inputs is likely to become less and less.* This falling off of extra returns is a consequence of the fact that the new "doses" of the varying resources have less and less of the fixed resources to work with.

■ ECONOMIES OF SCALE AND MASS PRODUCTION: A DIGRESSION

Before leaving this section we ought to take note of a phenomenon that is different from our controlled variation of one thing at a time.

Suppose we merely increase "scale of operations," i.e., increase all the factors at the same time in the same degree. In many industrial processes, when you double *all* inputs, you may find that your output is more than doubled; this phenomenon is called "*increasing* returns to *scale.*"

Our previous law of diminishing returns always refers to cases where *some* factors were varied while some remained fixed. Hence, this case of increasing returns to scale is not a direct refutation of the law of diminishing returns.

Increasing returns to scale, or so-called "economies of mass production," are often associated with one of the following advances: (1) the use of nonhuman and nonanimal power sources (water and wind power, steam, electricity, turbines and internal-combustion engines, internal atomic energy); (2) the use of automatic self-adjusting mechanisms (lathes, jigs, servomechanisms); (3) the use of standardized, interchangeable parts; (4) the breakdown of complex processes into simple repetitive operations; (5) the specialization of function and division of labor; as well as many other technological factors. The automobile-production assembly line and the historical development of modern textile spinning and weaving are examples typifying these diverse factors.

Upon thought, it will be evident that *each of these economies or savings comes into full play only if a large enough number of units is being produced to make it worth while to set up a fairly elaborate productive organization.* If only a few guns are to be produced, they might just as well be produced by hand; but if resources are available to produce many thousands, it will pay to make certain elaborate initial preparations that need not be repeated when still more units are to be produced. In such cases, where mere scale matters much, the tendency for land fixity to force diminishing extra returns to labor could be thwarted for a long time by an increase in the total labor scale involved.[6]

Economies of scale are very important in explaining why so many of the goods we buy are produced by large companies. We shall see that they are important in helping explain "the division of labor" and pattern of "specialization." They raise questions to which we shall return again and again in later chapters—as, for example, monopoly.

■ LABOR THEORY OF VALUE IN EDEN BEFORE DIMINISHING RETURNS

We are now in a position to explain why the *production-possibility frontier* has been made into a bowed-out or concave curve in all our diagrams. If the *p-p frontier* were a straight line, the relative costs of getting some extra guns in terms of sacrificed butter would always be the same. Economists would term this a case of "constant (relative) costs." But actually it is more common in life to meet the law of increasing (relative) costs.

■ *Definition:* The "law of increasing (relative) costs" prevails when in order to get equal extra amounts of one good, society must sacrifice ever-increasing amounts of the other good. A bowed-out or concave curvature of the *production-possibility frontier* depicts the law of increasing (relative) costs—as shown by the fact that when we want more farm goods (e.g., butter), their (relative) cost rises, as seen in Fig. 2-9(b) of the next page, by the steeper absolute slope at *C* than at *B*.

Why is this reasonable? We shall see that the law of increasing (relative) costs is related to, but definitely not the same thing as, the law of diminishing returns. We shall see that, along with the law of diminishing returns, economists must be able to assume that guns and butter use the factors of production, such as labor and land, in different proportions or intensities to deduce this law of (increasing) relative costs.

The famous "labor theory of value" was adapted by Karl Marx from such classical writers as Adam Smith and David Ricardo. There is no better introduction to it than to quote from Adam Smith's *The Wealth of Nations*. Smith employed the quaint notion of a Golden Age, a kind of Eden, wherein dwelt the noble savage before land and capital had become scarce and when human labor alone counted. He wrote:[7]

In that early and rude state of society which precedes both the accumulation of stock and the appropriation of land, the proportion between the quantities of labour necessary

---

[6]Accordingly, it might come about that, unlike our earlier simplified picture, we should have to pay two butter units for our first gun unit; but to get still another gun unit we should have to pay only one butter unit because of the efficiency of mass production. This would be a case of decreasing rather than increasing extra-costs-for-one-good-in-terms-of-another. When strong increasing returns to scale predominate, advanced treatises show that you have to redraw Fig. 2-3 to be "bowed in" (convex from below) rather than "bowed out" (concave from below), at least near each axis.

[7]Adam Smith, *The Wealth of Nations*, Book I, chapter VII.

for acquiring different objects seems to be the only circumstance which can afford any rule for exchanging them for one another. If among a nation of hunters, for example, it usually costs twice the labour to kill a beaver which it does to kill a deer, one beaver should naturally exchange for or be worth two deer. It is natural that what is usually the produce of two days' or two hours' labour, should be worth double of what is usually the produce of one day's or one hour's labour.

Note that the law of diminishing returns had no chance to operate in Eden. Why not? Because if you doubled the labor applied to an industry, be it beaver or deer hunting, you always had unlimited free land to add along with the varying labor. There simply was no fixed factor to become scarcer and scarcer for combining with a varying factor, as the law of diminishing returns requires.

Figure 2-9(a) shows that the *production-possibility frontier* between deer and beaver would have to be a straight line in the absence of any possible operation of the law of diminishing returns. Here is why. First, apply all society's labor—call it 100 units of *L*—to producing deer. If it takes 2 hours' hunting to produce 1 deer, that gives

Land scarcity spoils "labor theory," entails increasing costs:

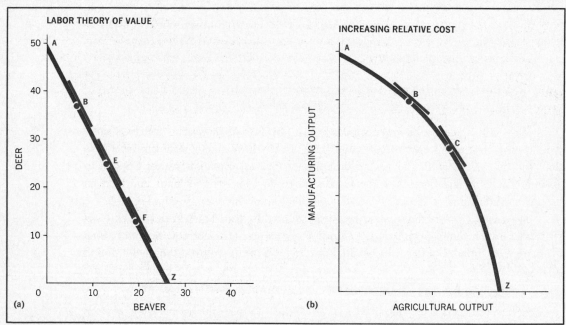

FIG. 2-9(a). In Eden, with land and other nonlabor factors superabundant, labor theory of value applies: labor hours alone can determine prices. Costs of getting extra beaver by sacrificing equal amounts of deer (i.e., by transferring deer labor) stay constant at 2 to 1 (equals 4 hours/2 hours); green slopes are of same steepness at all points, depicting constant (relative) costs.

FIG. 2-9(b). Now land is scarce; Agricultural product requires land along with labor; Manufactures require labor only. Equal sacrifices of Manufactures—from A to B and from B to C—transfer equal doses of labor to fixed farmland. Hence, diminishing returns of food result—as shown by steeper green slopes depicting relative costs at B and C.

50 deer in all at point A. But suppose it costs 4 hours' hunting for 1 beaver. Then applying all society's labor to beaver gives 25 beaver at Z.

Now suppose we divide society's labor fifty-fifty between the two industries. Half the labor applied to deer gives half 50 deer; half the labor applied to beaver gives half 25 beaver. This fifty-fifty point is shown at E, exactly halfway between A and Z along the straight line joining them. What is true for the fifty-fifty point would be true for the twenty-five–seventy-five point shown at B; likewise for every point on the straight line AZ. (Check your understanding of the point marked F.)

With the *p-p frontier* in Eden a straight line, the relative cost of getting an extra unit of one good by sacrifice of another is measured by a constant slope. Always 1 beaver costs 2 deer. Under competition, when labor alone is scarce, always

$$\frac{\text{Price of beaver}}{\text{Price of deer}} = \frac{4 \text{ labor hours}}{2 \text{ labor hours}} = 2$$

Adam Smith was right: in such an Eden, labor would get all the national income, and all goods would be priced proportional to their labor content alone. But Adam Smith realized this was unrealistic and soon went on to drop the labor theory of value in favor of a theory which makes price depend upon land-rent cost and capital-interest cost, as well as on labor-wage cost. Karl Marx, a century ago in *Das Kapital* (1867), unfortunately clung more stubbornly than Smith to the oversimple labor theory. This provided him with a persuasive terminology for declaiming against "exploitation of labor," but constituted bad scientific economics—as Parts Three and Four demonstrate.

To show that labor hours alone cannot explain price, let us use an example dear to the hearts of Ricardo and Smith. Back in Fig. 2-9(b), suppose that Manufactured goods do require labor alone and negligible land. But suppose that we have left Eden and Agricultural goods do require, along with labor, fertile land *that has grown scarce enough to have become private property*. Now we have the two ingredients to explain the law of increasing (relative) costs shown in the *p-p frontier*: The two industries use land and labor in different proportions; so transferring varying amounts of labor onto fixed Agricultural land will turn out to bring into play the law of diminishing returns. Let us see exactly how.

> Begin by using all labor to produce Manufactures, at A in Fig. 2-9(b). Now sacrifice equal amounts of Manufactures to get more Agriculture, going to B and C. How is this transformation accomplished? By transferring equal amounts of labor away from Manufactures. But note that these equal amounts of transferred labor are applied to a *fixed* total of Agricultural land. As equal amounts of varying labor are applied to a fixed land factor, each has less and less acres to work with and hence adds less and less of extra Agriculture product. We see then why each new Agriculture is procured at higher and higher costs in terms of Manufactures.

Once factors other than labor become scarce, there is no longer a constant 2-for-1 labor-cost ratio: instead, at each new point, you encounter steeper slopes on the *p-p frontier* and increasing extra costs.[8] The labor theory of value fails. *Q.E.D.*

___

[8]The common sense of this law of increasing (relative) cost does not depend upon one of the goods using labor alone. It depends only on having the two goods—call them guns and butter—differing in the proportions of factors they require. Thus, note that the first few guns can be produced in part

C. THE UNDERLYING POPULATION BASIS OF ANY ECONOMY: PAST AND FUTURE POPULATION TRENDS

■ THE MALTHUS THEORY OF POPULATION

The law of diminishing returns has an important and interesting application in the field of population. Around 1800, Thomas Robert Malthus, a young English clergyman, used to argue at breakfast against his father's perfectionist view that the human race was getting ever better. Finally the younger Malthus became so agitated that he wrote a book. His *Essay on the Principle of Population* (1798) was an instantaneous best seller. It went through several editions and for a century influenced the thinking of people all over the world (including Charles Darwin, the expositor of the famous doctrine of biological evolution). It is still a living influence today. Malthus' views depend directly on the law of diminishing returns, and continue to have relevance.

Malthus first took the observation of Benjamin Franklin that, in the American colonies where resources were abundant, population tended to double every 25 years or so. Malthus postulated, therefore, *a universal tendency for population—unless checked by food supply—to grow at a geometric progression.* Now, anyone with imagination knows how fast geometric progressions grow—how soon 1, 2, 4, 8, 16, 32, 64, 128, 256, 512, 1,024, . . . , becomes so large that there is not space in the world for all the people to stand.[9]

All this left members of the perfectionist school, such as the elder Malthus and William Godwin, unimpressed. So at this point Malthus in effect unleashed the devil of the law of diminishing returns.

As population doubles and redoubles, it is exactly as if the globe were halving in size, until finally it has shrunk so much that food and subsistence fall below that necessary for life. Because of the law of diminishing returns, food tends *not* to keep up with the geometric-progression rate of growth of population.

Mind you, Malthus did not say that population *would* increase at these rates. This was only its *tendency* if unchecked. He considered it an important part of his argument to show that, in all places in all times, checks operate to hold population down. In his first edition he put emphasis on *positive* checks that act to increase the death rate: pestilence, famine, and war. Later he backed down from this gloomy doctrine and held out hope for the human race through *preventive* checks operating on the

---

with the kind of resources that are no good for butter anyway. If more guns are wanted, we must use resources that are valuable for butter production; and if we insist upon having all guns, we must be prepared to take farmers and farmlands, which are very efficient in the production of butter, and transform them to the production of guns even though they can produce only very little in this sphere. Thus, increasing (relative) costs are to be expected in such a case. Even if resources could be divided into two uniform classes, such as homogeneous land and homogeneous labor, increasing costs would still result from the fact that guns and butter do not require the same proportion of these resources—butter taking more land, and guns requiring relatively more labor—as in the Ricardo example above.

[9] At 6 per cent compound interest, money doubles in value every 12 years. It has been estimated that the $24 received by the Indians for Manhattan island would, if deposited at compound interest, be today worth as much as all real property on the island. At 6 per cent, Sir Francis Drake's plunder of Spanish gold would today equal Britain's wealth.

birth rate. Although the birth-control movement is called neo-Malthusianism, Malthus, himself an early-nineteenth-century clergyman, advocated only *moral restraint* with prudential postponement of early marriages until a family could be supported. In fact, he preached that the struggle for existence was an illustration of the wisdom of Nature, keeping poor people from getting soft and lazy.

This important application of diminishing returns illustrates the profound effects a simple theory can have. Malthus' ideas had widespread repercussions. His book was used to support a stern revision of the English poor laws, whereby destitution was considered a result of laziness and unemployment a state to be made as uncomfortable as possible. His opinions also bolstered the argument that trade-unions could not improve the welfare of workers, since any increase in their wages would only cause workers to reproduce until there was again barely subsistence enough for all.

Despite the statistics covering many countries incorporated in his later editions, it is today recognized that his views were oversimplifications. In his discussion of diminishing returns, Malthus never fully anticipated the miracles of the Industrial Revolution. In the next century technological innovation *shifted* production-possibility frontiers rapidly *outward* and made possible better standards of living for more people, even though at the same time medical advances were prolonging human life and further lessening the positive checks to population. Nor did he anticipate that after 1870 in most Western nations, including the United States, family *fertility* as measured by actual number of children would begin to fall so far short of family *fecundity,* or biological reproductive capacity.

Nevertheless, the germs of truth in his doctrines are still important for understanding the population behavior of India, China, and other parts of the globe where the balance of numbers and food supply is a vital factor.

Table 2-3 shows how much world population has increased. This increase was made possible mainly through the declining death rate, resulting from scientific advances in medicine and from the improved living standards made possible by the Industrial Revolution. Life expectancy of a Western baby has doubled since 1800 to over 70 years at present, and standards of living far exceed those of any previous century.

Even more dramatic has been the reduction of death rates in low-income regions. Ceylon offers the dramatic case where control of mosquitoes by DDT greatly reduced malaria, cutting the death rate by 34 per cent in a single year! In India alone, one of the fruits of modern science has been a great increase in average life expectancy. In the last 20 years India's population grew by at least 120 million, an amount greater than the combined populations of France and England!

World population has more than tripled since 1800:

	1800	1940	1967
Europe (including all of U.S.S.R.)	188	572	680
North, South, and Central America	29	277	470
Asia, Africa, and Oceania	702	1,396	2,200
World	919	2,245	3,350

TABLE 2-3. POPULATION OF THE WORLD—in millions. (Sources: W. S. Thompson, *Plenty of People,* Ronald, New York, 1944; United Nations *Statistical Year Book.*)

Professor Kingsley Davis of California, an expert on population, has warned against the facile belief that it is primarily hunger (or even malnutrition) which makes life so short in poor societies. The role of disease is important as an independent factor: if inexpensive science greatly lengthens life without greatly increasing productivity and greatly changing preindustrial attitudes, the fears of Malthus take on a new relevance.

■ CONTROLLING POPULATION GROWTH

As we shall see in Part Six, much of the world is in a state of underdevelopment and poverty. If the birth rate were to continue at the high levels typical of the past—when you had to have six or more children in order to ensure that there would be a surviving child to carry on your line—population numbers would explode, and the law of diminishing returns would vitiate the gains from technical progress. Little wonder then that, wherever religions and ethical attitudes permit, there is beginning to be an active birth-control movement.

Education is, of course, basic. But nevertheless the new chemical means appropriate to the advanced Western nations—the so-called pill—are often inordinately expensive in poorer lands. A couple of dollars a month may seem like little in New York City; but in Java or El Salvador you could raise a family on that much. The American foreign-aid programs, when foreign nations have requested it, and when it is not in conflict with prevalent ethical beliefs, have provided assistance for programs of family planning. No doubt technological changes will vastly alter costs in this as in other areas.

All that needs stressing in a work on economics is the fact that there is an important relationship between population density and average standards of life.

■ DO AMERICA AND EUROPE FACE DEPOPULATION?

At the end of World War I men still feared the Malthusian curse of overpopulation. Books then had such alarming titles as *The World Faces Overpopulation* and *Standing Room Only!* But just as these books were coming off the presses, Western Europe and the United States were undergoing a profound revolution in population. This was understood only a generation later. The pendulum then swung to the other extreme; best sellers had flashy titles like *The Twilight of Parenthood* and *England without People.*

Since 1870—even earlier in France—birth rates began to drop in most countries of Western European civilization. After World War I, and especially after the Great Depression of the 1930s, the drop became precipitous; but the crisis in births was hidden for a time.

Observations that there was an excess of births over deaths gave a misleading feeling of security, because they ignored the fact that the United States and Western Europe *temporarily* had an unusually large number of women in the childbearing groups. Why this excess in these age groups? Because people in 1900 had larger families than people in 1935 were having. With so many women of the age to be mothers, prewar birth *totals* temporarily held up; and yet the number of births *per mother* was low—so low that, if the same prewar rates had continued, the future growth of the population would have eventually ended and turned into a decline.

Before World War II there was every reason for the population expert to despair for the future of the population of Western nations. Moreover, the problem did not appear to be directly economic. Everyone knew that the rich had fewer children than the poor. Before the war, Harvard and Vassar students were not reproducing themselves. Neither were Michigan State and Oberlin students, nor high school graduates and urban groups generally.[10]

■ OUR AMAZING POPULATION UPSURGE

Just then something remarkable happened to jar the expert. Nobody yet knows quite how to explain it. During and after World War II the pattern of fertility began steadily to climb, reaching new heights. Every year now brings more than 4 million babies.

Some of the reasons are, of course, obvious. With the war came prosperity, and the backlog of depression-deferred marriages began to melt. The Selective Service Act also had something to do with the increase in marriages. The number of bachelors and spinsters shrank; and the age of (first) marriage fell sharply, so that more girls marry at 18 than at any other age, with half married by shortly after 20, and with half the men married by age 22!

With many more recent marriages, it was only natural to expect the birth rate to leap upward. But more than that, people stepped up the rate at which they had children. Third and fourth children became very fashionable among the middle classes, a dramatic reversion from the pre–World War II situation.

A glance at a college faculty—young, old, and middle-aged—will show the changing trends in this regard: the associate professors have already had more children than retired professors, and the final score is not yet in. Paradoxically, poorer nations such as Japan and Italy, which used to have high birth rates, now restrict family size more than do the rich nations.

Table 2-4 shows that the richer countries of Western Europe had pre–World War II net reproduction rates[11] far below unity and now have rates above the critical

---

[10]Most authorities believe birth rates are to be explained by social rather than biological factors. Thus, the French Canadians, who have high birth rates, once came from just those rural regions of France with lowest rates. Second-generation Italian and Jewish city dwellers show greatly reduced rates, as do Negroes who move from the South to the North. Some of the highest net reproduction rates are among the white people in the Southern hillbilly regions. Ironically, the highest rates of all are to be found among—of all peoples—the American Indians, suggesting that we may yet give the country back to the Indians. Physiologists now dispute the notion that modern man is less fecund than his hungry ancestors.

[11]Demographers define the net reproduction rate (NRR) as "the *average* number of girl babies that will be born to a representative newly born girl in her lifetime." Thus, if 1,000 girls born in 1970 will, by 2020 A.D., have produced 1,600 girl babies, the NRR = 1,600/1,000 = 1.6; and were such a fertility rate to be maintained indefinitely, population would ultimately be growing at the rate of 60 per cent per "generation," i.e., about every 25 years, the average age of a mother when giving birth. (Explain exactly what NRR = 0.7 or = 1.0 means, showing why 1.0 is the watershed between decay and positive growth.)

Net reproduction rates make correction for changing age distribution:

United States			Belgium	0.90	1939
Total	0.98	1930–40		1.24	1961
	1.72	1960	Netherlands	1.15	1935–39
	1.56	1963		1.51	1963
White	0.96	1935–40	Australia	0.98	1935–39
	1.66	1960		1.57	1963
	1.51	1963	Palestine		
Nonwhite	1.14	1935–40	Moslems	2.17	1940
	2.04	1960	Jews	1.61	1945
	1.97	1963	Israel		
United Kingdom	0.78	1935–39	Jews	1.57	1963
	1.34	1963	Japan	1.49	1935–39
France	0.87	1935–37		0.92	1963
	1.37	1964	India	1.72	1931
Sweden	0.78	1935–39		1.54	1941
	1.18	1964	Soviet Union	0.78	1935–39
Germany				1.18	1964
Total	0.71	1933			
West	1.13	1962			

TABLE 2-4. NET REPRODUCTION RATES FOR VARIOUS COUNTRIES. An NRR (net reproduction rate) permanently greater than 1 means ultimate population growth. An NRR less than 1 means ultimate population decline. The NRR for the United States is now substantially above 1. (Source: *Population Index*, April, 1963, Office of Population Research, Princeton, N.J.)

level of unity. The United States has come to have a net reproduction rate that is one of the highest in the world or in recent history, and only recently has begun to show a change in trend.

■ TURN OF THE TIDE?

Since 1957, however, America has experienced a modest but steady fall in the birth rate. In part this was because of a temporary drop in the ratio of women of child-bearing age to total population. More significant for the longer-run trend is the fact that the fertility and net reproduction rates have been dropping slightly among married women of every age. National surveys of the number of children that women say they want still report 3.1, on the average. Nonetheless, the actual number being born has been slowly declining.

No doubt economic factors are involved here. Professor Richard Easterlin of the University of Pennsylvania has put forth an interesting hypothesis. He speculates that a young married couple will be less eager to have many children if their current income is falling far below that which their own families had a few years earlier. He points out that in the 1950s, when young people were scarce and their incomes relatively high, they hastened to have many children. In the late 1960s, when the vast crop of war babies has been coming onto the labor market and bidding down incomes, the comparison is less favorable. In Easterlin's view, this helps to explain the decline in NRR.

Finally, though, let us be clear on one thing: Birth rates are still quite high in America compared with what they are in other advanced nations.

■ ECONOMIC EFFECTS OF POPULATION GROWTH

The economic impact of population changes is already very noticeable. Our suburbs teem with children; our schools are overcrowded. The bulge of war births has already hit colleges: by 1975 college enrollment will almost double that of 1967! Ice cream and piano sales reflect the rise in youths.

Figure 2-10 shows the rising proportion of dependent children. For some time people of working age will decline in relative importance: caught between the growth of the dependent old *and* young, they will each have to support more nonworkers.

From the military manpower viewpoint, time may be working against the countries of Western Europe. Table 2-5 shows estimates of future populations for certain countries. Note the high estimate for the Soviet Union, where net reproduction rates have a long way to fall until they reach unity; note the low figures for Sweden and England.

The old and young are gaining on the productive age group:

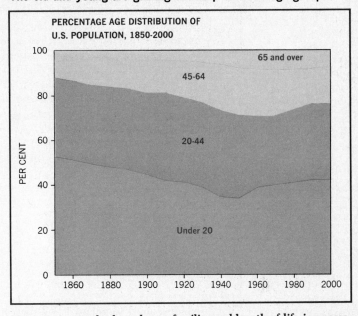

PERCENTAGE AGE DISTRIBUTION OF U.S. POPULATION, 1850-2000

FIG. 2-10. As couples have larger families and length of life increases, each person of working age will have more dependents to support. Note the rising flood of youthful workers, which could bring with it serious unemployment problems. (Source: U.S. Bureau of the Census.)

United States and Soviet populations gain relative to rest of Europe:

	1964	GROWTH, 1958–1964	1975	1980
United States	192	1.6%	229	247
United Kingdom	54	0.7%	57.5	59.2
France	48	1.3%	56	60
Soviet Union	228	1.6%	269	290
Sweden	7.7	0.6%	8.2	8.4
Italy	51	0.7%	54	56
Japan	97	1.0%	107	112

TABLE 2-5. ESTIMATED FUTURE POPULATION OF DIFFERENT COUNTRIES IN 1980 (in millions). Note the different rates of recent growth in the second column, with the U.S. and the Soviet growing fastest and Sweden and Italy slowest. (Source: United Nations *Statistical Year Book.*)

Is our population upsurge a good thing? Economics alone cannot answer such a general question. The joys and aches of family life are not to be measured in mere dollars and cents. Yet we can study certain economic aspects of population growth; and when we come to do so in later chapters, we shall find that the answers are rarely simple.

On the one hand, *growing* population makes for high money spending, as homes and factories are being replicated in like number. Therefore it may act against unemployment, and by the same reasoning, it could also aggravate inflationary threats. On the other hand, a considerably higher *level* of population threatens us with the law of diminishing returns. It fills our cars with people and fills our roads with cars; it pollutes the air with smog; it pollutes our water with filth; it spoils the countryside and ruins privacy.

Economic analysis has to weigh carefully so complex a matter as population change in order to help provide the citizen and statesman with the knowledge needed for understanding.

SUMMARY

A. PROBLEMS OF ECONOMIC ORGANIZATION

1 ■

Every economy must somehow solve the three fundamental economic problems: WHAT kinds and quantities shall be produced of all possible goods and services; How economic resources shall be used in producing these goods; and FOR WHOM the goods shall be produced, i.e., the distribution of income among different individuals and classes.

2 ■

Societies meet these problems in different ways—by custom, by instinct, by fiat and decree, and in our own society, largely by a price system.

3 ■

The basic problems are important because of the fundamental fact of all economic life: with limited resources and technology, standards of living are limited. Economic goods are *scarce* rather than free; society must choose among them, because not all needs and desires can be fulfilled.

B. TECHNOLOGICAL CHOICES OPEN TO SOCIETY

4 ■

With given resources and technology, the production choices open to a nation between two such goods as butter and guns can be summarized in the production-possibility frontier, or curve. This indicates the way in which one good can be transformed into another by transferring resources from its production to that of the other.

5 ■

Production-possibility frontiers can illustrate many basic economic processes: how we use relatively less of our resources for food necessities as we develop; how we choose between private market goods and public governmental goods; between current consumption and capital goods that enhance future capacity to produce. The *p-p frontier* can illustrate technical progress and pave the way for diminishing returns.

6 ■

The *law of diminishing returns* asserts that, after a point, as we add more and more of a variable input (such as labor) to a fixed input (such as land), the amount of extra product will fall off. This law is really a matter of proportions: the varying input has less and less of the fixed input to work with.

7 ■

Economies of mass production or of scale are often described as "increasing returns *to scale*." The word "scale" is a warning that all inputs are being varied simultaneously, with none held fixed as in the law of diminishing returns. Many modern processes do pass through an initial stage of increasing returns to scale.

8 ■

The *labor theory of value* can validly predict prices in terms of labor hours alone only in a hypothetical time when land and other nonlabor factors of production are abundant enough to be freely available. Once such factors as land become scarce, market price ratios depend on the whole mix of labor-wage, land-rent, and capital-interest costs.

The *p-p frontier* then ceases to be a straight line and becomes a curve which is concave (from below). *This depicts the law of increasing (relative) costs.* To get equal amounts of one good requires society to sacrifice more and more of the other. All this results when goods use factors of production in different proportions, and hence unbalanced transfers of productive factors bring the law of diminishing returns into play.

C. UNDERLYING POPULATION BASIS OF ANY ECONOMY

9 ■

Malthus' theory of population rests on the law of diminishing returns. He thought that a population, if unchecked, would tend to grow in geometric rate, doubling every generation or so. But each member of the growing population would have less natural resources and land to work with. Therefore, because of diminishing returns, income would have a tendency to fall so low as to lead to a stable population at a level of starvation and pestilence.

10 ■

For a century and a half after Malthus, populations grew by leaps and bounds everywhere. Numbers grew primarily because death rates fell sharply as a result of improved medical and public health technology; yet technological progress in industry more than offset the law of diminishing returns.

11 ■

After 1870 birth rates began to fall. Prior to World War II, advanced nations had net reproduction rates below 1 and faced depopulation. Since 1939 the middle classes have swung back toward a larger-family pattern, a trend predicted by few and one which has had momentous future consequences. Only recently has the tide been slowly turning.

QUESTIONS FOR DISCUSSION

1. Without looking at the next chapter, can you anticipate how a price system through supply and demand solves the three problems of economic organization?

2. Explain what economists mean by *"scarcity,"* by *free goods,* by *inefficiency.*

3. Draw society's *p-p frontier* if scientific inventions increased the productivity of given resources in butter production only, and not in guns.

4. If land were increased in a number of steps and labor were held constant, would the law of diminishing returns hold? Illustrate and tell why this would happen.

5. Describe and contrast (*a*) the law of diminishing returns; (*b*) the phenomenon of increasing returns to scale. How about (*c*) the law of increasing (relative) costs?

6. How many were there in your great-grandparents' family? In your parents' family? How many do you think there will be in your own family?

7. "Population pressure doesn't cause war, as is commonly believed. Careful study suggests cause and effect are just the reverse. Nations that want to expand try to persuade their citizens to grow in numbers so the nation will be militarily strong and will have a pretext for expansion." Discuss.

8. Review your understanding of the following concepts:

economic and free goods

substitution and law of scarcity

production-possibility frontier

law of diminishing returns

total versus extra product

productive factors or inputs

increasing returns to scale

labor theory of value

law of increasing (relative) cost

Malthusian population theory

age distribution of population

net reproductive rate (NRR)

3 Price Functioning of a "Mixed" Capitalistic Enterprise System

EVERY INDIVIDUAL ENDEAVORS TO EMPLOY HIS CAPITAL SO THAT ITS PRODUCE MAY BE OF GREATEST VALUE. HE GENERALLY NEITHER INTENDS TO PROMOTE THE PUBLIC INTEREST, NOR KNOWS HOW MUCH HE IS PROMOTING IT. HE INTENDS ONLY HIS OWN SECURITY, ONLY HIS OWN GAIN. AND HE IS IN THIS LED BY AN *INVISIBLE HAND* TO PROMOTE AN END WHICH WAS NO PART OF HIS INTENTION. BY PURSUING HIS OWN INTEREST HE FREQUENTLY PROMOTES THAT OF SOCIETY MORE EFFECTUALLY THAN WHEN HE REALLY INTENDS TO PROMOTE IT.
ADAM SMITH, *The Wealth of Nations* (1776)

■ THE MIXED ECONOMY

Most of our attention will be devoted to the special features of economic life found in twentieth-century industrial nations (with the exception of the Soviet system). In most of these countries there was a trend in the past few centuries toward less and less direct governmental control of economic activity; gradually feudal and preindustrial conditions were replaced by greater emphasis on what is loosely called "free private enterprise," or "competitive capitalism."

Long before this trend had approached a condition of full *laissez faire* (i.e., of complete governmental noninterference with business), the tide began to turn the other way. Since late in the nineteenth century, in almost all the countries under consideration there has been a steady increase in the economic functions of government. We must leave to historians the task of delineating the important factors underlying this significant and all-pervasive development. Suffice it to say this here

■ Ours is a "mixed economy" in which both public and private institutions exercise economic control.

Section A of this chapter shows how our mixed economy tackles the three problems of economic organization that must be met by any society. Section B describes some fundamental characteristics of the present economic order.

A. HOW A FREE ENTERPRISE SYSTEM SOLVES
THE BASIC ECONOMIC PROBLEMS

In a system of free private enterprise, no individual or organization is consciously concerned with the triad of economic problems set forth in Chapter 2: WHAT, HOW, and FOR WHOM. This fact is really remarkable.

To paraphrase a famous economic example, let us consider the city of New York. Without a constant flow of goods in and out of the city, it would be on the verge of starvation within a week. A variety of the right kinds and amounts of food is involved. From the surrounding counties, from 50 states, and from the far corners of the world, goods have been traveling for days and months with New York as their destination.

How is it that nearly 10 million people are able to sleep easily at night, without living in mortal terror of a breakdown in the elaborate economic processes upon which the city's existence depends? For all this is undertaken without coercion or centralized direction by any conscious body!

Everyone notices how much the government does to control economic activity— tariff legislation, pure-food laws, utility and railroad regulations, minimum-wage regulations, fair-labor-practice acts, social security, price ceilings and floors, public works, national defense, national and local taxation, police protection and judicial redress, zoning ordinances, municipal water or gas works, and so forth. What goes unnoted is how much of economic life proceeds *without* direct government intervention.

Hundreds of thousands of commodities are produced by millions of people more or less of their own volition and without central direction or master plan.

■ NOT CHAOS BUT ECONOMIC ORDER

This functioning alone is convincing proof that a competitive system of markets and prices—whatever else it may be, however imperfectly it may function—is not a system of chaos and anarchy. There is in it a certain order and orderliness. It works.

A competitive system is an elaborate mechanism for unconscious coordination through a system of prices and markets, a communication device for pooling the knowledge and actions of millions of diverse individuals. Without a central intelligence it solves one of the most complex problems imaginable, involving thousands of unknown variables and relations. Nobody designed it. It just evolved, and like human nature, it is changing; but it does meet the first test of any social organization—it can survive.

A dramatic example of the importance of a pricing system is Germany after World War II. In 1946–1947 production and consumption had dropped to a low level. Neither bombing damage nor postwar reparation payments could account for this breakdown. Paralysis of the price mechanism was clearly to blame: Money was worthless; factories closed down for lack of materials; trains could not run for lack of coal; coal could not be mined because miners were hungry; miners were hungry because peasants would not sell food for money and no industrial goods were available to give them in return. Prices were legally fixed, but little could be bought at such prices; a black market characterized by barter or fantastically high prices existed. Then in 1948 a "miracle" happened. A thoroughgoing currency reform set the price mechanism back into effective operation. Immediately production and consumption soared; again the WHAT, HOW, and FOR WHOM were being resolved by markets and prices.

The fact to emphasize is that such so-called miracles are going on all around us all the time—if only we look around and alert ourselves to the everyday functioning of the market. A revolutionist out to destroy the capitalistic system could ask nothing better than a great inflation or deflation that would paralyze the price mechanism.[1]

■ THE INVISIBLE HAND AND "PERFECT COMPETITION"

Students of economics have to avoid the error of thinking that a price mechanism must work chaotically if it is not controlled by somebody. Having learned this lesson, they must not go to the other extreme and become enamored of the beauty of a pricing mechanism, regarding it as perfection itself, the essence of providential harmony and beyond the touch of human hands.

Adam Smith, whose *The Wealth of Nations* (1776) is the germinal book of modern economics or political economy, was thrilled by the recognition of an order in the economic system. Smith proclaimed the principle of the "Invisible Hand"; every individual, in pursuing only his own selfish good, was led, as if by an invisible hand, to achieve the best good for all, so that any interference with free competition by government was almost certain to be injurious. While Smith did recognize some of the realistic limitations on this doctrine, it was not until later that economists discovered this truth: The virtues claimed for free enterprise are fully realized only when the complete checks and balances of "perfect competition" are present.

> ■ Perfect competition is defined by the economist as a technical term: "Perfect competition" exists only in the case where no farmer, businessman, or laborer is a big enough part of the total market to have any personal influence on market price; on the other hand, when his grain, merchandise, or labor is large enough in size to produce depressing or elevating effects on market prices, some degree of monopolistic imperfection has set in, and the virtues of the Invisible Hand must be that much discounted.

Actually, some of the praise of perfect competition is beside the point. As discussed earlier, ours is a mixed system of government and private enterprise; as will be discussed later, it is also a mixed system of monopoly and competition. A cynic might say of perfect competition what Bernard Shaw said of Christianity: The only trouble with it is that it has never been tried.

Historians quarrel over whether there ever was a golden age of free competition. And certainly, competition is not now perfect in the economist's sense. We do not even know whether, because of the fundamental nature of large-scale production and technology, consumers' tastes, and business organization, competition is becoming less or more intense. The statistics suggest at least a slight weakening of monopolistic concentration of power.

In any case, society need not accept as inevitable any trend toward big business, mergers, trusts, and cartels such as began to swell in the 1890s. The challenge is to work

[1] In the 1960s governments in the Soviet Union and Eastern European countries are rediscovering some virtues of a pricing system. Imitation is the sincerest form of flattery.

out laws and customs that help to improve the working of our less-than-perfect competitive system. The polar cases—*laissez faire* and totalitarian dictatorship of production—dramatize economic principles. Yet the relevant choice for policy today is not a decision between these extremes, but rather the degree to which public policy should do *less* or *more* in modifying the operation of particular private economic activities.

■ THE PRICE SYSTEM

Just how does the unconscious automatic price mechanism operate? The bare outlines of a *competitive* profit-and-loss system are simple to describe.

Everything has a price—each commodity and each service. Even the different kinds of human labor have prices, usually called "wage rates." Everybody receives money for what he sells, and uses this money to buy what he wishes.

If more is wanted of any one good—say, shoes—a flood of new orders will be given for it. This will cause its price to rise and more to be produced.

Similarly, if more of a commodity such as tea becomes available than people want to buy at the last-quoted market price, its price will be marked down by competition. At the lower price people will drink more tea, and producers will no longer produce quite so much. Thus equilibrium of supply and demand will be restored (as the next chapter and Part Three will show).

What is true of the markets for consumers' goods is also true of markets for *factors of production* such as labor, land, and capital inputs. If welders rather than glassblowers are needed, job opportunities will be more favorable in the welding field. The price of welders, their hourly wage, will tend to rise, while that of glassblowers will tend to fall. Other things being equal, this will cause a shift into the desired occupation. Likewise, an acre of land will go into sugar cultivation if sugar producers bid the most for its use. In the same way, machine-tool production will be determined by supply and demand.

In other words, we have a vast system of trial and error, of successive approximation to an *equilibrium system of prices and production.* We shall see later that the matching of supply and demand and of prices and costs helps solve our three problems simultaneously. Here are the bare outlines:

1. WHAT things will be produced is determined by the votes of consumers—not every two years at the polls, but every day in their decisions to purchase this item and not that. Of course, the money that they pay into business cash registers ultimately provides the payrolls, rents, and dividends that consumers receive in weekly income. Thus the circle is a complete one.

2. How things are produced is determined by the competition of different producers. The method that is cheapest at any one time, because of both physical efficiency and cost efficiency, will displace a more costly method.

The only way for producers to meet price competition and maximize profits is to keep costs at a minimum by adopting the most efficient methods. For example, synthetic rubber will be made from oil rather than alcohol if the price of the one is in a certain relation to the price of the other; or electric power will be generated by steam rather than atomic power if the price of coal is below some critical level. The large tractor-operated farm will displace the family-size farm if this leads to lower costs of production.

> *International example:* Bob Jones farms *extensively,* with much American land relative to each hour of labor; Pierre Reny farms *intensively,* using much labor to each hectare of French land. Who orders these sensible How decisions, which properly adjust to the fact that France is more densely populated than America? Congress? The Chamber of Deputies? The UN? Of course not. The price system is society's signaling device. Like a master who gives carrots and kicks to coax his donkey forward, the pricing system deals out profits and losses to get WHAT, How, and FOR WHOM decided.

8. FOR WHOM things are produced is determined by supply and demand in the markets for productive services: by wage rates, land rents, interest rates, and profits, all of which go to make up everybody's income—relative to everyone else and relative to the whole. (Of course, the character of the resulting distribution of income is highly dependent upon the *initial* distribution of property ownership, upon acquired or inherited abilities, and upon educational opportunities.)

Note this: Consumer votes do not by themselves determine WHAT goods are produced. Demand has to meet with a supply of goods; so business cost and supply decisions, along with consumer demand, do help to determine WHAT. Just as a broker may help arrange a match between buyer and seller, the auctioneer in the commodity market acts as the go-between who reconciles the consumer votes and business supplies that impinge on the market. (The next chapter explains how.) The profit seeker is society's agent to determine How, seeking least factor-costs for producing each good and being punished by ruthless competition if he fails to use best methods.

■ A PICTURE OF PRICES AND MARKETS

To amplify this highly simplified explanation, turn over to Fig. 3-1. It gives a bird's-eye view of the way market pricing reconciles public demand and supply with business supply and demand. Note that markets serve as the connecting device between the public and business. Twenty minutes of poring over this diagram may be worth hours of disconnected musing about economic pricing. (In Chapters 10 and 32, similar circular-flow diagrams will appear namely, Fig. 10-1 and Fig. 32-1.)

A competitive system is impersonal but not completely so. The consuming families face business enterprises on two fronts, with only prices in between. One front is the widely dispersed one, the retail market on which consumers buy thousands of small items from a score of different retail establishments; grocery, drug, and department stores; movie theaters; gasoline stations; and from electric-power companies, government post offices, landlords, railroad lines, and insurance companies.

On the other front—the market for labor and other productive services—relations are not always so peaceful. To the family breadwinner his wage is not simply another price; it is the difference between luxury and comfort, between comfort and privation. The laborer may feel inferior to the large corporation in bargaining power, and he may turn to collective bargaining through trade-unions. By doing this, he may at times be helping to restore competition, while at other times he may be causing conditions to deviate still further from perfect competition.

The competitive price system uses supply-demand markets to solve the basic economic problems—WHAT, HOW, and FOR WHOM:

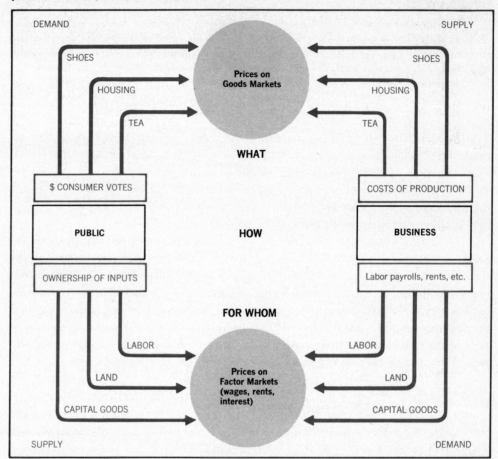

FIG. 3-1. All demand relations are shown in green; all the supply relations in brown. See how consumer dollar votes of demand interact in the upper goods markets with business cost-supply decisions, thus helping determine WHAT is produced. And how business demand for inputs or productive factors meets the public's supply of labor and other inputs in the lower factor markets to help determine wage, rent, and interest income—i.e., FOR WHOM goods are produced. Business competition to buy factor inputs and sell goods most cheaply determines How goods are to be produced. (WARNING: All parts of the diagram interact together. WHAT depends on the lower part, just as FOR WHOM depends on the upper part—carpenter wages depend on housing demand, and demand for yachts depends on oil-land royalties.)

■ ETHICAL ASPECTS OF INCOME DISTRIBUTION

The above picture of competition tending toward ideal efficiency, toward being on the production-possibility frontier and not inside it, is a highly oversimplified one. But even if the system worked perfectly as described above—which everybody knows is not the case—many would not consider it ideal. In the first place, goods go where there are the most votes or dollars. A rich man's dog may receive the milk that a poor child needs to avoid rickets. Why? Because supply and demand are working badly?

No. Because auction markets are doing what they are designed to do—putting goods in the hands of those who can pay the most, who have the most money votes. Defenders and critics of the price mechanism should recognize this fact.

Or suppose the invention of automatic machines should cause the competitive price of labor to fall, thereby reducing incomes of the poor. Would all ethical observers regard that as necessarily right or ideal?

Should the fact that a man inherited 500 square miles of range land, for which oil companies offer a million dollars per year, necessarily justify so large an income?

These questions are discussed repeatedly in Congress. Whether incomes should be completely determined by a competitive struggle—the survival of the survivors—is an ethical question that goes beyond the mechanics of economics.

> *A parable on the rationing role of efficient pricing.* There were in Flanders two kingdoms. In Zig, good King Jean commandeered the food brought to the city in time of famine, paying the peasants a just (but generous) fee and rationing supplies in fair shares for all. As the famine persisted, the dying citizens blessed the dying King.
>
> In nearby Zog, at a time of plenty each of a dozen merchants stealthily built (and stocked with cheap grain) a warehouse of food. When famine came, they sold the food at double the usual price, stripping people even of their watches and jewels. Some (but by no means all) of the jewels they then gave to less-hard-hit peasants to coax out still more food; and as the news spread, peasants came with food from as far away as Zig. The longer the famine, the higher the price Zogites paid for food, until finally the market rationed them to a minimal diet. By the time the famine ended, the whole city was in debt to the merchants, but alive; and each merchant was resentful that competition from his colleagues had kept him from increasing his fortune twentyfold, rather than only fourfold.

There is no simple moral to this tale. But there is a lesson in it on the mechanics of how a price system works (1) to ration out existing supplies of goods and (2) to cause resources to flow efficiently toward goods which people with money and ability to earn wages will pay for.[2]

■ IMPERFECTIONS OF COMPETITION

As we said earlier, one drawback to the picture of the price system as described above is the fact that, in the real world, competition is nowhere near "perfect." Firms do not know when consumer tastes will change; therefore they may overproduce in one field and underproduce in another. By the time they are ready to learn from experience, the situation may have changed again. Also, in a competitive system many producers simply do not know the methods of other producers, and costs do not fall to a minimum. In the competitive struggle one can sometimes succeed as much by keeping knowledge scarce as by keeping production high.

An even more serious deviation from perfect competition comes from *monopoly elements.* These—as we shall see later on—may result in wrong pricing, incorrect and wasteful resource allocation, and monopoly profits. We shall be reminded again and

[2]Cecil Woodham-Smith, *The Great Hunger: Ireland 1845–9* (Hamish Hamilton, London, 1962), relates the unbelievable details of how a laissez-faire Victorian government let millions of Irish children, women, and men literally starve when a fungus destroyed the potato crop.

again how strict is the economist's definition of a "perfect competitor"; the mere presence of a few rivals is not enough for perfect competition.

MONOPOLY ELEMENTS   The economic definition of "imperfect competitor" is *anyone who buys or sells a good in large enough quantities to be able to affect the price of that good.* To some degree that means almost all businessmen, except possibly the millions of farmers who individually produce a negligible fraction of the total crop. All economic life is a blend of competitive and monopoly elements. Imperfect (monopolistic) competition is the prevailing mode, not perfect competition. This is a fact, not a moral condemnation. A good approximation of perfect competition may be all one need hope for.

Of course, as we shall later see, a businessman cannot set his prices completely as he pleases and still make profits. He must take into account the prices of goods that are substitutes for his own. Even if he produces a trademarked coal with unique properties, he must reckon with prices charged for other coals, oil, gas, and insulation.

Businessmen, farmers, and workers both like and dislike competition. We all like it when it enables us to expand our market, but we label it as "chiseling," "unfair," or "ruinous" when the knife cuts the other way. The worker whose livelihood depends on how the market prices his labor may be the first to howl when competition threatens to depress wages. Farm groups, aware of what competition can do to agricultural prices, often bring pressure on the state to restrict production and thereby raise prices.

Some of the basic factors responsible for monopoly-creating bigness in business may be inherent in the economies of large-scale production. This is especially true in a dynamic world of technological change. Competition by numerous producers would simply not be efficient in many fields and could not last. Trademarks, patents, and advertising are often responsible for still other market imperfections. It would be humanly impossible, therefore, to attempt to create *perfect* competition by law. The problem is one of achieving reasonably effective "workable competition."

We shall proceed later to a more microscopic examination of supply and demand. After that discussion we shall be in a position to appraise the workings of the price system more judiciously. A competitive price system is one way of organizing an economy, but not the only way. Still it is of interest that some socialists plan to continue to use a price mechanism as part of their new society. A price system is not perfect, but neither are its alternatives.

■ ECONOMIC ROLE OF GOVERNMENT

It was said earlier that ours is not a pure price economy but a mixed economy in which elements of government control are intermingled with market elements in organizing production and consumption. The economic role of government is now so important that Chapters 8 and 9 are devoted to it.

An outline of its influence can be briefly indicated here. Democratic countries are not satisfied with the answers to WHAT, HOW, and FOR WHOM given by a completely unrestrained market system. Such a system might dictate that certain people starve from lack of income and that others receive inadequate or excessive incomes. Therefore the citizenry through their government step in with expenditure to supplement the real or money incomes of some individuals. Thus, government may provide hospital beds for citizens or the needy with monthly allowances in times of unemployment or old age. Minimum standards of life are widespread modern goals.

PUBLIC SERVICES AND TAXES   More than this, government provides certain indispensable *public* services without which community life would be unthinkable and which by their nature cannot appropriately be left to private enterprises. Government came into existence once people realized, "Everybody's business is nobody's business." Obvious examples are the maintenance of national defense, of internal law and order, and the administration of justice and of contracts.[3]

By and large, in its expenditure of money, government is behaving exactly like any other large spender. By casting sufficient votes in the form of dollar bids in certain directions, it causes resources to flow there. The price system then takes over and performs much as if these were private rather than public needs.

Actually, most government expenditure is paid for out of taxes collected. It is here that an important element of *coercion* enters. It is true that the citizenry as a whole imposes the tax burden upon itself; also, each citizen is sharing in the collective benefits of government. But there is not the same close connection between benefits and tax payments as holds when the individual citizen puts a nickel into a gum machine or makes an ordinary purchase. I need not smoke Luckies or buy nylon stockings, but I must pay my taxes.

LAWS AND FIATS   Moreover, a second important form of coercion is involved in the universal custom of passing governmental laws: thou shalt not sell false weight, thou shalt not employ child labor, thou shalt not burn houses, thou shalt not pour out smoke from thy factory chimney, thou shalt not sell or smoke opium, thou shalt not charge more than the ceiling price for food, and so forth. This set of rules gives the framework within which private enterprise functions; it also modifies the direction of that functioning. Together with government expenditure and taxation, the decrees of government supplement the price system in determining the economic fate of the nation.

It would be fruitless to debate whether public enterprise or private enterprise is the more important—as fruitless as to debate heredity versus environment. Without either, our economic world would be an entirely different one.

Finally, as we shall see in Parts Two and Six, it is part of the government's function to help stabilize acute and chronic cycles of unemployment and inflation and to help achieve economic growth.

[3] Here is a later example of government service: lighthouses. These save lives and cargoes; but lighthouse keepers cannot reach out to collect fees from skippers. "So," says the advanced economic treatise, "we have here a divergence between *private* advantage and money cost [as seen by a man odd enough to try to make his fortune running a lighthouse business] and true *social* advantage and cost [as measured by lives and cargoes saved in comparison with (1) total costs of the lighthouse and (2) extra costs that result from letting one more ship look at the warning light]. Philosophers and statesmen have always recognized the necessary role of government in such cases of 'external-economy divergence between private and social advantage.'" Much more on this subject will come in Chapter 8 and elsewhere.

B. CAPITAL, DIVISION OF LABOR, AND MONEY

There are three further important features of modern economic society:

1. Modern advanced industrial technology rests upon the use of vast amounts of *capital:* elaborate machinery, large-scale factories and plants, stores and stocks of finished and unfinished materials. Our economy has the name "capitalism" because this capital, or "wealth," is primarily the private property of somebody—the capitalist.

2. The present-day economic system is characterized by an almost incredibly elaborate degree of *specialization* and intricate *division of labor.*

3. Ours is a system that makes extensive use of *money.* The flow of money is the lifeblood of our system. It also provides the measuring rod of values.

All these features are interrelated, each with the other and all with the price mechanism described in Section A of this chapter.

Thus we shall see that, without the great facility for trade and exchange which money provides, an elaborate division of labor would be impossible. Money and capital become related through credit activities of the banking system and through the organized capital markets upon which securities can be transformed into money by sale or vice versa. Of course, the relationship between the price mechanism and money is immediate and obvious.

■CAPITAL AND TIME

No one has trouble seeing that production of economic goods can result from use of such inputs as labor and land (including in the latter term natural resources generally). These are often called *"primary* factors of production," for the reason that neither land nor (these days) labor is regarded as a result of the economic process, but instead exists by virtue of physical and biological rather than economic factors.[4]

Capital, which is the word often used to refer to capital goods generally, is a different kind of production factor. A capital good differs from the primary factors in that it is *an input which is itself the output of the economy.*

> ■ Capital goods, then, represent *produced* goods that can be used as factor inputs for further production, whereas labor and land are primary factor inputs not usefully thought of as being themselves produced by the economic system.

Part Four will show that, just as wages and rent are the factor-prices of primary labor and land, the 4 or 6 or 10 per cent interest rate per annum can be usefully regarded as the factor-price that rewards and rations society's scarce supply of various

[4] Some qualifications will be evident. Land can sometimes be made by drainage or filling in; this is true of much of Chicago's lake front and Boston's Back Bay. Natural resources such as minerals are laid down by nature, but it may take much economic effort to locate, use, and process them. Therefore they come to have some of the properties of capital goods. Even if one abandons in the Western world a Malthusian theory of population, whereby people seem to be given a cost of production not unlike that of machines, one realizes that the process of education consists in investing in people, thereby making them more productive factors of production. When you see a medical-school graduate, you are in a certain sense looking at a chunk of capital.

capital goods and investment projects. Because an interest rate is a percentage per unit of time (per year or month or decade), it calls our attention to another way of looking at capital—a way that stresses the special relationship between capital and time.

Let us survey this important economic role of capital. If men had to work with their hands on barren soil, productivity and consumption would be very low indeed. Thus, when an anthropologist asked of mourning tribesmen who had died, they replied, "What is death? We have lost the needle!" Over a long time our own economy has amassed a vast stock of equipment, factories and housing, inventories, and drained land.

Men learned very early that the simple, direct methods of production can be improved upon by using *time-consuming indirect methods*. We who are inside the economic system are not conscious of how roundabout productive processes have become. An outside observer would be struck with the fact that almost no one in our system seems to be producing *finished* goods. Almost everyone is seen to do work of a preparatory nature, with final consumption a distant future goal. The farmer spends his time in fattening hogs, the truck driver in carrying them toward market, and the packer in advancing them further toward the last stage of consumption. A steel worker prepares pig iron, part of which will become a hammer to build a house; another bit will become part of a pig-iron furnace; which in turn will prepare pig iron to be used in making further hammers and more pig-iron furnaces; and so forth.

■ THE NEED TO FOREGO PRESENT CONSUMPTION

The fact that it takes time to get things started and synchronized is important. It explains why society does not automatically replace all direct processes by more productive indirect ones, and all indirect processes by still more indirect processes. The advantage in doing so is balanced by the initial disadvantage of having *to forego present consumption goods* by diverting resources from current production to uses that will bear fruit only after some time.

To the extent that people are willing to save—to abstain from present consumption and wait for future consumption—to that extent society can devote resources to new capital formation.[5] And to the extent that people are unconcerned about the future, they may at any time try to "dissave"—to snatch present pleasures at the expense of the future. How? By diverting resources away from the endless task of replacing and maintaining capital and to the job of producing extra present-day consumption goods. (Turn back to Fig. 2-6 of Chapter 2, page 23, to review the process of foregoing current consumption in favor of capital formation which adds to future production possibilities.)

We may summarize as follows: Economic activity is future-oriented. By the same token, current economic consumption is largely the consequence of past efforts. Current productive efforts, so to speak, produce for the future, in order to repay the past for present consumption. Also, in progressive societies a fraction of current consumption is sacrificed to production of net capital formation, which will increase future production.

---

[5] We shall later see that, *sometimes* in our modern monetary economy, the more people try to save, the less capital goods are produced; and paradoxically, that the more people spend on consumption, the greater the incentive for businessmen to build new factories and equipment.

■ CAPITAL AND PRIVATE PROPERTY

Physical capital goods are important in any economy because they help to increase productivity. This is as true of Soviet communism as it is of our own system. But there is one important difference. By and large, private individuals own the tools of production in our capitalistic system.

What is the exception in our system—government ownership of the means of production—is the rule in a socialized state where productive property is collectively owned. The returns from such real capital goods accrue to the government, not to individuals directly. The government then decides how such income is to be distributed among individuals. The communist government also decides how rapidly resources are to be invested in new capital formation: the government decides by how much *present* consumption should be curtailed in order to add to the total of factories, equipment, and productive stocks of goods that are necessary if *future* output is to rise.

In our system individual capitalists earn interest, dividends, and profits, or rents and royalties on the capital goods that they supply. Every patch of land and every bit of equipment has a deed, or "title of ownership," that belongs to somebody directly— or if it belongs to a corporation, then indirectly it belongs to the individual stockholders who own the corporation. Moreover, each kind of capital good has a money market value; hence each claim or title to ownership of a capital good also has a market value. A share of common stock of General Electric is quoted at a certain price, a New York Central bond at its price; a mortgage on a house is valued at some amount; the deed to a house is appraised by the real-estate market at some price; and so forth.

It should be pointed out that the government does own a good deal of the national real capital, e.g., Hoover Dam and submarines. In addition, its agencies, such as the Small Business Administration (SBA), are important sources of capital loans for private individuals and business.

Also, we note that the *legal property rights of an individual are relative and limited.* Society determines how much of his property a man may bequeath to his heirs and how much must go in inheritance and estate taxes to the government. Society determines how much the owners of public-utility companies—such as electric and gas firms—can earn and how they must run their business.

Even a man's home is not his castle. He must obey zoning laws and, if necessary, make way for a railroad or slum-clearance project. Interestingly enough, most of society's economic income cannot be capitalized into private property. Since slavery was abolished, human earning power is forbidden by law to be capitalized. A man is not even free to sell himself: he must rent himself at a wage.

■ SPECIALIZATION, EXCHANGE, AND DIVISION OF LABOR

Turn now to the second characteristic feature of the present-day economy. The economies of mass production upon which modern standards of living are based would not be possible if production took place in self-sufficient farm households or regions. *Specialization* of function permits each person and region to use to best advantage any peculiar differences in skill and resources. Even in a primitive economy men learn that, rather than have everyone do everything in a mediocre way, it is better to start a *division of labor*—better for fat men to do the fishing, lean men the hunting, and smart men to make the medicine, each exchanging his goods for the goods he needs.

Besides resting on interpersonal differences in ability, specialization accentuates and creates differences. Hunting makes a man thin and good at stalking prey; a region with no resources especially adapted to weaving may still develop skills which give it advantages in weaving. (Specialization may involve some costs, breeding half men—anemic clerks, brutish stokers—and producing social alienation.)

Finally, specialization may pay, even with no natural or acquired differences in skills: often in this way alone can a large enough volume of activity be reached to realize all the economies of large-scale production mentioned in the preceding chapter. Two identical Indian twins might find it better for one to make all bows and the other all arrows—even if they had to draw lots to see which would make which—because only in this way could each be making enough to warrant introducing improved techniques.

> To illustrate the increased productivity of specialization, Adam Smith provided the classical example of pinmaking. One man could at best make a few dozen imperfect pins per day. But when a small group of men are subdivided with respect to function so that each performs simple repetitive operations, they can turn out hundreds of thousands of perfect pins per day.[6]

Moreover, the simplification of function made possible by specialization lends itself to mechanization and the use of labor-saving capital. At the same time it avoids the wasteful duplication of tools that would be necessary if every man had to be a Jack-of-all-trades; and it also saves time lost in going from one job to another. The modern conveyer system of automobile assembly illustrates the efficiency of specialization. Today automation is the watchword.

[6]Smith recognized that specialization and division of labor were limited by the extent of the market, i.e., by the volume that can be sold. Smith would have approved of the European Common Market, which aims to lower the internal tariff barriers to trade and create a market big enough to support fruitful mass production and specialization.

The following passage describing the extent of specialization in meat slaughtering is often quoted: "It would be difficult to find another industry where division of labor has been so ingeniously and microscopically worked out. The animal has been surveyed and laid off like a map; and the men have been classified in over thirty specialties and twenty rates of pay, from 16 cents to 50 cents an hour. The 50-cent man is restricted to using the knife on the most delicate parts of the hide (floorman) or to using the ax in splitting the backbone (splitter); and, wherever a less skilled man can be slipped in at 18 cents, $18\frac{1}{2}$ cents, 20 cents, 21 cents, $22\frac{1}{2}$ cents, 24 cents, and so on, a place is made for him, and an occupation mapped out. In working on the hide alone there are nine positions, at eight different rates of pay. A 20-cent man pulls off the tail, a $22\frac{1}{2}$-cent man pounds off another part where good leather is not found, and the knife of the 40-cent man cuts a different texture and has a different 'feel' from that of the 50-cent man. Skill has become specialized to fit the anatomy. . . .

"The division of labor grew with the industry, following the introduction of the refrigerator car and the marketing of dressed beef, in the decade of the seventies. Before the market was widened by these revolutionizing inventions, the killing gangs were small, since only the local demands were supplied. But when the number of cattle to be killed each day increased to a thousand or more, an increasing gang or crew of men was put together; and the best men were kept at the most exacting work." From J. R. Commons, *Quarterly Journal of Economics*, vol. XIX, 1904, pp. 3, 6.

■ SPECIALIZATION AND INTERDEPENDENCE

Clearly, however, specialization and division of labor involve one serious problem—that of *interdependence*. A single-celled low form of life such as the amoeba or paramecium may not be particularly good at doing anything complicated, but it can live alone and like it. In higher animals such as man, every cell will die if once the heart cells fail. When all goes well, the extreme specialization of cells is very efficient—but at the cost of extreme interdependence.

In modern economic society this process is carried to the nth degree. No one man makes the smallest fraction of the commodities that he consumes. In medieval times the artisan made one article and exchanged it for many others. Today a worker produces not even a single good; he may make only shoe tongues or simply turn bolt 999 on the Ford assembly line. Such may be his whole life work. In exchange for doing this he will receive an income adequate to buy goods from all over the world.

Thus, specialization involves complete mutual dependence. A bank in Austria fails, and the natives in Fiji, who carry water in empty Standard Oil cans and clothe their infants in Pillsbury flour bags, lose their livelihood—yes, and may even starve. In the backwash of a strike or war, a breakdown in transportation and the economic fabric of exchange reveals how perilously modern economic life depends upon exchange. Would we, if we could, turn the clock back to a simpler and poorer life? Or can we keep the advantages of division of labor by finding policies that prevent breakdown?

■ BARTER VERSUS THE USE OF MONEY

Along with capital and specialization, money is a third aspect of modern economic life. Without the use of money our present division of labor and exchange would be impossible. To be sure, we could imagine a state of *barter*, where one kind of merchandise is traded directly for another. In primitive cultures it is not uncommon for food to be traded for weapons, or aid in the building of a house exchanged for aid in clearing a field.

Even in the most advanced industrial economies, if we strip exchange down to its barest essentials and peel off the obscuring layer of money, we find that trade between individuals or nations largely boils down to barter—transforming one good into another by exchange rather than by physical transmutation.

Barter represents a great improvement over a state of affairs in which every man had to be a Jack-of-all-trades and master of none. A great debt of gratitude is owed to the first two ape men who suddenly perceived that each could be made better off by giving up some of one good in exchange for some of another. Nevertheless, simple barter operates under grave disadvantages. An elaborate division of labor would be unthinkable without the introduction of a great new improvement—the use of money.

In all but the most primitive cultures men do not directly exchange one good for another. Instead they sell one good for money, and then use money to buy the goods they wish. At first glance this seems to complicate rather than simplify matters, to replace a single transaction by two transactions. Thus, if I have apples and want nuts, would it not be simpler to trade one for the other rather than to sell the apples for money and then use the money to buy nuts?

Actually, the reverse is the case: the two transactions are simpler than one. Ordinarily there are always people ready to buy apples and always some willing to sell—at a price—nuts; but it would be an unusual *coincidence* to find a person with tastes exactly opposite my own, with an eagerness to sell nuts and buy apples. Such a coincidence would be as unlikely as the chance of flipping a dozen "tails" in a row. Even if the unusual should happen—as occasionally it must—there is no guarantee that the desires of the two parties with respect to the exact *quantities* and terms of the exchange would coincide.

To use a classical economic phrase: Instead of there being a double coincidence of wants, there is likely to be a want of coincidence; so that, unless a hungry tailor happens to find an undraped farmer, who has both food and a desire for a pair of pants, neither can make a trade.

Money does simplify economic life. But do not for a moment forget that, for society as a whole, a mere increase in the total of money will not enable people to consume more than the real products technically producible with the economy's existent totals of labor, land, and capital. And money can cause financial crisis.

■ COMMODITY MONEY, PAPER MONEY, AND BANK MONEY

If we were to reconstruct history along hypothetical, logical lines, we should naturally follow the age of barter by the age of commodity money.

Historically a great variety of commodities has served at one time or another as a medium of exchange: cattle (from which comes the Latin stem of "pecuniary" and also the words "capital" and "chattel"), tobacco, leather and hides, furs, olive oil, beer or spirits, slaves or wives, copper, iron, gold, silver, rings, diamonds, wampum beads or shells, huge rocks and landmarks, and cigarette butts.

Each of the above has some advantages and disadvantages. Cattle are not divisible into small change; but while it is being hoarded, such "money" is likely to increase by reproduction, giving the lie to the doctrine of Aristotle that "money is barren." Beer does not improve with keeping, although wives may. Olive oil provides a nice liquid currency that is as minutely divisible as one wishes. Iron will rust and is of so little value that one would need a cart instead of a pocketbook. The value of a diamond is not proportional to weight but varies with its square; therefore, if cut up into pieces it loses value. The yearly additions to (by mining) or subtractions from (by use in teeth or jewelry) the accumulated stock of *precious metals* are small in percentage terms; so the total amounts and value of these substances do not fluctuate wildly. Silver has luster but will tarnish in air. Gold keeps its attractive sheen but, unless mixed with an alloy, is soft. Gold's high specific gravity makes detection of counterfeiting and admixture easy; but through most of historical time, gold's scarcity value has been so great per ounce as to require inordinately minute coins for ordinary purchases.

Most kinds of money tended once to be of some value or use for their own sake. Thus, even wampum had decorative uses, and paper money began as warehouse or mint receipts for so much metal. But the intrinsic usefulness of the money medium is now the least important thing about it.

The age of commodity money gives way to the age of paper money. The essence of money, its intrinsic nature, is typified by paper currency. *Money, as money rather than a commodity, is wanted not for its own sake but for the things it will buy!* We do not wish to use up money directly, but rather to use it by getting rid of it; even when we choose to use it by holding it, its value comes from the fact that we can spend it later on.

Money is an artificial, social convention. If for any reason a substance begins to be used as money, all people will begin to value it, even if they happen to be tee-totalers or vegetarians or disbelievers in its intrinsic usefulness. As long as things can be bought and sold for a given substance, people will be content to sell and buy with it. Paradox: money is accepted because it is accepted!

The use of paper currency (dollar bills, fives, tens, . . .) has become widespread because it has many conveniences as a medium of exchange. Currency is easily carried and stored away. By the printing of more or fewer zeros on the face value of the bill, a great or small amount of value can be embodied in a light, transportable medium of little bulk. By the use of decimal points it can be made as divisible as we wish. By careful engraving, the value of money can be made easily recognizable and protected from counterfeiting and adulteration. The fact that private individuals cannot create it at will in unlimited amounts keeps it scarce, i.e., an economic, and not, a free good.

■ **Given this limitation in supply, modern currencies have value, i.e., can buy things, independently of any gold, silver, or government backing. The public neither knows nor cares—and need not know or care—whether its currency is in the form of so-called "silver certificates," Federal Reserve notes, or copper or silver coin. So long as each form of money can be converted into any other at fixed terms, the best is as good as the worst.[7]**

Finally, along with the age of paper money, there is the age of bank money, or bank checking deposits. Today at least nine-tenths of all transactions, by value if not in number, take place by checks. A professor will have his salary paid directly into his bank account, after income taxes have already been withheld at the source by his employer. His rent or dentist bills will be paid by check; his gasoline and hotel bills, by a credit card. Except for petty cash for lunches and carfare, he needs little cash.

This completes the discussion of the way in which money performs its essential functions. In Part Two, we shall examine in detail the monetary and credit operations of banks and the government to see how they bear on fluctuations in prices, production, and employment.

---

[7] A century ago it was the exception rather than the rule for bank notes and coins to exchange for each other at par. Each had different prices which varied from day to day, so that it was necessary for storekeepers to keep daily lists of values; and it became a profession in itself to change money, buying and selling it at a profit.

SUMMARY

A. PRICING AND THE MIXED ECONOMY

1 ■

The price mechanism, working through supply and demand in competitive markets, operates to answer the three fundamental problems of economic organization in our mixed private enterprise system. The system is not perfect, but it works to solve the WHAT, HOW, and FOR WHOM.

2 ■

The dollar votes of people affect prices of goods; these prices serve as guides for the amounts of the different goods to be produced. When people demand more of a good, a competitive businessman can make a profit by expanding production of that good. Under perfect competition, he must find the cheapest method of production, using labor, land, and other factors that are relatively cheap and economizing on the use of relatively expensive factors; otherwise, he will incur losses and be eliminated.

At the same time that the WHAT and HOW problems are being resolved by prices, so is the problem of FOR WHOM. The distribution of income is determined by competitive bidding up or down of factor-prices—wages of each kind of labor, rents of land, royalties of books, and various returns to capital. Anyone who possesses fertile well-located land or widely admired crooning ability will be supplied with many dollar votes for his use in the markets for consumer goods. Anyone without property or education and with skills that the market cares little about will receive a low annual income.

3 ■

Our economy is mixed in two senses: Governments modify private initiative; monopolistic elements condition the working of perfect competition.

B. CAPITAL, DIVISION OF LABOR, AND MONEY

4 ■

Capital goods—produced inputs such as machinery, housing, and inventories of goods in process—add tremendously to a nation's output. Roundabout, time-consuming methods take time to get started; hence, adding to the stock of capital goods requires a temporary sacrifice of present consumption.

5 ■

Under capitalism, capital goods are owned as private property; the incomes they produce belong to their owners. Under communism, the state owns capital goods. In no system are private-property rights unlimited.

6 ■

Specialization and division of labor characterize modern economies. This raises productivity, but at the cost of interdependence.

7 ■

Without exchange, division of labor could not be highly developed. Simple barter is inefficient and tends to be superseded by the use of money. Commodity money is in turn superseded by paper money and bank money. Unlike other economic goods, money is valued because of social convention; we value it indirectly for what it buys rather than for its direct utility.

QUESTIONS FOR DISCUSSION

1. During World War II, did we let consumers' dollar demand determine their sugar consumption? Why not? What did?

2. Could supply and demand for labor work out to give salesmen with a "gift of gab" five times the income of skilled surgeons? At other times could it operate to give surgeons twice the income of accountants?

3. Do you think that an "instinct of craftsmanship" and a "sense of social responsibility" could ever replace the "profit motive"? Read the chapter head's Invisible Hand quotation aloud. What do you think Smith is trying to say there? And here: "I have never known much good done by those who affected to trade for the public good." Dissect the Zig-Zag parable.

4. List a number of cases where the government modifies the working of an automatic price system. List cases where monopoly elements intervene.

5. Assuming it cannot borrow abroad, what must China do if it wishes to become an efficient industrialized nation in the next few generations?

6. "Lincoln freed the slaves. With one pen stroke he destroyed much of the capital the South had been able to accumulate over the years." Comment.

7. Would ice cubes make a good unit of money? What would?

8. What are some of the advantages of using checks on bank deposits rather than paper currency or metal coins? List any disadvantages.

9. Review your understanding of the following concepts:

mixed economy

demand-and-supply markets for
   goods and for factors of
   production

profit seeking, cost minimizing

price "rationing" **?**

perfect and imperfect competition

roundaboutness of production

abstinence and waiting, foregoing

dissaving by failure to maintain
   and replace capital goods

specialization, interdependence

division of labor, exchange

barter versus money pricing

commodity, paper, and bank-deposit
   money

4 Supply and Demand: The Bare Elements

YOU CAN MAKE EVEN A PARROT INTO A LEARNED POLITICAL ECONOMIST—ALL HE MUST LEARN ARE THE TWO WORDS "SUPPLY" AND "DEMAND." ANONYMOUS

EVERY SHORT STATEMENT ABOUT ECONOMICS IS MISLEADING (WITH THE POSSIBLE EXCEPTION OF MY PRESENT ONE). ALFRED MARSHALL

Chapters 2 and 3 introduced the three basic problems every economy must face. (1) WHAT shall be produced of the great variety of possible goods and services, and in precisely what quantities? (2) How shall society combine its different productive factors—land, labor, and so forth—to produce each good? (3) FOR WHOM shall goods be produced—that is, how shall the national product be distributed among the different people with their different labor skills and ownerships of land and capital goods?

Chapter 2 showed that a variety of systems could be thought of to solve these three problems. WHAT, How, and FOR WHOM might be determined by custom, instinct, or even by centralized, collective fiats. But Chapter 3 indicated that the modern mixed economy relies primarily on none of these to solve its basic problems. Instead it relies on a system of markets and prices.

The consumer is, so to speak, the king. Or rather, with every man a king, each is a voter who uses his money as votes to get the things done that he wants done. His votes must compete with other men's votes; and the people with the most votes end up with the most influence on what gets produced and on where those goods go.

Now our task is to see just how this spending of money votes—this system of "consumer sovereignty"—takes place.

■ THE MARKET MECHANISM

Let us take an example. You wake up this morning with an urge for a new pair of shoes. You would not think of saying, "I'll go down to the city hall and vote for the mayor most likely to give me a new pair of shoes. Of course, I mean a new pair of size 9, soft-leather, dark-brown shoes."

Or, to take an actual case from history, suppose men begin to get prosperous enough to afford meat every day rather than having to fill up on potatoes. How does their desire to substitute meat for potatoes get translated into action? What politician do they tell? What orders does he in turn give to farmers to move from Maine to Texas? How much extra rent does he decide will be needed to bribe landlords to take land from potato production to cattle grazing? And how does he ensure that people get what they want of pork and lamb as well as beef? And who is to get the choice cuts?

Why belabor the obvious? Everyone knows it never worked itself out that way at all. What happened was this. Consumers began to buy less potatoes and more meat. That raised the price of meat and cut the price of potatoes. So there resulted losses to the potato growers and gains to the ranchers. Ranch labor found it could hold out for higher wages, and many a potato digger quit his job for a better-paying job elsewhere. In time, the higher meat prices brought larger productions of beef, pork, and lamb. And the different parts of the cow—its horn, hide, liver, kidneys, choice tenderloin, and tough ribs—got auctioned off for what each part would bring.

To show that it is not some important government official or businessman who sets relative prices, see what actually happened when science discovered that liver was good for anemia. Kidneys, for reasons somewhat obscure, were previously dearer than liver. In fact, according to the records, you could hardly give liver away before this discovery. Now go to the butcher shop: price liver; and, if you can find any, also price kidneys. A veritable revolution has taken place; the price of liver has risen greatly relative to the price of kidneys, so as to ration the limited supply of liver among the eager demanders for it—all through the impersonal workings of supply and demand.

Similar revolutions are taking place in the economic market place all the time. As people's desires and needs change, as engineering methods change, as supplies of natural resources and other productive factors change, the market place registers changes in the prices and the quantities sold of commodities and productive services—of tea, sugar, and beef; of land, labor, and machines. There exists a *system of prices*, a concept that is far from obvious.

The purpose of this chapter is to show how supply and demand work themselves out in the competitive market for one particular good. We shall define a demand curve and then a supply curve. Finally, we shall see how the market price reaches its competitive equilibrium, where these two curves intersect—where the forces of demand and supply are just in balance.

A demand schedule relates quantity demanded to price:

	(1) PRICE ($ PER BU.) P	(2) QUANTITY DE- MANDED, MILLION BU. PER MONTH Q
A	$5	9
B	4	10
C	3	12
D	2	15
E	1	20

TABLE 4-1. DEMAND SCHEDULE FOR WHEAT. At each market price, there will at any time be a definite quantity of wheat that people will want to demand.

At a lower price, the quantity demanded will go up—as more people substitute it for other goods and feel they can afford to gratify their less important wants for wheat.

■ THE DEMAND SCHEDULE

Let us start with demand. It is commonly observed: The quantity of a good that people will buy at any one time depends on price; the higher the price charged for an article, the less the quantity of it people will be willing to buy; and, other things being equal, the lower its market price, the more units of it will be demanded.

> ■ Thus there exists at any one time a definite relation between the market price of a good (such as wheat) and the quantity demanded of that good. This relationship between price and quantity bought is called the "demand schedule," or "demand curve."

Table 4-1 gives an example of a hypothetical demand schedule. At any price, such as $5 per bushel, there is a definite quantity of wheat that will be demanded by all the consumers in the market—in this case 9 (million) bushels per month. At a lower price, such as $4, the quantity bought is even greater, being 10 (million) units. From Table 4-1 we can determine the *quantity demanded at any price*, by comparing Column (2) with Column (1).

A downward-sloping curve depicts demand:

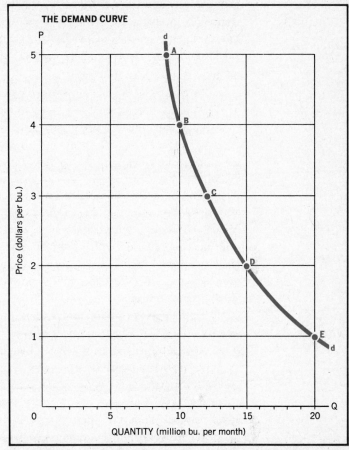

FIG. 4-1. Prices are measured on the vertical axis, and quantities demanded on the horizontal axis. Each pair of *Q*, *P* numbers from Table 4-1 is plotted here as a point, and a smooth curve passed through the points gives us the demand curve.

The fact that *dd* goes downward and to the right illustrates the very important "law of downward-sloping demand."

■ THE DEMAND CURVE

The numerical data of Table 4-1 can be given a graphic interpretation also. The vertical scale in Fig. 4-1 represents the various alternative prices of wheat, measured in dollars per bushel. The horizontal scale measures the quantity of wheat (in terms of bushels) that will be demanded per month.

A city corner is located as soon as we know its street and avenue; a ship's position is located as soon as we know its latitude and longitude. Similarly, to plot a point on this diagram, we must have two coordinate numbers: a price and a quantity. For our first point A, corresponding to $5 and 9 million bushels, we move upward 5 units and then over to the right 9 units. A dot marks the spot A. To get the next dot, at B, we go up only 4 units and over to the right 10 units. The last dot is shown by E. Through the dots we draw a smooth curve, marked *dd*.

This picturization of the demand schedule is called the "demand curve." Note that quantity and price are *inversely* related, *Q* going up when *P* goes down. The curve slopes downward, going from northwest to southeast. This important property is given a name: the *law of downward-sloping demand.* This law is true of practically all commodities: wheat, electric razors, cotton, ethyl gasoline, cornflakes, and theater tickets.

■ *The law of downward-sloping demand:* When the price of a good is raised (at the same time that all other things are held constant), less of it is demanded. Or, what is the same thing: If a greater quantity of a good is put on the market, then—other things being equal—it can be sold only at a lower price.

■ REASONS FOR LAW OF DOWNWARD-SLOPING DEMAND

This law is in accordance with common sense and has been known in at least a vague way since the beginning of recorded history. The reasons for it are not hard to identify. When the price of wheat is sky high, only rich men will be able to afford it; the poor will have to make do with rye bread, just as they still must do in poorer lands. When the price is still high but not quite so high as before, persons of moderate means who also happen to have an especially great liking for white bread will now be coaxed into buying some wheat.

Thus a first reason for the validity of the law of downward-sloping demand comes from the fact that *lowering prices brings in new buyers.*

Not quite so obvious is a second, equally important, reason for the law's validity: namely, each reduction of price may coax out some *extra purchases by each of the good's consumers;* and—what is the same thing—a rise in price may cause any one of us to buy less. Why does my quantity demanded tend to fall as price rises? For two main reasons. When the price of a good rises, I naturally try to *substitute* other goods for it (tea for coffee, for example). Also, when a price goes up, I find myself really poorer than I was; and I will naturally cut down on my consumption of most normal goods when I feel poorer and have less real *income.*

Here are examples of cases where I buy more of a good as it becomes more plentiful and its price drops. When water is very dear, I demand only enough of it to drink. Then when its price drops, I buy some to wash with. At still lower prices, I resort to still other uses; finally, when it is really very cheap, I water flowers and use it lavishly for any possible purpose. (Note once again that someone poorer than I will probably begin to use water to wash his car only at a lower price than that at which I buy water for that purpose. Since market demand is the sum of all different people's demands, what does this mean? It means that even after *my* demand stops expanding very much with price decreases, the *total* bought in the market may still expand as new uses for *new people* come into effect.)

To confirm your understanding of the demand concept, imagine there is an increase in demand for wheat brought about by a boom in people's incomes or by a great rise in the market price of the competing rye, or simply by an increased desire of people to spend their money on wheat. Show that this *shifts* the whole demand curve in Fig. 4-1 rightward, and hence upward; pencil in such a new curve and label it *d'd'* to distinguish it from the old *dd* curve. Note that such an increase in demand means that more will now be bought at each price—as can be verified by carefully reading off points from the new curve and filling in a new *Q* column for Table 4-1.

■ THE SUPPLY SCHEDULE

Let us now turn from demand to supply. The demand schedule related prices and the amounts *consumers* wish to buy. How is the supply schedule defined?

■ By the *supply schedule,* or *curve,* is meant the relation between market prices and the amounts of the good that *producers* are willing to supply.

Table 4-2 illustrates the supply schedule for wheat, and Fig. 4-2 plots it as a supply curve. Unlike the demand curve, the supply curve for wheat normally rises upward and to the right, from southwest to northeast.

At a higher price of wheat, farmers will take acreage out of corn cultivation and put it into wheat. In addition, each can now afford the cost of more fertilizer, more labor, more machinery, and can even afford to grow extra wheat on poorer land. All this tends to increase output at higher prices.

As will be seen in Part Three, our old friend the law of diminishing returns provides one strong reason why the supply curve would slope upward. If society wants more wine, more and more labor will have to be added to the same limited hill sites suitable for producing wine grapes. Even if this industry is too small to affect the gen-

The supply schedule, relating price to quantity produced, can also be plotted as a curve:

	POSSIBLE PRICES ($ PER BU.)	QUANTITY SELLERS WILL SUPPLY, MILLION BU. PER MONTH
A	$5	18
B	4	16
C	3	12
D	2	7
E	1	0

TABLE 4-2. SUPPLY SCHEDULE FOR WHEAT. At each *P*, there is listed the *Q* that producers will want to bring to market.

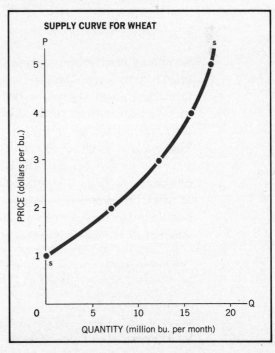

FIG. 4-2. Each *Q, P* pair of numbers in Table 4-2 is here plotted as a point. A smooth curve passed through them gives the upward-sloping supply curve *ss*.

Equilibrium market price is at the point where supply and demand match:

	(1) POSSIBLE PRICES ($ PER BU.)	(2) QUANTITY DEMANDED, MILLION BU. PER MONTH	(3) QUANTITY SUPPLIED MILLION BU. PER MONTH	(4) PRESSURE ON PRICE
A	$5	9	18	Falling
B	4	10	16	Falling
C	3	12	12	Neutral
D	2	15	7	Rising
E	1	20	0	Rising

TABLE 4-3. SUPPLY AND DEMAND SCHEDULES FOR WHEAT. Only at the equilibrium price of $3 will quantity demanded by consumers equal quantity supplied by producers. At any lower price, amount demanded would exceed amount supplied; at any higher price, amount supplied would exceed amount demanded.

eral wage rate for labor, each new man will—according to the law of diminishing returns—be adding less and less extra product; and hence the necessary cost to coax out additional product will have to rise. (Cost and returns are opposite sides of the same coin, as will be shown later.[1])

To depict an increase in supply, recall that this means an increase in the amounts that will be supplied at each different price. Now if you pencil the new supply curve into Fig. 4-2, you will see that it has shifted *rightward;* but for an upward-sloping supply curve, this change means the new $s's'$ curve will have shifted rightward and *downward* (not rightward and upward as in the case of a shifted downward-sloping demand curve). To verify that $s's'$ does depict an increase in supply, fill in a new column in Table 4-2 by reading off points from the new diagram carefully.

■ EQUILIBRIUM OF SUPPLY AND DEMAND

Let us now combine our analysis of demand and supply to see how competitive market price is determined. This combining is done in Table 4-3. Thus far we have been considering all prices as possible. We have said, "If price is so and so, sales will be so and so; if price is such and such, sales will be such and such; and so forth." But to which level will price *actually* go? And how much will then be produced and consumed? The supply schedule alone cannot tell us. Neither can the demand schedule alone.

Let us do what an auctioneer would do, i.e., proceed by trial and error. Can situation A in Table 4-3, with wheat selling for $5 per bushel, prevail for any period of time? The answer is a clear No. At $5, the producers will be supplying 18 (million) bushels to the market every month [Column (3)]. But the amount demanded by consumers will be only 9 (million) bushels per month [Column (2)]. As stocks of wheat

[1] While the exceptions to the law of downward-sloping demand are few enough to be unimportant in practice, we shall encounter in Part Three some interesting exceptions to the upward-sloping supply curve. Thus, suppose that a family farmer produces wheat and its price rises so much as to give him a much higher income. With wheat so lucrative, he is at first tempted to *substitute* some of his leisure time to produce more of it. But might there not reasonably come a time when he feels comfortable enough at his higher *income* to be able to afford to take things easier and work less?

pile up, competitive sellers will cut the price a little. Thus, as Column (4) shows, price will tend to fall; but it will not fall indefinitely to zero.

To understand this further, let us try the point E with price equal to only $1 per bushel. Can that price persist? Again, obviously not, for a comparison of Columns (2) and (3) shows that consumption will exceed production *at that price*. Storehouses will begin to be emptied; disappointed demanders who cannot get wheat will tend to bid the price up. This upward pressure on price is shown by Column (4)'s rising arrow.

We could go on to try other prices, but by now the answer is obvious.

■ The equilibrium price, i.e., the only price that can last, is that at which the amount *willingly* supplied and amount *willingly* demanded are equal. Competitive equilibrium must be at the intersection point of supply and demand curves.

Only at C, with a price of $3, will the amount demanded by consumers, 12 (million) bushels per month, exactly equal the amount supplied by producers, 12 (million). Price is at equilibrium, just as an olive at the bottom of a cocktail glass is at equilibrium, because there is no tendency for it to rise or fall. (Of course, this stationary price may not be reached at once. There may have to be an initial period of trial and error, of oscillation around the right level, before price finally settles down in balance.)

Figure 4-3 shows the same equilibrium in pictorial form. The supply and demand curves, superimposed on the same diagram, cross at only one intersection point. This point C represents the equilibrium price and quantity.

The equilibrium market price is where demand and supply curves intersect:

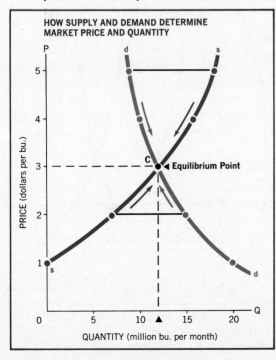

HOW SUPPLY AND DEMAND DETERMINE
MARKET PRICE AND QUANTITY

FIG. 4-3. At the C equilibrium intersection, the amount supplied just matches the amount demanded.

At any lower P, the excess of demand will force P back up; and at any P higher than the equilibrium, the amount supplied will be excessive and P will be forced back down to the equilibrium level.

At a higher price, the black bar shows the *excess* of supply over demand. The arrows point downward to show the direction in which price will move because of the competition of *sellers*. At a price lower than the $3 equilibrium price, the black bar shows that demand surpasses supply. Consequently, the eager bidding of *buyers* requires us to point the arrow indicators upward to show the pressure that they are exerting on price. Only at the point C will there be a balancing of forces and a stationary maintainable price.

Such is the essence of the doctrine of supply and demand.

■ EFFECT OF A SHIFT IN SUPPLY OR DEMAND

Now we can put the supply and demand apparatus to work. Gregory King, an English writer of the seventeenth century, noticed that when the harvest was bad, food rose in price; and when it was plentiful, farmers got a lower price. Let us try to explain what happens by our diagrams.

Figure 4-4(a) shows how a spell of bad weather reduces the amount that farmers will supply at each and every market price and thereby displaces the equilibrium point E. The *ss* curve has shifted to the left and has become *s's'*. The demand curve has not changed. Where does the new supply curve *s's'* intersect *dd*? Plainly at *E'*, the new equilibrium price where demand and the new reduced supply have again come into balance. Naturally, P has risen. And because of the law of downward-sloping demand, Q has gone down.

Diagrams show effects on price of demand and supply shifts:

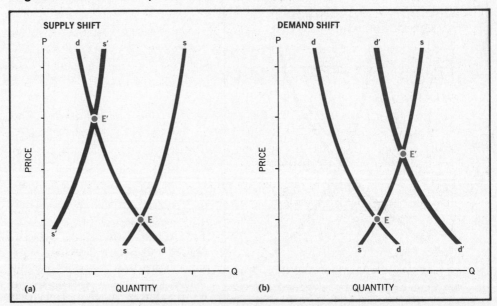

FIG. 4-4(a). If supply shifts leftward for any reason, the equilibrium-price intersection will travel up the demand curve, giving higher P and lower Q.

FIG. 4-4(b). If demand shifts rightward, the equilibrium will travel up the supply curve.

Suppose the supply curve, because of good weather and fertilizers, had increased instead. Draw in a new equilibrium E'' with lower P and higher Q.

Our apparatus will help us also analyze the effect of an increase in demand. Suppose that rising family incomes make everyone want more wheat. Then at each unchanged P, greater Q will now be demanded. The demand curve will shift rightward to $d'd'$. Figure 4-4(b) shows the resulting travel up the supply curve as enhanced demand raises competitive price.

■ TWO STUMBLING BLOCKS

It is well to pause here to consider two minor sources of possible confusion. These have puzzled students of economics in all generations. The first point deals with the important fact that in drawing up a demand schedule or curve, one always insists that "other things must be equal." The second deals with the exact sense in which demand and supply are equal in equilibrium.

"OTHER THINGS EQUAL" To draw up a demand schedule for wheat, we vary the price of wheat and observe what would happen to its quantity bought *at any one period of time in which no other factors are allowed to change so as to becloud our experiment.* Specifically, this means that, as we change wheat's P, we must not at the same time change family income or the price of a competing product such as rye or anything else that would tend to *shift* the demand schedule for wheat. Why? Because, like any scientist who wants to isolate the effects of one causal factor, we must try to vary only one thing at a time. True enough, in economics we cannot perform controlled experiments in a laboratory, and we can rarely hold other things constant in making statistical observations of economic magnitudes. This limitation on our ability to experiment empirically in economics makes it all the more important *to be clear in our logical thinking,* so that we may hope to recognize and evaluate important tendencies—such as the effect of P on Q demanded—when other tendencies are likely to be impinging on the situation at the same time.

The case of demand shift in Fig. 4-4(b) can illustrate this common fallacy based upon a failure to respect the rule that other things must be held equal in defining a demand curve. Suppose that the supply curve shifts little or not at all. But suppose the demand curve shifts up to $d'd'$ in good times when jobs are plentiful and people have the incomes to buy more wheat; and suppose in the more depressed phase of the business cycle, demand always shifts down to dd. Now take a piece of graph paper and plot what would actually be recorded in the statistics of the wheat market.

In good times you would record the equilibrium point E', and in bad times the equilibrium point E. Take a ruler and join the points E and E'. The fallacy to be avoided like the plague is expressed as follows: "I have disproved the law of downward-sloping demand; for note that when P was high, so was Q—as shown by E'. And when P was lowered, instead of that change increasing Q, it actually lowered Q—as shown by E. My straight line joining E and E' represents an upward-sloping, not a downward-sloping, demand curve; so I have refuted a basic economic law."

Being alerted beforehand, one detects the fallacy in this argument. For at the same time that P went up, other things were *not* held constant; rather, income was also raised. The tendency for a rise in P to choke off purchases was more than masked by the countertendency of rising income to raise purchases. Instead of testing our economic law by moving *along* the demand curve, the beginner has measured changes that result from the *shift* of the demand curve.

Why is this bad scientific method? Because it leads to absurd results such as this: "On the basis of my revolutionary refutation of the law of downward-sloping demand, I confidently predict that, in the years when the harvest is especially big, wheat will sell for a higher rather than a lower price." Not only will such reasoning lead to absurd predictions that would lose fortunes for a speculator or miller, but it also fails to recognize other important economic relationships—such as the fact that, when family incomes go up, demand curves for goods such as wheat tend to shift rightward.

MEANING OF EQUILIBRIUM   The second stumbling block is a more subtle one, less likely to arise but not so easy to dispel. It is suggested by the following.

"How can you say that the equality of supply and demand determines a particular equilibrium price? For, after all, *the amount one man sells is precisely what another man buys.* The quantity bought must always equal the quantity sold, no matter what the price; for that matter, whether or not the market is in equilibrium, a statistician who records the Q bought and the Q sold will always find these necessarily identical, each being a different aspect of exactly the same thing."

The answer to this must be phrased something like this:

You are quite right that measured Q bought and measured Q sold must be identical as recorded by a statistician. But the important question is this: At which P will the amount that consumers are *willing to go on buying* be just matched by the amount that producers are *willing to go on selling?* At such a price, where there is equality between the *scheduled* amounts that suppliers and demanders want to go on buying and selling, and only at such an equilibrium P, will there be no tendency for price to rise or fall.

At any other price, such as the case where P is above the intersection of supply and demand, it is a trivial fact that whatever goods change hands will show a statistical identity of measured amount bought and sold. But this measured identity does not in the least deny that suppliers are eager at so high a price to sell more than demanders will continue to buy; and that this excess of scheduled supply over scheduled demand will put downward pressure on price until it has finally reached that equilibrium level where the two curves intersect.

At this equilibrium intersection, and there alone, will everybody be happy: the auctioneer, the suppliers, the demanders—as well as the patient statistician, who always reports an identity between the measured amounts bought and sold.[2]

■ WHAT SUPPLY AND DEMAND ACCOMPLISHED: GENERAL EQUILIBRIUM

Having seen how supply and demand work, let us take stock of what has been accomplished. The scarce goods of society have been rationed out among the possible users

[2]A similar question of measured identity versus scheduled intersection could arise in the discussion of income determination in Chapter 12.

of them. Who did the rationing: a board? a committee? No. The auctioneering mechanism of competitive price did the rationing. It was a case of "rationing by the purse."

FOR WHOM goods are destined was *partially* determined by who was willing to pay for them. If you had the money votes, you got the wheat. If you did not, you went without. Or if you had the money votes, but preferred not to spend them on wheat, you did without. The most important needs or desires for goods—if backed by cash!—got fulfilled.

The WHAT question was being *partially* answered at the same time. The rise in market price was the signal to coax out a higher supply of wheat. It was the signal for men and other scarce resources to move into the wheat-production industry from alternative uses.

Even the How question was being *partially* decided in the background. For with wheat prices now high, farmers could afford expensive tractors and fertilizers and could bring poorer soils into use.

Why the word "partially" in this description of how the competitive market helped solve the three problems? Because this wheat market is but one market of many. What is happening in the corn and rye markets also counts; and what is happening in the market for fertilizer, men, and tractors obviously matters much.

■ We must note that the pricing problem is one that involves *interdependent markets,* not just the "partial equilibrium" of a single market.[3]

There are, so to speak, auctioneers operating simultaneously in the many different markets—wheat, corn, fertilizer, and land; labor, wool, cotton, mutton, and rayon; bond, stock, and personal loans. Each ends up at the equilibrium intersection point of his supply and demand schedules—wheat, corn, fertilizer prices, and land rent; labor wage, wool, cotton, mutton, and rayon prices; bond price and its interest yield, stock prices and dividend yield, interest charges on personal loans.

No market is an island unto itself: when wool P rises (because, say, of sheep disease abroad), it pulls up the P's of domestic labor, fertilizer, and land needed for expanded wool output; and it raises the P's of rival goods like cotton that some demanders will now turn to; it might well lower the P of wool spinners and of suit-company stock shares, since the latter must now pay more for their raw materials and may bid less eagerly for spinning labor.

The new general-equilibrium set of interdependent prices adjusts to the new situation. The price system meets the problem posed by the basic definition of eco-

---

[3] The alert reader will not have to be reminded that the competitive market gives goods to those with money votes and does so efficiently. But the distribution of the money votes depends on for how much you can sell your labor and property in competitive and imperfectly competitive factor markets, and it is affected in an important way by (1) how lucky you are, (2) how lucky your parents and in-laws were, and (3) the advantages and disadvantages of your genetic and acquired skills and aptitudes. If a student writes on a final exam, "FOR WHOM is decided (in part) by how people decide to use their money votes," he is not wrong. Indeed, he gets possibly 50 per cent credit. However, he will not get the other 50 per cent unless he adds, "The basic problem of FOR WHOM is the process by which the money votes *themselves* get determined, which is primarily not by supply and demand in a single good's market, but by supply and demand in the labor, land, and other interdependent factor markets of Part Four and factor supplies depend much on distribution of ownership."

nomics: the study of (1) how *scarce means with alternative uses*—limited land and labor that can be switched from one industry to another—are allocated, and (2) how to *achieve ends or goals*—as prescribed by the tastes for wool, nylon, food, and housing of sovereign consumers, possessed of factors of production that give them money-income votes for the market place. Each separate market, with its supply and demand curves, is doing its bit toward creating the general-equilibrium set of prices, which in our society resolves the basic economic problems of WHAT, HOW, and FOR WHOM.

■ PERFECTION AND IMPERFECTIONS OF COMPETITION

Our curves of supply and demand strictly apply only to a *perfectly competitive* market where some kind of *standardized* commodity such as wheat is being auctioned by an organized exchange that registers transactions of *numerous* buyers and sellers. The Board of Trade in Chicago is one such example, and the cotton exchanges in New York or Liverpool are others. The New York Stock Exchange, while it does not auction goods and commodities or productive services rendered by factors of production, does provide a market where shares of common stocks such as those of General Motors and Royal Dutch Petroleum are auctioned at each moment of the working day. Many corporate bonds are also bought and sold in the bond division of the Exchange.

The economists' curves of supply and demand are important ways of idealizing the behavior of such markets. They do not pretend to give an accurate microscopic description of what is going on during each changing moment in such a market place, as various brokers mill around on the trading floor while frantically giving hand and voice signals to the specialist who serves as auctioneer for each grain or company stock. Nonetheless, the tools of supply and demand do summarize the important average relationships resulting over a period of time from such organized trading.

As far as these fundamental tools of supply and demand are concerned, it matters little what kind of exchange the goods are traded on: whether hand signals or slips of paper are used; whether the auction is of the familiar kind, where the auctioneer calls out a *minimum* starting price and accepts higher and higher bids until only one high bidder is left to get the Renoir painting in question; whether there is a "Dutch auction," where the price starts high instead of low and moves downward at stated time intervals until an eager buyer, fearing that someone else will get in the bid first, finally gives the first bid and gets the merchandise; or whether the auctioneer asks for written bids and offers in order to be able to make up a table or chart like those of Table 4-3 and Fig. 4-3 and find the equilibrium intersection at one fell swoop.

Indeed, the market need not have a single auctioneer: all the bidding may well take place by telephone calls, as in the case of the market for United States government bonds, which is a much more perfect one than the corporate bond market on the floor of the New York Stock Exchange. The same can be true of stocks listed on the so-called "over-the-counter market," a market which is conducted throughout the country completely by telephone and by daily mailing of price-quotation lists by different brokers; for example, an important stock such as Bank of America, which is listed on this market, may actually behave more nearly like our competitive model than does some stock *inactively* traded on the floor of the New York Stock Exchange.

Needless to say, the requirements for absolutely perfect competition are as hard to meet as the requirements for a perfectly frictionless pendulum in physics. We can approach closer and closer to perfection but never quite reach it; yet this fact need not do serious damage to the usefulness of our employing the idealized concept. Actually, it matters little to the economic scientist that different grades of wheat will call for slight variations from the quoted market prices. It matters little, too, that dealers in foreign exchange, whose bids and offers determine whether the price of an English pound (or French franc) will be $2.79 rather than $2.80 (or 20.3 cents rather than 20.4 cents), use the telephone and cable rather than a trading floor with auctioneer or specialist dealer presiding. Nor does it matter in the case of standardized cotton goods, so-called "gray goods," that they are sold and bought in an informal way by many competing firms: so long as there are *numerous* buyers and sellers on each side, *well-informed* about quality and about each others' prices and having no reason to discriminate in favor of one merchant rather than another and no reason to expect that variations in their *own* bids and offers will have an *appreciable effect* upon the prevailing market price—so long as all this is true, the behavior of price and quantity can be expected to be much like that predicted by our supply and demand curves.

The various diagrams in Fig. 4-5 illustrate how the tools of supply and demand might be used to give a good approximate description of various economic situations other than that of a staple commodity such as wheat: there is pictured a competitive market for cotton gray goods; for a factor of production such as newly graduating

Supply and demand tools have many applications:

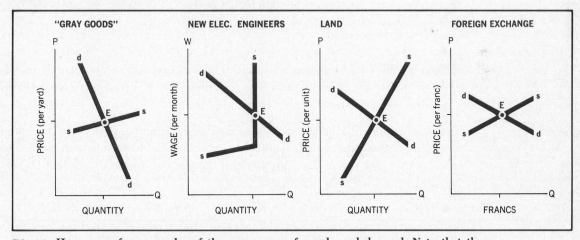

FIG. 4-5. Here are a few examples of the many uses of supply and demand. Note that these diagrams have straight lines rather than the curved lines of previous figures: in connection with supply and demand and many other diagrams, the economist often makes such simplified drawings merely because the eye takes them in rapidly; usually, this is a tolerably good approximation to the true empirical curves, but when this is not so, it is easy to modify the straight lines. (EXAMPLE: The supply of graduating electrical engineers is a relatively fixed number, and this is depicted in the vertical supply line in the second diagram; however, it is an exaggeration in view of the fact that, as the wage gets low enough, some graduates will take jobs in other fields and some will go to graduate school—which is the reason why the *ss* curve bends to the southwest at low wages.) Can you interpret the four cases?

electrical engineers, whose price is represented by a wage per month; for a bond or capital asset such as a corner lot of land; and finally, as will be explained later in the discussion of international trade in Part Five, a foreign exchange market in which the dollar price of an English pound, a French franc, or a single unit of any other foreign currency is determined by the bids of those who need foreign currency and by the offers of those who want to sell such currencies to get American dollars.[4]

To be sure, not all today's markets are anywhere near to being perfectly competitive in the economist's sense. We shall see later, in Part Three, that elements of monopoly power or of market imperfection may enter in, and these imperfections will require us to modify the competitive model. After we have learned how to handle such cases, we shall recognize that the world is a blend of competition and imperfections—which means that the competitive analysis, properly qualified, is still an indispensable tool for interpreting reality.

SUMMARY

1 ■

A basic problem of economics is how the mechanism of market pricing grapples with the triad of problems WHAT, HOW, and FOR WHOM.

2 ■

By the demand schedule we mean a table showing the different quantities of a good that people will—at any time and with other things held equal—want to buy at each different price. This relationship, when plotted on a diagram, is the demand curve.

3 ■

With negligible exceptions, the higher the price the lower will be the quantity demanded, and vice versa. Almost all commodities obey this "law of downward-sloping demand."

4 ■

The supply curve or schedule gives the relations between the prices and the quantities of a good that producers will—other things equal—be willing to sell. Most usually, supply curves rise upward and to the right: diminishing returns means that higher P is needed to coax out higher-cost extra Q.

5 ■

Market equilibrium can take place only at a price where the quantities supplied and demanded are *equal*. At any price higher than the equilibrium intersection of the supply and demand curves, the quantity producers will want to go on supplying will exceed

---

[4]Question 9 at the end of this chapter reproduces from a newspaper its financial reports for a single day, showing what might have been the market price quotations for grains, bonds, common stocks, and foreign exchange. After studying economics, one is in a better position to understand the basic forces underlying these price quotations; but only experience and study can make one reasonably expert at the hazardous game of forecasting. The stock market is discussed in this Appendix; Chapter 21's Appendix discusses the economics of speculation in organized commodity markets.

the quantity consumers will want to go on demanding; downward pressure on price will result as some sellers undermine the going price. Similarly, the reader can show why a price lower than the equilibrium price will meet irresistible upward pressure.

6 ■

Competitive pricing rations out the limited supply of goods to those with desire or need backed by money votes. Along with helping to decide FOR WHOM, it signals changes in WHAT shall be produced and in HOW goods shall be produced. But any one market only "partially" helps solve the WHAT, HOW, and FOR WHOM because of its interdependence with other commodity and factor markets in setting the general-equilibrium system of prices.

7 ■

Organized trading markets exist for a number of staple commodities such as wheat; they may also exist for some common stocks, bonds, and other financial items. There are still other markets that behave much like an auction market, even if there is no formal auctioneering procedure: so long as there are numerous well-informed suppliers and demanders, each too unimportant to have *by himself* an appreciable effect upon the price of the standardized good in question—so long as such conditions prevail, the tools of supply and demand will give an adequate approximation of the behavior of such markets. Yet, as will be seen later, a good deal of modern economic reality departs from the strict competitive model of the economist, and he must find tools applicable to monopoly and imperfect competition.

QUESTIONS FOR DISCUSSION

1. Although we should all like to escape the hardship implied by higher market price, show that rising market prices may perform some useful functions in time of scarcity. Show how such hardships might work themselves out in some different kind of economy.

2. Define carefully what is meant by a demand schedule or curve. State the law of downward-sloping demand—that there is some kind of *inverse* relation between P and Q, one going down when the other goes up.

3. Define the concept of a supply schedule or curve. Show that an increase in supply means a rightward and downward *shift* of the supply curve. Contrast this with the rightward and up-ward shift implied by an increase in demand. Why the difference? Treat cases of decrease.

4. What factors might increase the demand for wheat? The supply? What would cheap mechanical pickers do to cotton prices? To farm wages?

5. Spell out arguments to show that competitive price must settle down at the equilibrium intersection of supply and demand. Use too-high or too-low P.

6. "An increase (or decrease) in supply will lower (or raise) price. An increase (decrease) in demand will generally raise (lower) price. While we can predict that an increase in demand accompanied by a decrease in supply will be followed by a rise in price, we cannot guess without further information what will happen if we *simultaneously* increase demand and *increase* supply." Verify. Puzzle out this use of parentheses, common in economics, for alternatives.

7. "A simultaneous increase of demand and decrease of supply, as in question 6 above, is statistically impossible. Demand and supply are identically the same thing." Comment in terms of the section on Two Stumbling Blocks.

8. "If there is only one seller or only a few very large sellers, monopoly and imperfect competition theory will need to be considered rather than the tools of competitive supply and demand. If products are far from being standardized, then each brand-name seller may well have a degree of control over his price not enjoyed by the perfect competitor as defined by the economist." Verify. Make a check list of conditions needed for "perfect competition."

9. Try to puzzle out what the following newspaper reports mean.

WHEAT

	Open	High	Low	Close	Change	Season's High	Season's Low
July	182	183¼	181⅜	182–181¾	+¾ to ½	195	144⅝
Sept.	186	187½	185⅛	185¾–⅞	+½ to ⅝	197½	149⅜
Dec.	191½	193¼	190⅞	191¾–⅞	+⅞ to 1	202½	159½
Mar.	196	197	194¾	195¼–½	+¾ to 1	205½	164½
May	192	193½	191¼	192¼–½	+⅞ to 1⅛	202	176¾

CORN

	Open	High	Low	Close	Change	Season's High	Season's Low
July	134½	135½	133	133⅜–½	–1⅛ to 1	136½	122½
Sept.	137½	137⅝	135	135½–⅜	–1½ to 1⅝	138¾	120
Dec.	137⅜	138⅛	135⅛	135⅝–¾	–2 to 1⅝	140¾	118⅛
Mar.	141½	142½	139¼	139⅞–140	–1⅞ to 1¾	145½	123¼
May	143½	144½	141	141¾	–2⅛	147	129¼

1966 HIGH	1966 LOW	STOCKS AND DIV.	SALES IN 100s	OPEN	HIGH	LOW	CLOSE	NET CHGE.
			A					
16⅜	14	AbacusF .50t	28	14¼	14½	14¼	14½	+⅜
45⅝	35½	Abbott Lab 1	61	37⅝	38¼	37⅝	38⅛	+¼
33	23¼	ABC Con .80	23	24¾	25	24½	24½	...
34¼	31⅝	Abex Cp 1.60	17	32⅞	32⅞	32½	32¾	–⅛
54¾	45	ACF Ind 2.20	20	51⅝	52¼	51½	51¾	+½
57	42	Acme Mkt 2b	5	46	46¼	46	46¼	...

TREASURY BONDS

Rates	Maturities		Bid	Asked	Yield
3s	1966	Aug.	99.25	99.27	4.44
4¾s	1966	Nov.	99.28	99.3	4.90
3⅝s	1967	Feb.	99.4	99.6	5.00
1½s	1967	Apr.	97.26	98.2	4.22
3⅝s	1967	Nov.	98.2	98.6	5.02
1½s	1968	Apr.	94.26	95.2	4.50
2½s	1968–63	Dec.	94.12	94.16	4.89
4s	1969	Oct.	90.26	91.2	4.50
1½s	1970	Apr.	89.18	89.26	4.50
5s	1970	Nov.	100.0	100.4	4.94
4¼s	1985–75	May	92.22	92.30	4.81

	THURSDAY	WEDNESDAY	WEEK AGO	YEAR AGO
STERLING—$2.80 per pound ($2.78–$2.82)				
Spot	2.7787	2.7883	2.7903	2.7916
90 days'	2.7844	2.7853	2.7863	2.7780
BELGIUM—2.00 cents per franc (1.9851–2.0151)				
Spot	2.0085	2.0087	2.0068	2.0144
GERMANY (Fed. Rep.)—25.00 cents per mark (24.8138–25.1899)				
Spot	25.02¾	25.03	25.00½	25.99¾
90 days'	25.00	24.99¾	24.96¼	25.01½
INDIA—13.33 cents per rupee (13.20–13.46)				
Spot	13.35	13.35	13.35	20.94

10. Review your understanding of the following concepts:

demand schedule or curve
law of downward-sloping demand
supply schedule or curve
diminishing returns
equilibrium intersection
shifts of schedules
movements along a schedule
how supply and demand in one market "partially" solve WHAT, HOW, and FOR WHOM
general-equilibrium prices
imperfectly competitive situations

APPENDIX: Stock-market Fluctuations

To the public the most dramatic example of a competitive market is provided by Wall Street, where supply and demand bid up and down the prices of common stocks or equity shares each second. While it is true that only 22 million out of 190 million Americans own stocks under what the New York Stock Exchange calls "people's capitalism," everyone likes to read the financial headlines and envision the fireworks in world financial centers.

In the United States, during the fabulous stock-market boom of the "roaring twenties," housewives, Pullman porters, college students between classes—all bought and sold stocks. Most purchases in this wild "bull" market were "on margin"; i.e., the buyer of

$10,000 worth of stocks had to put up only $2,500 or less in cash and borrowed the difference pledging his newly bought stocks. What matter that he had to pay his broker 6, 10, or 15 per cent per year on his borrowing when in one day Auburn Motors or Bethlehem Steel might jump 10 per cent in value!

The most wonderful thing about a bull market is that it creates its own hopes. If people buy because they think stocks will rise, their act of buying sends up the price of stocks. This causes people to buy still further, and sends the dizzy dance off on another round. And unlike a game of cards or dice, no one loses what the winners gain. Everybody gets a prize! Of course, the prizes are all on paper and would disappear if everyone tried to cash them in. But why should anyone wish to sell such lucrative securities?

When the whole world is mad, 'tis folly to be sane. Suppose one were so wise or so naïve as to believe that the public-utilities holding companies were paper pyramids on cardboard foundations; or that Florida dream real-estate developments were midway between pine thicket and swamp; or that private foreign loans to South America and Europe were being frittered away in roads to nowhere or on public swimming pools? What could such a social misfit do? He would soon learn the first rule of property values: "A thing is worth what people *think* it is worth." But to be successful, this has to be applied in connection with the second rule, which is as hard to follow in practice as belling the cat or catching birds by putting salt on their tails: "Don't be the sucker left holding the bag."

When the black October crash of 1929 came, everyone was caught, the big-league professionals and the piddling amateurs—Andrew Mellon, John D. Rockefeller, the engineer in the White House, and the economics professor from Yale. The bottom fell out of the market. Brokers had to sell out the "margin" accounts of investors who could no longer pony up extra funds to cover the depleted value of their collateral,[1] sending the market down still further. Even those who did not buy on margin lost one-third of their capital by the end of the year, and five-sixths by 1932!

The bull market was over. The bear market had taken its place. And as the former had lived on its

[1] Frederick Lewis Allen's amusing and interesting chronicle of the 1920s, *Only Yesterday,* gives a detailed account of the role of the stock-market boom in American life.

dreams, so the latter was consumed by its own nightmares. Billions of dollars of security values were wiped out every month, taking with them not only the capital of gamblers out for speculative gains, but also the widow's mite supposedly invested for steady income. A "blue chip" stock like United States Steel fell from a 1929 high of 261 to a 1932 low of 21, while less respectable securities dropped off the board completely. Even though President Hoover and his administration were friendly toward business, in vain did they try to restore confidence by predicting "prosperity is just around the corner" and "stocks are excellent buys at their present levels."

Finally, after the great banking crisis of 1933, the stock market began to follow general business recovery. Figure 4-6 shows the movements of stock-market values over the whole period. Although stocks were bullish in 1936–1937 and again during World War II, it was not until the mid-fifties that they returned to anything like the peak levels of 1929. The boom in glamor growth stocks, which ended in the mid-1962 and mid-1966 collapses, confirmed the fact that human nature never changes much.

OUTGUESSING THE MARKET?

To the age-old question, Does the market follow business activity or business activity the market? no simple answer can be given. It is reasonably clear that business activity, national income, and corporate earnings determine stock prices and not vice versa; and also that the psychological effects of market movements no longer have primary importance. But still the market can occasionally *anticipate* changes in national income and total purchasing power. It then appears to be leading them when really it is following what it thinks they will be later.

HOW TO INVEST There are no simply stated foolproof rules for making money out of the stock market. Anyone who can accurately predict the future course of business activity will prosper; but there is no such person. At least four main classes of investors and speculators can be distinguished:

1. The group who simply buy and hold. Because the national economy has a long-term upward trend, they fare reasonably well over the long run. They might do a little better if they followed the statistical advice

The only thing sure about stock prices is that they will fluctuate:

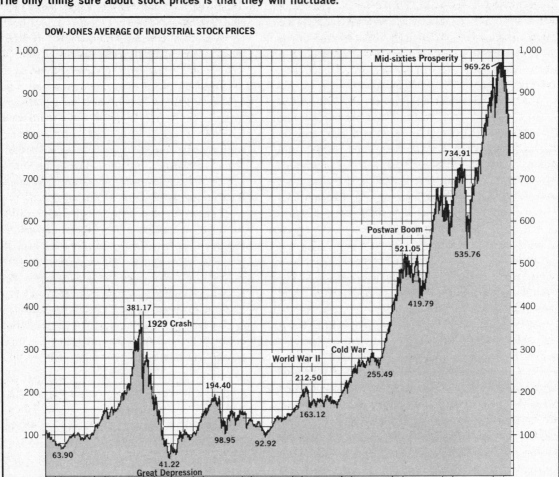

DOW-JONES AVERAGE OF INDUSTRIAL STOCK PRICES

FIG. 4-6. As money national income rises, from output and price-level growth, trend in common-stock prices is upward. But note the severe oscillations. (Source: Dow-Jones and Co., Inc.)

of investment services as to how to switch to companies of more favorable growth prospects. Surprisingly, though, representative studies show that the best mutual funds and investment counselors rarely do much better than the Dow-Jones average of 30 industrial stocks.

The effect of this holding group is neither to stabilize nor to destabilize prices; to the extent that they freeze shares off the market and limit the number of tradings, they tend to make the market "thinner." In a thin market there are so few transactions that the attempt to buy a few hundred shares of a stock may send its price up a few points because of the absence

of ready sellers around the ruling market price. An attempt to sell may depress the price a few points.

2. At the other extreme are the hour-to-hour, day-to-day ticker watchers, to be seen in every brokerage office. Generally speaking, they buy and sell, sell and buy. Usually, they make money only for their brokers.

The existence of this group has the effect of making the market less thin. Because of this group, any investor can expect to be able to liquidate his market holdings at any time at some price, although not at a price predictable in advance nor that he would like. Still, even this restricted "liquidity" enhances the attractiveness of securities traded on organized exchanges over and above the unlisted issues of smaller companies bought and sold by brokers over the counter.

3. In between are those speculators who play intermediate swings of many months or years. The least successful of these are the amateurs whose entrance into the market at the top when it is too late is supposed to be the signal for the "smart money" to leave. The most successful speculators are those who are able to avoid the extremes of enthusiasm of the mob and to discern underlying business conditions. This does not mean that they buy simply because a stock looks low and sell when it looks high. On the contrary, they buy when stocks look as if they will continue to rise. When a drop seems imminent, they sell short or, more conservatively, they simply go into cash or high-grade bonds. It takes cool nerves to sell short, because on the whole the market is overoptimistic. But if a single individual does it cleverly, he may achieve success in avoiding the losses of a bear market.

The behavior of such speculators is often destabilizing to prices. They "pile on" to a price rise and send it farther; they similarly *accentuate* a decline.

Thus, in the mid-1960s certain so-called "performance" mutual investment funds became prominent. They would buy electronic or airline glamor stocks just before these became glamorous. Then as people saw them buying, the public would be attracted to the same stocks. After the prices of these had been bid up, the performance funds would sell out to the public at a nice profit, moving on to new fields to conquer. The

evident perils in all this are well illustrated by a modern Wall Street story.

A broker phones me, telling me to buy XYZ at $2 a share. I buy 100 shares. He phones to say: "XYZ has risen to $3, better buy a couple of hundred more." I do. He calls again: "Better buy 300 at $5." Again I do; but when next he calls I finally refuse to buy and ask to sell. "What, sell XYZ," he says, "sell it *to whom?*" (*In joco veritas.*)

4. Finally, there are individuals who study special situations. From public or inside sources, they learn in advance of changes in the fortunes of particular companies: of rumored bankruptcies; of special stock dividends, split-ups, or mergers; of likely earnings and dividend announcements. When combined with the successful characteristics of the third group, members of this group—such as the elder statesman of two wars, Bernard Baruch—make the largest profit from the market. Since World War II some alert operators have been able to run $1,000 up to $10,000,000 or more—at the same time keeping profits in the form of less heavily taxed capital gains.

But the investor must take to heart Baruch's caution:

■ If you are ready to give up everything else—to study the whole history and background of the market and all the principal companies whose stocks are on the board as carefully as a medical student studies anatomy—if you can do all that, and, in addition, you have the cool nerves of a great gambler, the sixth sense of a kind of clairvoyant, and the courage of a lion, you have a ghost of a chance.

5 Business Organization and Income

THE BUSINESS OF AMERICA IS BUSINESS. CALVIN COOLIDGE

To understand our business civilization, we must first understand the organization and functioning of business enterprise. The first part of this chapter leads up to the analysis of the modern corporation, primarily by an extensive case study; the last half is concerned with the financial structure of corporations, particularly the modern large-scale, or "giant," corporation. The Appendix to this chapter presents a brief introduction to the fundamentals of accounting. Without some comprehension of accounting, there can be no deep understanding of the economics of enterprise.

■ BIG, SMALL, AND INFINITESIMAL BUSINESS

There are 5 million American business units in 1967. All but a small fraction of these enterprises are very small-scale units owned by a single person. Most businesses are here today and gone tomorrow, the average life expectancy of a business being only 6 years. Some will terminate in bankruptcy; many more will be voluntarily brought to a close with sighs of regret for dashed hopes and an expensive lesson learned; still others will come to a joyous end when their owner finally lands a good, steady job.

Faster than old businesses die, new ones are born. The present population of business concerns grew up as a result of the cumulative excess of business births over business deaths during previous years. As an economy grows, we can expect a steady excess of business births over deaths.

By number the tiny, transient, self-owned "individual proprietorship" is overwhelmingly the dominant form of American business. But in terms of dollar value, political and economic power, payrolls, and employment, some few hundred "giant corporations" occupy a strategically dominant position.

Let us glance briefly at the role in our economy of "infinitesimal businesses." There are more than 300,000 grocery-store owners in the United States, all trying to make a living. There are nearly a quarter of a million automobile service stations; more than 50,000 drugstores; and so it goes.

Some of these ventures are highly successful; but it is still true to say that most do not earn for their owners much more than they could get with less effort and risk by working for somebody else. Thus, chain stores do about 55 per cent of all the grocery business, the rest being divided among the independents. Most of these independents consist of the so-called "Ma and Pa" stores, doing less than $100 of business every day. These are often started by people who have only a few thousand dollars of initial capital—less than half the amount necessary for an adequate grocery store to do the $150-a-day business necessary if the owner is to earn even minimum wages for his effort. Such small-scale efforts are doomed from their very beginning. When the owner's initial capital is used up, they are finished. They illustrate why one-third to one-half of all retail businesses are discontinued within 2 years.

Of course, business fields differ in the amount of capital required. To build a modern service station costs more than $90,000, but to lease one from an oil company brings the initial capital down to around $5,000. Occupations with a high "rate of turnover of inventory"—such as vegetable stores—obviously require less initial capital than drugstores, hardware, or jewelry stores, where many items of stock will stay on the shelves for 3 to 5 years and where the average "turnover ratio" of annual sales to stock of inventory may be a good deal less than one.

Aside from the capital necessary to open a business, there is the tremendous amount of personal effort required. Self-employed farmers usually work from 55 to 60 hours per week during the peak summer months. Similarly, it has been estimated that the people who are their own bosses put in more hours per week than wage earners. Who, on his Sunday ride in the country, has not pitied some self-employed drudge, whose own efforts and those of all his family hardly suffice to cause him to break even?

Still, people will always want to start out on their own. *Theirs* may be the successful venture. Even if they never do succeed in earning more than a few thousand a year, there is something attractive about being able to make your own plans and do the variety of tasks that a small enterprise calls for.

■ THE SINGLE PROPRIETORSHIP

We gain insight into the principal forms of business organization—the single proprietorship, the partnership, and the corporation—by following the history of a particular business venture as it grows from a small beginning into a good-sized corporation. In the last part of this chapter, we shall turn to the subject of the giant corporation and its modern economic role.

Let us suppose you decide to start a business to produce toothpaste. You may have hit upon a good preparation in your chemistry class; or perhaps you simply looked up an old formula in the *Encyclopaedia Britannica*. To be a single proprietor you need not get anybody's permission; you simply wake up one morning and say, "Today, I am in business!" And you are.

You can hire as few or as many men as you wish, borrow whatever capital you can. At the end of the month whatever is left over as profits—after all costs have been met!—is yours to do with as you like. And there is nothing to stop you from going to the cash register at any time, taking out $800 if you can find it there, and giving it to your wife to buy a fur coat or a Chippendale chair. (Of course, as an individual, you must pay personal income taxes on all earnings.)

The losses of the business are all yours, too. If your sales fail to cover the costs you have incurred, your creditors can ask you to dig deeper into your personal assets: the bonds set aside for Junior's education, the old farmstead, and the rest. In legal terms, an individual proprietor has "unlimited liability" for all debts contracted by the business. All his property, with the exception of a small minimum, is legally attachable to meet those debts.

■ BUSINESS GROWTH AND THE NEED FOR SHORT-TERM CAPITAL

Suppose the business is prospering tremendously—perhaps because your low price has induced a chain of 5-and-10-cent stores to place a large order for tubes of paste to be marketed under its name. You are now making more money than you expected to; but you find yourself harder pressed for cash than ever before. Why? Because you are not paid in advance for your sales, whereas you must pay your workers and suppliers promptly on receipt of their services. For the moment you are putting out money and getting nothing for it, i.e., nothing except the certainty of future payment on the sales orders which you have booked, nothing but a miscellaneous batch of "goods in process"— unfinished toothpaste, empty tubing, and so forth.

To some extent, the stringency of cash can be relieved by your not paying for supplies until the end of the month or even longer. However, there is a limit to how far your suppliers will let you run up bills. Also, letting your so-called "accounts payable liabilities" pile up is an expensive way of raising capital, because goods are often billed at 2 per cent discount if paid within 30 days. When you do not take advantage of such discounts, you are, in effect, paying a very high interest rate—up to 24 per cent per year!

Where is such a single proprietor to borrow? A personal finance company will probably charge you something like 3 per cent per month or 40 per cent per year for a small personal loan; and even it will prefer to lend to a man with a steady wage that can be legally "attached" or "garnisheed" in case of nonpayment. If you own a home without a mortgage, a loan at 6 or 7 per cent might be raised upon it. To borrow in this way is clearly to risk your family's future well-being; but probably, if you are hopeful of your business future, you may go ahead and assume the risk.

Why can't the local banker be called upon for a commercial loan at 6 per cent? Ordinarily, a commercial bank will not provide "venture capital" for an unproven enterprise. The bank's president looks at your checking balance and finds it has always been near the vanishing point; this is natural, since as fast as payments have come in, you have had to write checks to stave off the ever-insistent claims of your creditors. Ordinarily, the bank likes to make 3-month loans to be used for peak-season needs and to be canceled during the rest of the year. It is idle to pretend that 3 months from now your growing business will be more liquid than now. At that time you will be applying for continuous renewal of the loan; you know it, and the banker knows it.

Even if the bank were emancipated from the older prejudice against "term loans" of some years' duration, it could not conscientiously provide capital to a business like yours. No matter how certain and glorious the future of the business appears to you, to the banker you are only one of numerous would-be entrepreneurs; and most, he knows, are destined for failure even in the best of times, and almost all would be wiped out if a really big depression came along. For the bank actually to protect the sums entrusted to it by its depositors, it would have to charge you an extra risk premium of perhaps 10 per cent or more,[1] in addition to, say, 6 per cent interest. Otherwise, the gains from successful ventures would not offset the losses of the unsuccessful.

There is one possibility of your getting a loan from the bank. The Small Business Administration (SBA) might join with the bank to make you a loan, thus coaxing the banker to make it. Or there might be a Small Business Investment Company, set up for tax advantages, that will lend you venture capital in return for eventual partial ownership. In some states, there are development commissions which have limited funds to help bring a business to town or keep it there.

Despite your makeshift attempts to raise capital, the business is still suffering from growing pains. You have exhausted all possibilities of raising further loan capital. Perhaps the time has come to look for a partner.

■ THE PARTNERSHIP

Any two or more people can get together and form a partnership. Each agrees to provide some fraction of the work and capital, to share some percentage of the profits, and of course to share the losses or debts. A purely oral agreement will do; but it is more businesslike and makes for less misunderstanding if you have a lawyer draw up some sort of formal partnership agreement.

In the case of the toothpaste business, suppose your brother-in-law is given a part ownership in the business in return for putting up $25,000 capital. Like you, he is to work for the company for, say, $5,000 per year as compared with your $8,000. You are to receive two-thirds of all profits or losses, computed after the partnership withdrawals are treated as costs; he gets one-third.

Your partner has put up $25,000 in cash. What have you brought into the venture? In the first place, you have, of course, some unfinished barrels of toothpaste to contribute, along with some uncollected accounts receivable for goods already delivered. This does not seem like much.

Actually, what you bring to the partnership is an intangible but valuable asset: the profitable sales orders and the know-how, or what is called "good will." In short, you are bringing with you a potential profit-earning power over all costs and drawings of, say, $12,000 a year. You are letting your partner have a $5,000-a-year job—which

---

[1] Another alternative has been used extensively in Germany but not in the United States or Britain: German banks buy part ownership in business and share in the profits. Such participation in ownership inevitably leads to management responsibilities by the banks and often to monopoly control of business by banking interests. For this reason, and others, such activity is legally forbidden to our banks, which are rarely sources of venture capital.

we shall assume is perhaps equal to what he can get elsewhere—and, in addition, for $25,000 he is purchasing a one-third slice of $12,000 every year.

To get this much per year from bond investments would cost him much more than $25,000. He would have to buy $100,000 worth of 4 per cent government bonds to get such a return, or $80,000 worth of 5 per cent private bonds. Aside from the risk element, your partner is getting a good buy for his $25,000, since he will annually collect some 16 per cent on his investment. So your two-thirds share is justified by the good will that you supply.[2]

■ "THIS IS THE WAY WE GROW"

And your business continues to prosper and grow. Each year, both partners agree to take out of the business only their stipulated drawings (which are like wages) and about a fifth of their share of profits, plowing the rest of the profits back into the business. Why do you decide to take out any profits from the business at all? Because you need the cash to pay your federal personal income taxes, which are levied not only on your salaries but also *upon your respective shares of the partnership's earnings.*

Why does a business like this grow? Here are some possible reasons: (1) Your toothpaste sales have risen as a result of your trade name's becoming advertised and better known and as a result of your sending out more salesmen. (2) As more toothpaste is produced, economies of large-scale production are realized so that you are able to cut your price. (3) A new factor of growth results from "vertical integration." You decide to buy a chemical factory to produce your own raw materials, and you also become your own wholesaler, thus operating three stages rather than only one "stage of production." (4) The company also grows by "horizontal integration": you take advantage of a profitable opportunity to buy out a number of competitors who produce similar toothpastes. (5) New "complementary products" such as soap and lipstick are added. You feel that bringing in the new lines under the same roof will help to spread the overhead expenses, and your salesmen feel that they might just as well get many orders as few when making a call. (6) Finally, your business may grow just because you are producing a better toothpaste.

■ NEW NEEDS AND SOURCES FOR CAPITAL

Once again, the enterprise finds itself in a paradox: the more successful it is and the faster it grows, the harder up it is for capital. The $25,000 of new "equity capital" brought into the business did not stay long in the form of cash. It was quickly transformed into circulating assets such as goods in process and office supplies. In part it went to pay off the most pressing liabilities.

The remainder was used as a down payment on a factory building and equipment. The difference between the down payment and the purchase price of the factory was secured by a mortgage loan on the property. The mortgage money was advanced

---

[2] Good will and capitalized earning power are discussed in the accounting Appendix to this chapter.

by a nearby life-insurance company and was to be amortized or paid off in install-ments over a period of 20 years, along with 6 per cent interest per year on the actual principal still unpaid at any time. In case the loan should not be paid, the holder of the mortgage of course has the right to foreclose the mortgage, i.e., to take over the ownership of the building and sell it for what it will bring. Since the down payment on the factory came to about one-fourth of its price, since this price was a bargain price to begin with, and since each year the insurance company will be getting back part of its principal, the risk it takes is not very great. The only way it could lose would be if there were a disastrous real-estate crash within the first few years.

Despite the continuous plowing of profits back into the business, growth still leaves you needing more capital. But now, having established your reputation, so to speak, new avenues of borrowing are open to you. Your banker will be glad to lend you money to tide you over the busy pre-Christmas period. A company, such as the Commercial Credit Corporation, will lend you money on the basis of your safe, but as yet uncollected, "accounts receivable" (i.e., sums owed you for goods already sold).

Suppose, when all is said and done, you need still more capital than you can raise by any kind of borrowing. The painful necessity arises of getting more "equity" capital by letting some new people share in the profits (and losses) of the business. (As a matter of fact, even if you could still find some institutions to borrow from, it would be unwise to do so. You have already superimposed too many liabilities and fixed charges on a narrow equity base. As long as things go well, it would be nice to earn 16 per cent profit on capital that costs you only 6. But if losses should occur, they will fall all the more heavily on you, the two partners, who are the residual owners.)

■ DISADVANTAGES OF THE PARTNERSHIP FORM

One possibility of getting more ownership capital is to admit new partners. There is no limit to the number you can admit; there have been partnerships in the brokerage and banking fields involving more than 100 people. However, every time a new partner is admitted, or one dies or resigns, a whole new partnership must be formed.[3]

As the number of partners increases, there comes to the fore a factor that has been soft-pedaled in our discussion up to now. Each partner is liable *without limit* to the full extent of his personal fortune for all debts contracted by the partnership. If

---

[3] More weighty is the real disadvantage stemming from the fact that a partnership can be dissolved whenever any party finds the existing arrangement unsatisfactory and wishes to withdraw. The law of partnerships also makes it impossible for any partner to sell his share to a new party without the consent of his partners; if agreement cannot be secured, the partnership may have to be wound up.

The reader may recall that the novelist William Dean Howells has his famous title character Silas Lapham, a rising self-made paint tycoon, present his partner with the ultimatum: "You buy me out or I'll buy you out." Silas' two excuses, that his were the real brains and energy responsible for the success of the business and that the proffered price exceeded his partner's original investment, were cleverly seen through by Mrs. Lapham. She pointed out that, without the partner's money at the critical time, the business could never have succeeded and that Silas' offer to sell was premised upon the knowledge that his partner was not in a position to buy the whole of the business.

he owns 1 per cent of the partnership and the business fails, then he will be called upon to foot 1 per cent of the bills and the other partners will be assessed their 99 per cent. But suppose they cannot pay any part of their assessment. Then the 1 per cent partner may be called upon to pay *for all*, even if it means selling his fine etchings or auctioning the family home.

This feature of *unlimited liability* reveals why partnerships tend to be confined to small, personal enterprises. According to the doctrine of "mutual agency" involved in the law of partnerships, each partner has broad powers to act as agent to commit the whole partnership. When it becomes a question of placing their personal fortunes in jeopardy, people are reluctant to put their capital into complex ventures over which they can exercise little control.

This explains why agriculture and retail trade are the only sectors of our economy where more than half of the business done is done by single proprietors and partnerships. In the field of investment banking, concerns like J. P. Morgan & Company used to advertise proudly "not incorporated" so that their creditors could have the extra assurance. But even these concerns have converted themselves into corporate entities.

Only recently did the giant brokerage concern Merrill Lynch, Pierce, Fenner & Smith incorporate. For a long time it had many major partners and scores of junior partners, illustrating that the barriers to running a large enterprise put up by the partnership form are not insuperable. Such giant partnerships now are rare.

■ Undoubtedly, unlimited liability and the red tape needed to ensure continuity are the main drawbacks to the partnership form.

■ THE CORPORATION

At this point, therefore—or even long before—you will probably decide to form a corporation rather than a partnership. Usually you will incorporate in the state in which you live and operate. However, if the corporation is sizable, you may prefer to establish token headquarters in some state such as Delaware or New Jersey, which have set up very easy rules to attract firms.

Centuries ago, corporation charters were awarded by governments very rarely and only by special acts of the king and legislature. Parliament or Congress would graciously permit a public-utility enterprise or railroad to form a corporation to do specific things and perform specific functions. The East India Company was such a privileged corporation. The early railroads here and abroad often had to spend as much money in getting a charter through the legislature as in preparing their roadbeds. Gradually, within the past century, this procedure began to seem unfair, and it became the practice to pass general incorporation laws granting almost anyone the privilege of forming a corporation for almost any purpose, without having to get a special vote of approval from the state legislature or from Congress.

Today, for a small fee a lawyer will draw up the necessary papers and will write into the corporate charter almost as wide powers and purposes as you could wish. Automatically, the state will grant the charter. Let us see how the incorporating procedure works in the case of your toothpaste company. You decide to issue 20,000 shares of common stock in the corporation: 6,600 going to you; 3,300 to your partner; 100 to your wife; and the other 10,000 to be sold to outside interests. Although each share is to have an initial stated value of $10, your lawyer has advised you to make them no-par shares, since "par value" has no particular significance anyway.

The 10,000 shares to be sold to the public are to be marketed through a local *investment banking* firm. These firms are simply merchandisers of securities; and as with any merchant, their profit comes from the difference between their buying and selling prices. Because yours is such a small business, they must drive a hard bargain, especially since they can claim that the costs of selling the securities are likely to be high. Thus the investment brokers may offer you $10 per share and plan to resell at a price of $12.50 per share. Had you been a large company, you might have held out for as much as $12.25—or even in some cases $12.40—out of the $12.50 selling price, because of the eager competitive bidding of the different investment banking syndicates.

For a large company the investment banker would probably have agreed to *underwrite* the new issue of 10,000 shares. This means that he would have guaranteed the purchase of the full 10,000 shares at a set price. If the market then refused to buy all these shares from the investment banker at his announced price, he, not you, would have to absorb the loss. But he probably regards you as too small and untried a business to justify his assuming the risk of underwriting. So he takes your issue on a "best effort" basis; and if he cannot sell all the shares, you end up raising less capital.

CORPORATION STRUCTURE   Fortunately, all goes well, and he pays you $100,000 in cash for the securities sold. Unlike the case of the partnership, you need not concern yourself with the people to whom he has sold the shares or with the fact that they may resell their shares. The names of the owners of the shares are registered with the company or its bank agent in case they get lost and so that you will know where to send the dividend checks or the announcements of stockholders' meetings.

Ordinarily, each share gives its owner one vote. Shares in the corporate earnings are also in direct proportion to the number of shares owned. Those with 100 shares get 100 votes and correspondingly higher dividends.

The outside owners of 10,000 shares have paid in $100,000 cash to the company. What have you and your partner paid in? Obviously not cash, but rather a sizable amount of earning assets: plant, equipment, goods in process, and perhaps good will, which is, as already seen, the capitalized value of the presumed "excess earning power" of the business, resulting from its trademarks, patents, know-how, and so forth.

Back in the old days before 1929, you and your investment banker might have evaluated the good will as liberally as you wished, possibly giving yourself 20,000 rather than 10,000 shares. This practice has been called "watering the stock." Today, you would have to submit any sizable new issue to the Securities and Exchange Commission (SEC), a regulatory agency set up as part of the New Deal in 1933. They would have to satisfy themselves that there are no misleading claims before permitting the new flotation. However, they do not pretend to pass judgment on or attest to the value of the stock. *Caveat emptor*—let the buyer beware—still prevails as a doctrine!

■ ADVANTAGES AND DISADVANTAGES OF THE CORPORATE FORM

PRIVATE ADVANTAGE   The corporation has solved most of the problems that bothered you about the partnership. It is an almost perfect device for the raising of large sums of capital. Of first importance, every stockholder now has *limited liability*. After paying $12.50 per share, the investor need not worry about his personal estate's being in jeopardy. If worse comes to worst and the business goes bankrupt, the most each shareholder could lose would be his original $12.50 per share. He cannot be assessed further.

Of secondary importance is the fact that the corporation is a fictitious legal person created by the state. It exists not by "natural right" but only at the pleasure of the state. The corporation, as distinct from its owners, can be sued in court and can sue. Any officer of the company, unlike any partner, is strictly limited in his legal ability to act as agent for the other owners and to commit them financially. Also, the corporation may have "perpetual succession" or existence, regardless of how many times the shares of stock change hands by sale or bequest and regardless of whether there are 10,000 different stockholders. No group of shareholders can force any other group to sell or retain their holdings, and only a majority vote rather than unanimity is needed to reach usual business decisions. Normally, the stockholders will be too many to meet for every decision; they will prefer to elect a board of directors consisting of a dozen or so members to represent them between annual meetings, in much the same way that democratic electorates select legislative representatives to act for them. As we shall see, the problem of keeping large corporations "truly democratic" is a hard one.

You will face one disadvantage to incorporation that has become increasingly serious in recent years. The federal government taxes corporate income. Thus, during World War II, a profitable corporation might have had to pay as much as 80 per cent of its income to the government in excess-profit taxation; the Korean conflict also brought an excess-profit tax. Most sizable corporations must pay almost half of each extra dollar of income. (This is in addition to the personal income tax that owners pay on dividends they get.)

The corporate tax is a rather high price for a small business to pay for limited liability and greater ease of raising capital. Yet there are also tax *advantages* offered by the corporate form. There is a loophole in our present law: *undistributed* corporate profits escape *personal* income taxes; only paid-out dividends are so taxed. A rich man who is taxed about 70 cents of every dollar of personal income can say, "Why pay such rates on partnership earnings? Let's incorporate, pay the lower corporate tax, and keep dividends low."[4]

Another loophole used to avoid the disadvantages of double taxation under the corporate form is where the owners of a closely held corporation vote most of its earnings to themselves and their relatives in the form of high salaries, pensions, and perquisites. The Treasury Department tries to check up on avoidance of taxes by such

---

[4] To some degree he is only putting off the evil day. For unless his lawyer can work out a lightly taxed "capital-gains deal," his dividends later will be taxable when he receives them. But in any case the delay in tax payment is worth money to him. Under new tax revisions, many people can win either way: they are given the option of being taxed as partnerships or as corporations.

padding of expenses; but it is always hard to know whether a given in-law is worth $20,000 a year and whether a trip to a Bermuda convention is truly a business rather than a personal expense.

SOCIAL ADVANTAGE   When Prime Minister Gladstone was shown electricity on a visit to Michael Faraday's laboratory, he asked, "What is the use of electricity?" Faraday gave the amusing reply, "I suppose some day, Sir, you may come to put a tax on it." Surely the advantage of the corporate form to society is not merely that the state can tax it.

■ Large-scale production is technically efficient, and a large corporation is an advantageous way for investors to pool the irreducible risks of business life. Without limited liability and the corporation, society could simply not reap the benefit that comes when large supplies of capital can be attracted to competing corporations that produce a variety of complementary products, pool risks, and best utilize the economies of sizable research units and managerial know-how. That is why the privilege of the corporate form is legalized.

■ HOW A CORPORATION CAN RAISE CAPITAL

Let us suppose your corporation continues to grow as a result of vertical and horizontal combination, new products, economies of mass production, advertising promotion, and so forth. Besides borrowing on promissory notes or mortgages, buying on credit, and relying on earnings not paid out in dividends, what new forms of financing are now available to you?

BONDS   First, you may issue bonds. These are nothing but special kinds of promissory notes, nicely printed on gilt paper, issued in $1,000 or other denominations so as to be readily marketable for resale. A bond is a security promising to pay a certain number of dollars every 6 months for a number of years until it matures. At that time the borrowing company promises to pay off the principal of the bond at its face value. (Often the company has the right to call in the bond a few years before its maturity date by paying the bondholders some previously agreed-upon price.) The dollar installments paid every 6 months, the interest earnings of the bond, are usually called the "coupon" payments, because the owner of most bonds cuts off a certain little corner of the bond certificate each 6 months and then mails it in to receive his interest payment.

Ordinarily, payments for the coupons and principal must be made on time, regardless of whether the company has been making earnings or not. Otherwise the company is in default of its obligations and can be taken to court like any debtor.[5] Of course, there is no particular reason why a partnership could not borrow by the use of bonds; but ordinarily it would not be well enough known to succeed in interesting a lender. For that matter, a small corporation can rarely raise capital by issuing bonds.

[5] Income bonds, whose interest is payable only if there are large enough earnings, are not uncommon. Mortgage bonds, secured by property, are often encountered. Convertible bonds, which can be exchanged for a stated number of common shares, are a popular hybrid.

COMMON STOCKS   Issuing bonds and issuing common stocks are opposite methods of financing. The common stockholder is providing "equity" capital. He shares in profits and in control of business decisions, but he must also share in all losses. His is a more risky venture, because he can never receive any dividends until the fixed charges owed to the bondholder are paid off. The bondholder gets a limited but steadier income. Unless the corporation is bankrupt or in danger of being so, the bondholder ordinarily has no legal control over the decisions of the business; but a wise management will take care to stay on good terms with all sources of future capital.

PREFERRED STOCKS   Between bonds and common stocks are so-called "preferred stocks." These pay *at most* a stated dividend—say, a stipulated 4 per cent of the face value per share—no matter how profitable the business becomes. The preferred stockholder is more likely to get his dividend even when profit is small than is the common stock-holder, because legally he stands next in line after the bondholder and before the common stockholder. The latter gets no dividends if the preferred stock fails to receive its full dividend.

Often "cumulative" preferred stock is issued. This means that, if for 5 years of depression there has not been enough in the way of earnings to pay any of the 4 per cent dividends on the preferred stock, when good times come back again the "cumulated" $20 (= 5 × $4) of unpaid preferred stock dividends must be made good before the common stockholders can begin to receive any dividends. Often, too, preferred stock is "callable" and "convertible." The first term means that at some previously stated value, say $103, the company can buy back its outstanding preferred stock. The second term refers to the right given the preferred stockholder of converting each share into shares of common stock at some stipulated ratio.[6]

■ ADVANTAGES OF DIFFERENT SECURITIES

From the standpoint of the investor, bonds, preferred stocks, and common stock usually form a sequence of increasing risk and decreasing security—balanced by an increased chance of making high earnings or capital gains. Today, a "gilt-edge" bond may yield about $4\frac{1}{2}$ per cent, a good preferred stock about 5 per cent. Because common stocks may rise in value and give capital gains, they now often have a spread of dividend yields that begins even lower than bonds: some "growth stocks" like IBM yield much less than the safest government bonds. To test his understanding of these three forms of securities, the reader should make sure that he understands why common stocks tend to be better investments in time of inflation than the other two.

It would be a mistake to leave the reader with the impression that bonds are perfectly safe investments. On the contrary, during depressions many companies went bankrupt and defaulted on their bonds, paying off only a few cents on the dollar. The

---

[6] Also, some preferred stocks are made more attractive by being "participating." This means that, once profit exceeds some agreed-upon figure, they share with the common stockholder in further profits. But this form is rare. When one corporation owns stock in another, it pays tax on only 15 per cent of the dividends; this explains why corporations are important holders of preferred stocks.

basic risk in all corporate investment is a possible loss of earning power, which will greatly reduce the value of its assets. Often a company will undergo reorganization in which the stockholders may be squeezed out completely; the courts may appoint a "receiver" or trustee to run the business, and the bondholders may be given bonds (or even stocks!) equal only to some fraction of their original investments. Moreover, certain bondholders may have prior claims over holders of other bonds. Many investors in railroad securities have learned of these possibilities the hard way.

From the corporation's view, bond debt creates low but inflexible fixed charges. These may be embarrassing in bad times. Preferred stock is slightly better with respect to flexibility; equity capital, best of all.[7]

■ THE GIANT CORPORATION

While one should not infer that all corporations go through three stages, we have now carried our successful toothpaste enterprise far enough up the ladder of success. The rest of this chapter will be concerned with the economic position and power of the very large modern corporation and the problems that it creates for the American economy.

A list of the 200 largest nonfinancial corporations reads like an honor roll of American business, almost every name being a familiar household word. Among the industrial companies will be United States Steel, Bethlehem Steel, and the Aluminum Company of America; Standard Oil of New Jersey, of California, of Indiana; the Texas Company; General Motors, Chrysler, and Ford; Swift and Armour meat packing; American Tobacco (Luckies) and R. J. Reynolds (Camels); The Great Atlantic & Pacific Tea Company, Sears, Montgomery Ward, F. W. Woolworth, and J. C. Penney; National Dairy (Kraft), Borden; Procter & Gamble, Lever Brothers; and many others.

Among the railroads are such old stand-bys as Pennsylvania, New York Central, Southern Pacific, and many others. The public-utility list is headed by A T & T. If we go on to add the largest financial organizations, we bring in such giants as the Bank of America (California), First National City Bank (New York), the Chase Manhattan Bank, the Continental Illinois National Bank (Chicago), and the First National Bank of Boston; the Metropolitan Life Insurance Company, Prudential Life, Equitable Life; etc. Altogether there are now more than 100 companies with assets above the billion-dollar mark!

The tremendous concentration of economic power involved in giant corporations may be gauged from the following facts: Alone they own 40 per cent of the total assets of all nonfinancial corporations, more than a third of all banking assets, and 85 per cent of all life-insurance assets. The largest 200 corporations hold between a fifth and a fourth of income-producing national wealth. They employ one out of every eight workers. The 500 largest United States industrial corporations have more than half the sales in manufacturing and mining and get more than 70 per cent of the profits. Five corporations each handle more money than any one of our 50 states does.

[7]Interest charges can also be deducted from the corporation earnings for tax purposes. There is an incentive, therefore, other things being equal, to use debt rather than stock financing. However, other things have not been equal, and the practice in the past 20 years has been to grow by plowing back earnings and to issue enough bonds to keep the debt-to-equity ratio about the same. New stock issues have not kept pace.

Their power did not grow overnight. After 1900, their percentage importance steadily mounted. Throughout the 1930s and up to World War II, relatively speaking, they just about held their own.

Large size breeds success, and success breeds further success.[8] But there are also economic and political barriers to largeness. Recent economic research shows the falsity of the widespread view that the giants are gulping up more and more of modern industry. Statistics suggest that, relatively, the giants have probably lost a little ground since 70 years ago, when the "trust movement" had not yet run afoul of the Sherman Antitrust Act (1890). And just as a hotel may be always full—but with different people—so do we find the list of biggest corporations to be a changing one, but at a very slow rate.

■ DIVORCE OF OWNERSHIP AND CONTROL IN THE LARGE CORPORATION

Let us examine the internal workings of one of these giant corporations. *The most striking feature is the diversification of ownership among thousands and thousands of small stockholders.* In 1967 more than 3,000,000 different people had shares in A T & T. To be sure, half these people had less than 10 shares each; one-quarter of the shares were held in blocks of less than 100 shares; and no single owner has as much as 1 per cent of the total. The Stock Exchange has a goal of "people's capitalism," in which the masses have appreciable ownership of society's capital. Now more than 20 million people do own some common stocks; but less than 1 in 10 gets an appreciable return yet.

In a path-breaking study,[9] Berle and Means pointed out that this wide diversification of stockholding has resulted in a *separation of ownership and control.* Recent studies show that in the typical giant corporation, all management together—officers and directors—hold only about 3 per cent of the outstanding common stock. The largest single minority ownership groups typically hold only about a fifth of all voting stock. Such a small fraction has been deemed more than enough to maintain "working control."[10]

■ LEADERSHIP AND CONTROL OF THE LARGE CORPORATION

The problem of keeping a large corporation truly democratic is a difficult one. Until recent years, a dozen stockholders would turn up for the annual meeting. More recently,

[8] The statistical evidence on profits suggests that profits increase with size but that the very biggest firms in an industry sometimes seem to show a slight dropping off of relative profits compared with the next to the largest. A larger percentage of small firms than of large firms falls in the class of firms making losses.

[9] A. A. Berle, Jr., and Gardner C. Means, *The Modern Corporation and Private Property* (Commerce Clearing House, New York, 1932). See R. A. Gordon, *Business Leadership in the Large Corporation* (Brookings Institution, Washington, 1945), Chap. II. R. J. Larner in a 1966 *American Economic Review* study has shown that the Berle-Means thesis on separation of ownership and control is even truer in the 1960s than in 1929: whereas 6 of the 200 largest corporations were privately owned (80 per cent or more of stock) in 1929, in 1963 there were none; and 84.5 per cent of the firms today had no group of stockholders owning as much as 10 per cent!

[10] You can even pyramid control by owning one-fifth of a million-dollar company, which owns one-fifth of a five-million-dollar company, and so forth. Such a pyramid of so-called "holding companies" can give control over billions to small ownership at the base.

many hundreds have been attending some meetings, often drawn by free chicken salad and, it must be confessed, by the chance to heckle management or watch the show.

Decisions at the annual meeting are really settled by use of "proxies." Each stockholder is asked to mail in a proxy permitting the management to exercise his votes. Some do not reply; but enough usually do to establish a quorum and a comfortable plurality for management. The SEC has tried to improve the democratic structure of corporations by insisting that motions to be decided at the annual meeting be indicated on the proxy statement so that stockholders can indicate their preferences; also, rival groups must be permitted mailing access to the stockholders, and so forth.

Prior to recent years, most managements could be said to be self-perpetuating. Whether the corporation runs well or poorly, whether the managers work efficiently or not, the typical small stockholder could do little about it. He could rubber-stamp approval or relieve his feelings by not voting. In either case management went undisturbed.

Recently there has been a slight change. Thanks to the SEC rules, some challenging minority groups have attempted—and successfully attempted!—to oust the in-group and put themselves in as new managers. Thus, the late Robert Young ran a tremendous campaign—using all the devices of modern publicity—to oust the New York Central railroad officers. And he did succeed in winning majority support. Similar battles have taken place in connection with the New Haven railroad and Montgomery Ward.

In a sense, therefore, we can hope that democratic control of corporations by stock owners has increased. But competent observers still insist that, barring blatant incompetence, management can count on remaining in office; and often the proxy battle is fought to determine which minority group shall control.[11]

■ A MANAGERIAL REVOLUTION?

Who makes corporate decisions? Primarily, the increasingly important class of *professional managers*. The old-time captain of industry, for all his creativeness and ability to calculate the risks necessary to build up a great enterprise, often had something of the buccaneer in his makeup and an irresponsible "the-public-be-damned" attitude. In company after company, the original founder has been replaced by a new type of executive, usually having a different surname. If he should be a completely self-made man, he will nevertheless probably have acquired special training and management skills. The new professional executive is more adept at public relations and in the handling of people. He is necessarily more the "bureaucrat," often interested as much in preserving the *status quo* as in taking extreme risks.

Typically, the dominant man will be the president of the corporation. As he begins to feel his years, he may be made chairman of the board of directors. The chairman of the board is often an elder statesman who, together with a small executive or steering committee of the board of directors, gives advice and approval to the actions of the president and his many vice-presidents.

[11] A dissatisfied stockholder can always sell his shares and buy into another company. If enough stockholders do so, the company will find it hard ever to raise capital by selling a new issue; the fall in its share prices may depress the value of "stock options" issued to company executives as a tax-loophole bonus and could galvanize other stockholders into a proxy revolt.

The exact role of the board of directors varies from company to company and from group to group. Some directors are simply well-known men selected to give prestige. Others possess special knowledge and take an active part in determining policy. On the whole, it would be going too far to say that most boards of directors act simply as rubber stamps to approve the decisions already taken by the officers of the company. But it is true that, so long as management possesses the confidence of the board, that body will usually not actively intervene to dictate specific policies. This is the same administrative procedure usually followed by the board of trustees of a philanthropic foundation or college, and is not too unlike the parliamentary system of ministerial responsibility in Great Britain and elsewhere.

Generally speaking, there will be no clash of goals between the management and stockholders. Both will be interested in maximizing the profits of the firm. But in two important situations there may be a divergence of interests, not infrequently settled in favor of management. First, insiders may vote themselves and their friends or relatives large salaries, expense accounts, bonuses, retirement pensions, and stock options at the stockholders' expense.[12]

A second conflict of interest may arise in connection with undistributed profits. The managers of every organization have an understandable tendency to try to make it grow and perpetuate itself. The psychological reasons are subtle and by no means always selfish. In some cases when profits are plowed back into a company, there is reason to suspect that the same capital could better be invested by the stockholders elsewhere or spent upon consumption. Indeed, the case occasionally arises when a company would be well advised to wind itself up and pay back its capital. But a cynic might doubt that management is likely to vote itself out of existence and out of jobs.

■ THE EVIL OF MONOPOLY

In view of all the above facts, it is not surprising to find that most important American industries are characterized by a few large corporations whose share of the output of that particular industry is vastly greater than their numerical importance would warrant. Figure 5-1 gives a list of some large American industries and depicts their degree of concentration by showing the relative proportion of total industry employment controlled by the first four dominant corporations and by the next four.

In Part Three we shall analyze some of the problems raised by monopoly and imperfect competition. In the past century, particularly since the 1890 Sherman Antitrust Act, there has been great concern over the breaking down of free competitive markets under the encroachment of large-scale enterprise. In recent years officials of

---

[12] Other conflicts can involve outright cheating: executives may take bribes, throw business to their own companies, or violate SEC rules by using inside knowledge and spreading false rumors to make market profits on the company's stock. A recent president of Chrysler had to resign when it was discovered he had secret ownership in a supplying firm. An insurance executive came under fire for joining privately in a tax deal with a company the insurance company had dealings with. Such cases are rare, but not rare enough.

General Electric, Westinghouse, and other electric suppliers were even sent to jail for colluding on monopoly price setting.

From an economic point of view it does not much matter which of the following monopolistic devices cause price to be too high: (1) mergers of competing firms, (2) cooperative "pools" or "cartel agreements," (3) so-called "trusts" (involving selected "trustees" who "coordinate" pricing policy), (4) interlocking directorates, (5) "holding-company" control, (6) tacit collusion and trade-association action, (7) government "fair price" legislation (Robinson-Patman Act, etc.) and government-sponsored "commodity agreements" (wheat, rubber, cotton, etc.).

Too high a price, wastage of resources, and creation of monopoly profits are economic evils, however brought about and whatever the legal technicalities of the matter. This we shall study in Part Three, but a brief preview can be presented here.

Under perfect competition, dollar resources are drawn into the production of goods people most want to buy. The most efficient engineering knowledge and economic combination of land, labor, and capital are brought about by ruthless Darwinian competition. But if firms have monopoly powers:

1. They can earn at the expense of other factors of production more than their facilities would be worth under perfect competition.

2. Having plenty of monopoly carrots already, the monopolist may not be motivated by the prospect of still more carrots to introduce all possible technical efficiencies that will reduce his costs to the minimum—and he will certainly be protected somewhat from the harmful kicks of perfectly competitive rivals.

3. The price that monopolists charge can be higher than minimum competitive costs (and along Chapter 4's *dd* curves, output will be smaller than it would be under lower competitive pricing).

4. Too-low output in the monopoly industry means that labor and land and other resources must go too much into other industries where their output is worth less, or may even go into nonemployment (e.g., the basic decision, whether I should work an extra hour per week or day, is distorted, since under monopoly I shall not be able to

Some industries are dominated by a very few sellers:

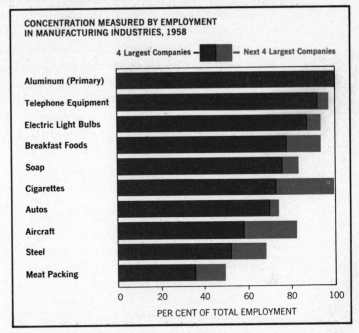

FIG. 5-1. In aluminum, autos, steel, and many other industries, a few firms get most of the business. This is in contrast to the notion of perfect competition among innumerable small sellers (e.g., farmers), each too small to affect the market price. But MIT's expert M. A. Adelman thinks concentration was probably even greater back in 1900. (Source: U.S. Bureau of the Census.)

buy for a dollar the extra goods that are truly made possible by my doing an extra dollar's worth of work).

5. In some ways worst of all, the practice of charging a monopoly (or imperfectly competitive) price may, as is shown in Part Three, result in too many barbers standing around, doing too little—and because of the entry of other imperfectly competitive barbers, the consumer may pay too high a price *without* the monopolist barbers' ending up making any more than they would under perfect competition! How can everybody lose? Because Chamberlinian monopoly has produced inefficiency and underutilized capacity, leaving us well *inside* the production-possibility frontier depicted in Chapter 2![13]

■ THE CURSE OF BIGNESS?

Is bigness itself a bad thing? Undoubtedly there is much popular hostility toward large corporations. Even if they could do so, General Motors or United States Steel would be most reluctant to swallow up competitors until they accounted for, say, nine-tenths of their respective industries. They would fear the effect on public opinion. Is this antagonism toward big business directed toward bigness itself? Or against the alleged evils of monopoly that are often supposed to be associated with bigness? What should public policy be toward a "benevolent, well-behaving, efficient" giant corporation?

The so-called "A & P" case provides an example. This chain of food stores is noted for its low prices. Yet the Department of Justice prosecuted it under the antitrust acts. Leaving aside certain minor irregularities that the company may have engaged in, the basic issue was clearly posed: Shall it be a crime to grow large as a result of efficiency and continued maintenance of low, competitive prices? The federal courts seemed almost to answer, Yes.

Another example shows that policy problems are not easy. In the mid-fifties there was a rash of mergers; e.g., in the auto industry Nash combined with Hudson, and Studebaker with Packard. Often there was a "tax angle" to the merger; but in some cases, firms merged in order to try to become more efficient, so as to be able to compete with General Motors and Ford. Do such mergers—even though they undoubtedly increase the size of the merged units—really reduce competition rather than increase it? (Was the Attorney General wrong in forbidding a merger between Bethlehem and Youngstown steel companies? Was the Interstate Commerce Commission right in permitting the C & O railroad to merge with the B & O?)

To produce an atomic bomb, the government turned to the Du Pont Company and gave it a cost-plus-one-dollar contract. The scientific know-how of General and Western Electric is invaluable for peace as well as war. In the words of Schumpeter, a world-famous economist who died in 1950:[14]

[13]Undertakers provide a case in point: People generally, including poor people, pay in some regions an average of $700 per complete funeral! But so many undertaking establishments come into existence that—as in New York—each handles only about one funeral per week, or 56 per year, to be exact!
[14]J. A. Schumpeter, *Capitalism, Socialism, and Democracy* (Harper, New York, 1942). Whatever the merits of the Schumpeter thesis, it is still true that there have been great productivity changes in competitive agriculture; that many basic inventions come from independent persons or small com-

The modern standard of life of the masses evolved during the period of relatively unfettered "big business." If we list the items that enter the modern workman's budget and from 1899 on observe the course of their prices not in terms of money but in terms of the hours of labor that will buy them—i.e., each year's money prices divided by each year's hourly wage rates, we cannot fail to be struck by the rate of the advance which, considering the spectacular improvement in qualities, seems to have been greater and not smaller than it ever was before. . . . Nor is this all. As soon as we go into details and inquire into the individual items in which progress was most conspicuous, the trail leads not to the doors of those firms that work under conditions of comparatively free competition but precisely to the doors of the large concerns—which, as in the case of agricultural machinery, also account for much of the progress in the competitive sector— and a shocking suspicion dawns upon us that big business may have had more to do with creating that standard of life than keeping it down.

This suggests that the future problem may not be one of choosing between large monopolistic corporations and small-scale competitors, but rather that of devising ways to improve the social and economic performance of large corporate aggregates. To keep the tremendously creative abilities of the modern large-scale corporation working toward the public good—that may have to be the goal for the years ahead. We shall return to the problem of the maintenance of "effective and workable competition" after an analysis in Part Three of prices and cost under perfect and imperfect competition.

SUMMARY

1 ■

The present population of American businesses has grown up as a result of a cumulative excess of business births over business deaths. The great majority of businesses consist of infinitesimal single proprietorships, largely in retail and service establishments. Their turnover is rapid.

2 ■

One should understand how an enterprise grows, its needs and avenues for short-term or long-term capital, and the advantages and disadvantages of the corporate form over the single proprietorship and partnership.

3 ■

One should also be acquainted with the fundamental legal rights involved in the corporation and with the general features of bonds and of preferred and common stocks.

-----

panies; and that there is no evidence of an upswing in inventiveness during the 1890s, a decade of monopoly concentration. Reference should be made to J. Kenneth Galbraith's doctrine of "countervailing power" in *American Capitalism* (Houghton Mifflin, Boston, 1952). It is there argued that big units do characterize American life, but that "big labor" checks big business, and vice versa; that big Sears and A & P check their big suppliers, and so a kind of a tolerable equilibrium is achieved, albeit not one of a competitive type. Part Three studies E. H. Chamberlin's imperfect competition.

4 ■

Problems created by the separation of ownership and control and by the concentration of economic wealth and monopoly power in the modern giant corporation deserve serious study. (Part Three will discuss imperfect competition and antitrust policies.)

Accounting is a great help to the understanding of economics, and its fundamental principles are presented briefly in the Appendix to this chapter.

QUESTIONS FOR DISCUSSION

1. Imagine you are starting a business of your own. Write its case history.

2. Compare the advantages and disadvantages of (*a*) the single proprietorship, (*b*) the partnership, and (*c*) the corporate form of business organization.

3. List ways of raising capital for small, medium, and large businesses.

4. What are the advantages and disadvantages of different securities?

5. Discuss the structure of the large modern corporation.

6. What is meant by calling ours the age of the "Managerial or Bureaucratic Revolution"? Does this apply outside government?

7. Give examples of conflict of interest between stockholders and management. Of coincident interests. Of problems of democratic control.

8. Defend "bigness as such." Attack it. What evils might accompany it?

9. What are the economic evils of monopoly? Give examples.

10. Review your understanding of the following concepts:

single proprietorship
partnership
corporation
unlimited and limited liability
investment banking
Securities and Exchange Commission (SEC), SBA
corporate, personal income tax

bonds, common and preferred stocks
proxy, minority control
director, executive, bureaucrat
forms of monopoly control
merger, collusion
evils of monopoly
possible dynamic advantages of bigness

APPENDIX: Elements of Accounting

In this "age of accounts" a little literacy in accounting has become a prime necessity.

THE BALANCE SHEET

A student of economics must have some understanding of the two fundamental accounting statements: the Balance Sheet and the Statement of Profit and Loss (or the so-called "Income Statement").

The Balance Sheet is presented in a report, usually annually. It represents an instantaneous "still picture" of the condition of the enterprise on some particular day, usually the last day of the year. Corresponding to the dollar value of every asset—tangible or intangible—

there must necessarily be an exactly equal total amount of claims or ownership. The value of a $20,000 house is exactly matched by somebody's claim to its ownership consisting, say, of $15,000 owed a creditor and $5,000 owned by its owner.

This is the fundamental identity underlying every Balance Sheet:

■ Value of assets = value of total claims or
                    ownership
               = value of liabilities (owed)
                + value of proprietorship
                  (owned)

or

         Assets = Liabilities + Net Worth

Let us illustrate this by considering a simple Balance Sheet, as shown in Table 5-1; this lists Assets on the left and on the right Liabilities and Net Worth for a new company whose operations have just begun.

A blank space has been deliberately left next to the Common Stock Net Worth item because you should realize that the only correct entry compatible with our fundamental Balance-Sheet truism is $200,000. A Balance Sheet must always balance—because Net Worth, i.e., ownership of the "residual claimants," always adjusts itself to make a balance.

To illustrate this, suppose a thief steals all the cash, and a fire burns up one-fourth the inventory. The accountant will learn of this sad news without turning a hair. "Total Assets are down $40,000 all told; Liabilities remain unchanged. Very well, I must write

down Net Worth by $40,000, to only $210,000." Such is his way of keeping score.

A number of interesting facts are revealed by even this simple Balance Sheet. First, it is customary to divide up Assets according to whether they will be convertible into cash by normal operations within a year or not, the first category being called Current Assets and the second Fixed Assets. The Liabilities can also be subdivided into Current and Long-term Liabilities, depending upon whether they come due in less than a year.

Here is something to be noticed about a Balance Sheet: Although its two sides must balance *in total,* yet no single item on one side is matched by an item on the other side. Thus, Bonds do not correspond in value to the Equipment or Buildings, nor do Capital items correspond to Cash. The only correct statement about a Balance Sheet is that creditors have a general claim of a definite value against the enterprise, and owners have a residual claim against the rest.

Most of the specific items listed are more or less self-explanatory. Cash consists of coins, currency, and money on deposit in the bank. Cash is the only asset whose value is exact rather than an estimate. All other valuations involve some guesswork, albeit careful guesswork. Moreover, all accounting valuations must be made relative to the actual intended purpose or use of the asset in question. If a business is a going concern and not in the process of liquidation, the accountant will be careful not to value doubtful assets at the low figure they would bring at a forced sale; he rather

A Balance Sheet is a point-of-time picture showing that Assets = Liabilities + Net Worth:

ASSETS		LIABILITIES AND NET WORTH	
		Liabilities	
Current Assets:		**Current Liabilities:**	
Cash	$ 20,000	Accounts payable	$ 20,000
Inventory	80,000	Notes payable	30,000
Fixed Assets:		**Long-term Liabilities:**	
Equipment	130,000	SBA note	50,000
Buildings	170,000	Bonds payable	50,000
		Net Worth	
		Capital:	
		Preferred stock	50,000
		Common stock	. . . . . .
Total	$400,000	Total	$400,000

TABLE 5-1. BALANCE SHEET OF PEPTO-GLITTER, INC., AS OF DECEMBER 31, 1970.

will value them at their worth to the company in its normal operation.

Inventory, consisting in the case of our toothpaste company of sugar, chemicals, tubing, raw materials, and other goods in process, can be valued in many different ways. Many conservative companies use original cost of the inventories or present market value, whichever is lower. Especially difficult problems arise when the prices of materials vary from month to month. Should we figure the chemical cost of the toothpaste at the original price of the ingredients actually used, which of course were bought some time ago when prices were different? Or should we figure, as our cost, the price that must *now* be paid for the chemicals to replace those being used up? An elementary discussion cannot go into these two possible methods of inventory valuation.[1] Obviously, it will make a great difference in stated profits during a time of inflation or deflation which of these two methods is used. It also will make a difference in income taxes. Therefore the government is compelled to say, "Use whichever method you wish, but having made up your mind, stick to it." So much for inventories.

If we assume that the Equipment and Buildings items were bought just at the end of 1970, then their Balance-Sheet values will be listed equal to their purchase price. This follows a fundamental accounting rule or convention: "At time of purchase a thing is presumed worth what the enterprise pays for it." However, as we shall see in connection with the Income Statement and the next year's Balance Sheet, hard problems are involved in deciding how to evaluate exactly equipment and buildings that have depreciated through use and age.

On the Liabilities side, Accounts Payable are, as their name implies, the sums owed for goods bought and charged. Notes Payable are promissory notes owed to the banks or to a finance company. The SBA Note listed under the Long-term Liabilities is a 5-year loan advanced by, or guaranteed by, the federal Small Business Administration. The Bonds Payable are a long-term loan, floated at a 3 per cent coupon rate, and not due for 15 years. (NOTE: What appears as a Liability to this company may show up as an Asset to someone else; thus the creditors who own these bonds will carry them as left-hand-side Assets, "Bonds Receivable.")

[1] Accounting texts refer to them as "First-in-first-out" (FIFO) and "Last-in-first-out" (LIFO) and analyze them in detail.

Turning now to Net Worth items, we find that 500 shares of $100, 4 per cent, cumulative (nonparticipating) preferred stock have been issued; and 20,000 shares of no-par common stock were issued at $10 each.

This completes our first glance at a simple Balance Sheet.

THE STATEMENT OF PROFIT AND LOSS, OR INCOME STATEMENT

Now let time march on. During the following months, the firm is profitably engaged in producing and selling toothpaste. To show its flow of income over the 12 months of the year, we must turn to its Income Statement, or—as many companies prefer—the Statement of Profit and Loss, Table 5-2.

This is a statement which reports the following: (1) Pepto-Glitter's revenues from sales in 1971, (2) the expenses to be charged against those sales, and (3) the profit remaining after expenses have been deducted. That is,

Total Profit = Total Revenue minus Total Costs
(the fundamental identity of the Income Statement).

You will understand it better if at first you disregard the figures in the Manufacturing Cost of Goods Sold section (the indented figures) and look only at those in the right-hand column. Sales were $240,000; and the cost of manufacturing the goods sold came to $170,000. After deducting another $14,000 for Selling and Administrative Costs, $56,000 remained in Net Operating Profit. Out of this, a total of $23,500 in interest and taxes had to be paid, leaving $32,500 in Net Earnings after Taxes. Dividends of $2,000 preferred and $10,500 common were paid, leaving $20,000 of net profit (Addition to Surplus) retained in the business.

Now turn to the indented Manufacturing Cost of Goods Sold section, which lists the costs incurred in this part of the business. The firm's outlays for materials, labor, and miscellaneous expenses are listed, together with an item for Depreciation. (Depreciation is worth a section to itself, and we shall consider it soon.) The sum of these four items ($175,000) is the Total Manufacturing Cost. Then follows what may seem a puzzling adjustment. The value of the inventory on January 1 is added, and that of the year-end inventory is deducted. The result, which differs from Manufacturing Cost by $5,000, is the Manufacturing Cost *of Goods Sold*. What is the difference between these terms, and why this inventory adjustment?

The flow of income over the year is shown by the income statement:

Net Sales (after all discounts and rebates)		$240,000
Less: Manufacturing Cost of Goods Sold:		
Materials	$ 50,000	
Labor Cost	100,000	
Depreciation Charges	20,000	
Miscellaneous Operating Cost	5,000	
Total Manufacturing Cost	$175,000	
Add: Beginning Inventory	80,000	
	$255,000	
Deduct: Closing Inventory	85,000	
Equals: Manufacturing Cost *of Goods Sold*	$170,000	170,000
Gross Profit (or Gross Margin)		$ 70,000
Less: Selling and Administrative Costs		14,000
Net Operating Profit		$ 56,000
Less: Fixed Interest Charges and State and Local Taxes		6,000
Net Earnings before Income Taxes		$ 50,000
Less: Corporation Income Taxes		17,500
Net Earnings after Taxes		$ 32,500
Less: Dividends on Preferred Stock		2,000
Net Profits of Common Stockholders		$ 30,500
Less: Dividends Paid on Common Stock		10,500
Addition to Surplus		$ 20,000

TABLE 5-2. INCOME STATEMENT OF PEPTO-GLITTER, INC., FROM JANUARY 1, 1971, TO DECEMBER 31, 1971.

Pepto-Glitter began the year with inventory of $80,000 in raw materials and finished goods. During the year, it built up inventories by an extra $5,000. In this case, it would be false to attribute all the manufacturing cost to *the goods actually sold.* Some of these costs are really attributable to goods to be sold *in the future.* To neglect this fact would be to overstate the Manufacturing Cost of Goods Sold in this year; it would mean subtracting too much from this year's Net Sales and understating this year's Profits.

If there had been no change in the amount of inventory, then all would be simple: Manufacturing Cost and Manufacturing Cost of Goods Sold would be identical.

On the other hand, what if we had had less inventory on hand at the year's end than at the beginning? Pretty clearly, we shall be fooling ourselves if we do not recognize that the cost of the goods we have sold this year ought really to be *greater* than the money we have paid out to labor and to other firms. We shall have neglected the cost element of used-up and unreplaced inventory.

Summary: To reach a valid figure for Manufacturing Cost of Goods Sold, we must adjust the Manufacturing Cost figure thus:

If the Closing Inventory shows an increase over the Beginning Inventory, deduct that increase; if the Closing Inventory has decreased, add that decrease.

Instead of subtracting $5,000 directly from the $175,000 total manufacturing expense, the accountant does it in two steps. Rather than working with the difference between the two, he first adds the total Beginning Inventory, then subtracts the Closing Inventory. This procedure has the advantage of being standardized; it is the same whether inventory is up or down, whereas a single change-in-inventory figure would in some cases be a subtraction, in others an addition. And the accountant's method also reveals the change in inventory relative to the size of the total inventory.

Note that items in Table 5-2 differ from Balance-Sheet items of Table 5-1. Income items refer to *flows* over time: moving-picture action. Balance-Sheet items refer to *stocks* at an instant of time: still pictures.

DEPRECIATION

At first, one may wonder why any Depreciation Charges have been made for 1971. The buildings and equipment were newly bought at the beginning of the year, and surely they will not have worn out already. (It will, of course, be necessary to spend money on men to maintain the equipment and keep the factories painted; but their wages are already included in Labor Cost or Miscellaneous Operating Cost and are not included in Depreciation Charges.)

Here is where the farseeing wisdom of the accountant comes to the fore. He points out that not a cent may have to be spent upon replacement of equipment for 10 years, at which time all the machines may suddenly have to bought anew. It would be nonsense to charge nothing to depreciation for 9 years and fool yourself into thinking you are making a nice profit and then suddenly in the tenth year have to charge off all the value of the machines at once and think you have incurred a great loss in that year.

Actually, he points out, the equipment is being used up all the time. A truer, undistorted picture of net income or profit will be reached if the costs of the equipment are spread more evenly over its lifetime. The value of equipment declines as a result of age and use; it depreciates from its price as new to its final scrap value. In recognition of this, the accountant depreciates the value of fixed capital items by some *gradual* formula. Of the various proposed methods, here are two widely used ones.

The first is called "straight-line depreciation." Suppose that you have a truck whose cost new is $10,100 and whose economic life is 10 years; after this its physical life may continue but its economic life will be over, because of its unreliability and maintenance costs. Suppose that its scrap value at the end of 10 years is $100. According to the straight-line method, you will each year charge off to depreciation one-tenth of the lifetime decline in its total value, $10,000 (new price minus scrap value). Thus, $1,000 will be entered in Depreciation Charges every year.

A second method of more rapid early depreciation has become fashionable, especially since the recent tax laws permit generous use of it. Instead of writing off a new asset steadily by the straight-line method, firms can use the "declining-balance method," or—what is somewhat similar in its generosity toward fast

early depreciation—the "sum-of-the-digits" method. Only the first will be described in this brief treatment.

Disregarding scrap value as negligible, consider the 10-year $10,000 truck. Instead of taking one-tenth its value for depreciation in the first year, the tax law lets you charge off, under the declining-balance method, twice that amount, or 2×10 per cent = 20 per cent in its first year. So you get a much larger deduction for tax purposes. Evidently you cannot go on charging off that amount for each year of life, since that would leave you with zero value by the halfway point, at the end of 5 years. What the declining-balance method does is to let you take off 20 per cent of *remaining* value or balance each year. In the second year, then, you take off 20 per cent of the $8,000 of remaining value, or $1,600. In the third year you take off 20 per cent of what is left, namely, of $6,400. So the process goes. It can be calculated that by the time the asset has reached half the length of its useful life, you have been permitted to write off for tax purposes almost two-thirds its value—rather than one-half, as under the straight-line method. It is later in life that the declining-balance method begins to be less generous in order to compensate for its early generosity.[2]

Although depreciation is usually figured by some apparently exact formula, every accountant knows that the estimates are really very rough, being subject to large and unpredictable errors and involving arbitrary corrections and assumptions. He comforts himself with two thoughts: (1) A rough method of depreciation, like an imperfect watch, is often better than none at all. (2) Mistakes in depreciation will ultimately "come out in the wash" anyway.

Let us see why a mistake in depreciation ultimately tends to correct itself. Suppose that the truck lasts 15 years rather than the predicted 10. We have then been overstating our depreciation *expenses* during the first 10 years. But in the eleventh and later years there will be no depreciation charged on the truck at all, since it has already been written down to its scrap value by the end of the tenth year. Our profits

[2] A quite different method, called the "service-unit method," or "unit-of-production method," can be mentioned only briefly here. According to this we should estimate the number of miles, loads, or service units that the truck will perform in its life. Thus, if the truck goes a million miles in 10 years and its loss of value during that time is $10,000, then each mile used up represents about 1 cent.

in these later years tend, therefore, to be overstated by about as much as they were understated in the earlier years. After 15 years, everything is pretty much the same after all. That is, except for taxes. Different methods of depreciation result in a different apparent distribution of earnings over time, and therefore in a different pattern over time of corporation income taxes. Naturally, a businessman prefers a method of depreciation that will make his income average out more steadily over time, so as to keep his effective tax rate as low as possible and permit him to cancel off losses against profits; and he also likes a fast method (such as the declining balance) that enables him to put off the evil day of taxes as far as possible.

This explains why so many corporations took advantage of the government's emergency offer to let them amortize (or depreciate) their defense plants and equipment over 5 years. They were glad to be able, by charging high depreciation expenses, to reduce their stated profits during the defense emergency when their profits were enormous. They much preferred to take advantage of this "accelerated depreciation" plan so as to shift their profits from those emergency years to later

years when it was hoped that corporation tax rates would be lower.

The Treasury will not let a corporation manipulate its Depreciation Charges as to avoid taxes. The company may select any reasonable method; once having made its choice, it must stick to it. Many people are today worried about the harmful effects of taxation on "venture capital." They argue, we shall get more investment in new tools and create more jobs if the Treasury is more liberal in letting companies depreciate their equipment rapidly, thereby saving on taxes. In the 1960s the Kennedy Administration introduced an "investment tax credit," which actually gives a subsidy to firms that invest in new equipment. This tax credit can be turned on and off to stabilize investment.

THE RELATION BETWEEN THE INCOME STATEMENT AND THE BALANCE SHEET

Now we must relate the description by the Income Statement of what has happened during the year to the Balance Sheets at the beginning and end of the year. Table 5-3 shows the Balance Sheet of our toothpaste

After the year's operations, we get a new balance sheet:

ASSETS			LIABILITIES AND NET WORTH	
			Liabilities	
Current Assets:			**Current Liabilities:**	
Cash		$ 17,000	Accounts Payable	$ 10,000
Inventory		85,000	Notes Payable	17,000
Sinking Fund to Replace Equipment		5,000	Reserve for Taxes	21,000
(U.S. government bonds)				
Fixed Assets:			**Long-term Liabilities:**	
Equipment	$130,000		SBA Note	50,000
Less: Allowance (or Reserve)			Bonds Payable	50,000
for Depreciation	15,000			
		115,000		
Buildings	$170,000		*Net Worth*	
Less: Allowance (or Reserve)			**Capital Stock:**	
for Depreciation	5,000		Preferred Stock	50,000
		165,000	Common Stock	200,000
Intangible Assets:			**Surplus:**	20,000
Patents		10,000		
Good Will		21,000		
Total		$418,000	Total	$418,000

TABLE 5-3. BALANCE SHEET OF PEPTO-GLITTER, INC., AS OF DECEMBER 31, 1971.

corporation at the end of its first year of operation. It has prospered. Net Worth, the difference between Total Assets and Total Liabilities, has increased between the beginning and end of the accounting period by $20,000—from $250,000 to $270,000. The amount of this increase, as seen by comparing Balance Sheets, just equals the earnings or profits *available* to the common stockholders but not paid out to them in dividends, or as we saw at the bottom of the Income Statement, just equal to $30,500 minus $10,500, or $20,000 of undistributed profits.

Some Net Worth item must be written up by $20,000. It would clearly never do to increase the Preferred Stock Capital Account, because such stockholders are not the residual claimants to the profits of the corporation and no new stock has been sold. Conceivably, one could add the $20,000 to the Common Stock Capital Account. However, this is not done. Instead, the Common Stock Capital Account is left at its original par or issued value.

It is more informative to create a new account called Surplus—or sometimes Earned Surplus or Earnings Retained in the Business—to show how much of the increase in "book value" or Net Worth has resulted from accumulated undistributed earnings plowed back through the years.

In many ways Surplus is a misleading word. It sounds like something extra or unnecessary, or too often like a spare chunk of cash which the company's workers or stockholders might hope to stage a raid against. Actually, Surplus is distinctly not an Assets account, much less a pool of liquid cash. It simply indicates a part of the ownership—over and above Liabilities to creditors and original subscribed capital ownership—in the polyglot Assets of the corporation. A glance at Table 5-3 shows us that the $20,000 of Surplus is not matched by an equivalent amount of cash on the Assets side.

We must again issue a warning against trying to link specific items on the two sides of the Balance Sheet. Only the final totals correspond. It is not even possible to say exactly how the $20,000 plowed back into the business, or added to Surplus, was used. An addition to Surplus must be associated with an increase in Assets and/or a decrease in Liabilities—that is all we can say.

It would be an equal mistake to think that the profits of a corporation accrue in the form of cash, so that on the last day of the year, just before the board

of directors decided upon its dividend rate, there was some $30,500 of cash on hand, available either for the stockholders or to be reinvested in the business. In the case of our toothpaste company, the very handsome profit earned was largely embodied in the form of new Assets and lowered Liabilities; not very much more than $10,500 could have been paid out as cash dividends without forcing serious changes in the financial decisions of the company—decisions such as to borrow more, to grow more slowly, to sell off some of the equipment and inventory at a loss, or to operate with a ludicrously low cash balance.

SUMMARY OF ELEMENTARY ACCOUNTING RELATIONS

Before taking a last look at the new complexities introduced in the 1971 Balance Sheet over that of 1970, we may briefly summarize the relationship between Balance Sheets and Income Statements:

1. The Balance Sheet indicates an instantaneous financial picture: it is like a measure of the stock of water in a lake.

2. The Income Statement shows the flow of sales, cost, and revenue over the year or other accounting period: it measures the flow of water in and out of the lake.

3. The change in total Net Worth between the beginning and the end of the period—as shown by comparing the new and old Balance Sheets—is also to be understood from an examination of the changes in Surplus as appended at the end of Table 5-3's Income Statement: the change in the lake's level over the year we can relate to the flows during the year. (If new common stock is sold, that will be revealed by comparing the two Balance Sheets.)

There do remain, however, certain shifts in the Balance-Sheet items from their previous levels in the earlier period to which the intervening Income Statement gives us no clue. A closer look at the December 31, 1971, Balance Sheet will therefore prove instructive, although enough has been said already to introduce the reader to the fundamentals of accounting.

RESERVES AND FUNDS

The new Balance Sheet looks much like the old for the most part; but some new items are present for the first time. The last of these new items, Surplus, we have already explained. Among the Liabilities there is a new item called Reserve for Taxes of $21,000. It is not hard to understand. The taxes that the corporation will have to pay the government are as much short-term Liabilities as the Accounts Payable or Notes Payable.

Taxes Payable might have been a better title, since the word "Reserve" suggests a pool of cash, which it decidedly is not. Instead, the Reserve for Taxes is simply an earmarking of part of the Total Assets of the company for a special creditor—a reminder that the owners' Net Worth is less by the amount of owed taxes. We shall soon see there are three main kinds of "Reserves," and no one represents a pool of cash or liquid Assets.

Let us turn to the Assets side for new items.[3] The first stranger, entitled "Sinking Fund to Replace Equipment," is listed midway between the Current and Fixed Assets. It is an asset consisting of, say, 5 per cent government bonds which are to be held for the purpose of ultimately providing part of the money to buy new machines when the old ones are to be replaced. Although the corporation could change its mind and use the Sinking Fund bonds for another purpose, it presumably will not choose to do so. The nature of this Sinking Fund is understandable; it is simply a pool of liquid Assets set aside for a specific future purpose.

Turning to the Fixed Assets, we find ourselves in for a surprise. From our previous discussion of the Depreciation Charges of the Income Statement, we should have expected the Buildings and Equipment items to total $280,000. Why? Because at the beginning of the year they added up to $300,000, because no new equipment was bought during the year, and because the Income Statement told us that $20,000 of depreciation accrued during the period as part of the necessary costs of production.

Why, then, are these Fixed Assets carried on the new Balance Sheet at the old $130,000 and $170,000 figures? Looking more closely, we see that they really are not. From the $130,000 nominal Equipment valua-

tion, there is subtracted an Allowance (or Reserve) for Depreciation, so that really only $115,000 is carried for Equipment. Similarly, from the $170,000 original value of the Buildings, there is subtracted a $5,000 Allowance for Depreciation. Our faith in the accountant's sanity is restored; but we may still wonder why he goes through this roundabout procedure of stating "two" as "four minus two" instead of simply as "two."

Actually, he has his good reasons. An honest accountant knows his Depreciation estimate is only the roughest of guesses. Were he simply to guess and put down the final figure of $115,000 for Equipment, the public would not know how much reliance to place upon the figure. So he puts down $130,000 of original value, which is firmly rooted in the solid fact of original cost; and he then carefully isolates his own guessed-at Allowance for Depreciation. Then the public is in a better position to evaluate the reliability of the final $115,000 figure. The roundabout procedure does no harm, and may do good.

Now we know the precise meaning of Allowances (or Reserves) for Depreciation. They are not sums of money; they are not sinking funds of liquid Assets that can be spent on replacement. They are *subtractions from overstated Assets figures*. Thus, the Allowance for Depreciation of Buildings of $5,000 is an explicit correction of the original value of the Buildings, which would be an overstatement of the value left in them. This correction must be made to keep Assets and Net Worth from both being artificially inflated.

It must be made regardless of whether at the same time any money is or is not being set aside into sinking funds to replace the Depreciation asset. Note that there is no Sinking Fund for Buildings and that the Sinking Fund to Replace Equipment is only one-third as large as the estimated Allowance for Depreciation of Equipment. As a matter of fact, American businesses rarely set aside any considerable sums of money in replacement sinking funds. This is because liquid gilt-edge bonds earn at most only a few per cent interest, whereas capital invested in the firm's own activities usually brings in much more.[4]

---

[3] Neither this Balance Sheet nor the previous one contains a frequently met Current Assets item called Prepaid Expenses. Often an enterprise will pay its rent or buy some supplies a number of months in advance. Very properly, the enterprise is regarded as possessing on its Balance Sheet an equivalent asset.

[4] Where, then, will the money be coming from to replace any particular machine or building if no sinking funds have been set aside? Ordinarily, the equipment can be purchased with sales dollars earned by other equipment that is not cur-

We have met two kinds of Reserves: (1) a Liability Reserve, like that for taxes, which is really simply a liability of fairly certain amount, and (2) an Asset Valuation Reserve like that for Depreciation (or allowance for estimated uncollectible bills), which is really simply a subtraction from an overstated asset. A third so-called "Surplus Reserve," which is also not to be confused with a sum of money, may be mentioned: Sometimes a firm takes part of its Surplus and sets it aside under a different name so the stockholders will not be tempted to lobby for higher dividend payments. For example, our toothpaste company might earmark half of its $20,000 Surplus account into a Reserve for Research and Development. This $10,000 Reserve would no more consist of cash or liquid funds than does Surplus itself, or than does any other kind of Reserve. It should never be confused with a fund.[5]

We have now outlined the fundamentals of accounting, and the rest of the Appendix deals with some further developments.

INTANGIBLE ASSETS

Only one further new category of Assets can still be found on the December 31, 1971, Balance Sheet. To illustrate that an asset need not be a tangible commodity, a piece of equipment, or a sum of money, a patent has been introduced into the picture. Suppose it is a patent on a profitable new chemical process, giving us exclusive production rights for 17 years.

Such a patent is obviously worth money. Of course, as 5, 10, 12, and 16 years pass, the patent will be coming near to the end of its 17-year life and will be declining in value. Therefore, some depreciation formula will be applied to it just as if it were a truck.

---

rently calling for replacement expenditure. The selling price of the output of such other equipment contains an accounting allowance for depreciation expense, and a corresponding sum of money is available for investment elsewhere in the business. Speaking somewhat loosely, we may say that each asset not needing replacement lends its Depreciation Charges to those which need replacement, knowing that it too will be taken care of when the need arises.
[5] The problem of Reserves becomes even more complicated in connection with contingencies that may or may not occur. Thus Reserve for Depression Contingencies or for Renegotiation would fall halfway between true Liability and Surplus Reserves.

GOOD WILL AND MONOPOLY EARNING POWER

So much for Patents as an illustration of an intangible asset. Let us suppose that, at the same time we bought the patent, we also took over a rival toothpaste company. This horizontal combination will presumably add to our monopoly position and earning power. Therefore we were willing to buy the company for more than its trifling Assets—which happened to consist solely of a little inventory—were worth. Perhaps part of the purchase price went as profits to those who promoted this little monopolistic merger.

An example of the capitalization of earning power is J. P. Morgan's formation of the giant United States Steel Company at the turn of the century. He bought out the Andrew Carnegie steel plants and combined them with half a dozen other holdings. But in economics, as in atomic physics, the whole is equal to more than the sum of its parts.

After Morgan had put the pieces together, he found himself with some 130 million dollars of extra capital value!

Who was hurt by this transaction? Certainly not Carnegie or Morgan. Even the people who bought the stock had no right to complain that it had been "watered," since for many years they got more than a fair return on their investments. To have sold them the stock for its actual cost (without water) would be (1) to make them a free gift of the enlarged profits of the concern, and (2) to give them the privilege of reselling the stock at the higher price that its earning power could earn for it in a competitive stock market. (In terms of standards at the time, there was nothing illegal or unethical about this merger.)

Our practical-minded accountant, however, is not concerned with such matters of public policy and political economy as whether the consumer will or will not now pay higher prices. He will tell our toothpaste company or J. P. Morgan the same thing: "If you paid a certain sum of money for some assets, they must presumably be worth that much to you. If the assets don't exist, they must be created. 'Good Will' is their name." But since this term has come into bad repute in recent years, it is often lumped in with some other assets.

The intangible asset Good Will is thus the difference between what a company pays in buying out another company and what it gets in identifiable Assets.

CONCLUSION

Finally, some interesting relations between economics and accounting can be briefly mentioned. (1) All Balance Sheets depend on valuation of Assets, which is one of the basic questions of the capital and interest theory discussed in Part Four. (2) Our national-income statistics are founded on the accounting data of sales, cost, and so forth, as Chapter 10 shows. (3) As we shall see in a later discussion of how firms set price, accounting cost data play an important role in price determination.

The accountant deals with money magnitudes; the economist tries to probe deeper to the underlying real magnitudes. Especially in periods of great inflation or deflation, the accountant realizes that his ordinary methods may give strange results.

One example is the problem of changing price levels and depreciation. Suppose prices are rising sharply. If I sell my goods for enough to cover labor and other costs and also to cover depreciation, you might think I am breaking even. What would an accountant say who figures depreciation on the basis of the past low prices originally paid for my machines and building? He, too, would say I am breaking even. But in fact I can be said to have been selling my goods at a *real* loss; for when my machines and buildings have worn out, I shall not have enough money to *reproduce them* at the new higher price level. The same is true of a merchant who sells off his inventory at less than replacement cost.

So we must beware of fictitious money overstatements of real profits during rising prices and of fictitious understatements of profits during falling prices. (Later, in national-income statistics, you will note that profits are "adjusted" for inventory revaluations.)

SUMMARY TO APPENDIX

Instead of a lengthy recapitulation, here is a check list of accounting concepts that you should understand:

1 ■

The fundamental Balance-Sheet relationship between Assets, Liabilities, and Net Worth and the breakdown of each of these into Current and Fixed Assets, Current and Long-term Liabilities, Capital and Surplus.

2 ■

The character of the Income Statement (or Profit-and-Loss Statement) and the relationship between undistributed profit and Surplus changes on the new Balance Sheet.

3 ■

The whole problem of Depreciation, both in its income-statement aspect as a necessary expense, which need not be an expenditure, and in its balance-sheet treatment as a deduction from a purposely overstated asset; also the logic of the principal depreciation methods. Although any errors in calculating depreciation tend to cancel out eventually, recent tax concessions that allow rapid depreciation, do improve the cash position of corporations.

4 ■

The difference between a Fund or a pool of liquid Assets and three kinds of so-called "Reserves"; also the meaning of intangible Assets like Patents and Good Will.

QUESTIONS FOR DISCUSSION

1. Describe the Balance Sheet's right-hand side. Its left-hand side. What items must match from the "fundamental identity"?

2. You are a banker deciding whether to lend money to the toothpaste company. Why be especially interested in current items?

3. Write out a list of many different Assets. Give the nature of each in a few lines. Do the same for Liabilities.

4. Is an Income Statement a "still picture" at an instant of time? Why not?

5. In 1971 a company has 10 million dollars of net sales and 9 million dollars of costs of all kinds (including taxes, interest, etc.). It rents its equipment, its inventory does not change in the year, and it has no preferred stock. It pays no dividends. Draw up its simplified Income Statement.

6. The same company as in question 5 owes no money, having been completely equity-financed years ago. Fill in the year-end Balance Sheet at the end of this section.

7. Redo problems 5 and 6, making the following changes: In addition to the other expenses, its buildings depreciate by 2 million dollars; also its inventory has fallen off by 3 million dollars.

Draw up an Income Statement showing its loss for the year, and adjust its 1971 Balance Sheet accordingly.

8. Describe two methods of calculating Depreciation, and explain tax advantages.

9. Differentiate between three different kinds of Reserves. Which, if any, are "Funds"? Which cash? Describe intangible Assets.

10. Guess how much you would pay for a business that is sure of yielding a net profit of $15,000 per year with little risk of principal. Suppose its Total Assets exclusive of Good Will were valued at $100,000. What would you guess for Good Will?

11. Review your understanding of the following concepts:

Balance-Sheet identity
Income-Statement identity
Assets, Liabilities, and Net Worth
Current versus Fixed Assets
Surplus, earnings, dividends
Manufacturing Cost of Goods Sold
Manufacturing Cost, inventory change
Depreciation (as expense and reserve)
intangible Assets—Patents and Good Will
Asset and Liability Reserves versus Sinking Fund

ASSETS			LIABILITIES AND NET WORTH		
	1970	1971		1970	1971
			Liabilities	0	0
			Net Worth	$50 million	....
Total	$50 million	....	Total	....	....

6 Affluence and Poverty: Individual and Family Income

F. SCOTT FITZGERALD: YOU KNOW, ERNEST, THE RICH ARE DIFFERENT FROM US.
ERNEST HEMINGWAY: YES, I KNOW. THEY HAVE MORE MONEY THAN WE DO.

Everyone realizes the importance of income. The expression "Clothes make the man" would be more nearly right if it were "Income makes the man." That is to say, if you can know but one fact about a man, knowledge of his income may prove to be the most revealing. Then you can roughly guess his political opinions, his tastes and education, his age, and even his life expectancy. Furthermore, unless a family has a steady stream of money coming in every week, month, and year—even though it has saintly endurance—that family is sick. Not only its materialistic activities, but its nonmaterialistic activities—the things that convert existence into living—must suffer: education, travel, recreation, and charity, to say nothing of food, warmth, and shelter.

It is a commonplace to state that the American standard of living and level of family income are the highest in all the world. But few people realize just how small the average American income really is, or how great is the range between the highest and the lowest incomes.

This chapter gives some basic facts about incomes and wealth, here and abroad. America has been described by Harvard's J. Kenneth Galbraith as The Affluent Society. And the mixed economies of Western Europe are following hot on our heels. Yet pockets of poverty remain: and as we shall see, this kind of poverty is new in history and different from that found in most other parts of the earth.

■ THE DECLINE OF POVERTY

It is now well over a century since Karl Marx and Friedrich Engels in 1848 issued the Communist Manifesto containing the lines: "Workers of the world unite! You have nothing to lose but your chains." While some of Marx's predictions about the future of industrial capitalism were proved correct in the intervening years, one of his most famous has proved to be quite wrong. His assertion that *the rich will become richer and the poor will become poorer* cannot be sustained by careful historical and statistical research. In Europe and America there has definitely been a steady secular improvement in minimum standards of living, whether measured by food, clothing, housing, or length of life. This fact about capitalism is clear from statistics soon to be given.

It used to be fashionable for economic historians to dwell on the evils of the Industrial Revolution and the poverty-ridden condition of the masses in the disease-producing cities. In point of fact, no Dickens novel did full justice to the conditions of child labor, length of the working day, and conditions of safety and sanitation in early nineteenth-century factories. A work week of 84 hours was the prevailing rule, with time out at the bench for breakfast and sometimes supper, as well as lunch. A good deal of work could be got out of a six-year-old child; and if a man lost two fingers in a machine, he still had eight left.

However true their lurid picture of industrial factory towns, the earlier historians erred in thinking that conditions were worse than in the preindustrial era. The earlier "putting-out," or domestic, system, in which wool or yarn was provided to workers for them to spin or weave in their homes, brought the worst conditions of the sweatshop into the home. The whole family was figuratively forced to run on the treadmill.

Furthermore, poverty is never so obvious in the country as in the industrial cities, where it forces itself on the observer. The idyllic picture of the healthful, happy countryside peopled by stout yeomen and happy peasantry is a mirage in most parts of the world. Even today, New York's Hell's Kitchen or Harlem, Boston's South or North End, "behind the Yards" in Chicago or its black belt hardly overshadow the poverty and squalor of our rural problem areas: the Tobacco Road of the deep South, hillbilly regions of the Appalachian Plateau, dust bowls, and ghost mining towns.

Modern historians therefore emphasize that the conditions of the industrial present, inadequate as they may seem, are nevertheless great improvements over the previous periods of commercial enterprise and agrarian feudalism.

■ TWO WORLDS?

Most of Asia and Africa are even today at lower levels of living than were the Western countries before the Industrial Revolution. Figure 6-1 shows how fortunate the United States growth in output has been. A great economic statistician, Simon Kuznets of Harvard, has recently shown that the leading Western nations have for decades been averaging rapid rates of growth of output per head. How rapid a growth? Study the front-leaf chart to learn the story.

What about the progress of the poorer countries? We lack data to give firm answers. Professor Kuznets has made shrewd guesses and inclines to the view that their productivity growth has been lagging behind. He makes the important observation:[1]

[1] Simon Kuznets, "Quantitative Aspects of the Economic Growth of Nations: I," *Economic Development and Cultural Change*, vol. V, 1956, p. 25.

. . . the presently developed countries were already in advance of the "rest of the world" when modern industrialization began—and the latter only increased the disparity.

Table 6-1 shows the wide international spreads of income per head. In the United States itself, the South has much lower incomes than the Northeast and the West Coast. States such as Mississippi have scarcely attained per capita incomes equal to those reached in Pennsylvania and New York back in 1900 or those found in France today. But it is interesting to note that the regional differentials in income are gradually narrowing and changing. The South and West grow faster than the average; and older regions, such as the Middle Atlantic states, are reverting toward the average.

■ DISTRIBUTION OF INCOME IN THE UNITED STATES

A poll of students will show that they are not very sure about what their own family incomes really are. Usually it turns out they have a slightly exaggerated notion of their fathers' earnings. And despite the recent (quite justified) claim of a prominent club-

Higher productivity gives us more product and more leisure:

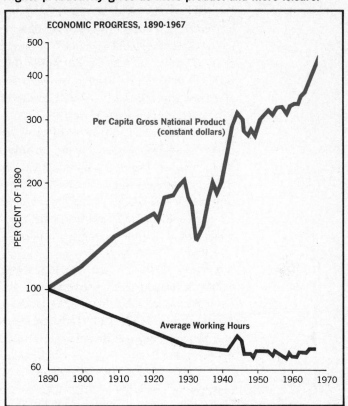

FIG. 6-1. Technological improvements, better capital goods, and more highly skilled labor have raised production faster than the growth of population. NOTE: This is a "ratio," or "semilog," chart; the vertical scale is arranged so that equal vertical distances depict equal percentage rather than equal absolute changes. EXAMPLE: 400 is as far above 200 as 200 is above 100. (Source: U.S. Department of Commerce.)

Americans enjoy highest standard of living in world:

United States	$3,272	Italy	$969
Sweden	2,282	Ireland	909
Canada	2,258	Japan	716
Switzerland	2,200	Poland	530
Denmark	1,861	Argentina	523
France	1,807	Mexico	454
West Germany	1,773	China (Taiwan)	189
United Kingdom	1,700	Togo	90
U.S.S.R.	1,060	India	88

TABLE 6-1. PER CAPITA INCOME OF DIFFERENT COUNTRIES, 1964. All estimates have been converted into U.S. dollars at exchange rates designed to reflect actual purchasing powers; but all figures should be regarded as rough approximations, particularly in countries at drastically different stages of development. (Source: AID and Center for International Studies, MIT.)

woman that "women spend 70 per cent of the national income, and we soon hope to get hold of the rest," an astonishing number of wives have no conception of their husbands' paychecks. In addition, there are some people so inept at keeping records and with such variable earnings that they do not themselves know how much they make. Even where income is known within the family, there is a quite natural reticence to reveal it to outsiders; thus investigators who made a survey of the birth-control habits of native white Protestants of Indianapolis often found it harder to get financial data than intimate personal information.

In the absence of statistical knowledge, it is understandable that one should form an impression of the American standard of living from the full-page magazine advertisements portraying a jolly American family in an air-conditioned mansion, with a Buick, a station wagon, a motor launch, and all the other good things that go to make up comfortable living. Actually, of course, this sort of life is still beyond the grasp of 85 per cent of the American public and even beyond most families from which the select group of college students comes.

THE SOBER TRUTH   In the late 1960s, at the pinnacle of American prosperity, the per capita income in the United States is about $55 per week. Such an average figure is derived by pretending that all the income in the United States is divided equally among every man, woman, and child. Of course, income is distributed far from equally; and there is no guarantee that an attempt to divide it equally would leave the total unchanged.

If the members of a classroom, or of the whole country, write down their family incomes on cards, these cards may be sorted into different income classes; i.e., some cards will go into the $0-to-$1,999 class, some into the $2,000-to-$3,999 class, and so forth. In this way we get the *statistical frequency* distribution of income. At one extreme will be the very poor, who have drawn a blank in life; at the other, the very rich. In between fall the vast majority.

Table 6-2 summarizes recent statistics on this subject. Column (1) gives the *income class interval*. Column (2) shows the percentage of families and individuals in each income class. Column (3) shows the percentage of the total of all income that goes to the people in the given income class. Columns (4) and (5) are computed from (2) and (3), respectively. Column (4) shows what percentage of the total number of families and individuals belongs to each income class *or below*. Column (5) shows what percentage of total income goes to the people who belong in the given income class or have still lower incomes.

This table shows it would be a great mistake to think that the poor and the rich are equally distributed around the middle. The Biblical statement, "For the poor ye have always with you," gives no inkling of their vast numbers. Abraham Lincoln pointed up this fact picturesquely in his statement, "The Lord prefers common people. . . . He made so many of them."

A glance at the income distribution in the United States shows how pointed is the income pyramid and how broad its base. "There's always room at the top" is certainly true; this is so because it is hard to get there, not because it is easy. If we

Few families in America reach income level of $15,000:

(1)	(2)	(3)	(4)	(5)
INCOME CLASS	PERCENTAGE OF ALL FAMILIES AND INDIVIDUALS IN THIS CLASS	PERCENTAGE OF TOTAL INCOME RECEIVED BY FAMILIES AND INDIVIDUALS IN THIS CLASS	PERCENTAGE OF FAMILIES AND INDIVIDUALS IN THIS CLASS AND LOWER ONES	PERCENTAGE OF INCOME RECEIVED BY THIS CLASS AND LOWER ONES
Under $2,000	11	2	11	2
$ 2,000–$ 3,999	18	7	29	9
4,000– 5,999	18	12	47	21
6,000– 7,999	17	15	64	36
8,000– 9,999	12	13	76	49
10,000– 14,999	15	22	91	71
15,000 and up	9	29	100	100
Total	100	100		

TABLE 6-2. DISTRIBUTION OF INCOMES OF AMERICAN FAMILIES AND INDIVIDUALS, 1964. Half of these families and individuals are below the median income of $5,700. The average (or arithmetic mean) income each would get if total income were distributed exactly equally is about $7,900. More families and individuals have incomes around the modal $5,000 level than around any other income. (Source: U.S. Department of Commerce.)

made an income pyramid out of a child's blocks, with each layer portraying $1,000 of income, the peak would be far higher than the Eiffel Tower, but almost all of us would be within a yard of the ground.

The middle, or "median," income class (which divides the upper from the lower half of the people) corresponds to a modest income—only about $5,700 in the 1964 table. The median income falls short of the average (or "arithmetic mean") income of $7,900. This is primarily because the distribution of incomes is always a skewed one, with a long tail of incomes stretching out above the mean.

■ HOW TO MEASURE INEQUALITY AMONG INCOME CLASSES

How great is the spread of incomes, and how shall we measure the degree of inequality of income distribution?

From Table 6-2, we can estimate that roughly half of all Americans fall in the middle-income range $3,600 to $9,800. This means that one-fourth fall below $3,600 and an equal number have incomes above $9,800. Of course, the fact that there are the same number of individuals and families in the above-$9,800 group as in the below-$3,600 group does not mean that they each receive the same percentage of the total income. Actually, the lowest fourth of the people receives less than *half of half* of the income received by the highest fourth (as Fig. 6-2 shows).

This suggests how to go about the task of getting a numerical measure of the degree of inequality of income distribution. We can ask, What per cent of all income goes to the lowest 10 per cent of the population? What to the lowest 20 per cent?

Incomes are distributed with neither absolute equality nor absolute inequality:

PERCENTAGE OF PEOPLE	PERCENTAGE OF INCOME		
	ABSOLUTE EQUALITY	ABSOLUTE INEQUALITY	ACTUAL 1964
0	0	0	0
20	20	0	5
40	40	0	18
60	60	0	32
80	80	0	54
95	95	0	81
100	100	100	100

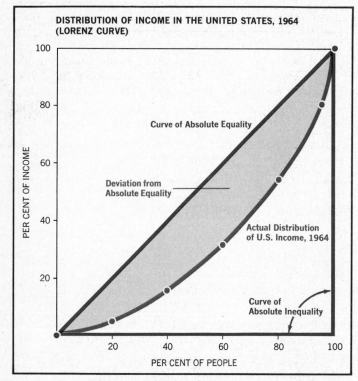

DISTRIBUTION OF INCOME IN THE UNITED STATES, 1964 (LORENZ CURVE)

Curve of Absolute Equality

Deviation from Absolute Equality

Actual Distribution of U.S. Income, 1964

Curve of Absolute Inequality

PER CENT OF INCOME

PER CENT OF PEOPLE

FIG. 6-2. By plotting from the table above, we can see that the actual distribution-of-income curve lies between the two extremes of absolute equality and absolute inequality. The shaded area of this Lorenz chart (as a percentage of half the square's area) measures relative inequality of income. (How would the curve have looked back in the roaring 1920s when inequality was greater? In a 1984 welfare state that narrows income differences?)

The lowest 50 per cent? The lowest 95 per cent? And so forth. Such data can be derived from Columns (4) and (5) of Table 6-2 on the previous page.

If incomes were absolutely uniformly distributed, the lowest 20 per cent of the population (which in this case would mean *any* 20 per cent) would receive exactly 20 per cent of the total income; the lowest 80 per cent would receive 80 per cent of the income; and the highest 20 per cent would also get only 20 per cent of the income.

This is depicted by the so-called "Lorenz curve" in Fig. 6-2. It plots percentage of people, ranked from the poorest up, on the horizontal axis and percentage of total income they receive on the vertical axis.

The second column of the table in Fig. 6-2 gives data for the diagonal line of absolute equality. So much for the case of absolute equality.

At the other extreme, we have the hypothetical case of absolute *inequality*, where everybody (say, 99 out of 100 people) has no income, except for one person who has *all* the income. This is shown in the third column of the table. Why those numbers? Because the lowest 0, 20, 80, and 99 people have no income at all. But the lowest 100 do include the last man; and all the people, of course, have all the income. The lowest curve on the Lorenz diagram—the brown, right-angled line—represents this limiting case of absolute inequality.

Any actual income distribution, such as that of 1964, must fall between these extremes. Its Lorenz curve is given in Fig. 6-2 by the indicated intermediate green curve, with the shaded area indicating the deviation from abso-

Inequality differs among nations and is different for income than for wealth:

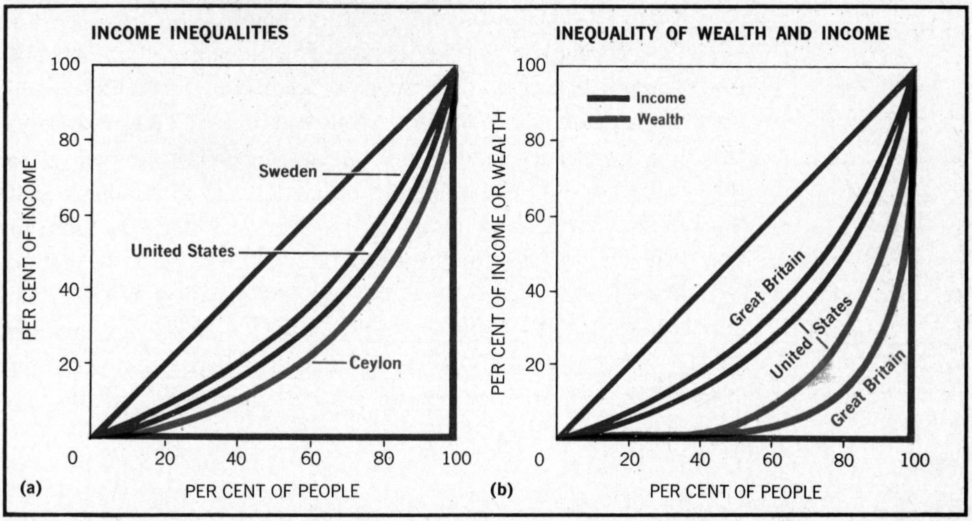

FIG. 6-3(a). Advanced economies show less inequality of income distribution than do preindustrial economies—contrary to dire predictions of scientific socialists that the rich get richer and the poor get poorer under capitalism. The mixed economy shows greater equality.

FIG. 6-3(b). Holdings of wealth tend to be more concentrated than do incomes earned annually. The United States and the United Kingdom have similar equality of incomes; but British wealth is much more concentrated than American.

lute equality, and hence giving us a measure of the degree of *inequality* of income distribution.[2] (This figure repays careful study.)

■ TRENDS OF INEQUALITY

What is happening to the degree of inequality of incomes in modern nations? Is it getting greater, as pessimists feared? By calculating Lorenz and other curves, scholars find that inequality is definitely less in America than it was back in 1929, but little different today from the end of World War II. A glance at Fig. 6-3(b) will show that the United Kingdom and the United States have rather similar degrees of inequality of incomes, the major difference apparently not being attributable so much to differences in social

[2] There are still other ways of measuring the degree of inequality of income. One of the most interesting of these we can mention but not discuss in detail here. The Italian-born Swiss professor of economics Vilfredo Pareto was often called, with somewhat questionable accuracy, the ideological precursor of fascism. By using a certain logarithmic chart called the "Pareto chart," he found that the "upper tail" of the income data of many different countries and many different times fell along straight lines of almost the same slopes. He came to believe this to be a fundamental natural law. According to Pareto's Law, *there is an inevitable tendency for income to be distributed in the same way—regardless of social and political institutions and regardless of taxation.* In the past 70 years, more careful studies have refuted the universality of Pareto's Law, as well as its inevitability. Thus, in Great Britain, in the period following World War II, income taxation had gone so far as to leave only 70 people with incomes of more than $24,000 after taxes were paid!

philosophy as to the fact that there is a larger fraction of subsistence farmers and low-paid Negro workers in the American economy.

Before industrialization, was there a golden age of greater equality of distribution? Fragmentary historical data suggest otherwise. Have developed societies generally greater inequality than underdeveloped nations? Casual tourist observation often suggests the reverse: the extremes of poverty and wealth appear greater in poor countries than in industrialized ones. The limited statistics available do confirm this view; thus, the Lorenz curve for a country like Ceylon in Fig. 6-3(a) will show greater inequality than will such a curve for the United States, the United Kingdom, or the Netherlands.

Which country today has the greatest equality? No one knows how to compare the inequality in the Soviet Union[3] or China with that in mixed economies. If we confine ourselves to the noncommunist world, it has been suggested that the new state of Israel may lead the list. Sweden and other mixed economies have low inequality, as the comparison in Fig. 6-3(a) shows.

■ DISTRIBUTION OF WEALTH

A Lorenz curve of distribution of *wealth* ownership shows considerably more inequality than does a curve of *income* distribution. Figure 6-3(b) shows how great is the difference between the wealth and income curves. Whereas the United Kingdom and the United States have similar inequality of incomes, note that the United Kingdom has much greater inequality of wealth than does the United States. In part this is because certain peers and tycoons in Britain own tremendous concentrations of land and other property. But study of the data shows that much of the difference comes from the fact that many Americans of quite modest incomes do have positive net worth (i.e., assets minus liabilities), whereas this is less common among the lower-income British.

Turn back to Fig. 3-1 on p. 44. It shows that the FOR WHOM problem is determined by (1) the price that people can get for the factors they supply—land, labor, machinery, and general capital goods, and (2) the amounts of these factors that they start out with. If labor could be ignored, the distribution of incomes would tend to be that determined by the distribution of wealth: at the same interest return, twice the wealth yields twice the income. Hence, property incomes show great Lorenz inequality.

The earnings from work—wages, salaries, earnings of unincorporated entrepreneurs—are evidently less unequally distributed. But of course they are not uniform, as the following sections show.

[3] A very careful study of wage inequalities in Russia's communistic economy, Abram Bergson, *The Structure of Soviet Wages* (Harvard University Press, Cambridge, Mass., 1944), showed inequalities and dispersions between the best-paid and the poorest-paid workers surprisingly like those of our own society. Shostakovich, other top Soviet musicians, and top scientists probably make more there than do Stravinsky, Teller, and similar persons in America. The inequality of political privilege among Soviet bureaucrats, military officers, Communist party members, and the Soviet public at large is not susceptible to precise numerical measurement. Employment incomes in mixed economies like Australia and Sweden were found in a 1965 study to be slightly more equal than in Poland.

■ INCOME DIFFERENCES AMONG OCCUPATIONS

What single profession seems to make the most money? In recent years it has without question been the doctors. They have forged well ahead of lawyers. Doctors have mean earnings of about $28,000 and median earnings of about $23,000; lawyers have mean and median earnings of $19,000 and $13,000. Why these high doctor earnings? Primarily because the costs of training doctors are so high and the capacities of our medical schools are so low; as a result, we train not many more doctors than we did in 1910, even though the demand has greatly increased. Medical societies are also accused of helping to keep doctors' incomes up by various devices, including the insistence on high quality standards.

Dentists, engineers, and schoolteachers are estimated to have median incomes of about $16,000, $13,000, and $6,000, respectively. College teachers as a class have a median salary of about $8,500 for a 9-month academic year ($10,000 if they also teach summer school, but only half have this opportunity). Full professors at the largest universities get twice these amounts; professors of physics and engineering average higher incomes than do professors of Greek and botany. While teachers' salaries have been improving recently, it is ministers who are lowest paid of all professionals. Their median salary is still not up to $5,000! And even with special perquisites, the final figure is unbelievably low.

Do incomes increase with age? Not in the lowest-paid manual jobs. For such work, a man is at his best in his early twenties; after that he goes downhill. In the professions and in business executive jobs, earnings do increase with age: doctors and lawyers reach their prime after fifty; both can hope to work beyond the normal retirement ages. A junior executive with an A.B. or business degree will begin training at $850 a month; if he is very successful, he may retire as chairman of the board, earning, say, $125,000 a year and with stock bonuses and retirement provisions.[4]

On the other hand, many corporations and institutions have been fixing inflexible retirement ages of sixty-five. With improvements in life expectancies, this poses a problem of long years of wasteful and unhappy retirement. The ultimate solution seems to be along these lines: Let each man taper off slowly rather than abruptly, other factors besides chronological age being decisive.

■ IS COLLEGE WORTH WHILE?

How do education and training affect lifetime income? Are they worth their cost? The evidence answers, Decidedly yes. Men who never finish eight grades of school earn scarcely $3,800 annually; college graduates do three times as well. Unemployment among school dropouts exceeds that of graduates by a growing margin.

Even if you have to borrow at 7 per cent interest, put off years of gainful employment, live away from home, and pay for food and books, your lifetime earnings in

[4] Salaries of top officers do increase with the size of the firm, but by no means in strict proportion. Statistics suggest that the head of Corporation A, twice the size of Company B, will *not* get twice the salary that the head of B gets, but only about 30 per cent more.

Lawyers and doctors show great income inequalities, professors and army officers less:

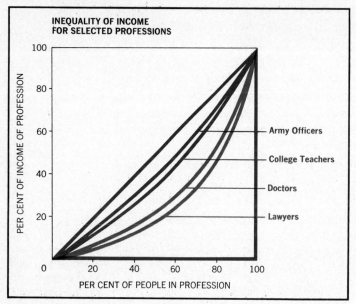

FIG. 6-4. Why would the curve for *salaried* doctors and lawyers fall in the middle of the four curves shown? Why would you expect dentists to have a curve just above doctors? How might the curve for speculators in common stocks look? (Source: G. J. Stigler, National Bureau of Economic Research, New York, 1956.)

the professions that are open only to college graduates will probably turn out to be more than compensatory. (Good grades help: A *Time* study showed, in its own argot, that "greasy grinds" end up with slightly higher pay than do "big men on campus"; both outearn the anonymous face in the college crowd.)

Money is not everything—better to be uneducated, poor, and happy than to be well-off and miserable? The Governmental Commission on Mental Illness and Health reported a 1960 survey of how people with different education compared mentally. Were college graduates worried and depressed in comparison with those of little schooling? Surprisingly, the answer was, Definitely not. College graduates reported greater happiness and less mental illness. True, they were more introspective; but coupled with this went a greater sense of well-being and satisfaction. Their perspectives were broader and aspiration levels higher; and when they worried, their worries tended to be over genuine rather than imagined troubles.

Figure 6-4 shows how professions differ in inequality of earnings. Can you guess why the order of inequality is self-employed lawyer, . . . , salaried army officer?

Education is one of society's most profitable investments. Human capital yields a return as great as or greater than capital in the form of tools and buildings. That is why Professor T. H. Schultz of Chicago has urged undeveloped and developed countries to spend more on education and training.

■ DIFFERENCES IN ABILITY AND INCOMES

In Part Four we shall study in detail the economic principles underlying the distribution of income. Our common sense enables us to anticipate part of its analysis and suggests that one factor helping to explain differences in income must be differences in people.

These differences in people may be physical, mental, temperamental, or even moral. They may be associated with biological inheritance through the genetic cells or with social and economic environment. They may be permanent—like being a blonde—or acquired, like educational advantage. These differences may even involve such conventionalities as the possession of a union card, and one's propensity to drop aitches in speaking or to pronounce "oil" with an "r" and "girl" without one.

These differences provide us with part of the answer. Physical traits (such as height or hip girth) and measured mental traits (such as intelligence quotient or tone perception) appear to be not so different among people as are the differences in income distribution. Often, the scientist who measures individual traits finds that they are "normally" distributed, with most people in the middle and fewer people at each end, as represented by the brown bell-shaped curve of Fig. 6-5. (If their IQ scores depart from the normal distribution, psychologists often rescale them so as to be in agreement!) Incomes—even those from work rather than property—are distributed *skewly*, as shown by the green curve with a very long tail off in the direction of the highest-paid individuals.

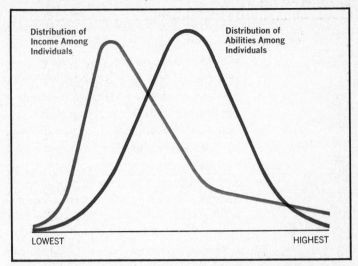

Are abilities more normally distributed than market incomes?

Distribution of Income Among Individuals

Distribution of Abilities Among Individuals

LOWEST   HIGHEST

FIG. 6-5. Heights, intelligence quotients, and many measured human traits seem to follow a so-called "normal" bell-shaped statistical distribution. Market incomes seem to be more skewed, highest incomes being more than a hundred times the lowest (as in green curve).

Actually, there is nothing particularly sacred about the so-called "normal curve." If heights of cubes (not people) are normally distributed, then their volumes will be skewed off to the right. Moreover, careful examination of census data on incomes suggests that each kind of wage income may tend to approximate roughly a bell-shaped distribution curve of modest symmetry. But when we add together the distributions of earnings for women as well as men, for property owners as well as workers, for lucky speculators, and other diverse groups, the great "skewness" of the whole distribution does emerge. Moreover, if we follow each wage earner over a period of years, a pattern of dispersion will emerge, one of the important factors causing differences among individuals being the different degrees of unemployment they suffer.

Perhaps a warning is in order at this point against jumping to the conclusion that there is something *necessary* and *inevitable* about this dispersion of income. Within the framework of our competitive society, fundamental changes in education have already made significant changes in inequality. Moreover, as no one knows better than the man at the top, our system of progressive income taxation has already greatly changed the relative take-home and—what is more important—the "keep-at-home" of the high- and low-paid; and presumably this will continue to be an abiding feature of American life.

■ ECONOMIC STRATIFICATION AND OPPORTUNITY

America has always been considered the land of opportunity, where anyone with ability might get ahead in the world. The success legend of Horatio Alger, Jr.'s, "poor but proud" hero who worked his way to the top and married the boss's daughter—

or vice versa—has no doubt been overdrawn. But it did have elements of truth as compared with the situation in older countries, where an aristocratic tradition lingered and where free schooling beyond the primary grades was never established.

For example, the "old school tie" and, more important, the Oxford accent were until recently almost indispensable to political and social advancement in Britain; even with the free scholarship system, few members of the lower or middle class could jump this hurdle. In this country, few people even recognize a "prep school" accent, and variations in speech are geographical rather than social. The American secretary is almost indistinguishable in appearance from the blueblood debutante.

Moreover, ours has been rather a materialistic civilization in which success is interpreted in business terms. Because "money talks," it is easier for outsiders to break into the upper crust than it would be in a culture that puts greater emphasis upon tradition. The *nouveaux riches* of one generation, such as the Vanderbilts a century ago, become the social arbiters of the next.

RECRUITMENT OF THE ELITE   Nevertheless, careful questionnaire investigation of the social origins of successful businessmen, namely, the directors and officers of corporations, turns up some surprising facts. The typical American business executive does not come off a farm or out of a workingman's home; more likely his father was also a businessman or possibly in one of the professions. Table 6-3 summarizes some typical research studies made by Taussig and Joslyn and others.

Does this mean that American economic society is hardening along caste lines?[5] Taussig and Joslyn are not sure. They point out that two diametrically opposite explanations are possible:

(1) In the past there was high social mobility in America: all the cream rose to the top, leaving naturally less gifted people at the bottom. (2) There are strong, and perhaps growing, barriers to circulation between the economic classes.

Taussig and Joslyn incline rather to the first view, feeling that "you can't keep a good man down." Many sociologists would disagree. They would emphasize the thou-

---

[5] When the first edition of this book was written, the author inclined toward the view that it was becoming increasingly difficult to go from the bottom to the top. Now he is not so sure. Recent careful studies of the origins of business leaders back before 1900 suggest that the present may compare favorably with the good old days, which may not have been so good after all. Increasingly, as organizations become bigger, the elements of nepotism and personal favoritism seem to become less important, and the increasing emphasis upon civil-servant-like quasi-objective tests of performance suggests greater mobility among the elite. Perhaps we are becoming a "meritocracy."

The arithmetic of "transition probabilities" can be made to yield the following results. Divide society into two classes, so that I am either a U in the Upper class or a *non-U* in the Lower. If a child's chance to move out of his parents' class is as great as to stay in, then $\frac{1}{2}$ the children, grandchildren, great-grandchildren, and descendants generally of a U parent will be U's. But if there is social stratification so that a child has only $\frac{1}{4}$ chance of moving into a class different from his parents, $\frac{3}{4}$ ($= \frac{1}{2} + \frac{1}{4}$) of the children of U's will be U's. However, it can be deduced that only $\frac{5}{8}$ ($= \frac{1}{2} + \frac{1}{8}$) of grandchildren of U's will be U's; and only $\frac{9}{16}$ ($= \frac{1}{2} + \frac{1}{16}$) of their great-grandchildren. Evidently, the chance of remote descendants of U's being also U's goes ultimately down to $\frac{1}{2}$, with 50 per cent of the excess above the $\frac{1}{2}$ equality level being wiped out at each new generation. Hope for the *non-U*'s means despair for the U's only if a fair race is deemed a tragedy. For more on transition probabilities, see W. Feller, *An Introduction to Probability* (Wiley, New York, 1957).

Anyone can climb the ladder of success, but it helps to start high:

OCCUPATION OF FATHER	PERSONS LISTED IN Who's Who, 1912, PER CENT	AMERICAN MILLIONAIRES, LIVING IN 1925, PER CENT	AMERICAN BUSINESS LEADERS, 1928, PER CENT	AMERICAN BUSINESS LEADERS, 1952, PER CENT	AMERICAN BUSINESS LEADERS UNDER 50, 1952, PER CENT
Businessman	35.3	75.0	60.0	61.8	67.8
Professional man	34.3	10.5	13.4	13.5	14.8
Farmer	23.4	7.3	12.4	12.7	11.1
Laborer	6.7	1.6	12.5	7.8	2.5
Other	0.3	5.6	1.7	4.2	3.8
Total	100.0	100.0	100.0	100.0	100.0

TABLE 6-3. SOCIAL ORIGIN OF SUCCESSFUL LEADERS IN AMERICA. Though laborers far outnumber businessmen in the population at large, most successful businessmen had a businessman father. What trends do you see in this table? How would you explain them? (Sources: F. W. Taussig and C. S. Joslyn, *American Business Leaders*, Macmillan, New York, 1932; *Fortune*.)

sand and one subtle psychological, social, economic, and educational disadvantages of the children of less fortunate families; that equal ability is not always able to give rise to equal achievement.

Whichever view is right, the implications for policy are the same. Human beings are a nation's most important form of social capital—a high-yielding form, moreover, in which we have invested too little in the past. Talent, wherever it may be, is worth seeking out and nurturing.

■ AFFLUENCE FOR WHOM?

In the 1960s America dropped the complacent notion that it had already become an affluent society with no more economic problems. The last act of President John F. Kennedy, before his tragic 1963 assassination, was to map out a war against poverty. President Lyndon B. Johnson carried forward and expanded this gigantic social program. Here is a brief outline of the fight against poverty.

The Economic Opportunity Act (1964), proposed by Kennedy, established the Office of Economic Opportunity (OEO) under R. Sargent Shriver. The OEO, building upon earlier work by the Ford Foundation and the Mobilization for Youth Program in New York City, set up Community Action Agencies to coordinate federal, state, and local programs in cities. The Neighborhood Youth Corps, Job Corps, and Work Experience Programs were started by OEO in 1965 to furnish job training in schools and camps and to provide literacy programs for adults. VISTA, the domestic Peace Corps, was initiated, and project Head Start was begun to give underprivileged preschool children preparation to break the vicious circle of environmentally inherited poverty.

By 1976, 200 years after the Declaration of Independence, Sargent Shriver prophesied that poverty could be finally terminated in the United States. What does such a grandiloquent prophecy mean?

The minimum-subsistence budget moves with the economy:

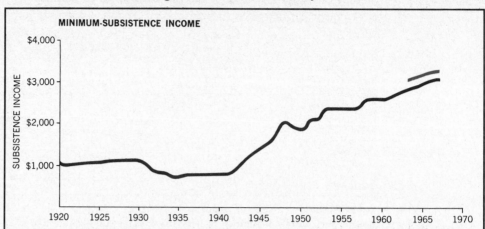

FIG. 6-6. The brown line shows how the social-service worker's minimum-income welfare budget for a family of four has risen with economic growth. The cost-of-subsistence budget, $3,300 in 1967, is shown in green, and is in close agreement with the welfare budget.

Even after allowing for cyclical price-level changes, society's estimate of "minimum subsistence" income moves up in prosperity, down in recession. World War II and postwar high employment much reduced the percentage of population living in poverty; but since 1945 our standards have risen as fast as our incomes; the challenge remains to reduce numbers in poverty further and raise earning abilities. (Sources: Oscar Ornati, New School of Social Research, and U.S. Department of Health, Education, and Welfare.)

■ DEFINITION OF POVERTY

Let us see how large the group is that is stuck below an adequate income level, and which minorities are likely to be in this group.

Economists have tried to calculate "minimum-subsistence" incomes in two different ways: First, they have taken over from social-service welfare workers carefully calculated budgets purporting to measure the cost of a minimum-subsistence income. Second, as a check, OEO economists have noted that poor families generally spend about one-third of their income on food; and hence from calculations by the Department of Agriculture of the cost of a subsistence food budget in different places, they can, by multiplying by 3, get estimates of needed minimum-subsistence income.

The two methods agree fairly well, and Fig. 6-6 shows how the cost of such a minimum-subsistence budget for a family of four[6] has risen in half a century. It is to be stressed that most of the rise comes because, as the nation as a whole gets more prosperous, the definition of minimum requirements is raised. What Americans consider

---

[6]Statistical budgetary data throw light on the age-old question, Can two live as cheaply as one? According to the Bureau of Labor Statistics, the answer is No. Even if one works in the home, it costs a married couple about $100/70$ times what it costs a single person to live, on the average. There are advantages, however; and this amount is still less than it costs two to live singly. Each child in the family adds to the cost of living. Thus, if it costs 70 to live alone and 100 to live with a wife, it will cost about 130 with one child, 160 with two, and so forth, for each additional child.

poverty would be regarded as affluence in Asia, and most families behind the Iron Curtain would be deemed poor if our budget requirements were extrapolated to them.

What do these standards come to? In 1967 the cost of the "subsistence" budget might be about $3,300 for a family of four, and includes only the bare necessities: no movies, little meat, no dental care, no newspapers, little clothing, and so forth. A "minimum-comfort" budget, hardly luxurious, costs about $5,500 and allows for adequate diet, occasional recreation, some tobacco and books, and so forth.

■ THE POSITION OF MINORITIES

No discussion of the inequality of incomes would be complete without mention of the position of economic minorities. In a real sense this is the concern of everyone, because we all belong to some minority. Yes, even the Smiths, or for that matter, the Lodges and the Cabots. What are the characteristics of the people who live in families with less than minimum-subsistence income? Table 6-4 shows at a glance the relative economic position of the white and nonwhite population. Surveys show that female-headed households, or those headed by an unemployed male, are most likely "to be poor." Nearly half the nonwhite population has less than minimum-subsistence income! The United States population is only 11.6 per cent nonwhite, but the poor are 30.6 per cent nonwhite. Other groups with high poverty incidence are farmers, the aged, children, and Southerners. Consider the odds against an aged Negro in the rural South. Many of the poor are untrained, stuck in economically stagnant areas, isolated in city ghettos, and so forth. Yet, many are also active job seekers in the urban labor markets.

Negroes get less income and education and have more unemployment than whites:

	WHITE	NONWHITE
Income		
Median income of families	$6,858	$3,839
Per cent of households in poverty	17.1	43.1
Per cent of families with incomes of $10,000 or more	24.1	8.3
Education		
Median years of school completed by men 25 years or older	12.0	9.0
Per cent of persons 20–24 years old who complete high school	76.3	50.2
Per cent of persons over 25 who are college graduates	9.9	5.5
Unemployment rates (per cent)		
Adult men	2.9	6.0
Adult women	4.0	7.4
Teenagers	12.2	25.3

TABLE 6-4. SELECTED MEASURES OF DISCRIMINATION AND INEQUALITY OF OPPORTUNITY, 1965. Because they have less education, Negroes get less good jobs. The resulting lower income makes them less able to afford a good education. The incidence of unemployment compounds the inequality and shows that minorities have a particular interest in full-employment programs. Education is not a cure-all. A Negro college graduate earns less in a lifetime than does a white high school graduate! (Source: Council of Economic Advisers)

Careful, competent observers have asserted that outright sexual discrimination, in the sense of paying men higher rates for the same kind and volume of work, is not a common practice. Similarly it has been asserted that racial discrimination in the sense of unequal pay for the same work is not common.

How can we reconcile these statements with the economic inequalities which every sophisticated person knows prevail between the sexes and races, as shown in Table 6-4? The answer to the paradox lies partly in the fact that discrimination usually takes the more subtle and more effective form of *not admitting women to the same jobs as men and barring Negroes from skilled labor, executive, and sales positions.*

Undoubtedly this explains much of the story. However, other competent observers maintain that women and Negroes on exactly the same job do often receive less pay. Women grade school teachers often receive lower pay than men. In a large electrical-goods plant, job-evaluation experts divide all factory work into two parts: women's jobs and men's jobs. The lowest pay of the men begins about where the women's highest pay leaves off; yet both management and the union will admit, off the record, that in many borderline jobs the productivity of the women is greater than that of the men.

Now, it cannot be denied that there are physical and temperamental differences between men and women; for example, a woman could not win the heavyweight wrestling championship or set a record for the 100-yard dash. On the other hand, the female sex is the stronger sex in the sense of life expectancy and also, perhaps, in being capable of sustained, painstaking effort. It is equally obvious that there are differences of skin color and hair texture between colored and white races.

REDUCING DISCRIMINATION   Whatever one's views are about the biological and environmental differences between the races and sexes—and the views of the scientists who have studied the question most are quite different from those of the man on the street—it is absolutely clear to any observer that there are numerous jobs which either sex or either race can do equally well and is prevented from so doing. This is shown by the experience of wartime and boom, when the usual barriers were lowered.

Similarly, the older worker in ordinary times finds himself at a disadvantage in our society. A man may be thrown on the scrap heap by the age of fifty when many of his best years are still ahead. It is not true that an older worker is the first to be fired; usually his experience or seniority helps to protect him. But once he is fired, it is much harder for him to become reemployed. Paradoxically, the humanitarian measures adopted by corporations to aid older workers—such as retirement pension schemes—are one reason for corporations' refusing to hire older men, since it then becomes more expensive to hire them.

From the horror of World War II, a few salutary lessons were learned. Women, Negroes, and older workers showed that they were capable of holding down better jobs and earning more money than was thought possible before the war. The experience of the federal and state Fair Employment Practices Commissions has not been that prejudice can be legislated out of existence overnight, but that steady improvement is possible if the people really want it. Nor can all the blame be placed upon bigoted employers. Organized labor must incur some of the onus for Jim Crow legislation.

The Civil Rights Act (1964) set up the Equal Employment Opportunities Commission, which has been making some steady progress in lessening discrimination—discrimination against women and discrimination against nonwhites.

■ CONCLUSION

Of course, the millennium will not arrive in 1976 or on any other date. New times will define new challenges. Ideas that seem impractical now—such as a guaranteed minimum income of $3,000 a year, implemented through the device of a negative income tax[7] or some other method—will be taken as a matter of course by our posterity.

Some experts in the field put the matter thus:[8]

> The U.S. has arrived at the point where poverty could be abolished easily and simply by a stroke of the pen. To raise every individual and family in the nation now below a subsistence income to the subsistence level would cost about $10 billion a year. This is less than 2 per cent of the gross national product. It is less than 10 per cent of tax revenues. It is about one-fifth of the cost of national defense.

SUMMARY

1 ■

Factual studies of the American distribution of income show that median incomes are lower than popularly believed. Even though incomes today are higher than in any other country or time, they are still not high in comparison with common notions as to what represents comfortable modern living.

2 ■

The view that the poor are becoming poorer in modern industrial nations will not stand up under careful factual examination. Since the Industrial Revolution, average standards of life in Western Europe and America seem definitely to have been showing a rising secular trend, tending to outstrip the underdeveloped nations. Even within the United States, the differentials in living standards are very great; there is a trend, however, toward narrowing the old differentials between North and South.

3 ■

The Lorenz diagram is a convenient device for measuring the spreads or inequalities of income distribution. It shows what percentage of total income goes to the poorest 1 per cent of the population, to the poorest 10 per cent, to the poorest 95 per cent, and so forth. The modern distribution of American income appears to be less unequal than in 1929 or than that in underdeveloped countries, but it still shows a

[7] Diverse economists—such as Yale's New Frontiersman, James Tobin, and Chicago's Milton Friedman, adviser to candidate Barry Goldwater—have advocated a negative income tax!
[8] J. N. Morgan, M. H. David, W. J. Cohen, and H. E. Brazer, *Income and Welfare in the United States* (McGraw-Hill, New York, 1962), pp. 3–4.

considerable measure of inequality. An interesting question is to try to relate the skew distributions of income to the more "normal" differences in human mental and physical abilities.

4 ■

Minority groups—such as the aged, women, Negroes, and various ethnic groups—pose important economic problems for any democracy. At the borders between economics and sociology, we run into interesting questions concerning the "circulation of the elite." Such popular clichés as "shirt sleeves to shirt sleeves in three generations" appear to have but a partial basis in fact. There is a strong positive correlation between income and social status of a person's parents and grandparents and his own, but the exact direction of causation is hard to establish.

5 ■

Within the affluent society the public war against poverty goes unceasingly on. As each rampart is conquered, higher standards of performance are set by society for itself. The vicious circle by which poverty is environmentally inherited has to be broken if the antipoverty war is to be permanently won.

QUESTIONS FOR DISCUSSION

1. Let each member of the class write down on a slip of paper an estimate of his own family's income. From these, draw up a frequency table showing the distribution of incomes. What is the median income? The arithmetic mean or average income?

2. How much do you think it takes for a childless married couple to live comfortably in your community? How would the money be spent?

3. Were your parents better off than their parents? What does this suggest with respect to the advantages and disadvantages of capitalism and the modern mixed economy?

4. Formulate some of your own ethical beliefs concerning how unequal incomes should be for people of different abilities and needs. How do you justify these beliefs? Would a nineteenth-century American agree? A Russian? A Fiji Islander? What is the relevance of the Bureau of Labor Statistics report that those in the under-$1,000 income class give 3.3 per cent of their income to church and charity while those in the over-$10,000 class give 2.6 per cent?

5. Review your understanding of the following concepts:

income distribution	normal and skew distributions
mean, median, and modal income	social stratification
per capita incomes	minimum budget
Lorenz curve of income and wealth	war against poverty

7 Labor and Industrial Relations

MR. HENNESSEY: BUT THESE OPEN-SHOP MIN SAY THEY'RE F'R UNIONS.
MR. DOOLEY: SHURE, IF PROPERLY CONDUCTED. NO STRIKES, NO RULES, NO CONTRACTS, NO SCALES, HARDLY INY WAGES AN' DAM FEW MIMBERS.   FINLEY PETER DUNNE

Almost everybody is at some time in the labor force. Half of our hours awake are spent on the job. Earnings from work—wages, salaries, and unincorporated earnings—constitute fully four-fifths of the total of national income. It is no wonder that the late Sumner Slichter of Harvard said—with pardonable exaggeration—that ours is a *laboristic* rather than a capitalistic society.

This chapter surveys the important role of labor unions in American life, paving the way for the more detailed discussion of wage determination in Part Four.

■ WHO BELONGS TO UNIONS?

Over 18 million Americans belong to a union. Almost one-third of the nonagricultural working force is thus made up of union men. If we excluded white-collar workers, foremen, and executives, the proportion would be higher still. In certain important industries, such as rail and other transportation, basic steel, autos, mining, and clothing, practically all eligible workers belong to unions. Few large firms escape being organized by unions.

Figure 7-1 shows the growth of union memberships since 1900: the slow, steady advance up to World War I; the upsurge during that war and immediately thereafter; and the rather sharp decline and leveling off during the 1920s. It shows the explosive acquisition of new members during the New Deal recovery years following the Great Depression; the continued rapid growth during World War II; and finally, the stagnation in recent years.

To what unions do workers belong? Here are the seven largest, with size of membership: the Teamsters (TCWH), 1,500,000; the United Steel Workers (USA), 1,000,000; the United Auto Workers (UAW), 1,200,000; the Machinists (IAM), 800,000; the Carpenters (CJA), 800,000; the Electrical Workers International Brotherhood (IBEW), 800,000; the Mine Workers (UMW), 600,000.

Unionism spurted in the Depression and during World War II, but has been stagnating recently:

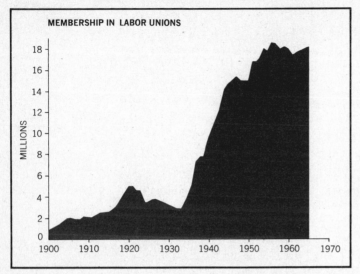

FIG. 7-1. Of nonfarm workers, 30 per cent belong to unions, as against but 11 per cent in 1933. The outlook for union growth looks bleak: "Automation" means a trend toward less blue-collar production-line workers, and white-collar workers are hard to organize. The South, a region traditionally hard to organize, grows relatively fast; public and legislative hostility toward unionism, based on suspicions of union power, is on the rise. (Source: U.S. Department of Labor.)

With two exceptions, they all belong to the merged American Federation of Labor and Congress of Industrial Organizations, i.e., the AFL-CIO. The Teamsters, under their leader James R. Hoffa, were expelled from the federation because of corruption. The United Mine Workers, under John L. Lewis and later leaders, have been in and out of the AFL and the CIO.

Statistics of membership understate the influence of unions. Many nonunion people are covered by union agreements on wages, hours, and working conditions. If you took a solemn oath never to join a union or work under a union agreement, you would have to give up all hope of being a factory worker in many sectors of manufacturing industries. *In every single manufacturing industry,* at least 20 per cent of all wage earners are under union agreements—even if they are not actually union members. You would have to give up a career in mining; in construction; in transportation. Where could you go? You could avoid unions on the farm, in government service, in finance, and in trade. Or go South: attempts to organize workers have met strong resistance there. Fully two-thirds of all union men now live in 10 industrial states.

Besides outright trade-unions, there are many organizations of professional people—like the American Medical Association (AMA) to which 200,000 doctors belong, and the National Education Association (NEA), to which 1,000,000 teachers belong—which in fact are important forces lobbying for higher incomes and specified working conditions. You would be naïve to think that the AMA and the NEA are not important influences on the interplay of supply and demand, even though economic betterment is not stressed in their official constitutions.

■ NATIONAL AND LOCAL UNIONS

There are three layers in the structure of American unions: (1) the *local* union, (2) the *national* union,[1] and (3) the *federation* of national unions.

To a member, the *local* is the front line of unionism. He joins the local in his

---

[1]Many unions have Canadian chapters and are called "international unions."

plant or town. He pays his dues to it. Usually, the local union signs the collective bargaining agreement determining his wages and work conditions.

But the local is only a single chapter or lodge of the national union. Thus, a linotypist in Chicago belongs to the local union located there, but this is one of hundreds of local chapters of the International Typographical Union, whose headquarters is in Colorado Springs. Part of the local dues—one-half or less, usually—goes to the national union; the bylaws and practice of the local cannot transcend the broad policies laid down at the national level. The president and other officers of the local are probably local workers; but the important office of business agent is a full-time job, the salary for which is often paid by the national union. The trend is increasing for the national unions to lend a hand in collective bargaining by the local.

Altogether there are about 180 autonomous national unions. We have seen that seven of these have more than half a million members. More than half the national unions have between 10,000 and 200,000 members each; and a quarter of the national unions have less than 5,000 members each.

The number of local union chapters or lodges is no less than 74,000. Some have as few as a dozen men. A few giant locals cover thousands of men. For example, the Ford local of the UAW is the largest of all. It alone has 30,000 members! The vast majority of locals number from 50 to 1,000 workers.

■ NATIONAL UNIONS AND THE FEDERATION

The AFL-CIO is a loose federation made up primarily of national unions as members. It is dependent upon these member national unions for financial support. Like the Big Five nations on the Security Council of the United Nations, the national unions have insisted upon their "sovereignty" and right of veto and their right to "exclusive jurisdiction" over workers in their area. Most of the headaches and fights come from such jurisdictional disputes.

The public thinks of the federation as being the most important part of the labor movement; but it is not. It acts as spokesman for labor; yet its own power is strictly limited. Thus Walter Reuther wields more real power in his capacity as head of the United Auto Workers than he does as vice-president of the AFL-CIO. Former teamsters' boss Dave Beck had more to fear from government action than he did from criticisms of his financial peccadilloes by the AFL-CIO. As a federation the AFL-CIO strongly disapproves of union discrimination against Negroes, but it has no power short of expulsion to act against those few member unions which still have restriction rules written into their constitutions. When the United Electrical Workers and 10 other left-wing unions were expelled for being Communist-infiltrated, this was considered a precedent-breaking action.

The AFL-CIO has been quite active in politics in recent decades, supporting candidates favorable to labor. Nominally nonpartisan, organized labor has usually supported Democratic candidates; but there have been some notable exceptions. And a few labor leaders do generally support Republican presidential candidates. Figure 7-2 gives an organization chart for the AFL-CIO. The state and city federations shown

American labor finally reunited in the 1955 AFL-CIO merger:

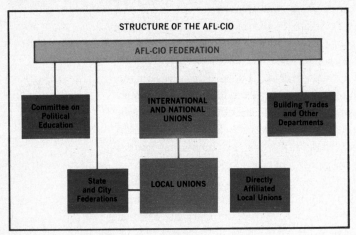

FIG. 7-2. The national and local unions remain the important units in our federated labor structure.

thereon lobby at these levels of government and cooperate in producing radio programs, parades, and election or strike solidarity. The chart also shows a few local unions that attach directly to the federation rather than to any national union. Usually, these locals are in new fields just being organized or in fields that fall between the jurisdiction of the constituent national unions. The departments usually are coordinating bodies made up of unions in similar areas, such as building.

■ THE URGE TO UNIONIZE

Aside from the medieval guilds to which craftsmen and their apprentices belonged, how did present-day unions first begin? Why were men tempted to join such organizations? What general functions are they supposed to perform?

In past centuries wages were low everywhere. Productivity was then low, so that no way of dividing the social pie could have given the average man an adequate slice. But workers often felt that they were at the particular mercy of the boss; they felt poor, uninformed, and helpless to hold out economically against the employer, with his greater staying power in any conflict. Shops were organized on dictatorial principles, and orders were passed down from on high; the worker was but a cog in the machine, a dehumanized robot. Such was the worker's image of the situation as revealed in historical records.

Men gradually discovered that in numbers there is strength. One hundred men acting in concert seemed to have more bargaining power than all had by acting separately. Workers began to meet in taverns and chapels. They formed fraternal societies for mutual contacts, entertainment, and discussion. Gradually such early unions began to offer mutual death benefits and various other forms of insurance, and promoted self-education. They also began to propose standard wage rates that members were to insist upon getting paid.

Naturally, employers fought back. They, too, learned that strength came from formal cooperation, in which each employer backed up the other and refused to hire men on the "blacklist" of known labor agitators. Not unexpectedly, employers invoked the powers of the law against labor conspiracies and group actions. Later they hired gunmen and spies to fight unions.[2]

That is the background of the modern American union. Unlike many abroad,

[2]The chief weapons used by employers to fight unions have been (1) discriminatory discharge of union members, (2) the blacklist, (3) the lockout, (4) the "yellow-dog" contract (agreement in advance not to join a union), (5) the labor spy, (6) the strikebreaker and armed guards, and (7) the "company union." Also, employers have used the courts to fight against unions.

American unions exist primarily for *economic* betterment: to try to get higher wages, shorter hours, more vacations, easier work rules, fringe benefits such as pensions and health insurance, democratic rights for men on the job, and so forth.

While economic goals are the major preoccupation and reason for the existence of unions today, unions do also perform purely social functions. Union men bowl together. Through their union they join in campaigns for blood donations, charity, and civic uplift. Just as a man belongs to his lodge, his church, the American Legion, and his boat club, so may he feel the necessity of union affiliation. (This is not to deny that a coworker down the line may never do more than pay his union dues; or that still another worker, whose wage is also determined by collective bargaining, may detest the whole idea of organized labor.)

■ BRIEF HISTORY OF THE AMERICAN LABOR MOVEMENT

Although American labor was late in becoming organized, the beginnings go back well into pre-Civil War times. Local craft unions of highly skilled, strategically placed workers (printers and others) were the first to be formed; and periodically, in boom times or in times of industrial unrest, these would combine in city and national federations for political and reform purposes. But not until the 1880s, when the AFL was formed, did the American labor movement assume its characteristic present-day form.

THE KNIGHTS OF LABOR   In the last third of the nineteenth century, out of the populist revolt against "big interests," the Knights of Labor emerged. At first it was a secret society which all but "lawyers, bankers, gamblers or liquor dealers, and Pinkerton detectives" could join. Later, secrecy was dropped; and by 1886, the high-water mark, the Knights had some 700,000 members. The Knights represented an attempt to form *one great labor union* to speak for all labor. But it was a heterogeneous collection, throwing together "craft unions" of skilled workers, "industrial unions" of all workers in a given plant or industry, and mixed assemblies of any who cared to join.

The Knights were much interested in political reform and agitation. Some officials were more interested in "uplift" and radical political changes than in day-to-day increases in hourly wages. After a few unsuccessful strikes, the Knights declined in membership as rapidly as they had grown. America did not seem susceptible to such a political labor movement, and the organization of the Knights of Labor was too loose to give it any staying power.[3]

THE AMERICAN FEDERATION OF LABOR   In 1881, and formally in 1886, the present-day labor movement took its form in the birth of the American Federation of Labor. For almost half a century, until his death in 1924, Samuel Gompers dominated this organiza-

---

[3]Again, around the time of World War I, the IWW (Industrial Workers of the World, or "Wobblies") tried to organize the whole working class for the overthrow of capitalism. It had limited success in its efforts to organize unskilled migratory workers, loggers, and metal-mine workers. It had greater success in inducing panic in Wilson's Attorney General Palmer, who in 1920 threw suspected radicals in jail in defiance of civil liberties. But nothing came of the IWW, and it soon faded away into complete ineffectiveness.

tion and gave the movement its characteristic pattern. Gompers himself was brought to this country as a child by immigrant parents. He was active in developing the Cigar Makers' Union and in founding the AFL as a rival organization to the Knights of Labor. Though early interested in socialistic uplift movements, he soon realized that no movement opposed to capitalism would flourish on American soil.

Gompers' main principles were simple:

1. He insisted on "business unionism," aiming at day-to-day higher wages and better working conditions, not engaging in the class struggle to alter the form of society. Labor was to get more and still more by evolution, not by violent revolution.

2. He committed the AFL to the principle of *federalism,* with each national union having autonomous sovereignty and "exclusive jurisdiction" over its craft specialty. This meant that the AFL would not tolerate "dual unionism": two unions could not try to organize the same workers; and a group of workers could not break away from a recognized national union.

3. Finally, he insisted on *voluntarism,* with the government not to interfere in collective bargaining, either in favor of or against labor. In politics he favored rewarding labor's friends and punishing its enemies, but he would not commit labor to any one political party.

Thus, the AFL was a polar opposite of the Knights of Labor in almost every respect. As the Knights dwindled in importance, the AFL grew. It has continued to grow. One might say that the philosophy of the AFL turned out to be the dominant philosophy of the American labor movement.

THE UNFAVORABLE TWENTIES   After World War I, the AFL had about 5 million members and seemed to be riding high; but during the 1920s, labor met determined opposition from the National Association of Manufacturers (NAM) and other business groups. The "open shop" was declared to be the "American plan." Moreover, the 1920s was a "new era" of eternal prosperity. As John J. Raskob, business executive and Democratic party leader, said, anyone could easily get rich by saving $15 a week and investing it in the stock market. (He added that not only was it possible for people to become rich—it was their *duty* to become rich as well.) Also, the 1920s was one of those rare high-employment periods when prices were not rising; so discontent over the cost of living was not operating to encourage unionization.

The AFL itself was rather stagnant. At Gompers' death, John L. Lewis and other strong men tried to get his job. William Green was elected as a compromise candidate and was president until his death in 1952. On the whole he voiced the viewpoint of "craft unions," made up of skilled workers of one occupation. Lewis, on the other hand, was associated with the "industrial unions," made up of all workers in a given industry or plant.

RECOVERY AND THE FORMATION OF THE CIO   By the depths of the Depression, the AFL had fallen to less than 3 million members. But with recovery, a new era for unionism was in the offing. The Depression had soured the American public on many of the slogans of the 1920s and had excited class antagonisms. Even before Roosevelt's New Deal, the electorate and the courts began to modify their opposition toward unions.

But within the AFL itself, the old insistence on the exclusive jurisdiction of national unions stood in the way of organization of the great mass-production industries. For example, before Judge Gary of United States Steel crushed the great 1919 steel strike, an unwieldy committee of some two-score craft unions was set up to conduct the strike. To this day the Carpenters' and Machinists' unions have never been able to settle some of their differences.

Astute observers in 1933 saw the handwriting on the wall: industrial unions were to play an important part in the future. John L. Lewis of the UMW, the late Sidney Hillman of the Amalgamated Clothing Workers Union, and other leaders formed in 1935 the Congress of Industrial Organizations (CIO) with Lewis as president. Helped by new government attitudes, legislation (especially the Wagner Act of 1935), and court decisions, a whirlwind campaign followed; in it the important mass-production industries, such as automobiles, steel, rubber, and oil, were organized, despite the bitter oposition of the principal companies in these industries.

By this time the AFL had learned the important lesson of industrial unionism. It, too, began to organize on an industrial basis; but its craft unions remained dominant.

UNIONS IN THE LATE 1960s   Labor's dream of a united movement was finally realized in 1955. The AFL-CIO was formed, with AFL's George Meany as its first president. The union movement seems now to have settled down, with few new industries left to be organized.

A new breed of man seems to be moving to the top. Back in the days when unions were being born and were fighting for their lives, colorful men such as John L. Lewis, Philip Murray, and Dan Tobin were the leaders. The new men who are replacing them are often men with gifts as *administrators*. With millions of members and literally hundreds of millions of dollars in their welfare funds, the unions are in need of men who can administer and who can deal persuasively with Congress, management, and the public.

■ COMMUNISM AND CORRUPTION IN UNIONS

Boring in by Communists used to be something of a problem for the union movement. Thus, in the 1920s David Dubinsky led a successful effort to purge the communist influence from his union, the International Ladies' Garment Workers. During the 1930s the Communists attempted to influence policy in many unions. Although usually forming only a tiny percentage of membership, they exercised an influence beyond their numbers because they acted as a unit, using Machiavellian tactics to achieve their goals. They provided zealous labor organizers, and Lewis himself in his factional disputes for a time tolerated their help. In the United Electrical Workers (until 1949, CIO), the National Maritime, and the longshoremen's unions, the struggles between the "Commies" and anti-Communists were especially severe; and in the International Fur and Leather Workers (CIO) Communists did get control.

After 1949 there was a showdown. In addition to expelling the UEW and half a dozen other unions, the CIO in 1950 expelled Harry Bridges' West Coast longshoremen's union as a Communist-infiltrated union. In the mid-fifties, laws against Communists became stiffer and stiffer. Except in a dozen or so unions, the Communists never attained any considerable power. Theirs was almost entirely a minority influence resting on their cleverness in strategy and in identifying themselves with popular labor causes. Whatever one may think of the economic wisdom of its policies, American labor is red-white-and-blue, not red.

Gangsterism has had only a minor role in the union movement. After the repeal of prohibition, corrupt gunmen did work their way into a few urban unions (e.g., the longshoremen around New York). Such union officials were as ready to sell out labor for a bribe as to fight in labor's interests. Labor had some success in cleaning its own house; in cities where there is effective law enforcement, the evil of labor gangsterism is pretty well under control.

One trouble spot does remain: fraud and mismanagement of the sizable union funds are not yet completely at an end. Teamster Dave Beck got rich speculating with union funds, and other misuses of union welfare funds have been turned up by congressional investigating committees. "Jimmy" Hoffa, Beck's successor, long successfully defied the AFL-CIO, congressional committees, court-appointed monitors, and minorities in the Teamsters Union. Because teamster members believed that "Jimmy delivers the goods for us," Hoffa remained in control even after courts had found him guilty.

Stirred by public revelations of graft, Congress overcame labor opposition and passed the Labor-Management Reporting and Disclosure (Landrum-Griffin) Act (1959). Among other things, this requires filing of union financial reports, limits union loans to officials to $2,000, and prohibits nonwage payments by employers to union representatives. The Act also provides a "Bill of Rights" for union members, which guards against rigged elections and summary disciplining of members by the union.

■ HOW DEMOCRATIC ARE UNIONS?

In Chapter 5 we discussed the problems involved in democratic control by stockholders of corporation management. Similar problems arise in connection with unions. It is true that union officials are elected to office and all union members are given equal votes. But officers once elected often stay in power for a considerable time, and between annual conventions the union is usually run by a small executive board. Men such as John L. Lewis and Walter Reuther have on the whole been popular with members; but if a member disagreed with the general policies laid down by such leaders he might not get very far.

The average union member does not participate very actively in policy formation. However, according to the late Sumner Slichter, who must still be regarded as one of the most astute students of the American labor movement:[4]

> This does not mean the rank and file lack influence. Their influence is great, but influence is not participation. If democracy simply means strong rank and file influence, most unions are democratic. The typical situation in a union is similar to that found in most organizations, churches and clubs of all sorts. There is a minority which is sufficiently interested in the affairs of the organization to attend business meetings and to

[4] S. H. Slichter, *The Challenge of Industrial Relations* (Cornell University, Ithaca, N.Y., 1947), p. 111.

participate actively in discussing problems. In the case of unions this minority usually asks the officers to press for stiff demands—stiffer than employers would be willing to grant without a long fight, stiff enough to force many employers out of business. In order to avoid trouble, the great majority of the union would settle for much less than the active minority demand.

Quite naturally the professional leader feels on the spot. If he disappoints the active minority too deeply, his leadership will be challenged. If he gets the inactive majority into too much trouble, he may provoke revolt also. He compromises, as, of course, he must. Usually he is more interested in placating the active minority than the inactive majority because he knows that the support or opposition of the active members is more important than the support or opposition of the inactive members. The record shows that union officials lose their jobs, not for being too radical for the majority, but for being too conservative for the minority.

■ HOW COLLECTIVE BARGAINING WORKS

Let us examine how collective bargaining is carried on.[5] Consider a production-line worker in a factory that has just been organized. An AFL-CIO union has petitioned the National Labor Relations Board (NLRB) for an election to determine the exclusive bargaining agent in this plant. The worker marks a secret ballot in favor of the union, and it wins more votes than an existing so-called "company union" which has no outside affiliations and which management prefers to deal with. The NLRB then certifies the new union as the collective bargaining agent for the plant, limiting any other union from negotiating directly with management.

A day is set for the new union representatives to meet with representatives of management at the bargaining table. Seated at the table will probably be a vice-president in charge of industrial relations; with him will be attorneys from a law firm that specializes in the labor field. On the union side will be the local business agent of the union and a small committee of union officers, and handling the negotiations will be an expert from union headquarters. He may be neither a lawyer nor a professional economist, but the economic research staff of the union helps him prepare an extensive brief backing up the union's demands.

Hourly wage rates are not the only issue in bargaining. In addition, the union may ask for a dues "checkoff" (whereby union dues are automatically deducted from the payroll of union members). The union may bargain for a "union shop," requiring all employees to become union members within 30 days after employment. Pension and health-insurance demands may be discussed at the bargaining table. In many industries where piece rates prevail, the structure of rates is an important subject for negotiation; the exact work load—how many looms each man will attend, and similar matters—may be discussed, and the general problem of how rapidly technological improvements shall be adopted will enter into the final contract. The seniority rights of workers and a grievance procedure for handling cases of discharge—these and many other problems will come into the collective bargaining.

Indeed, management has become worried over the inroads that organized labor has been trying to make into what it regards as its prerogatives. Many employers claim

[5] Chapter 29 includes a more analytical discussion of the collective bargaining process.

they can no longer run their business the way they feel is best. They find it hard to hire whom they will, fire for just cause, determine work methods, and decide on the order in which people will be laid off. They feel that every new decision occasions a meeting of a new committee; and time that could better be spent on production must be devoted to labor relations. They claim the worker acts as if he has a *right* to any job he has held for some time. Such critics complain that many unions oppose incentive wage schemes, insist upon rigid seniority, discourage efficient work methods, and seriously limit the autonomy of management. A recent casebook on collective bargaining devotes more space to issues arising from workers' rights in jobs than to any other single subject.

But at last the contract, covering many pages of fine print, is signed. Everything is set down in black and white, including provisions for grievances that arise during the life of the contract; often, too, there are provisions for the *arbitration* of issues that arise under it, each side agreeing in advance to accept the decision of an impartial outside arbitrator. The usual life of a contract is one or more years, with provisions made for reopening negotiations for a new contract under specified conditions.

Collective bargaining is a complicated business—a matter of give and take.

Many business leaders have learned to agree with the statement by Cyrus S. Ching,[6] formerly vice-president of United States Rubber Company and subsequently head of Federal Mediation and Conciliation:

> Where we are dealing with organized labor, we are going to get about the type of leadership that we are ourselves.

And many businessmen recognize the grain of realism in the statement by Philip Murray, who headed the CIO:[7]

> Employers generally get the kind of labor relations they ask for. If the unions indulge in "excesses," then the employer as a rule has no one but himself to blame for it. For instance, if he engages the services of labor espionage agencies such as the Railway Audit, Pinkerton's or others, if he stocks up his plant with tear gas, hand grenades, submachine guns, blackjacks, rifles, and other implements of war, if he hires high-priced Wall Street lawyers to harass the union before the Labor Board and in the courts, if he distributes to his foremen anti-union literature and lets it be known to them that any harm they can do to the union would be forgiven by him, if he contributes to anti-labor organizations such as the notorious Johnstown Citizens' Committee, if he quibbles over words, if he refuses to consent to an election or to sign a contract when he knows the union has a majority, if after a contract has been forced from him he delays and hampers the settlements of grievances, if he continues to discriminate against union members, then labor will answer in kind and nine out of ten businessmen, viewing it from afar, will say, "Ah, another excess."

No one should get a false impression that all management has been antiunion. Violence makes the headlines, while patient cooperation goes unnoticed. In most industries there has long been a successful pattern of fruitful cooperation between labor and management. To highlight this fact, the National Planning Association has pub-

---

[6]Cyrus S. Ching, "Problems in Collective Bargaining," *Journal of Business*, University of Chicago, 1938, Part 2, p. 40.

[7]P. Murray and M. L. Cooke, *Organized Labor and Production* (Harper, New York, 1940), pp. 259–260.

lished studies describing cases of successful labor relations. These reports describe "how historically hostile groups can co-exist on a basis of reasonable equality of position in the enterprise, and at the same time be participants in a common endeavor from which both seek security, opportunity, and sustenance."[8]

Thus, the West Coast pulp and paper industry, whose leading member is the Crown Zellerbach Corporation, has had 35 years of healthy labor relations. The Nashua Corporation has maintained relations with no less than seven AFL unions for 35 years without strikes. And the Hickey-Freeman Company, a men's-clothing manufacturer, has dealt with unions for 50 years without a strike; for 35 years no grievance ever went as far as arbitration. Many historic problem areas in labor relations, like the West Coast longshoremen, have settled down in recent years to relatively peaceful dealings.

These are not cases where peace has been maintained because the management or the union was soft. Hard bargaining on both sides is likely to accompany a good management-labor relationship; apathy on both sides or one-sided dominance postpones solutions and ultimately leads to breakdowns. In healthy cases, each side has a respect for the rights of the other. The two sides are not in love, but they are compatible.

■ ROLE OF GOVERNMENT IN COLLECTIVE BARGAINING

Although unions are relatively free in this country in comparison with their control in collectivist countries, government has played an important role in their historic development. Two hundred years ago, when labor first tried to organize in England and America, the common-law doctrines against conspiracy in restraint of trade were used against their members. Well into this century, unions and their members were convicted by courts, assessed for damages, and harassed by various injunctive procedures. Repeatedly the Supreme Court struck down acts designed to improve working conditions for women and children and other reform legislation involving hours and wage rates.

In 1890 the Sherman Antitrust Act made monopolistic restraints of trade illegal. It did not mention labor unions; but in the next 20 years, the Sherman Act was used increasingly by the courts to curb the activities of unions. If a union struck for ends which in a judge's opinion were undesirable, he might rule against it. And many traditional means used by unions were declared by judges to be illegal even if in pursuit of a legitimate end.

The AFL, though against labor's taking an active role in politics, was forced into the political arena; and in 1914, labor was successful in getting the Clayton Antitrust Act passed. Although hailed as "labor's Magna Carta" and designed to remove labor from prosecution under the Sherman Act, this did not end legislative and judicial opposition to the labor movement.

PROLABOR LEGISLATION   After 1930 the pendulum swung toward support of union bargaining. Particular landmarks of legislation involved the Railway Labor Act (1926), which accepted the basic premise of collective bargaining; the Norris-La Guardia Act

[8] *Fundamentals of Labor Peace*, Case Study 14, (National Planning Assoc., Washington, 1953).

(1932), which virtually wiped out injunctive interference of the federal courts in labor disputes; the Walsh-Healey Act (1935), which provided that minimum wage standards be required on all government contracts; and the Fair Labor Standards Act (1938), which set a minimum wage (to reach $1.60 per hour by 1968) for most nonagricultural workers engaged in interstate commerce, barred child labor, and called for time-and-a-half pay for hours in excess of 40 per week.

The biggest landmark of all was the National Labor Relations (Wagner) Act (1935). It stated bluntly: "Employees shall have the right to self-organization, to form, join, or assist labor organizations, to bargain collectively through representatives of their own choosing, and to engage in concerted activities, for the purpose of collective bargaining or other mutual aid or protection" (Sec. 7). Moreover, it set up the National Labor Relations Board (NLRB) to make sure that employers do not engage in "unfair labor practices" against labor.[9] The NLRB also goes into plants and holds elections to see what organization is to be regarded as the collective bargaining representative for all the workers. It can, and does, issue "cease and desist orders" against employers, enforceable by the courts after appeal; and it often makes employers reinstate with back pay employees unjustly discharged.

Without such favorable governmental attitudes, it is doubtful that the union movement could have grown to its present status.

ANTIUNION TRENDS   After World War II the electorate became fed up with strikes and rising prices. Labor was no longer considered the underdog; and people felt that the Wagner Act had been one-sided, favoring labor and putting all the penalties upon the employer. Congress passed the Labor-Management Relations (Taft-Hartley) Act (1947).[10] This is a *two-edged* labor relations law that—unlike the Wagner Act—prescribes standards of conduct for unions as well as employers. The hand of the worker who does not want to join a union is also strengthened, and so are rights of a member within the union as against the officers. Among its principal features are the following:

> Strikes which "imperil the national health or safety" may be suspended by an 80-day court injunction requested by the Attorney General. Unions must give 60-day notice before any strike.
>   Unfair union labor practices are defined, and unions' behavior limited. Unions can be sued and held responsible for acts of their agents. The "closed shop," which requires all employees to be union members, is limited, and states are given a free hand to pass stronger laws. Secondary boycotts and jurisdictional strikes are made illegal. Political activity and financial contributions by unions are restricted; the free-speech rights of the employer are reaffirmed and strengthened.

[9]The term "unfair labor practices" as used in the Wagner Act was a broad one referring to employers' activities that interfere with employees' rights to self-organization. Examples of such employer practices are (1) firing men for joining a union, (2) refusing to hire men sympathetic to unions, (3) threatening to close an establishment if employees join a union, (4) interfering with or dominating the administration of a union, or (5) refusing to bargain with the employees' designated representatives. NOTE: Workers always had various rights to organize, but legislation of the 1930s explicitly encouraged and expanded those rights.

[10]The Landrum-Griffin Act (1959), which was set up to cope with corruption, was discussed earlier.

■ CURRENT BARGAINING PROBLEMS

The key issues facing America and other nations as the 1970s approach are these:

1. Organized labor tries to improve its money wage rates, in the hope that this will not induce a commensurate rise in prices which leaves *real wages* little or no better off. Because the strike is labor's ultimate bargaining weapon, and the right to refuse a wage increase even though this brings on a strike is the employer's ultimate weapon, work stoppages provide the major headlines in labor relations.

2. In an age of rapid technical change and much talk of "automation," union men are often more concerned about *job security* than about mere money wage gains. What good is a raise in pay for a job that no longer exists?

3. Modern mixed economies seem to be subject to a new disease—a tendency for anything like an approach to full employment to lead to "creeping inflation."

STRIKES   The power to strike is central in present-day collective bargaining. Contrary to common impressions, this power is, as shown in Fig. 7-3, used sparingly: the number of days lost from work on account of the common cold is by far greater than that from all work conflicts.

Chapter 29, which discusses wage determination in detail, points out that, without the right to strike, a union's powers to bargain would, for better or worse, be substantially altered. Time and again concessions have been wrung out of an employer only by the realistic threat of forcing upon him the heavy financial losses involved in a prolonged shutdown. And, of course, workers also suffer grievous financial losses and demoralization from a long shutdown. Yet many a time employers have successfully refused union demands by a determined willingness to "take" a painful strike rather than accede.

When strikes involve key industries (such as steel) or key functions (such as the railroads or the docks) or take place on a nationwide scale in an important sector like autos, at this point the public interest becomes overriding. Two men are not free to engage in a fight if that does harm to other people. Just as the rights of private property and of personal freedoms are not absolute and must be reconciled when they come into conflict with the rights of others and of the public generally, so too must the rights of "free collective bargaining" be subject to limitation and coordination with social necessities.

These are not academic questions. In 1919 Governor Calvin Coolidge said

Work stoppages reached their peak just after World War II:

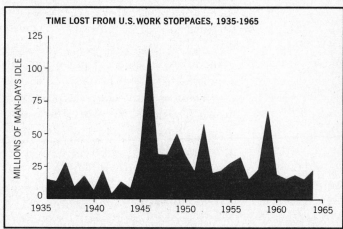

FIG. 7-3. While time lost from strikes is measured in millions of man-days, as a per cent of total labor-days worked, it never has reached 1½ per cent and has averaged less than ½ per cent. (Source: U.S. Department of Labor.)

in connection with the Boston police strike, "There is no right to strike against the public safety, by anybody, anywhere, any time."

In fact, the government will not today let a crippling strike long persist. Again and again, Presidents Truman, Eisenhower, Kennedy, and Johnson were forced to use Taft-Hartley injunction procedures or other devices to suspend strikes in crucial areas.[11] The President often appoints blue-ribbon committees to help end serious strikes. In the future, unionization among government and quasi-public workers—teachers, defense and atomic-energy employees—is bound to make the problem of avoiding pivotal work stoppages more acute.

PRODUCTIVITY RESTRAINTS   Unions become especially concerned when new techniques threaten the job security of their members. The word "sabotage" arose when laborers threw their wooden shoes (*sabots*) into the works of the new machines brought in by the Industrial Revolution to replace workers. "Featherbedding" refers to any rules imposed on employers merely for the purpose of keeping up the demand for workers: use of small shovels, limitation on number of bricks laid per day, requirement that use of music recordings be accompanied by a stand-by orchestra that does nothing but draw pay, requirement of a fireman (i.e., coal shoveler) on a diesel engine under the pretense that he is needed for safety reasons.

Entrenched unions have power to enforce uneconomical makeshifts. The railroads have been a flagrant example. As Chapter 29 will show, there are limits on how much unions can raise wages, but their powers are particularly great in keeping wages up within dying industries. Elsewhere, they are sometimes helpful in the orderly introduction of improved production techniques.

WAGE-COST CREEPS   Repeatedly we shall be discussing the problems involved in inflation. Few modern countries have been able for long to enjoy simultaneously (1) reasonably full employment and (2) reasonably stable price levels. Part of the difficulty will be found to arise in the realm of monetary and fiscal policy. Part may come from a tendency for wage rates to be sticky against downward adjustments, but to be only too prone to rise in excess of productivity improvements even before full employment is approached.

Some of this wage pressure seems to be associated with our system of free collective bargaining. In good times workers ask for, and get, steady wage increases. Unsuccessful strikes only slow down the process. Under voluntary or compulsory arbitration the chances are not even that the rate will be raised or be cut; it is almost sure to be raised. Those directly concerned deem it cheaper to buy labor peace by granting wage awards averaging more than is compatible with steady prices.

---

[11]If anything, the state seems prone to interfere quickly, urging compulsory arbitration proposals: a rail strike, which might reduce the national product by 25 per cent, has to be distinguished from a newspaper strike that hampers the dissemination of news and advertising or from an auto strike that puts off new-car purchases and sends ripples of reduced spending throughout the system. The case of rails is much more fraught with public interest than the others, serious as they may seem to be.

■ DYNAMIC LABOR CHANGES

There remain unsolved problems in the field of labor. This is not a static field, as the trends in Fig. 7-4 show. As society develops, it demands relatively less labor in food production, thus forcing labor to go from agriculture to industry. We move from the "primary-good" stage to the "secondary-good" stage. As incomes rise still further, manufactured goods finally begin to drop in relative importance. People desire services rather than material goods; how to sell and deliver what is produced becomes important. And manufactured goods can be produced by fewer and fewer people; of those still employed in factories, more and more wear white collars and perform such services as filing, computer tending, and typing.

Population changes are important. Half the women now work, particularly after they are 35 with no dependent infants. Baby booms during and after World War II swell the ranks of youths looking for jobs. Automation calls for new skills, emphasizing training rather than mere strength or mechanical supervision. All the principles of economics have to be brought into play to understand and facilitate this process of never-ending adaptation and readjustment.

The occupational structure of labor changes greatly over the years:

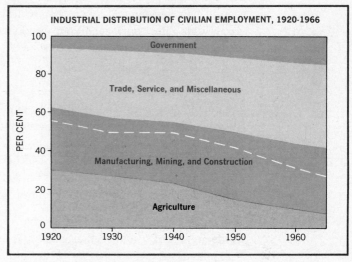

FIG. 7-4. Offsetting the steady decline in agricultural employment is the rise in government and service employment.

Manufacturing itself, after first growing, ultimately declines in relative importance. Workers in manufacturing are divided by the broken white line into blue-collar production workers below the line and white-collar workers above the line. Note the relative decline since 1950 in production workers compared with white-collar workers. (Source: U.S. Department of Labor.)

SUMMARY

1 ■

Labor unions occupy an important but not expanding role in the American economy, in terms of both membership and influence. Their present structure is in three layers: (*a*) local unions, (*b*) national unions, and (*c*) federation of unions (AFL-CIO), the first two being the most important.

2 ■

By the 1880s, the typical American pattern of federated, nonpolitical, gradualistic business unionism had been established. Since 1933, the CIO and finally the AFL have modified the pattern in the direction of *industrial* unionization of whole mass-production industries rather than relying solely upon *craft unionization* of skilled workers.

3 ■

After a union has been recognized by an NLRB election as the exclusive bargaining agent, management and labor representatives meet together to negotiate a contract fixing wage rates, work conditions, productivity standards, degree of union recognition, seniority rights, and grievance procedures.

4 ■

Right up until the middle 1930s there was bitter opposition to unions. But finally, the pendulum of government swung to support of collective bargaining, and since the Wagner Act (1935) most manufacturing industries have become unionized. The result has been less violence, but still vigorous collective bargaining between the opposing groups. After 1947 Congress felt it had become one-sided in favor of labor and passed the Taft-Hartley and Landrum-Griffin Acts to correct the balance. Strike threats in crucial industries always invoke governmental action.

5 ■

Aside from strikes and featherbedding, a major post–World War II problem has been the relation of wage increases to the price level. If patterns of "successive rounds of general wage increases" are established that go far beyond the 3 to $3\frac{1}{2}$ per cent yearly rise in productivity, the price level is almost sure to rise in an inflationary manner and "cost-push" inflation will become a serious problem.

QUESTIONS FOR DISCUSSION

1. Describe the structure of America's organized labor. Describe the layers of the union movement. Which are the largest unions in your locality?

2. Historically, American unions have followed the principles associated with Samuel Gompers. What are these? How have they been modified since 1933? How do you explain the fact that American labor has not been more active in politics along the lines of European socialists?

3. Give some contrasting examples of peaceful collective bargaining.

4. Describe the swing of the pendulum in the attitude of legislatures and courts toward organized labor before and after the Wagner Act.

5. Should policemen have the right to strike? Postmen? Milkmen? Anyone?

6. "Wage rates tend to be sticky as far as downward moves are concerned." Why might this be increasingly true? Interpret the phrase "inflationary wage-cost push."

7. Review your understanding of the following concepts:

national and local union	strike, lockout, work stoppage
AFL-CIO federation	union corruption, communism
UAW, UMW, NLRB	Wagner, Taft-Hartley Acts
collective bargaining	featherbedding
business versus revolutionary unionism	wage-cost push on prices
craft versus industrial unions	automation and occupational trends

8 The Economic Role of Government: Expenditure, Regulation, and Finance

DEMOCRACY IS THE RECURRENT SUSPICION THAT MORE THAN HALF THE PEOPLE ARE RIGHT MORE THAN HALF THE TIME.   E. B. WHITE

The activities of the State are becoming an increasingly important part of the study of modern economics. This is reflected in the quantitative growth of government expenditure, of redistribution of income by government, and of direct regulation of economic life. So in this chapter we survey government expenditure. In the next chapter we survey government taxation and local and state finance.

■ THE GROWTH OF GOVERNMENT EXPENDITURE

Before World War I, federal, state, and local government expenditure amounted to little more than one-twelfth of our whole national income. During World War II, it became necessary for the government to consume about half of the nation's greatly expanded total output. Within half a century, the cost of all government in the United States rose from a minute 3 billion dollars spent in 1913 to almost 200 billion dollars per year in the late 1960s.

For more than a century, national income and production have been rising. At the same time, in almost all countries and cultures, the trend of governmental expenditure has been rising even faster. Each period of emergency—each war, each depression—expands the activity of government. After each emergency is over, expenditures never seem to go back to previous levels.

Nor is the end in sight. Government expenditure receded from its World War II peak, but it did not drop to the prewar levels of less than 10 billion dollars, levels which used to be considered alarmingly high. In the years ahead, regardless of whether the Republican party or the Democratic party holds office, the upward trend seems likely to continue.

Government spending has risen faster than gross national product all this century:

FIG. 8-1. Government expenditures include federal, state, and local annual expenditures. Note the relative trends. Also note that this is a "ratio," or "semilog," chart, with vertical distances arranged to reflect percentage changes. (Source: U.S. Departments of Commerce and Treasury.)

Figure 8-1 shows the historical trend of total government expenditure and federal debt relative to the growth of gross national product. And Table 8-1 points up the fact that rich countries tend, relatively, to spend more on government than do poor countries. (Also refer back to Fig. 2-5, page 22.)

These are the facts about public finance. Some may deplore them, some may approve them—but there they are. They make clear the increasingly important economic role of government.

■ THE GROWTH OF GOVERNMENT CONTROLS AND REGULATION

The increase in collective expenditure is only part of the story. Besides larger direct participation by government in national production, there has been a vast expansion in its laws, regulations, and executive fiats governing economic affairs.

Perhaps nineteenth-century America came as close as any economy ever has to that state of *laissez faire* which Carlyle called "anarchy plus the constable." The result was a century of rapid material progress and an environment of individual freedom. There were also periodic business crises, wasteful exhaustion of irreplaceable natural resources, extremes of poverty and wealth, corruption of government by vested interest groups, and at times the supplanting of self-regulating competition by monopoly.

No longer does modern man seem to act as if he believed "That government governs best which governs least." Gradually, and in the face of continuing opposition, the methods of Alexander Hamilton were applied to the objectives of Thomas Jefferson. The constitutional powers of government were interpreted broadly and used to "secure the public interest" and to "police" the economic system. Utilities and railroads were brought under state regulation; after 1887, the ICC (Interstate Commerce Commission) was set up to regulate rail traffic across state boundaries. The Sherman Antitrust Act and other laws were invoked after 1890 against monopolistic combinations in "restraint of trade." Regulation of banking became thoroughgoing; after 1913, the Federal Reserve System was set up to serve as a central bank, controlling member commercial banks; and since 1933 most bank deposits have been insured by the Federal Deposit Insurance Corporation (FDIC).

Pure food and drug acts were passed following the revelations of the muckraking era of the early 1900s. Loan sharks came under regulation in many states. The abuses of high finance, before and after 1929, gave rise to ever more stringent regulation of financial markets by the Securities and Exchange Commission (SEC) and other bodies.

POLITICAL EVOLUTION With the passage of time, the radical doctrines of one era became the accepted and even reactionary beliefs of a later era. State and federal legislation was expanded to include minimum-wage laws; compulsory workmen's accident compensation insurance, compulsory unemployment insurance and old-age pensions; maximum-hour laws for children, women, and men; regulation of factory conditions, compulsory collective bargaining, and fair-labor-relations acts. Private property is never wholly private, free enterprise not wholly free.

To understand the trend toward greater governmental authority one must maintain a sense of historical perspective. Each new step generated strong political feelings on both sides. Thus the "square deal" doctrines of the Republican Theodore Roosevelt, which today would cause no fluttering of pulses, were once considered dangerously radical. Our Republic cannot, and would not if it could, turn the clock back to the conditions of the nineteenth century as represented by Henry Ford's Greenfield Village and McGuffey's Reader. Still, it would be wrong to think these historical processes inevitable—to join Omar Khayyám in his mournful chant:

> The Moving Finger writes; and having writ,
> Moves on: nor all your Piety nor Wit
> Shall lure it back to cancel half a Line,
> Nor all your Tears wash out a word of it.

A democracy generally gets the kind of government it wants.

Unfortunately, not until long after the event will history tell us—and perhaps not then—whether or not a given expansion of governmental authority was a good or bad policy; whether it deserves the approval of all who are genuinely interested in conserving and improving the good elements in our system. And in politics as elsewhere, it is only too true that the road to hell is paved with good intentions.

But past history does seem to suggest this: Unyielding conservatism defeats its own purpose. Steel without "give" will break suddenly under strain. Brittle economic

Government share of national product is biggest in wealthy, developed countries:

DEVELOPED COUNTRIES	RECENT AVERAGE TAX, PER CENT	LESS DEVELOPED COUNTRIES	RECENT AVERAGE TAX, PER CENT
West Germany	35	Ecuador	19
France	30	Burma	18
Sweden	30	Colombia	14
United Kingdom	26	Peru	12
Canada	24	Philippines	10
United States	24	Jamaica	09
Australia	22	Nigeria	09
Japan	21	India	09

TABLE 8-1. GOVERNMENT RECEIPTS AS PERCENTAGES OF GROSS NATIONAL PRODUCT. Governments of poor, underdeveloped countries show a persistent tendency to tax and spend less, relative to national product, than do those of more advanced countries. With higher income comes greater interdependence and less need to spend on private necessities. (Source: J. L. Williamson, *Manchester School of Economics and Social Studies*, 1961, pp. 43–56. Data include all tax and nontax receipts of all levels of government.)

systems without the flexibility to accommodate themselves in an evolutionary manner to accumulating tensions and social changes—however strong such systems may appear in the short run—are in the greatest peril of extinction, as science and technology are constantly changing the natural lines of economic life. If a system is to continue to function well, social institutions and beliefs must be able to adjust themselves to these changes. And without a sense of historical perspective, neither radicals nor conservatives nor middle-of-the-roaders can effectively advance their own true long-run interests.

Before applying economic analysis to the nature of governmental activity, we must get a broad picture of what that activity now is.

■ FEDERAL, STATE, AND LOCAL FUNCTIONS

Each American is faced with three levels of government: federal, state, and local. It will surprise most people to learn that, of the three, the states have always been the least important with respect to government expenditure. This is still true.

Prior to World War I, local government was by far the most important of the three. The federal government did little more than pay for national defense, meet pensions and interest on past wars, finance a few public works, and pay salaries of judges, congressmen, and other government officials. Most of its tax collections came from liquor and tobacco excises and tariff duties levied on imports. Life was simple. Local governments performed most functions and depended primarily on property taxes.

In Fig. 8-2, we see how the picture has changed since World War I. Though nondefense federal spending grows relatively less than the total of state and local, the federal government is still far ahead in total spending.

Local and state spending has been rising faster than federal nondefense spending:

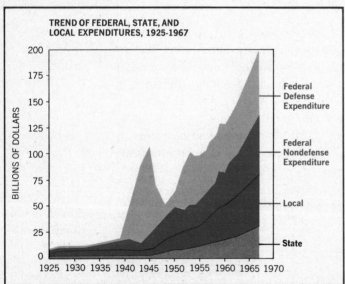

FIG. 8-2. Federal expenditure rose sharply in the Great Depression, and even more during World War II. Defense expenditure has remained high; but it is local and state expenditure on schools, sewers, and roads that shows the steepest civilian trends. (Source: U.S. Department of the Census and U.S. Commerce Department.)

■ FEDERAL EXPENDITURE

The United States government is the biggest business on earth. It buys more typewriters and more cement, meets a bigger payroll, and handles more money than any other organization anywhere. The numbers involved in federal finance are astronomical: not millions or hundreds of millions, but billions (i.e., thousands of millions). Such magnitudes convey no meaning to the human mind. We all know what it means to be a mile from home, but

Most federal expenditure goes to pay for defense and past wars:

	ESTIMATE, BILLIONS OF DOLLARS	PERCENTAGE OF TOTAL
1. National security	$ 61.4	42.4
2. Veterans benefits and services	6.4	4.4
3. Interest on public debt	10.2	7.0
4. International affairs and science	4.4	3.0
5. Space research and technology	5.3	3.6
6. Natural resources	3.0	2.0
7. Agriculture and agricultural resources	3.6	2.5
8. Health, labor, welfare, and education	42.1	29.1
9. Commerce, transportation, and housing	7.8	5.4
10. General government and other	.8	.6
Total expenditure	$145.0	100.0

TABLE 8-2. ESTIMATED FEDERAL EXPENDITURE IN FISCAL YEAR 1967. The first five items are 60.4 per cent of total expenditure. Hence, purely civilian expenditure for domestic peacetime purposes is about two-fifths of the total. In the prewar era the proportions would have been reversed. These figures are from the Budget Bureau's "consolidated cash budget," and include expenditures of $31.3 billion from social security and retirement trust funds and $4 billion from the highway trust funds.

the assertion that the sun is 93 million miles from the earth or that there are enough molecules in a glass of water to make a string of pearls from here to kingdom come always leaves us unimpressed. Perhaps public expenditure will have more meaning if we remember that each billion dollars amounts to about $5 per American man, woman, and child. A current federal annual budget of about 140 billion dollars would be equivalent, then, to about $700 per capita—about 2 months of the average annual income.

Table 8-2 gives the estimated importance of different categories of federal expenditure in the fiscal year 1967, i.e., from July 1, 1966, to June 30, 1967.

In the main, the first five items represent the costs of past and future wars. Together they account for two-thirds of all federal expenditure, as well as for most of the increase in federal expenditure over prewar levels. Naturally, these are estimates—subject to change when international tension changes.

Much of the sixth item goes to the support of conservation programs, TVA, the St. Lawrence Seaway project, and so on. The other items are largely self-explanatory, representing aid to the farmer; welfare aid to the needy, aged, and handicapped under the Poverty, Medicare, and other programs; and expenditure on labor, education, and health. The final category includes the costs of running Congress and the courts, as well as the general expenses of the executive branch of the government.

It needs emphasizing that the bulk of federal expenditure and debt is the consequence of hot and cold war, not of depression and welfare programs.

■ THE CHANGING FUNCTIONS OF GOVERNMENT

The last quarter of a century has witnessed great political changes. How great have been the economic changes? How great have been the departures from the traditional capitalistic system? We can tackle these questions by considering government activity under five headings:

DIRECT CONTROLS   As noted, there has been an increase in the amount of government *control*. Much of this regulation can hardly be dignified by the title of "planning," and market prices still run most activities. Economic analysis of government interference deserves discussion later and will be met in later chapters.

SOCIAL CONSUMPTION OF PUBLIC GOODS   As we have also seen, the increase in government expenditure means that as a nation we are consuming more of our national product *socially* rather than individually through private money purchases. Rather than pay to ride on the public roads as we do to ride on railroads, we pay for such valuable services by taxes.

Note that socially consumed goods and services are *largely produced by free private enterprise*. The government pays for a hospital or typewriter, but these are produced by free private enterprise. And so it is with most government expenditure on productive goods. This is not what the original socialists meant by socialism—government ownership and operation of factories and land.[1]

STABILIZING FISCAL AND MONETARY POLICY   As will be seen in Parts Two and Six, an important function performed by modern governments involves the control of runaway price inflation and the prevention of chronic unemployment and stagnant growth. Two principal weapons are used.

A central bank—which is a bank for bankers and which is given the power to issue currency—either is directly in the executive branch of government or, more commonly, is a public not-for-profit organization ultimately responsible to the legislature. We shall study how our version of it, the Federal Reserve Banks and Board, exercises *money and credit policies* designed for high production and price stability.

Since the beginning of recorded history, governments have had constitutional authority over money. But only in the last 40 years has it become widely recognized that *fiscal policy of government*—variations in expenditure and tax totals, which create a surplus or deficit rather than a balanced budget—has profound effects on unemployment, total production, money and real incomes, and the level of prices. Bad fiscal policy can make the business cycle worse. Stabilizing fiscal policy can moderate the ups and downs of business. Now that governments are large, claiming to have *no* fiscal policy is like claiming to be dead: left to themselves, budgets will definitely not balance; a policy of trying to balance the budget in every month, year, decade, or over the whole business cycle—any one of these involves deliberate social policy choice.

Later chapters will study monetary and fiscal policy in depth.

GOVERNMENT PRODUCTION   There has been little expansion in this direction in recent decades. Historically, our government has performed certain direct productive operations, and not others. The post office and parcel post have long been a function of government, while private management has operated telegraph service and railway express. Airports, but not railway terminal facilities, are usually governmentally owned. Munic-

[1] See the discussion of socialism, communism, and fascism in the final chapter of this book.

ipalities now often provide water, sometimes gas and electric utilities, but rarely telephone service. (Abroad telegraph and telephones are typically publicly operated.)

The reasons for drawing the line at one place rather than another are partly historical and are to some degree changing; but, economically, the distinction is not completely arbitrary. Thus, the courts have held that, in the special case of "public utilities affected with public interest," there is limited possibility of effective competition among many independent producers, so they must be publicly regulated or owned; but one would not expect the production of soap or perfume to be natural candidates for governmental operation.

Whatever the merits of the arguments on each side, it is well to examine the facts to see how much government ownership of production has been introduced these last 30 years. Under the New Deal itself, there was but one direction in which such expansion took place, namely, the power field. (EXAMPLES: Tennessee Valley Authority, Bonneville Dam in the Northwest, Hoover Dam in the Southwest, rural electrification, and so forth.) Unlike Canada, or Sweden, or Britain, we have never had national ownership of railroads, coal mines, steel mills, airlines, or radio and television broadcasting.

If words are used in their traditional meanings, it is not incorrect to call TVA "creeping socialism." The fact to note is how little of that sort of thing has, for better or worse, taken place in recent years.[2]

The atomic-energy program was a post–New Deal development: It shows how poorly traditional "black-and-white" words and concepts are adapted to describe the gray territory of modern life. When the government pays General Electric a negligible fixed fee to start and run a vast nuclear industry, is this private or public enterprise? Private, in that the workers are GE employees and not civil servants. But the government puts up all the money, and certainly audits all major decisions. So the whole development of the atomic and hydrogen bombs could by some be called "galloping socialism." (For peacetime atomic energy, the government is relinquishing some of its monopoly. But decisions about secrecy, about fusionable and fissile materials, about patents, will keep nuclear energy subject to public supervision.)

In connection with this fourth category, which involves the use of human and other resources directly by the government, we should recognize that there has been a substantial rise of the federal payroll and in the number of government employees. Many of the latter are in the Washington executive offices, in regional laboratories, in the armed services, and so forth. Even if they are not producing private goods and services in competition with private industry, such resources are being directly used by the government; as we shall see, it behooves us all as citizens that they be used wisely and in right amounts relative to the importance of our various national needs.

WELFARE EXPENDITURES   Finally, we turn to an activity of government that has expanded tremendously since 1929 and that will continue to loom large in the decades ahead, namely, government welfare expenditure, which transfers purchasing power

[2] It is noteworthy that the war plants built by the government were, almost without exception, sold to private industry or shut down. Government arsenals do, in some measure, still produce war matériel, but this is exceptional.

to the needy or worthy without regard to their providing a service in return. Payments are made to veterans, old people, the handicapped, pensioned workers and their families, and unemployed people. This category of "transfer expenditure" deserves further discussion. Because of it our system is sometimes called the "welfare state."

■ TRANSFERS AND TAXES IN THE WELFARE STATE

A government check received by a veteran or needy person differs economically from that received by a postal clerk or by a man who produces typewriters. It is important to understand why, because our later discussion of national income will involve this same distinction between items that are "transfers" and items that are parts of national production or of national income.

We shall see later that governmental payments to a postal clerk and stenographer or to a missile and typewriter producer are counted as parts of national income and output. Why? Because they do cover services rendered, they do use up resources and production, and they do provide collective direct or indirect consumption to the citizens of the United States. Whether they are financed by taxes, by the sale of postage stamps, or by any other means, the government uses its dollars to provide services for citizens' use. Such dollars are as much part of national income as the dollars used by a railroad company to provide transportation services for its customers.

A blind widow's pension is something else again. Socially, it may be one of our most desirable expenditures, but nevertheless it is not part of national output or national income. Why? Because the widow does not render any concurrent services to the government or its citizens in exchange for the pension. She does not provide any labor, land, or capital. The pension does increase her purchasing power, does permit her to live more adequately and to buy goods and services from other individuals. These goods and services that she buys are part of the national income and output; but they are *attributable* to the people and private factories that have produced them, not to her.

Transfer expenditures have grown greatly in recent years. They grew partly as a result of the Depression, which made relief expenditures necessary, but they grew mostly because new minimum standards of health, nutrition, and security have been set up by the collective conscience of the American people. Society now rules that children shall not have rickets because of the bad luck or weakness of their parents, that poor people shall not die young because of insufficient money for operations and needed care, that the old shall be able to live out their years with some minimum of income. A political movement has even grown up to give every family a guaranteed income of at least $3,000 per year, on the theory that America is the first affluent society that can afford finally to end poverty.

Are welfare expenditures anticapitalistic? We shall later see that, "on the first round," these expenditures do not directly consume goods and services; but by swelling the purchasing power of their recipients, they do create orders and jobs for free private enterprise "on the second round." The thing to note is that *the production induced by this process is both privately produced and privately consumed.*

Unless these expenditures are financed by new money or by bond borrowing, larger taxes will have to be levied on the public, and it is for this reason that they are usually called "transfer expenditures." Often the more fortunate citizens are paying for consumption of the less fortunate; and doubtless within reasonable limits, most people will feel that this is not improper.

In connection with welfare programs of the government, mention should be made of the fact that various redistributions of income among citizens are accomplished by the form in which the government allocates the burden of the taxes it levies on different groups and classes. The next chapter shows that there is a tendency in modern states for the well-to-do to be taxed absolutely and relatively more heavily than those below the median income.

Thus, suppose there were no program of direct governmental transfers. But suppose the government made the very rich pay all the taxes for national defense and most of the taxes for civilian programs. Is it not evident, then, that it would be altering the inequality in the distribution of the after-tax disposable incomes that different classes have to spend on bread, cars, and anything else?

■ Along with transfer programs, one must include in the activities of the modern welfare state any redistributions of income it brings about by the way it differentiates in its tax system between the various income classes.

For the rest of this chapter, we can try to use some of the tools of economic analysis to understand the nature of the various governmental programs already surveyed.

■ GRAPHICAL ANALYSIS OF GOVERNMENT ACTIVITY[3]

The production-possibility concept of Chapter 2, particularly Fig. 2-5 on page 22, gives insight into the nature of government activity. Turn over to Fig. 8-3(a) which indicates how society can choose between (1) *private* goods (bread, shoes, dictionaries), which families buy voluntarily out of their after-tax incomes at prices set by markets, and (2) *public* goods (battleships, services of policemen and civil servants, defense, weather forecasts), which we consume collectively and which involve government expenditure (financed by taxes, deficit borrowing, printing of money).

What determines the actual E_1 position, which represents about one-quarter of the total produce devoted to *public* goods and three-quarters to *private*? It is quite evident that legislative decision puts E_1 where it is and also determines in the background the exact composition of the social expenditure as divided between the three levels of government. What about the composition of the private sector at the point E_1? On reflection, one realizes that it does indeed depend on governmental decision making, but only in the following respects: (1) Welfare transfers by government help to determine the distribution of spendable incomes of people in the private community, money which they can spend voluntarily for different goods purchasable in the market. (2) Tax legislation by our representatives decides how to allocate the tax burden among different individuals and classes; such decisions impinge in a similar way on the allocation, in the background, of E_1's private goods among persons. Aside from transfer and tax influence, the private consumption of goods is determined by volun-

---

[3] The next two sections are separable from the rest of the chapter and could be skipped.

Cutting out waste is not the same as cutting scope of government:

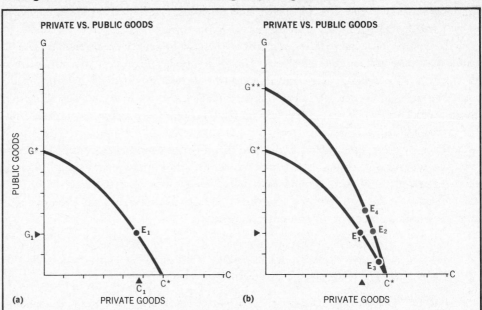

FIG. 8-3(a). Along society's production-possibility curve giving choices between private and public expenditure on goods and services, we begin at a point such as E_1.

FIG. 8-3(b). Cutting out waste and increasing governmental efficiency pivots the production-possibility curve up from old G^* to new G^{**}. This permits the previous level of government to be reached at E_2 with less sacrifice of private goods. (Cutting down on scope without change in efficiency would mean, however, moving down on the old curve to E_3.) At E_4 the populace has decided to allocate the new affluence that efficiency has brought among new extra goods of both private and governmental type.

tary market decisions of individuals—as they decide to buy white rather than rye bread, beef rather than pork, boats rather than autos, and Scotties rather than Kleenex.

Suppose international tension ended, thereby permitting us to cut down greatly on government expenditure and on taxes so as to leave people with more money to spend individually. Provided the economic system were made to run smoothly without significant unemployment, you should be able to show that the point E_1 would then move down the *p-p frontier* in Fig. 8-3(a), toward more private and less social spending.

Suppose the electorate agrees with Galbraith's *The Affluent Society*, and decides it would prefer to enjoy less private consumption of cars and such and enjoy more social consumption of roads, parks, schools, and hospitals. You should be able to show the upward and leftward movement of E_1 as it climbs the production-possibility frontier.

■ WASTE IN GOVERNMENT AND SCOPE

Our diagram helps to disentangle a common confusion. Government expenditure can be reduced in two quite different ways: First, the people can succeed in making their public activities more *efficient*. They can abolish graft and waste and insist on better planning of programs and on more efficient administration. This is sometimes called "cutting out fat without cutting muscle."

Second, they can change the *scope* of government, reducing public expenditure by having the government drop many of the functions it performs. The government can build fewer roads, provide less weather information, cease to do research, or abandon conservation activities.

Figure 8-3(b) helps keep the problem of efficiency in government distinct from the problem of scope of government. Its new curve C^*G^{**} shows the result of a successful program of increasing the *efficiency* of government activity: we can now get a greater quantity of government goods and services for the same sacrifice of resources from the private economy; so the old C^*G^* curve can be thought of as shifting upward to a higher G^{**} point, pivoting around the same old C^* point.[4]

Where, then, is the new E_2 point if the electorate wants to leave the scope of government unchanged? Now E_2 will be due right of old point E_1, with same G_1 level of social consumption but with private goods now increased as shown. (This came about in the background in something like the following way: the savings in efficiency resulted in tax reduction large enough to give people the extra income sufficient to use up all the resources released by government.)

As an alternative to the above case, suppose people succeed in reducing government expenditure solely by cutting down on the *scope* of government activity. Then there will have been no change in efficiency and no new curve. On the old C^*G^* curve, the nation moves down and to the right to E_3.

Consider still another alternative. Suppose everyone favors efficiency and we do succeed in getting the new curve. But now the electorate decides it will use its greater affluence for *both* private and additional social wants. If it decides to spend its extra real income on something from both categories, then it will move up and to the right to the point marked E_4.[5] (Please reread Fig. 8-3.)

What does this economic analysis suggest for practical policy? Students of administration seem generally to believe that the government is not less efficient relative to

[4] There is an alternative way of treating an increase of government efficiency: instead of shifting the *p-p frontier* outward, we could say that an increase in efficiency moves us from *inside* the frontier out to it. Both methods have advantages and disadvantages.

[5] Sometimes one hears the view that no government can tax and spend more than 25 per cent of the national income without creating disaster; or that the United States defense program has been as much as the economy can stand economically. If there were an absolute real limit, the transformation curves would have a corner at about E_1 and would move off horizontally to the left. There appears to be no evidence of any such discontinuity. The possibility that inflation might be the consequence of going northwest of some critical E point is a quite different argument; after study of Part Two, one can appraise such an allegation. (An advanced treatise would discuss the fact that as society taxes to transfer from private to social consumption, some distortions of incentives and efficiency are likely to result; in changing the division of the pie, you may alter its size. This means that the C^*G^* curve in Fig. 8-3 is already inside a C^*G^{**}-like curve that an engineer from Mars could demonstrate the economy was *physically* capable of producing. This constitutes one of the genuine costs of government, and sensible electorates will want to give it due weight in deciding whether this should lower or expand government's proper scope.)

private industry these days than it was in decades past. Auditing procedures, mechanization of public operations, and quality of those who take and pass civil-servant tests are believed by observers to be of such a satisfactory level that the vast increase in public expenditure has to be traced to the many new functions and expanded scope of government activity rather than to new inefficiencies. At the same time, informed men of good will are agreed on the desirability of increasing efficiency (in both the public and private sectors). What is necessarily a more controversial and philosophical problem has to do with the scope of governmental activity. It is here that representative government must respond to the desires of the citizenry.

■ SOCIAL AND PRIVATE WANTS: EXTREME *LAISSEZ FAIRE*

Let us return from graphs to the basic issues. *Why is governmental use of goods and services ever required at all?* What light can economic analysis throw on this?

In the first place, suppose all goods could be produced efficiently by perfectly competitive enterprise at any scale of operations. And suppose that all goods were like loaves of bread, the total of which can be definitely divided up into separate consumptions of different individuals, so that the more I consume out of the total, the less you consume. And suppose that there were neither altruism toward other people nor envy of them. And suppose that each person had equal initial access to human and natural resources, had equal opportunity in every sense, and could carry on his activities independently of others, much as in frontier days.

If *all* these idealized conditions were met, would there be any need whatsoever for a mixed economy? Why should there be any government functions at all? Indeed, why speak of a society at all, since the world could then be regarded as an array of independent atoms with absolutely no organic connections among them? Clearly, such a case of zero government is at one extreme pole.

Yet even in this case, if there were to be a division of labor between people and regions, and if a pricing system such as that described in Chapters 3 and 4 and in Part Three were to work, the need would soon grow for government courts and policemen to ensure honesty, fulfillment of contract, nonfraudulent and nonviolent behavior, freedom from theft and external aggression, and guarantee of the legislated rights of property. This would be *laissez faire* with minimal government—and a good system it might be if the ideal conditions presupposed for it were truly present.

■ SOCIAL WANTS IN REAL LIFE

Each and every one of the idealized conditions enumerated above is lacking in some degree in real life as mankind has always known it. Abilities, opportunities, and ownership of property exhibit disparities, depending on biological and social history. It is a fact that many kinds of production can take place most efficiently only in units too large for "perfect competition" as defined exactly by the economist; and many other imperfections mar the simplicity of the scenario. All this forms the subject of analysis throughout this book—analysis designed to provide perspective for the important compromises that a free society must make. But here, in a chapter on public expenditure, we shall concentrate on the factors that call for governmental activity.

Let us consider national defense. Nothing is more vital to a threatened society than its security. But national defense, regarded as a commodity, differs completely from the case of a private commodity like bread. Ten loaves of bread can be divided up in many ways among individuals in a group; but national defense has to be provided more or less automatically for all. Most individuals will appreciate it, much as they appreciate quantities of bread; but even among them some would be more willing, if necessary, to give up more bread for a given level of defense than others would. Some, who are pacifists, may profess that defense expenditure does not interest them particularly; while still others, who are "subversives," may actually experience pain from the social good and would require much bread to bribe them into voluntarily voting for national defense.

Could *laissez faire*, with no political voting and coercion, give the group the national defense desired by the majority? Evidently not. If I knew that I was going to benefit anyway from the defense you had paid for, why should I come into the market place and exercise a dollar demand for it? Patriotism would of course motivate me; but it would show itself in the way that I and my neighbors voted and in the way we acquiesced to the coercive fiats legislated by our responsive government, rather than in our day-to-day private purchasing.

To be sure, the example of national defense is a dramatic and extreme case. But when you think of the night policeman, the presiding judge, the appropriation for a park concert, or the damming of a river upstream to prevent floods downstream—indeed, when you think of government activities in general—you find the same common element:

■ The benefits from a social good, unlike those from a purely private good, are seen to involve *external consumption effects on more than one individual*. If a good can be subdivided so that each part can be competitively sold separately to a different individual with no external effects on others in the group, it is not a likely candidate for governmental activity.

In Part Three more will be said about external effects: so-called "external diseconomies," such as the smoke from my factory chimney which contaminates the air for all; and "external economies," such as the advantage your fruit trees get from the straying bees I raise to help pollinate my own fruit trees. It is enough here to give examples of government activities justifiable because of external effects.

Take our earlier case of a lighthouse to warn against rocks.[6] Its beam helps everyone in sight. A businessman could not build it for a profit, since he cannot claim a price from each user. This certainly is the kind of activity that government would naturally under-

---

[6] The analysis of this section owes much to the nineteenth-century analysis of Knut Wicksell and other economists and to the important recent treatise by Richard A. Musgrave, *The Theory of Public Finance* (McGraw-Hill, New York, 1959). In the lighthouse example, one thing should be noticed: The fact that the lighthouse operators cannot appropriate in the form of a purchase price a fee from those it benefits certainly helps to make it a suitable social or public good. But even if the operator were

take. It would meet Abraham Lincoln's test: "The legitimate object of government is 'to do for the people what needs to be done, but which they can not, by individual effort, do at all, or do so well, for themselves.'"

Or take the case of government provision of research on corn farming. No one competitive farmer is large enough to do it; and he also knows he cannot retain the monetary advantage of the research financed by him. Nevertheless, there is great benefit to the group and to society from learning about and adopting any improvements that might be uncovered by research on farming. As a result of these considerations, because of a clear *externality* in the use of knowledge, no prudent private firm can be expected to invest its scarce dollars up to the point of best advantage to the group as a whole. Therefore governmental activity in this area, whether in its own laboratories or by commissioning of private or university research, may well be a desirable act of representative democracy. (Where a government project, like an atomic pile, involves external *dis*economies, policy makers will have to take them into account.)

This concludes our brief economic analysis of the nature of government activity. In Part Three the discussion will go beyond the questions of government finance and will develop the economic principles that determine when a government might prudently intervene in *laissez faire* to restrain monopoly, regulate it where it is inevitable, and use tax or subsidies to offset distorting external diseconomies and economies. The next chapter will discuss public finance as it relates to the tax systems of the federal, state, and local governments and will discuss expenditures of the states and localities and their coordination with the federal government.

SUMMARY

1 ■

The economic role of government has been a generally expanding one. More and more activities in our complex, interdependent society have been coming under direct regulation and control.

2 ■

A larger fraction of the total output here and abroad has been going to collective consumption of *public* rather than *private* goods.

3 ■

An increasing part of the national income is being "transferred" by taxation and government welfare expenditure from the relatively rich to the relatively poor.

---

able—say, by radar reconnaissance—to claim a toll from every nearby user, that fact would not necessarily make it socially optimal for this service to be provided like a private good at a market-determined individual price. Why not? Because it costs society zero extra cost to let one extra ship use the service; hence any ships discouraged from those waters by the requirement to pay a positive price will represent a social economic loss—even if the price charged to all is no more than enough to pay the long-run expenses of the lighthouse. If the lighthouse is socially worth building and operating—and it need not be—a more advanced treatise can show how this social good is worth being made optimally available to all. Parts Three and Four go deeper into all this.

4 ■

There has been in America, however, no trend toward state ownership of industry and of society's means of production.

5 ■

Since World War I, federal expenditure has far outstripped local and state expenditure. During the Depression of the 1930s, expenditures on relief, public works, and similar matters expanded the federal budget. But the post–World War II budget remains many times prewar levels because of increased defense and space outlays, interest on the public debt, and aid to veterans.

6 ■

The production-possibility frontier of Chapter 2 can help distinguish between reducing government expenditure (*a*) by reducing governmental waste or (*b*) by reducing governmental scope of activity.

7 ■

Economic analysis of private goods consumable solely by individuals points up the contrast with *public* goods which involve "external consumption effects" on more than one individual in the group. National defense, research, conservation, lighthouse operation, and similar activities must pass the test of involving such "external effects" if they are to be easily justifiable as government activities.

QUESTIONS FOR DISCUSSION

1. Name things which government does now that it did not do in the past.

2. Between now and 1975, how would you expect the government's share in the national income to develop? Why? What factors affect your answer?

3. How much does the increasing economic cost of government reflect decreasing efficiency? How would you go about making a scientific study of this?

4. "The radical doctrines of three decades ago are the conservative doctrines of today." Is this ever true? Always true? Give favorable cases and exceptions.

5. "Government expenditure on goods and services represents public goods, many of which are produced by market-operated private enterprise." Appraise.

6. "To bring back the federal budget to anywhere near the pre–World War II level, veterans' programs and defense will have to be the main items cut." Discuss.

7. Define, giving examples, transfer payments and redistributive taxes.

8. Review your understanding of the following concepts:

government spending	welfare state, socialism
public debt and budget	transfer expenditures
laissez faire versus controls	private versus public goods
fiscal policy	efficiency and scope

9 The Economic Role of Government: Federal Taxation and Local Finance

THE POWER TO TAX . . . IS NOT ONLY THE POWER TO DESTROY BUT ALSO THE POWER TO KEEP ALIVE. UNITED STATES SUPREME COURT

Discussion of public finance continues in this chapter with an analysis of taxation. Then follows a survey of the federal tax system, of expenditure and taxation at the state and local levels, and of the interrelations among the different branches of government. Finally comes the problem of tax incidence—upon whom does the burden of each tax ultimately fall? How does the tax burden on rich and poor compare with their respective benefits from government expenditures?

■ ECONOMIC NATURE OF TAXATION

FINANCING REAL EXPENDITURES The state needs money to pay its bills. It gets the dollars to pay for its expenditures primarily from taxes. However, what the state really needs to build a battleship or run a lighthouse is not so much money as real economic resources: steel and watchmen—in short, the use of society's scarce supplies of labor, land, and capital goods.

> ■ In deciding how to tax themselves, therefore, the people are really deciding how resources needed for social wants shall be taken from all the various families and from the enterprises they own and be made available for governmental goods and services.

ALTERING DISTRIBUTION OF INCOMES The state also spends on *welfare transfers,* which go to particular individuals in the community for them to spend on their private needs and wants. Again, money is a veil that cloaks the *redistribution* of command over real goods and services which results from action by the state to tax some and give to others.

Recall also that, even if there were no direct welfare transfers, the state is alter-ing the distribution of incomes that results from *laissez faire.* In deciding who shall be made to pay for the resources spent on social goods and services, the electorate can vote taxes that will fall heavily on the rich rather than on the poor; on the energetic rather than the lethargic; on the owners of tangible resources such as land and prop-erty, rather than on the owners of labor power.

■ Thus taxation supplements transfers in affecting the distribution of private incomes.

In the distant past, taxes were levied by those in power against those out of power purely in terms of expediency. A nobleman at the court of Louis XIV might get off scot-free, while a merchant in Marseilles or a peasant in Normandy was sorely burdened. When scholars tried to form more rational guides to taxation, what princi-ples finally emerged?

BENEFIT VERSUS SACRIFICE PRINCIPLES   Of the many principles concerning optimal taxa-tion, two major groups can be distinguished:

1. There is the general notion that different people should be taxed in propor-tion to the "benefit" they can be expected to receive from public activity.

2. There is the general principle that people should be taxed in such a way as to lead to a desirable pattern of "sacrifice"; or what is really the same thing, that taxa-tion should be arranged to accomplish whatever the good society regards as the proper *redistribution* of market-determined incomes.[1]

Such general principles are important; but they do not avoid difficult decisions with respect to just what is the desirable structure of taxes.

For instance, consider benefit taxation. If you and I were *exactly* alike, then the benefit we receive from the armed services, the public roads, and general govern-mental services would be the same; so we ought to pay equal taxes. Similarly, take redistributional taxation. If we were exactly alike, then the amount of sacrifice we each ought to make would again be equal. No one then will quarrel with the *dictum:*

■ Those who are essentially equals should be taxed equally.

EQUALITY FOR EQUALS AND INEQUALITY FOR UNEQUALS   This notion of equal treatment of equals was important in the past and has importance today. If Man A and Man B are alike in every respect except that A has red hair, that is presumably not a legiti-mate reason for taxing them differently—any more than, in a rule of law, the fact that A is a friend of the Prime Minister or President should relieve him from taxation.

[1]Economists who think the utilities of different persons can be added together to form a total social utility speak of taxing to produce maximum total utility, or to produce some specified pattern of utility sacrifice. Thus, if each extra dollar brings less and less satisfaction to a man, and if the rich and poor are alike in their capacity to enjoy satisfaction, a dollar taxed away from a millionaire and given to a median-income person is supposed to add more to total utility than it subtracts. See Chap-ter 22 and also Fig. 21-7 for more on this.

As we shall see, the existence of loopholes in tax laws shows how necessary it is not to forget the above dictum.

However, a corollary to this dictum *once again raises* all the hard problems:

■ If equals are to be taxed equally, then there is a presumption that unequals are to be taxed unequally.

On the basis of neither the general-benefit criteria nor the optimal-sacrifice criteria does this corollary by itself resolve society's policy issues.

Imagine that Man A and Man B are alike in every respect except that B has ten times the property and income of A. Does that mean that B should pay the same *absolute* tax dollars for police protection as A? Or that he should pay the same *percentage* of his income as tax to defray police expense? Or that opulent B, inasmuch as the police have greater need to spend their time in protecting the property of the well-to-do, will not have paid his fair share of police expense unless he pays a *larger fraction of his income* in taxes?

The general philosophy of benefit or sacrifice taxation similarly leaves unanswered the question of the best tax formula. It is one thing to say that the rich have greater "ability" to pay taxes than the poor, that their "sacrifice" is less when they pay a dollar of taxes than when the poor pay a dollar. This still leaves open the question: *How much* differently should unequals in incomes be taxed?

■ PRAGMATIC COMPROMISES IN TAXATION

How have modern mixed societies tended to resolve these difficult philosophical questions? Democracies have generally adopted pragmatic solutions that will please neither the zealots in favor of benefit notions nor the zealots in favor of thoroughgoing redistributional-sacrifice notions.

Where various public services at the local and national levels are peculiarly for the benefit of recognizable groups, and where those groups have no special claim for favorable or unfavorable treatment by virtue of their average incomes or other characteristics, modern governments generally rely on taxes of the benefit type. Thus, local roads are usually paid for by local residents; taxes collected on gasoline may on the whole be devoted more specifically to road construction than to schools or libraries.

PROGRESSIVE AND REGRESSIVE TAXATION   On the other hand, extensive reliance has been placed on *graduated income taxes.* A man with $20,000 of income is taxed more than a man with $10,000 of income—even if the former claims to benefit very little from government expenditures. Not only does the higher-income man pay larger income tax, but he in fact pays a *higher fraction* of his income. This graduation of the rate of tax is in contrast to a strictly "proportional tax" that makes each man always pay exactly the *same proportion* of his income, and in even greater contrast to a so-called "regressive" tax, which takes a larger fraction from low incomes than it does from high.

PAYROLL AND BUSINESS TAXES   States and localities often charge organizations license fees for their privilege of acting as a corporation, running a tavern, and so forth. Some states tax the net income of a corporation as well, and collect miscellaneous other fees from business enterprises.

In addition, all states have been bribed by the offer of federal aid into collecting a wage tax up to 3 per cent of payrolls in occupations covered by social security. The proceeds are used to provide "unemployment compensation benefits or insurance" when workers become unemployed.

PERSONAL INCOME AND INHERITANCE TAXES   More than half the states imitate the federal government, but on a much smaller scale, by taxing individuals according to the size of their incomes. Such a method of taxation has already been discussed in connection with federal finance. A few important states, such as Illinois, do not rely at all on this relatively progressive tax.

Inheritance taxes on individuals who inherit bequests of property upon death of a relative or friend are self-explanatory. They differ only in minor detail from estate taxes that are levied on the dead giver's estate. Gifts too are taxed, since wealthy people have every incentive to distribute their wealth before death to escape taxation.

Both the federal and the state governments share in estate and inheritance taxes. The federal government tries to act to prevent states such as Florida from advertising to old folks, "Come here to die and avoid all inheritance taxes." The federal government gives up part of its revenues to any state that passes such a tax law and accepts a state tax receipt as part payment of a citizen's taxes. State laws vary widely, however.

The inheritance and estate tax is called a progressive tax. The poor widow's inheritance usually pays no tax at all because of liberal exemptions, while the rich man's estate pays at a progressive rate. Social reformers attach great importance to death taxes for the purpose of preventing the development of a permanent moneyed caste, living not on its effort and intelligence, but on its property inherited from one generation to the next. Yet, in the late 1960s, the right to "split income," to make gifts, to set up complex "trusts," and to bequeath tax-free insurance policies— all these have reduced death-tax collections to a low level. (This is also happening in Great Britain.)

There are other miscellaneous revenues. Some localities sell natural gas and electricity. Some, especially in Nevada, tax slot machines and racetrack betting. All collect some revenue from assessments on property owners who benefit from specific sewage and road improvements.

■ INTERGOVERNMENTAL GRANTS-IN-AID AND DEBT-FINANCE

An important revenue source is the financial aid that states receive from the federal government and that localities receive from the states.

Having access to more revenue sources, the federal government has increasingly been making grants to the states, and in lesser degrees to the localities. These are primarily for highways, public welfare assistance, and education. They help in part to offset the great regional differences in real incomes, as between North and South.

Similarly, within the states there have been grants-in-aid to the localities—primarily for schools, highways, and public assistance (relief, old-age pensions, and so forth). Only in this way can the poorer parts of each state maintain certain minimum standards of schooling, roads, and living. In this way well-to-do suburbanites who have fled the city are made to share the burden.

Despite these grants-in-aid, there remain sizable differentials in minimum standards. It still matters where one is born.

When all is counted in, it is not true that the total of state and local expenditures equals the total of their revenues. The difference represents new borrowing or debt repayment. Prosperity during World War II swelled state tax revenues. At the same time it became impossible to build new schools and highways. As a result, most states were then able to run a surplus and retire part of their previously accumulated debt.

But since the war, states and localities have again been increasing their debts. Their costs have risen as new school and highway projects have been undertaken. Veterans' bonuses, too, have added to state debts. As the 1970s approach, it will be states and localities that are subjected to the greatest financial strains.

Between World War I and World War II, most state and local borrowing tended to behave perversely, acting to accentuate rather than dampen the business cycle. During the prosperous 1920s, when the federal government was retiring part of its war debt, states and localities floated tremendous amounts of bonds, in order to build needed highways and schools at the high prices then prevailing for cement and carpenters. When the Depression of the 1930s came, state and local governments retrenched activities and on balance reduced their debts. Even though they do not have the federal government's advantage of having a money-creating Federal Reserve, states and localities should be able to act in a less destabilizing manner in the future.

■ CONCLUSION: THE THORNY PROBLEM OF TAX INCIDENCE

In ending this survey of taxes and other revenues, let us note a few warnings. Even if the electorate has made up its mind about how the tax burden shall be borne by individuals, the following difficult problems remain:

Who ultimately pays a particular tax? Does its burden stay on the person against whom it is first levied? One cannot just assume that the person Congress says a tax is levied on will end up paying that tax. He may be able to *shift* the tax: shift it "forward" on his customers, by raising his price as much as the tax; or shift it "backward" on his suppliers, who end up charging him less than they would have done had there been no tax.

Economists therefore say: We must study the final *incidence* of the tax—the way its burden ultimately gets borne, the totality of its effects on commodity prices, factor-prices, resource allocations, efforts, and composition of production and consumption.

Tax incidence, thus, is no easy problem and requires all the advanced tools of economics to help toward its solution.

> EXAMPLE: Does a tax on wheat raise the price to the consumer by as much as itself, so that the incidence is on the consumer? Or does the tax raise the price by half itself or not at all, so that the incidence is partially on the producers? Does it change oat prices? And does the tax kill off all or much of wheat production, so that it is having incidence effects beyond those which show up in money prices and wages and even beyond the burdens that you can allocate among the different citizens?)

Parts Three and Four will develop some of the important tools that one needs to begin to tackle this thorny problem. Economists are not yet in agreement on final results. Some think the corporate income tax falls mostly on the consumer; some argue it falls mostly on stockholders or capitalists.

Figure 9-4 reports on a valiant statistical attempt to determine how progressive or regressive our over-all tax and expenditure system is. Experts agree that the results of such a study can be only approximate, since no one knows just how a corporate or other tax gets shifted. Even an expert is not a magician capable of making a controlled experiment in which he (1) measures things without taxes, then (2) measures things with taxes, and finally (3) determines tax incidence as the difference between these situations.

Experts try to answer the question, Who pays the taxes and gets the benefits?

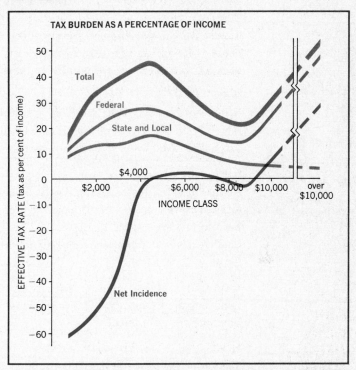

FIG. 9-4. The brown curves show taxes as percentages of income. Because the federal government levies payroll and excise taxes on the poor, even its tax structure is not progressive until one gets to the most prosperous one-fifth of the populace. However, as the green curve of "net incidence" shows, after we take account of the favorable impact on the poor of government expenditure, the pattern is "progressive" and the green curve generally rises with income. This means government has a balancing or equalizing effect upon the dispersion of real income. (Source: W. Irwin Gillespie in R. A. Musgrave, ed., *Essays in Fiscal Federalism*, Brookings Institution, Washington, D.C., 1965 pp. 136–162.)

Note the sag in progression of tax around the median income level. The affluent do get taxed to help the poor, but the man in the middle is something of a forgotten man when it comes to tax burden. But, as the green curve in Fig. 9-4 shows, when we consider which income classes benefit from government expenditure, the needy do show a more favorable "net incidence" than the affluent. With a negative income tax and federal revenue sharing, net incidence would be even more progressive.

SUMMARY

1 ■

Taxes give the government the resources it needs for its public activities. Taxes also finance welfare transfer expenditures that change the distribution of income; and the over-all way taxes are levied affects the final distribution of incomes among people.

2 ■

Notions of "benefit" and "sacrifice or redistribution" are two principal theories of taxation. Justice implies taxing equals equally, unequals unequally. Direct and progressively graduated taxes on incomes are in contrast to indirect and regressive excises.

3 ■

About three-fourths of federal revenue comes from personal and corporation income taxes. The rest comes from "regressive taxes" on payrolls and excises. The personal income tax, except for loopholes and erosion of the tax base, is steeply progressive, tending to redistribute income from rich to poor.

4 ■

State and local expenditures have been rising in the postwar period: the principal items are education, highways, public welfare, and the ordinary police and safety functions of government.

5 ■

The property tax is the most important source of local revenue. Sales taxes and excises are important for the state. In the postwar period, states and localities have been spending more than they tax, thereby increasing their debts.

6 ■

The federal government gives large grants to the states, primarily for highways, matching grants-in-aid for social welfare, and education. The states help the localities—primarily in education, highways, and public assistance.

7 ■

The incidence of a tax is its ultimate division of burden, its total effect on prices and other economic magnitudes. Those upon whom a tax is levied may succeed in shifting part of its burden forward or backward. The economists' tools of Parts Three and Four will help in tackling this difficult problem. Progression in benefits seems to offset the regressive sag of our tax structure at middle income levels.

QUESTIONS FOR DISCUSSION

1. Make a list of different taxes in order of their progressiveness. What is the importance of each at the federal, state, and local level?

2. List different state and local expenditure categories in order of quantitative importance. Compare with federal expenditure categories of Chapter 8.

3. How do you think different government functions should be allocated among the three levels of government? How about revenues and grants-in-aid?

4. Should a citizen in Massachusetts be taxed to help a citizen in Arkansas? To help a citizen in Vermont? In Massachusetts? In Mexico or India?

5. "Since people don't change their smoking habits as a result of taxation, and since the poor smoke, a tax on cigarettes is really no different from a tax on bread." Do you agree? If so, what ought to be done?

6. From Table 9-2, calculate the personal income tax paid by a typical doctor, lawyer, teacher, stenographer, mechanic, and carpenter.

7. In the next decade there will be a political move to get the federal government to introduce a comprehensive sales tax or some other nonpersonal tax. Evaluate the pros and cons.

8. "More kids and cars mean local expenditure and debt." Evaluate.

9. Review your understanding of the following concepts:

benefit and sacrifice notions	grants-in-aid, public debts
direct and indirect taxes	budget surpluses and deficits
progressive and regressive	tax incidence and shifting

10 National Income and Product

THE TIME HAS COME, THE WALRUS SAID,
TO SPEAK OF MANY THINGS.
OF SHOES, AND SHIPS, AND SEALING WAX,
OF CABBAGES—AND KINGS.   LEWIS CARROLL

One of the most important concepts in all economics is national income. This chapter's discussion of national income can serve as the unifying summary of Part One's introduction to the *basic economic processes and institutions* of modern mixed societies. Alternatively, this analysis of national income, its anatomy and accounting structure, can be regarded as the introduction to the treatment of macroeconomics of Part Two— the study of the physiological forces that determine total employment, production, real income, and the price level. The concept of national income is indispensable preparation for tackling the great issues of unemployment, inflation, and growth.

■ THE YARDSTICK OF AN ECONOMY'S PERFORMANCE

What is national income? It is the loose name we give to the money measure of the over-all annual flow of goods and services in an economy. Often, instead of it, we use the almost equivalent, precise term "national product" or "net national product" (NNP);[1] or the slightly different concept of "gross national product" (GNP).

If you asked an economic historian just what the Great Depression really meant, his best brief answer would be: "From a 1929 NNP of 95.8 billion dollars there was a drop to a 1933 NNP of 48.8 billion dollars. This halving of the money value of the flow of goods and services in the American economy caused hardship, bank failures, riots, and political turmoil."

■ In brief, national income or product is the final figure you arrive at when you apply the measuring rod of money to the diverse apples, oranges, and machines that any society produces with its land, labor, and capital resources.

[1] We shall have occasion below to note the special and narrow use of the term "national income" by the U.S. Department of Commerce.

■ TWO MEASURES OF NATIONAL PRODUCT: AS GOODS-FLOW OR EARNINGS-FLOW

How do we measure the net national product, NNP? The general idea is simple. Figure 10-1 shows the circular flow of dollar spending in an economy with no government and no accumulation of capital or net saving going on.

FLOW-OF-PRODUCT APPROACH Each year the public consumes goods and services: goods such as apples, oranges, and bread; services such as manicures. The public spends dollars for these consumer goods, as in the upper loop of Fig. 10-1. We add together all the consumption dollars spent for these final goods to arrive at the total of NNP.

Thus, in our simple economy, one can easily calculate national income or product as the sum of the annual flow of final goods and services: (price of oranges × number of oranges) + (price of apples × number of apples) + ⋯.

Why use market prices as weights

Net national product is measured as flow of output or as equal flow of costs:

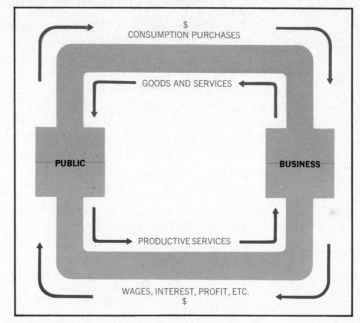

FIG. 10-1. In the upper loop, people spend their money on final goods: the total dollar flow of these per year is one measure of net national product, NNP.

The lower loop measures the annual flow of costs of output: the earnings that business pays out in wages, rent, interest, dividends, and accrued profits. With profit properly reckoned as a residual, the two measures of NNP must always be identical.

in evaluating and summing diverse physical commodities and services? Because, as we shall see in Part Three, market prices are reflectors of the relative desirability of diverse goods and services.

■ The *net national product*, or "national income evaluated at market prices," as it is technically named, is definable as the total money value of the flow of final products of the community.[2]

EARNINGS OR INCOME APPROACH There is a second, equivalent way to calculate NNP in so simple an economy. Go to the lower loop in Fig. 10-1: What is the total cost of output which business is paying out to the public? It is paying out wages, interest, rents, and profit. Why? Because these factor earnings of land, labor, and capital are the *costs* of production of the flow of product. (NOTE: Here the economist, unlike the accountant, does count profit as a cost or earning item.)

[2]In our first, simplest model, the only final product is private consumption expenditures. But in a moment we shall see that government expenditures on goods and services and private net investment are also to be included.

The statistician can measure the annual flow of such factor earnings or income in the lower loop.[3] In this way, he will *again* arrive at the NNP.

■ Net national product is also definable, from a second viewpoint, as the total of factor earnings (wages, interest, rents, and accruing profits) that are the costs of production of society's final goods.

Now we have calculated NNP by the upper-loop flow-of-product approach and by the lower-loop earnings-flow approach. Which is bigger? Answer: They will be *exactly* the same.

Here is the reason for this identity. Recall that we have included "profit" in the lower loop—along with wages, interest, and rents. What exactly is profit? Profit is what you have left over from the sale of product (your oranges, apples, bread, and manicures) *after* you have paid the other factor costs. So *profit automatically is the residual that takes on the size needed to make the lower-loop approach via earnings* exactly *match the upper-loop approach via flow of goods.*

This all reflects the useful device of double-entry which accountants use to keep the two sides of their books in perfect balance.

■ To sum up: NNP, or net national product, is measurable as the flow of product; but it is also convenient for the statistician to measure it via the earnings approach in the lower loop. With the proper definition of profit and its inclusion as an economic earning and cost, each approach will yield exactly the same NNP.

An example will show how to go from business accounts to national accounts in the simplest case, without government and investment, and where all final products are produced from land, labor, and capital in 10 million identical one-stage firms or farms.

INCOME STATEMENT OF TYPICAL FARM

OUTPUT ATTRIBUTABLE TO FARMING		EARNINGS	
Sales of goods (wheat, apples, etc.)	$1,000	Costs of production	
		Wages	$ 800
		Rents	100
		Interest	25
		Profit (residual)	75
Total	$1,000	Total	$1,000

Adding all the 10 million farms gives the NNP account easily in this trivial case.

NATIONAL PRODUCT ACCOUNT (in millions!)

UPPER-LOOP FLOW OF PRODUCT		LOWER-LOOP EARNINGS OR INCOMES	
Final output (10 × 1,000)	$10,000	Wages (10 × 800)	$ 8,000
		Rents (10 × 100)	1,000
		Interest (10 × 25)	250
		Profit (10 × 75)	750
NNP total	$10,000	NNP total	$10,000

Note that the definition of profit makes the firm's two sides balance; hence the two NNP approaches must still match after summation.

[3] When we leave our simple model, taxes will have to be included here.

We deflate by a price index to correct for our rubber money yardstick:

DATE	(1) MONEY NNP, BILLIONS OF CURRENT DOLLARS	(2) INDEX NUMBER OF PRICES	(3) REAL NNP, IN BILLIONS OF 1929 DOLLARS $(3) = \frac{(1)}{(2)} \times 100$
1929	96	*100*	$\frac{96}{100} \times 100 = 96$
1933	48	75	$\frac{48}{75} \times 100 = 64$

TABLE 10-1. SAMPLE CALCULATION OF REAL NNP. Using price index of Column (2), we deflate Column (1) to get real NNP, Column (3). (RIDDLE: Can you show that 1929's real NNP was 72 billion dollars in terms of 1933 prices? HINT: With 1933 as a base, 1929's price index is 133⅓.)

■ REAL VERSUS MONEY NATIONAL PRODUCT: USING A PRICE INDEX TO "DEFLATE"

We saw that NNP uses the measuring rod of money prices in the market to combine diverse apples, oranges, and other goods to a single total figure. But one would hardly choose to measure things with a rubber rather than a wooden yardstick—one that stretched in your hands from day to day.

This is one of the problems economists have to solve when they use money as their measuring rod. Everyone knows that inflations and deflations can send most prices up or down. Or, as the economist puts it, "The value of money does change between years like 1929 and 1933, or 1939 and 1967."

What can be done about this? Economists can repair most of the damage due to the changeability of our measuring rod by using an index number of prices.[4] A 1929–1933 comparison will illustrate the process by which one uses a price index number to "deflate" a "current money NNP," converting it into a "real NNP in terms of dollars of unchanged 1929 purchasing power."

Table 10-1 gives the actual 1929 and 1933 NNP figures to the close approximations of 96 and 48 billion dollars. It shows a halving of money NNP. But the government estimates that prices of goods and services dropped on the average about 25 per cent in the Depression. Using 1929 as a base of 100, this means the 1933 price index was about 75. So our 48-billion-dollar 1933 NNP was really worth more than half the 96-billion-dollar NNP of 1929.

How much more? Table 10-1 divides through by the price index number to "deflate" and shows that *real NNP" fell only to two-thirds the 1929 level:* thus in terms of dollars of 1929 purchasing power, it fell down to 64 billion dollars. Hence, part of the halving shown by the money NNP was due to the optical illusion of the changing price yardstick.

---

[4]Computing a price index would be easy if all prices were to change by the same percentage. When all P's triple, the index rises from 100 to 300; when all halve, it drops to 50. If P's increase in different degrees, but all end up between double and triple their base, the index is certainly between 200 and 300. Just where? Evidently we need some kind of *average* of the price changes, each being *weighted* in accordance with its approximate economic *importance*. The official indexes are good approximations, but some basic problems remain: getting an accurate sample of prices; allowing for quality improvements; deciding which average to use (arithmetic or geometric mean, median, etc.); defining relative-economic-importance weights, in a statical and in a changing world.

How rising prices spuriously inflated our net national product:

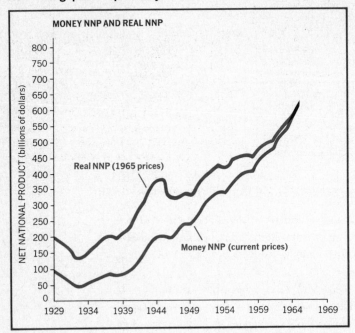

FIG. 10-2. The rise in money NNP since the Depression and World War II exaggerates the rise in real NNP: because the price index has generally been rising since then, we must use it to deflate the money NNP in order to arrive at the real NNP trends.

Figure 10-2 shows the history of money NNP (expressed in the actual dollars and prices that were current in each historical year). Then, for comparison, the real NNP expressed in 1965 dollars is shown. Note that part of the increase in money NNP is really spurious, being due merely to inflation in the last 30 years of our money yardstick's price units.

■ AVOIDING "DOUBLE COUNTING" OF INTERMEDIATE GOODS

Returning to current money figures, we can now show how to handle "intermediate" goods (which are not truly *final* goods) and thus avoid counting anything two, three, or more times.

IGNORING INTERMEDIATE GOODS   We do want to count bread in NNP, but we must *avoid also counting in the dough that goes to make the bread.* That would indeed be double counting, since the only reason we want the dough is for the final bread. Turn back to the two-loop Fig. 10-1. You could find bread (and manicures) there; but you won't find any dough, flour, or wheat. Where are they? These are so-called "intermediate products" that are produced during all the stages leading up to the final bread product, and they are hidden in the block marked "business." That is as it should be. We don't want intermediate products to be double-counted along with final product.

USING "VALUE ADDED" TO AVOID DOUBLE COUNTING   Some students say:

I can see that, if you are careful, your upper-loop approach to NNP will avoid including intermediate products. But I'm a little uncertain whether or not you might find yourself in some difficulty when you use the lower-loop approach. After all, doesn't the Commerce Department gather income statements from the accounts of business firms? Won't it then be picking up what millers pay to farmers, what bakers pay to millers, and what grocers pay to bakers? Won't this result in double counting or even triple and quadruple counting of some items that go through several stages of production?

This is a legitimate question. Fortunately, we can give it a satisfactory answer. The statistician making lower-loop earnings or factor-cost measurements is always very careful to use what he calls the "value-added" approach.

The value-added approach refuses to include *all* the expenses shown on each

NNP is the sum of value added of all the separate stages:

STAGE OF PRODUCTION	(1) SALES RECEIPTS		(2) COST OF INTER- MEDIATE MATE- RIALS OR GOODS		(3) VALUE ADDED (WAGES, PROFIT, ETC.) (3) = (1) − (2)
Wheat	5	−	0	=	5
Flour	8	−	5	=	3
Baked dough	17	−	8	=	9
Delivered bread	25	−	17	=	8
	55	−	30	=	25 (sum of value added)

TABLE 10-2. BREAD RECEIPTS, COSTS, AND VALUE ADDED (in cents per loaf). To avoid double counting, we carefully calculate value added at each stage, subtracting all the costs of materials and intermediate products not produced in that stage but bought from other business firms. Note that every intermediate product appears both in Column (1) and with opposite sign in Column (2); hence it is canceled out.

firm's business income statement in the lower-loop factor earnings. Which expenses are excluded? All purchases of materials and services from *other* firms are excluded, because those dollars will get properly counted in NNP from the reports of *other* firms.

EXAMPLE: Pepto-Glitter Co. buys electric power from the Edison Co. This expense on the Pepto income statement is *not* included in value added. Why should it be? It is not a wage, interest, rent, or profit payment. In fact, it is not a payment to any Pepto-Glitter productive factor; hence it never shows up in the lower loop at all. It stays inside the business block, where it and all other such expenditures by a firm on intermediate goods are carefully subtracted from Pepto's receipts. What is left? Pepto's true value added—which is exactly the sum of *its* wage, interest, rent, and profit costs.

Mind you, the electric power was produced by the Edison workers—and by the Edison interest, rent, and profit receivers. So do not fear that this electrical activity will get overlooked by the NNP statistician. It will not. He will pick it up as the value added of the Edison Co. This is as it should be: we want to count each thing once, not twice or three times.

Table 10-2 illustrates by means of the several stages of a loaf of bread how careful adherence to the value-added approach will enable us to subtract the intermediate expenses that show up in the income statements of farmers, millers, bakers, and grocers—ending up with the desired equality between (1) net value of final bread and (2) the lower-loop factor-costs embodying the sum of the value-added data of all stages. All this can be summarized as follows:

■ *Value-added approach.* To avoid double counting, we take care to include in net national product only final goods, and not the intermediate goods that go to make the final goods. By resolutely sticking to the *value added* at each stage, taking care to subtract expenditures on the intermediate goods bought from other firms, the lower-loop earnings approach properly avoids all double counting and records wages, interest, rent, and profit exactly one time.

Our earlier example with a million farmers can now have added to it a million second-stage manufacturers, who buy wheat and farm goods and add value to them by processing them into bread and other final products by the use of labor, land, and capital. Alongside the farmer's income statement we have the manufacturer's income statement.

INCOME STATEMENT OF TYPICAL MANUFACTURER

OUTPUT ATTRIBUTABLE TO MANUFACTURING		EARNINGS	
Sales of goods	$5,000	Costs of value added	
Minus goods bought from other firms	1,000	Wages	$3,500
		Rent	100
		Interest	100
		Profit (residual)	300
Total	$4,000	Total	$4,000

To get total NNP for society, we can add the left-hand sides of the 10 million farmers *and* 10 million bakers; or to get lower- rather than upper-loop NNP, we add the right-hand items for *all* these 20 million firms.

NATIONAL PRODUCT ACCOUNT (in millions)

UPPER-LOOP FLOW OF PRODUCT		LOWER-LOOP EARNINGS OR INCOMES	
Final output (finished bread, etc.)		Wages (8,000 + 35,000)	$43,000
[50,000 = 10,000 + (50,000 − 10,000)]	$50,000	Rent (1,000 + 1,000)	2,000
		Interest (250 + 1,000)	1,250
		Profit (750 + 3,000)	3,750
NNP total	$50,000	NNP total	$50,000

■ NET INVESTMENT, CAPITAL FORMATION

So far we have banished all capital growth from our discussion. We talked of people as wanting to currently consume bread, apples, oranges, and manicures.[5] In real life, however, people often want to devote part of their income to saving and investment. Instead of eating bread *now,* they may want to build new machines to help produce more bread for *future* consumption, or they may want to add to the inventory of bread, dough, flour, and wheat. In short, we must recognize that the final goals of people do include net investment or capital formation, not simply current consumption.

If people are using part of society's production possibilities for capital formation rather than consumption, the economic statistician recognizes that he must include such output in his upper-loop flow of NNP. So really, we must modify our original definition to read:

■ **Net national product is the sum of *all* final products, such as consumption goods and services, and including also *net* investment.**

This net investment (or net capital formation) will include the net additions to our stock of (1) buildings, (2) equipment, and (3) inventories.

WARNING: To economists, investment always means real capital formation—production of added goods in inventories, of new plants, houses, and tools. To the layman, investment means merely using money to buy an outstanding share of GM stock, to buy a corner lot,

[5]Indeed, the economic statistician counts in the NNP all consumption items that people want to spend *their* incomes on. He draws the line at illegal expenditures, e.g., opium consumption or prostitution. During World War II when black-market operations were important, he found it necessary in some countries to supplement his statistics with estimates of black-market money transactions.

to open a savings account. It is important not to confuse these meanings: If I take $1,000 from my safe and now put it in the bank, the economist says that neither investment nor saving has gone up from this act alone. Only if some physical capital formation takes place is there investment; only if society consumes less than its income, devoting resources to capital formation, is there saving.

■ NET INVESTMENT EQUALS GROSS INVESTMENT MINUS DEPRECIATION

How does the economist get accurate figures on net investment?

First he has to make estimates of inventories and of their changes. Harder still is his task of estimating net investment in buildings and equipment.

Why can't he just jot down *all* the buildings built and *all* the machines produced, add them in with his calculated net inventory change, and let it go at that? He does indeed make such a calculation. But the resulting figure is too large—too gross. Recognizing this he gives a new name to the result, namely, "gross investment" rather than "net investment."

Why the word "gross"? The statistician uses this word to emphasize that he has not yet made any allowances for the using up of capital, i.e., no allowance for capital depreciation. (Recall the accounting appendix of Chapter 5.)

One would not think much of a statistician who estimated the change in human population by ignoring deaths. If he just added up gross births, without subtracting a good estimate for deaths, he would get an exaggerated notion of the net change in population. The same holds for economic equipment and buildings: net change is always gross births (of capital) minus deaths (or capital depreciation). This can be summed up in the definition:

■ Net investment always equals gross investment minus depreciation.

Table 10-3 gives typical figures relating net and gross investment. They differ only by depreciation; and fortunately, this is a sluggish item that changes slowly over a period of a few years. That is why many forecasters, who really are interested in net

To get net investment, subtract depreciation from gross investment:

INVESTMENT COMPONENTS	1929	1932	1946	1965
New construction	$ 8.9	$7.0	$14.0	$ 52.7
Producers' durable equipment	5.6	3.8	10.2	44.8
Change in business inventories	1.7	−6.2	6.4	9.1
Gross private domestic investment	$16.2	$4.6	$30.6	$106.6
Allowances for depreciation or capital consumption (also = difference between GNP and NNP)	−7.9	−7.4	9.9	−59.6
Net private domestic investment	$ 8.3	$ −2.8	$20.7	$47.0

TABLE 10-3. GROSS AND NET INVESTMENT (in billions of dollars). After subtracting capital depreciation from Gross private domestic investment, we get Net private domestic investment—to which net foreign exports can be added later. (Source: U.S. Department of Commerce.)

investment, are satisfied to work with the gross investment figures, which are easier to find in the newspapers and official statistics.

■ GROSS NATIONAL PRODUCT VERSUS NET NATIONAL PRODUCT

Gross investment can be estimated fairly accurately, involving no difficult depreciation estimate. For this reason governments and the United Nations sensibly decided to calculate a gross national product figure *first* rather than a net national product figure.

> ■ **Gross national product (GNP) is defined as the sum of final products such as consumption goods and gross investment (which is the increase in inventories plus gross births or production of buildings and equipment).**

Table 10-3 suggests it will be easy enough to get NNP from GNP after we know what is the total depreciation figure that is to be subtracted from GNP.[6]

The official statistics do present NNP data at stated intervals. Generally, though, they concentrate on GNP, for the good reason that depreciation cannot be quickly and accurately measured each quarter. Even if the economist—as in later chapters—likes to talk about NNP, he is content to work with GNP data, knowing that the two concepts do move together closely during any period that is not too long.

■ GOVERNMENT EXPENDITURE ON GOODS AND SERVICES

Until now we have ignored government. We have talked about consumers but ignored the biggest consumer of all, namely, the federal, state, and local governments. Somehow NNP and GNP must somehow take into account the billions of dollars of product that a nation collectively consumes. How?

After some debate, the income statisticians of the United States and United Nations decided on using the simplest method of all. To the flow of (1) consumption product and (2) investment product, they simply add (3) *all* government expenditure on goods and services. (Repeatedly in the next few chapters, you will see $C + I + G$, which stands for these three components.)

Here are examples. Along with bread consumption and net investment in NNP, we include in it government expenditures on jet bombers. We include government expenditure on the services of jet pilots, judges, policemen, national-income statisticians, firemen, and agricultural chemists.

In short, all the government payroll expenditures on its employees plus the goods (typewriters, guns, and airplanes) it buys from private industry are included in this third great category of flow of product, labeled G and called "government expenditure on goods and services."

Figure 10-3 pictures NNP and its three major components.

[6]Here is a convenient rule of thumb: NNP is usually about ten-elevenths of GNP, depreciation nowadays being about one-eleventh of GNP. Figure 10-4 will soon bear this out.

EXCLUSION OF TRANSFER PAYMENTS
Does this mean that every dollar the government pays out is included in NNP? Definitely not. If you get an old-age pension from the government, we call that a "transfer payment" and do not treat it as part of NNP. Why not? Because it is not a government expenditure on goods and services of this year. Or if your aunt gets a widow's assistance payment, that welfare expenditure is also deemed a transfer item. The same goes for pensions to the blind, veterans, and other welfare recipients. These transfers are not payments for *current* productive services.

Many other government transfer items[7] could be mentioned, but we can conclude with one big item: interest on the public debt. The interest paid on federal bonds was included years ago in NNP, but the fairly universal custom now is for countries to treat this as a transfer item. This is not now included in G, on the argument that it is not a payment for current goods and services.[8] (As will be seen on page

NNP is sum of consumption, investment, and government expenditures on goods and services:

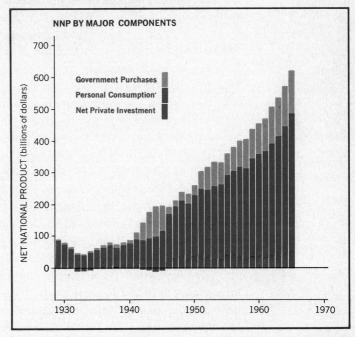

FIG. 10-3. Though consumption dominates NNP, note the World War II and postwar growth in government expenditure and in investment. Note that in the Great Depression and the war, gross private investment fell short of replacement needs, and net private investment was negative. (Source: U.S. Department of Commerce.)

189, interest paid by consumers on their borrowings has been treated since 1965 by the Commerce Department statisticians as a transfer item. Why? Because this is not regarded as a payment for current productive services—exactly the same argument used for treating government debt interest as a transfer item.)

Do not think that the Treasury's budget fails to take account of all government transfer payments. The budget back on page 153 did include these: the government

---

[7] The name "transfer payment," as used in Chapter 8 and here, is a little misleading. If you tax me to give a relief dole to my unemployed neighbor, that does sound like a "transfer." But suppose you print a new green 20-dollar bill to give him, or borrow by selling bonds to make relief payments. He gets money that is not transferred from anybody else. Economists still call the relief payments transfers, regardless of how they are financed.

[8] How to treat government items in NNP is still somewhat controversial. (1) Some experts argue that G should be broken down into government current consumption and government net investment (increase in its buildings, equipment, and inventories), just as private product is so broken up. And some nations do this. (2) Some experts say, too, that part of G is really "intermediate" rather than "final" product—much like dough rather than bread—in that it may merely contribute to final private product already counted in (e.g. weather information for farmers who help give us our daily bread). But few nations make estimates of how much such double counting may be involved in the G figures.

surplus does equal taxes minus the sum of G *and* transfers. The official budget also includes some purely bookkeeping expenses. But do not confuse the usual budget with national-income accounts, which are related but distinct.

TREATMENT OF TAXES   In using the flow-of-product approach to compute NNP as $C + I + G$, we need never worry about taxes or how government finances itself. Whether the government taxes, issues interest-bearing IOUs, or prints new noninterest IOU greenbacks, the statistician computes G as the value of government expenditure on goods and services (evaluating these items at their actual cost to the government, wherever the money came from; and private $C + I$ at actual market prices.)

It is all very well to ignore taxes in the upper-loop flow-of-product approach. But what about in the lower-loop earnings or cost approach to NNP? In this lower loop, we do indeed have to take account of all taxes.

Consider wages, for example. Part of what my employer pays me in wages I have to give to the government in the form of personal income taxes. So these direct taxes do definitely get included in the wage component of the lower loop, and the same holds for direct taxes (personal or corporate) on interest, rent, and profit.

Or take the sales and other indirect taxes that manufacturers and retailers have to pay on a loaf of bread (or on the wheat, flour, and dough stages). Suppose these indirect taxes total 5 cents; and suppose wages, profit, and other value-added items add up to 25 cents in cost to the bread industry. (We do not care how much of this 25 cents goes to direct taxes.) What will the bread sell for in the upper loop? For 25 cents? Of course not. The bread will sell for 30 cents, equal to 25 cents of factor-costs plus 5 cents of indirect taxes.[9]

Hence we definitely do always include taxes in the lower-loop cost approach to NNP and GNP.

Now that the government has been brought into the picture, a final comprehensive definition can be given.

■ GNP and NNP are definable as the sum of three major components: personal consumption expenditure on goods and services, plus government expenditure on goods and services, plus investment expenditure—where it is understood that in GNP gross investment expenditure on all new machines and construction are included, whereas in NNP only the net investment expenditure is included, there having been subtracted from the gross births of capital goods an appropriate depreciation allowance to take account of deaths, or using up of capital goods.

GNP and NNP are each definable, not only as an upper-loop flow of product, but also as a lower-loop total of costs: to factor-costs such as wages, interest, rents, and profit (always carefully excluding double counting of intermediate

[9]This is plainly so by definition of our residual profit and from the fact that residual profit is treated as a cost; but this result definitely says *nothing at all* about whether the tax is passed forward to the consumer or backward to the factors, whose wages and other returns might have been higher had there been no taxes. Chapter 20 analyzes such a "tax incidence" problem of the sort described in Chapter 9.

goods bought from other firms by the value-added technique), there will have to be added all the indirect business taxes that do show up as an expense of producing the flow of products; and in the case of gross national product there will also be included depreciation expense, whereas the net national product will be less by the amount of this estimated expense.

The two loops yield identical magnitudes by definition (i.e., by careful adherence to the procedures of "double-entry" bookkeeping).[10]

■ AMERICA'S NNP AND GNP

Armed with an understanding of the concepts involved, we can turn the page to the actual data in the important Table 10-4, a table which merits lengthy study.

FLOW-OF-PRODUCT APPROACH   Look first at Table 10-4's left side. This gives the upper-loop flow-of-product approach to NNP. Distinguishing between domestic and foreign investment, we have four components. Of these, C and G and their obvious classifications require little comment.

Net private domestic investment does require one comment. Its net figure of 47.0 billion dollars was arrived at in the way already described: from estimated gross private domestic investment of 106.6 was subtracted the estimated value of depreciation of 59.6, just as in Table 10-3 of this chapter.

The final international item will be discussed further in the Appendix to this chapter and later in Chapter 33. Except for some complications that arise from government transfer expenditures abroad (2.8 billion dollars, constituting parts of foreign and other aid), the 7.0 billion dollars net export of goods and services could be interpreted as our net foreign investment, which has to be added to net domestic investment to arrive at the total of investment. In any case, along with C, G, and domestic I, net exports do represent a fourth component of the flow of product.[11]

Adding up the four components on the left gives the important total NNP of 621.6 billion dollars. This is the harvest we have been working for: the money measure of the American economy's over-all performance for 1965.

Finally, note that if we add depreciation back into the figures, we have the GNP of 681.2 billion dollars—which is bigger because it contains gross rather than net investment in its measure of product.

LOWER-LOOP FLOW-OF-COST APPROACH   Now turn to the right-hand side of the table. Here we have all the value-added items plus taxes.

[10]Statisticians must always work with incomplete reports and must fill in some gaps by estimation. As will be seen in a moment, approximate guesses of the two definitions can differ somewhat by what is officially reported as the "statistical discrepancy." Along with the civil servants who are each heads of units called wages, interest, and so forth, there is actually a man with the title "head of the statistical discrepancy." If data were perfect, he would be out of a job; but as real life is never so, his task of reconciliation is one of the hardest of all. (In the presentation of the balance of international payments given in Chapter 33 a similar "errors and omissions" item will appear.)

[11]EXAMPLE: Of 100 chocolates of NNP, suppose 80 go to C, 10 to G, 6 to domestic I in the form of added inventory, and 4 are exported abroad with nothing being imported from abroad.

Here are the two ways of looking at NNP and GNP in actual numbers:

FLOW-OF-PRODUCT APPROACH			EARNINGS AND COST APPROACH		
1. Personal consumption expenditure		$431.5	Wages and other employee supplements		$392.9
Durable goods	$ 66.1		Net interest		17.8
Nondurable goods	190.6		Rent income of persons		18.3
Services	174.8		Indirect business taxes and adjustments°		62.8
2. Government purchases of goods and services		136.1	Income of unincorporated enterprises (adjusted)		55.6
3. Net private domestic investment (106.6 − 59.6)		47.0	Corporate profits before taxes (adjusted)		74.2
4. Net export of goods and services (39.0 exports − 32.0 imports)		7.0	Dividends	$19.2	
			Undistributed profits	25.3	
			Corporate profits taxes	31.2	
			Reported profits (unadj.)	$75.7	
			Inventory valuation adjustment	+1.5	
Net National Product		**$621.6**	**Net National Product**		**$621.6**
Depreciation (or capital consumption allowance)		59.6	Depreciation (or capital consumption allowance)		59.6
Gross National Product		**$681.2**	**Gross National Product**		**$681.2**

TABLE 10-4. NET NATIONAL PRODUCT, 1965 (in billions of current dollars). The left side measures flow of product (at market prices). The right side measures flow of costs (factor earnings plus indirect taxes). GNP, which includes Depreciation, is also shown. Be sure you understand the main items. (Source: U.S. Department of Commerce. The starred item includes the "statistical discrepancy" and arises from imperfect measurement of upper- and lower-loop data.)

A few explanations are in order. Wages[12] and other employee supplements include all take-home pay and fringe benefits, and they also have in them the withheld and other income or payroll taxes that wage earners have to pay.

Net interest is a similar item. (Note again, interest on government bonds is not included as part of G or NNP, being treated as a transfer.)

Rent income of persons requires only one explanation. If you own your own home, you are treated as paying rent to yourself. This is a so-called "imputed" item and makes sense if we really want to measure the housing services the American people are enjoying and do not want the estimate changed every time a tenant buys the house he has been renting. Admittedly, this imputed item has to be estimated, since no one reports rental receipts on his own home.

Indirect business taxes, as we earlier saw, do have to be included in the lower loop if we are to match the upper loop. Any direct taxes on wages, interest, or rents were already included in those items.

[12]The late Sir Arthur Bowley of the London School of Economics noted how remarkably constant over almost a century is wages' share of national income. No one is sure why this should be so. (The wages' share does rise at the expense of profit during recession; in recent decades the wage share has perhaps shown a slight upward creep, as seen in Chapter 37.)

Lastly, turn to profit. This should come last because it is the residual determined as what is left over after all other items have been taken into account. There are two kinds of profits: profit of corporations and profit of unincorporated enterprises, i.e., proprietorships and partnerships. "Income of unincorporated enterprises (adjusted[13])" represents the latter. This includes much farmer and professional income. As we shall see in Chapter 32, really a good deal of this is a return to farmers and self-employed people for the labor, capital, and land they provide for their own businesses; but the statisticians count it all as profit.

Finally, "corporate profits before taxes (adjusted)" is shown. Its 74.2 billion dollars includes corporate profits taxes of 31.2 billion dollars. The remainder then goes to dividends or to undistributed corporate profits, which is what you leave or "plow back" into the business, and is called "net corporate saving."

Again, on the right side, the flow-of-cost approach gives us the same 621.6 billion dollars of NNP and the same GNP figure of 681.2 billion dollars, which was arrived at by adding back in the gross item of depreciation. The right and left sides do agree.

■ THREE RELATED CONCEPTS: DISPOSABLE, PERSONAL, AND NATIONAL INCOMES

Table 10-4 summarized the fundamentals of national-income accounting. For purposes of broad economic understanding, our task is over. But a businessman, citizen, or statesman who wants to follow carefully what is happening from month to month and quarter to quarter in the American economy or abroad will benefit from a brief discussion of three other concepts that are measured and reported on by the U.S. Department of Commerce and similar official units elsewhere.

Disposable income, personal income, and (narrowly defined) national income are useful rearrangements of the above data.

Disposable income. How many dollars per year do private individuals and families have available *to them* to spend? The concept of disposable[14] income tries to answer this question. Broadly speaking, to get disposable income, one subtracts all taxes direct or indirect from NNP, subtracts all corporate earnings that were not paid out in dividends but retained as net corporate savings, and adds in transfer payments of welfare or interest-on-federal-debt type. The result is, so to speak, what actually gets into our hands and is left there for us to dispose of as we please.

[13]The term "adjusted" refers to an inventory valuation adjustment of the following type: If money prices change *within* the year, our yardstick for measuring profits is faulty. Part of the reported profit is simply a markup (or markdown, if the price level is falling within the year) of inventory. The statistician uses within-the-year price changes to estimate the amount of such overreporting of profits. Actually in 1965 wholesale prices were rising, so there had to be an inventory valuation adjustment of −1.5 billion dollars that gets subtracted from reported corporate profits of 75.7 billion dollars to give a more meaningful adjusted figure of 74.2 billion dollars. (In 1962, when prices fell, the adjustment was positive and *added* to reported corporate incomes.)

[14]As is discussed in detail on page 189 of the Appendix, the Department of Commerce has altered the definition of disposable income: since 1965, the amount of money that families have to divide between consumption and saving falls short of the officially reported *DI* by the amount of interest consumers pay on loans. Throughout this book, therefore, the official *DI* has been adjusted by subtracting consumer interest from it, and the resulting *DI (adj.)* or *DIA* is used as "disposable income."

Disposable income is an important series of data because, as will be seen in Part Two, it is this sum (suitably adjusted) that people divide between consumption spending and net personal saving. Thus, in recent years people have been spending about 94 per cent of adjusted disposable income on consumption and about 6 per cent on net personal saving. It is this series that will be watched eagerly by a department-store head and a policy maker apprehensive over inflationary pressure or too little consumption spending.

Personal income. Unfortunately, *DI* data are available only every 3 months. For those who want up-to-date monthly information, the government publishes the series called "personal income." Like *DI*, *PI* removes corporate saving from NNP and adds back all transfers and consumer interest. If it excluded *all* taxes, *PI* would be identical with *DI*. Some taxes, however, are hard to estimate in a hurry, on a month-to-month basis. *PI* does eliminate some taxes that can be estimated fairly accurately in the short run: corporate income taxes and certain other payroll taxes; but it does *not* try to estimate the income taxes of people, and thus it does differ slightly from disposable income. However, if we did have a monthly estimate of *DI*, there is every reason to think that it would change in about the same percentage as *PI* most of the time. Therein lies the principal importance of personal income: it is a quickly available monthly figure that is an excellent substitute for disposable income and is thus an indicator of what is happening to family well-being and spending.

National income, narrowly defined. We have followed the common practice and used the term "national income" to refer generally to all the concepts of this chapter —NNP, GNP, and so forth. Mention should be made of a narrower sense in which the U.S. Department of Commerce defines the term. In the narrow sense, national income is simply NNP with all indirect business taxes (excises, cigarette stamps, gasoline taxes, and all sales taxes of any kind) taken out. But note that all direct taxes have been left in, as well as corporate income taxes.[15] (Figure 10-5 in the Appendix presents visually the relation among the different concepts.)

Figure 10-4 plots three of the important national-income concepts, GNP, NNP,

The different national-income aggregates tend to move together:

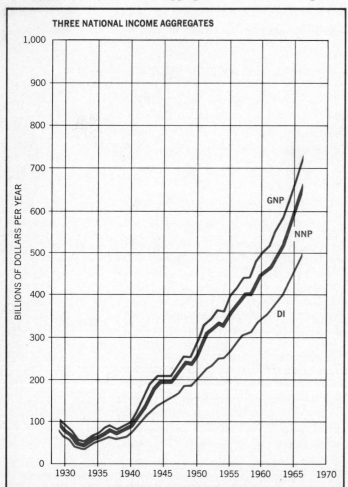

THREE NATIONAL INCOME AGGREGATES

FIG. 10-4. NNP averages about ten-elevenths of GNP. Because of taxes and corporate saving, the disposable income of people is smaller still. (Source: U.S. Department of Commerce.)

[15] If NNP can be called "net national product evaluated at market prices," then this version of national income can be called "net national product evaluated, not at market prices, but at the factor-costs (exclusive of indirect taxes) of that output."

and *DI*, and shows how much alike are their movements and how predictably slow are their drifts apart. That is why most people are content to watch GNP alone, occasionally supplementing it with data on disposable income.

This chapter has now given us the tools to chart the progress and health of an economy. It is a culmination of the introductory survey that is the task of Part One. It is a prelude to the subject of Part Two, the analysis of the macroeconomic forces that determine the level, trend, and cyclical fluctuations of the national income and of the general level of prices.

SUMMARY

1 ■

Net national product, NNP, is definable as a dollar flow of total product for a nation: the sum of consumption plus net investment (domestic and foreign) plus government expenditure on goods and services. $NNP = C + I + G$.

2 ■

By use of a price index, we can "deflate" NNP in current dollars to arrive at a more accurate measure of "real NNP, expressed in dollars of one base-year's purchasing power." Use of such an average price index (of consumer-goods, investment-goods, and government-goods prices) is an approximate way of allowing for the rubber yardstick implied by changing levels of prices.

3 ■

Because of the way we define residual profit, we can match the flow-of-product measurement of NNP by the lower-loop flow-of-cost measurement. This uses factor earnings, carefully computing *values added* to eliminate double counting of intermediate products. And after adding all (before-tax) wage, interest, rent, and profit income, it adds to this total all *indirect* tax costs to business. (NNP definitely does *not* include transfer items such as receipt of interest on government bonds, receipt of welfare pensions, or consumer-loan interest.)

4 ■

Net investment is positive when people are devoting part of society's resources to creating more inventory and more buildings and equipment than are currently being used up in the form of depreciation. Net investment equals gross investment minus depreciation. As depreciation is hard to estimate, the statisticians have more confidence in their measures of gross than of net investment.

5 ■

For the foregoing reason, the official statistics put greatest stress on gross national product rather than net. GNP = NNP + depreciation, always. Since depreciation is sluggish and rarely varies much from one-eleventh of GNP (or one-tenth of NNP), we can generally use GNP and NNP interchangeably.

6 ∎

Disposable, personal, and (narrowly defined) national income are three additional official measurements. *NI* is simply NNP with indirect business taxes (gasoline, sales, and other nonincome taxes) removed. *PI* is simply a convenient monthly approximation to movements in *DI* and the other series that are available only on a quarterly basis. Disposable income is what people actually have left to spend on consumption or to save after all tax, corporate saving of undistributed profits, transfer adjustments, and adjustments for consumer interest have been made.

More information about national-income accounting is given in the Appendix to this chapter. Also given are some selected figures on the nation's recent economic history: the Federal Reserve Board's important production index, which comes out monthly; and data on employment and unemployment. These vital aggregates chart a nation's economic health.

QUESTIONS FOR DISCUSSION

1. Compare the two-loop flow of money of Fig. 10-1 with Fig. 3-1 on page 44 which shows the way a pricing system solves society's WHAT, HOW, and FOR WHOM.

2. "You can't add apples and oranges." Show that money lets us do this.

3. Convince a skeptic that services do count as well as material goods—that we want most goods for the consumption services they provide us (e.g. cars and rides).

4. Making a guess how prices have changed since 1965, test your knowledge of the deflating process by penciling in, on Fig. 10-2, recent money NNP and recent real NNP. How might you deflate for population change? If the United Kingdom has 1966 NNP of 30 billion pounds, and if £1 buys what $3 will buy, how would you express U.K. NNP in U.S. 1966 dollars?

5. R. Crusoe produces upper-loop product of $1,000. He pays $750 in wages, $125 in interest, and $75 in rent. What must his profit be? Calculate NNP in the upper-loop and lower-loop way and show they must agree exactly.

6. From a recent *Federal Reserve Bulletin* or *Survey of Current Business* (Commerce Department), recalculate Table 10-4 for a later year than 1965. Explain the various items.

7. Distinguish between government transfer expenditure and the *G* that goes into NNP = *C* + *I* + *G*. To get disposable income, why remove all taxes from NNP and add in transfers? What about undistributed corporate profit?

8. Review your understanding of the following concepts:

NNP in two equivalent views	NNP = *C* + *I* + *G*
1970 money NNP in current dollars, and 1970 real NNP in 1965 dollars	government transfers, indirect and direct taxes
intermediate goods, double counting, value added	net exports of goods and services
gross investment − depreciation = net investment	dividends, undistributed profits
	income of unincorporated enterprise
GNP − depreciation = NNP	valuation adjustment
	NI, *PI*, and *DI*

APPENDIX: The Official National-income Data

The main text of this chapter has expounded the basic principles of national income. Here some special problems are elaborated.

A FEW BRAIN TEASERS

Readers often like to worry about fine points. Here are a few sample cases.

1. Services of a housewife do not get counted in the NNP. So if a man marries his housekeeper, the NNP may go down! Or if a wife arranges with her neighbor for each to clean the other's house in return for $4,000 a year, then the NNP would go up by $8,000.

This item is not omitted for logical reasons, but rather because it would be hard to get accurate estimates of the money value of a wife's services. So long as the number of women working at home does not change much in relative importance, the ups and downs of NNP will be about the same whether or not we include this item or similar items such as home-grown vegetables and other do-it-yourself activities.

All this illustrates an important rule of approximate measurement in economics. *Often it does not matter which definition of measurement you use, so long as you stick to one definition consistently.*

2. For many items it is hard to know whether to put them in the intermediate or final class. EXAMPLES: A painter's ladder is certainly not to be charged as a final consumption item. Like bread dough, it is an intermediate expense item that has already been counted in as part of the fine homes he helps to create.

What about his overalls? His carfare from one job to another? His carfare from home to work? The coffee he buys a prospective customer? The coffee he himself drinks? The ball game he takes a prospective customer to, in his campaign for more business? Would you treat the last differently if he himself likes baseball?

Each of these items can raise an argument. Each has an element of intermediate business expense in it, and each an element of consumption. The tax collector and the national-income statistician do not always agree on the treatment of these, and we can raise questions about each one's decisions. (EXAMPLE: The tax collector will not let anyone deduct his commuting costs to work *in town;* but out of town he may be able to. The ladder is clearly deductible from taxable

income and from NNP; but the overalls are not if it can be shown that wearing them saved an ordinary suit's wearing out. So it goes. Close decisions and arbitrary ones.)

3. Gifts that are not disguised payments for work done or for goods and services are not included in NNP. They are like government transfers that we have already discussed. The same goes for the allowance a father gives his son. But what about the fee he pays the son for mowing the lawn? In logic it should be in NNP, but it rarely is.

4. If I buy an old painting, a corner lot, or a used car from someone else, that transaction is not a final transaction to be put into NNP. He and I have just exchanged assets: money for picture. Nothing has been produced.[1] So this is more in the nature of a special kind of transfer.[2] It illustrates an important fact: the total dollar volume of all intermediate transactions greatly exceeds the volume of the final transactions that we call national income or product. The loops of Fig. 10-1 include only a minority of the transactions that are taking place within the business and public blocks of that diagram.

Note, too, that we try not to let capital gains due to mere price changes enter into NNP. If Wall Street bids up my Ford stock, I may feel rich and spend more of my *DI.* But that windfall gain is not attributable to current economic activity, and the statistician tries to keep it out. For similar reasons he makes the inventory valuation adjustment in corporate profits.

5. Should interest paid by consumers be included in disposable income, *DI,* in consumption expenditure, *C,* and in NNP? Before 1965 the official statistics did include consumer interest in *C* and NNP. But after 1965 the Commerce Department, with the approval of the United Nations Statistical Office, decided that this was not an item reflecting *current* (as against *past*) production. Hence, by a close but reasonable decision, net consumer interest payments (along with personal

---

[1] If a broker earns a fee for arranging the deal, that fee is counted as part of NNP. Just as some men produce satisfactions in the form of bread, brokers and salesmen produce satisfactions in the form of bringing transactors together.

[2] Do not confuse this kind of transfer with the government transfers we have talked about.

How the official statistics of national income are interrelated:

ITEM	1929	1933	1939	1945	1950	1955	1960	1964	1965
Gross national product	103.1	55.6	90.5	212.0	284.8	398.0	503.8	631.7	681.2
Less: Capital consumption (Depreciation)	7.9	7.0	7.3	11.3	18.3	31.5	43.4	56.0	59.6
Equals: **Net national product**	95.2	48.6	83.2	200.7	266.5	366.5	460.4	575.7	621.6
Less: Indirect business taxes	7.0	7.1	9.4	15.5	23.3	32.1	45.2	58.5	62.7
Business transfer payments	0.6	0.7	0.5	0.5	0.8	1.2	1.9	2.5	2.6
Statistical discrepancy	0.7	0.6	1.3	4.0	1.5	2.1	−1.0	−1.4	−1.6
Plus: Subsidies less current surplus of government enterprises	−0.1	0.0	0.5	0.8	0.2	−0.1	0.2	1.3	1.0
Equals: **National income**	86.8	40.3	72.6	181.5	241.1	331.0	414.5	517.3	559.0
Less: Corporate profits and inventory valuation adjustment	10.5	−1.2	6.3	19.2	37.7	46.9	49.9	66.6	74.2
Contributions for social insurance	0.2	0.3	2.1	6.1	6.9	11.1	20.7	28.0	29.2
Excess of wage accruals over disbursements	0.0	0.0	0.0	0.0	0.0	0.0	0.0	0.0	0.0
Plus: Government transfer payments	0.9	1.5	2.5	5.6	14.3	16.1	26.6	34.2	37.1
Net interest paid by government and consumers	2.5	1.6	1.9	4.2	7.2	10.1	15.1	19.1	20.6
Dividends	5.8	2.0	3.8	4.6	8.8	10.5	13.4	17.3	19.2
Business transfer payments	0.6	0.7	0.5	0.5	0.8	1.2	1.9	2.5	2.6
Equals: **Personal income**	85.9	47.0	72.8	171.1	227.6	311.0	401.0	496.0	535.1
Less: Personal taxes	2.6	1.5	2.4	20.9	20.7	35.7	51.0	59.4	66.0
(Federal)	1.3	0.5	1.2	19.4	16.5	29.7	42.5	50.7	54.8
(State and local)	1.4	1.0	1.2	1.5	4.2	6.0	8.5	8.7	11.2
Equals: **Disposable personal income**	83.3	45.5	70.3	150.2	206.9	275.3	350.0	436.6	469.1
Less: Consumer interest payments plus transfers to foreigners	1.9	0.6	0.8	0.9	2.8	5.1	7.8	10.7	11.9
Equals: **Disposable income adjusted**	81.4	44.9	69.5	149.3	204.1	270.2	342.2	425.9	457.2
Less: Consumption expenditures	77.2	45.8	63.9	119.7	191.0	254.4	325.2	401.4	431.5
Equals: **Personal saving**	4.2	−1.1	0.6	29.6	13.1	15.8	17.0	24.5	25.7

TABLE 10-5. GROSS AND NET NATIONAL PRODUCT, NATIONAL INCOME, PERSONAL INCOME, AND DISPOSABLE INCOME (in billions of dollars). Read this together with Fig. 10-5 to understand the official data most easily. (Sources: U.S. Department of Commerce; *Economic Report of the President*; note that detail may not add to totals because of rounding.)

transfer payments to foreigners, a smaller item) are no longer in C and NNP.

But consumer interest is still in the official Department of Commerce disposable income, *DI*, figures. This seems debatable to the author. Certainly if we want to work with the money income actually available to be spent on C or on personal saving, we must work with disposable income adjusted—i.e., with consumer interest and personal transfer payments to foreigners subtracted out. (For 1965 this subtracted item came to almost $12 billion.)

Inasmuch as later chapters discussing national-income determination will be interested only in those elements of *DI* which enter NNP, we shall adjust the Commerce Department's *DI* by subtracting consumer interest and transfer abroad, so that

$$DIA = DI - \text{Int.} - \text{Trans. A.} = C + S$$

where C is consumption expenditure in current production and S is personal saving. To get an idea of the size of these elements of *DI*, carefully read the bottom five lines of Table 10-5.

THE OFFICIAL STATISTICS

Figure 10-5 summarizes the relations of the different United States government statistics on national income or product. Many find careful study of this summary and of Table 10-5 a great aid to understanding.

Table 10-6, along with national-income data, gives the other principal aggregates which business and public officials watch closely.

One could go on giving borderline cases, but we conclude with only one more. In measuring NNP we are not interested in consumption and investment goods merely for their money value: money is the measuring rod used to give some approximate figure to the underlying "satisfactions" or "benefits" or "psychic income" that comes from goods. Strictly speaking, then, each time I play a phonograph record, shouldn't that get into the NNP at its fair market value? In principle, Yes. And if I have put a dime in a juke box, it may in fact get directly into the NNP; but playing it at home will not get it directly into the NNP.

How to picture relations among official national-income data:

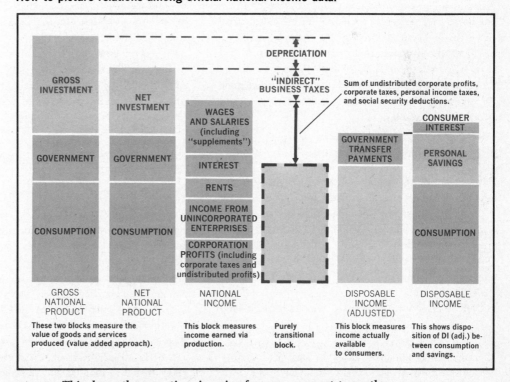

FIG. 10-5. This shows the operations in going from one concept to another.

Indirectly, this enjoyment of a psychic pleasure does tend to get in the NNP to the extent that I wear out the record by playing it. Hence, as I replace my records, my consumption purchases at the store give a rough money measure of my enjoyments—but only a rough measure.

The statistician admits this, defending his practice by saying that a man's house is his castle and no accountant can enter his abode to measure his actual current consumptions; instead, he settles for treating a thing as consumed when it enters his abode. This all works well enough, except in one case.

More and more these days we spend our consumption dollar on durable consumers' goods. (This was seen in the breakdown of consumption into services, durable goods, and nondurable goods in Table 10-4.) Actually, then, in the years that we are building up our home inventories of such durable goods, our true psychic consumption is being overstated by our retail purchases; and vice versa in the years when we run home inventories down.

Some purists say, "In NNP, let's try to estimate actual home consumption of services or durables and put that in C, not the mere retail purchases of the year." The Commerce Department thinks this too hard a job to do, but for special purposes economists have tried to make (from gas and mileage records, for example) more accurate estimates of auto consumption than are provided by new car sales.[3]

Fortunately, in the long run, the two methods tend to come to much the same thing, particularly if society is not growing too fast.

INTERNATIONAL ASPECTS OF INCOME

Here is the place to give a few details on how net foreign investment was arrived at.

From the beginning we agree to mean by United States NNP the income or product accruing to all "permanent residents" of the United States. This includes American citizens temporarily abroad and also unnaturalized immigrants who live permanently in the United States.

Note that, if an Englishman owns an acre of land

in this country, his income therefrom is to be included in the United Kingdom NNP and not in ours. Similarly, if Americans receive dividends from British companies, this is part of the American income and not the British, being treated as payment for a property service that we have exported.

The previous paragraph shows that it is a considerable task to allow for international aspects of income. We must take account of exports, imports, dividends paid in and out of a country, and much more. As we shall see in the discussion of international finance in Part Five, a balance of international payments between the United States and the rest of the world can be drawn up of all such items. There is no need at this point of our national-income discussion to anticipate all the details of this subsequent discussion. We are interested only in the bare logic of the task of finding out the magnitude of net export of goods and services, which is the final component of NNP.

To get net export of goods and services we must calculate the surplus of all the goods and services we provide to foreigners over what they provide to us. Thus calculate (a), the total of our exports to them (wheat, shipping, . . .), plus our earnings from factors of production we own abroad (dividends and interest payable to us). Also calculate (b), the total of what we import from them and must pay them for their ownership of productive factors located in this country. The surplus of (a) over (b) represents our net export figures. We shall see that, just as net domestic investment can provide jobs and expand the economy, so can net exports as well.

THE IDENTITY OF MEASURED SAVING AND INVESTMENT

To pave the way for the discussion of intersecting saving and investment schedules in Chapter 12, we can here show that the national-income statistician defines the saving he measures as exactly the same thing as the investment he measures. This equality of measured saving and measured investment is an identity of double-entry bookkeeping and holds by definition.

What is the measure of investment? Forgetting government, we know I is the output in the upper loop that is not C. What is the measure of saving S? Again forgetting government and corporate saving, we know that S is that part of the lower-loop disposable

---

[3] It is interesting that in the case of a house, the most durable consumers' good of all, the officials do actually follow this principle: they do not take expenditures on a house as its C, but estimate the house use separately and count it as C.

These aggregates chart the nation's economic health:

YEAR	GROSS NATIONAL PRODUCT	NET NATIONAL PRODUCT	NATIONAL INCOME	DISPOSABLE INCOME (ADJ.)	NET SAVING AS PERCENTAGE OF DISPOSABLE INCOME (ADJ.)	GOVERNMENT EXPENDITURE ON GOODS AND SERVICES AS PERCENTAGE OF GNP	FEDERAL RESERVE BOARD INDEX OF INDUSTRIAL PRODUCTION (1957–1959 = 100)	CIVILIAN LABOR FORCE, THOUSANDS	UNEMPLOYMENT AS PERCENTAGE OF CIVILIAN LABOR FORCE
1929	103.1	95.2	86.8	81.4	5.8	8.2	38	49,180	3.2
1931	75.8	68.0	59.7	63.0	4.1	12.2	26	50,420	15.9
1933	55.6	48.6	40.3	44.9	−2.0	14.5	24	51,590	24.9
1935	72.7	65.4	57.2	57.8	3.7	13.9	31	52,870	20.1
1937	90.4	83.3	73.7	70.3	5.4	13.1	40	54,000	14.3
1938	84.7	77.4	67.4	64.7	0.8	15.3	31	54,610	19.0
1939	90.5	83.2	72.6	69.5	3.8	14.7	38	55,230	17.2
1940	99.7	92.2	81.1	74.7	5.1	14.1	44	55,640	14.6
1941	124.5	116.3	104.2	91.6	11.9	19.8	56	55,910	9.9
1942	157.9	148.1	137.1	116.0	23.8	37.8	70	56,410	4.7
1943	191.6	181.3	170.3	132.7	25.1	46.2	84	55,540	1.9
1944	210.1	199.1	182.6	145.5	25.6	45.8	83	54,630	1.2
1945	212.0	200.7	181.5	149.3	19.8	38.5	70	53,860	1.9
1946	208.5	198.6	181.9	158.4	9.6	12.9	59	57,520	3.9
1947	231.3	219.1	199.0	168.0	4.4	10.9	66	60,168	3.6
1948	257.6	243.0	224.2	186.9	7.2	12.2	68	61,442	3.4
1949	256.5	239.9	217.5	187.2	5.0	14.7	65	62,105	5.5
1950	284.8	266.4	241.1	204.1	6.4	13.3	75	63,099	5.0
1951	328.4	309.2	278.0	223.6	7.4	17.9	81	62,884	3.0
1952	345.5	322.3	291.4	234.8	7.7	21.6	84	62,966	2.7
1953	364.6	338.9	304.7	249.3	7.4	22.4	91	63,815	2.5
1954	364.8	336.8	303.1	252.7	6.5	20.4	86	64,468	5.0
1955	398.0	366.5	331.0	270.2	5.9	18.7	97	65,848	4.0
1956	419.2	385.2	350.8	287.3	7.2	18.7	100	67,530	3.8
1957	441.1	404.0	366.1	302.2	6.9	19.5	101	67,946	4.3
1958	447.3	408.4	367.8	312.3	7.1	21.1	94	68,647	6.8
1959	483.7	442.3	400.0	330.3	5.8	22.1	106	69,394	5.5
1960	503.8	460.3	414.5	342.2	5.0	19.8	109	70,612	5.6
1961	520.1	474.9	427.3	356.3	5.9	20.7	110	71,603	6.7
1962	560.3	510.4	457.7	376.7	5.7	20.9	118	72,011	5.6
1963	590.5	537.9	481.9	394.9	5.0	20.7	124	72,975	5.7
1964	631.7	575.7	517.3	435.9	5.6	20.4	132	74,233	5.2
1965	681.2	621.6	559.0	457.2	5.6	20.0	143	75,635	4.6

TABLE 10-6. PRINCIPAL ECONOMIC AGGREGATES (all income data in billions of current dollars). Forecasters like to use the production index because it moves more sensitively than income data. Statesmen worry about unemployment. (Sources: U.S. Department of Commerce; Federal Reserve Board; *Economic Report of the President*.)

income, or NNP, that is not spent on C. To summarize:

$$I = \text{upper-loop NNP minus } C$$
$$S = \text{lower-loop NNP minus } C$$

But the two loops must give the same measure of NNP. So $I \equiv S$: the identity between measured saving and investment.

Our task will be done once we bring the corporation and the government into the picture. Investment is just as before. But now saving S must be split into three different terms: (1) net personal saving, which

people do out of their disposable incomes; (2) net corporate saving, that part of corporate incomes which they fail to pay out as dividends; finally (3) net government surplus (or "saving"), which represents the algebraic excess of its tax revenues over its expenditure on goods and services *and* on transfers.

Our identity of measured S and I now has to be written in terms of the three components of total S.[4]

$$I \equiv \text{NPS} + \text{NCS} + \text{NGS}$$

---

[4]The eager reader can test his grasp of this fundamental identity (which must hold at all times whether or not an economy is in equilibrium or is galloping to or from an equilibrium) by going back to the discussion (page 189) of how disposable income (*adj.*) is defined in terms of NNP − taxes − NCS + transfers, and how NPS = *DIA* − *C*. These relations combined with the $C + I + G$ breakdown of NNP can be used to give an algebraic demonstration of our identity.

Thus, from the definition of *DIA*,
$$\text{NNP} \equiv DIA + \text{NCS} + Tx - Tr$$
Adding and subtracting G and splitting up *DIA* gives
$$\text{NNP} \equiv C + [\text{NPS} + \text{NCS} + (Tx - Tr - G)] + G$$
$$\equiv C + [\text{NPS} + \text{NCS} + (\text{NGS})] + G$$
But recall the upper-loop definition
$$\text{NNP} \equiv C + [I] + G$$
So we do indeed verify the saving-investment identity
$$[I] \equiv [\text{NPS} + \text{NCS} + \text{NGS}]$$

Part 2 Determination of National Income and its Fluctuations

11 Saving, Consumption, and Investment

WE ARE ALL KEYNESIANS NOW. MILTON FRIEDMAN

In Part One the groundwork was laid for an understanding of the concept of national income. Now we can go beyond the anatomy of the problem to its physiology. What causes national income to rise? To fall? Why is NNP what it is at any time, rather than something larger or smaller? What causes inflation?

This chapter provides an introduction to what is called the "modern theory of income analysis." The principal stress is upon the *level of total spending as determined by the interplay of the monetary forces of saving and investment.*

Although much of this analysis is due to an English economist, John Maynard Keynes (later made Lord Keynes, before his death in 1946), today the broad fundamentals of "the new economics" are increasingly accepted by economists of all schools of thought, including, it is important to notice, many who do not share Keynes' particular policy views and who differ on technical details of analysis.[1]

The income analysis here described is itself neutral: it can be used as well to defend private enterprise as to limit it; as well to attack as to defend government fiscal intervention. When business organizations like the United States Chamber of Commerce, the Committee for Economic Development, or the Chase National Bank use the apparatus of saving and investment, it is absurd to think this implies that they are "Keynesian," in the sense of belonging to that narrow band of enthusiasts associated with some of the policy programs that J. M. Keynes himself espoused during the Great Depression.

In recent years 90 per cent of American economists have stopped being "Keynesian economists" or "anti-Keynesian economists." Modern economists are "post-Keynesians,"

[1]Keynes himself was a many-sided genius who won eminence in the fields of mathematics, philosophy, and literature. In addition, he found time to run a large insurance company, to advise the British Treasury, to help govern the Bank of England, to edit a world-famous economic journal, and to sponsor ballet and drama. He was also an economist who knew how to make money, both for himself and for King's College, Cambridge. His 1936 book, *The General Theory of Employment, Interest and Money*, created the greatest stir in economic thinking of the century and will live as a classic.

keen to render obsolete any theories that cannot meet the test of experience. The new generation has worked toward a synthesis of whatever is valuable in older economics and in modern theories of income determination. The result might be called "neoclassical economics" (or a "neoclassical synthesis") and is accepted in its broad outlines by all but a few extreme left-wing and right-wing writers.

■ THE CLEAVAGE BETWEEN SAVING AND INVESTMENT MOTIVATIONS

The most important single fact about saving and investment activities is that in our industrial society they are generally done by different people and for different reasons.

This was not always so; even today, when a farmer devotes his time to draining a field instead of to planting and harvesting a crop, he is saving and at the same time investing. He is "saving" because he is abstaining from *present* consumption in order to provide for larger consumption in the *future*—the amount of his saving being measured by the difference between his net real income and his consumption. But he is also "investing"; i.e., he is undertaking net capital formation, improving the productive capacity of his farm. Not only are saving and investment the same things for a primitive farmer, but his reasons for undertaking them are the same. He abstains from present consumption (saves) only because he wants to drain the field (to invest). If there were no investment opportunity whatsoever, it would never occur to him to save; nor would there be any way to save for the future, should he be so foolish as to wish to.

In our modern economy, net capital formation or investment is carried on by business enterprises, especially corporations. When a corporation or a small business has great investment opportunities, its owners will be tempted to plow back much of its earnings into the business. To an important degree, therefore, some business saving does get motivated directly by business investment.

Nevertheless, saving is primarily done by an entirely different group: by individuals, by families, by households. An individual may wish to save for a great variety of reasons: because he wishes to provide for his old age or for a future expenditure (a vacation or an automobile). Or he may feel insecure and wish to guard against a rainy day. Or he may wish to leave an estate to his children or to his children's children. Or he may be an eighty-year-old miser with no heirs who enjoys the act of accumulating for its own sake. Or he may already have signed himself up to a savings program because an insurance salesman was persuasive. Or he may desire the power that greater wealth brings. Or thrift may simply be a habit, almost a conditioned reflex whose origin he does not himself know.

■ **Whatever the individual's motivation to save, it usually has little to do with society's investment opportunities.**

This truth is obscured by the fact that in everyday language "investment" does not always have the same meaning as in economics. We have defined "net investment," or capital formation, to be the net increase in the community's real capital (equipment, buildings, inventories). But the plain man speaks of "investing" when he buys a piece of land, an old security, or any title to property. For economists these are clearly *transfer* items. What one man is buying, someone else is selling. There is net investment only when *additional real capital* is created.

In short, even if there are no *real* investment opportunities that seem profitable, an individual may still *wish* to nonconsume—to save. He can always buy an existing security asset; he can accumulate, or *try* to accumulate, cash.

■ THE VARIABILITY OF INVESTMENT

Thus, we are left with our proposition:

> ■ Saving and investing are often desired by different individuals and for independent reasons. While it is families who primarily decide to save, net capital formation takes place largely in business enterprise.

The amount of investment is highly variable from year to year and decade to decade. This capricious, volatile behavior is understandable when we come to realize that profitable investment opportunities depend on *new* discoveries, *new* products, *new* territories and frontiers, *new* resources, *new* population, *higher* production and income. Note the emphasis on "new" and on "higher." Investment depends on the *dynamic* and relatively unpredictable elements of *growth* in the system and on elements outside the economic system itself: technology, politics, optimistic and pessimistic expectations, "confidence," governmental tax and expenditure, legislative policies, and much else.

> ■ This extreme variability of investment is the next important fact to be emphasized.

We shall see that an industrial system such as our own can do many wonderful things. It can mobilize men, tools, and know-how to respond to any given demand for goods. Over time it can improve upon its own response.

But there is one thing it cannot always do.

> ■ Unless proper policies are pursued, a laissez-faire economy cannot guarantee that there will be exactly the required amount of investment to ensure full employment: not too little so as to cause unemployment, nor too much so as to cause inflation. As far as total investment or money-spending power is concerned, the laissez-faire system is without a good thermostat. For decades there might tend to be too little investment, leading to deflation, losses, excess capacity, unemployment, and destitution. For other years or decades, there might tend to be too much investment, leading to periods of chronic inflation—unless prudent and proper public policies in the fiscal (i.e., tax and expenditure) and monetary (i.e., Federal Reserve central bank) fields are followed.

Nor is there an Invisible Hand guaranteeing that the good years will by themselves equal the bad, or guaranteeing that scientists will discover just in the nick of time precisely enough new products and processes to keep the system on an even keel. From 1855 to 1875 railroads were built all over the world. In the next two decades nothing quite took the place of this activity. The automobile and public utilities produced a similar revolution in the 1920s. In the 1930s plastics and radio had no comparable effect on total net investment. In the years immediately following World War II, much of the time we were plagued by too much investment spending relative to the resources released by those acts of renouncing consumption which economists call "saving." Then in the Eisenhower years of the 1950s, America experienced sluggish growth, with increasing unemployment. By the mid-1960s inflation problems were back.

Thus we see that the instabilities are not all on the downward side. Economic history is, alas, a history of inflations. Anyone who comes of age in 1967 has seen prices double in his own lifetime. Unless proper policies are followed, he can look forward to gyrating prices for the rest of his life.

While a realist must recognize that an economy like ours of 1929 or of the 1970s will not *by itself* maintain stability of prices and full employment, critics should still recognize that there are certain elements in a pricing economy that can work toward stability if given a chance to operate and if helped by vigorous public stabilizing actions. As we shall see later, the structure of interest rates—which determines how costly and hard it is to get credit for investing activities—can be helped by Federal Reserve monetary policy to play a stabilizing role in moderating investment fluctuations. Also, to a considerable extent the frictions that keep various prices inflexible and sticky in a modern mixed economy can be offset by public actions and by the sense of security stemming from the belief that the worst gyrations of the unlucky past can be prevented from coming to pass again.

This, then, is one of our most important economic lessons.

■ Where the stimulus to investment is concerned, the system is somewhat in the lap of the gods. We may be lucky or unlucky; and one of the few things you can say about luck is, "It's going to change." Fortunately, things need not be left to luck. We shall see that perfectly sensible public and private policies can be followed that will greatly enhance the stability and productive growth of our economic system. They cannot expect to wipe out business fluctuations 100 per cent. We would not want them to, even if they could. But they can try to reduce the range of wild fluctuations in prices and employment—a process which the following chapters discuss.

The next chapters will show how investment and saving determine the equilibrium level of national income. First, we must understand the important budgetary patterns, reflecting how people consume and save at different income levels.

■ BUDGETARY EXPENDITURE PATTERNS

No two families spend their money in exactly the same way. Yet statistics do show that there is a predictable regularity—on the average—in the way people allocate their expenditures on food, clothing, and other major items. Literally thousands of budgetary investigations have been made of the ways that people at different levels of income spend their money; and there is remarkable agreement on the general, qualitative patterns of behavior.[2] What are they? Figure 11-1 tells the story.

[2] Figure 11-1's behavior patterns are called "Engel's Laws," after the nineteenth-century Prussian statistician Ernst Engel (not to be confused with Karl Marx's friend Friedrich Engels). The average behavior of consumption expenditure does change fairly regularly with income; but averages do not tell all the story. Within each income class, there is spread around the average.

Poor families must, of course, spend their incomes largely on the necessities of life: food, shelter, and, in lesser degree, clothing. As income increases, expenditure on many food items goes up. People eat more and eat better. They shift away from cheap, bulky carbohydrates to more expensive meats and proteins—and to milk, fruit, vegetables, and labor-saving processed foods.

There are, however, limits to the amount of extra money that people will spend on food when their incomes rise. Consequently, the *percentage* importance of food expenditure declines as income increases. (Actually, there are a few cheap, but filling, items such as spaghetti or sausage whose consumption decreases absolutely with income increase. These are called "inferior goods" in Part Three.)

After you get out of the very poorest income class, your proportion of income spent on shelter is pretty constant for a wide range. This is expressed in a familiar rule of thumb: One week's salary should cover one month's expenditure on rent and house utilities. The other rule of thumb—that you should pay about 2 years' income for a house—has a hollow ring these days.

Family expenditures show regular income patterns:

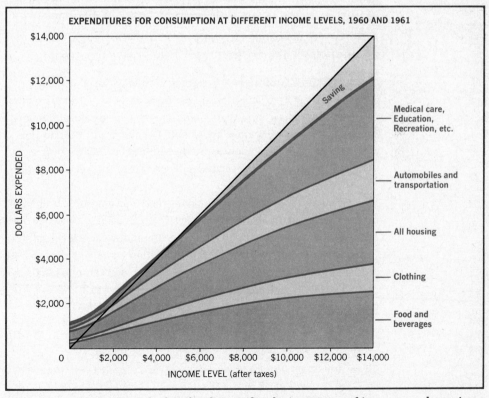

FIG. 11-1. Careful sampling of urban families verifies the importance of income as a determinant of consumption expenditure. Notice the drop in food as a percentage of higher incomes. Note also the rise in saving, from below zero at low incomes to substantial positive levels. (Source: U.S. Bureau of Labor Statistics and U.S. Department of Agriculture.)

Most saving is done by families with incomes above the average:

(1) DISPOSABLE INCOME AFTER TAXES	(2) NET SAVING (+) OR DISSAVING (−)	(3) CONSUMPTION
$ 4,000	$ − 170	$4,170
5,000	− 110	5,110
6,000	0	6,000
7,000	+ 150	6,850
8,000	+ 400	7,600
9,000	+ 760	8,240
10,000	+ 1,170	8,830
11,000	+ 1,640	9,360
12,000	+ 2,150	9,850

TABLE 11-1. POSTWAR PROPENSITY OF FAMILIES TO SAVE AND CONSUME. The break-even point at which people cease to dissave and begin to do positive saving is here shown at $6,000. How much of each extra dollar do people around this income level devote to extra consumption? How much to extra saving? (Answer: About 85 cents and 15 cents.)

Expenditure on clothing, recreation, and automobiles increases more than proportionately to after-tax income, until high incomes are reached. Of course, luxury items, by definition, increase in greater proportion than income; and in many ways, as we shall soon see, saving is the greatest luxury of all, especially at very high incomes.

■ THE PROPENSITY TO SAVE AND PROPENSITY TO CONSUME

An important use of after-tax income is saving for the future rather than consuming now. This facet is what interests us most. It is a matter of common observation that rich men save more than poor men, not only in absolute amounts but also in percentage amounts. The very poor are unable to save at all. Instead they "dissave," i.e., spend more every year than they earn, the difference being covered by going into debt or using up previously accumulated savings. Thus, income is a prime determinant of saving, as shown in Table 11-1.[3]

Table 11-1 gives data on saving and consumption indicative of family patterns in the 1960s, the so-called "propensity to consume" and "propensity to save." Column (2) shows the net saving that accompanies each level of disposable income. The "break-even point," where the family neither saves nor dissaves, instead consuming all its income, falls at $6,000. Below this, as at $5,000 or $4,000, they actually consume more than their income; they dissave (see the −$110 and −$170 data). Above $6,000 they begin to do positive saving (see the +$150 data).

Column (3) shows the consumption pattern at each income level—the so-called "propensity to consume." Since each dollar of income is divided between the part

[3] These data do not depict long-run behavior of each family when its income moves from a *permanent* low level to a *permanent* high level. Transitorily, saving rises much; but as people get accustomed to higher "permanent income," consumption rises and saving becomes more moderate. Surprising as it may seem, statistics show that people with $12,000 of *permanent* income save about the same fraction of their income as do people with $6,000 of *permanent* income.

consumed and the remaining part saved, Columns (3) and (2) are not independent: they must always exactly add up to Column (1). (Check that they do.)

Economic analysis is interested not simply in the total figures of saving and consumption, but in the *extra* saving and consumption that each *extra* dollar of income brings. Thus, as income goes from $6,000 to $7,000, the extra $1,000 of income is divided between $850 of extra consumption and $150 of extra saving—split up 85 and 15 per cent, so to speak. (Where did these numbers come from? You get them from $6,850 minus $6,000 and from $150 minus $0. And verify that the division between consumption and saving of extra income dollars beyond $7,000 is, respectively, 75 and 25 per cent, then 64 and 36 per cent. . . . Does it seem reasonable to you that richer people will consume a little less of each extra income dollar than will poorer?[4])

Family propensity-to-save and propensity-to-consume patterns have been rather stable. (Workers, however, have generally seemed to save less than the self-employed.)

To understand how saving and investment determine the level of national income and employment, we must continue to study in detail (1) the propensity-to-save schedule, relating saving and income, and its twin brother (2) the propensity-to-consume schedule, relating consumption and income.

■ THE PROPENSITY-TO-CONSUME SCHEDULE IN DETAIL

Table 11-2, on the next page, rearranges these same data in more convenient form. First, identify its similarity to Table 11-1. Then disregard its Columns (3) to (5), and notice how consumption expenditure goes up at each higher level of income.

This same consumption-income relation can be shown even more vividly in diagrammatic form. In Fig. 11-2 the total of consumption expenditure in Column (2) is plotted against family disposable income of Column (1); through the resulting circles *A, B, C, D, E, F, G,* and *H,* a smooth curve has been drawn.

■ This relation between consumption and income is called the *consumption schedule,* or *propensity-to-consume schedule,* or often simply the *propensity to consume.* It is a basic, important concept whose general properties we must study.

It will help you to understand its properties if, first, you look at the 45° line also shown in Fig. 11-2. Inasmuch as the vertical axis of consumption has been drawn to the same scale as the horizontal axis of income, any point lying on the 45° helping line has the following simple property: Its indicated consumption expenditure—measured by the vertical distance of the point from the horizontal axis—is exactly equal to 100 per cent of its indicated level of disposable income—measured by the horizontal distance of the point from the vertical axis. (Use your eye to verify that any point *not*

---

[4]Students at first find it hard to understand that, even when family income is below the break-even point and saving is negative, nonetheless each *extra* income dollar goes partly into positive extra saving and partly into positive extra consumption. To convince yourself, compare row 2 of Table 11-1 with row 1. Adding $1,000 to $4,000 of income gives $5,000. The extra income makes consumption go from $4,170 to $5,110, a gain of $940, with $60 of extra saving.

How we depict important consumption-income and saving-income patterns:

1st, A table presents the propensity-to-consume schedule:

	(1) DISPOSABLE INCOME (AFTER TAXES)	(2) CONSUMPTION EXPENDITURE	(3) MARGINAL PROPENSITY TO CONSUME (MPC)	(4) NET SAVING (4) = (1) − (2)	(5) MARGINAL PROPENSITY TO SAVE (MPS)
A	$ 5,000	$5,110		$ −110	
			$\frac{890}{1,000} = 0.89$		$\frac{110}{1,000} = 0.11$
B	6,000	6,000		0	
			$\frac{850}{1,000} = 0.85$		$\frac{150}{1,000} = 0.15$
C	7,000	6,850		+150	
			$\frac{750}{1,000} = 0.75$		$\frac{250}{1,000} = 0.25$
D	8,000	7,600		+400	
			$\frac{640}{1,000} = 0.64$		$\frac{360}{1,000} = 0.36$
E	9,000	8,240		+760	
			$\frac{590}{1,000} = 0.59$		$\frac{410}{1,000} = 0.41$
F	10,000	8,830		+1,170	
			$\frac{530}{1,000} = 0.53$		$\frac{470}{1,000} = 0.47$
G	11,000	9,360		+1,640	
			$\frac{490}{1,000} = 0.49$		$\frac{510}{1,000} = 0.51$
H	12,000	9,850		+2,150	

TABLE 11-2. PROPENSITY TO CONSUME AND PROPENSITY TO SAVE. Each dollar of income not consumed is saved. And each extra dollar of income goes into extra consumption or extra saving—giving us important concepts we need: MPC and MPS. (NOTE: $890 = 6,000 − 5,110. How about $850?)

on the 45° line cannot possibly be equidistant from the two axes. Reread the description of the 45° line.)

THE "BREAK-EVEN" POINT The 45° line will tell us right away, therefore, whether consumption spending is equal to, greater than, or less than the level of income. The point on the consumption schedule where it intersects the 45° line shows us the level of disposable income at which families just break even. This break-even point is at B; here, consumption expenditure is exactly equal to disposable income; the family is borrowing nothing and on balance saving nothing. Similarly, *anywhere else* on the propensity-to-consume curve, the family cannot be just breaking even. To the right of point B, the curve lies below the 45° line; the long green arrow in Fig. 11-2 shows that the vertical distance (consumption expenditure) is less than the horizontal distance (disposable income). If the family is not spending all its income, then it must be saving the remainder. The 45° line tells us more than that; it enables us to find *how much* the family is saving. Net saving is measured by the distance from the propensity-to-consume curve up to the 45° line, as shown by the appropriate saving arrow.

Similarly, to the left of point *B*, our 45° helping line tells us that the family is for the moment somehow spending more than the income it receives. The excess of consumption over income is its "net dissaving" and is measured by the vertical distance between the two curves. To review:

■ When the propensity-to-consume schedule lies above the 45° line, the family is dissaving. Where the two curves meet, the family is just breaking even. Where the propensity to consume lies below the 45° line, the family is performing net positive saving. And the amount of dissaving or saving is always measured by the distance between the two curves.

THE "PROPENSITY-TO-SAVE SCHEDULE" This means that we can easily derive from the consumption schedule in Fig. 11-2 a new schedule: the propensity to save, or as it is sometimes called, the "saving schedule."

Graphically, this is shown in Fig. 11-3. Again we show disposable income on the horizontal axis; vertically we now show what the family *does not* spend; i.e., we show its net saving, whether negative or positive in amount.

This propensity-to-save curve comes directly from Fig. 11-2. It is simply the distance between the 45° line and the propensity-to-consume schedule. At a point such as *A* in Fig. 11-2, the fact that the family's savings were negative was indicated by

2d, A schedule graphs the propensity to consume:

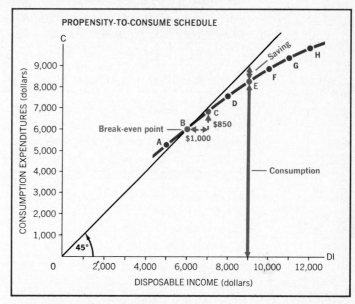

FIG. 11-2. The curve through *A*, *B*, . . . , *H* is the consumption schedule, or the propensity to consume. Its slope at any point, measured by forming a little triangle and relating altitude to base, is the MPC, the marginal propensity to consume. The 45° line helps locate the break-even point and helps our eye measure net saving. Can you see how? (Source: Table 11-2.)

3d, The saving schedule is the exact twin of the consumption schedule:

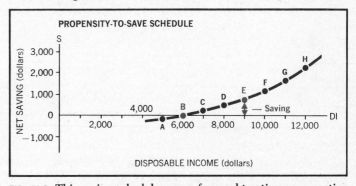

FIG. 11-3. This saving schedule comes from subtracting consumption from income. (Graphically, we vertically subtracted the consumption schedule from the 45° helping line.) Note that the break-even point *B* is at the same $6,000 level as in Fig. 11-2. Why? Measure MPS by the curve's slope at any point. Does MPS + MPC = 1 everywhere? (It had better!)

the propensity-to-consume schedule lying above the helping line. Figure 11-3 shows this fact of negative saving directly, and similarly for the positive saving that begins when family income pushes past point B.

■ THE MARGINAL PROPENSITY TO CONSUME

In the next chapter, we shall be attaching much importance to the *extra* amount that people will want to spend on consumption if given an *extra* dollar of income. Economists are so interested in this concept that they have given it a special name, the "marginal propensity to consume," or MPC. (The word "marginal" is used by the economist to mean "extra"; thus, marginal cost will later be defined as extra cost of producing an extra unit of product; marginal utility as extra utility; marginal revenue as extra revenue; and so forth.)

Column (3) back in Table 11-2 shows how we compute the marginal propensity to consume. From B to C, income rises by $1,000, going from $6,000 to $7,000. By how much does consumption rise? Consumption grows from $6,000 to $6,850 or by $850. The extra consumption is therefore .85 of the extra income. Out of each extra dollar of income, 85 cents goes to consumption and 15 cents goes to saving. We therefore can say that the marginal propensity to consume, or MPC, is .85 between B and C, which agrees with Column (3) of Table 11-2.

You can easily compute MPC between other income levels. In Table 11-2, MPC begins at .89 for poor people and finally falls to .49 at higher incomes.

Now we know how to compute MPC numerically. What is its geometric meaning? It is a numerical measure of the steepness of slope of the consumption schedule.[5] Look again at Fig. 11-2. Near points B and C a little triangle is drawn. As we move to the right from B by $1,000, in order to stay on the schedule, we must go up by $850; this gives a numerical slope $850/$1,000, or .85. NOTE: If higher incomes have a lower MPC, the family consumption schedule will look slightly bowed (convex from above, concave from below).

■ THE MARGINAL PROPENSITY TO SAVE

Along with the marginal propensity to consume goes a Siamese-twin concept, the "marginal propensity to save," or MPS. This is defined as *the fraction of each extra dollar that goes to saving instead of to consumption.*

[5]By the numerical slope of the line XY, we always mean the numerical ratio of the length ZY to the length XZ. See the accompanying drawing. If XY were a curve, we could find the slope at any point on it (1) by placing a ruler tangent to it, and (2) applying the procedure of this triangle to that tangential line.

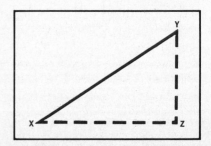

Why are MPC and MPS related like Siamese twins? Since each extra dollar of income must be divided between extra consumption and extra saving, it is obvious that, if MPC is .85, then MPS must be .15. (What would MPS be if MPC were .6? Or .99?) A comparison of Columns (3) and (5) of Table 11-2 confirms our common-sense feeling that at any income level, MPC and MPS must always add up to exactly 1, no more and no less.[6]

■ BRIEF REVIEW OF DEFINITIONS

For the record, let us jot down the main definitions now learned:

■ 1. The propensity-to-consume schedule (or consumption schedule) relates in a table or a curve the level of consumption to the level of income.

2. The propensity-to-save schedule (or saving schedule) relates saving to income. Since what is saved is the same thing as what is nonconsumed, saving and consumption schedules are Siamese twins in the sense that

Saving + consumption = disposable income

3. The "break-even point" is the income level where net saving is zero. Below it, there is dissaving, or negative saving; above it, positive net saving. Graphically, the break-even point is where the 45° helping line intersects the consumption schedule, or where the saving schedule intersects the horizontal axis.

4. The marginal propensity to consume (MPC) is the amount of *extra* consumption generated by an *extra* dollar of income. Graphically, it is given by the slope of the consumption schedule—a steep slope meaning a high MPC and a flat one meaning a low MPC.

5. The marginal propensity to save (MPS) is the *extra* saving generated by an *extra* dollar of income, or the slope of the saving schedule. Because the part of each dollar that is not consumed is necessarily saved, MPS = 1 − MPC always. Hence, higher income that lowers MPC must raise MPS, implying a concave (from below) consumption schedule and a convex saving schedule.

■ THE COMMUNITY'S OVER-ALL CONSUMPTION SCHEDULE

So far we have been talking about the consumption patterns shown by families of different incomes. To study what determines a nation's income, we are interested in a propensity-to-consume schedule slightly different from the family-budget schedule. We are interested in the "national propensity-to-consume schedule," relating total

---

[6] You can also verify from Fig. 11-3 that the numerical steepness of slope of the propensity-to-save schedule is the geometric expression of MPS. This shows: The saving schedule will always have the opposite curvature to that of the consumption schedule; as MPC falls, MPS must rise. And since every extra dollar divides up between positive extra consumption and extra saving, it follows that neither the consumption nor the saving schedule *anywhere* has a slope as steep as the 45° line, which by definition has a slope of 1. Remember, we are here discussing *marginal* propensities. Thus, at point A, the family is spending more than its income; but that does not alter the fact that, at A, its *marginal* propensity to consume out of *extra* income is less than 1. (These family data show more exaggerated curvature than would seem realistic in the late 1960s for *permanent* income levels.)

4th, National consumption did move with national income:

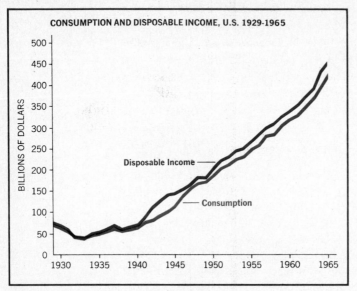

FIG. 11-4. Good forecasts of consumption come from income data. Can you see how great saving became during World War II's goods shortage and rationing? (Source: U.S. Department of Commerce.)

consumption to total "disposable (after-tax) income."[7] This is because we are interested in how the total of *all* consumption spending in the United States changes as the total of our spendable income rises.

While aggregate income is not the only factor determining aggregate consumption, common sense and statistical experience tell us that it is one of the most important factors. Note in Fig. 11-4 how closely consumption seems to follow yearly disposable income; the only exceptional period is that of World War II, when goods were scarce and rationed and people were urged to save.

Figure 11-5 shows this relationship between consumption and disposable income in the form of a "scatter diagram" for the years 1929 to 1966. Each dot marks the magnitude for each year. The resulting scatter of points shows no particular curvature, so a straight-line consumption schedule was drawn in. The actual data fall near, but not exactly on, the "fitted" consumption schedule,[8] reminding us that economics is not, like physics, an exact science. A good rule of thumb is this: Out of each dollar available for consumption C or for saving S, 94 cents goes for C and 6 cents goes for S.

■ QUALIFICATIONS

We are now prepared for the theory of income determination. We have introduced the crucially important concepts of consumption and saving schedules that will be used in the next chapter. But warnings are in order.

The national consumption schedule must be in some sense an aggregation of the family schedules. Yet even if we knew that the family schedules were perfectly reli-

[7] As mentioned in Chapter 10, the disposable income (adjusted) used here and from now on differs from that of the Commerce Department in that here we subtract interest paid by consumers in order to arrive at the adjusted sum consumers have left over to divide between consumption and saving.
[8] So that no reader may think there is great accuracy in this line, let it be mentioned that it was fitted by stretching a black thread from the lower corner through all the data (excepting those for World War II) at what appeared a reasonable position. As in the case of supply and demand curves in Chapter 4 and Part Three, it will be convenient to go back and forth between drawing propensity-to-consume schedules as curved lines or more simply as straight lines when that does no gross violence to the actual facts.

able, we should still have to know something about the distribution of increased incomes before we could get the new point of total consumption of the national schedule. So long as the national-income rise is associated with the distribution of extra income that is typical for such a rise, then we shall be moving along on an unshifted national consumption schedule *CC*.

Aside from the distribution of income, there is a second factor that must be taken into account in any attempt to relate the family and national patterns. Suppose my income were to go from $5,000 to $40,000 a year. Would I spend and save my money in the same way that the budget studies showed $40,000-a-year people spend their money? Not necessarily. Especially at the beginning, I would be *nouveau riche* and have different patterns of behavior.[9]

A third reason why it is difficult to go from the family to the national consumption schedule is suggested by the expression "keeping up with the Joneses." Fifty years ago, if your family had $2,000 worth of purchasing power, you would have been quite well off and above the break-even point of zero saving. But today many people have incomes above that level. Because man is a social animal, what he regards as necessary comforts of life depends on what he sees others consuming. So today, with $2,000 of income, you would be desperately poor and unable to make ends meet. This fact that one man's consumption depends upon the incomes and consumption of others means that we cannot expect the final national pattern to be the simple sum of the separate family patterns. It also means that we must expect the consumption schedule to be shifting upward each decade as living standards rise. Hence, in Fig. 11-5, one would be foolish to push the line back to the income of 1900 or forward to 1999. It is a succinct description of history, rather than necessarily the best guess of the consump-

[9] Modern theoretical and statistical researches by Professors James S. Duesenberry, Milton Friedman, and Franco Modigliani suggest strongly that if people were generally to get a prescribed percentage increase in their incomes that was permanent, they would probably add more to their long-run consumption expenditure than would be indicated by budget studies recorded for a single year such as 1950 or 1970. This warning, which appeared earlier in footnote 3, is worth repeating.

5th, The national consumption schedule in statistical form:

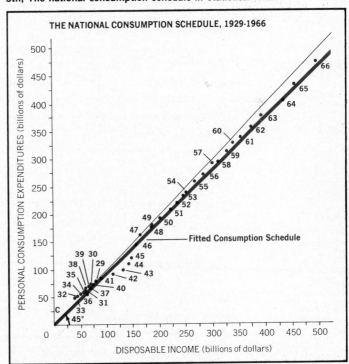

FIG. 11-5. The curve *CC* approximately fits the statistical points for all years except the World War II period. Can you verify its MPC slope of about .94? (Source: Fig. 11-4.)

tion schedule a bank or government economist would use in estimating next year's consumption.

A number of other important qualifications will occur to the reader. The national consumption schedule will shift as prices change and total population grows. Statisticians sometimes try to allow for this by working with per capita consumption and per capita income, expressed in real terms by means of a deflating price index of the sort discussed in the last chapter.[10]

We can think of still other reasons why the propensity-to-consume schedule might shift around. Thus, at the end of World War II, many economists made a famous wrong prediction. They neglected the fact that people came out of the war hungry for goods and with greatly increased amounts of liquid assets (such as government bonds and bank deposits); for this and other reasons, the consumption schedule turned out to be at a higher level than many pessimistic predictions had indicated.

Again we are reminded that no social science can have great exactitude. We shall have to use tools such as the propensity-to-consume curve—or curves of supply and demand—which we know are subject to error and which tend to shift over time rather than remain stable.

The last chapter showed that the national-income accounts *always measure* an identity between saving and investment. This chapter showed that the *motives* and *desires* behind saving and investment are generally quite distinct—which certainly raises the suspicion that the total flow of dollar spending is not guaranteed to proceed at exactly the same rate year in and year out. The hard facts of history confirm this suspicion: at times the economy experienced overexuberant demand and inflation; at times—and they used to be of considerable duration—it experienced considerable unemployment and excess capacity; in the absence of determined public programs of fiscal and monetary controls, only at rare times have economies enjoyed full employment and steady price levels.

The next two chapters investigate how the forces of saving and investment interact to produce an equilibrium level of national income, which can be at high or low employment and which can be conducive to price stability or to price inflation.

SUMMARY

1 ■

Motivations making people want to engage in saving and to engage in investing are different. History shows there is no automatic tendency for the same number of dollars to get spent always at the same rate. Hence, our modern mixed economy would be

---

[10]Thus, instead of working with simple, total dollar C, statisticians may correct it for Price and Population, by working with doubly deflated $C/(\text{Price} \times \text{Population})$; likewise, they may replace DI by its doubly deflated $DI/(Pr \times Po)$, to get *per capita real* income.

subject to inflationary and depression swings if proper public fiscal and monetary policies did not act to help stabilize the economy and reinforce its spontaneous internal
mechanisms that strive to achieve stability.

2 ■

Income is one of the most important determinants of consumption (food, clothing, total)
and saving. The propensity to consume is the schedule relating total consumption to
total income. Because any dollar of income is either saved or consumed, the propensity-
to-save schedule is the other side of the propensity-to-consume picture.

3 ■

The characteristics of family or national propensity-to-consume and propensity-to-save
schedules are summarized in the brief review of definitions on page 205 and must be
thoroughly understood prior to the analysis of income determination in the next chapter.

4 ■

We could aggregate the family consumption schedules to get the national propensity-
to-consume schedule, (a) if we knew the distribution of income for each level of disposable income, (b) if families always stuck to the same consumption-income patterns
in the short run and the long, (c) if we could forget the fact that one man's consumption is influenced by the income levels of his neighbors, and (d) if price levels,
population, corporate saving, and taxes could be neglected.

    The statistical data suggest that total consumption expenditure follows rather
closely the changes in total disposable income. But in using the propensity-to-consume
concept for the discussion of income determination in the next chapter, we must beware
of forming an exaggerated notion of the accuracy and empirical stability of such a
theoretical concept.

QUESTIONS FOR DISCUSSION

1. Summarize familiar budget patterns. Food, clothing, luxuries, saving.

2. What are some of the reasons why people save? What are some of the forms in which they
keep their assets?

3. Exactly how were the MPC and MPS in Table 11-2 computed? Illustrate between *A* and *B*.
Explain why it must always be true that MPC + MPS = 1.

4. I consume *all* my income. Draw my consumption and saving schedules.

5. Do you think the break-even point is the same in New York as in Mississippi? What do
you think is the current break-even point in your community? List a number of ways a person
can incur negative net saving for a while.

6. "Along the consumption schedule, income changes more than consumption does." Why?
Show that this is even more true on the saving schedule.

7. What factors must be taken into consideration if we want to aggregate family budgetary propensity-to-consume schedules to arrive at a national propensity-to-consume schedule? What would happen to the amount consumed out of 800 billion dollars of income if the degree of inequality of income were increased? To the amount saved? What if total taxes out of the 800 billion dollars were to increase? If people were to have more government bonds and bank deposits, how would that affect saving out of the 800 billion dollars?

8. Contrast the meaning of this chapter's beginning quotation with the following 1966 letter to the editor of *Time Magazine* by Professor Milton Friedman of the University of Chicago.

> Sir: You quote me [Dec. 31] as saying: "We are all Keynesians now." The quotation is correct, but taken out of context. As best I can recall it, the context was: "In one sense, we are all Keynesians now; in another, nobody is any longer a Keynesian." The second half is at least as important as the first.

9. Review your understanding of the following concepts:

family motives for saving

business motives for investing

volatile investment decisions

consumption and saving schedules

propensity to consume or to save

MPC and MPS

break-even point and 45° line

after-tax, or disposable, income

permanent versus transitory income

national consumption schedule versus
family schedule

12 Income Determination: The Simple Theory

GIVEN THE PROPENSITY TO CONSUME AND THE RATE OF NEW INVESTMENT, THERE WILL BE ONLY ONE LEVEL OF EMPLOYMENT CONSISTENT WITH EQUILIBRIUM. J. M. KEYNES (1936)

Economists are agreed that the important factor in causing income and employment to fluctuate is investment. Whether we are to face a situation of inflationary bidding up of prices or shall live in a frigid state of mass unemployment depends, as will be seen, upon the level of investment.

There is no need to emphasize the importance of the problem of income determination. In World War II and the early postwar years, nations were plagued by problems connected with too high a general money demand, shortages, and price increases.

From 1953 until the early 1960s, the American economy suffered from a growth in unemployment and an insufficiency of total money demand. Figure 12-1 shows how the economy, spurred on by the tax cut proposed by President Kennedy and passed in 1964, moved back toward the full-employment growth path in the middle 1960s. Memories are short, and there is danger that we shall forget the tremendous costs that were associated with the mass unemployment of the prewar Great Depression. It is scarcely an exaggeration to say that the economic costs of that depression were of the same general magnitude as the costs of all the economic resources which had to be used up in World War II itself. Figure 12-1 also reminds us that the American economy, because of failure to maintain full-employment growth, has lost hundreds of billions of dollars worth of goods and services in recent decades.

This chapter and the next one outline the modern theory of income determination. Because the problems are so important and because the analysis is so useful, the present chapter stresses the fundamentals—how saving and investment, or what is the same thing, how consumption and investment interact to determine the equilibrium level of national income at full employment, below full employment, or with over-full-employment inflationary conditions.

Once the tools of this chapter are mastered, we are ready to understand the next chapter's analysis of inflation and deflation, of how government expenditure and gov-

Cost of sluggish growth rivals that of war:

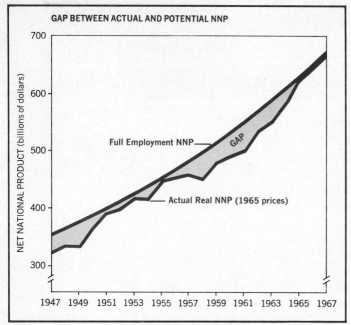

FIG. 12-1. The *green* area shows the gap between what we actually produced in recent years and what our economic system was capable of producing at reasonably high employment and capacity utilization. Public policy in 1960s aimed to reduce this "gap."

ernment tax policy can alter the income equilibrium, and of the interesting "multiplier" principle that shows how one dollar of new primary spending can create additional dollars of secondary respending.

■ USING THE CONSUMPTION AND SAVING SCHEDULES

The last chapter gave a simplified picture of the propensity-to-consume and the propensity-to-save schedules for the community. As discussed, they are drawn up on the basis of our knowledge of the thriftiness of different families, the distribution of incomes between families, and so forth. (At the beginning, we shall make the further simplifying assumptions that there are no taxes, undistributed corporate profits, transfers, or government expenditure of any kind to worry about; hence, we do not have to concern ourselves for the moment with any distinction between net national product and disposable income, and we can use the word "income" to refer to either. Also, we shall initially neglect any changes in the price level.)

Examine Fig. 12-2 closely. Each point on its consumption schedule shows how much the community will *want to continue to consume* at that level of disposable income. Each point on the saving schedule shows how much it will want to continue to save at that income level. Recall that the two schedules are clearly related: since $C + S =$ income always, the CC and SS curves are Siamese twins that will add up always to the 45° line.

■ HOW INCOME IS DETERMINED AT THE LEVEL WHERE SAVING AND INVESTMENT SCHEDULES INTERSECT

We have seen that saving and investment are dependent on quite different factors: Saving tends to depend in a "passive" way upon income, while volatile investment often depends upon "autonomous" factors of dynamic growth.

For simplicity, first suppose investment opportunities are such that net investment would be exactly 60 billion dollars per year regardless of the level of NNP. This means that, if we now draw a schedule of investment against NNP, it will have to be a *horizontal* line—always the same distance above the horizontal axis. Turn over to Fig. 12-3, where this investment schedule is labeled *II* to distinguish it from the *SS* saving schedule. (*II* does *not* mean Roman numeral two.)

The saving and investment schedules intersect at *E*, which corresponds to a level of NNP equal to the distance from 0 to *M*.

■ This intersection of the *saving and investment schedules is the equilibrium toward which national income will gravitate.* Under our assumed conditions, no other level of income can perpetuate itself. The remaining pages of this chapter are devoted to the single task of explaining this important truth.

Let us see why the equilibrium income must eventually be at *E*, the point of intersection between the investment and saving schedules. We consider three cases.

The first case is that in which the system is *at E* itself, where the *II* schedule of what business firms *want* to invest and keep investing just intersects the *SS* schedule of what families *want* to save. Consequently, everyone will be content to go on doing just what he has been doing. Firms will not find inventories piling up on their shelves, nor will they find sales so brisk as to force them to produce more goods. So produc-

Society's national income determines its consumption and saving:

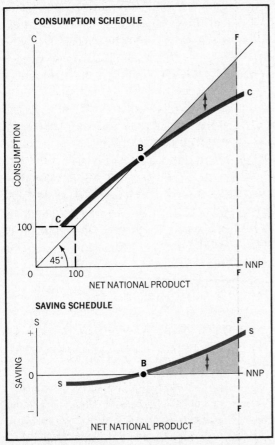

FIG. 12-2. *CC* is the propensity-to-consume and *SS* is the propensity-to-save schedule for the community. Note that these are closely related: the break-even point *B* is shown on the upper diagram where *CC* intersects the 45° line and on the lower diagram where *SS* intersects the horizontal axis. Can you explain why the vertically aligned arrows *must* be equal?

The broken line *FF* depicts the full-employment NNP. Mark what consumption and saving would be at that level. (The curvature is slightly exaggerated here to help identify the two schedules. The two points marked 100 should help emphasize the important property of the 45° line: it depicts a vertical distance equal to exactly 100 per cent of the horizontal distance.)

We can show equilibrium determination of national income in the following equivalent ways:

1st, By intersection of saving and investment schedules:

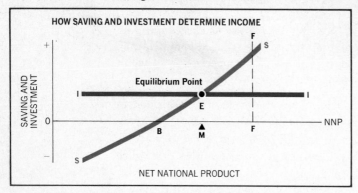

HOW SAVING AND INVESTMENT DETERMINE INCOME

SAVING AND INVESTMENT

NET NATIONAL PRODUCT

FIG. 12-3. *E* marks the spot where investment and saving curves intersect. Equilibrium is at intersection of *SS* and *II* curves because at no other level of NNP could the desired saving of families continually match the desired investment of business.

tion, employment, and income spending will remain the same. NNP in this first case does truly stay at the point *E*; and we can rightly call that "equilibrium."

The second case is where the system is *first* at an NNP *higher* than at *E*, so that it begins east of *E*, at an income level where the *SS* schedule is higher than the *II* schedule. Why can't the system stay there indefinitely? Because at such an income level, families are saving—are refraining from spending on consumption—*more* than business firms will be *willing to go on investing*. Firms will thus find they have too few customers and that their inventories are piling up against their wishes, and they will not want to go on being forced into such undesired

inventory investment. What can they do about it? They can certainly cut back production and lay off workers. This moves NNP gradually downward, which means westward in Fig. 12-3. Where does the system stop being in such disequilibrium? Only when it gets back to *E*, the equilibrium intersection point. There the longer-run tendency to change has disappeared.

The third case should be mastered by the reader. Show that if NNP were *below* its equilibrium level, strong forces would be set up to move it eastward back to *E*. (HINT: At any NNP level where families' *intended* saving falls short of business firms' *intended* investment, the result is consumption of more goods than are being currently produced. What does this mean? It means that business will find itself having to sell inventory off its shelves faster than its production line is producing such goods. Once businessmen notice that they are being forced into less investment, i.e., into more *in*voluntary inventory *disinvestment*, than the *II* curve shows they want, what will they do? They will then expand production and hire new men. This will complete the demonstration that the system does move back eastward until it gets to *E*.)

All three cases then lead to the same summary:

■ The only equilibrium of national income is at *E*, where the saving and investment schedules intersect. At any other point, the *desired* saving of families will not match the *desired* investment of business, and this discrepancy will cause businessmen to change their production and employment levels in such a way as to return the system to the equilibrium intersection.

Before we go on, a warning is in order. An equilibrium level like *E* is a point where the system tends to stay. But there is nothing necessarily optimal about every equilibrium point. Note the vertical dotted line *F* in Fig. 12-3 that depicts full-employment income. Note the fact that the *E* equilibrium shown is at a level of NNP lower than that corresponding to *F*'s full employment.

During a great depression, a capitalistic system may be firmly stuck at a point of very great unemployment. It is then at the *E* given by its low *II* schedule. No one would make the mistake of thinking that such a deep-unemployment equilibrium point is in any sense a good thing. Instead, the government would intervene in the economic system to try to shift the curves until a new equilibrium point *E'* was attained at a desirable level.

■ INCOME DETERMINATION BY CONSUMPTION AND INVESTMENT

There is a second way of showing how income is determined, other than by the intersection of the saving and investment schedules. The final result is exactly the same, but our understanding and confidence in the theory of income determination will be increased if we work through this second approach.

This second approach is called the consumption-plus-investment rather than the saving-investment approach. The *C + I* approach[1] takes advantage of the Siamese-twins property of the saving and consumption schedules. Thus it must always lead to

exactly the same equilibrium income as does the saving-and-investment approach. This is shown by the fact that when you line up Fig. 12-4 vertically under Fig. 12-3, you always find that in both charts *E* marks exactly the same NNP equilibrium.

The *C + I* approach has the advantage of concentrating on *total spending:* spending for consumption goods plus spending for investment goods. The *C + I* approach vertically adds the *II* schedule of business' *desired* investment to the *CC* consumption schedule of families' *desired* consumption spending.

Only where these two *desired* amounts of spending add up to equality with the value of NNP being produced will there be equilibrium.

With what must the combined *C + I* schedule intersect to depict this equilibrium? Figure 12-4 introduces a 45° line to provide our looked-for inter-

[1] When government is brought into the picture, *C + I* will become *C + I + G*.

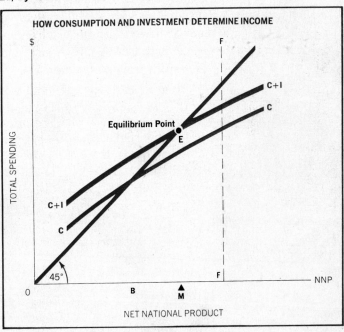

2d, By intersection of *C + I* schedule with 45° line:

HOW CONSUMPTION AND INVESTMENT DETERMINE INCOME

FIG. 12-4. Adding *II* to *CC* gives the *C + I* curve of total spending. At *E*, where it intersects the 45° line, we get the same equilibrium as in the saving-and-investment diagram. (Note the similarities between this figure and Fig. 12-3: the investment added to *CC* is the same as *II* of Fig. 12-3; *B* and *F* each come at the same place on the two diagrams, *and so must the E intersection.*)

section point. The 45° line, we have seen, has the useful property that it lays out in the vertical direction a distance always exactly equal to the income shown on the horizontal axis. So the 45° line is admirably designed to depict the total expense that firms are incurring for the productive factors required to produce national output, and which they must be getting back if they are to feel safe to continue hiring the same number of men and producing the same level of NNP.[2]

We can summarize the $C + I$ method of income determination thus:

■ The equilibrium level of national income is at the intersection of the $C + I$ schedule of desired total spending with the 45° line depicting value of total output.[3] This equilibrium E corresponds exactly to the saving-and-investment equilibrium because of the Siamese-twins relation between the consumption and the saving schedules.

We shall see in the next chapter that the $C + I$ approach has great advantages in helping to analyze government expenditure and fiscal policy. It easily turns itself into an exactly similar $C + I + G$ approach.

■ ARITHMETIC DEMONSTRATION OF INCOME DETERMINATION: A DIGRESSION FOR A THIRD RESTATEMENT

A thoughtful reader may still want to know more about *why* the equilibrium level of income will have to be at the intersection of the saving and investment schedules. What forces will push income to that level and no other?

An arithmetic example may help verify this important matter. Table 12-1 shows an especially simple pattern of the propensity to save against income. The break-even level of income where the nation is too poor to do any net saving on balance is assumed to be 620 billion dollars. Each change of income of 90 billion dollars is assumed to lead to a 30-billion-dollar change in saving and a 60-billion-dollar change in consumption; in other words, MPC is for simplicity here assumed to be constant and exactly equal to $\frac{2}{3}$ with MPS = $\frac{1}{3}$. For this reason, the saving propensity schedule SS in Fig. 12-5 takes on the especially simple form of a perfectly straight line.

What shall we assume about investment? For simplicity, let us suppose again that the only level of investment that can be voluntarily maintained indefinitely is exactly 60 billion dollars, as shown in Column (4) of Table 12-1.

─────────────────────

[2] As the intermediate texts would put it: If the system is not at this intersection, there will be *unintended* inventory investment or disinvestment and/or *unforeseen windfall* profits or losses. As a result, there cannot be equilibrium; but rather a chain of new decisions will be set up to expand or contract output, and possibly to raise or lower prices. So the system will move in disequilibrium until it ends up at the intersection point of equilibrium. Those same intermediate texts point out that *measured S* and *measured I* stay identical even during the worst disequilibrium, by virtue of some people's experiencing unintended losses or gains and/or experiencing unintended investment or saving. (Remember, too, that economists include profit in total business expense.)

[3] Some writers like to call the $C + I$ curve an aggregate *demand* curve, and the 45°-line curve an aggregate *supply* curve. Then, using Chapter 4's language, they say: The equilibrium level of income is where the aggregate demand and supply curves intersect.

3d, The tendency toward equilibrium is shown by arithmetic table:

(1) LEVELS OF NNP AND DI	(2) SCHEDULED CON-SUMPTION	(3) SCHEDULED OR PLANNED OR MAIN-TAINABLE SAVING (3) = (1) − (2)	(4) SCHEDULED OR PLANNED OR MAIN-TAINABLE INVEST-MENT	(5) EXPENSE INCURRABLE BY BUSINESS TO PRODUCE NNP (5) = (1)	(6) SCHEDULED SPENDING THAT WOULD PERMANENTLY COME BACK TO BUSINESSES (6) = (2) + (4)	(7) RESULTING TENDENCY OF INCOME
$980	$860	$120	$60	$980 >	$920 ↓	Contraction
890	800	90	60	890 >	860 ↓	Contraction
800	740	60	60	800 =	800	Equilibrium
710	680	30	60	710 <	740 ↑	Expansion
620	620	0	60	620 <	680 ↑	Expansion
530	560	−30	60	530 <	620	Expansion

TABLE 12-1. INCOME DETERMINATION BY SAVING AND INVESTMENT (in billions of dollars). The green row depicts the equilibrium NNP, where the 60 billion dollars that businessmen will be willing to continue to invest is just matched by families' intended saving. (In higher rows, firms will be forced into unintended inventory investment and will respond by cutting production and NNP back to equilibrium. Interpret the lower rows' tendency toward expansion.)

Now, Columns (5) and (6) are the crucial ones. Column (5) shows how much total expense business firms undergo at each level of national production for wages, interest, rent, *and* profit. This is the NNP of Column (1) copied once again into Column (5), because our repeated discussions in Chapter 10 showed that upper- and lower-loop measurements must be the same.

Column (6), on the other hand, shows what business firms would in fact be *getting back* in the long run in the form of scheduled or voluntary consumption spending plus scheduled or voluntary investment.

When business firms as a whole are temporarily producing a high total product, higher than the sum of what consumers will buy and what business as a whole wants to be investing in equipment and inventory accumulation, businesses will find themselves forced involuntarily to pile up inventory of unsalable goods. At the same time their total sales revenue will be so low as to be putting disagreeable downward pressure on their profit position. With scheduled SS above II, therefore, they will want to contract their operations, and NNP will tend to fall. (Contrariwise, when II > SS and inventories are being involuntarily depleted and profit margins improving, they will increase their employment, and production and NNP will rise.)

When business firms as a whole are temporarily producing at an expense greater than what they can recover, they will want to contract their operations, and NNP tends to fall. When they are getting back more than their current expense for production, they increase their production and NNP rises.

■ Only when level of scheduled saving in Column (3) exactly equals scheduled investment in Column (4) will business firms stay continually in aggregative equilibrium. Their sales will there be just enough to justify continuing their current level of aggregate output. NNP will neither expand nor contract.

This same story is shown in Fig. 12-5. NNP can be read in either of two ways: on the horizontal axis or (from the nature of a 45° line) as the equivalent vertical distance from that axis up to the helping 45° line. The line *SS* represents the saving schedule; the line *II* represents the scheduled level of investment that can be maintained over time. Consumption can also be seen in the figure. Since income not saved is consumed, consumption is always the vertical distance from the saving schedule to the 45° line.

Now we can use Fig. 12-5 to confirm what has just been shown by the arithmetic of Table 12-1. No level of income can *long persist* if it is higher than the equilibrium level given by the *scheduled* saving and investment intersection at 800 billion dollars. To the right of the intersection point *E*, the expense incurred by businesses would exceed the *amount received back* by businesses in the form of maintainable consumption plus maintainable investment.

Graphically, this is shown by the following: The amount continuously paid out by business is the whole distance up to the 45° line, i.e., from *Q* to *R*; but the amount that would continuously be received back by business would be only the sum of voluntary investment *QK* and consumption *JR*. There is a gap of *JK*.

4th, A graph reinforces table's story of restoring equilibrium:

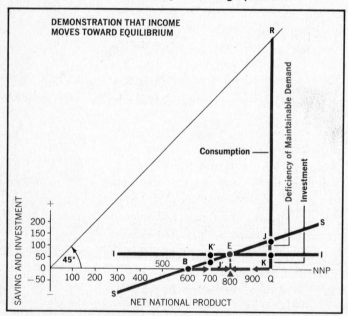

FIG. 12-5. Only at *E* is there no gap between scheduled saving and investment. A gap like that shown at *JK* will soon cause firms to cut their production, which explains the westward green arrow pushing NNP back to *E*'s equilibrium level.

Show that the opposite gap at *J'K'* will mean that firms find their sales so great as to deplete their inventories; interpret the eastward green arrow showing that firms expand production to push NNP back to *E*.

Businesses face a real dilemma. For a while they could keep their prices high and let unsold goods pile up on their shelves, but that would not represent an equilibrium situation and could not persist. Or for a while they could lower prices on their goods and sell below needed cost with less profits; but that, too, could not last.

Thus, it is completely clear that income cannot *permanently* be maintained higher than the equilibrium level —*the level where the amount of saving that people want to do is matched by the amount of investment businessmen are willing to maintain*. A persistent gap of the *JK* type must, through attempts to cut down losses and excessive inventories, result in a contraction of employment and net national product back toward the equilibrium point, where there is no gap. Therefore the green arrow near *Q* points leftward back toward the equilibrium level.

A similar argument shows why income will tend to rise from any place to the left of the equilibrium-intersection level. Indicate on the diagram the relation between business expense and what business can permanently receive back. Show that there will be a favorable gap (as at $J'K'$): Businesses either will be selling so much as to be depleting inventories on their shelves or will be temporarily raising their prices and earning extra profits. In either case, they will be tempted to expand their employment and production. And when they do, the result will be a rise in income back toward the equilibrium-intersection level.[4] Thus ends our digression.

■ THE SIMPLIFIED THEORY OF INCOME DETERMINATION RESTATED

Figure 12-6 pulls together in a simplified way the main elements of income determination. Without saving and investment, there would be a circular

Dynamic investment pumps national income up and down:

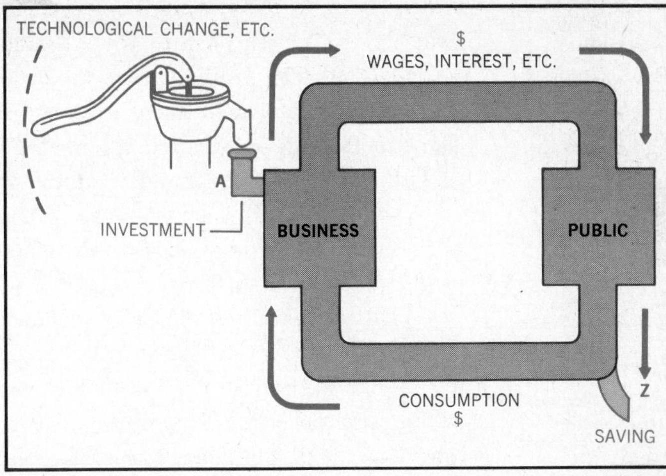

FIG. 12-6. Technological change, population growth, and other dynamic factors keep the investment pump handle going. Income rises and falls with changes in investment, its maintainable equilibrium level being realized only when intended saving at Z continues to match intended investment at A.

flow of income between business and the public: above, business pays out wages, interest, rents, and profits to the public in return for the services of labor and property; and below, the public pays consumption dollars to business in return for goods and services.

Realistically, we must recognize that the public will wish to save some of its income, as shown at the spigot Z. Hence, businesses cannot expect their consumption sales to be as large as the total of wages, interest, rents, and profits. Why not? Because dollars saved do not come back *as consumption sales.*

Some monetary cranks think that this saving necessarily means unemployment and depression. Such a view is simply incorrect. If there happen to be sufficiently profitable investment opportunities, business firms will be paying out wages, interest, and other costs *in part for new investment goods* rather than 100 per cent for consumption goods. Hence, to continue to be happy, business needs to receive back in

---

[4]The recorded income statistics never show the gap depicted by *JK* and by Column (6) minus Column (5). Why not? Because these are gaps in people's *scheduled* quantities. They show levels that cannot continue to persist. On the other hand, the *measurable* statistics of saving and investment are definitionally equal no matter what income is doing: thus, when inventory is *involuntarily* piling up, the Commerce Department statistician cares not that its identity of investment and saving is the result of *unintended* investment. Why should it? It need never go beyond the anatomy of the problem. But we—interested in dynamic physiology of income determination—are vitally interested in schedules. (NOTE: In the last few pages, words such as "voluntary," "scheduled," and "maintainable" were repeated and stressed. This was done to call attention to the difference between a magnitude permanently persisting as a schedule, and the actual amounts measured after the fact in any disturbed short run. In the supply and demand schedules of Part Three, the same problem will recur; Chapter 4 showed that the wheat bought is always numerically identical with the wheat sold, but only at equilibrium market price do the *scheduled* amounts intersect.)

consumption sales only *part* of the total income paid out to the public—only that part which involves the cost of current consumption goods. The *saving* that the public wants to make will do no harm to national income so long as it is not greater than what business can profitably continue to be *investing*.

In Fig. 12-6, investment is shown being pumped into the income stream at A. The handle of the pump is being moved by (1) technological invention, (2) population growth, and (3) other dynamic factors that affect the profitability of investment.

When the investment pump is going at a rapid, steady pace, NNP is high and is at its maintainable equilibrium rate where scheduled saving at Z just balances scheduled investment at A.

This demonstrates that the pessimistic monetary cranks who think that saving is always disastrous are plain wrong. But there is also a second misconception: some go to the opposite extreme and insist that saving and investment can never, in our modern mixed economy with all its frictions and rigidities, cause income to be too high or too low. They make the fatal error of automatically, and without regard to banking policy and fiscal policy, connecting the pipe at Z with the pipe at A.

Many books have been written on this subject of equilibrium income determination, and it is only in the last few decades that economists have learned how to separate the truth and falsity of both extremes. The next 100 pages will deal with this important question, in its relation to income, banking, and business-cycle policy. More specifically, the next chapter will discuss the multiplier, and also fiscal policy's effect on "inflationary or deflationary gaps."

SUMMARY

1 ■

The motives that make people want to save are often different from those that make businesses want to invest. Net investment tends to depend on such autonomous elements as new population, new territory, new inventions, new tastes, and other growth elements. Consumption and saving tend to behave in accordance with passive schedules plotted against national income.

2 ■

People's wishes to save and the willingness of businesses to invest are brought into line with each other primarily by means of changes in income. The equilibrium level of national income must be at the *intersection* of the saving and investment schedules SS and II, or what is exactly the same thing, at the *intersection* of the consumption-plus-investment schedule C + I with the 45° line.

3 ■

If incomes were temporarily above the equilibrium level, business would find itself unable to sell all it was producing at prices that fully covered required costs of production. For a short time inventories might pile up involuntarily and sales at a loss or untenable profit margin might take place, but eventually employment and production would be cut back toward the equilibrium level. The only equilibrium path of income that can be maintained is at the income level where families will voluntarily continue to save exactly as much as business will voluntarily continue to invest.

4 ■

To sum up for the simplified case of this chapter: Investment calls the tune; investment causes income to rise or fall until voluntary, scheduled saving has adjusted itself to the level of maintainable investment.

QUESTIONS FOR DISCUSSION

1. Can you recall from the last chapter how the *CC* and *SS* schedules are in a Siamese-twins relationship, with MPC + MPS = 1 always? Why does the break-even point come at the same level of income (which will be on the horizontal axis in the lower part of Fig. 12-2 and on the 45° line in the upper part)?

2. If there were always zero net investment, can you show that equilibrium would take place at the break-even point? (HINT: Income must fall to that low permanent level at which the amount that people would want to go on saving was zero—namely the break-even point.)

3. If the *SS* schedule had been lower in the late 1950s, or the *II* schedule had been higher, show that Fig. 12-1's wasteful gap would have been much smaller.

4. The saving-and-investment diagram and the 45° line (or *C* + *I*) diagram are two different ways of showing how national income is determined. Describe each. Show their equivalence.

5. Reconstruct Table 12-1 assuming that net investment is equal to (*a*) 90 billion dollars, (*b*) 120 billion dollars. What is the resulting difference in national income? Is this greater or smaller than the change in investment? Why? When *I* drops 30 (or 1) below 60, how much must NNP drop?

6. Which side do you suspect is right in the following argument:

Pessimist: "Automation means that people will not have enough purchasing power to create jobs for all."

Optimist: "Provided society can shift down the *SS* schedule enough or shift up the *II* schedule enough, their equilibrium intersection can be made to take place at the full employment *FF* level no matter how fast science is improving technology."

7. Review your understanding of the following concepts:

consumption schedule *CC*	equilibrium intersection and forces
saving schedule *SS*	moving you when you are not in
45° helping line	equilibrium
break-even point	intended maintainable saving
C + *I* schedule	and investment versus
equivalent intersection of *SS* and *II*;	measurable identity of saving
or *C* + *I* and 45° line	and investment

13 Income Determination: The Multiplier and Fiscal Policy

THE AGE OF CHIVALRY IS GONE; THAT OF SOPHISTERS, ECONOMISTS, AND CALCULATORS HAS SUCCEEDED. EDMUND BURKE

The last chapter set forth the essentials of the modern theory of income determination. Here we must go on to discuss a number of important qualifications and applications.

First, in Section A, we shall explore the relations between externally caused investment movements and the level of income—the so-called "multiplier." Then we look at the relations between thriftiness and unemployment in depressed times—the so-called "paradox of thrift." To show that the theory of income determination is not merely an exercise in depression economics, we proceed to work out the analysis of both "inflationary gaps" and "deflationary gaps."

In Section B, we stop being the detached observers of whatever it is that happens. Like the doctor who puts to work the objective findings of physiological science, we put to work the theory of income determination to show how government fiscal policy— expenditure and taxation—can influence and stabilize the level of national income.

A. INVESTMENT AND INCOME

■ THE "MULTIPLIER"

Let us first show this:

■ An increase in private investment will cause income to expand; a decrease in investment will cause it to contract.

This is not a very surprising result. After all, we have learned that investment is one part of net national product; when one of the parts increases in value, we should naturally expect the whole to increase in value. That is only part of the story. Our theory of income determination gives us a much more striking result.

■ **Modern income analysis shows that an increase in net investment will increase national income by a multiplied amount—by an amount greater than itself! Investment dollars—like any independent shifts in governmental, foreign, or family dollar spending—are high-powered, double-duty dollars, so to speak.**

This amplified effect of investment[1] on income is called the "multiplier" doctrine; the word multiplier itself is used for *the numerical coefficient showing how great an increase in income results from each increase in investment.*

Some examples will make this terminology clear. Let there be an increase of investment of 10 billion dollars. If this causes an increase of income of 30 billion dollars, then the multiplier is 3. If instead the resulting increase in income were 40 billion dollars, then the multiplier would be 4.

■ *Definition:* **The multiplier is the number by which the change in investment must be multiplied in order to present us with the resulting change in income.**

No proof has yet been presented to show that the multiplier will be greater than 1. But by using ordinary common sense one can see why, when I hire unemployed resources to build a $1,000 garage, there will be a *secondary* expansion of national income and production, over and above my primary investment. Here is why.

My carpenters and lumber producers will get an extra $1,000 of income. But that is not the end of the story. If they all have a marginal propensity to consume of $\frac{2}{3}$, they will now spend $666.67 on new consumption goods. The producers of these goods will now have an extra income of $666.67. If their MPC is also $\frac{2}{3}$, they in turn will spend $444.44, or $\frac{2}{3}$ of $666.67 (or $\frac{2}{3}$ of $\frac{2}{3}$ of $1,000). So the process will go on, with each new round of spending being $\frac{2}{3}$ of the previous round.

Thus a whole endless chain of secondary consumption responding is set up by my primary $1,000 of investment spending. But, although an endless chain, it is a dwindling chain. And *in toto* it adds up to a finite amount. By either grade school arithmetic, in which we add the successive numbers until the decimals become insignificant, or by high school geometric progression,[2] we get

---

[1]Our later analysis will show that the multiplier can apply to government and other shifts in spending; but in this section we stick to the simplifying assumption of shifts up and down of a horizontal investment schedule only, leaving the government out of the picture and not letting the CC schedule shift and thereby itself initiate amplified multiplier effects.

[2]High school algebra says the formula for an infinite geometric progression is

$$1 + r + r^2 + r^3 + \cdots + r^n + \cdots = \frac{1}{1-r}$$

as long as the MPC, r, is less than 1 in absolute value. If the MPC were changing along a curved schedule, in the multiplier formula we should have to use an MPC at an income level somewhere between the old and new level. Footnote 10 in this chapter handles a nonhorizontal II case.

$$
\left.\begin{array}{c}
\$1{,}000.00 \\
+ \\
666.67 \\
+ \\
444.44 \\
+ \\
296.30 \\
+ \\
197.53 \\
+ \\
\vdots
\end{array}\right\} = \left\{\begin{array}{c}
1 \times \$1{,}000 \\
+ \\
\dfrac{2}{3} \times \$1{,}000 \\
+ \\
\left(\dfrac{2}{3}\right)^{2} \times \$1{,}000 \\
+ \\
\left(\dfrac{2}{3}\right)^{3} \times \$1{,}000 \\
+ \\
\left(\dfrac{2}{3}\right)^{4} \times \$1{,}000 \\
+ \\
\vdots
\end{array}\right.
$$

$$
\begin{array}{cc}
\$2{,}999.9999 & \dfrac{1}{1 - \frac{2}{3}} \times \$1{,}000, \text{ or } 3 \times \$1{,}000 \\
\text{or} & \\
\$3{,}000 &
\end{array}
$$

This shows that, with an MPC of $\frac{2}{3}$, the multiplier is 3, consisting of the 1 of primary investment plus 2 extra of secondary consumption respending.

The same arithmetic would give a multiplier of 4 if the MPC were $\frac{3}{4}$, for the reason that $1 + \frac{3}{4} + (\frac{3}{4})^{2} + (\frac{3}{4})^{3} + \cdots$ finally adds up to 4. If the MPC were $\frac{1}{2}$, the multiplier would be 2. The size of the multiplier thus depends upon how large the MPC is; or it can be expressed in terms of the twin concept, the MPS. If the MPS were $\frac{1}{4}$, the MPC would be $\frac{3}{4}$, and the multiplier would be 4. If the MPS were $\frac{1}{3}$, the multiplier would be 3. If the MPS were $1/X$, the multiplier would be X.

By this time it is plain that the simple multiplier is always the upside-down, or "reciprocal," of the marginal propensity to save. Our simple multiplier formula is

$$
\text{Change in income} = \frac{1}{\text{MPS}} \times \text{change in investment}
$$

$$
= \frac{1}{1 - \text{MPC}} \times \text{change in investment}
$$

In other words, the greater the extra consumption respending, the greater the multiplier. The greater the MPS "leakage" into extra saving at each round of spending, the smaller the final multiplier.

■ GRAPHICAL PICTURE OF THE MULTIPLIER

Up to this point, we have discussed the multiplier in terms of common sense and arithmetic. Will our saving-investment analysis of income give us the same result? The answer must of course be, Yes.

Suppose, as back in Table 12-1 (page 217), the MPS is $\frac{1}{3}$ and a new series of inventions comes along and gives rise to an extra 30 billion dollars of continuing investment opportunities, over and above our previous 60 billion dollars. Then the increase in investment should raise equilibrium NNP from 800 billion to what? To 890 billion dollars if the multiplier is indeed correctly given as 3 by our previous analysis.

Figure 13-1 confirms this result. Our old investment schedule *II* is shifted upward by 30 billion dollars to the new level *I'I'*. The new intersection point is *E'*. And lo, the increase in income is exactly three times as much as the increase in investment. This is because an MPS of only ⅓ means a relatively flat *SS* saving schedule. As the green arrows show, the horizontal income distance is three times as great as the "primary" vertical saving-investment distance, the discrepancy being equal to the secondary "consumption responding."

The saving-and-investment diagram has many applications. It shows how:

1st, Each dollar of investment can be "multiplied" into three dollars of income:

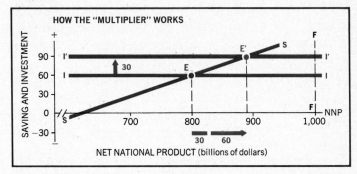

FIG. 13-1. New investment shifts *II* up to *I'I'*. *E'* gives the new equilibrium income, with income increasing 3 for each 1 increase in investment. (Note that the broken horizontal green arrow is 3 times the length of the vertical green arrow that shows the shift in investment, and is broken to show 2 of consumption responding for each 1 of investment.)

In short, income must rise enough to bring out a volume of voluntary saving equal to the new investment. With an MPS of ⅓, income has to rise by how much in order to bring out 30 billion dollars of new saving to match exactly the new investment? By exactly 90 billion dollars,[3] verifying our multiplier arithmetic.

■ HOW THRIFTINESS OR SHIFTS IN THE CONSUMPTION SCHEDULE AFFECT INCOME

We have seen that investment affects incomes. Let us now consider changes in thriftiness. Won't an increase in thriftiness shift the *SS* saving schedule upward? And won't

the new *S'S'* schedule intersect an unchanged *II* schedule in a new equilibrium *E'*? With a new lower NNP?

The answers to these three questions are, Yes, yes, and yes. Figure 13-2

[3]Table 12-1 on page 217 will also verify this answer. In Column (4), we now put in 90 billion dollars instead of 60 billion dollars of investment. The new equilibrium level of income now shifts one row up from the green equilibrium row. The multiplier can also work downward: thus a decline of 1 billion dollars in investment spending will induce an endless chain of negative items, leading ultimately to a 3-billion-dollar *reduction* in equilibrium income. (Check by cutting *I* from 60 to 30.)

2d, Changes in thriftiness, or a shift in *CC*, will change income in a multiplied way:

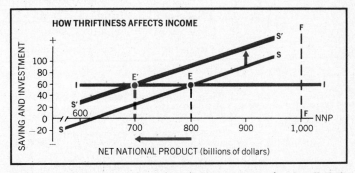

FIG. 13-2. A desire to consume less at every income level will shift the saving schedule upward. With *II* unchanged, equilibrium drops to the *E'* intersection. Why? Because income has to fall until people feel poor enough to again want to save what the system can invest.

shows that an upward shift in the saving schedule—and, what is the same thing, an equivalent downward shift in the consumption schedule—will tend in the absence of any change in the investment schedule to *lower equilibrium* NNP.

Common sense tells us why. If people consume less out of their incomes and if business will not willingly invest more, sales will fall and production must soon be cut. Cut how far? Until so much national income has been destroyed as to make people feel poor enough that they will finally end up not trying to save more than business will go on investing.

Perhaps this point seems obvious. But Fig. 13-2 tells us something more surprising. It shows that a $1 upward shift in the saving schedule will kill off $3 of income. Contrariwise, a $1 downward shift in the saving schedule, which means a $1 upward shift in the consumption schedule, will produce a similar multiplier $3 increase in income.

■ In short, just as investment dollars are "high-powered dollars" that have multiplier effects on income, those consumption dollars are also high-powered that represent a genuine *shift* in the propensity to consume and to save!

We shall meet many examples of this. Thus, Section B shows how reducing taxes can increase consumption and thereby expand income by more than that consumption shift. Or, for a second example, take the case of a famous Harvard economics professor of a past generation, Frank W. Taussig. During the Great Depression he went on the radio to urge everyone to save less, to spend more on consumption. What did he have in mind? That was before the modern theory of income determination was known, but he presumably meant that such spending would on the first round give jobs and incomes to people; that their respending on consumption would create second-round jobs and income; and that it would continue thus in a multiplier chain.

A last example will arise in connection with the next section's so-called "paradox of thrift." The following summary paves the way for it.

■ If scheduled investment holds constant, an upward shift in the saving schedule —which means an equal downward shift in the consumption schedule—will kill off national income in a multiplier way until income falls low enough to bring people's new desired saving again into equality with investment opportunities. Thus an *attempt* to save may not lead to more saving in some situations, but instead may then simply reduce national income.

■ INDUCED INVESTMENT AND THE PARADOX OF THRIFT

Until now we have always treated net investment as an autonomous element, absolutely independent of national income. All our investment schedules have been drawn as horizontal lines, their level being always the same regardless of NNP. This simplification can now be relaxed.

Any practical businessman will tell you that he is more likely to add to his plant or equipment if his sales are high relative to his plant capacity. In the short run (before businessmen have had time to adjust their capital stock to a changed plateau of income), it is reasonable for us to draw the *II* schedule in Fig. 13-3 as a rising curve. *An increase in employment and national product may* induce *a higher level of net investment.*

As before, the equilibrium level of (maintainable) national income is given by the intersection of the investment and saving schedules, or by *E* in Fig. 13-3. So long as the *SS* curve always cuts the *II* curve from below, businessmen's action must finally bring the economy back to the equilibrium level.[4]

Induced investment means that anything which increases national income is likely to be good for the capital-goods industries; anything hurting national income is likely to be bad for them.

3d, Higher income will induce businessmen to want higher investment:

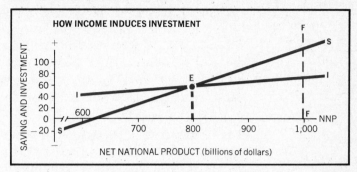

FIG. 13-3. Now we drop the assumption of a horizontal *II* schedule. Now *II* slopes upward, showing intended investment less than 60 billion dollars at low NNP and more than 60 billion dollars at high NNP. Equilibrium is still at *E*, where *SS* intersects *II* from below.

This throws new light on the age-old question of thrift versus consumption. It shows this:

■ An increased desire to consume—which is another way of looking at a decreased desire to save—is likely to boost business sales and increase investment. On the other hand, a decreased desire to consume—i.e., an increase in thriftiness—is likely to reduce inflationary pressure in times of booming incomes; but in time of depression, it could make the depression worse and reduce the amount of actual net capital formation in the community. *High consumption and high investment are then hand in hand rather than opposed to each other.*

This surprising result is sometimes called the "paradox of thrift." It is a paradox because most of us used to be taught that thrift is *always* a good thing. Ben Franklin's *Poor Richard's Almanac* never tired of preaching the doctrine of saving. And now along comes a new generation of financial experts who seem to say that the old virtues may be modern sins in depressed times.

Let us for the moment leave our cherished beliefs aside and try to disentangle the paradox in a dispassionate, scientific manner. Two considerations will help to clarify the whole matter.

The first is this. In economics, we must always be on guard against the logical fallacy of composition. That is to say, what is good for each person separately need not always be good for all; under some circumstances, private prudence may be social folly. Specifically this means that the *attempt* of each and every person to increase his saving may—under the conditions to be described—result in a reduction in *actual* saving by all the people in the community. Note the italicized words "attempt" and

---

[4] If the two curves crossed in the opposite way, the little arrows back in Fig. 12-5, page 218, would point out instead of in and we should have unstable equilibrium; then the economy would rush away—in either direction—from the intersection neighborhood. A physical analogy may help: An egg on its side is in "stable equilibrium"; given a slight disturbance, it returns to equilibrium. An egg on its tip is in "unstable equilibrium"; a light touch topples it.

"actual"; between them, in our imperfect mixed economy, there may be a world of difference when people find themselves thrown out of jobs and with lowered incomes.

The second clue to the paradox of thrift lies in the question of whether or not national income is at a depressed level. If we were at full employment, then obviously the more of our national product we devoted to current consumption, the less would be available for capital formation. If output could be assumed to be always at its maximum, then the old-fashioned doctrine of thrift would be absolutely correct—correct, be it noted, from both the individual and the social standpoints. In primitive agricultural communities, such as the American colonies of Franklin's day, there was truth in Franklin's prescription. The same was true during World Wars I and II, and it is true during periods of boom and inflation: if people then become more thrifty, less consumption will mean more investment.

But according to statistical records, full employment and inflationary demand conditions have occurred only at intervals in our nation's history. Much of the time there were some wasting of resources, some unemployment, and some insufficiency of demand, investment, and purchasing power. When this is the case, everything can go into reverse. What once was a social virtue may then become a social vice. What is true for the individual—that extra thriftiness means increased saving and wealth—may then become completely untrue for the community as a whole.

Under conditions of unemployment, the *attempt to save* may result in *less*, not more, saving. The individual who saves cuts down on his consumption. He passes on less purchasing power than before; therefore someone else's income is reduced, for one man's outgo is another man's income. If one man succeeds in saving more, maybe it is because someone else is forced to dissave. If one man succeeds in hoarding more money, someone else must do without.

Thus, when there is stubborn unemployment, consumption and investment can be complementary, not competitive. What helps one helps the other. The attempt to cut down on consumption (to save) then only results in a reduction of income until everyone feels poor enough no longer to try to save more than can be invested. Moreover, at lower levels of income, less, and not more, capital goods will be needed. Therefore *investment will actually be less*. (As will be seen again and again, with prudent public and private policies, our system will be restored to proper operation, so that the paradox of thrift can be robbed of its applicability.)

Let us clinch our common-sense understanding of this paradox by combining Figs. 13-2 and 13-3 into Fig. 13-4.

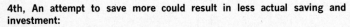

4th, An attempt to save more could result in less actual saving and investment:

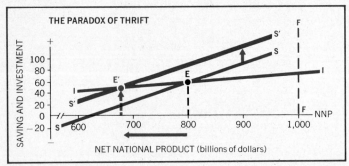

FIG. 13-4. The shift of SS upward to S'S' depresses income; and the drop of income kills off some investment, moving us southwest along the sloping II schedule. (If the system were straining at the full-employment level of F, the effect of increased thriftiness might be different.)

An increase in thriftiness or the desire to save will shift the SS curve upward to S'S'. Note that the new intersection E' is now at a lower level of income. Because of induced *disinvestment*, the drop in income does also mean lower investment. Thus both income and investment have actually decreased! The attempt to save more in depression times has resulted in less actual saving.[5]

If true, this is an important lesson. It will never again be a satisfactory measure to urge men in time of depression to tighten their belts, to save more in order to restore prosperity. The result will all too likely be the reverse—a worsening of the vicious deflationary spiral. At such a time, many of the usual arguments go into reverse. An economic lobbyist of the capital-goods industries would, if he has their selfish interests at heart, advocate less thriftiness in depressed times, so that the consumption schedule will be pushed upward, and so that attempts to save—which then really lead only to decreases in income—will be discouraged. For only then will investment and sales of heavy capital goods flourish.[6]

Later, we shall see that the modern neoclassical synthesis can rid the paradox of thrift of its terrors.

■ THE DEFLATIONARY GAP

The multiplier is a two-edged sword. It will cut for you or against you. It will amplify new investment, as we have seen. But it will also amplify negatively any *de*crease in investment. Thus, if investment opportunities drop by 30 billion dollars in our earlier examples, then national income will have to fall by three times as much—by 90 billion dollars. If net investment drops away to zero, income will have to fall to the break-even point where the community is made poor enough to stop all net saving.

This reminds us once again that there may be nothing particularly good about what we have called the equilibrium level of national income. If investment is low, the equilibrium level of income will involve much unemployment and waste of national resources. The only level of national income that we are entitled to regard as a desirable goal is that near to full employment; but we shall end up at such a level of high employment only if investment opportunities happen to match full-employment saving.

> ■ Unless this full-employment saving is "offset" by private investment (or by public policies), the nation cannot continue to enjoy full employment. There is then said to be a "deflationary gap," its size being measured by the deficiency of investment compared with full-employment saving.

[5] At the end of the summary on page 227, pencil in the words: "Sometimes the attempt to save may even reduce actual saving!" Note also that induced investment makes the multiplier bigger; in addition to a secondary chain of induced consumption spending, there will be a reinforcing chain of secondary *induced investment* spending. See footnote 10 in this chapter.

[6] We have seen that this line of argument does not apply in conditions of full employment. It also requires some slight modifications to allow for the fact that thriftiness, by lowering income, may also lower interest rates and promote investment, or it may depress wages and prices and thereby increase the real purchasing power of people's money holdings enough to destroy their initial thriftiness. These qualifications are discussed later; in our imperfect mixed economy, with wage and price levels sticky and inflexible, they seem rather unimportant considerations during deep depression.

When C + I spending that would be generated at full employment differs from the full-employment NNP, we call:

1st, Any spending deficiency a "deflationary" gap:

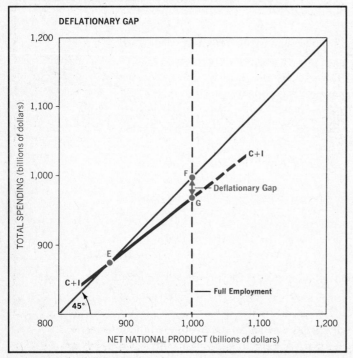

FIG. 13-5. The deflationary gap is always measured at the full-employment NNP level. It is the vertical distance there between the 45° line and the *C + I* schedule, that is, *FG*. Such a deflationary gap will depress income in a multiplied way. (Later, after government is introduced, we'll relabel *C + I* as *C + I + G*.)

We can picture the deflationary gap on a consumption-plus-investment graph, Fig. 13-5. Suppose that 1,000 billion dollars represents the full-employment income. Suppose that, at this income level *F*, the scheduled total of *C + I* adds up to only 960 billion dollars, as shown at *G*. *This leaves a 40-billion-dollar deflationary gap between G and F*. Since obviously we cannot then remain at full employment, what will happen? Will income drop by only 40 billion dollars? Clearly not. It must drop by some greater multiple of the original deflationary gap. If each dollar of reduced income results in a cut of $\$\frac{2}{3}$ in consumption spending, income will have to fall until it has dropped three times as much as the original deflationary gap (see point *E* in Fig. 13-5).[7]

■ THE PROCESS OF PRICE INFLATION

Instead of a deflationary gap, we may have an inflationary gap. If scheduled investment tends to be greater than full-employment saving, then more goods will be demanded of business than it can produce, and prices will begin to rise. Figure 13-6 shows how we measure the inflationary gap as a vertical distance: The new *C' + I'* curve lies *above* the 45° line at the full-employment level by the distance *FG'*, giving us an inflationary gap of 30 billion dollars.

■ If full-employment saving falls short of scheduled investment at full-employment, there is said to be an "inflationary gap," its size being measured by the excess of the *C + I* schedule above the 45° line's full-employment level (which is the same thing as the excess of full-employment scheduled *II* over *SS*).

[7] What can be done about this? If we continue to leave the government out of the picture, we must have either an increase in investment or an increase in consumption. By how much must the level of investment or of the consumption schedule shift upward if full employment is to be restored? By the full 120 billion dollars of lost income? No. Because of the multiplier, to wipe out a deflationary gap, the *C + I* schedule need shift upward only by the amount of the gap itself, not by any multiple of the gap. (In a saving-investment diagram like Fig. 13-3 you measure the deflationary gap by the vertical distance between the *SS* and *II* schedules at the full-employment income *FF*.)

Now what will result from the 30 billion gap? Can production rise by 90 billion dollars to give a new equilibrium at E'? Plainly not. Everyone is already fully employed, and factories are producing at their practical capacity points. The region to the right of the vertical full-employment line through F is a never-never land. It shows us what we should like to be able to produce, but not what we are actually able to produce. Although an inflationary gap is the opposite of a deflationary gap, its effects upon employment and production are of a slightly different qualitative nature. A deflationary gap can move production leftward, down to 90 or even 70 per cent of a full-employment level; but an inflationary gap cannot possibly move employment rightward to 150 per cent of full or maximum employment. The economic system cannot move in *real terms* very far to the right of the broken full-employment line.

The excess in purchasing power can result only in price increases and

2d, Any spending excess an "inflationary" gap:

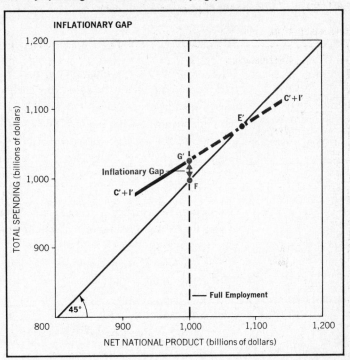

FIG. 13-6. FG' measures the inflationary gap. People are trying to buy more than can be produced, and thereby they are inflating the price level. (With all prices changing, the spending schedules are likely to shift upward, so it would be a mistake to regard E' as an actually attainable equilibrium point.)

an inflationary spiral; money national income will rise because of "paper" price-tag changes, but real national product cannot go above its maximum full-employment level. Unfortunately, the upward movement of prices will continue for as long as there is an inflationary gap,[8] i.e., until we are lucky enough for investment or consumption demand to fall off or smart enough as a nation to adopt corrective policies that will wipe out the inflationary gap.

Far from being "depression economics," modern income analysis has many of its most important applications in connection with the process of inflation and what can be done about it. During and after World War II, the concept of the inflationary gap was indispensable in indicating the quantitative magnitude of taxation needed to keep decontrolled prices from rising; and without understanding the rudiments of income

[8]The process does not end with higher prices. The new higher price level will not equilibrate total supply and demand once and for all. On the contrary, since the higher prices received by businesses become in turn somebody's income—that of worker or property owner—demand again shifts upward and prices will continue to rise. Attempts of labor to secure higher wages as compensation for the soaring cost of living may only cause the inflationary spiral to zoom at a dizzier speed. (Lord Keynes formulated this theory of inflation in 1939.)

analysis, we cannot follow the important economic issues discussed in Congress and the public press.[9]

B. FISCAL POLICY IN INCOME DETERMINATION

When there is a large inflationary or deflationary gap, the government is called upon to do something about the price rise or the widespread unemployment. Tax and government expenditure policies—the general name for which is "fiscal policy"—will change the equilibrium level of income. So we must now explicitly introduce government fiscal policy into the picture to see exactly how income determination is affected. As you might guess, we now consider a $C + I + G$ spending schedule to show the equilibrium that results when government is in the picture.

It will simplify our task if in the beginning we analyze the effects of government expenditure with taxes held constant. When taxes come into the picture, we can no longer ignore the distinction between disposable income and net national product. But with the tax revenue first held constant, they will differ always by the same amount; and taking account of such taxes, we can still plot the CC consumption schedule against NNP rather than against DI.

In Chapter 10 we learned that net national product consists of three rather than two parts; namely,

NNP = Consumption expenditure + private net Investment + Government
expenditure on goods and services

$$= C + I + G$$

Therefore, on our 45°-line diagram in Fig. 13-7, we must now superimpose upon the consumption schedule not only private investment but also government expenditure G. This is because public road building is economically no different from private railroad building, and collective consumption expenditure involved in maintaining a free public library has the same effect upon jobs as private consumption expenditure for movies or rental libraries.

We end up with the $C + I + G$ schedule showing the amount of total spending forthcoming at each level of NNP. We now must go to the intersection with the 45° line to read off the equilibrium level of national product. At this equilibrium NNP level, the total the nation wants to spend on all goods is just equal in value to the full costs of production of these goods.

Figure 13-7 shows that government expenditure, taken by itself and disregarding taxes, has a multiplier effect upon income just like that of private investment. The reason is, of course, that a chain of *respending* is set into motion by the road builders, librarians, and other people who receive primary income from the government.[10]

---

[9]See later chapters in Parts Two and Six for further discussion of inflation, which includes along with the present kind of "excess-demand," or "demand-pull," inflation the possibility of "creeping cost-push inflationary tendencies."

[10]Our saving-investment diagram will give the same answer as the 45°-line diagram. The increase in government expenditure means an equivalent increase in the government deficit if taxes do not increase. Net saving must always equal private investment + government deficit. Therefore we add the deficit on top of the II curve and get our new greater equilibrium level of national income

To show the effects of an extra 20 billion dollars of G, shift $C + I + G$ in Fig. 13-7 up to $C + I + G'$ and show that the new E' will record a multiplier response of NNP to the government spending.

■ TAXATION AND SHIFTS OF CONSUMPTION SCHEDULE

Now let us turn to the depressing effects of taxes on the equilibrium NNP level. Without graphs, our common sense tells us what must happen when the government (1) takes away more from us in taxes while (2) at the same time holding its expenditure constant. Extra taxes will mean we have lower real disposable incomes, and lower disposable incomes mean we shall cut down on our consumption spending. Obviously, if investment and government expenditure remain the same, a reduction in consumption spending will then reduce net national product and employment; or if we already are having an inflationary gap, the new taxes will help close the gap and wipe out excessive inflationary price increases.

Government expenditures act like consumption and investment in determining national income:

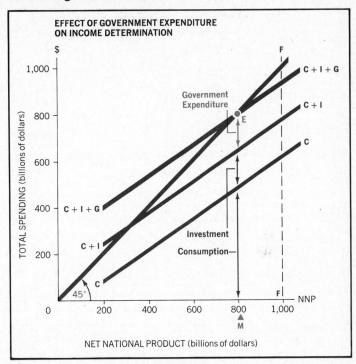

FIG. 13-7. On top of consumption spending and investment spending, we now add government spending on goods and services. This gives us the $C + I + G$ schedule. At E, where this intersects the 45° line, we find equilibrium. (What if G increases or decreases? Can you show the multiplied changes in income?)

Our graphs can confirm this reasoning: $I + G$ is unchanged, but now the increase in taxes will lower disposable income, thereby lowering consumption and shifting the consumption schedule downward; so in all, the $C + I + G$ schedule will shift downward, and its new intersection with the crucial 45° line must definitely be at a lower equilibrium level of NNP.

Figure 13-8 shows and explains how tax receipts shift the CC schedule downward. With CC down, $C + I + G$ in Fig. 13-7 will be down, and equilibrium NNP must drop.

REMARK: Now we know something that common sense did not immediately tell us. To offset a 20-billion-dollar upward shift in $I + G$, we must increase tax collections by *more* than 20 billion dollars. Figure 13-8 shows needed taxes as 30 billion when MPC $= \frac{2}{3}$.

at the intersection with the SS curve. In more advanced discussions, we could employ Fig. 13-7 to show how induced investment or government expenditure (i.e., induced by a changed level of income) will enter into the multiplier. The final change in income resulting from a unit upward shift in the $C + I + G$ schedule will always turn out to be $1 \div (1 - K)$, where K is the slope of the $C + I + G$ schedule, and might be called the "marginal propensity to spend (inclusive of induced C, I, and G effects)."

Higher taxes will cut disposable income and consumption:

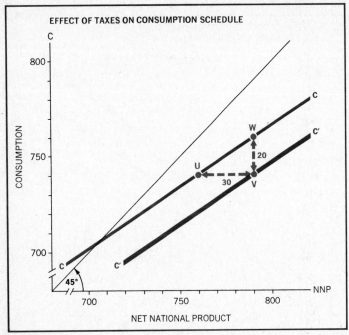

FIG. 13-8. Each dollar of tax lowers the *CC* schedule. Why? Because *CC* is shifted to the right by exactly the amount of the tax. (Example: First NNP = 760 at *U* with zero tax; *DI* = 760 also. *CC* shows consumption at *U* of about 740. Now add tax of 30; NNP at *V* must equal 760 + 30 if *DI* is to remain 760 and consumption 740 there. So *UV* arrow shows *C′C′* is shifted rightward by exact amount of the tax.) A rightward *CC* shift means a downward *CC* shift. But the downward shift is only two-thirds of the rightward shift if *CC's* slope of MPC = ⅔. (Verify *WV* = ⅔*UV*.)

With *CC* lowered, so will *C* + *I* + *G* in Fig. 13-7 be lowered. Show the drop in income there caused by such a tax increase.

This means that (1) when increased government defense spending is added to a full-employment economy with a balanced budget, then (2) taxes will probably have to be increased by *more than enough to balance the budget* if we are determined to avoid an inflationary gap.[11]

What was more important in connection with the massive Kennedy-Johnson tax cut of 1964, a reduction in tax rates will *raise* the equilibrium level of national income. We can easily reverse the above analysis to explain why tax reductions help to fight a sluggish recession. Each dollar of tax reduction leads, through an upward and leftward shift in *CC*, to an increase in people's disposable income by a dollar and to almost a dollar increase in initial consumption spending.

■ Hence, dollars of tax reduction are almost as powerful a weapon against mass unemployment as are increases in dollars of government expenditure.

Such a program may involve a larger budget deficit than an expenditure program would; but it also means that there is expansion of the private rather than government sector of the economic system. Both the United States and Japan used this tax-cut mechanism in the mid-sixties to increase their employment and income levels, a remarkable example of modern fiscal policy at work.

■ QUALIFICATIONS TO SAVING AND INVESTMENT ANALYSIS

The theory of income determination sketched in the last two chapters is a powerful tool.[12] It helps us to understand the ups and downs of the business cycle. It helps us

[11] Advanced treatises call this phenomenon the "balanced-budget multiplier theorem." This very useful, but highly simplified, doctrine says: A *balanced* rise in *G* and *T* will raise NNP by just that amount; a balanced cut of $1 in *G* and *T* will cut NNP by $1. So it is not merely the budget deficit, *G* − *T*, that has NNP effects.

[12] Advanced discussions show corporate saving can be handled graphically much like taxes.

to understand how foreign lending (which is one part of total net investment) affects domestic employment and income. It helps us to understand how governmental fiscal policy can be used to fight inflation and unemployment. All these topics are developed in later chapters.

But it would be a mistake to think that an economist can be made out of a parrot, simply by teaching him the magic words "saving" and "investment." Behind the scenes of these schedules a great deal is taking place.

It should be noted that an increase in the public's holding of government bonds and other wealth may shift the consumption schedule upward. Or rising living standards (resulting from advertising and the invention of new products) may shift the consumption schedule up, just as it has in the past.

In short, it is an oversimplification to regard investment as always an autonomous factor, and consumption as always a passive factor depending upon income. True, this is a fruitful oversimplification. But as we have already seen, some of net investment may be "induced" by income changes in the short run; and, as we shall see, changes in interest costs, availability of credit, and stock of money can alter the swings in investment. Furthermore, consumption also will sometimes shift autonomously even though income has remained constant. And the reader can verify by experimenting with the saving-investment and the 45°-line diagrams, the truth of our earlier assertion that such shifts in the consumption or saving schedules do have multiplier effects upon national income—*exactly* like the multiplier effects of changes in investment.

After the survey of our business-cycle history in the next chapter, the following chapters will discuss money and banking, to show how interest-rate and credit changes may cause the investment schedule to shift.

SUMMARY

A. INVESTMENT AND INCOME

1 ■

Investment (and any autonomous schedule shift) has a multiplier effect on income. When investment changes, there is an equal *primary* change in national income. But as these primary income receivers in the capital-goods industries get more earned income, they set into motion a whole chain of additional *secondary* consumption spending and employment.

If people always spend about $\frac{2}{3}$ of each extra dollar of income upon consumption, the total of the multiplier chain will be

$$1 + \tfrac{2}{3} + (\tfrac{2}{3})^2 + \cdots = \frac{1}{1 - \tfrac{2}{3}} = 3$$

The multiplier works forward or backward, amplifying either increases or decreases in investment. The simplest multiplier is numerically equal to the reciprocal of the MPS; this is because it always takes more than a dollar's change in income to bring forth a dollar's change in saving.

2 ■

The *attempt* to save more is quite different from the achievement of increased saving for society as a whole. The "paradox of thrift" shows that an increase in thriftiness may reduce already depressed income and, through induced effects on investment, may actually result in *less* net investment. Only when employment remains full or unchanged are consumption and investment necessarily competing; only then are private virtues always social virtues.

The moral is not for each individual to squander his money during a depression, trying to be patriotic. Instead, through proper national policies, we must re-create a high-employment environment in which private virtues are no longer social follies.

3 ■

In short, we must avoid both inflationary and deflationary gaps, so that full-employment saving and investment just match without inflation. We measure the size of the deflationary or inflationary gap as (*a*) the vertical discrepancy at full-employment income between the saving and investment schedules, or what is exactly the same thing, as (*b*) the vertical distance between the $C + I$ (or $C + I + G$ when government is in the picture) schedule and the 45° line.

B. FISCAL POLICY AND INCOME DETERMINATION

4 ■

An increase in government expenditure—taken by itself with taxes and investment unchanged—has expansionary effects on national product much like those of net investment. The schedule of $C + I + G$ shifts upward to a higher equilibrium intersection with the 45° line.

5 ■

An increase in taxes—taken by itself with investment and government expenditure unchanged—depresses the equilibrium level of national product. The schedule of consumption plotted against NNP is shifted downward and rightward by taxes; but since extra dollars go partly into saving, the dollar drop in consumption will not be quite so great as the dollars of new taxes. Therefore, to combat a given inflationary or deflationary gap, we may require an even larger change in taxation.

6 ■

The art of economics consists in recognizing both the core of truth in the simple theory of income determination and also its needed qualifications. In later chapters we shall see how interest rates and other factors may cause shifts in the schedules that determine levels of national income.

We leave to the final chapters of Part Two the analysis of government monetary and fiscal policy. In the intervening chapters we turn to an analysis of the wild dance of the business cycle, of money, banking policy, and interest.

QUESTIONS FOR DISCUSSION

1. Describe in a few paragraphs (a) the common sense, (b) arithmetic, (c) geometry of the multiplier. What are the multipliers when MPC = 0.9? 0.8? 0.5? When MPS = 0.1? 0.8?

2. Work out the chain of spending and respending when MPC = 4. Explain the economics of the arithmetic.

3. "Even if the government spends a billion dollars on 'wasteful' armaments, during a depression that may help create jobs and several billions of new useful production." Discuss.

4. Give arguments for and against thriftiness. Contrast carefully (a) the individual and the community viewpoint and (b) boom and depression.

5. Describe effects upon income of (a) government expenditure, (b) taxes, (c) our sale of more goods and services to foreigners than they sell us (i.e., positive net foreign investment).

6. "The purpose of fiscal policy is to help wipe out inflationary or deflationary gaps. Thus, if $C + I + G$ is too high, we have an inflationary gap; and we raise taxes to shift the new $C' + I' + G'$ schedule downward, thereby wiping out the inflationary gap." Explain. Show what you would do to taxes to fight a deflationary gap. To government expenditure.

7. If cold-war military expenditure could be ended, how would we be able to restore full employment? Explain your alternative programs in terms of shifts of the $C + I + G$ schedule.

8. Review your understanding of the following concepts:

multiplier impacts of investment

primary and secondary spending

multiplier effects on income of consumption or saving shifts

induced investment

paradox of thrift

inflationary, deflationary gaps

cumulative inflation

underemployment equilibrium

$C + I + G$ schedule

fiscal policy (expenditure and taxes)

G effect on equilibrium

tax effect on CC and equilibrium

qualifications to the analysis

14   Business Cycles and Forecasting

THE FAULT, DEAR BRUTUS, IS NOT IN OUR STARS—BUT IN OURSELVES. . . . WILLIAM SHAKESPEARE

We have examined the economic forces operating to determine the level of national income—the balance of saving and investment. We now turn to the problem of how the level of national income has fluctuated, and how economists try to forecast the future. It is typical in modern economics to follow bold theoretical formulation by careful description of the empirical facts of life.

■ PROSPERITY AND DEPRESSION

Business conditions never stand still. Prosperity may be followed by a panic or a crash. National income, employment, and production fall. Prices and profits decline, and men

Are business cycles calming down?

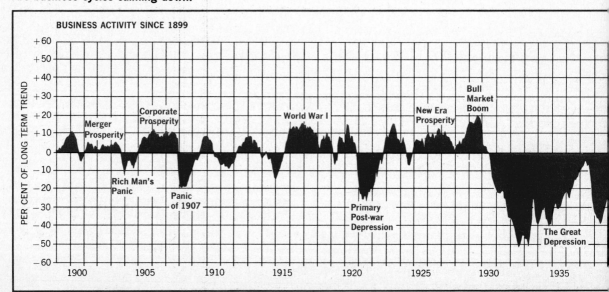

BUSINESS ACTIVITY SINCE 1899

are thrown out of work. Eventually the bottom is reached, and revival begins. The recovery may be slow or fast. It may be incomplete, or it may be so strong as to lead to a new boom. The new prosperity may represent a long, sustained plateau of brisk demand, plentiful jobs, buoyant prices, and increased living standards. Or it may represent a quick, inflationary flaring up of prices and speculation, to be followed by another disastrous slump.

Such, in brief, was the so-called "business cycle" that used to characterize the industrialized nations of the world for the last century and a half at least—ever since an elaborate, interdependent *money economy* began to replace a relatively self-sufficient precommercial society. Is the business cycle a thing of the past, a museum piece? This we must study.

No two business cycles are quite the same. Yet they have much in common. They are not identical twins, but they are recognizable as belonging to the same family. No exact formula, such as might apply to the motions of the moon or of a simple pendulum, can be used to predict the timing of future (or past) business cycles. Rather, in their rough appearance and irregularities, business cycles more closely resemble the fluctuations of disease epidemics, of the weather, or of a child's temperature.

From these introductory remarks, it will be clear that business fluctuations are simply one further aspect of the economic problem of achieving and maintaining high levels of jobs, production, and progressive growth.

■ MEASURING THE BUSINESS CYCLE

Figure 14-1 shows how the economic system was plagued with the uncertainties of the business cycle throughout our history as a nation, although fortunately rarely with so sustained and costly a slump as the post-1929 Great Depression. With surprisingly few

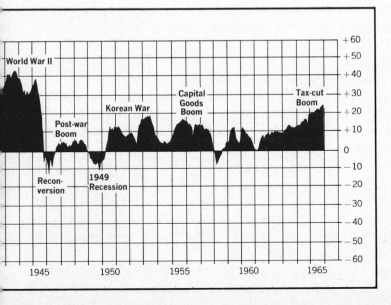

FIG. 14-1. For 25 years now we have had no significant depressions. But it was not always so in our history. (Source: Cleveland Trust Co.)

variations, the same pattern of cyclical fluctuations was long repeated in England, Germany, and other foreign nations. But it is a strange fact that the United States, supposedly one of the youngest and most vigorous of nations, always tended to have greater average amounts of unemployment and greater variation in unemployment than most other countries. Not only was this true in 1933, when our percentage of unemployment rivaled even that of Germany, but it appears to have been the case for almost as far back as we have any records or indications. Only in the last 25 years have we avoided deep unemployment, but still our rates exceed those abroad.

Figure 14-2 shows a number of post–World War II economic "time series," presented together for comparison. Note the all-pervasive common pulse of the business cycle: the recessions of 1948–1949, 1953–1954, 1957–1958, and 1960–1961 are shown as green shaded stretches. These fluctuations show up in production, unemployment, incomes, and even in such particular series as stock-market prices and building. Moreover, if data had been included on such noneconomic matters as marriages, births, and malnutrition, we could have seen the heavy hand of the business cycle in them too. Even political elections follow the business cycle: in slumps, the ins go out. Thus the 1960 Eisenhower recession helped elect President Kennedy, just as the Hoover depression of the 1930s helped elect Franklin Roosevelt.

Let us first stick to the facts and statistics. Later we can attempt to devise hypotheses and explanatory theories to account for the facts.

■ STATISTICAL CORRECTION FOR SEASONAL VARIATION AND FOR TRENDS

First, of course, we must remove from our statistical data irrelevant, disturbing factors such as seasonal patterns, and also certain so-called long-term "trends." If Sears' sales go up from November to December, 1960, we cannot conclude from this that the 1960 recession shown in Fig. 14-2 does not exist. Retail trade goes up every Christmas, just as Cape Cod hotels tend to be crowded in summer. The statistician attempts to remove the "seasonal influence" by carefully studying previous yearly patterns. If he finds that every December tends to involve about 150 per cent as much business as the average month of the year, and every January only 90 per cent, then he will take the actual raw monthly data and divide all the December figures by 1.5, all the January figures by 0.9, and so forth for each month. After this has been done, the statistician will end up with a time series of monthly department-store sales which have been "seasonally adjusted." These will show what we expected all along, that business was really still declining throughout all the last months of 1960, because December's improvement was less than the seasonal norm.

Another kind of problem arises when we examine the fluctuations through time of such a rapidly growing time series as electric-power production or personal income. (This last can be seen at the bottom of Fig. 14-2.) Such a growing series did not decline in any recession. But the recession is evident there, nevertheless. It rears its ugly head in the form of a *slowing down of the rate of growth* of the time series as compared with its normal or long-term "secular trend."

If we draw a smooth trend line or curve, either by eye or by some statistical

Most economic activities move up and down together:

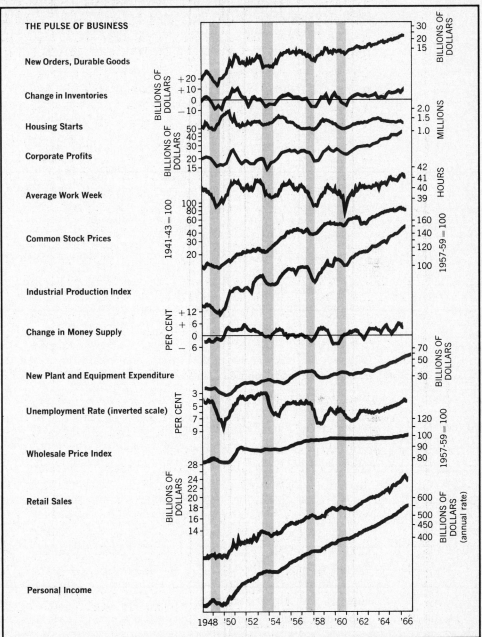

THE PULSE OF BUSINESS

New Orders, Durable Goods

Change in Inventories

Housing Starts

Corporate Profits

Average Work Week

Common Stock Prices

Industrial Production Index

Change in Money Supply

New Plant and Equipment Expenditure

Unemployment Rate (inverted scale)

Wholesale Price Index

Retail Sales

Personal Income

FIG. 14-2. The green-shaded stretches show years of recession, in contrast to the unshaded periods of expansion. The top curves tend to represent investment items, which seem to be "early movers" and originators of causal movements. The bottom curves show less volatile elements like consumption. Note how rare and short recessions have become in the post–World War II era. Similar charts for mixed economies abroad—Germany, Japan, Sweden, and France—would show same tameness of mid-century cycles. (Source: U.S. Census Bureau.)

formula, through the strongly growing components of NNP, we discover the business cycle in the twistings of the data above and below the trend line. If we measure the vertical deviations from the trend line and plot them on a separate diagram, we get a reasonably clear picture of the business cycle.[1] Let us take a look at it.

■ THE FOUR PHASES OF THE TRADITIONAL CYCLE

Early writers on the business cycle, possessing little quantitative information, tended to attach disproportionate attention to *panics* and *crises* such as the collapse of the South Sea Bubble in 1720, the panic of 1837, the Jay Cooke panic of 1873, the Cleveland panic of 1893, the "rich man's panic" of 1904, and, of course, the cataclysmic stock-market crash of "black Tuesday," October 29, 1929. Later writers soon began to speak of two phases of business: prosperity and depression, or boom and slump, with peaks and troughs marking the turning points in between.

Today, it is recognized that not every period of improving business need take us all the way to full employment. For example, throughout the decade of the 1930s there was a measure of recovery from the 1932–1933 trough levels, but we could by no means speak of the period as one of true prosperity. And from 1953 to 1965 unemployment never dropped to a 4 per cent plateau.

The cycle used to be broken up by many economists into four phases, the two most important ones being called the periods of "expansion" and "contraction or recession." The expansion phase comes to an end and goes into the recession phase at the upper turning point, or so-called "peak." Similarly, the recession phase gives way to that of expansion at the lower turning point, or so-called "trough." Thus, the four phases are supposed to keep repeating themselves as in the oversimplified picture shown in Fig. 14-3. Note that the emphasis here is not so much on *high* or *low* business activity as on the dynamic aspects of *rising* or *falling* business activity. (But do not forget the unemployment gap and the importance of growth trends.)

Each phase of the cycle passes into the next. Each is characterized by different economic conditions[2] and requires special explanatory principles. But let us continue with more facts before attempting analysis and theorizing.

How long have the traditional economic cycles been? This depends upon how many minor cycles you wish to count. Most observers have no trouble in agreeing on the major cycles, which were about 8 to 10 years in length. Everyone agrees that the late 1920s represent a period of prosperity and the early 1930s one of depression, and similarly with other past major business cycles. Not all economists, however, attach importance to the shorter minor cycles that are to be seen in economic charts. In 1924 and 1927, there were small dips in business activity. Shall we call the 1920s, therefore,

---

[1] The reader may be referred to any standard textbook on statistics for these technical procedures. However, cautious judgment must be exercised in using the mechanical tools of statistics. A beginner, carelessly "eliminating a trend," may throw out the baby along with the bath water if not careful, or at least distort the true appearance of the infant.

[2] For example, during expansion we find that employment, production, prices, money, wages, interest rates, and profits are usually rising, with the reverse true in recession.

three different (minor) cycles or one major prosperity period? In 1948–1949, 1953–1954, 1957–1958, and again in 1960–1961, we suffered mild recessions. Should these count as cycles?

In an elementary introduction of this type, it is perhaps best to stick primarily to major business cycles. For our purposes we may accept the summary that Harvard's illustrious Alvin Hansen gave to pre–World War II economic history:[3]

The business cycle, like the year, has its seasons:

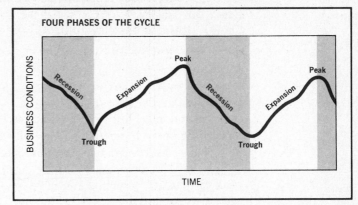

FIG. 14-3. Cyclical expansions follow recessions, with turning points in between. The National Bureau of Economic Research has dated these phases for America's history and for many other countries. Not every peak reaches "prosperity" in the sense of low unemployment. Nor does every threatened recession materialize.

> The American experience indicates that the major business cycle has had an average duration of a little over eight years. Thus, from 1795 to 1937 there were seventeen cycles of an average duration of 8.35 years. . . .
>
>   Since one to two minor peaks regularly occur between the major peaks, it is clear that the minor cycle is something less than half the duration of the major cycle. In the one hundred and thirty-year period 1807 to 1937 there were thirty-seven minor cycles with an average duration of 3.51 years.
>
>   . . . It appears that the building cycle averages somewhere between seventeen and eighteen years in length, or almost twice the length of the major business cycle. . . .
>
>   . . . American experience indicates that with a high degree of regularity every other major business boom coincides roughly with a boom in building construction, while the succeeding major cycle recovery is forced to buck up against a building slump . . . the depressions which have fallen in the interval of the construction downswing are typically deep and long. And the succeeding recovery is held back and retarded by the unfavorable depressional influence from the slump in the building industry.

The long swings in building construction and other series, which average anywhere between 15 and 25 years in length, are often called Kuznets cycles, being named for the scholar who first noticed them in 1930.[4] Work by A. F. Burns, S. Kuznets, M. Abramovitz, and other National Bureau scholars suggests that these pervasive swings have been associated with fluctuations in immigration and natural rates of popu-

---

[3] Alvin H. Hansen, *Fiscal Policy and Business Cycles* (Norton, New York, 1941), pp. 18–24.

[4] Kuznets cycles should not be confused with alleged very long waves, whose complete cycle length is about half a century. Thus, from the end of the Napoleonic Wars in 1815 to the middle of the nineteenth century, prices tended to fall and times tended to be unusually hard, on the average. After the Californian and Australian gold discoveries of around 1850, and as a partial result of the Civil and Crimean Wars, prices tended to rise. A new long cycle of falling prices followed the 1873 depression and lasted until the 1890s, when there was a great increase in gold production following the African and Alaskan gold discoveries. Whether these long waves are simply historical accidents due to chance gold discoveries, inventions, and political wars, it is still too soon to say. The interested reader may be referred to J. A. Schumpeter, *Business Cycles* (McGraw-Hill, New York, 1939), Chaps. 6 and 7, where long cycles are called "Kondratieffs."

lation growth, in railroad building and capital imports, and in the rate of growth of the money supply. Scholars have noted them abroad too. Kuznets cycles are of interest because they seem to involve three factors: variations in the supply trends of labor and other resources available to the economy; variations in productivity trends relating to the efficiency with which those supplies can be used; and, what is still provisional but important, variations in the average intensity with which resources get used—in other words, variations in rates of unemployment.

Was the notable sluggishness of the American economy in the last part of the 1950s a reflection of our passing through a less favorable phase of the Kuznets cycle? Or, as some then thought, was it a forerunner of some more ominous trend? Or merely the natural relaxation after a postwar sprint?

In any case, remember that fiscal and monetary policies can compensate for adverse phases of the Kuznets cycle—which modern man does not regard as one of those disasters, like earthquakes and volcanoes, which science can do nothing about.

■ A FIRST CLUE TO BUSINESS FLUCTUATIONS: CAPITAL FORMATION

Hansen's emphasis on construction gives us our first clue to the causation of the business cycle. Certain economic variables always show greater fluctuations than others in the business cycle. Thus, if we plot pig-iron production and cigarette consumption side by side, we hardly notice the business cycle in the latter. But in the pig-iron series there is little else to see but the business cycle. Why? Because cigarettes are nondurable consumers' goods, and in both good and bad times people are going to smoke the same amount. Pig iron, on the other hand, is one of the principal ingredients of capital and durable goods of all kinds: of plant equipment and durable machinery, of industrial and residential construction, and of automobiles, washing machines, and other durable consumers' goods.

> Check this by reexamining Fig. 14-2. Note how volatile are the top three investment series, in contrast to the last two series of retail sales and personal income. Note that production and profit fluctuations coincide with investment fluctuations.

By their nature, durable goods are subject to violently erratic patterns of demand. In bad times their new purchase can be indefinitely postponed; in a good year, everyone may suddenly decide to stock up on a 10-year supply of the services of durable goods.

> ■ Our first clue to the nature of the business cycle lies, then, in the fact that it is the durable- or capital-goods sector of the economy which shows by far the greatest cyclical fluctuations.

Their swings are wide compared with those of the economic time series which represent primarily consumption of services, of nondurables, and the *services of* durable goods. Except for a few short, choppy surface disturbances in such series, the latter tend to follow the general flow of income in a rather passive fashion. Ordinarily, consumption movements seem the effect rather than cause of the business cycle; in contrast, there is good reason to believe that the movements of durable goods represent key causes in a more fundamental sense.

■ HOW SAVING AND INVESTMENT SCHEDULES APPLY

It is comforting to find that statistical analysis supports the emphasis in previous chapters on the crucial importance of the capital investment process. The income-determination theories of the last chapter do indeed help in understanding economic history. Here are but a few reminders:

1. Wars have always been great disrupters of an economy. How do they transmit their economic effects? Plainly, they lead to great swings in the G component of the $C + I + G$ schedule, and this causes even greater swings in the over-all level of production and incomes. Inflationary gaps appear at full-employment NNP, leading to wartime price inflation.

2. In minor cycles of the postwar type, it is common for considerable fluctuations in the rate of inventory investment to occur. In the years of expansion, inventory accumulation is at a positive rate as merchants seek to rebuild their stocks and accommodate them to the growing level of sales. When merchants veer from a positive rate of inventory accumulation to a negative rate, the I component in the $C + I + G$ schedule goes down: then the production line is cut back, men are put on fewer average hours per week or are laid off, wages and profits fall, and all this gets registered in a multiplier drop in NNP or in its failure to grow along a normal trend.

3. When there are longer waves in railroad building and construction, the I component in the $C + I + G$ schedule causes the whole schedule and its equilibrium to go through slow swings of considerable amplitude.

4. While it is an oversimplification to say that the consumption schedule never shifts over time, S. Kuznets and R. Goldsmith have made National Bureau of Economic Research studies indicating the over-all stability of saving behavior relative to income over a long period. Their general finding is that, aside from short-term cycles, the percentage saved out of income has been remarkably the same over the last century.

The one situation in which we cannot regard consumption purely as a passive and predictable force comes in those times when consumer demand for autos and other durable goods fluctuates. (E.g., the record auto sales of 1962–1965 helped much to accelerate the long Kennedy-Johnson expansion of the 1960s.) Such *shifts* in the *CC* schedule also contribute to movements in the $C + I + G$ intersections, which, like any other shifts in autonomous factors, involve double-duty multiplier reactions.

■ A FEW THEORIES OF THE BUSINESS CYCLE

When it comes to explanations of why the income schedules shift, an industrious student could easily compile a list of separate theories of the business cycle that would run into the dozens.[5] Each theory seems to be quite different; but when we examine

[5] We may mention just a few of the better-known theories: (1) the *monetary* theory—attributes the cycle to the expansion and contraction of bank credit (Hawtrey, Friedman, et al.); (2) the *innovation* theory—attributes the cycle to the clustering of important inventions such as the railroad (Schumpeter, Hansen, et al.); (3) the *psychological* theory—treats the cycle as a case of people's infecting each other with pessimistic and optimistic expectations (Pigou, Bagehot, et al.); (4) the *underconsumption* theory—claims too much income goes to wealthy or thrifty people compared with what can be

them closely and throw out those which obviously contradict the facts or the rules of logic, or which just appear to be conveying an explanation when really they are not saying anything at all—when we do all this, we are left with relatively few different explanations. Most of them differ from each other only in emphasis.

One man believes the cycle to be primarily the result of fluctuations in total net investment, while another prefers to attribute the cycle to fluctuations in the rate of technological inventions and innovations, which act on business *through* net investment. A third man says that the root of the cycle is to be found in the fact that the creation of deposit money by our banking system causes investment spending to expand and contract so as to create boom and bust.

These sound like three different theories, and in most advanced textbooks they might be given the names of three different writers, but from our standpoint they are but three different aspects of the same saving-investment process. As we shall see, this does not mean there is perfect agreement among all theories of the cycle or that there are not some important differences in emphasis among different writers.

■ EXTERNAL AND INTERNAL FACTORS

To classify the different theories, we may first divide them into the two categories of primarily *external* and primarily *internal* theories.

■ **The external theories find the root of the business cycle in the fluctuations of something *outside* the economic system—in sunspot cycles, in wars, revolutions, and political events, in gold discoveries, in rates of growth of population and migrations, in discoveries of new lands and resources, and finally in scientific and technological discoveries and innovations.**

The internal theories look for mechanisms *within* the economic system itself which will give rise to self-generating business cycles, so that every expansion will breed recession and contraction, and every contraction will in turn breed revival and expansion, in a quasi-regular, repeating, never-ending chain.

If you believe in the sunspot theory of the business cycle—and no respectable economists today do—then the distinction between external and internal is rather easy to draw; although even here, when you come to explain how and why disturbances on the surface of the sun give rise to the business cycle, you begin to get involved in the internal nature of the economic system. But at least no one can seriously argue that the direction of causation is in doubt, or that the economic system causes the sunspots to fluctuate, instead of vice versa. However, when it comes to such other external factors as wars and politics, or even births and gold discoveries, there is always some doubt as to whether the economic system does not at least react back on the so-called

---

invested (Hobson, Sweezy, Foster and Catchings, et al.); (5) the *overinvestment* theory—claims too much rather than too little investment causes recessions (Hayek, Mises, et al.); (6) the *sunspot-weather-crop theories* (Jevons, H. L. Moore). The interested reader should consult G. Haberler, *Prosperity and Depression* (Harvard University Press, Cambridge, Mass., 1958, 4th ed.), or other business-cycle texts for further information.

"external" factors, thereby making the distinction between external and internal not such a hard and fast one. Still, no one will deny that any such "feedback" effects take us outside the traditional boundaries of economics, and this is our justification for distinguishing between external and internal theories.

■ PURELY INTERNAL THEORIES

As against the crude external sunspot theory, we may describe a simple example of a possible crude internal theory.

"ECHO" WAVES OF REPLACEMENT   If machinery and other durable goods all had the same length of life (say, 8 or 10 years), then we might try to explain a business cycle of the same length by this fact. If a boom got started—never mind how—then there would be a bunching of new capital goods all of the same age. A few years later, before these goods had worn out, there would be little need for replacement. This would cause a depression. But after 8 or 10 years all the capital equipment would suddenly wear out and would all have to be replaced, giving rise to an inflationary boom. This in turn would give rise to another complete cycle, with new echoing cycles of depression and boom every decade. Thus, as a result of self-generating "replacement waves," we might have a purely internal business-cycle theory.

Actually, not all equipment has the same length of life; and identical automobiles produced on the same day will certainly not all be replaced at the same time. Consequently, any bunching of equipment expenditures will tend over time to spread itself out, at most giving rise to weaker and weaker replacement peaks. Twenty-five years after the Civil War one might have noted a deficit of births because of that conflict; but another generation later and the dip would be hardly noticeable; and today it is just as if there had never been that particular violent disturbance of population. Replacement waves, therefore, are like the vibrations of a plucked violin string: they tend to dampen down and die away, unless there is a new disturbance.

PSYCHOLOGICAL SELF-GENERATING CYCLES   The laws of physics guarantee that friction will lessen any purely autonomous physical fluctuations. In social science, there is no law like the conservation of energy to prevent the creation of purchasing power. Therefore a much better example of a self-generating cycle than replacement waves would be the case where people became alternately optimistic and pessimistic, each stage leading as inevitably to the next as the manic stage of some people leads to the depressive stage. We cannot rule out such an internal theory. Nor can we be satisfied with it as it stands, for it says and explains little.

■ COMBINING EXTERNAL AND INTERNAL ELEMENTS

Everyone has observed how a window or a tuning fork may be activated into pronounced vibration when a certain note is sounded. Is this vibration externally or internally caused? The answer is, Both. The sounded note is certainly an external cause; but the window or tuning fork responds according to its own internal nature, coming into strong resonance, not with any sounded note, but only with one of a certain definite pitch. It takes the right kind of trumpets to bring down the walls of Jericho.

Similarly, we may look upon business cycles as not unlike a toy rocking horse that is subjected to occasional outside pushes. The pushes need not be regular; great technical innovations never are. But just as the wooden horse rocks with frequency and amplitude that depend partly on its internal nature (size and weight), so too will the economic system respond to fluctuations in external factors according to its *internal* nature. Both external and internal factors are important in explaining cycles.

SYNTHESIS Most economists today believe in a combination of external and internal theories. In explaining the major cycles, they place crucial emphasis on fluctuations in *investment* or *capital* goods. Primary causes of these capricious and volatile investment fluctuations are found in such external factors as (1) technological innovation and (2) dynamic growth of population and of territory. With these external factors, we must combine the internal factors that cause any initial change in investment to be amplified in a cumulative, multiplied fashion—as people who are given work in the capital-goods industries respend part of their new income on consumption goods and as an air of optimism begins to pervade the business community, causing firms to go to the banks and the securities market for new credit accommodation.[6]

Also, it is necessary to point out that the general business situation definitely reacts in turn on investment. If high consumption sales make businessmen optimistic, they are more likely to embark upon venturesome investment programs. Inventions or scientific discoveries may occur independently of the business cycle, but their appreciable economic introduction will most certainly depend on business conditions. When NNP moved to a new postwar plateau some 50 per cent higher than prewar, it was reasonable to expect that a considerable volume of capital formation (new machines, added inventories, construction) would be induced. Therefore, especially in the short run, investment is in part an *effect* as well as a cause of income movements.

In the longer run, no matter how high a plateau of income is maintained, the stock of capital goods will become adjusted at a higher level and new net investment will drop off to zero unless there is (1) a growth of income, (2) a continuing improvement of technology, or (3) a never-ending reduction in interest rates.

The first of these processes, showing how investment demand may be induced by *growth* of sales and income, has been given a rather high-sounding name—the "acceleration principle." Almost all writers bring it in as one strand in their final business-cycle theories. Let us examine how this internal cyclical mechanism works itself out and interacts with other factors.

---

[6]With two dice you can manufacture something that looks a little like a business cycle. Record the results of successive tosses—as in the number sequence 7, 4, 10, 3, 7, 11, 7, 2, . . . Then take five-period moving averages—such as the successive numbers $(7 + 4 + 10 + 3 + 7)/5 = 6\frac{1}{5}$, $(4 + 10 + 3 + 7 + 11)/5 = 7$, . . . etc. A plot of these will look not too different from NNP or price fluctuations! Explanation: The random numbers are like exogenous investment shocks; the moving average is like the economic system's (or the wooden horse's) internal smoothing reactions of $C + I + G$ type.

The acceleration principle shows how variations in a system's growth rate will induce variations in its level of investment:

TIME	YEARLY SALES	STOCK OF CAPITAL	NET INVESTMENT *NI*	GROSS INVESTMENT *GI* (*NI* + REPLACEMENT)
First phase				
First year	$ 6	$ 60	$ 0	1 machine at $3 = $3
Second year	6	60	0	1 machine at $3 = $3
Third year	6	60	0	1 machine at $3 = $3
Second phase				
Fourth year	$ 9	$ 90	$30	(1 + 10) machines at $3 = $33
Fifth year	12	120	30	(1 + 10) machines at $3 = $33
Sixth year	15	150	30	(1 + 10) machines at $3 = $33
Third phase				
Seventh year	$15	$150	$ 0	1 machine at $3 = $3
Fourth phase (to be filled in by reader)				
Eighth year	$14.7	$____	− $ 3	____ machines at $3 = $____

TABLE 14-1. ILLUSTRATION OF THE ACCELERATION PRINCIPLE (in millions of dollars).

■ THE ACCELERATION PRINCIPLE

According to this law, society's needed stock of capital, whether inventory or equipment, depends primarily upon the level of income or production. Additions to the stock of capital, or what we customarily call *net* investment, will take place only when income is growing. As a result, a prosperity period may come to an end, not simply because consumption sales have gone down, but merely because sales have *leveled off* at a high level (or have continued to grow, but at a lower rate than previously).

A simplified arithmetical example will make this clear. Imagine a typical textile-manufacturing firm whose stock of capital equipment is always kept equal to about ten times the value of its yearly sales of cloth.[7] Thus, when its sales have remained at 6 million dollars per year for some time, its balance sheet will show 60 million dollars of capital equipment, consisting of perhaps 20 machines of different ages, with one wearing out each year and being replaced. Because replacement just balances depreciation, there is no *net* investment or saving being done by the corporation. *Gross* investment takes place at the rate of 3 million dollars per year, representing the yearly replacement of 1 machine. (The other 3 million dollars of sales may be assumed to be wages and dividends.) The first phase of Table 14-1 shows this.

Now let us suppose that, in the fourth year, sales rise 50 per cent—from 6 to 9 million dollars. Then the number of machines must also rise 50 per cent, or from 20 to 30 machines. In the fourth year, 11 machines must be bought—10 new ones in addition to the replacement of the worn-out one.

[7] To keep the discussion simple, we use the exaggerated ratio 10:1 and ignore changes in interest rates or degree of utilization of capacity. The reader can include inventory change and plant change along with equipment change in the analysis.

Sales rose 50 per cent. How much has machine production gone up? From 1 machine to 11; or by 1,000 per cent! This *accelerated* effect of a change in consumption or other final items on investment levels gives the acceleration principle its name.

If sales continue to rise in both the fifth and the sixth years by 3 million dollars, then we shall continue to have 11 new machines ordered every year.

So far, the acceleration principle has given us no trouble. On the contrary, it has given us a tremendous increase in investment spending as a result of a moderate increase in consumption sales. But now we are riding a tiger.

■ **According to the acceleration principle, consumption has to continue to keep increasing in order for investment to stand still!**

If consumption should stop growing at so rapid a rate—if it should level off in the seventh year even at the high level of 15 million dollars per year—then net investment will fall away to zero, and gross investment will, for many years, fall back to 1 machine (see Table 14-1). In other words, a drop of zero per cent in sales has resulted in a 90 per cent drop in gross investment and a 100 per cent drop in net investment. (See the third phase of Table 14-1, and fill in the fourth phase with 0 and $147 at appropriate spots.)

The acceleration principle can work in both directions. Should sales now drop below 15 million dollars, gross investment would drop away to nothing for a long time; in fact, the firm would want to disinvest by selling some of its used machinery.

It is clear that a depression can set in just because sales have stopped growing so rapidly, even if not dropping off absolutely but only leveling off at a high rate.

■ INTERACTIONS OF ACCELERATOR AND MULTIPLIER

Needless to say, the curtailment of production in the machine-producing industries will curtail income and spending on food and clothing and will lead to still further "multiplier" changes in spending. This might ultimately cause textile sales to stop growing altogether, or even to decline. This in turn will cause a further accelerated drop in net investment.

■ **Thus, we may be in a vicious circle where the acceleration principle and the multiplier interact to produce a cumulative deflationary (or inflationary) spiral.**

Our example used machines. Does that mean the acceleration principle is not involved in the inventory "recessions" (such as 1920–1921, 1937–1938, 1948–1949, 1953–1954, 1957–1958, 1960–1961)? Not at all. The same principle—that stocks of capital goods tend to be held in some proportion to sales per unit time—is valuable to help explain short inventory cycles.

This analysis can also explain how a downturn can result from the previous expansion itself. Suppose, in a situation of unemployment, we get income growing again. The rising income induces, via the accelerator, new investment. The new investment induces, via the multiplier, further rises in income. Hence, the rate of growth of output may be "self-warranting."

know little more about a one- or five-dollar bill than that it is inscribed with the picture of an American statesman, bears the signature of one or another government
official, and—most important of all—that each has a numeral showing its face value.

Examine a ten-dollar bill or some other paper bill. You probably find it says "Federal Reserve Note."[4] Also, it announces itself as "legal tender for all debts, public and
private," and contains the further, and nonsensical, statement that it "is redeemable
in *lawful money* at the United States Treasury or at any Federal Reserve Bank." Why
italicize "lawful money"? Because there is no such thing other than "legal tender" bills
under discussion, namely, Federal Reserve notes and so forth. In short, your old wrinkled
ten-dollar bill is redeemable into a crisp new bill, into two fives, or into ten ones if
you prefer! But that is all.[5]

■ Today, all American currency and coin is essentially "fiat" money. It is money
because the government decrees it is money, and because we all accept it. Metal-
lic backing has no real meaning anymore (except, as will be seen later, when it
serves to limit the total supply of fiat money).

Before 1933, it was not uncommon for good little boys and girls to be presented
on their birthdays with five- or ten-dollar gold pieces; and gold certificates were often
seen in circulation. These certificates were warehouse receipts promising the bearer
redemption in gold upon application to the United States Treasury. But in 1933, when
Congress raised the buying price of gold from about $21 to $35 an ounce, all gold—
except that tied up in wedding rings and dental fillings—was called in. This was done
so that holders or hoarders of gold could not make a 67 per cent profit as a result of the
devaluation of the dollar. At the same time, all gold certificates were called in. Congress
ruled that these certificates were not to be exchanged for gold upon being called in,
but simply for ordinary paper dollars. A few absent-minded people still have not turned

---

[4] Some one-dollar bills bear the words "Silver Certificate." Anyone who knows much about American
politics and history realizes that some paper currency is called "silver" certificates only because a few
Western senators from mining states could persuade Congress to give silver mining a continuing
subsidy by buying up quantities of silver for monetary use. Otherwise, silver has absolutely no *monetary*
significance; many countries are abandoning it even for small coins, and it is finally losing its hold on
the Orient. In 1963 silver for teeth, electronics, and photography rose in price to approach the point
where melting dollars and turning in bills for metal became profitable. So Congress dropped the farce
of requiring part of our money to take the form of silver certificates. Presumably these will one day
become as obsolete as the buffalo and spittoon.

Two-dollar bills, long considered to be bad luck, were so-called "United States Notes"—rem-
nants of the greenbacks used to finance the Civil War. After 1966 they ceased to be issued. Some
five-dollar bills are also United States Notes. Occasionally you may run into a bill that says "Federal
Reserve Bank Note" or even a "National Bank Note" containing the name of some nearby national
bank; these too are being gradually retired from circulation.

[5] A Cleveland businessman wrote to the Treasury asking for some "lawful money" in return for a
ten-dollar bill. He received two polite letters, but no satisfaction. Actually, since 1934 the old distinction between "legal tender" and other money has ceased to have meaning. Since then, if you
bring a thousand dollars' worth of pennies in to settle a tax bill or contract, they are as legally acceptable as anything else; earlier a creditor could have insisted on certain currency specified as "legal
tender."

in their gold certificates, but once these are brought to a bank, they will be retired from circulation forever and replaced by other bills.[6] In 1960 President Eisenhower prohibited the holding of gold by American citizens even abroad.

From the standpoint of understanding the nature of money, it is perhaps simpler that gold certificates and coins no longer exist. The modern student need not be mis-led, as were earlier generations of students, by some mystical belief that "gold backing" is what gives money its value. Certainly gold, as such, has little to do with the problem. Every expert knows that the popular conception "money has more value if it is ex-changeable into gold" exactly reverses the true relation. If it were not that gold has some monetary uses, gold's value as a metal would be much less than it is today. We should have cheaper inlays and wedding rings, and South African and Russian miners would be poorer.[7]

The sensible reason why a staunch conservative today wants to go back to gold-coin money is not that he thinks gold is needed to give money its value. Rather, he knows that governmental actions can today strongly affect the value of money, and he is convinced that *governments cannot be trusted to refrain from abusing this power;* so he favors taking away from the Congress, the Executive, and the Federal Reserve System their power in these matters and prefers to put his trust in the vicissitudes of mine discoveries rather than in fallible or allegedly corrupt representative governments.

As we shall see in subsequent chapters and in the international discussions of Part Five, gold still does have a limited influence on how big our total money supply can be. Herein lies its true role in twentieth-century economics.

> ■ **Limitation in the supply of money is the necessary condition if it is to have value. If currency is so unlimited in amount as to become practically a free good, people would have so much of it to spend as to bid up all prices, wages, and income sky high. That is why constitutional powers over money and banking are never given to private groups but are always vested in government.**

■ WHY CHECKABLE DEMAND DEPOSITS ARE CONSIDERED TO BE MONEY

There is also a third category of what economists call money. This involves so-called "demand deposits"—made up of bank deposits subject to checking on demand.

If I have $1,000 in my checking account at the Cambridge Trust Company, that deposit can be regarded as money. Why? Because I can pay for purchases with checks

---

[6] The courts also upheld a statute that invalidated contracts calling for payment in gold; only payment in terms of dollars was permitted. Otherwise, creditors would have made a 67 per cent profit on the revaluation and debtors would have lost 67 per cent. As we shall see in Chapter 17, the 12 Federal Reserve Banks still hold gold certificates of a special type.

[7] That gold affects prices only through its ability to *limit or to expand the volume of paper money and total spending* was overlooked by foolish European chancellors of the exchequer who, after World War I, tried to stop inflation by *accumulating* new gold reserves through the purchase of gold on the open market with newly *printed* money! Of course, the effect was just the opposite. Only after they had reversed the process and used their gold to buy up and burn outstanding paper money did they enjoy any success.

drawn on it. The deposit is like any other medium of exchange, and, being payable on demand, it serves as a "standard of value," or "unit of account," in the same sense that $1,000 worth of quarters do; i.e., both the deposit and the quarters are convertible into standard money or cash at fixed terms, dollar for dollar and penny for penny.

■ **Possessing the essential properties of money, bank demand deposits might just as well be counted as money. And they are.[8]**

Actually, as was noted in the discussion of money in Chapter 3, bank money is quantitatively more important than currency because most transactions are made by check. The convenience of checks for mailing, for paying the exact sum of money due, for providing a receipt in the form of the canceled check voucher, for protecting against loss when stolen or misplaced (while unendorsed or, for that matter, endorsed)—all these advantages are obvious and explain the widespread use of bank money.

Table 15-1, on the next page, illustrates the quantitative importance of the three components of money: coin, currency, and demand deposits. The total of these is called M_1, money as narrowly-defined.

■ TIME DEPOSITS, LIQUID ASSETS, AND OTHER NEAR-MONEY

Along with the total of money narrowly-defined, M_1, Table 15-1 also shows the total of money broadly-defined, M_2. Included in this broader definition of money are all kinds of saving and time deposits, whether in commercial banks, mutual savings banks, saving and loan associations, credit unions, etc. Although you cannot write checks on such time deposits, you can usually cash them in on short notice.

Suppose you have $10,000 on demand deposit and your brother has $5,000 on time deposit and $5,000 on demand deposit, will your saving and consumption schedules be very different ones? At equal incomes, is he likely to save a much larger percentage than you? Perhaps not; and that is why M_2 is important. Time or savings deposits—in commercial banks, mutual savings banks, and federal savings and loan associations—have gained mightily on demand deposits in recent years.

Because it is difficult to draw a hard and fast line at any point in the chain of things that do have a direct bearing on spending, the exact definition of M, the money supply, is partly a matter of taste rather than scientific necessity.

A century ago, demand deposits would not have been included in M. Today economists would include demand deposits, since even the most stubborn adherent of the old narrow concept has to admit that the existence of checking accounts does economize on the use of currency and thus acts much like an increase in the effective amount of currency. And a growing number of economists would argue along the same lines for inclusion of interest-bearing savings deposits in the measurement of the money supply.[9]

---

[8] My balance on deposit in the bank is usually called money—not the checks I write.

[9] Some scholars have even attempted to include government bonds in money, rather than give them zero weight and exclude them; such writers prefer to give them some fractional weight and add them into a total called "effective" money supply, M_3.

Demand deposits form three-fourths of our total money supply:

KINDS OF MONEY	MARCH, 1939	MARCH, 1946	MARCH, 1960	MARCH, 1966
Coin	$ 0.6	$ 1.3	$ 2.3	$ 4.2
Paper currency (outside of banks):				
Federal Reserve notes	4.3	23.9	26.8	36.3
Silver certificates and				
U.S. notes	1.6	2.3	2.4	0.9
Other currency (largely in				
process of being retired)	0.3	0.6	0.2	0.1
	6.2	26.8	29.4	37.3
Bank money:				
Demand deposits of all banks				
(adjusted to exclude government				
deposits, etc.)	26.1	76.2	108.8	130.3
Total M_1	$32.9	$104.3	$140.5	$171.8
Time and saving deposits (includes				
mutual savings banks, postal				
savings, savings and loan agencies,				
certificates of deposit)	30.0	59.1	158.2	316.3
Total M_2	$62.9	$163.4	$298.7	$488.1
U.S. government bonds held by				
individuals and business				
(excluding banks, insurance				
companies, etc.)	12.0	83.2	84.3	90.3
Total "near-money" and money	$74.9	$246.6	$383.0	$578.4

TABLE 15-1. MONEY SUPPLY OF UNITED STATES AND "NEAR-MONEY" IN BILLIONS. If to coin, currency, and demand deposits, we also add time and saving deposits, we get a broader and more rapidly growing concept of money—often called M_2 in contrast to M_1. (Source: *Federal Reserve Bulletin.*)

Economists are not all agreed on nomenclature in this field. Many would go so far as to append to M_1 and M_2 a category of liquid-wealth items called "near-money."[10] At the least, they would include in near-money the total of government bonds which anyone could present for redemption or sell for cash in the open market (albeit not at a stable price predictable long in advance). These near-money items have many of the properties of money. True, you do not pay your monthly expenses directly with government bonds, and so we hesitate to call such an item "money." Still, the fact that you have such an easily cashable asset means that your current spending habits are probably affected in much the same way as they would be if you owned a larger bank deposit instead of the government bonds.

Table 15-1 shows that all the different kinds of money are many times as great

[10] It would not be illogical to subtract out from people's liquid assets their current liabilities (charge accounts, installment loans, etc.). Along with income, perhaps their resulting "net worth" would be the single most important determinant of their spending.

now as before World War II. For the most part, this book will follow the most common practice and define the total money supply thus:

■ *M* is the sum of coin and currency in circulation outside the banks, plus checkable demand deposits (after various routine adjustments have been made in this magnitude). Along with this narrow definition of *M* (which we may call M_1), it is sometimes useful to work with a broader definition (called M_2), which includes time and saving deposits in addition to coin, currency, and demand deposits.

See Fig. 15-2 for the more rapid growth of the broad measure M_2 in recent years.

Consumer prices show a rising long-term trend:

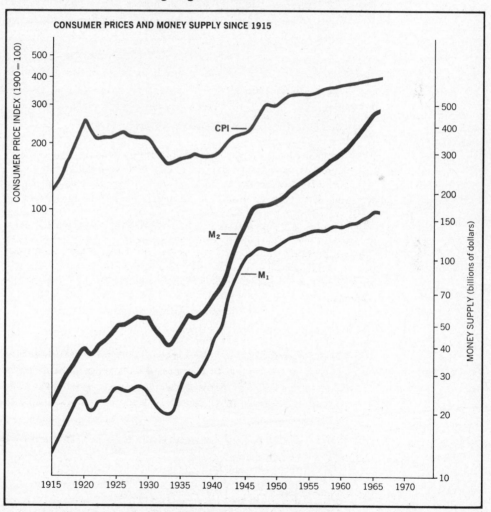

FIG. 15-2. Both prices and the money supply show generally similar movements. But money supply has grown faster than prices because of rise in real output. (Sources: U.S. Department of Commerce, *Federal Reserve Bulletin*, and Milton Friedman and Anna J. Schwartz, *A Monetary History of the United States, 1867–1960*, Princeton University Press, 1963.)

■ THE DEMAND FOR MONEY

What are the functions of money? Here are some old ones from Chapter 3 and some new ones:

1. Money is a *medium of exchange* enabling us to transact our national income and product without recourse to hopelessly inefficient barter.

2. Money is the *unit of account* in which we express prices for current transactions, and also for future or deferred transactions (such as when I borrow $1,000 today and agree to pay back $1,200 three years from now).

3. Money is a safe *way of holding* at least part of one's *wealth*—safe against the ups and downs inherent in stocks, land, homes, and bonds. When all these are going down in price, the canny hoarder of money is the most successful speculator in the community. (When prices rise, however, many money holders suffer.)

4. Money holding is a necessary *precaution* against having a sudden expense occur or an unexpected delay in a receipt due from someone else. Similarly, it enables one to take advantage of a bargain in goods or in securities that might suddenly come up.

All these functions are worth paying for. And we each do incur a cost in holding a coin, a bill, or a demand deposit—namely, the *sacrificed interest and profit yield* that might be obtained from purchase of earning assets.

> General Electric works just as hard to keep down its unnecessary cash as it does to keep down its unnecessary steel inventory and wastage. The business manager of a famous cartoonist was aghast to find that he had kept $120,000 idle in a demand deposit, earning no interest for years, and all merely because he never read his mail!

It is clear from the above that there are two main motives for holding money: (1) for the convenience of ordinary *transactions* needed at each level of income, and (2) to fill a prudent *precautionary* need arising from the uncertainties of safety and return from other forms of wealth, and the uncertainties of timing of expense outpayments and receipt inpayments.

At the turn of the century Alfred Marshall in Cambridge, England, and Irving Fisher in Yale summarized the factors involved in the demand for money thus:

> ■ *Demand for money.* The higher their annual incomes, the more dollars of business people will want to transact: with various allowances for economies of scale, men hold M at any time about in proportion to their *income* rate per year or month. This *transaction demand* for money will be a little lower when the interest rates offered on good bonds, savings deposits, and other close money substitutes rise above the 1 or 2 per cent level; but once people are holding minimal balances at each income level for transactions, the demand for such transaction M becomes rather inelastic to interest-rate changes.
>
> Men also hold M as a precautionary store of wealth, not wanting to put all their eggs in the basket of risky assets and wanting to be prepared for bargains or sudden expenses. This *precautionary* (or "asset") *demand* for money will be much affected by factors other than income: total wealth; level of sacrificed interest and profit yields; optimism, pessimism, and plain uncertainty about the future; expected changes in prices of goods and assets and expected changes in interest rates, all the speculative elements that any investments depend on.

The elements in the second paragraph of this summary are in Marshall and Fisher, but were not much emphasized until the 1930s, when Keynes and practical bankers noted that transaction demand could not account for massive changes in cash holdings. The pre-1930 discussions emphasized the M-and-income link by using the concept of "velocity of circulation of money," and to this we now turn.

■ VELOCITY OF CIRCULATION OF MONEY

It is historical fact that as dollar NNP has grown, so has M. With M now six times as large as before World War II, dollar NNP is even more than six times as large as its earlier figure. Nor is this merely history. If NNP grows from its present level of almost a trillion dollars to reach two trillion dollars a quarter of a century from now, the betting odds are that M will be nearly double its present amount then—a fair bet even before we know whether changes in M will be "cause" of changes in NNP or "effect."

Why should there be any connection? M is a stock magnitude, something you can measure at an instant of time like any other balance-sheet asset. NNP is a flow of dollar income *per year*, something that you can measure only from income statements that refer to the passage of time between two dates.

A new concept can be introduced to describe the Fisher-Marshall ratios between two such different magnitudes: it is called the "velocity of circulation of money" per year and is written as V.

■ *Definition of velocity:* The rate at which the stock of money is turning over per year to consummate income transactions is called the velocity of circulation of money (or more exactly, the *income* velocity). If the stock of money is turning over very slowly, so that its rate of dollar income spending per year is low, V will be low. If people hold less money at each instant of time relative to the rate of NNP flow (price of apples × apples + price of oranges × oranges + ⋯), then V will be high. The size of V can change over time with changes in financial institutions, habits, attitudes, expectations, and relative distributions of M among different kinds of institutions and income classes; but these changes in V need not be abrupt, volatile, or completely unpredictable. By careful integration with behavioral schedules of investment and saving (or $C + I + G$), modern economists can give appropriate weight to the relationships between money and other stock variables, on the one hand, and various employment, production, and income flows, on the other.

In every case, this formal definition of the velocity of circulation of money holds:

$$V \equiv \frac{\text{NNP}}{M} \equiv \frac{p_1 q_1 + p_2 q_2 + \cdots}{M} \equiv \frac{\text{sum } pq}{M} \equiv \frac{PQ}{M}$$

with the understanding that there can be choice of which aggregate measure of income (NNP, GNP, NI, . . .) one uses to define a particular income velocity. Here P stands for the average price level and goes up and down with an index of the price level, while Q stands for real (as distinct from current dollar) national product and has to be computed statistically by the mentioned process of "deflating" NNP with a price index.

Here is a helpful example. Table 15-1 shows that M in early 1966 was about 172 billion dollars. NNP and GNP were then at annual rates of about 670 and 730 billion dollars per annum. So 670 per year divided by 172 gives us an income velocity of about 3.9 per year. This expression means that each unit of money was used for NNP transactions four times a year; or putting this in an equivalent way, at any one time during the year people in the economy were holding money that amounted to 3 months' average income.[11]

■ THE QUANTITY EQUATION OF EXCHANGE: AN IDENTITY

After economists have invented the concept of velocity of circulation of money, they can rearrange its formal definition to get a new identity called the "quantity equation of exchange":

$$MV \equiv PQ$$

This comes merely from shifting M from the denominator of our last definition's right-hand side over to the numerator of the other side. By definition of V, the left-hand side in this new equation is equal to NNP, the rate of current national income or product per year. But the right-hand side, by virtue of what we have already defined P and Q to be, also is definitionally the same thing as NNP.

> EXAMPLE: If there were only a single good in the NNP, a billion baskets of bread selling at a price of $5 each, then $\text{NNP} \equiv PQ = 5$ billion dollars per year; when there is more than one commodity, we sum all such $p \times q$ products; and if all their q's stayed unchanged and all their p's doubled, then the average price level as denoted by P would double, naturally giving us a 10- rather than 5-billion-dollar NNP.[12]

All the definitional equations have been written with the three-bar identity symbol rather than with the more common two-bar equality symbol. This is to drive home the fact that they are what logicians call a "tautology"—statements which by themselves tell us nothing about reality but which would hold true by definition even if the United States reverted to barter, or if its M halved while its NNP grew tenfold. Although it is important to remember that the equation of exchange is such a tautology, it is not legitimate to infer from this fact that it must thereby be useless. It may, or may not, be a useful way of separating out for individual analysis the factors apt to lead to empirical relations which do best describe actual economic life. Subsequent chapters will show that careful description of income determination by $C + I + G$ schedules and how they are interrelated by changes in banking policy can also be expressed in terms of the magnitudes in the equation of exchange, and vice versa.

[11] Economists sometimes calculate V for *all* transactions including transfers, intermediate goods, and everything. From recent statistics of bank checking transactions (or debits), one finds that urban bank deposits outside of New York City turn over some 32 times a year, and New York City deposits turn over some 85 times a year. Plainly, such velocity figures are much greater than income velocity. (Problem: verify GNP V to be 4.2 per year, above.)

[12] Some find the following "explanation" of this necessary equality helpful. Every income transaction involves sale receipts equal to $p \times q$, which leads to the PQ totals on the right. But it is M that is used in such transactions. How much in a year? The stock M times its average velocity per year. Thus, value equals value, and the two sides must be the same.

■ THE QUANTITY THEORY OF MONEY AND PRICES: A HYPOTHESIS

THE CRUDE QUANTITY THEORY   If 1967 M is six times 1939 M, then an adherent of what can be called the "crude quantity theory of money and prices" would have to predict that the 1967 price level P should be almost exactly six times 1939 P. The fact that prices have only doubled in that period would be a refutation of this crude notion that the price level moves in direct proportion to the money supply. Arithmetically, the crude quantity theory might be written as $P = kM$, where k is a positive proportionality constant that depends on units used; thus, if P and M are measured by index numbers which were 100 in the same base year, k could be replaced by 1.0 or omitted. Note that this is not intended to be an irrefutable definitional identity, but rather a useful empirical relationship about k's constancy.

The idea behind the crude quantity theory is simple. If the government effects a thousandfold increase in M, then one can predict that there will be a galloping inflation in which P rises a thousandfold. Crude as this notion is, there is some usefulness to it. Thus when the head of the German central bank denied that its printing truckloads of currency had anything to do with the 1921–1923 trillionfold increase in prices, his statement was nonsensical. If he had said, "I am just a civil servant, forced, by the clamor of the populace in a defeated nation with grave external and internal disorganization, to take part in an upward race between P and M"—if he had said this, we could feel sorry for him. But who can seriously deny the elementary fact that a vastly larger bidding of German marks for a limited supply of goods had to send prices expressed in marks skyward?

■ Rudimentary as it is, then, the crude quantity theory linking P directly to M is useful to describe periods of hyperinflation and various long-term trends in prices, such as those in Spain and Europe after New World gold was discovered.

Since galloping inflation can put an intolerable strain on a democratic society, it is well to preach the crude quantity theory in season and out of season—not because in its crudest form it is in season very often, but because it is so urgently needed in those disorganized times when its message is in season.

A SOPHISTICATED QUANTITY THEORY   Few people still subscribe to the crude quantity theory. But we should not use its inadequacies to damn the whole idea that money can have important effects on macroeconomic magnitudes such as investment, employment, production, and prices.

The next few chapters will show how *monetary policy* does have an important influence on the *total of spending*. That analysis can be translated quite easily into the language of V and M, even though it was not fashionable to do so a couple of decades back. Since there has been something of a revival of interest in the quantity theory by a number of competent American economists in recent years, it is worth taking an eclectic approach here and reviewing the fundaments of a sophisticated quantity-theory approach, leaving until later a more extensive reconciliation of the various approaches.

The proof of the pudding is in the eating, and the test of all theories is their correspondence with the facts. Figure 15-2 shows that consumer prices and the supply of money have both generally grown, but by no means in perfect concordance.

Economists such as Chicago's Milton Friedman are not surprised to find M growing sixfold while P merely doubles; for they believe that only in time periods when real output remains roughly the same—say, at a high-employment level—can one expect M and P to be directly related. It is not so much M and P as M and NNP (or PQ) that they expect to be related. This belief is based upon the hypothesis that the velocity of circulation V can be predicted to be reasonably constant, or if not constant, at least subject to predictable changes.

■ While it is a fact that NNP has climbed somewhat faster than M since 1939, this rise in velocity has been a gradual one and perhaps one that might have been expected from the fact that 1939 was still a depressed year and still a time of very low interest rates and abnormally low V. Historically, one observes that V has exhibited a downward trend in the long run, moving down somewhat as real income has grown. The short-run cyclical swings in V are quite the opposite: when production and interest rates have gone up, V has tended also to have a short-run rise; when output has fallen in the short run, V has fallen too.

A sophisticated quantity theorist cannot be accused of believing that V is a fundamental constant of nature. What he does believe is that controlling the behavior of M will help much to control NNP, for the reason that the resulting changes in V will either be so small or so predictable as to make one confident that dollar NNP will still move in the same direction as M. Qualitatively, this is in agreement with almost any modern theory of income determination, and the only possible argument concerns the confidence with which one can predict the quantitative potency of effects on NNP of changes in M.[13]

So, from every point of view, the discussions in the ensuing chapters—how commercial banks can create demand-deposit M as the Federal Reserve Board affects

[13]There is general agreement, too, that whenever the dollar NNP gets pushed too high, there will be a strong tendency for P to rise. Where there is not so much agreement is on the degree to which inflexibilities in our mixed economy can keep wages and prices up in slack times; if so, *employment* and *production* will drop with the total of dollar NNP rather than having the drop in dollar NNP simply transmit its effects to lower wages and lower prices. And as we shall see, there is still controversy concerning the importance of a *cost-push* mechanism making for a price creep, as against inflationary effects of *excess dollar demand* alone. Later we shall attempt to appraise the measure of truth in both views. [It may be mentioned here that the *crude* quantity theory would be correct, if in the following rearrangement of the tautological equation of exchange $P \equiv (V/Q)M$, the expression in parentheses were a strict constant. Thus, if both V and Q changed little, or if their changes were always largely self-canceling, the crude theory would be correct. But once scholars agree that V may change appreciably when the economy goes from a 1929 high-interest prosperity to a 1939 low-interest depression, and that Q may fall from a full-employment 1929 level to a level that is far below full employment in some later year, they realize that a more sophisticated theory of money, production, interest rates, and prices must be studied. A rather crude form of rejection of the significance of M was provided by the Radcliffe Committee Report published in 1959 by the British government. After arguing (correctly) that PQ is affected by over-all "liquidity" and bears no simple proportionality to M, they incorrectly inferred that induced changes in V are as likely as not to offset fully contrived changes in M. The presumption in *all* modern theories is that a continued rise in M *will* definitely tend to expand PQ. Radcliffe's *non-sequitur*: "Money alone matters" is false; ergo "money doesn't matter."]

their reserve positions, how a central bank such as the Federal Reserve itself operates, how monetary policy fits with income determination and with stabilizing fiscal policies—are of tremendous importance.

SUMMARY

A. PRICES

1 ■

It is unrealistic to expect that expansions in investment and other spending will have effects solely on employment and output. Changes in price levels must be expected as well. The effects and causes of a general rise in prices and wages (i.e., inflation) and a general fall in prices (i.e., deflation) are vital.

2 ■

Historically, prices have shown their greatest swings in times of war. But in this century the trend in prices seems to have been more of a one-way climb: the absence of a drop in prices after World War II is perhaps a sign that modern mixed economies are no longer likely to tolerate lengthy periods of unemployment, soft business conditions, and falling prices.

3 ■

Inflations and deflations are never of the balanced type in which all prices and wages move in the same percentage relation, with no one helped and no one hurt by the process. Inflations typically favor debtors, profit seekers, and risk-taking speculators. Unforeseen inflation hurts creditors, fixed-income classes, pensioners, and conservative and timid investors. The old rather than the young are its prime victims.

4 ■

Aside from redistributional effects of inflation out of a fixed level of production, mild inflations like those found throughout most of capitalism's history have been regarded as being a little more likely to keep employment high and business brisk than mild deflations do. But the cause of the inflation may make a difference, and the threat that a mild creep of prices could break into a trot or gallop shows that complacency about price rises could be harmful.

    If the processes were *foreseen* and steady, there would not be much difference between three possible long-term patterns that various economists favor: (1) steady prices, with money and real wages rising with productivity; (2) gently rising prices, with money wages rising even faster than real wages and productivity; (3) slowly falling prices, with money wages constant and real wages rising as every consumer's dollar buys more and more goods—a pattern perhaps not feasible in rigid mixed economies.

B. THE MONEY SUPPLY AND ITS VELOCITY OF CIRCULATION

5 ■

In addition to coins, currency, and demand deposits—whose sum is the money supply M—there are also very important other liquid-asset items: time or savings deposits (which pay interest and are *de facto* withdrawable at short notice, and which many economists include in a broad definition of money, M_2), "near-money" such as government bonds (which anyone can quickly liquidate into cash, at a price that depends on market forces at the time). However defined, M has increased mightily over the decades.

6 ■

The demand for money consists of a *transactions* demand importantly related to income, and a *precautionary* (or asset) demand much dependent on interest and profit rates, (and on wealth, volatile expectations, risk aversion, and speculative price expectations).

7 ■

The (income) velocity of circulation of money is defined as the ratio of dollar NNP flow to the stock of M. While V is definitely not a constant, its movements are subject to some regularity and predictability; and from its

$$V \equiv \frac{NNP}{M} \equiv \frac{PQ}{M}$$

definition comes the quantity-theory-of-exchange *identity*

$$MV \equiv PQ$$

8 ■

The crude quantity theory of money and prices regarded P as almost strictly proportional to M. Useful as this view is in hyperinflation and for certain long-term trends, few would today uphold it in this crude form. It is generally agreed that action by the government and banks to affect the supply of money, its availability to investor borrowers, and the interest cost of such borrowings can have important effects on the total of *consumption* + *investment* + *government* spending, and thus on prices and wage levels. Subscribers to a sophisticated quantity theory and national-income theorists will all attach importance to the next chapters on banking and fiscal policy.

QUESTIONS FOR DISCUSSION

1. If sure of inflation ahead, what might you do to protect yourself? List some of the happenings that accompany galloping and mild inflation.

2. Explain what is meant by "near-money" and how it got its name.

3. If we printed and spent 100 billion dollars in new greenbacks, what do you think would happen to prices? Is there some truth, then, to the crude quantity theory? Differentiate between the crude and sophisticated quantity theorists in terms of how they regard $MV \equiv PQ$.

4. Show that the Marshall-Fisher-Keynes summary implies nonconstant V.

5. Review your understanding of the following concepts:

inflation, hyperinflation

redistribution and employment effects
   of price-level trends

real versus money wage

deflation and technological cost-price
   reduction

fractional coins, token money

demand versus time deposits

M_1, M_2, near-money

velocity definition

equation of exchange, $MV \equiv PQ$

crude quantity theory, $P = kM$

16 The Banking System and Deposit Creation

... ONE RULE WHICH WOE BETIDES THE BANKER WHO FAILS TO HEED IT,
... NEVER LEND ANY MONEY TO ANYBODY UNLESS THEY DON'T NEED IT. OGDEN NASH

The importance of ~~bank deposits~~ as part of the community's money supply has been established. This chapter continues with two distinct topics. First, we examine briefly the important facts and functionings of the modern banking system, showing how the present-day commercial bank gradually began to keep only "fractional cash reserves" against its deposits. Second, we see just how the banking system "manufactures" bank deposits—the most important component of our money supply.

A. NATURE AND FUNCTIONING OF THE MODERN BANKING SYSTEM

Today there are over 13,000 banks in the United States that accept checking deposits. Only about a third of these are national banks, the rest being under state supervision. All national banks are automatically members of the Federal Reserve System, and in addition most of the larger state institutions are also members. Although this still leaves more than half of all the banks not members of the Federal Reserve System, they are sufficiently small in size so that their deposits are only about one-sixth of the total.[1] Moreover, since 1933, almost all commercial banks, state or national, have had their deposits insured by the FDIC (Federal Deposit Insurance Corporation). The FDIC insures each deposit up to the sum of $15,000.

Unlike England or Canada, where a few large banks with hundreds of branches are dominant, the United States has tended to rely upon many independent, relatively small, localized units.[2] Until fairly recently, almost anyone could open a bank with

---

[1] Many state banks that are not full-fledged members nevertheless do belong to the Federal Reserve clearinghouse system and can use this service in handling checks of other banks.

[2] In California, the Bank of America has numerous branches all over the state, just as the Chase Manhattan Bank has branches all over New York City, and just as a few holding companies control many banks in Minnesota and Wisconsin. But by and large, the old American distrust of "big finance" has caused legislatures to hamper multiple-branch banking regardless of its cost-saving efficiencies.

relatively limited capital. It is not surprising, therefore, that the American history of bank failures and losses to depositors used to be a grievous one. Indeed, only about one-half the banks in existence in 1915 are still solvent; even in prosperous 1929, long before the Great Depression, no less than 659 banks with estimated total deposits of 200 million dollars failed. Since establishment of the FDIC, a bank failure has become a rare—but not impossible!—event.

■ The primary economic function of commercial banks is *to hold demand deposits and to honor checks drawn upon them*—in short to provide us, the economy, with the largest component of the money supply.

A second important function of commercial banks is to lend money to local merchants, farmers, and industrialists.

Banks also perform a variety of other functions in competition with other financial institutions. They usually hold savings or time deposits. Unlike demand deposits, these pay interest; although theoretically withdrawable only after 30 days' notice, they are in fact usually withdrawn (by their owners) on demand. (Recall that some economists include saving and time deposits in a broad M_2 definition of the money supply.) In this function, the commercial banks are, in parts of the country, competing with the so-called "mutual savings banks," which accept only time deposits; almost anywhere in the country the commercial banks are competing with cooperative building and loan societies and federal savings associations. In selling money orders or travelers' checks, the banks are competing with the post office, Western Union, and American Express. In handling "trusts" and estates, they overlap with investment counselors and other fiduciaries. Even in lending money to individuals and businessmen, the banks are competing with finance companies and with so-called "factors," that provide corporations with working capital. In buying bonds, mortgages, and securities, they compete with insurance companies and other investors.[3] Large banks even do computing and counseling for corporations.

In summary, the commercial banks are by no means our only financial institutions. By definition, however, they are the only organizations able to provide "bank money," i.e., checkable demand deposits that can be conveniently used as a medium of exchange. Therein lies their primary economic importance. Their second, related function is that of credit: they help manufacture short-term credit for businesses and families; they make long-term mortgage loans; and despite the older view that banks should lend only seasonally, they increasingly provide intermediate-term credit through "term loans" of over a year's duration.

■ CREATION OF THE FEDERAL RESERVE SYSTEM

In 1913, the Federal Reserve Act was passed by Congress and signed by President Wilson. It sprang from the panic of 1907, with its alarming epidemic of bank failures: the country was fed up once and for all with the anarchy of unstable private banking. After half a dozen years' agitation and discussion by both parties, the Federal Reserve System was formed—in face of strong banker opposition.

[3] Massachusetts, Connecticut, and New York savings banks even sell life insurance.

The country was cut into 12 Federal Reserve districts, each with its own Federal Reserve Bank. Their initial capital was subscribed by the commercial bank members of the Federal Reserve System, and so *nominally* each Federal Reserve Bank is a corporation owned by the "member banks." All are coordinated by the seven-member Board of Governors of the Federal Reserve System in Washington—popularly called the "Federal Reserve Board."

There is also a 12-man Federal Open Market Committee, with five representatives of the 12 districts as well as the seven-man Board of Governors. This has, with pardonable exaggeration, been called "the most powerful group of private citizens in America," for as we shall see, the Open Market Committee administers the single most powerful weapon of modern monetary policy.

The present-day realities of the Federal Reserve System can be summarized as follows.

■ **The Federal Reserve Board in Washington, together with the 12 regional Federal Reserve Banks, constitutes our American "central bank." Every modern country has such a central bank, as for example the Bank of England, the Bank of France, and the Deutsche Bundesbank of Germany.**

A central bank is a bank that the government sets up to help handle its transactions, to coordinate and control the commercial banks, and, most important, to help *regulate the nation's money supply* and credit conditions.

Although nominally a corporation owned by the commercial banks that are members of the Federal Reserve System, in fact the Federal Reserve (or the "Fed" as it is universally called by the financial press, with no disrespect intended) is a *public* agency. It is directly responsible to Congress; and whenever any conflict arises between its making a profit and the public interest, it acts according to the public interest without question. Its member banks receive fixed and nominal dividends from it; but so profitable is the Fed that its dollars of profit above a certain level go *entirely* to the United States government. The Federal Reserve authorities, meaning by this term the regional and Washington officials, never think of its stockholders, the member commercial banks, as the dictators of their actions, but instead regard the Fed as a public or quasi-public body. (So the men on the Federal Open Market Committee are *not* private citizens even though their paychecks do not come from the federal government.)

While the President appoints Federal Reserve Governors for 14-year terms, the Board considers that its allegiance is primarily to Congress and not to the executive branch. Here is a case where the American practice is different from that of most countries. E.g., in Britain, the Bank of England has not only been nationalized, but well understands that it must in the last analysis be subservient to the will of the Cabinet, with a right to protest publicly but a duty to coordinate its policies with those of the Cabinet.

Prior to an "accord" signed in 1951 by the Treasury Department and the Fed, there was considerable pressure by the President and the Treasury on the actions of the Fed. In recent years the Fed has generally (but not always!) cooperated with the President; ultimately it feels its primary responsibility is to Congress.

■ BANKING AS A BUSINESS

Banking is a business much like any other business. The commercial bank is a relatively simple business concern. A bank provides certain services for its customers (depositors and borrowers) and in return receives payments from them in one form or another. It tries to earn a profit for its stock owners.

A member bank's balance sheet shows certain assets, certain liabilities, and certain capital ownership. Except for minor rearrangements, the bank's published balance sheet looks, on the whole, much like the balance sheet of any other business, and rather simpler than most. The only peculiar feature about the consolidated bank balance sheet shown in Table 16-1 is the fact that such a large portion of the banks' liabilities are payable on demand; i.e., they are deposits subject to checking. And its vital reserves are, as we shall see, created and controlled by the central bank.

This fact is intriguing to the economist because he chooses to call such demand liabilities money; but to the banker it is a familiar condition which has long since been taken for granted. He knows well that, although it would be possible for every depositor suddenly to decide to withdraw all his money from the bank on the same day, the probability of this is quite remote. Each day, as some people withdraw their money, others normally make deposits tending to cancel the withdrawals. In a growing community new deposits more than offset the withdrawals from an average bank.

This, however, need not be strictly true at any one moment, in any one day, or in any one week. By chance alone the amount of withdrawals might exceed deposits for some period of time—just as a coin may land with heads turned up rather than tails for a consecutive number of tosses. For this reason, the banker would voluntarily keep a little cash handy in his vaults and perhaps a "reserve deposit" at a nearby Federal Reserve Bank.

> ■ *Normally, the vault cash in the bank's own vaults and its reserves at the Reserve Bank*—as far as prudent protection from withdrawals is concerned and disregarding involuntary *legal requirements* to be mentioned soon—*need be only a small fraction of the bank's total deposits;* and the same mathematical law of large numbers that makes life insurance possible assures the banker that the larger his bank and the more numerous his independent depositors, the smaller this fraction need be.

Demand deposits are important bank liabilities:

ASSETS		LIABILITIES	
Reserves	22.7	Capital accounts	24.9
Loans and discounts	169.8	**Demand deposits**	**153.5**
U.S. government		Time deposits	121.0
securities	45.0	Other liabilities	14.0
Other securities	36.8		
Other assets	39.1		
Total	313.4	Total	313.4

TABLE 16-1. CONSOLIDATED BALANCE SHEET OF ALL MEMBER BANKS, JANUARY 1, 1966 (in billions of dollars). Reserves and demand deposits are the two key items of interest to our later economic analysis. Reserves are this large primarily because of legal requirements and not to provide against expected withdrawals. (Source: *Federal Reserve Bulletin.*)

■ HOW BANKS DEVELOPED OUT OF GOLDSMITH ESTABLISHMENTS

All these facts are so much taken for granted by every modern banker that he is hardly aware of them. But it was not always so. According to superficial but useful history, commercial banking began with the ancient goldsmiths who developed the practice of storing people's gold and valuables for safekeeping. At first such establishments were simply like parcel checkrooms or warehouses. The depositor left his gold for safekeeping, was given a receipt, later presented that receipt, paid a small fee for safekeeping, and got back his gold.

Quite obviously, however, money is wanted only for what it will buy, not for its own sake. Money has an anonymous quality, so that one dollar is just as good as another, and one piece of pure gold as good as another. The goldsmiths soon found it more convenient *not* to have to tag the gold belonging to any one individual so as to be able to give to him upon request exactly the same piece of gold that he had left. Instead, the customer was quite willing to accept a receipt for an amount of gold or money *of a given value,* even though it was not the identical particle of matter that he actually left. This "anonymity" is important. Therein lies a significant difference between today's bank and a checkroom or warehouse. If I check my bag at Kennedy Airport and later see someone walking down the street with that same suitcase, I call my lawyer and sue the airline. If I mark my initials on a $10 bill, deposit it in my bank account, and later notice it in the hands of a stranger, I have no grievance against the bank management. They have only agreed to pay me on demand any old $10 of legal tender.

But let us return to the goldsmith establishments, which are supposed to typify the first embryonic commercial banks. What would balance sheets of a typical establishment look like? Perhaps like Table 16-2.

We assume the company has long since dropped its activities as a smith and is principally occupied with storing people's money for safekeeping. Over past time, 1 million dollars has been deposited in its vaults, and this whole sum it holds as a cash asset. To balance this asset, there is a current deposit liability of the same amount. Actually, such a business need have no other assets (except the negligible value of its office space and vaults). But its owners could have—on the side, so to speak—subscribed $50,000 of capital to be lent out at interest or buy securities like stocks or bonds. On the asset side this is shown under the heading Loans and Investments; it is balanced on the right-hand side by a like sum in the Capital and Surplus account.

The first goldsmith bank held 100 per cent cash against its demand deposits:

ASSETS		LIABILITIES AND NET WORTH	
Cash	$1,000,000	Capital and surplus	$ 50,000
Loans and investments	50,000	Demand deposit liability	1,000,000
Total	$1,050,000	Total	$1,050,000

TABLE 16-2. BALANCE SHEET OF EARLY BANK.

At this primitive stage, the bank would be of no particular interest to the economist. These investment and capital items have nothing to do with the bank's deposits; if all the bank's loans and investments should go sour and become worthless, the loss would fall completely on the stockholders who have agreed to take that risk in the hope of making a profit. Every depositor could still be paid off in full *out of the 100 per cent cash reserves* held by the bank. The bank would still cover its overhead and clerical expenses by making its customers pay storage charges. These would presumably vary with the length of time the customer left his money for safekeeping, the average amount of his money requiring safekeeping, and the number of times the turnover of his account made a clerk wait on him and keep records.

Economists could ignore such a bank's operations. The bank money[4]—the demand deposits created jointly by the bank's willingness to accept a demand obligation and the customer's willingness to hold a deposit—would *just offset* the amount of ordinary money (currency or coin) placed in the bank's safe and withdrawn from active circulation. The process would be of no more interest than if the public decided to convert some dollar bills into an equivalent amount of dimes. One might then say that the banking system has a *neutral* effect on spending and prices—not adding or subtracting from *total M* or its velocity.

■ MODERN FRACTIONAL RESERVE BANKING

Let us return to our early goldsmith-banker to see how modern banks gradually evolved. If he were an alert fellow, he would soon notice that, although his deposits are payable on demand, they are not all withdrawn together. He would soon learn that, although 100 per cent reserves are necessary if the bank is to be liquidated and all depositors are to be paid off in full, such reserves are not at all necessary if his bank is a "going concern." New deposits tend to balance withdrawals. Only a little till money, perhaps less than 2 per cent, normally seems needed in the form of vault cash.[5]

At first he probably thought this discovery too good to be true. Then perhaps he recalled the story of a rival bank whose dishonest clerk ran off with 95 per cent of its cash reserve—which was never discovered for a dozen years. No one ever had occasion to go to the back rooms of the vault because all withdrawals were financed by recently deposited money held in the front vaults.

We can imagine our intelligent banker—at first cautiously—beginning to acquire bonds and other earning assets with some of the cash entrusted to his care. Everything

---

[4] The economist would consider the demand deposit as money as soon as the custom grew up for depositors to pay for the goods they bought by giving the storekeeper a little note to the bank saying, "Mr. Goldsmith, pay to the order of Sears, Roebuck $2.99, (signed) John Q. Doe." In other words, as soon as the use and acceptability of checks became customary.

[5] If the bank could pay off its depositors with one of its own checks (or as in former times with one of its paper bank notes), it might not have to keep any till money at all. By judiciously limiting the rate at which it was making loans and investments, the bank could ensure that the checks it received from other banks plus cash deposited were just matched by its outpayments. An occasional temporary outward drain of funds could be met by permitting the bank to pay by check what it owed to other banks for the few hours or days until some part of its asset portfolio could be liquidated or until it contracted its operations so as to get a surplus of inpayments over outpayments.

works out all right: depositors are still paid off on demand, and the bank has made some extra earnings. Gradually, the banker no longer feels it necessary to conceal from his depositors what he is doing. If a depositor complains, the banker retorts, "Your money is safe. If you don't like my way of doing business, you are at liberty to withdraw your funds. Besides, haven't you noticed that the new method of fractional cash reserves has enabled me to *lower my service charges to you?* Also, it has enabled me to give a helping hand to our local businessmen who need more capital to buy new tools, buildings, and inventories. Such capital formation benefits consumers because they get better goods for lower prices. It also creates jobs for workers."

Little wonder, therefore, that banks should want to maximize their profits by putting most of the money deposited with them in earning assets and keeping only fractional cash reserves against deposits.

> ■ Indeed, as long as business confidence remains high and bank managers are judicious in their loans and investments, there is no reason why the bank should keep much more than 2 per cent cash reserves against deposits.

But what if the banker makes a mistake in his investments? Since nobody's judgment is perfect and all investments involve some element of speculative risk, this is certainly a possibility to reckon with. To lessen the chance of extreme losses, the banker can try to diversify his investments, not putting all his eggs in one basket. Besides, a conservative bank will have a considerable amount of capital put up by the stockholders. For example, capital stock may have been issued equal to 10 per cent of demand deposits. Then, even if all the bank's assets are in earning investments rather than in nonearning cash, depositors are protected against all capital losses that do not exceed 10 per cent of the bank's investment portfolio. Ordinarily, this will be sufficient, as long as it keeps to high-grade bonds, mortgages, and conservative business loans.

There is one last requirement the bank must meet if we are to give it an A+. The management must watch the general trend in the size of its deposits to make sure that its locality is not becoming a "ghost town" and that it is not losing deposits steadily over time. Were that the case, the bank's investment portfolio would have to be arranged to hold securities and loans that could be gradually liquidated and converted into cash to meet depositors' withdrawals.

Even if the bank is not a declining business, prudent managers must still protect themselves against a *temporary* surge of withdrawals. To hold cash against such a contingency would be costly, since cash earns no yield. They will usually decide, therefore, to hold in their portfolios as "secondary reserves" some securities that always have a ready market and can be liquidated at short notice.

Short-term government bonds serve this purpose admirably. Called "bills," "notes," or "certificates," they vary little in value and can be liquidated simply by not buying new ones as the old ones come due every 90 days or 12 months. Even long-term government bonds, with 30 years of life before they mature, provide liquidity in the sense that in normal times they can always be transferred[6] to some other buyer at some quoted market price—albeit a varying price.

---

[6] There is a saying "You can sell government bonds even on Sunday."

Reserve requirements vary, depending on the location of the bank:

KIND OF BANK	RESERVE RATIOS REQUIRED, PER CENT	
	AGAINST DEMAND DEPOSITS	AGAINST TIME DEPOSITS
Reserve City Banks (large and medium cities, Chicago, New York City)	16½	6
Other member banks (small-town or country)	12	6

TABLE 16-3. LEGAL RESERVE RATIOS FOR FEDERAL RESERVE MEMBER BANKS, JANUARY, 1967. These required reserve ratios have the purpose of controlling the volume of demand deposits and money supply. Congress gives the FRB the right to vary these rates within broad limits. (New York City and Chicago now are treated like other Reserve cities.)

The important thing here is not the *date of maturity* of the bond or loan, but rather how "shiftable" it is to some other investment institution. A 90-day loan to a local merchant, which is nonshiftable, is in this sense less liquid than a 90-year gilt-edge bond traded on a securities exchange.

■ LEGAL RESERVE REQUIREMENTS

The above precepts of sound banking practice are quite simple and understandable. They are a little harder to carry out in practice than to state in principle; but the same is true of most prescriptions for wise living.

If we compare a "going and growing" bank with any corporation, the surprising thing is not how little cash reserves the banks keep, but that they keep any at all (in excess of minimal till-money requirements). As long as financial skies are sunny, *we have seen that the same profit-maximizing logic which compels the abandonment of a system of 100 per cent reserves argues in favor of negligible reserves!*

Yet, if we turn to the facts, we find that a prudent modern bank is expected— and required by law!—to keep a substantial portion of its assets in nonearning cash. About a sixth or seventh of all demand deposits must be kept by banks immobilized in such nonearning reserve form. For the most part, a member bank holds these reserves on deposit with its regional Federal Reserve Bank; but in recent years the Fed gives each member bank the right to count as part of its reserves any cash it finds convenient to hold in its own vaults.

Table 16-3 indicates the level of required reserve ratios.[7] Roughly, they are about one-sixth against demand deposits, depending on the category of the bank. Because one-fifth gives rounder numbers to work our numerical examples with, for the most part we shall refer to 20 per cent reserve ratios, it being understood that such a figure is only for expositional convenience and would have to be lowered a little to correspond

[7] The 6 per cent ratio against time and saving deposits, strictly speaking, applies in 1967 only to a bank's total time deposits over $5 million; below $5 million, as in a small bank, the required reserve ratio is 4 per cent; and the same is true against ordinary passbook saving accounts.

with practice in the late 1960s (as contrasted to some earlier decades when one-fifth was truly a better approximation than one-sixth).

It is to be emphasized that *these legal reserve ratios are required of member banks of the Federal Reserve System for purposes of controlling their behavior.* The many, but unimportant, banks that are not members of the Federal Reserve System do not voluntarily keep such large amounts of nonearning cash as a precaution against withdrawals. Many experts think *all* banks should be subject to these same legal ratios, and if nonmember banks became important in total deposits, Congress might so legislate.

These legal reserve requirements need to be explained since they are so important a mechanism by which the FRB controls bank money.

ARCHAIC GEOGRAPHICAL REQUIREMENTS   Why should the size of a town affect the legal reserve requirement? Before the Federal Reserve was created, the city banks held the precautionary reserves of smaller town banks. When a crisis came, the smaller banks tried to withdraw cash from the city banks. Therefore in the early days of the Federal Reserve System it seemed logical to make city banks, especially in the central reserve cities, New York and Chicago, hold higher reserve requirements.

Those days are past. Now it is the Federal Reserve Banks, not the big city banks, that hold the reserves of member banks. A new law has finally removed all extra reserve requirements for New York and Chicago. Logically, all member banks might some day be given the same required reserve ratio.

LEGAL RESERVE REQUIREMENTS TOO HIGH?   Many bankers think wistfully about how much they could earn on loans or bonds if they were free to use part of the money they are forced to keep as legal reserves against their own deposits. They argue thus:

> Money we are required to keep as legal reserves doesn't earn us one red cent. So why do we have to keep such high legal reserves? One-sixth of our deposits is more than is really needed for safety. After all, our withdrawals never bunch up much; the laws of statistics take care of that. Besides, if we ever needed more, we could sell off some government bills or could turn to the Fed for help or could borrow temporarily from some other bank. We bankers think that legal reserves of as little as 10 per cent—some of us would say 5 per cent!—is all that prudence requires in this age of insured deposits.

In part these bankers are right. Years ago the legal reserve requirements for the city and country banks were lower: they ranged between 13 and 17 per cent against demand deposits and 3 per cent against time deposits. After the mid-thirties Congress gave the Reserve Board the right to double these ratios, and the Board used its discretion to do this in a number of gradual steps.

But why did the Board raise the legal requirements? And why did it later ask Congress for authority to raise them still further? Because of the belief that such high legal ratios are needed to assure depositors of being able to withdraw their money when they want to? No.

■ **The main function of legal reserve requirements is *not* that of making deposits safe and liquid, payable on demand. What, then, is it? Their vital function is to** enable the Federal Reserve authorities to be able to *control* the amount of demand deposits—or bank money—that the member banks can create. By imposing fixed legal reserve requirements, the Fed can limit the growth of bank deposits.

We shall soon learn just how this all works.

■ THE GOVERNMENT STANDS BEHIND THE BANKS

Banks are much safer than they used to be before the Depression. If this has little to do with legal reserve requirements, to what is it due?

> ■ Banks are safe today because all realize that it is a vital function of government to stand behind them (and its Federal Deposit Insurance Corporation) should a depression and panicky "run" on the banking system ever recur.

No banking system with fractional reserves—i.e., none which keeps less than 100 per cent of its deposits in cash—can ever turn all its deposits into cash on a moment's notice. So every fractional reserve system would be a "fair-weather system" if government did not stand ready to back it up. If panic ever again came, Congress, the President, and the Federal Reserve Board would all act, even using their constitutional powers over money to print the money needed to meet a national emergency!

Had this been said and done back in the black days of the early 1930s, history might have been different. Our country might have been spared the epidemic of bank failures[8] that created fear and crisis for the capitalistic system. With the American people of both political parties realizing that the government stands behind the banking system, it is highly improbable that a panic could ever get started. Here is a case where being prepared to act heroically probably makes it unnecessary to do so.

■ KEEPING EACH BANK SAFE: A CHECKLIST

Just because the peril of a nationwide bank run has been overcome does not mean that each banker can stop worrying about *his* bank's safety. Numerous important reforms have been introduced in recent decades to increase the safety of the individual bank's deposits. Here, in summary, are successive steps taken by government to alleviate the instability of laissez-faire banking:

1. *Regulation of bank formation and activity.* For decades, either state or federal authorities have set down conditions under which banks could be formed—the minimum amount of capital they must have, etc. Bank examiners periodically scrutinize bank assets and pass on the bank's solvency, always keeping in mind that an ounce of prevention is worth a pound of cure.

2. *Formation of Federal Reserve System.* The next great step forward was the establishment of a central bank, whose emergency function is to stand as a Rock of Gibraltar in time of panic, to be ready to use the full monetary powers of the govern-

---

[8]Some 8,000 banks with 5 billion dollars of deposits became insolvent in 1930–1933. To keep all banks from collapse, Franklin Roosevelt's first act was to close them by declaring a "bank holiday" until they could be officially reopened with confidence restored.

ment to stem collapse of the banking system. The normal vital function of a central bank is to control money supply and credit conditions.

3. *Government insurance of bank deposits.* One of the most important government bank reforms is also fairly recent. Following the bank crisis of 1933, the FDIC was belatedly set up to insure the safety of all bank deposits.[9] All banks that are members of the Federal Reserve System *must* belong, and most state banks also belong. In return for a yearly payment made by the banks, which varies with their total deposits, their customers are, as we have seen, completely protected against any loss up to $15,000, even if the bank should go bankrupt.

The importance of this measure can hardly be exaggerated. From now on most banks will be closed by bank examiners and government authorities, not by the panicky behavior of depositors whose fears bring on the very contingency they are most afraid of. A single bank need no longer fear that its reputation, like that of a good woman, is compromised simply by being brought into question.

B. THE CREATION OF BANK DEPOSITS

■ CAN BANKS REALLY CREATE MONEY?

We now turn to one of the most interesting aspects of money and credit, the process called "multiple expansion of bank deposits." Most people have heard that in some mysterious manner banks can create money out of thin air, but few really understand how the process works. Few understand that all our money arises out of debt and IOU operations. Actually, there is nothing magical or incomprehensible about the creation of bank deposits. At every step of the way, one can follow what is happening to the banks' accounts. The true explanation of deposit creation is simple. What is hard to grasp are the false explanations that still circulate.

According to these false explanations, the managers of an ordinary bank are able, by some use of their fountain pens, to lend several dollars for each dollar deposited with them. No wonder practical bankers see red when such power is attributed to them. They only wish they could do so. As every banker knows, he cannot invest money that he does not have; and money that he invests in buying a security or making a loan soon leaves his bank.

Bankers, therefore, often go to the opposite extreme. They sometimes argue that the banking system cannot (and does not) create money. "After all," they say, "we can invest only what is left with us. We don't create anything. We only put the community's savings to work." Bankers who argue in this way are quite wrong. They have become enmeshed in our old friend the fallacy of composition: what is true for each is not thereby true for all.

> ■ The banking system as a whole can do what each small bank cannot do: it *can* expand its loans and investments many times the new reserves of cash created for it, even though each small bank is lending out only a fraction of its deposits.

[9] In the late 1960s, there were more than 100 million depositors in FDIC banks; the $15,000 limit insured about 97 per cent of all depositors, of whom 98 per cent were *fully* insured.

Our answer, then, to the basic question is in the affirmative: Yes, the banking system and the public do, between them, create about $5 of bank deposits for each new dollar of reserves that is created for the banks. Let us see how.

■ HOW DEPOSITS ARE CREATED: THE FIRST-BANK STAGE

We begin with a brand-new deposit of $1,000 brought to a bank. Where it came from is not important. It could have been from a widow's hoard, from abroad, or more realistically, from someone's having just sold a bond to the regional Federal Reserve Bank (which may have paid for it by printing off twenty 50-dollar bills). To avoid ambiguity, let us suppose it arose from the government's giving a veteran $1,000 of newly printed money, which he deposited in his local bank. We shall see that *in the end* the banking system is going to manufacture $5,000 of new demand deposits out of this, thus taking in $1,000 of one kind of M (currency) and converting it into $5,000 of another kind of M (checkable demand deposits)—for a net gain of $4,000!

FIRST-BANK STAGE   Now, if banks were to keep 100 per cent cash-reserve balances, like the old goldsmiths, they could not create any extra money out of a new deposit of $1,000 left with them. The depositor would simply be giving up $1,000 of currency for a $1,000 checking deposit.

The change in the bank's balance sheet, as far as the new demand deposit is concerned, would be as shown in Table 16-4(a).[10]

Multiple-bank deposit creation is a story with many successive stages:

1st, A new deposit is added to the original bank's balance sheet:

ASSETS		LIABILITIES	
Reserves	+$1,000	Deposits	+$1,000
Total	+$1,000	Total	+$1,000

TABLE 16-4(a). ORIGINAL BANK IN INITIAL POSITION.

The bank has not created this deposit *alone*. The customer had to be willing to make the deposit. Once he took the initiative, the bank was also willing to accept his checking account. Together the bank and the public "created" $1,000 of bank money, or deposit. But there is no multiple expansion yet, no 5 for 1 or anything else. So long as the banks keep 100 per cent reserves, the growth of bank M is just offset by the decline of currency-in-circulation M.

[10] For simplicity, all our tables will show only the *changes* in balance-sheet items. To simplify the arithmetic, we use reserve ratios of 20 per cent, which are a little larger than the legal rates of Table 16-3. Hence, wherever an expansion of 5:1 is mentioned, the meticulous reader can choose to think of a 6:1 or 7:1 expansion. If M_2 inclusive of saving deposits were studied, the expansion ratio would of course exceed 7:1. (Important reminder: When bankers refer to their loans and investments by "investments" they mean their holdings of securities. They do not mean what we mean by I in $C + I + G$, namely, net capital formation for the community.)

Suppose now that the bank does not have to keep 100 per cent reserves. Suppose that the law requires it to keep only 20 per cent legal reserves. (It can always keep larger reserves if it wishes to; but if there are many outstanding, relatively safe, interest-yielding government bonds or numerous profitable lending opportunities, the bank will not find it profitable to keep much more reserves than the law requires.)

What can the bank now do? Can it expand its loans and investments by $4,000 so that the change in its balance sheet looks as shown in Table 16-4(b)? The answer is definitely, No. Why not? Total assets equal total liabilities. Cash reserves meet the legal requirement of being 20 per cent of total deposits.

2d, Of course the bank cannot then loan out four times the amount of the deposit:

ASSETS		LIABILITIES	
Reserves	+$1,000	Deposits	+$5,000
Loans and			
investments	+ 4,000		
Total	+$5,000	Total	+$5,000

TABLE 16-4(b). IMPOSSIBLE SITUATION FOR SINGLE SMALL BANK.

True enough. But how did the bank pay for the investments or earning assets that it bought? Like everyone else, it had to write out checks to the men who sold the bond or signed the promissory note. If all such would promise not to cash the bank's check—or what is the same thing, to hold all such money frozen on deposit in the bank—then, of course, the bank could buy all it wanted to without losing any cash.

But, in fact, no one will borrow money at 6 or 7 per cent just to hold it all in the bank. The borrower spends the money on labor, on materials, or perhaps on an automobile. The money will *very soon*,[11] therefore, have to be paid out of the bank. And if—as is likely—the bank is but one of many banks serving that city, county, state, and country, only a fraction of the sums withdrawn will ever come back to the original bank in another customer's deposit.

This loss of cash by a bank expanding its investments is even more clearly seen if the bank buys a bond rather than making a local loan. When my Boston bank buys a government bond, what are the chances that the man who sells the bond will happen to have an account with it? The likelihood is negligible. Probably he lives in New York City; or Ames, Iowa. So my bank knows it will soon have to pay out *all* the money it places in bonds. A bank cannot "eat its cake and have it, too." The New England bank cannot buy a bond and keep its cash at the same time. Table 16-4(b) gives, therefore, a completely false picture of what an individual bank can do.

Does this mean that Table 16-4(a) tells the end of the story? Must the bank, therefore, behave like the 100 per cent reserve goldsmith bankers?

[11]If the bank made loans of $800 to its own customers, and they kept them on deposit, then for a brief period it would have deposits of $1,800. But as its borrowers spent their money, and unless the people who got that money were local customers who put the money back on deposit in this original bank, it would soon find itself forced toward the position of Table 16-4(c).

3d, But what it can do is loan out four-fifths of the deposit:

ASSETS		LIABILITIES	
Reserves	+$ 200	Deposits	+$1,000
Loans and			
investments	+ 800		
Total	+$1,000	Total	+$1,000

TABLE 16-4(c). ORIGINAL BANK IN FINAL POSITION.

Of course not. Although the bank cannot jack its deposits up to five times its cash reserve, it certainly can *reduce its cash* down to one-fifth of its deposits. Nothing is easier. For, as just seen, all it has to do is acquire $800 worth of earning assets—bonds, loans, or mortgages. In a day or so it will lose practically all this cash as its checks come back for payment. Now its balance sheet will be as shown in Table 16-4(c).

As far as this first bank is concerned, we are through. Its legal reserves are just enough to match its deposits. There is nothing more it can do until the public decides to bring in some more money for deposit.

Before leaving the single small bank, note this important fact: It has created money! How? Clearly *it* retains from the public only $200 of cash M; and it has added $1,000 of bank-deposit M to the public's total. Thus, its activity has created a net increase of $800 in money supply.

■ CHAIN REPERCUSSIONS ON THE OTHER BANKS

But the banking system as a whole cannot settle down yet. The people who sold the bonds or borrowed from the bank will presumably deposit the proceeds in some other bank or pay them to someone else who will make such a deposit. Our original bank has thus lost $800 *to some other banks* in the system.

SECOND-GENERATION BANKS   If we lump these other banks all together and call them "second-generation banks," their balance sheets now appear as shown in Table 16-4(d). Of course, these banks are scattered all over the country. (Our original bank might even constitute a small part of the second generation as a few of its checks fell into the hands of its own depositors.) To these banks the dollars deposited are just like any other dollars, *just like our original deposit;* these banks do not know, and do not care, that they are second in a chain of deposits. They do know, and they do care, that they are now holding too much nonearning cash. Only one-fifth of $800, or $160, is legally needed against $800 deposits. Therefore they can, and will, use the other four-

4th, The money loaned out by the original bank is soon deposited in other banks:

ASSETS		LIABILITIES	
Reserves	+$800	Deposits	+$800
Total	+$800	Total	+$800

TABLE 16-4(d). SECOND-GENERATION BANKS IN INITIAL POSITION.

5th, Four-fifths of this new deposit will be loaned out by the second-generation bank:

ASSETS		LIABILITIES	
Reserves	+$160	Deposits	+$800
Loans and			
investments	+ 640		
Total	+$800	Total	+$800

TABLE 16-4(e). FINAL POSITION OF SECOND-GENER-ATION BANKS.

fifths to buy $640 worth of loans and investments. Hence, in a few days, their balance sheet will have reached equilibrium as shown in Table 16-4(e).

So much for the second-generation banks. They too have created money. Thus far, the original $1,000 taken out of hand-to-hand circulation and put into the banking system has given rise to $1,000 (first-generation deposits) plus $800 (second-generation deposits). The total of money has increased, and the end is not yet in sight. Here's why.

LATER-GENERATION BANKS   The $640 spent by the second-generation banks in acquiring loans and investments will go to a new set of banks called the "third-generation banks." The reader should by now be able to fill in their balance sheets as they look initially [see Table 16-4(f)]. Evidently, the third-generation banks will at first have *excess reserves* of an amount equal to four-fifths of $640, or $512. After this has been spent on loans and investments—and only then—the third-generation banks will reach the equilibrium of Table 16-4(g).

The total of bank-deposit M is now $1,000 plus $800 plus $640, or $2,440. This is already almost $2\frac{1}{2}$: 1 expansion of the original cash deposit. But a fourth generation of banks will clearly end up with four-fifths of $640 in deposits, or $512; the fifth generation will get four-fifths of $512, or $409.60; and so on; until finally, by the twenty-fifth round, we shall have all but a penny of the sum of the infinitely many generations.

FINAL EQUILIBRIUM   What will be the final sum: $1,000 + $800 + $640 + $512 + $409.60 + ⋯? If we patiently work out the sum by arithmetic, we shall find that it

6th, And similarly the four-fifths ratio applies to third-generation banks:

ASSETS		LIABILITIES	
Reserves	+____	Deposits	+____
Loans and			
investments	____		
Total	+____	Total	+$640

TABLE 16-4(f). INITIAL POSITION OF THIRD-GENERATION BANKS.

ASSETS		LIABILITIES	
Reserves	+$128	Deposits	+$640
Loans and			
investments	+ 512		
Total	+$640	Total	+$640

TABLE 16-4(g). FINAL EQUILIBRIUM OF THIRD-GENERATION BANKS.

7th, Through this chain process the banking system eventually creates total deposits equal to five times the original new reserves:

POSITION OF BANK	NEW DEPOSITS	NEW LOANS AND INVESTMENTS	RESERVES
Original banks	$1,000.00	$ 800.00	$ 200.00
2d-generation banks	800.00	640.00	160.00
3d-generation banks	640.00	512.00	128.00
4th-generation banks	512.00	409.60	102.40
5th-generation banks	409.60	327.68	81.92
6th-generation banks	327.68	262.14	65.54
7th-generation banks	262.14	209.72	52.42
8th-generation banks	209.72	167.77	41.95
9th-generation banks	167.77	134.22	33.55
10th-generation banks	134.22	107.37	26.85
Sum of first 10 generation banks	$4,463.13	$3,570.50	$ 892.63
Sum of remaining generation banks	536.87	429.50	107.37
Total for banking system as a whole	$5,000.00	$4,000.00	$1,000.00

TABLE 16-4(h). MULTIPLE EXPANSION OF BANK DEPOSITS THROUGH THE BANKING SYSTEM. (From the 7th generation on, all data have been rounded off to two decimal places.) Note that in every generation each *small* bank has "created" new money in the following sense: It ends up with final bank deposit five times *the reserves it finally retains.*

leads to $4,999.999 \cdots$ and "finally" to $5,000. Table 16-4(h) shows the complete effect of the chain of deposit creation; and we can also get the same answer in two other ways, by common sense and by elementary algebra.[12]

Common sense tells us the process of deposit creation must come to an end only when no bank *anywhere in the system* has reserves in excess of the 20 per cent reserve ratio to deposits. In all our previous examples no cash reserves have ever leaked out of the banking system, but have simply gone from one set of banks to another set of banks. Everyone will be at equilibrium only when a consolidated balance sheet for all the banks together—for the first, second, and hundredth generation—looks as shown in Table 16-4(i). For if total new deposits were less than $5,000, the 20 per cent ratio would not yet be reached and equilibrium would not yet have been everywhere attained.

If the reader will compare Table 16-4(i) with Table 16-4(b) previously judged "impossible," he will see this:

■ The whole banking system *can* do what no one bank can do by itself. It can expand its deposits to five times the *initial* new deposit. *Bank money has been created 5 out of 1—and all the while each bank has invested and lent only a fraction of what it has received as deposits!*

[12]This can be proved by algebra as follows:
$$\$1,000 + \$800 + \$640 + \cdots = \$1,000[1 + \tfrac{4}{5} + (\tfrac{4}{5})^2 + (\tfrac{4}{5})^3 + \cdots]$$
$$= \$1,000 \left(\frac{1}{1 - \tfrac{4}{5}}\right) = \$1,000 \times 5 = \$5,000$$

Just as the old multiplier made income rise threefold to generate the one-third of itself equal to the new dollar of *I*, here deposit *M* must rise fivefold so that 20 per cent of it will match the new dollars of reserves that started the chain.

8th, Now we can see that all banks together can do what is impossible for one alone:

ASSETS		LIABILITIES	
Reserves	+$1,000	Deposits	+$5,000
Loans and			
investments	+ 4,000		
Total	+$5,000	Total	+$5,000

TABLE 16-4(i). CONSOLIDATED BALANCE SHEET SHOWING FINAL POSITION OF ALL BANKS TOGETHER.

Who creates the multiple expansion[13] of deposits? Three parties do so jointly: the public by always keeping its money in the bank on deposit; the banks by keeping only a fraction of their deposits in the form of cash; the public and private borrowers who make it possible for the banks to find loans and attractive earning assets to buy with their excess cash. (There is also a fourth party, the central bank, which by its activities determines how much will be the new reserves to come to the banking system. It will be the task of the next chapters to survey and explain this process.)

9th, When a deposit is drawn out, a multiple contraction begins to take place:

ASSETS		LIABILITIES	
Reserves	−$ 200	Deposits	−$1,000
Loans and			
investments	− 800		
Total	−$1,000	Total	−$1,000

TABLE 16-5(a). EQUILIBRIUM POSITION OF ORIGINAL BANK LOSING A DEPOSIT.

Before leaving this section, test your knowledge of credit creation by tracing in detail what happens when the regional Federal Reserve Bank permanently kills off $1,000 of reserves by selling a government bond to a widow who withdraws cash from her demand deposit account to pay for it: (1) Her local bank loses $1,000 of reserves and $1,000 of deposits. But it previously held only 20 per cent cash reserves or $200 against her deposit. Clearly, it must have given up to her some of its legally necessary cash reserves held against its other demand deposits. Show that its total reserves are now below the legal minimum. (2) Therefore it must sell $800 worth of investments or call in that many loans. The first-generation bank will be in equilibrium only when its balance sheet finally looks as shown in a newly constructed Table 16-5(a).

But in selling its securities, our original bank has drained $800 from a second generation of banks; and they in turn, by liquidating securities and loans, drain reserves

---

[13] In effect, each small bank creates $1M$ out of $\frac{1}{5}M$, but not $5M$ out of $1M$. (NOTE: Whenever $1 of new reserves produces $5 of new demand deposit money, the *net* creation of M is only $5 − $1 = $4. So when one writes a 5:1 expansion expression, it means that there is associated with this a 4:1 *net*-creation-of-M expansion.)

There is nothing paradoxical in the fact that total bank deposits are several times greater than the amount of paper cash in existence anywhere; the same is true of the total of government bonds and real-estate values. Deposits are something that banks *owe* their customers; cash is *left* in a bank, but it does not *remain* in that bank. Throughout its lifetime a dollar may have been *left* in many banks, just as it may be used over a long period of time to buy hundreds of dollars of merchandise. The one thing to keep firmly in mind is that bank deposits are one of the three forms of modern money and, quantitatively, the most important.

from a third. And so it goes—until the widow and Fed's withdrawal of $1,000 of reserves from the banking system have produced a chain "killing off" $5,000 worth of deposits throughout the whole system and $4,000 of bank-earning assets. The student should follow through each stage: Table 16-5(b), Table 16-5(c), ...

You should also be able to show how an initial deposit of $1,000 can result in $10,000 of bank deposits if banks keep only 10 per cent reserve ratios, as they did in the 1920s. And since the reserve ratios of Table 16-3 average below 20 per cent, you might show that 6:1 is a more accurate figure than 5:1.

■ A "MONOPOLY BANK"

In all the above processes, it was assumed that no cash leaked out of the banking system into someone's mattress or into permanent hand-to-hand circulation. The banking system was then in the enviable position of finding that its checks were always deposited somewhere within itself.

This condition being so, it is easy to see that a single "monopoly bank" with many branches, which served the whole nation and represented the consolidated banking system, would be able to do *at once* what we have said each small bank cannot do. Its balance sheet could quickly go to the condition shown in Table 16-4(b) or (i). It could write checks freely to pay for securities or loans, knowing that the people to whom they are paid would always redeposit their proceeds in the one and only monopoly bank.[14]

■ SIMULTANEOUS EXPANSION OR CONTRACTION BY ALL BANKS

In the previous section we saw how the banking system can reach the limits of its expansion through many successive rounds or generations. If we allow half a week for checks to clear at each stage and for decisions to be made, then 5 to 8 weeks might be needed for the process to work itself out through more than a dozen rounds.

As a practical matter, it is not necessary to follow the chain of each dollar deposited through its successive rounds. Here is why. A rise in reserves will usually affect almost all the banks at the same time. They all receive some new deposits at about the same time. They all have excess reserves in the first instance, and all together make loans or buy securities. When a single small bank, all by itself, writes checks to acquire securities, these checks go to other banks and it loses cash. But when all write checks simultaneously and in balance, there will tend to be a cancellation of new checks deposited and paid out in each bank. No one bank need lose cash reserves.

Hence, without going through the successive generations of the previous section, all banks together can simply and blithely expand their loans and investments—so long as each does not jeopardize its reserve position—until deposits are finally brought into

[14] In countries like England, where there is a "Big Five" group of branch banks, or like Canada, where there are a few large banks, or in states like California, where there are a few great multiple-branch banks—in such cases a bank may be able to lend out more than its legal excess reserves, knowing that part of the money will come back *to itself* in later "generations." However, these so-called "derivative," or "self-returning," deposits are not important for the U.S., and calling attention to them can confuse beginning students, as it did economists of half a century ago, when this process was still novel.

a 5:1 relation to reserves. Then the banking system has reached the limit of its ability to create money.

One could follow through the similar process by which all banks *simultaneously* contract money 5:1 for each dollar of reserve withdrawn from the banking system, and one could also show how a monopoly bank would contract.

■ TWO QUALIFICATIONS

Finally, two qualifications to the ideal condition must be made. We have shown that $1,000 of new reserves put into a bank can ultimately result in an increase of $5,000 of bank deposits. This assumed that all the new money remained somewhere in the banking system, in one bank or another at every stage, and that all banks could keep "loaned up" with no "excess reserves."

1. *Leakage into hand-to-hand circulation.* It is quite possible, however, and even likely, that somewhere along the chain of deposit expansion some individual who receives a check will not leave the proceeds in a bank but will withdraw it into circulation or into hoarding outside the banking system. As a matter of fact, in boom times when bank deposits are expanding, there is usually at the same time an increased need for pennies, dimes, and paper currency.

The effects of such withdrawals on our analysis are simple. When $1,000 stayed in the banking system, $5,000 of new deposits were created. If $100 were to leak into circulation outside the banks and only $900 of new reserves were to remain in the banking system, then the new deposits created would be $4,500 ($900 × 5). *The banking system can always amplify in a 5:1 ratio whatever amount of new reserves is permanently left with it.*

2. *Possible excess reserves.* Our description of multiple deposit creation has proceeded on the assumption that the commercial banks stick fairly close to their legal reserve ratios. But there is no reason why a bank cannot choose to keep an *excess* over the legally required amount of reserves. Thus, suppose the original bank receiving a new $1,000 deposit had been satisfied to hold $800 of it in excess reserves. Then the whole process would have ended right there, with no multiple expansion of deposits. Or if banks were always to keep 5 per cent excess reserves, on top of the 20 per cent legal requirement, we'd have a chain of expansion of deposits $[1 + \frac{3}{4} + (\frac{3}{4})^2 + \cdots]$ rather than $[1 + \frac{4}{5} + (\frac{4}{5})^2 + \cdots]$, with only a 4:1 instead of a 5:1 expansion of deposits.

Back in the 1930s excess reserves—i.e., reserves over and above legally required reserves—were substantial, since bankers were then leary of loan opportunities and even of relatively safe government bills that were paying only $\frac{1}{8}$ of 1 per cent interest. Had the Fed then given the banking system $1,000 of new reserves, perhaps half might have gone into excess reserves. Today excess reserves are less important, as large banks find attractive uses even for one-day funds. It is primarily country banks that still keep some excess reserves.[15]

[15] A "Federal Funds" market has grown up in which banks lend reserves to each other daily. This has lowered average excess reserves. When the Federal Funds rate rises above the "discount rate," as it did sharply in 1966, you can be sure credit is very tight and hard to get.

The level of excess reserves depends more on the attitudes of banks toward the interest rates they can earn than on their fears that withdrawals will catch them unawares. When short-term interest rates become very low, and a banker finds that keeping an extra million dollars in idle reserves would not much change his earning position, he is not very anxious to get rid of all excess reserves. But as profit opportunities improve, he becomes more aggressive in putting his idle reserves to work earning him a return.

■ The possibility that the excess reserves of banks can change over time is an important reminder that there is nothing mechanical and completely accurate about using a 5:1 or any other *fixed* ratio for money creation.

Accordingly, there is nothing automatic about deposit creation. Four factors are necessary: the banks must somehow receive new reserves; they must be willing to make loans or buy securities rather than hold new excess reserves; someone must be willing to borrow or to sell securities; and the public must choose to leave its money on deposit with the banks, not depleting them of reserves.

SUMMARY

A. THE MODERN BANKING SYSTEM

1 ■

The American banking system consists primarily of relatively small-scale unit banks, chartered by the national government or by the states. Although less than half are members of the Federal Reserve System, member demand deposits include six-sevenths of the total of all deposits.

2 ■

The functions of commercial banks are numerous and overlap with those of such other financial institutions as mutual savings banks, federal savings and loan associations, finance companies, and insurance companies. But in their function of providing demand deposit M, the commercial banks perform a unique and important economic role. Their deposits constitute the single most important component of our money supply or medium of exchange. Also the banks are important sources for credit.

3 ■

The Federal Reserve System (or Fed) consists primarily of (*a*) member banks, (*b*) the 12 regional Federal Reserve Banks, and (*c*) the Board of Governors (or Federal Reserve Board) in Washington. Although nominally corporations owned by the member banks, the Federal Reserve Banks are, in fact, almost branches of the federal government, possessing wide powers and being concerned with the public interest rather than profits. Responsible to Congress, in practice their activities are not independent of Treasury and executive administration policy. It is the primary responsibility of the Reserve authorities to control the money supply in order to help achieve full employment with stable prices (and backstop the banking system in time of crisis).

4 ■

Modern banks gradually evolved from the old goldsmith establishments in which money and valuables were stored. It finally became general practice to hold far less than 100 per cent reserves against deposits, the rest being put into securities and loans for an interest yield. Fractional-reserve banking had evolved.

5 ■

If the government did not stand ready to use its emergency powers to protect the banking system, an attempt by all depositors at the same time to withdraw their money would ruin any fractional-reserve banking system; but knowing the government is ready to act, people will never put it to the test.

The member banks are required to keep legal reserves (on deposit with their regional Reserve Bank or in vault cash) in proportion to their deposits. (The geographical differences in required ratios are archaic and are diminishing.) These legal reserve requirements are *not* primarily to protect deposits but to permit the Federal Reserve to control the total supply of M and keep credit conditions conducive to proper overall spending.

B. THE CREATION OF BANK DEPOSITS

6 ■

If banks kept 100 per cent cash reserves against all deposits, there would be no net creation of money when currency was taken out of circulation and deposited in the banking system. There would be only a $1:1$ exchange of one kind of money for another kind of money.

7 ■

Modern banks are required to keep legal reserves of only about one-sixth or less of their demand deposits, depending on the size of the city. Consequently, the banking system as a whole—together with public or private borrowers and the depositing public—does create deposit money almost $6:1$ for each new dollar taken out of circulation and left on deposit somewhere in the system—or $5:1$ in our simplified examples.

8 ■

Each small bank is limited in its ability to expand its loans and investments. It cannot lend or invest more than it has received from depositors; it can lend only about four-fifths as much. Its deposits are five times its cash, only because its cash decreases, and not because its deposits increase; but it does create 1 unit of bank money for the $\frac{1}{5}$ of reserves it retains.

9 ■

The system as a whole can expand at once, as each small bank cannot. This can be seen if we examine a monopoly bank in a closed community. The checks written by such a bank always come back to it; therefore the only restriction upon its ability to expand its investments and deposits (its assets *and* its liabilities in double-entry bookkeeping) is the requirement that it keep one-fifth cash-reserve ratios against deposits. When deposits have expanded until they are five times the new reserves, the monopoly bank is "loaned up" and can create no further deposits until given more reserves.

10 ■

In present-day America, there is no monopoly bank. Nevertheless, the same 5:1 expansion of bank deposits takes place. The first individual bank receiving a new $1,000 of deposits spends four-fifths of its newly acquired cash on loans and investments. This gives a second group of banks four-fifths of $1,000 in new deposits. They, in turn, keep one-fifth in cash and spend the other four-fifths for new earning assets; this causes them to lose cash to a third set of banks, whose deposits have gone up by four-fifths of four-fifths of $1,000. Obviously, if we follow through the successive groups of banks in the dwindling, never-ending chain, we find for the system as a whole new deposits of

$$\$1,000 + \$800 + \$640 + \$512 + \cdots$$

$$= \$1,000 \times \left[1 + \frac{4}{5} + \left(\frac{4}{5}\right)^2 + \left(\frac{4}{5}\right)^3 + \cdots \right]$$

$$= \$1,000 \left(\frac{1}{1 - \frac{4}{5}} \right) = \$1,000 \left(\frac{1}{\frac{1}{5}} \right) = \$5,000$$

Only when each of the $1,000 of new reserves supports $5 of deposits somewhere in the system will the limits to deposit expansion be reached. Then the system is loaned up; it can create no further deposits until it is given more reserves.

11 ■

In practice, it is not necessary to wait for the successive rounds in the chain of $1,000, $800, $640, . . . , to work themselves out. Usually, many banks tend to get new reserves at about the same time. If all expand their loans and investments approximately in balance, their outpayments will tend to cancel each other. Thus, each loses cash; and all together can rather quickly expand their assets and deposits to the 5:1 limit.

12 ■

As a minor qualification to the above discussion, we must note that there will be some leakage of the new cash reserves of the banking system into circulation *outside* the banks. Therefore, instead of $5,000 of new deposits created, as in the previous examples, we may have something less than that—the difference being due to what is withdrawn from the system. A second qualification results from the fact that a bank may keep *excess reserves* above legally required reserves. While big city banks do not hold much excess reserves in prosperous times, others may hold varying amounts of excess reserves, depending upon interest rates and precautionary expectations. So there is nothing automatic about a 5:1 or other fixed-gear ratio.

In this chapter we have seen how bank deposits are kept at about five times the legal reserves of the banking system. In Chapter 17 we shall learn how the Federal Reserve Banks make bank reserves go up when an expansion of the total money supply is desired. When a contraction of the quantity of money is in order, the Federal Reserve authorities pull the brakes. Instead of pumping new reserves into the banking system, they draw off some of the reserves. We shall see that in so doing they are able to reduce the quantity of money, not 1 for 1, but (as just shown) 5 for 1.

QUESTIONS FOR DISCUSSION

1. Suppose that all banks kept 100 per cent reserves. How different would they be? What function do legal reserves perform? What are "excess reserves"?

2. Assume a 10 per cent reserve ratio. Trace the process of multiple bank expansion, duplicating Tables 16-4(a) to (i). Reverse the process.

3. Do bankers create deposits? Who does? If a banker receives a new deposit and new reserves, is he always able to find borrowers? Can he always expand his holdings of government securities?

4. "Banks borrow from their depositors at zero or low interest rates and invest most of the proceeds in higher-yielding loans and investments. They use the difference to pay their expenses, to provide us with low-cost mediums for monetary transactions, and to reward their stockholders for taking on the risks of declines in earning-asset values. They constitute an efficient method of allocating the saving and newly created M of the community to worthy local enterprises. One can scarcely imagine a better system than this, particularly with the recent reforms that insure depositors from loss and make psychological bank runs improbable." Appraise.

5. "My bank's books always balance. I merely *pass on* to investors the savings that my depositors bring me. Who dares say a banker can create M or demand deposits?" Do you dare?

6. "The Fed should create new reserves indefinitely, as long as we bankers can find good productive loans to make, because then each new M will be balanced by new product Q and prices won't rise and the community will get a higher real NNP indefinitely." This view was widely supported by the founders of the Fed in 1913. Can you see where the implied elasticity of M could be harmful in a world of fluctuating $C + I + G$ schedules? (HINT: Banks would expand M in booms and contract M in recessions: inflationary gaps might get worse.)

7. Review your understanding of the following concepts:

national, state banks; member banks, FDIC-insured banks	legal reserve ratio requirements
	chain of generations
Board of Governors, 12 Federal Reserve Banks, Fed	deposit creation for a monopoly bank versus a system of many small banks
bank balance sheet	simultaneous expansion by all banks
goldsmiths and fractional-reserve banking	excess reserves, leakage of reserves
	qualifications to multiple deposit creation

17 Federal Reserve and Central Bank Monetary Policy

THERE HAVE BEEN THREE GREAT INVENTIONS SINCE THE BEGINNING OF TIME: FIRE, THE WHEEL, AND CENTRAL BANKING. WILL ROGERS

The Federal Reserve is a central bank, a bank for bankers and for the government. Every central bank has one prime function:

■ *It operates to control the economy's supply of money and credit.* If business is getting worse and jobs are getting scarce, the Federal Reserve Board will try to expand money and credit. But if spending threatens to become excessive, so that prices are rising and there are many job vacancies, then the Federal Reserve authorities (the Fed) will do all that is possible to step on the brakes and contract money and credit. Monetary policy "leans against the wind" of prevailing deficient or excessive aggregate demand spending, to promote optimal real growth and price-level stability. All mixed economies rely on such a central bank.

In a nutshell that is the function of central banking. In this chapter we shall survey the weapons that the Fed uses to expand or contract money and credit.

■ HOW MONETARY POLICY WORKS TO CONTROL SPENDING

What is the exact process by which the Reserve authorities affect general spending? Here are five steps:

1. As shown in the last chapter, commercial or member banks must have reserves to support their assets and deposits. (So important are these "reserves" that we shall capitalize the word for the rest of this chapter.)

The first step of the Fed, therefore, when it wants to put on the monetary brakes, is to act to cut down on the Reserves available to the banks.

2. *Each dollar contraction in bank Reserves forces about a $5 contraction in total bank money, i.e., in total demand deposits.* (Recall the last chapter's analysis of multiple deposit creation in a fractional-reserve banking system.)

3. *The contraction in total money makes credit generally "tight," that is, both dearer*

and less available. We shall see that less *M* will raise interest rates. Just as important, less *M* will make credit less *available* to people.

Interest rates will rise for mortgage borrowers; for local governments that want to build schools and roads; and for businessmen anxious to build plants, buy new equipment, or add to inventory. Reinforcing higher interest cost will be credit's decreased availability. Thus, if you want to build a house, it matters to you that the interest rate has risen from 6 to 7 per cent. If you are like most families, it matters even more that you may now find it hard to get a mortgage with a low down payment. You may find your banker's manner a shade cooler; and he may discourage you from buying the $25,000 house that you really prefer to the $18,000 one you have been considering. When *M* is scarce, turndowns on loans become common. (During the Viet Nam boom, all this happened. Housing starts plummeted for lack of credit.)

4. *With credit expensive and hard to get, private and public investment will tend to fall.* Why this downward shift in the *I* and *G* schedules?[1] Because people's decisions as to whether it is profitable to build a new house or plant, order a new machine, and hold more inventory usually depend upon how they can finance such investment spending. If they have to pay a high interest rate or find it very hard to get loans, they often scale down their investment plans. The same holds for state and local governments. The old road gets patched up and that new road postponed when the town finds it cannot float its bonds at any reasonable interest rate. The gymnasium and library are cut out of the new school plans when the citizens learn their tax rate is going up because it now costs 5 per cent to borrow, instead of 4 or 3½ per cent.

5. *Finally, the pressure on credit and on investment spending will, through the downward shift in the I + G schedule, have downward effects on income spending, prices, and jobs.* The multiplier analysis of Chapter 13 showed how such a drop in investment will depress income spending sharply.

If the Fed has been right in its diagnosis of inflationary conditions, the drop in money income will be just what the doctor ordered to help the situation. *M* contraction will have succeeded in reducing the inflationary gap.

■ RECAPITULATION

This five-step sequence—from the Fed's changing the commercial banks' Reserves, to 5:1 changes in total *M*, to changes in credit's interest cost and availability, to changes in private and public investment spending, and finally to multiplied changes in money income—is vital. By rereading the italicized parts of the previous section, you can consolidate your understanding of it. Better still, psychologists tell us we learn fastest by participating. The previous section was explained in terms of a time when the Fed wants to *contract* business activity. Tackle the problem of how things proceed when the Fed wants to *expand* business activity.

---

[1] Later chapters (particularly Chapter 30) show that higher interest rates tend to depress the market value of wealth items: land, bonds, buildings, equipment. With their total wealth less and installment credit hard to get, people's *CC* schedule may also be shifted down along with their *II* schedules.

Suppose you are Chairman Martin of the Fed's Board of Governors at a time when the economy is mildly depressed. Suppose you are called to testify before a congressional committee—as Martin so often is—to explain to an interrogating senator just how your *expansionary* acts would operate. Retrace these detailed steps.

The Fed expands Reserves; member banks then engineer something like a 5:1 expansion in demand deposits; increase in society's M is associated with "easier money conditions," i.e., lower interest rates on loans, bonds, and mortgages and, equally important, more easily available credit to would-be investors and government spenders. There results an increase in I, G, and perhaps even in durable-goods C installment spending. And finally, there follow multiplier effects of the shift in the $C + I + G$ schedule on income, employment, and possibly price levels.

■ BALANCE SHEET OF THE FEDERAL RESERVE BANKS

Now that we have surveyed the process of monetary policy with a telescope, let us study the mechanism in some detail. We shall not attempt to look at Federal Reserve policy under a microscope, since that is the job of an intermediate course in money and banking; but we do want to get a general idea of exactly what weapons the Fed can use to affect bank Reserves.

Look at Table 17-1. This lists the combined balance sheet of the 12 Reserve Banks. The first asset consists mostly of gold certificates, i.e., warehouse receipts from the Treasury to the Fed for so much gold. United States government securities make up most of the rest of the assets—the significance of this item will be explained soon. The smaller Discounts, Loans, and Acceptances item is primarily loans or advances to member banks. (The interest rate the Fed charges banks for such loans, or "discounts," is called the "discount rate," which is usually about the same in all 12 Reserve Districts.)

The right-hand side lists the usual capital accounts: original capital subscribed by the member banks plus accumulated surplus. This would be much greater for so profitable a business were it not for the already mentioned fact that the Federal Reserve gives all its excess profits back to the Treasury.

Federal Reserve notes and deposits underlie our money supply:

ASSETS		LIABILITIES AND NET WORTH	
Gold certificates and other cash	$13.6	Capital accounts	$ 1.1
U.S. government securities	40.8	Federal Reserve notes	37.1
Discounts, loans, and acceptances	0.3	Deposits:	
Miscellaneous other assets	8.0	**Member bank Reserves**	**18.4**
(primarily "uncollected		U.S. Treasury	0.7
items")		Foreign and other	0.5
		Miscellaneous liabilities	4.9
Total	$62.7	Total	$62.7

TABLE 17-1. COMBINED BALANCE SHEET OF 12 FEDERAL RESERVE BANKS JANUARY 1, 1966 (in billions of dollars). By (a) controlling its earning assets (government securities and discounts), the Fed (b) controls its liabilities (deposits and Federal Reserve notes), thereby (c) controlling the economy's money supply (currency and demand deposits) and affecting NNP.

Federal Reserve notes are the Fed's principal liabilities. These are the various dollar bills we all carry in our wallets. These IOUs cost the Fed no interest, and it is highly privileged to have been granted by Congress this power to issue currency.

Little comment is needed on several of its deposit liabilities: United States government deposits, foreign central bank deposits, and miscellaneous.

Of vital importance, though, are the member banks' reserve balances kept on deposit with the Federal Reserve Banks and shown as FRB liabilities. Along with small amounts of vault cash, these are the Reserves we have been talking about. They provide the basis for multiple deposit creation by the member banks.

We shall see that the Fed, by altering its holding of government securities and discount assets, can create changes in the Reserves of the commercial banks—thereby starting off our earlier-mentioned five-step sequence. The total of its government securities plus discounts is often called "Reserve Bank Credit"; and observers watch carefully in weekly newspaper reports the changes in this important figure which reflect the desire of the Fed to expand or contract credit. (Later, Fig. 17-2 will show how these important balance-sheet items have changed in recent years.)

■ DISCRETIONARY MONETARY POLICIES BY THE FEDERAL RESERVE:
OPEN-MARKET OPERATIONS

To initiate the five-step stabilization sequence, the Federal Reserve has three main weapons, which are, in order of their present importance, (1) open-market operations, (2) discount-rate policy, (3) changes in the legal reserve ratio requirements of the member banks. (We shall review its five minor weapons later in this chapter.)

> ■ By selling or buying government bonds in the open market (mostly in New York City), the Reserve authorities can tighten member bank Reserves or loosen them. These so-called "open-market operations" are the Fed's most important stabilizing weapon.

At frequent intervals, even as you read this book, the Open Market Committee is meeting to decide whether to pump more Reserves into the banking system by buying Treasury bills (i.e., short-term bonds) or longer bonds, or whether to tighten things up a little by selling government securities. It is a never-ending job.

To see how an open-market operation changes Reserves, let us suppose that the Fed thinks the economic winds are blowing up a little inflation. Its Open Market Committee holds the usual secret meeting. They say: "Let's sell 1 billion dollars of government bonds from our portfolio to contract Reserves and over-all credit." The motion is unanimously carried. To whom are the bonds sold? No one knows: to the open market. The dealers in government bonds—there are about half a dozen big ones—will not reveal the names of the buyers. But you can guess that they are primarily insurance companies, commercial banks, and big business firms.

The buyer will most likely pay for the bonds by a check to the Fed drawn on his bank account. The Fed will present this check for payment to his member bank. That member bank will lose an equivalent amount of its Reserve balances with the Federal

Open-market sale cuts Reserves and cuts deposits 5:1:

(a) First, producing this change in the Federal Reserve Banks' balance sheet:

FEDERAL RESERVE ASSETS		FEDERAL RESERVE LIABILITIES	
U.S. securities	−$1.0	Member bank Reserves	−$1.0
Total	−$1.0	Total	−$1.0

(b) Finally, producing this change in the member banks' balance sheet:

MEMBER BANK ASSETS		MEMBER BANK LIABILITIES	
Reserves	−$1.0	Demand deposits	−$5.0
Loans and investments	− 4.0		
Total	−$5.0	Total	−$5.0

TABLE 17-2(a) and (b). CHANGE IN FEDERAL RESERVE AND IN MEMBER BANK BALANCE SHEETS (in billions of dollars). When an open-market sale kills off 1 billion dollars of Reserves, it induces a 5-billion-dollar drop in total demand deposits. The member banks must call in loans and sell off their "investments" (i.e., their securities) up to 4 billion dollars.

Reserve. Table 17-2(a) shows the final effect on the Federal Reserve balance sheet. The open-market sale has cut down on the Fed's assets and liabilities. (It has also initially cut down on member bank Reserves and their demand deposits owed to the bond buyer.)

Actually, this shows only the *initial* potency of open-market sales. In all likelihood the 1-billion-dollar sale of government bonds will result in a 5-billion-dollar cut in the community's money supply. We've seen why before.

Reserves go down by 1 billion dollars, and that tends to set off a 5-billion-dollar contraction of deposits. Table 17-2(b) shows the member banks' position after Reserves have been extinguished by the open-market operation. In the end, the Fed's open-market sale has put 5:1 downward pressure on bank-deposit M.

> To test your understanding of open-market operations, consider the reverse process. Suppose incomes and jobs are at too low a level. What will the Open Market Committee want to do? Buy government bonds on the open market and thereby create new Reserves for the member banks? Produce thereby a 5:1 expansion in M, thus making credit cheaper and more easily available to investors, and consequently encouraging an upward shift in C + I + G and a multiplier increase in NNP? Confirm all this.

■ DISCOUNT-RATE POLICY: A SECOND WEAPON

The Federal Reserve Banks also make loans to the member banks. These we call "discounts." When its discounts are growing, the banks are borrowing from the Fed, which is thereby helping bank Reserves to grow. When the Fed's discounts are dropping, it is helping bank Reserves to contract.[2]

[2] When the Federal Reserve System was started, it was thought that discount policy would be most important of all. The idea was to have member banks "rediscount" their customers' promissory notes, sending them over to the Reserve Banks in return for new cash. That way the neighborhood banks would never run out of money to accommodate worthy farm and business borrowers. It did not work

Unfortunately, the Fed is not free to pursue a discount policy exactly the way it wants to. It cannot send salesmen out to drum up more discounts whenever it wants to expand them. All it can do is wait for banks to come to it. All it can do is name the "discount rate," which sets its interest charge in each of the 12 Federal Reserve districts for such discounts or advances.

True, it can expect to get more business by lowering the discount rate or can discourage the volume of its discounts by raising the discount rate. But as far as discount policy is concerned, the Fed must play the passive role. It can sit and wait. It can veto. It can make its rate attractive. But it certainly cannot set its amount of *discounts* at precisely the figure it wants. Only in its open-market operations can it take the active role. But do not overlook the power of a veto. A bank knows it must not abuse the privilege of being able to discount; it must not continually use this source of funds. By being able to say No, the Fed has some power to put contractionary pressure on its discounts.

CHANGING THE DISCOUNT RATE   On New York's Wall Street, Chicago's LaSalle Street, and Boston's State Street, everyone keeps careful watch on the discount rate that the Fed charges for its discounts. Thus, on the Thursday when the discount rate is raised, stocks and bonds will usually fall in price. Even London and Paris find their interest rates and investment spending influenced by announced changes in our discount rate.

The discount rate is usually set to *follow* the market. After open-market sales have been forcing interest rates up, banks will more and more try to borrow from the Fed at the not-yet-raised discount rate. To discourage such a growth in its discounts and advances, the Fed will eventually have to raise the discount rate to bring it back into normal alignment with the market.

And when the Fed does raise the discount rate, very many in the market will say: "Aha, the Board still thinks the wind is blowing in the inflationary direction." Changes in the discount rate, as well as being reflections that follow the tightness of credit, can also have important reinforcing *causal* effects upon the credit market. The effective interest rate banks charge customers—such as the "prime rate" charged biggest corporate borrowers—may soon get forced up to maintain their differential above the discount rate.

These patterns are reversed when the Fed wants easier credit. The discount rate is lowered to reflect the ease already apparent in the market, and the announcement of its being lowered usually serves to ease the market further. Thus, in August, 1960, when the discount rate was cut from $3\frac{1}{2}$ to 3 per cent, stocks and bonds soared in price. By contrast, the December, 1965, announcement of a discount-rate rise caused bonds and stocks to plummet downward; now people realized the Fed would keep money tight to fight the Viet Nam demand-pull inflation.)

---

out that way, for two reasons. First and most important, today experts realize that the last thing a healthy economy wants is an *elastic* money supply that will *automatically* expand when business is good and contract when it is bad. That way lies disastrous *reinforcement* of business cycles and inflation. Second, banks find that they prefer to borrow from the Fed on the basis of their numerous government securities rather than on their customers' promissory notes. Since 1935, most borrowing is on government securities, and that is why we now speak of the "discount rate" rather than of the old-fashioned "rediscount rate." (In England, they speak always of "bank rate.")

■ CHANGING RESERVE REQUIREMENTS: A DRASTIC AND
INFREQUENTLY USED WEAPON

The Federal Reserve Board is given by Congress the limited power to raise or lower the
required legal reserve ratio that the member banks must keep against their deposits. If
the Fed wants to make credit tight very quickly, it can raise the required reserve ratios
for the city and country banks to the 22 and 14 per cent statutory limits. (If it wanted
credit still tighter, it would have to ask Congress to raise these limits, just as it would
have to if it wished to raise the 6 per cent time-deposit requirement.)

If the Fed wants to ease credit conditions, it can do the reverse. It can cut legal
reserve ratios, doing this again and again until the banks are down to 10 and 7 per cent.
To go lower than that would require a new act of Congress. And, as in 1962, the Fed
can lower the required reserve ratios behind time deposits.

■ Changing reserve requirements is a powerful tool: it is used sparingly—a
change comes only every few years, not every day as in the case of open-market
operations. It could be used more often; but open-market operations can produce
about the same effects.

Exactly how does an increase in required reserve ratios operate to tighten credit?
Suppose the banks had built up deposits in a 5:1 fashion as a result of the required ratio
having been 20 per cent, with excess reserves being negligible. Now suppose the Fed
wants to tighten credit and Congress lets it raise the required ratio to 25 per cent. Even
if it does nothing by way of open-market operations or discount policy to change bank
Reserves, the member banks now have to contract their loans and investments greatly—
and their deposits as well.

Why? Because (as the last chapter showed) now the bank deposits can only be in
a 4:1, not a 5:1, ratio. So there will have to be a drop by one-fifth in all deposits.

This painful cut will start to take place quickly. For as soon as the Board signs the
new fiat raising requirements to 25 per cent, banks will find themselves deficient with
respect to Reserves. They will have to sell some of their bonds and call in some loans.
The bond buyers will use up their demand deposits, and the borrowers whose loans are
called will use up their demand deposits to pay back such loans. The process ends
only after banks have brought down their deposits to 4 rather than 5 times their
Reserves.

Table 17-3 shows how their combined balance sheets might look before and after
the change. You may be sure that so great a change in so short a time would result in
very high interest rates, in unavailable credit, in great cuts in I (and possibly in local G),
and in great reductions in national income and employment. Hence, this powerful weapon
of changing reserve requirements is rarely used.[3]

---

[3] In 1936–1937 reserve requirements were sharply raised. But at that time banks found loans and bonds
so unattractive that they were already holding heavy "excess reserves," i.e., holding more idle cash
than the law required. So raising legal requirements did not have the great effects in lowering M or
raising interest rates that it would have today. It should also be pointed out that such a sudden squeeze
on banks' reserve positions would undoubtedly today cause them to borrow at the "discount window"
even at a higher discount rate for some temporary period at least.

Raising Reserve requirements forces member banks to contract:

Before: when 1:5 prevails

MEMBER BANK ASSETS		MEMBER BANK LIABILITIES	
Reserves	$20	Demand deposits	$100
Loans and investments	80		
Total	$100	Total	$100

After: when 1:4 prevails

MEMBER BANK ASSETS		MEMBER BANK LIABILITIES	
Reserves	$20	Demand deposits	$80
Loans and investments	60		
Total	$80	Total	$80

TABLE 17-3. EFFECT OF RISE IN LEGAL RESERVE RE-QUIREMENTS FROM ONE-FIFTH TO ONE-FOURTH. The same base of Reserves now supports only 4:1, not 5:1, of deposits. What will be happening on Main Street in the transition?

■ MINOR WEAPONS: QUALITATIVE VERSUS QUANTITATIVE CONTROLS

The Fed also has used five further minor weapons: (1) "moral suasion," (2) selective controls over "margin requirements" for loans to buy stocks, (3) control over maximum interest rates banks can pay on time deposits, (4) selective credit controls over installment contracts and consumer credit, (5) selective controls over the terms of housing mortgage contracts. (The last two powers Congress let lapse in the early 1950s.)

MORAL SUASION   This refers to "jawbone control": the Reserve officials express their displeasure if banks are not doing what is wanted of them. Bankers are called in for heart-to-heart talks. An appeal to community spirit is made. Vague threats concerning future availability of credit may be made, and bank examiners may become especially zealous in going over the books.

Many economists doubt that slaps on the wrist will keep competitive bankers from doing what they want to do. Nevertheless, it is a tenable belief that moral suasion does have some significant effects, especially in the short run and especially when banks are heavily reliant on the privilege to "discount" at the Fed. After all, bankers are sensitive to public opinion just like anyone else. And bankers find it only prudent not to get in the bad books of the Fed (as their extraordinary compliance with the 1966 voluntary program of control over foreign loans by banks did demonstrate).

SELECTIVE CONTROLS: MARGIN REQUIREMENTS   A selective or qualitative credit control is contrasted with an over-all quantitative credit control that operates merely by affecting over-all bank Reserves and over-all credit tightness. Selective credit controls can be very important in countries that have considerable central planning and supervision by the government of the detailed actions of business. To build a house there, you may need a permit; similarly, to float a new stock or bond issue.

The banks, particularly if, as in England, there are a few great ones, may be called in by the Chancellor of the Exchequer. He may say: "Look here. We want you to favor export industries in making your loans. And favor necessities. And cut back your total loans by 10 per cent before Christmas."

Such selective credit controls can be very powerful indeed. However, in normal peacetime it is the American custom not to rely on these detailed interferences with the pricing process—with one exception. The Federal Reserve is given power to set "margin requirements" that limit how much people can borrow in order to buy and carry listed common and preferred stocks. Thus, I could in 1967 borrow 30 per cent from my broker but had to put up the other 70 per cent myself. In 1958 I could borrow only 10 per cent, and in 1962, as much as 50 per cent.[4]

INTEREST-RATE CEILINGS   When any bank can earn 4 per cent or more on safe short-term government bonds (or even more on riskier loans), it stands to gain when it can owe people demand deposits at a zero interest rate. Under competition, free banking would result in banks then bidding up the interest rate paid on demand deposits to a positive level. (That is what used to happen in the 1920s: Our grandfathers often got paid 5 per cent on their checking deposits! Or they could often draw checks on their saving or time deposits.)

But during the Great Depression Congress made it illegal for banks to pay interest on checking accounts. This was for two reasons: Banks could earn practically nothing then on safe government bonds, and the industry felt that its earnings would be better if rivals were kept by law from bidding positive interest on demand deposits; aside from this cartel reason, many experts jumped to the conclusion that overcompetition among banks had given rise to unsound lending practices, which led to the mass bank runs and failures.

This depression-born stricture against interest on demand deposits still stands. It explains why people and corporations have been putting less and less of their idle funds into demand deposits, keeping their check balances to a minimum and merely replenishing them from their savings accounts when they get too low. (And it explains the 1960s' rapid rise in the broadly defined M_2 money supply compared with the narrower M_1 definition including only deposits payable on demand. See Fig. 15-2, p. 267.)

From the mid-thirties to the late fifties, the Fed also put low ceilings on the interest rates member banks could pay on *time* deposits. As long as competitive rates to be earned on government bonds remained low, this did not matter much. But when federal savings and loan associations could afford to pay 4, 5, and more per cent, people stopped leaving their money in commercial bank savings accounts. They switched to nonmember banks and to S&Ls; in the case of firms, they switched to the Treasury bill market. The big New York banks were especially hard hit when their foreign depositors began to withdraw deposits and to buy securities directly themselves.

[4] Back in the boom market of 1929, there were no rules at all: one could borrow 70, 80, or even 90 per cent of the value of any stock he bought. Little wonder that, once the crash came, brokers began to phone their clients for them to put up more "margin to cover the declining value of their stocks." Since many clients were already operating on a shoestring, they could not pony up the extra margin. Result: The broker had to sell their stocks; so just when stocks were already weak, the forced selling by low-margin holders added to the avalanche.

In recent years, therefore, spurred on by the fear that foreign governments and firms would withdraw their money, the Fed has raised the rates banks can pay on time deposits (to as much as 5 or $5\frac{1}{2}$ per cent, under so-called "Regulation Q"). Critics feared that raising such ceilings would make money tighter. Actually, the reverse happened in 1962–1965, as competitive economic theory predicted it would: the member banks retained more funds than they otherwise would have, and the shift toward more time deposits at first had the good effect of keeping down the long-term interest rates so important for construction and investment loans, while permitting the Fed to tighten short-term rates so important to dissuade money from going abroad and worsening our gold problem.

After 1965 a new problem began to arise. During the 1960s the large New York banks pioneered a new kind of time deposit—the so-called "certificate of deposit." This was a negotiable instrument that would enable a corporation to deposit $100,000 or $1,000,000 for 90 days (in 1966, say, at $5\frac{1}{2}$ per cent per annum); however, if at the end of a few days the firm should change its mind, it could sell the "C-D" to some other corporation and yet lose little or no interest. What was the result in 1966 when credit became very tight in order to help calm down the Viet Nam-induced inflationary gap? Investors started to withdraw their funds from West Coast saving and loan associations to put them into Eastern C-Ds. A few S&Ls were on the verge of bankruptcy after they began to lose funds; they now had to pay $5\frac{3}{4}$ per cent or more on time deposits, whereas they had obligated themselves to lend money on long-term mortgages that brought in a net yield of less than that!

To Congress it appeared that the competitive scramble for funds led to unwise and risky loans by banks and S&Ls desperate to hold onto their deposits. Therefore, Congress has led the Federal Reserve to use Regulation Q to limit interest rates that banks can pay on low-denomination C-Ds. Inasmuch as the government insures deposits in banks and in S&Ls, it has a burning interest in how competition works out in this area. But diddling maximum rates to protect S&Ls may not work long. Even if commercial banks are kept by fiat from offering competitive interest rates, depositors can withdraw funds from S&Ls and invest directly in higher-yielding Treasury bills.

CONTROL OVER INSTALLMENT TERMS   Besides moral suasion and direct controls over margin borrowing and deposit terms, the Fed for many years had the power to set limits on installment contracts. Thus, in the years of the Korean conflict, the Fed made you put so much down when you bought cars, furniture, and other goods; and this same so-called "Regulation W" also required you to pay up on your charge accounts before buying more goods on credit. Regulation W seems to have been very effective, and the same has been true of similar regulations in Britain and elsewhere. But it became unpopular, and after the Korean crisis this power was allowed to lapse.

CONTROL OVER MORTGAGE TERMS   Congress had long empowered the Federal Reserve to set terms for mortgage down payments and the number of years for amortization. This so-called "Regulation X" gave the Board powerful leverage over the pace of house-construction expenditure. By raising down payments and shortening the span of mortgages, the Board could choke off housing. By doing the reverse, it could help step up the pace of construction.

This strong weapon of mortgage control was allowed by Congress to lapse in 1953. The Fed, with its philosophy of over-all quantitative controls rather than selective fiats, was perhaps not too sorry to see this power go; but it soon learned that

Nature abhors a vacuum. If the central bank will not wield these powers, somebody else will. Financial intermediaries have burgeoned.

Thus, much housing is subsidized by the government: the Veterans Administration (VA) guarantees mortgage loans, and so does the Federal Housing Authority (FHA). Also, there is the Federal National Mortgage Association ("Fannie Mae"), which buys mortgages to make credit for housing more available. The federal savings associations can borrow from the Federal Home Loan Bank, a government agency which threatens to become practically a second central bank, not always coordinated with the Federal Reserve.[5]

■ INTERNATIONAL GOLD MOVEMENTS AND RESERVES

Until now we have been speaking as if all the movements in total M originate in actions of the Federal Reserve aimed to change bank Reserves in the direction desired by the authorities. There is, however, an external force that affects our M, namely, gold movements. These are primarily gold exports to or from abroad. Such movements tend to induce changes in M even when the Fed has done nothing. But it should be realized that the three weapons of its monetary policy can enable the authorities to *offset* any such changes in M that are thought to be against the national interest.[6]

Part Five will deal with international trade in detail; here we need only touch upon the banking aspects of gold flows. When American exporters are selling more goods abroad than importers are importing, and consequently foreigners are paying us by shipping gold here, we shall see that the deposit of such gold in our banking system will give rise to the familiar 5:1 expansion process—just as in our earlier examples where a widow, or a seller of bonds to the Fed, or anyone else brought new Reserves to deposit in a member bank.

When, as has been more the custom in recent years, America is losing gold to pay for the excess of her total imports (including government dollars spent on military and foreign aid) over her total exports, there will then be a loss of gold and of Reserves by our banking system. Unless the Federal Reserve Board chooses to offset this loss of Reserves by some action, what must then happen to M? The money supply will be contracted in a 5:1 fashion.

[5] These government agencies, which have no connection with the Federal Reserve, have often done what you might expect—they have worked at cross-purposes to the Board. Nowadays, public policy takes special interest in certain sectors of the credit market. It does not seem content to let interest rates find their own level in each market; it seeks to encourage activities such as housing and small business and to discourage others such as stock speculation. (Earlier we saw that finance and insurance companies perform many functions similar to the banks. But they are not under the tight reserve requirement and other controls exercised over the member banks. Some experts think that monetary policy would gain in potency and fairness if some controls over financial intermediaries were introduced. Others say, "After all, they don't directly create M, and in any case putting pressure on the banks does put pressure on the intermediaries at one stage removed.")

[6] However, if the Fed now offsets the effect on M of a gold drain and thereby postpones the process of corrective adjustment, it must be prepared to countenance that loss and maybe more loss of America's gold in the future, as we shall later see in Part Five.

THE OLD GOLD STANDARD   Before 1933 the analysis of gold movements was simple. We Americans had gold coins, just as England did before 1914. And, since coins are not very handy to do business with, we had gold certificates. These were nicely printed gold-and-black bills that were warehouse receipts, issued by the Treasury, which gave you the right to $10 or $20 worth of gold.

What happened before 1933 when the United States sold more exports than she bought imports, paying the difference by importing gold bars? These bars of gold were exchanged at the nearest Treasury office for gold coin or for gold certificates. The exporter then took these to his commercial bank, and then would begin one of our familiar multiple expansions of deposits. (This was 10:1 then rather than 5:1, because before 1936, member banks had to maintain a legal reserve ratio of only about one-tenth their deposits. You can show how deposits had to *contract* in a 10:1 fashion when America *exported* gold to pay for the surplus of our imports over exports. Chapter 33 gives more details.)

SINCE 1933   Today things are somewhat different. When the New Deal Congress decided to raise the price of gold from about $21 an ounce to $35 an ounce, it called in all the gold and all the gold certificates. (The Supreme Court did approve the constitutionality of this use of congressional power over the currency.) Congress called in the gold at $21 an ounce so that those who held it would not make a profit from the revaluation of gold. And just in case any future Congress should raise the price of gold again and face the same problem, a law was passed forbidding Americans to hold gold domestically—except in jewelry, dental fillings, and old coins. (Recall earlier discussions.)

Yet it still is true that whenever we export more than we import and get paid in gold, the Treasury and Fed will convert that gold into new money. But now it does not convert it into gold coins that you can hold or into gold certificates that private individuals can hold. What the Treasury now does is to use the Federal Reserve Banks as its agent to accomplish a similar result.

Essentially, here is how the process works. Any gold you have earned for America by exporting goods (or mining with pan and pick) comes to the Federal Reserve Bank of New York. It gives $35 an ounce for the gold—by check, not in gold certificates, which it is illegal for the public to hold. You deposit this check, and when your bank sends it to the Federal Reserve, it gets in return a new Reserve balance equal to your original gold. Like the pre-1933 case, this new Reserve created by the gold can today also start a multiple deposit expansion.

What does the Federal Reserve do with the gold? It is only an agent in the process. It turns the gold over to the Treasury to be put in Fort Knox, Kentucky; and the Fed receives in return those gold certificates you saw in the Federal Reserve Bank balance sheet (Table 17-1). The process is now complete.[7]

[7] NOTE: The Fed has added a gold-certificate asset and an equal member-bank Reserve liability. The government now holds physical gold and has issued a gold certificate against this; the banks end up with new Reserves, 4:1 loans and investments, and 5:1 demand deposit liabilities. (The Fed deals in gold primarily with foreign central banks, not with private citizens. So it is generally not you, the exporter, who walks into the New York FRB with gold in a satchel. But the result is quite the same, and the gold shipped from the importing country's central bank does give our banks new Reserves.)

■ GOLD AS A CONSTRAINT ON MONETARY POLICY

This completes the discussion of how international gold movements can themselves affect our money supply. Such international influences on our *M* can be offset by planned Federal Reserve open-market operations acting in the opposite direction. All over the world, central banks have often chosen to offset the influences of international gold movements. In particular, for 25 years after 1933 the United States was in the position of having so much gold that she could determine domestic policy, completely ignoring her international balance of payments and blithely offsetting any gold movements she wanted to.

As we shall see in Part Five, dealing with international trade, this freedom no longer holds. When the Federal Reserve wants to lower interest rates in order to pursue a domestic stabilization policy of expansion, it must now take into account the following fact: if short-term interest rates are lowered here relative to those abroad, many foreigners will want to move their funds to higher-interest-rate markets abroad. There will be a resulting drain of "cool money" and gold from our shores; and, although we still have much gold, we can no longer afford to ignore such a drain. In the future, unless the Fed can directly affect long-term rates of interest rather than merely short-term ones, we may find ourselves in an era when fear of gold loss will require greater reliance on stabilizing fiscal policies than on stabilizing monetary policies.

■ THE PYRAMID OF CREDIT

Figure 17-1 summarizes the relation between the commercial or member banks and the public; between these banks and the Federal Reserve Banks; and between the Reserve Banks and the Treasury. At the bottom of the pyramid is a relatively small amount of gold held by the United States Treasury, about 13.7 billion dollars' worth in mid-1966. With minor exceptions not worth noting, this gold is matched by gold certificates in the coffers of the Federal Reserve Banks.

Moving up the pyramid from the Treasury to the Federal Reserve Banks, we find their total liabilities and total assets to be 62.7 billion dollars, so that Federal Reserve Bank gold certificates are about 22 per cent of their total liabilities and about 36 per cent of their Federal Reserve note liabilities (which provide us with our currency). The Federal Reserve Banks since 1965 are legally required to hold at least 25 per cent of these note liabilities in the form of gold certificates. (This Federal Reserve gold-reserve ratio should not be confused with the member bank 1:5 reserve ratio.) The Fed must stay well above *its* legal ratio if it is to be perfectly free to act in *both* an expansionary and a contractionary direction. Should the Fed begin to get close to this legal 25 per cent ratio as we lose gold, Congress could do what it did during the war and again in the 1960s—pass a law lowering or eliminating the requirement, so as to restore two-way freedom to the Fed.[8]

[8] Some experts think that, by declaration of an emergency each 30 days, the Fed could go below this required gold ratio. In 1913 the founders of the Federal Reserve System thought this gold-reserve requirement would be important. They took it so seriously that part of the blame for the 1920 price collapse must be attributed to the fact that no one dreamed that Congress could lower the gold requirement at a time when the Fed was threatening to go below the 35 and 40 per cent ratios that then

The Federal Reserve provides our currency and bank Reserves:

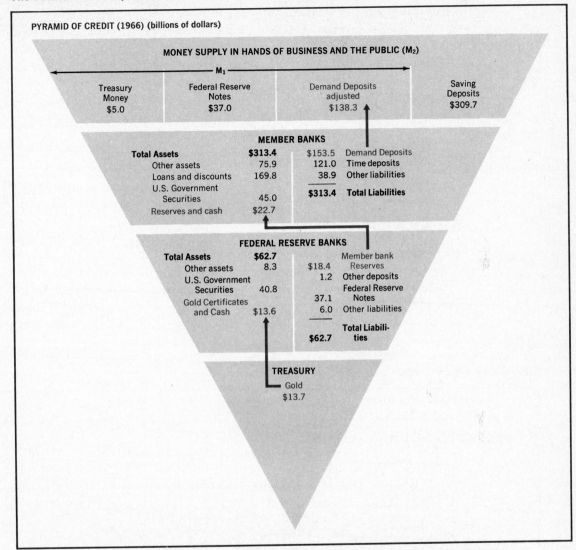

PYRAMID OF CREDIT (1966) (billions of dollars)

MONEY SUPPLY IN HANDS OF BUSINESS AND THE PUBLIC (M₂)

M_1

Treasury Money	Federal Reserve Notes	Demand Deposits adjusted	Saving Deposits
$5.0	$37.0	$138.3	$309.7

MEMBER BANKS

Total Assets	$313.4	$153.5	Demand Deposits
Other assets	75.9	121.0	Time deposits
Loans and discounts	169.8	38.9	Other liabilities
U.S. Government Securities	45.0	$313.4	Total Liabilities
Reserves and cash	$22.7		

FEDERAL RESERVE BANKS

Total Assets	$62.7		Member bank
Other assets	8.3	$18.4	Reserves
U.S. Government Securities	40.8	1.2	Other deposits
			Federal Reserve
Gold Certificates and Cash	$13.6	37.1	Notes
		6.0	Other liabilities
		$62.7	Total Liabilities

TREASURY

Gold
$13.7

FIG. 17-1. The small amount of gold at the bottom of this pyramid could be dispensed with entirely if Congress passed a law repealing all gold-reserve requirements on the Federal Reserve. Notice that the liabilities of one stage correspond to the assets of the next-highest stage. Total saving deposits include those of savings and loan and other noncommercial banks. (Sources: Tables 15-1, 16-1, and 17-1, and the 1966 *Federal Reserve Bulletin*.)

legally prevailed. The founders of the system would look at today's pyramid of credit and say: Each dollar of gold can give rise to at least a 20:1 deposit expansion, i.e., 5:1 at the member bank level times 4:1 at the Fed level. This is misleading in that the Fed does not adhere to its 1:4 ratio and each new dollar of gold results directly only in a 5:1 deposit expansion—and not even that, if the Fed wants to offset it. In a future emergency, foolish *adherence* to such a 4:1 rule could conceivably force us off the gold standard. Today experts realize that *all* our gold is to be available for international, not domestic, purposes.

Besides gold certificates, the Federal Reserve Banks hold about 8.3 + 40.8 billion dollars of loans and investments, primarily in short-term government bills.

Matching their total assets, the Reserve Banks' biggest single liability consists of Federal Reserve note currency. This is held largely by the public.

The other principal liability of the Reserve Banks is Reserves of the member banks. Pyramided upon 18.4 billion dollars of Reserves is the volume of bank deposit money held by the public. To show all the saving deposits held by the public, we have added to the top layer deposits in S&Ls, mutual saving banks, etc.

■ FINANCE IN THE POST–WORLD WAR II PERIOD

The pyramid of credit gives us a still picture. To see changes that have been taking place in recent years, refer to Fig. 17-2, which depicts the important economic variables published each month in the *Federal Reserve Bulletin*.

At the top is currency in circulation. It grew mightily in World War II and has since shown persistent growth. Demand deposits would be too large to show on the same chart, but they would show a pattern of somewhat slower growth.

Member bank reserve balances, which together with vault cash constitute Reserves, show a similar but less dramatic pattern. Our major interest is to explain how these Reserves change. Part of the explanation will come from the behavior of the gold stock.

How "Reserve Bank Credit" determines our money supply:

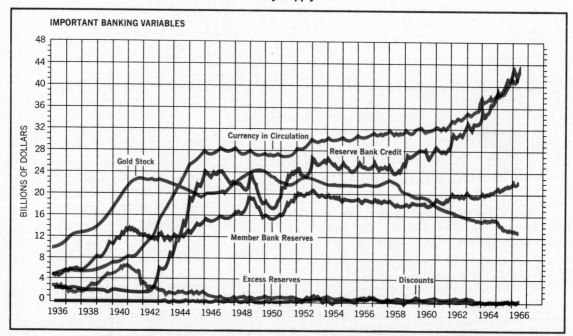

FIG. 17-2. Money in circulation and Reserves underlying bank *M* have followed Reserve Bank Credit pretty closely. The Fed has not let gold flows call the tune.

But not much: the Fed has not let un-dulations and declines in our gold hold-ings show up as changes in Reserves.

To explain Reserves we must turn to Reserve Bank Credit, namely, to the sum of the Fed's government securities and discounts. Notice that the Fed has been using open-market purchases to lift Reserve Bank Credit by more than enough to offset our loss of gold, thus keeping member bank Reserves from falling after 1958.

See Figs. 17-2 and 17-3 for the vol-ume of *discounts*. Their total is small in comparison with government securities; but their change in some years is sig-nificant in comparison with that year's net open-market purchases or sales. In the short run, these discounts operate at cross-purposes to open-market opera-tions. Thus, note how discounts grew in 1966, just when the Fed was trying to tighten credit. Some economists, there-fore, are critical of discount policy. But defenders say, "If it weren't for the safety valve of the discount privilege, the Fed wouldn't dare to have so tight a policy of open-market sales. Just as car brakes enable cars to go *faster,* the exist-ence of discounting enables the Fed to pursue a sterner open-market policy."

Excess reserves, as shown in the top chart of Fig. 17-3, have been pretty small in recent years.[9] When discounts get above excess reserves—so that so-called "net free reserves" are negative— you can be pretty sure money is tight.

The Fed seeks to control banks' reserve positions:

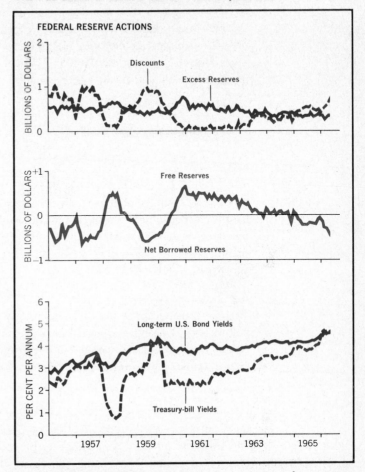

FIG. 17-3. When discounts exceed excess reserves, net free reserves turn negative (becoming net borrowed reserves). Usually, this means credit is tight and interest rates are high.

When business slackens and the Fed pursues easy-money policies, it gives banks much excess Reserves in order to encourage expansion of M and $C + I + G$. By lowering or raising the discount rate relative to short-term market interest rates (such as Treasury-bill rates), the Fed can encourage or discourage discounts.

[9] In the mid-thirties you would have seen a tremendous bulge in excess reserves. Gold flowed here in great amounts; but with banks wary of loans and of further government securities, the result was no multiple expansion—merely a piling up of excess reserves. The Board, nervous always about inflation (even during the slump itself!), feared that these excess reserves might suddenly become the base of deposit expansion. So, as we have seen, they doubled reserve requirements, to bring excess reserves under control. In brisk times, when banks can find attractive earning assets, excess reserves do not become substantial. As the federal funds market has developed, even the small country banks have cut down on their level of excess reserves.

The middle of Fig. 17-3 plots the important concept *net free reserves*. It tends to be negative when "money is tight" and interest rates are high and to be positive when the Fed eases credit. Thus, as business expanded from 1963 to 1967, the Fed, by engineering declining net reserves, let the money market tighten itself.

This chapter has now laid the base for the discussion of the interplay between monetary policy and income determination in the next chapter.

SUMMARY

1 ■

The Federal Reserve is a central bank, a bank for bankers. Its duty is to control the community's supply of money. Its five-step mode of action goes thus: (1) it contracts bank Reserves, which (2) causes multiple contractions in total deposits, which (3) makes credit expensive (high interest rates) and hard to get, which (4) depresses private and public investment spending, which (5) puts a multiplied damper on money income and prices.

2 ■

The powerful weapons the Fed uses are (*a*) open-market operations, (*b*) discount-rate policy, and (*c*) changes in legal reserve requirements. Minor weapons used at times by central banks are moral suasion and selective controls over time-deposit interest ceilings, margin borrowing, installment sales, and mortgage credit terms.

3 ■

Unlike its neutral acquiescence to change in gold supplies, sales by the Fed of government securities to the open market represent a positive act which reduces its assets and liabilities and which reduces the Reserves of the member banks, and hence their base for deposits. Open-market purchases do the opposite, ultimately expanding *M*. Powerful day-to-day open-market operations should be understood by every student of monetary policy.

4 ■

Gold outflows will reduce Reserves and *M* unless offset by FRB open-market purchases of bonds (as was done in recent years). Gold inflows have opposite effects.

5 ■

The main facts of finance, as shown by the still picture of the credit pyramid or by the charts of changing Reserves and money supply, are to be understood in terms of this chapter's analysis.

QUESTIONS FOR DISCUSSION

1. In what Federal Reserve district are you? Where is the nearest branch?

2. Trace the effects of a 1-billion-dollar open-market purchase. An open-market sale.

3. Trace the effects of a doubling of reserve requirements; a halving. Which alters bank earnings more: open-market or reserve-requirement action?

4. List the weapons of monetary control of the Reserve authorities. How powerful are they to control (a) M, (b) interest rates, (c) prices, and (d) employment and unemployment?

5. You find gold in a mine. Describe the resulting steps. (Use balance sheets.)

6. "Gold movements affected prices only because we used them as a barometer, signaling us to expand or contract the total of money supply. Of course, the gold standard was a stupid system; but it was wiser to tie ourselves to such an imperfect system than to trust corrupt legislatures whose tendency is always to print inflationary paper money." Discuss.

7. Discuss the following 1939 statement of the Reserve Board: "The Federal Reserve System can see to it that banks have enough reserves to make money available to commerce, industry, and agriculture at low rates; but it cannot make the people borrow, and it cannot make the public spend the deposits that result when the banks do make loans and investments."

8. Some people say, "Measure monetary tightness by heights and rises in interest rates." Some say, "Measure tightness by growth in net borrowed reserves." Others say, "Measure tightness only by what is happening to the growth rate of M_1 or M_2." Eclectics say, "Use all three measures and more." What do you say?

9. Some University of Chicago economists believe that the Federal Reserve (and any central bank that uses discretionary judgment) is unnecessary. Instead, simply ensure that M grows every year at a specified rate (e.g., 4 per cent). Would you agree? What if judgment can offset with M variations in V and shortfalls of Q?

10. Review your understanding of the following concepts:

the five-step sequence	moral suasion, interest ceilings
Reserves and excess reserves	margin requirements
availability and cost of credit	selective controls
gold certificates	pyramid of credit
Federal Reserve notes	Reserve Bank Credit
open-market purchases and sales	net free reserves (+ or −)
discount rate, discounts	net borrowed reserves (− or +)
legal reserve ratio requirements	offsets to gold movements

18 Synthesis of Monetary Analysis and Income Analysis

ABOUT THIS TIME THERE WAS A CRY . . . FOR MORE PAPER-MONEY. . . . I WAS ON THE SIDE OF AN ADDITION, BEING PERSUADED THAT THE FIRST SMALL SUM STRUCK IN 1723 HAD DONE MUCH GOOD, BY INCREASING THE TRADE, EMPLOYMENT, AND NUMBER OF INHABITANTS IN THE PROVINCE, SINCE I NOW SAW ALL THE OLD HOUSES INHABITED, AND MANY NEW ONES BUILDING. . . . THE UTILITY OF THIS CURRENCY BECAME BY TIME AND EXPERIENCE SO EVIDENT, AS NEVER AFTERWARDS TO BE MUCH DISPUTED. . . . THO' . . . THERE ARE LIMITS BEYOND WHICH THE QUANTITY MAY BE HURTFUL. BENJAMIN FRANKLIN

Chapters 12 and 13 showed how saving and investment schedules intersect to determine the level of national income. And the last chapters have shown how changes in Federal Reserve policy affect the community's stock of money.

This chapter relates these two analyses. Monetary analysis is seen to fit in well with the modern theory of income determination. And the stage is set for stabilization policy—(1) central bank monetary policies; (2) government fiscal policies (public expenditure and taxation, with the implied budget deficit or surplus). These monetary and fiscal policies have to be coordinated to achieve the goal of a progressive economy enjoying reasonable price stability and lives up to its production potentialities.

This chapter shows how stabilization policies work and interact. We leave more detailed study of fiscal policy issues for the remaining chapter of Part Two.

■ MONEY, LIQUIDITY PREFERENCE, MARGINAL EFFICIENCY, MULTIPLIER

The last chapters showed that M expansion by the central and commercial banks can shift upward the $C + I + G$ intersection point of Chapter 12. What is the same thing, an increase in M shifts upward the SS-II intersection point of Chapter 12, as follows:

■ When the Fed increases the money supply, M, this primarily affects investment, shifting II upward. Its expansion of M bids up bond prices and thus bids down interest rates and makes credit loans more easily available to investors. Therefore, it has become more profitable to undertake new investment projects. In the simplest case, the sequence is this:

$$M \text{ up} \rightarrow i \text{ down} \rightarrow I \text{ up} \rightarrow \text{NNP up, up}$$

It can be illuminated by new graphs.

Chapter 15 (page 268) showed that the demand for money, along with depending positively on the level of income transactions, also depends inversely on the interest and profit yields sacrificed in order to have the safety and convenience of holding M. To get more M held by the community, the Fed must therefore bid down interest rates enough to make people find it advantageous to economize less on their cash balances and hold more M. The so-called "liquidity-preference schedule" of Fig. 18-1(a) shows how an increase in M resulting from monetary policy (open-market purchases, etc.) leads initially to a reduced interest rate—from A's 6 per cent to B's 4 per cent.

Figure 18-1(b) picks up the story to show how reduced interest rates (and what does not show on the graph but is lurking in the background, namely, greater *availability* of credit) make more investment profitable. On Fig. 18-1(b)'s so-called "marginal efficiency of investment schedule," the drop in interest rate induces the rise in investment from A' to B'.

Central bank affects money, interest, investment, and output:

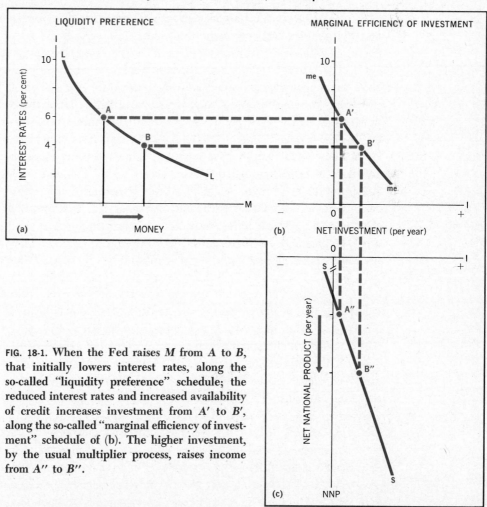

FIG. 18-1. When the Fed raises M from A to B, that initially lowers interest rates, along the so-called "liquidity preference" schedule; the reduced interest rates and increased availability of credit increases investment from A' to B', along the so-called "marginal efficiency of investment" schedule of (b). The higher investment, by the usual multiplier process, raises income from A'' to B''.

Figure 18-1(c) is merely Chapter 12's saving-investment diagram, page 214, turned on its side to line it up with Fig. 18-1(b)'s investment axis. Note that the interest rate drop from A to B led to the investment rise from A' to B', and this (through the multiplier) has led to the NNP rise from A'' to B''.

To clinch understanding of this vital sequence, consider the following reverse case where monetary policy is contracting to wipe out an inflationary gap:

■ Monetary contraction (open-market sales, increased legal reserve ratios, etc.) bids up interest rates and decreases credit availability. This depresses investment spending, and via the multiplier depresses income by even more. The basic sequence is now

$$M \text{ down} \rightarrow i \text{ up} \rightarrow I \text{ down} \rightarrow NNP \text{ down, down}$$

Retrace the reverse BA, $B'A'$, and $B''A''$ sequence in Fig. 18-1 to see how money and income determination interact.

DEPRESSION MODEL   This reconciliation of the theories of money and of income determination is, of course, oversimplified and needs some qualifications. For example, it does not emphasize what can happen in severe depression when the liquidity-preference curve is practically horizontal because interest rates are already so low that people are quite indifferent whether they hold M or the near-M government Treasury bills the Fed wants to swap for M. In such a rare, but possible, case, the potency of monetary policy is at least temporarily very low. This is summarized in the aphorism "The central bank can pull on a string (to curb booms), but it can't *push* on a string (to reverse deep slumps)." Indeed, in such depressed times the profit expectations of businessmen are likely to be so low that they would not employ men and machines on new investment projects even if you let them borrow temporarily at a zero interest rate. In this case, the marginal-efficiency schedule of Fig. 18-1(b) is practically vertical; and again the chain of monetary action loses potency. (It is these "depression models" which are often, but wrongly, associated with the name of Keynes; and if they were his sole cases, his ideas would only rarely be of great interest.)

CLASSICAL CASE   The opposite classical case, equally extreme, occurs when the liquidity schedule is practically vertical, so that each unit of M is under a strong compulsion to circulate at a constant velocity; or where the marginal-efficiency schedule is so horizontal that the slightest reduction in interest rate is enough to wipe out any deflationary gap and the slightest rise in interest is enough to wipe out any inflationary gap. As most economists interpret the history of the last few centuries, this extreme case is not deemed realistic. They cannot agree with the extreme classical view known as "Say's Law of Conservation of Purchasing Power." The Appendix to this chapter discusses this matter further. It is enough here to characterize Say's Law as alleging:

There cannot be any such thing as a saving-and-investment problem. What is not consumed is surely destined to be spent on investment goods, without the possibility of any snag. Hold M constant (or growing in an announced trend) and *laissez faire* will take care of the problems of depression and boom without any fiscal or monetary policy actions.

QUALIFICATIONS Eschewing polar cases, we must notice the point raised by experts in corporate finance. They point out that many firms, particularly large ones, finance their investments out of retained earnings and the cash flow generated by their own operations. Many avoid going to the banks or outside markets for borrowings or stock flotations. (EXAMPLE: The great Du Pont Company has not borrowed a cent for more than 30 years, and yet it has been an important source of progress in the chemical field.)

To the degree that investment depends upon internal funds that are insulated from market fluctuations in interest rate and credit availability, the potency of monetary policy is just that much less: it then takes greater action by the Fed to produce the same effect. One could go on to give other bits of evidence used to play down the importance of monetary policy (as, for example, the fact that when investors are uncertain about the future, small changes in safe-asset interest rates may have little effect upon the high profit rates investors require as inducement to undertake investment).

Qualifications are not all in the direction of playing down the importance of M. We have noted in passing that credit policy does have some influence on G and C in $C + I + G$. Higher market evaluations of land, plant, and equipment, and of securities generally, may shift CC up. In the long run, if the increase in M comes, let us say, from gold mining or Treasury printing (and not merely from a swap by the Fed's Open Market Committee of M for near-M), the new M adds directly to people's net worth, and this does lead them, other things equal, to spend more on C, on I, and on G.[1]

■ FISCAL POLICY AND INCOME DETERMINATION

Aside from the central bank, the government has another major way of affecting current spending. This we have seen in Chapter 13. As part of its *fiscal policy* the government can expand its expenditures: build useful public roads and schools, hire more civil servants, increase defense expenditure, do a hundred and one useful (or foolish) things to expand total spending. This could be shown in a saving-investment diagram like Fig. 18-1(c).

But better still, we can show it as an upward shift in the G component of the $C + I + G$ schedule that was used as an alternative way to show income equilibrium. Figure 18-2(a) recapitulates the demonstration on page 232 of how an expansion of public expenditure G leads to an expansion of income.

The same type of chart[2] can show, in Fig. 18-2(b), the other side of fiscal policy—

---

[1] Some economists used to hope that higher interest rates would stimulate saving and kill consumption; i.e., they hoped an interest rise would shift up the SS schedule in Fig. 18-1(c), thereby reinforcing the effect of a downward shift in II. Experience, and the analysis of Chapter 31, suggest that outside the area of installment-financed consumer durables, these effects are probably weak and cannot be much counted on. (WARNING: The B points in Fig. 18-1 are final equilibria only if the Fed now creates just enough further M to satisfy enhanced *income* needs; otherwise, we repeat the cycle with LL shifted by changed NNP level, finding final equilibria somewhere between the A and B points. See the Hicks-Hansen diagrams in the Appendix for a rigorous handling of this problem.)

[2] The treatment here recapitulates the treatment on page 233 of Chapter 13 and best handles the effects of personal income taxes. For more complicated analysis of indirect and other taxes, also taking account of tax effects on investment, see intermediate texts.

Fiscal policy means government expenditure and tax policy:

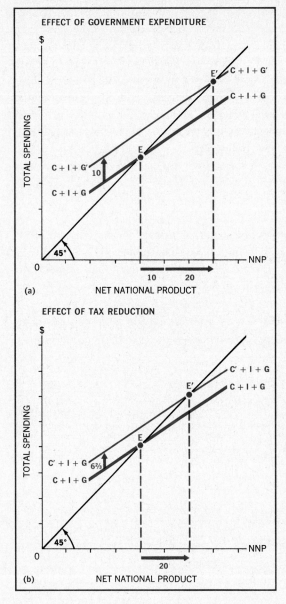

FIG. 18-2(a). An increase in government expenditures on goods and services will shift $C + I + G$ up to $C + I + G'$, raising income to E'. Moreover, the usual multiplier is involved.

FIG. 18-2(b). Lowering taxes has similar expansionary effects on income, as was seen after the 1964 Kennedy-Johnson tax cut. Lower tax collection gives you more disposable income out of NNP, and hence shifts the consumption schedule upward. We go from E to E' as a result of the new $C' + I + G$ schedule. (Dollar for dollar, tax reduction is a little weaker than G increase. Why? Because some tax rebate is saved rather than used to shift *CC* up. A cut in taxes of 10 shifts *CC leftward* that much, but *upward* only by $\frac{2}{3} \times 10 = 6\frac{2}{3}$ when the MPC is $\frac{2}{3}$. Recall Fig. 13-8.)

changes in tax collections. To raise NNP the fiscal authorities cut taxes: this gives people higher disposable income, and since they have a propensity to consume out of extra income, this means they will consume more.

How can we show the increased consumption on Fig. 18-2(b)? We can show the effect of reduced taxes as an upward shift of the *CC* schedule, which is plotted against NNP and is a major component of the pictured $C + I + G$ schedule. With taxes lower, we subtract less from each level of NNP to get the corresponding level of disposable income. So, with higher disposable income corresponding to each NNP, we must show higher consumption—hence the higher *CC* curve.

We may summarize the effects of fiscal policy:

■ Increased *G* raises income by raising the *GG* component of *C* + *I* + *G*. Reduced taxes raise the *CC* component of the *C* + *I* + *G* schedule. Both together—which also means deficit financing or a reduction in the budgetary surplus—result in an even greater upward shift of the *C* + *I* + *G* schedule and of equilibrium income. In the reverse case of contractionary fiscal policy, the final *C* + *I* + *G* schedule shifts downward.

Here is a good test of one's understanding of the mechanics of fiscal policy:

Show the effect on NNP of the massive 1964 tax cut; and then see what the effect would have been if there had been a matching cut in *G*, as some people then recommended.

■ THE SYNTHESIS AT WORK: TECHNOLOGICAL UNEMPLOYMENT?

To appreciate how modern tools of income and monetary analysis really work, let us here apply them as a case study to one of the great problems of our day.

A notable feature of our time is the development of "automation." Will this "new industrial revolution," in which machinery plays a new role, be a curse or a blessing to mankind? In particular, does it not confront the modern economy with the threat of mass unemployment?

Our tools enable us to give an optimistic answer; but our optimistic answer is quite different from the old-fashioned one, which simply *asserted that inventions would necessarily create new jobs just as fast as they killed off old ones.* Such a view was based upon an uninformed faith, and it was not persuasive. Sometimes experience accorded with it; sometimes experience went against it. In short, it made the outcome depend merely on luck. Our contemporary optimistic answer is truly more optimistic.

WHAT AUTOMATION IS   The word "automation" was coined in 1947 by Del Harder, vice-president of Ford Motor Company, to apply to "automatic handling of parts between progressive production processes." At about the same time John Diebold, a management engineer, shortened the word "automatization" into automation. Diebold stressed the use of control devices that operate by means of "feedback."

Automation has still other meanings. Giant electronic calculators, which are a millionfold faster than hand machines, have simplified data processing and record keeping. One pretty machine does the work of a hundred even prettier girls. Some modern digital computers can beat a good player at checkers, but none can yet beat a champion. None can yet play a really fine game of chess; at simple games such as ticktacktoe, the machine plays a perfect game. Numbers recorded on magnetic tape can make a milling machine or lathe turn out intricate copies of a master pattern.

DISPLACEMENT OF LABOR?   Whether one thinks automation is something absolutely new or represents a great postwar quickening of developments already known in principle, everyone admits it is a force to reckon with. Automation will presumably increase productivity; otherwise it would not be installed. Does this mean it will reduce the total need for labor and create mass unemployment? Back in the depression of the 1930s, long before we knew the term "automation," there was much fear of "technological unemployment." Should we again worry that modern man will become obsolete?

The late Norbert Wiener, MIT mathematician and one-time prodigy, who coined the name "cybernetics" (from the Greek word for "helmsman"), has pronounced on this subject in the following dramatic way:[3]

> The industrial revolution has . . . displaced man and the beast as a source of power. . . . The factory of the future . . . will be controlled by something like a modern high-speed computing machine. . . . We can expect an abrupt and final cessation of the demand for the type of factory labor performing repetitive tasks . . . an intermediate transitional period of disastrous confusion. . . . Industry will be flooded with the new tools to the extent that they appear to yield immediate profits, irrespective of what long-time damage they can do. . . . It is perfectly clear that this will produce an unemployment situation, in comparison with which the present recession and even the depression of the thirties will seem a pleasant joke.

THE FORWARD LOOK   Any increase in productivity will indeed, *if output does not increase,* throw men out of work. In the Great Depression men readily believed total product would remain the same, that desired output would fail to grow with the growth of productivity. This view makes you look at unemployment in the following way: "Why did those unemployed workers over there lose their jobs? Which machines displaced them?" And so forth.

Modern students of income determination take a more fruitful tack. They say:

■ Regardless of why those men lost their jobs, why aren't there enough *new* jobs for them? What fiscal and monetary policies are needed to create the new dollar purchasing power necessary for them to be hired anew?

"Satchel" Paige, a great baseball player, once said: "Never look backward; someone may be gaining on you." This is good advice in economics, too. Do not look back to find what caused past layoffs; look forward to see what you have to do to restore high employment. This is much more efficient.

Better still, this approach means you do not have to decide whether the pessimists are right who argue that inventions will kill off more jobs than they create. Why care? *In every case we know that high employment without inflation will require monetary and fiscal policies of the correct magnitudes and mixed economies know what needs doing.*

GRAPHICAL RESTORATION OF HIGH-EMPLOYMENT EQUILIBRIUM   To apply this fruitful approach, we can use our consumption + investment + government spending schedule and look for income equilibrium where the $C + I + G$ schedule just intersects the 45° helping line. Figure 18-3 illustrates this.

[3] N. Wiener, *The Human Use of Human Beings* (Cambridge, Mass., 1950), pp. 180, 181, 186, 188, 189.

The income-determination diagrams before and after automation:

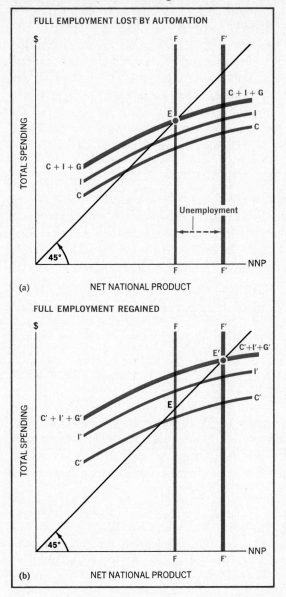

FIG. 18-3(a). If inventions raise productivity 30 per cent, *FF* shifts 30 per cent rightward to *F'F'*. Were *C*, *I*, and *G* not to change, the intersection would still be at *E*, but now with mass unemployment. (Under *laissez-faire* no one can predict what the net final effect of such inventions on *C* + *I* + *G* would be.)

FIG. 18-3(b). An expansionary monetary policy will raise *I*. Expansionary fiscal policy will lower taxes, raise disposable incomes, and shift up the consumption schedule; and it can increase *G* to *G'*. Full-employment equilibrium will be restored at *E'*, where *C'* + *I'* + *G'* has been shifted upward the right amount.

Suppose that automation makes labor 30 per cent more productive. This means that the same full-employment labor force could produce 30 per cent more real national product; hence, the *FF* full-employment line of Fig. 18-3(a) is now shifted rightward 30 per cent to *F'F'*. Let us make the worst possible assumptions: (1) that government leaves its expenditure *G* as it was; and that the new machines are so cheap and short-lived that they can be introduced just by using up the depreciation allowances of the wearing-out machines, so that (2) net investment *I* is no greater than before; finally, that automation gives people the same things for less but does not whet their appetites for new gadgets, which means that (3) the propensity-to-consume schedule (and propensity to save) will be exactly the same as before in terms of disposable income.

In short, we assume the $C + I + G$ schedule has none of its components shifted as a result of automation. Then the schedule must continue to intersect at the same E point as before. Whereas this E point was previously a full-employment equilibrium, it now represents a point of mass unemployment. A large fraction of the populace is now out of work completely, and many are working only part time. Were this the case, who can doubt that unions and the government would agitate to cut the length of the working week and to sabotage new methods and machines?

NEW ECONOMICS TO THE RESCUE   Even this worst case can be cured by proper therapy. Here is how. Let the Federal Reserve fight this slump by making credit much cheaper and much more freely available. (Recall open-market purchases, lowering of reserve requirements, and lowering of discount rates.) What will this do to the I schedule? Push it up. At the same time, let the government cut down on the heavy taxing it was doing in the previous full-employment situation. This will increase people's disposable incomes, will increase their consumption spending, and thus shift upward the C part of the $C + I + G$ schedule. (Maybe I will get further shifted, too.) Without increasing government expenditure directly, we can thus shift the $C + I + G$ schedule far enough upward until the new $C' + I' + G'$ schedule intersects the 45° line at the new full-employment level E'. Alternatively, a public-works program or other expansion of G could be used to help shift $C + I + G$ up to the target level, if the people feel they need public services more than extra private consumption.

Figure 18-3(b) shows how these upward shifts have restored the full-employment equilibrium. By proper policy we have converted the machine from a curse to a blessing. People now enjoy 30 per cent more output. They are not forced into bread lines. They are not made to work short hours and do not have to take Mondays off because the limited work has to be shared. They do not have to throw their cigarette cases into the works of the new machinery to protect their jobs and take-home pay.

You should be sure you know how to use the same diagram to handle the case where automation or new inventions spontaneously increase investment a great deal and tempt people onto an upward-shifted consumption schedule. You can then show how the desired E' equilibrium could come about spontaneously. Indeed, to test your powers, you should analyze the extreme case where automation causes too great a burst of investment and consumption spending. You should then show how contractionary monetary and fiscal policy would be needed to wipe out the resulting inflationary gap and to bring the new $C + I + G$ schedule back to the proper intersection.

Of course, the higher dollar demand engineered by fiscal and monetary policy cannot be expected to provide the same kind of jobs using exactly the same skills and paying exactly the same wage rates. Inevitably there will still be important transitional problems for particular workers, firms, and regions. Programs of retraining and of increasing labor mobility and flexibility are vital (as Chapter 29 discusses), along with policies to ensure proper aggregate dollar demand.

■ THE NEOCLASSICAL SYNTHESIS

Critics used to regard the classical principles of economics as out of date. Looking at the long bread lines and the men selling apples on street corners, they said:

> Why speak of scarcity? Or efficiency? Or growth? Or fairness? Throw away your tools of supply and demand, your finespun theories of market pricing. Tear up the rule book. We live in a new era in which everything is upside down: attempts to save kill off investment; a hurricane or war is a blessing in that it creates jobs and gives food to the starving unemployed.

What is the modern economist's answer to all this? He says:

■ You are right to question the classical principles. All principles should be subjected to the closest examination with respect to both their logic and their factual relevance. The classical arguments were oversimple, and they admittedly did not allow for the facts of nineteenth- and twentieth-century life. But experience since 1932, and careful logical reasoning, suggest that you had better discard your own false inferences. Everywhere in the free world, governments and central banks have shown they can win the battle of the slump if people want them to. They have the weapons of fiscal policy (expenditure and taxes) and of monetary policy (open-market operations, discount-rate policy, legal reserve ratio policy) to shift the various schedules that determine national income and employment.

Just as we no longer meekly accept disease, we no longer need accept mass unemployment. That being so, you will find that the classical principles will again apply; but now they apply because our macroeconomics has validated their premise of adequate demand—not because the world is lucky enough to have them apply automatically and at all times.

This is a brave answer, and essentially—most careful economists would today say—an accurate answer. But let us not be too boastful of our modern conquest of instability. Let us quietly add the following qualifications:

■ The worst consequences of the business cycle, which Chapter 14 showed plagued capitalism from its beginning, are probably a thing of the past; but that does not mean that the cycle is gone. We still shall have minor inventory fluctuations, still shall have transitions from war to peace and from one kind of boom to another. The difference will be this: the age-old tendencies for the system to fluctuate will still be there, but no longer will the world let them snowball into vast depressions or into galloping inflations—no longer will we let our banking system fail and our nation go through the most painful debt deflation and bankruptcy.

And let us admit that all the political pressures in a democracy do work to make a drastic slump unlikely. But can we be so sure that the same pressures will operate to prevent mild inflation? Even if fiscal and monetary policies could prevent such chronic mild inflation of a couple of per cent per year, are you sure that they will be used to do so? And is it clear that the citizens in a democracy like America will, in peacetime, refuse to countenance persistent unemployment rates like 5 and 6 per cent?

Finally, in the appendix to this chapter and in Chapter 38, the discussion of the new problems confronting America in the 1970s will examine this question: In our mixed economy is there a new kind of inflation, one not merely to be understood in terms of the aggregate demand tools of Part Two, but requiring as well the study of "cost-push" forces that produce a creeping inflation?[4]

SUMMARY

1 ■

Monetary policy by the central bank is an important way of shifting the saving and investment schedules, or the total schedule of consumption-plus-investment-plus-government-spending.

2 ■

Along the downward-sloping "liquidity-preference schedule," higher M induces a lower interest rate—enough lower to persuade people to hold all the new M. Along the downward-sloping "marginal efficiency of investment schedule," lower interest rate and more available credit make it profitable for new investment projects to get done. Along the familiar saving-investment multiplier-type diagram, the induced increase in I leads to higher production and incomes. (If there is a deep-depression inelasticity of investment response to interest and/or a deep-depression horizontality of LL representing indifference to money holding, the effect of M will fall to nil. In quantity-theory language, then and *only* then will the contrived rise in M be completely negated by a compensating fall in V, leaving NNP $= P \times Q$ quite unchanged.)

3 ■

Fiscal policy means governmental tax and expenditure policy. It, too, affects income determination by shifting the spending schedules. Higher expenditure on goods and services directly raises the G component of the $C + I + G$ schedule and thus raises its equilibrium intersection. Taxes work in reverse: *reduced* tax rates, by shifting the CC schedule leftward and upward, push *up* the $C + I + G$ schedule; increased tax rates have the opposite, contractionary effect; and in either case, tax changes are, dollar for dollar, a little less potent than changes in government expenditure on goods and services.

4 ■

The important case of technological invention shows how, by combination of fiscal and monetary policies, a modern economy can ensure the restoration of high-employment equilibrium even in the worst case where automation is reducing the need for men to do any given amount of work and is not bringing in its train any spontaneous expansion of dollar demand elsewhere.

---

[4] At the end of this chapter's Appendix, there is an analysis of "cost-push" inflation and the need for an "incomes policy."

5 ∎

Modern democracies have the fiscal and monetary tools, and the political will to use them, to end chronic slumps and galloping inflations. This gives us the neoclassical synthesis: the classical principles of microeconomic pricing of later chapters are thus validated by successful marriage with the macroeconomic tools of these chapters.

QUESTIONS FOR DISCUSSION

1. Relabel Fig. 18-1(a), (b), and (c) to show tight monetary policies. Trace out the steps.

2. Wipe out a 1975 automation-created deflationary gap by (*a*) fiscal policy alone, (*b*) monetary policy alone, and (*c*) any blend of them. Which path leads to full employment with slowest growth (i.e., least capital formation for the future)?

3. "Fiscal and monetary authority should be in one agency, or at least be coordinated. Otherwise they may conflict, one undoing what the other is trying to accomplish." Criticize.

4. Use Fig. 18-2 to show that increasing *G* and taxes at the same time will tend to have canceling effects on income. Difficult question: Can you follow the intricate reasoning which has argued that, dollar for dollar, changes in *G* are a little more potent than changes in taxes—so that a balanced-budget decrease in *G* is likely to be somewhat deflationary?

5. The tools that handle automation problems can handle any threat of unemployment that might come from sudden peace and disarmament. Explain how, thereby anticipating Chapter 39's argument.

6. Explain what the neoclassical synthesis is. Qualify it.

7. Review your understanding of the following concepts:

$M \to i \to I \to$ NNP   liquidity-preference schedule
shift of $C + I + G$: through   marginal-efficiency schedule
   monetary policy and through   leftward *CC* shift from tax cut
   tax and expenditure changes   automation and unemployment
tax versus expenditure potency   neoclassical synthesis

APPENDIX: Mechanisms of Money and Income Determination

This is a brief discussion of how money, interest, investment, income, prices, and velocity of circulation are interrelated. Classical views that there can never be unemployment, and depression versions of the Keynesian system, will turn out to be alternative poles of such an analysis. And what most economists would consider to be the most realistic description of how our economy works and what are the potencies of policy weapons will fall somewhere on the continuum between these extreme poles.

The topics will be covered in this order: velocity interrelations; classical models; liquidity preference and income determination; and models of "cost-push," or "sellers' inflation."

BEHAVIOR OF VELOCITY

Instead of the chain $M \rightarrow i \rightarrow I \rightarrow$ NNP (or its even further elaboration to take account of wealth-capitalization effects and effects on G and C schedules), some proponents of a sophisticated quantity theory prefer to short-circuit the process and use the concept of velocity. They write

$$M \rightarrow MV \equiv \text{NNP}$$

■ This asserts that an increase in M, unless *offset fully* by an induced shift in V of the type that neither they nor the believers in the four-link chain consider likely, will serve to increase dollar NNP with all the implied effects on the product $P \times Q$.[1]

These different modes of language can formally represent the same facts, just as an account in English or an account in French can be given of any sequence of events. In a sense, therefore, reasonable men will not argue about terminology and semantics.

At a deeper level, however, those who prefer one terminology usually think that certain hypotheses about the real world are more fruitful than certain others. Thus, those who like to use MV usually have more definite views about the probable behavior of V, and its invariance under a wide range of alternative conditions, than do those who like to use the $C + I + G$ approach explicitly. While the bulk of economists today incline toward the latter view, there is no need to be dogmatic about the matter. If the day ever arrives when the proponents of the velocity approach can prove by their researches that theirs is the more convenient tool, pragmatic scholars will welcome all its help.

CLASSICAL PRICE FLEXIBILITY

More basic than the question of whether to use or not use the terminology of either school is the contrast between a *frictionless* system in which all market prices are *flexible* and the *realistic* world of a mixed economic system that exists here and elsewhere in the West. Many classical economists thought unemployment to be quite impossible because in their frictionless models whatever is not spent in one direction gets automatically spent in another.

SAY'S LAW   This view, called Say's Law, after the 1803 French writer J. B. Say, has been much debated because of the ambiguous form in which it was expressed. Thus, Say and other classical writers felt that overproduction was impossible by its very nature, since all value relations were relative—shoes being comparable with spoons at some proper relative price; they felt that what a worker saves gets spent as truly on employing men in the machinery trades as what the worker spends on giving work in the food or other consumers' industries; they had at least a vague supposition that the interest rate in a flexible capital market would always find a level at which (full-employment) saving and investment schedules would intersect; they, or their more sophisticated followers, had the notion that, if only the money wage would fall flexibly far enough, it would always bring out job offers for every willing worker. So went the rather vague arguments.

In the years since 1800, there were often short periods of considerable unemployment, and on a few occasions there were longer periods of considerable unemployment or of underemployment. So economists wanted to go beyond the simpler formulations of Say's Law: to deny some of its implicit presumptions about flexible prices and wages, or to abandon it and work from alternative hypotheses.

Today it is clear that the alternative approaches are perfectly capable of being reconciled, so that there is only a difference of degree and of realism between them, not a difference of kind. A. C. Pigou of Cambridge University showed in 1943 how his older cherished beliefs could be related to what he had first thought were Keynesian heresies; his reconciliation goes as follows.

PIGOU EFFECTS   Let there be a certain M in the system that consists of coins or of imperishable paper currency. Suppose that initially there is unemployment because the SS and II schedules intersect to the left of the full-employment level. Suppose interest rates are in equilibrium on every bond and security market, with auctioneers finding matching supply and demand bids.

---

[1] Some proponents would think V will stay constant after a sizable change in open-market operations; others would not think this a necessary assumption. Some, impressed by the empirical fact that in past short-term upswings, rises in M and V have tended to coincide, might choose to extrapolate this *post hoc* experience. Others would set up more complicated hypotheses, depending on the environment upon which the open-market operation impinged. Many will agree with our later liquidity-preference theory, whose Hicks-Hansen diagrams can be thought of as a theory of velocity.

And just to complete the simplified discussion, suppose there is no central banker or fiscal authority to do anything about the situation.

A sophisticated follower of Say would now assert: "There is just one flaw in this equilibrium. Men who want to work at going wages are not employed. To be fair, whether or not this is realistic, you should also imagine an auctioneer for the labor market. His wage rate expressed in money must be allowed to fall whenever there is excessive labor supply."

Pigou agrees. He lets the wage rate fall. Money wages being an important cost of production, for all the reasons discussed in Parts Three and Four, this drop will result in considerable lowering of all prices. When prices and wages are low enough, what will happen to the SS and II intersection? Suppose I am a typical man who previously owned an acre of land, a machine, and $100 in cash. (I also may have owed on a mortgage or may have held someone's IOU stated in terms of money; but for the community as a whole, such interpersonal money liabilities and assets have to *cancel* out. Recall also that there are no government bonds in the picture to worry about.)

For dramatic effect, suppose that wages fall to one-thousandth (.001) of their previous level; suppose, although it is unnecessary except for simplicity to stick to the same number, that prices of all things also fall to .001 of their previous levels. This means that my acre of land and machine will fall to .001 of their previous value. Everything falls in value—except one item. My $100 bill is still a $100 bill. But now, in terms of its real purchasing power, I own the equivalent of what was $100,000 before. I am rich!

Will I spend the same amount on consumption and on saving out of *income* levels that are the same as before either in money or in real terms? I will not. I am rich.

■ At some point, because of the enhanced *real wealth effect* of the increased purchasing power of the hard money in the economic system (induced by a large enough wage and price fall), *CC* schedules will shift up and *SS* schedules equivalently downward. The new *SS* and *II* intersection can thus be moved up to the full-employment level. So, even if there were no favorable effects of the price-level or interest change on the *II* curves, *by getting money wages and prices far enough down, the condition of*

"full employment" could theoretically be achieved. QED.

Pigou thus vindicated abstract classical principles by recourse to this "hard-money effect," which economists today call the "Pigou effect" in his honor.[2] But being a realistic observer of the difficulties of getting wages to move flexibly downward in a mixed capitalistic society, and having lived through eras in which the dynamic process of debt deflation led to bankruptcy, riots, slump, and even revolution, Pigou hastened to point out that he did not recommend such hyperdeflation to cure capitalism's unemployment. He much preferred to accomplish the same thing by increasing dollar *M*; and actually, he adhered to the general notions of Part Two of this book. The fact that he often liked to use the word "velocity" in his Keynes-like theory shows that mere semantic matters are indeed of limited importance.

CRUDE QUANTITY THEORY IN THE CLASSICAL MODEL   Recall now the crude quantity theory, which held that prices must always be proportional to the amount of money—so that doubling *M* must exactly double *P*. For many situations in the real world—with its sticky prices, boom, depression, and thousands of changes always going on to confound the experiment—we saw that the crude quantity theory was not a good predicting device. But if we confine our attention to the perfectly frictionless model of the classical type used by Pigou and others in the above discussion, we can find an important nucleus of truth in the crude quantity theory; and we can understand better the reasons why it has a degree of predictive value during galloping inflations and over certain long time intervals.

Recall Pigou's fantastic but happy equilibrium which has made the representative man feel rich enough to save as little as society can invest at full employment. Now suppose his $100 bill had been a $10 bill. Do you see that merely by having all prices go down still another nine-tenths, the equilibrium could be *exactly restored*, with every relative price and wage just the

[2] Mention may be made here of a non-Pigou, non-Say, non-Keynes version of full employment originated by Professor Nicholas Kaldor of Cambridge. He is widely interpreted to believe that, within broad limits, any change of *I* will induce just enough shift of the *share* of income accruing to thrifty profit receivers to produce a long-run full-employment intersection of SS and II always. If only it were valid, such a view would be important. If only . . . .

same as before and every physical commodity and input the same as before? *Cutting M to one-tenth has cut P to exactly one-tenth* in this classical model.

In this abstract model the crude quantity theory has come into its own. In the tautological equation of exchange $MV \equiv PQ$, there has not been the slightest reason for the Q or V to have changed (waiving all dynamic questions of how the system gets into the new equilibrium and "forgets" all its past price levels). So P does equal kM, where k is the ratio V/Q, whose numerator and denominator will have been constant in this abstract example, however much they may vary in reality.

This long-period full-employment frictionless classical model has the further property that no change in interest rates can come from the balanced change in M. As David Ricardo argued, if all prices and wages change in exactly the same proportion, so that what used to be called 4 pence is now 2 pence, then any asset that used to pay 5 per cent per annum in the form of 50 pence on 1,000 pence will now be paying 5 per cent in the form of 25 pence on 500 pence.

It should not be necessary to stress that the real world as we know it is a far cry from the abstract model. This is true especially in the short run; in the longer run, to the degree that all price adjustments get made and other disturbances are ruled out, the abstract model fits somewhat better. The art of economics is to know how to blend the elements of absurdity and of relevance of such a model in interpreting living events and policy.

PERMANENT PUBLIC DEBT   Even in the extreme classical model, all P's would not be proportional to M alone! Interest-bearing public bonds, which correspond to no government capital formation and which no taxpayer rationally expects to have to help retire *in his lifetime,* have effects similar to those of the noninterest *IOUs* we call M. Thus, the Pigou effect from hyperdeflation involves an increase in the real value of such bonds *along with* an increase in the real value of hardmoney M. Since a rational taxpayer will reckon that he *will* have to help pay taxes to keep up the interest payments (during his lifetime) on the public debt, $1 of such debt will not have the potency to produce as much spending as will $1 of M. Even so, believers in a crude quantity theory for an extreme classical model *should* reformulate their theory to say:

Doubling M *and* permanent public debt will, other things equal, double all P's and leave all relative P's,

physical quantities, and interest rates unchanged in the new long-run equilibrium. *Doubling M alone represents a nonneutral change* whose substantive effects are the greater the shorter is taxpayer life expectancy and the higher is the interest rate.[3]

LIQUIDITY PREFERENCE AND INCOME

We have seen that the amount of money people will hold depends upon the interest rate and is a declining function of it in the sense that you must contrive lower yields on securities to coax people to be willing to hold more money. Figure 18-1(a) showed this liquidity-preference link between money and interest.

But as already noted, there is a transactions motive for holding money along with the store-of-wealth or asset reason for holding money. So part of the money held can be said to depend upon the level of income: this so-called "active" component of the money supply is a function of the level of NNP, rising as NNP rises. Indeed, if velocity were a strict constant for *all* money and not just for this idealized active-money component, there would be no room at all for a nonvertical liquidity-preference curve LL in Fig. 18-1(a).

This dependence of money on income as well as on interest was not depicted in the important sequence of Fig. 18-1(a), (b), and (c). The chapter's first footnote warned us that the diagram did not take into account the full feedback effect of the transactions demand for money induced by a successful expansion of NNP contrived by an increase in M. We can here make good this deficiency, and verify that the chapter's story is essentially correct, even if oversimplified in the telling; now we consider what is known as a Hicks-Hansen diagram, named for Sir John Hicks of Oxford and Alvin Hansen of Harvard.

The brown curve labeled IS in Fig. 18-4 recapitulates in a single income–interest-rate diagram the story told by Fig. 18(b) and (c), quite independently of (a). We see back on page 317 that when we change the interest rate we do end up changing the NNP level, as shown here on the brown curve. In Fig. 18-1, this took place in two steps: (1) the marginal-efficiency step of 18-1(b) in which changing interest rate changed investment in the opposite direction; and (2) the old multiplier relation, inherited from our saving-investment

[3] WARNING: Doubling M and PD does not mean you can add $M + PD$ and treat that magnitude as if P's were proportional to it. Rather it is the case that $(2M, 2PD)$ implies $2P$.

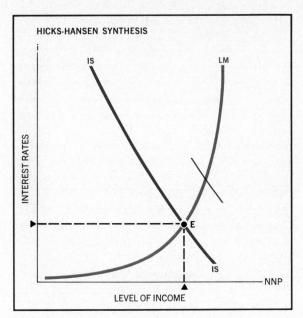

FIG. 18-4.

analysis of Chapters 12 and 13, in which the change in investment resulted in an amplified change in income in its same direction, owing to primary spending and secondary responding. We call this result of the two steps the *IS* relation, because it shows the resulting correspondence between interest rate and income when scheduled saving and scheduled investment have been kept equal. (Recall this is the definition of maintainable NNP equilibrium.)

The new element in Fig. 18-4 is the green *LM* schedule. This relationship between the interest rate and the level of income is labeled *LM* because it is the complete liquidity-preference relationship between money and income after we have taken into account *both* the dependence of money holding on interest *and* on income. I.e., we have recognized the *transaction* motive for "active money," which depends primarily on income; and also what page 268 called the *precautionary* (or "asset") store-of-wealth motive for holding money, which depends upon the interest rates that investors speculate could be earned on alternative stores of wealth (bonds, stocks, land, real capital goods—earning assets in general). Figure 18-1(a) reflected this.

It is important to emphasize that the *LM* schedule is drawn up on the proviso that the total amount of *M* is fixed. Why then does *LM* slope upward? Because an eastward increase in NNP will require more active *M* for transactions, leaving less *M* for people to hold as a

wealth asset. The smaller amount of *M* for wealth holding can only be rationed out at a higher (or northward-moving) interest rate, which is needed to coax people more into securities and more *out* of money.

■ Now we must combine the marginal-efficiency-multiplier brown curve *IS* with the green liquidity-preference curve *LM*, to show that their interaction does determine the equilibrium level of income and of interest rate for each given total of *M*. *E* shows the equilibrium intersection. There and only there has the existing amount of money produced just low enough interest rate and just high enough investment to lead to a maintainable level of income: at this indicated NNP and *i* rate, the existing *M* supply just covers the transactions and holding demand for money. QED.

What if the Fed engineers an *increase* in *M*? What will that do to the *LM* curve? Now with more money to be held at each level of income, the interest rate will have to be bid down. Hence, the *LM* curve clearly shifts downward (and therefore *rightward*). What about the *IS* curve? In this simplified version, *IS* does not have the money supply in it anywhere; *IS* stays unshifted by an *M* change. The downward shift of *LM* moves the equilibrium NNP upward and the equilibrium interest rate downward (just as, in Chapter 4, page 64, an increase in supply *ss* intersected an unchanged demand curve *dd* in a higher *Q* and lower *P*).

By contrast to monetary policy, which shifts the *LM* curve, fiscal policy shifts the *IS* curve. How? An increase in government expenditure *G* (just like an increase in any component of a *C + I + G* schedule) will shift the *IS* schedule *rightward*. Why? Because it leads to a higher income level at the same interest rate. Thus, you can show that expansionary fiscal policy leads to a new *E* higher on the unshifted *LM* curve, with equilibrium income and interest rate higher. (The reader should test himself by penciling in on Fig. 18-4 a new *LM* curve for central bank contraction and a new *IS* curve for fiscal contraction. Contrast the new *E* intersections where the interest rate is concerned.)

Figure 18-5 shows at the ends of the *LM* curve the extreme "classical" pole and the extreme "depression" (or so-called "liquidity-trap") pole.[4] Where *LM* turns

[4] Sometimes the "depression model" is called the "Keynesian model" but most authorities agree that this is bad terminology, since Keynes' *General Theory* covered all cases from the beginning and not merely that of the Great Depression.

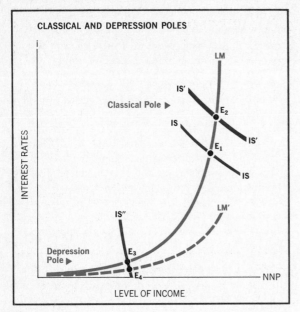

CLASSICAL AND DEPRESSION POLES

FIG. 18-5.

Chapter 39 will point out that one of the major topics being discussed by economists in the 1960s is the question of a possible price creep which takes place even while there is considerable unemployment and excess capacity, and which does not seem to originate in any particular inflationary gap in the $C + I + G$ or MV relations. "Demand-pull" on prices versus "cost-push" are terms that dramatize such discussion.

A few words here will lay the analytical foundation for some of that discussion.

Begin by assuming imperfections in labor and other markets. Set up the hypothesis that wage rates are, for a variety of reasons, relatively inflexible as far as downward movements are concerned, so that Pigou effects become uninteresting. Suppose further that wage rates get set by the interplay of employers and employees (with or without important intervention by unions) so as to be moving upward in money terms at a percentage rate per annum that is only weakly responsive to the degree of unemployment in the labor sector. An extreme example would be wage rates per hour going up 5 per cent a year everywhere, by imitation and spontaneous thrust. Finally, suppose that the technological improvement in labor productivity occurs at the rate of, say, 3 per cent per year.

What will be the outcome? If business generally can set its prices so as to keep labor's share of total NNP at about the same fraction of three-fourths, then the resulting pattern of prices is determined. As wage rates grow by 5 per cent per annum, prices generally will grow at the rate of 2 per cent per annum, the 3 per cent difference being attributable to the technological increase in real productivity. [Real wages thus rise by only 3 per cent, not by the attempted 5 per cent; rising P accounts for the shortfall; note also that real profits (or nonwages) rise by the same 3 per cent per year if the three-quarter–one-quarter division remains unchanged.]

Note that so far nothing has been said about saving and investment schedules or about behavior of M and V. Thus, if there happened to be a zero inflationary gap and a zero deflationary gap, prices would in this model still rise by 2 per cent per year. Our theory of income determination would still be relevant whether it were of a $C + I + G$ or MV type, but not relevant to determine stable P; it would be merely a theory to determine Q.

almost vertical, no shift in the IS curve can increase NNP: that is because money's velocity has reached its limit. (Note the constancy of NNP at E_1 and E_2.) At this classical pole, then, fiscal policy would accomplish little unless accompanied by central banking change in the money supply. Few modern economists think present-day mixed economies operate in such an extreme classical region. (In any case they would probably combine fiscal policy with monetary policy where such a threat became serious.)

At the other extreme, at vanishingly low interest rates such as prevailed in the late 1930s, the LM curve might turn horizontal. If the Fed engineered an increase in M by open-market purchases which involved swapping a close-money-substitute Treasury bill for M itself, the Fed would merely succeed in shifting the LM curve rightward, leaving its horizontal part virtually unchanged. At such a pole, and particularly where extreme inelasticity of the depression marginal-efficiency curve makes IS virtually a vertical line, monetary policy is practically impotent to affect NNP. (Note the virtual identity of the E_3 and E_4 intersections.)

The Hicks-Hansen diagram succeeds not only in synthesizing fiscal and monetary policy, the theory of income determination, and the theory of money; in addition it helps synthesize the classical and Keynesian theories of macroeconomics by providing us with a definite and general theory of the velocity of money.

[Thus, if at the higher price level the schedules determining the inflationary gap of Chapter 13 shifted up exactly in balance so there were still a zero gap, then real Q would rise at the 3 per cent per year rate at which our full-employment output can grow by virtue of technical improvements. But if the new higher level of P meant that the schedules could not shift upward so nicely, but instead began to intersect with a *deflationary* gap, then the cost-push process would have generated unemployment, and real Q would be growing slower than the 3 per cent technologically possible. Or in a third case, if M were held strictly constant throughout, but the rise in P was accompanied by a concomitant rise in V that happened to be large enough, then there might now be some demand-pull inflation aggravating the cost-push; i.e., the new spending schedules would have shifted up so much as to create an inflationary gap. If we had started out with full employment, real Q could not rise as fast as the percentage increase in dollar NNP, since only a 3 per cent rise in productivity and product is now possible.]

This describes the simplest theory of cost-push. Perhaps the name "sellers' inflation" would be better, in that there need be no greater degree of causation proceeding from wage rates than from profit rates; and the process need not come from unilateral union pressure but rather from the interacting institutional framework in which *all* prices and wages are finally determined as a result of producer, worker, and consumer psychology and administered decisions.

There is nothing *logically* wrong with such a simple model granted its hypotheses. A few will simply deny that there is any realism at all in such hypotheses and claim that the real world acts very much like the classical model if you examine it properly. Others will swallow these hypotheses hook, line, and sinker. An eclectic middle group will grant much validity to them but will prefer to modify them in a more realistic manner to elaborate on how they work themselves out in each microsector of the great macroaggregates.

Figure 18-6, which is sometimes called a "Phillips diagram," after A. W. Phillips of the London School of Economics, can be used to depict a modified cost-push model of demander-seller inflation. On the horizontal axis is the percentage of unemployment. On the black left-hand vertical scale is the algebraic percentage change per annum in average prices; on the right-hand green scale is the accompanying percentage change in

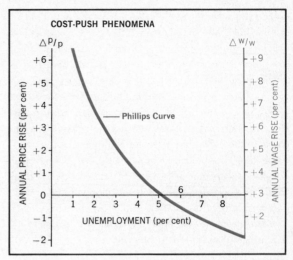

FIG. 18-6.

money wage rates per hour. These two scales differ only by the postulated amount of productivity increase per year (so that the price change of 2 per cent per year would correspond to a wage change of 5 per cent per year if productivity grew by 3 per cent per year and its fruits were shared in the same old proportions by labor and nonlabor).[5]

The indicated "Phillips curve" shows by its downward slope that increasing the level of unemployment can moderate or wipe out the upward price creep. There seems to be a dilemma of choice for society between "reasonably high employment with maximal-growth-and-a-price-creep," or "reasonably-stable-prices with considerable unemployment;" and it is a difficult social dilemma to decide what compromises to make.

Be it noted that the MV and $C + I + G$ approaches to aggregate dollar spending are still applicable *off-stage*, but one needs the information of the Phillips curve to translate the resulting product $P \times Q$ into its separate components. In the simplest classical world of solely demand-pull inflation, the Phillips curve would be a vertical line at the minimal unemployment level: Q would then always correspond to full employment, and P would float in free labor markets to whatever level total money spending would determine. In a limiting model of depression unemployment, where

[5] A higher rate of productivity growth will show itself in an equal upward shift of the green curve and scale. Thus, with productivity growing at 4 per cent per year, a 5 per cent wage increase would correspond to only a 1 per cent annual price rise. A profit squeeze could be similarly shown.

wage rates were inflexible against any downward movements but costs do not rise until full employment is reached, the Phillips curve would be the horizontal axis until minimal unemployment was reached; and it would then shoot up vertically as in classical cases.

One can expect the putative Phillips curve for different mixed economies to be different, depending upon their institutional patterns and psychological outlooks. Thus, in the 1950s, the curve for West Germany seemed more like the limiting cases mentioned above than did the American, British, or Swedish curves. So in the latter countries you then heard more concern about cost-push creeps of inflation.

Many economists think an important problem of modern life can be technically put thus:

■ How can a mixed economy, without relying unduly on inefficient direct wage and price controls, give itself a Phillips curve in which closer approaches to high employment can be made without engineering a considerable price creep?

Will antitrust legislation of the type discussed in Chapter 26 help? Union busting? Exhortation? Programs to improve labor mobility and training? Temporary creation of considerable unemployment in order to rid people of inflationary expectations and militant bargaining demands? Issuance of Presidential guideposts?

This will truly be an important, but terribly difficult, problem of the 1970s. Chapter 39 will call it the problem of an "incomes policy" for the mixed economy.

SUMMARY TO APPENDIX

1 ■

The causal interrelations between M, i, I, and NNP could also be expressed in MV language. So long as one expects any induced changes in V to be such as not *fully* to offset the original change in M, then changing M can in one step be described as changing NNP. Semantics alone would be involved, were it not true that special hypotheses about V may seem tenable to those who use this concept.

2 ■

In a perfect classical world without frictions and with an inflexible hard-money public-debt base, Pigou proved in the 1940s that a sophisticated version of Say's Law could be asserted. For policy and realistic description, he preferred not to rely on hyperdeflation to produce such "Pigou effects." Pushing such a full-employment model to its logical limits, however, does enable one to reaffirm the crudest quantity theory in which P becomes strictly proportionate to M and public debt (the degree

of the proportion varying only when extraneous real changes take place).

3 ■

Policy dilemmas arise in a nonclassical cost-push, or sellers' inflation, model. If wage and price levels are determined institutionally, then unemployment can persist. Also, postulating a tendency for wage rates to rise in the presence of persisting unemployment can lead to a creep of P even in the absence of any inflationary gap of the demand-pull type. Or if both demand-pull and cost-push elements are present, monetary and fiscal policy aimed at creating a zero inflationary gap may not end the price creep; to end it, varying amounts of unemployment may be needed, depending upon how unlucky a nation is in its Phillips curve relating percentage price change per year and percentage of unemployment or how successful it is in finding an "incomes policy" to reconcile full employment and price stability.

QUESTIONS FOR DISCUSSION

Review your understanding of the following concepts:
Say's Law and classical models
Pigou effects
crude quantity theory
induced changes in V
public-debt effects
Phillips curve and "incomes" policy dilemmas

liquidity preference:
   M dependence on both NNP and i
   Hicks-Hansen LM and IS intersection
   depression and classical poles
cost-push, or sellers' inflation

19 Fiscal Policy and Full Employment without Inflation

THE CONGRESS DECLARES THAT IT IS THE CONTINUING POLICY AND RESPONSIBILITY OF THE FEDERAL GOVERNMENT TO USE ALL PRACTICABLE MEANS . . . FOR THE PURPOSE OF CREATING AND MAINTAINING . . . CONDITIONS UNDER WHICH THERE WILL BE AFFORDED USEFUL EMPLOYMENT OPPORTUNITIES . . . FOR THOSE ABLE, WILLING AND SEEKING TO WORK, AND TO PROMOTE MAXIMUM EMPLOYMENT, PRODUCTION, AND PURCHASING POWER. EMPLOYMENT ACT OF 1946

We have seen in earlier chapters that the behavior of saving and investment determines the level of national income and employment. We have seen that investment and other spending often fluctuate widely from year to year. History shows how painful and wasteful the business cycle has been in the past. Today everyone is in agreement that we must succeed in laying to rest, the ghost of instability, chronic slump, and snow-balling inflation.

What prescription follows from our economic diagnosis? No single answer can be given; there is no single cure-all for the economic ills of society. Business, labor, and agriculture must of course attempt to pursue price and wage policies aimed at maintaining a stable, high-employment economy. The Federal Reserve System can also do much, by way of interest and monetary policy, to moderate instability. But while all these measures are being used, powerful help is still needed from the weapon of public *fiscal policy* (i.e., governmental tax and expenditure policies). Fiscal policy alone is not a cure-all, but it is an important part of any economic program.

Be warned that the subject matter of this chapter is still in a controversial stage. Even economic experts are not in full agreement on all the issues connected with budget deficits and the public debt. And yet it is fair to say that the differences in doctrine among economics scholars pale into insignificance in comparison with the wide gulf that persists between the opinions of these experts and the ideological views on fiscal policy held by the public and politicians. Gradually, however, informed lay opinion is becoming less archaic on such questions as the following:

Must the budget be balanced every year? Should it be? Should it be balanced only over a complete business cycle rather than every year? Can a growing economy prudently incur a deficit most of the time?

Is the growth of *debt, per se,* a good or bad thing? How different is public from private debt in this respect? If I as a private person overspend and incur debt, I invite disaster and bankruptcy. Is the same really true of a government that is financing a chronic debt by borrowing from its own citizens? Is a budget deficit necessarily inflationary? Or is it, in recession times, only antideflationary?

As will be seen in this chapter, experienced researchers into the facts and the analytical principles of public finance have today, all over the world, quite different answers to these questions from those of the man in the street or our forefathers. The problem for an introductory text is to explain the logic and experience underlying modern doctrines, not to indoctrinate the student into any one view. An objective analysis of the issues—both the pros and cons—should be helpful in giving each person the materials from which he can form his own opinion on these matters.

A. SHORT-RUN AND LONG-RUN FISCAL POLICY

By a positive fiscal policy, we mean the process of shaping *taxation* and *public expenditure* in order (1) to help dampen down the swings of the business cycle and (2) to contribute toward the maintenance of a growing, high-employment economy free from excessive inflation or deflation.

The World War II and postwar years have shown fiscal policy to be a powerful weapon. Indeed, some would argue that it is like the nuclear bomb, too powerful a weapon to let men and governments play with; that it would be better if fiscal policy were never used. However, it is absolutely certain that, just as no nation will sit idly by and let smallpox decimate the population, so too, in every country fiscal policy is brought into play whenever depressions gain headway. And in time of clear inflation, there always appears a consensus of economists in favor of contractionary fiscal policy.

There is no choice, then, but to attempt to lead fiscal policy along economically sound rather than destructive channels. Every government has a fiscal policy, whether it realizes it or not. The real issue is whether this shall be a constructive one or an unconscious, bumbling one.

■ THE TASK OF FISCAL POLICY

Without fiscal and monetary policy, the economic system might in a particular year be threatened with a deflationary gap. Suppose private consumption and investment spending were too weak to provide adequate employment. What action would then be called for?

The Federal Reserve would use expansionary monetary policy to try to stimulate private investment. To the degree that its efforts were not fully successful, the fiscal authorities would still be faced by a deflationary gap. This would be the signal for Congress and the President to introduce tax and public-expenditure policies designed to help reachieve stable full employment.

Similar action would be called for in the case where private investment amd consumption decisions were threatening the economy with an inflationary gap. With prices rising and employers vying desperately for nonexistent workers, the Fed would initiate contractionary credit programs aimed to reduce the inflationary gap. But if the saving-investment or $C + I + G$ intersections still threatened the economy with a sustained inflationary gap, it would then be the duty of Congress and the President to initiate higher tax rates and/or lower-public-expenditure programs in the attempt to restore a high-employment equilibrium without inflation.

■ In summary, fiscal policies dealing with taxes and public expenditure, in cooperation with stabilizing monetary policies, have for their goal a high-employment and growing economy—but one without price inflation. The fiscal and monetary authorities "lean against the prevailing economic winds," thereby helping provide a favorable economic environment within which the dynamic forces of private initiative can have the widest opportunity for achievement.

■ OUR IMPORTANT "BUILT-IN STABILIZERS"

One might get the impression from the above remarks that fiscal policy helps stabilize the economy only so long as government officials are carefully watching trends, are successfully anticipating future developments, and are meeting promptly to take decisive actions. Such "discretionary fiscal policies," involving the making and changing of explicit decisions, are important; fortunately, they are but part of the story.

The modern fiscal system has great inherent *automatic stabilizing* properties. All through the day and night, whether or not the President is in the White House, the fiscal system is helping to keep our economy stable. If in 1972 a recession got under way while Congress was out of session, powerful automatic forces would go instantly into action to counteract it before there were committee meetings or the exercise of special intelligence of any form.

What are these mysterious stabilizers? They are primarily the following:

1. *Automatic changes in tax receipts.* We saw in Chapters 8 and 9 that our federal tax system depends progressively on personal and corporate incomes. What does this mean for stability? It means that as soon as income begins to fall off, and even before Congress makes any changes in tax rates, the tax receipts of the government also fall off. (Today, for each 10-billion-dollar drop in NNP, total tax receipts drop by about $3\frac{1}{2}$ billion.)

Now, reductions in tax receipts are just what the doctor prescribes in case of a dip in income. So our present tax system is a mighty and rapid built-in stabilizer.

NOTE: Taxes stabilize *against upward* as well as downward movements. In times of inflation, this is a good thing; but when built-in rises in taxes stand in the way of healthy real growth, we call it "fiscal drag"—a subject discussed on page 343.

A century ago, writers thought that *stability* of tax revenue was a good thing, and they would have looked with disapproval on the present-day tendency for tax receipts to rise and fall with national income. Today, most economists believe that the truth is just the reverse. Thus, to dampen a boom, a budgetary surplus is desirable. There are two ways to produce such a surplus: by a reduction in government expenditure, yes; but also by an increase in tax receipts. To fight a recession, there are likewise two ways open: raising expenditures, or cutting tax rates. Indeed, from the standpoint of free private enterprise, tax changes represent the more conservative policy. How lucky we are, therefore, that our present tax system has to some degree "automatic flexibility," with its receipts tending to rise in inflationary times and to fall in times of depression. This is a powerful factor stabilizing the economy and moderating the business cycle.

2. *Unemployment compensation and other welfare transfers.* In the last 35 years we have built up an elaborate system of unemployment compensation. Soon after men are laid off, they begin to receive payments from the unemployment compensation funds. When they go back to work, the payments cease; and the taxes collected to finance unemployment compensation rise when employment is high. During boom years, therefore, the unemployment reserve funds grow and exert stabilizing pressure against too great spending; conversely, during years of slack employment, the reserve funds are used to pay out income to sustain consumption and moderate the decline.

Other welfare programs—such as relief payments outside the social security system—also show an anticyclical automatic behavior of a stabilizing type.

3. *Farm-aid programs.* The various parity programs to aid agriculture, which we shall discuss later in Part Three, act like built-in stabilizers. When dollar spending drops off and farm prices fall, the federal government pays out dollars to farmers and absorbs surpluses. When inflation brews and prices soar, the government warehouses put forth farm goods and absorb dollars, thus cushioning any movement.[1]

4. *Corporate savings and family savings.* Not all the applause goes to the government. Our private institutions also have built-in stabilizers. Thus, the custom of corporations' maintaining their dividends, even though their incomes change in the short run, does cause their retained savings to act like a shock absorber or built-in stabilizer.[2] And to the extent that families try to maintain previous living standards and are slow to adjust their living standards upward—to this extent, they too help stabilize. (To the extent that they rush out to spend extra income on down payments or hysterically cut down on consumption when economic clouds arise, they hinder stability.)

Still other stabilizers could be mentioned, but these are the main ones.[3]

■ LIMITATIONS OF AUTOMATIC STABILIZERS

Before leaving the subject of automatic stabilizers, we should stress two things. First, the built-in stabilizers are our first line of defense, but are not by themselves sufficient

[1] By pushing up the prices of raw materials, parity formulas can also have an "escalating," or destabilizing, effect; and to the extent that they simply limit supply at all times, they redistribute and lower rather than stabilize income. Defense stockpiling of metals is at times stabilizing, at times not.
[2] To the extent that corporate investment is itself linked to corporate saving, this stabilizing influence is negated. A rise in the wages/profits ratio is a [partial] stabilizer on dips, as Cambridge's Nicholas Kaldor insists.
[3] Many experts advocate increasing the stabilizers by having Congress pass a law making tax *rates* vary *automatically* with changes in various aggregative price and income indexes. But Congress so far has not been willing even to vote discretionary power over tax rates to the President, as the 1960 Commission on Money and Credit had recommended.

to maintain full stability. Second, reliance on them in preference to discretionary programs raises some philosophical and ethical questions. Let us examine these points.

The automatic tendency for taxes to take away a fraction of each extra dollar of NNP means that the size of the "multiplier" is cut down. Each dollar swing in investment—whether caused by sunspots, inventions, or anything else—will now have its destabilizing effect on the system reduced *but not wiped out completely*. Instead of such disturbances having their effects on NNP multiplied three or more times, there will now—because of the automatic stabilizing effect of taxes—be a multiplier effect of only 1.5 or 2 times.[4]

■ In short, a built-in stabilizer acts to reduce *part* of any fluctuation in the economy, but does not wipe out 100 per cent of the disturbance. It leaves the rest of the disturbance as a task for fiscal and monetary discretionary action.

Philosophically, some reformers dislike the need to have human beings decide policy. They speak of a "government of laws and not of men." They advocate setting up automatic rules and mechanisms that would go into action without ever depending on human decisions. At the present time an automatic gyropilot can keep an airplane pretty stable while the pilot catches a nap; but when something unusual comes up, the human pilot must still take over. No one has yet found a gadget with all the flexibility of man. Similarly in the social field: we have not yet arrived at a stage where any nation is likely to create for itself a set of constitutional procedures displacing the need for discretionary policy formation and responsible human intelligence.

■ DISCRETIONARY FISCAL POLICY

The principal weapons of discretionary fiscal policy—programs which involve explicit public decision making—are (1) varying public works and other expenditure programs, (2) varying transfer expenditure programs, and (3) varying tax rates cyclically.

PUBLIC WORKS   When governments first began to do something active about depressions, they tended to initiate work on public investment projects for the unemployed. Often these were hastily devised, and in that they aimed primarily to create work for people, they often were rather inefficient; e.g., road building using as little machinery as possible to make the work stretch, leaf raking during the depression by the WPA relief workers, trumped-up pork-barrel projects of low utility and lacking careful planning. The extreme case is the mythical program where men dig holes and then refill them.

---

[4] Intermediate texts show that in the simple multiplier formula $1/(1 - \text{MPC})$, we have to cut MPC down to .65 MPC now that .35 of each NNP dollar goes to taxes and only .65 to disposable income. What effect on the multiplier does this attenuation of MPC have? In the case of a multiplier of $3.0 = 1/(1 - \frac{2}{3})$, it cuts the $\frac{2}{3}$ down to .433 and the final multiplier down to only 1.8. (The propensity of corporations to distribute only a fraction of their earnings has similar attenuating effects on the multiplier; but their tendency to let a rise in income induce I and their tendency to increase their I merely because they have some retained profits will work to increase the multiplier. Transfer expenditures on welfare, which tend to fall when NNP rises, act like taxes to reduce the multiplier.

The day is long past when a modern nation will let its economy collapse to the point where its only rescue must come from hastily contrived and wasteful public-works spending. The modern emphasis has, rightly, shifted away from such "make work" projects. Indeed, where a recession is expected to be a short one, economists today would wish to rely much more on a temporary reduction in tax rates than on an increase in public works.

Why this shift away from public works as a recession cure? Men now realize that it takes a long time to get a post office started or to put into effect a road-building and slum-clearance program. Plans must be made; blueprints drawn; land acquired by purchase and court condemnation; existing buildings razed; and then new structures and roads constructed. All this may take five or more years; and, at the least, half of this time may elapse before any sizable amount of money will get spent on labor and materials. Suppose the recession turns out to last a year at most, followed by two years of steady advance. Then, just in the third year, when the economy may have gone all the way from too little demand to too much demand, there will suddenly come onto the market the government spending that was intended to help a recession. Such timing would of course make fiscal policy an aggravator of instability not a reducer.

The above remarks should not be construed as an argument against public works. Slum clearance, urban rehabilitation, road building, and public construction might be deemed by the American people to represent the most urgent use of their social resources. If that were the case, such programs should be pushed hard; but—and this is the point—they should not be pushed hard under the guise of a program designed merely to achieve short-run stabilization. They should be carried out for their own sake and over that long period of time which is necessary if they are to be done well and efficiently.

Of course, the case will often arise where the economy is in a recession and where it may be possible to move ahead the date of carrying out a long-term public expenditure program that the people had already agreed ought to get done anyway. An intelligently planned shelf of blueprints for desirable public-works projects, even though some costs would be involved in arranging them ahead of time and keeping them up to date, could much improve fiscal timing. As Secretary of Commerce and President, Herbert Hoover long advocated this, and since 1931 we have had such laws.

WELFARE EXPENDITURES   We saw that existing welfare programs, such as unemployment compensation and old-age retirement payments, do act as automatic stabilizers, rising automatically when incomes fall and needs increase.

In addition to such built-in stabilizers, it is possible for the government to institute various discretionary programs of transfer expenditures that will stabilize further. Thus, the government could refrain from giving some pending veterans' bonus in inflationary times and push forward such disbursements in depressed times. If it intends to lower parity farm payments, Congress might hope to time the change to coincide with a boom period. Most important, in times of prolonged unemployment, the federal government has moderated the decline by aiding the states in prolonging the period for which the jobless can get paid unemployment compensation. It is precisely in times of sustained unemployment that the present system is most deficient, and it is in such times that there will be minimal harmful effects on job mobility and incentives from increasing unemployment disbursements.

A major drawback in using welfare transfer programs for short-run stabilizing purposes is the political fact that it may not be easy to terminate such emergency programs after times have become good again.

VARIATION OF TAX RATES   If there is good reason to think that a recession will be brief, a temporary cut in income tax rates can be a very good way of keeping disposable incomes from falling and of preventing a decline from snowballing. Under our withholding system, the moment Congress or the executive branch decides the economy needs stimulus through tax reduction, employers can begin to withhold less from salary paychecks. Varying tax rates can be used also to help control an inflationary gap and long-run sluggishness.

Aside from the obvious political difficulty that it takes Congress a long time to debate and act to make tax changes, there is a minor weakness in the case for heavy reliance on discretionary varying of tax rates for stability purposes. An objection to temporary suspension of tax rates to counter a recession comes from the political fact of life that in a democracy it may be hard to get tax rates back up after the emergency decline is over. Political sentiment to fight unemployment is often easier to mobilize than sentiment to fight inflationary gaps and more-than-full employment. (In long slumps this may be good.) At a time of demand-pull inflation, such as 1966 when Vietnam spending coincided with a plant and equipment boom, the so-called "New Economics" plumps for an increase in tax rates. That is why President Johnson asked Congress in September, 1966, to suspend temporarily the 7 per cent investment tax credit and also the accelerated depreciation given for new construction. That is why he was urged by economists inside and outside the government to raise corporate and personal income tax rates temporarily.

While advantages and disadvantages are claimed for various alternative fiscal programs, the observer should not let them blind him to the basic fact that in the last 30 years the proneness of the American economic system to chronic slump and major instability has been drastically reduced. When William Howard Taft was President in 1912, federal finance was much more like what it had been in the 1800s than like what it has since become!

■ SURPLUS AND DEFICIT FINANCING: STAGNATION, EXHILARATION, AND CONTRIVED GROWTH

When an inflationary gap calls for contractionary fiscal policy, the principle of a balanced budget will almost certainly be violated by the need for higher tax rates and reduction of expenditure. Similarly, a successful attempt to offset a deflationary gap almost certainly will put the budget into a deficit.

If the business cycle were around some "normal" level, most people would not worry too much so long as the boom-time budgetary surplus were always matched by the depression budgetary deficit. With such regularity, *the budget would be balanced over the business cycle* even though not balanced in every single year or month. There would be no secular trend upward in the public debt, nor downward.

But how can one be sure that the cycle will be so regular? What if America is in for what Harvard's Alvin Hansen called "secular stagnation"—which means a long period in which (1) slowing population increase, (2) passing of the frontier's free land, (3) high corporate saving, (4) the vast piling up of capital goods, and (5) a bias toward capital-saving inventions will imply depressed investment schedules relative to saving schedules? Will not an active fiscal policy designed to wipe out such deflationary gaps then result in running a deficit most of the time, leading to chronic growth in the public debt?

Contrariwise, suppose population is proliferating, new inventions are zooming, and investment is generally excessive relative to full-employment saving. If this threatens to go on most of the time, will not active fiscal policy require a budgetary surplus most of the time? Hence, will not such a condition of "secular exhilaration" lead to a long-term decline in the public debt?

A new, third possibility looms for the 1970s. Suppose a democracy is concerned to accelerate its own rate of growth. Suppose its representative government wishes to increase the fraction of its full-employment income that gets devoted to capital formation rather than to consumption. If public policy succeeds in stepping up net investment by militant easy credit or other policies, how can consumption spending be cut down to prevent excessive dollar demands from precipitating inflation? Primarily by having the government pursue an austere fiscal policy: raising tax rates and cutting down on marginal expenditures, thereby contriving a *chronic* budget surplus to offset easy money. In brief, one cannot set in advance the optimal trend of surplus or deficit.

■ THE NEW ECONOMICS AT WORK

For ten years after World War II, total demand was exuberant, real economic growth was unusually rapid, and by 1953 unemployment was down to what seems in retrospect a glorious minimal amount. During the 1950s unemployment became higher at each successive peak: $2\frac{1}{2}$ per cent in 1953, 4 per cent in 1957, 5 per cent in 1960. Real growth was sluggish in the Eisenhower years: businessmen complained of a "profit squeeze"; and critics of the mixed economy began to wonder whether it was not subject to the debilitating disease of "structural unemployment" that could not be cured by macroeconomic measures. Long-term stagnation had again reared its ugly head.

At this point President Kennedy introduced the "New Economics" into American public policy. Elected in 1961 on the pledge to "get the country moving again," he realized that this would require fiscal actions and not just words. In the first years of the 1960s, the United States government for the first time in its history *explicitly tried to add to a recession deficit in the interests of higher employment and better growth.*

At first, the New Frontier fiscal actions took the form primarily of an increase in government expenditure. But by the end of 1962 President Kennedy had become convinced that the country needed a massive tax cut. To cut taxes when there was already a budget deficit was indeed "new" economics. Only after a long campaign of education did businessmen, laborers, and the man in the street generally become persuaded of the following precepts:

■ 1. To the extent that a tax cut succeeds in stimulating business, our progressive tax system will collect extra revenues out of the higher income levels. Hence, a tax cut *may* in the long run imply little (or even no) loss in federal revenues, and hence no substantial increase in the long-run public debt.

2. There is no need to balance the budget, or try to balance it, in every year. By the time of his death, President Kennedy had become convinced that in a growing economy prudent policy does not even require that the budget be balanced over a decade, or over a complete business cycle. So long as continuous deficits do not result in the public debt growing faster than GNP grows, good economic health can prevail. For the economy, "balance" means full employment and healthy growth with no wasteful gap between our potential and our actual real output, and also no inflationary gap.

At first the nonexpert public remained skeptical about these new doctrines. But when President Johnson, after Kennedy's tragic assassination, persuaded Congress to introduce a massive tax cut early in 1964, it worked well enough to impress even the most skeptical. What were the effects of the more than ten-billion-dollar tax cut? Scientists have studied this experiment more carefully than almost any other in our economic history, and here are their main conclusions.

■ The cut in taxes did not prove impotent to change consumption and investment spending, as extremists had argued. Nor did it succeed miraculously in producing full employment overnight, as other extremists had argued.

Instead, the tax cut resulted in just about the gradual rise in consumer spending that the propensity-to-consume concept had predicted. It also had the expected direct stimulus on investment spending. And then the multiplier doctrine worked very much as modern economic textbooks had suggested it would. Moreover, Federal Reserve actions reinforced the fiscal actions with the appropriate monetary policies needed for a steady return toward full employment.

In economics, of course, controlled experiments are not possible. Other things will not remain constant, and by 1966 the unplanned upswing in Vietnam military expenditures caused the economy to overshoot the goal of full employment and enter into a period of demand-pull inflationary gap.

■ "FISCAL DRAG"

In concluding this discussion of deficits and surpluses, and before taking up the issue of the public debt, we should notice some new principles which were developed in the 1960s and which formed the intellectual cornerstone of the Johnson-Kennedy programs. First, there is the important concept of "fiscal drag." Second, there is the related concept of the "full-employment budgetary surplus (or deficit)" as contrasted with the actual surplus or deficit experienced at whatever NNP actually happens to be.

We have seen that a progressive income tax structure results in vast increases in tax revenues when incomes grow. Thus, every year that the American economy shows 5 or 6 per cent growth in money NNP, the government collects about 10 billion extra dollars of revenue. Every year!

If inflation is taking place, this built-in stabilizer is a great thing—just what the doctor ordered. But suppose the economy is in a normal healthy state of full employment without inflationary or deflationary gap? Then a collection of 10 billion new dollars of tax revenue can prove a *deflating* influence that may kill off full employment. And in this case we call it "fiscal drag," and know that we must get rid[5] of it either by cutting taxes, raising federal expenditures, or giving financial aid to the states and localities, with their burgeoning social needs and inflexible tax systems.

■ *Definition:* "Fiscal drag" is the name for the automatic growth in tax revenues in an economy with a progressive tax structure and steady overall growth. Unless needed to fight an inflationary gap, fiscal drag has to be offset by (1) federal expenditure increase on public goods deemed vital, (2) tax-rate cuts that increase people's disposable incomes and expenditures on the private sector, (3) revenue sharing with the states and the localities, or (4) combinations of all of these.

■ THE FULL-EMPLOYMENT BUDGET SURPLUS

As a way of dramatizing this ever-recurring problem of fiscal drag, economists have learned not to look at the actual budget deficit. When, as in 1961, we had 7 per cent unemployment and a large gap between our actual output and our full-employment potential, we were of course running a budget deficit.[6]

But modern economists make a new calculation, asking: "Suppose we were now at high or full employment, say with only 4 per cent of the labor force unemployed and with firms at their desired 95 per cent of capacity. With all the higher tax revenues that such an increase in NNP would bring, what then would our budget deficit be?"

Figure 19-1 shows by the green curve that in the early 1960s there was really a "full-employment surplus," even though the brown line indicates an actual budget deficit at that time.

■ To summarize, the "full-employment budget surplus or deficit" measures what *would* be the budget position *if* the economy were at full employment and the legislated tax and spending structures were in effect. Unless tax rates are cut or expenditures increased, there would be in every healthily growing economy an increase in the full-employment surplus and a resulting fiscal drag.

By now we have come a long way from the old-fashioned views of the man in the street. Economic emphasis has been put on the economy's healthy growth without inflation and not on the balancing of the budget. But is this sound economics? Can the

---

[5] As will be seen in Part Six, if there is no international constraint on expansionary monetary policy, fiscal drag can be offset by inducing higher private investment to accelerate national growth.

[6] This was true whether you used the official "administrative budget," or the so-called "cash budget," or the more informative "budget on national-income account."

The new economics introduces new concepts: full-employment budget and fiscal drag:

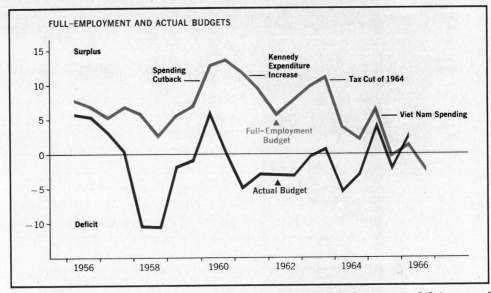

FIG. 19-1. Even though the brown curve shows that the actual budget was in deficit most of the time from 1958 to 1965, the green curve shows that there was a surplus in the full-employment budget (which measures what the story would be if output and tax receipts were at the full-employment level). Growth of the economy would have enlarged the full-employment surplus every year and produced "fiscal drag," if the Kennedy-Johnson Administrations had not deliberately raised expenditures at the beginning of the 1960s and deliberately cut taxes in the mid-1960s. To fight a 1966-type demand-pull inflation, can you show that you want to contrive fiscal drag by raising the full-employment surplus through judicious tax-rate increases? (Source: Federal Reserve Bank of St. Louis and Council of Economic Advisers.)

economic system prudently bear the implied burden of the public debt? To that vital question we turn for the remaining section of this chapter.

B. THE PUBLIC DEBT AND MODERN FISCAL POLICY

As a result primarily of World War II, the public debt of the federal government is over 325 billion dollars—about one-third of a trillion dollars. What are the various economic problems created by such a debt? Are there any false problems associated with it? What are the important noneconomic factors that must be reckoned with in any discussion of this vital political issue?

In appraising the burdens involved in a public debt, we must carefully avoid the unscientific practice of making up our minds in advance that whatever is true of one small merchant's debt is also necessarily true of the government's debt. Prejudging the problem in this way comes perilously close to the logical fallacy of composition; and instead of permitting us to isolate the true—all too real—burdens of the public debt, it may only confuse the issue.

No beginner can be expected to master all the intricacies involved in correct appraisal of the public debt. He will see from the following discussion that modern economists give great attention to the debt's true burden but diagnose its problems in a way significantly different from the approach the layman used to take.

■ BURDENS AND BENEFITS OF THE PUBLIC DEBT

The man in the street, if asked to make a list of important economic problems, will usually put the size of the public debt near the top of his list. A panel of economic experts, in this country or anywhere in the free world, will usually put the debt toward the bottom of any such list, and indeed some will actually include it on the credit side as a positive blessing.

Why this difference of opinion? And why is it that in countries like Germany, Britain, Japan, and Holland, statesmen, editors, and the citizenry never even know what their current budgetary deficits (as we measure the concept) are? These are interesting psychological questions that do not belong primarily in a course on economics. It is our task here to make sure we understand in an objective and dispassionate way the *economic* effects of debts, deficits, and surpluses. The facts agreed on by economic scholars can be briefly summarized in the main body of this chapter. The Appendix will present a survey of the analysis that underlies the economics of public debt, and of popular analogies.

As the Appendix shows,

■ The main way that one generation can put a burden on a later generation is by using up currently the nation's stock of capital goods, or by failing to add the usual investment increment to the stock of capital.

Thus, the bulk of our 325 billion dollars of federal debt came from World War II. The primary burden of that war came from the need *then* to eat up capital goods without replacing them in order to maximize our effectiveness against the enemy and shorten the conflict. (Hence, it was the prohibition against car manufacture or building construction and repair that produced this real burden, and not the happenstance that Congress decided to finance part of the war effort on a loan-deficit basis rather than on a full tax-as-you-go basis.)

Looking to the future, we can say that increases in public debt which are incurred in time of full employment and involve no government capital formation, but which do require that private investment be held down (by Federal Reserve policy or by inflation itself), do in fact represent a "burden." On the other hand, incurring debt when there is no other feasible way to move the $C + I + G$ equilibrium intersection up toward full employment actually represents a *negative* burden on the immediate future to the degree that it induces more current capital formation than would otherwise take place!

There is a second aspect of the American public debt that needs stressing. An *external* debt (owed to foreigners), as the Appendix shows in detail, does involve a net subtraction from the goods and services available to the American people, to the degree that we have to send goods abroad to pay interest on that debt. An *internal* debt (owed by the government to its own citizens) is quite a different matter. Certainly one cannot blithely ignore an internal debt on the ground that "we all owe it to ourselves." There definitely are problems involved in an internal debt, but what needs stressing is the way in which they differ from those of an external debt.

The principal problems of an internal debt have to do with the transfer payments of interest that must be made to some people and the taxes that are levied upon all people for this purpose. To the degree that the people involved are different and that the interest receivers are wealthier, more thrifty, or deemed less in need of income, there will be redistributional effects to reckon with. But even if the same people are taxed to pay on the average the same amounts they receive in interest, there will still be the distorting effects on incentives that are inescapably present in the case of any tax. (The Appendix shows that taxing Peter to pay Peter interest may make Peter work less hard or harder—and either of these may be a distortion of efficiency and well-being.[7])

The existence of a large outstanding public debt may also have an influence on interest-rate levels. Some writers fear that channeling investment funds into the purchase of government bonds will raise the rate of interest to private borrowers. Thus, if people want to hold a certain total of assets to provide for their old-age retirement, the existence of government bonds may substitute for ownership of deeds to machinery and buildings. Alexander Hamilton, the spokesman of the conservative Federalist party, held just the opposite opinion. He felt that, rightly managed and in the right amounts, a public debt would be "a national blessing" because it would provide a secure gilt-edge asset that would give businessmen an income and enable them to trade for smaller profits. Notice, too, the beneficial effects of interest payments to banks, colleges, widows, and other *rentiers*. If there were no public debt, or if interest rates were to fall substantially, (1) charitable institutions would have to be supported by public and private current contributions more than by interest on endowments, (2) social security and annuities would have to take the place of *rentier* interest, and (3) service charges by banks would have to be relied upon instead of public bond interest.

Still other effects are analyzed in the Appendix. But in general, when economists evaluate the magnitude and trend of the public debt, with rare exceptions, they agree that its present level does not merit the psychological excitement that used to be accorded it and that often still is. They also agree, however, that *recklessness* concerning deficit spending and debt formation could become an important social evil if it emasculates all public self-discipline, and they point to numerous historical instances. This is a case where the economist has a duty to lay all the arguments before the citizen, allowing him to form his value judgments concerning appropriate policies.

■ EFFECTS ON PRIVATE INVESTMENT

Never forget that there is a tremendous amount of emotion involved in people's attitudes toward the debt, and this we must not dismiss lightly. Like sex or religion,

[7] But recall that back on page 143, debt interest is listed as barely one-fourteenth of the total tax level.

the public debt is a subject we all love to discuss. Many people used to predict the end of the world when the debt reached one-hundredth, one-tenth, and one-fifth of its present level; each year when the dire disaster had not appeared, they renewed their predictions for subsequent years.

Such attitudes may affect private investment. If private investment could be assumed constant, then in unemployment times public expenditures would admittedly have favorable primary effects upon income and employment; more than that, the consumption respending of income would give rise to the familiar multiplier chain of favorable secondary effects. But what if private investment is frightened off by government expenditure or by the deficit?

This is certainly possible. Businessmen may say, "With that man in the White House spending recklessly, we're going to abandon even the little private investment we had planned." Or a private utility company may curtail investment because it fears the threat of public dam projects. Or when government spending gives people money to buy in retail stores, the effect in time of deep depression may simply be to permit merchants to work off inventory of surplus merchandise; if they don't reorder production goods, the public expenditure has been just neutralized by induced private *disinvestment* (in inventory), and the multiplier chain is stopped dead in its tracks.

On the other hand, there may be expansive effects on private investment that are just the opposite of these unfavorable repercussions of government finance. When current production is at a low ebb and there is excess plant capacity, no prudent businessman feels like undertaking new capital formation. If the government is able to boost retail sales and the production of consumption goods, then businessmen will have the financial ability and at least some motive to renew equipment and build new plants.[8] Sometimes purely psychological fears about the public debt and deficit could *accentuate* an inflation situation, even one with its origin outside the fiscal sphere.

Where there are two such opposing tendencies—expansive and contractionary effects upon private investment—facts rather than arguments must be our guide. Although economics does not permit us to make controlled experiments to settle the point conclusively, the bulk of the statistical data seems to suggest that private investment tends on the whole to move sympathetically with the level of national income. The cash register calls the tune, and in a free enterprise society, rightly so.

PROOF OF THE PUDDING   Many Congressmen have said, "Deficit financing was tried in the Great Depression and proved to be a failure." MIT's E. Cary Brown studied the fiscal facts of the 1930s to see whether this was true. His careful measurement of the actual statistics of NNP, G, and deficits showed that the historical facts agreed remarkably well with multiplier theory: despite the hysterical criticisms of the New Deal deficits as being gigantic, they in fact were what we would consider small today in relationship to the existent deflationary gap—much too small for any scientist to predict that they would restore full employment; but the fiscal actions of the 1930s did, *per dollar,* produce the expansionary effects predicted by multiplier theory.

[8] An example of this was provided by the discussion in Chapter 14 of the acceleration principle relating induced investment to the upward change in sales.

■ THE QUANTITATIVE PROBLEM OF THE DEBT

To assess the importance of the present public debt, we must turn to the facts. Do interest payments on it swallow up most of the national income? How does the total of all interest payments, public and private, compare with past years and with the experience of other countries? What about the future?

To see how the present debt compares with the past and with Britain's debt, look at Table 19-1. It shows for selected times and places the size of national debts and their relationship to size of national income and interest payments. Thus, in 1965 our national debt of about 320 billion dollars represented little more than one-half year of national income, and its interest payments represented only about 2 per cent of net national product. Note that England in 1818, 1923, and 1946 had an internal debt estimated at more than twice national income, and her interest on the debt as a percentage of national income far exceeded anything that we need look forward to; yet the century before World War I was England's greatest century—greatest in power and material progress. Furthermore, as the table shows, her national debt was not substantially reduced; but with the steady growth of her national income, the debt and its charges shrank to almost nothing in relative magnitude!

In the light of these statistics and by careful qualitative analysis, the reader must form his own judgment as to whether the national debt can be rationally regarded as

Growing debt holds little peril for a dynamically growing economy:

(1) YEAR	(2) NATIONAL DEBT	(3) INTEREST CHARGES ON NATIONAL DEBT	(4) NATIONAL INCOME	(5) SIZE OF DEBT IN YEARS OF NATIONAL INCOME (5) = (2) ÷ (4)	(6) INTEREST CHARGES AS A PERCENTAGE OF NATIONAL INCOME (6) ÷ 100 = (3) ÷ (4)
United States (billions):					
1965	$321.4	$11.43	$559.0	0.6	2.0
1945	278.7	3.66	181.5	1.5	2.0
1939	47.6	0.95	72.6	0.7	1.3
1929	16.3	0.66	86.8	0.2	0.7
1920	24.3	1.02	79.1	0.3	1.3
1916	1.2	0.02	38.7	0.0+	0.0+
1868	2.6	0.13	6.8	0.4	1.9
Britain (millions):					
1964	£30,250	£620	£26,500	1.1	2.3
1946	24,000	500	8,100	3.0	6.2
1923	7,700	325	3,950	1.9	8.2
1913	625	20	2,400	0.3	0.8
1818	840	31	400	2.1	7.7

TABLE 19-1. NATIONAL DEBT AND INTEREST CHARGES RELATIVE TO NATIONAL INCOME. The 40-billion-dollar debt that so worried people in the 1930s looks small against the subsequent rise in our income. (Sources: *Economic Almanac*, U.S. Department of Commerce; U.S. Treasury; United Nations; *Colwyn Report; Statistical Abstract of United Kingdom*. Data rounded off.)

a problem of the first magnitude in comparison with the problems of national defense, the nuclear bomb, unemployment, and inflation. Whether productivity will continue to rise in the future, whether labor and management can learn to bargain collectively without strikes and inflation—to many observers these seem much more important than the debt itself.

GROWTH IN THE ECONOMY   In dispassionately analyzing the growth of the debt, there is one error we must avoid: *We must not forget that the real national product of the United States is an ever-growing thing.*

Our population grows lustily. As to productivity, there is no indication that man-hour efficiency and new techniques have begun to slacken off. Upon this, "stagnationists" and "exhilarationists" both agree. What seemed like a big debt in 1790 would be nothing today. What our children will come to regard as a big debt, our great-grandchildren will deem relatively unimportant.

This explains why England and France, in the crucially formative years of the capitalistic system and the Industrial Revolution, were able to go on—not only decade after decade, but century after century—with their budgets in balance less than half the time. Figure 19-2 shows that the growth of our economy since 1945 has drastically reduced the ratio of United States public debt to gross national product. (This, properly, excludes FRB and Treasury holdings; but the point would be the same if these exclusions had not been made.) This fact of growth explains why, in the United States, where real national product grows at about $3\frac{1}{2}$ to $4\frac{1}{2}$ per cent per year, the public debt might increase by another 300 billion dollars in 20 years without its relative percentage burden growing at all.

While private debt outstripped NNP growth, public-debt ratio fell steadily after World War II:

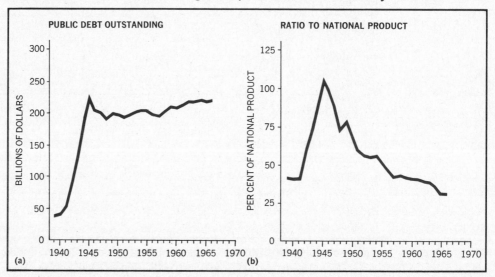

FIG. 19-2. Most of the federal debt held by the public came from wars. In the last 25 years, its ratio to the growing GNP or NNP has declined steadily. (Source: U.S. Treasury. FRB and government holdings of bonds are excluded from the total of federal debt.)

This would give the wildest believer in government spending an average deficit of 15 billion dollars per year before he would have to turn to such even more unorthodox financial expedients as printing money or selling interest-free bonds to the Federal Reserve Banks. Moreover, before turning to such expedients, he would still have open to him the now familiar process of keeping down interest rates on government bonds by a conventional easy-money banking policy. This raises a sobering question.

Could a nation fanatically addicted to deficit spending pursue such a policy for the rest of our lives and beyond? Study of the mechanics of banking and income determination suggests that the barrier to this would not be financial. The barrier would have to be political; and the effects of such a policy depend crucially upon whether it impinges on an economy that is already inflationary or deflationary. And if the electorate and Congress learn the half-truth that expenditure is expansionary, while forgetting the fact that unpleasant taxes may be necessary to curb undue expansion, then the long-term outlook may be in the direction of rising prices.

Now we have looked carefully at the facts about the public debt here and abroad and have given the economic principles that underlie the burdens of a public debt. We have seen that there are certain definite problems involved, but that laymen often have mixed-up notions as to what are and are not genuine burdens. (The Appendix discusses private- and public-debt analogies.)

There are many major problems ahead for our economy: inflation, slump, conservation and congestion, adequate growth, international balance of payments, and scores of others. Prudent fiscal and monetary policies impinge on them all; but in a sober man's list of grave problems, the present magnitude of the public debt does not come near the top.

■ CONCLUSION: A GRAND NEOCLASSICAL SYNTHESIS

The Employment Act of 1946 stated that the government felt a responsibility to help keep employment high and to moderate cyclical instability, and many have suggested that it be amended to mention explicitly a similar government concern for reasonable stability of the price level. Even if there were no such legislative proclamations, it is a fact all over the world that the populace of modern mixed economies require their representative governments to pursue economic policies that attempt to keep employment high, growth strong, and prices stable.

Part Two has presented the economic tools of macroeconomics: how the various schedules determine levels and movements in incomes and prices; and how monetary and fiscal policies can shift those schedules so as to avoid deflationary and inflationary gaps and promote growth. In Part Six certain special problems connected with the modern era—growth, demand-pull and cost-push inflation, and so forth—will be discussed in greater detail.

We may conclude here on the optimistic finding of our macroeconomic analysis. It represents neither the classical faith that *laissez faire* must by itself lead to utopian stability nor the pre–World War II pessimism that classical principles have become inapplicable to the modern world. Instead we end with what can fittingly be called a "neoclassical synthesis," which shows how appropriate monetary and fiscal policies can ensure an economic environment which will validate the verities of microeconomics—that society has to choose among its alternative high-employment production possibilities, that paradoxes of thrift and the fallacies of composition will not be permitted to create cleavages between private and social virtues or private and public vices.

■ *Neoclassical synthesis:* **By means of appropriately reinforcing monetary and fiscal policies, our mixed enterprise system can avoid the excesses of boom and slump and can look forward to healthy progressive growth. This fundamental being understood, the paradoxes that robbed the older classical principles dealing with small-scale "microeconomics" of much of their relevance and validity will now lose their sting. In short, mastery of the modern analysis of income determination genuinely validates the basic classical pricing principles; and the economist is now justified in saying that the broad cleavage between microeconomics and macroeconomics has been closed.[9]**

With good conscience we can turn to the analysis in Part Three of how the great social aggregates of national income and employment *get determined in their detailed parts* and to Part Four's analysis of *income distribution.*

SUMMARY

A. SHORT- AND LONG-RUN FISCAL POLICY

1 ■

When private investment and consumption spending create an inflationary (or deflationary) gap, it is the task of fiscal and monetary policy to offset the gap in the attempt to preserve price stability, high employment, and growth.

2 ■

Fiscal weapons refer to taxation and expenditure policies. In this connection, the modern economy is blessed with important "built-in stabilizers." Requiring no discretionary action, tax receipts change *automatically* when income changes, thereby reducing the size of the multiplier and serving to wipe out part of any disturbance. (The same stabilizing effect is created by unemployment compensation and other welfare transfers that automatically grow as income falls, as well as by farm-aid programs and the propensity of corporations to pay out in dividends only part of their current earnings.)

3 ■

Because the automatic stabilizers never *fully* offset the instabilities of an economy, scope is left for discretionary programs. Public works and other expenditure on goods and services can involve such time lags in getting under way as to make their use to combat short recessions undesirable. Discretionary variations in transfer expenditures and in tax rates—politics aside—have greater short-run flexibility.

---

[9]Naturally, one can point out many needed qualifications to this optimistic formulation. But events of recent decades and the most painstaking economic research in universities, industry, and government justify our concentrating on the doughnut—not on its hole.

4 ■

When men began to drop the notion that the government's budget had to be balanced in every year or month, they first thought that it would be in balance over the business cycle—with the boom-time surpluses just matching the depression deficits. It is today realized that only by coincidence would the prosperity years just balance in their intensity the depression years.

If, as a few believe, we are in for "secular stagnation," with private saving and investment schedules tending much of the time to produce deflationary gaps, fiscal policy will probably succeed in maintaining stable high employment only by having a long-term increase in the public debt. If, as others believe, we are in for "chronic exhilaration," with demand so brisk as to lead much of the time to inflationary gaps, then active fiscal policy will probably mean a bias toward surplus financing and a secular downward trend in the public debt. Perhaps the majority of economists feel there is no need to try to predict what the distant future has in store, being prepared to advocate programs that the developing situation calls for. Moreover, long-term surplus financing could be coupled with long-term easing of credit and special encouragements to capital formation in order for a mixed economy to move its high-employment production in the direction of investment and rapid growth and away from current consumption.

5 ■

To get a better measure of changes in discretionary fiscal policy, economists supplement knowledge of the actual budget surplus or deficit with the hypothetical "full-employment budget surplus or deficit," which measures what the existing tax and spending structure would entail *if* NNP were at the full-employment level. In a growing economy, there would automatically be a steady growth in the size of the full-employment surplus and resulting "fiscal drag"—unless offset by expenditure increases, tax cuts, or sharing of tax revenues with states and localities. In time of inflation, automatic fiscal drag is a good thing; and if national policy is for faster growth, expansionary monetary policy can offset it and give us more rapid capital formation (and a lower-consumption economy) at full employment.

B. THE PUBLIC DEBT AND MODERN FISCAL POLICY

6 ■

The public debt does not burden the shoulders of a nation as if each citizen were made to carry rocks on his back. To the degree that we now follow policies of reduced capital formation which will pass on to posterity less capital goods, we can directly affect the production possibilities open to them. To the degree that we borrow from abroad for some transitory consumption purpose and pledge posterity to pay back the interest and principal on such external debt, we do place upon that posterity a net burden, which will be a subtraction from what they can later produce. To the degree that we bequeath to posterity an internal debt but no change in capital stock beyond what would anyway have been given them, there may be various internal transfer effects as one group in the community receives a larger share of the goods then produced at the expense of another group. At any one time there is no "net burden" of such internal transfers quite like the net subtraction involved in the external-debt payment, but there can be important transfer effects between people of different ages then alive and certain effects within each generation's lifetime on how much they will receive of consumption and at what ages. And the process of taxing Peter to pay Paul, or taxing Peter to pay Peter, can have definite costs: these can involve various distortions of production and efficiency, but should not be confused with actually sending goods abroad.

Aside from the above "real" effects, there may also be psychological effects upon the minds of men, and men's resulting actions must of course be regarded as real. Moreover, the fact that there are more rather than less bonds being owned by people in the community can be expected to have quite real effects on their propensity to save and consume out of income. Each person regards his government bond as an asset, but the future taxes to service these bonds he does not count in fully as a current personal liability, even though all society will have to pay taxes equal to such debt service. (This is not irrational from his viewpoint, since the tax rates he will be subject to have little to do with his personal holding of the debt, as the Appendix discusses.)

This summary point has been written at some length to indicate the complexity of the problem. We see that a debt does have important impacts on the economy, even if they are not primarily those that orators and editors preach about.

It is important, also, to know roughly what the size of the post–World War II federal debt is in relation to national income and interest charges, in order to assess the present, both in terms of the past and in terms of the future. The growth of the debt must be appraised in terms of the growth of the economy as a whole. Since 1945 the ratio of public debt to private debt and national product has been substantially declining.

7 ■

A full- (or high-) employment program has as its goal a level of total spending that is neither too little nor too great—so that the saving and investment schedules intersect in the region of full employment. The Employment Act of 1946 represents an important innovation in our Republic, affirming responsibility of the government for employment opportunities and setting up executive and congressional machinery for policy action.

8 ■

To the extent that reinforcing monetary and fiscal policies are efficacious in stabilizing the worst excesses of boom and slump, we need no longer fear the clash between private and social virtues or the various paradoxes of a depressed economy. Mastery of the modern tools of income determination at the macroeconomics level will turn out to validate the basic truths in the classical doctrines of pricing and scarcity at the micro-economic level. This is the optimistic "neoclassical synthesis."

QUESTIONS FOR DISCUSSION

1. "No nation can avoid having a fiscal policy. With the government such an important part of the present-day economy, it is almost impossible even to define a 'neutral fiscal policy.' It is even harder to give rational reasons for preferring such a policy to an active fiscal program aimed at preventing inflation and deflation." Examine this statement critically.

2. List various "built-in stabilizers." Show how they work.

3. What phase of the business cycle (if any) are you now in? What tax and expenditure policies would seem appropriate? Qualitatively, how would you vary the relative mix of taxes (income-tax rates and exemptions, sales taxes, property taxes) to fight unemployment or inflation?

4. From the early 1870s to the middle 1890s, depressions were deep and prolonged, booms were short-lived and relatively anemic, the price level was declining. What long-run fiscal policy should have been followed in that quarter of a century? Would your answer be the same for the following 20 years leading up to World War I, a period of rising prices and prosperity?

5. Comment on the 1840 views of the historian Macaulay:

> At every stage in the growth of that debt the nation has set up the same cry of anguish and despair. At every stage in the growth of that debt it has been seriously asserted by wise men that bankruptcy and ruin were at hand. Yet still the debt went on growing; and still bankruptcy and ruin were as remote as ever. . . .
> The prophets of evil were under a double delusion. They erroneously imagined that there was an exact analogy between the case of an individual who is in debt to another individual and the case of a society which is in debt to a part of itself. . . . They made no allowance for the effect produced by the incessant progress of every experimental science, and by the incessant efforts of every man to get on in life. They saw that the debt grew; and they forgot that other things grew as well. . . .

6. Show briefly why "burden of the debt" is a complicated economic issue.

7. Formulate and evaluate the "neoclassical synthesis."

8. Review your understanding of the following concepts:

inflationary and deflationary gap

tax receipts and tax rates

government expenditure on goods and transfers

built-in stabilizers and the reduced multiplier

discretionary policy problems

fiscal drag

the full-employment budget surplus

internal versus external debt

present versus future generations and bequeathal of real capital

debt/income ratios here and abroad, today, yesterday, and tomorrow

chronic stagnation, exhilaration, and trends in the public debt

Employment Act of 1946

neoclassical synthesis

APPENDIX: False and Genuine Burdens of the Public Debt

According to a popular image, the public debt, prorated over the population, is like a load on each man's back. According to this same image, when Congress adds a dollar to the debt by running a current deficit of a dollar, that is like just one more rock added to the load our children or grandchildren will already have to carry on their backs.

This image is misleading in two ways. First, it exaggerates the burdens that are truly involved. Second, by giving a mistaken view of the debt burden, it lays itself open to refutation and thereby to the mistaken conclusion that there are, after all, no burdens connected with the public debt. In other words, superficial and wrong analysis offers genuine comfort neither to the conservative nor to the liberal ideological groups in a democracy.

As a preview to a judicious appraisal, see how vulnerable the foregoing image is.

A DIALOGUE

Suppose all debt came from World War II. This war is over. Suppose all America's families (1) share equally in ideal nondistorting taxes, (2) hold equal shares of public-debt bonds, (3) all live forever (as individuals or as a cohesive family). With no debt held abroad, (4) "we all owe it to ourselves."

"Then such bonds are not rocks on our shoulders, or even paperweights. If we unanimously voted to abolish the bonds, there would be no real difference. If an enemy bombed our homes and factories, that would be a genuine personal and national burden. But if an enemy bombed our bond lockboxes out of existence, that would merely save us the red tape of taxing ourselves to pay each of us back in bond interest just what the extra tax took away."

So goes the argument. Notice how simple the above refutation is. And how clever in taking the wind out of the sails of those who use the oversimplified rock-burden image. Moreover, the refutation is—granted its assumptions—logically rigorous.

Has the refutation proved that the war involved no grievous burden? It has been cunningly silent on that matter. The Devil's Advocate who produced the refutation would, if pressed by a Tireless Truthseeker, have to concede much.

DEVIL'S ADVOCATE: Yes, the war did involve a grievous economic burden at the time. We had to work hard and long hours. We had to cut wartime consumption to the bone: do with little meat, no cars, no travel—make do with few of the things that make life enjoyable rather than merely tolerable.

TIRELESS TRUTHSEEKER: With severe rationing controls, the contemporaneous wartime burden of sacrificed consumption would, according to your view, be much the same even if the war had been financed by pay-as-you-go wartime taxes instead of deficit?

D.A.: Precisely. Postwar canceled tax receipts, instead of bonds, would make no difference.

T.T.: But surely, we used up capital goods during the war by not replacing them. The enemy had to be fought with current 1941–1945 goods and not with 1967 goods. By using up capital goods *then*, we could throw more resources into the war effort. And that did put a real burden *on us in the postwar period* since we inherited less capital goods at war's end. In the postwar period

we've had to consume less in order to rebuild those capital goods; and we've had to consume less than we could have if 1941–1945 had given us the normal peacetime increase in capital goods.

D.A.: True. But wartime rationing produced that result. If no wartime deficits and bond indebtedness had been created, that *genuine burden* on the postwar group due to the war would still have had to take place.

T.T.: I feel there must be a catch somewhere. Your argument sounds too facile.

1. I can't help feeling that the existence of the public debt leads (*a*) to tax distortions as we collect taxes to pay its interest, and (*b*) to a lower consumption schedule when poor people with higher MPC pay taxes for bond interest to wealthier people with a lower MPC.

2. Moreover, people don't live forever, and it is not irrational of them to feel wealthier because of the public debt (since they need count on paying taxes for debt interest only through their remaining lifetime). This increase in the *CC* propensity to consume could be at the expense of net capital formation in a full-employment postwar year, requiring contractionary *M* policy that hurts investment.

3. Besides, a small part of our public debt (about 1 in 20) is external and held abroad: sending them goods to cover the interest payments does constitute a definite subtraction from our NNP available for domestic consumption and investment.

4. While it may be true that transfers of purchasing power—between individuals living at one time, between individuals at different ages of their life spans, and between individuals alive today and yet unborn—can be engineered by the government without using the device of the public debt at all, yet I can't help believing that society is led by the presence of the debt to make some transfer decisions that it probably wouldn't otherwise have made.

5. If the decision to have a deficit in depression times (or in times when the international balance of payments makes expansionary monetary policy infeasible) merely prevents unemployment, then I admit the implied deficit adds to, rather than subtracts from, the capital stock bequeathed to the postdepression times. (Maybe 50 billion dollars of the depression deficit and some of the 1958–1964 deficit were such a blessing.) But when a decision to have a deficit leads to a compensating cut in private capital formation through inducing more restrictive FRB monetary policy than would otherwise

be the case, I say that such a way of increasing the public debt does *itself* put a real burden on the backs of later citizens.

6. Of course, I admit that floating a public debt to add to useful government capital is as legitimate as floating private debt to build useful private capital—because in each case the new paper assets are matched by real income-creating assets.

7. But in a well-run full-employment system, I have to regard loan finance for *current* public consumption as putting a kind of burden on the future through its effective cutting down on net capital formation at the time, and subsequently through its wealth stimulus on consumption that may be competitive with investment.

D.A.: I've never denied anything you are saying. I merely assumed away most of your genuine burdens. If I may say so, you are now shifting over to the side of the angels and are beginning to analyze the true and false burdens of the public debt—and not merely using vivid analogies that obscure rather than illuminate the truth, the whole truth, and nothing but the truth.

SUMMARY OF DEBT BURDENS AND BENEFITS

1. CAPITAL-BEQUEATHED BURDEN   The principal way one generation puts a burden on itself later or on a later generation is by bequeathing it less real capital than would otherwise have been the case. Any growth of public debt that has this effect—as in the case of full-employment borrowing for current public consumption that has to be offset by contractionary monetary policy which will lower investment—most definitely does involve a genuine "burden."

2. EXTERNAL-DEBT BURDEN   Any public debt that is externally held does involve a current burden on the citizens at home, since in the end they have to send goods abroad corresponding to the interest payments and debt service. (Of course, if the original borrowing from abroad resulted in equivalent fruitful capital goods here, their fruits will cover the external-debt service; so the net effect of such external borrowing, taken as a complete package, would be favorable to our economy.)

3. TRANSFER EFFECTS   Taxing Peter to pay Paul bond interest, even if they are the same person, is certain to cause some harmful distortions of personal and business decisions. (EXAMPLE: Paul is taxed 10 per cent of his income to pay himself $1,000 of bond interest. He is under the illusion, and rightly so as

an individual, that he can work less and cut down on his tax; but if all do so, we simply have to increase the tax rate. Result: We all end working less because taxes on each individual matched by exactly equal interest payments to him do not economically cancel out!)

Correlated with public-debt operations, but not always in an intrinsic way, are certain transfers that take place between different individuals living at the same time, between the same individual at different periods of life, and between successive generations.[1]

4. WEALTH STIMULUS TO CONSUMPTION   The existence of public debt, for reasons already seen, makes the average man feel wealthier. For good or evil, it raises his propensity-to-consume schedule: this may, in a poorly functioning system, be a great thing to reduce unemployment and increase both consumption and investment. Or in a system where employment can be counted on to remain full by virtue of price flexibility, luck, or monetary management, the increase in C may be at the expense of I and reinforce the less-capital-bequeathed burden.

5. EFFECTS ON INTEREST AND MONEY POLICY   A large debt gives the Fed great leverage for massive open-market operations to achieve stabilization—unless, as in 1946–1951, the central bank is pressured by the government to sacrifice the goal of stabilization to the dubious goal of keeping down the interest charges on the public debt. Many experts believe that the existence of a broad market in government securities makes possible extensive open-market operations of a stabilizing

---

[1] EXAMPLES: Twin Jane Day worked hard in World War II; twin Rose did not. Because our government used deficit financing, Jane ended up in 1945 with bonds rather than tax receipts. (Jane may have been motivated to work harder by the bribe of postwar command over goods.) Since 1945 Jane has been receiving a larger share of consumption than Rose; Rose is being taxed more than would otherwise have been the case in order to help pay interest and principal to Jane. Moral: A public debt can definitely involve *internal transfer effects* between individuals of the same or different ages.

Even if Jane Day had died in 1955, she could have consumed more in 1945–1955 by selling off her bonds. The burden of *this* extra consumption could be imposed on those born after 1955 (1) by causing a reduced capital stock after 1955 due to lowered investment in 1945–1955, but also (2) by having an intermediate generation of young postwar workers (employed in 1945–1955 and who have bought Jane's bonds out of their personal saving) supported in their old age by the 1980 workers who will then pay taxes on the public debt.

type and tends to enhance the effectiveness of monetary policy. Debt management by the Treasury and Fed by a proper policy of open-market operations in bonds of all maturities that was properly carried out could enhance the stability of a modern system.

6. EFFECTS ON DISCIPLINE AND IDEOLOGY It would be a tragedy if people, in giving up their irrational fears of deficit spending, were thereby led to call the sky the limit. Unlimited spending can produce inflation, chaos, and waste.

It is to be hoped that the discipline of rationality can replace the discipline of superstition and misunderstanding.

PRIVATE AND PUBLIC ANALOGY

"How can the government go on running up debt? If I or my wife lived beyond our means and ran a debt, we'd soon learn what trouble is." The person speaking has overlooked the fallacy of composition: What is true for each unit may be false for the whole of society.

"Why do conservatives complain about the size of the public debt? Private debt has grown tremendously faster in the postwar period than public debt, and you don't hear complaints about that. All credit involves debt. The pyramid of credit could be called the pyramid of debt. If people are to have liquid assets, other people or institutions must have liabilities—d--t to the squeamish." The speaker here is also trying to use analogies with private finance, but this time to the advantage of a program for large deficits.

Both analogies are in principle suspect. Each contains some element of truth, but every strand of such arguments needs critical testing.

Thus, it is true that private debt is more than twice the public debt, and that it more than doubled in the last twenty years, while federal debt grew little in absolute amount and has actually dropped from being 62 per cent of all debt in 1945 to being only 20 per cent in the late 1960s. But it is also true that the private assets to back up that private debt have gone up too. And it is true that one could imagine an economy—not ours!—where everything was financed by *equity* issues without fixed debt.

With the warning that no analogy is conclusive, we present an analogy between a private corporation like the American Telephone and Telegraph Company and the United States government.

A T & T AND THE U.S.A.

A T & T has grown all this century. It has floated new debt throughout this century, with never an end to it. If our economy remains healthy, A T & T will undoubtedly have a rising bond debt for the rest of this century. This is prudent finance, not unsound finance. It is prudent to buy that bond debt, but not for the reason that the company has plants and equipment bought from that debt financing and which it could liquidate in a pinch. There is no one to whom A T & T could sell such specialized items in an emergency, since they are good only for the telephone business in which A T & T has complete local monopolies.

Why is never-ending growth in A T & T debt prudent? It is prudent because *the dollar receipts the company can earn from its telephone services are sure to grow along with the population and GNP.* The interest on the debt, and the occasional refunding (but not retirement) of the debt, can be paid for out of the revenues of the telephone company's customers. If they all became impoverished, say, by atomic war, A T & T would have to go bankrupt and not repay its debt. But in a growing economy, no going concern proceeds on the assumption that all the people will go bankrupt.

What does the federal government use to pay its debt interest and refundings? Obviously, *it is the taxable capacity of the country's national product that any government can rely on.*

So long as the money NNP (or GNP) grows at 4 or 5 per cent from now until kingdom come, the public debt of the federal government can grow at those rates, ultimately passing one, two, or any number of trillion dollars. No inflation need result if the process takes place in balance. And no bankruptcy or increase in relative tax burden. And no embarrassment to the Secretary of the Treasury. Like life itself, there is no end to the process.

The above analogy is given only for those who feel a psychological need for reassuring analogies and as an antidote to misleading pessimistic analogies. It says nothing about the great harm governments can do if they spend their taxed or borrowed funds rashly and feed fuel to inflationary gaps when such exist. It says nothing about the proper scope and efficiency of government, because those issues were already clarified in Chapter 8. It says nothing about the proper rate of capital formation and rate of current consumption.

Part 3 The Composition and Pricing of National Output

20 Determination of Price by Supply and Demand

THE END IS EASILY FORETOLD,
WHEN EVERY BLESSED THING YOU HOLD
IS MADE OF SILVER, OR OF GOLD,
  YOU LONG FOR SIMPLE PEWTER.

WHEN YOU HAVE NOTHING ELSE TO WEAR
BUT CLOTH OF GOLD AND SATINS RARE,
FOR CLOTH OF GOLD YOU CEASE TO CARE
UP GOES THE PRICE OF SHODDY.

GILBERT AND SULLIVAN, *The Gondoliers*

Part One of this book described the modern economic system and discussed the nature of national income. Part Two gave the modern theory of income determination: it showed why and how incomes, job opportunities, and levels of price fluctuate; it showed how money and banking fit in with income analysis; and most significantly, it showed how fiscal and monetary policy can keep the aggregate system working tolerably well. Today such analysis is called macroeconomics.

■ PREVIEW

Now Parts Three and Four analyze *micro*economics, which deals with the following important questions: What determines the relative prices of particular goods? What determines the quantitative breakdown of the national-income aggregates into various kinds of goods and services?

In order to understand the *system* of market prices which strikes an equilibrium among people's tastes for different goods and the scarcities of total resources that can produce them, Part Three studies in detail the tools of supply and demand that Chapter 4 introduced briefly.

Part Four follows with a closely related supply-and-demand analysis of what determines the prices of factors of production. Why are wages growing? Why does the share of land rent in the economy move in this way or that? What determines interest? Why have unskilled wages been falling relative to white-collar wages? Such problems constitute the subject of "distribution of income" in Part Four.

We shall see that the concepts of supply and demand as they are developed further in this chapter are vital tools for mastering the analysis of varied branches of microeconomics. (As a matter of fact, the supply-and-demand tools are indispensable in explaining the international trade problems of Part Five and the current economic issues of Part Six.)

■ MICROECONOMICS VERSUS MACROECONOMICS?

Macroeconomics deals with the big picture—with the macro aggregates of income, employment, and price levels. But do not think that microeconomics deals with unimportant details. After all, the big picture is made up of its parts. Mere billions of dollars would be meaningless if they did not correspond to the thousand-and-one useful goods and services that people really need and want. And who would be impressed by a vast national income if its distribution among human beings was a matter of caprice and pointless inequality?

There is really no opposition between micro- and macroeconomics. Both are vital. You are less than half-educated if you understand one while being ignorant of the other. We cannot even say which comes first: some books begin with one; some with the other. And surveys show that even books like this one, which begin with macroeconomics, are used by about 40 per cent of the courses to teach microeconomics first.

Thirty years ago our society had such poor mastery over its macroeconomics as to make people naturally give less emphasis to microeconomics. With millions starving because of a slump, who could get excited about whether mutton or pork was in a proper relative-price configuration? Or who thought much about white-collar wage trends relative to unskilled wages, when the unemployed tramped the street in shirts so faded you could not tell their color?

Today we hope all that is changed. Man has gained considerable mastery over his macroeconomic problems, and hence it is natural for the classical problems of microeconomics to move again to the forefront of his attention.

■ REVIEW OF FUNDAMENTALS OF SUPPLY AND DEMAND

Chapter 3 discussed how a system of pricing and of markets performs the task in any mixed economic system of determining WHAT shall be produced, How goods shall be produced, and FOR WHOM they are to be produced. Then Chapter 4 introduced the basic concepts of supply and demand: their description in terms of schedules of numbers and in terms of intersecting curves. It will be assumed that each reader has this material fresh in his mind, or has gone back to review what was learned earlier, or will stop and take time to master it now.

Our task here is to put the tools of supply and demand to work: to show how they help explain changes in price, in the short run and in the long run; to help predict what effect a tax will have on competitive price; to evaluate various policies that interfere with the laws of supply and demand.

We shall make repeated efforts to see what it is that market pricing is accomplishing in terms of the *efficiency* with which the economy fulfills its basic functions.

All through Part Three new tools of economic analysis will be introduced and the old tools will be gradually developed. But it would be a mistake for any reader to become enamored of tools for their own sake. It is the application of the tools to the richness of modern economic life that makes them exciting. Experience shows that one cannot understand the economic world of the present and the future without having at his command a systematic method of analyzing it. And the testimony of generations of students is that, however far away they later move from formal schooling and examinations, their understanding of the basic economic processes is forever keener, once they have mastered the elementary tools of economic analysis.

REVIEW   Glancing back at the supply-and-demand diagram in Fig. 4-3 (page 63), we see how equilibrium P comes at the intersection of competitive dd and ss curves. We note that any departure above equilibrium creates an "oversupply" condition leading back to equilibrium, and that any fall in P below equilibrium creates an "excess demand" that bids P back up to restore the equilibrium.

The succeeding diagram, Fig. 4-4(a) on page 64, shows how a shift in supply, such as might be brought about by a bad harvest, will be likely to increase the equilibrium price P and decrease the equilibrium quantity Q. The new E' intersection point is found to be higher on the unshifted demand curve—just far enough up to cut consumption down to the depressed harvest level.

This illustrates well an important principle, the law of downward-sloping demand —the fact that the demand curve slopes down toward the southeast, in reflection of the observation that people will buy more at lower prices and buy less at higher ones. Likewise, Fig. 4-4(b) shows how an upward shift of the demand curve leads to a higher equilibrium price.

A. ELASTICITY OF DEMAND AND SUPPLY

Second-graders, it is found, know that an increase in supply, whether because of an abundant harvest or for whatever reason, is likely to depress price. So it is no surprise that Gregory King, the English writer of the seventeenth century mentioned on page 64, should have remarked on this fact. But that same writer observed a fact perhaps less obvious: his studies convinced him that farmers as a whole received *less* total revenue when the harvest was good than when it was bad!

This fact, that high agricultural Q tends to be associated with low $P \times Q$, is one that every President of the United States has had to reckon with in facing the farm problem. To understand it and to lay the groundwork for the discussion of farm problems in Chapter 21, we must in this chapter consider and master a new and important economic concept, "elasticity of demand." Henry Ford, and any businessman tempted to cut his price in order to sell more goods and make more profit, is also interested in the concept of elasticity. And when the ICC lets a railroad raise its prices in order to cut down on passenger-service losses, the elasticity concept is crucially involved.

■ ELASTICITY OF DEMAND

Various goods differ in the *degree* to which Q bought responds to changes in each respective P. Wheat Q may go up much less than 1 per cent for each 1 per cent cut in wheat P; Henry Ford's Q may rise far more than 1 per cent for each 1 per cent reduction in its *P*; in between is the borderline case of a good whose *Q* would just halve whenever its *P* doubled, where the percentage changes are just in balance.

Elasticity of demand is a concept devised to distinguish these three cases. Thus, the first case of weak percentage response of wheat *Q* is put into the category of "inelastic demand." The second case of great percentage response is put in the category of "elastic demand." The borderline case is called "unitary elasticity of demand."

Here is how the economist goes about defining the three cases:

The crucial thing to concentrate on is the *total dollar revenue* that buyers pay to sellers. If consumers buy 5 units at $3 each, what is total revenue? It is not given by the $3 *P* alone; nor by the 5-unit *Q*. Total revenue is always, by definition, price times quantity, or the $15 product $P \times Q$. By arithmetic multiplication, total revenue can always be calculated for each point in a demand schedule or diagram.

Elasticity of demand is important primarily as *an indicator of how total revenue changes* when a fall in *P* induces a rise in *Q* along the demand curve.

■ *Definition of elasticity of demand:* This is a concept devised to indicate the degree of responsiveness of *Q* demanded to changes in market *P*. It depends primarily upon *percentage* changes and is independent of the units used to measure *Q* and *P*. Elasticity ends up qualitatively in one of three alternative categories:

1. When a cut in *P* raises *Q* so much as to *increase* total revenue $P \times Q$, we speak of *elastic* demand—or of elasticity of demand *greater than unity*.

2. When a cut in *P* results in an exactly compensating rise in *Q* so as to leave total revenue $P \times Q$ exactly *unchanged*, we speak of *unitary elasticity of demand* —or of elasticity of demand that is numerically *exactly equal to unity*.

3. When a percentage cut in *P* evokes so small a percentage increase in *Q* as to make total revenue $P \times Q$ fall, we speak of *inelastic* demand—or of elasticity of demand that is *less than unity* (but not less than zero).

Figure 20-1 gives a graphic example of the three cases. In each case, *P* is halved from *A* to *B*, but it would be just as much in order to have used a very small percentage change in *P*. Perhaps at a first glance, it will be easiest to begin with the borderline case of unitary elasticity of demand.

In Fig. 20-1(b), the doubling of *Q* exactly matches the halving of *P*, with the result that the total revenue collected remains unchanged at $1,000. This can be shown graphically by comparing certain rectangular areas. How? Price and quantity can be easily read off the curve at any point; but how do we read off total revenue, which is their arithmetic product $P \times Q$? When we recall that the area of a rectangle is always equal to the product of its base times its altitude, the answer is easy:

Total revenue at any point is always as shown by the area of the rectangle which that point makes with the two axes. (Check that the shaded rectangle at *A* does have a base equal to *Q* and an altitude equal to *P*.) Hence, if our eye watches how the area of each point's rectangle changes as we cut price and move down the demand curve, we can know in which of the three categories of elasticity such a movement happens to fall.

Clearly, in the middle diagram, the areas are remaining exactly the same because of offsetting changes in their *Q* bases and *P* altitudes; consequently, this is the case

Elasticity of demand comes in three cases, depending on how total revenue moves:

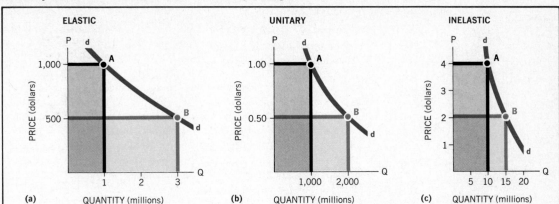

FIG. 20-1. In cutting P from A to B, we raise, leave unchanged, or lower the rectangle of total revenue, depending on whether demand is elastic, unitary elastic, or inelastic. That is, elasticity depends on percentage response of Q to each percentage change in P.

neither of elastic nor of inelastic demand, but rather is the borderline case of unitary elasticity of demand.

The reader can now verify that Fig. 20-1(a) does correspond to *elastic* demand, with total revenue going up when P is cut and elasticity hence greater than unity. And Fig. 20-1(c) does correspond to the opposite case of *inelastic* demand, with total revenue falling off when P is cut and elasticity less than unity. [Which diagram best represents the Gregory King finding that smaller harvests meant higher total revenues for farmers? Which best represents the early belief of Henry Ford, that if only he could reduce his cars' P, he would encounter a tremendous increase in cars sold? Surely, 20-1(c) and 20-1(a), respectively.]

■ NUMERICAL MEASUREMENT OF ELASTICITY: A DIGRESSION[1]

The general notion of elastic, inelastic, and unitary elasticity as an indicator of the percentage responsiveness of quantity to price and as an indicator of how total revenue behaves is now clear. But some readers will be curious to know how these qualitative cases can be given exact numerical measurement by economists. What does it mean to say that the elasticity of demand is 1.0? 2.3? 0.5? To answer this question, we give the following definition for a coefficient of elasticity E between two different price points on a demand curve:

$$\text{Elasticity coefficient } E = \frac{\text{per cent that } Q \text{ has risen}}{\text{per cent cut in } P}$$

Note that the movements along P and Q are in opposite directions because of the law of downward-sloping demand. Note, too, the use of *percentages*, which brings in the

[1]In a short course the next two sections can be skipped.

nice property that the units of a good or of money—bushels or pecks of wheat, dollars or pennies—do not affect elasticity.[2]

Do not get bogged down in numerical details of E calculation. Now that you have mastered the general idea of elastic, inelastic, and unitary demand, you can proceed to the following numerical examples.

Always there is a slight ambiguity about percentage changes. Suppose a grocer buys bread for 15 cents and sells for 25. Is that the $66\frac{2}{3}$ per cent markup that comes from relating the change of 10 to the lower base 15? Or is it the 40 per cent change that comes from relating 10 to the higher base 25? No one answer can be said to be right, and no one definitely wrong. Fortunately, when it comes to very small percentage changes, as from 100 to 99 or from 100 to 101, the difference between $\frac{1}{100}$ and $\frac{1}{99}$ becomes hardly worth talking about. For small changes, it does not matter much how you calculate the percentage changes; but for larger ones it may make quite a difference, and no single answer can be declared to be the right one.

What is a good rule to use? Long experience suggests this: As good a rule as any is to relate the price change to neither the higher nor the lower of the two P's, but to their average. Thus, is a cut from 101 to 99 a change of $\frac{2}{99}$ or $\frac{2}{101}$? By our convention, it is neither: we call it a change of $\frac{2}{100}$, because the average of 99 and 101 is $(99 + 101)/2 = \frac{200}{2} = 100$.

Dividing percentage price cut into percentage quantity rise gives numerical elasticity:

P	$-\Delta P$	Q	ΔQ	$\frac{P_1 + P_2}{2}$	$\frac{Q_1 + Q_2}{2}$	$E = -\frac{\Delta Q}{\Delta P} \times \frac{(P_1 + P_2)/2}{(Q_1 + Q_2)/2}$
6		0				
	2		10	5	5	$\frac{10}{2} \times \frac{5}{5} = 5 > 1$
4		10				
	2		10	3	15	$\frac{10}{2} \times \frac{3}{15} = 1$
2		20				
	2		10	1	25	$\frac{10}{2} \times \frac{1}{25} = .2 < 1$
0		30				

TABLE 20-1. NUMERICAL CALCULATION OF ELASTICITY COEFFICIENT. Each P cut, $-\Delta P$, is related to the average P, $(P_1 + P_2)/2$; each Q rise, ΔQ, to the average Q, $(Q_1 + Q_2)/2$; the resulting ratio gives numerical E, a measure expressed in percentage (dimensionless) units, not in absolute slope units.

Table 20-1 is self-explanatory: it shows how to calculate E for three movements along a dd curve. We shall be seeing that most dd curves start out elastic at high P and end up inelastic at low P, passing through unitary elasticity at an intermediate position where total revenue $P \times Q$ is at its maximum.

[2]Units will affect the slope of the demand diagram, just as the draftsman can make a curve look steep or flat in slope by changing the scale of one of his axes. So the purpose of the next section is to help you avoid confusing slope and elasticity. As Fig. 20-1(b)'s curve with $E = 1$ shows, it is not a straight line with constant slope that corresponds to a curve of constant elasticity, but rather one whose slope varies in order to keep the percentage changes in the same ratio. (Mathematicians call the unitary-elastic curve a ["rectangular"] hyperbola.)

Absolute slope and percentage elasticity are not the same:

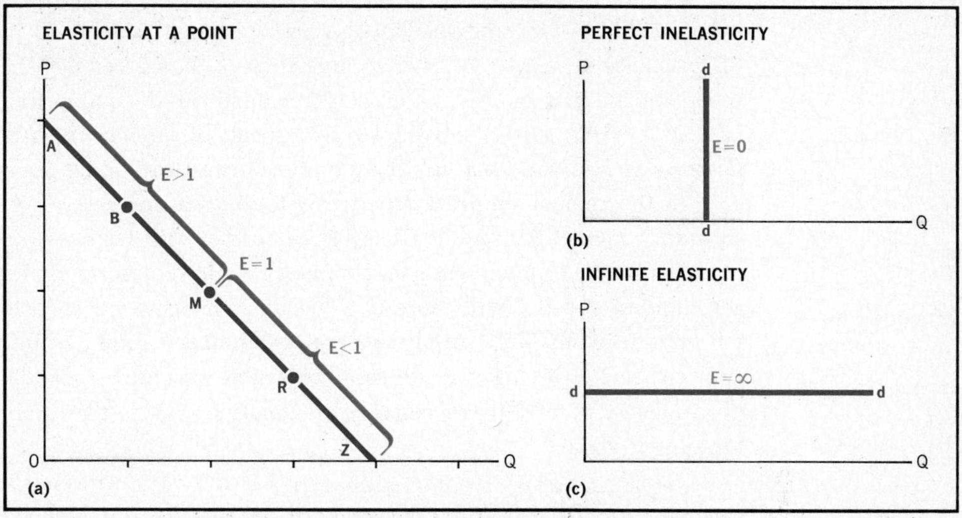

FIG. 20-2. All points on *dd*'s straight-line demand in (a) have same absolute slope; but above the midpoint price, demand is elastic; below it demand is inelastic; at it demand is unitary. Only in the case of perfectly vertical or horizontal curves, as in (b) and (c), can you infer inelasticity and elasticity from slope alone.

■ GRAPHICAL MEASUREMENT OF ELASTICITY: A DIGRESSION

Students tend to make a simple mistake: They often confuse the slope of a curve with its elasticity; they think a steep slope on *dd* must mean inelastic demand, and a flat slope must mean elastic demand. This is not quite true. Why not? Because slope of *dd* depends upon *absolute* change in P and Q, whereas elasticity was seen to depend upon *percentage* changes.

The straight line *dd* in Fig. 20-2(a) illustrates the fallacy of confusing slope and elasticity. Everywhere it has the same absolute slope. But toward the top of the line, where (1) P is high and its percentage change low and (2) Q is very low and its percentage change therefore almost infinitely great, our numerical formula for E results in a very high elasticity.

Thus, above the midpoint M of any straight line, demand is elastic, with $E > 1$; at the midpoint, demand is of unitary elasticity, with $E = 1$; below the midpoint, demand is inelastic, with $E < 1$.[3]

When many people make the same mistake, there is usually a reason. The limiting cases of *completely vertical* and *completely horizontal* demand curves, shown in Fig. 20-2(b) and (c), do validly portray the limiting cases *completely inelastic* and *infinitely elastic* demands. But do not think that the in-between cases, where most of reality falls, can have their elasticities depicted by slope alone.

Now, we go back to the mainstream of demand and supply.

[3]Intermediate books tell how to calculate E at any one point on a straight line: E equals the length of the line segment below the point divided by the length of line segment above it. Since M is halfway, the formula there gives $E = 1$, unitary elasticity. At B, it gives $\frac{3}{1} = 3.0$; at R, $E = \frac{1}{3} = .33$. Knowing

■ ELASTICITY OF SUPPLY

What we did for demand, we can also do for supply. Economists introduce the concept of "elasticity of supply" to give an indication of the percentage increase in the amount of Q supplied in response to a given percentage rise in competitive P. (Note that in the case of a *rising* supply curve, we now speak of an *increase* in P, rather than of a *decrease* in P as was done in the case of a downward-sloping demand curve.)

If the amount supplied is perfectly fixed, as in the case of perishable fish brought to today's market for sale at whatever price they will fetch, we face the limiting case of perfectly *inelastic,* or vertical, supply. If we have a horizontal supply curve, so that the slightest cut in P will cause Q to become zero and the slightest rise in P will coax out an indefinitely large supply, we are at the other extreme of infinitely *elastic* supply. Between such extremes, we call supply elastic or inelastic depending upon whether the percentage rise in Q is respectively greater than or less than the percentage rise in P bringing it about.[4]

Supply elasticity is a useful concept but not quite so useful a concept as demand elasticity, for the reason that elasticity of demand has the major additional function of telling us what is happening to total revenue.

---

how to calculate E for a straight line enables you to calculate it for any point along a curved dd. (1) Draw with a ruler the straight line tangent to the curve at your point (e.g., at B in Fig. 20-3); (2) calculate the E for the straight line at that point (e.g., E at $B = \frac{3}{1}$); (3) identify your resulting E as the correct elasticity for the dd curve at your chosen point. Question 7, page 383, proves the truth of the geometrical rule for calculating E.

NOTE: E at a point can be shown to be mathematically equivalent to the following limit: $\dfrac{-\Delta Q}{Q} \div \dfrac{\Delta P}{P} = -\dfrac{P}{Q}\dfrac{\Delta Q}{\Delta P} \rightarrow -\dfrac{P}{Q}\dfrac{dQ}{dP}$ as ΔP goes to zero, taking ΔQ with it and making it immaterial which of the P's and Q's or their averages we use to compute percentage changes. Intermediate texts show that, when you plot dd on double-log paper, it becomes correct to identify slope with elasticity—because double-log paper does measure percentage changes.

[4]A numerical coefficient of supply elasticity E_s is defined thus: E_s = (percentage change in Q)/(percentage change in P). Figure 20-4 shows three straight-line supply curves: at A the line going through the origin has elasticity of exactly 1.0; the steeper curve is inelastic, with elasticity coefficient less than 1; and the flatter curve is elastic, with elasticity coefficient greater than 1. (If—as we shall see can happen—the supply curve actually bends up backward, elasticity of supply as here defined could actually become negative.) Also, for a supply curve with curvature, one can reckon its elasticity at a point A' by drawing a straight line with a tangential ruler and seeing which curve of Fig. 20-4 it resembles; or plot it on double-log paper and study its slope at A'.

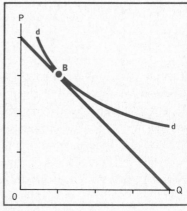

FIG. 20-3.

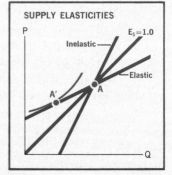

FIG. 20-4.

There is, however, an important fact that supply elasticity can help describe. A given change in price will tend to have greater and greater effects on amount supplied as we move from the momentary situation to a short-run period of time and on to the long-run period. This means:

■ Elasticity of supply tends to be greater in the long run, when all adjustments to the higher price have been made, than in shorter periods of time.

■ MOMENTARY, SHORT-RUN, AND LONG-RUN EQUILIBRIUM

Alfred Marshall, Cambridge's great economist at the turn of the century, helped forge these tools of supply and demand. We can review our understanding of equilibrium and at the same time advance our knowledge if we survey Marshall's important emphasis on the *time element* of the problem.

He distinguishes at least three time periods: (1) *momentary* equilibrium, when the supply is fixed; (2) *short-run* equilibrium, when firms can produce more within given plants; and finally (3) *long-run* equilibrium (or "normal price"), when firms can abandon old plants or build new ones and when new firms can enter the industry or old ones leave it.

Let us imagine that the demand for a perishable good, such as fish that cannot be preserved, increases from dd to $d'd'$. With the amount of fish supplied unchanged, the stronger demand will sharply bid up the momentary price of fish. This is shown on the next page in Fig. 20-5(a), where the fixed supply curve $s_m s_m$ runs up to the new demand curve $d'd'$ to determine the new sharply higher momentary equilibrium price shown at E'. The price has had to rise so much in order to *ration* the limited supply of fish among the now eager demanders.

But with so high a price prevailing in the market, skippers of the fishing boats will be motivated to hire more men and to use more nets. Even if they do not have the time to get new boats built, they will in the short run begin to bring to the market a greater supply of fish than they did at the old momentary equilibrium. Figure 20-5(b) shows the new $s_s s_s$ short-run supply schedule, and shows that it intersects the new demand curve at E'', the point of short-run equilibrium. Note that this equilibrium price is a little lower than the momentary E' price. Why? Because of the extra supply of fish induced in the short run by more intensive use of the same number of boats.

Figure 20-5(c) shows the final long-run equilibrium, or "normal," price. The higher prices that long prevailed have coaxed out more shipbuilding and attracted more trained sailors into the industry. Where the long-run supply curve $s_L s_L$ intersects the demand curve $d'd'$ at E''' is the final equilibrium reached after *all* economic conditions (including number of ships and shipyards) have adjusted to the new level of demand.

Note that the long-run equilibrium price is not as high as the short-run equilibrium price, and not nearly as high as the momentary equilibrium price. Yet it is a little bit higher than the price that prevailed previously when demand was lower. Marshall would call this a case of "increasing cost" and would regard it as the normal one to be met in most sizable competitive industries. Why normal? Because when a large

Effect of demand increase on price varies in the three time periods:

1st, The new momentary equilibrium raises P to ration out the unchanged supply:

2d, Short-run equilibrium coaxes out increased supply from existing plants:

3d, Normal long-run equilibrium comes when new plant, all resources, and costs get adjusted:

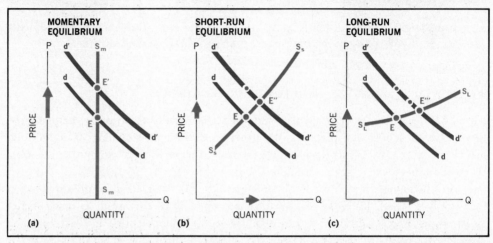

FIG. 20-5. Marshall distinguishes three different time periods, depending upon whether supply elements have time to make (a) no adjustments, (b) some adjustments of labor and variable factors, (c) full adjustment of all factors and all costs to price. (The upward slope of $s_L s_L$ puts this case in the "increasing cost" category discussed in the text. What would $s_L s_L$ be like in the "constant cost" case? Why might a very small industry have constant costs?)

industry (which has already achieved the economies of large-scale production) expands, it must coax men, ships, nets, and other productive factors away from other industries by bidding up their prices and thus its cost. So the long-run supply curve $s_L s_L$ will usually be sloping gently upward as in Fig. 20-5(c). Only if the industry is small compared with the total of all other users of its factors will Marshall's $s_L s_L$ curve in Fig. 20-5(c) be horizontal—which is called the case of "constant cost."[5]

The reader can test his understanding of all the foregoing discussion by now assuming a downward shift in the demand curve back to *dd*. Show what happens in the new momentary run; in the short run; and in the long run. The Appendix to this chapter presents various cases of supply and demand. Chapter 23 will give in greater detail the factors underlying the various supply curves.

B. APPLICATIONS AND QUALIFICATIONS OF SUPPLY AND DEMAND

Other things being equal, as economists are fond of saying, there is a unique schedule of supply or demand in any period of time. But other things will not remain equal. The demand for cotton is declining over the years because of reductions in the price of synthetics. The supply schedule of gasoline is shifting because technological progress permits more to be produced at the same cost. As costs and tastes change, as incomes vary, as the prices of rival products (coffee in relation to tea) or of cooperating products

[5] See the cases in the Appendix.

(sugar in relation to tea) change, our schedules will shift. What will be the effects on consumption, production, and price? That we must now study.

All beginners in the field of economics must beware of a common error. They must take care not to confuse an increase in *demand*—by which is meant a *shift* of the whole curve to the right and upward, as more is now bought at each same price—with an increase in the *quantity demanded* as a result of moving to a lower price *on the same demand curve*. By "demand" is meant the whole demand curve; by "supply" is meant the whole supply curve; by an "increase" in demand or supply is meant a *shift* of the whole curve in question to the right. To indicate a single point on a demand curve, we speak of the "quantity bought" or the "quantity demanded" *at a particular price*. A movement *along* the same curve is "a change in the quantity demanded as a result of a price change." It does not represent any change in the demand schedule. The need for this warning will appear in a moment.

■ INCIDENCE OF A TAX

We can illustrate the case of a shift in the entire curve by referring to supply and demand schedules for a good like wheat. Fig. 20-6 shows an equilibrium price at *C* of $3 per bushel before a tax is imposed.

Let us now introduce a new factor, which will disturb this equilibrium. In particular, assume that the government imposes a sales tax on wheat. On each and every sale, the producer is required to pay a tax of $1 per bushel of wheat.

A tax on wheat falls both on consumer and producer:

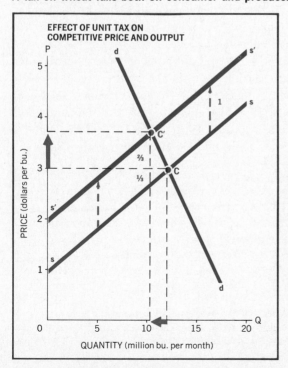

FIG. 20-6. A $1 tax shifts *ss* up $1 everywhere to give parallel *s's'*. This intersects *dd* in new equilibrium at *C'*, where price to consumer has risen $⅔ above old *C* equilibrium and where price to producer has fallen by $⅓. The thick green arrows show change in *P* and *Q*. (Had *dd* been very elastic and flat relative to *ss*, most of the $1 tax would have fallen on the producer. Had *ss* been completely horizontal, the whole $1 tax would have been shifted forward onto the consumer.)

What is the final effect, or what economists call the "incidence," of the tax? Is its burden shifted back completely onto the producer who must pay it in the first instance? Or may it be shifted forward in part to consumers? The answer can be derived only from our supply and demand curves.

There is no reason for the demand curve of the consumers to have changed at all. At $3, consumers will still be willing to buy only 12 (million) bushels; they neither know nor care that the producers must pay a tax.

But the whole supply curve is shifted upward and leftward: leftward because at each market price the producers will now supply less as a result of the tax; upward because, to get the producers to bring any given quantity to market, say, 12 (million) units, we must give them a higher market price than before—$4 rather than $3, which is higher by the exact amount of the $1 tax.

The student should be able to fill in a new supply column, resembling Column (3) in Table 4-3, page 62, but with each price raised by $1. Here in Fig. 20-6, the demand curve dd is unchanged, but the supply curve ss has been shifted up everywhere by $1 to a new vertically *parallel* supply curve s's'.

Where will the new equilibrium price be? The answer is found at the intersection of the new demand and supply curves, or at C', where s's' and dd meet. Because supply has decreased, the price is higher. Also, the amount bought and the amount sold are less. If we read the graph carefully, we find that the new equilibrium price has risen from $3 to about $3⅔. The new equilibrium output, at which purchases and sales are in equilibrium, has fallen from 12 (million) per month to about 10.6 (million) bushels.

Who pays the tax? Well, the wheat farmers do in part, because now they receive only $2⅔, ($3⅔ − $1), rather than $3. But the consumer also shares in the burden, because the price received by the producer has *not* fallen by as much as the tax. To the consumer, the wheat now costs $2⅔ plus the $1 tax, or $3⅔ in all. Because consumers want wheat so badly, they pay ⅔ of the tax, and producers pay ⅓ of the tax.[6]

To check his understanding of the above reasoning, the student should consider the case of an opposite shift in supply. Let the government pay producers a subsidy of $1 per bushel of wheat instead of taxing them this amount. Shift ss down to the new curve s''s''. Where is C'', its intersection with dd? What is the new price? The new quantity? How much of the benefit goes to the producer? How much to the consumer?

■ *Summary.* A sales tax on a good will raise its price most and reduce its quantity least when supply and demand curves are most *inelastic.* (When they are elastic, Q changes much and P changes little.)

The tax is shifted forward onto the consumer when dd is very inelastic. It is shifted backward onto the producer when ss is relatively the more inelastic. Only with the apparatus of supply and demand can the economist analyze the incidence of various different taxes—import tariffs, cigarette and liquor excises, payroll and corporation taxes, etc.

---

[6]There is another and equivalent way to handle this tax problem. If the consumer were thought of as paying the tax in the first instance, you could subtract $1 everywhere from his dd curve. The new d'd' will intersect ss at the same new Q, and the same $2⅔ and $3⅔ prices will prevail. It goes without saying that all these figures are hypothetical.

■ A COMMON FALLACY

By now the student has mastered supply and demand. Or has he? He knows that a tax will have the effect of raising the price that the consumer will have to pay. Or does he know this? What about the following argument of a kind often seen in the press and heard from the platform:

> The effect of a tax on a commodity might seem at first sight to be an advance in price to the consumer. But an advance in price will diminish the demand. And a reduced demand will send the price down again. Therefore it is not certain, after all, that the tax will really raise the price.

What about it? Will the tax raise the price or not? According to the editor's written word and the senator's oratory, the answer is, No. Evidently, we have here an example of the treachery of words. One of the four sentences in the quotation is false because the word "demand" is being used in the wrong sense. The student has already been warned against confusing a movement *along* an unchanged curve with a shift in the curve. Actually, the correct answer[7] would be more or less as follows:

> A tax will raise the price to the consumer and will lower the price received by the producer, the difference going to the government. At the higher price a smaller quantity will be bought by consumers. This is as it should be, because producers are also supplying a smaller quantity at the lower price which they receive. Thus the amounts willingly bought and sold are in balance where the new supply and demand schedules intersect, and there will be no further change in price.

■ IS THE LAW OF SUPPLY AND DEMAND IMMUTABLE?

Competitive price and quantity are determined by supply and demand. But does not price depend on other factors, such as the amount of gold production or whether there is a war going on? Actually, price does depend on many such factors. However, they are not *in addition* to supply and demand, but are included in the numerous forces which determine or *act through* supply and demand. Thus, if new gold production gives everyone higher incomes, it will shift demand curves and raise prices. But it is still true that competitive price is determined by supply and demand.

At this point a thoughtful reader should be moved to voice protest. Little has been said about price as being determined by cost of production. Should not this be listed as a third factor in addition to supply and demand? Our answer is the same.

■ **Competitive price is affected by cost of production only to the extent that this cost affects supply.**

If God sends nutritious manna from heaven without cost but in limited supply, then its price will not be zero but will be given by the intersection of the demand and supply curves. On the other hand, if it would cost $50,000 to print the national anthem on the head of a pin, but there is no demand for such a commodity, it simply

---

[7] H. D. Henderson, *Supply and Demand* (Cambridge, London, 1922), p. 27, explains this.

will not be produced and would not command $50,000 if it were produced. (What the market price of something nonexistent should be called is left to the reader's pleasure.)

This does not mean that cost of production is unimportant for price determination. Under competition it is especially important. But its importance shows itself *through its effects upon supply*. Businessmen produce for profit. If they cannot get a price high enough to cover their past costs, then they will not like it. Nevertheless, once the crop is in, so to speak, there is not much they can do about it under competition. They have no choice but to minimize their short-term losses. But they will not continue *in the future* to supply goods at prices that fail to cover the *extra* costs incurred to produce these goods. Thus supply depends intimately on cost, especially on what Chapter 23 and later chapters will call "extra" or "marginal" cost; and so too must price.

Moreover, to say that price equals cost does not in itself tell us which is the cause of which. In many cases where an industry uses a productive factor highly specialized to itself (e.g., baseball players, opera singers, vineyard land), *price determines cost rather than vice versa*. Grain land is dear because the price of grain is high. Apartment buildings sell for little because rents are low. This type of relationship was overlooked by the Massachusetts dairy farmers who petitioned during World War II for a higher milk price "because the price of cows is high." If their request had been granted, they would soon have observed the price of cows chasing the milk price upward.[8]

USEFUL CATEGORIES   Thus, supply and demand are not ultimate explanations of price. They are simply useful catchall categories for analyzing and describing the multitude of forces, causes, and factors impinging on price. Rather than final answers, supply and demand simply represent initial questions. Our work is not over but just begun.

This should help to debunk the tendency of neophytes to utter sagely, "You can't repeal the law of supply and demand. King Canute knew he could not command the ocean tide to retreat from his throne on the seashore. No more can government get around, or interfere with, the workings of supply and demand."

It would be better not to have learned any economics than be left with this opinion. Of course the government can affect price. It can do so by affecting supply or demand, or both. In Chapter 21 we shall examine how government programs for restricting farm production can raise price and income by cutting down on supply. Similar programs by government cartels have been pursued all over the world: Brazil has burned coffee to raise its price; Britain during the 1920s tried artificially controlling the price of rubber; sugar and cocoa are still under international control.

These governments have not violated the law of supply and demand. They have worked (not always to good purpose) through the law of supply and demand. The state has no secret economic weapons or tricks. What is true for the state is also true for individuals. Anyone can affect the price of wheat as long as he has money to throw on the market or wheat to hold off it.

[8] Where a factor of production is inelastic in supply, as in all these cases, its cost is "price-determined" rather than "price-determining" and its return is called an "economic rent." See Case 3 in the Appendix and also footnote 2 of Chapter 28.

Trade-unions often influence wages, or try to, by directly or indirectly affecting the supply of labor. Anyone with a somewhat distinctive commodity may try by advertising to increase the demand for his product and, by restricting supply, to raise price above his extra costs of production. It should be emphasized, however, that as soon as individual producers grow in size and become important enough to affect the price of the things they sell, they then cease to be perfect competitors in the strict sense, and their behavior has to be analyzed in terms of a blend of monopoly and competition, i.e., in terms of imperfect competition as described in Chapters 25 and 26.

■ PRICES FIXED BY LAW

There is one genuine interference with supply and demand whose effects we must analyze. The government sometimes sets by law a maximum price or a minimum wage. During World War II, ceilings were placed on items in the cost of living. In 1968, a floor of $1.60 is to be put under hourly wages of most workers. These interferences by law are quite different from government actions, previously described, which work through supply and demand.

PRICE CEILINGS AND RATIONING   Consider, say, the market for sugar, which has ordinary curves of supply and demand such as we have repeatedly met in this chapter. Suppose that the government through an Office of Price Stabilization (OPS) establishes an order prohibiting sugar from rising above 7 cents a pound (retail). Now, because of prosperity or bad crops, let demand be so high and supply so small that the equilibrium price would have been 20 cents a pound if the government had not intervened. This high price would have contributed to "profiteering" in that industry, it would have represented a rather heavy "tax" on the poor who could least afford it, and it would only have added fuel to an inflationary spiral in the cost of living, with all sorts of inflationary reactions on workers' wage demands. So go the arguments of the would-be price fixers.[9]

Therefore the government, through Congress and the OPS, decides to hold the line on prices. It passes a law putting a maximum price on sugar at the old level of 7 cents a pound. The line JK in next page's Fig. 20-7 represents the legal price ceiling. Now what will happen?

At the legal ceiling price, supply and demand do not match. Consumers want thousands of pounds of sugar in excess of what producers are willing to supply. This is shown by the gap between J and K. This gap is so large that there will not long be enough sugar on grocers' shelves or in the warehouse to make up the difference. Somebody will have to drink bitter coffee. If it were not for the maximum-price law, this somebody would gladly bid the price up to 8 or 9 cents or more, rather than do without sugar. As in our earlier discussion (Fig. 4-3, page 63), we could have shown this

---

[9]Most economists would, in normal peacetime, favor controlling inflation by the tools of macroeconomics—fiscal and monetary policies—rather than by simply legislating price ceilings that lead to chaotic rationing of the "shortages," and often to black markets and law evasion.

A legal maximum price, without rationing, leaves a gap between demand and supply:

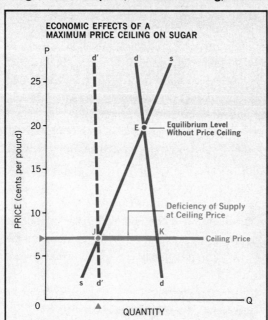

FIG. 20-7. Without a legal price ceiling, price would rise to *E*. At the artificial ceiling price, supply and demand do not balance and some method of rationing, formal or informal, is needed to allocate the short supply and bring the effective demand down to *d′d′*.

by putting an upward-pointing arrow perpendicular to *JK*. Such an arrow would not stop pointing upward until price had been bid up to the equilibrium level of 20 cents.

But it is against the law for the consumer to bid a higher price. Even if the consumer should be so unpatriotic, the seller could not legally take the higher price. There follows a period of frustration and shortage—a game of musical chairs in which somebody is left without a seat when the music stops playing. The inadequate supply of sugar must somehow be rationed. At first, this may be done by "first come, first served," with or without limited sales to each customer. Lines form, and women have to spend much of their time foraging for food. But this is no solution, since somebody must be left at the end of the line when the sugar is gone.

The price mechanism is stymied and blocked. Nonmonetary considerations must determine who is the lucky buyer and who the unlucky one: the warmth of the smile that the customer flashes on the grocer, her previous standing at the store in question, the amount of other things the customer is willing to buy, or the accident of being in the store when the sugar is put on the shelves.

Nobody is happy, least of all the harassed grocer. Were it not for the community's elementary sense of fair play, the situation would soon become intolerable. Patriotism is more effective in motivating people to brief acts of intense heroism than to putting up day after day with an uncomfortable situation. It is no wonder that black markets occasionally develop; the really surprising thing is how infrequently they do occur.

■ If for political or social reasons market price is not to be permitted to rise high enough to bring demand down to the level of supply, the ultimate solution may require outright allocation of *ration* tickets.

Once rationing is adopted, most people heave a sigh of relief, because now sellers need not turn people away and buyers can count upon getting their fair quota of the limited supplies. Of course, there are always a few women and cranks, longer on intuition than brains, who blame their troubles on the mechanism of rationing itself rather than on the shortage. "If only the government could print more ration tickets," they sigh. Such people are like the ignorant ancient kings who used to slay the messengers bringing them bad news. Their complaints need not be taken seriously; they only serve to add spice to the human comedy.

Just how do ration coupons work out in terms of supply and demand? Clearly, the OPS tries to issue just enough of them to lower the demand curve *to d'd', where supply and the new demand balance at the ceiling price.* If too many coupons are issued, demand is still too far to the right and we encounter the old difficulties, but in lesser degree. If too few coupons are issued, stocks of sugar will pile up and *P* will fall below the ceiling price. This is the signal for liberalizing the sugar ration.

One goes to an insane asylum to learn to appreciate normal human behavior. So, too, the breakdown of the price mechanism during war gives us a new understanding of its remarkable efficiency in normal times.

Goods are always scarce, in the sense that there is never enough to give everyone all he wishes. Price itself is always rationing scarce supplies: rising to choke off excessive consumption and in order to expand production; falling to encourage consumption, discourage production, and work off excessive inventories.

MINIMUM FLOORS AND MAXIMUM CEILINGS   Even in peacetime, when there arises any kind of emergency or state of general shortage and inflation, political pressures for wage and price freezes develop. Experience has taught most economists, whether they be liberals or conservatives, that such emergency measures work very well in short emergencies but create more and more distortions the longer they are in effect. Economists therefore, in contrast to politicians, tend to recommend that such direct fiats be reserved for emergency periods and not squandered on minor peacetime situations.

Nevertheless, as Adam Smith well knew when he protested against the devices of the mercantilist advisers to the earlier kings, most economic systems are plagued by inefficiencies and inequities stemming from inexpert interferences with the mechanisms of supply and demand. Here is a brief list of such interferences (shown in Fig. 20-8).

1. *Minimum wage rates.* These often hurt those they are designed to help. What good does it do a Negro youth to know that an employer must pay him $1.60 per hour, if the fact that he must be paid that amount is what keeps him from getting a job?

2. *Rent ceilings.* Everyone hates a landlord and loves a farmer. To protect the poor from being gouged by landlords, maximum rentals are often fixed by law. These fiats may do good; but they may also do harm. Thus, France had practically no residential construction from 1914 to 1948 because of rent controls. If new construction had been subjected to such controls after World War II, the vigorous boom in French residential building since 1950 would never have taken place.

3. *Usury laws.* Interest rates have always been an object of suspicion. No longer is lending at interest a crime, but in many places a maximum rate is set by law. Unfor-

When government by fiat sets maximum or minimum prices, troublesome discrepancies between supply and demand may emerge:

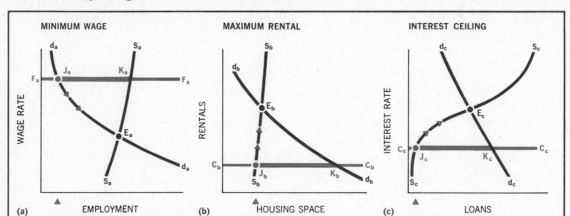

FIG. 20-8(a). Setting minimum-wage floor at F_aF_a, high above free-market equilibrium rate E_a, results in forced equilibrium at J_a. The too-high floor freezes workers into unemployment from J_a to K_a. Lowering the minimum wage will move us down along dd, as shown by green arrows, increasing employment. (If dd is elastic, total wage payrolls rise though hourly rate falls!)

FIG. 20-8(b). Setting maximum rental ceiling at C_bC_b, far below free-market equilibrium at E_b, causes fringe of unsatisfied renters between forced equilibrium at J_b and K_b. Raising the ceiling rate moves the system up s_bs_b, as shown by green arrows: new construction provides more living space, and old quarters are used more efficiently.

FIG. 20-8(c). Setting maximum interest rates at C_cC_c, far below free-market equilibrium rate E_c, results in drying up of available funds. Desperate borrowers at J_cK_c turn to loan sharks. Raising interest ceiling moves system toward more loans, as shown by green arrows on s_cs_c.

tunately, the ceiling is often far below what would be set by the competitive supply-and-demand market, after account is taken of riskiness and administrative expense connected with small loans. The result? Funds dry up completely. The cheap money you can't get does you little good. Veterans who tried to get mortgages learned this in the 1950s; college students trying to get tuition loans from the banks learned this in 1966.

■ EFFICIENCY OF SUPPLY-DEMAND PRICING AND "EQUITY"

We do not study competitive pricing for the beauty of the subject. Nor for its realism alone, since often monopoly elements spoil the competitive picture. We study it for the light it throws on *efficient* organization of an economy's resources. The pathology of interference with supply and demand helps to bring out the remarkable efficiencies produced by perfect competition.

Why then do politicians and the populace keep interfering with the mechanism? Because man does not live by efficiency alone. He is interested in the question: Efficiency for what? And for whom? Most of these floors and ceilings are set in the name of "equity"—to help some group deemed deserving at the expense of some other group deemed already affluent and amply well-off. Just as Robin Hood "robbed the rich to help the poor," these devices try to create or restore a distribution of real income considered more equitable. Their advocates are willing to pay some price in the form of lower efficiency and higher waste to bring about a "fairer" distribution of income.

■ MONOPOLY INTERFERENCES WITH SUPPLY AND DEMAND

Aside from governmental interferences, there are serious monopolistic interferences with supply and demand. Competitive supply and demand is one way of organizing an economy. It is one way of getting the job done, but of course it is not the only way. Certainly, if one or a few producers could get monopoly control of an industry, they could move the final outcome away from the competitive equilibrium point. As we shall see later, a monopolist can reduce output and make the consumers travel up their demand curves to higher prices.

Is such an interference with supply and demand a "good thing"? If the monopolist were a more worthy soul than the rest of us, or if he were much poorer and had greater need for money than the rest of us, some might rise to defend his act of raising price. Or if he took our money and devoted it to better causes (charity, scientific research) than we should do, some might still defend him as a modern-day Robin Hood.

Chances are, however, that anyone in a position to contrive a monopoly will be at least as well off as his customers, and there is not much reason to think he would be of finer clay than anyone else. And though Robin Hood may have been all right in his day, in our day we tend to think it is the government that ought to do any subsidizing of worthy causes, not self-appointed monopolists; and we hope government can be more efficient in financing its good causes out of tax revenues than any monopolist could ever be. So what probably needs emphasis is this:

■ Any *haphazard* interference with competitive supply and demand is likely— save in some exceptional circumstances—to be a bad rather than a good thing.

Thus, a monopolistic interference in Industry A reduces its output needlessly relative to Industry B. The fact that it produces such scarcity is reflected in the higher P_A/P_B ratio it creates, relative to the citizenry's desires for the goods and to their true relative costs as measured along the production-possibility frontier or by undistorted competitive costs. The monopoly may also lead to a bad distribution of income in that it may give extra income to one who already has as much income as he deserves.

■ At this point monopoly's *restriction in output* relative to that of competitive industries perhaps needs more stressing than its distortion of the income distribution. For what if we taxed away the monopolist's ill-gotten gains?[10] We should then have rectified the income-distribution distortion of monopoly. But the community would still be left enjoying less of the consumption goods that it really wants and can produce.

---

[10]Or what if many monopolists entered the industry, with all keeping their price too high but with total business so divided up among them that none ends up making any exorbitant monopoly profit? Then the evil effect on the income distribution would not exist, but the resulting wasteful pattern of overcapacity in the industry and too high price could persist until doomsday. More on this when Chapter 26 treats imperfect competition along the lines of Harvard's E. H. Chamberlin.

Like sin, monopoly is one of those things most people are against. Therefore one need not labor the point that monopoly interferences with supply and demand are probably a bad thing. Still, it is better to know analytically why.

■ GOVERNMENT INTERFERENCES WITH SUPPLY AND DEMAND EVALUATED

In conclusion let us appraise government interferences. Surely the government means well and its interferences are not to be as harshly judged as those of a monopolist?

Well, that all depends. If the government happens to know better than people what is really good and evil, its interferences may improve matters. An example might be opium. We do not treat the consumer as a sovereign who can decide how much opium he will spend his money votes on. Where opium is concerned we adopt a paternalistic attitude, treating the consumer a little the way we treat the insane, minors, and other "incompetents."

But where eight-cylinder cars or cigarettes are concerned, we usually are content to let the consumer spend his own dollars in his own way. We recognize that advertising has given us one set of tastes, which may not be intrinsically better than some other set, but in the interests of freedom we do treat the consumer as sovereign.

As we have seen, the matter becomes more complicated if the sellers or the buyers in a market happen to be especially rich, or especially poor, or especially "deserving," or especially "undeserving." For example, imagine an artificial case where 1 million very rich producers sell milk in competitive markets to 50 million very poor people. Some people would then be tempted to approve of any interference that lowered milk price. "That leads to what we call a fairer income distribution," they might say.

Without foisting his ethical judgments on others, the economist can remind us:

> ■ **Interfering with the competitive supply-and-demand mechanism is an inefficient[11] way of correcting the income distribution. Whatever distribution you**

[11]The fact that buyers and sellers are different people who may have different incomes or worth hides the truth that the competitive equilibrium point has certain allocative efficiency properties in solving the WHAT and How economic problems. So consider a simplified case where I trade only with myself. I have 10 hours of leisure worth exactly $2.50 per hour to me. I can produce 1 Q unit with each hour of work or sacrificed leisure. Suppose the first Q unit is worth exactly $4 to me, and successive Q units are worth $3, $2, $1, and $0. Figure 20-9 shows *my* supply and demand for Q. Equilibrium is at E, where I consume exactly 2 of Q. I get $4 + $3 of "satisfaction" from them (as shown by light shading) and 8 times $2.50 from my 8 hours left of leisure (as shown by heavy shading), or $27 of satisfaction in all, as shown by the sum of the areas. You can show that any disturbance which makes me work 1 hour too much, or too little, kills off 50 cents of my satisfaction. Distortion of a second hour kills off $1.50 of satisfaction; each further distortion takes a heavier and heavier toll, as shown by the growing discrepancy between *dd* and *ss*. (See Figs. 22-4, 26-4, and 32-2, for more on "consumer's surplus," which can be used to demonstrate monopoly harm or price-control harm.)

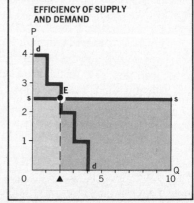

FIG. 20-9.

Parity is ratio of prices farmer gets to prices he pays:

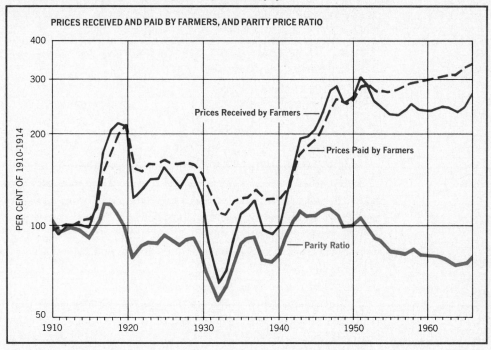

FIG. 21-1. If the change since 1909–1914 in prices farmers receive for their products just matched the change in the prices they pay for goods, the parity-price ratio curve would be at 100. Its being recently around 80 shows that prices received by farmers have not risen as much as have prices they have to pay.

tion, cities might grow smaller and smaller; the rural share of total population would grow larger and larger. What does the law of diminishing returns tell us such an eventuality would mean? It would mean a great reduction in the productivity of each man-hour spent on the farm. The land would become crowded with many people, each producing little and each unable to buy many of the comforts of life with his produce.

Does this sound far-fetched? It is a true picture of about two-thirds of the globe. In Asia especially, standards of living are pitifully poor. With three out of every four persons engaged in producing the food necessary for life, only one out of four can be producing the comforts of life. Contrast this with the United States, where each producer is efficient enough today to feed 35 other people and feed them well.

TECHNOLOGICAL CHANGE AND PATTERNS OF TASTE   Besides the differential in birth rates, there are two other reasons why agriculture is a problem area:

Technological progress has been greatly reducing the number of people needed to produce any given total of food and fiber. Use of the tractor, the combine, the cotton picker, irrigation, fertilizer, selective breeding of hybrid corn and livestock, and numerous other examples come to mind.

Coupled with the improvement in labor-saving technique is the unshakable fact that, *as we get richer, we do not want to expand our food consumption by as much as we want to expand our consumption of city products*. This has been shown by almost every statistical investigation here and abroad. Hence,

■ Birth rates, tastes, and technology dictate that agriculture must go on exporting people to industry.

■ AGRICULTURE'S LONG-RUN DECLINE: GRAPHICAL ANALYSIS

SUPPLY AND DEMAND CURVES   One single diagram is more useful in explaining the sagging trend of farm prices than libraries of orations and editorials.

In Fig. 21-2 let the point E represent the initial equilibrium of supply and demand at some earlier period. Now see what happens to these curves as the years go by. We know that dd will shift rightward as population grows and as higher real incomes make people want to consume more food at the same price; but we know that basic foods are the kinds of necessities which do not grow in the family budget at all proportionately to increases in real income, and we realize that United States population no longer grows at the prodigious percentage rates of the nineteenth century. So the rightward demand shift to d'd' is of modest amount.

What about supply? Though many make the mistake of thinking of farming as a backward business, statistical records show that productivity in American agriculture

One diagram goes far to explain the farm problem:

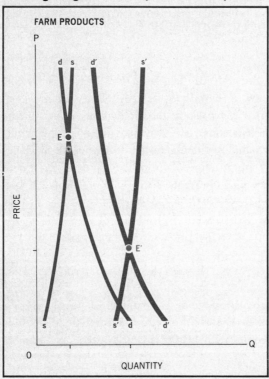

FIG. 21-2. As the years go by, the increase in demand for farm products generated by population and income growth tends to be less than the vast increase in supply generated by technological productivity improvements. Thus free prices fall. With both schedules highly inelastic, prices fall hard, farm incomes deteriorate. And small shifts in inelastic curves generate large price fluctuations.

has increased at a pace even faster than in industry. So each new improvement helps to shift the *ss* curve a great deal to the right.

What, then, must be happening to the new equilibrium E' that would prevail in the market if the government did not intervene? Certainly a shift in supply that outstrips the shift in demand must lead to a downward trend of market prices (relative, of course, to the general price level, so that effects of over-all inflation are disregarded). Naturally, this declining price trend means financial pressure and hardship on those farmers and rural workers whose efficiency has not undergone tremendous increase; and it means that there will be considerable pressure for people to leave the countryside for jobs in industry. It also means that consumers are paying lower prices for the raw-material component of their foods[1] and that the economy is reallocating its resources toward the things that are now most demanded in our growing society.

And, as we know, it means strong political pressures for government aid to agriculture.

THE PRODUCTION-POSSIBILITY FRONTIER   This basic tool can illuminate the decline in agriculture. Turn back to Fig. 2-4, page 22. The figure shows that tremendous technological change has shifted out the *p-p frontier;* the even greater productivity in food production—from use of tractors, fertilizers, hybrid seeds, and insecticides—is indicated by the strong eastward shift that flattens the whole curve. What does this flattening of the curve imply for the trend of farm prices relative to industrial prices? It means that a larger amount of food can be got from the same resources relative to nonfood. So food costs and prices must, in free markets, fall relative to nonfood.

A second reason for this price trend can also be seen back in Fig. 2-4. Food is a necessity whose expenditure drops relative to higher and higher incomes. As the nation grows richer, it does not move from *A* out northeastward toward *B*; it moves almost due northward to an even flatter part of the technically flattened new *p-p frontier.* No wonder food prices drop in competitive markets.

■ INSTABILITY IN AGRICULTURE

Farming is an up-and-down industry. Corn, wheat, beef, pork, and other farm products are sold in highly competitive markets whose prices change yearly, daily, hourly, and by the minute. The farmer swings at the very end of our seesawing economy. Good times bring him great percentage increases in income. Depressions cause his cash income to drop away to very little. The farmer particularly benefits from wartime

[1] Even though the price the farmer gets for the food he sells will fall, the retail price need not fall so much—or may even rise in the years ahead. Why? Agricultural experts claim this is not so much because railroads, packers, and supermarkets extort an undue share of the food dollar as that we consumers today want our food more and more fabricated (e.g., frozen, cut, cleaned, cooked, minutely packaged, premixed for baking, and so forth) and that greater technological progress may be taking place in producing raw food than in processing and marketing it. In the late 1960s the farmer gets but 40 cents of the retail food dollar, as compared with about 50 cents in the years of high farm prices right after World War II.

demand conditions; and unlike most of the community, the farmer can ride out an inflationary period of skyrocketing prices. But since 1947 farm income has been sliding downward relative to other incomes, both in total and in per capita terms.

If we look closely at farm statistics, we note a surprising fact.

■ Farm *incomes* fluctuate between boom and bust to a greater degree than nonfarm incomes, but farm *production* is remarkably more stable than industrial production.

Even the weather, which is a great threat to stability of income in any one farm region, does not cause sizable fluctuations in total farm crops over the whole nation. During the last quarter century, industrial production had an average year-to-year variation of about 9 per cent, while agricultural production had less than 3 per cent.

No wonder the farmer feels he is at the mercy of a fluctuating market. His supply curves are relatively inelastic for many reasons: (1) When P is low, his own effort to increase output may increase, as he desperately tries to maintain family income; (2) many of his costs go on anyway, whether he produces much or little, and he can save but little extra cost by cutting his Q.

The amount of farm products demanded, in addition to growing little when income rises, is also quite inelastic in response to price changes.

What, then, is the result of (a) relatively inelastic demand coupled with (b) relatively inelastic supply when (c) both curves are quite shiftable?

To answer this, take a sheet of paper and construct price and quantity axes. Then draw on it a quite vertical supply curve intersecting a quite vertical demand curve, much as in Fig. 21-2. Now shift either curve the least little bit. Do you see how great are the resulting shifts in P? Could anyone like having his living standards dependent on a tiny shift of supply and demand, when a whopping change in family income results?

Figure 21-1 showed that fluctuations in the prices received by farmers are greater than the fluctuations in the prices of the things they must buy. In the Great Depression days of the 1930s, prices received by farmers dropped about twice as far as did prices elsewhere. Even in the prosperous 1920s the farmer did badly; and, to make things worse, he then carried a heavy burden of mortgage debt left over from the war boom.

■ GOVERNMENT AID TO AGRICULTURE

Agriculture may be the unlucky stepchild of nature, but it is often the favored foster child of government. From the beginning of time, the public seems always to have hated a landlord and loved a farmer. So there is fairly widespread support among the electorate at large for aid to the farmer even though the voting strength of the farm bloc itself has shrunk considerably.

Prior to 1929, the principal government aid to agriculture came through our public land policy aimed at getting acreage into the hands of settlers, and through the elaborate practical and scientific aids to improved agricultural methods and conservation. The work done in agricultural experiment stations, at the so-called "state land-grant colleges," is well known; and in every farm district, the government-paid county agent is an important source of help toward efficient farming.

But in 1929, under the Hoover administration, the Federal Farm Board was set up. A new era of direct aid to farmers began. Subsequently, under various alphabet agencies (the AAA, the CCC, etc.), the government stepped in to "interfere with the natural laws of supply and demand" to increase the stability and level of farm incomes.[2] Both political parties have pledged themselves to a continuation of such activities; the powerful Farm Bureau Federation, the Grange, and the Farmers' Union maintain close contact with Washington to make sure Congress knows farmers' wishes.

THE PARITY CONCEPT   The years 1909 to 1914 are often looked back upon as the golden age of agriculture. So, over the years, there was increasing political pressure to have the government somehow guarantee to the farmer prices as relatively favorable as then prevailed. This is the root notion of "parity"—the simple feeling that if a bushel of wheat or farm goods sold for enough in 1909–1914 to buy a certain market basket of city goods and services, then in the 1960s it should still be able to buy the equivalent of that same market basket.

Parity, as shown back in Fig. 21-1, perhaps sounds simple; and perhaps rather fair—especially since we all like farmers and their votes. Why, then, the fight over it?

Deeper analysis shows that, as demand and supply change over a long period of time, the attempt to peg price at an arbitrary high level results in an avalanche of surplus farm goods. (Show the gap between the $s's'$ and $d'd'$ of Fig. 21-2 at prices kept higher than E'; and show how that gap will grow over time.) The dollar costs of aid become astronomical. The distortions of production become cumulatively greater and greater. Thus, until the mid-1960s the government storage bins were bursting, and even the mothball fleet of abandoned warships has had to be used for storage; grain has even had to be stored on the ground itself.

The reason for this farm surplus, we have already seen. More rapid technical progress in the farm than in town means that an hour of rural labor now produces many more bushels of food than it did in 1909–1914; and if an hour of city labor does not now produce relatively as many more market baskets of industrial goods, why should these city and farm items still swap at the same "parity" terms?[3] In short, the real costs of production have gone down immensely since then; so pegging prices at the old levels calls forth a supply much larger than will be bought in the market at the parity prices. For the efficient farmers, parity maintenance means incomes running into six figures. And it keeps inefficient farmers from going to higher-productivity occupations.

Farmers boast of their independence; and when they come to the government for help—as they most certainly do—they claim they do not want a handout, but rather that they want to "earn" their subsidies. But actually, in some of the years following World War II, more than half of what the farmers collected in the market place for

[2] Also, the Farm Credit Administration (FCA) and the Rural Electrification Administration (REA) are government agencies set up to help the farmer borrow at low interest rates and enjoy electric power.

[3] Even if productivity were to grow at about the same rate in the two areas from now on, it would still be necessary to have some differential in earnings on and off the farm in order to coax the socially desirable shift of labor to production of those goods and services which expand in people's demand more rapidly than do food and fiber.

certain crops—such as peanuts, sorghum grain, and others—resulted from government aid programs!

Then along came a food shortage in the mid-1960s: soybean crop failure in China; poor wheat harvests in Russia; hungry mouths in India and elsewhere. After our government had forced and bribed farmers to limit acreage and production, the world suddenly faced a scarcity of food. This illustrates the need to understand the shiftings of demand and supply once the State steps in to interfere with market mechanisms.

■ FORMS OF GOVERNMENT AID

What are the economic mechanisms by which government can help, or seem to help, the farmer? They are principally five in number:

1. Outright gift or relief payments, given to needy farmers who have established their need and misery

2. Programs by the government that aim to increase the demand for farm products or cut their real cost of production

3. Crop-limitation programs (such as acreage allotments or crop quotas to each farm) that aim to cut down on supply and raise price

4. Purchase-loan storage programs to guarantee or support prices

5. Finally, purchase-and-resale differential subsidy plans connected with the names of Eisenhower's Secretary of Agriculture Benson and Truman's Secretary Brannan

GIFTS AND RELIEF   There is nothing complicated about outright gifts or transfer payments, which might well be adjoined to our Social Security system. The farm pressure groups do not particularly want such aids, even though in strictest economic logic they may be the most defensible of all: If our Republic wants to alleviate the burden on farmers and provide minimum standards, outright gifts will clarify exactly what is involved and what it costs, thereby enabling the electorate to decide rationally what it wants to accomplish.

Less than a fifth of our farms correspond to the public image of a "family farm" earning a decent living. Most farms by number are poverty enterprises. Only one out of three farms produces over $10,000 of sales per year; and they produce four times as much as the 2 million poorest farms! As it is now, billions of dollars of farm subsidies per year trickle down only in small fractions to those in greatest need: the Southern sharecropper who lives in credit peonage, the less fortunate tenant farmers, owners of small marginal farms, and paid farm laborers.

DEMAND PROMOTION AND RESEARCH   Little need be said about attempts by the Department of Agriculture to find new chemical uses of farm products or to send out circulars telling people to improve their diets. (The Department may also get Congress to provide funds to finance cheap school lunches and other demand-raising programs.) Such activity goes a long way back in our history, as does government aid to land-grant colleges' experimental work to increase farm productivity. Not only will the Agriculture Department send a farmer a pamphlet on baking an angel-food cake or running a Halloween party; it will also send a county agent to teach him good conservation methods, how to keep records, and how best to till his soil. Some observers think it odd that while one branch of the government is trying to get the farmer to produce less, another branch is trying to improve his productivity.

Probably the most important promotion of demand for farm products has come from Public Law 480 (the Agriculture and Trade Redevelopment and Assistance Act, 1954). This permits underdeveloped countries like India, Pakistan, and Egypt to buy our wheat and other grains. But they do not have to pay dollars for these goods; at worst they can pay the United States government in their own currencies (rupees, pounds, etc.). These "counterpart funds" are of limited usefulness to our government, although some of this local currency may be used for American propaganda purposes, cultural activities, or exchange fellowships.

Of course, our farmers get paid for their grain in American dollars that come from the budget and, indirectly, from the general taxpayer. In effect, the government is subsidizing agriculture by shifting the *dd* curve for food upward and to the right; then it proceeds to "dump" these goods abroad where they are much needed, as part of our foreign-aid program. All this is to the good; but we should ponder the warnings of Harvard's Hendrik Houthakker:

> The program has been popular with American farmers, who regard it as a legalized form of dumping. One danger which has appeared recently is that some countries (especially India) have become so dependent on food imports from the United States as to create artificial shortages in the United States. . . . This may be good for farmers, but it does not help in maintaining stable domestic prices or in improving the balance of payments. An unintended result of Public Law 480 has been that the United States now exports much of its farm products to nations that cannot pay, while its competitors (especially Canada) sell for cash to the more solvent customers.

■ ECONOMICS OF THREE MAIN AID PROGRAMS

To understand the remaining three programs, our economic tools of supply and demand are absolutely necessary. Let us see how each case works.

CASE 1. CROP RESTRICTION   If farmers produce a smaller total Q, they will each receive a higher P. Because the demand for farm products is generally inelastic, limiting total Q will actually raise the total revenues received by farmers—as the last chapter showed. Not only do farm owners get higher revenue; they can also save some cost outlays if they produce a smaller rather than larger output.

Of course, the consumers will be hurt by scarcity of goods and by higher prices, just as they would be if flood or drought created a scarcity of foodstuffs. In deliberately restricting farm Q, society is deliberately shifting economic resources away from places that produce the extra goods which people's dollar votes in the market place show they really want. Either those resources go into idleness, as occurs with land no longer culti- vated, or they may go into secondary uses for which they are ill-fitted and which involve producing items that people do not much want.

A silver lining is provided by the fact that soil conservation and flood control may be achieved if land gets a rest or is put into forests and pasture. And to the degree that some of the benefits from the monopolistically contrived higher prices accrue to poverty-stricken farm families, there may be certain Robin Hood–like social gains to offset the social costs: current suffering may be alleviated; and some of the benefit may be used to get the young people out of low-productivity agriculture.

On the other hand, some of the desirable long-run shifts and economic adjustments may be slowed down by the farm aid programs. And it can be shown that many of the methods used to cut down on Q—such as holding wheat acres down to a quota, but leaving farmers free to use tremendous doses of fertilizer to expand production on the quota land—will lead to inefficient use of resources in producing the reduced Q. In terms of the production-possibility frontier of Fig. 2-4, not only are people pushed farther north on the frontier than their true food and nonfood tastes would dictate, but in addition, society is pushed *inside* the producible frontier by the inefficient methods of Q restriction.

Does the situation described above mean that farm aid is bad? Not necessarily, since noneconomic ethical and political issues are also involved. But it does suggest that each bit of benefit to some farmers is being bought at a greater sacrifice to the rest of the community than is economically and technically necessary. It does suggest that society look around for more efficient methods.

Regardless of sermons or partisan debate, advocates of any view will want to

A cut in farm supply raises price and total revenue:

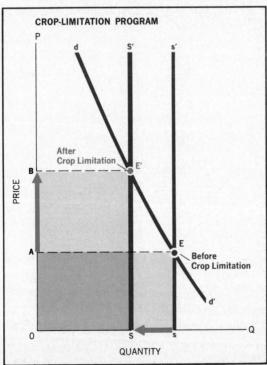

CROP-LIMITATION PROGRAM

FIG. 21-3. Before government intervenes, the *ss'* supply curve intersects the inelastic *dd'* curve at the low price shown at E. As an individual competitor, each farmer has no motive to do anything to improve the situation. But if all together can get government to put monopolistic limits on their total Q, they can benefit.

When production controls cut supply from *ss'* to *SS'*, P rises to E'. Because demand is inelastic, total gross farm income is thereby increased. (Recall that $P \times Q$ revenues at E and E' are measured, respectively, by the *OsEA* and *OSE'B* rectangular areas. Let your eye confirm that the gain in E' height over E outweighs the rectangle's loss in width; with elastic demand, the reverse would have been true.)

Government loans or purchases support price by acquiring unsold surplus:

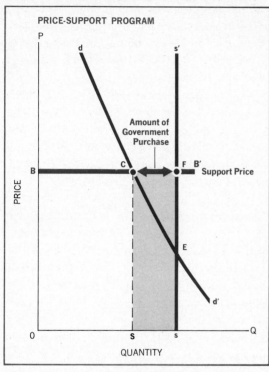

FIG. 21-4. The government keeps price at indicated floor or support price *BB'* (near or at parity) by acquiring for storage unsellable surplus shown by *CF*. The shaded area shows the total cost to the government of raising market price from *E* to *F*. Note that domestic consumers pay the higher price and get no current benefit from the *CF* part of the crop.

understand the mechanics of how *Q* output restriction works. Figure 21-3 tells its own story, which can be summarized as follows:

■ If the demand for farm products is inelastic rather than elastic, then a program of crop reduction will result in higher total receipts to the farmer. And since he also saves a little on total costs when he produces less, his net revenue goes up by even more than his total receipts do.

CASE 2. PARITY PRICE THROUGH LOAN SUPPORT OR GOVERNMENT PURCHASE   This case is a little harder. Now government guarantees the farmer a price higher than would have prevailed in the market. This "price floor" is shown by the green line *BB'* in Fig. 21-4. At so high a price, consumers will not buy all the crop supplied. Consumers will be on the demand curve at the point *C*. But farmers are supplying the full amount shown by the point *F*. If government does nothing, price must fall to *E*, which is below the parity price.

So what does the government have to do? By outright purchase or through some kind of loan red tape, it must acquire the unsold portion between *C* and *F*, marked with an arrow. This will go into storage, or be dumped abroad (as part of foreign aid, perhaps), or be left to rot. What, then, has the final result been?

The government has increased the price received by the farmer from *E* to *F*. But unlike the previous case, the farmers can now sell as much as they want to; so the increased price is gravy to them, representing a clear increase in their incomes. The consumers are now paying a higher price and buying less; to them Case 2 is just as bad as Case 1.[4] Who, then, is footing the bill for the extra income now received by the farmers? Obviously, the government: The Treasury is having to shell out an amount of dollars equal to the part of the crop they must buy times the full market price. (In terms of area, the Treasury's expense is shown by the shaded area *SCFs*. Can you explain why?)

Of course, if the demand curve *dd'* were in later years to shift upward so that it intersected the supply curve at *F* or above, then the Treasury would not have to do anything to ensure parity. Indeed, it might in such a prosperous year exactly reverse the above procedure; instead of buying part of the crop to add to storage, it might take food out of storage and sell it. The interested reader can draw a new *dd'*, to see how such an "ever-normal granary" program of stabilization purports to work.

CASE 3. SUBSIDIZED PRODUCER-CONSUMER PRICE DIFFERENTIAL   This is the hardest case of all. It involves paying an artificially high price to farmers, but reselling food to consumers at whatever low price the market will set. Although originally proposed by Truman's Secretary of Agriculture Brannan for perishable goods, this resale proposal was also advocated by Eisenhower's Secretary Benson with respect to butter and was passed by the Republican Congress with respect to wool.

Here the farmer is again guaranteed the *BB'* parity price, just as in Case 2. But Fig. 21-5 shows the new fact that food, instead of being left to rot in storage, is to be resold to the public for current consumption at whatever market price it will bring.

How is the farmer to receive the parity price if market price proves to be below that figure? The Department of Agriculture *simply writes him a check for the difference.* In effect, then, it is much as though the government had bought the crop at the parity price—as in the loan support of Case 2—but had then sold it on the open market for whatever price it would bring.

Every bit produced, as shown by the *ss'* supply curve, will now go to the consumer. Consumption will end up at the original point *E*. Why? Because the "law of supply and demand" tells us that, for consumers to buy the full crop, price must fall to the point where the demand curve intersects the market supply. But producers are promised the parity price for their entire crop. So the price they are to receive is indicated by *F* (just as in Case 2). Who pays the difference? The government—by sending each primary producer a check, whose amount per bushel is shown in Fig. 21-5 by the vertical arrow *EF*.

How much does this cost the government? The answer is clear, once we realize that the government must pay the difference between the producer's and consumer's price *on each and every unit produced!* (In terms of area, the expense to the government is the shaded rectangular area *ABFE*. Here the shaded rectangle goes all the way leftward to the price axis, whereas back in Case 2 the shaded rectangle of government expense went all the way downward to the quantity axis.)

---

[4]Such *Q* as is being produced is presumably being produced efficiently. In this case, unlike Case 1, society is not inside its production-possibility frontier. It is merely too far southeast on Fig. 2-4's *p-p frontier* producing more food than spontaneous dollar votes call for.

Benson-Brannan plan pays farmers gap between actual consumer's price and producer's supported price:

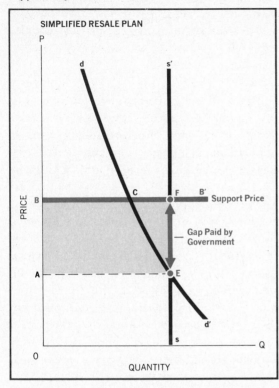

SIMPLIFIED RESALE PLAN

FIG. 21-5. The government lets price to consumer fall to E. It then makes up, by direct payments to farmers of *EF* per bushel, the difference between the low market price and the desired support price. Farmers end up with total price return shown at *F*. The shaded area shows the cost to government of the direct payments involved in such a two-price system.

An important but tricky question is the following: Will the Benson-Brannan plan of Case 3 cost the Treasury more or less than the plan of having the government withhold from the consumers part of the crop as outlined in Case 2? The answer turns out to depend upon our old friend the elasticity of demand and upon nothing else.

Look at the problem this way: Under either plan the *producers* are equally well off, being at F in both cases and receiving the same total income. Remember, too, that under either plan the producer's revenue can come from only two sources: the total revenue paid by the consumers plus the government's contribution. Hence, to answer the question, "Which plan costs the government more dollars?" we need only answer the much simpler question, "Which plan collects the greater total revenue from consumers: the plan where the consumers pay a high price and buy little, or the plan where consumers pay a low price and buy much?"

But note: this is nothing but the question we have met repeatedly in connection with the definition of elasticity. A point high up on the demand curve, such as C, will collect more total revenue than a point low down, such as E, provided the demand is *inelastic* in that interval. If demand were *elastic*, then the reverse would be true.

So now we can answer the question of relative cost as follows:

The Benson-Brannan plan of making more food available to consumers will currently cost the Treasury more money than will a purchase-for-storage-or-destruction program provided the demand curve is *inelastic*. If it had been *elastic*, the reverse would have been true. (Of course, wasteful storage costs militate against Case 2.)

From the standpoint of political economy, a plan which brings price to the consumer more nearly down to the social cost of producing food would have much to be said for it even if it should happen to result in costing the Treasury more money. If farmers are to get the same income in one way or the other, the important thing to us consumers is not so much how we divide our payments between market purchases and taxes as that food be produced and consumed up to the point where marginal utilities and costs are more nearly in balance.[5]

■ ISSUES IN FARM AID

In the early New Deal days, the emphasis was on crop reduction. Acreage was cut, but technical progress and intensive cultivation often kept Q from declining. Later, the emphasis shifted from Case 1 to price supports through purchase or loan. These Case 2 programs became colossally expensive as rightward shifts of the supply curves made the free-equilibrium price fall further and further below 100 per cent or 80 per cent of parity. Government warehouses bulged (except during war and cold-war periods, when the surplus turned out to be a godsend). Grain rotted;[6] the mere cost of holding and storing became great.

The Republican administrations of the 1950s, with the backing of the associations of larger commercial farmers, favored lowering price supports far below parity and closer toward free-market levels. The Kennedy-Johnson Administration favored a mixture of crop reduction, loan support, and direct subsidies: in return for generous price supports, farmers were to vote to limit their production quotas severely—a reversion to the Case 1 methods of the 1930s. The resulting rise in their income was thus to be financed in effect primarily by a hidden excise tax on food (in the form of higher prices for scarcer food supplies) rather than by glaring expenditure items in the federal budget.

On the other hand, farmers have warred among themselves: the very large commercial farmers want freedom to produce; the smaller farmers want protection. All farmers seem to want handouts, but do not like them to be obvious, preferring that they appear in the guise of market "earnings."

As 1970 comes into view, the basic outlook for American agriculture seems to be improving. Chronically bad crops in Russia and China, plus the flowing of resources all over the world into more prosperous industry, have created recognition of the important role that efficient American and Canadian commercial farms have in helping feed the world. As we shall see in Part Five's discussion of international trade, America does enjoy what is called a "comparative advantage" in the production of food and fiber on highly capitalistic large-scale farms.

■ WHAT ECONOMIC ANALYSIS CAN SUGGEST

As other chapters in Part Three demonstrate, there is often a strong case for sticking to the competitive market's outcome. The main exception is (1) when the people helped

---

[5] If ss' were drawn more realistically so as to be somewhat upward-sloping, we should have the evil of slightly too much Q being coaxed out by the too-high government subsidy; consumers would be getting too much farm Q at a price to them below true social costs of resources used.

[6] Admittedly, we gave some of the surplus to our poor, through school lunch, stamp, and other programs. And, as already seen, we shipped food and fiber abroad under Public Law 480.

by government interference are for some reason strongly preferable to those who are hurt and (2) when it can be shown that there is no better way of helping them out of general taxes. How does this apply to the farm problem?

Many tough-minded economists would argue that much of our government aid now goes to very prosperous commercial farmers, with too little filtering down to the really poor farmers, whose poverty makes them most deserving. (In 1966, 95 per cent of economists sampled criticized farm aid!) They favor new programs which give whatever aid it is decided to give to farmers in a more efficient way—so as to leave the rest of us with more than we now get. Such programs would involve more pinpointing of the aid given to those who actually merit it from the standpoint of need.

Such a turnabout would involve more reliance on market forces in determining food and fiber prices. As prices fell, consumers generally would be able to afford more food, and especially more of the expensive protein foods such as milk and meat. The United States would be better able to export the food and fiber she is well suited to produce. Commercial farmers would feel pressure on them to become more efficient, and many of the remaining family farmers would find their incomes so low in agriculture as to be speeded into industry. The really poor farmers would receive welfare aids under such a program—not so much because they are farmers, but for the same reason that government aid is given to any who are poverty-stricken and need rehabilitation.

The economists who argue along this line say:

■ In terms of resource allocation, the American people so little value an extra unit of food relative to other things, and our technology so easily permits us to produce an extra unit of food, that it is most worthwhile for us to equate supply and demand for food at low prices—low enough to coax resources out of agriculture and into industry, where they will produce things for which there is a demand in the form of consumers' money votes unbuttressed by artificial government aids.[7] Resources should both be forced out, and attracted out, of agriculture. The transitional distress should be alleviated by outright subsidies which will not involve inefficient distortion of production and which should be made to taper off after a set number of years. Human suffering merits the same aid anywhere.

■ THE LONG-RUN SOLUTION?

Does all this sound cruel and heartless—hard-boiled? It is perhaps a bit extreme in giving too little weight to the argument that a civilization is happier when it seeks to protect any group in it from sudden and drastic changes in status.

Nonetheless, this economic analysis succeeds in pointing out the only ultimate solution. That solution, as suggested in the quotation from Vanderbilt's expert agricultural economist W. H. Nicholls, is to reduce our surplus of farmers. No doubt this has to be done gradually. And it is actually happening all the time: each year there are fewer and fewer people in agriculture.

Before mourning over this century-old trend, consider the following parable:

[7] Footnote readers can refer to page 380 for a graph of the argument that uninterfered-with pricing has a property of being "efficient," even if not necessarily "equitable."

Back in Andrew Jackson's day, the American people discovered that cheap Western land was depressing farm prices. So they introduced an AAA program. Later the Whigs stepped up this program, and in the Grant administration, following the Civil War, the program was stepped up still further.

To restore the golden age of 1820, the government bought and burned crops. This became so expensive that it also had to set acreage quotas. By 1860 each farmer had to leave an acre fallow for each acre he cultivated. By 1900 he could cultivate only 1 acre in 10. By 1970, so rapid was technological innovation that he could cultivate only 1 acre in 30. And even then, the government found itself taxing one-third the Net National Product for purchases of crops to burn. Yet America's 50 million people—her population could not grow much under such a regime!—were so dedicated to helping agriculture that they cheerfully voted the burden. And why not? More than half of the working force had to farm on the 1 acre in 30 in order to support the other half. The average income per head was, in 1984, about that prevailing in Japan, a country not lucky enough to have a wonderful farm aid program.

Everybody was happy. Except for one thing. Americans feared that with so low an income they would be unable to equip a strong army against the Enemy, who each year foolishly encouraged his own farm and city productivity and who looked with longing eyes on all 30 out of each 30 lush North American acres.

Of course, this is a rather silly parable. It overstates the case, and that is not fair. And yet . . . and yet . . . for all its overstatement, are there not some important economic insights to be gleaned from it?[8]

SUMMARY

1 ■

Although the rural birth rate is higher than the urban, a persistent cityward migration means that the percentage of the population engaged in agriculture is declining. Improvements in agricultural techniques mean that supply increases greatly and that the same total of food can be produced with fewer workers; also, as incomes increase, the increase in demand for food is less than proportionate.

So free-equilibrium prices tend to fall. Farm income tends to be both low and unstable; as a result, government adopted a variety of programs to support farm-product prices and maintain farm incomes.

2 ■

Pegging prices at any ancient parity formula, despite its superficial plausibility and fairness, utterly disregards basic changes in demand and real costs of production. As time passes, such a parity will produce prices differing sharply from "natural competi-

[8] All this will remain for a long time a political issue. No one will begrudge the farmer his desire to be free from wildly fluctuating prices. In the Appendix we shall see how private speculators on an organized exchange are supposed in traditional economic theory to be able to iron out any *foreseeable* fluctuations. The question remains whether, gifts aside, we can expect the government to make better forecasts of the uncertain future than private speculative markets can, and whether we can expect the government, through its storage program, to be better than private markets in stabilizing prices.

tive" levels here and abroad. The result: huge surpluses, with the wrong goods being produced and with growing distortions of efficiency.

3 ■

Aid programs involving direct gifts or promotion of demand and of cost research require no deep economic analysis. But the tools of supply and demand are needed to understand the three aid programs: (1) crop limitation by acreage or other allotments, (2) government price support by purchase-loan storage programs, (3) resale to consumers at competitive market prices of food bought at a pegged price, with the government footing the bill for the differential. (Hybrids of all three are frequently legislated.)

4 ■

Because high and inflexible parity support causes storage to grow astronomically and sends the government's aid costs skyward, Case 2 in practice leads to more and more of Case 1. (Farmers like 2 and accept 1 only as a necessary evil; consumers dislike 1 and 2, but like 3.)

5 ■

The long-run solution must involve maintenance of prosperity outside agriculture, so that people can continue to move to the lines of highest productivity and so that demand for agriculture will be optimally high. But mere prosperity in industry is not enough. The 1920s and 1960s show that the city and town can prosper while the country's economic position deteriorates.

   In the long run, resources have to be helped to move out of low-efficiency rural uses and into more productive uses. That means a continuation of the trend toward fewer but more efficient farmers, and a need for short-run aids to speed the reconversion and to ease its human burdens. It also means flexible pricing practices that permit efficient American farms to help feed the world.

QUESTIONS FOR DISCUSSION

1. Contrast long-term and cyclical patterns of agriculture and industry.

2. Describe government indirect and direct farm aids. Explain "parity."

3. Why might limiting a farm's acreage in one crop not reduce the total of it much? How would it affect noncontrolled crops? Fertilizer demand?

4. Use the *p-p frontier* concept to evaluate effects and harm from farm aid.

5. Debate the merit of taking a dollar from the 17 in 18 people outside farming and giving it to the 1 in farming. Distinguish ways of giving him the dollar.

6. What does Professor Dudley Johnson of the University of Washington mean here? "Major premise: Society should help poor people. Minor premise (of doubtful validity as stated): Farmers are poor people. (Dubious) Conclusion: Therefore society should help farmers. Actually, if society is to subsidize individuals, it should not be done on the basis of their occupations, but because they are *poor—i.e.*, aid on an *income* basis."

7. Review your understanding of the following concepts:

inelastic farm demand and supply

farm technology and declining percentage of income spent on food

free-farm-price trends

parity, 1909–1914 golden age

Public Law 480

Q limitation; *P* support; direct payments with consumer and producer *P*'s different

pros and cons of free farm prices

long- and short-run solutions

comparative advantage in food

APPENDIX: Economics of Speculation, Risk, and Insurance

Here we apply the tools of supply and demand to analyze price relations across space and time and the important problems involved in risk, speculation, and gambling. We deal not only with the purchase and sale of actual commodities such as corn or cotton, but also with the purchase and sale of something more mysterious—of bits of paper.

These bits of paper are called "commodity futures": they are contracts that brokers deal with on organized commodity exchanges like the Chicago Board of Trade or the New York Cotton Exchange. You and I may buy or sell such commodity futures even though we have never seen any *real* cotton or corn. As speculators in such futures, the last thing in the world we should want to happen would be for a truck to roll up to our door seeking to deliver real honest-to-goodness corn or cotton.

Yet, as we shall see, even though speculators never touch the real thing, they may under certain conditions be helping to even out the consumption of the crop between harvest times and to carry over the proper amount of grain and fiber between seasons.

In his autobiography, the elder statesman Bernard Baruch said that ten years after he heard Professor George B. Newcomb lecture on supply and demand at C.C.N.Y., he had made more than a million dollars from speculation—implying that those lectures may have had something to do with it. Certainly, this Appendix is not designed to make you rich, and if you skip it, your knowledge of the rest of the book need not suffer much. But speculation is a fascinating topic and can serve as an example of important applications of supply and demand. Inevitably, it is a complicated subject which no elementary book can pretend to treat completely.

GEOGRAPHICAL PRICE PATTERNS

In a well-organized competitive market, there tends to be at any one time and place a single prevailing price. This is due to the action of professional speculators or "arbitragers" who keep their ear to the market and, as soon as they learn of any price differences, buy at the cheaper price and sell at the dearer price, thereby making a profit for themselves—at the same time tending to equalize the price.[1]

Two markets at a considerable distance from each other may have different prices. Wheat in Chicago may sell for a few cents more per bushel than identical wheat in Kansas City, because of shipping, insurance, and interest charges involved in transportation. If ever the price in Chicago should rise by more than the few cents of shipping costs, speculators will buy in Kansas City and ship to Chicago, thereby bringing the price up in Kansas City and down in Chicago to the normal maximum differential.

Nobody legislates these patterns. They follow from supply and demand.

SPECULATION AND PRICE BEHAVIOR OVER TIME

In an ideal competitive market there tends to be a definite pattern of prices *over time* just as there is over space. But the difficulties of predicting the future make this pattern a less perfect one: we have an equi-

[1]On the floor of the Chicago Board of Trade, the important market for grain, some hundred important "pit scalpers," or dealers, are said to make all their profits on price changes within each day, closing out all their transactions every night and sleeping peacefully until the next day. Specialists on the floor of the Stock Exchange act similarly.

For a good to be stored, expected price rise must match storing cost:

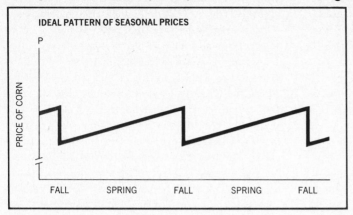

IDEAL PATTERN OF SEASONAL PRICES

P

PRICE OF CORN

FALL   SPRING   FALL   SPRING   FALL

FIG. 21-6. Ideally, P is lowest at harvest time, rising gently with accumulated storage costs until the next harvest. This flexible pattern tends to even out consumption over the seasons—as compared with a harvest glut's causing very low autumn price and summer scarcity's causing sky-high price.

librium that is constantly being disturbed but is always in the process of re-forming itself—rather like the ocean's surface under the play of the winds.

STABILIZING SEASONAL PATTERNS   Consider the simplest case of a grain, like corn, that is harvested at one period of the year. This crop must be made to last all the year if privation is to be avoided. Since no one passes a law regulating the storage of grain, how is this desirable state of affairs brought about? Through the attempts of speculators to make a profit.

A well-informed speculator who is a specialist in this grain realizes that, if all the grain is thrown on the market in the autumn, it will fetch a very low price because of the glutting of the market. On the other hand, months later, with almost no grain coming on the market, price will tend to skyrocket.

The above description tells what would tend to happen were it not for the action of speculators. Speculators realize that by (1) purchasing some of the autumn crop while it is cheap, (2) withholding it in storage, and (3) selling it later when the price has risen, they can make a profit. This they do. But in doing so, they increase the autumn demand for grain and raise its autumn price; and they increase the spring supply of grain and lower its spring price. At the same time that they are equalizing the price over the year, they are also equalizing the supply coming on the market in each month—which is as it should be.

Moreover, if there is brisk competition among speculators, none will make an excessive profit over the costs that he incurs (including, of course, the wages necessary to keep him in this line of activity). The speculator himself may never touch a kernel of corn or a bale of cotton, nor need he know anything about storage, ware-

houses, or delivery. He merely buys and sells bits of paper. But the effect is exactly as described above.

Now there is one and only one monthly price pattern that will result in neither profits nor losses. A little thought will show that it will not be a pattern of constant prices. Rather, the ideal price pattern will involve lowest prices in the autumn and then gradually rising prices until the peak is reached just before the new corn comes in. The price must rise from month to month to compensate for the storage and interest costs of carrying the crop in storage—in exactly the same way that the price must rise over space from one mile to the next to compensate for the cost of transportation.[2] Figure 21-6 shows the behavior of prices over an ideal yearly cycle.

STABILIZING FORESEEABLE FLUCTUATIONS   Not all fluctuations in activity can be so accurately forecast as the seasonal harvesting of a crop. No one can predict with confidence next year's weather or the likelihood of a recession in the near future. But to the extent that speculators can form any accurate guesses today about the future *scarcity* of a commodity, they will tend to buy it now for *future* delivery, thereby causing (1) a withdrawal of present supply, (2) an increase of present price, (3) an increase in amount stored, (4) an increase in future supply, (5) a reduction in future price—or in all a relative stabilization of price and consumption over time. The reader should try to

---

[2]Do I, as a warehouse storer, need a crystal ball to tell me price will rise enough to pay me to store corn today? No. The market today will quote me a future price—for delivery of corn some months hence—and when this future price sufficiently exceeds the current spot price for physical corn, I get the signal to store corn.

visualize the opposite process by which speculators stabilize prices when they correctly foresee an exceptionally large future crop and a low future price: how they then begin to "sell short"[3] for future delivery, tending to depress current prices, raise present consumption, and lower carry-over of stocks.

SPREADING OF RISKS   Aside from their possible influence toward stabilizing prices, speculators have another important function. By being willing to take risks on their own shoulders, they enable others to avoid risk.

For example, a warehouse owner must carry large inventories of grain in the course of his business. If the price of grain goes up, he makes a windfall capital gain; if down, he incurs a windfall loss. But let us suppose that he is content to earn his living by storing grain and wishes to forego all risk taking. This he can do by a process called "hedging." This complicated procedure is rather like a man who bets on Army to win the Army-Navy game and then washes out this transaction, or covers it, by placing an equal bet on the Navy. Whichever side wins, he comes out the same, his left hand winning what his right hand loses.

To get a notion of how the complicated process of hedging works out, here is a highly simplified example. Suppose I am buying and storing corn in the late fall. I am a specialist in running a warehouse and wish to stick to my last rather than become involved in the risky business of taking speculative bets as to whether the price of corn will change between now and next spring, when I expect to stop storing corn and to sell it. In effect, I should really like to sell it now for an agreed-upon price that will compensate me for my 9-cent-per-bushel storage expenses between now and

later delivery time. If a speculative market exists, that is precisely what I can do by the device of hedging.

How do I hedge? For each 5,000 bushels of corn I buy in November to put into storage until next May, let us suppose I have to pay $1 a bushel to local Illinois farmers. I look up the price quoted today, November 30, on the Chicago Board of Trade for next May corn futures and see that this quotation is $1.09. I realize that this 9-cent excess over today's price will give me a fair return for my expenses of storage and that is why I am glad to store. I now hedge by *selling* a 5,000-bushel May corn-future contract. (The brokerage commission on this "short sale" transaction will be less than $\frac{1}{2}$ cent per bushel; my broker will require that I put up less than 10 cents per bushel as "margin" to ensure that I fulfill my contractual obligation, and he will neither know nor care whether I actually have some physical corn with which I might make later delivery.)

Now I am hedged. I happen to own 5,000 bushels of physical corn in storage. I also have sold 5,000 bushels of May corn futures.

What will happen if slack corn demand and a tremendous winter wheat crop cause the price of corn to fall to 90 cents by next May?

My brother, who owns a warehouse and bought corn in the fall as I did *but did not hedge,* will now lose 10 cents per bushel. Indeed, he is worse off than that, because he is also out the 9 cents that it costs him to keep his warehouse going (watchmen's pay, and so forth). So he has really lost 19 cents per bushel *in toto*.

What about me, the cagy hedger? I do lose 10 cents a bushel *on my physical corn* because of the unforeseen change in price. But when, as May arrives, I look in the paper for the Board of Trade quotation on my May future, I am relieved to see that it has fallen from $1.09 all the way down to 90 cents—at which price I buy in, or "cover," my futures. Thus, *on short sale of my futures* I have gained 19 cents, or exactly as much as I (and my brother) have lost *in toto* on the sale of physical corn. *The hedge has protected me from all price fluctuations:* my left futures pocket has gained what my right physical-corn pocket lost. I am left with my 9-cent costs well covered. The speculator who made my hedge possible took price risks off my shoulders.[4]

[3] There is nothing mysterious about selling short. I simply put in an order to my broker in which I agree, in return for a certain price *now*, to deliver *at some later date* an amount of grain. Usually, at the time of putting in the order, I do not have the grain on hand. But I legally fulfill my contract by later "covering," i.e., buying the grain and making delivery. If I later have to pay a higher price in covering than I now receive when selling short, then I take a loss. But if I have guessed right and prices do fall in the intervening period, then I "buy in" for less than I have sold and make a profit.

Selling short in the stock market works out similarly, except that I am free to cover and make future delivery of the stock at any time I please. Meanwhile, the man who has bought the stock receives his stock shares. How? As a result of the fact that my broker, obligingly, lends me the stock certificates to make delivery. Later, when I cover, I buy in some stock and turn over the certificates to my obliging broker.

[4] To check your understanding, work through the case where a war scare sends up the price of physical corn in the May market to, say, $1.19. Now my unhedged brother, in addition to his 9-cent return as a warehouseman, makes an additional windfall risk profit of 10 cents per bushel. What about me?

To the extent that speculators forecast accurately, they provide a definite social service. To the extent that they forecast badly, they tend to aggravate the variability of prices. Were it not for the detailed statistical information provided by the Department of Agriculture and private agencies, the traders of the Chicago Board of Trade would find themselves at the mercy of every idle rumor, hope, and fear. For speculation is often a mass contagion, like the inexplicable dancing crazes that swept medieval villages, the Dutch tulip mania that sent the price of a single bulb higher than that of a house, the South Sea Bubble in which companies sold stock at fabulous prices for enterprises which would "later be revealed."

GAMBLING AND DIMINISHING MARGINAL UTILITY[5]

The defenders of speculation resent the charge that it represents simply another form of gambling, like betting on the horse races or buying a lottery ticket. They emphasize that an uncertain world necessarily involves risk and that someone must bear risks. They claim that the knowledge and the venturesomeness of the speculator are chained to a socially useful purpose, thereby reducing fluctuations and risks to others. (We have just seen that this is not always the case and that speculation may indeed be destabilizing; but certainly, no one can deny all validity to the above claims.)

Why is gambling considered such a bad thing? Part of the reason, perhaps the most important part, lies in the field of morals, ethics, and religion; upon these the economist is not qualified to pass exact judgment. There is, however, a substantial economic case to be made against gambling.

First, it involves simply *sterile transfers of money or* *goods* between individuals, creating no new money or goods.[6] Although it creates no output, gambling does nevertheless absorb time and resources. When pursued beyond the limits of recreation, where the main purpose after all is to "kill" time, gambling subtracts from the national income.

The second economic disadvantage of gambling is the fact that it tends to promote *inequality* and *instability of incomes.* People who sit down to the gaming table with the same amount of money go away with widely different amounts. A gambler (and his family) must expect to be on the top of the world one day, and when luck changes—which we have seen to be the only predictable thing about it—he may almost starve.

LAW OF DIMINISHING MARGINAL UTILITY AND CHANCE But why is inequality of income over time and between persons considered such a bad thing? One answer is to be found in the widely held belief that the gain in utility achieved by an *extra* $1,000 of income is not as great as the loss in utility of foregoing $1,000 of income. Where that is the case, a bet at fair odds involves an economic loss: the money you stand to win balances the money you may lose; but the satisfaction you stand to win is *less* than the satisfaction you stand to lose.

Similarly, if it could be assumed that individuals are all "roughly the same" and are ethically comparable, so that their utilities can be added, then the dollars gained by the rich do not create as much "social welfare" or total utility as the dollars lost by the poor. This has been used not only as a criticism of gambling, but as a positive argument in favor of "progressive" taxation aimed at lowering the inequality of the distribution of income.[7]

On my physical wheat which I bought at $1 and sell for $1.19, I gain; but I lose 10 cents on having to buy in my May futures at 10 cents more than I sold it for. So I end up making my 9-cent warehouse return and no more—regardless of what can happen to corn price fluctuations.

Actual hedging of millers, farmers, and storers can become more complicated. Also, it could happen that, in order to coax out speculators, the quotation in November of the May future would on the average have to sell for a little less than the $1.09 such physical corn can be expected to sell for in May; this means that the risk-bearing speculators require a premium for the insurancelike risk taking they are providing—a premium (called "normal backwardation") that, like any cost, must be borne by producers and ultimate consumers.

[5] Some of this material leans on the later discussion of marginal utility, beginning on page 417.

[6] Actually, in all professional gambling arrangements, the participants lose out on balance. The leakage comes from the fact that the odds are always rigged in favor of the "house," so that even an "honest" house will win in the long run. Moderate gambling among friends may be considered as a form of consumption or recreation activity whose cost to the group as a whole is zero. Oddly, some people who do not trust their ability to save do use steady purchase of lottery tickets as a way to cut down on current consumption and put themselves in the position of occasionally accumulating larger sums of money. In some past and present societies, the enhancement of inequality of income distribution by gambling may have made a roundabout contribution to social thrift and capital formation.

[7] The issue of incentives must also enter into forming any decision on policy, since discussions elsewhere show that redistributing the national pie may lessen its total.

Just as Malthus saw the law of diminishing returns as underlying his theory of population, so is the "law of diminishing marginal utility" used by many economists to condemn professional gambling. According to this theory (discussed in next chapter) as money income increases, each new dollar adds something to utility, but less and less. Similarly, each extra unit of any good that can be bought with money contributes less and less satisfaction or utility. When we get as much of a good as we wish (e.g., air), it becomes a "free good" because still further units add nothing new to our utility.

WHY IDEAL STABILIZATION BY SPECULATORS IS OPTIMAL

We can now use the tools of marginal utility to show how ideal speculation would maximize total utility over time. Suppose every consumer has a utility schedule that holds for each year independently of any other year. Now suppose that in the first of two years there was a big crop—say, 3 units per person—and in the second a small crop of only 1 unit per person. If this crop deficiency could be foreseen, how should the consumption of the two-year 4-unit total be spread over the two years?

If we agree, for simplicity, to neglect all storage, interest, and insurance charges and all questions of

utility commensurability over time, we can prove that *total utility for the two years together will be maximized only if consumption is equal in each year.*

Why is uniform consumption better than any other division of the available total? Because of the law of diminishing marginal utility. Here is the reasoning:

Suppose I consume more in the first year than in the second. My last unit's marginal utility in the first year will be low, and then it will be high in the second. So if I carry some crop from the first to the second year, I shall be switching from low to high marginal utilities—and that will maximize my total utility.

But is not that exactly what the following ideal speculation pattern would accomplish?

If speculators can neglect interest, storage, and insurance charges and happen to forecast accurately next year's low crop, what will they do? They will figure it pays to carry goods over from this year's low price resulting from the high crop, hoping instead to sell at next year's scarcity price. But as each speculator subtracts from this year's supply and adds to next year's, what must finally happen? Equilibrium can be reached only when the two prices have been equalized! Then there will be no further incentive to carry over more crop.[8] (Of course, a small payment for the speculator's

---

[8] A graph can illuminate this argument. If utility could be measured in dollars, with each dollar always denoting the same marginal utility, the demand curves would look just like the marginal utility schedule of page 418. The two curves of Fig. 21-7 show what would happen if there were no carry-over—with price first determined at A_1, where s_1s_1 intersects dd, and second at A_2, where the lower supply s_2s_2 intersects dd. Total utility of the green shaded areas would add up only to $(4 + 3 + 2) + 4$, or \$13 per head. But with optimal carry-over to the second year of 1 unit by speculators, P's and Q's will be equalized at E_1 and E_2, and now the total utility of the green areas will add up to $(4 + 3) + (4 + 3)$, or \$14 per head. (Show that the gain in utility of \$1 is measured by the light block, which represents the excess of the second unit's marginal utility over the third unit's marginal utility; one can show that equality of marginal utilities is optimal.)

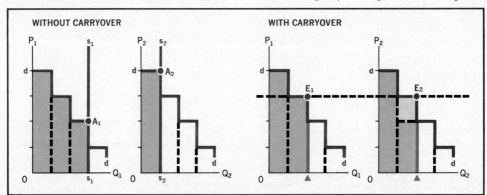

FIG. 21-7. The green areas measure total utility enjoyed each year. Carrying one unit to the second year equalizes Q and also P, and increases total utility by amount of light block.

effort might have to be included—but we have agreed to waive all costs just to keep the example simple.)

Do not for a moment get the impression that real flesh-and-blood speculators can guess the future correctly. They often make mistakes and often are prey to rumors and mass enthusiasms. So the process is not as ideal as here pictured. Still, to the degree that speculators can intelligently foresee the future—and those who have a terrible batting average may get eliminated fast as their capital is lost—they (and for that matter, *farsighted* government agencies, too) may help to provide a useful stabilizing function.

ECONOMICS OF INSURANCE

We are now in a position to see why insurance, which appears to be just another form of gambling, actually has exactly opposite effects. For the same reasons that gambling is bad, insurance is economically advantageous.[9] Whereas gambling creates risks, insurance helps to lessen and spread risks.

In buying fire insurance on his house, the owner seems to be betting with the insurance company that his house will burn down. If it does not—and the odds are heavily in favor of its not burning—the owner forfeits the small premium charge. If it does burn down, the company must reimburse the owner to the tune of the agreed-upon loss. (For the obvious reason of removing temptation from hard-up home owners who like fire engines and excitement, the face value of the policy tends to be something less than the money value of the property insured.)

What is true of fire insurance is equally true of life, accident, automobile, or any other kind of insurance.

[9]The astute reader will note (1) that economics proves that those subject to diminishing marginal utility should not gamble and should insure, but that a man with *increasing* marginal utility will maximize his expected utility by gambling and by noninsuring; and (2) that any economist who uses observations on a person's reaction to situations involving probabilities as his test of how marginal utility varies for that person may end up with the following circular reasoning: those who gamble should gamble; those who insure should insure. So the case for prohibiting gambling must rest on extraneous ethical or religious grounds; or must be withdrawn; or must be based on the notion that society knows better than individuals what is truly good for them; or must be based on the notion that we are all imperfect beings who wish in the long run that we were not free to yield to short-run temptations. Some political economists feel that moderate gambling might be converted into socially useful channels.

Actually, at the famous Lloyd's of London, which is a place for insurance brokers to come together, you can arrange to insure a ball team or vacationer against rain, dancers against infantile paralysis, a hotel keeper against a damage suit from the widow of a man killed in a fight with another man who bought a drink in the hotel's cocktail lounge, and you can get numerous other bizarre policies. But by the common law, Lloyd's may refuse to bet $10,000 with me that it will not snow on Christmas, since I do not have an "insurable interest" of that amount and the bet would be unenforceable in the courts. But a ski-resort owner, who stands to lose that much if it does not snow, would have such an insurable interest and could certainly buy such a policy. Economic theory shows that the difference between these two cases is that insuring the latter stabilizes income while the former destabilizes it.

The insurance company is not gambling, because what is unpredictable and subject to chance *for the individual* is highly predictable and uniform *in the mass*. Whether John C. Smith, age twenty and in good health, will live for 30 more years is a matter of chance, but the famous *law of large numbers* guarantees that out of 100,000-odd twenty-year-olds in good health, only a definite proportion will still be alive at the end of such a period of time. The life-insurance company can easily set a premium at which it will not lose money. Certainly, therefore, the company is not gambling.

What about the buyer of insurance? Is he gambling? The reverse can be shown to be true: the man who does not insure his house is doing the gambling. He is risking the whole value of his house against the small premium saved. If his house does not burn down in any year, he has won his bet; if it does, as occasionally must happen, he loses his bet and incurs a tremendous penalty.

At this point, a sporting man will say, "So what? Of course, a man gambles when he doesn't buy insurance. But the odds on such a bet are not unfavorable. In fact, they are favorable, because we know that the insurance company is not in business for its health. It must keep records, it must support insurance salesmen, and so forth. All this costs money and must be 'loaded' onto the insurance premium, detracting from the perfect mathematical odds of the buyer and making the odds for the nonbuyer a little better."

To which a rational man will reply: "When I am among friends, I don't mind a small game of chance for relaxation even at slightly unfavorable odds. But when a big bet is involved, even if the odds are favorable, then I pass. I insure my house because I hardly miss the premium each year; but if it burned down without being covered, I'd feel the loss an awful lot. When I insure, my living standards over time and my income remain the same, come what may. When I don't insure, I may be up for a while, but I risk going way down."

Obviously, the law of diminishing marginal utility—which makes the satisfaction from wins less important than the privation from losses—is one way of justifying the above reasoning.[10] *This law of diminishing marginal utility tells us that a steady income, equitably divided among individuals instead of arbitrarily apportioned between the lucky and unlucky people whose house did or did not burn down, is economically advantageous.* (Also, when a family chooses to buy hospital and medical insurance, it may express the belief that this will be relatively painless forced "saving against a rainy day." This self-imposed "compulsory-saving" feature is another benefit of insurance.)

WHAT CAN BE INSURED

Undoubtedly, insurance is a highly important way of spreading risks. Why, then, can we not insure ourselves against all the risks of life? The answer lies in the indisputable fact that certain definite mathematical

[10] Figure 21-7 of this Appendix can show all this. Change the titles "Without Carryover" and "With Carryover" to "Without Insurance" and "With Insurance" to see the gain in utility from insuring. To prove the loss from gambling, relabel once again the left-hand figure "After Gambling" and the right-hand one "Before Gambling." To illustrate that equal incomes maximize the sum of utility of two ethically commensurable people, relabel Fig. 21-7 still once again to read "Before Redistribution" and "After Redistribution."

conditions are necessary before sufficiently exact actuarial probabilities can be determined.

First, we must have a *large number of events.* Only then will a pooling of risks and a "cancellation of averages" be possible. The bank at Monte Carlo knows there is safety in numbers. The lucky streak of an Arabian prince one night will be canceled by his next night's losings or by the losings of a fake Balkan countess. Once in a blue moon someone may "break the bank"; but in a few more lunar cycles the "house" will more than break even.

But large numbers are not enough. No prudent fire-insurance company would confine itself to the island of Manhattan even though there are thousands of buildings there. *The uncertain events must be relatively independent.* Each throw of the dice, each chance of loss by fire, should stand relatively by itself. Obviously, a great fire like that of Chicago in 1871 or of the San Francisco earthquake would subject all the buildings in the same locality to the same risk. The company would be making a bet on one event, not on thousands of independent events. Instead, it must diversify its risks. Private companies cannot, without government aid, bear the risks of nuclear-bomb insurance. Nor is it possible to buy unemployment insurance from a private company. Depressions are great plagues which hit all sections and all classes at one and the same time, with a probability that cannot be computed in advance with any precision. Therefore only the government, whose business it is to take losses, can assume the responsibility of providing unemployment compensation.

There still remain, and probably always will, numerous risks of personal and business life. No one can insure the success of a new beauty shop, a new mousetrap, or a hopeful opera singer. Without error there cannot be trial; and without trial there cannot be progress.

SUMMARY TO APPENDIX

1 ■

The intelligent profit-seeking action of speculators and arbitragers tends to create certain definite equilibrium patterns of price over space and time. To the extent that speculators moderate price and consumption instability, they perform a socially useful purpose. To the extent that they provide a market and permit others

to hedge against risk, they perform a further useful function.

But to the extent that speculators pile on to price changes and cause great fluctuations in stock and commodity prices, and in foreign-exchange rates, they do social damage.

2 ◼

The economic principle of diminishing marginal utility is one way of showing why consumption and price stability is good, and why gambling is economically un-

sound and insurance is sound. There are fundamental differences among what can be insured by private rather than social agencies and what can scarcely be insured at all.

QUESTIONS FOR DISCUSSION

1. How does ideal speculation work to stabilize seasonal prices? To spread risks?

2. "Insurance reduces total risk; gambling increases the total. Therefore the former is good and the latter is bad." Explain.

3. "I love the thrill of gambling, of risking all on the turn of a card. What do I care for odds or economic principles?" Can economic science pass judgment on whether such a person should gamble or not?

4. Can you reverse the reasoning concerning the desirability of gambling and insurance so that it will apply to two individuals with increasing rather than decreasing marginal utility of income?

5. If $1 of gain is worth less than $1 of loss, show that people will prefer to hold a portfolio of diversified securities.

6. List some important differences between private and social insurance.

7. Review your understanding of the following concepts:

   spatial P equality but for transport costs
   ideal seasonal price pattern
   hedging, speculation, and short-sale
   law of diminishing marginal utility
   consumption stability versus instability
   gambling versus insurance
   social versus private insurance

22 The Theory of Demand and Utility

WHAT IS A CYNIC? A MAN WHO KNOWS THE PRICE OF EVERYTHING, AND THE VALUE OF NOTHING.
OSCAR WILDE

In a competitive market, price is determined by the schedules of supply and demand. But what principles of economics lie behind the demand schedules? What principles behind the supply schedules?

In this chapter we shall investigate briefly the economic principles of *total utility* and *marginal utility* which underlie the market demand schedule, leaving to later chapters a survey of the cost concepts which underlie the competitive supply schedule and the behavior of monopolists.

■ SUMMING INDIVIDUAL DEMANDS TO GET MARKET DEMAND

The demand curve for a good such as tea is arrived at for the whole market by summing up the amounts of tea that will be demanded by each consumer. Each consumer has a demand curve along which the quantity demanded can be plotted against the price of tea. It generally slopes downward and to the right, dropping from northwest to southeast. If all consumers were exactly alike in their demands and there were 1 million consumers, then we could think of the market demand curve as a millionfold enlargement of each consumer's demand curve.

But people are not all exactly alike. Some have high incomes; some low. Some greatly desire tea, while others prefer coffee or concerts. What must we do to the demand schedules or curves of each consumer to arrive at the total market demand curve?

All we have to do is calculate the sum total of what all the different consumers will consume at any given price; we then plot that total amount as a point on the market demand curve; or if we like, we may set the total down in a demand table like that first seen in Chapter 4.

■ *Summary.* We sum individual demands at each price to end up finally with the market demand curve. (Figure 22-1 adds demand curves "horizontally.")

414

To get market demand, we add all consumers' demand curves:

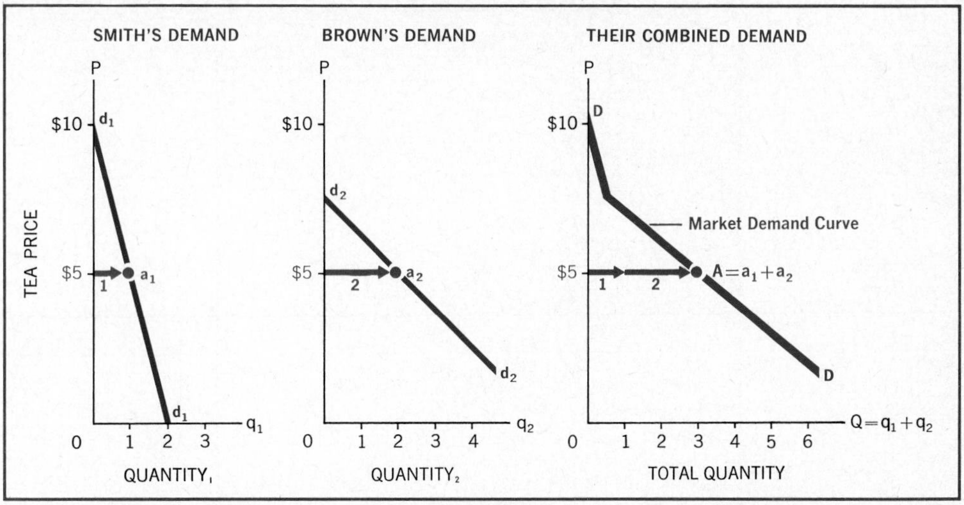

FIG. 22-1. At each price, such as $5, we *horizontally* add quantities demanded by each man to get market quantity demanded.

◼ DEMAND SHIFTS FROM INCOME AND OTHER CHANGES

Factors other than changes in the price of tea can change the quantity demanded of tea. We know from budget studies, from historical experience, and from thinking about our own behavior that an increase in money income is a factor that will normally tend to increase the amount we are willing to buy of any good. Goods that are necessities tend to be less responsive to income changes, and goods that are luxuries tend to be more responsive; a very few abnormal goods, called "inferior" goods, may actually go down in quantity bought when we get enough income to be able to afford to replace them in the budget by other goods. (Potatoes, rye bread, bologna, soup bones and offal, lard, and oleomargarine might be examples of inferior goods, but the species is so rare that we can generally neglect it in our discussions.)

Let us now show what all this means in terms of our old friend the demand curve. This curve is, of course, simply the graphical picture of the response of quantity bought of a good to the change in its *own* price. But quantity bought may change also as a result of changes in the *prices of other goods* or as a result of a change in the consumer's *income*. The demand curve is drawn on the assumption that these other things do not change. But what if they do? Then the whole demand curve will *shift* to the right or to the left.

Figure 22-2 illustrates such changes. Given a certain income and established prices for all other goods, we can draw the consumer's demand for tea. First, assume price and quantity are at point A. Suppose now that his income rises. Even though the price of tea is unchanged, he will in all probability buy more tea than before; hence the demand curve will have shifted to the right, say, to d'd', with A' indicating his new total purchase of tea. If his income should fall, then we may expect a reduction in

Demand curve shifts with change in income or in another good's price:

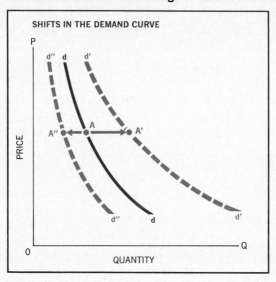

FIG. 22-2. Higher income will shift *dd* to *d'd'*. (Explain why; and why lowering income will shift *dd* to *d''d''*.) Similarly, a rise in price of coffee, which is a substitute for tea, might shift tea's *dd* out to *d'd'*. (What would a cut in coffee price do? Can you explain why a great rise in price of lemon, a complementary good used with tea, might shift *dd* leftward to *d''d''*?)

quantity bought—there *must* be a reduction if income falls far enough. This downward shift we illustrate by *d''d''* and by *A''*.

Income is only one of many factors that the position of the demand curve depends upon. An increased taste or a fashion for tea would also shift the demand to the right, and a decreased taste would have the opposite effect. Advertisers seek to shift the *dd* curve. Even if each person consumed the same amount of a good, a growth in population would have the effect of increasing the total market demand for a product. If people think that a boom is about to get under way, they may increase their purchases now in order to beat the gun.[1] Still other factors operate all the time to shift demand.

■ CROSS RELATIONS OF DEMAND

Everyone knows that raising the price of tea will decrease the amount demanded of tea. We have seen that it will also affect the amounts demanded of other commodities. For example, a higher price for tea will lower the demand for a commodity such as lemon; i.e., it will shift the whole demand schedule of lemon downward. But it will also increase the amount demanded of coffee. Probably it will have little or no effect on the demand curve for salt.

We say, therefore, that tea and coffee are rival, or competing, products, or *substitutes*. Tea and lemon, on the other hand, are cooperating, or *complementary*, com-

---

[1] In fact, when I see in today's paper that the price of tea is going up, I may rush out to buy more: this may seem superficially to be an exception to the law of downward-sloping demand, but (as discussed on page 387, footnote 3) it can be reconciled with that law when we realize that I am buying more because of the *rising* price of tea and because I want to be able to buy less of it tomorrow when its price will have stabilized at a high level. Despite this *dynamic* effect of *changing* prices, it remains true that at a steady high price for tea, I shall consume less than at a steady low price.

modities, or complements. In-between pairs such as tea and salt are said to represent *independent* commodities. The reader will of course be able to classify such pairs as beef and pork, turkey and cranberry sauce, automobiles and gasoline, truck and rail-road freight, oil and coal.

Besides showing effects of income changes, Fig. 22-2 also illustrates the effect of changed prices of other goods. A fall in the price of coffee may well cause our con-sumer to buy less tea; the demand curve shifts to, say, *d″d″*. But what if the price of lemon were to fall? The change may be small or nonexistent. But if there is any change, it will be in the direction of *increased* tea purchases—a rightward shift of *dd*. Why this difference in response? Because coffee is a rival, a *substitute* product for tea; lemon is a cooperating, a *complementary*, commodity to tea.

■ THE LAW OF DIMINISHING MARGINAL UTILITY

Return to the law of downward-sloping demand, which is so basic that we have to investigate the economic principles operating in the background to justify and explain it. Within the last century economists hit upon the fundamental notion of "marginal utility," and it was from this analysis that they felt able for the first time to derive the demand curve and explain its properties. There is space here only to sketch the basic notions underlying such theories, and there is no pretense of presenting the kind of complete discussion and criticism that appears in specialized treatises on advanced economic theory.

As a customer you will buy a good because you feel it gives you satisfaction or "utility." A first unit of a good gives you a certain amount of psychological utility. Now imagine consuming a second unit. Your total utility goes up because the second unit of the good gives you some additional utility. What about adding a third and fourth unit of the same good?

A century ago economists proclaimed an important law that sounds like the law of diminishing returns; but instead of referring to the extra output added by successive doses of an input (as in Table 2-2 on p. 25), this is a law about the behavior of psy-chological utility as you add more and more of a good. It can be described by words, by a table of numbers, and by two curves.

■ *The law of diminishing marginal utility.* As you consume more of the same good, your *total* (psychological) utility increases. However, let us use the term marginal utility to refer to "the extra utility added by one extra last unit of a good." Then, with successive new units of the good, your total utility will grow at a slower and slower rate because of a fundamental tendency for your psycho-logical ability to appreciate more of the good becomes less keen. This fact, that the increments in total utility fall off, economists describe as follows:

As the amount consumed of a good increases, the *marginal utility* of the good (or the extra utility added by its last unit) tends to decrease.

Column (2) of Table 22-1 shows that *total utility* enjoyed increases as *Q* grows, but at a decreasing rate. Column (3) measures *marginal utility* as the increment of

The law of decreasing marginal utility can be shown by numbers or curves:

(1) QUANTITY OF A GOOD CONSUMED	(2) TOTAL UTILITY	(3) MARGINAL UTILITY
0	0	
		4
1	4	
		3
2	7	
		2
3	9	
		1
4	10	
		0
5	10	

TABLE 22-1. ALTHOUGH *TOTAL* UTILITY RISES WITH CONSUMPTION, IT DOES SO AT A DE-CREASING RATE. This means that marginal utility—the extra utility added by each last extra unit of the good—will be de-creasing. From this psychological fact, older economists prepared their demon-stration of the law of downward-sloping demand.

FIG. 22-3. The green blocks show the extra utility added by each new unit. The fact that total utility increases at a decreasing rate is shown on the right by the declining steps of marginal utility. If we make our units smaller and smaller, the steps in total utility are smoothed out and total utility becomes the smooth brown curve. Now *smoothed marginal utility is shown in (b) by the green downward-falling smooth curve, and* marginal utility becomes indistinguishable from the *slope* of the smooth curve of (a).[2]

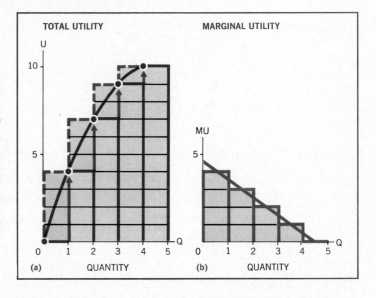

total utility resulting when one last unit of the good is added; the fact that marginal utilities in the table are declining exemplifies the law of diminishing marginal utility.

Figure 22-3(a) pictures how total utility increases, but at a decreasing rate. Figure 22-3(b) depicts marginal utilities—increments of utility (not the total of utility itself). Whether we work with sizable units of the good and measure utilities by blocks and steps, or whether we smooth the drawings by use of the brown and green curves to reflect continuously divisible units, the law of diminishing marginal utility means that

[2] NOTE: It will be found that the sum of all the marginal utilities in Table 22-1's Column (3), if reckoned above some point, must equal the amount of total utility in Column (2) at that point. [Thus, 4 + 3 + 2 does give us the 9 shown in Column (2). What does 4 + 3 give?] In terms of Fig. 22-3(b), the area under the marginal utility curve, as measured by blocks or by area under the smooth curve, must add up to equality with the numerical height of the total utility curve shown in (a)—it being understood that we make our comparison at a specified quantity level. All this portrays the fact that total utility is the sum of all the marginal (or extra) utilities added from the beginning.

the relations in Fig. 22-3(b) must slope downward and—what is exactly the same thing—that the total utility relations in Fig. 22-3(a) must look concave from below, reflecting total utility's growth becoming less and less.

> The validity of the law of diminishing marginal utility seemed probable to economists of an earlier generation as they looked into their own minds for their own psychological reactions to extra consumption. These findings of *introspection* seemed strengthened when they learned about numerous laboratory experiments by psychologists of the 1850s.
>
> Suppose you blindfold a man and ask him to hold out his hand, palm up. Now place a weight on his palm; he certainly will notice it. As you add more units of weight, he notices their addition too. But after his palm is carrying a good deal of weight, you can add just as big a weight as you did in the beginning, and yet this time he will reply that he is not conscious of any addition. In other words, the greater the *total* weight he is already carrying, the *less* will be the effect of an extra or *marginal* unit of weight.
>
> When older economists learned that perception of sound, light, and other sensations seemed to show a similar Weber-Fechner law of decreasing marginal effect, this gave them even greater confidence in the economic law of diminishing marginal utility.[3]

■ THE PROCESS OF RATIONAL CHOICE

What is the fundamental equilibrium condition that has to be satisfied if a consumer is spending his income on the variously priced goods so as to make himself truly best off in terms of utility or well-being? Certainly he would not expect that the last egg he is buying brings him exactly the same marginal utility as the last lamb chop he is buying. For lamb chops cost much more apiece than eggs. On reflection, it would seem more reasonable that he should keep buying a good which costs twice as much per unit as another until it ends up in his equilibrium bringing him just twice as much in marginal utility.

In short, if he has arranged his consumption so that every single good is bringing him marginal utility just exactly *proportional* to its price, then it would seem that he could not better himself by departing from such an equilibrium. This same fundamental condition can be stated as follows:

> ■ "Marginal utility proportional to respective price" means that there must be exact equality among the *ratios* of each good's marginal utility divided by its price. These *MU/P* ratios for each good are called the marginal utility *per dollar*

<hr>

[3] The modern generation, however, has found that the exact way in which one measures utility is not particularly important to explain the money demand curve. Some economists would still use introspection. Others would want to observe whether you had to give a man 2 to 1 odds to get him to wager on the toss of a fair coin the loss of a new hat against the winning of a second new hat; and they would conclude from this that the marginal utility of the second hat decreases to half the marginal utility of the first hat. Such economists thus hope to measure his marginal utility "behavioristically" rather than introspectively. Probably the majority of economists in advanced graduate theory today would feel that what counts for consumer demand theory is whether certain situations have more total utility than others. These economists would not care to look for any numerical measure of utility beyond such "greater or less than" comparison; they would use the "indifference curves" of the Appendix to this chapter. By any of these three methods, the general properties of the market demand curve can be securely established. (NOTE: Demand theory never has any need to make interpersonal comparisons of utility that involve adding or comparing utilities of different minds.)

that the consumer gets from spending his money on that good. So final equilibrium will require that there be *equality* of each and every good's *marginal utility per dollar.*

For those who like numerical examples, the next section digresses to work out a food and clothing case (and can be skipped at a first reading).

■ NUMERICAL EXAMPLE OF OPTIMAL CHOICE

Let's apply this MU/P reasoning to an actual two-good choice. Table 22-2 supposes that the good previously considered in Table 22-1 is called clothing. Clothing price, P_1, is assumed to be \$1. Column (2) of Table 22-2 lists clothing's marginal utility per dollar, MU_1/P_1: thus, the first dollar spent on clothing brings you 1 clothing unit and $MU/P_1 = 4$. A second dollar spent on it brings in a marginal utility of only 3 utils. Why? Because of the law of diminishing marginal utility. Total utility has gone up from 4 to 7 (but not to 8!). What would a third and fourth dollar spent on clothing alone bring? Evidently they bring marginal utilities per dollar of 2 and 1, with total utility from 4 clothing units ending up at 10 utils (as back in Table 22-1).

To have a problem of choice, you must be confronted with at least two goods. So Column (3) brings into the picture a new good, food. It also is assumed to cost \$1; that is, $P_2 = \$1$. Being a necessity, food starts out with a very high MU_2 per dollar, namely 10. And at first its MU_2/P_2 drops very little, being 9 for the second unit. But once you are fed, your MU_2 and MU_2/P_2 drop very rapidly—to $1\frac{3}{4}$ for the third unit of food and to $\frac{3}{4}$ for the fourth unit.[4]

Now to choose. Start out with daily income of only \$1. Your best buy is food: 1 unit. Why? Because 10 utils from a dollar spent on food is better than 4 utils from a dollar spent on clothing.

Now consider \$2 of income. Again, all goes for food. The second food unit brings you 9 utils, which still beats the 4 utils that could come from the first clothing unit.

But now get \$3 of income. At last you have enough to buy a luxury: 1 unit of clothing along with your 2 of food. (Why a first unit of clothing rather than a third of food? Because $MU_1/P_1 = 4 > MU_2/P_2 = 1\frac{3}{4}$. Q.E.D.)

Table 22-3 shows your budget pattern of food-clothing purchases at different income levels. How was it derived? Verify that you did maximize your total utility from all sources only if you always followed the rule of picking that unit of a good which gives you the larger MU/P. (Can you fill in the \$7 blanks as 3 food and 4 clothing? Why?)

So much for the important budgetary patterns of expenditure at different incomes with prices fixed. Can we derive the usual *demand curves with respect to price* from the utility data of Table 22-2? Yes, we can. Imagine that the price of food has halved, to $P_2 = 50$

---

[4] WARNING: Goods 1 and 2 in Table 22-2 are assumed to have *independently* addable utilities. If they had been rival goods, like tea and coffee, the MU of the third tea unit would go down when you got one more coffee unit. If they had been complementary goods, like tea and lemon, the MU of the third tea unit would go up when you got one more lemon unit. The $MU_1/P_1 = MU_2/P_2$ rule would still hold in maximizing equilibrium; but you couldn't get these from *separate* columns. You would need the Appendix's indifference contours to handle such a case, or more complicated analysis.

You maximize utility by choosing items with greatest marginal utility per dollar:

(1) UNIT OF GOOD	(2) GOOD 1, CLOTHING MU_1/P_1	(3) GOOD 2, FOOD MU_2/P_2
1	4	10
2	3	9
3	2	$1\frac{3}{4}$
4	1	$\frac{3}{4}$

TABLE 22-2. MARGINAL UTILITIES PER DOLLAR WHEN EACH GOOD HAS $P = \$1$. Food, being a necessity, has its MU_2 falling faster than MU_1 of clothing falls. In choosing how to spend each last dollar, the rule that gives you most total utility is this: Select any item whose MU/P is largest; if $MU_1/P_1 = MU_2/P_2$, you can be indifferent. (Hence, successive dollars of income go for food first, food second, clothing third, clothing fourth, ... —because $10 > 9 > 4 > 3$. . . .)

TABLE 22-3. INCOME BUDGETARY PATTERN OF DEMAND. By choosing items in Table 22-2 with highest MU/P (i.e., marginal utility *per dollar*), you find your optimal equilibrium pattern of demand.

INCOME (PER DAY)	$1	$2	$3	$4	$5	$6	$7	$8
Clothing (demanded)	0	0	1	2	3	3	____	4
Food (demanded)	1	2	2	2	2	3		4

cents. We want to show that, at unchanged income levels and with P_1 held at $1, the cut in P_2 will indeed increase the quantity demanded of Q_2.

Clearly Table 22-2's clothing column of MU_1/P_1 remains unchanged at 4, 3, 2, 1. But food's column now is $MU_2/\$\frac{1}{2}$ instead of $MU_2/\$1$; this means that the numbers 10, 9, $1\frac{3}{4}$, . . . would have to be *doubled* to read 20, 18, $3\frac{1}{2}$, ...

Now let us make our controlled experiment. Hold income constant at $1 per day and P_1 at $1, but cut P_2 to 50 cents. Now for each dollar we can buy 1 clothing unit, as before, or 2 food units. Because the new numbers 20 and 18 are both greater than 4, our first two half-dollars will both be spent on food. Consequently, comparing this 2-of-food result with the first entry in Table 22-3, which had shown only 1 of food bought, we see that the price reduction of food has definitely caused its quantity bought to increase— even though it is a necessity. (Actually, its price elasticity, as calculated by any of the formulas for Chapter 20, happens by accident to turn out to be unity, since the same total receipts are spent on it at both prices.)

We shall omit the calculations to show how any other level of income would be spent in the new situation,[5] and how any other cuts in the price of P_2 do tend to increase Q_2 bought.

■ EQUILIBRIUM CONDITION: EQUAL MARGINAL UTILITIES PER DOLLAR
FOR EVERY GOOD

After our digression for a numerical example, we restate the basic principle.

■ A consumer with a fixed income and facing given market prices of different goods can come into his equilibrium of maximum satisfaction or utility only when the following holds:

[5] See Figs. 22-9 and 22-10 in the Appendix for a rigorous derivation of demand responses to income and price changes. Appendix footnote 5 discusses some problems due to lumpiness of units, as does page 433's footnote 6.

Law of equal marginal utilities per dollar. Each good—such as sugar—is demanded up to the point where the marginal utility per dollar (or penny) spent on it is exactly the same as the marginal utility of a dollar (or penny) spent on any other good—such as salt. If any one good gave more marginal utility per dollar, the consumer would gain by taking money away from other goods and spending more on that good—up to the point where the law of diminishing marginal utility brought its marginal utility per dollar down to equality. If any good gave less marginal utility per dollar than the common level, the consumer would buy less of it until the marginal utility of the last dollar spent on it had risen back to the common level.[6]

This fundamental condition of consumer equilibrium can be written in terms of the marginal utilities and prices of the different goods as follows:

$$\frac{MU\ Good\ 1}{P_1} = \frac{MU\ Good\ 2}{P_2} = \frac{MU\ Good\ 3}{P_3} = \cdots = \text{common } MU \text{ per dollar of income}$$

The logical meaning of this condition rather than the rote memorizing of a formula is, of course, what matters. One should be able to justify this equilibrium situation by the following common-sense reasoning:

Why can I not be in equilibrium with sugar's marginal utility twice its price and salt's marginal utility three times its price? Because the last unit of money spent on salt is giving me more utility than the last unit of money spent on sugar. What must happen, then, if I transfer a little money from sugar, where it is yielding a relatively low marginal utility, and move it to salt, where it yields a relatively high marginal utility? Evidently, I shall gain the difference in these two marginal yields. So I shall make the switch. But now my further purchase of salt has brought *down* the marginal utility from the last dollar spent on it. (Remember the fundamental law of diminishing marginal utility!) And my consuming less sugar has brought *up* the marginal utility of money spent on it. So I am indeed moving toward equality, and I shall go on gaining a little total utility until I am at equilibrium with proper marginal equality.[7]

Nor need all this apply just to spending money. Suppose you have only a certain number of hours to spend on study for examinations. If you are so uncreative as to seek merely to maximize your grade average, how should you allocate your time? By spending equal hours on each course? Not necessarily. You have to shift from history to chemistry, from German to economics, until you are getting *the same marginal grade advantage from the last minute spent in each alternative use.*[8] The same marginal rule can show you how to allocate your time on a pleasant weekend. Our marginal equilibrium condition is not merely a law of economics; it is a law of logic itself.

[6] At a few places in economics the indivisibility of units is important and cannot be glossed over. Thus, Cadillacs do not come like peas, and their indivisibility may matter. Suppose I buy one but definitely not two Cadillacs. Then the marginal utility of the first car is enough larger than the marginal utility of the same number of dollars spent elsewhere to induce me to buy this first unit. The marginal utility that the second Cadillac would bring is enough less to ensure I do *not* buy it. When indivisibility matters, our equality rule for equilibrium can be restated as an inequality rule.
[7] The validity of this equilibrium condition can be made quite independent of how, or whether, we measure utility *numerically*. Only relative marginal utilities matter.
[8] This does not mean that you study to get the same 89 grade in all classes. Your average may be maximized with grades of 93, 92, 90, and 81, but with each marginal hour of study adding one-tenth of a grade point to any subject.

A final remark may be in order at this point. A consumer is not expected to be a wizard at numbers or graphs, nor need he be, to approximate the demand behavior of this chapter. He can even make most of his decisions unconsciously or out of habit. As long as he is fairly consistent in his tastes and actions, all he has to do to make the present analysis relevant is to avoid repeating those mistakes which he found in the past did not give him the goods and services he most wanted and to avoid making wild and unpredictable changes in his buying behavior. If enough people act in this way, our scientific theory will provide a good measure of approximation to the facts.

■ SUBSTITUTION- AND INCOME-EFFECTS: A DIGRESSION

The concept of marginal utility has lent credence to the fundamental law of downward-sloping demand. A different way of looking at the same problem makes no mention of marginal utility explicitly; but it does lead rigorously to the desired result, and does provide an interesting insight into the factors that tend to make the response of quantity to price very great or very little.

SUBSTITUTION-EFFECT   The first factor explaining diminishing consumption when price rises is an obvious one. If the price of tea goes up while other prices do not, then tea has become relatively dearer. It pays, therefore, to *substitute* other goods for tea in order to maintain one's standard of living most cheaply. Thus tea becomes a relatively dearer source of stimulation than before, and less of it will be bought and more of coffee or cocoa. Similarly, a rise in price of movies relative to stage plays may cause the consumer to seek less of his amusement in the dearer direction. The consumer is doing here only what every businessman does when rises in the price of one productive factor cause him to adjust his production methods so as to substitute cheap inputs for the dear inputs. By this process of substitution, he is able to produce the same output at least total cost. Similarly do consumers buy satisfaction at least cost.

INCOME-EFFECT   In the second place, when your money income is fixed, being forced to buy a good at a higher price is just like having a decrease in your real income or purchasing power, particularly if you have been buying a great deal of the raised commodity. With a lower real income you will now want to buy less tea. Thus, unless a good is an "inferior" good like bologna or oleo, the income-effect will *reinforce* the substitution-effect in making the demand curve downward-sloping.[9]

---

[9] Income- and substitution-effects not only explain the downward slope of demand but also explain a possible, albeit extremely rare, exception to that law. When the 1845 Irish famine greatly raised the price of potatoes, families who consumed a lot of potatoes merely because they were too poor to consume much meat might have ended up consuming *more* rather than less of the high-P potatoes. Why? Because now they had to spend so much on potatoes, the necessary of life, as to make it quite impossible to afford any meat at all and hence were forced to become even more dependent than before on potatoes. In brief, the substitution-effect was here overcome by the perverse income-effect applicable to a peculiar "inferior" good, such as the potato, which tends to *decrease* in the poor man's budget when incomes *rise*. This *curiosum* is attributed to Sir Robert Giffen, a Victorian economist. (NOTE: In the case of ordinary inferior goods on which we spend little money, the perverse income-effects will not outweigh the substitution-effects and produce the odd Giffen case.)

Of course, the quantitative importance of each of these effects varies with the good in question and with the consumer. Under some circumstances the resulting demand curve is very *elastic:* as where the consumer has been spending a good deal on the commodity and where ready substitutes are available—for example, a drunkard's demand for gin. But if a commodity, such as salt, involves only a small fraction of the consumer's budget, is not easily replaceable by other items, and is needed in small amounts to complement more important items, then demand will tend to be *inelastic.*

■ THE PARADOX OF VALUE

The preceding theories help to explain a famous question that troubled Adam Smith in *The Wealth of Nations*. He asked, How is it that water, which is so very useful that life is impossible without it, has such a low price—while diamonds, which are quite unnecessary, have such a high price?

Today even a beginning student can give a correct answer to this problem. "That's simply explained," he will write on an examination. "The supply and demand curves for water are such that they intersect at a very low price, while the supply and demand curves for diamonds are such that they intersect at a high price." (Today he could add that water is no longer all that cheap.)

This is not an incorrect answer. Adam Smith could not have given it because supply and demand curves as descriptive tools had not yet been invented, and were not to be for 75 years or more. But after he had mastered the lingo, old Adam Smith would naturally ask the question, "But *why* do supply and demand for water intersect at such a low price?"

The answer is by now easy to phrase. It consists of two parts:

Diamonds are very *scarce,* the cost of getting *extra* ones is high; and water is relatively *abundant,* with its cost low in many areas of the world. This first part would have seemed reasonable to even the classical economists of more than a century ago, who would probably have let it go at that, and would not have known how to reconcile these facts about *cost* with the equally valid fact that the world's water is more *useful* than the world's supply of diamonds. In fact, Adam Smith never did quite resolve the paradox. He was content simply to point out that the "value in use" of a good—its total contribution to economic welfare—is not the same thing as its "value in exchange"—the total money value or revenue for which it will sell. Smith had not arrived at the point where he knew how to distinguish *marginal* utility from *total* utility!

Today, we should add to the above cost considerations a second truth:

The *total* utility of water does not determine its price or demand. Only the relative marginal utility and cost of the *last* little bit of water determine its price. Why? Because people are free to buy or not buy that last little bit. If water is priced higher than its marginal utility, then that last unit cannot be sold. Therefore the price must fall until it reaches exactly the level of usefulness of the last little bit, no more and no less. Moreover, because every unit of water is exactly like any other unit and because there is only one price in a competitive market, *every unit must sell for what the last least useful unit sells for.* (As one student put the matter: The theory of economic value is easy to understand if you just remember that the tail wags the dog: concentrate on *marginal* and not on *total* utility.)

■ Now we know that the more there is of a commodity, the less the relative desirability of its *last* little unit becomes, even though its *total* usefulness always grows as we get more of the commodity. So, it is obvious why a large amount of water has a low price. Or why air is actually a free good despite its vast usefulness. The many later units pull down the market value of all units.

■ CONSUMER'S SURPLUS

The foregoing discussion emphasizes that the accounting system which records the "total economic value" or revenue of a good (price × quantity) differs from the measurement necessary to record "total welfare." The total economic value of air is zero; its contribution to welfare, very great.[10] Similarly, if we increase the quantity produced of a good, we obviously increase the community's welfare; but if it is a good like wheat, whose demand is inelastic, we do at the same time destroy some economic value.

■ Thus, there is always a sort of gap between total utility and total market value. This gap is in the nature of a *surplus*, which the consumer gets because he "receives more than he pays for."

Nor does he benefit at the expense of the seller. In a swap, one party does not lose what the other gains. Unlike energy, which cannot be created or destroyed, the well-being of all participants is increased by trade.

It is easy to see how this surplus arises. Each unit of a good that the consumer buys costs him only as much as the last unit is worth. But by our fundamental law of diminishing marginal utility, the *earlier* units are worth *more* to him than the last. Thus, he enjoys a surplus on each of these earlier units. When trade stops benefiting him and giving him a surplus, he stops buying.

As final clinching evidence that the consumer always receives a surplus, we may cite the fact that a ruthless seller could present the consumer with an ultimatum—what is called an "all-or-none" offer: "Either you pay me an extra amount of money for the whole block of the good that you are consuming, or you must go without all the units, from first to last. Take it or leave it!" The consumer would certainly be willing to pay extra rather than do altogether without the good of this discriminating monopolist.

How is the concept of consumer surplus used? It is sometimes needed to help make correct social decisions. Suppose a new branch road would cost the locality $100,000. Being free to all, it is expected to bring in no dollar revenues, and all the utility it gives to each user will represent his consumer's surplus. (To avoid extraneous interpersonal difficulties, let us assume there are 1,000 users all exactly alike in income and in their benefit from the road, and all equally worthy.) If each such similar man

---

[10] Or, as Smith would say, its value in use is very great; its value in exchange, negligible.

enjoys $100 (the road's per capita cost) or more of consumer's surplus from the road, they should all vote to build the road. If the consumer's surplus of each is less than $100, it is uneconomical for them to tax themselves for this public project.

Many ingenious ways have been suggested for measuring consumer's surplus, but they are of no particular significance here.[11] The important thing is to see how lucky the citizens of modern efficient communities really are. The *privilege of being able to buy a vast array of goods at low prices cannot be overestimated*.

This is a humbling thought. If ever a person becomes arrogantly proud of *his* economic productivity and *his* level of real earnings, let him pause and reflect. If he were transported with all his skills and energies intact to a primitive desert island, how much would his money earnings buy? Indeed, without capital machinery, without rich resources, without other labor, and above all without the technological knowledge which each generation inherits from society's past, how much could *he* produce? It is only too clear that all of us reap the benefits of an economic world we never made. As L. T. Hobhouse said:

> The organizer of industry who thinks that he has "made" himself and his business has found a whole social system ready to his hand in skilled workers, machinery, a market, peace and order—a vast apparatus and a pervasive atmosphere, the joint creation of millions of men and scores of generations. Take away the whole social factor and we have not Robinson Crusoe, with his salvage from the wreck and his acquired knowledge, but the naked savage living on roots, berries, and vermin.

SUMMARY

1 ■

The market demand curve for all consumers is derived by adding *horizontally* the separate demand curves of each consumer. A demand curve can shift for many reasons, such as the following: Normally, a rise in income will shift *dd* rightward, thus increasing demand; a rise in the price of a substitute or competing good (coffee for tea, and so forth) will also create such an upward shift in demand; a rise in the price of a

---

[11]In the special case where money provides a firm measuring rod of utility, consumer's surplus is easily measured and depicted. In Fig. 22-4, when the consumer buys *OM* sugar at *ON* price for each, he pays the total revenue indicated by the brown rectangular area *OMEN;* but that much sugar gives him total utility (expressed in money) which is the whole area *OMER;* the green triangular area *NER* left over is his consumer's surplus, and it obviously will be greater the lower the price becomes.

This geometrical concept is useful in illustrating how taxes, farm quotas, and monopolistic interferences create social inefficiency and loss.

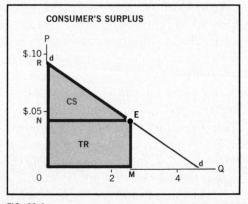

FIG. 22-4.

complementary good (such as lemon in its relation to tea) will represent a cross effect that shifts the *dd* curve downward and leftward. Still other factors—such as changing tastes, population, or expectations—can increase or decrease demand.

2 ■

The concepts of total and marginal utility were introduced to explain the law of downward-sloping demand. The fact that total utility rises with each new marginal addition of a good but at a decreasing rate of growth can be expressed in a different way. With equal additions to a good's quantity, its marginal utility (which is the increment of utility coming from adding a last extra unit of quantity) tends to decrease.

3 ■

To get the most total utility, the consumer must achieve a fundamental marginal condition for demand equilibrium: A consumer has not maximized his well-being until he has succeeded in *making equal the respective marginal utilities per dollar spent on each and every good.* (BEWARE: The marginal utility of a $25-per-ounce bottle of perfume is not equal to the marginal utility of a 10-cent glass of cola; but their marginal utilities divided by price per unit—that is, their marginal utilities per last dollar, MU/P— are to be equalized in optimizing equilibrium.)

   This is a fundamental rule of logic that transcends demand theory: If you want to allocate any limited resource among competing uses, whenever the marginal advantage in one use happened to be greater than in another, you can benefit by transferring from the low-marginal-advantage use to the high—until a final equilibrium is reached at which all have become equal.

4 ■

Without using the marginal utility concept explicitly, we can gain new insight into the factors making for downward-sloping demand by analyzing the effect of a price rise into (1) its *substitution-effect* component and (2) its *income-effect* component. When P for a good rises, I tend to maintain the same level of well-being by *substituting* other goods for the good that has just become dearer. Reinforcing this decrease in a good's Q that arises out of substitution is the income-effect: Since I ordinarily buy less of the good in question when my family income is lower, the rise in its price—which has produced a *drop in my real income* or purchasing power—thus induces a further cut in consumption as the result of my now having a lower real income.

5 ■

Adam Smith's paradox of value—that a commodity important for welfare may sell for less in the market than one less important—is clarified by the distinction between the concept of marginal and total utility. The scarcity of a good, as determined by its cost and supply conditions, interacts with the market demand for the good as determined by the usefulness of its *marginal* unit (not the usefulness of the *total* stock of the good).

6 ■

The fact that market price is determined by marginal rather than total utility is dramatized by the concept of *consumer's surplus.* Since we pay in the market the same price for each unit that the marginal unit is worth to us, we reap a consumer's surplus on all the previous units. This consumer's surplus reflects the benefit we gain from being able to buy at low prices, rather than being confronted by a ruthless monopolist who insists we pay him for the whole of our consumption just what that total is worth to us. However difficult it may be to quantify consumer's surplus, advanced treatises show it is a concept relevant for many social decisions—such as deciding when the community should incur the heavy initial expenses of a road or bridge.[12]

Without reading the Appendix, we can go from the utility background of demand to the next chapter's cost background of supply.

QUESTIONS FOR DISCUSSION

1. As you add horizontally the demands of more and more people, the aggregate market curve begins to look flatter and flatter on the same scale. Show that this merely reflects the fact that the same cut in price induces more new sales from many buyers than from few. (NOTE: Elasticity need not change. Guess why.)

2. List several goods in order of their responsiveness to higher income.

3. Which of the following goods do you think could be classified as complementary, substitute, and independent goods: beef, ketchup, lamb, applesauce, cigarettes, gum, pork, butter, paperbacks, taxis, and oleomargarine? Illustrate the resulting shift in the demand curve for one good when price of another good goes up. How would a change in income affect the demand curve for butter? The demand curve for oleomargarine?

4. Explain the difference between marginal and total utility. State the law of diminishing marginal utility. Be sure you understand what it means in terms of numbers and diagrams.

5. Why is it nonsensical to say, "In equilibrium, the marginal utilities of all goods must be exactly equal"? Reword to give a correct statement and explain.

6. If you wanted to avoid using the marginal utility concept, show that you still can justify the law of downward-sloping demand by reasoning that involves (1) substitution-effect and (2) income-effect.

7. How much would you be willing to pay rather than give up *all* movies? How much do you spend on movies? Calculate consumer's surplus.

8. Review your understanding of the following concepts:

market versus individual demand

demand shifts from income and
   other changes

substitute, complementary, and
   independent goods

income-effect and substitution-effect

law of diminishing marginal utility

equating marginal utility of last dollar
   spent on each good, $MU_1/P_1 = MU_2/P_2$

value in use versus value in exchange

paradox of marginal versus total utility

consumer's surplus

---

[12]See page 615's footnote on this topic.

APPENDIX: Geometrical Analysis of Consumer Equilibrium

It is instructive to show graphically, and without using the language of numerical utility, exactly what the consumer's equilibrium position looks like.

THE INDIFFERENCE CURVE

We start out by considering a consumer who buys only two commodities, say, food and clothing, at definite quoted prices. We suppose the consumer can tell us whether (1) he prefers a given combination or batch of the two goods, say, 3 units of food and 2 of clothing, to some second combination or batch, say, 2 units of food and 3 of clothing, or (2) he is "indifferent" as between the two combinations.

Let us suppose that, actually, these two batches are equally good in the eyes of our consumer—that he is indifferent as to which of the two he receives. Let us go on to list in Table 22-4 some of the other combinations of goods between which he is likewise indifferent.

Figure 22-5 shows these combinations diagrammatically. We measure units of clothing upon one axis and units of food upon the other. Each of our four

combinations or batches, A, B, C, D, is represented by its point. But these four are by no means the only combinations that would leave our consumer just indifferent as between them. Another batch, such as 1½ units of food and 4 of clothing, might be ranked as equal to any of A, B, C, or D above, and there are many others.

■ The curved line of Fig. 22-5, linking up the four points, is an "indifference curve." *Every* point thereon represents a different combination of the two goods; and the indifference curve is so drawn that, if our consumer were given his choice of any point on it, he would not know which one to choose. All would be equally desirable to him, and he would be indifferent as to which batch he received.

It should be noted that this indifference curve is of convex curvature viewed from below. As we move downward and to the right along the curve—a movement which implies increasing the quantity of food and reducing that of clothing—the slope of the curve becomes flatter. The curve is drawn so because this illus-

Food-clothing batches which give equal utility are "indifferent":

	FOOD	CLOTHING
A	1	6
B	2	3
C	3	2
D	4	1½

TABLE 22-4. INDIFFERENCE COMBINATIONS. Getting more of one good compensates for giving up something of the other. The consumer likes situation A exactly as well as B, C, or D.

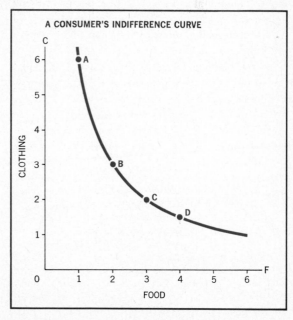

FIG. 22-5. The food-clothing combinations that yield equal satisfaction can be plotted as a smooth "indifference curve" (or so-called "equal-utility contour"). This is convex (from below) in accord with the law of substitution, which says: As you get more of a good, its "substitution ratio," or "indifference slope," diminishes.

trates a property which seems most often to hold true in real life and which we may call the "law of substitution":

■ **The scarcer a good, the greater its relative *substitution* value; its marginal utility rises relative to the marginal utility of the good that has become plentiful.**

For example, the consumer who is at position *A* in Table 22-4 is willing to give up 3 units of clothing in order to get a second unit of food; thus, at *A*, he would swap 3 of his 6 clothing units in exchange for 1 extra food unit. But when he has moved to *B*, he would sacrifice only 1 of his remaining clothing supply in order to obtain a third food unit—a 1-for-1 swap. For a fourth unit of food, he would sacrifice only $\frac{1}{2}$ unit from his dwindling supply of clothing.

If we join the points *A* and *B* of Fig. 22-5, we find that the slope of the resulting line (neglecting its negative sign) has a value of 3. Join *B* and *C*, and the slope is 1; join *C* and *D*, and the slope is $\frac{1}{2}$. These figures—3, 1, $\frac{1}{2}$—are simply the "swapping terms" that we noted just above.

But to move from *A* to *B* is to move a considerable distance along the curve. What about the swapping terms for smaller movements? If the consumer is at *A* and we consider a movement to the intermediate position (not shown in Table 22-4) of $1\frac{1}{2}$ food and 4 clothing, the swapping ratio would be 4. And it is clear that, as the movement along the curve grows smaller, the closer the swapping terms come to the actual slope of the indifference curve.[1]

So the slope of the indifference curve is the measure of the terms on which—for very small changes—the consumer would be willing to exchange a little of his supply of one good in return for a little more of the other. And an indifference curve which is convex in the manner of Fig. 22-5 conforms to the law of

---

[1] By the arithmetic slope of the indifference curve, we mean this: To find the slope of the curve at, say, point *B*, take a ruler and place it so that it is just tangent to the curve at *B*—it touches the curve, but does not cross it either above or below *B*. Mark the points at which the ruler's edge crosses the two axes. The slope is the ratio of the distance cut off on the vertical axis to the distance cut off on the horizontal axis; e.g., at *B*, the slope is $\frac{6}{4}$, or $1\frac{1}{2}$. Intermediate texts refer to the slope of the indifference curve at any point as the "substitution ratio," or "the marginal rate of substitution," or the "*relative* marginal utility ratio" at that point.

substitution earlier noted. As the consumer's food goes up—and his clothing goes down—food must become relatively cheaper and cheaper in order for him to be persuaded to take a little extra food in exchange for a little sacrifice of clothing. The precise shape and slope of an indifference curve will, of course, vary from one consumer to the next; but for this introductory discussion, it seems reasonable to assume that the general convex shape of the curve in Fig. 22-5 is typical.

THE INDIFFERENCE MAP

Table 22-4 is but one of an infinite number of possible tables. We could have started out with a still higher level of satisfaction or indifference and listed some of the different combinations that belonged to it in the mind of our consumer. One such table might have begun with 2 food and 7 clothing; another with 3 food and 7 clothing. Each table could be portrayed graphically; each has its corresponding curve. Figure 22-6 shows four such curves; the old curve of Fig. 22-5 is now labeled U_3. This figure is analogous to a geo-

Every point lies on one of the many indifference curves:

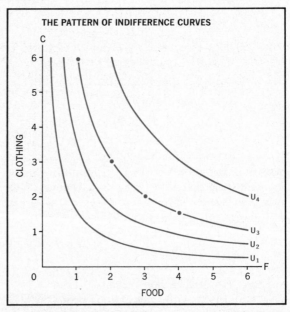

FIG. 22-6. The curves labeled U_1, U_2, U_3, and U_4 represent indifference curves, or equal-utility contours. (Why is it better to be on a farther-out indifference curve?) U_3 is the indifference contour of Fig. 22-5.

Fixed income and market P's imply limited consumption possibilities:

FOOD	CLOTHING
4	0
3	$1\frac{1}{2}$
2	3
1	$4\frac{1}{2}$
0	6

TABLE 22-5. ALTERNATIVE CONSUMPTION POSSIBILITIES. The costs of these budgets (reckoned as $\$1.50F + \$1C$) all add up to $6 income.

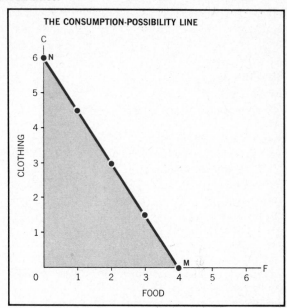

THE CONSUMPTION-POSSIBILITY LINE

FIG. 22-7. *NM* is the consumer's consumption-possibility budget line. When he spends just $6 daily, with food and clothing prices $1.50 and $1, he can choose any point on this line. (Why is its slope $\$1.50/\$1 = \frac{3}{2}$?)

graphical contour map. A person who walks along the path indicated by a particular height contour on such a map will find that he is neither climbing nor descending; similarly, the consumer who moves from one position to another along a single indifference curve enjoys neither increasing nor decreasing satisfaction from the change in the flow of goods he is getting. Of course, only a few of the possible indifference curves or equal-utility contours are shown in Fig. 22-6.

Note that, as we increase both goods and hence move in a northeasterly direction across this "map," we are crossing successive indifference curves; we are reaching higher and higher levels of satisfaction. Unless the consumer is satiated, he would be enjoying increasing satisfaction from receiving increased quantities of *both* goods. Hence, curve U_3 stands for a higher level of satisfaction than U_2; U_4, for a higher level of satisfaction than U_3; etc.

THE CONSUMPTION-POSSIBILITY BUDGET LINE

Now let us set the consumer's indifference map aside for a moment and give him a fixed income. He has, say, $6 per day to spend, and he is confronted with fixed prices for each food and clothing unit—$1.50 for food, $1 for clothing. It is clear that he could spend

his money on any one of a variety of alternative combinations of food and clothing. At one extreme, he could buy 4 food units and no clothing; at the other, 6 clothing units and no food. Table 22-5 illustrates some of the possible ways in which his $6 could be allocated.

Figure 22-7 shows these five possible positions on a diagram with axes similar to those of Figs. 22-5 and 22-6. Each position is indicated by a small dot, and it will be noted that they all lie on a straight line, which is labeled *NM*. Moreover, any other attainable point, such as $3\frac{1}{3}$ food units and 1 clothing unit, would lie upon *NM*. *NM* sums up all the possible positions that our consumer could occupy in spending his $6 of budget income.[2]

The slope of *NM* (neglecting its sign) is $\frac{3}{2}$, which is necessarily the ratio of food price to clothing price; and the common sense of line *NM* is clear enough. Given these prices, every time our consumer gives up

---

[2] This is so because, if we designate quantities of food and clothing bought as F and C, respectively, total expenditure on food must be $\$1\frac{1}{2}F$ and total expenditure on clothing, $\$1C$. If daily income and expenditure is $6, the following equation must hold: $\$6 = \$1\frac{1}{2}F + \$1C$. This is a simple linear equation, the equation of the budget line *NM*. NOTE:
Arithmetic slope of $NM = \$1\frac{1}{2} \div \$1$

$\qquad\qquad\qquad\quad = $ price of food $\div$ price of clothing

1½ clothing units (thereby dropping down 1½ vertical units on the diagram), he can gain 1 unit of food (i.e., move east 1 horizontal unit). Or what is the same thing, he can exchange 3 clothing units for 2 food units. We can call NM the consumer's "consumption-possibility" (or "budget") line.

THE EQUILIBRIUM POSITION OF TANGENCY

Now we are ready to put our two parts together. The axes of Fig. 22-7 were the same as those of Figs. 22-5 and 22-6. We can superimpose the consumption-possibility budget line NM upon the consumer's indifference map, as in Fig. 22-8. He is free to move anywhere along NM. Positions to the right and above NM are barred to him unless he has more than $6 of income to

Equilibrium is where consumer has reached highest satisfaction level:

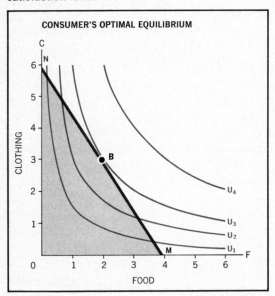

CONSUMER'S OPTIMAL EQUILIBRIUM

FIG. 22-8. At B the consumer reaches highest indifference curve attainable with his fixed income. B represents tangency of consumption-possibility budget line with highest indifference curve. (Why? If slopes were unequal, NM would intersect a U contour and he could cross over onto higher satisfaction levels.) At tangency point B, substitution ratio equals price ratio P_F/P_C. This means that all goods' marginal utilities are proportional to their prices, with marginal utility of the last dollar spent on every good being equalized—as demonstrated in the chapter's main text.

spend; and positions to the left and below NM are unimportant, since we assume that he will want to spend the full $6.

Where will the consumer move? Obviously, to that point which yields the greatest satisfaction; or, in other words, to the highest available indifference curve, which in this case must be at point B. At B, the consumption-possibility line just touches—but does not cross[3]—the indifference curve U_3; at this point of tangency is found the highest utility contour he can reach.

Geometrically, the consumer is at equilibrium where the slope of his consumption-possibility budget line is exactly equal to the slope of his indifference curve. And as already noted, the slope of the consumption-possibility line is the price of food ratio to clothing.

■ We may say, then, that equilibrium is attained when the consumer's *substitution* ratio is just equal to the ratio of food price to clothing price.[4]

CHANGES IN INCOME AND PRICE

Our understanding of the process will be furthered by considering the effects of (1) a change in money income and (2) a change in the price of one of the two goods.

1. Assume, first, that the consumer's daily income is halved, the two prices remaining unchanged. We could prepare another table, similar to Table 22-4, showing the consumption possibilities that are now open to him. Plotting these points on a diagram such as Fig. 22-9, we should find that the new consumption-possibility budget line occupies the position N'M' in Fig. 22-9. The line has made a *parallel* shift, toward the southwest.[5] The consumer is now free to move only along this new budget line. Again he will move to the highest attainable indifference curve, or to the point B'. A simi-

[3]At any point on NM other than B, NM is crossing indifference curves. And as long as the consumer can keep crossing indifference curves, he can keep moving to higher ones.

[4]The substitution ratio, or slope of the indifference curve, can be shown to be nothing but the ratio of the marginal utility of food to the marginal utility of clothing. So our tangency condition is just another way of stating that a good's price and its marginal utility must be proportional in equilibrium—the consumer there getting the same marginal utility from his last penny spent on food as from his last penny spent on clothing (in agreement with page 422).

[5]The equation of the consumption-possibility line is now $3 = $1½F + $1C.

When income or a P changes, we find new equilibrium:

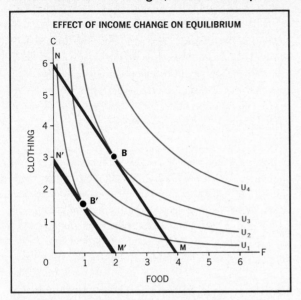

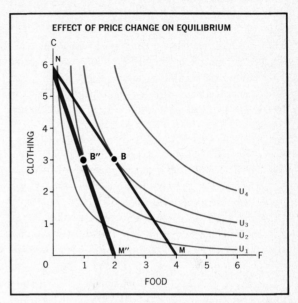

FIG. 22-9. An income change shifts the consumption-possibility budget line in a parallel way. Thus, halving income to $3 shifts NM to N'M' moving equilibrium to B'. (Show what doubling income to $6 does to equilibrium. Pencil in a new tangency point.)

FIG. 22-10. A rise in the price of food makes the consumption-possibility budget line rotate from NM to NM''. New tangency equilibrium is at B'', with less food and either more or less clothing. (Can you handle a change in P_C?)

lar tangency condition for optimal equilibrium again applies.[6]

2. Now let us return our consumer to his previous daily income of $6, but then assume that the price of food rises from $1.50 to $3. Again we must examine the change in the consumption-possibility budget line. This time we shall find that it has pivoted on the point N and is now NM'',[7] as in Fig. 22-10.

[6] Join B' and B by a smooth curve to generate the important budgetary income-expenditure patterns of Fig. 11-1, page 200, or Table 22-3, page 421. The Appendix and most of the chapter assume goods come in minutely divisible units. If the student were to try to write down the new table like 22-2 for $P_2 = 50$ cents and derive from it a new budget-income table like 22-3, he would find that the lumpiness of the units presents a little problem. By working with pennies instead of dollars, and with hundredths of a unit of food instead of units, he could reduce this problem to a minimum. Or another trick might be used: To spend $1.50 per day, we might let him spend $2 on even days and $1 on odd days, averaging out to $1.50. Likewise, by having him buy 1 of clothing on every other day and 0 on the other day, he could manage to consume fractional amounts of clothing on the average.

[7] The equation of the consumption-possibility line is now $6 = $3F + $1C.

The common sense of such a shift is clear. Since the price of clothing is unchanged, the point N is just as available as it was before. But since the price of food has risen, point M, which meant 4 food units had been purchasable, is no longer attainable. With food costing $3 per unit, only 2 units can now be bought with a daily income of $6. So the new consumption-possibility line must still pass through N, but it must pivot around N and pass through M'', which is below M. (The new line has a slope of $3/1$. Why?)

Equilibrium is now at B''; we have a new tangency situation in that equilibrium. Higher food price has definitely reduced food consumption; higher P_F may change clothing consumption in either direction. (The dd demand curves of this chapter were derivable by plotting the P_F, Q_F data you can read off from the B to B'' shift.)

To clinch his understanding, the interested reader should work out the cases of (1) an increase in income and (2) a fall in the price of clothing or food. (He should also connect all the tangency points generated by income changes in order to get the Engel's budgetary patterns of Chapter 11.)

SUMMARY TO APPENDIX

1 ■

An "indifference curve" or "equal-utility contour" depicts the points of equally desirable consumption. The indifference contour is usually drawn convex from below, in accordance with the empirical law of diminishing relative marginal utilities (or of substitution ratios).

2 ■

If a consumer has a fixed money income, all of which he spends, and is confronted with market prices of two goods, the consumption-possibility budget line upon which he is free to move is a straight line. The steepness of the line's slope depends on the ratio of the two market prices; how far out it lies depends on the size of his income.

3 ■

The consumer will move along this consumption-possibility line until he reaches the highest indifference curve attainable. At this point, the consumption-possi-

bility line will touch, but not cross, an indifference curve. Hence, equilibrium is at the point of *tangency*, where the *slope of the consumption-possibility line* (the ratio of the prices) exactly equals the *slope of the indifference curve* (the substitution ratio or relative-marginal-utility ratio of the two goods).

4 ■

A fall in income will move the consumption-possibility line inward, usually causing less of both goods to be bought. A change in the price of one good alone will, other things being equal, cause the consumption-possibility line to pivot so as to change its slope. In any case, whatever change has occurred, a new equilibrium point of highest satisfaction will be reached. It is a new point of tangency, where the marginal utility per dollar has become equal in every use. By comparing the new and old equilibrium points, we trace out the usual *dd* demand curve.

QUESTIONS FOR DISCUSSION

1. Explain why, since an indifference curve will go through any point on an indifference map, two such curves never cross.

2. If the consumer is at a point on his consumption-possibility line where it crosses an indifference curve, explain why he cannot have reached equilibrium. How will he move?

3. Can *you* generate the ordinary *dd* food demand curve from Fig. 22-10? The *dd* for clothing?

4. Give Robinson Crusoe (or Utopia) a production-possibility curve between food and clothing like the

curve of Chapter 2. Give him the indifference curves like those of this Appendix. Can you depict the basic equilibrium of any economy from the resulting tangency and interpret its price aspects?

5. Review your understanding of the following concepts:
indifference curves or contours
slope or substitution ratio
consumption-possibility budget line
optimal tangency equilibrium:
P_F/P_C = substitution ratio
parallel and pivoted shifts

23 Competitive Supply

COST OF PRODUCTION WOULD HAVE NO EFFECT ON COMPETITIVE PRICE IF IT COULD HAVE NONE
ON SUPPLY. JOHN STUART MILL

The last chapter looked behind the market demand curve for its base in terms of the marginal utilities of individuals. It showed how the demand curves of the different individuals in the market place can be summed to form the aggregate market demand schedule.

In this chapter we look behind the supply curve of the industry to find its base in the costs of the different competitive firms. A new concept—that of "marginal" or "extra" cost—is seen to be crucial.

We are interested in competitive supply not merely as a descriptive device. Here in this chapter, we are also interested in showing that the marginal cost concept has a crucially important role to play in appraising how efficient or inefficient any particular price and production pattern is. (We leave to the following chapter a detailed view of the different kinds of costs that are important in economics.)

■ SUMMING ALL FIRM SUPPLY CURVES TO GET MARKET SUPPLY

Figure 22-1 showed how we add horizontally all individual demand curves to get the aggregate market demand curve. The same applies to supply.

Suppose we are dealing with a competitive market for fish. How much of this commodity will be brought to market at each different level of market price? Firm A will bring so much to market at a particular price; Firm B will bring so much at this same price; Firm C will bring the amount shown on its supply curve; and so it goes. The total Q that will be brought to market at a given market P will be the sum of all the q's which firms will want to supply at that price. And similarly at any other price.

■ *Summary.* To get the aggregate *SS* supply curve for a good, we must add horizontally the *ss* supply curves of the independent producers of that good.

This is illustrated for two firms by Fig. 23-1. Recall that the firms' momentary-run supply curves are defined as the inelastic supplies in a time period so short that no variability in output is possible:

To get market supply curve, we add all firms' supply curves:

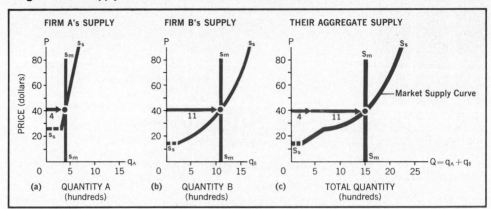

FIG. 23-1. At each price, such as $40, we add quantities supplied by each firm to get total market quantity supplied. This applies to any number of firms. In fact, if there were a thousand identical firms, the market supply curve could be made to look just like the supply curve of each firm by a careful thousandfold change of horizontal scale in the third diagram; if no horizontal scale change is made, aggregate supply must look flatter than each firm's.

■ To get the industry's vertical momentary supply curve $S_m S_m$, add horizontally, at the same P, all firms' vertical momentary supply curves.

Now recall from Chapter 20 (page 369) that Marshall's short run is defined as that period of time in which the firm is stuck with certain fixed commitments, but in which some variable factors of production can be altered so as to produce more output along the various firm's supply curves:

■ Again, to get the industry's short-run supply curve $S_s S_s$, add horizontally at the same P the short-run supply curves of the fixed number of firms which exist in that short run.

Our problem is to see how a firm's supply curve is determinable from its costs.

■ HOW TO DETERMINE MAXIMUM-PROFIT COMPETITIVE SUPPLY

It is evident that costs are vital determinants of how much a firm will be willing to supply. It would supply nothing if market P were too low to cover its out-of-pocket expenses, and would supply much if P were very high. To decide how much to supply at each market P, the firm will want to know the *extra* cost to it of each extra unit of q. Thus, consider Firm A in Fig. 23-1, which is shown supplying 4 (hundred) units at a market price of $40 per unit. Why does $q = 400$ and not 401 or 399?

At first you might be tempted to reply: "Firm A has no choice but $q = 400$ because that is all it can sell at $40—no more, no less." What is wrong with such an answer? It overlooks the fact that this is a model of *perfect competition*.

■ *Definition:* A perfect competitor is too small and unimportant to affect the market price. Like a wheat farmer, he is a "price taker" who can sell *all* he

Marginal or extra cost can be shown numerically by subtraction:

(1) QUANTITY PRODUCED, q	(2) TOTAL COST TC	(3) MARGINAL COST MC
399	$15,960.05	
		$39.95
400	16,000.00	
		40.05
401	16,040.05	

TABLE 23-1. TYPICAL CALCULATION OF MAR-GINAL COST. The difference in total dollar cost from producing an extra unit is found by subtracting adjacent items of total dollar cost in Column (2). At $q^* = 400$, $MC = \$40$ to a high degree of approximation.

wishes to at the ruling market price. In terms of elasticity of demand, a perfect competitor faces a (virtually) horizontal dd demand curve for *his* product—his elasticity of demand being infinite.[1]

Granted that a perfect competitor can sell any q he chooses at the going P, how does he pick his best q supply response? A perfect competitor picks the quantity he will supply by referring to his marginal cost curve, so that $P = MC$. Why? He will do this because he is interested in maximizing the total profit he can earn. Profit is the difference between the total revenue he receives from selling his output and the total cost incurred in producing that output. He increases his total profit so long as the *extra* revenue brought in from the last unit sold is greater than the *extra* cost which that last unit entailed. Total profit reaches its peak—is maximized—when there is no longer any extra profit to be earned by selling extra output. The last little unit he produces and sells is just in balance as far as extra revenue and extra cost are concerned. What is that extra revenue? It is price per unit. What is that extra cost? It is marginal cost.

Specifically, in Fig. 23-1(a), why might you choose to produce quantity $q^* = 400$ at $P = \$40$? Only one answer is correct: Because the 401*th* unit would involve you in extra (or so-called "marginal") cost of just over $40; and the 399*th* unit involved you in extra cost of just under $40; so that the 400*th* unit of q involves an *extra* or *marginal cost* just exactly equal to price P of $40.

Table 23-1 shows how we calculate marginal (or extra) cost: By subtracting the $16,000 total cost of producing $q^* = 400$ units from the $16,040.05 total cost of producing $q = 401$, we find $MC = \$40.05$ for producing 1 more unit beyond q^*; to produce 1 less unit involves a difference of $MC = \$39.95$, or $\$16,000 - 15,960.05$. So at

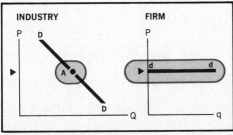

FIG. 23-2.

[1] Figure 23-2 shows the contrast between the industry demand curve DD, relating P to the sum of firm demands $Q = q_1 + q_2 + \cdots$, and the dd curve facing any one small competitor. If there are thousands of firms in the industry, the draftsman will have to train a microscope on point A of the industry DD curve to show how this sloped curve will reappear as the horizontal dd curve to the Lilliputian eye of the firm.

q^* itself we may, by disregarding the trifling differences caused by the trifling lumpiness of units, make the estimate $MC = \$40$.

■ *Definition:* Marginal Cost at any production level q is the total cost of producing one extra unit more (or less);[2] it comes from subtracting total dollar costs of adjacent outputs.

■ DIMINISHING RETURNS AND INCREASING MARGINAL COSTS

Why can you expect Marginal Cost to be ultimately a rising curve? This takes us back to the law of diminishing returns of Chapter 2, pages 23 to 26. Behind the dollar costs of the firm lies the production relationship between the firm's output and the labor and other inputs it hires. This will be discussed in depth in Chapter 27, but here we can indicate the general logic of the situation.

Suppose some factor is held fixed in the short run we are considering: it could be fixed land or, in manufacturing, it could be fixed plant capacity. Suppose that we get our varying amounts of q by hiring varying amounts of some input such as labor. If we can always buy labor at the same wage per unit, the only reason why our marginal or extra costs of getting more q should rise would be because the extra product added by each successive unit of labor is going down. Hence, if we do get diminishing returns to the varying labor factor, we shall certainly get increasing Marginal Cost.

■ Costs and productivity returns are merely opposite sides of the same relationship.

■ THE IMPORTANT MARGINAL COST CURVE

Just as we can calculate MC for $q^* = 400$, we can calculate it for any and every q. Table 23-1 put a microscope on cost behavior around 400 and 401 units. To see the big picture,[3] let us stand off and see how the Marginal Cost curve behaves at *all* levels of output.

Figure 23-3 shows that Marginal Cost is related to Total Cost in the same way that Fig. 22-3, page 418, related marginal utility to total utility. From Fig. 23-3(b), you will see this:

■ *MC* tends to be U-shaped: ultimately it is rising, even though there may be an initial phase in which *MC* is falling.

We can test our understanding of all this by asking why MC is U-shaped. Why does MC often decline at first, as shown in Fig. 23-3(b)? Recall that the law of diminishing returns tends *ultimately* to hold: at the beginning, it might be negated by a strong

---

[2] *Warning: MC* is usually *not* the same as average cost per unit, which we get by dividing total cost by number of units produced: *MC* is extra cost, or incremental cost, or differential cost; or, as we have seen from the use of the word "marginal" in connection with *extra* utility, the appropriate name is indeed Marginal Cost.

[3] Figure 23-3 and Table 23-2 measure q in units of hundreds; hence, $q = 300, 400, 401, 500$ in Table 23-1 would show here as $q = 3, 4, 4.01, 5$, etc.

Marginal Cost is to Total Cost as marginal utility is to total utility:

(1) OUTPUT (IN HUNDREDS) q	(2) TOTAL COST TC	(3) MARGINAL COST MC
0	$ 55	
		$30
1	85	
		25
2	110	
		20
3	130	
		30
4	160	
		50
5	210	

TABLE 23-2. CALCULATING MARGINAL COST. To find the MC of producing the fifth unit, we subtract $160 from $210 to get $50. At $P = 40, it will not pay to produce the fifth unit, but it will pay to produce the fourth unit. (Compare this table with marginal utility Table 22-3 on page 418.)

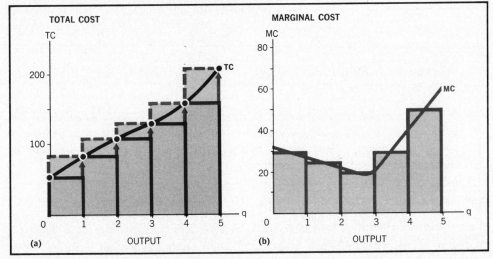

FIG. 23-3. In (a) a smooth curve has been drawn through the points of TC. In (b) a smooth MC curve has been drawn through the steps of extra cost. Ultimately MC is rising, but it may at first fall, giving the curve a U-shaped contour.

tendency toward increasing returns, owing to the economies of large-scale production associated with indivisibility of the productive process and the chance to introduce more elaborate division of labor as scale expands. If at first we have *increasing* returns, we must at first have *declining* rather than increasing Marginal Cost.[4]

[4]It is instructive to examine the behavior of Marginal Cost in the long run. Suppose we consider so extended a period of time that nothing can be regarded as fixed. Old plants can wear out and be replaced. New plants can be designed and built. Old land obligations can expire. New land contracts can be made. And so forth. In the long run we may be able to buy *all* the factors of production in balance at unchanged prices. Now what will happen to long-run costs, particularly long-run MC, if the firm has no fixed factors and can enjoy "constant returns to scale"? (This is defined as a state

Profit-maximizing competitor has supply curve determined by Marginal Cost:

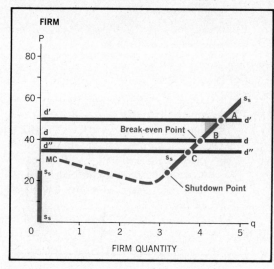

FIG. 23-4. If you can sell all you wish at *P* given by horizontal *d'd'*, your Maximum-profit equilibrium comes at its intersection with the *MC* curve at *A*: your maximum profit is positive; and the green-shaded triangle shows you would lose some profit if you produced less than at *A*, since your extra revenue of *P* would exceed your extra cost, *MC*.

If *P* dropped to *d''d''* level, you maximize profit at *C*: *P = MC* there minimizes your unavoidable short-run loss. If *P* falls below Shutdown point, your revenue fails to cover out-of-pocket expenses and you will shut down. If *P* is at Break-even point *B*, your maximized profit (inclusive of normal return to your labor and capital) is just zero: new firms will not enter, and old ones will not leave.

We can summarize the relationship between the productivity laws of returns and the laws of Marginal Cost:

■ A tendency for varying factors to show diminishing returns when applied to fixed factors implies a tendency for *MC* to be rising. If at first there is increasing returns, there will at first be declining *MC*—ultimately to be followed by diminishing returns and increasing *MC*.

■ DERIVING THE FIRM'S SUPPLY CURVE FROM ITS *MC* CURVE

We say that a competitive firm is at its Maximum-profit position when it is definitely producing all units with *MC* less than *P*, and is not producing further units for which *MC* is definitely greater than *P*. Evidently, its equilibrium of maximum profit comes when it follows the rule

Price = Marginal Cost   or   *P = MC*

This means that the firm's supply curve is given by its rising *MC* curve as shown in Fig. 23-4. Thus, at the indicated horizontal *d'd'* level of $50, the firm will find its Maximum-profit supply response at the intersection point *A*. (To check this, note that the loss of profit from producing a little less than at *A* is shown by the green-shaded triangle, depicting the surplus of *P* over *MC* on the last little units.)

---

where there is no reason for diminishing returns to operate, since *all* factors grow in balance, and where all economies of large-scale production have already been realized.) *Answer:* If long-run constant returns to scale holds, then doubling all inputs will exactly double their total dollar costs and will at the same time exactly double total output. Hence, there will be constant Marginal Cost, *MC* being horizontal rather than rising or falling. (See page 459 of Chapter 24 for the long-run envelope cost curves.)

Alternatively, suppose the firm were faced by a horizontal *dd* at $40. Its Maximum-profit supply response is shown at the intersection point *B*. It happens, as our original cost Table 23-1 shows, that the firm just breaks even, covering all its long-run costs at this point.

Or suppose the firm faced *d"d"*. At this price below $40, the firm cannot break even; but it does *minimize its short-term losses* there at the *C* intersection with the *MC* curve (as you can show by penciling in a green-shaded triangle like that at *A*).

■ Thus, we see that the firm's rising *MC* curve does indeed constitute its competitive supply curve.

■ TOTAL COST AND SHORT-RUN SHUTDOWN CONDITIONS

Recall that earlier the "short run" was defined as that period of time in which certain equipment, resources, and commitments of the firms are fixed; but it is a period long enough for the firm to vary its output by hiring more or fewer variable factors of production, such as labor, raw materials, and so forth. It is certainly not a precise period of time which will be the same for all industries. Even within an industry, we can be asking questions about "short-run" periods of different duration. At one ultrashort extreme, so many decisions have already been frozen as to make the resulting Marginal Cost curve practically a vertical and inelastic line. Or at the other extreme, we can permit so much time to pass as to let more and more of the equipment have a chance to wear away or be replaced, thereby making the resulting Marginal Cost curve almost as flat as it will be in the longest run when *no* fixities are possible except those associated permanently with the management of the firm itself.

Now consider a firm making its short-run decisions. It has a certain "fixed cost": this is defined as the total of costs that will go on anyway because of its fixed commitments that are already frozen in the short run; examples would be bond interest, rentals, overhead salaries, franchise taxes, and so forth. The rest of its "total cost" is called "variable cost": this is defined as the sum of all costs that vary with output; examples are cost of materials, wages for workers on the production line, and so forth. Chapter 24 will discuss all these in detail.

But now consider the firm facing lower and lower *P*. It always has the option of producing nothing at all. How much will it then lose? With its revenue zero and all its fixed cost going on anyway, its shutdown loss will exactly equal its fixed cost. When *P* falls so low as to give it less revenue than the variable cost it incurs from producing positive *q*, the firm will prefer to shut down completely: why should it produce if that means it incurs loss greater than its fixed cost, as will most certainly be the case when *P* has fallen so low as to bring it revenue less than the variable cost it must expend? So the following rule holds:

■ *Shutdown point.* At the critically low market price, where the firm just recovers its variable cost by producing, it will be on the verge of shutting down. Below that point, it will produce nothing at all.

Above that *P*, it *will* produce along its short-run Marginal Cost curve. For, at such $MC = P$ points, the firm will be getting something toward covering its fixed cost; and either it will be getting maximized positive profits, or at least will be minimizing its losses (and in that sense maximizing its profit).

The location of the Shutdown point was shown in Fig. 23-4. The MC curve continues down below that point, but it does not correspond there to a supply curve.

■ TOTAL COST AND LONG-RUN BREAK-EVEN CONDITIONS

Once I am stuck with certain fixed cost commitments, I will be willing to produce in the short run along my MC curve above the Shutdown point—even though I am not earning enough to cover *all* my costs. But only at some higher point on my MC curve will I be earning enough to cover *all* the costs that have to be met if I am to stay in business after the short run is over and I have regained my long-run freedom (1) to renew my old commitments or (2) to move to another industry.

There is, then, a critical "Break-even point" below which *long-run P* cannot remain if I am to stay in this business. If every other firm were exactly like me, the long-run supply would dry up completely below this critical Break-even level which covers all costs of staying in business.

Now let us suppose further that entry into the industry is absolutely free in the long run, so that any number of firms can come into the industry and manage to produce in exactly the same way and at exactly the same costs as the firms already in my industry. Under such conditions of free "replication," it is obvious that long-run P cannot remain above this same critical Break-even point at which they all cover their long-run total costs—including in these (1) all labor, materials, equipment, taxes, and other expenses; (2) all wages payable to the identical managers at the level determined competitively by the bidding in all industries for people of such talents and industriousness; and (3) the interest yield that any of them could get on the amounts of capital that they tie up in this industry instead of investing it elsewhere.

■ Long-run Break-even condition: This comes at a critical P where the identical firms just cover their full competitive costs. At lower long-run P, firms would leave the industry until P had returned to the critical equilibrium level; at higher long-run P, new firms would enter the industry replicating what existing firms are doing and thereby forcing market price back down to the long-run equilibrium P where all competitive costs are just covered.[5] Thus

$P = MC$ = minimum competitive costs, the long-run equilibrium condition

---

[5] If investors tend to be overoptimistic and repeatedly produce an oversupply in the industry so as to create permanent losses on the average, full competitive costs might be defined compatibly with such chronic losses resulting from repeated miscalculations. [WARNING: The full competitive costs to which both P and MC get equated in the long run will be seen, in Chapter 24, to be average (or unit) costs. Average cost will be defined as Total Cost divided by the number of q units produced, and it corresponds to the man in the street's rough notion of costs. Although average and marginal costs will be shown in the next chapter to be related, they are not at all the same thing. Only at the long-run Break-even point, where average cost is at a minimum, will it be found to equal MC. Figure 24-1(b), page 455, will show this to be no coincidence (and also will show that the Shutdown point comes at the bottom of the U-shaped "average variable cost" where that just equals MC).]

■ IMPLICIT- AND OPPORTUNITY-COST ELEMENTS: A DIGRESSION

It is important to stress that the "full competitive minimum costs" which have to be just covered by normal price include more than accountants usually include in costs. Economists include a normal return to management services, as determined competitively in all industries; and a normal return to capital, as determined competitively everywhere by industries of equal riskiness. In the above sense we may say that "normal profits" are included in costs and that "excess profits" are competed away by entry of new firms, and "abnormal losses" are eliminated by long-run exit of firms.

IMPLICIT-COST ELEMENTS   The return to a factor of production is economically important regardless of how it happens to be owned. To the economist, the returns that go to factors of production owned by the firm itself are so important as to deserve a new name: in contrast to wages that are *explicitly* paid to outside labor, we defined the concept of "implicit wages" as the return to the labor provided by the owner himself; and similarly, implicit rent and interest would be the returns to the land and capital provided by the owner himself rather than hired from outside owners.

Through miscalculation, a person may fail to receive his implicit wages in the short run; on the other hand, he may in the short run be getting more than the needed implicit return, the difference being a transient profit that has not yet been competed away. If he owns some special factors of production, like rich ore land, exceptional know-how, or fertile soil, his accounts may show a high return even in the long run, but we realize this is not so much profit as a return to that special factor of production he is lucky enough to own.[6]

OPPORTUNITY-COST ELEMENTS   Related to the above discussion is an even broader notion about cost. The man in the street can clearly recognize costs that are actual cash payments; the accountant must go well beyond that. But the economist goes even further. He realizes that some of the most important costs attributable to doing one thing rather than another stem from the *foregone opportunities* that have to be sacrificed in doing this one thing. Thus, Robinson Crusoe pays no money to anyone, but realizes that the cost of picking raspberries can be thought of as the sacrificed amount of strawberries he might otherwise have picked with the same time and effort. This sacrifice of doing something else is called "opportunity cost." Note that it exists even if he loves to spend that hour in doing both kinds of picking and recognizes not the slightest disutility or sweat in performing that type of work.

How does this apply to industry supply and the firm's Break-even costs? In this way: The long-run Break-even level of costs includes, in addition to explicit cost outlays, those implicit costs that accrue to factors which might otherwise be used in alter-

---

[6]If he happens to own very fertile land and persists in cultivating it by uneconomical methods, he will be paying for his folly or stubbornness by foregoing the high return such land is capable of yielding; in dollars, the land becomes worth more to others than to him, and if he refuses to rent or sell it, he is as surely spending his sustenance to please his own tastes as he would be doing if he sold the land and spent the proceeds on wine, song, or being a country squire. A young person with high IQ and versatile talents who stays in a dull dead-end job or dying industry is similarly squandering his economic potential.

native ways. If my labor in wheat could have been used in rye or even in some other man's wheat patch, then its value in those uses has to be met[7] or I shall not continue to supply it to my own wheat patch. For these reasons, full competitive cost intimately involves opportunity cost. The latter is an important concept, which covers much more territory than does the notion of implicit costs. The prices of labor and other factors that competitive farmers in an industry are forced to pay out explicitly depend importantly on the foregone opportunities for use in other industries or for leisure; and this means that all competitive costs involve opportunity costs in the background.

The terminology of economists is not uniform in this connection, but the concept of opportunity cost is important and we shall run into it again and again.

■ LONG-RUN INDUSTRY SUPPLY AND FIRMS' BREAK-EVEN POINTS

Now we can return to the behavior of industry supply as firms can enter or leave the industry. We resume the story begun in Fig. 23-1's short run. Figure 23-5(b) pictures industry's long-run supply in relation to the supplies of firms—actual firms and *potential* firms.

Figure 23-5(b) shows the long-run horizontal supply curve $S_L S_L$ that would result if we can postulate conditions of replicability and absolutely free entry at precisely the level of the firm's Break-even point in Fig. 23-5(a), which is essentially a reproduction of Fig. 23-4. This horizontality also depends on a postulate that should now be made explicit: It assumes that this industry (1) is very small compared with the total of other industries, or (2) uses *all* the factors of production (land, skilled and unskilled labor, and so forth) in proportions very near to those of the rest of the economy that is contracting as this industry is expanding. Both of these assumptions assure that expansion of this industry (and contraction of other industries) does not significantly alter the prices of any of the productive factors that the identical producers (and potential producers) are using in this industry—so that even a vast increase in demand for this industry will leave all our cost curves unchanged.

If this additional postulate were not made, the long-run expansion of this industry as more firms come into the market and as each firm expands its output would produce an increase in the market prices of those factors of production that are in peculiarly heavy use in this industry. (EXAMPLE: If wine production were much expanded, those special hillsides needed for vineyard production could not be drawn away from other uses at constant rental rates.) What would be the effect upon the $S_L S_L$ supply curve when an increase in industry Q raises the prices of those factors of production peculiarly important in this industry? It would certainly be to *shift upward* the marginal and other cost curves of the new and old firms. And the final result would be that the long-run supply curve of the industry will slope upward from the horizontal.

---

[7] The *best* alternative use is of course the proper one to use in reckoning opportunity cost. If alternatives exist along an infinite and smooth continuum, such opportunity cost will set a tight limit on costs to this industry. If alternatives come in steps, then the next-best alternative may give us only a lower limit on factor-price, leaving a possible area in which it has to be determined by the "rent" analysis of Part Four.

Short-run and long-run industry supply depends on firms' costs:

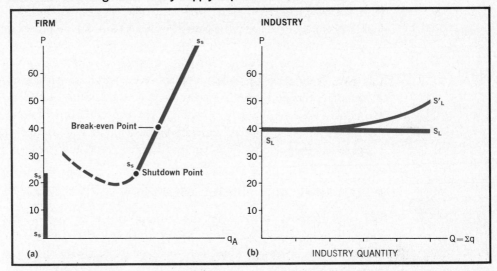

FIG. 23-5. With details omitted, Fig. 23-4 is shown again here in (a). In (b) the industry supply curve is shown. With entry and exit free and any number of firms able to produce on identical unchanged cost curves, the long-run SS curve will be horizontal at each firm's Break-even level. If industry cannot attract all the factors it uses at unchanged factor-prices, the $S_L S_L'$ supply curve will have to slope upward as each firm's cost curves are all shifted upward.

The law of diminishing returns is likely to become involved in the increasing-cost case.[8] As discussed in Chapter 2 and on page 370, if the sizable industry needs a specific factor—say, able seamen—more intensively than do the rest of industries, expanding its Q will put special upward pressure on that factor's relative price. To be sure, the scarcity of this factor can be partially compensated for by adding other factors to it. But remember what happens when the industry has to add variable factors to a relatively fixed one. They experience diminishing returns. The industry gets less from them, and that sends its long-run costs up. That this industry's $S_L S_L'$ curve is upward-sloping comes from the fact that expansion of its Q relative to other industries' outputs makes its factor-costs (and therefore its price) rise relative to theirs, fulfilling the expectation implied by the curvature of the production-possibility frontier of Chapter 2.

The relative rise in this industry's P and in its peculiar-factors' prices is a fact, but it also can be termed a desirable fact. Why? Not because the consumers who must pay more for this good are undeserving, nor because owners of the peculiarly scarce productive factors are especially deserving of higher incomes. Then why? Because any expansion of Q ought to be accomplished *efficiently* with least possible sacrifice of other Q's: the especially scarce factors have now to be severely rationed and be given more of other factors to work with; this will come about, not by a planning board's edict, but by a rise in the prices of this good and its peculiar factors, which will both signal the news of what must be done for efficiency and actually induce people to make the substitution needed if society is not to be inefficiently inside its *p-p frontier*.

---

[8] The discussion here concerns the *industry* level and does not merely repeat the earlier analysis relating the firm's rising MC to its short-run experience of diminishing returns. Even if each small firm had horizontal long-run MC, when *all* firms expand, their factor prices will rise and thereby *shift up* each MC curve, thereby causing the industry to travel up the $S_L S_L'$ curve.

It will be noted that in industries where $S_L S_L'$ slopes upward, owners of mines, land, know-how, and any other productive factors peculiar to this industry will earn a higher income (or what will be called "rent") from those factors as the industry's output expands.

If you do not like their earning such an extra return, you might take some of this away from them by taxes or other devices. But any special price ceilings placed on them in order to keep them from reaping such a return will definitely interfere with the equality-of-marginal-cost condition that is needed for maximal social efficiency—and such egalitarian legislation should be passed only if no better way of achieving this purpose can be found and the game is deemed worth the candle it will cost.

■ DECREASING COSTS AND THE BREAKDOWN OF PERFECT COMPETITION

Economic textbooks of years ago used to supplement the cases of horizontal supply and upward-sloping supply by a third case in which Marginal Costs of the firms were falling rather than rising and in which this was thought to create an industry long-run supply curve that sloped gently downward. Actually, if we review our argument of page 440 telling us why a maximizing firm will want to produce where $MC = P$, we find that the argument *fails completely* in the case where the firm's MC curve is a downward-sloping one. For if you move to the right of a point on a falling MC curve, you find that your additional P per unit is in excess of the now lower MC; and so in the case of decreasing Marginal Cost, the firm will expand its output more and more beyond the MC curve to gain extra profit.

Under decreasing Marginal Cost, the first firm to get a head start will find its advantage increasing the greater it grows. As it forces other firms to contract their q's, their disadvantage will become aggravated as they are forced to travel back up their falling MC curves.

The result must be obvious:

■ **Under persisting decreasing costs for the firms, one or a few of them will so expand their q's as to become a significant part of the market for the industry's total Q. We shall then end up (1) with a single monopolist who dominates the industry; (2) with a few large sellers who together dominate the industry and who will later be called "oligopolists"; or (3) with some kind of imperfection of competition that, in either a stable way or in connection with a series of inter-mittent price wars, represents an important departure from the economist's model of "perfect" competition wherein no firm has any control over industry price.**

As this chapter's Appendix will show, when the firms in this industry all expand together, they could create what are called *external economies* (or *diseconomies*). Thus, a school for fishermen might become feasible only at high industry Q; and this training might cause a downward shift of every firm's cost curves as the industry total Q rises. The result could be an industry $S_L S_L$ curve that slopes downward due to *external* economies. But this does not deny the fact that ("internally") decreasing cost for a firm destroys perfect competition.

■ A FINAL WORD ON EFFICIENCY OF MARGINAL COST PRICING

A coldly objective scientist, who wanted to know nothing beyond how to describe and analyze competitive supply behavior and who had not the slightest interest in society's welfare, would consider the Marginal Cost concept extremely important. But what about a person who was concerned also with human happiness and with the social efficiency of a pricing system? He would find the equating of price to Marginal Cost even more interesting. His deeper studies would prove the following remarkable truth:

■ Only when prices of goods are equal to Marginal Costs is the economy squeezing from its scarce resources and limited technical knowledge the *maximum* of outputs. Only when each source of industry output has had its rising *MC* equated to *any* other source's *MC*—as will be the case when each *MC* has been set equal to the common *P*—can the industry be producing its total *Q* at *minimum Total Cost*. Only then will society be out on its production-possibility frontier and not inefficiently inside the frontier.

This equal-marginal-cost dictum is as applicable to a communist, socialist, or fascist society as it is to a capitalistic society. Unless wheat cultivation has been pushed in different parts of the Soviet Union so as to equalize Marginal Costs (including transportation), the planners there will be failing to achieve the abundance of wheat and other goods that could be theirs with more efficient allocation of resources. (Perhaps it is not surprising to learn from reading the recent debates in their own economic journals that they are gradually becoming aware of this basic fact of logic and economics.)

Treatises on welfare economics give rigorous proofs of this rule and indicate the exceptions that might arise when its basic premises are not valid. Here it is desirable merely to sketch the nature of the reasoning needed to establish this optimality conclusion. The reasoning proceeds as follows:

Suppose industry output was being produced so that there was greater Marginal Cost from one firm or source and less from another. Then surely it would pay us to cut back a little on the high-marginal-cost source and instead produce that extra little from the low-marginal-cost source. Why? Because we could thereby save for the industry or society the divergence between these Marginal Costs. So we do the transferring, and now reexamine the situation. If the *MC*'s are still unequal, we repeat the process. The final outcome is at a position where *MC*'s for a commodity are equal from every source. Then we are at equilibrium with *minimum Total Costs* for society, since no longer can we save money by taking advantage of *MC* divergences.

Although the foregoing reasoning is couched in terms of money, it can be reworded to apply to the saving of labor, sweat, horsepower, scarce minerals, or anything else. It even applies to a firm deciding how to allocate its total *q* among its different plants. It applies to a varying or fixed number of firms.

Because Marginal Cost has this optimality property, it can with some care be used as a yardstick to detect inefficiency in any institutional setup. Thus, if perfectly competitive industries did not exist at all, or if they were rarer even than they are today, one would still derive great benefit from defining and studying the concept of Marginal Cost.

This completes our discussion of competitive supply. The Appendix deals with further aspects of cost and supply: so-called "external economies and diseconomies"; and efficient *MC* pricing for peak loads. And at this point, the many cases of competitive supply and demand given in Chapter 20's Appendix could be fruitfully restudied or be studied for the first time.

SUMMARY

1 ■

In a competitive market, aggregate supply of a group of independent firms comes from adding horizontally their separate supply curves. When the number of firms is variable, as in the longer run when new firms can enter the industry and old ones leave it, we must take account of such changing numbers in the adding process.

2 ■

The short run is defined as that period of time in which some of the firm's productive factors and costs are fixed and some are variable. For a firm we can define Marginal Cost as its extra or incremental cost of producing an extra unit of output, and can compute the instantaneous rate of Marginal Cost at each output from a smoothed schedule or graph of costs.

3 ■

Trends of costs and of productivity returns are reverse sides of the same coin: when the law of diminishing returns ultimately holds, the *MC* curve ultimately rises; when there is an initial stage of increasing returns, *MC* initially falls; if *all* factors of production could be brought in balance at unchanged prices and output were to then show constant returns to scale, long-run Marginal Costs could be horizontal forever.

4 ■

A perfectly competitive firm is defined as one which is able to sell all it wants to at the posted market price. To maximize its (algebraic) profit, it will move along its (horizontal) demand curve until it reaches its rising Marginal Cost curve. At this intersection, $MC = P$, and the firm is maximizing its profits or minimizing its losses. So the industry supply curve from a given number of firms will come from adding horizontally their relevant Marginal Cost curves.

5 ■

Out-of-pocket costs (or avoidable, variable costs) must be taken into consideration in determining a firm's short-run "Shutdown point." Below some critical P the firm will not even be recovering in price revenues the variable cost that could be saved completely if it shut down; so rather than end up losing more than its fixed cost, it will shut down and produce nothing at lower P's.

In the long run all the commitments of the firm will expire, and it will decide to stay in business only if price at least covers all its long-run costs—whether they be actual out-of-pocket payments to labor, lenders, material suppliers, or landlords; or whether they be "implicit" wages (defined as the "opportunity costs" of its owners'

and also in diagrams:

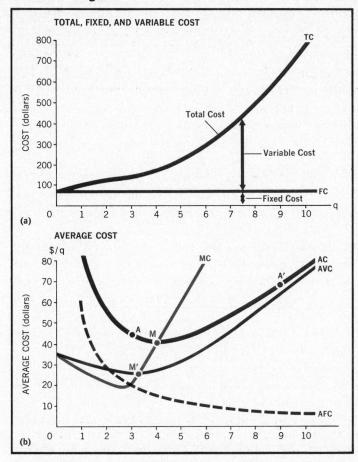

(a)

TOTAL, FIXED, AND VARIABLE COST

COST (dollars)

Total Cost

Variable Cost

Fixed Cost

TC

FC

(b)

AVERAGE COST

$/q

AVERAGE COST (dollars)

MC

AC
AVC

A'

A M

M'

AFC

FIG. 24-1(a). The total Fixed Cost curve is horizontal by definition. Adding on top of it the rising total Variable Cost gives the rising Total Cost curve.

FIG. 24-1(b). The green curve of Marginal Cost falls and ultimately rises, as in Chapter 23. *MC* is shown as a smooth curve after the steps of incremental cost are smoothed out; the numbers from the smooth *MC* curve are given in white in Column (5) of Table 24-1 (and correspond to the slope of Fig. 24-1(a)'s *TC*).

By dividing *TC* by *q*, we can plot Average Cost: $AC = TC/q$. *AFC* comes from FC/q, and *AVC* comes from VC/q. At any point, we can add these two brown curves and also get the *AC* curve at that point.

Note that *MC* intersects *AC* at *AC*'s minimum. This is no coincidence. To the left of *M*, *MC* is less than *AC* and hence is pulling *AC* down. To the right, $MC > AC$ and hence is pulling *AC* up. At the *M* minimum point, $MC = AC$; hence *AC* is horizontal there, being neither raised nor lowered by the equivalent *MC*. Also, *MC* cuts the *AVC* U at its bottom.

between any two outputs is the same as the jump in *VC*. Why? Because *FC* stays constant at $55 throughout and cancels out in any such comparison. (Fill in by subtraction the missing *VC* data of the third column.)

■ *Definitions.* "Total Cost" represents lowest aggregate dollar expense needed to produce each level of output *q*. *TC* rises as *q* rises.

"Fixed Cost" represents the total dollar expense that goes on even when a zero output is produced. It is often called "overhead cost" and usually includes contractual commitments for rental, maintenance, depreciation, overhead salaries and wages, etc. It is a sunk cost that is quite unaffected by any variation in *q*; in the time period for which it is sunk, the only rule is this: Disregard Fixed Cost because *FC* cancels completely out of every decision.

"Variable Cost" represents all items of *TC* except for *FC*—as, for example, raw materials, wages, fuel, etc. Always, by definition,

$$TC = FC + VC$$

(Note that *TC* and *VC* always show exactly the same increments as *q* changes, because *FC* is a strict constant.)

Figure 24-1(a) shows the rising *TC* curve, broken down into its constant *FC* and rising *VC* components.

■ MARGINAL COST AGAIN

We saw in Chapter 23 how Marginal Cost is defined as the increment of Total Cost that comes from producing an increment of one unit of *q*. (Recall that "marginal," whether applied to utility, cost, or anything else, always means "extra" in economics.)

The green *MC* numbers in Column (5) of Table 24-1 come from subtracting the adjacent *TC* numbers in Column (4). Thus *MC* is $30 in going from 0 to 1 unit of *q* (i.e., $85 − $55 = $30).

MC is seen to be $110 − $85 = $25 in going from *q* = 1 to *q* = 2. *MC* is $20 for the third unit of *q*, $30 for the fourth, and thereafter rising steadily until it is shown as $150 in going from *q* = 9 to *q* = 10. (What is it in going from *q* = 5 to *q* = 6? Pencil in your answer in green.)

Instead of getting *MC* from the *TC* column, we could as easily get the *MC* number by subtracting each *VC* number of Column (4) from the row below it. Why? Because Variable Cost always *grows* exactly like Total Cost, the only difference being that it must —by definition—start out from 0 rather than from the constant *FC* level. (Check that 30 − 0 = 85 − 55, and 55 − 30 = 110 − 85, ...)

Figure 24-1(a) and (b) shows the behavior of Total Cost (in brown) and Marginal Cost (in green). Note that the *q* axes of the graphs are just lined up so that the eye can see the correspondence between *TC* and *MC*.[2]

This example shows *MC* to be U-shaped—at first falling, but ultimately rising. We saw why on page 438: At first there may be great economies in using some or all of the productive factors on a larger scale; and so *MC* at first falls down to a minimum positive

---

[2] As on page 438, we have assumed that units can be made indefinitely small, so that the smoothed-instantaneous *MC* values can be plotted and read off to give the white numbers of Table 24-1, Column (5). To help understand the smoothed-instantaneous *MC* at a point *q*, see Fig. 24-2 below. It helps to clarify the distinction already mentioned between *MC* as an increment of cost for a finite step

between two points of *q*, and *MC* as a smoothed-out instantaneous rate depicting the tangential slope at which *TC* is rising at one given *q* point. The distance from *a* to *b* represents one extra unit of output. The distance from *b* to *a'* represents the resulting increase in Total Cost, which is the first and simplest definition of incremental Marginal Cost. The second definition is given by the slope of the Total Cost curve at point *a*—and what mathematicians call $d(TC)/dq$—or what is the same thing numerically, by the distance from *b* to *c*. In the limit, as the size of the extra units becomes small and we reexamine the ratios in the new smaller triangle, the discrepancy between the two definitions becomes relatively negligible. (I.e., $ba' \div bc$ approaches one.)

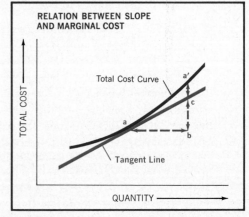

RELATION BETWEEN SLOPE AND MARGINAL COST

TOTAL COST

Total Cost Curve

Tangent Line

QUANTITY

FIG. 24-2.

number before again rising. If we stick to the short run where some factors of production are fixed, ultimately the old law of diminishing returns will operate to reduce the extra product that comes from adding equal physical and dollar increments of the varying factors on to the fixed factors. So the cost of getting extra product will ultimately become more expensive, and the short-run curve of Marginal Cost will ultimately be rising.

Marginal Cost has many uses. We saw in the last chapter that the rising MC curve of the firm provides us with the rising short-run ss supply curves which we sum horizontally to get the industry's short-run SS supply curve. In the next chapter we shall see that the firm will find its Maximum-profit equilibrium by nicely balancing its extra cost against its extra revenue (i.e., by finding an intersection of its Marginal Cost curve and what will be defined as its "Marginal Revenue" curve).

■ AVERAGE, OR UNIT, COST

But first turn to Column (6) of Table 24-1. This gives Average Cost (per unit), which is simply the Total Cost divided by the number of q units produced.

$$\text{Average Cost} = \frac{\text{Total Cost}}{\text{output}} = \frac{TC}{q} = AC$$

In Column (6), when only 1 unit is produced, Average Cost has to be the same as Total Cost, or $85/1 = $85. But for $q = 2$, $AC = TC/2 = $110/2 = 55, as shown. Note that Average Cost is, at first, falling lower and lower. (We shall see why in a moment.) But AC reaches a minimum of $40 at $q = 4$, and then slowly rises.

Figure 24-1(b) gives a careful plotting of U-shaped AC, nicely arranged below the TC it came from. We can now break down Average Cost into its two components, fixed and variable. Earlier we had the breakdown of TC into FC and VC. By dividing each of the last two by q, we get Average Fixed Cost, $AFC = FC/q$ of Column (7); and Average Variable Cost, $AVC = VC/q$ of Column (8).

AVERAGE FIXED COST   Since total Fixed Cost is a constant, dividing it by q gives in Column (7) a steadily falling Average Fixed Cost curve. The brown-dashed AFC curve in Fig. 24-1(b) looks like a unitary demand curve, or hyperbola that approaches both axes: it drops lower and lower, approaching the horizontal axis as the constant FC gets spread over more and more units. If we allow fractional and zero units of q, AC starts infinitely high, as the finite FC is spread over tinier and tinier units of q.

AVERAGE VARIABLE COST AVC of Column (8) and Fig. 24-1(b) at first falls and then ultimately rises. We could have predicted this U-shaped behavior of AVC from the U-shaped behavior of MC. When MC at first falls, each new q is pulling down the Average Variable Cost calculated over all the items.

THE POINTS OF MINIMUM AVERAGE COST   Figure 24-1(b) is an important economic diagram. Fix it on your eye's retina. Note particularly the typical U shape of the AC curve.

The AC curve is always pierced at its minimum point by the rising MC curve. This is no coincidence. And now we can explain why this has to be the case.

Competitors are in long-run equilibrium where price equals minimum average cost:

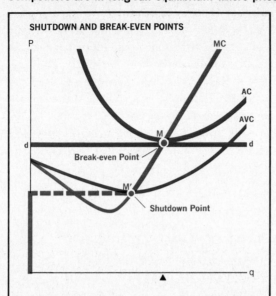

FIG. 24-3. The Break-even point is at *B* where *dd* is tangent to *AC* and *AC* is at its minimum. The short-run Shutdown point is similarly at the bottom of the *AVC* curve.

■ Any average curve is pulled downward when *MC* is less than *AC*: if the last increment of cost is less than the average of all previous ones, it must pull the average down! But when *MC* gets as big as *AC*, *AC* no longer is pulled down; it now turns sideward or level. Then, if *MC* rises above the *AC*, it must of course pull *AC* up. So at the point where rising *MC* = *AC*, and only at that point, shall we find the point of minimum *AC*.[3]

■ *Summary.* So long as Marginal Cost is below Average Cost, it is pulling Average Cost down; when *MC* gets to be just equal to *AC*, *AC* is neither rising nor falling and is at minimum *AC*; after *MC* is above *AC*, it is pulling *AC* up. Hence:

At bottom of U-shaped *AC*,   *MC* = *AC* = minimum *AC*

Likewise, the *MC* curve cuts the *AVC* curve at the bottom of its U, pulling it down before this point because *MC* < *AVC* and pulling it up beyond that point because *MC* > *AVC*.

Now that we know how the *MC* curve intersects the *AC* and *AVC* curves where their U's bottom out, we can describe exactly how the firm's Shutdown and Break-even points of Fig. 23-4, page 440, had been determined. The Break-even point of long-run no-profit competitive equilibrium is seen here in Fig. 24-3 to be at the bottom of the U-shaped *AC* curve, in accordance with

P = *MC* = minimum *AC*, in long-run equilibrium

Likewise, the Shutdown point would come at *M'*, once the horizontal *dd* of the firm

---

[3]Here is an explanation of the *MC* and *AC* relationship in terms of college grade averages. With *MC* below *AC*, Average Cost keeps being pulled down by the lowered cost of the final unit—just as one's cumulative grade average is pulled down when one's incremental average in the junior year is less than one's cumulative average up to that time. Only when one's "marginal or current" grade average crosses above or below one's cumulative grade average will the latter reverse its direction.

In the long run, a firm can choose its best plant sizes:

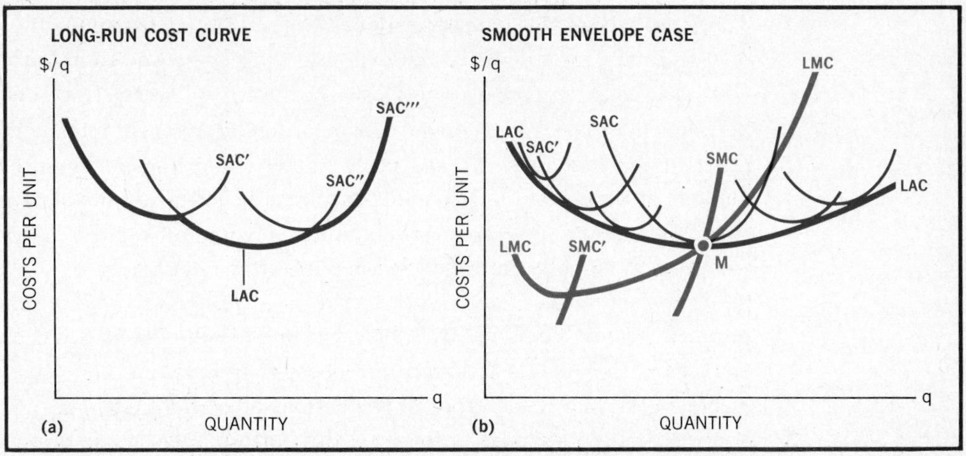

FIG. 24-4. In the long run, the firm can alter its plant size and number of plants. In (a) its *LAC* is the brown "envelope" or lower frontier of the three possible choices of plant. In (b) there is an indefinite number of choices and we get *LAC* as a smooth brown envelope. In the usual manner we can derive from the brown *LAC* curve its green marginal curve, *LMC*.

had fallen to a level of *P* so low as to just cover minimum *AVC*. A price below this level would cause the firm to produce zero output.

■ LONG-RUN-PLANNING ENVELOPE CURVE

Industry *Q* was shown earlier to be able to rise in the long run as new firms are added. Similarly, the *q* of any firm can rise in the long run by shifting from one plant size to another or by utilizing multiple plants. Figure 24-4(a) shows the firm's long-run average cost curve as *LAC*, the heavy brown lower limit of its short-run *AC* (*SAC* not *AVC*!) curves. Figure 24-4(b) shows the same lower limit in the case where the firm has choice of infinitely many smooth *SAC* curves: now *LAC* is the U-shaped smooth "lower-envelope" curve; and *its* well-behaved *LMC* provides the firm's long-run Marginal Cost curve, emerging from the *LAC* minimum point with a gentler slope than the short-run *SMC* curve there.

If entry is really free, not only has perfect competition the nice property of ensuring that each firm ends up on an efficient curve and at the minimum point on it, but in addition the Invisible Hand ensures that the industry gets its *Q* from the proper number of firms as some are squeezed out or attracted in.[4]

---

[4] If indivisibilities require that $Q = nq^*$, where q^* is the optimal quantity each firm should produce at the bottom of its U, and if *DD* is large enough to make *n* so large that we can ignore the ratio $[(n + 1) - n]/n$, then it can be proved that the no-profit no-loss condition of ruthless competition will achieve n^*, the most efficient number of firms to minimize *TC* for the industry's *Q*. For why force more expensive extra output from an existing number of firms if it can be got cheaper by replication of firms? And why not be sure that each of the identical firms produces neither too much nor too little, instead producing that Break-even *q* where $P = MC$ and where likewise *P* equals the lowest Average Cost per unit that will keep the firm in business in the long run? (There are certain problems connected with the discreteness of firm sizes that will be discussed in Fig. 24-5.)

■ TASKS ACCOMPLISHED AND TASKS YET TO COME

The main task of this chapter is done. The important concepts of cost have been introduced: Total Cost, and its breakdown into total Fixed and total Variable Costs; Marginal Cost; all the different Average Costs (per unit), *AC*, *AFC*, and *AVC*; the interrelations between marginal and average concepts, including their intersection at the minimum point of the U-shaped average curve; finally, long-run envelope cost, *LAC*, when the number of plants and all elements can be adjusted to the level of production.

We are now prepared to handle the Maximum-profit equilibrium of Chapter 25's complete monopoly. And then in Chapter 26 we can go on to consider such important patterns of imperfect competition as the case of oligopoly and of sellers of differentiated products whose numbers are great because of the freedom of anyone to enter the market. Such analysis is important because it helps us understand and appraise the inefficiencies that result from imperfections of competition—and to formulate goals of antitrust policy designed to improve the performance of the mixed economy.

But before we leave the analysis of cost, we must note how *different patterns of cost and returns crucially affect the viability of perfectly competitive markets;* and how the pattern of costs relative to the pattern of interrelated demands must crucially determine the type of market structure prevailing in the real world.

■ COST PATTERNS AND STRUCTURE OF MARKET IMPERFECTION

At the end of Chapter 23 we saw that decreasing cost is incompatible with perfect competition. If every, or even *any*, firm in an industry could always bring down its Marginal and Average Cost in the long run merely by expanding its output q, it would soon expand to become an important fraction of the industry. In short, it would expand to become some kind of monopolist, ceasing to be a price taker and now having some measure of control over the price it gets. As soon as it has control over price, it will cease to follow the $P = MC$ rule for profit maximization. (Chapter 25 will show why.) And as soon as somebody in the system raises Price above Marginal Cost, a critic is able to find a flaw of inefficiency in the economic organization of society.

Figure 24-5 illustrates some patterns of costs which lead to a breakdown of perfect competition. In Fig. 24-5(a) the firm is shown to have Average and Marginal Costs that fall forever. It displays "increasing returns to scale": as q grows, the firm finds more elaborate ways of specializing its equipment; it organizes its work gangs in larger and more efficient units; it can afford ever larger boilers and machines, which display greater net efficiency. All this without end. No matter how big is the demand for its product—no matter how far out the industry *DD* curve happens to lie, the most efficient operating size for this one firm will be greater, and peaceful competitive coexistence of thousands of price takers will be quite impossible.

Perhaps the pattern of unlimited decreasing cost is unrealistic. Perhaps *ultimately* the economies of scale will all have been achieved, and the cost curves will level out or turn up. Figure 24-5(b) illustrates such a case: the firm's long-run *MC* and *AC* curves do finally turn up. But, alas, they do not turn up soon enough to avoid the breakdown of perfect competition. For note where the industry total demand curve *DD* now lies:

To avoid monopoly, costs must turn up soon:

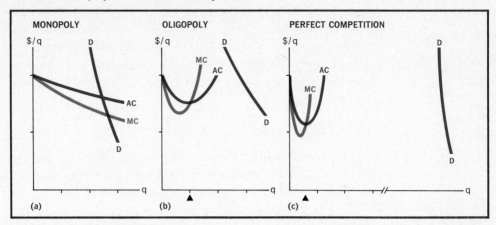

FIG. 24-5. When costs fall indefinitely, as in (a), any one firm can expand to dominate the industry. In (b) costs eventually turn up, but not soon enough relative to total industry demand *DD*. Coexistence of numerous perfect competitors is impossible; some kind of few-seller oligopoly is likely. In (c) total industry demand *DD* is so vast relative to efficient scale of any one seller as to permit viable coexistence of numerous perfect competitors. [What if firms contrive to differentiate their product in (c), fragmenting the market and moving *DD* far to the left, ending up in some kind of Chamberlinian imperfect competition—like (b) or (a)?]

it does not provide a big enough market to enable *numerous* firms to coexist at the efficient level of cooperation called for by the indicated cost curve. We shall still end up in some kind of monopoly (or few-seller oligopoly) situation.

In Fig. 24-5(c), the outlook is more favorable for perfect competition. Why? Because the industry *DD* is so great compared with the optimum size of each firm, we can hope to replicate the large number of firms needed for truly perfect competition.

As Adam Smith said, "Specialization is limited by the extent of the market." He meant by this that you often cannot use the most efficient known methods when serving a *small* market. And this provided him with good ammunition for attacking the mercantilistic interferences by governments of his time that served to fragment the *DD* demands into many smaller *DD* demands—one for each country or county. He might have gone on to add this:

> If you are *still* in the stage where efficient specialization is being limited by the extent of the market, then you are not yet in the state appropriate for perfect competition; instead, not-yet-exhausted economies of scale leave you in some area of imperfect or monopolistic competition. In such a case there is all the more reason for society to promote measures that will extend the market.

One more important point. Suppose we begin in the Fig. 24-5(c) situation where *DD* is large enough relative to the efficient size of firm operation to permit coexistence of numerous viable competitors. But suppose something arises to fragment the aggregate *DD* demand into much smaller separate demands for the different firms. Then perfect competition will be dethroned. Since the new *DD* curve confronting any firm or segment of the market will be moved far to the left, we are really back in Fig. 24-5(b) or even 24-5(a).

Such a case arises when restrictive tariffs are used to fragment markets and create a monopolistic situation. "The tariff is the Mother of trusts," is a slogan from American history showing that even the man in the street understands the point. And one of the purposes of the Marshall Plan for reconstructing Europe was to help create the Common Market, so that *DD* curves would become large enough relative to efficient production levels to promote vigorous and effective competition.

■ DIFFERENTIATION OF PRODUCTS

What is not so obvious is that the *DD* demand curves for an industry can be deliberately fragmented into smaller segments by the profit-seeking activities of firms. This is what Harvard's Edward Chamberlin called "differentiation of product."

CONTRIVED PRODUCT DIFFERENTIATION   Each seller tries to make his product a little different from that of any other sellers. He avoids the price competition of classical "perfect competition." Instead, he introduces brand quality competition, precisely because it is a profitable form of imperfect competition.

> EXAMPLE: He makes his cider more sour (or more sweet). He advertises to make you think his cider is different, whether or not it is; or more important, he advertises so that you will attach significance to such differences as are there.

What is the result when everybody successfully differentiates his product? The result is that the *DD* curves of Fig. 24-5(c)'s model of perfect competition are moved so far to the left as to become like those of the models of monopoly or oligopoly shown in Fig. 24-5(a) and (b). Fortunately, each firm is not able at will to differentiate its product successfully to any degree that it wishes.

Chamberlin would agree with much that has been said here. But he would resent the implication that all product differentiation is an artificial, contrived thing whose only purpose is to increase monopoly power and bilk the consumer. Rather, he would insist that people's tastes differ: different people want different degrees of sourness of cider; and even the same person may not want all his units of cider to be of the same sourness. Creating a great variety of differentiated products is often, Chamberlin insists, a genuine catering to basic human wants and needs. Chamberlin does not agree that we would be better off if we all agreed to wear a few basic styles of clothes, each of which is produced in long and efficient factory runs.

In effect, Chamberlin is reemphasizing the importance of decreasing costs in making perfect competition unviable. He is saying, "Once we replace a homogeneous output Q of the industry (or what is the same thing, the homogeneous output q of a typical firm) by a whole complex of somewhat different $Q_1, Q_2, \ldots$, then the demands will just not be big enough to permit you to have many different producers at the bottom of their efficient U-shaped cost curves." Chamberlin is arguing, "You think that as *DD* grows in Fig. 24-5(b), with population or for any other reason, society will move from the imperfect-competition model of (b) to the perfect-competition model of (c). But you are wrong. With the bigger scale of *DD* will come a bigger opportunity for making more, and more minute, differentiations of product."

NATURAL PRODUCT DIFFERENTIATION   Even if we do not agree with Chamberlin's implication that the world is perpetually assigned to the realm of imperfect competition regardless of increases in scale, we must concede that he does have a valid and important point. His general *Weltanschauung*—that the economic world cannot be properly understood in terms of the simple models of perfect competition or complete monopoly, but must be interpreted in terms of a richer theory that involves phenomena not to be described as mere blends of these polar cases—is made more convincing by the following considerations:

■ Products are often differentiated by natural as well as man-made causes. Space itself, and the transport costs associated with it, provides one important example.

Consider the steel industry. It involves very large-scale production. Yet this is a big country. So you might argue that we can tolerate numerous replications of the most efficient-sized plant. But what follows? The United States does not constitute one single market for steel. Because of transport costs, each region and each part of each region provide us with relevant *DD* curves to compare with the efficient large-scale U of cost. It would be ridiculous to think that even New York City could have the dozens or hundreds of independent integrated steel producers needed for the market model of perfect competition.

Similarly with electric-power production. In order to reach minimum Average Cost, one might today want to build a generating plant of more than 2 million kilowatts of capacity. But that efficient size is already much too big for perfect competition to prevail. Any *compact region* that had ten such competing plants would be plagued with dreadful overcapacity.

We may conclude as follows:

■ Patterns of returns in which costs still decline relative to the effective size of the market imperil the realism of perfect competition and of $P = MC$ efficient social pricing. This problem is accentuated by man-made or natural differentiations of product which lower the effective *DD* levels of demands relative to the bottom of the U levels of efficient production, making competitive coexistence of numerous competing units simply nonviable.

We now realize the importance of Chapter 25's discussion of monopoly, and Chapter 26's treatment of antitrust policy and of other patterns of imperfect competition.

SUMMARY

1 ■

Total Cost can usefully be broken down into its Fixed and Variable Cost components. *FC* cancels out of all decisions relevant to the period for which it is truly fixed.

2 ■

Marginal Cost is the increment of Total Cost resulting from one increment of q. (If our units are divisible, *MC* can be defined as the slope of the smooth *TC* curve at any q point, since this slope gives a close approximation to the extra cost of producing one more small q increment.)

3 ■

Average (total) Cost, AC, is the sum of ever-declining Average Fixed Cost and of usually U-shaped Average Variable Cost. AC is U-shaped, being intersected at its bottom by the rising MC curve. Similarly, AVC is cut by MC at its bottom.[5]

4 ■

In the long run, when all fixed commitments expire and a firm is free to plan to operate any number of plants, the long-run cost curves LTC and LAC must represent the lower-envelope frontier of best choice of plant for each level of ouput. This frontier will be a smooth envelope, containing at any point a tangential short-run cost curve, if potential plant sizes are smoothly continuous. Usually the long-run curve LAC, and its associated marginal curve LMC, will be U-shaped: ultimately it will rise if not all factors of production (including management) are expandable at constant prices; and at very small outputs, indivisibilities in the inputs or the methods of combining them will cause costs initially to fall.

5 ■

Market structure—perfect competition, monopoly, few-seller oligopoly, etc.—always depends crucially on the behavior of costs. Unless total market demand DD is very large compared with efficient bottom-of-the-U scale of production, coexistence of numerous perfect competitors will not be viable. As Chamberlin points out, man-made and natural causes of product differentiation constantly threaten fragmentation of DD market size, and hence point up the importance of antitrust policy and of analysis of patterns of imperfect competition.

QUESTIONS FOR DISCUSSION

1. Make a list of cost elements: wages, salaries, fuel, rentals, etc. Divide them into the Fixed and Variable categories.

2. Explain the difference between Marginal Cost and Average Cost. Why should AFC always look much like MC? Why is MC the same when computed from TVC as from TC?

3. To the \$55 of Fixed Cost of Table 24-1, add \$90 of additional FC. Now calculate a whole new table, with the same VC as before but new FC = \$145. What happens to MC, AVC? To TC, AC, AFC? Can you verify that minimum AC is now at $q^* = 5$ with $AC = \$60 = MC$? (You can check MC and TC of your table against Chapter 25's Table 25-3.)

4. Explain why MC cuts AC and AVC at the bottom of their U's. Recall, in connection with the last chapter, that minimum AVC can be shown to provide the short-run Shutdown point, and minimum AC to provide the long-run Break-even point.

5. Explain how the long-run envelope cost curve is defined as the lower frontier of all short-run curves. Illustrate with (a) the case of a few plant sizes, and (b) the case of infinitely continuous plant sizes.

6. Relate the rising MC curve to the law of diminishing returns. Contrast the falling part of the curve with that law.

[5] See no. 8 in the Questions for Discussion section for useful rules about AC and MC curves.

7. Review the reasoning which shows that decreasing cost imperils the perfection of competition. Summarize in your own words the Chamberlin argument, which claims differentiation of product lowers the relevant *DD* relative to the bottom-of-the-U level of efficient operation, thereby jeopardizing perfect competition.

8. Extra-credit Problem: With the help of the adjoining diagram, puzzle out the meaning of the following rules. *First Rule:* If a Marginal Cost curve is below its associated Average Cost curve, it is pulling the *AC* curve down; if *MC* is above *AC*, it is pulling *AC* up; if *MC = AC*, *AC* must be horizontal. *Second Rule:* If *AC* is a straight line, as in (a), (b), or (c), *MC* will be a straight line starting from the same vertical intercept point but with twice the slope of *AC*. (Note: This tells us how to find the *MC* point above or below the *AC* point on *any* non-straight-line *AC* curve. At a chosen *q* in (d), merely draw the tangent straight line to *AC*; from that line's vertical intercept, draw an *MC* line with twice the slope; read off from this last line the *MC* value at your chosen *q* level. Of course, you must draw two new straight lines for every different *q* level.)

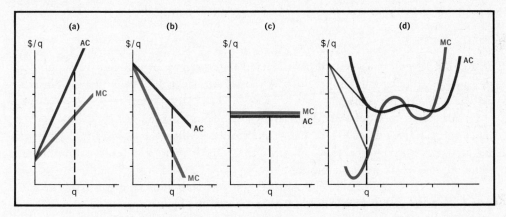

9. Can you connect the following reasoning with footnote 1 at the beginning of this chapter? Technologists tell the firm that it can produce *q* = 2 units by using much land and little labor *or* by using much labor and little land. It must therefore have taken into account the market prices of land and labor services and have come up with the lowest-expense production decision. That least-cost total is shown in the *q* = 2 row as $110. So Table 24-1 was drawn up on the assumption that factor-prices are known and constant: if they all went up, Total Cost in every row would go up; more than that, if land's rent rose relative to labor's wages, the accountants would tell the engineers to economize on the use of land by substituting labor for it wherever possible. (What if the technologists found a way of producing the same *q* with less factor inputs? You will realize that this would lower the *TC* cost numbers in Table 24-1 and shift down the *TC* curve in Fig. 24-1.)

10. Review your understanding of the following concepts:

Total Costs: Fixed and Variable

$TC = FC + VC$

$AC = TC/q = AFC + AVC$

Marginal Cost (incremental and smoothed)

long-run envelope of cost, *LAC* and *LMC*

increasing cost and diminishing returns

decreasing cost and market imperfection

product differentiation: man-made, natural

25 Equilibrium of the Firm: Profit Maximization under Monopoly

BOTH MONOPOLISTIC AND COMPETITIVE FORCES COMBINE IN THE DETERMINATION OF MOST PRICES. EDWARD H. CHAMBERLIN

In the last several chapters we have studied the workings of competitive supply and demand in considerable detail. For the most part, we have been studying the case called "perfect competition."

Perfect competition means something very definite to the economist. As we saw, the economist means by it something *much stronger* than the man in the street and the businessman do when they talk of "strong rivalry and keen competition among different business firms and industries."

The special case of perfect competition is very important. But it is only one case, and economists pay it so much attention because of the light it throws on the *efficiency* of resource use. Certainly, it cannot faithfully represent many of the facts about modern industries. The real world—as we know it in America, Europe, or Asia—contains significant mixtures of monopoly imperfections along with elements of competition. The real world, then, is for the most part to be classified in the realm of "imperfect competition": it is neither perfectly competitive nor perfectly "monopolistic."

The remaining chapters of Part Three, therefore, will give us the tools to analyze imperfect as well as perfect competition. They will show what modifications have to be made in any conclusions that were based on an analysis of perfect competition. We shall see that the way a pricing system succeeds in solving the basic problems of WHAT, HOW, and FOR WHOM is affected to an important degree by any elements of monopolistic imperfection that may be involved in numerous modern industries.

Part A of this chapter gives an overview of patterns of imperfect competition and of real-world market structure. It also presents a new important tool—the concept of marginal revenue. Part B portrays the equilibrium analysis of an idealized monopoly firm, to show how it achieves maximization of profit by balancing its marginal cost and marginal revenues. We then are ready to appraise at the end of this chapter the inefficiency inherent in imperfection of competition, and to develop in the Appendix the principles of public regulation.

466

A. OVERVIEW OF MARKET STRUCTURE AND THE CONCEPT OF MARGINAL REVENUE

■ PERFECT COMPETITION CONTRASTED WITH IMPERFECT COMPETITION

Figure 25-1(a) reminds us that, to an economist, a perfect competitor is defined as a firm that has no control over price—in the sense that it faces an essentially horizontal *dd* curve along which it can sell as much or as little output as it likes.

Remember how strict this definition of perfect competition is. Think of any commodity that comes to mind: razor blades, toothpaste, steel, aluminum, potatoes, wheat, cigarettes, tobacco, nylon, cotton. Which fit in with our strict definition? Certainly not razor blades or toothpaste or cigarettes. Who ever heard of an auction market for blades, toothpaste, or cigarettes?

Neither aluminum nor steel meets the definition of perfect competition. For a long time there was only one aluminum company, Alcoa (Aluminum Company of America); and even today there are only Alcoa, Reynolds, Kaiser, and one or two others. Contrast this with the case of thousands, if not millions, of cotton and wheat farmers.

What about steel? United States Steel and Bethlehem are the industry giants. Together with Republic Steel, Jones & Laughlin, and the few others that constitute Little Steel, they produce a large fraction of the total market. It is true that one plant's steel output may be much like another's, but it is not true that Bethlehem and Republic are so weak that each could never depress the price of steel by throwing on the market as much as it could comfortably produce.

When you go down the list, you will find that only potatoes, tobacco, wheat, and cotton come within our strict definition of perfect competition. Nylon must compete with cotton; that is very true. But in the economist's strict sense, nylon is not a product supplied under "perfect competition," nor is each of its few producers a "perfect competitor" in the economist's sense of the term.[1]

[1]Sometimes economists use various synonyms for perfect competition: they often call it "pure competition," in contrast to "impure, or imperfect, or monopolistic competition"; or they occasionally call it "atomistic competition," to convey the notion of numerous small firms which combine like a multitude of tiny atoms to make up the industry. Occasionally, too, an economist will say: "By perfect, I mean really perfect. The wheat market isn't 'perfect competition' unless everyone in it is perfectly *informed* about all the future, there being nowhere any *uncertainty*." However, that is not the sense used here for perfect competition. The price of wheat will fluctuate in a

The acid test for imperfect competition is slope of firm's demand:

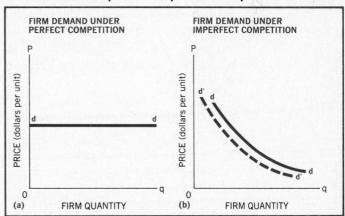

FIG. 25-1. The perfect-competitor firm can sell all it wants to along its horizontal *dd* curve, never depressing market price. But the imperfect-competitor firm will find that its demand curve slopes downward as its increased *q* forces down the *P* it can get. And unless it is a sheltered monopolist, a cut in its rivals' *P*'s will appreciably shift its own *dd* leftward to *d'd'*.

■ IMPERFECT COMPETITION DEFINED

But suppose the single firm finds itself facing a demand curve which slopes appreciably downward as in Fig. 25-1(b)—which means that when it insists on throwing more on the market, it definitely does depress price along its *dd* curve—then the firm is classified by the economist as an "imperfect competitor."

> ■ *Definition:* "Imperfect competition" prevails in an industry or group of industries wherever the individual sellers are imperfect competitors, facing their own nonhorizontal *dd* curves and thereby having some measure of control over price. (This does not mean that a firm has absolute monopoly power over the price it can charge; as we shall see, there are varying degrees of monopolistic imperfection in different imperfectly competitive markets.[2])

Mind you, we are not saying that the owner of an imperfectly competitive firm is of poor character, that he beats his wife, or fails to pay his bills. Nor does the fact that a firm is an imperfect competitor mean that it is not keenly seeking to outsell and outadvertise its rivals. Intense commercial rivalry and "perfect competition" are not at all the same thing; indeed, Farmer Jones, perfect competitor, will do no advertising at all. Why should he? He can sell all the wheat he can produce without depressing market price. But American Tobacco Co., producer of Lucky Strike cigarettes and an imperfect competitor, will spend much of its energies in trying to outsell Chesterfield, the snuff industry, and even the candy industry.

■ IMPERFECT COMPETITION: MONOPOLY, OLIGOPOLY, AND DIFFERENTIATED PRODUCTS

MONOPOLY How imperfect can imperfect competition get? The extreme case would be that of a *single* seller with practically complete monopoly power. (He is called a "monopolist," from the Greek word *mono* for "one" and *polist* for "seller.") He is the only one producing in his industry, and there is no industry producing a close substitute for his good. (In Fig. 25-1(b), a change in another firm's price would shift his *dd* curve negligibly.)

Exclusive monopolies, like public utilities or telephones, are usually regulated by the government; and even they must usually take account of the potential competition

---

way that no one can now foresee, but as long as no seller can appreciably influence wheat price, we shall agree to call the wheat market perfect. (Naturally, once you bring government control programs into the wheat picture, as in Chapter 21, you are bringing monopolistic imperfections into this perfect-competition setup.)

[2] The standard book on all this is E. H. Chamberlin, *Theory of Monopolistic Competition* (Harvard University Press, Cambridge, Mass., 1963, 8th ed.). Chamberlin prefers the term "monopolistic competition" for what is here called "imperfect competition," but that may give the impression to the layman that there is something especially nasty, or illegal, in not being a perfect competitor, which is not Chamberlin's view. Also, confusion can result from the fact that "monopolistic competition" is sometimes used as a name for Fig. 26-3's special large-group case of symmetric sellers of differentiated products, a nomenclature avoided in this book.

of alternative products—oil for gas, or cables for telephones. This shows how relatively unimportant complete monopolies are.

OLIGOPOLY   This horrible-sounding word means "few sellers" (and comes from the Greek *oligos,* meaning "few"). Oligopolists are of two types.

First, an oligopolist may be one of a *few* sellers who produce an *identical* (or almost identical) product. Thus, if A's steel is much the same as B's, then the smallest price difference will drive the consumer from A to B. Neither A nor B can be called a monopolist. Yet, if the number of sellers is few, each has a great effect on market price.

This first kind of oligopoly is thought to be common in a number of our basic industries where product is fairly homogeneous and size of enterprise is large—as in the aluminum and nylon industries. Another example would be that of moving freight between New York and Chicago by any of the three or four alternative rail routes. In the old days when rail rates were unregulated, there would be periodic price wars in which each railroad undercut the other in an attempt to gain more of the business: sometimes it would become cheaper to move freight from New York to Chicago than to move it from New York to Buffalo; and occasionally it might be cheaper to move freight from New York to Buffalo via Chicago, with all the implied wasteful cross-haulage.

The second kind of oligopoly is typified by the case where there are *few* sellers who sell *differentiated* (rather than identical) products. The Big Three in the auto industry are examples: three producers dominate the industry, but the Fords, Chevrolets, and Plymouths that they make are somewhat differentiated products. In the cigarette industry, a few large sellers own the numerous brands and types (filter, king-size, and regular) that compete for and get the bulk of the business. In heavy machinery, such companies as General Electric, Westinghouse, Allis-Chalmers, and others illustrate the case of an oligopoly that has few sellers and some differentiation of product.

MANY DIFFERENTIATED SELLERS   This is the last in our list of imperfect competitors. Here there are many sellers, but now they do *not* produce *identical* products as in the case of many perfect competitors. Instead, they produce "differentiated products," i.e., products which differ somewhat in real qualities or which the buyer thinks differ in real qualities. My toothpaste is a little different from yours; and if I raise my price above yours, I may still hope to sell a good deal to those consumers conditioned by my advertising or by past use of my product.

Advertising, brand names, trademarks, patents, and custom may explain why there is product differentiation. Or it may merely be that a given barber shop or grocery store is in a locality near to certain consumers: the fact of this nearness may give it a measure of monopoly power; and yet, if its price gets too high, it will find itself losing trade to more distant competitors. (In Fig. 25-1(b), when your rivals cut their *P,* your *dd* curve shifts downward appreciably.)

All these categories of market structure overlap. They range in degree from perfect competition, to a large number of differentiated sellers, to the two kinds of oligopoly, and finally to the limiting case of monopoly.

■ BRIEF SUMMARY OF KINDS OF COMPETITION AND MARKET STRUCTURE

Table 25-1 presents a brief picture of the various possible categories of imperfect and perfect competition. It merits close study, for we shall later examine each of its cases.

The remainder of this chapter will analyze the principles of profit maximization, concentrating mostly on the limiting case of a complete monopoly. As has been mentioned, few firms in real life enjoy anything like a complete monopoly: usually some other products will be partially substitutable for the ones you sell. If for some unnatural reason you were in a position of practically unchecked monopoly, we can be sure that the modern mixed economy would make you subject to public regulation. The example of public regulation of such utilities as electricity, gas, and telephones comes immediately to mind; and by the end of the chapter we shall be in a position to understand the proper principle of monopoly regulation.

The tools useful to understand Maximum-profit equilibrium for the complete monopoly—namely marginal cost and marginal revenue—turn out to be the tools needed

Most industries are imperfectly competitive—a blend of monopoly and competition:

KIND OF COMPETITION	NUMBER OF PRODUCERS AND DEGREE OF PRODUCT DIFFERENTIATION	PART OF ECONOMY WHERE PREVALENT	DEGREE OF CONTROL OVER PRICE	METHODS OF MARKETING
Perfect competition	Many producers; identical products	A few agricultural industries	None	Market exchange or auction
Imperfect competition:				
Many differentiated sellers	Many producers; many real or fancied differences in product	Toothpaste, retail trade	Some	Advertising and quality rivalry; administered prices
Oligopoly	Few producers; little or no difference in product	Steel, aluminum		
	Few producers; some differentiation of products	Autos, machinery		
Complete monopoly	Single producer; single product without close substitutes	A few utilities	Considerable	Promotional and "institutional" public-relations advertising

TABLE 25-1. TYPES OF COMPETITION.

to understand Maximum-profit equilibrium in the more realistic cases of oligopoly and various forms of imperfect competition. They lay the groundwork for study of antitrust policy.

■ PRICE, QUANTITY, AND TOTAL REVENUE

What is the Maximum-profit output q that a monopolist tries to produce in any situation? What is the accompanying Maximum-profit price P that it should charge? It turns out that old and new *marginal* concepts provide the key to the common-sense trial-and-error procedure of maximizing profit. The final results will agree with common sense, after analysis discloses the good sense in common sense.

As far as costs are concerned, all the tools that we shall need have already been developed in Chapter 24's discussion. Here, therefore, we can begin with the sales revenue side of things. From the firm's demand curve dd, we know the relation between P and the q it can sell. Table 25-2 indicates this relationship for a hypothetical firm in Column (2). And Fig. 25-2(a) depicts, in brown, the dd demand curve for this monopolist (who is given, for simplicity, a straight-line demand curve). Column (3) of Table 25-2 shows how to get the firm's Total Revenue by multiplying $P \times q$: thus 0 units bring in $TR = 0$; 1 unit brings in $TR = \$180 \times 1$; 2 units bring in $\$160 \times 2 = \$320$. $TR = P \times q$ always.

Total Revenue at first rises with q, since the reduction in P needed to sell the extra q is moderate in this first elastic range of the demand curve. But when we get to some intermediate point on dd, TR reaches its maximum—at $q = 5, P = \$100$, and $TR = \$500$. Increasing q beyond this point brings you into inelastic demand regions, and now the percentage cut in P needed to sell 1 per cent more q is so much greater than 1 that it cuts down on TR. Figure 25-2(b) shows TR to be dome-shaped, rising from zero to a maximum of \$500 and falling back to zero when P has become vanishingly small.

Already Table 25-2 illustrates an important fallacy: "A firm out to maximize its profits will always charge what the 'traffic will bear.' That means charging the highest possible price." This statement is wrong. A profit maximizer may not be an altruist; but that does not mean he is a fool. To charge the highest possible price is to sell no q at all and to get no TR at all! Even if we reinterpret this doctrine to mean charging the highest price at which anything at all can be sold, it is obvious that selling but one unit even at a high price is not the way to maximize your profit. Even if we neglect (for a moment) all costs, the correct interpretation of charging what the traffic will bear must mean that we find the best compromise between a high P and a high q if we are to get the best profit. In Table 25-2, it is at $q = 5$ that $P \times q = TR$ is at a maximum: this is the point where demand elasticity turns into demand inelasticity.

Before proceeding now to introduce the important concept of Marginal Revenue, we can note the fact that the *price* at which each q is sold could be called *Average Revenue* to distinguish it from Total Revenue. Thus, we get $P = AR$ by dividing TR by q (just as we earlier got AC by dividing TC by q). Verify that if Column (3) had been written down *before* Column (2), we could then have filled in Column (2) by division.

Marginal Revenue numbers come from demand-schedule P and q data, and also

(1) QUANTITY q	(2) PRICE $P = AR = \dfrac{R}{q}$	(3) TOTAL REVENUE $R = P \times q$	(4) MARGINAL REVENUE MR
0	$200	$ 0	+200
			+180
1	180	180	+160
			+140
2	160	320	+120
			+100
3	140	420	+80
			+60
4	120	480	+40
			+20
5	100	500	0
			−20
6	80	480	−40
			−60
7	60	420	−80
			−100
8	40	320	−120
			−140
9	20	180	−160
			−180
10	0	0	

TABLE 25-2. TOTAL AND MARGINAL REVENUE. From demand curve data, Total Revenue is easily computed. To get green Marginal Revenue, we increase q by a unit and calculate the difference in Total Revenue it brings. Note MR is at first positive, but after demand turns inelastic, MR becomes negative. Price never becomes negative, but MR lies below P because of loss owing to the necessity to lower price on previous units if the new unit of q is to get sold. (White data of instantaneous Marginal Revenue come from smoothed MR curve of Fig. 25-2(a).)

■ MARGINAL REVENUE AND PRICE

We need a test to determine whether Total Revenue is gaining or losing as we increase q. Marginal Revenue is the convenient concept for this purpose.

　■ *Definition:* "Marginal Revenue" is defined as the increment of Total Revenue (plus or minus) that comes when we increase q by an increment of one unit. MR is plus when demand is still elastic, minus when demand is inelastic, and just crosses zero when demand turns from being elastic to being inelastic. (If units of q are divisible, the MR steps of Fig. 25-2(a) can be replaced by a smooth MR curve.)

The green numbers of Marginal Revenue are shown in Column (4) of Table 25-2; they are calculated by subtracting the TR we get by selling q units from the TR we get by selling $q + 1$ units, the difference being our extra revenue or MR. Thus, from $q = 0$ to $q = 1$, we get $MR = \$180 - 0$. From 1 to 2, MR is $\$320 - 180 = \$140$.

MR is positive until we arrive at $q = 5$, and negative from then on. That does not mean you are giving goods away at a negative price. Actually, Average Revenue, which is P, continues to be positive. It is merely that, in order to sell the sixth unit of q, you

Marginal Revenue curve comes from demand curve:

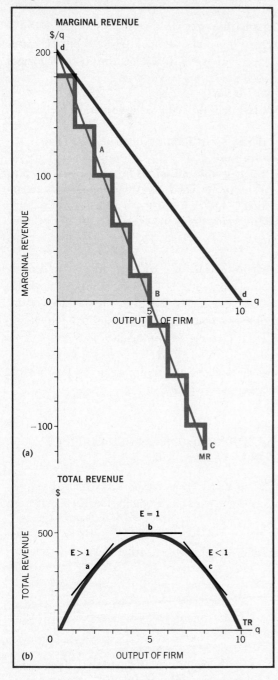

FIG. 25-2(a). The green steps show the increments of Total Revenue from each new unit of output as calculated from Table 25-2 (or from the *TR* of Fig. 25-2(b) below). *MR* falls below *P* from the beginning, actually dropping twice as fast as the straight-line *dd* curve. *MR* becomes negative when *dd* turns inelastic. Smoothing the incremental steps of *MR* gives the green *MR* curve, which in the case of straight-line *dd* will always have twice as steep a slope as *dd*.

FIG. 25-2(b). Total Revenue is dome-shaped, rising from zero (where $q = 0$) to a maximum (where *dd* has unitary elasticity) and then falling back to zero (where $P = 0$). *TR*'s slope gives instantaneous *MR*, just as its jumps give incremental *MR*.

must reduce the price so much on *all* the units as to end up getting less *TR*—which is what the negative *MR* is telling you.

This warns us: Do *not* confuse Marginal Revenue with Average Revenue or Price. The table shows they are different. Review Fig. 25-2(a) and note that the plotted green steps of *MR* definitely lie below the brown *dd* curve of *AR*. *MR* has already turned negative when *dd* is only partway down toward zero.

> ■ Generally, Marginal Revenue is less than the price, as indicated by the fundamental formula
>
> Marginal Revenue of *n*th unit = difference in Total Revenue in going from $n - 1$ to *n* units
>
> = price of *n*th unit minus *loss in revenue* on previous units resulting from induced *P* reduction
>
> In Column (4) of Table 25-2, the white numbers of smoothed *MR* are also seen to be less than Column (2)'s *P*'s.

Only under perfect competition, where the sale of extra units will never depress price at all, is the loss-in-revenue term zero. Only then will Price and Marginal Revenue be identical. Graphically, a straight-line *MR* curve always has twice the steepness of the *dd* curve. But if *dd* is horizontal, as in perfect competition, so then must *MR* be: thus, a perfect competitor's *dd* and *MR* coincide as the same horizontal line!

This completes our analysis of Marginal Revenue and equips us for the task of finding Maximum-profit equilibrium of the firm.

B. MAXIMUM-PROFIT MONOPOLY EQUILIBRIUM: DIVERGENCE OF PRICE AND MARGINAL COST

Now suppose the firm wants to maximize its Total Profit. To do this it must bring in, along with the Total Revenue information it gets from its demand side, the Total Cost information described in Chapter 24.

> ■ *Definition.* Total Profit equals Total Revenue minus Total Cost:
> $$TP = TR - TC = P \times q - TC$$
> To maximize its profit the firm must seek out the equilibrium price and quantity, P^* and q^*, that gives it the largest difference, $TR - TC$. Common sense tells us this will occur only where the firm's extra (or marginal) revenue has just come into balance with its extra (or marginal) cost.

We may now bring all our relevant facts together in a supertable, Table 25-3. Total Profit is, of course, the column of greatest interest in this table.

What quantity q^* will maximize Total Profit, and at what price? The easiest way to solve this problem is to compute Column (5), Total Profit, which is simply the difference between Total Revenue and Total Cost. Running our eyes down this column tells us:

Equating Marginal Cost to Marginal Revenue gives the firm its Maximum-profit output and price:

(1) QUANTITY q	(2) PRICE P	(3) TOTAL REVENUE TR	(4) TOTAL COST TC	(5) TOTAL PROFIT TP	(6) MARGINAL REVENUE MR	(7) MARGINAL COST MC	
0	200	0	145	−145	+200	34	
					+180	30	MR > MC
1	180	180	175	+5	+160	27	
					+140	25	
2	160	320	200	+120	+120	22	
					+100	20	
3	140	420	220	+200	+80	21	
					+60	30	
4	120	480	250	+230	+40	40	MR ≐ MC
					+20	50	
5	100	500	300	+200	0	60	
					−20	70	
6	80	480	370	+110	−40	80	
					−60	90	
7	60	420	460	−40	−80	100	
					−100	110	MR < MC
8	40	320	570	−250			

TABLE 25-3. SUMMARY OF FIRM'S REVENUE, COST, AND MAXIMUM PROFIT. Total and Marginal Cost of production are now brought together with Total and Marginal Revenue. The Maximum-profit decision is where $MR = MC$, with $q^* = 4, P^* = \$120$, and maximum profit $TP = \$230 = \$120 \times 4 - \$250$. (NOTE: For convenience, the white MR and MC numbers are put in to give the smoothed instantaneous values at each q point itself: disregarding these, we could get the same result.)

The optimal quantity is 4 units, with a price of $120 per unit. After taking account of Total Cost, we see that no other situation will give us as much profit as the $230 at $q^* = 4$.

Another way of arriving at the same result is to compare Marginal Revenue, Column (6), and Marginal Cost, Column (7). (MR is computed from the TR column, as in Table 25-2. Recall from the last chapters that MC is similarly calculated from TC.)

As long as a step toward extra output gives us more Marginal Revenue than Marginal Cost, our profit is increasing and we continue to produce more output. But whenever Marginal Cost exceeds Marginal Revenue, we contract output. Where is equilibrium?

■ Maximum-profit equilibrium is where Marginal Revenue and Marginal Cost are equal.

$MR = MC$,   the Maximum-profit point

This second way of finding the optimum point by comparing Marginal Cost and Marginal Revenue is neither better nor worse than the first method of simply examining Total Profits. They are really exactly the same thing.

■ GRAPHICAL DEPICTION OF FIRM'S MAXIMUM-PROFIT POSITION

The curves of Fig. 25-3 illustrate these procedures. In Fig. 25-3(a), MC intersects MR at E, the Maximum-profit point, where $q^* = 4$. We run up vertically from E to the dd curve to G, where $P = \$120$. The fact that G lies *above* F, the point on the AC curve at $q^* = 4$, guarantees a positive profit. (We cannot read directly the amount of Total Profit unless we calculate the area of the shaded rectangle.)

The same story is told in Fig. 25-3(b) with total curves. Total Revenue is dome-shaped. Total Cost is ever-rising. The vertical difference between them is Total Profit, which begins negative and ends negative. In between, TP is positive, reaching its maximum of \$230 at $q^* = 4$, where the green slopes of the TR and TC are equal and parallel: if these MR and MC slopes were pointing inward, we should gain a little extra profit by contracting q. At $q^* = 4$, things are just right. This is verified by the Total Profit curve, whose green slope is horizontal at its peak: TP's slope is clearly the difference $MR - MC$, and this slope should definitely have a zero value at the maximum.

And note this important consequence.

■ *Excess of P above MC.* For the firm with some monopoly power, maximizing profits by equating Marginal Revenue to Marginal Cost leads to a price that is above Marginal Cost. The canny seller *contrives an artificial scarcity of his product* so as not to spoil the price he can get on the earlier premarginal units.

■ PERFECT COMPETITION A SPECIAL CASE OF IMPERFECT COMPETITION

This completes our discussion of Marginal Revenue and Marginal Cost as tools to maximize profit. It will add to your confidence in the result if you find that the general $MR = MC$ rule is consistent, when applied to a perfect competitor, with Chapter 23's $P = MC$ rule for a profit-maximizing perfect competitor. Is it? Yes, indeed. Here is why:

■ For a small perfect competitor, Marginal Revenue works out to be exactly the same thing as price. With no need to cut your P to sell an extra unit of q, the incremental Marginal Revenue it brings you is precisely the P received for that last unit, with no loss on previous units being subtracted.[3] Hence, $MR = MC$ and $P \equiv MR$ do lead to the special rule for profit maximizing by a perfect competitor:
$$P = MR = MC \qquad \text{at a perfect competitor's Maximum-profit point}$$

This completes our survey of how a rational firm will find its maximum-profit equilibrium. The analysis applies to firms under monopoly, oligopoly, or anything else.

■ BYGONES AND MARGINS

While economic theory does not necessarily make you a successful businessman, it does introduce you to some new ways of thinking. Here is one instance.

---

[3] If you redraw Fig. 25-3(a) for a perfect competitor, make dd horizontal and coinciding with MR. Then proceed to find the MR and MC intersection as usual (which gives the old MC supply story of Chapter 23). In the new Fig. 25-3(b), TR merely becomes a straight line, rising from the origin, but the slopes of TR and TC must still match at the Maximum-profit equilibrium point.

Graphs of marginal and total curves show Maximum-profit equilibrium:

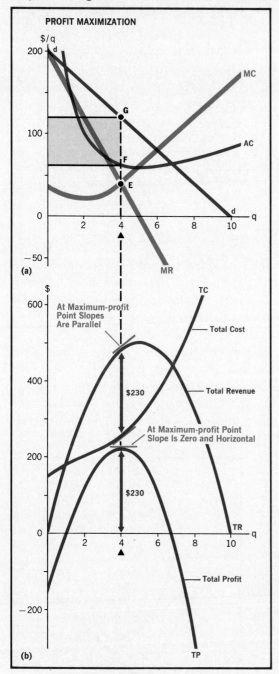

(a)

(b)

FIG. 25-3(a). At E, where MC intersects MR, equilibrium position of Maximum profit is found. Any move from E will lose some profit. Price is at G above E; and since P is above AC, the maximized profit is a positive profit. (Can you understand why the shaded rectangle measures Total Profit?)

FIG. 25-3(b). This tells the same story of maximizing profit as above, but uses total concepts rather than marginal concepts. Total Profit is given by vertical distance from TC up to TR. This is at a maximum where the two curves have equal and parallel slopes, $MR = MC$.

The economist always stresses the "extra," or "marginal," costs and advantages of any decision. He says:

Let bygones be bygones. Don't look backward. Don't moan about your sunk costs. Look forward. Make a hard-headed calculation of the *extra* costs you'll incur by any decision and weigh these against its *extra* advantages. Cancel out all the good things and bad things *that will go on anyway,* whether you make an affirmative or negative decision on the point under consideration.

This disregarding of bygones is extremely important, and most successful decision-makers practice it intuitively, even if they have not had a formal course in economics. Here is an application of this principle:

> The King taxes a monopolist a flat sum for his match-monopoly franchise—say $100 per day, no matter what he does. How will this affect the new Maximum-profit P and q? If you have grasped the tools of this chapter, you will discover that a flat-sum tax will not shift either the *MR* or *MC* curve. If the monopolist successfully maximizes his profits before and after the tax and if nothing else changes and if he stays in business, *the flat-sum tax will have absolutely no effect on price or output,* but will be borne completely by the monopolist! (Can you verify?)[4]

■ HOW IMPERFECTION OF COMPETITION AFFECTS RESOURCE ALLOCATION

In the next chapter we shall study some of the important cases of imperfect competition. This will involve us in important public questions that lie in the field of "antitrust policy." As preparation, let us see again how imperfections of competition affect the efficiency with which a free-price system solves the important problems of WHAT, HOW, and FOR WHOM.

Suppose that, under free pricing, firms do definitely face a sloping demand curve so that their Marginal Revenue is below their price. Then, to the degree that such imperfect competitors intelligently pursue their self-interest, will they still be led by Adam Smith's Invisible Hand to perform the acts needed to promote the general interest?

No, they will not. There is now a flaw in the picture. When a businessman takes account of Marginal Revenue, he is making sure "he will not spoil the market." He is *contriving* to keep his commodity *scarce* lest he depress his own receipts. Naturally, he is not keeping the commodity completely scarce; that would yield him zero revenue. But he is

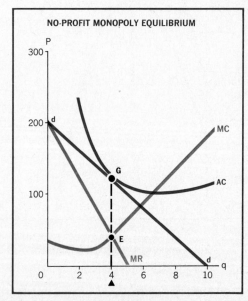

FIG. 25-4.

[4]Suppose the King put a flat-sum tax of $230 on Fig. 25-3's monopolist to wipe out all his profit. The new Fig. 25-4 shows the story. *MR*, *MC*, and *dd* are exactly as before. (Why?) But now *AC* has been shifted up because of the added Fixed Cost. Only at the price of *G*, where the *dd* curve is tangent to the new *AC* curve, can the firm break even: everywhere else it makes a loss; maximizing profit by finding $MR = MC$ now means avoiding loss. (But see the Appendix for a demonstration that taxing away monopoly profit does still leave society with a discrepancy between price, or marginal utility, and Marginal Cost.)

desisting from cutting his price down to his Marginal Cost. Unlike the perfect competitor on the farm who throws all his q on the market up to the point where his MC equals the P he gets, the imperfect competitor holds back enough q to keep his MC at MR, *which is below his P.*

How does this divergence between price and Marginal Cost affect the goodness or badness of the way the economy is organizing its production and distribution? We have already met this complex question, and will do so again.

First, the imperfect competitor may be earning more than he would if the government somehow made him compete like a perfect competitor. If so, is that a good or a bad thing? Is he a more worthy man than most? Is he poorer than most, and more in need? (And will he use his gains to subsidize the arts, or to pay for vulgar display? Will he use any monopoly profits to sponsor new industrial research? Or to sponsor research in ways to convince consumers that his product is better than other firms' product?)

When the man in the street thinks of the monopoly problem, he gives most weight to the above type of questions—to the way it affects the FOR WHOM problem of distribution.[5] Yet, *even if it has no harmful effect on income distribution, imperfection of competition could still represent an important economic evil.*

To see this, imagine that all money votes are distributed properly and that A is the only imperfect competitor in the system. Everyone else is a perfect competitor, who keeps his MC equal to his P. Price is the signal that consumers use to indicate how much they value various goods. Costs, and particularly Marginal Cost, are the indicators of how much of society's valuable resources each good's production utilizes: our scarce land, our sweaty labor, and other resources that could produce other goods. Everywhere else, competitive firms are giving people what they most want and are producing right up to the point of $P = MC$, where goods are shown to be worth what they cost.

But take the imperfect competitor A—the one deviant. What is he doing? A is not forcing people to buy from him. But the fact that A faces a sloping demand curve shows he does have some control over P. How is he using that power? Does he produce goods up to the point where their social cost—as measured by his MC—is equal to what the last unit of the good is worth to society—as measured by market P resulting from consumer money votes? No.

■ The imperfect competitor is contriving to keep things a little scarce. He is contriving to keep P above MC because in that way he sets $MR = MC$ and thereby maximizes his profit. So society does not get quite as much of A's good as it really wants in terms of what that good really costs society of produce![6]

[5] As the next chapter shows, imperfect competition might result in no one's making a profit if there is "free entry" into the Chamberlinian industry in question. Yet P might still stay above MC, and so the result might still be tremendous wastage of resources because we have too many corners with too many gasoline stations, each with too many idle attendants (who in the end are not even well rewarded for being imperfect competitors). To be sure, more gas stations could mean shorter walks for people out of gas and more consumer convenience generally; but who is to say that the optimal amount of such differentiation-of-product convenience is being provided under any particular regime of imperfect competition?

[6] As Fig. 20-9, page 380 showed, it is a social inefficiency when monopolists' outputs are too small and competitors' outputs get expanded beyond their optimal amounts.

Do not think A is a villain. If he did not intelligently try to maximize his firm's profits, he might be displaced by the stockholders or be sued. Even if A owned the company and chose to lower P to MC, he would be shunting money from his wife and kids to the public at large. While there is no law against his being such an altruist, such a Santa Claus, the betting odds are against this. And in any case such an optimal solution to the problem *by chivalry* has nothing to do with Adam Smith's Invisible Hand—which insisted that *self*-interest (not altruism) would perform the miracle of providing for the general interest.

The clue to the Invisible Hand paradox is this: Adam Smith would have to rely on strictly defined "perfect competition" to get his result. As soon as we have imperfect competition in the real world, we have left the Garden of Eden and there arises the problem of how to minimize the evil and wastes involved in such imperfections of competition. Chapter 26 analyzes the main forms of imperfect competition and surveys the antitrust policies of modern governments. And the brief Appendix to this chapter indicates the economic principles that should underlie public regulation of monopoly and imperfect competition and should underlie antitrust philosophy.

SUMMARY

A. OVERVIEW OF MARKET STRUCTURE AND THE CONCEPT OF MARGINAL REVENUE

1 ■

Most market situations in the real world can be thought of as falling on a line somewhere between the limiting extremes of perfect competition and complete monopoly. Imperfect competition involves some control by each of its firms over its own price, by virtue of the fact that there are not *a very large number of rivals* who sell *exactly the same product* as it does. (Note the italicized words.) Oligopoly—few sellers of similar or differentiated products—and many sellers of differentiated products are important cases.

2 ■

From the firm's demand curve, we can easily derive its Total Revenue curve. From the schedule or curve of Total Revenue we can easily derive its Marginal Revenue—the extra revenue resulting from the sale of an extra unit of output. Ordinarily, Marginal Revenue will fall short of price because of the *loss on all previous units* of output that will result when we are forced to drop our price in order to sell an extra unit of output.

B. MAXIMUM-PROFIT MONOPOLY EQUILIBRIUM: DIVERGENCE OF PRICE AND MARGINAL COST

3 ■

A firm will find its Maximum-profit position where the last little unit it sells brings in extra revenue just equal to its extra cost. This same result can be shown graphically by intersecting MR and MC curves, or by the equality of the slopes of the Total Revenue and Total Cost curves. In any case, *Marginal Revenue = Marginal Cost* must hold at the equilibrium position of maximum profit.

4 ■

Economic reasoning leads to an emphasis upon marginal advantages and disadvantages —to a cancellation of bygones and factors that go on no matter how you make a decision.

5 ■

Imperfection of competition, by putting P above MC for some goods, acts as one extra deterrent to Adam Smith's Invisible Hand, which tried to convert mankind's selfish interest to a best solution of society's WHAT, HOW, and FOR WHOM problems.

QUESTIONS FOR DISCUSSION

1. List distinguishing features of perfect and imperfect competition.

2. "A corporation charges what the traffic will bear." Interpret.

3. What is the numerical value of MR when dd has unitary elasticity?

4. Relate MR to P, at $q = 4$ or 6 in Tables 25-2 and 25-3, showing loss on previous units.

5. Figure 25-3(a) and (b) describes the Maximum-profit equilibrium position. Explain in detail that it really shows two different ways of describing exactly the same fact, namely, that a firm will stop when the extra cost of a further move just balances its extra revenue.

6. Here is a hard question. "If a monopolist is big enough to affect the P for the good he sells, he may also be big enough to affect the price of materials and the labor he buys. (He becomes what is called a 'monopsonist'—or 'single buyer.') In computing MC as it *looks to him*, he will debit against the last unit of q the rise in wage forced on all the *previous* units of labor by his need to hire more labor. Private pecuniary MC, so computed, is higher than the true MC society wants P equated to for efficiency." Interpret this if you can (but if you cannot, don't worry).

7. Review your understanding of the following concepts:

perfect versus imperfect competition	$MR = P$, $P = MC$, for perfect competitor
monopoly, oligopoly, product differentiation	bygones versus relevant alternative
rivalry versus perfect competition	opportunities
MR in relation to P	imperfection of competition and Smith's
$MR = MC$ condition at Maximum-profit	Invisible Hand

APPENDIX: Ideal Regulation of Monopoly Pricing

Figure 25-5 repeats a monopoly equilibrium like that of Fig. 25-3(a). The monopolist is seen to be (1) making a profit, as shown by the green-shaded rectangle near G; and (2) charging a P above MC, as shown by the EG discrepancy.

Suppose a public-utility commission is set up to regulate the monopolist. Or suppose the antitrust department of the government threatens to arrest him. If the regulators decide to make him charge a price that will wipe

out his excess profits, they will move him to H, the intersection of his dd and AC curves. Here $P = AC$, and price covers only normal costs.

How good is this solution? Economically speaking, it probably does represent something of an improvement.

First, the owner of the monopoly is probably no more deserving, or poorer, than the consumers. So there is no reason to let him transfer monopoly profits from them to him. By wiping out monopolistic profit, we probably

Under unregulated monopoly, price is set too high:

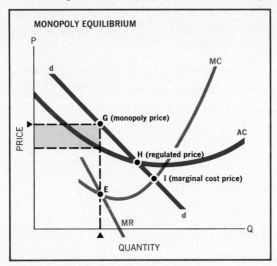

FIG. 25-5. Maximum-profit equilibrium for the unregulated monopolist is at *G*, directly above the intersection of *MR* and long-run *MC*, with *P* above *MC* and with monopoly profit shown by the shaded rectangle.

Public-utility regulation of the monopoly would set its price down to the *H* intersection of demand with long-run average cost; this wipes out excess profit; more important, it brings price down closer to the Marginal Cost level at *I*, where marginal social costs and benefits are appropriately balanced.

Ideally, *P* should be forced all the way down to *MC* at *I*, with the chronic loss being covered by permanent government (lump-sum) subsidy.

have a more "equitable distribution of income." (WARNING: Value judgments that go beyond technical economics are involved in such a conclusion.)

Second, the regulators have lowered the discrepancy between price and Marginal Cost in making the monopolist cut his *P* from *G* to *H*. Why deem this an improvement? Because (equity considerations aside and assuming that dollars truly reflect social utilities and social costs) the expanded *q* units are worth more to people in marginal utility than their extra or Marginal Cost. *Proof:* Between *G* and *H*, *dd* lies above the *MC* curve.

IDEAL PRICING If *P* = *MC* is such a good thing, why shouldn't the regulators go all the way and make the monopolist lower *P* until he is at *I*, the intersection point of the *dd* and *MC* curves?

Actually, requiring *P* = *MC* is the ideal target for optimal welfare. But with a decreasing-cost situation like this one—and we saw in Chapter 24, Fig. 24-5, page 461, that much of monopoly, oligopoly, and other forms of imperfect competition come from decreasing-cost cases—setting *P* = *MC* while *AC* is still falling will involve the firm in a *chronic loss*. (Remember: Falling *AC* means *MC* < *AC*; or *P* = *MC* < *AC*.)

How can society achieve its ideal of *P* = *MC*, where the marginal utility of output just matches its Marginal Cost at the equilibrium amount? The answer involves a permanent government subsidy to the decreasing-cost producer. Where does the subsidy come from? From the general budget (and ideally from taxes collected on a "lump-sum" basis so that people's marginal decisions are not distorted by attempts to minimize taxes.)[1]

----

[1]Some qualifications are given in advanced treatises. (1) If lump-sum taxes are not politically feasible, the evil from *P* = *MC* must be balanced against the distortion from taxation. (2) As Fig. 32-2 will show, a decision has to be made whether the money needed to subsidize the *I* point could not be used better elsewhere, with this *q* set equal to zero. (3) If the consumers of this good are especially "deserving"—or if this should be a good that society deems even more worthwhile than the valuations that consumers themselves act on—there may be a case for even greater subsidy. (Reverse the argument if the good is opium or is something bought only by those who already have too large a share of society's income.) (4) See Fig. 26-3, where it is shown that a flat-sum tax could wipe out the monopolist's profit but leave you with the socially inefficient *P* − *MC* discrepancy. (5) If in many other industries *P* > *MC*, it may not be optimal to bring *P* all the way down to *MC* in this industry alone.

26 Imperfect Competition and Antitrust Policy

THE WHOLE LOGIC OF PRIVATE ENTERPRISE RESTS ON THE FUNDAMENTAL ASSUMPTION OF
ACTIVE COMPETITION IN FREE MARKETS. IF SUCH A SYSTEM IS TO BE PRESERVED, IT IS
ESSENTIAL THAT COMPETITION BE KEPT ACTIVE AND MARKETS FREE. COMMITTEE ON CARTELS AND
MONOPOLY OF TWENTIETH CENTURY FUND

The last chapter paved the way for us now to get a bird's-eye view of the market structure of modern-day industry. How do firms go about setting their prices? What is the role of the theoretical tools developed to analyze profit maximization? What are some of the important patterns of imperfect competition? Part A deals with these subjects.

Part B then takes up the basic problem, What issues for public antitrust policy do patterns of imperfect competition raise?

A. ANALYTICAL PATTERNS OF IMPERFECT COMPETITION

■ DO FIRMS MAXIMIZE PROFITS?

To what degree do businessmen actually try to maximize their profits? To what extent do they succeed if they do try to? It is not easy to give precise answers to these questions. Certainly, this much is true:

■ If a firm is absolutely reckless in calculating costs and revenues, then the Darwinian law of survival of the fittest will probably eliminate it from the economic scene. Therefore those firms which do manage to survive cannot be completely oblivious to the maximization of profits.

But this does not necessarily mean that every oligopolist or monopolist is seeking desperately to squeeze the last ounce of profit from every transaction. As soon as the firm becomes of any considerable size and begins to enjoy some control over price, it can often afford to relax a little in its maximizing activities.

Moreover, it is probably good business to take the long view and not concentrate on purely immediate gains. Many acts of altruism and apparent generosity can be amply defended in terms of public relations and the maximization of long-run profits.

Consider a firm that is maximizing its profits in a fairly sensible manner. Does this mean that it is calculating elaborate geometrical curves of cost and revenue and from them deriving elaborate measures of marginal cost and revenue? Obviously not, as you will soon learn if you inquire about current business practices. But even if the firm is not itself tackling the problem with conscious awareness of the particular marginal tools of the theoretical economists, *to the extent that it is truly making a pretty fair guess as to where its highest profits are realized,* it will be succeeding in making marginal revenue and marginal cost approximately equal. It does this without curves, just by feeling its way to the optimum by trial and error.

■ MARKUP PRICING

One reason why business is a challenge is the fact that best guesses must be made in terms of incomplete information. It is no small task for a business to make an estimate of the demand curve for its products. A railroad can only guess whether a cut in fares will bring many more customers. Because other things do not remain equal, a firm has no exact way to judge the demand elasticity for its many products.

Many observers claim that modern business firms—even the largest—cannot in real life accurately determine marginal revenue and marginal cost. They cannot determine their optimum price and output with neat exactitude. Yet the day's work must somehow get done. Prices must be set on their products. Here is where average, or unit, cost is often thought to play an important role. The argument goes as follows:

> Put yourself in the position of the president of a company producing many products. Prices are partly at your disposal. Your last year's sales are known to you, but your next period's sales can only be guessed even if you leave prices unchanged. Not knowing the extent or elasticity of demand for your products, you will be unable to determine marginal revenue. What will you do?
>
> Probably, you call in your accountants and sales managers and ask, "What is our likely volume if we stay on our toes and keep our share of the market?" In answering, the sales force has to guess at the probable level of business activity, consumers' needs, results of market surveys, and much else.
>
> After they have made their estimates, you turn to the cost experts and probably ask for the average cost of producing each product in question at those levels of output. There will be plenty of headaches in aiming at any sort of figure. For example, how should the administrative and plant overhead costs be allocated between different products? Or if a given process simultaneously creates joint products like meat and hides, how should the costs be allocated between them? Or if a building will last for many years, how much should be charged against current operations?
>
> Headache or no headache, it is the practice of accountants to come out with some sort of answer as to average costs. Management must now decide by how much to mark up price over the cost figure. Depending upon its estimate of the consumers' reaction and the pricing policy of its competitors, the firm may perhaps decide on a 5, 10, 30, or 110 per cent markup.[1] Whether aware of it or not, the businessman is making some kind of implicit guess about his demand elasticity in setting his markup.

[1] General Motors, one of the world's most successful enterprises, has used such markup methods for 40 years. Note that the average costs used prior to markup will for most firms *not already* include a return on the firm's own capital.

In bad times, when price competition is particularly keen, businessmen may even set prices at less than "full costs" because they realize that fixed expenses will go on whether or not production is at a low level. But price will never be set below average *variable* costs unless the item in question is being used as a "loss leader" to attract other business now and in the future, or unless the firm is willing to incur temporary losses in order to crush a rival and drive him out of business completely.

Many investigators of actual business pricing policies have testified that corporations often do follow the above-described practice of quoting administered prices on a "cost and markup" basis, hoping thereby not only to recover their "full cost outlays," but also to make a return on their investments. This theory therefore seems realistic. But the theory is not very informative. It stops tantalizingly short of telling us *why* the average markup is 40 per cent in one industry and 5 per cent in another; it cannot tell why, before World War II, General Motors in the auto industry was able to earn 30 per cent on the book value of its invested capital while Ford, almost as large, could earn but $\frac{1}{2}$ of 1 per cent. Demand and cost just have to be regarded as lurking in the background of any business case.

Careful reading of the foregoing account suggests that it is compatible with the principles outlined in Chapter 25. So long as the percentage markup is subject to the pressures implicit in *MC* and *MR* analysis, markup pricing may hinge on the same conditions as in the simplified theory.

■ BREAK-EVEN POINTS AND "ADMINISTERED PRICES"

Businessmen often speak of their break-even points. You will hear them complain that union wage demands since World War II have raised the level of their break-even points to a dangerous degree, so that, if there is any slackening of the peak levels of sales, profits may soon turn into losses. What might I, a hypothetical businessman, mean by my "break-even point"?

Suppose that I have already fixed upon the price to be charged. Probably I used some sort of markup rule to do so, guessing at the most profitable price range, but it does not much matter how I made the decision.

If I am like most firms, I shall not be changing my *P* every day. Probably I name a so-called "administered price" and—subject to varying discounts and other reflections of demand elasticity—I stick to it until further notice.

So long as my *P* is above *MC* and *AVC*, it is clear that my profits will grow with sales. As a matter of fact, at small outputs I shall not even be earning enough to cover fixed costs; but as sales increase, this loss will dwindle, and I shall reach a point where I just cover fixed and variable costs. My sales have now reached the break-even point.

Beyond this break-even point, my profits will begin to materialize. Anything I can do to increase sales will be all the more to the good. I am quite unlike a perfect competitor on the farm: he can always sell all he wants to produce at the market price. As an imperfect competitor, with $P > MC$, I am glad to sell more q at the market price. That is why I advertise and hire salesmen. And that willingness to sell more marks me as no perfect competitor.

■ OLIGOPOLY: COMPETITION AMONG THE FEW

Table 25-1, page 470, gave a classification of different forms of market structure. It is important enough to warrant reproducing again here as Table 26-1.

Monopoly (one seller) is a rare case. Duopoly (two sellers) happens occasionally, particularly in geographically distinct markets where a couple of steel makers or a couple of railroads dominate the market. More common still is the case of oligopoly (few sellers). We saw in Chapter 5, page 91, that most large-scale industries are dominated by a few giant firms: In automobiles, the Big Three saturate most of the market; in steel, a few big firms dominate; and so it goes in the cigarette, aluminum, aircraft, meat-packing, soap, and telephone industries.

An economic theory of oligopoly has been developed to try to account for the facts of *administered* prices which change infrequently, and to account for the prevalence of markup pricing. Let us consider the case of three or four dominant firms. Already we know that the pattern of costs and returns is likely to be such that the optimal size of efficient production—at the bottom of the U-shaped long-run *AC* curve of page 461

Most industries are imperfectly competitive—a blend of monopoly and competition:

KIND OF COMPETITION	NUMBER OF PRO-DUCERS AND DEGREE OF PRODUCT DIF-FERENTIATION	PART OF ECONOMY WHERE PREVALENT	DEGREE OF CONTROL OVER PRICE	METHODS OF MARKETING
Perfect competition	Many producers; identical products	A few agricultural industries	None	Market exchange or auction
Imperfect competition:				
Many differentiated sellers	Many producers; many real or fancied differences in product	Toothpaste, retail trade		
Oligopoly	Few producers; little or no difference in product	Steel, aluminum	Some	Advertising and quality rivalry; administered prices
	Few producers; some differentiation of products	Autos, machinery		
Complete monopoly	Single producer; single product without close substitutes	A few utilities	Considerable	Promotional and "institutional" public-relations advertising

TABLE 26-1. TYPES OF COMPETITION AND MARKET STRUCTURE. (Source: Table 25-1, page 470.)

Oligopoly means few sellers of the same or differentiated products:

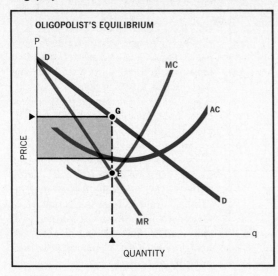

FIG. 26-1. After experience with disastrous price wars, each of the few rivals who dominate a given market is almost sure to recognize that price cutting begets canceling-out price cutting. So the typical oligopolist will estimate his demand curve *DD* by assuming others will be charging similar prices (and by taking into account the potential entry of new oligopolists).

and elsewhere—will be *very large relative to the total market demand*. That is why the three or four firms do not become thirty or forty, or three hundred, or three thousand.

Thus, it probably costs a billion dollars to produce an integrated steel plant. Kaiser Steel is the only integrated producer on the West Coast. If steel could be produced at the scale that wheat is produced, there would be thousands of West Coast steel companies, and Kaiser would have to fear much more competition than it now gets from Japanese imports and shipments from the eastern United States.

Figure 26-1 shows the large-scale operation of a typical oligopolist. The most acute case threatening instability of oligopolistic competition is that in which the different firms produce virtually *identical* or *homogeneous* products. If Firm A's sulphuric acid undersells Firm B's by even $1 a cartank, A will get practically all the business. In this case, we oligopolists are practically sure to recognize our "mutual interdependence"[2]— namely, that we must end up charging about the same prices, and that any initial advantage I get in undercutting your price will be lost when you are induced to cut your price in return. That is why the *DD* demand curve shown for Corporation A in Fig. 26-1 is *not* drawn up on the assumption of "other things (including rivals' prices) being held constant"; instead A's *DD* is just exactly as inelastic as the whole industry's *DD*, since it is A's prorated one-third or one-fourth of the shared market.

[2]A century of theorizing by economists about what Mind A thinks Mind B will do if *he* thinks A will do such-and-such culminated in J. von Neumann and O. Morgenstern, *The Theory of Games and Economic Behavior* (Princeton University Press, Princeton, N.J., 1953, 3d ed.). This mathematical theory, while it cannot clear up all the philosophical problems of how two omniscient minds will act against each other in an interdependent world, does offer many fine insights for political warfare as well as economics. (EXAMPLES: A teacher picks quiz questions *at random* from a book; a watchman makes his rounds at random, not in a discernible pattern. Facing you as a smart rival, I shall work hard to maximize my *most vulnerable* defense, knowing you will find out the weakest link in my chain. I bluff at poker, not simply, as some think, to win a pot with a weak hand, but rather to ensure that all players do not drop out when I bet high on a good hand.)

A kinked or cornered demand curve can explain rigidity of oligopolists' administered price:

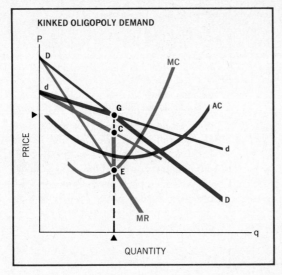

FIG. 26-2. The *DD* curve through *G* is the demand curve when all sellers move prices together and share total market. However, *dd* is the more elastic demand curve when this firm alone changes its price and loses sales to its rivals. Below *G*, as others match your price cut, *DD* prevails. Above *G*, when rivals do not match your price increase, *dd* prevails. Geometrically, the different demand curves generate different *MR* curves, with the *EC* vertical discontinuity (or "kink") resulting from the corner at *G*. Considerably shifting *MC* curves will still lead to intersection on *EC*, and hence unchanged oligopoly price and quantity at *G*.

Where is the Maximum-profit equilibrium for the oligopolist? It is shown in Fig. 26-1 at *E*, the intersection of his *MC* and *MR* curves, with *P* at *G* on *DD* just above *E*. If you turn back to page 477, you see that this oligopoly equilibrium looks much like the simple monopoly equilibrium of Fig. 25-3(a).

INFLEXIBLE, ADMINISTERED PRICING   But there is an important difference under oligopoly. A monopolist might be expected to change his price every time his *DD* or *MC* curve shifts, which could be every year, every quarter, every month. We need an economic theory to explain the more inflexible price quotations administered typically by oligopolists. We deduce the needed theory from the fact that rivals may behave one way when you *cut* your price—namely, matching your cuts and thwarting your hope for new business; and they behave another way when you *raise* your *P* above the customary level—namely, holding their prices constant in order to pick up some of your customers. In consequence, you have little motive to change your price in either direction. Instead you "administer" your price in a rigid fashion.[3]

Figure 26-2 illustrates the "kinked" or "cornered" demand curve that economists postulate to explain rigid price behavior. The equilibrium price *G* is shown in both diagrams at about that markup level over costs which the oligopolists think will be best for them in the long run.[4]

But at *G* there is a kink in the effective demand and marginal revenue curves of Oligopolist A. Why? Because if he cuts his *P* below *G*, his rivals will follow him, and

---

[3] The remainder of this section can be skipped if desired.

[4] Actually, it would be realistic for them to draw up their *DD* curves allowing for entry of *potential* rivals who might be tempted into the industry if they collude on so high a *P* as to make it profitable for new firms to come in. In consequence, each firm's *DD* might be somewhat more elastic than that for the whole industry.

characterized by rather large numbers of firms. Apparently, complaints arise from frictions between firms, while giant companies that dominate a field and exercise quiet monopoly power tend to be overlooked. Some cynics, decades ago, even argued that the antitrust laws encourage bigness, because in practice they are so much harsher on agreements *between* firms than on what the economist would consider the same price–marginal cost discrepancies engineered by *intrafirm* practices that require no furtive meetings at midnight or incriminating letters.

Too often the law—as drawn up by Congress, enforced by the Department of Justice, and adjudicated by the courts—regards various vigorous forms of competition that tend to reduce the discrepancy between price and marginal cost as crimes rather than benefits. The legal mind is not so much concerned with the distortion of prices, which it has no means of measuring, as it is with the methods by which prices are set. Yet the economic and legal minds do seem today to be coming closer together.

As to the future evolution of antitrust policy, there are two opposing philosophies. Carl Kaysen, formerly of Harvard and now Director of the Institute for Advanced Studies in Princeton, together with Donald F. Turner, one-time professor at Harvard Law School and now President Johnson's head of the Antitrust Division, believe the test should be whether a firm has "market power per se," stemming from its monopolistic market *structure*. Independently of its *conduct*, Kaysen and Turner would say there is a prima-facie case for breaking up such a company. At the opposite pole is the view that an updated "rule of reason" should be applied to every case. If even the biggest monopoly is found to display marvelous Schumpeterian innovation, it should be left undisturbed by antitrust litigation. Evidently there is an unresolved conflict here, and all that can be said at this point is that economists tend on the whole to lean toward the market-structure viewpoint.

■ FINALE: WORKABLE COMPETITION

Our discussion of antitrust has concentrated on United States experience, for the very good reason that this country has been a pioneer in such legislation. For many years countries such as Britain, Germany, and Japan, as well as other European nations, appeared to us to take a very lax view of the legality of monopolistic arrangements. After World War II, American occupational authorities in Japan and Germany tried to introduce legislation in those countries to break up their old combines. For a while this seemed to succeed. Then, as those nations began to stand on their own feet, there was some backsliding. However, the Common Market countries have been strengthening their antitrust statutes, and it remains to be seen in what spirit the letter of the regulations will be interpreted. And Britain has belatedly begun to adopt antitrust practices. (Many nations, like the United States in the Webb-Pomerene Act, 1918, lighten their antitrust rules for their own exporters, many more exempt them completely.)

While no one would claim that American antitrust legislation and enforcement has been completely logical or has come anywhere near complete success, one has but to look abroad to realize how much worse off our economy might have been were it not for the omnipresent threat of legal prosecution. American enterprise is kept on the defensive and would never dream of adopting the flagrant devices that are all too common in most places. Harvard's Richard Caves has compared American antitrust action to traffic laws. Most citizens do not consider breaking the traffic laws mortal sins. And the police tend to act only against the most flagrant offenders—the driver who goes 80 in a school zone. But the fact that the policeman may be there, ready to make an arrest, does keep drivers generally more in conformity with the laws of the road. "The guilty flee where no man pursueth." And so, often, do the innocent. To cynics, part of the efficacy of the antitrust laws may even result from their arbitrariness: like the emperor who would take out a general at random and shoot him—"in order to encourage the others"—the antitrust program hangs like the sword of Damocles over every businessman, limiting his temptation to exercise monopoly power.

By *laissez faire* one does not automatically get perfect competition. To reduce imperfections of competition, a nation must struggle perpetually and must ever maintain its vigilance.

Repeatedly, in Part Three, we have stressed the basic problem of how a pricing system solves society's questions WHAT, HOW, FOR WHOM. This frames the rational goal of antitrust policy.

We cannot expect competition to become everywhere "perfectly perfect," in the strict sense of the economist. But what we can strive for is what the late J. M. Clark of Columbia University years ago called "workable competition." By public and private policies we can hope to improve the efficiency with which market prices reflect underlying individual needs, desires, and wants against the background of true costs of goods—costs in terms of alternative goods that could be produced and in terms of used-up scarce productive factors which involve sweat and disutility.

Part Four will be concerned with identical problems that arise in connection with the pricing of land, labor, and capital. Again, the function of such pricing in solving society's problems is the focal point of interest.

SUMMARY

A. ANALYTICAL PATTERNS OF IMPERFECT COMPETITION

1 ■

Few business firms are able to develop exact curves of cost and revenue. This does not mean that they are oblivious to profit maximization. Through trial and error, they may be doing a tolerably good job of keeping alive as a business entity and of achieving long-run optimum profits.

2 ■

Under imperfect competition, a firm may have to make rough guesses in setting its price. Often it will use some kind of *markup* over an estimate of unit cost. Nonetheless, the demand for inputs is a *derived demand*—derived indirectly from the final demand by the consumer. The problem is complicated by the fact that the demand for factors is a *joint demand*—joint because the factors interact in producing final product.

3 ■

The relationship between quantities of available inputs—land, labor, machines, fertilizer—and quantity of output is called the production function. By varying one factor in successive small increments, we define its marginal-physical-product. Diminishing returns implies falling *MPP* of any factor if other factors are held fixed. But when *all* inputs increase *in balanced proportion,* the J. B. Clark model of competition presupposes that there will be exactly *constant* returns (i.e., constant-returns-to-scale).

4 ■

Competition of numerous free landowners and labor-owners will ensure that total product gets allocated among the factors by each having its factor-price equal to its marginal-product. That will allocate *exactly* 100 per cent of the product. Any factor, not just labor alone, can be the varying factor: because each of it gets paid only the *MP* of the last hired, there is enough of a residual surplus left (from the triangle of excess-of-early-over-last-*MP*'s) to pay the other factors their exact marginal-products. Hence, the Clark neoclassical theory of distribution, although simplified, is logically complete and a true picture of idealized competition.

5 ■

Ambitious attempts to measure an aggregate production function for the whole of American manufacturing seem to provide rough corroboration for the theories of production and marginal-products. In this century, technological progress has been shifting the productivities of both labor and capital upward. At the same time capital has been growing faster than the labor supply, with the following implications: (*a*) the increase of capital per worker has shifted his productivity wages up even faster than technological change would alone; (*b*) the tendency of each unit of capital to encounter diminishing returns has just about been canceled by technological innovations; (*c*) the relative shares of labor and property incomes have remained at about three-quarters and one-quarter despite the vast institutional changes in union organization and in automation of production. (Chapter 37's growth theory will return to this.)

6 ■

If he is given ruling market prices of all factors and is given engineering, technical information about the effects of factor changes on final product, the businessman can simultaneously solve the two problems (*a*) of substituting the different factors for each other so as to realize the Least-cost combination—at which he has *equalized the marginal-physical-product per dollar spent on every factor used*—and (*b*) of finally determining which of all possible outputs is his Maximum-profit position, where *MR = MC*.

7 ■

An exactly equivalent condition of factor equilibrium is the following: *equality* of marginal-*revenue*-products to factor-prices. Why must this hold in the Maximum-profit equilibrium? Because any businessman with common sense will stop hiring any factor at the point where what its marginal-physical-product will bring in to his firm in actual dollars of marginal revenue begins to fall short of the market price he must pay to hire as much or little as he wants.

8 ■

Our analysis has shown why, when a factor-price rises, the quantity of it that is demanded will tend to fall. Higher labor price will cause other factors to be substituted for it in producing each output; and higher labor cost probably means that the Maximum-profit output will be at a lower level where MR equals a now higher MC. What is the same, the marginal-revenue-product demand curve for the factor tilts downward because of technical diminishing returns, reinforced by spoiling of the monopolist's market. (This last fact reminds us that monopolists produce too little and hire too few factors.)

In the next few chapters we shall apply these principles to show how supply and demand operate in the factor markets to determine rents, wages, and other factor-prices. The Appendix to this chapter provides a review of the theory of production for those interested in a more geometrical approach.

QUESTIONS FOR DISCUSSION

1. Give examples of derived demand and joint demand.

2. Explain the "production function concept" and various marginal-products.

3. Explain Clark's distribution theory, varying land in a new version of Fig. 27-2.

4. Define marginal-revenue-product, distinguishing it from marginal-physical-product. Give a common-sense explanation to show that Maximum-profit is not attained unless each factor-price exactly equals its marginal-revenue-product.

5. Convince a skeptic of the truth of the rule that to reach a Least-cost point you must equalize the marginal-productivity-per-dollar spent on every factor. Show this to be true even when we have not yet decided on the Maximum-profit output.

6. Suppose NNP grows in a mixed economy faster than labor supply in every decade. If, contrary to Karl Marx's predictions, wage share stays about the same fraction of NNP, show that real wage rates must rise.

7. Review your understanding of the following concepts:

For Whom, How, factor pricing, distribution theory
derived demand
joint demand
production function
diminishing returns
aggregate production function
symmetry of land and labor

MP rectangle, residual triangle
marginal-product, marginal-physical-product, marginal-revenue-product, marginal-physical-product-per-last-dollar spent on each factor
substitution rule of Least-cost
$MR = MC$ and Maximum-profit q
monopoly output and misallocated factors

APPENDIX: Graphical Depiction of Production Theory

The production theory of this chapter can be graphically presented. Table 27-1 is a numerical example of a simple production function relating output to two inputs, labor and land. It is the form of a two-way table, looking like a baseball schedule or a mileage chart of distances between cities.

Along the left-hand side are listed the varying amounts of land, going from 1 unit up through 6. Along the bottom are listed amounts of labor also happening to go from 1 through 6. Output corresponding to the specified land row and labor column is listed inside the table.

If we are interested in knowing exactly what output there will be when 5 units of land and 2 units of labor are available, we count up 5 units of land and then go over 2 units of labor. The answer is seen to be 448 units of product. Similarly, we find that 3 units of land and 6 of labor will produce 600 units of output. Thus, for any combination of labor and land, the production function tells us how much product we shall

have (using, of course, the best methods of the technical engineer).

THE LAW OF DIMINISHING MARGINAL-PHYSICAL-PRODUCT

The law of diminishing returns can be nicely illustrated by Table 27-1.

First recall that we have given the name "marginal-physical-product of labor" to the extra production resulting from *one* additional unit of labor, land being held constant. At any point in Table 27-1 the marginal-physical-product of labor can be derived by subtracting the given number (representing product at that point) from the number on its right lying in the same row. Thus, when there are 2 units of land and 4 units of labor, the marginal-physical-product of an additional laborer would be 48, or 448 minus 400 in the second row.

By the "marginal-physical-product of land" we mean, of course, the extra product resulting from one

The production function summarizes technology:

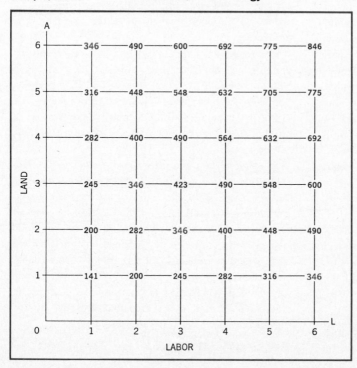

TABLE 27-1. PRODUCTION FUNCTION RELATING AMOUNT OF OUTPUT TO VARYING COMBINATIONS OF LABOR AND LAND INPUT. When you have 3 land units and 2 labor units available, the engineer tells you your maximum obtainable output is 346 units. Note the different ways to produce 346 and to produce 490.

additional unit of land, labor being held constant. It involves a comparison of adjacent items in a given column. Thus, when there are 2 units of land and 4 units of labor, the marginal-physical-product of land is shown in the fourth column as 490 − 400, or 90. The reader should be able to compute the marginal-physical-product of labor or land at any point inside the table.

Having defined what we mean by the marginal-physical-product of an input, we are now in a position to restate the law of diminishing returns:

■ As we hold a fixed input constant and increase a variable input, the marginal-physical-product of the variable input will decline—at least after a point.

To illustrate this, hold land constant in Table 27-1 by sticking to a given row, say that corresponding to land equal to 2 units. Now let labor increase from 1 to 2 units, from 2 to 3 units, and so forth. What happens to product at each step?

As labor goes from 1 to 2 units, product increases from 200 to 282 units, or by 82 units. But the next dose of labor adds only 64 units, or 346 − 282. Diminishing returns has set in. Still further additions of a single unit of labor give us, respectively, only 54 extra units of output, 48 units, and finally 42 units. The reader should check some other row to verify that the law of diminishing returns holds there too. He should also verify that the same law holds true when labor is held constant and land is added in a number of steps. (Examine the changes in product in any *column*.)

At this point, it is well to recall the explanation given for diminishing returns. In Chapter 2, it was attributed to the fact that the fixed factor decreases *relative* to the variable factor. Each unit of the variable factor has less and less of the fixed factor to work with, and it is only natural that extra product should begin to fall off.

If this explanation is to hold water, there should be no diminishing returns when both factors are increased in proportion. When labor increases from 1 to 2 and land *simultaneously* increases from 1 to 2, we should get the same increase in product as when both increase simultaneously from 2 to 3. This can be verified from Table 27-1.[1] In the first move we go from 141 to 282,

and in the second move the product increases from 282 to 423, an equal jump of 141 units.

Also, this explanation of diminishing returns in terms of the proportions of the inputs would lead us to expect that increasing land will improve the marginal-physical-product of labor. Again this can be verified from our table: The fifth unit of labor adds 48 units of product when there are only 2 units of land; but at 3 units of land, a fifth unit of labor adds 58 units of product.

LEAST-COST FACTOR COMBINATION FOR A GIVEN OUTPUT

The numerical production function shows that the engineer is not able to tell us definitely how any given output is to be produced. There is more than one way to skin a cat. And there is more than one way to produce any given output. Thus, the green numbers in Table 27-1 show that the output $q = 346$ can be produced in any one of the ways shown in Table 27-2.[2]

As far as the engineer is concerned, each of these combinations is equally good at producing an output of 346 units. But the accountant, interested in keeping profits of the firm at a maximum and costs at a minimum, knows that only one of these four combinations will give Least-cost. Just which one will depend, of course, on the respective prices of the two factors of production.

Let us suppose that the price of labor is $2 and the price of land $3. Then the sum of the labor and land costs in situation A will be $20 (= 1 × $2 + 6 × $3). And costs at B, C, and D will be, respectively, $13, $12, $15. At these stated input prices, there is no question but that C is the best way of producing the given output.

If either of the input prices changes, the equilibrium proportion of the inputs will always change so as to use *less* of the input that proportionately has gone up most in price. This is just like the substitution-effect of Chapter 22. Thus, if labor stays at $2 per unit but land falls to $1 per unit, the new optimal combination will be B, where more land is substituted for reduced labor and where total cost is only $7. The reader should verify this by computing the new total expense of all other combinations and seeing that they are higher. (Pencil in missing costs in Table 27-2.)

---

[1] Not all production functions met within real economic life would have these special properties of so-called "constant returns to scale." Recall from Chapter 2 the discussion of increasing returns to scale, or economies of mass production.

[2] You can and should make up a similar table for output equal to 490 or some other number.

How we graphically find Least-cost point:

1st, Factors can be substituted to produce the same output:

	LABOR L	LAND A	TOTAL COST WHEN $P_L = \$2$ $P_A = \$3$	TOTAL COST WHEN $P_L = \$2$ $P_A = \$1$
A	1	6	$20	——
B	2	3	13	$7
C	3	2	12	——
D	6	1	15	——

TABLE 27-2. EQUAL-OUTPUT FACTOR COMBINATIONS. More labor can be substituted for less land to produce 346 units. When $P_L = \$2$ and $P_A = \$3$, calculate total of wage cost plus land cost to verify that their combination gives lowest cost $12 at C. Show that lowering P_A to $1 causes land to be substituted for labor as you move from C to B.

Exactly the same sort of thing can be done for any other output; as soon as all input prices are known, we can experiment until we have found the Least-cost input combination. (To guarantee your understanding of the principles involved, work out the optimum production decision and cost for output equal to 490 units when price of labor is $4 and price of land is $3. See that 3 labor and 4 land units will turn out to produce Least-cost of $24 for $q = 490$.)

EQUAL-PRODUCT AND EQUAL-COST CONTOURS: GRAPH OF LEAST-COST POSITION

The common-sense numerical analysis of the way in which a firm will combine inputs to minimize costs can be made more vivid by the use of diagrams. From the production schedule we can draw a picture of the different input combinations that will produce a given output. Figure 27-3 is the exact counterpart of Table 27-2. In it the smooth curve indicates the different combinations of labor and land that yield an output of 346 units. This could be called a "production-indifference curve" by analogy with the consumer's indifference curve of the Appendix to Chapter 22. But a more expressive name would be to call it an "equal-product" curve. (You should be able to draw in on Fig. 27-3, as a dotted curve, the corresponding equal-product curve for output equal to 490. You should realize that an infinite number of such equal-product contour lines could be drawn in, just as a topographical or weather map could be covered with an indefinitely large number of equal-altitude or equal-pressure contour lines.)

Given the price of labor and land, the firm can evaluate the total cost for points A, B, C, and D or for any other point on the equal-product curve. Obviously, it will be maximizing its profits only when it has found that optimum point on the equal-product curve at which it reaches Least-cost.

2d, Equal-output factor combinations can also be graphed:

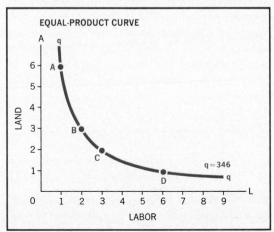

FIG. 27-3. All the points on the curve represent the different combinations of land and labor that can be used to produce the same 346 units of output.

3d, Equal-cost contours are parallel lines:

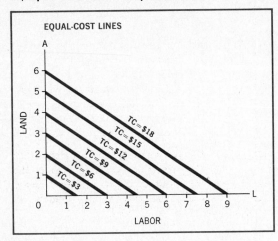

FIG. 27-4. Every point on a given line represents the same total cost. The lines are straight because of constant factor-prices, and they all have a numerical slope equal to the ratio of labor price to land price, $2/$3, and hence are parallel.

Purely as a graphical trick, the firm might try to save itself much tedious arithmetical computation by evaluating once and for all the total cost of every possible factor combination of land and labor. This is done in Fig. 27-4, where the family of parallel straight lines represents all possible equal-cost curves when the price of labor is $2 and the price of land $3.

To find the total cost for any point we have simply to read off the number appended to the equal-cost line going through that point. The brown lines are all straight and parallel because the firm is assumed to be able to buy all it wishes of either input at constant prices. The lines are somewhat flatter than 45° because the price of labor P_L is somewhat less than the price of land P_A. More precisely, we can always say that the arithmetic value of the slope of each equal-cost line must equal the ratio of the price of labor to that of land[3]—in this case $\frac{2}{3}$.

[3] The careful reader will notice the parallel between the geometry of this section and that of the analysis of consumer equilibrium in the Appendix to Chapter 22. Each equal-cost line indicates all the possible different quantities of labor and of land that the firm might buy for any given cost outlay. Each line is straight since its equation is $TC = \$2L + \$3A$. In the Appendix to Chapter 22, the consumer is buying goods, not factor services; otherwise his "consumption-possibility line" exactly parallels the equal-cost lines we are now discussing. We can explain, similarly, why the slope of an equal-cost line equals the ratio of the two prices involved.

But note this difference: The consumer was assumed to have a fixed budget; hence, he had but one consumption-possibility line. The firm is not limited to any particular level of costs; so it must consider many equal-cost lines before discovering its Least-cost equilibrium.

It is now easy to recognize the optimum equilibrium input position of the firm at which total costs are minimized for the given output. The single green equal-product curve has superimposed upon it the family of brown equal-cost lines. This is shown in Fig. 27-5. The firm will always keep moving along the green convex curve of Fig. 27-5 as long as it is able to cross over to lower cost lines. Its equilibrium will therefore not be at A, B, or D. It will be at C, *where the equal-product curve touches (but does not cross) the lowest equal-cost line.* This is, of course, a point of tangency, where the slope of the equal-product curve just matches the slope of an equal-cost line and the curves are just kissing.

We already know that the slope of the equal-cost curves is P_L/P_A. But what is the slope of the equal-product curve? This slope is a kind of "substitution ratio" between the two factors, and it depends upon the *relative* marginal-physical-products of the two factors of production—just as the rate of substitution between two goods along a consumer's indifference curve was earlier shown to equal the ratio of the marginal, or extra, utilities of the two goods (Appendix to Chapter 22).

LEAST-COST CONDITIONS

Thus, our Least-cost equilibrium can be defined by any of the following equivalent relations:

■ 1. The ratio of the marginal-physical-products of any two inputs must equal the ratio of their factor-prices. That is,
Substitution ratio, or

4th, We move on equal-product curve to Least-cost line:

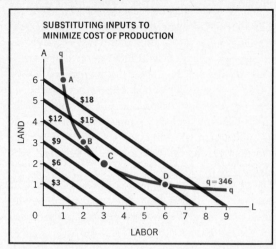

FIG. 27-5. Where the equal-product curve touches (but does not cross) the lowest total-cost contour is the Least-cost optimum position. This tangency means that factor-prices and marginal-physical-products (or "substitution ratios") are proportional.

$$\frac{\text{marginal-physical-product of labor}}{\text{marginal-physical-product of land}} = \frac{\text{price of labor}}{\text{price of land}}$$

■ 2. The marginal-physical-product-per-dollar received from the (last) dollar of expenditure must be the same for every productive factor. That is,

$$\frac{\text{Marginal-physical-product of } L}{\text{Price of } L}$$
$$= \frac{\text{Marginal-physical-product of } A}{\text{Price of } A} = \cdots$$

Relation 2 is discussed in detail in the main body of the chapter. (It could also be derived from relation 1 by transposing terms from one numerator to the other denominator, i.e., by "interchanging means," as is always algebraically permissible.)

But the student should not be satisfied with any such abstract explanation. He should always remember the common-sense economic explanation which shows how a firm will redistribute its expenditure among inputs if any one factor offers a greater return for each last dollar spent on it. Finally, we may state the above Least-cost relations in the following form:

■ 3. Input prices and their marginal-physical-products must be proportional, the factor of proportionality being marginal cost.[4]

[4]Why are these marginal-physical-products-per-dollar each equal to the reciprocal of marginal cost, or to $1/MC_q$? Because extra output per dollar is nothing but the upside-down of extra dollars per unit of product, which is what we always have meant by *MC*.

MC of output × marginal-physical-product of labor = Price of labor
MC of output × marginal-physical-product of land = Price of land
and so on for any number of inputs.

The Least-cost relationships 1, 2, and 3 are all equivalent. Each holds at every point along the Total Cost curve, *whatever the output*. They do *not* tell the firm where it should finally produce.

MARGINAL-REVENUE-PRODUCT CONDITION OF MAXIMUM-PROFIT

But now we add the Maximum-profit condition that $MR = MC$; and we recall the definition of marginal-revenue-product as equal to marginal-physical-product times marginal revenue. Then we can combine the Least-cost relations of item 3 just above and the Maximum-profit relationship to reach our final equilibrium condition:

Marginal-revenue-product of labor = Price of labor
Marginal-revenue-product of land = Price of land
and so on for any number of factors.

■ Thus, our graphical analysis has arrived at the same final result as our common-sense reasoning of this chapter—which tells us that we shall stop hiring more of a factor only at the point where the marginal-revenue-product it brings just matches its market price. This is what lies behind the firm's demand curve for a productive factor.

FIXITY OF PROPORTIONS

An important qualification must sometimes be made. We have calculated the marginal-physical-product of any one input by (1) holding all the other inputs constant and then (2) increasing the input in question by 1 unit. The resulting increase in physical product was then measured, and that was identified as the factor's marginal-physical-product. But in some technological processes the factor inputs work very intimately together, so that, when you increase only one of them, holding the others constant, you get *zero extra product;* and when you decrease one factor alone, you lose *the whole product* produced by both together; only when you change them both *in combination* do you seem to get a nice smooth curve of marginal-physical-product.

Certainly, such discontinuities can sometimes happen, but perhaps they do not occur quite so often as some critics have claimed. Thus, critics often point out examples where one man is always using one shovel or where it seems to take a certain amount of gold to produce a watchband and no amount of labor can substitute for this gold. But actually, in any digging operation, extra shovels must usually be kept on hand; and if shovel prices were very high and wages were low, workers on different shifts might use the same implements so that the shovel requirements could be kept to a minimum; also, we might in time change the size of the shovels or introduce bulldozers, thereby changing the proportions of the factors. Or in the above case of the gold watchband, there will almost certainly be some waste of metal in the form of shavings and dust; and if wages were low enough relative to the price of gold, it would pay us to hire more men to produce the same number of watchbands out of less gold—the labor being, in effect, a substitute for the use of more gold.

Numerous other arguments and examples could be given in reply to those who stress fixity of factor proportions and discontinuities in substitutability and marginal-products. Nonetheless, in some technical processes, there may not be continuous substitutability between the various inputs, and so the calculated marginal-physical-products may become very erratic and lumpy.

It was once thought that lack of substitutability would spoil the economic theory of production; but that is fortunately not so.

To see the case of fixed proportions, we would have to replace the smooth green contour of Figs. 27-3 and 27-5 by a green L-shape equal-product contour. Regardless of how high or low the positive P_L/P_A ratio is, the Least-cost point of "tangency"—where the green contour touches but does not cross the minimal brown line of *TC*—comes always at the corner of the L. Hence, the Least-cost condition is even more easily found in the fixed-proportions case. (There now will be *no* substitution when one factor becomes dear relative to another, for the reason that no technical substitutability is possible.)

The derived demand of firms for factors is still well determined, but with the difference that there may be inelastic stretches and some discontinuities in the factor-input demand curve. In Fig. 27-2, a vertical *dd* curve would spoil the simple Clark tale of rectangle and residual triangle.

Fortunately, dropping the one-good assumption of Clark and replacing a single Q by many goods (Q_1, Q_2, . . .) can sometime restore determinacy of distribution. Let's see why.

INTERCOMMODITY SUBSTITUTION AND QUALIFICATIONS

It is not hard to show what happens when we drop the simplified case of a single product. As any factor, such as unskilled labor, becomes more plentiful, its marginal-revenue-product and rental will tend to fall. Not only will more of it tend to be substituted for other factors in each line of production, but in addition, those special goods which happen to use much of this factor in their production will fall in price more than will prices generally. This relative price drop will tend to cause consumers to use more of such cheapened goods, and in this way the derived demand for the factor will become even more elastic.

Thus, *in addition to intracommodity technical substitutability between factors, there is also intercommodity substitutability resulting from differential price effects.* This suggests how distribution will be determined even when the continuous-substitutability assumptions of the marginal-product theory of production break down. If factors must be used in fixed proportions, their derived demands are still perfectly well determined. These demands, together with supply relations, help determine all prices. Intercommodity substitutions now become extremely important, as do the supply conditions for the factors.[5]

Finally, note this. To understand the different aspects of the problem of distribution is to begin to understand much of the history of the classical and modern theories of distribution and of competitive pricing. But it does not tell us much about the cases of imperfect competition: (1) where there may be economies of scale that lead to a few firms' gaining semimonopoly power and (2) where consumers may develop a special preference for products that can be produced only by factors owned by a single firm. As Chapter 31 shows, in these cases the firms may earn "monopoly profits" or "monopoly rents" which the attempted competition of other firms may not take away from them. To "natural scarcity" is then being added artificial "contrived scarcity,"

[5] An example illustrates how intercommodity substitutions can determine factor-prices even in the worst case of fixed-proportions, e.g., where 1 unit of land *and* 1 unit of labor are needed to produce a unit of wine and where 1 unit of land *and* 2 units of labor are needed to produce a unit of bread. Assume that wine sells for $10 per unit and bread for $12. Bread differs from wine by $2 in price and cost; and in terms of inputs, it differs by what? By 1 extra unit of labor. Hence wages must be exactly $2 per unit (= $12 − $10), and land use must be priced at $8 per unit (= $10 − $2, or $12 − 2 × $2). So from commodity prices we can obtain factor-prices—even in this fixed-proportions case.

You will realize that the prices of wine and bread had also to be determined by supply and demand and will depend in part upon how much income goes to hungry laborers and thirsty machine owners and upon the initial supplies of the factors. For example, imagine that we started with a supply of 200 acres of land and 300 laborers, and let us summarize the resulting general equilibrium.

If we had started with factors in a 1:1 ratio—say, 200 of each—and *if* we required them to be fully employed, they would *all* have to go into wine production. We could not possibly produce any bread and still keep all our factors employed. Similarly, if our factor totals had been in a 1:2 proportion—say, 200 acres of land, 400 laborers—we should have to produce nothing but bread to preserve full employment.

But we start with a halfway ratio—200:300. Common sense and simple algebra tell us that we must then split our land half and half between the two industries, thereby using up the total of both factors in producing 100 wine units and 100 bread units. The prices of these supplies of goods would then be determined by the interplay of competitive supply and demand for the two goods and for the two factors, and thus we end up at the above equilibrium prices for goods and services. (NOTE: A factor-price can be made zero by some demand and supply patterns, but this "free factor" possibility is neglected for simplicity. And so is the case where one $Q = 0$.)

brought about by someone's holding in his supply for fear of "spoiling the market."

COMPETITIVE EQUILIBRIUM A GOOD THING?

We have now completed a sketch of how the marginal-product theory "distributes" total product between two factors—land and labor—in a simplified world.

We have simply been observing how hard-boiled competition would work itself out under simple conditions. Just as the jungle has its laws without regard to right and wrong, so does the competitive market have its brute facts.

But did you notice one efficient thing that happened? Without a planning board, *society got its food produced in the most efficient way.* How did that happen? Well, efficiency certainly requires that the homogeneous land and labor be everywhere combined for food in exactly the same proportions. (PROOF: Suppose society were using much labor on half its land, and little labor on the other half. The law of diminishing returns tells us that the marginal-product of the workers will be less on the dense than on the sparse half. So we can get some extra Q by shifting men to the sparse acres with higher MPP. Maximum output comes when marginal-products are equal on both halves, i.e., when labor and land are combined in the same proportions on both halves. QED.)

Ruthless competition with only the commercially fittest surviving did bring about the desirable equality everywhere of factor proportions and marginal-products. How did it do this? By landlords' seeking maximum rents; by workers' seeking maximum wages; by market prices' being forced to lowest costs of production. These were the vital processes. (WARNING: A tendency toward "increasing returns to scale" would have killed off perfect competition and have brought in monopoly to spoil the whole story. Note also that if different acres were of different qualities, we would no longer use the same proportion of labor on each; instead the desirable equality of marginal products of transferable labor would be achieved by using relatively more laborers on the better lands—a sensible result!)

We shall see again, in Chapter 32, that competitive pricing can help solve efficiently the How problem of any society. We shall see that charging a rent for God-given land is necessary if such scarce land is to be rightly allocated.

28 Pricing of Factor Inputs: Rents of Land and Other Resources

THE PRICE OF PIG,
IS SOMETHING BIG;
BECAUSE ITS CORN, YOU'LL UNDERSTAND,
IS HIGH-PRICED, TOO;
BECAUSE IT GREW
UPON THE HIGH-PRICED FARMING LAND.

IF YOU'D KNOW WHY
THAT LAND IS HIGH,
CONSIDER THIS: ITS PRICE IS BIG
BECAUSE IT PAYS
THEREON TO RAISE
THE COSTLY CORN, THE HIGH-PRICED PIG.

H. J. DAVENPORT

The last chapter showed how each firm decides on its demand curve for any factor of production that it wants as an input for its production function. This chapter will show in detail how the demand curves of all firms and industries are added together to form the aggregate market demand for any factor of production. Such a demand curve, together with the supply curve for the factor, will be found to determine its market price; in this way a market economy determines the distribution of income to owners of the different factors of production.

The interesting special case of the rents to lands and other resources serves to illustrate these general principles. The following chapters will provide still other important applications to wages, interest, and profit.

■ AGGREGATE MARKET DEMAND CURVES FOR OUTPUT AND FOR EACH INPUT

Figure 28-1 shows how the demand for a given input, such as fertile cornland, must be regarded as derived from the consumers' demand curve for corn. This assumes, of course, that we hold constant the prices of such cooperating inputs as fertilizer, labor, and farm machinery. The last chapter showed this: At each land-rent price prevailing in the market place, any small farmer must decide on the Least-cost combination of the various inputs, and he must also decide on the Maximum-profit scale of his output to throw onto the market. Therefore each farmer will want to hire more and more of cornland up to the point where its marginal-revenue-product is equal to its market rental. At that point, the last unit just brings in an amount equal to its extra cost. That is why it is the equilibrium point at which the farmer ceases to demand more or less.[1]

■ FACTOR-PRICE DETERMINATION BY SUPPLY AND DEMAND

Until now we have worked only with the demand curve for a factor, taking its market price as given to the demanders. But obviously it is *all the firms together* that determine the factor's market price that each small firm faces. Now we must see how the total demand curve of all firms for the factor, together with its total supply curve, will interact to determine the equilibrium price tending to rule in the market place.

Figure 28-2 repeats the total derived demand curve for cornland *dd*; it was arrived at by adding together the demand curves of all the firms.

Demand for factors is derived from demand for the goods they produce:

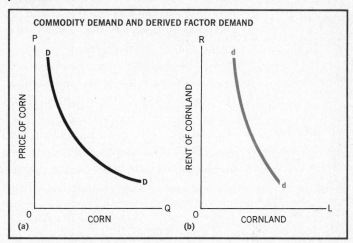

FIG. 28-1. The green curve of derived demand for cornland comes from the brown curve of commodity demand for corn. Shift the brown curve up and up goes the green curve. (Make the brown commodity curve more inelastic and vertical, and in part the same tends to happen to the green factor curve.)

Now it is one of the peculiarities of land that, unlike most things, its total supply is relatively fixed by nature and in general cannot be augmented in response to a higher price for it or diminished in response to lower land rentals. (This is not strictly true. Land can sometimes be created by drainage, and the fertility of existing land can be depleted by overcropping.)

■ Nonetheless, we can accept the complete fixity of land's supply as its characteristic feature. By tradition, we may confine our discussion to the "original and inexhaustible gift of nature" whose total supply is by definition *completely inelastic.* It was the price or return to such a factor that the classical economists of the last century called "rent."

---

[1] We are dealing with a competitive industry in which the single farmer is too small to affect the market price of corn. In such a competitive industry, no one need worry about spoiling the market for the previous units of corn being sold; consequently, marginal revenue and price are the same thing. It follows that marginal-revenue-product will be exactly the same thing as marginal-physical-product times corn price. For such a special perfectly-competitive case, economists often use the special name "value of the marginal product" instead of marginal-revenue-product.

Five principles governing elasticity of this factor demand will perhaps seem reasonable. Demand for a factor tends to be the more inelastic (1) the more inelastic is the demand for the product; (2) the less important is the fraction of total cost of this factor ("It is important to be unimportant"); (3) the less other factors can be technically substituted for this factor; (4) the more inelastic are the supplies of other factors; and (5) the more inflexible is the administered price at which the firm continues to sell its product. (Skilled electricians meet all the first four requirements: little is spent on them; they are indispensable; other labor, such as carpenters and masons, is inelastically supplied; and the demand for new structures is quite inelastic.)

This differs from ordinary usage in which rent or rental is the money paid for the use over a period of time of anything—of a house, truck, and so forth. (For the rest of Part Four we shall use the word "rent" to refer to the return to a factor whose supply is completely inelastic and "rental" to refer to money paid for the services, over a period of time, of any factor.)

In Figure 28-2, the supply curve for land *ss* is made to be completely inelastic because of the fixity of its supply. The demand and supply curves intersect at the equilibrium point *E*. It is toward this factor-price that the rent of land must tend. Why? Because if rent rose above the equilibrium price, the amount of land demanded by all firms would be less than the existing amount that would be supplied; some property owners would be unable to rent their land at all; therefore they would offer their land for less and thus bid down its rent. By similar reasoning, the rent could not long remain below the equilibrium intersection. If it did, you should be able to show how the bidding of unsatisfied firms would force the factor-price back up toward the equilibrium level. Only at a competitive price where total amount demanded of land exactly equals the total supply will there be equilibrium. It is in this sense that supply and demand determine any factor-price.

Note that the man who owns land does not have to be a particularly deserving citizen in order to receive this rent. A virtuous and poor landowner will be given exactly the same rent by competition as will a wealthy wastrel. It is the productivity of the acre of land that is being paid for, and not the personal merits of the landowner.

Even this productivity of the land is not something absolute. For example, what would happen if the price of corn were to fall greatly because people began to desire

Fixed land must work for what its demanders will bid:

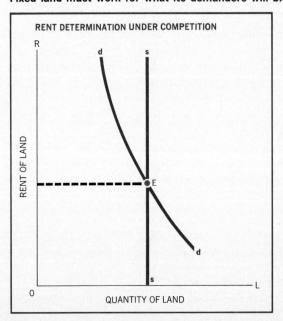

RENT DETERMINATION UNDER COMPETITION

R

d   s

RENT OF LAND

E

d

s

0   L

QUANTITY OF LAND

FIG. 28-2. Perfect inelasticity of supply characterizes the case of so-called "pure economic rent." We run up *ss* curve to factor demand curve to determine rent. (Aside from land, we can apply rent considerations to oil and mining properties, and anything in inelastic supply.)

other goods? Then the derived demand for cornland would shift drastically downward and to the left. What will happen to the rents received by landowners? After a time, rents must sink down to a new equilibrium intersection. The land is not less productive in a technical sense than it was before, and the landlords are neither more nor less virtuous than they were before. But factor demand-and-supply intersection has changed.

A factor of production like cornland is said to earn a "pure economic rent" (1) when its total supply is regarded as perfectly inelastic; and (2) when we can assume that the land *has no other uses*, such as in the production of sugar or rye. Adam Smith's great follower in England, David Ricardo, noted in 1815 that the case of such an inelastically supplied factor could be described as follows:

■ It is not really true that the price of corn is high because the price of corn land is high. Actually the reverse is more nearly the truth; the price of corn land is high because the price of corn is high!

Land's total supply being inelastic, it will always work for whatever is given to it by competition. Thus the value of the land is completely derived from the value of the product, and not vice versa.[2]

■ RENT AND COSTS: IMPLICIT VERSUS EXPLICIT RETURNS

Some economists went so far as to say: "Rent does not enter into the cost of production."

As a digression let us see why. The last section shows that there is a grain of truth in this. But still it is very dangerous terminology. If you were a farmer trying to go into the corn-raising business, you would certainly find that the landlord has to be paid like anybody else. You would certainly include rent in your cost of production; and if you could not pay it, you would go out of business.

Even if you were a farmer who owned your own land, it would be a mistake to think that rent does not enter into your costs of production. After you had paid all your other bills, including wages to yourself at least as great as what you could earn elsewhere in the market, there would have to be left an amount at least equal to the market rental value of your land. For what if there were not? Then you would soon find that it would be better for you to rent out your farm on the open market and hire out your own labor to somebody else.

Sometimes economists call rent paid by a man to himself "implicit" rather than "explicit" rent. Very clearly, implicit rent is as much a part of long-run competitive costs as are any other costs, and the same can be said of the implicit wages or implicit interest earned on any other factors that you could sell rather than use personally. The reader is urged to refer to the discussion of opportunity cost in Chapter 23 (page 443), which bears on this point.

---

[2] Land is not the only factor whose return may be considered as economic rent. For an example where most of a wage payment is a "pure rent," see page 550. And in the short run, the supply of a machine or plant may be entirely fixed; thus a hydroelectric plant takes a long time to build, still longer to wear out. The return to any factor in temporarily fixed supply is sometimes called a "quasi rent"— "quasi," because in the long run, its supply need not be fixed. Those farmers in World War II who petitioned OPA for higher milk price because of higher wartime cow prices, without knowing it, illustrated rent and quasi-rent doctrines.

■ RENT AND COSTS: RELATIVITY OF VIEWPOINT

Let us continue our theoretical digression.

When some economists claim rent does not enter into society's cost of production, what are they driving at? They are saying:

Since rent is the return to an inelastically supplied factor that would still be supplied to the community even at much lower prices, the direction of causation goes as follows: "The prices of goods really determine land rent—rather than having land rent determine the prices of goods."

But at this point we must avoid our old enemy "the fallacy of composition." What appears as a cost of production to each and every small firm using a particular kind of land may, as we have seen, be to the whole community merely a derived price-determined rent expense rather than a price-determining one. More than that, suppose the land is specialized and can be used only for the production of one industry. If a grade of land is inelastically supplied to one industry and, having no place else to go, will always work for whatever it can earn there, its return may appear to every small firm as a cost like any other. But as scientific observers of the whole industry, we still must recognize that the land return is a price-determined rent and not a price-determining cost.

Now let us move on to an alternative case. Suppose this land can be used for a variety of industries: for corn growing, rye growing, buckwheat growing, cattle grazing, and so forth. Then to each small industry (such as buckwheat growing), land's return will definitely appear as a necessary expense that the consumers of buckwheat will have to pay as cost before they can get their buckwheat. One small industry is just like any one small firm in this case: although the total of land is *inelastic* in supply for *all* uses, to any *one* small firm or industry it is in completely *elastic* supply.

■ To conclude: Whether rent is or is not a price-determining cost depends upon the viewpoint: that of a small firm, small industry, large and even exclusive-user industry, or whole economy. What is a price-determined rent return to a factor which is inelastic in supply to the whole community or dominant industry may, to each firm and to any small industry that is only one of many potential users, appear as a price-determining cost.[3]

■ HENRY GEORGE'S SINGLE-TAX MOVEMENT: TAXATION OF LAND "SURPLUS"

In the last part of the nineteenth century, a western frontier still existed in this country. As more and more people came here from Europe, each acre of land had more and more people to work with. In a sense, therefore, the land became more productive. In any case its competitive rental value certainly tended to rise. This created handsome

---

[3] The Davenport verse opening this chapter hints at such a conclusion. To cover cases like this, economists invented the technical expression "opportunity cost." (Again see Chapter 23's discussion.) To each owner of land, using it in his own business is wise only if its marginal product there will be sure to cover his "opportunity cost" or cost foregone in not selling it in the market for others to use. Similarly, a competitive industry can employ a factor only if its derived worth there at least measures up to the opportunity cost of using it elsewhere. In the terminology of Chapter 2's production-possibility frontier: The cost of guns is the foregone (or opportunity) cost of not producing butter with the same resources; gun cost can be measured in terms of sacrificed butter even if every factor were in inelastic supply, involving no disutility and earning price-determined or "residual" rents that are quite unnecessary to elicit the factors' supply and effort.

profits for some of those who were lucky or farsighted enough to get in on the ground floor and buy land early.

Nor was this true only in agriculture. Men still alive in the Middle West can remember when towns first began. They will tell you how they might have been rich if their fathers had recognized 90 years ago that the corner of State and Madison would eventually become the center of town and grow tremendously in value as a result of the great increase in urban populations. Urban sites with good locations earn rents in the same sense that fertile areas do. Many people began to wonder why lucky landowners should be permitted to receive these so-called "unearned land increments."

Henry George, a printer who thought much about economics, crystallized these sentiments in the single-tax movement. This movement had a considerable following three-quarters of a century ago or more, and there are still some adherents to it; but it is not likely that anyone running on the single-tax ticket will again come so close to being elected mayor of New York City as George did in 1886. Nor is it likely that anyone will soon come along and write so persuasive a bible for the movement as Henry George did in his *Progress and Poverty,* a book which sold millions of copies.

This is not the place to attempt any assessment of the merits and demerits of George's political movement. But one important principle of distribution and taxation can be illustrated by his valid central tenet:

■ Pure land rent is in the nature of a "surplus" which can be taxed heavily *without distorting production incentives or efficiency.*

Let us see why. Suppose that supply and demand create an equilibrium land rent, as in Fig. 28-3 at *E*. Now what would happen if we were to introduce a 50 per cent

Tax on fixed land is shifted back on landlords, skimming off pure rent:

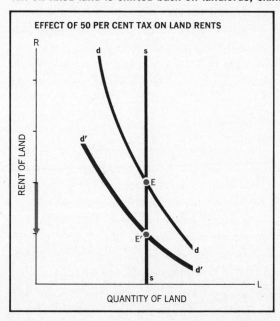

EFFECT OF 50 PER CENT TAX ON LAND RENTS

FIG. 28-3. A tax on fixed land leaves rentals paid by users unchanged at *E* but reduces rent retained by landowners to *E'*. (What can the landowners do but accept less return?)

tax on all land rents? Mind you, we are not taxing buildings or improvements; for that certainly would affect the volume of construction activity. All we are supposed to be taxing is the yield of the naturally fixed supply of agricultural and urban land sites, assuming that this can somehow be identified.

There has been no shift in the total demand curve for land; firms are still willing to pay the same amount as before for the same amount of land. Hence, with land fixed in supply, the market price that they pay must still be at the old intersection E. Why? Because supply has not changed and neither has demand. Because at any higher price than before, some land would have to go without any demanders. Hence, competitive rents could not permanently be raised to land users.

Of course, what the farmer pays and what the landlord receives are now two quite different things. As far as the landlords are concerned, once the government steps in to take its cut of 50 per cent, the effect is just the same as if the net demand to the owners had shifted down from dd to $d'd'$. Landowners' equilibrium return *after taxes* is now only as high as E', or only half as high as E. The whole of the tax has been shifted backward onto the owners of the factor in inelastic supply! The landowners will not like this. But under competition there is nothing they can do about it, since they cannot alter the total supply and the land must work for whatever it can get. Half a loaf is better than none, or even than one-fourth of a loaf.

Whether or not it is a fair thing to take away part of the return of those who own land is quite another question. Perhaps many voters will feel that such owners are not less deserving than are investors who have put their money into other things; perhaps many will feel that no one should have the right to benefit from nature's windfall gifts of oil, minerals, or soil fertility.[4] But these are political questions that are not to be discussed at this stage. What is relevant is to point out that a similar 50 per cent tax put upon a different factor of production whose total supply is *not* completely inelastic would certainly produce definite effects on the factor-prices charged in a competitive market. To some extent this tax would distort the pattern of production, and it would shift part of the burden *forward* onto the users of the factor and onto consumers. Thus, if the same acre of land were to be taxed differently when used for wheat rather than corn production, this would certainly have distorting effects on the price of wheat relative to that of corn.

■ SUPPLY AND DEMAND FOR ANY FACTOR

The competitive determination of land rent by supply and demand is only one instance of the general analysis applicable to *any* factor of production. How is the rental value per week of a tractor to be determined in a competitive market? We first sum up the derived demands of all business firms for tractors. (Of course, these derived demands have behind them marginal-revenue-product considerations of the last chapter; but this behind-the-scenes relation need not concern the observer of the aggregate market demand for this factor.) Along with the dd curve shown in Fig. 28-4, we must also have

---

[4] In most countries, unlike America, the owner of land is not permitted to claim the full reward from lucky mineral discoveries on "his" terrain.

Factor supply and derived demand together determine income distribution:

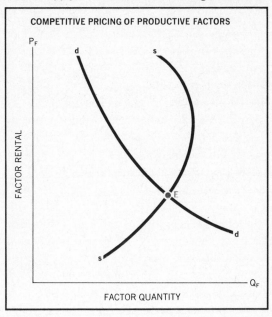

COMPETITIVE PRICING OF PRODUCTIVE FACTORS

P_F

FACTOR RENTAL

FACTOR QUANTITY

Q_F

FIG. 28-4. Land's share in national income rises when its rent is bid up. Skilled and unskilled labor shares are determined, in competitive markets, by interplay of factor supply and demand. The same would hold for any factor.

a supply curve such as *ss*. But there is now no reason why the supply curve should be perfectly vertical. It may now be positively elastic, rising upward toward the northeast. (EXAMPLE: The case of tractor supply, dependent on rising marginal costs of production.) Alternatively, if the factor of production were labor, it might be that people would feel they could afford to work *fewer* hours when wages rise, so that the *ss* curve might eventually bend backward and northwestward from the vertical, rather than rising forward.

In any case, whether the supply curve is vertically inelastic, positively elastic, or negatively elastic, there will be an *ss* curve as in Fig. 28-4.

■ Where the derived demand curve intersects the factor supply curve, the final equilibrium factor-price will be set. And if the demand curve for the factor shifts upward, its market price will tend to rise; on the other hand, if the supply offered of any factor increases, so that the supply curve shifts rightward, then the factor-price will tend to fall.

In a competitive market economy, therefore, factor-prices and the distribution of income are not determined at random. There are definite forces of supply and demand operating to create high returns to scarce factors that are very useful in producing the things wanted by people with purchasing power. But the price will drop if more of any factor should become available, or if other close substitutes for it are found, or if people stop wanting the goods that this factor is best suited to make. Competition gives, and competition takes.

■ FACTOR PRICING AND EFFICIENCY: RENT AND FACTOR-PRICES AS DEVICES TO RATION SCARCE RESOURCES

Competitive supply and demand helps determine the For Whom problem of society. Whether or not we like its answer to this distribution question—and in the case of rent, Henry George certainly did not—we have to admit that it does contribute to an *efficient* solution of the How problem for society.

Thus, as a result of supply and demand in markets for goods and for factors, in America where land is plentiful and labor scarce, we find extensive agriculture. In Europe or Asia, where people are plentiful relative to land, we find intensive agriculture.

Why? Because of government planning? No, not necessarily.

Rather it is the *signaling* of market pricing that results in efficient How. Land has to be auctioned off at a low price here; labor auctioned off at a high price here. So every farmer, seeking his Least-cost combination lest he go bankrupt, substitutes land for labor. Contrariwise abroad, cheap labor gets substituted for land. (More than that: with labor scarce here, we find that fussy vegetables, which require much care, get priced relatively higher than those which lend themselves to extensive methods. So the resulting high commodity prices tend to make us *substitute the cheaper goods* in our diet for the more expensive labor-intensive ones. Abroad the opposite commodity substitutions take place. Hence, the pricing system signals best commodity substitutions as well as best factor substitutions!)

Do you now believe that charging rent has a function—even if you later tax part of it away? Then you are ready to appreciate examples showing how troubles in the real world come from the fact that there is no way to charge the appropriate rents.

Item: The sea is free to all. So everyone fishes in it until the fish are all killed off or decimated. If society could somehow charge rents for commercial fishing licenses, we might in the long run all be better off—including fishermen! Refer to the discussion of external diseconomies in Chapter 23's Appendix, and show that letting workers overrun Iowa farmland at zero rents would lower society's efficiency in using those acres.

Item: Our roads get very crowded on weekends and during rush hours. We usually cannot charge tolls or rents. If we could, we might coax shoppers and people who are getting little pleasure from driving to do their driving at some less crowded time.

Item: Even if policemen can inspect and make collections from parking meters at a negligible fraction of the cost of the revenue collected by parking meters, it may be socially desirable to keep the tolls of such meters high enough to create a rational use of limited curb space.

Other examples of how charging rent leads to efficient How—even though it may lead to For Whom considered ethically dubious—could be given. But the point has been made.

■ CONSERVATION AND LAND TENURE

Ricardo and Henry George emphasized the original, unaugmentable, and indestructible gift of Nature. Actually, much of the land we use *has* been augmented by man: it has been drained, filled, and fertilized by investment effort quite like that which builds machines and plants. Equally important, Nature's gifts *can* be destroyed. There are now deserts where green acres once flourished. There are used-up mines; deforested timber lands; eroded and depleted topsoils. Part of the rental element in the sale of Minnesota copper ore was a return of capital for this exhaustible resource. More and more we must go abroad for the raw materials to feed our machines.

Charging rents for use of resources may slow down their rate of depletion and serve to ration out such scarce, exhaustible resources. But in a freely competitive system, the self-interest of owners may well lead to the rapid using up of natural resources. The resulting depletion is not merely to the owner, who is left with nothing more to sell or rent. Unsightly and unhealthy slag piles may also be created. There may be short-term and long-term regional unemployment. There may be deforestation that causes floods and soil erosion downstream. All these "external diseconomies" create a presumption toward public concern and toward governmental regulation or coordination.

AIR AND WATER POLLUTION   Civilization pollutes the atmosphere, rivers, lakes, and even seas. Urbanization and irrigation deplete water reservoirs and depress the level of the water table below ground. Fresh water becomes a vital scarcity, and regions fight over the disposition of scarce water: Colorado versus California; northern versus southern California; Illinois versus Michigan versus Canada. That is one reason why huge dam projects are undertaken publicly—TVA in Tennessee, Bonneville and other projects in the Northwest and Canada, the Aswan dam on the Nile, the Volta in Ghana: for irrigation, conservation, electric power, and defense purposes.

As we shall see in Chapter 38's discussion of underdeveloped nations, at the village and farm level, inefficient systems of land tenancy may keep society inside its production-possibility frontier and even depress that frontier. Absentee landlords will not put money into the land; tenants on short and uncertain tenure have every incentive to mine the land and to refuse to make needed long-term improvements; credit is lacking for productive investment; and peasants who pay 40 per cent interest to money-lenders in order to tide them over until the new harvest alleviates starvation can hardly be expected to make capital investment in the land or even maintain it.

Thus, the choice is not between ideal perfect competition and public regimentation. It is between imperfect *laissez faire* and imperfect public coordination; between inefficient government fiats and rational democratic programming.

This is why most of the mixed economies put some limits on freedom to use land. They make zoning restrictions and draw up regional and urban plans. They employ the right of eminent domain, in which owners are made to sell their land at publicly determined prices. Parklands, owned by government, are used to create "external economies" and common consumption benefits. In Britain, Italy, France, Sweden, and elsewhere, limitations are put on the windfall capital gains that can be secured by those lucky enough to own farmland where a new city is to be located or those clever enough to speculate successfully on future developments.

■ CONCLUSIONS

The same general principles determining land rent also determine the prices of all inputs: capital goods, natural resources, or labor. Thus the rentals of threshing machines or of trucks are determined in essentially the same way. We might even go so far as to say that wages are the rentals paid for the use of a man's personal services for a day or a week or a year. This may seem a strange use of terms, but on second thought, one recognizes that every agreement to hire labor is really for some limited period of time. By outright purchase, you might avoid ever renting any kind of land. But in our society, labor is one of the few productive factors that cannot legally be bought outright. Labor can only be rented, and the wage rate is really a rental.

The next chapter deals with the peculiar problems of wages and labor markets. Chapter 30 will analyze the problems of capital and interest, which will be seen to be important in determining the supply of durable goods available for rental and use.

SUMMARY

1 ■

Factor demand curves are derived from commodity demand curves. An upward shift in the latter causes a similar upward shift in the former; and inelasticity in commodity demand makes for inelasticity of derived factor demand.

2 ■

We add up for all the firms their derived demands for a factor in order to get the aggregate demand curve. This, together with the specified supply curve of the factor, can be expected to determine an equilibrium intersection. At the equilibrium market price for the factor of production, the amounts demanded and supplied will be exactly equal—only there will factor-price have no tendency to change. Anywhere above the equilibrium price, suppliers will tend to undercut the market and to cause price to fall; anywhere below the equilibrium price, shortages will cause demanders to bid the price upward, restoring the equilibrium.

3 ■

The unchangeable quantity of natural land is an interesting special case where the supply curve happens to be perfectly vertical and *inelastic*. In such a so-called *pure* rent case, competition will still determine an equilibrium market rental. But in this case, we are faced with a cost element that is more price-*determined* than price-*determining;* the land rent is more the result of the market prices for the finished commodities than their cause. (Yet we must not forget that, to any small firm, or to any industry too small to affect appreciably the total demand for land, rent will still seem to enter explicitly or implicitly into the cost of production just like any other expense. To such a small industry, rent reflects the opportunity cost of using land elsewhere and appears to be as much price-determining as any other cost element.)

From the standpoint of the community as a whole, the rent of an inelastically supplied factor will be reckoned in the national income at its full dollar value, like anything else. But below the veil of money, it still remains true that this factor would be willing to work for less if it had to, and in that sense its return is in the nature of a "surplus" rather than in the nature of a reward necessary to coax out the factor supply.

This provides the basis for Henry George's "single-tax" program, proposing to tax the unearned increment of land value—and without any shifting forward of the tax to the consumer or distorting effects on production.

4 ■

Whatever some may feel about the ethical nicety of its answer to the FOR WHOM problem, proper factor pricing does under perfect competition contribute to efficient solution of society's How problem. Indeed, *not charging rents* may cause inefficient overcrowding and bad choice of use in many situations.

   Because land utilization is fraught with "neighborhood and externality effects," zoning fiats and public controls on land use are common. Exhaustibility of natural resources, conservation, and distorting forms of land tenure raise special problems of economic analysis for land.

5 ■

The general principles of supply and demand can also be used to explain the competitive price determination of all services other than those of land. In common everyday usage, we speak of rent or rental as the price paid for the use of any input, whether the factor's supply curve is inelastic or not. The rental of all inputs—including the wages that have to be paid for the use of the services of human beings and the rentals of durable machines—is determined in a competitive system by supply and demand.

QUESTIONS FOR DISCUSSION

1. Define the "pure rent" case. Explain the sense in which price of such a factor is "price-*determined*" rather than "price-*determining*." Show that, nonetheless, an increase in supply of the rent-earning factor will depress its return and lower prices of goods that use it much.

2. What was the Henry George single-tax movement all about? Use a diagram to show the effect of taxing pure rent. Apply this to a ballplayer's inelastic supply.

3. "Value of the marginal-product" is defined as $MPP \times$ price of the product; "marginal-revenue-product," as $MPP \times$ marginal revenue. Which of these two values is lower for a firm in an imperfectly competitive industry? In a perfectly competitive industry? ($MPP =$ marginal-physical-product.) Do you understand footnote 1's use of these concepts?

4. The East as well as West Coast now faces problems of smog. Probably the auto is a prime factor. What interferences with freedom will this require?

5. Review your understanding of the following concepts:

derived demand	supply-and-demand equilibrium
inelastic supply of God-given land, pure rent	factor-price equilibrium
single tax, backward shifting of land tax, unearned increment	price signaling of efficient factor and commodity substitutions
price-*determined* expense versus price-*determining* expense	How, FOR WHOM, and rents
	resource exhaustibility and conservation
	land zoning and public policies

29 Competitive Wages and Collective Bargaining

THE LABOURER IS WORTHY OF HIS HIRE. NEW TESTAMENT

A man is much more than a commodity. Yet it is true that men do rent out their services for a price. This price is the wage rate, and of all prices it is by far the most important. For the vast majority of the population, the wage is the sole determinant of family income. And when we remember that much of the income of farmers and of nonincorporated enterprises is in actuality a form of labor income, we realize that wages must constitute almost 80 per cent of the national income.

What is supposed to determine wages under competitive conditions? This is the first problem we shall tackle, in Section A below. Then in Section B, we shall investigate the effect of deviations from competitive conditions, analyzing the economics of collective bargaining between trade-unions and employers.

A. WAGE DETERMINATION UNDER PERFECT COMPETITION

Wage rates differ enormously. The average wage is as hard to define as the average man. An auto executive may earn $500,000 a year at the same time that a clerk earns $7,000 and a farmhand $3,000. In the same factory, a skilled machinist may earn $160 a week, while an unskilled man gets $80. Part of any theory of wages must explain these differentials.

But important as these wage *differences* are, we must not overlook the general wage *level*. Wages of virtually every category of labor are higher than they used to be half a century ago. Wages are higher in the United States than for similar categories of labor in Europe; and they are higher in Europe than in Asia. Economics endeavors to provide understanding of such basic facts.

■ REAL WAGE DETERMINATION FOR A SINGLE GRADE

Let us begin by examining the simplified case of wages paid for similar jobs to laborers who are all exactly alike in skill, effort, and every other respect. Then competition will

542

Favorable resources and technology explain high American wages:

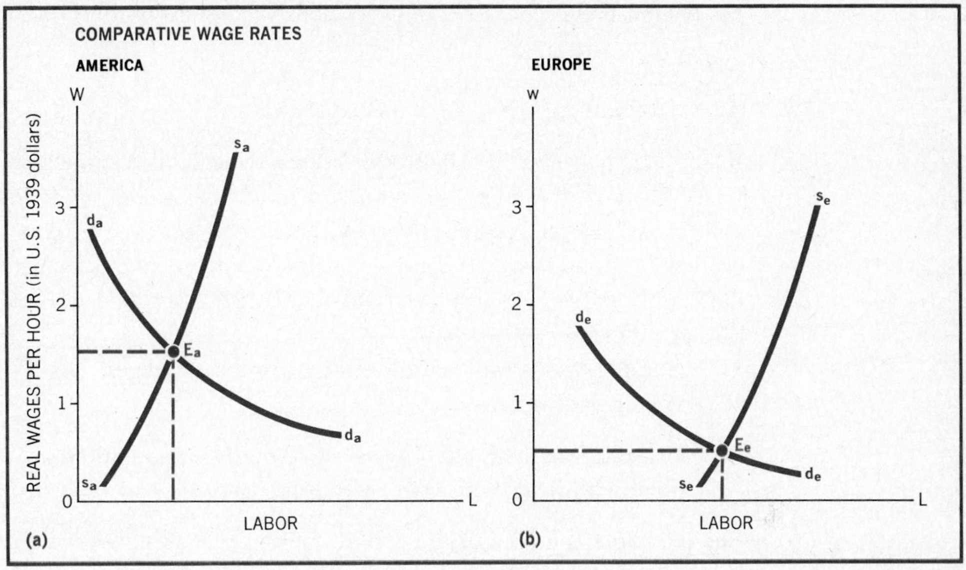

FIG. 29-1. Supply and demand determine a higher competitive wage in America than in Europe.

cause their wage rates per hour all to be exactly equal. No employer would pay more for the work of one man than he would pay for his identical twin, and no worker would be able to ask more for his services.

How is this single market wage determined? If we know the supply and demand curves for these laborers—as in Fig. 29-1(a)—then the competitive equilibrium wage must be at E, the intersection point. If the wage rate were higher than E, spirited bidding by frustrated employers would restore the equilibrium.

We are interested in *real wages*—in what the wage will buy—and not just in the money wage. Therefore, in our illustrations, we express wages in money units whose purchasing power over goods is held constant at the level of some particular year and place, e.g., in terms of American dollars of 1939 or 1967 purchasing power. By definition, an index of the real wage represents an index of actual money wages deflated (or divided) by an index of the price level. (EXAMPLE: Money wage rates doubled since 1950; however, since prices increased $33\frac{1}{3}$ per cent in that period, real wages increased by only one-half; i.e., $200/133\frac{1}{3} = 1\frac{1}{2}$.)

Imagine that Fig. 29-1(a) represents the state of affairs in America and Fig. 29-1(b) that in Europe. Why are wages so much higher in America than in Europe? Is it because we have unions and they do not? Or because we have passed higher minimum-wage laws than they? Experts doubt that these factors can explain the difference. In any case, such factors have been ruled out in our simplified competitive case. A true answer would be:

■ Supply and demand are such in America, compared with Europe, as to lead to a higher real wage here.

But *why* are supply and demand such as to lead to high American wages? What lies behind these schedules? Why is labor's marginal product so high here?

■ RESOURCES, CAPITAL, AND TECHNOLOGY

In the first place we recall that the derived demand schedules for labor slope downward. The law of diminishing returns suggests that adding more and more labor to the same American natural resources and land area will tend to diminish labor's marginal productivity and wages. Suppose you let American population increase so as to shift the supply curve *ss* far to the right in Fig. 29-1(a). Then the wage might fall to the European level or even lower.

One important explanation of high American wages, therefore, lies in the sphere of economic geography:

■ Compared with the size of our working population, we are generously supplied with land, with coal, with iron, with oil, and with water power.

The per capita supplies of these vital sinews of modern industrial production are less in Europe and still less in many other regions.

But economic geography does not tell the whole story. Two regions may be exactly alike in endowment of natural resources; but if one uses superior technological methods, its productivity and real wages may be much higher than the other's. In part, using superior technological methods involves better know-how, better applied science, better economic laws and customs, better management, and better work methods; in part, it involves relative abundance of capital goods—of man-made machinery, materials, and plants.

Just why America developed a superiority in know-how and capital availability is not well understood by economic historians. Our lead seems to be narrowing slightly, as know-how spreads abroad. But the truth of this superiority is not in doubt.

■ IMMIGRATION AND RESTRICTIONS OF LABOR SUPPLY

This raises the question, Why don't Europeans move from their low-wage area to our higher-wage area? People *did* migrate to this country in great numbers during the three centuries prior to World War I. A few came to seek religious freedom, many because they liked our system of government, but by far the greatest number came to better their economic condition.

After World War I, laws were passed severely limiting immigration. Only a trickle of immigrants has been admitted since then. This is a first example of interference with the free play of competition in the wage market. By keeping labor supply down, immigration policy tends to keep wages high. Let us underline this basic principle:

■ Limitation of the supply of any grade of labor relative to all other productive factors can be expected to raise its wage rate; an increase in supply will, other things being equal, tend to depress wage rates.

The law of diminishing returns makes it easy to understand why the trade-unions have favored restrictions on immigration. The same analysis helps to explain why they have pressed for (1) a shorter and shorter working week and more days of vacation per year; (2) restrictions on child labor, encouragement of early old-age retirement, and exclusion of women from some areas of labor; and (3) restrictions on degree of effort and speed-ups. The old labor jingle

> Whether you work by the week or the day,
> The shorter the work the better the pay

expresses the hope that workers can travel upward on the demand curve for labor.[1]

■ THEORY OF THE OPTIMUM POPULATION

At this point we must be careful not to overstate the law of diminishing returns. Working against it, for a range at least, is a counterlaw: *the law of increasing returns to scale*, or of *economies of mass production*.

One of the reasons the United States is so prosperous is that ours is so *large* a free-trade area. Modern technology increasingly requires larger and larger plants: unless you can produce a thousand electric refrigerators per day, you will not realize the full economies of large-scale mass production. Before the Common Market brought down trade barriers in Europe, a small country with a limited domestic market found it difficult to have an efficient domestic industry.

This raises a question: Would the United States be better off in the 1970s if our population were cut by one-half? If you apply the law of diminishing returns uncritically, the answer is, Yes. But in view of the counterlaw of increasing returns, the answer is in doubt.

This discussion suggests a rather interesting theory of population. Why not have the best of both situations? Why not take advantage of increasing returns per capita as well as of diminishing returns? Specifically, why not aim at letting population grow up to the exact point where increasing returns end and decreasing returns begin? This point will give the highest level of real wages or real incomes, and is called the "optimum population." Figure 29-2, on the next page, illustrates how the optimum is defined at the very top of the productivity curve.

■ THE IRON LAW OF WAGES: MALTHUS AND MARX

In Chapter 2, we encountered the Malthusian theory of population, and will meet it again in Part Six. According to this theory, you should draw in on Fig. 29-1(a) a *horizontal* long-run supply curve of labor. This should be drawn in at the wage level corresponding to the lowest standard of living at which people will just reproduce their numbers. A century and a half ago, economics was called "the dismal science"

---

[1] Union policy today is by no means uniform in pressing for these restrictions upon supply. In recent years, many unions have revised their views on retirement age, now opposing compulsory retirement at sixty-five. The AFL-CIO helped pass the 1965 immigration reforms that lessened sociological and ethnic discrimination. Many unions still featherbed, but some encourage high productivity.

Incomes reach a peak where population is not too large or small:

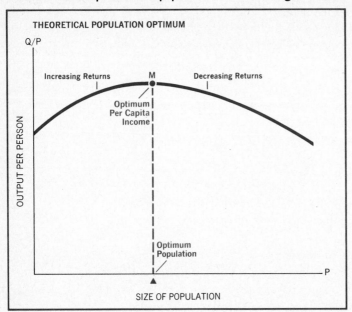

FIG. 29-2. At the point where decreasing per capita returns begins, output per person is at its very highest. Unfortunately, economists are unable to estimate just where the optimum is for a modern nation.

because many classical economists believed wages tended toward the bare minimum of subsistence. Our survey of rising living standards and growing populations showed how unrealistic for the West is this notion of a bare-minimum long-run supply curve of labor.

A quite different version of the iron law of wages was provided by Karl Marx. He put great emphasis upon the "reserve army of the unemployed." In effect, employers were supposed to lead their workers to the factory windows and point to the unemployed workers out at the factory gates, eager to work for less. This, Marx thought, would depress wages to the subsistence level.

Let us try to show this on our diagrams. Figure 29-1(a) is redrawn as Fig. 29-3. Suppose that the wage is at $2 per hour in 1939 prices (over $5 in 1967 prices). Employment is at the level indicated by the point A. At this high wage, there would indeed be unemployment, as alleged. The amount of unemployment would be represented by the distance between the labor supplied and demanded AB. In our simple, idealized model of competition, such unemployment could certainly be expected to put downward pressure on wages.

But does the basic Marxian conclusion follow? Is there any tendency for real wage rates to fall to a *minimum subsistence level* such as *mm* in Fig. 29-3? None at all. There is absolutely no reason why in our simple model real wage rates should ever fall below the equilibrium level at *E*. In a country well endowed with capital and natural resources, this competitively determined equilibrium wage might be a very comfortable one indeed. In a less fortunate country, we should expect it to be lower. Thus we reach an important principle:

■ If competition in the labor market were really perfect, there would be no necessary tendency in an advanced country for wages to fall to any minimum subsistence level.

Employers might prefer to pay low wages. But that would not matter. In a competitive market they are unable to set wage rates as they would *like*. As long as employers are numerous and do not act in collusion, their demands for any grade of labor will bid its wage up to the equilibrium level at which the total forthcoming labor supply is absorbed. The workers may aspire to still higher wages, but under competition they do not get what they would *like* either; as long as they do not act collusively to limit the labor supply, their wishes will not serve to make wages rise above the competitive level.

■ LUMP-OF-LABOR FALLACY AND THE THIRTY-HOUR WEEK

It would be wrong to think that diminishing returns alone explains why unions pursue policies to restrict labor and effort. There is a related and still more powerful reason why workers fight for shorter hours. They fear unemployment; they tend to think the *total amount of work to be done is constant* in the short run. So what happens if a foreigner is put to work? Or a woman comes into the labor market? Or an old man refuses to retire? Or a fellow worker works too efficiently? Or a machine replaces a man? Or men work overtime? Each of these looms up as a threat to a worker's job and livelihood.

This attitude, that there is only a fixed amount of work to be done, is sometimes called by economists the "lump-of-labor fallacy." We must give this notion its due. To a particular group of workers, with special skills and status and stuck in one region, the introduction of technological change may represent a real threat. Viewed from their personal standpoint, the lump-of-labor notion may not be so fallacious.

Karl Marx exaggerated power of reserve army of the unemployed:

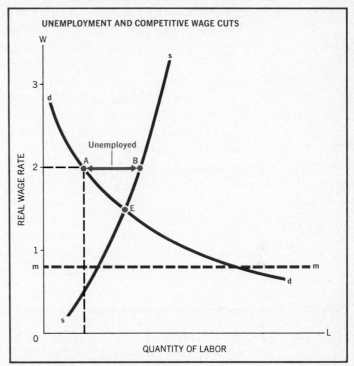

FIG. 29-3. Contrary to Marx, the "reserve army of the unemployed" —as shown by *AB*—need not depress real wages to the *mm* "minimum-subsistence" level. It can only depress competitive wages from *A* to *E*. If labor supply became so abundant that *ss* intersected *dd* at *mm*, the wage would be at a minimum level, as in many underdeveloped regions; but institutional or legal changes can do little when marginal productivity remains abysmally low.

True enough, in a great depression, when there is mass and chronic unemployment, one can understand how workers generally may yield to lump-of-labor philosophy. But the lump-of-labor argument implies that there is only so much useful remunerative work to be done in any economic system, *and that is indeed a fallacy.*

■ If proper monetary, fiscal, and pricing policies are being vigorously promulgated, we need not resign ourselves to mass unemployment. Although technological unemployment is not to be shrugged off lightly, its optimal solution lies in offsetting retraining policies that create adequate job opportunities and new skills, rather than in restrictions on production. Retraining is to be coupled at the macroeconomic level with expansionary fiscal and monetary policies.

There are, of course, still other arguments for or against cutting standard working hours from, say, 40 per week to 30. As our standards of living and productivity rise, it is only natural that we should feel we can afford more leisure. Historically, working hours have been progressively shortened, as we have already seen. Saturday work will no doubt become rarer and rarer in American industry. Probably there will be a trend toward increased vacations with pay—not so much because the vacation will improve workers' productivity as that people get enjoyment from summer and winter vacations. Taking more time off will probably be one of the ways in which we shall choose to enjoy the fruits of technological progress. No doubt, too, our grandchildren will choose to work a still shorter week; but that should reflect choice, not necessity.

Still, at this stage of history would American workers really wish to purchase 10 extra hours of leisure per week if this meant foregoing a sizable fraction of real and money income—say, 20 per cent of what potentially might be earned? One wonders. As our economy approached full employment in the 1960s, agitation for the 30-hour week declined. This suggests that the unemployment rather than the leisure argument really carried most weight. Moreover, when a union leader favors a shorter week, he at the same time asks that there be no cut in take-home pay. What worker could be against a free present of more leisure? A few pages later we shall investigate the degree to which unions can squeeze higher wages out of employers. But there is no doubt that legal shortening of hours would imply lower real wages than a full-employment economy is capable of providing.

■ GENERAL SUPPLY CURVE OF LABOR

Return now to the case of perfect competition. What is the supply curve of labor like? How does the wage rate affect population? Affect people's desire for a longer or shorter average working day? Influence the number of people *not* in the labor force (via age of retirement, years of schooling, and women workers)? Will higher wages motivate people to work more effectively or make them feel they can afford to relax?

These questions show that the supply of labor involves at least four dimensions: (1) population, (2) proportion of the population actually in the labor force, (3) average number of hours worked per week or year by workers, and (4) quality and quantity of effort and skill that workers provide.

These four labor-supply dimensions all depend on sociological as well as economic forces.[2] The third, though, is of particular economic interest.

"SUBSTITUTION-EFFECT" VERSUS INCOME-EFFECT   What effect will wage rates have on the number of hours worked per year? We have already touched on this earlier. A diagram may help to make the issues clear. Figure 29-4 shows the supply curve of total hours that a group of people will want to work at each different wage. Note how the supply curve rises at first in a northeasterly direction; then at the critical point *c*, it

[2]The labor force sometimes tends to grow in deep depression: when a husband is thrown out of work, his wife and children may seek jobs. Tending to cancel this is the fact that women and other workers are, under prosperous conditions, attracted into jobs by plentiful employment opportunities. The labor force grew less from 1957 to 1967 than demographers had expected: apparently the high level of unemployment discouraged new entrants. When full employment finally reappeared, new entrants were coaxed back; experts estimate that every time aggregate demand policies create 10 new jobs, 3 additional persons will enter the labor market, until the over 5 million persons who were discouraged by the stagnant 1950s all have come back.

At a high enough wage we can afford to work less:

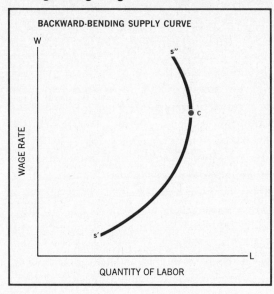

FIG. 29-4. Above the critical point *c*, raising the wage rate reduces amount of labor supplied. (Income-effect overcomes substitution-effect: at higher income, one feels he can afford more leisure even though each extra hour of leisure is costing him more than before.)

begins to bend back in a northwesterly direction. How can we explain why higher wages may either *increase* or *decrease* the quantity of labor supplied?

Put yourself in the shoes of a worker who has just been offered higher hourly rates and is free to choose the number of hours worked. You are torn two different ways: On the one hand, you are tempted to work some extra hours because now *each hour of work is better paid.* Each hour of leisure has become more expensive—hence you are tempted to substitute extra work for leisure. But working against this so-called "substitution-effect" is an opposing "income-effect."[3] With the wage rate higher, you are, in effect, a richer man. Being richer, you will want to buy more clothes, more insurance, better food, and more of other consumer goods. But most important for the present problem, *you will tend also to buy more leisure!* Now you can afford to take Saturday off, have a week's vacation in the winter or an extra week in the summer.

Which will be more powerful, the substitution-effect or the income-effect? Or will they just balance each other and cancel each other out—so that the supply curve neither rises forward nor bends backward, but rises perfectly vertically and inelastically? There is no one answer. It depends upon the individual. In Fig. 29-4, from *s'* to *c* the substitution-effect outweighed the income-effect. But from *c* to *s''*, the income-effect was the more important.

[3] See Chapter 22 for a discussion of "substitution-effects" and "income-effect" in connection with consumption, and Case 4 of the Appendix to Chapter 20. The income-effect of a wage increase is defined as its tendency to make you feel richer and able to afford more pleasurable leisure. Its substitution-effect is its tendency to make you want to react to the higher price of leisure—higher because of the higher hourly wage you now forego to get each hour of leisure—by substituting for leisure the new goods your higher pay will buy. The two effects of a wage change oppose each other; when the income-effect wins out over the substitution-effect, labor's supply curve bends back.

■ RENT ELEMENTS IN WAGES OF UNIQUE INDIVIDUALS

Generally, one could expect that, after people receive a comfortable margin over what they consider to be conventionally necessary, further increases in wage will not bring forth further hours of work. This was tested by a tax lawyer who studied his professional and business friends in New York City to learn the effect on them of heavy graduated taxes. Somewhat to his surprise, he discovered that taxes seemed to make them work harder so as to maintain their previous standards of living. Apparently, the short-run income-effect of reduced after-tax wages was more powerful than the substitution-effect. But probably most powerful were their nonmoney drives—desire for achievement and liking for their work. A Harvard Business School study gathered similar evidence, as did a recent study of English accountants and solicitors.

As we shall see in Chapter 31 on profits, the most harmful effects on incentives of our increasingly high tax rates seem to involve risk taking and venture capital rather than any connection with the supply of effort by gifted people. Most of the high earnings of outstanding individuals can probably be classified as "pure economic rent." Babe Ruth earned $100,000 a year playing baseball, something he liked to do anyway. Outside the field of sports it is doubtful if he could have counted on earning more than, say, $5,000 a year. Between these two limits his supply curve was almost completely *inelastic,* and so economists can term the excess of his income above the alternative wage he could have earned elsewhere *a pure rent,* logically like the rent to nature's fixed supply of land as discussed in the last chapter.

■ EQUALIZING DIFFERENCES IN WAGES

Let us now turn from the problem of supply of labor in general to investigate the vital problem of *differentials in competitive wages* among different categories of people and jobs. Supply conditions now become all-important in explaining the tremendous wage differentials observed in everyday life.

> ■ When you look more closely at the differences among jobs, some of the observed pay differentials are easily explained. Jobs may differ in their unpleasantness; hence wages may have to be raised to coax people into the less attractive jobs. Such wage differentials that simply serve to *compensate for the nonmoney differences among jobs* are called "equalizing differences."

Steeplejacks must be paid more than janitors because people do not like the risks of climbing flagpoles. Workers often receive 5 per cent extra pay on the 4 P.M. to 12 P.M. "swing shift" and 10 per cent extra pay for the 12 midnight to 8 A.M. "graveyard shift." For hours beyond 40 per week or for holiday and weekend work, $1\frac{1}{2}$ times the base hourly pay is customary. And when you observe a doctor who earns $30,000 a year, you must remember that at least a part of this is an equalizing difference needed to induce people to incur tuition costs and endure the lack of pay for years.

Jobs that involve dirt, nerve strain, tiresome responsibility, tedium, low social prestige, irregular employment, seasonal layoff, short working life, and much dull training all tend to be less attractive to people. To recruit workers for such occupations you must raise the pay. On the other hand, jobs that are especially pleasant or attractive find many applicants, and remuneration is bid down. Many qualified people like white-collar jobs, and so clerical wages are low.

To test whether a given difference in pay is an equalizing one, ask people who are well qualified for both jobs: Would you take the higher-paying job in preference to the lower? If they are not eager to make such a choice, then it is fair to conclude that the higher-paid job is not really more attractive when due weight is given to all considerations, nonmonetary and monetary.

■ NONEQUALIZING DIFFERENTIALS: DIFFERENCES IN LABOR QUALITY

If all labor were homogeneous, we have seen that every observed competitive wage differential could be explained as an equalizing difference. But turn to the real world. True, some of the observed differentials can be regarded as equalizing. Yet everyone knows that the vast majority of higher-paid jobs are also *more pleasant*, rather than less pleasant. Most wage differentials cannot therefore be of the equalizing type. What, then, are they due to?

Are they perhaps due to the fact that competition is imperfect? Undoubtedly, some observed differentials are of this type. Studies show that workers do not have anything like perfect knowledge of job opportunities. Trade-unions or minimum-wage laws or a monopoly by the workers in a particular occupation can also explain part of the existing nonequalizing differentials. If you removed these obstructions due to monopolistic or imperfect competition, enough people would flow into some of the higher-paid jobs to bring pay in these jobs into equality with that prevailing elsewhere. We shall analyze these interferences with competition in a moment.

> ■ But never forget that many of the observed differentials in wages have little to do with the imperfections of competition; they would still persist if there were no monopoly elements. Even in a hypothetically perfect auction market, where all the different categories of labor were priced by supply and demand, equilibrium would necessitate tremendous differentials in wages.
>
> This is because of the tremendous *qualitative* differentials among people.

No one expects the competitive wage of a man to be the same as that of a horse. Then why expect one man to receive the same competitive wage as another man or woman? A zoologist may call us all members of the same *Homo sapiens* species, but any personnel officer who is trying to equalize the marginal-physical-product per dollar expended in every direction knows that people vary much in their abilities and contributions to a firm's dollar revenue.

There are more than 80 million people in our labor force. There is no single factor of production called labor; there are thousands of quite different kinds of labor. If you are hiring men to shovel railroad trains out of a blizzard, it will probably pay you to lump together as one indistinguishable factor of production all adult males of certain ages who appear to be reasonably healthy, muscular, and sober.

Thus, the labor market will always group people into certain general classifications for purposes of wage determination. But even after groupings are made, many distinguishable categories of labor remain, with wide dispersion of their wage rates.

■ "NONCOMPETING GROUPS IN THE LABOR MARKET"

A century ago, economists began to call these different categories of labor "noncompeting groups in the labor market." Instead of being a single factor of production, labor was recognized to be many different factors. Economists expected that as many different wage rates would result as there were noncompeting groups. Their instinct was sound, but there is some danger of misunderstanding their terminology.

In the first place, we must not think that in a perfectly competitive labor market the so-called "noncompeting groups" would disappear. We should still have different categories of labor—just as in the wheat market we have winter wheat, spring wheat, grade 2 red wheat, etc. Second, no one can doubt that these different groups are in some sense competing with each other. Just as I decide between hiring a horse and a tractor, so must I decide between hiring a very skilled, fast-working, high-paid worker and a lower-paid, less skilled one.

The essential point, then, is this: The different categories compete with each other; yet they are not 100 per cent identical. They are *partial rather than perfect substitutes* for each other.

Workers can to some degree cross over from one category into another. If welders' wages were to become $100,000 a year, I might study the art and quit being a teacher. Or if I did not, others would. Therefore, even when the wages of the different categories of labor are different, quantitative wage differences are still subject to the laws of supply and demand. "Cross elasticity" of supply becomes very important: The wage you must pay to recruit foundrymen depends on what the nearby auto plant is paying men on the assembly line.

Or take the case of skilled surgeons. They receive high pay in all countries compared with butchers. Why? Because their work is important? Only in part on this account. For suppose that (1) every year as many babies were born with the capacity necessary for a surgeon as with the capacity necessary for a butcher, (2) we knew how to train surgeons in no time at all, and (3) a surgeon's activities and responsibilities were not regarded as less pleasant or more taxing than those of a butcher. Then do you really think that surgeons would continue to receive higher earnings than butchers? And if you think the sanctity of human life is the key explanation, how do you account for the fact that the best plastic surgeons are higher-paid than the best heart surgeons?

■ GENERAL EQUILIBRIUM OF LABOR MARKET

In real life as we know it, things are not black or white. There is some mobility between different jobs; differences in wages will tend gradually over a long period of time to encourage greater and greater mobility; nor is it necessary for all workers to be mobile—a few movers are enough.

But there will still remain certain permanent barriers to mobility that depend

Competitive wage structure shows great variety of patterns:

SITUATION	RESULT
1. People all alike—jobs all alike.	No differentials.
2. People all alike—some jobs differ in disutility.	Equalizing wage differentials.
3. People differ, but each type of labor is in unchangeable supply ("noncompeting groups").	Wage differentials that are "pure economic rents" or "surpluses."
4. People differ, but there is some mobility between groups ("partially competing groups"; "cross elasticity" important).	General equilibrium pattern of wage differentials as determined by general demand and supply (includes 1–3 as special cases).

TABLE 29-1. COMPETITIVE WAGE DETERMINATION.

upon the irreducible differences in biological and social inheritance. Hence, wage differentials will persist even in the long run.

How big will these differentials be? Suppose we made it easy for people to get the education they are fitted for and to travel from one region to another where their skills can be better used. And suppose we provided people with the best possible information about job opportunities and about their personal potentialities. Then differentials would be much reduced. But for such differentials as remain, how exactly are they determined? The answer is provided by supply and demand.

■ *The market will tend toward that equilibrium pattern of wage differentials at which the total demand for each category of labor exactly matches its competitive supply.* Then and only then will there be general equilibrium with no tendency for further widening or narrowing of wage differentials. Table 29-1 sums up our conclusions.

B. IMPERFECTIONS OF THE LABOR MARKET AND COLLECTIVE BARGAINING

Real-world labor markets are far removed from the ideal model of perfect competition. You can grade wheat into neat market categories, but you cannot do that with human beings. No auctioneer allocates workers to the highest bidders. Studies of areas such as New Haven, Connecticut, show that workers often have only the most imperfect knowledge of nearby wage rates.

WAGE STICKINESS   Two tests indicate that the labor market is imperfect. When there is a considerable increase in unemployment—as in the sluggish 1950s—do wage rates drop as they would in a competitive market? History answers, No.

You may be every bit as capable as someone who has a job, and yet there is no way that you can take his job away by underbidding him. Just imagine going to Ford or any large corporation when the next depression comes, brandishing your degrees and certificates of IQ and excellence, and offering to work for less than they are paying. Could you get a job that way?

WAGE POLICY OF FIRMS   The fact that a firm of any size *must* have a wage policy is additional evidence of labor market imperfections. In a perfectly competitive market, a firm need not make decisions on its pay schedules; instead it would turn to the morning newspaper to learn what its wage policy would *have* to be. Any firm, by raising wages ever so little, could get all the extra help it wanted. If, on the other hand, it cut the wage ever so little, it would find no labor to hire at all in a perfectly competitive labor market.

But just because competition is not 100 per cent perfect does not mean that it must be zero. The world is a blend of (1) competition and (2) some degree of monopoly power over the wage to be paid. A firm that tries to set its wage too low will soon learn this. At first nothing much need happen; but eventually it will find its workers quitting a little more rapidly than would otherwise be the case. Recruitment of new people of the same quality will get harder and harder, and slackening off in the performance and productivity of those who remain on the job will become noticeable.

Availability of labor supply does, therefore, affect the wage you set under realistic conditions of imperfect competition. If you are a very small firm, you may even bargain and haggle with prospective workers so as not to pay more than you have to. But if you are any size at all, you will name a wage for each type of job, then decide how many of the applicants will be taken on; and in terms of the number of applicants who respond, you may alter your wage rate over time. Even in the absence of unions, you will find it a perplexing task to decide on an optimal wage policy.

EQUALITY OF BARGAINING POWER?   One of the reasons given in the past for starting trade-unions was the feeling that unorganized workers, facing financially strong employers, lacked "equality of bargaining power." By union organization it was hoped that a greater equality of bargaining power could be restored. But exactly how one goes about measuring equality or inequality of bargaining power remains a difficult research task for the economic theorist.

It is safe to say that prior to the formation of labor unions, the labor market was not a perfectly competitive one in the economist's sense of the term. And after the formation of unions it continues to differ from the perfectly competitive model. Moreover, a number of the features of labor markets usually associated with unions are also present even where there are no unions. Thus, large companies that have no union will typically introduce a standard trend-rate of pay and be slow to change it, even though the number of workers locally unemployed might go up or down. In years of labor market slack these firms raise their wage rates as much as unionized trades do, despite the fact that competitive theory would expect them then to be cutting rates.

■ THREE WAYS UNIONS SEEK TO RAISE WAGES

Leaving the oversimplified picture of perfect competition behind, we can use economic theory to analyze how trade-unions operate. How might unions hope to raise wages in a particular industry?

There are three main methods of raising wages, all interrelated: (1) Unions can wholly "noncompeting groups," it is nonetheless true that there are innumerable categories of partially competing groups. When the relative wage of one category rises, there are substantial cross-elasticity effects on labor supply as some people switch to the improved-pay occupation. The final pattern of wages would, in a perfectly competitive labor market, be determined by the general equilibrium of the interrelated schedules of supply and demand, as shown in Table 29-1's final category.

B. IMPERFECT COMPETITION AND COLLECTIVE BARGAINING

1 ■

Labor markets are not perfectly competitive in real life. With unions or without them, employers usually have some control over wages, but their wage policy must be conditioned by the available supply of labor.

2 ■

Unions affect wages by (a) restricting labor supply, (b) bargaining for standard rates, and (c) following policies designed to shift upward the derived demand schedule for labor—(b) being most important.

3 ■

Relative increases in wages will in most industries result in less employment there. This is based on the assumption of a movement *along* a given demand schedule (i.e., no demand shifts from higher productivity).

4 ■

At the collective bargaining table the following are some of the determining factors around which argument is likely to center: (1) cost and standards of living, (2) ability to pay and profits, (3) productivity trends and improvement factors, (4) "going wages" paid elsewhere in the locality and in the industry, (5) the influence of higher wages on purchasing power and on the level of costs, (6) the "national pattern" as determined by "key bargains" in important industries, (7) continuous increases based upon improvement factors from long-term technical improvements, and (8) Presidential guideposts for wages and prices or other aspects of an "incomes policy." Economic theory cannot tell just what the final wage bargain will be, it being theoretically indeterminate.

5 ■

Usually a compromise settlement will be possible, without government intervention, formal arbitration, or a strike. But the *threat* of strike is ever-present and conditions the whole bargaining procedure. In vital industries, however, the interest of the public transcends the individual interests and rights of the disputing parties; consequently, voluntary collective bargaining is on trial in such strategic areas and is subject to government controls whenever damaging work stoppages occur.

6 ■

Historically, the extent to which unions have succeeded in raising wages is in doubt. Since 1933 union membership has greatly increased, but in this same period wage differentials seem to have remained about the same in absolute terms. There seems to have been here and abroad a narrowing of percentage wage differentials. While it is true that *recently unionized* industries seem to show slightly greater wage increases since 1933, the quantitative difference is not great and it is not clear which is cause and which effect. Heavily concentrated and expanding industries may have been targets for unionization, and the high wages may have been the result of factors associated with or causing unionization rather than of unionization as such.

7 ■

A final warning is in order: We must beware of the fallacy of composition in ascribing to the *demand curve for labor in general* the shape characteristic of the *demand curve for one small category of labor*. Wages are more than costs; they also constitute much of the income of consumers and react heavily back upon the demand for products of business. A general change in money wage rates can be expected to have important effects on prices. It is even possible that real wages will not change at all. To the extent that a general wage change is balanced by an equivalent percentage change in *all* prices, little substantive effect upon unemployment may result.

8 ■

Structural unemployment could be helped by fiscal and monetary measures as well as by retraining and relocation programs—provided the guideposts of a rational "incomes policy" could be achieved. These would be an achievable goal if "incomes policy" could be integrated with fiscal and monetary programs that optimize aggregate demand. Only then could the conflict between full employment and price stability disappear.

QUESTIONS FOR DISCUSSION

1. Explain narrowing of wage differentials from competition of like people.

2. What factors of technology, economic geography, and legislation help to determine the level of real wages? Show how diminishing returns and countertendencies are linked with the theory of optimum population.

3. Define and contrast "equalizing and nonequalizing differences in wages." Which concept is exemplified by high wages that contained much "pure economic rent"? What about non-competing groups?

4. Give a list of imperfections in the labor market. Show that not all are related to monopoly power or to trade-union organization.

5. Give three ways unions try to influence wages, as described in this chapter. Contrast the first two, and gauge their importance. Do the same for the third method.

6. "Unions can raise real and money wages in a particular industry, but the result will be less employment." Evaluate, utilizing the elasticity of demand for labor.

7. What is the public interest in voluntary collective bargaining?

productivity. On the other hand, modern societies necessarily are engaging in monetary and fiscal policies—and it is these public policies that to an important degree do shape the resulting pattern of high-employment consumption and investment.

This power over the community's rate of capital formation should constitute a sobering responsibility for the voters in any modern democracy.

SUMMARY

1 ◼

We can apply *primary* factors of production, land and labor, in indirect ways by introducing *intermediate* productive factors called *capital goods*. It is taken as a technological fact that this "roundaboutness" yields a *net productivity* over and above all replacement costs, expressible as an annual interest percentage and subject to the usual law of diminishing returns. (Read again the exact definition of net productivity.)

2 ◼

To get the capitalized value of an asset, the interest rate is needed. It is also the device society uses to select investment projects that are most urgent and economical. When interest is high, only projects with highest net productivities can qualify. Gradually, after much past capital formation has invoked the law of diminishing returns, the interest rates will be falling. This provides the signal for introducing capital projects with lower net productivities.

3 ◼

Thrift, in the sense of *abstaining* from consuming past capital accumulations and *waiting* for future consumption goods rather than consuming now, interacts with the technical net productivity of capital goods to determine the developing pattern of interest rates and capital formation. Even outside a collectivist world, government monetary and fiscal policies play an important role in this process.

4 ◼

Even a planned state which is not run for private profit or gain would have to use some device like an interest rate as a sieve to determine which of the many possible investment projects represent the best use of the resources available today after present consumption needs have been determined. "Come the revolution"—come *laissez faire*—Nature's law of diminishing returns is likely still to be in business.

5 ◼

Consumption loans, while they are of minor importance today, do have some influence on the rate at which the community accumulates capital rather than consumes. Like the subjective factors of thrift, abstinence, waiting, foresight, impatience, and so forth, (1) personal borrowings do interact with (2) the technological fact of opportunity to invest in long-lived projects that yield a net productivity.

Critics of interest had in mind the occurrence of consumption loan transactions in highly imperfectly competitive markets where the poor might be regarded as being at the mercy of the rich lender's bargaining power. Today no one would be in favor of usurious overcharges that take advantage of the poor man's inadequate access to competitive loan markets; but economists and philosophers recognize that the net productivity of capital is the technological fact most basic to modern-day interest: when you lend me money, you are giving up the opportunity to invest in land, machines, bonds, and stocks—foregone opportunities of which interest is the rough measure.

6 ■

Important qualifications of the oversimplified traditional capital theory include the following: Lack of perfect foresight means that the capital net productivity is very shiftable as expectations, technology, and income levels change. Also, a classical theory that ignores deviations from full-employment income does need modification.

7 ■

Fortunately, we can adopt a *neoclassical synthesis* of the valid elements of the traditional classical capital theory and the modern theories of income determination and effective demand. According to this rather optimistic—and somewhat oversimplified!—view, a great variety of compensating monetary and fiscal policies can succeed in maintaining inflationless, reasonably full employment. Stable employment being assumed, Fig. 30-2 gives the needed qualification to the traditional theory; and it reveals that public policy has great responsibility for determining whether the composition of the full-employment national income will be heavily weighted toward investment or toward consumption; this means that the central bank and the legislature between them shape the environment within which private thriftiness is translated into social thriftiness.

QUESTIONS FOR DISCUSSION

1. Give some examples of efficient roundabout processes. Of "produced" or "intermediate" inputs.

2. Contrast three "prices" of capital: (*a*) rental of a capital good, (*b*) market price of the capital good, and (*c*) interest yield on the value of the good.

3. Irving Fisher wrote a book with the title *The Theory of Interest*. He gave it the subtitle *As Determined by Impatience to Spend and Opportunities to Invest*. Explain what these mean. Defend the following: "Fisher should have added 'and as affected by government monetary and fiscal policies.'"

4. "The interest rate was simply a bourgeois device for exploitation." Discuss.

5. Protestant, Catholic, and Jewish organizations today issue mortgages to build local places of worship, and they invest any surplus funds in bonds, or possibly, as in the case of the Church of England, in equity stocks. How might they ethically distinguish this from "taking usury"?

6. How do innovations and expectations affect traditional interest theory?

7. Interpret the "neoclassical synthesis." Contrast full employment involving "tight money" and "easy fiscal policy" with an opposite full employment.

8. Explain the rule for calculating present discounted value of a perpetual income stream.

9. Review your understanding of the following concepts:

net productivity of capital

indirect, roundabout methods and
   diminishing returns

capitalization by $V = \$N/i$

interest rate per annum

choosing among investment projects

zero interest under any ism

abstinence and waiting

uncertainty and technological change

austere fiscal policy and easy monetary
   policy, or opposite

neoclassical synthesis and public
   responsibility for rate of capital
   formation

APPENDIX: Theoretical Aspects of Interest, Money, and Policy

Here, very briefly, can be mentioned some elaborations and qualifications of this chapter's discussion.

PRODUCTIVITY OR IMPATIENCE?

Some people like to find a single cause for everything, and such people ask: "Is interest caused by the productivity of capital? Or by the fact that savers must be paid for the unpleasant task of 'abstinence' or 'waiting'? Which is more important: opportunity to invest or impatience to spend?"

   Our previous argument shows this is a false antithesis. *Both* factors operate to determine the time path of interest: the impatience to spend, or the tendency to prefer the present to the future, limits the growth rate and attained size of capital; and the productivity factor tells us what is the interest or net productivity that can be earned as we have various amounts of diverse capital goods. Just as both blades of a scissors are needed to cut—so that you cannot say that one blade rather than the other is doing the actual work—similarly, both factors, impatience *and* productivity, interact to determine the behavior of interest rates.[1]

----

[1] Those who have mastered the indifference-curve graphs of the Appendix to Chapter 22 can use Fig. 30-3 to see that positive interest is caused by two factors: (1) a vertical bias of the *AB* production-possibility frontier between present and future consumption goods, and (2) a general vertical bias of the typical consumer's indifference contours between present and future consumption goods. Hence, the tangency-equilibrium at *E* has a slope steeper than 1.0, corresponding to positive interest. The experienced reader will recognize that these can be related to Böhm-Bawerk's three famous causes for interest. His third cause, technological superiority of roundabout processes, and his first cause, the expectation by the typical consumer that his future dollars will have lower marginal utility

DETERMINATION OF THE INTEREST RATE

Can our account of interest determination avoid the use of Fig. 30-1's simplifying concept of a stock of homogeneous capital? Yes, in a number of ways, some of which are too complex to explain in an introductory

----

because his income will be higher in the future (as a result of technological progress or of the productivity of roundaboutness), relate to factor (1). Böhm's second cause—systematic time preference by consumers for present rather than future goods, for rational reasons of life's uncertainties or for irrational reasons—relates to (2). (Suppose we were to rule out factor (1) by making *AB* "symmetrical around the 45° line" and rule out factor (2) by making the indifference curves "symmetrical around the 45° line." Having thus ruled out net productivity and time preference, we should find that the equilibrium interest rate must then be zero.)

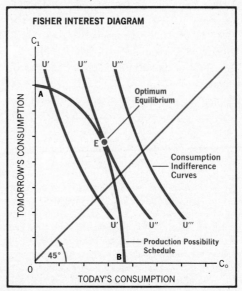

FIG. 30-3.

work. Thus, we may work with a variety of different physical capital goods and processes, being careful never to add their heterogeneous units together, noting that the sum of their capitalized market values does depend (in a virtuously, and not viciously, circular way) on the market interest rate, and never forgetting that it is machines and not hunks of dollars which enter into physical production functions. If the realistic problem of uncertainty about the future and the risks thereby implied could be ignored, advanced treatises can show rigorously how an equilibrium interest-rate pattern can be defined in such a heterogeneous model.

This is clearly not the place for such refinements. But it is desirable to mention that a theory of equilibrium interest rates can be given which avoids the homogeneous-capital assumptions of Fig. 30-1.

The key to a simple approach comes from Fisher's diagram, Fig. 30-3, in footnote 1 of page 585, which states the following fundamental fact about the whole theory of interest.

Society can exchange present consumption goods for future consumption goods at a trade-off rate depicted by the rate of interest.

LONG-RUN EQUILIBRIUM   How long could this accumulation process of sacrificing current consumption go on? Just as Fig. 30-1 suggested, it can go on until the interest rate is zero, or until people want to do no net saving. At the zero rate of interest, if we could ever quite reach this point on the horizon, the plateau of consumption would be as high as is technically possible with the given labor, land, and primary resources. It would be a kind of "golden age."[2]

In real life three or more things keep us from reaching the golden age:

1. People may be so impatient that at some interest rate like 3 per cent, they won't want to do net saving.

2. Inventions will come along and offset diminishing returns by shifting upward all curves *like dd* in Fig. 30-1.

3. There is always riskiness in a dynamic society: long before the pure interest rate reaches zero, the profit-rate-inclusive-of-premium-for-risk may have hit a floor below which investment lags. We must examine this important matter.

AN UNCERTAINTY FLOOR TO RISKY RETURNS AND INVESTMENT?

It may be that under conditions of perfect certainty, persistent thrift can lead to no floor for interest except that of zero. But what about the real world where a measure of uncertainty must always be feared for any actual investment project? Can it not be the case that investors will dislike the task of taking risks on their shoulders? That they will insist on a rate of return on such investments which includes a certain definite positive percentage premium? Thus, even if the rate of interest to be earned on perfectly safe holdings were forced down to zero, might not people still insist on a 5 per cent after-tax return on a risky investment in a machine or in the purchase of land that produces an uncertain yearly rental?

This floor at 5 per cent, or at some positive level above zero, might be a realistic problem to contend with. And if it were to materialize, some serious problems for full-employment policy might one day arrive. Here is why: Suppose that Federal Reserve expansionary policies lowered the rate of interest on very safe short-term government bonds toward zero; this could be expected to bring the rates of return on risky enterprises down from, say, 12 per cent to 8 per cent. And since at the lower rate many new investment projects would now pay, an upswing in investment spending might result that, through the mechanism of the familiar multiplier process, would lift output, income, and employment.

But suppose all this were not enough to reestablish full employment. Then the Federal Reserve could do more of the same. But by no amount of expansionary moves could it reduce the safe interest rate below the floor of zero. And it might well be the case that a zero floor on safe holdings could pull the rates on risky investment down only to their floor of 5 per cent—and no farther. Then it would be quite conceivable that the sticky 5 per cent floor would bar further reduction in

---

[2] Advanced books show that this golden rule must be modified if primary resources such as labor are *all* growing at 3 or 5 per cent per year. Then the golden age of maximal per capita consumption comes when the interest rate has been brought down also to 3 or 5 per cent: then the young earners in society, who are saving for their old age, are just enough more numerous than the retired earners, who are eating up what they had earlier saved; and then there is just enough net saving and investing to keep all capital goods growing in full proportion to the growth in primary labor. Then we have an equilibrium, a nice moving equilibrium with balanced growth. (If land will not grow at all, Malthus reminds us that this Eden must come to an end in the absence of inventions.)

rates needed to coax out a pace of current job-giving investment big enough to restore full employment.

Therefore it is conceivable that an impasse, a kind of Day of Judgment for our mixed system with its inflexible wage and price levels, might arrive when conventional measures to stimulate investment could not restore full employment and let our optimistic neoclassical synthesis work itself out smoothly and fully.[3]

While this pessimistic possibility may not now be at hand, a prudent society has to keep it in mind. And if that unhappy day should ever approach, more extensive remedial programs (such as insurance of loan risks or new institutions to provide venture capital) would have to be imaginatively explored.

MARKET CAPITALIZATION OF ASSETS EQUALS THEIR PRESENT DISCOUNTED VALUE

Here we can go beyond page 571's simple case of perpetual annuities to the general case. Under conditions of absolute certainty, anyone can borrow or lend as much as he wishes at the single competitive market rate of interest. Every asset must be yielding that same

[3] Without risk the problem of placing my assets is easy. I put all my wealth in Bank A if it offers me $5\frac{3}{4}$ per cent while Bank B offers only 5 per cent. I put all my wealth in building stores or tools if they offer more than Bank A's $5\frac{3}{4}$ per cent. So long as I know I can get any safe positive interest return, I hoard no money, keeping only minimal balances for transaction purposes. Without any risks, so long as interest yields remain positive, we should never run out of investment opportunities and into unemployment problems on this account.

With risk, if I obey the law of diminishing marginal utility of Chapter 22, the Appendix of Chapter 21 showed that I shall avoid gambling and want insurance (since a gain in my wealth will be worth less to me than an equivalent *dollar* loss). Now I refuse to put all my eggs in one basket: I put some money in both banks in case one should fail; I prefer $5,000 in General Motors and $5,000 in General Foods to $10,000 in either one alone; I buy many independent stocks for my portfolio; I particularly buy both war and peace stocks so as to be hedged against the worst that can happen. For safety's sake I always hold some idle cash even though it pays no interest. When the pure interest rate is below 2 per cent, I would just as soon hoard cash equal to a large fraction of my wealth or just as soon hold less. This is why Part Two's problem of great unemployment can persist—when a low investment schedule intersects the saving schedule at a point of low-employment NNP, and with profit and interest rates already at their bottom, there is relatively little that conventional banking policy can do in such unlucky times. Then we thank Providence for fiscal policy!

market rate of interest. This equality of yield results from the way competitors bid up or bid down the market price of any asset—whether it be a bond, stock, patent, going business, corner lot, or any earning stream of net rentals whatsoever.

What exactly is the formula for the capitalized market value of *any* asset?

Under absolute certainty, every asset will be capitalized *by the price bids of buyers and sellers* in the market place at the *present discounted value* of all its future net receipts. These dollar receipts cannot simply be added up regardless of the date when they are received. The farther off in the future a given dollar receipt is, the less it is worth today. Why?

Because the positive market rate of interest means that all future payments must be *discounted*. A building far off looks tiny because of spatial perspective. The interest rate produces a similar shrinking of time perspective. Even if I knew you would pay $1 to my heirs 999 years from now, I should be foolish to advance you more than a cent today. To see why, let us review the arithmetic of this discounting process.

At 6 per cent interest I can set aside about 94 cents today, and it will grow to $1 within the year. Hence, the *present discounted value* of $1 payable a year from now is today only 94 cents (or to be exact, $100/1.04 = 94\frac{36}{106}$ cents). The present discounted value of $1 payable in 2 years' time is only about 89 cents, or $1/(1.06)^2$. Similarly, any tables of compound interest will show how to compute present discounted values.[4]

■ The way to arrive at any asset's present discounted value is straightforward. Let each dollar stand on its own feet; evaluate the present worth of each part of the stream of future receipts, giving due allowance for the discounting required by its payment date. Then simply *add together* all these separate present discounted values. Thus we have arrived at the asset's capitalized market value, or what is called its "present discounted value."

[4] The general rule for present discounted values is the following: To figure out the value today of $1 payable t years from now, ask yourself how much must be invested today at compound interest to grow into $1 at the end of t years. Now we know that at 6 per cent compound interest any principal grows in t years proportionally to $(1 + 0.06)^t$. Hence, we need only invert this expression to arrive at the final answer. Therefore the *present discounted value* of $1 payable t years from now is only $1/(1 + 0.06)^t$. What if the interest rate were 8 per cent per annum? Or i per cent?

Future dollar receipts are discounted to get their present value:

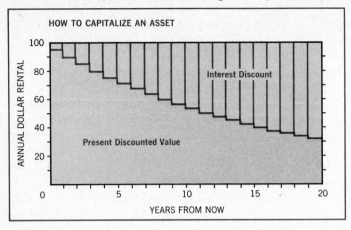

FIG. 30-4. The present value of a machine giving net annual rentals of $100 for 20 years (with interest rate prescribed at 6 per cent) is shown by the lower area. The upper area has been discounted away. (Why does raising the interest rate depress the market price of an asset such as a machine or bond?)

Figure 30-4 shows this graphically for a machine that earns steady net annual rentals of $100 over a 20-year period and has no scrap value at the end. Its present value is not $2,000, but only $1,147. Note how much the later dollar earnings are scaled down or discounted because of the time perspective we have been talking about. The total area remaining after discounting (the green-shaded area) represents the total of the machine's *present discounted value*—its capitalized market value.[5]

[5]Can you now verify our $V = \$N/i$ perpetuity formula? In high school algebra we learn to sum a convergent geometric progression

$$1 + K + K^2 + \cdots = \frac{1}{1 - K}$$

for K any fraction less than 1. If you set $K = \dfrac{1}{1 + i}$, you can with a little work verify our capitalization formula for a permanent income stream: write out *all* the discounted terms

$$\frac{\$N}{1 + i} + \frac{\$N}{(1 + i)^2} + \cdots$$

$$= -\$N + \$N \left\{ 1 + \frac{1}{1 + i} + \left(\frac{1}{1 + i} \right)^2 + \cdots \right\}$$

$$= -\$N + \$N \frac{1}{1 - \dfrac{1}{1 + i}} = \frac{\$N}{i} \quad \text{[QED]}$$

But note that common-sense economics gives us an equally convincing proof: At interest i, $\$N/i$ is the only sum *whose earnings will exactly match* the $\$N$ per year of income.

(A FINE POINT: Sometimes you cannot be sure just which of two machines is the more "durable" one that will be brought into use at a lower interest rate. Suppose Machine A yields $100 of output one period from now and $132 of output three periods from now. Let Machine B yield $230 units of output

ACTING TO MAXIMIZE PRESENT DISCOUNTED VALUE
Our formula tells us how to write down in our balance sheets the value of any asset once we know how that asset will be used. But note that an asset's future receipts usually depend on our business decisions: Shall we use a truck 8 or 9 years? Shall we overhaul it once a month or once a year? Shall we replace it with a cheap nondurable truck or an expensive durable one?

There is one golden rule for giving correct answers to all investment decisions:

■ Calculate the present discounted value resulting from each possible decision. Then always act so as to achieve the maximum present discounted value. That way you will have more wealth, to spend whenever and however you like.[6]

_____

two periods from now, and let it cost the same as A. Which is more durable? More capital-intensive? We can't say. At low rates of interest, present discounted value or *PDV* of A exceeds *PDV* of B, since $100 + 132 > 230$. At very high rates of interest, *PDV* of A exceeds *PDV* of B, since the second and third periods' outputs are discounted away to almost nothing. But at intermediate interest rates, between 10 and 20 per cent per period, calculation shows *PDV* of B exceeds *PDV* of A, and B will be chosen. This "reswitching" phenomenon spoils any simple diminishing-returns story, as advanced treatises show.)

[6]This rule shows that business decisions in an ideal capital market would be independent of the decider's personal consumption-saving time preference. Why? Because it is always better to be able to sell out now for a larger money sum than for a smaller sum, no matter how you decide to spend on consumption. In imperfect markets, personal time preference may matter.

MONEY, INTEREST, AND PUBLIC POLICY

Our final brief task is to suggest how the classical theory of interest fits in with the modern theory of effective demand and money.

Do changes in the amount of money affect the interest rate?

If you believed that employment was always full and that changes in money always resulted via a strict "quantity theory" in proportional changes in *all* prices, then interest rates would indeed be independent of monetary policy. This extreme classical version of neutral money is today believed applicable to short-run events by nobody. (Some economists would, as we saw earlier, grant it a measure of long-run validity, even today: refer back to Chapter 15's discussion of the "crude quantity theory.")

In Part Two we saw that an alternative to holding earning assets is holding money as an asset. Suppose people make no change in their current propensities to save and consume out of a given income when faced by a given interest-rate structure. But suppose they do decrease their desire to hold cash. Then they bid for existing stocks, bonds, and titles to earning assets. This raises capital values and immediately *lowers interest rates;* it also may set capital to growing at a more rapid rate; but only after a time period of higher investment can the volume of real capital goods be appreciably increased. Unless offset by contractionary fiscal policy, all this will raise employment and/or expand wages and prices.

Note that the central bank can create exactly the same chain of events by engaging in expansionary monetary policies. (Recall from Chapter 17 the open-market operations, reserve-rate and discount-rate changes, ...)

How do we reconcile this increase in investment that results from no change in personal thriftiness with classical notions? We do so by recognizing that moving interest downward and relaxing credit generally may raise employment and income and thereby increase achieved capital formation—thus sending us down capital's schedule of net productivity at a faster rate.

SYNTHESIS OF CLASSICAL THEORY OF INTEREST WITH THEORY OF INCOME DETERMINATION: REVIEW

The neoclassical synthesis referred to earlier shows how private and public thrift patterns interact. It shows that private thrift need no longer be feared lest it cause a depression and paradoxically abort itself. It deals with a well-running system that is kept near inflationless full employment by matching central bank and fiscal policies.

Thus, if we desire a high-investment full-employment condition, the central bank uses its "bag of tricks" to increase investment. Of course, given the community's private thrift patterns and technological-expectational investment patterns of the moment, we can stay at the full-employment level aimed at by the central bank only if Congress adopts a compensating fiscal policy.

What are the requirements of this compensating fiscal policy? Taxes and expenditure must be just contractionary enough to affect disposable incomes enough to cut the consumption propensity down to equality with full-employment product minus investment. (Describe what central bank and fiscal authorities must do to create full employment with high consumption.[7])

---

[7] See the Hicks-Hansen diagrams in the Appendix to Chapter 18. We can be, and stay, at full employment by having contractionary fiscal policy shift the *IS* curve rightward whilst expansionary central bank policy shifts the *LM* curve rightward. (Can you show how to engineer a high-consumption low-investment full employment by reversing this prescription?)

SUMMARY TO APPENDIX

1 ■

Technical opportunities to invest (to swap present consumption for future consumption goods) interact with people's subjective preferences (about how much to add to the accumulated stocks of past capital formation) to determine the interest rate. As in all markets, *both* supply and demand factors act.

2 ■

Avoiding the highly useful device of homogeneous stock of physical capital, we can still have a complete interest theory along Fisher lines. The interest rate equals terms of trade at which we can get next-year's consumption goods for today's—106 chocolates next year for 100 today means a 6 per cent interest rate per annum.

3 ■

The formula for capitalizing the asset value of a perpetual constant income can be extended when receipts are neither constant nor perpetual. Each dollar payable t years from now is worth only its "present discounted value" of $\$1/(1 + i)^t$. So for *any* net receipt stream $(N_1, N_2, \ldots, N_t, \ldots)$,

$$PDV = \frac{N_1}{(1 + i)} + \frac{N_2}{(1 + i)^2} + \cdots + \frac{N_t}{(1 + i)^t} + \cdots$$

4 ■

Under conditions involving no uncertainty and no technical innovations, if the community insisted on accumulating more and more capital, diminishing returns might finally force capital's net productivity and the interest rate indefinitely down toward zero. Under real-life conditions of great uncertainty, there is the possibility that the floor on risky returns would be considerably higher than the floor of zero return on risk-free loans. So we cannot rule out the pessimistic possibility of a future Day of Judgment, where the authorities would have to supplement the orthodox methods by which the central bank eases interest rates if they are to succeed in coaxing out the volume of job-creating investment needed to keep employment high or full.

5 ■

The classical assumption that changes in the amount of money merely change the nominal price level and leave all relative prices, interest rates, and production and employment levels unchanged is in need of drastic modification in today's world, where wages and other prices are sticky in the short run, where wages may be hard to get down even in the long run, and where the degree of unemployment may vary considerably.

Increases in money (or decreases in people's desire to hold idle money) will often bid up security prices, lower interest rates, raise investment, and expand real and/or money incomes.

6 ■

But the classical analysis can be usefully applied if we make the neoclassical assumption that central bank and fiscal policies will be so meshed as to preserve stable high-employment levels without undue inflation. (The central bank, so to speak, sets interest to achieve the desired investment level, and the fiscal authorities regulate taxes and expenditures to validate the needed thrift. Of course, both policies are to be *simultaneously* applied.)

QUESTIONS FOR DISCUSSION

1. After the H-bomb was discovered, my time preference for present over future consumption increased. After having learned that my uncle will bequeath me a fortune a decade from now, the same happened. Was this rational? Thinking of a lobster dinner tonight, I offer you $6 on Saturday for $5 now. Is this irrational?

2. Two communities have the same technological production functions. Why might they show different interest-rate patterns in history?

3. Give reasons why lower interest rates might increase investment demand.

4. What might higher M do to interest? Why? What does higher income do? Explain why *independent* mone- tary and fiscal policies need not lead to full employment. Show that there is more than one investment rate compatible with full employment because of changing mix of policies.

5. Review your understanding of the following concepts:
abstinence, impatience, waiting
opportunity to invest
present discounted value
interest rate and planning
uncertainty
technical progress
public policy and capital growth
neoclassical synthesis

31 Profits and Incentives

THE WORLD WILL ALWAYS BE GOVERNED BY SELF-INTEREST. WE SHOULD NOT TRY TO STOP THIS, WE SHOULD TRY TO MAKE THE SELF-INTEREST OF CADS A LITTLE MORE COINCIDENT WITH THAT OF DECENT PEOPLE. SAMUEL BUTLER

In addition to wages, interest, and rent, economists often talk about a fourth category of income: profit. Wages are the return to labor; interest the return to capital; rent the return to land. What is profit the return to?

The answer that economists give is a complex one. This chapter will show that the word "profits" has many different meanings in everyday usage. From these different possible meanings, the economist, after careful analysis, ends up relating the concept of profit to dynamic innovation and uncertainty, and to the problems of monopoly and incentives.

We shall first discuss the main notions of profit. The usual profit figures bandied about will not check with any of these, as we shall see. Then, after analyzing the main notions, we shall conclude the chapter with a summary of the role profit and loss play in the market pricing solution to society's problems WHAT, HOW, and FOR WHOM.

■ REPORTED PROFIT STATISTICS

When a United Nations or U.S. Department of Commerce statistician gives newspaper reporters a figure involving profits, what does he usually include?

Certainly he includes *corporation earnings*—whether they are paid out as dividends or retained as undistributed profits. (In some reports he includes and in some he excludes corporate profit taxes, and sometimes he "adjusts" corporate profits for changes in evaluation of inventories due to price-level changes. So you must be careful in using published statistics.) He may also give another figure that has the flavor of profits about it, namely, *income of unincorporated enterprises* (farmers, self-employed, doctors, partnerships, and so forth).

We understand how he arrived at such a statistical figure of profits for a corporation or unincorporated enterprise. From the sales revenue of the firm, he subtracted its costs: cost of materials, wage payments to employees, bond interest, land rents, and the rest. What is left goes into the figures as profit.

■ FIRST VIEW: PROFIT AS "IMPLICIT" FACTOR RETURNS

To the economist, such statistical profits are a hodgepodge of different elements. Obviously, part at least of reported profits is merely the return to the owners of the firm for the factors supplied *by them*. Part may be the return to the personal work provided by the owners of the firm—by the farmer and his family, by the doctor, by the partners, or by corporate executives who also happen to be principal stockholders. Part may be the rent return on self-owned natural resources; part the equivalent of interest on the owner's capital. (Recall Chapter 23's discussion, page 443.)

This shows us the first fact about profit:

> ■ Much of what is ordinarily called profit is really nothing but interest, rents, and wages under a different name. *Implicit* interest, *implicit* rent, and *implicit* wages are the names economists give to this part of profit, i.e., to the earnings of *self-used* factors.

■ SECOND VIEW: PROFIT AS THE REWARD TO ENTERPRISE AND INNOVATION

Suppose we lived in a dreamworld of perfect competition, where we could read the future perfectly from the palms of our hands and where no innovations were permitted to disturb the settled routine of things. Then the economist says there would really be no profits at all! Here is what he means.

The statistician might still be reporting some profit figures to the press; but we know that, under these ideal equilibrium conditions, the *implicit returns* to the labor and property supplied by owners *would exactly swallow up all the profits reported.* Why? Because owners would hire out their factors on the market if they did not get equal rewards from using them in their own businesses. And because people who previously were hiring out their labor and property services would soon go into business for themselves if they knew they could earn more in that way.

Perfectly free entry of numerous competitors would, in a static world of perfect knowledge, bring price down to cost and squeeze out all profits above and beyond competitive wages, interest, and rent.[1]

We do not live in such a dreamworld. We never shall. In real life somebody must act as boss and decide how a business shall be run. Competition is never "perfectly perfect." Somebody must try to peer into the future to decide whether there will be a demand for shoelaces or what will be the price of wheat. And in the world as we know it, there is a chance for a man with a brand-new idea to invent a revolutionary machine or a softer soft drink—to promote a new product or find a way to lower costs on an old one.

Let us call the man who does any of these things an *entrepreneur,* or *innovator.* Although it is hard to draw the line, let us distinguish him from the bureaucratic executive or manager who simply keeps an established business running. Many economists—

---

[1]If people like running their own business, they may gladly take lower implicit wages. If, by contrast, people dislike having to boss other people and to take responsibility for management decisions, then management wages may have to be higher.

such as the late Joseph Schumpeter, Harvard's Austrian-born economist—do not think of the wages of management as profit: they think of the wages of management as wages—implicit or explicit, and high as they may be in the competitive market for gifted managers. But they think of *profit as the return to innovators, or entrepreneurs.*

Today it is easier for us to understand this distinction than it used to be half a century ago. We are all acquainted with huge corporations run by managers who own less than 1 per cent of the common stock. Even though these executives run the business, they are paid wages much like anybody else. Management of this type is a skill not different in kind from other skills, such as being able to keep books or supervise production. People who possess this skill are bid for in the market place, and like any other factor, they move into those jobs where they will receive the highest wages.

The innovator is different. Though he may not always succeed, he is trying to carry out new activities. He is the man with vision, originality, and daring. He may not be the scientist who invents the new process, but he is the one who successfully introduces it. Maxwell developed the scientific theory of radio waves, Hertz discovered them experimentally, but Marconi and Sarnoff made them commercially profitable. On the other hand, De Forest, who discovered the triode tube, also sought to put his inventions to commercial use; yet he went broke a number of times and on each occasion disappointed the hopes of investors who had put money into his enterprises. Many try; a few succeed.

■ The dollars earned by the successful innovators are defined by some economists—like Schumpeter—as profit. Usually, these profit earnings are temporary and are finally competed out of existence by rivals and imitators. But as one source of innovational profits is disappearing, another is being born. So altogether, these innovational profits will continue to exist.

■ THIRD VIEW: RISK, UNCERTAINTY, AND PROFIT

If the future were perfectly certain, there would be no opportunity for a bright young man to come along with a revolutionary innovation; everything would already be known. This shows that innovators' profits are closely tied up with risk and uncertainty. Frank Knight, a famous University of Chicago economist of the last 45 years, has an important theory that *all true profit is linked with uncertainty.*[2] Innovators' profits, discussed in the preceding section, represent one important category of uncertainty-induced profit.

In examining any profit figures, we must always keep uncertainty and risk in mind. We saw in earlier chapters that some low-grade risky bonds may appear to be yielding 9 per cent at the same time that high-grade safe bonds yield only 5 per cent. But if the chances are that 1 out of 20 low-grade issues will default on their principal in the coming year, then you are fooling yourself if you think that these bonds are a better buy. Actually, the extra 4 per cent may be no more than enough to cover the risk of default.

[2]Frank H. Knight, *Risk, Uncertainty and Profit* (London School of Economics and Political Science, Series of Reprints of Scarce Tracts, No. 16, 1933).

While people who buy lottery tickets face uncertainty, the promoter of the lottery faces no risk. He knows *he* will come out ahead. Similarly, a large insurance company may rely on mathematical laws of probability to reduce its relative riskiness. Why? Because the different risks tend to be canceled by each other if the numbers are large enough. To the extent that we can eliminate uncertainty by pooling risks, the problem of profits fails to arise. It arises only for the irreducible minimum of riskiness that remains.

In some years, the total losses may be greater than the total profits. Then risk bearers as a whole have paid out to labor, to capitalists, and to landowners more than those factors would have earned if the future had been certain. In another year, the algebraic total of Knight-defined profits may turn out to be positive—so that the factors of production have then received less than they would have if the future were certain. A big question is this:

Are risk bearers on the whole overly optimistic? As a class do they lose money and subsidize the other factors of production? Or are risk bearers as a class overly "pessimistic"—as claimed in most economics textbooks—so that profits represent a net positive payment for the service of risk bearing? Many economists think that businessmen on the whole act as if they dislike mere riskiness, and hence they must on the average be paid a positive premium or profit for shouldering risks.

We summarize the notion of profit as the reward of risk bearing thus:

■ If people generally act like risk averters, feeling that the marginal utility of the dollars they gain is less than that of the dollars they lose, they will prefer smaller steady incomes to erratic incomes even when those average out to a higher figure. Therefore economic activities that involve much uncertainty and risk, which will fall on the people who engage in them, will be forced by competitive entry and exit of risk takers to pay, over the long run, a positive profit premium to compensate for aversion to risk. The yield on capital invested in such industries will involve, in addition to pure interest corresponding to safe investments, an extra element corresponding to positive profit. (Other productive factors, such as labor in risky trades, may also have profit premiums as the necessary bait to keep them in the trade in question.)

■ FOURTH VIEW: PROFIT AS A "MONOPOLY RETURN"

We have noted three aspects of profit: (1) profit as *implicit* rents, wages, and interests; (2) profit as the temporary return to daring but unforeseen *innovations;* and (3) profit as the divergence—thrown up by the fact of *uncertainty*—between what people had *expected* to happen and what actually happened, tending to average out positive if people dislike risk and must be paid a positive premium to shoulder it.

If you point out the above to a person who feels vaguely critical toward profit, you may confuse him and make him uncertain as to what it is that he is against. His hazy notion of a capitalist as a fat man with a penchant for arithmetic, who somehow exploits the rest of the community, calls attention to a fourth possible meaning of profit, namely, *profit as the earnings of monopoly.* Like most people, he may have an exaggerated notion of how much of each dollar spent on an automobile or a pork chop goes to profit receivers—according to any of our definitions. Most likely, he thinks that about 50 per cent of each dollar goes to wealthy monopolists; the prosaic truth is that, even in terms of the catchall statistical definition, corporate profits after taxes are less than *one-fifth* of corporations' wage payrolls (even after personal taxes).

PERFECT COMPETITION REDEFINED   Still, if we are to be objective, we must not close our eyes to this fact: In the world as we know it competition is not "perfect" as rigorously defined by the economist. Some elements of monopolistic imperfections do certainly exist. Perfect competition means that each seller has *absolutely no control* over price; it means that his demand curve is perfectly horizontal and *infinitely* elastic; it means that no person is able to control any significant fraction of the total of any category of productive resource.

We have seen in Chapter 25 and elsewhere that perfect competition is a far cry from the real world. Most firms, outside farming, can raise or lower their prices without losing or gaining *all* the customers in the market. Instead, their demand curves are somewhat sloped, and there is a discrepancy between price and marginal revenue. Most markets are imperfectly competitive—a blend of competition and monopoly. (So common a condition is by no means necessarily illegal or immoral but, as already seen, competitive imperfections have distorting effects on WHAT, HOW, and FOR WHOM.)

Now let us return to the fourth view of profits. When we examine the ownership of productive factors, we see that no two factors are quite alike. Your abilities as a worker and those of your neighbor are somewhat different. If we define your precise pattern of abilities as a separate factor of production, then we must admit that you do own and control an appreciable fraction of the total of that unique factor of production—100 per cent, in fact. Or you may be the sole owner of the patent to a particular process, or own the only site where the river narrows down to its most suitable place for a bridge. Or there may be no acre of Iowa land quite like yours.

Let us see how this ties in with imperfect competition. Your neighbors are a little different from you, certainly. But probably they are enough like you that the hourly wage rate for your services would not be appreciably higher even if you *withheld* some from the market. You really do not possess any appreciable monopoly power because the demand for the factor you own is for practical purposes infinitely elastic.

The same is true of your acre of good Iowa cornland. If you let half of it stand idle, the price of corn would not be affected; and the derived price for each acre of your land would be unchanged, even though you and your family know that there is really no other farmstead quite like it.

And note this: If the land is sufficiently fertile, you will, of course, be making quite a living off your farm. Perhaps you may even be in the top 2 per cent of the income distribution. Even though competition is perfect, this rent return to the land you own *cannot* be competed away by rival farmers. As long as the Good Lord made only a limited amount of fertile Iowa farmland, it will earn a rent for its owner— regardless of how he originally acquired title to the land. *Competitively determined rents are the results of a natural scarcity.*[3]

---

[3] If there is great inequality in the distribution of ownership of factors of production, then even under the most perfect competition (where pure profit is zero) there can still result a very rich, possibly idle, minority of plutocrats surrounded by masses of lower-income people.

■ "CONTRIVED SCARCITIES" VERSUS "NATURAL SCARCITIES"

It is quite a different matter if the demand for one of your factors of production is negatively inclined rather than infinitely elastic. (Let us review what this means: It means that, when you raise your price, you still can sell *some* of your factor; this is the sense in which you have some monopoly control over price.) If you are the sole owner of an important patent, it will pay you to charge a price so as to limit its use. If audiences swoon to your singing as to nobody else's, then you will have to remember that the more you sing, the lower will be the price the market will pay for your singing. If you own the best site for a bridge, then you must be careful not to sell anyone else the lot next to it; otherwise he will be able to offer the bridge builders a site nearly as good as yours, and this will limit the dollars you can derive from yours. Part of the rent you earn on Nature's bridge site has a monopoly element in it by virtue of your withholding its use for fear of spoiling your dollar market.

What does all this add up to? It means that, *as soon as there is an appreciable deviation from perfect competition, it will pay you to take account of the fact that you will spoil the market the more you offer of your factor.*

Any prudent firm takes account of the loss on all previous units resulting when it sells an extra unit of product, and it is its marginal revenue—lower than price because of the loss on previous units—which a prudent firm concentrates on. Again with you as the owner of a factor: you are interested in the *marginal,* or *extra, revenue* that the factor brings you. You will not withhold all the factor from the market—that would bring you in *no* revenue at all. Nor will you provide so much of the factor that it becomes a free good and brings in no revenue. As a quasi-monopolist, or imperfect competitor, what should you do? You will withhold just as much of that service as will bring its marginal revenue down to zero.[4]

Our principle is this: *Under imperfect competition, it pays people to limit the supply of their factors somewhat.* By definition, natural scarcities are such that nothing can be done about them. But under imperfect competition, we encounter in addition so-called "contrived scarcities."

■ MONOPOLY EARNINGS AS THE RETURN TO "CONTRIVED SCARCITIES"

Hence, the fourth view of profits as a monopoly return is often reformulated in the economic textbooks to read as follows:

■ *Part of what is called profit is the return to a contrived scarcity.* This return takes the form of rent, wages, or interest, depending on the nature of the factor in question and on the contractual relations set up to handle the particular situation. (For example, an investor may buy the bridge-site land at the full capitalized value of its monopoly earning power. To him, the return will seem to be interest.) So monopoly profits are inextricably tied up with wages, interest, and rent.

[4]Of course, there may be some discomfort to you in rendering the service, or you may have the opportunity of selling the service in some other market—as in the case where you could use your bridge site to grow corn. In these cases, you will obviously equate marginal revenue to some defined positive marginal *cost* rather than to zero.

Wherever contrived scarcities exist, they distort the optimum pattern of resource use. They may also create high earnings for the people involved. But high earnings do not always follow. Thus, under imperfect or monopolistic competition, there may be many taxicabs or grocery stores. Each owner may have a sloping demand curve and may be setting a price in excess of marginal cost. Yet there may be so many imperfect competitors that none of them is earning more than he could get in a perfectly competitive industry. Wiping out the imperfections and illegally contrived scarcities might improve the pattern of production, but it still might or might not have much effect on relative distribution of income (see the Chamberlinian Fig. 26-3, page 490).

■ ETHICAL ATTITUDES TOWARD PROFITS

Any sampling of public opinion shows some hostility toward profit. A statistician recently asked a random sample of businessmen if they "tried to maximize their profit." To a man, they all denied this firmly, perhaps because they pictured a profit maximizer as some kind of chiseling extortionist or miser. But then the investigator asked the same businessmen whether they thought any change in their present price policies could be counted on to make them better off in the long run. To a man, they all replied that they were already doing as well as they could hope to do!

It is misleading to talk about "a profit system." Ours is a *profit-and-loss* system. Profits are the carrots held out as an incentive to efficiency, and losses are the kicks that penalize using inefficient methods or devoting resources to uses not desired by spending consumers. This metaphor of carrots and kicks is ancient, but apt.

Within the framework of law and custom—where it is both illegal and uncustomary to put sand in sugar—what does the pursuit of profit mean? It means that the businessman, like anybody else, is trying to get as much as he can for the resources at his disposal. (This is not different from what a worker is doing when he changes occupations or joins a union.) If competition is perfect, the businessman will end up with no *excess profits*. If competition worked perfectly, the attempt by all to reap excess profits would result in none succeeding. Competitors would have to run hard in order to stay in the same place! This is a paradox, but it is true nonetheless.

Would the competitive disappearance of profits mean that the businessman's land, acumen, sweat, and financing would go without reward? No, certainly not. Even under perfect competition, his factors would earn wages, interest, and rent. Much of the hostility toward profit is really hostility toward the extremes of inequality in the distribution of money income that comes from unequal factor ownership; this should be kept distinct from hostility toward profit created by imperfections of competition.

■ THE IMMEASURABILITY OF "PROFIT": TAX EFFECTS

How large are these four different categories of profit? We have no way of knowing. It would be nice if we could say that so many billion dollars of the reported total of profit is implicit wages, so many billions implicit interest, and so many billions implicit rents and, of the remainder, so much is innovator's profit and so much is the algebraic total due to uncertainty generally. It would be nice, too, if we could divide the total of all factor incomes into two separate parts: (1) the return to so-called contrived scarcities and (2) the competitive rent return to so-called natural scarcities.

But probably we shall never be able to do this with precision. And what good would it do us if we could? Well, for one thing, some reformers believe that, if only Congress could easily identify every situation of an illegally contrived scarcity, it might act to bring about a more efficient use of resources. Or some citizens may think that, if Congress could identify the temporary profits due to innovation, it might try to tax them more heavily. And some may agitate for reversal of the present light treatment of capital gains and propose that Congress tax the profits arising from uncertainty more heavily than it taxes ordinary income.

But even if you are opposed to high profits, realize that taxing profits will raise problems. Such legislation will have many effects on the economic system, and we had better examine these effects hardheadedly before making up our minds as to how far to go in this direction.

TAXING PROFITS   Let us examine some of the effects of taxing each of the four different kinds of profit.

1. Suppose you pass a law taxing a corporation's implicit interest more heavily than the explicit interest it pays out to bondholders. What are the consequences likely to be? To answer this, we do not have to conjecture in a vacuum, for the American corporation income tax is just such a law.

Standard Oil must pay the government almost half of each dollar earned on the capital supplied by its stockholders; on the capital it raises through bond flotations, it does not have to pay corporate taxes. (That is, Standard Oil can deduct from its taxable income each dollar of bond interest, but it *cannot* deduct any dollars paid out in dividends or plowed back as undistributed profits.) What is the result? If Standard Oil is otherwise indifferent between bond or stock financing, it will tend to rely on bonds in order to make its capital earnings show up as explicit rather than implicit interest. (The reader may work out the following similar problem: When I quit my job for a week in order to paint my house, I switch from explicit to implicit wages and the latter is not taxed as personal income. What tendencies can you predict?)

If hostility to profit makes you tax implicit returns, you should realize that this will change (and sometimes distort) people's decisions.

2. The case of taxing innovators' profit is even clearer. Taxing a retired innovator's income may seem to have no distorting effects. But we must not forget the young innovator who can then no longer look forward to reaping a tidy sum from his new ideas. He may decide to take that civil service job or remain thirteenth vice-president of a bank. You cannot tax the results of an old innovation without somewhat affecting the prospects of an as-yet-unborn innovation.[5]

3. If Congress taxes risky activities more heavily than routine activities, what can any reasonable person expect to happen? People will naturally tend to avoid ven-

---

[5] Incidentally, this provides a partial defense of patents. Society deliberately gives a man a monopoly; this contrivance permits him artificially to keep something *partially* scarce. But society hopes the offered bribe of temporary monopoly will encourage the invention of things that would otherwise be 100 per cent scarce.

turous fields and to gravitate toward routine, steady ones. Yet all of us—rich and poor alike—have a great stake in promoting vigorous exploration of new ways of doing things. Not only has scientific and technological innovation been the secret of our material progress, but in addition the investment associated with venturesome projects is just what the doctor orders to avoid depression and mass unemployment.

As Chapter 9 showed, our present income tax already discriminates against venture capital. It is true that income taxation is being improved by introducing systems of "averaging income" over more than one year; but until further reforms are made, it remains partially a case of "heads I lose, tails the government wins." The losses brought to me by uncertainty cannot be fully offset against my gains, and taxing profits still more heavily would increase the harmful effects on venture capital.

This conclusion, that our ordinary income tax on personal and corporate income discriminates against risk taking, has to be substantially qualified when we take into account present light taxation of capital gains. Tax experts know that many investors, particularly high-income investors, deliberately seek out risky investments: oil drilling, common-stock buying, new growth companies, patents, and so forth. Why? Because they expect that the lucky gains from such ventures will be taxed at less than half rate, while many of their costs can be charged off against high-taxable income.[6]

The above capital-gain loopholes are today widely used.[7] Hence, some say that our present tax system, far from penalizing risk taking, improperly encourages people to do too much of this. And others say, "We can't have too much risk taking if we want to make progress. Capitalism breathes through those tax loopholes." No simple answers can be given in this controversial field.

4. In advocating taxation of monopoly profits you may think you are on more solid ground. But how can you decide what fraction of any company's profits are attributable to these so-called contrived rather than natural scarcities? In 1920 the American Viscose Company dominated the rayon field with its patents, and it earned 156 per cent on its capital. Perhaps the courts might identify cases like this as monopoly profit, perhaps not. But such simple cases are the exception, since we have seen that returns to alleged contrived scarcities are intermingled with all factor returns. Monopoly profits may already have been capitalized and may appear in the guise of interest, or they may take the form of high wages.

Moreover, the best cure for monopoly may not be to transfer its earnings to the state, as the Bourbons and other despots used to do with their salt and match taxes.

[6]Thus, a 1966 movie star borrows from a bank to drill for oil; he knows his interest will be paid 70 cents on the dollar by the government through his tax savings; he knows he can deduct his intangible drilling expenses on the same 30-to-70-cent basis; he knows too that when he finds oil, he can sell it and pay only 25 per cent long-term capital-gain tax—or, holding on to the successful oil well, he can collect tax-free $27\frac{1}{2}$ per cent oil-depletion allowance.

[7]A 1953 Harvard Business School study suggests that the rich men it examined were able to keep their tax rates down to 50 per cent on the average, and that taxes pushed some toward venturesome investment. "Appreciation-minded investors . . . may have been so stimulated by the tax structure to seek out investments offering unusually large capital gains potentialities, such as promising new ventures, as actually to increase the flow of capital to such situations." J. K. Butters, L. E. Thompson, L. L. Bollinger, *Effects of Taxation: Investment by Individuals.*

If a factor is not naturally scarce, why keep it artificially scarce? Where the government can recognize illegal monopoly, it should deal with it by court action or by public-utility regulation. It would often be sounder policy to wipe out excessive monopoly profits by price cuts than to transfer them by taxation.

■ INCENTIVES, SURPLUSES, AND EQUITY: PROFIT NOT NECESSARILY A SURPLUS

Voters often favor measures that tax the rich relatively more than the poor and that tend to reduce inequality of income.

Within the framework of constitutional government, it is the privilege of the electorate to press for what they regard to be ethically the good life. But in weighing what they consider to be the ethical advantages of a more equal distribution of income, the public should rationally face what may be some of the concomitant effects on venturesomeness, efforts, and thriftiness.

The prevailing hostility toward so-called "profits" shows that there is a fifth—deceptive—definition of profit in the back of most people's minds.

■ Many people think of profits as an *unnecessary surplus* that factors earn.

Our earlier discussion of the rent earned by inelastically supplied land shows that "taxable surpluses" may indeed occasionally exist. And in the case of *any* factor of production, it must be clear that every time you raise prices in order to coax out the last or marginal unit, you are in part creating a kind of extra surplus for all the factors already employed.[8] (Thus, in World War I, the government raised the price of copper in order to bring poorer mines into operation; in doing this sensible thing, it created high earnings for the more efficient mines.)

Every factor income, therefore, has in it both elements of (1) *surplus* and (2) *incentive payment*. But that does not mean you can take the 800 billion dollars of national income and divide it up into two parts—say, 150 billion dollars of taxable surplus and 650 billion dollars of incentive payments. *The two are hopelessly intertwined;* and unless you were to make a study of each and every factor or commodity unit and were to name a discriminatingly different price for each unit—as was done by OPA for the copper industry in World War II—you would have no way of hitting at the surplus without at the same time doing damage to incentives.

This fifth notion of profit as an easily taxable surplus must therefore be handled with care.

■ A SERMON ON PROFIT AND WHAT, HOW, AND FOR WHOM

Back in Chapter 3 we surveyed how a price system helps solve society's basic problem of WHAT, HOW, and FOR WHOM. In Part Three we studied the tools of supply and demand that determine competitive market price. And we examined important effects of monopolistic imperfections of competition.

[8] Alfred Marshall termed this "producers' surplus," which is closely analogous to the "consumers' surplus" of Chapter 22.

It is fitting here, prior to the next chapter's complete review, to summarize the role of profit and loss in the over-all pricing process.

1. Each person seeks his own advantage. Workers seek highest wages; landlords, highest rents; capitalists, highest interest returns. Some of these factor returns will be implicit returns. Still other returns may arise from innovation and/or uncertainty, and for those reasons they may be called profit.

2. In the most general sense, profit seeking is simply seeking of self-advantage. Does this all lead to a jungle—"red in tooth and claw," and chaotic? Not if there are complete checks and balances. These checks and balances are most complete if competition is perfect; incomplete, if it is imperfect. Adam Smith's Invisible Hand cannot be counted on under monopolistically imperfect competition.

3. Where competition is perfect, or nearly so, there results a pattern of order, of efficiency. But not, mind you, any proven condition of utopia, with the poor become prosperous and the rich brought down near the mean.

Of course, shirkers get low incomes. And earnest people, born stupid and with weak muscles, also get low incomes for all their earnestness. Smart go-getters get high incomes. Highly intelligent altruists, who seek the well-being of other people, themselves get low incomes. Smart girls, born of smart and lucky fathers, get high incomes. Stupid girls, born of smart and lucky fathers, get high incomes. Those who get a good education from five to twenty, or four to twelve, stand to gain at the expense of those who do not. So it goes.

4. Where a democracy does not like the For Whom pattern that results from *laissez faire*, it puts in tax changes, school and other expenditures, fiats, and subsidies to change the pattern. This helps some incomes, hurts others.

These redistributions are acquired at a cost. What cost? The cost of distortions of incentives, distortions which somewhat lessen the efficiency of the most efficient market system. There are costs, too, in tax collection and transfer.

5. Profits and losses signal the advantages of activities. When a man is doing what some buyers in society want, he finds his wage or profit return rising. So he keeps on doing this. If he overdoes it, he gets penalized. Or, through no fault of his own, he gets penalized when someone better comes along. He may then get kicked into the next best thing for him to do.

PROFIT AS A COORDINATING DEVICE Where knowledge is imperfect, a man may make money by correctly guessing the future. If he thinks wheat will be scarce in Kansas, he ships wheat there; or grows more wheat there; or makes a bet about wheat's scarcity on the board of trade, and by making this bet may activate someone else to grow more wheat, eat less, or ship more—or he may just gain from another bettor.

In a free pricing system, each man may use his initiative to create a new product or process. If his guess about the future is wrong, he stands to lose. And so do all the people who guessed that he was right—his workers who gave up other jobs, his capitalist backers, and so forth. If he turns out right, he strikes it rich; and his rival may go to the poorhouse. Any entrenched way of doing things can, under the freest competition, be bested and changed.

Profits and high factor returns are the bait, the carrots dangled before us enter-

prising donkeys. Losses are our penalty kicks. Profits go to those who have been efficient in the past—efficient in making things, in selling things, in foreseeing things.
Through profits, society is giving the command over new ventures to those who have
piled up a record of success.

To understand this last point, imagine a bureaucratic board that awards money
to people who apply to it for new projects. If a man was very successful in his last
five projects, the board is likely to act favorably on his new application. Well, profits
that a man with high innovating abilities has piled up from the past automatically
give him the go-ahead signal in his future enterprises. (But in life, and in the case of
the bureaucratic board, how do you get your first start?)

■ Profits are the report card of the past, the incentive gold star for the future,
and also the grubstake for new ventures.

6. Under perfect competition a man could get ahead only by doing things of
value to himself or someone else. With knowledge perfect, he could not spread lies
about fake uranium mines and make money that way or from false advertising claims.
A perfect competitor would not cut down on his output in equating marginal revenue
to marginal cost ($MR = MC$). Instead he would have no control over market price
and would be doing what the utopian Invisible Hand says everyone has to do if the
pricing system is to be 100 per cent efficient; namely, he would be equating price to
marginal cost ($P = MC$). And he could not be making monopoly profits from contrived
scarcity, because under perfect competition there are no monopoly positions.

And if a pricing system were really utopianly perfect in its working, no activity
would be pouring smoke into the air without being made to share the cost that such
smoke imposes on the rest of the community. No one would refuse to do basic research
for fear that he could never tap its full advantage to society and thereby recover his
own private research costs. All "external" benefits or costs connected with every activity would be correctly counted in. So when each maximized his own advantage, the
checks and balances of perfect pricing would ensure that the benefit of all with money
votes was being efficiently achieved.

7. The above remarks show that you would be wrong to say: The trouble with
perfect competition is that it has never been tried. For could it ever be tried? Can we
institute perfection? Monopoly aside, can we banish "external effects"? Obviously, no
one can institute perfection. And obviously, no one can identify the existing world with
perfect competition, or identify a government-do-nothing world of *laissez faire* with
perfect competition.

To the degree that public action can (1) lessen monopolistic imperfections, (2)
increase imperfect knowledge, and (3) bring total social benefits and costs into closer
alignment with private benefits and costs—to this degree will there be a creative
economic role for the state. Of course, all such action has costs, and these must be
carefully weighed in judging extension of government and retention of old functions.

Our sermon on pricing is over. Taking into account the real world as we know it,
students of the modern economy realize why it has to be—from its very nature—a

mixed economy. Competitive pricing must carry most of the burden of solving society's WHAT, HOW, and FOR WHOM. But constructive public policies are needed to keep the system competitive and provide the favorable environment in which private initiative can achieve the common good.

SUMMARY

1 ■

Profit is a highly miscellaneous category. In national-income statistics, it is the total of lumped-together corporate earnings and the income of unincorporated enterprises. But economically we must distinguish four profit concepts.

2 ■

Much of what is called profit is really *implicit* interest, rent, and wages payable for the productive factors provided by the owners of the business.

3 ■

The special category of *high temporary earnings resulting from innovation* is often termed profit by many economists. Routine management earns wages, they say, but profit may accrue to genuine entrepreneurship.

4 ■

Uncertainty is the all-pervading fact of life. It makes innovation possible and also creates positive and negative divergences between what factors expect to earn and what they actually end up earning. Knight and other economists define profit and loss as the *unforeseeable discrepancies created by uncertainty.* If people are generally averse to risk and erratic returns and resist being overoptimistic, a positive premium of profit will be required to coax out their limited supply of risk bearing.

5 ■

Still another definition of profit is the return accruing as the result of some kind of monopoly position. This concept is sometimes varied to describe profit as part of the return resulting from a "contrived scarcity."

6 ■

The taxation of any of these categories of profit can be expected to have definite reper-cussions, some undesirable from any viewpoint. A fifth notion of profit as *an identifiable and taxable surplus rather than incentive payment* is oversimple. If the public wishes to pursue what it calls equity or an ethically more desirable distribution of income, let it face and weigh any resulting distorting effects on incentives.

7 ■

Profit or advantage seeking does, under perfectly competitive pricing conditions, lead to efficient HOW. If the distribution of initial wealth, abilities, and opportunities were made ethically optimal (and were continually adjusted to changing relative prices), and if there were no externalities or monopolistic imperfections of technology and markets, then the checks and balances of perfect competition could lead to a "best" solution of WHAT, HOW, and FOR WHOM.

In a mixed economy, public policies try to provide needed correctives and checks and balances and try to help align social and private benefits—in short, try to promote the best environment within which private initiative can function.

QUESTIONS FOR DISCUSSION

1. Define "implicit" factor earnings. Contrast with other profit concepts.

2. Give cases of innovation; of risk taking. How will taxes affect them?

3. What is meant by perfect competition? By imperfect competition? Can you specify a monopoly profit that all will think bad? Can you identify natural and contrived scarcities?

4. Discuss ethical and incentive aspects of taxing so-called profits or higher incomes generally. (E.g., corporate income tax favors bond finance. So?)

5. "Profit seeking is ugly. Even if it were efficient—and I deny that it works out that way—I'd be against it. Give me medieval charity or Zuñi brotherhood, but deliver me from the market." Do you disagree?

6. "If the Lord gives a man strength, brains, and energy, then he's been given much. So he deserves lower material income—not higher." Contrast with "To each according to his ability—according to his marginal-product."

7. Chapter 40 reports the evolution of the Soviet Union toward use of some measurements of profitability. How might one account for such a trend?

8. Review your understanding of the following concepts:

reported statistics of profits

implicit versus explicit factor returns

wages of management

reward for risk taking

innovation, uncertainty

capital gain, ordinary income

probability, large-number of risks

imperfections of competition, monopoly

contrived versus natural scarcity

rent and surplus, incentive payments

initial distribution of wealth

external effects, and divergence of private and social benefit and cost

ethical questions and value judgments

32 Epilogue to Microeconomic Pricing

TRUTH CAN NEVER BE TOLD SO AS TO BE UNDERSTOOD AND NOT BE BELIEVED.   WILLIAM BLAKE

Parts Three and Four are now completed. Let us review the broad principles of *value* and *distribution*.

■ SURVEY OF THE INTERDEPENDENT PRICING PROCESS

We have seen:

1. How competitive supply and demand operate in a *single* market, in both the short and long run.

2. How the relative marginal utility (or indifference) preferences of men lie behind their respective demand curves.

3. How marginal costs lie behind the competitive supply curves.

4. How the technical production function relating output to factor inputs lies behind the total and average cost curves, which have been minimized by the firm's demanding inputs until their marginal-physical-products are proportional to factor-prices.

5. How these marginal-physical-products and marginal-revenue-products, summed for all firms, provide the "derived demands for the factors."

6. How these derived demands for land, labor, or capital goods interact with their market supplies to determine factor-prices such as rent, wages, rentals, and so forth.

7. How primary resources like labor and land are used to make produced capital goods, which are in turn used in roundabout ways to increase society's final output; how this "net productivity of capital" is reflected in the rate of interest, which, in the absence of technical change, is generally subject to diminishing returns much as labor and land are subject to that law; and how competitive markets evaluate all assets at their "present discounted values," using interest yields to screen out best investments.

8. Finally, how pursuit of profit and avoidance of loss furnish the motive force behind the whole competitive process; how, paradoxically, under static conditions free of uncertainty and innovational change, competitive profits (other than implicit factor

returns and wages of management) would tend to zero; but how the persistence of risk coupled with a general aversion to risk taking, on the ground that dollar gains have less marginal utility than dollar losses, would lead to profit return as a positive premium for risk bearing.

■ SIMULTANEOUS MUTUAL DETERMINATION

Notice how, in the listing of the eight steps above, each follows from the preceding one—from step 1 to step 2 and then step 3, until finally we come to step 8. In the textbook chapters they follow in about the same order.

But in real life, which comes first? Is there any order and sequence, with prices being determined in single markets on Monday, consumers evaluating preferences on Tuesday, businessmen reckoning costs on Wednesday and marginal-products on Thursday? Obviously not. All these processes are going on at one and the same time.

That is not all. These different processes do not go on independently side by side, each in its own little groove, careful not to get in the way of the other. All the processes of supply and demand, of cost and preference, of factor productivity and demand—all these are really different aspects of one vast simultaneous *interdependent* process.

Thus, the supply curve for wheat given in the first chapter of Part Three is itself the resultant of the cost calculations given at the end of Part Three, of the production considerations given at the beginning of Part Four, and of the wage and rent and interest determinations given at the end of Part Four. Actually, you can take any one of the 8 steps in the outline and draw arrows connecting it causally *with every other step.*

Figure 32-1 tries to give a summary picture of the interdependent system which economists call "general equilibrium." Recall the circular-flow diagram on national income (Fig. 10-1, page 171), showing plumbing pipes carrying dollars clockwise from business to families and from families to business. That gave what economists call the "aggregative," or "macroeconomic," picture of the nation's grand economic totals.

Now turn to Fig. 32-1. It also gives the circular flow of dollars. But this time we take a microscopic approach—what economists call the "microeconomic" picture. Now we do not talk about the grand total of factor incomes; instead we show derived demand by business for skilled labor, unskilled labor, good vineyard land, and for every other factor of production. Nor do we speak of total consumption: we specify; we show the consumer's demand for coffee, tea, shoes, and for each and every commodity or service.

Note that in the lower loop we have for each factor *both* a supply and a demand. (QUERY: Which of these schedules comes from business? Which from consumers? Match green and brown colors.) And in the upper loop, you see *both* a business supply and consumer demand for each good.

Thus, we can give an optimistic answer to the logical purist who poses the embarrassing question: "Your economic system isn't determinate until you have found conditions to determine a price *and* a quantity for each output and for each input. Do you have enough simultaneous conditions (or equations) to make your interdependent equilibrium system determinate?"

WHAT, HOW, and FOR WHOM is determined by general equilibrium pricing:

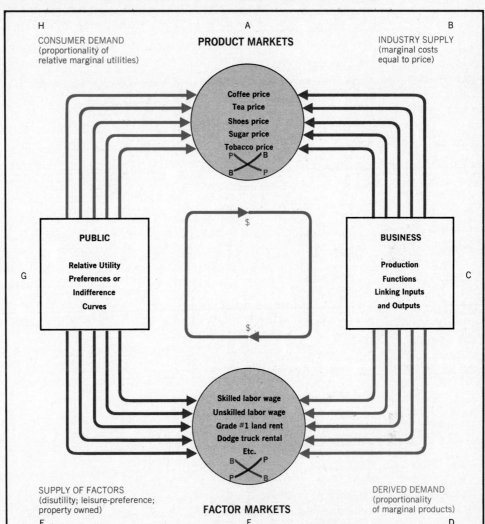

FIG. 32-1. The clockwise money flow is broken up to show consumer demand meeting industry supply at *A* to determine equilibrium price and quantity of each good. Similarly, derived factor demands of business meet public's supply of factors at *E* to determine equilibrium factor-prices and amounts. (Interpret what is going on behind *B*, *D*, *F*, and *H*—and inside *C* and *G*—and compare this with the WHAT, HOW, and FOR WHOM of Fig. 3-1, on page 44.)

Fortunately, we can answer: "We do have for each output or input *both a supply and a demand condition.* So we can hope that the system will, by trial and error in the market place, finally settle down—if left undisturbed!—to a determinate competitive equilibrium."[1] And we can add: "The final competitive equilibrium is an 'efficient'

---

[1] Leon Walras, a French economist three-quarters of a century ago, is usually credited with the discovery of general equilibrium. But W. S. Jevons of England, C. Menger of Austria, Alfred Marshall of England, J. B. Clark of America, Vilfredo Pareto of Italy, and Knut Wicksell of Sweden all made significant contributions; and even in Adam Smith you can hunt out the germ of the idea.

one. Output is being maximized, inputs minimized; people who like apples are not being given oranges, etc. From so efficient a final point, you can no longer make everyone better off. You can help Joe only by hurting Tom."

Figure 32-1 is the final development of the figure on page 44 of Chapter 3, where we first asked how a price system goes about solving WHAT, How, and FOR WHOM. Only after mastering the tools of Parts Three and Four are we able to present this culmination of our original inquiry.

■ IMPERFECTIONS OF COMPETITION

This survey proceeded on the basis of some heroically abstract assumptions: no monopolies, no imperfections, no dynamic innovations or unforeseen disturbances, no governmental distortions, and so forth. Figure 32-1, therefore, is like the no-friction model of the physicist; it is not a picture of the real world as we know it when we step outside the library and rub elbows with real live breathing people on the street.

Yet, even though every engineer knows he must meet friction, he does find the frictionless model a valuable tool in throwing light on complicated reality. So it is with our ideal competitive model. In the long run, many imperfections turn out to be transient. *The competitive model, therefore, may suggest in its oversimple way some interesting hypotheses that turn out to have a measure of long-run validity!*

> EXAMPLE: An invention cuts cost of aluminum; the competitive model says price will fall and pressure will be put on use and price of steel. The sophisticated student of imperfect competition says the real world is not perfectly competitive, so no hard-and-fast conclusion can be drawn. Still, bet with him that the above result will happen *in the long run*—and probably you will win his money. A sure thing? No, but often a good bet.

Even if we agree that the perfect-competition model does give some approximate descriptions of reality, we cannot be satisfied with such crude approximations. Forty years ago an economics textbook would have had to confine itself to the case of perfect competition, and let it go at that. Thanks to the pioneering work in the theory of imperfect and monopolistic competition over the last generation, economists now have the tools (marginal revenue, etc.) to analyze oligopoly, monopoly, differentiation of products of numerous sellers, collective bargaining, and various intermediate cases. (Recall Chapter 26 and Table 25-1, page 470.)

We have seen that prices are often inflexibly administered, changing rarely and being subject only to minor hidden discounts, which is in contrast with the minute-to-minute volatility and year-to-year gyrations of competitive prices. We have seen that two union men may work in the same city or block at different wage rates for comparable work; that interference by a union with wage setting may correct a previous monopoly condition of unequal bargaining, or may increase the departure from the model of perfect competition. We have seen Chamberlinian cases where free entry may squeeze out profits while still leaving price above minimum average costs.

There is no need, therefore, to warn against overemphasis on the elegant model of perfect competition as a description of economic reality.

■ A WORD ON WELFARE ECONOMICS

Even if perfect competition were a poorer descriptive tool than it is, students of economics would still want to study it intensively and master its principles. This is so for a reason unconnected with mere description. The competitive model is extremely important in providing a benchmark for appraising the *efficiency* of an economic system.

For the most part in any science, scholars discuss what *is* and what will be under this or that situation. The task of positive description should be kept as free as is humanly possible from the taint of wishful thinking and ethical concern about what ought to be. Why? Because scientists are cold-blooded robots? No, rather because experience shows again and again that a more accurate job of positive description will be achieved if one tries to be objective. (Experience also shows that, try as we may, we humans never succeed in separating completely the objective and subjective aspects of a discipline. Indeed, the very choice of what scientists choose to measure, and the perspective from which they observe and measure it, and the reactions the observer produces in that which is observed—all these make the distinction between *is* and *ought*, between objective and subjective issues, at bottom a matter of degree rather than kind. Recall, for example, Chapter 1's bird-antelope paradox.)

The citizenry, unlike the specialist, are in the end perhaps most interested in problems of "norms," of what *ought* to be done, of policy rather than mere description. That citizenry is best served by the scientist who can give it the most accurate description of what is, and of what the consequences of different policy actions will be.

Very briefly then, in this epilogue, let us again devote a few lines to implications for economic welfare that have been developed in Parts Three and Four.

First, we have seen repeatedly that a regime of perfectly competitive pricing would have certain efficiency properties if conditions were really present for the maintenance of perfect competition. Therefore Adam Smith, in his talk about an Invisible Hand, which led the selfish actions of individuals toward so harmonious a final result, did have some point. Smith never could state or prove exactly what that point was, but modern economics can state this property of ideal competitive pricing:

> ■ Under perfectly perfect competition, where all prices end up equal to all marginal costs, where all factor-prices end up equal to values of marginal-products and all total costs are minimized, where the genuine desires and well-being of individuals are all represented by their marginal utilities as expressed in their dollar voting—*then* the resulting equilibrium has the efficiency property that "you can't make any one man better off without hurting some other man."

What does this mean exactly? It means that a planner could not come along with a slide rule and find a solution, different from the laissez-faire one, which could improve the welfare of everyone.[2]

---

[2] If *A* is the competitive equilibrium, there is no point *B* the planner could devise which could be approved over *A* by a *unanimous* vote. Some would be hurt in going to *B*, some might gain; but the gainers could never find it worthwhile to give big enough bribes to win the losers over to approving the move to *B*. Graduate treatises call this a case of "Pareto optimality," named after Pareto's work at the turn of the century as elucidated in our time by Harvard's Abram Bergson.

What does it not mean? It does not mean that actual *laissez faire*, with the imperfections of competition that will go with it, leads to efficiency or necessarily even to a close approximation to efficiency. It does not mean that the people who are deemed by various religious or ethical observers to be most worthy, most deserving, or most needy will necessarily get their ethically best share of goods and services. Laissez-faire perfect competition *could* lead to starving cripples; to malnourished children who grow up to produce malnourished children; to perpetuation of Lorenz curves of great inequality of incomes and wealth for generations or forever. Or, if the initial distribution of dollar-wealth votes, genetic abilities, conditioned motivations, and training happened to be appropriate, perfect competition might lead to a rather egalitarian society characterized by uniformity greater than might please many an aristocratic ethical tradition.

In short, Adam Smith, in the famous passage quoted on page 39, had no right to assert that an Invisible Hand channels individuals selfishly seeking their own interest into promoting the "public interest"—as these last two words might be defined by a variety of prominent ethical and religious notions of what constitutes the welfare of a nation. Smith has proved nothing of this kind, nor has any economist since 1776.

REDEFINING THE INVISIBLE-HAND DOCTRINE   If Smith were alive today, he would agree with all this; and one ventures the guess, from his biography, that he would probably reword his doctrine pretty much along the following lines.

1. Only if abilities and dollar-wealth votes were originally distributed in "an ethically optimal" manner—and kept so distributed by nondistorting, nonmarket interventions—could even perfectly competitive pricing be counted on (*a*) to produce an efficient configuration of production out on society's production-possibility frontier (and not inside it), and (*b*) to give people what they really deem is best for them, in accordance with their dollar votes that now reflect equally significant social utility. (Note that Smith has not committed himself as to which ethical system is the right one: this is not the business of a technical economist to pronounce on in his professional capacity.)

2. Admittedly, the demands of people in the market place sometimes do not reflect their true well-beings as these would be interpreted by even the most tolerant and individualistic of ethical observers. (EXAMPLES: A dope addict's craving for opium even at the expense of his food or his children's food; a child's desire for a seventh lollipop; a diabetic's craving for sweets; a spendthrift's mortgaging his house for a sports car.) As a pragmatist, Smith would say, "People are entitled to make their own mistakes in many matters, but it is arrogant to think that anyone who is not a minor or a lunatic is in every respect a sovereign will; as men conscious that we were born not perfect and as inhabitants of a post-Freudian world, we shall sparingly and for good cause want democratically to place restrictions on our own behavior. So again, laissez-faire perfect competition would not inevitably be the ideal."

Then, after emphasizing the need for tolerance and the virtues of freedom, Smith might strike a more technical note.

3. Where there are monopolistic imperfections that produce deviations from ideal competitive marginal-cost pricing—and in situations of strong increasing returns and decreasing costs, such deviations are practically inevitable—of course there is a

prima facie case that laissez-faire pricing is not efficient. Public scrutiny, to see whether democratic controls would make the situation better or worse, has to be presumed in such quasi-monopoly situations.[3]

■ CONCLUSION

The reader is warned that all the above issues of welfare economics can be given varying interpretations and can lead to controversial debate which present-day science cannot presume to settle. Conservatives may legitimately interpret the above principles in terms of their version of the good society. Middle-of-the-roaders may do the same for theirs. And radicals may call for small or large reforms of the present structure of a mixed economy by giving their interpretation of these principles. That means the reader may do so, too.

The following Appendix gives in greater depth a view of the efficiency aspect of the system of interdependent economic pricing under capitalism or socialism.

[3]Smith would add that wherever there are "external economies and diseconomies," such as were analyzed in the Appendix of Chapter 23 and in the discussion of public versus private goods in Chapter 8, there is a *prima facie* case for study to see whether zoning laws, taxes or subsidies, and government expenditure and regulation should be initiated in some degree. Where the checks and balances of perfect competition are not operative, the Darwinian struggle for existence is not led by an Invisible Hand to any kind of an optimum.

APPENDIX: Review of Commodity and Factor Pricing: General Equilibrium and the Parable of Ideal Welfare Pricing

PARABLE OF UTOPIAN PRICING

We economists are twitted that our books always harp on Robinson Crusoe. True enough: we do find that the economic decisions of a single man furnish a dramatic way of simplifying our basic principles. But these days we have an even more dramatic device for illustrating the fundamental facts of economic life: we use the example of a fully collectivized society. This retains the same simplicity of ultimate decision making, but at the same time it gives us social interactions between people that the Crusoe model lacks. The contrast between such a model and our realistic everyday world is, of course, enormous. And therein lies its value. By examining the logic of such a model, we get new insight into the nature of our own pricing system.

Let us, therefore, examine how our economic analysis of pricing can be applied to a completely artificial planned society of the kind never seen in Russia or anywhere else. Call it Utopia or call it Hades. In analyzing the problem of pricing in a planned socialist state, we kill two birds with one stone:

1. We get one of the best possible reviews of the over-all working of a perfect *capitalistic* price system.

2. We get an introduction to "welfare economics," the study of what is considered right and wrong about any economic system. This depends, of course, upon ethical points of view, themselves necessarily a-scientific. But the economist, as a disinterested observer, may help to throw light on how successfully an economic system realizes any suggested ethical *goals.*[1]

[1]For example, he may be personally opposed to an equal distribution of income, but that does not prevent him from measuring the degree of success in reaching this common ethical goal or of the costs involved.

A DILEMMA FOR CENTRALIZED PLANNING

The earlier chapters of this book have shown how a system of market prices operates to solve the basic economic problems of WHAT, HOW, and FOR WHOM. To drive home what all this really means, try a mental experiment. Suppose you were given the job of making the blueprints for a completely planned economic system. How might you begin?

First, let us suppose you are interested in giving people what they want, not in telling them what they ought to want. Obviously, you cannot give them everything they want: land, labor, capital goods, and technological knowledge are limited in amount. So you must make compromises and choices.

You may say: This is merely a complicated mathematical problem, calling for the use of lots of high-powered electronic high-speed calculating machines. But remember that we shall have to deal with the millions of items that are to be found in department stores, with thousands of grades of productive factors, and with numerous individuals and families. The number of unknowns of the mathematical problem will be in the millions, and the number of steps to its solution in the billions of billions. No known set of computing machines can even begin to tackle such a problem.

You are stumped. And discouraged. Perhaps you will lower your sights and stop being a perfectionist. Instead of giving people exactly what they think they want, you may decide that there will be only a few types of, say, shoe styles and sizes, so that the calculation problem will be simplified. Or you may start to give people goods that *you* find it convenient to give them.

One thing is clear: If centralized planning means that one centralized person must have in his mind all the myriad intricacies of detail, then it is an impossible job to do with any efficiency. So you will naturally begin to experiment with various devices to decentralize the job. And quite probably you will end up by introducing a *pricing* system in many ways like that of capitalism. How might such a system work?

PRICING IN A UTOPIAN STATE: CONSUMPTION-GOODS PRICES

In your new society, the consumer will still have *freedom of choice* and will not have dictated to him the relative amounts of different commodities which he is to "enjoy." As in the capitalist system, each person will receive a sum of money or abstract purchasing power to spend among different commodities as he wishes. Thus, vegetarians will not have to eat meat, and those who most prefer meat will be able to do so.

How will relative prices between salmon and ham or any other consumers' goods be set by the socialist state? Generally speaking, prices will be set with the same double purpose as in a capitalist society: (1) just high enough to ration out the existing supplies of consumers' goods, so none are left over and none are short; and also (2) just high enough to cover the socially necessary extra costs of producing the goods in question—or, in technical terms, prices are to be set equal to relative "marginal utilities" and "marginal costs."

THE DISTRIBUTION OF INCOME

So far the process has worked much like the capitalistic system. Almost by definition, however, socialism means a society in which most land and capital goods or nonhuman resources of all kinds are owned collectively by society and not individually by people. In our society, an Astor who owns 500 parcels of New York City land, each of which produces $60,000 of net rents per year, will receive an income of $30 million per year—which may be 10,000 times what a night watchman is able to earn, and 2,000 times what the average skilled engineer can earn. In a society where most property is owned collectively and not distributed with great inequality among different individuals, an important source of inequality of income would be absent.

Many people profess to hold the ethical and philosophical belief that different individuals' wants and needs are very much alike, and that the present market mechanism works inadequately because the rich are given so many more votes in the control of production than the poor—which makes the market demand for goods a faulty indication of their true social worth. Such people with a relatively equalitarian philosophy will welcome a great reduction in the spread of incomes between the lowest 90 per cent of all families and the highest 10 per cent. They may argue that taking away $1,000 from a man with an income of $100,000 and giving it to a man with an income of $2,000 will add to social well-being (by taking dollars from a place deemed low in marginal social utility to a place deemed higher). After the distribution of income between families has been determined correctly, according to society's fundamental (a-scientific) value judgments, then and only then will it be true that the dollars coming on the market will be valid indicators of the value of goods and services; and only then will they be serving to direct production into the proper channels and goods into the right hands. Hence, lump-sum taxes and transfers will be used in Utopia to give ethically proper income distribution. So goes the argument.

How is what is considered the proper ethical distribution of income to be achieved aside from the negative act of wiping out unduly high property owning and the appropriate lump-sum taxing of individuals?

Perfectionists have two answers: (1) in part by letting people get some of their income in the form of wages; but (2) in part by having these wages supplemented by receipt of a lump-sum *social dividend payment* or negative *tax.* This cash payment would presumably be nearly the same for most average families; but even in an equalitarian society, there might be differences to compensate for numbers of children, age, and health.

It is an ethical rather than a scientific question as to just how large, relatively, each person's final income ought to be. As a science, economics can concern itself only with the best means of attaining given ends; it cannot prescribe the ends themselves.

Indeed, if someone decided that he preferred a feudal-fascistic kind of society, in which all people with little black mustaches were to be given especially high incomes, the economist could set up the pricing rules for him to follow to achieve his strange design best. He would be told to determine his social dividend payments to achieve the required optimal distribution of income, after which each dollar coming on the market could be regarded as correctly representing (that eccentric philosopher's) true social values.

The social dividend differs from a wage because it is to be given to every individual *regardless of his own efforts.* That is why it is called a "lump-sum" dividend or transfer.[2] (Any bonus based upon productivity or effort is to be treated as a wage.)

We have not yet seen how wages are to be determined, but before doing so, let us first turn to another important problem.

[2]If the state is providing public goods for the people which require greater use of resources than the state owns, most of the social dividends may have to be negative—lump-sum taxes rather than transfers.

PRICING OF NONHUMAN PRODUCTIVE RESOURCES AND INTERMEDIATE GOODS

What should be the role of land and other nonhuman productive resources as an element of cost in such a utopia? Some people would say that such nonhuman resources should not enter into cost at all; that only human sweat and skill are the true source of all value; and that any extra charges based upon the cost of land or machinery represent a capitalistic surplus which the owners of property are able to squeeze out of the exploited laboring masses by virtue of the private monopoly of ownership of the means of production. This view is sometimes loosely spoken of as the "labor theory of value," which we already met in Fig. 2-9, page 28. It is usually identified with Karl Marx, the intellectual father of communistic socialism. Learned scholars dispute over just what Marx meant by the "labor theory of value" and whether he meant it to apply to a socialist economy in the short or long run.

We need not enter into this dispute. However, it is important to note that, in its simple form, *the labor theory of value will lead to incorrect and inefficient use of both labor and nonlabor resources in even the most perfect socialist society.*

So long as any economic resource is limited in quantity—i.e., *scarce* rather than free—the socialist planners must give it a price and charge a rent for its use. This price need not, as in the case of the Astor millionaire under the capitalistic system, determine any individual's income. It can be a purely bookkeeping or accounting price set up by the planners, rather than a market price. But there must be a price put upon the use of every such resource.

Why? First, we must price nonhuman resources to ensure that society is deciding How goods shall be produced in the best way, so that we really end up on the true production-possibility frontier of society and not somewhere inside it. It would be absurd to get rid of the capitalistic system with its alleged wastes due to unemployment, and then, by stupid planning, end up far inside society's true production potentialities.

Related to the above point is the second need for all resources to be given a value if correct prices are to be charged to consumers for those final goods that use up a great deal of scarce resources. In other words, for society to find itself in the best of all possible positions on the production-possibility frontier, we must price such consumption goods as food and clothing to reflect their true relative (extra or marginal) costs of using up *all* scarce resources. Otherwise, the free choice exerted by consumers on their dollar spending will not truly maximize their own and society's preferences.

THE EXAMPLE OF LAND RENT

The foregoing two reasons are difficult to grasp. However, let us try to make the necessity for nonlabor pricing clear by considering a single land example. Suppose there are twins in a farming utopia. What if one were to produce wheat on an acre of good land, and the other were to produce less wheat by the same year's work on an acre of bad land. If they are identical twins, working equally hard, we would certainly have to agree that their wages ought to be the same.

Now, if wages were to be treated as the only cost, in accord with the labor theory of value, then the same price could not be charged for the two different outputs of wheat, even though the kernels of wheat were identical. The good-land wheat would have involved lower labor costs and will have to sell for less than the poor-land wheat.

This, of course, is absurd. A well-wishing social planner might try to get around the dilemma by charging the same price for both, losing money on the poor-land wheat and gaining on the other. Or what is almost the same thing, he might say, "To keep the costs of the two wheats the same, let us pay the twin on bad land lower wages; but then let us make the richer brother share his wages with the poorer."

Such a solution is not absurd, but it falls short of achieving the desired best results: maximum production and equal pay for equal human effort. In particular, *it fails to shift more labor onto the more productive land.*

The only correct procedure is to put an accounting price or rent tag on each land, with the good land having the higher tag. The prices of both kinds of wheat will be equal, because the land cost of the good-land wheat will be just enough higher than that of the poor-land wheat to make up the difference.

Most important of all, the socialist production manager must try to minimize the combined labor and land cost of producing each kind of wheat. If he does so according to the marginal-product principles discussed in Part Four, he will accomplish something undreamed of by the simple believer in the labor theory of value.

He will find it pays to work the good land more intensively, perhaps with the time of $1\frac{1}{2}$ men until the extra product there has been lowered by the law of diminishing returns so as to be just equal to the extra product of the $\frac{1}{2}$ man's time on the poor land. Only by putting a price upon inert sweatless land are we using it, and sweating breathing labor, most productively! The price or rent of land rises in order to ration its limited supply among the *best* uses.

Note, too, that the most finicky humanitarian will have nothing to complain of in our solution. By transferring labor from one acre to the other until labor's marginal productivity has been made equal, we get the largest possible total production of wheat.[3]

The two brothers are paid the same wages because they have worked equally hard. But their wages are not high enough to buy all the wheat, since part of the cost of the wheat has come from (bookkeeping) land charges. However, the people through their government own the land equally. The land's return does not go to any property owner but is available to be distributed as a lump-sum social dividend to both brothers and to others according to their ethical deserts.

By putting a proper accounting price or rent on land, society has more consumption than was otherwise possible!

If we turn now to the production of more than one consumer's good, it will be obvious that their cost prices must be made to reflect the amount of socially limited land and machinery which they each use up. Field crops like wheat require little labor and much land compared with garden crops like tomatoes. If we price each good on the basis of labor costs alone, wheat will sell for too little, and too much land will be forced out of tomato production. All will be worse off.

MARGINAL-COST PRICING

One last point concerning the final determination of a product's cost and price. After the costs of all necessary factors of production have been added together to arrive at total cost, the planning authorities must set

---

[3] As earlier discussions of marginal productivity have shown, *total product will be at a maximum only when labor has been transferred from the land where its marginal-product is low to the good land where its marginal-product is high.* Every such transfer must necessarily yield us extra product, until finally no further increases in output can result when the marginal-products have been equalized in the two uses.

their prices at the marginal cost of production. Or more accurately, the socialist managers of a plant must behave like a perfect competitor: they must disregard any influence that their own production might have on market price and must continue to produce extra units up to the point where the last little unit costs just as much as its selling price.

For many industries, such as railroads, where unit costs are constantly falling, setting marginal costs equal to price will imply that *full* average costs are not covered. In a noncapitalistic society the difference would be made up by an (accounting) lump-sum grant from the state; for if a railroad system is worth building, it is worth being utilized well.[4]

[4] The long-run question as to whether to build a railroad in the first place may involve an "all-or-none decision," which cannot be made step by step. In such a case, there must still be a balancing of the extra (or marginal) advantage and extra cost to society of the enterprise. But for such a big step, price is no longer a good indicator of total welfare, since—as we saw in Chapter 22—there is always an element of consumer's surplus in the total amount of goods a person consumes over what he has paid for them.

Figure 32-2 pictures a case where *dd*, which we assume reflects true marginal utilities to society, everywhere lies below decreasing long-run *AC*. So pricing at long-run *MC* can never recover full long-run social costs. Yet, with the *a* area a little larger than the *b* area, the total-utility area under *dd* is greater than the total-cost area under *LMC*. So society should produce at *E*, giving a lump-sum subsidy to cover the inevitable loss or somehow getting people to pay more for their earlier units that yielded great consumer surplus. (EXAMPLES: A railroad line to a country region; a monorail for urban commuters.) If *dd* shifted down enough to make $a < b$, the

SUMMARY OF RESOURCE PRICING

Correct social planning requires that all scarce resources, whether human labor or not, be given accounting prices at least. The final costs of consumers' goods should include the sum total of *all* extra costs necessary to produce each good, or in short, should equal *marginal cost*. The demand for consumers' goods is really an indirect demand for all productive resources, a demand which can be kept in proper check only by putting appropriate valuations on productive resources.

Otherwise, society's valuable nonhuman—and human!—resources will be incorrectly allocated and the market pricing of finished goods will not lead to maximum consumers' satisfaction. It is to be emphasized that the accounting prices of land and other nonhuman resources need not, in a socialist state, be part of the incomes of anyone. In the language of the visionary critic of private enterprise: no one is "exploited" by having a property owner skim off part of the final product. Instead, the contribution of capital and land to production is given to people in the form of government goods and the algebraic *social dividend*.

THE ROLE OF THE INTEREST RATE IN UTOPIA

We have seen that the interest rate has an important function in a capitalistic, socialistic, or any other kind of economic system. Capital goods have a "net productivity." As long as resources can be invested for the present or the future, it will be necessary to make important decisions with respect to capital. Shall we apply present land and labor to the production of a corn crop this year or to apples 15 years from now? Shall we have grape juice today or wine 10 years hence? Shall we replace a worn-out loom with a new expensive one which yields its services over a period of 20 years or buy a cheap one that will last only 14 years? Every one of these questions can be answered only by using an interest rate to relate future and present economic values. Without such an interest rate, the existing stock of fixed and circulating capital cannot be devoted to its best uses; and whatever amount of

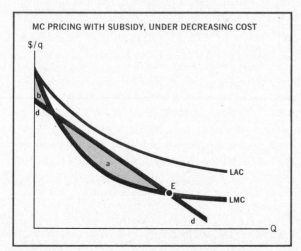

MC PRICING WITH SUBSIDY, UNDER DECREASING COST

$/q

LAC

E

LMC

Q

FIG. 32-2.

whole project should be abandoned. Even if *dd* shifted up a bit, so that part of it lay above *LAC* and price *could* cover all costs, *P* still should be kept down to *LMC* for efficient pricing. (All this needs qualifications if dollars do not represent true and constant marginal utility and true social costs, as in a world of many monopolies and in making big decisions.)

national income society has decided to invest in capital formation cannot be embodied in the best form without such an interest rate.

The interest rate acts as a sieve or rationing device: all projects that can yield 10 per cent are undertaken before any projects that yield only 8 per cent.

It should be added that many economic writers on socialism do not think that the rate of interest should also determine—as it does in our economy, to some degree—the rate at which capital growth is to take place at the expense of current consumption. The decision as to how much should be saved would be determined by the state "in the light of national and social needs," and not by the "haphazard" notions of individuals with respect to the future. But the level of social saving and capital growth once having been determined, the interest rate must be used to allocate scarce "capital supplies" optimally and to determine the priority of alternative projects.[5]

WAGE RATES AND INCENTIVE PRICING

We must now return to the problem of how the utopian planners would set wage rates, and then we are done. If the amounts of labor of all kinds and of all skills were perfectly fixed, there would be no reason why labor should not be given accounting prices just like any other productive factor. Workers would receive no wages at all. They would then receive all the national income in the form of an enlarged *social dividend.*

However, if heterogeneous people are to be free to choose their own occupations and given the choice of working a little harder and longer in return for extra consumption goods, then it will be necessary to set up a system of *actual market wages* at which people can sell their services set just high enough to equate demand and supply. Wages may differ depending upon how the irksomeness of the job affects voluntary labor supplied; and unlike now, the pleasanter jobs may then be the lower-paid, and the ditchdiggers or garbage collectors may have to be higher-paid to attract people into these jobs. Occupations that require much training and skill will receive high pay, but much of that pay may be spent by the state in providing the education

necessary to acquire those skills. Piece rates might be used, and a worker with a 20 per cent higher productivity will be receiving higher (pretax and pre-social-dividend) wages. Workers will in every case be offered wages equal to their marginal, or extra, productivity.

Therefore, it is not necessarily true that all incomes will be at a dead level in the utopian society. They will differ somewhat as a result of two distinct factors: (1) society's appraisal of the "needs and worth" of different individuals—as reflected primarily in the size of the individuals' lump-sum *social dividends*—and (2) the need for wages to differ to provide incentives and to compensate people for extra disutility and effort. Incomes need not differ, however, because of inequality in the ownership and inheritance of property and genetic talents. Wage rents (like Babe Ruth's) could be heavily lump-sum-taxed, exactly like Henry George's surplus land rents.

SUMMARY OF UTOPIAN PRICING

1. A utopian system could make use of four different kinds of pricing: (*a*) consumer-goods prices, (*b*) wage and incentive rates, (*c*) accounting prices of intermediate goods or produced inputs, and (*d*) final lump-sum dividends (when positive, transfers; when negative, taxes). The first three prices would be determined by supply and demand.

2. To give people free choice among consumers' goods, market prices would be set for such goods. Similarly, to provide freedom of choice of occupation, to give people incentives, and to provide compensation for differences between occupations, wage rates would get set to correspond to (marginal) productivities and disutilities.

3. Accounting prices would have to be set on all nonhuman productive resources to ration them in their best uses where their (relative) marginal productivities are equal and highest. Similarly, there would have to be a rate of interest to ration the existing and growing stock of capital among its best uses. Any consumption good would be produced up to the point where the full marginal cost of production (necessary to keep all resources from other uses and from leisure) is just equal to the price.[6]

---

[5] There is no logical reason why individuals who are willing to forego present for future consumption should not be permitted to do such voluntary extra saving and receive an interest return equal to the net productivity of capital.

[6] The decentralized managers of industries could generally achieve this by seeking to maximize their net algebraic profits, measured in accounting points or actual dollars, but with *all P's*

4. Lastly, the final distribution of income would be made to correspond to what society regards as the ideal distribution pattern by means of payment of a lump-sum social dividend to people, depending upon "need, wants, and deservingness," but not—like a wage—on effort or performance. In Utopia, it might be felt that a much more nearly equal distribution of income will be necessary before the dollar votes of consumers can be expected to reflect true social preferences. However, this is a nonscientific, ethical question; and we could use the same economic principles to make blueprints for an *ine*galitarian utopia.

5. None of these processes except the last requires detailed comprehensive planning by a central agency. Mathematicians would not have to be called in to solve thousands and thousands of simultaneous equations. Instead, the decentralized planners would proceed by successive approximation, by trial and error—setting provisional market and accounting prices and cutting them or raising them, depending upon whether available supplies are piling up or running short.

It would be naïve to think that any actual society would succeed in reaching the ideal equilibrium positions described above. Errors of foresight would inevitably be made. Existing vested interests, anxious to preserve their security in a dynamic world of change, would resist and sabotage such change in the same qualitative fashion as they have done in historical societies. Even where politicians and the electorate do not pay much attention to the incentive mechanisms outlined in the preceding pages, the importance of this discussion is that it teaches us how to appraise the mechanical efficiency of pricing in a *non*socialist society.[7]

WELFARE ECONOMICS IN A FREE ECONOMY

On the basis of the above principles of pricing, we are in a position to see what friendly and unfriendly critics think is wrong in our system, or not necessarily right from various ethical viewpoints. Critics list the following possible deviations from the social optimum:

1. The existing distribution of property, income, education, and economic opportunity is the result of past history and does not necessarily represent an optimum condition according to the ethical philosophies of Christianity, Buddhism, paganism, the American creed, or other ideologies. Defenders of the capitalist system point out that such deviations from the optimum distribution can be corrected by appropriate tax policies, if that is desired. There are, however, some costs to be incurred in our capitalistic system from such policies because of taxation effects upon incentives, risk taking, effort, and productivity.

2. The widespread presence of monopoly elements in our system and the limited appearance of perfect competition mean that production is rarely being pushed to the optimum point of equality of marginal cost to price; because the elasticity of demand is not infinite to imperfect competitors, production is pushed only to the point of equality of marginal cost to marginal revenue. Because of the fear of "spoiling the market," monopoly price is then too high and monopoly output is too low relative to competitive outputs.

This is related to a further Chamberlinian evil under imperfect competition when entry of new firms into an industry is very easy. There may then tend to be an inefficient division of production among too many firms; the *P* charged is too high, but through wasteful use of resources, no one need be making any profits.[8]

---

taken as given parameters. (NOTE: Under cost conditions suitable for viable *laissez faire,* such behavior is actually policed by competition, but where bureaucrats "play the game of competition," there may be a hard administrative problem to make sure they do act in the prescribed price-taker manner.)

[7] A brief history of welfare pricing doctrines may be of interest. From Smith's time at least, men saw beauty in the laissez-faire mechanism and inferred that it must have teleological significance in giving efficiency. But they were often uncritical, and often they overlooked the assumption that dollar votes were to be distributed in the ethically desired way; and they could not prove what they believed. Around 1900 Pareto showed that an ideal socialism would have to solve the same equations as competitive capitalism. Around 1920, Ludwig von Mises, perhaps unaware of Pareto's proof, set forth the challenging view that rational economic organization was *logically*

impossible in the absence of free markets. Fred Taylor of Michigan, A. P. Lerner of England and N.Y.U., and Oscar Lange of Poland answered Mises with the view that socialism could conceptually solve the problems of economic organization by a decentralized process of bureaucratic trial and error—"playing the game of competition" and "deliberately planning not to plan." F. A. Hayek has argued that this answer overlooks the problem of giving *each man the initiative* to better the existing order and that only with actual free enterprise do you efficiently utilize the dispersed information which each of us may possess. See Chapter 40 for the movement in Soviet Russia to depend more on prices and profitability.

[8] Another evil, discussed in Chapter 23, is the fact that individual firms, in making their decisions, do not take into account some possible effects of their production decisions on other

3. Finally, of course, as shown in Part Two, under a laissez-faire system, there may be great wastes due to unemployment and the business cycle. Consumers, labor, farmers, and business, together with public fiscal

and monetary policy, must be mobilized in a never-ending war against this greatest of social scourges— poverty which has no real cause but stems only from an intricately misbehaving monetary society.

---

firms or industries. In digging his oil well, Pat does not mind that he may be robbing Mike's oil pool; and the same with Mike—with the result that less oil is obtained in the end, and with more cost. Because of such so-called "external disecono-mies or economies" apparent "private marginal costs" do not reflect true "social marginal costs"; and certain lines of activity deserve to be contracted and others to be expanded. Compare A. C. Pigou, *Economics of Welfare* (Macmillan, New York,

1932). The paradox that really perfect competition would dis-courage people from inventing (since they would know their profits would disappear) can be understood in terms of external economies: my pecuniary reward from an invention may be much less than its social value after it has been widely imi-tated. Governmental activities are needed when "public goods" involve external benefits to more than one person at the same time, as shown in Chapter 8. See too, Chapter 23's Appendix.

SUMMARY TO APPENDIX

1 ■

In a pure unmixed competitive society, the economic problems of WHAT shall be produced, How, and FOR WHOM are solved in an interdependent manner by the impersonal workings of profit-and-loss markets. Each variable depends upon every other, but all tend to be simultaneously determined at their general equilibrium values by a process of successive approximations and readjustments.

2 ■

Unless a utopian economy were uninterested in effi-ciency and economizing, or in freedom of choice of goods and jobs, it would have to institute a system of pricing. However, some prices would be purely account-

ing or bookkeeping figures; in addition, the final deter-mination of the distribution of income would involve an outright social dividend or tax, in various lump-sum amounts to people as determined by explicit a-scientific ethical decision of government and society.

3 ■

From the standpoint of welfare economics, it is seen that our own capitalistic system may depart from what is considered a social optimum in three main ways: through improper distribution of income, monop-oly and externalities, and unemployment.

Each one of these evils can be ameliorated by appro-priate policies, within the framework of the mixed economy.

QUESTIONS FOR DISCUSSION

1. Summarize how a pricing system works to solve the three fundamental economic problems. Illustrate their interdependence.

2. Discuss the four kinds of prices in a utopian state.

3. What do you deem to be imperfections in our eco-nomic order? Virtues? What defects would plague a collectivist society?

4. Review your understanding of the following con-cepts:

interdependence, general equilibrium
determinate final equilibrium

efficient final equilibrium
labor theory of value versus proper
    pricing of nonhuman resources
interest rate in capitalism and socialism
social dividend: lump-sum tax or transfer
wage rents, incentive wages
accounting prices versus actual prices
monopoly restrictions
"external" divergences between social
    and private benefits and costs
welfare economics, ethical distribution
    questions, value judgments

Part 5   International Trade and Finance

33 The Balance of International Payments

In the earlier chapters of this book we took international trade more or less for granted. Here in Part Five we wish to analyze explicitly the interesting economic problems arising as soon as an economy engages in foreign trade.

This chapter and its Appendix deal with the monetary mechanisms involved in international trade. Then the next two chapters concentrate on the basic real factors which underlie international trade and which are often obscured by the monetary veil that covers all international transactions. These basic real factors are involved in any rational appraisal of the problems raised by tariffs and other barriers to the international division of labor. In the final chapter all these principles are put to work to help you understand the contemporary international economic scene.

International trade is important for the following basic reason:

■ Foreign trade offers a "consumption-possibility frontier" that can give us more of all goods than can our own domestic production-possibility frontier!

EXAMPLE: Men in Malaya give us rubber; we give Englishmen wheat; Englishmen give Malayans cotton shirts. *Each of us ends up consuming more than he could produce alone.* The world is out on—and not inside—its true production-possibility frontier. That is the essence of foreign trade. So simple. And yet so hard for congressmen and voters to grasp and remember.

Our task in Part Five is to study the mechanics of international trade and finance: foreign exchange rates; balance of international payments; foreign lending and giving; tariff duties on imports, and import quotas; the so-called "principle of comparative advantage," which tells what kinds of trade will take place and why; and finally, the international economic problems of the 1960s and 1970s—such as the drain of American gold, the European Common Market, foreign aid, the International Bank, and the International Monetary Fund.

These are anything but abstract economic problems. They are the news that is breaking on tomorrow's front page.

A. MECHANISMS OF FOREIGN EXCHANGE AND TRADE

■ FOREIGN EXCHANGE RATES

First, how does trade take place? If I buy maple sugar from Vermont or pig iron from Pittsburgh, I naturally want to pay in dollars. Also, the farmer and steel producer expect to be paid in dollars, for the reason that their expenses and their living costs are all settled in dollars. Within a country, economic transactions seem simple.

If, however, I wish to buy an English racing car directly, matters are more complicated. I must ultimately pay in British money, or what is called "pounds sterling," rather than in dollars. Similarly, an Englishman must somehow get dollars to an American producer if he wants our merchandise. Most Americans have never seen a British pound note. Certainly they would accept pounds only if they could be sure of converting them into American dollars.

Clearly, therefore, exports and imports of goods between nations with different units of money introduce a new economic factor: the foreign exchange rate, giving the price of the foreigner's unit of money in terms of our own.

Thus, the price of a British pound was about $2.80 in 1967. There is also a foreign exchange rate between American money and the currencies of each and every country: 20.4 cents for the new French franc;[1] less than $\frac{1}{6}$ cent for an Italian lira; etc.

Given the foreign exchange rate, it is now simple for me to buy my English car. Suppose its quoted price is £1,000 (i.e., 1,000 British pounds). All I have to do is look in the newspaper for the foreign exchange rate for pounds. If this is $2.80 per pound, I simply go to a bank or post office with $2,800 and ask that the money be used to pay the English car exporter. Pay him what? Pounds, of course, the only kind of money he needs.

Whether I use the post office or a bank or a broker is of no particular importance. In fact, it is all the same if the English exporter sends me a bill requesting payment in dollars or if he deals with me through an American garage. In any case, he ultimately wants pounds, not dollars, and will soon trade the $2,800 for £1,000. (Needless to say, we are neglecting all commission charges and the cost of money orders.)

You should be able to show what a British importer of American grains has to do if he wants to buy, say, a $5,600 shipment from an American exporter. Here pounds must be converted into dollars. Why, when the foreign exchange rate is $2.80 per pound, will this cost him £2,000?

---

[1] There are also foreign exchange rates between the pound and the French franc. But these rates between other countries need not interest us much, particularly since, in a free competitive market, the pound-franc rate can be simply calculated from the pound-dollar and franc-dollar rate, because sharp-eyed international arbitragers see to it that relative "cross rates" do not get out of line: thus a pound must sell for a little less than 14 (= $2.80/$.20) francs. Of course, these 1967 examples have to be modified when official exchange rates are altered.

The businessman or tourist does not, as an individual, have to know anything more than this to get his imports or exports transacted. But the true economics of the problem cannot be grasped until we find out *why* the foreign exchange rate is at the level it is. What economic principles determine foreign exchange rates?

■ STABLE EXCHANGE RATE UNDER THE CLASSICAL GOLD STANDARD

There are three important cases to study:

1. The working of some kind of pure or modified *gold standard*.

2. The case of *free foreign exchange rates,* available to every person in either country, but fluctuating from day to day according to *market demand and supply* (quite like the case of wheat, which is available to all at a price that fluctuates from day to day, depending upon competitive supply and demand).

3. The case of *controlled* international trade, where each transaction requires a government license and where the foreign exchange rate may be different for different kinds of transactions, being set according to the will of the state.

The gold-standard case has been historically most important; in modified form, it prevails today; and chances are, some variant of it will prevail in the next quarter of a century. It is also one of the easiest cases to master.

GOLD BARS   Suppose people everywhere insisted on being paid in bits of pure gold metal: weight alone would count, and its shape—whether round like a ball or a coin, or irregular like a sliver, or cylindrical like a broom handle—would not matter so long as there were a guarantee of its purity and weight. Then buying pig iron in Pittsburgh would merely require payment in gold at a price expressed in ounces of gold; and buying a bicycle in Britain would involve the same kind of payment. By definition, there would be no foreign exchange rate problem.

GOLD COINS   Since slivers and blobs of gold are inconvenient to carry and to assay for purity and for weight, it became customary for the state—in those days, the prince—to stamp out in coin form a specified number of ounces of gold carrying the seal of the state to guarantee purity and weight. (The edges were milled, so that removal of the edges would reveal light weight and fraud. Even so, since gold is soft and rubs off, merchants and banks weighed the coins.)

With gold coins as the exchange medium, would not foreign trade still be like domestic trade? Yes, essentially. But with some minor differences: If we used ounces and France used grams to measure weight, you would merely have to have a table of units' conversion. And the same problem would arise if Queen Victoria chose to make her coins about $\frac{1}{4}$ ounce of gold (the "sovereign") and President Buchanan chose to make his $\frac{1}{20}$ ounce of gold (the dollar). In that case, the pound sovereign, being five times as heavy as the dollar, would naturally have an exchange rate of $5 to £1.

Now that is essentially how the pre-1914 gold standard actually worked. Of course, local pride tended to keep us using our coins and the English using their coins. But anyone was free to melt down our coins and get them converted into English coins (at very nominal costs). So except for the trifling costs of melting down, shipping across the ocean, and recoining, all countries on the gold standard had essentially stable exchange rates whose par values, or parities, were determined by the gold content of their local money unit.

> *Minor qualifications.* Gold being quite inconvenient to carry around for spending purposes, inevitably governments issued paper certificates which were pledged to be redeemable in gold metal. People had the right to turn in gold for certificates and certificates for gold, and they often exercised that right. Also, in those days ocean transport was slow and costly: so there were "gold points" around the true mint parities within which the pound and dollar exchange rates could fluctuate. Thus, if it cost 2 cents to ship an ounce of gold either way across the Atlantic Ocean (inclusive of insurance and interest costs), could the exchange rate depart a little from $5? Yes. In New York, the quoted price of a pound could rise to as much as $5.02 before it would pay to get gold bars and ship them to London to be exchanged for pounds; a price higher than $5.02 could not prevail because enough gold would be flowing to keep the price no higher than the upper gold point. It should be evident that the pound could fall below the mint parity of $5 by 2¢ to $4.98. When the exchange rate got down to this lower gold point, it would be cheaper for gold to be shipped from Europe to America. All this actually happened (except that $5 is substituted here for the correct pre-1914 parity of $4.87 to simplify the arithmetic, and the shipping costs are exaggerated for dramatic effect). Before 1914, the foreign exchange rate of the pound and dollar stayed essentially constant, varying but a trifle from these weight-determined mint parities until the gold points were touched and gold had to flow in the indicated direction.

THE HUME GOLD-FLOW EQUILIBRATING MECHANISM   Now that the mechanics of the problem are understood, we probe deeper to answer this question:

Under the gold standard, what kept America from buying more goods from England than England bought from us—which, after all, would have required us to keep shipping gold in final payment? Why wouldn't we be drained of all our gold?

This is a good question, and the mercantilist writers, who preceded Adam Smith and his friend the noted philosopher David Hume, gave a plausible but superficial answer. The mercantilists said:

"A country will lose its gold unless the Prince introduces tariffs and quotas to cut down on imports of goods; and unless he gives subsidies to encourage exports; and unless he forbids skilled workmen to take their knowledge abroad and makes sure that all shipping takes place in our own boats, however dear they may be." As an afterthought, almost too obvious to require mention, they said: "Of course, losing gold is a terrible thing for a nation. Don't ask why. Everyone knows it to be one of the worst tragedies that can happen to a nation."

David Hume in 1752, and economists ever since, have given the answer to this line of reasoning. First he noted that it could not be true that everyone would all the time be losing gold under free trade. Where would it go—into Davy Jones' locker? And he demonstrated that it is no tragedy at all if a country goes permanently from having 10 million ounces of gold to having 5 million, or even 1 million. *If* having double the amount of gold means merely that *all* prices are exactly doubled, no one in the country is the least bit better or worse off. So, losing half or nine-tenths of a nation's gold is nothing to worry about if it merely ends up with an equivalently reduced price level.

Here it is well to recall the crude quantity theory of money and prices discussed in Chapter 15. David Hume, along with John Locke and earlier writers, was one of the first to enunciate and hold to this theory concerning the proportionality of all prices to the stock of M (in this case, gold).[2]

Now comes the second and important part of Hume's classical refutation of mercantilism and defense of free trade. He asserted that there was a four-pronged mechanism that tended always to keep the international balance of payments of countries on the gold standard in equilibrium. Briefly, the Hume mechanism is this:

■ Whenever one country imports too much and begins to lose gold, its loss of gold reduces its price and cost level, thereby (1) decreasing its imports of foreign goods that have become relatively dear, and (2) increasing exports of its home-produced goods that have become relatively cheap.

The other country, which had been having a so-called "favorable balance of trade," in which it was sending more goods abroad than it was importing and merely receiving barren gold in exchange, now has (via the quantity theory) its price and cost levels of goods raised. This is a further reason (3) for its now-expensive exports to go down in physical amount and (4) for its citizens to buy more of the now-cheap goods of the first country.

The result of this four-pronged gold-flow price-level mechanism is to improve the balance of payments of the country which was losing gold and worsen that of the country with the favorable balance of trade—until equilibrium in international trade is established at relative prices that keep imports and exports in balance with no net gold flow. The equilibrium is stable and self-correcting requiring no tariffs and other state interference.

■ MODIFIED MODERN GOLD STANDARDS

The classical mechanism is oversimplified. But it does contain an essential germ of truth. Some realistic qualifications are needed; and these will both strengthen and weaken the classical account.

SILVER VERSUS GOLD AND BIMETALLISM   There is of course nothing sacred about gold. Platinum, silver, lead, or paper napkins would do, provided they had convenience for exchange, could not be falsified, and were sufficiently limited in supply to keep the price level from becoming astronomical. Actually, in the last centuries, silver has been more commonly the standard than gold; and England stumbled onto the gold standard two centuries ago without realizing it. So great was her prestige that France, the United States, and the rising empires of Germany and Japan had all by 1900 adopted the gold

---

[2] He admitted that the equilibrium predicted by the quantity theory would not take place instantaneously; indeed, he was one of the first to recognize that a period of rising M and rising prices, when it was first happening and was not foreseen, would give profits to businessmen by causing their prices to rise more than their costs; he thought this would be good for full employment and capital formation in the short run.

standard. The gold standard's real heyday was but a brief half century before 1914; and in that time several crises caused it to break down (as, for example, when the Civil War forced us to leave gold for more than a decade).

Had Hume lived, he would have been worried about one aspect of gold. If physical production in the countries on the gold standard was increasing in the years 1875 to 1895 at the rate of 5 per cent per year, the gold supply would have to increase by 5 per cent per year to keep prices stable according to the quantity theory of money. With more countries going on the gold standard and the California and Australia gold rushes giving out, gold mining was not producing this much gold; as a result, all over the world price levels were sagging in the last third of the nineteenth century.

This gave rise to much social unrest. In an ideal world of perfect price and wage flexibility, where the quantity theory worked smoothly both down and up, falling prices should not have mattered much. But as Hume himself insisted, prices and wages tend to be sticky downward; and falling price levels tend to lead to labor unrest, strikes, unemployment, and radical movements generally. Precisely that happened in the United States and other countries during the 1875–1895 era of Populism. (Recall Chapter 7's account of the rise of the Knights of Labor.) Since gold seemed to be squeezing prices downward, there was a clamor on the part of farmers and workers for use of silver to supplement gold. This culminated in the historic speech by William Jennings Bryan in favor of "bimetallism" at the 1896 Democratic Convention, where the "Boy Orator of the Platte" warned against crucifying mankind on a cross of gold.[3]

FRACTIONAL-RESERVE BANKING, AND THE GOLD-EXCHANGE STANDARD With Germany and Japan going on the gold standard, the deflationary pressure on prices would have been even worse had it not been for growing methods of economizing on gold. Modern banks, which hold only fractional reserves, began to develop: the demand deposit M they created meant that not quite so much gold was needed to keep up with growing total output. Moreover, most of the countries on the gold standard did *not* keep 100 per cent gold reserves to back up the token coins and paper currency they issued. Thus, if the typical country held only one-fourth gold against its paper money, only a quarter as much gold would have to be mined to support the same world price level.

---

[3] Bimetallism would mean that the Treasury would exchange dollars for *either* gold or silver, at some agreed-upon ounce ratio, such as 16 ounces of silver to each ounce of gold. Unless all countries agreed on the same 16:1 ratio, there would be a one-way movement of each metal to the place where it was most valued; and the place where gold was most valued would be on the gold standard, while the place where silver was most valued would be on the silver standard. As a result, with every change in the relative supplies and demands for the two metals, there would be an ensuing fluctuation in the foreign exchange rates between the two countries. (The percentage size of the fluctuation could be only two-sixteenths if their respective bimetallic parities were 16:1 and 18:1. Even if all countries went on the same 16:1 ratio, any tendency for mines to pour out the two metals at substantially different rates would lead to the free market's bidding their price ratios to some figure other than 16:1; and in this case, by a form of what is known as Gresham's Law—"Cheap money drives out good"—the result would be that the cheapest metal in the market place would all be given to the treasuries of the different countries, and in effect the world would be on a single standard again—that of the cheapest metal. Today no one, not even a Kansas farmer, favors bimetallism.)

Another development helped economize on gold. Many countries, particularly small ones (like the Philippines), kept their money exchangeable at fixed rates with respect to gold. But they held little or no gold. Instead, they would hold the money of some big country (like the United States) which was on the gold standard. So long as the small country could stay on such a "gold-exchange standard," the effect would be much like the pure gold standard, but with great economizing on gold.

Fortunately for those who favored the gold standard, the deflationary pressures eased some when gold was discovered in the Klondike and South Africa in the mid-nineties and when the cyanide process greatly increased the output of gold mines. Together with the increasing leverage attained by having smaller and smaller fractional reserve ratios and more and more gold-exchange standards, the increase in mining enabled the world to keep on the gold standard and stave off deflation up until the 1929 crash. But this did involve a strain on international liquidity, and some experts actually attribute that slump to an increasing shortage of world liquidity.

All this is very relevant for our own day. For, as we shall see in Chapter 36, there are experts today who think that the world will soon face an international liquidity shortage; and to prevent this, they advise that new monetary arrangements be made—using the International Monetary Fund, inventing new currency units called "cru" or "bancor" or anything else, or simply raising the price of gold in terms of most of the world's currencies.

Before leaving this topic, let us consider what Hume would have thought of the modifications in his pure gold standard. He probably would have issued the warning:

"If money managers and central banks *offset* the movements of gold generated by trade imbalances, they will put off the day of corrective-price-level equilibrium; and putting off that day will keep gold flowing out just that much longer and that much more. And, if fractional reserves are too small and everything is leveraged too much, disaster in the form of bank runs and exhaustion of gold reserves may take place, with the result that one or more countries will be forced off the gold standard. And if new world currencies are created in excessive supply, world inflation could follow."

■ FLEXIBLE EXCHANGE RATES

Having seen how a gold standard works, we turn now to the case where supply and demand are left free to determine the foreign exchange rate. In the absence of any tie to gold, the pound in the 1940s might have had an average price of $4 or $5, and in this decade, an average price of $2.80. Who knows, perhaps next decade it could be at $4.50, or $3 or $1.50, once floating exchange rates become the rule.

The forces of supply and demand will determine the answer. If Americans want to buy so many English goods at the existing $2.80 level and Europeans want so few American goods, then we might be demanding more pounds as needed foreign exchange than they will be wanting to supply us with. What then will happen? If there is no longer a gold standard, one cannot get gold and ship it over so as to keep the foreign exchange rate within narrow gold points around the $2.80 parity. Instead, our urgent demand will bid up the foreign exchange rate. How far? Just far enough so that, at the new higher price of (say) $3 for the pound, our total demand for foreign exchange will be brought again down into equality with their enhanced supply of foreign exchange.

Two main steps are involved: (1) With the pound rate more expensive, it will cost more to import British bikes and our physical demand for them will fall off in the usual fashion. (2) With the dollar now cheaper, our goods will cost less to Europeans and they will want to demand more of our export goods. (If we look at these two effects, from both their viewpoint and our own, we have something like the four-pronged action of Hume. But with certain important differences. Our whole *domestic* price level need not change, and neither need theirs. The change in foreign exchange rate can itself bring about directly enhanced relative dearness and cheapness of export and import price levels.)

The familiar curves of supply and demand developed in Chapter 4 and Part Three are used in Fig. 33-1 to show equilibrium determination of flexible exchange rates.

America's *dd* curve comes from our desire for foreign exchange rate to buy import goods, to make tourist visits, to hire shipping and insurance services, to finance our troops abroad and our foreign-aid grants, to pay the dividends and interest we owe to foreign owners of our securities and property; and also to finance long-term investment abroad by American firms or stock buyers, and short-term investment in foreign near-term bonds or savings accounts.

What is behind their demand for dollars—which shows up as the *ss* supply curve of the pound-foreign-exchange they offer us? The exactly similar items in their balance of payments: desire to import our export goods, need to pay us dividends, etc.

Demand bids up, supply bids down a free foreign exchange rate:

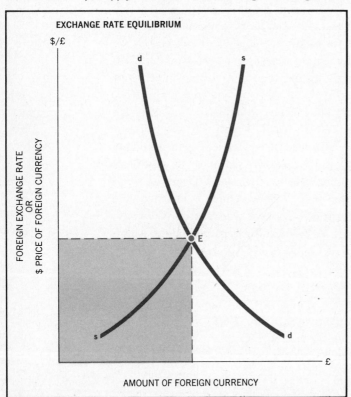

FIG. 33-1. Behind our *dd* is our desire to import British goods, buy British securities, visit the Bard's grave, and so forth. Behind their *ss* supply of pounds to be traded for dollars is their desire for our export goods and other items. If the rate were above *E*, there would be an excess of foreign currency that they would want to supply us over what we should want to demand. Such an excess of supply would bid the rate back down to *E*, where the market of foreign currency for dollars is just cleared.

■ At the *dd* and *ss* intersection, the flexible foreign exchange rate will get set, having then no tendency to rise or fall from this equilibrium level.

What will happen if tomorrow we send more troops abroad, travel abroad more, find new bargains in their catalogues and expand our dollar demand for their goods, and are forced by domestic inflation to raise our export-goods prices? Such changes will obviously shift our *dd* upward and rightward and also their *ss* leftward and upward. With what resulting intersection? With a new higher equilibrium level of the exchange rate; as described above, just enough higher to coax out more American exports and choke off imports from Europe. The exchange rate at which we buy foreign currencies has risen; the dollar's relative value has fallen.

A classical economist like Hume would understand all this very well. In fact, he (and Ricardo around 1817 and Sweden's Gustav Cassel around 1917) would offer this clue to the equilibrium level of a flexible exchange rate:

■ *Purchasing-power parity.* Let America and Europe be at equilibrium, say, at $2.80 per £1. Now let America double *all* her prices by domestically inflating her *M*; and let Europe keep her *M* limited enough to produce a steady price level. Then, other things being equal (such as employment remaining full and there being no inventions, crop failures, tariffs, or change in tastes), the new *dd* and *ss* intersection will come at twice the old $2.80 rate, namely, at $5.60 per £1.

Hume's reasoning would be classically simple. With all wages and prices here exactly doubled (and *M* doubled here to finance them), we can buy exactly the same physical imports and sell exactly the same physical exports at the new exchange rate that has doubled like everything else. (It is just as if every American old dollar is now called two American dollars, period.)[4]

DEPRECIATION, APPRECIATION, AND DEVALUATION   A doubling of the pound is a halving of the dollar. By definition, the fall in the price of one currency in terms of one or all others is called a "depreciation." A relative rise in the price of a currency in terms of another currency is called an "appreciation." Evidently, the pound has appreciated in our example, and the dollar has undergone a large depreciation.

The term "devaluation" is often confused with the term "depreciation." Devaluation usually is defined to mean a rise in the price of gold: thus, in 1933, Roosevelt devalued the dollar, raising the price of gold from about $21 an ounce eventually to its present price of $35 an ounce. When the Swiss or French stayed on the gold standard at their previous parities, the devaluation of the dollar meant depreciation of the dollar relative to the undevalued French franc and Swiss franc; but relative to the Canadian dollar and Philippine peso, which devalued equally with us, there was neither depreciation nor appreciation. (Check that the French franc then underwent appreciation.)

■ *Devaluation defined.* When gold officially goes up in price relative to a currency—as from $21 an ounce to $35—we say the currency has been devalued.
  Depreciation defined. When the price of a foreign currency rises relative to a given currency—e.g., when the price of the German mark rose 5 per cent

[4]Cassel and other writers developed the doctrine of purchasing-power parity to predict how much World War I currencies would depreciate when internal inflation sent their price levels up by 100 or more per cent. His long-run predictions worked out better than his short-run predictions, but neither had perfect accuracy. In the real world, unlike the classical model, other things did not stay equal.

in 1961, from $0.238 to $0.250 per mark—we say the (domestic) currency has depreciated, and of course the foreign currency has had a relative appreciation.

If *all* countries *simultaneously* raised the price of gold by 30 per cent, there would be no depreciation or appreciation, but there would be a devaluation.

■ EXCHANGE-RATE MECHANICS CONCLUDED

We have now surveyed the fundamentals of foreign exchange rates. Although money prices are quoted in international trade, in the longest run there must really be an international *barter* of goods and services against goods and services. Under a stable exchange-rate system like that of the modified gold standard, gold flows are supposed to lead to price-level adjustments big enough to restore equilibrium on the export and import side. Under flexible exchange rates, it is fluctuation in the foreign exchange rate that alters the relative costs and prices of foreign and home goods enough to restore an equilibrium balance in the international trade.

Generally, a depreciation of the currency which has been running an international deficit can be expected[5] to help restore the equilibrium. Although this happens less frequently, equilibrium could be restored by having the surplus country *appreciate* its currency—an example would be the 5 per cent appreciation of the mark and guilder engineered by the Germans and Dutch in 1961, or the World War I appreciation of the Swedish *kroner*.)

If prices and wages lack the flexibility to make the needed trade adjustments under the gold standard, the deficit country may find itself forced into a devaluation; this rise in the price at which it will buy and sell gold will imply a depreciation of its currency relative to any currency that remains at the old gold parities.[6] If all countries devalue together and in balance—to restore international liquidity or for any other reason—no appreciation or depreciation of currencies relative to each other takes place.

The remaining section of this chapter will go behind the demand and supply curves of international trade to examine each item involving foreign exchange payments and see how they all combine.

[5] There is a theoretical possibility that the relative price changes brought about by depreciation of the dollar could make the deficit worse rather than better if international demands turn out to be very inelastic rather than elastic. In such cases, lowering the prices of American export goods will not expand our physical sales much; therefore Englishmen will actually offer fewer pounds for dollars rather than more pounds. Similarly, if the American demand for British goods should be very urgent and inelastic, raising British prices may force us to demand more pounds rather than less. Thus, the price reaction to a depreciation of the dollar may be a perverse rather than an equilibrating one: The dollar would have to depreciate still further until demands ceased to be so inelastic; paradoxically, currency *appreciation* might in this perverse case wipe out a country's import deficit.

[6] At the end of this chapter's Appendix, there is discussed a compromise proposal that has some of the stability advantages of the gold standard's fixed exchange rates, and some of the flexibility advantage of floating exchange rates set by market forces of supply and demand. It is called the "sliding peg," and it permits limited changes in the exchange rate each year; over several years an orderly change in parity can then be achieved.

B. BALANCE OF INTERNATIONAL TRADE AND CAPITAL MOVEMENTS

■ THE BALANCE OF INTERNATIONAL PAYMENTS

The time has come to explain exactly what we mean when we speak of a country's "balance of international payments." We mean the statement that takes into account the values of all goods, all gifts and foreign aid, all capital loans (or "IOUs"), all gold coming in and going out, and the interconnections among all these items that lie behind Fig. 33-1's curves.

The balance of international payments summarizes these important relations. If you understand it, you have a fairly good grasp of foreign trade.

The U.S. Department of Commerce keeps records and makes official estimates of all international transactions during a year: merchandise exported and imported, money lent abroad or borrowed, gold movements, tourist expenditures, interest and dividends received or paid abroad, shipping services, and so forth. They all go to make up the "balance of international payments"—which is simply a double-entry listing of all items, drawn up in such a way that it must always show a balance.[7]

The balance of international payments is listed in three sections:

I. Current account
   Private:
       Merchandise (or "trade balance")
       Invisibles:
           Transportation (shipping services, etc.)
           Travel expenditure (tourists, etc.)
           Income on investments (interest, dividends, etc.)
           Private gifts (immigrants' remittances, etc.)
           Miscellaneous services
   Governmental:
       Government export of military goods to allies
       Unilateral grants of U.S. government (aid programs, military aid)
II. Capital movements
   Long-term:
       Private
       Government
   Short-term:
       Private
       Government
III. Gold movements (out and in)

BALANCE ON CURRENT ACCOUNT   The totality of items under section I is usually referred to as the "balance on current account." This important magnitude summarizes the

---

[7] Smuggling and some innocent items elude the record keepers, so it is necessary to introduce a miscellaneous category of omitted items, as in NNP's "statistical discrepancy."

difference between our total export of goods and services and our total import of goods and services.

In a moment, we shall see how any surplus or deficit balance on current account is "financed"—or, more precisely, is offset—by gold and capital movements under sections II and III. But before doing this, we shall describe briefly the major current items under the headings Private and Governmental.

Centuries ago, when *merchandise* items predominated, writers concentrated on them alone. If merchandise exports were greater in value than merchandise imports, they spoke of a "favorable balance of trade"; if imports exceeded exports, of an "unfavorable balance of trade." This is not a good choice of terms, for we shall see that a so-called "unfavorable" balance of trade may be a fine thing for a country.

In addition to such so-called "visible" merchandise items, we must not forget the important role played these days by the "invisibles." These consist of such items as shipping and insurance services which we provide for foreigners or which they provide for us, American tourist expenditures abroad, our earnings from abroad, and the gifts that immigrants send back home. On reflection, one realizes that an invisible item such as an American's expenditure for a drink in Paris has the same effect on the final balance of payments as does his import of French wine to be drunk here at home in America. And when we provide shipping insurance service, that acts like an export.

DEBITS AND CREDITS   A good way to decide how any item should be treated is to ask the following question: Is the item like one of our merchandise exports, providing us with more foreign currencies? Such an export-type item is called a "credit item" and gives us a supply of foreign money. Or is the item like one of our merchandise imports, causing us to use up our stock of foreign currencies and making it necessary to get more foreign currency? Such an import-type item is called a "debit item" and gives us a demand for foreign money.

To show how this rule works, ask the following question: How shall we treat interest and dividend income on investments received by Americans from abroad? Clearly, they are credit items like exports, in that they provide us with foreign currencies. The reader can reverse the argument to show that the interest and dividends which foreigners receive from us must be treated like debit items—like imports, they use up our foreign currencies.

At this point a close look at Table 33-1 will be helpful. It presents official data on the balance of international payments of the United States for 1965. Note its three main divisions into current, capital, and gold items; in addition, it has an item (line 21) to account for statistical errors and omissions. Each row is numbered to make reference easy. Then, after each item has been listed by name in Column (a), we list in Column (b) the credits, i.e., the amounts of those items that are like exports in earning us foreign currencies. Next, in Column (c), we list the debits, i.e., the amounts of the items that use up foreign currencies because of our need to pay for imports, and so forth.

Thus, in 1965 our merchandise exports gave us credits of 26,285 million dollars, but our merchandise imports gave us debits of only 21,492 million dollars. The net

These figures summarize international transactions:

NO.	(a) ITEMS	(b) CREDITS	(c) DEBITS	(d) NET CREDITS (+) OR DEBITS (−)	
	I Current				
	Private:				
1	Merchandise (adjusted)	$26,285	$21,492	+$4,793	
	Invisibles:				
2	Transportation	2,400	2,648	−248	
3	Travel expenditures	1,212	2,458	−1,246	
4	Income on investments (interest, dividends, etc.)	6,450	1,130	+5,320	
5	Private remittances		612	−612	
6	Miscellaneous services	1,112	375	+737	
7	Current private balance				+$8,744
	United States governmental:				
8	Exports of military goods and services (+)	1,624			
	Military aid payments (−) to allies		1,624	0	
9	Other military transactions	815	2,838	−2,023	
10	Other grants and payments		2,187	−2,187	
11	Miscellaneous government transactions	786	1,039	−253	
12	Current government transactions				−$4,463
13	Net balance on current account				+$4,281
	II Capital account, net exports of our IOUs (+) or net imports (−)				
	Long-term loans (−) or borrowing (+)				
14	Private			−4,423	
15	Government			−1,790	
16	Net long-term foreign investment				−6,213
17	Net balance on current account + long-term loans (the "basic deficit in U.S. balance of payments")				−$1,932
	Short-term loans (−) or borrowing (+)				
18	Private			+925	
19	Government			+1	
20	Net investment in short-term debt				+926
	III Net gold exports (+) or imports (−)				+1,665
21	Errors and omissions				−659
22	Offset to basic U.S. "deficit"				+$1,932
23	Over-all net balance of international payments				0

TABLE 33-1. UNITED STATES BALANCE OF INTERNATIONAL PAYMENTS, 1965—in millions of dollars. Although our current balance or private account exceeded $8 billion, that was not large enough to cover our $4½ billion of government aids and our $6 billion of long-term private investment. Result: gold loss of $1.665 billion. (Source: Adapted from U.S. Department of Commerce data.)

difference between credits and debits is in this case +4,793 million dollars. It is shown listed in the last column, Column (*d*), of the first row. (Be sure you know why the algebraic sign is shown + rather than −.) Even today one hears this export merchandise surplus called by the misleading title "favorable balance of trade."

The reader can interpret each line of the invisible items. He will know why the American tendency to travel abroad results in a negative—or net debit—entry under travel expenditures. He will also know why gifts by private Americans to relatives or charities abroad serve to use up foreign currencies and are listed as debits in line 5. (Of course, in their balance of payments, foreign countries would think of *our* debit as *their* credit, and of these last two items as "making more *dollars* available.")

Table 33-1 shows that as far as the private current items are concerned, the final effect of invisible items was to reinforce greatly our surplus of credits over debits—primarily because of our interest and dividends from abroad.

The whole net credit balance of the first seven private rows more than offsets the governmental items of the next five rows. Government military transactions and various foreign-aid grants and payments[8] resulted in the balance of −4,463 million dollars in line 12, enough to wipe out much of the positive private balance and make the final "net balance on current account" (line 13) equal to +4,281 million dollars.

In computing the net balance on current account, we have completed the first great block of Table 33-1. How must a nation offset its net balance on current account? Either by gold as in section III of the table or by net borrowing as in section II. *For it is a tautology that what you get you must either pay for or owe for.* And this fact of double-entry bookkeeping means that the whole table of the balance of international payments must show a final definitional balance. (Statistical errors and omissions, as in the case of the GNP statistical discrepancy discussed in Chapter 10, must of course be reckoned with if the double-entry bookkeeper is not given all the accurate facts; but this should not affect the *logic* of the perfect balance.)

CAPITAL MOVEMENTS   We can now turn to capital movements: the long-term and short-term loans *private* citizens make or receive from foreign private citizens (e.g., when General Motors builds an automobile plant abroad or when I buy a French bond or deposit funds in a Swiss bank; or when Belgians buy New York real estate or United States Treasury bonds); and long-term and short-term *government* loans and credits through various direct or intermediate channels.

It is easy to decide which are credit and which debit items in the capital accounts if you use the following rule: Always think of America as exporting and importing *capital securities*—or, for short, exporting and importing IOUs. Then you can treat these exports and imports like any other exports and imports. When we lend abroad,

[8] It will be seen that direct government gifts of equipment to, say, the German army would appear in line 8 as a self-canceling item in that it was produced here at home and simply left with the Germans as a gift; if counted as an export credit, it also is matched by the debit act of giving. Other military transactions, such as pay to the Germans for petrol for our troops there or their maintenance, and other United States government foreign programs would show up in lines 9 through 11.

is it a credit or debit? Obviously, we are importing IOUs—and imports always give rise to debits. Therefore it is a debit.

Similarly, when we are borrowing from abroad on balance, this creates a net credit. If you do not follow this rule, you will find yourself getting confused: when we lend abroad you will be tempted to think of us as exporting capital abroad and thereby earning a credit. This is wrong: we are then importing IOUs, and these imports are debit *offsets* enabling us to be paid for a surplus of credit exports on current account.

Line 16 shows that in 1965 America was a net long-term foreign lender: we were doing more long-term lending or investing abroad (directly by firms or through security portfolio buying) than foreigners were lending or investing here. We were the net importers of long-term IOUs by −6,213 million dollars.

BASIC DEFICIT   Now let us depart from a simple consideration of current, capital, and gold items. Let us investigate the important concept of America's "basic deficit." Certain short-term capital movements take place to make up for, and offset, our inability to generate enough credit items. So we exclude such short-term items in order to discover where we really stand on a longer-term basis.

Line 17 totes up the score of *all* our current transactions and long-term capital movements. So great were current government debits and long-term private investment debits as to give America a so-called net "basic deficit" of −1,932 million dollars.

It is somewhat dangerous to speak of a "deficit in the balance of payments," for, as we have just seen, the whole balance of payments must always be in tautologically perfect balance because of the identities and conventions of double-entry bookkeeping. What, then, do newspapers and congressmen mean when they refer to the American deficit in the balance of payments for the years 1958–1967? They probably[9] have reference to something like line 17, which is the sum of the current account deficit and the long-term investment deficit. It is this basic deficit that must definitely be paid for either by gold or by having foreigners choose to acquire liquid American assets on short-term capital account, knowing they can always change their mind and ask for gold if they decide that other financial markets offer them a higher interest rate on short-term funds than does New York City.

GOLD MOVEMENTS   The basic deficit of lines 17 and 22 is offset in part by our shipment of gold abroad. As shown in section III, 1,665 million dollars of gold had to go abroad. Why did so much gold have to go abroad, since line 20 shows that our total short-term borrowing of 926 million dollars should have helped to finance our basic deficit? The answer lies in line 21's innocent-looking "errors and omissions" item.

[9]This "basic deficit" should not be confused with two other international deficits to be encountered later in Chapter 36, and which appear more commonly in official government statistics. The "basic deficit" used here was developed in President Kennedy's first official 1961 message and in W. S. Salant and others, *The United States Balance of Payments in 1968* (The Brookings Institution, Washington, D.C., 1963). For 1965 the Official Settlements balance was −1.3 billion dollars, as opposed to the −1.9-billion-dollar basic deficit of Table 33-1.

Experts suspect that almost all this 659-million-dollar item represented short-term capital flight abroad that never got recorded. (EXAMPLE: If I deposit money in Switzerland during a vacation trip, that is perfectly legal, but does not get recorded.) If these error items had been included in line 20, it would have shown a net export of short-term IOUs of only 267 million dollars. And we could then say that this total of our 1,665 million dollars of gold exports and our net export of 267 million dollars of short-term capital (derived by combining lines 20 and 21) covered our basic deficit of 1,932 million dollars.

After paying out this gold, we finally achieve the formal balance shown in line 23. The balance of international payments taken as a whole is built out of double-entry debit and credit items, so that it will always show this formal balance. This was true even of the period from 1946 to 1949 when we were gaining gold and liquid assets from abroad (during the so-called "dollar-shortage" when European factories were noncompetitive with ours). This formal balance holds true even in recent times—when there has seemed to be the opposite of a dollar shortage, namely, a "chronic deficit" in the American current and long-term capital balance which is being matched by an outflow of gold and the short-term dollar obligations that foreigners were piling up instead of taking all in gold.

■ STAGES OF A COUNTRY'S BALANCE OF PAYMENTS

Historically, the United States has gone through the four stages typical of the growth of a young agricultural nation into a well-developed industrialized one. A review of this history may be useful to consolidate understanding.

1. *Young and growing debtor nation.* From the Revolutionary War era until just after the Civil War, we imported on current account more than we exported. England and Europe lent us the difference in order to build up our capital structure. We were a typical young and growing debtor nation.

2. *Mature debtor nation.* From about 1873 to 1914, our balance of trade appears to have become favorable. But growth of the dividends and interest that we had to pay abroad on our past borrowing kept our balance on current account more or less in balance. Capital movements were also nearly in balance, our new lending just about canceling our borrowing.

3. *New creditor nation.* In World War I, we expanded our exports tremendously. At first, private American citizens made loans to the warring Allied powers. After we got into the war, our government lent money to England and France for war equipment and postwar relief needs. We emerged from the war a creditor nation. But our psychological frame of mind had not adjusted itself to our new creditor position. We passed high tariff laws in the 1920s and in 1930. Because we refused to import, foreigners found it difficult to get the dollars to pay us interest and dividends, much less repay principal.

So long as we remained in this third stage of being a new creditor country—so long, that is, as we kept making *new* private foreign loans all through the 1920s—everything momentarily appeared all right on the surface. We could continue to sell more than we were buying, by putting most of it "on the cuff." The rest of the world met our export surplus by sending us gold and by sending us IOUs. As long as Wall Street bankers could interest Main Street investors in foreign bonds, everything seemed rosy. But by 1929 and later, when Americans would no longer lend abroad, the crash finally came. International trade broke down. Debts were defaulted. America, as much as the rest of the world, was to blame.

4. *Mature creditor nation.* England reached this stage some years ago, and as in all such cases, her imports exceeded her exports. Before we feel sorry for her because of her so-called "unfavorable" balance of trade, let us note what this really means.

Her citizens were living better because they were able to import much cheap food and in return did not have to part with much in the way of valuable export goods. The English were paying for their import surplus by the interest and dividend receipts they were receiving from past foreign lending.

Fine for the English. But what about the rest of the world? Were they not worse off for having to send exports to England in excess of imports? Not necessarily. Normally, the capital goods that England had previously lent them permitted them to add to their domestic production—to add *more* than had to be paid out to England in interest and dividends. Both parties were better off. Nineteenth-century foreign lending was twice blessed: it blessed him who gave and him who received. Of course, international trade and finance did not always operate quite so smoothly. Some investments proved unwise. Political problems of colonies and nationalism complicated the situation. And the whole process went awry and broke down after World War I.

By virtue of our cold-war foreign-aid and defense commitments, America finds herself needing the income from previous investments to meet her current requirements from abroad. We need huge current surpluses to cover aid and investment programs.

■ BASIC SIGNIFICANCE OF INTERNATIONAL CAPITAL MOVEMENTS

Return now to the problem of capital movements. If political problems of nationalism and domestic problems of unemployment did not enter the picture, the fundamentals of international lending would be easy to understand. We could easily cut through the fog of money and finance and concentrate on the real aspects in terms of goods and resources.

How does capital grow within a country? By our diverting labor, land, machinery, and other resources away from the production of current consumption goods. Instead, we plant trees, drain rivers, or build new machinery and buildings. All these add to our future income and consumption.

We are postponing present consumption for future consumption; in fact, for an even *greater* amount of future consumption. Where does the increase in future consumption come from? As Chapter 30 showed, *capital goods have a "net" productivity.* This constitutes the real aspect of the interest rate.

Different parts of the world have different amounts of resources: labor, minerals, climate, know-how. Were it not for ignorance or political boundaries, no one would push investment in North America down to the point of 5 per cent returns *if elsewhere there still existed 10 per cent opportunities.* Some capital would certainly be invested abroad. This would give foreign labor higher wages, because now the foreign worker has more and better tools to work with. It would increase foreign production. By how much? Not only by enough to pay for the constant replacement of used-up capital goods but, in addition, by enough to pay us an interest or dividend return on our investment. This interest return would take the form of goods and services which we receive from abroad and which add to our standard of living. An all-wise scientist would probably approve of the process. It would make sense to him because capital is going into the regions where its productivity is highest.

When would we be repaid our principal? So long as we are earning a good return, there is no reason why we should ever wish to have it repaid. However, the once-backward country may finally become rather prosperous. It may wish to pull in its belt as far as consumption is concerned and to use its savings to buy out our ownership in its factories, farms, and mines. But suppose that we are rich, with plenty of savings and with so much capital at home that our rate of interest is low. We might not particularly wish to sell out or be repaid. We might raise the selling price of our farm and factory holdings abroad. In other words, we might be content with a smaller percentage interest return. Thus, there is no necessary reason why a country should ever be paid off for its past lending, unless it has become relatively poorer.

When nationalism rears its head, matters change. Within the United States, interest and dividends may stream from South to North and West to East until doomsday. A few people may grumble about absentee ownership; but the courts and police are there to see that property rights are respected. Not so between nations. When a country is poor, it may be anxious to borrow. After it has become richer, it becomes unhappy to have to pay dividends and interest abroad. It chooses not to remember that its prosperity stemmed in part from its past borrowing. More than an economic burden is involved; politically, countries do not like the principle of absentee ownership by "furriners." They are prone to insist upon getting rid of their international liabilities—paying them off at a fair or unfair price, or often by outright default.

Economics and politics mix in ways too complicated to discuss in this book. Some say "trade follows the flag." Others say the flag follows trade. Some say the pursuit of economic gain is the primary motive behind the imperialistic search for colonies. Others claim that national power (offensive and defensive) is an end in itself; that economic well-being is sacrificed to this end; and that economic resources are sought for their contribution to military strength (offensive and defensive) rather than for their contribution to economic well-being. According to this view, without wars and nationalism, anyone could invest and trade anywhere, and sensible people should prefer to live in small countries unhindered by costly military establishments and colonial administration. At the opposite extreme is the view that victory in battle, rather than comfortable living, is the only worthy end in life; that the foreigner is of no importance compared with the fatherland; that he can be stripped of his goods and land, and be made to work for the conquerors. The world of the last few centuries lies somewhere between these extreme cases.

■ FINANCIAL VERSUS REAL ASPECTS OF FOREIGN LENDING

Let us turn from politics back to economics to see how foreign investment takes place in financial terms. Money throws a veil over the real aspects of capital movements. Usually, a foreigner borrows *money* from us rather than capital goods directly. He gives us an IOU in the form of a bond, note, or stock certificate. We give him dollars. If he simply holds the dollars or puts them in an American bank or invests them in an

American security, there has not yet been a net capital movement. We have some form of his IOU; he has some form of ours. In the capital-movements section of the balance of payments, the difference cancels out. Only when the foreign borrower uses the receipts of the loan to import goods (or gold) in excess of his exports to us does a real and a financial capital movement take place.

When the time comes for interest payment, the foreigners must sell us more goods than they buy in order to get the extra dollars to remit to us. Our balance of international payments then will show an import trade surplus, balanced by the invisible credit item, interest and dividends.

Should a nation feel glad or sorry when it is exporting more than it is importing? If we never had to worry about unemployment, we would certainly regret having to give away goods that might better serve our own well-being. Only the consolation of later receiving goods in return could serve to compensate us for this present loss. Altruism aside, if we could look into a crystal ball and see that the investment was sure to go sour later and never be repaid either in principal or interest, then we should certainly conclude that the capital movement was a bad and not a good thing.

A century ago, John Stuart Mill properly stressed that *it is imports and not exports that add to a nation's well-being.* Before World War II, countries were handling the problem of maintaining full employment so badly that they began to put the cart before the horse and to treat exports as if they were an end for their own sake. Fortunately, nations are learning how proper monetary and fiscal policies can restore to validity the fundamental principles of classical economics. And to this degree Mill's sensible stress on imports comes back into its own.

SUMMARY

A. MECHANISMS OF FOREIGN EXCHANGE AND TRADE

1 ■
Buying or selling abroad presupposes a foreign exchange rate between home and foreign currencies. Two countries on a gold standard have a stable foreign exchange rate set by the stable parity prices at which they each buy and sell gold—whether gold bars, coins, or fractional reserve banking and gold-exchange standards are used.

2 ■
Classical economists (such as David Hume) relied on gold movements to alter relative price levels, (a) raising exports and (b) curbing imports of the deficit country, and (c) cutting exports and (d) raising imports of the surplus country.

3 ■
Once stable exchange rates under a gold standard were abandoned, flexible foreign rates would get set by interaction of supply and demand schedules for foreign exchange. The adjustment now involves changes in export and import prices and not necessarily absolute price levels.

B. BALANCE OF INTERNATIONAL TRADE AND CAPITAL MOVEMENTS

4 ■

The balance of international payments refers to all the transactions that use up foreign exchange or make foreign exchange available to us. It relates the total of our exports of goods and services to our imports. Our exports of goods, services, gold, or IOUs are credit items, making foreign currencies available to us. Our imports of those items are debits, using up foreign currencies.

5 ■

Our net balance on current account comes from adjusting our merchandise trade balance for "invisible" service items and from taking into account our unilateral government aid programs. It and net long-term capital movements constitute the "basic deficit" which has to be offset by gold shipments and short-term capital movements.

6 ■

As a nation passes from the "young debtor" to the "mature creditor" stage, its payments go through a characteristic sequence of stages.

7 ■

No problem in international finance is more important than that of understanding the real and the monetary aspects of capital movements in their effect upon the industrial development of nations.

QUESTIONS FOR DISCUSSION

1. Contrast free and stable foreign exchange rates. Explain each.

2. What are the gold points exactly? Suppose transport costs diminish.

3. Draw up a list of items that belong on the credit side of the balance of international payments and another list of items that belong on the debit side. What is meant by a "favorable balance of trade"? By the balance on current account? By the "basic deficit"? Why the term "invisible items"? What is the difference between short- and long-term capital movements?

4. Construct hypothetical balance sheets for a young debtor country, a mature debtor country, a new creditor country, and a mature creditor country.

5. "Foreign lending causes war. Foreign giving postpones war. Free foreign trading prevents war." Comment.

6. Review your understanding of the following concepts:

gold standard versus free exchange rate
debits and credits
currency depreciation and devaluation
balance of international payments,
    trade balance, invisibles, current
    account, government aid items
"favorable balance"

America's "basic deficit"
gold movements
IOUs, capital movements
net foreign investment
historical capital movements, financial
    and real, in politics and in
    economics

APPENDIX: Income and Unemployment Aspects of International Trade

FOREIGN-TRADE MULTIPLIER

The classical mechanism of Hume depended primarily on relative prices. It seems to have assumed, essentially, that employment is always full: that in the long run, trade simply moved a society from one point on its domestic production-possibility frontier to another; that foreign trade never moved society inside its p-p frontier or pushed it outward toward that frontier from an initial underemployment equilibrium.

Yet we saw in Part Two that a laissez-faire system is not automatically always at full employment. That cannot be guaranteed unless stabilizing monetary and fiscal policy is brought to bear on it (or unless there is more ideal flexibility of wage and price levels than modern mixed economies have.)

What, then, will be the effects of international forces on the $C + I + G$ equilibrium of Part Two? One can guess that additional exports and foreign investment will have the same expansionary effects on domestic production and employment as will additional domestic investment.

That guess is correct: similar multiplier effects are involved. New exports do have exactly the same multiplier effects on output and prices. They raise incomes directly, but in addition they set up a chain of further spending and respending.

Thus, 1 billion dollars' worth of new export orders to New England machine-tool factories will create 1 billion dollars of primary jobs and income. Then workers and owners may respend perhaps two-thirds of their new income on the consumption products of Indiana and California; two-thirds of this extra income is in turn respent. The process finally comes to a halt only when the total adds up to

$$3 = 1 + \tfrac{2}{3} + (\tfrac{2}{3})^2 + \cdots = 1/(1 - \tfrac{2}{3})$$

—i.e., to 1 billion dollars of initial expenditure plus 2 billion of extra secondary consumption expenditure.

Besides introducing a multiplier effect of exports into the picture, international trade has a second important effect. Our higher American NNP will increase our imports, let us say, by one-twelfth out of every extra dollar. This means that our chain of induced domestic purchasing power will peter out faster than

in the above example. At each step, these imports act as "leakages," just like the marginal propensity to save.[1]

Therefore, out of the original 1 billion dollars of income in the export industries, perhaps only

$$\tfrac{7}{12}\,(= \tfrac{2}{3} - \tfrac{1}{12})$$

rather than $\tfrac{8}{12}$ will be respent on *American* consumption goods (in Indiana, California, and so forth). And so it will go at each stage. The whole multiplier will now add up to only

$$1 + \tfrac{7}{12} + (\tfrac{7}{12})^2 + \cdots$$

or only to

$$2\tfrac{2}{5} = 1 \div (1 - \tfrac{7}{12}) = 1 \div \tfrac{5}{12}$$

instead of to 3. Note that $\tfrac{1}{12}$ of our extra $2\tfrac{2}{5}$ billion dollars of generated income—or $\tfrac{1}{5}$ billion dollars in this case—tends to go abroad for extra imports. A general rule can be stated:

■ Exports raise domestic income, but with a multiplier reduced by our induced imports. So long as some fraction of income at every stage is leaking into domestic saving, a new dollar of exports will raise income, but can never lift it by enough to call forth a full dollar of new imports.[2]

In conclusion, we may say that variations in income generated by international trade will often go part way to effecting the needed adjustments; but they do not obviate the need for some price or exchange-rate reductions, since a spontaneous increase in demand for our exports can never create a large enough induced

[1] Applying the foreign-trade multiplier analysis to a small city or country, you will find that secondary multiplier effects upon the workers of that region are almost negligible, since most extra income leaks out to other regions.

[2] Suppose that each extra dollar of income is always split up into the three fractions: c for American consumption goods; b for America's propensity to import goods from abroad; a for the remaining amount going into saving. Then let exports go up by 1 unit. The multiplier tells us that our income will go up by $1/(1 - c) = 1/(b + a)$. Multiplying this extra income by the fraction b, we get induced imports of $b/(b + a)$, which is certainly less than our original 1 of new exports—to the extent that the marginal propensity to save a is positive.

If there is any induced domestic investment, it can be thrown in with c, and our result will still hold for any "stable" system with positive "leakage" a.

expansion of our imports to cancel out all final effects on the balance of payments between us and abroad.[3]

OVERVALUATION OF CURRENCY AND UNEMPLOYMENT

Consider two countries. Call them A and E for America and Europe. Although England is not identical with Europe, let the respective currencies be called dollars ($) and pounds (£). If German marks were familiar to readers, their use would provide greater realism. Let A and E begin in long-run foreign exchange equilibrium with $2.80 per £1.

Now let productivity in Europe grow faster than in America. If all money wages and profits grew in E as quickly as productivity, there need be no lasting disturbance to the equilibrium: thus, doubling productivity and money wages and factor payments in E will leave her prices just as they were in relation to A's unchanged prices. The real income level in E has grown relative to that of A, perhaps closing some of the gap between them. But so long as Engel's laws imply that A's goods are as much in demand at higher income levels as E's, there need be no disturbance of the equilibrium. A is not hurt or helped by E's improved real income.

However, it is more realistic to assume that money wage and other factor costs do not *at once* grow abroad as fast as productivity does, even though they grow much faster than in relatively stagnant A. Now E's goods are bargains. Although A has not had domestic wage or other inflation, A's goods are now relatively dear. What is the effect? E's exports expand physically and (probably) in value; A's exports dwindle physically and (probably) in value. If payments were in balance before, now A runs a chronic international deficit.

We can say: Before at $2.80 per £1, the dollar was neither undervalued nor overvalued; now at $2.80, the dollar is definitely an "overvalued currency," running

a chronic deficit and having too high a cost level. This results from the more rapid technical change abroad, which partially closed the gap between their technology and ours and lowered their relative costs.

The deficit disequilibrium in A's balance on current account will probably be aggravated by a tendency for A's investor to want to invest in E, where profitability is likely to be very high as a result of (1) rapid growth in E; (2) rapid technical change in E; (3) great opportunity for A firms to profit from applying their "know-how" in E.

EFFECTS OF OVERVALUATION

1. If A previously had full employment, her loss of export production (and perhaps of domestic production displaced by cheap imports) implies a multiplier drop in employment and real NNP.

2. She cannot use Federal Reserve easy money to stimulate domestic *I*, for fear that low interest yields will drive cool money to seek higher yields in E.

3. If A uses militant fiscal policy, expanding *G* expenditure and cutting tax rates to expand *C* and *I*, she can overcome her unemployment; but the resulting increase in NNP will wipe out the drop in A's imports from E that resulted from A's income drop (and which had *partially* relieved the international deficit).

4. If E previously had full employment, she now is threatened with overemployment, with demand-pull and cost-push inflation. If E previously had some slack, she would be delighted with her good fortune to have become an *undervalued* currency nation, with the extra NNP and employment thereby implied.

5. Actually, now that E is quoting prices low relative to those A is quoting, the disturbed-equilibrium terms of trade have moved against E and in favor of A. E is, so to speak, throwing away goods to A. Not only is A getting cheap goods—the goal of rational nonmercantilistic nations—but she is also, for the moment, getting some goods in return simply for her shipping out barren gold or mere IOUs.

CORRECTING OVERVALUATION
What can correct the situation? A can wait for inflation in E to raise E's prices and end the undervaluation of E's currency. If E's productivity continues to show miracles of growth, the wait may be a long and grueling one.

Or, in premodern times, A could try to deflate her own wage and cost level by 10 or 20 per cent. This seems not very practical in a mixed economy of rather rigid administered prices and wages: blood has often

---

[3] But it is not quite correct to say, as some books used to do, that these income effects are always *reinforcing* to the classical relative-price adjustments of Hume and others. (EXAMPLE: A runs a deficit with E. A depreciates its currency relative to E. This causes relative price changes, which, let us say, are by themselves just enough to cure the trade deficit. But now assume A's output can expand, and that the expansion in A's exports causes a multiplier expansion in her income *and some increase in her imports from* E. Note that such an income effect has now made it necessary for an *additional* change in relative prices.)

run in the streets of nations trying to adjust to an over-valued currency by internal cost deflation.

Or A might pray for a miracle that would increase her productivity. Exhortation by the government and by each of us to have us all work harder and more skillfully will no doubt be forthcoming in abundance.

Or A might *de*preciate the dollar.[4] When the pound has risen from $2.80 to $3 or $3.50, there may again be equilibrium, with neither currency overvalued. Such a realignment of exchange rates would create certain political problems, domestic and foreign: interferences with the gold standard, crises of confidence at home, retaliation from E if E is enjoying having an under-valued currency, etc. Hence, let us suppose that for the years in question depreciation is simply not feasible.

If A's gold is large enough to meet the chronic drain and E's willingness to take A's IOUs is sufficiently great, the disequilibrium situation may go on for a long time. Perhaps in that time luck will shift the winds of demand in A's favor; or A's productivity might grow; or A may become a more profitable place for investors in either country to want to place their long-term funds; or the government in A may, reluctantly, cut down on its troop and its aid expenditures abroad.

A country with an overvalued currency will be under great internal pressure to interfere with free trade. Employers and workers will clamor for protective tariffs and quotas. Congress will consider preventing costly tours abroad, curbing free flow of capital abroad, intro-ducing comprehensive exchange controls, initiating export subsidies, tying up foreign aid, and requiring purchase of military equipment at home even at prices twice as high. The President will exhort business to moderate profitable investments abroad by a "voluntary" program, and will even introduce so-called "interest equalization taxes" which place perhaps a 15 per cent tax on long-term foreign loans.

Most chronically overvalued currencies in history have resulted in suspension of freely convertible cur-rencies and in controlled international trade. More-over, once the overvaluation of the currency has been handled in this way, there is no possibility of removing the controls: once controls are ended, the international payments deficit reappears. History is replete with cases of premature dashes toward convertibility, which ended in fiascoes and return to controls.

[4]Or E might *ap*preciate the pound.

THE ACHILLES' HEEL OF CLASSICISM   What needs emphasis here is the economics of overvaluation. We shall discover that all the discredited notions of the mercantilists—fear of gold drain, insistence on import curbs and export subsidies, wish to export unemploy-ment abroad, desire to give goods away cheaply rather than dearly, etc.—make some sense in the case of an overvalued currency. The skillful classical arguments of Hume, Smith, and Samuelson no longer carry the day because their major premise of equilibrium currency valuation is explicitly denied.

The next two chapters will elucidate the pro-and-con arguments for tariffs and will demonstrate the basic theory of comparative advantage that justifies mutually advantageous geographical division of labor and trade. If prices and wages were everywhere perfectly flexible and/or exchange rates could be counted on to be neither overvalued nor undervalued, the arguments of these chapters would be unanswerable. Here is an example:

Chapter 34 points out that the veil of money and foreign exchange merely covers the true barter nature of trade. It says, "One country cannot undersell the other in *all* goods, but only in those in which it has a comparative advantage, being undersold by the other country in those goods in which that country has a comparative advantage." That is absolutely true in a Ricardian model where the wage ratio between the two countries moves flexibly so that the resulting foreign exchange rate is neither overvalued nor undervalued.

But it is still quite obvious that if one country insists on pricing its goods sky high in money terms (because of sky-high wage rates *or* profit markups), it can certainly price itself out of the market, bringing upon itself an overvalued currency, unemployment, and international deficits. After all, any one of us can do that by insisting on $100,000 per hour; and any region, such as New England, could be undersold by the South in everything if it insisted on prices that cleared no markets. So this can certainly happen internationally as well as intranationally.

DETERIORATING TERMS OF TRADE   Modern analysis can cast light on the truth and untruth both in mer-cantilism and in classicism. Here, for example, is an aspect of America's possible overvaluation that could be discovered only by analytical economics.

Suppose that the productivity miracle in E involves a significant increase in her ability to produce the goods that A was previously exporting or producing for home

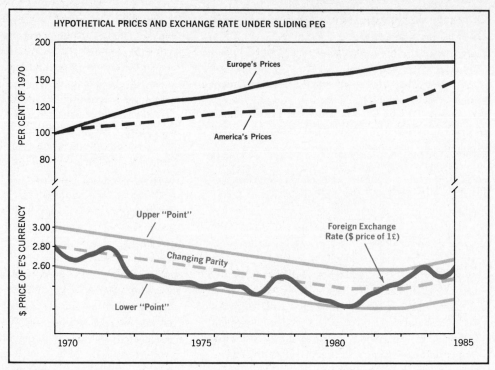

FIG. 33-2.

consumption. Again A has an overvalued currency, just as in the previous case of across-the-board unbiased productivity advance in E. Again A has unemployment stagnation. Again equilibrium can be restored by depreciation of A's $1 relative to E's £1. But with this important difference:

Under unbiased technical change abroad, A's new equilibrium terms of trade could be presumed to be about what they had been before. However, with technological change abroad biased toward improvements designed to narrow the gap between productivity in those goods where we were enjoying comparative advantage, there is a strong presumption that the new equilibrium will involve a permanent deterioration of our terms of trade.

We are actually (somewhat) impoverished by the technical advance abroad, or at least slowed down in our rate of material progress by this event. How can we be hurt if *our* productivity has not deteriorated? Because worsened terms of trade cause us to lose some of the "consumer satisfaction" we were before gaining from international trade.

The universe was not made such that what helps

one *must* help all; often what helps one thereby hurts another. In this case A, who is already quite rich, may find solace in the fact that E is becoming less poor, and may not regret too much the slight sacrifice implied for A.

Chapter 36 shows that the foregoing analysis has relevance to the world of the 1950s and 1960s. It all did happen that way!

A SLIDING PEG?

We have seen that stable exchange rates promote fruitful trade. We have also seen that a flexible, freely floating exchange rate, determined by momentary supply and demand as in Fig. 33-1, prevents long-term balance-of-payments disequilibrium of the kind that will be discussed in Chapter 36. A number of economists[5] have therefore suggested as a new reform measure an inter-

[5] J. M. Keynes proposed widening of the gold points in the 1920s. In the 1960s, A. W. Phillips, J. E. Meade, and J. Black of the United Kingdom proposed a sliding peg; and a large number of American experts endorsed the combined scheme in a 1965 petition. Chapter 36 will return to this subject.

esting compromise between exchange-rate stability and flexibility.

■ 1. The "gold points," which surround the parity exchange rate, are to be widened (and freed from any dependence on a fixed price of gold or the cost of shipping gold).

Thus instead of holding fluctuations of the £-$ rate within the range $2.80 ± .02, let it now freely move with supply and demand within the range of, say, $2.80 ± .20. I.e., in any year the pound rate might fall from $3 to $2.60 if Europe's import debits were threatening to exceed her export credits.

Within the widened range, equilibration would take place as a result of permitted, orderly rate adjustments (appreciation or depreciation).

■ 2. Over a period of years, the midrange parity, around which the widened limits are drawn, would be permitted to rise or fall by, say, 1 or 1½ per cent per year.

Why? So that if Europe's cost structure were showing a long-term tendency to rise more than ours, the threatened fundamental disequilibrium could be averted. (Merely widening the upper and lower points would give only limited relief: for, if Europe's costs and prices rise

chronically, the exchange rate would always be at the $2.60 floor; only by gradually lowering that floor could the growing dearness of Europe's exports be offset by long-term, orderly depreciation of the pound.)

The slowness of the long-term slide in the exchange-rate peg should go far to discourage speculators from "piling on" to a one-way movement, thereby aggravating it and making it even more disorderly.

Figure 33-2 shows how the scheme might work in a hypothetical future period.

Note that in the early years, European prices (costs, wages, etc.) are rising faster than American prices (these are shown in brown above). By the "purchasing-power parity" doctrine of this chapter, that should depress the pound rate toward its floor. (Of course, monetary ups and downs of supply and demand change the green exchange rate within the widened limits.) Since Europe's relative price rise is chronic and not temporary, the green tracks all move in one direction, at 1½ per cent per year. In a decade, an orderly 15 per cent exchange-rate adjustment has been made! Best of all, the process can be a two-way street. If, much later, American prices outsoar European, it can be the dollar's turn to depreciate: now the pound appreciates toward the ceiling limit, and the tracks gradually rise.

34 International Trade and the Theory of Comparative Advantage

THE BENEFIT OF INTERNATIONAL TRADE—A MORE EFFICIENT EMPLOYMENT OF THE PRODUCTIVE FORCES OF THE WORLD. J. S. MILL

Again and again we have seen how specialization increases productivity and standards of living. Now we must show exactly how this works out in the field of international trade, going behind the facade of international finance.

Why did the United States specialize a century ago in the production of agricultural goods and exchange these for the manufacturing output of Europe? Why is she today able to export highly complex mass-produced goods to the far corners of the globe? Why is the agriculture of Australia so different from that of Austria or Belgium? How great would the costs of complete self-sufficiency be to a modern country? How do all countries benefit from trade?

The key to the correct answers to such questions, and many more, is provided by the theory of comparative advantage or comparative cost. Developed more than a century ago by David Ricardo, John Stuart Mill, and other English followers of Adam Smith, the theory of comparative advantage is a closely reasoned doctrine which, when properly stated, is unassailable. With it we can identify gross fallacies in the political propaganda for protective tariffs aimed at limiting imports. With it we can identify the germs of truth that sometimes pop up in the heated claims for tariff protection.

■ DIVERSITY OF CONDITIONS BETWEEN REGIONS OR COUNTRIES

For simplicity, therefore, let us imagine two countries or continents, each endowed with certain quantities of natural resources, capital goods, kinds of labor, and technical knowledge or know-how. The first link in the comparative-cost chain of reasoning is the *diversity in conditions of production between different countries.*

Specifically, this means that the production possibilities of the different countries are very different. Although people could try to produce something of every commodity in any region, it is obvious that they would not succeed; or if they did succeed, it would only be at a terrific cost. With hothouse procedures and forcing methods, wine grapes could perhaps be grown in Scotland; but the cost in terms of economic resources would be exorbitant, and the resulting product would be scarce fit to drink.

■ Even if by chance two countries can both produce the same commodities, they generally find that it pays for each to concentrate its production especially on some goods and trade them for other goods.

If we consider trade between, say, the northern temperate zones and the southern tropics, the foregoing proposition will seem true and trite. Of course, resources near the equator are more productive in the growing of bananas, and northern resources are better designed for wheat growing. Everyone can readily see that in this case specialization and trade will increase the amount of world production of both goods, and also each country's ability to consume both goods.

It is not so immediately obvious, but it is no less true, that

■ International trade is mutually profitable even when one of the countries can produce *every commodity* more cheaply (in terms of labor or all resources) than the other country.

One country may be *absolutely more efficient* in the production of *every* good than is the other country; and this means the other country has an absolute disadvantage in the production of every good. But so long as there are differences in the *relative* efficiencies of producing the different goods in the two countries, we can always be sure that even the poor country has a *comparative advantage* in the production of those commodities in which it is relatively most efficient; this same poor country will have a *comparative disadvantage* in those other commodities in which its inefficiency is more than average. Similarly, the rich, efficient country will find that it should specialize in those fields of production where it has a comparative advantage, planning to import those commodities in which it has a comparative disadvantage.

Thus, trade between America and Europe in food and clothing is mutually advantageous even if America can produce both these items more efficiently (in terms of all economic resources). Moreover, barter between America and Asia is especially advantageous to us even though the Indian laborer receives only a fraction of the real wages going to productive American labor. We shall see in a moment why this is so.

A traditional example used to illustrate this paradox of comparative advantage is the case of the best lawyer in town who is also the best typist in town. Will he not specialize in law and leave typing to a secretary? How can he afford to give up precious time from the legal field, where his comparative advantage is very great, to perform typing activities in which he is efficient but in which he lacks *comparative* advantage? Or look at it from the secretary's point of view. She is less efficient than he in both activities; but her relative disadvantage compared with him is least in typing. Relatively speaking, she has a comparative advantage in typing.

So with countries. Suppose America produces food with one-third the labor that Europe does, and produces clothing with one-half the labor. Then we shall see that America has a comparative advantage in food and a comparative disadvantage in clothing—this, despite the fact that America is absolutely most efficient in everything. By the same token, Europe has a comparative advantage in clothing.

■ A SIMPLE CASE: EUROPE AND AMERICA

Let us illustrate these fundamental principles of international trade by a simplified example. Consider America and Europe of a century ago, and concentrate on only two commodities, food and clothing. In America land and natural resources were then very plentiful relative to labor and capital; but in Europe, people and capital were plentiful relative to land.

This contrast is best seen if we look at the *intensive* agriculture of a country such as Belgium. There, in order to get the greatest possible output, small plots of land have to be cultivated assiduously by many people using much fertilizer. Compare this with the extensive agriculture of early America: here one family cultivated many acres, and national product was maximized by each man's "spreading himself thin" over the virtually free land. A Belgian would have thought this wasteful. But in view of the relatively high cost of our labor or capital and the low cost of land, it was prudent.

Of course, if surplus population could have all migrated from Belgium to the United States, the law of diminishing returns implies that real wages here would fall toward equality with rising wages there; and high land rents there would fall toward equality with rising rents here.[1]

But suppose that immigrants from abroad are to be kept out of the United States in order to keep labor scarce here and wages high. From this same selfish point of view, should the United States also impose a protective tariff designed to keep out imports from abroad? Or should it not? To answer this important social question we must measure carefully the amounts of food and clothing that will be produced and consumed in each country (1) if there is no international trade and (2) if trade, according to comparative advantage, is permitted to follow its own course.

■ THE LAW OF COMPARATIVE ADVANTAGE

David Ricardo, stockbroker and self-made millionaire, expert on the theory of land rent and of currency, came up in 1817 with the beautiful proof that international specialization pays for a nation. This is the famous theory of comparative advantage, or, as it is sometimes called, the "theory of comparative cost." This very important theory repays close attention.

For simplicity Ricardo worked with only two countries; we shall call them America and Europe, and assume they are both about the same size. For simplicity he worked with only two goods; we shall call them food and clothing. For simplicity Ricardo chose to measure all costs in terms of hours of labor; we shall do the same, recognizing that more advanced treatises and the Appendix to this chapter can give some of the needed qualifications when our simple assumptions are relaxed. The germ of truth in the principle of comparative advantage will still remain.

---

[1] Actually, this would have tended at the same time to increase *total world production*. Why? Because the transfer of workers from their poor Belgian farms to rich American farms would increase their productivity and total world product.

UNCOMMON SENSE   Using common sense, people will probably agree that trade between America and Europe is likely to be mutually profitable in a first simple case where European labor has greater productivity in one good and American labor has greater productivity in another.

In this case, to produce a unit of food in America requires a smaller number of labor days than is needed in Europe to produce it, while to produce a unit of clothing takes a smaller number of labor days in Europe than in America. The man in the street needs no Ricardo to tell him that in such a case America will probably specialize in food production, exporting some food for Europe's clothing exports.

But Ricardo showed much more than this. He showed that even if American labor (or resources generally) were more productive than Europe's *in both* food and clothing, trade is still likely to be mutually advantageous.

Table 34-1 illustrates this principle of comparative advantage. In America a unit of food costs 1 day's labor and a unit of clothing costs 2 days' labor. In Europe the cost is 3 days' labor for food and 4 days' labor for clothing. By forming the proper two ratios of these four crucial numbers, Ricardo is able to prove conclusively that America and Europe will *both* benefit if America specializes in food and exports it for the clothing exports that Europe specializes in.

Before examining this, listen to the European in the street as he says:

> *Mon Dieu!* Trade could never be profitable for us with that American colossus. Her efficiency will enable her to undersell us in every line—food and clothing. We need import tariffs to protect the honest European worker.

Now listen to what is being said here in America by the man in the street and the congressmen who have not grasped the law of comparative advantage:

> The European wage level most assuredly will be far below that of this most prosperous (and productive) nation on earth. If we subject the American workers to the unbridled competition of the European, who subsists on less per day than we do, the real wage of the American worker must drastically fall. A protective tariff against cheap imports is desperately needed to maintain the American standard of living.

What Ricardo shows is that both arguments are wrong. The European and American workers *both* can get higher real wages by international trade. Prohibitive tariffs on either or both sides will reduce real wages in both places. (And we may add in our

Comparative advantage depends only on productivity ratios:

PRODUCT	IN AMERICA	IN EUROPE
1 unit of food	1 day's labor	3 days' labor
1 unit of clothing	2 days' labor	4 days' labor

TABLE 34-1. AMERICAN AND EUROPEAN LABOR REQUIREMENTS FOR PRODUCTION. Even though America's 1 and 2 are, respectively, less than Europe's 3 and 4, we have *comparative* advantage in food and Europe has it in clothing. Why? Because our 1 ÷ her 3 is less than our 2 ÷ her 4 (or equivalently, because our 1:2 is less than her 3:4).

day that there are better tools than protective tariffs to make sure that there are plenty of job opportunities and stable price levels in both places; namely, proper fiscal and central-bank monetary policies.)

BEFORE TRADE   If we start with a prohibitive tariff that has prevented all international trade, Table 34-1 shows that the real wage of the American worker for a day's work will be 1 unit of food or $\frac{1}{2}$ unit of clothing. The European worker is even less well off and gets for a day's labor before trade only $\frac{1}{3}$ unit of food or $\frac{1}{4}$ unit of clothing.

Evidently, under competition in each isolated continent, the price ratios of food and clothing will be different in the two places because of the difference in relative labor cost ratios. In America clothing will be 2 times as dear as food because it takes twice as much labor. In Europe clothing will be only $\frac{4}{3}$ times as dear as food.

AFTER TRADE   Now we repeal the protective tariff and make trade free. The relative prices of clothing and food must now come to a common level, just as the water in two connecting pipes must come to a common intermediate level once you remove the barrier between them. Why?

Competitive merchants buy where things are cheap and sell where they are dear. With clothing relatively more expensive in America, merchants will soon ship clothing from Europe to America and ship food from America to the European markets, where it has been relatively dear. Our clothing industry will feel the keen price competition of imports, and if the figures in Table 34-1 do not change, it will lose *all* its workers to the American food industry. The opposite will happen in Europe: workers will leave the food industry for the clothing industry, in which it has a comparative advantage.

America as a whole has benefited. Like any merchant who will buy electric power from another firm if he cannot produce it as cheaply himself, America has taken advantage of the fact that clothing does cost us less by barter than by domestic production. The same goes for Europe's benefit from specializing in clothing and getting her food more cheaply by barter.

> *Example of benefit.* Each unit of American labor still gets the 1 unit of food it produces here. But now 1 American food trades for *more* than $\frac{1}{2}$ unit of clothing. How much more? Certainly not more than the $\frac{3}{4}$ ratio set by Europe's costs. The common ratio after trade will be somewhere between $\frac{1}{2}$ and $\frac{3}{4}$. American labor gains in clothing by any degree that it exceeds $\frac{1}{2}$. Similarly, European labor gains in bartering clothing for food by any degree that the ratio falls short of $\frac{3}{4}$. (See the Appendix for elaborations.)

Granted that Ricardo has proved that both countries have benefited from trade in accordance with comparative advantage, what about the workingman in each place? Table 34-1 can show that his real wages have improved in both places. Now the American worker's day of labor will buy him the same food as before, but he gets *more* imported clothing for a day of labor and can now afford to consume more of *both* goods. Likewise, the European worker can get more of the cheapened food for a day of his labor, and inasmuch as he gets the same real wage in clothing, his budget is also better off. It is the expanded *world* production of both goods, which specialization and trade created, that makes it possible for *everyone* to be better off.

■ *The principle of comparative advantage restated:* Whether or not one of two regions is absolutely more efficient in the production of every good than is the other, if each specializes in the products in which it has a *comparative advantage* (greatest *relative* efficiency), trade will be mutually profitable to both regions. Real wages of productive factors will rise in both places.

An ill-designed prohibitive tariff, far from helping the protected factor of production, will instead reduce its real wage by making imports expensive and by making the whole world less productive through eliminating the efficiency inherent in the best pattern of specialization and division of labor.

This simple principle provides the unshakable basis for international trade.

■ OTHER CAUSES OF INTERNATIONAL TRADE

DECREASING COSTS If economies of mass production are overwhelmingly important, costs may decrease as output expands. This would strengthen the case for international exchange of goods. In fact, decreasing costs are a second great factor—in addition to differences in comparative costs—explaining why specialization and trade are profitable. For, as was discussed in Chapters 3 and 24, large-scale specialization is most fruitful when there is a widely expanded market.

In fact, even if there were no differences in comparative costs between two countries, it might pay for them to toss a coin to decide who was to produce each of two goods subject to increasing returns or decreasing costs. Complete specialization would increase world production of both goods. This may be illustrated by our example in Chapter 3 of the identical Indian twins who, despite their similarity, still find it advantageous to specialize to reap the efficiencies of "mass" production. The European Common Market (France, West Germany, Italy, Belgium, The Netherlands, Luxembourg) hopes to reap the advantages of such an extended division of labor.

Moreover, there is one very practical aspect of international trade to be observed under decreasing cost. Peculiarly under such conditions, perfect competition is likely to break down and be succeeded by monopoly, or imperfect competition. By excluding foreign competition, protective tariffs only serve to consolidate the position of the monopolist. This is recognized in the old slogan, "The tariff is the mother of trusts." Freer international trade is often an efficient way of breaking up monopoly positions.[2]

DIFFERENCES IN TASTES OR DEMAND Here is a third possible cause for trade. Even if costs were identical in the two countries and were increasing, trade might take place as the result of differences in *tastes.*

Thus, it might pay both Norway and Sweden to produce fish from the sea and meat from the land in about the same amounts. But if the Swedes have a relatively great fondness for meat and the Norse for fish, then a mutually profitable export of meat from Norway and fish from Sweden would take place.

[2]Still, one must admit that decreasing-cost situations might under free trade lead to bigger monopolies, and that decreasing-cost situations may have in them some of the valid elements of the "infant-industry" argument to be met in the next chapter.

Supply and demand here and abroad determine export P's:

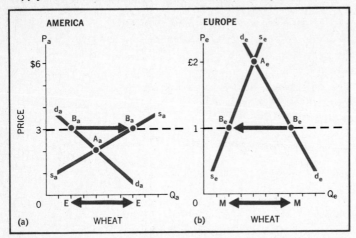

FIG. 34-1. With zero trade, American wheat price is at A_a, below European price at A_e. With free trade, goods flow from low- to high-price place, finally equalizing P's at that level where the export arrow just matches the import arrow.

Both parties gain from this trade. The sum total of human happiness is increased, just as it is when Jack Spratt trades fat meat for his wife's lean. Both get some "consumer's surplus" from the swap.[3]

We have now gone beyond the financial facade of international trade to the real fundamentals. Now we can handle the remaining two chapters of Part Five.

■ FOREIGN-TRADE SUPPLY-AND-DEMAND CHARTS[4]

The foregoing theory of comparative advantage stripped international trade down to its barter essentials. It said nothing about dollars, pounds, or foreign exchange rates. How does the matter appear to the perfect competitors in one small food or clothing industry in America? Why does competitive P settle down so that America exports this item of wheat but not that item of cloth? How do the supply and demand curves look in the competitive market for a small clothing item exported by Europe—say, linen cloth?

Figure 34-1 first takes up the case of an American export good, wheat, in the simplest case where every European unit of money—call it a pound—is always worth exactly $3. Figure 34-1(a) shows the American demand and supply curves $d_a d_a$ and $s_a s_a$ for wheat expressed in dollars (which, by a 1:3 scale change, can also be read in pounds). Figure 34-1(b) shows the European supply and demand for wheat as $d_e d_e$ and $s_e s_e$ (in pounds, with vertical scales nicely aligned so as to be read in dollars or pounds).

Suppose trade in wheat were prohibited by quotas, tariffs, or sky-high transport costs. Where would equilibrium be in each country? Under such an assumption of no trade, equilibrium would be at the separate intersection points A_a and A_e: Wheat's price (per bushel) in America would be $2, or £⅔; its price in Europe would be $6, or £2. Both markets are cleared; exports and imports are, of course, zero.

Now open up trade in wheat. If there are zero transport costs, quotas, and tariffs, both markets must have the same price. Why? Because sharp-eyed arbitragers could buy where wheat was cheap and send it for sale where it was dear. With what result?

---

[3] Even two individuals with identical amounts of two goods and the same tastes may in rare instances trade. Two sailors, each with a fifth of rye and a fifth of gin, might toss a coin to decide which is to have two fifths of gin and which two fifths of rye. You can reason out why the same might be true of herring and chocolate, but not of corned beef and cabbage. Such cases of trade are oddities.

[4] The next two sections are quite independent of the rest of this chapter, except for points 5 and 6 in the Summary. The next chapters do not require them or this chapter's Appendix.

Evidently, P_e would fall and P_a rise until equality was achieved. How much would the price changes be? That would depend on the slopes of each country's *dd* and *ss* curves.

■ **The condition for the free-trade equilibrium is that the new price should coax out an import demand abroad just equal to our export supply.**

Free-trade equilibrium is at the $3 and £1 level, where America's export arrow *EE* or B_aB_a just matches (and opposes in direction) Europe's import arrow *MM* or B_eB_e. No other equilibrium can persist.

Figure 34-2 shows exactly the same phenomenon for the case of Europe's clothing export, linen. Who decides that linen will be Europe's export and wheat will be America's?

Supply and demand here and abroad determine import P's:

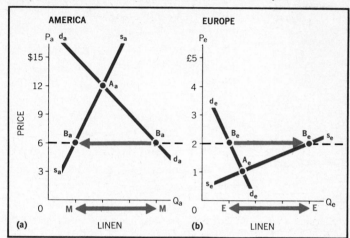

FIG. 34-2. Lower European *P* at zero trade means linen will be imported from Europe when trade is permitted. Common *P* is where imports and exports match. (Quotas, tariffs, or transport costs will make *P*'s unequal.)

The levels of the no-trade equilibria intersections decide: goods flow uphill toward higher prices under free competition! (Because A_e is below A_a, Europe exports linen.)

The reader could draw a new figure for the case where the no-trade *P*'s happen to start out equal and where free trade leads to zero trade. This is a rare razor's-edge case of coincidental levels. However, in real life, there are always transport costs that impede trade. Thus, although bricks may seem to be cheaper in America, if the difference between the no-trade equilibrium intersections is less than the substantial *costs of shipping* heavy and bulky bricks, each country will produce its own bricks and there will be neither exports nor imports. Goods try to flow uphill toward higher prices, but transport-cost or tariff impediments can inhibit their flow.

This supply-and-demand analysis is a simple extension of that given in Chapter 4 (or Part Three). It is useful. But note that we should have to go to Ricardo's deeper analysis of comparative advantage to explain *why* the wheat prices will be such as to give America a money-cost advantage in exporting this food item. That same analysis of basic comparative advantage is needed to explain why the clothing item, linen, will have *dd* and *ss* intersections causing Europe to export it.[5]

■ EFFECTS OF TARIFFS AND QUOTAS

PROHIBITIVE TARIFF   Figure 34-2 can be used to illustrate the effect of an American tariff (or "custom tax") on the import of linen. If we tax linen imports by more than

[5] As economists put this matter: Marshall's supply and demand curves depict only "partial equilibrium." They must be anchored on "general equilibrium" analysis, of which Ricardo's is a special case.

the difference in prices ($9 $\equiv$ £3 = $12 − $3) shown between the no-trade A_a and A_e intersections, how much linen will get sent here? Absolutely none: the tariff of more than $9 will be a prohibitive one, shutting out all imports. Why? Because any importer who tries to buy linen at the European A_e price of $3 (or £1) can sell it here for at most $12 (or £4). But the tariff the importer has to pay would come to *more* than that difference! Hence, such a tariff kills off *all* the advantage of specialization and trade.

SOCIAL COST OF TARIFFS   What happens to our domestic linen industry? The tariff gives it a higher price than under free trade. The effect of a tariff that "protects" against imports is to raise the price to the domestic consumer.[6]

But does not the government collect in tariff revenue about what the consumers now pay in extra prices? Our special example of a prohibitive tariff points up the neg-ative answer that can be generally given. Here consumers pay more but the govern-ment collects nothing! This needs emphasis, and shows how foolish it is to try to measure a tariff's height and capacity for doing harm by the tax revenue it brings in. Also, any tariff that limits imports will make consumers pay a higher P for all the domestically supplied output, and *none* of this shows up in government revenue.

The higher P lowers the satisfaction and well-being of consumers. Whom does it benefit? The suppliers of this particular industry do benefit. If linen were a monopoly industry here, the monopolist would benefit and could afford to lobby for tariffs. Some of the benefit would trickle down to his employees and to owners of resources especially fitted for linen production. Even if, as in Fig. 34-2(a), there is perfect competition, the productive factors specialized for the protected industry stand to get some benefit (higher P for linen, more jobs, higher wage rates, higher economic rents on factors inelastically supplied to that industry).[7] When the wife of one of these specialized employees complained about the high cost of linen and of living generally, resulting from a high-tariff program, her husband could reprimand her: "Stop complaining. We get more than we give as a result of the tariff. It's the rest of the community that ex-periences the net harm from the cessation of linen imports."

In wheat and other nonprotected industries, wives and husbands can both legiti-mately complain about this linen tariff. Indeed, let us consider (1) the harm done to consumers, (2) the revenue collected by government, and (3) the benefit received by suppliers. What is the net effect, on the supposition that both rich and poor, worthy

---

[6] The price rise need not be as great as the tariff itself; it will be that great only if the industry abroad is so large compared with our use of the product that one or both of their ss and dd schedules can be regarded as practically horizontal, our imports being too small to affect their prices appreciably.
[7] Indeed, if $s_a s_a$ were completely vertical, all the money newly extorted from the consumer would be transferred to the producers in extra rent: this would presumably be a switch from not particularly unworthy consumers to not particularly worthy producers. But with $s_a s_a$ having some positive elasticity, the higher P will coax out extra domestic Q; this will represent a definite social inefficiency, to the degree that resources are drawn from fields where America has a comparative advantage into pro-tected industries where she has a comparative disadvantage. In the extreme case of a horizontal $s_a s_a$, where factors are indifferent between this and other industries, *all* the tariff's benefits to producers are frittered away in inefficient resource allocation, and not even those in the industry derive a selfish benefit at the expense of the hard-hit consumers.

and unworthy, are involved? It is shown in the Appendix to this chapter that the harm of a prohibitive tariff outweighs its gain, in this sense:

■ A system of prohibitive tariffs puts a society inefficiently *inside* the consumption-possibility frontier that would be available if the efficiencies of international exchange and division of labor were utilized. This is absolutely true of the world as a whole, and absolutely true for a country that cuts off all imports and becomes self-sufficient.[8]

QUOTAS   The effect of a prohibitive tariff could be achieved by imposing a zero quota on all imports. The prices would find their A_a and A_e levels in both markets as in the no-trade cases already discussed. Consumers here will be hurt; and in the sense described above, they will be hurt more than producers are helped.

Suppose the quota is set, not at zero, but, say, at half the level of free-trade imports. The reader can verify that, in the special case of Fig. 34-2's straight-line curves, the American P will rise half the distance between the free-trade B_a price and the no-trade A_a price. (In Europe P will fall halfway.) Only at these new respective P's of $9 and £1½ will the arrow of Europe's linen export match our import arrow. (Verify.)

The quota has produced a price difference between here and abroad. As just said, that equilibrium difference is defined as just large enough to make exports and imports match. (NOTE: A tariff on each unit import of linen, which was exactly equal to this price difference, could have achieved the same equilibrium.[9])

There is thus no essential difference between tariffs and quotas. Except this: A nonprohibitive tariff at least gives revenue to the government, in part offsetting the net harm done to the importing country by the restriction on imports. A quota, on the other hand, puts the profit from the contrived price difference into the pocket of the importer lucky enough to get a quota license. He can afford to wine and dine the officials who give out import licenses; or if they are not already his kinfolk or political cronies, he can afford to bribe them.

---

[8] It is also true with rare (and unimportant) exceptions for a country that levies prohibitive tariffs on a subset of its goods. The exceptions apply to a country large enough to affect appreciably the relative prices of the goods it imports. By levying sufficiently small, shrewdly gauged tariffs, it might exploit its monopoly power to "make the foreigner pay" for its tariff. [This is an esoteric point, which could be illustrated by means of utility-disutility areas under the schedules in Fig. 33-2(a). But readers of Chapter 25's discussion of marginal revenue (and the loss taken on all earlier units when an extra unit of q is sold by a monopolist) can understand the point thus: The last little unit of import under free trade brings us zero marginal benefit; that is why it is the last unit. If we impose a tiny tariff to keep it out, we do force a reduction in the P we pay on *all* previous units imported. So we could benefit a little from such a move (unless the $s_e s_e$ and/or $d_e d_e$ curves were horizontal). However, Europe could do the same to our wheat, and when all play this game, there is some presumption that world inefficiency will make all (or most) worse off.]

[9] This gives the clue to how to compute the equilibrium prices for any tariff rate between the prohibitive and zero levels. In Fig. 34-2, shift the exporting country's whole diagram upward by the amount of the tariff (so that its vertical-scale prices now differ from the importing country's vertical scale by the amount of the duty). Then move a horizontal ruler up and down until you have located exactly equal export and import gaps between the respective schedules.

This is why economists generally regard tariffs as a lesser evil than quotas. "At the least," they advise, "if you must introduce inefficient restrictive quotas, be sure that the government auctions off the scarce import-quota licenses so that the Treasury gains the swag and so that bureaucracy is not put under the strain of corruption and exercise of arbitrary power and caprice."

■ The harmful effects of a nonprohibitive tariff or quota are of the same type as, but lesser in degree than, those of prohibitive tariffs or quotas. Generally, there is net harm done to the citizenry as it is forced to curb its consumption of the goods it desires most and to channel resources from lines of true comparative advantage to economically inefficient uses.

TRANSPORTATION COSTS   The economic costs of moving bulky and perishable goods also lessen the extent of profitable regional specialization.

The effects are like those produced by the passage of artificially restrictive tariff legislation. Many of these effects are harmful to national economic welfare (to be discussed in the next chapter). In the case of transportation costs, the evil is unavoidable, whereas protective tariffs or artificial barriers to interregional trade within a nation are squarely the responsibility of man.

This ends two sections of digression on particular markets' price equilibria under trade and tariffs. We now return to our discussion of basic comparative advantage.

■ QUALIFICATIONS AND CONCLUSIONS

Of course, comparative advantage holds for any two countries and goods, not just for America and Europe and food and clothing. (Ricardo used England and Portugal and cloth and wine in his examples.) The following Appendix shows how the principle of comparative advantage can be generalized to handle any number of goods; and more advanced books show how it can handle any number of countries or regions. Instead of using simple labor cost examples, we could easily measure costs in terms of "doses" of labor, land, and capital goods of fixed proportions. We can also allow for changing factor proportions and diminishing returns. For this and more, see the Appendix.

Perhaps a more serious defect of comparative advantage is its static assumptions. The theory is stated in terms of barter and relative price ratios. It disregards all stickiness of prices and wages, all transitional inflationary and overvaluation gaps, and all balance-of-payments problems. It pretends that when workers go out of one industry they always go into another more efficient industry—never into chronic unemployment. No wonder this abstract theory sold at a discount during the Great Depression. Recently its prestige has been coming back. To the extent that we can in the future count on the successful neoclassical synthesis, which mobilizes modern theories of monetary and fiscal policy to banish chronic slumps and inflations—to that extent will the old classical theory of comparative advantage come back into social relevance.

If theories, like girls, could win beauty contests, comparative advantage would certainly rate high in that it is an elegantly logical structure. Indeed, one must admit that it is a highly simplified theory. An oversimplified one, as far as our rushing out to make immediate applications to real life is concerned. Yet, for all its oversimplification, the theory of comparative advantage provides a most important glimpse of truth. Political economy has found few more pregnant principles. A nation that neglects comparative advantage may pay a heavy price in terms of living standards and potential growth.

SUMMARY

1 ■

As soon as there are diversities of productivities within a country, specialization and exchange become profitable. The same holds for nations: international exchange is an efficient way for us to transform one good into another, more efficient than having to rely solely on domestic production.

2 ■

Without much study of economics, people see that trade is mutually beneficial between the tropics and the temperate zones—or between two countries where one is more efficient in producing one good and the other is more efficient in producing the other good. But it takes the important Ricardian principle of *comparative* advantage to see that trade is no less mutually beneficial between two countries (or as in the case cited of the lawyer and stenographer, between any two units) even when one of the countries happens to be absolutely more efficient in every industry than is the other.

As long as there is a difference in *relative* efficiency, there will be powerful benefits derived from *specializing* in those goods in which there is a comparative advantage, *trading* them for goods in which the other nation has a comparative advantage.

3 ■

The law of comparative advantage not only predicts the geographical pattern of specialization and direction of trade; it also demonstrates that *both* countries are made better off and that the real wages (or returns to the factors of production taken as a whole) are improved by trade and the resulting *enlarged* totals of world production. Prohibitive tariffs that recreate *autarky* (i.e., national economic self-sufficiency) will hurt real wage and total factor returns—not help them.

4 ■

Decreasing costs (economies of scale) are an important cause of specialization and regional trade. Differences in tastes can also cause trade.

5 ■

In supply-demand markets for one small good, completely free trade will equalize prices, causing the good to be exported from the place with lowest zero-trade price. The equilibrium common P is at the level equating physical exports to physical imports.

6 ■

A tariff or quota, by lowering imports, will cause a rise in domestic P and a fall in foreign P. (So long as some imports continue, the P's will differ by the amount of the tariff.) The harm done to the domestic economy, from higher P and decreased home consumption, and from wastage of resources on goods lacking comparative advantage, will generally exceed the benefit to producers. Transport costs also cut down on trade and well-being.

7 ■

The important law of comparative advantage must be qualified to take into account certain interferences with it. Thus, if money wage rates are rigid in both countries or if fiscal and monetary policies are poorly run in both countries, then the blessing of cheap imports that international specialization gives might be turned into the curse of unemployment.[10] With proper public policies, modern nations can achieve a neoclassical synthesis which need not sacrifice the great benefits from trade, but rather can recreate the environment in which the principle of comparative advantage will apply.

QUESTIONS FOR DISCUSSION

1. "Buying a good cheaper abroad than we can produce it at home is to our advantage." Is this consistent with comparative advantage? Show that it indeed is.

2. Are real wage levels, like water in connecting pipes, brought to the same level by completely free international trade? Why not? Are international prices? Why?

3. What happens if two countries are exactly alike in productivity and efficiency? Explain. Justify the slogan *"Vive la différence!"*

4. What if (1,2; 3,4) in Table 34-1 became (1,2; $1\frac{1}{2}$,3)? Can you show that all trade is killed off? And that this certainly hurt America? Show that if it instead had become (1,2; $1\frac{1}{2}$,4), Europe would export food.

5. Can a country once have a comparative advantage, say, in electric generating equipment, and then lose it? What then *will* happen? Should it?

6. Why might a new continent have a comparative advantage in food?

7. "If some goods continue to be imported, the sum of the rise in domestic P and the fall in foreign P must equal the new tariff." Show why.

8. Review your understanding of the following concepts:

personal and regional diversity and specialization	barter versus home production
	international price equilibrium
absolute efficiencies versus comparative advantage	quota and tariff equilibrium
	prohibitive tariffs and real wages

---

[10]See the Appendix to the previous chapter for a demonstration that overvaluation of a country's currency can undercut these basic classical principles.

APPENDIX: Comparative Advantage Amplified and Qualified

Our discussion of comparative advantage has until now followed Ricardo and measured all costs in terms of labor. Modern economists know that the theory is still valid even if you do not want to assume a labor theory of value.

The production-possibility, or transformation, frontier that we used in Chapter 2 to discuss guns and butter is the tool that enables us to dispense with labor units: users of the production-possibility curve choose to measure the cost of clothing in terms of the food we must sacrifice to get more clothing. (This is sometimes so-called "opportunity cost.")

The first part of this Appendix follows through in detail the America-Europe food-clothing case, showing the irrelevance of absolute labor costs.

AMERICA WITHOUT TRADE

In Chapter 2, we saw that every economy has a production-possibility (or transformation) schedule indicating how much of one commodity, food, can be produced if all resources are diverted to it; also how much of the other commodity, clothing, can be produced if all resources are diverted to its production; and how either good can be transformed into the other.

For simplicity, let us suppose food can always be transformed into units of clothing in America at the *constant ratio* of 10:3. For each 10 units of food sacrificed, we can always get 3 units of clothing. We further assume that, when all resources are diverted to food production, America will have altogether 100 (million) units of food.[1]

Then, clearly America can, if she chooses, have 90 units of food and 3 units of clothing, 80 and 6, . . . , or finally 0 of food and 30 of clothing. We may put this in the form of a schedule, as shown in Table 34-2.

This may be plotted in Fig. 34-3, just as was done in Chapter 2, Fig. 2-3 (page 21). The solid line *AK* is the production-possibility curve. This new production-possibility curve is a straight line, whereas the earlier one was rounded, being concave when looked at from below. The straight-line production-possibility schedule has been introduced in order to keep the argument simple—to relieve the student from having to remember many different cost ratios. As will be seen later, this will not seriously affect the validity of the argument. The few qualifications needed are made later.

So far we have been talking only about production. However, if the United States is isolated from all trade, what she produces is also what she consumes. Let us suppose, therefore, that the emphasized quantities for *H* in Table 34-2 and Fig. 34-3 represent the amounts produced and consumed by America in the absence of trade; or in numerical terms, America then produces and consumes 30 units of food and 21 units of clothing.

Why was this particular combination decided upon rather than one of the other possibilities? We know from earlier chapters that in a competitive system nobody "decides" upon this, but that the price mechanism, operating through supply and demand for goods and services, determines WHAT shall be produced, How, and FOR WHOM. Well, the indicated quantities are the WHAT. Very little need be said here about the How, except for the obvious remark that agricultural food production will require more land relative to labor than will more highly fabricated clothing output. As to the FOR WHOM, we need only remark parenthetically that scarcity of labor in the United States will mean rather high wages for workers, while superabundance of land here will mean low rents (per acre) for landlords.

Let us proceed to introduce Europe into the picture. Before doing so, it will pave the way for the later argument to interject a question. What would happen if some American (like Eli Whitney, inventor of the cotton gin, for example) should make a clever invention, allowing each 10 units of food to be transformed into 6 rather than 3 units of clothing? Would America be potentially better off? The answer is, obviously, Yes. The production-possibility curve has shifted outward and upward and is now shown by the broken line *AK'* in Fig. 34-3. (Show that America could now go from *H* northeast to a new point *H'* and have *more of both* food and clothing.)

---

[1] Note that labor is never mentioned in the following discussion. But if you wanted to relate this discussion to Ricardo's labor treatment, you could merely change the numbers in Table 34-1 from (1,2; 3,4) to (3,10; 8,10), or more generally to ($3a$, $10a$; $8b$, $10b$), where a and b are arbitrary positive numbers depending only on units and absolute efficiencies.

America can produce food or clothing, consuming before trade what she produces:

AMERICA		
POSSIBILITIES	FOOD, MILLIONS OF UNITS	CLOTHING, MILLIONS OF UNITS
A	100	0
B	90	3
C	80	6
D	70	9
E	60	12
F	50	15
G	40	18
H	30	21
I	20	24
J	10	27
K	0	30

TABLE 34-2. PRODUCTION-POSSIBILITY SCHEDULE OF AMER-
ICA (10:3 CONSTANT-COST RATIO).

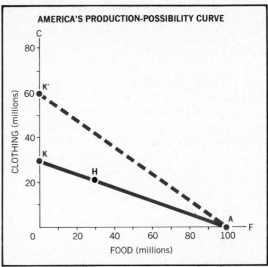

FIG. 34-3. The constant-cost line *AK* shows America's domestic production possibilities. The new line *AK'* indicates an increased ability to produce clothing and means that America can move northeast from *AK*, enjoying more of both goods.

EUROPE WITHOUT TRADE

We can now do for Europe exactly what was done above for America, but with an important difference. Europe's plentiful endowment of labor relative to land would give her a different cost or transformation ratio between food and clothing. She might have a comparative advantage in clothing rather than in food. For her, each 10 units of food may be transformable into, say, 8 units of clothing. She gets 5 more than was true of the United States because of her comparative advantage in clothing. However, in terms of food, America gets $^{10}/_{3}$, or 3.33 units, for each unit of clothing sacrificed, while Europe's comparative disadvantage in food production gives her only $^{10}/_{8}$, or 1.25 units, for each sacrificed unit of clothing. *The important thing to concentrate upon is the difference in the two cost ratios: 10:3 for America and 10:8 for Europe.*

We shall still keep the two continents isolated from each other. What is Europe's exact production-possibility schedule? Let us suppose that Europe's population is so large and her land area such that before trade she was at *c*, producing and consuming 50 units of food and 80 units of clothing. This fact, plus the

constant-cost ratio 10:8, tells us all we have to know in order to draw up Europe's complete production-possibility schedule as in Table 34-3. Check this against the production-possibility frontier of Fig. 34-4.

THE OPENING UP OF TRADE

Now, for the first time, let us admit the possibility of trade between the two regions. Food can be bartered for clothing at some *terms of trade*, i.e., at some *price ratio*.[2] To dramatize the process, let us suppose that in mid-ocean there stands an impersonal auctioneer whose business it is to balance supply and demand— offers of clothing and offers of food. He does this by calling out to both countries an exchange rate or price ratio between food and clothing. Until supplies and demands are balanced, he keeps the bidding going. When he finally hits on the equilibrium price level *at which supply and demand balance*, he raps his gavel three times and says, "Going, going, *gone!*"

[2] Terms of trade (or an exchange ratio) of, say, 10 food for 6 clothing means that clothing is more expensive than food, with the price ratio, (clothing price)/(food price) = $1^{2}/_{3} = {}^{10}/_{6}$.

Probably, he will suspect in advance that Europe is going to specialize in clothing production, in which she has a comparative advantage, and that she will wish to export part of her clothing production in exchange for food imports. But he has no idea what the final exchange ratio, or terms of trade, between food and clothing will be—whether it will be 10:3, 10:8, 10:5, 10:6, or anything else. For that matter, if the auctioneer is very new at the game, or very stupid, he may think that the final equilibrium exchange level, or terms of trade, will be 10:1 or 10:12.

Actually, neither of these last two can be the final exchange ratio. He would soon learn this from bitter experience. For let him tell America and Europe that they can get all the clothing they want in exchange for food at the rate of only 1 unit of clothing for every 10 units of food. What will America do? By producing at home, she can get 3 units of clothing for each 10 of food. Clearly, she will not be persuaded into trading food for clothing on those terms; she would rather remain self-sufficient.

That is only half the story. Why should not America go to the other extreme and export clothing in exchange for food imports? Each 1 unit of clothing gets her 10 units of food from the auctioneer. What will 1 unit of

clothing get at home in domestic food production? Obviously, from Table 34-2 and Fig. 34-3, only $\frac{10}{3}$, or 3.33, units of food. At 10:1, therefore, we should certainly shift all our resources to clothing production; we should export some surplus clothing for food imports.

Now, what about Europe? At home she gets only $\frac{10}{8}$, or 1.25, units of food for each unit of clothing. At 10:1, she too will want to trade clothing for food. We see, therefore, what a green hand the auctioneer was. By calling out 10:1, he brings a flood supply of clothing on his head and only demands for food. Since he has no supplies of either good up his sleeve, he must now change his tactics. He must raise the price of food relative to the price of clothing. He had better try the ratio 10:2, or perhaps even 10:9. You are now in a position to reason why neither of them will do: why 10:2 will still induce a tidal wave of clothing and, on the other hand, why 10:9 represents the opposite error, in which there is a tornado of food.

Clearly, *the final exchange ratio cannot be outside the original two-country limits of* 10:3 *and* 10:8! Anywhere between is a possibility—with America following her comparative advantage and specializing in food, and Europe following her comparative advantage and specializing in clothing.

Europe's production possibilities favor clothing, in which she has comparative advantage:

EUROPE		
POSSIBILITIES	FOOD, MILLIONS OF UNITS	CLOTHING, MILLIONS OF UNITS
A	150	0
B	100	40
C	50	80
D	0	120

TABLE 34-3. PRODUCTION-POSSIBILITY SCHEDULE OF EUROPE (10:8 CONSTANT-COST RATIO).

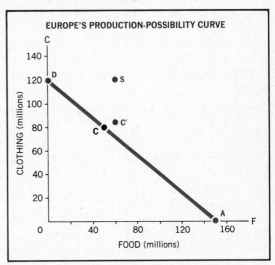

FIG. 34-4. Before international trade, Europe is on her domestic production-possibility curve at *C*, consuming just what she produces. (Disregard the points *C'* and *S* until later in the chapter.)

RECAPITULATION

Let us stop to consolidate and review.

1. If nature endows two regions unequally with factors of production, the *relative* cost of transforming one commodity into another domestically will probably be different for the two areas. (E.g., a land-rich area will have a comparative advantage in food and other land-intensive goods. A labor-rich area's comparative advantage will be in labor-intensive goods.)

2. Under free trade, goods will exchange for each other at a price ratio somewhere *intermediate* between the original domestic cost ratios of the two countries.

3. Each country will specialize in the commodity in which it has a comparative advantage and export its surplus of that product for imports from abroad.

4. Each country is made better off by trade and specialization: if America can get, say, 6 units of clothing for each 10 units of food traded, she is certainly better off than when she domestically transforms 10 units of food into only 3 units of clothing; Europe does better when she trades 6 units of clothing for 10 units of food than when she domestically transforms 8 of clothing into 10 of food. The same would be true if we had picked any trading ratio other than 10:6—so long as it is between the limits 10:3 and 10:8.

5. Trade is *indirect* production. It is efficient production. Efficient production is always better than inefficient production. (Note that advantages of trade have nothing to do with *relative wage rates*. Under free trade, a country's wage tends to be pulled up to the higher levels of productivity of its export industry, not down to the low-efficiency level of its import industry.)

EXACT DETERMINATION OF THE FINAL PRICE RATIO

Just where between the domestic cost ratios will the terms of trade settle down? Some of Ricardo's immediate followers were foolish enough to say, "Split the difference between the two countries' cost ratios, and pick 10:5½ as the equilibrium ratio."[3]

Actually, as John Stuart Mill, the third great classical economist (after Smith and Ricardo), showed a little later, *the exact final level of the terms of trade between the two cost ratios will depend upon the strength of world supply and demand for each of the two commodities.* If people have an intense desire for food relative to available supplies of food and clothing, the price ratio will settle near the upper limit of 10:8; if clothing is much demanded by both countries, the final price ratio will settle nearer to 10:3.[4]

Mill did what our auctioneer would have to do. He drew up a schedule showing supply and demand at *each possible price ratio:*[5] how much food America would wish to export and how much food Europe would want to import; and at the same time, how much clothing Europe would be willing to export at each price ratio in comparison with the amount of clothing America expected to import. At one, and (usually) only one, intermediate price ratio, exports and

---

[4] Also, if America were very small relative to Europe, so that its supplies made hardly a "dent" on the market, then the price ratio might even stay at 10:8. America would then be specializing in food and importing clothing, but all America's food exports would amount to so little that Europe would still have to produce some food for herself. This is possible only at a price of 10:8. America would in this case get all the gains from international trade. It pays to have a large (different!) neighbor.

[5] Chapter 22's indifference curves can be used to summarize each country's tastes for food and clothing. Together with the *P-P* curves, these could derive the reciprocal demand curves of Mill, shown in Fig. 34-5. Unlike ordinary *dd* and *ss* curves,

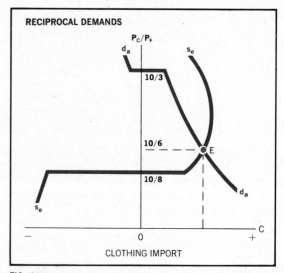

FIG. 34-5.

---

[3] Or would they have said halfway between 10:3 and 10:8, at 110:48, which corresponds to 10:4$^{4}\!/_{11}$? Both are silly.

C is trading against *F*, not against money; hence, relative prices P_C/P_F, rather than money P_C, are plotted. (If tastes and incomes vary within each country, aggregate indifference curves would be replaced by more elaborate analysis.)

imports will balance. At this equilibrium price, exports and imports will "mesh" (or match), quantitatively as well as qualitatively; the auctioneer and Mill will heave a sigh of relief, and trade will continue indefinitely until tastes or technology have changed.

For our numerical problem it has been assumed that the equilibrium terms-of-trade ratio is 10:6, a little "nearer" to Europe's pretrade ratio than to America's.

America concentrates her production completely on food. In Fig. 34-6 on the next page, America is productionwise at A. But since she can now trade freely at 10:6, America is no longer limited to her old production-possibility curve. By trading, she can now move on the solid line AK' *just exactly as if a fruitful invention had been made.* Is America made potentially better off by trade? Indeed she is. Just where she will stop on this solid line, which we may call her new *consumption*-possibility curve, depends upon the workings of her internal price system. We assume that this causes her to stop at the point H', where 40 units of food and 36 units of clothing are consumed. The green arrows show America's exports (+) and imports (−).

All this is summarized in America's rows in Table 34-4. This table should be studied carefully. To understand it thoroughly is to understand the doctrine of comparative costs.

As a result of specialization and trade, America has become better off; she has more food and more clothing to consume. The same is true of Europe. What is the black magic by which something seems to have been got for nothing? In Table 34-4 the rows marked World, which represent the sum of the American and European rows, show this: *World production of both goods has been stepped up by specialization and trade.*

Actually, the sixth row gives the data the auctioneer would be most interested in. He is assured that equilibrium has been reached by two facts shown there: (1) World consumption of each product is identical with world production—no more, no less; and (2) the amounts that each country exports are just balanced by the amounts that the other country wishes to import. Thus the price ratio 10:6 is the right one.[6]

This completes our explanation of comparative advantage. You might test your full understanding by filling in on Fig. 34-4 for Europe everything that has already been filled in for America on Fig. 34-6. Why does Europe's new consumption-possibility line, made possible by trade, pivot around the point D on the vertical axis? Draw in the arrows to S representing the amounts exported (+) and imported (−) as was done in Fig. 34-6. Note that Europe's arrows match America's but are opposite in sign. Why is this quantitative meshing of exports and imports necessary at equilibrium?

The eager reader could add labor measurements and wage data to the example. But the thing to note is that comparative advantage, not absolute labor advantage, is the all-important condition.

MANY COMMODITIES

Very briefly, we now show what happens when we remove some of the oversimplifications in the foregoing discussion. The conclusions are not essentially changed, and even the changes in details are minor.

First note that until now we have simplified the discussion by considering only two commodities, food and clothing. Obviously, food stands for many different items (beef, milk, etc.), and likewise for clothing. Moreover, the advantages of exchange are equally great when we consider the thousand and one commodities that can and do enter into international trade.

As is shown in advanced treatises,[7] when there are many commodities producible in two countries at constant costs, they can be arranged in order according to their comparative advantage or cost. For example, the commodities automobiles, flax, perfumes, watches, wheat, and woolens might be arranged in the comparative-advantage sequence shown in Fig. 34-7. This means that wheat costs are lowest relative to all other commodities in America; Europe has its greatest

---

[6]The auctioneer could have made up a whole book of such tables, each page corresponding to a different price ratio. Generally, only one page is the right one, however, because at all other prices the algebraic total of exports and imports would not cancel out. Thus, at 10:7, America's desire for clothing imports would surpass Europe's willingness to export clothing.

The world as a whole would be trying to consume more clothing than had been produced. Since the auctioneer has no inventories to draw upon, he would have to turn the pages toward a higher price for clothing and a lower price for food. On the right page the price ratio would be an equilibrium one: exports would balance imports, at the E intersection.

[7]For example, G. Haberler, *Theory of International Trade* (Macmillan, New York, 1937). Haberler also pioneered the use of *P-P frontiers* in trade theory.

America specializes in food and imports clothing:

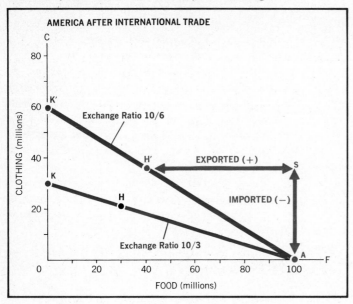

FIG. 34-6. The line *AK* represents America's domestic production-possibility curve; the line *AK'*, her new consumption-possibility curve when she is able to trade freely at the price ratio 10:6 and in consequence has decided to specialize completely in the production of food (at *A*). The green arrows from *S* to *H'* and *A* to *S* show the amounts exported (+) and imported (−) by America. As a result of free trade, she finally ends up at *H'* with more of both goods than before at *H*.

International trade makes larger world production possible:

AREA COMPARED	EXCHANGE RATIO OF FOOD FOR CLOTHING P_c/P_f	FOOD PRODUC-TION	FOOD CON-SUMP-TION	FOOD EXPORTS (+) OR IMPORTS (−)	CLOTHING PRODUC-TION	CLOTHING CON-SUMP-TION	CLOTHING EXPORTS (+) OR IMPORTS (−)
Situation before trade							
America	10:3	30	30	0	21	21	0
Europe	10:8	50	50	0	80	80	0
World	none	80	80	0	101	101	0
Situation after trade							
America	10:6	100	40	+60	0	36	−36
Europe	10:6	0	60	−60	120	84	+36
World	10:6	100	100	0	120	120	0
Gains from trade							
America	——	——	+10	——	——	+15	——
Europe	——	——	+10	——	——	+ 4	——
World	——	+20	+20	——	+19	+19	——

TABLE 34-4. SUMMARY SHOWING SPECIALIZATION AND GAIN FROM TRADE ACCORDING TO COMPARATIVE ADVANTAGE.

comparative advantage in perfumes; its advantage in watches is not quite so great; and so forth.[8]

From the beginning we can be almost sure of one thing. The introduction of trade will cause America to produce wheat, and Europe perfume. But where will the dividing line fall? Between automobiles and flax? Or will America produce flax and Europe confine herself to watches, woolens, and perfumes? Or will the dividing line fall on one of the commodities rather than between them, so that, say, flax might be produced in both places at once?

You will not be surprised to find that the answer depends upon the comparative strength of international demand for the different goods. If we think of the commodities as beads arranged on a string according to their comparative advantage, the total demand-and-supply situation will determine where the dividing line between American and European production will fall.

And an increased demand for automobiles and wheat, for example, may tend to turn the terms of trade in the direction of America and make us so prosperous that it will no longer pay us to continue to produce our own flax. Also, there is the possibility that a new scientific discovery permitting America to grow flax on the desert might rearrange the order of the comparative advantages of the different commodities and alter the pattern of specialization and trade.

MANY COUNTRIES

So much for the complications introduced by many commodities. What about many countries? Europe and America are not the whole world, and even they include many separate so-called "sovereign nations."

Introducing many countries need not change our analysis. As far as any one country is concerned, all

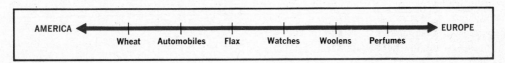

FIG. 34-7.

[8]This ordered array of goods might have arisen from the numerical data of Table 34-5, which are presented only for the curiosity of the more advanced reader and which are not essential for the above discussion. As before, it is not necessary to measure costs in terms of money or labor, but only in terms of the relative commodities into which any good can be "transformed." Suppose that we choose to measure the costs of every good in both countries in terms of woolens—selected arbitrarily because it comes last alphabetically. Then our data might be arranged alphabetically as in Table 34-5. This means that in America one must give up the production of 1,000 units of woolens to get 1 automobile, while in Europe the cost of 1 automobile is the sacrifice of 3,000 units of wool production. Therefore the comparative cost of automobiles relative to woolens is in Europe three times that in America, and so forth for the other goods.

Obviously, Europe's relative cost advantage is greatest in perfumes and least in wheat; in between, the commodities are arranged as shown in Fig. 34-7. The fact that the figures in the last column are predominantly greater than 1 in no way reflects on the efficiency of Europe; it merely comes from the accidental fact that we chose woolens as our common denominator in which to express costs. Had we selected wheat or watches, the opposite would have been the case, and yet none of our results would be any different—except for a "scale factor" (such as converts inches to feet or yards).

TECHNICAL NOTE: Anyone who feels he must bring in labor productivities can write the respective American requirements

in labor days as A, B, C, . . . , and Europe's as a, b, c, ... The whole analysis can then be worked out in terms of com-

(1)	(2)	(3)	(4)
GOODS	AMERICAN COST RATIO, IN TERMS OF WOOLENS	EUROPEAN COST RATIO, IN TERMS OF WOOLENS	COMPARATIVE EUROPEAN COSTS, IN TERMS OF AMERICAN COSTS (4) = (3) ÷ (2)
Automobiles	1,000	3,000	3.0
Flax	0.8	1.6	2.0
Perfumes	5.0	3.0	0.6
Watches	50	75	1.5
Wheat	0.2	0.8	4.0
Woolens	1.0	1.0	1.0

TABLE 34-5.

parative ratios of the form A/B, C/B, . . . , and a/b, c/b, . . . ; to explain trade patterns it is never necessary to compare absolute advantages between countries A/a, B/b, ... Of course, if he wants to compare money and real wages, these absolute advantages are necessary: by extending the analysis of Table 34-1, it can be shown that the ratio of European to American real wage must fall between the least and greatest of A/a, B/b, . . . ; just *where* between depends on the working out of reciprocal demands.

the other nations with whom she trades can be lumped together into one group as "the rest of the world." The advantages of trade have no special relationship to state boundaries. The principles already developed apply between groups of countries and, indeed, between regions within the same country. In fact, but for historical accident, they would be more applicable to trade between our Northern and Southern states than to trade between the United States and Canada.

From the standpoint of pure economic welfare, the slogan "Buy American" is as foolish as "Buy Wisconsin" would be, or "Buy Oshkosh, Wisconsin," or "Buy South Oshkosh, Wisconsin." Part of our great prosperity comes from the fortunate fact that there are no restrictive customs duties within our 50 states, which form one great free-trade area.

There is, however, one new aspect introduced by the existence of many countries. America may find it very profitable to trade indirectly with Europe. America sells Europe much, including finished commodities such as machinery. It buys little from Europe; but it does buy rubber and raw materials from the East Indies. They in turn do not usually buy goods from America; however, they do buy clothing and other goods from Europe. Thus, we have a very advantageous triangular trade, as shown in Fig. 34-8. The arrows indicate the direction of exports.

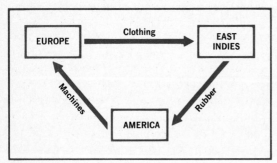

FIG. 34-8.

What would happen if all countries tried to sign bilateral trade agreements, so that America could not and would not buy from the Indies unless they bought an equal amount from us? And suppose the same bilateralism held for every two nations? Clearly, trade would be cut down severely. Imports would balance exports, but at the level of which is the lower. Each region would end worse off.

INCREASING COSTS

Returning again to two countries and two commodities, we must now drop the assumption that costs are constant. The production-possibility curves of Figs. 34-3, 34-4, and 34-6 should have been bowed, as they generally were in Chapter 2. It is no longer possible to specify a single cost figure for each country.

On the whole, America is better endowed for food production than Europe; still, after a great amount of American food is produced, the cost of *extra* food will begin to exceed that of Europe. Even after American competition has drastically lowered the price of food relative to clothing, a little of the best land in Europe will be able to hold its own in food production. Similarly, that first little bit of American clothing production which can be achieved at low costs will continue even after international trade has reached an equilibrium level. However, any attempt to expand American clothing production further would entail higher extra costs and competitive losses.

We may summarize the modifications in international trade made necessary by increasing costs:

■ As a result of international trade, each country will tend to specialize, as before, in the commodity in which it has the greatest comparative advantage; and it will export some of that commodity in exchange for the other country's surplus exports. But because of increasing relative costs, specialization need not be complete: something of both commodities may still be produced in either country, because even the less favored commodity may have low enough costs to compete when its production is small.[9]

[9] For the geometrically minded, Fig. 34-9 may be helpful. It shows America's condition before and after trade when increasing costs prevail. The production-possibility curve is now bowed out. Before international trade, America is consuming and producing at H. The domestic price ratio is 10:3, just equal to the ratio of extra costs of getting (at H) a little more clothing for a little sacrificed food. This is shown by the slope of the AK curve at H.

After trade, when the common price ratio is 10:6, American production shifts to B, toward less clothing but not away from clothing altogether. The new production point B will be reached as a result of competition, because the slope of the curve there—i.e., the ratio of costs of extra clothing for extra food—is 10:6, or just equal to the common international price ratio. At B, and only there, will the value of America's national product (evaluated at the 10:6 price ratio) be at a maximum.

INTERNATIONAL GOODS MOVEMENTS AS A SUBSTITUTE FOR FACTOR MOVEMENTS

Having acknowledged the law of increasing costs described in Chapter 2 and elsewhere, we now examine implications of the related law of diminishing returns within each country.

After international trade takes place, resources in Europe flow from food to clothing production. Because clothing requires relatively much labor and little land,

the pressure of population on the limited land of Europe is relieved. Land is no longer relatively so dear; rents fall compared with wages. In America the reverse happens after trade: concentration upon food production, in which labor is economized and land heavily utilized, tends to raise rents relative to wages.

In each case the free international movement of goods has effects which are partly like those following from the free international movement of factors of production. Just as the movement of labor from Europe to America would relieve the scarcity of labor in America and of land in Europe, so the movement of clothing from Europe to America and of food from America to Europe tends to make the superabundant factor in each country less abundant and the scarce factor less scarce.

The person who has most clearly emphasized how commodity trade partially relieves the scarcity in all countries of the less abundant factors of production is the Swedish economist and statesman Ohlin (pronounced O'Lean).[10] He has made this important addition to the classical doctrine of comparative cost:

Free movements of labor and capital between countries will tend to equalize wages and factor-prices. *However, even without any movements of productive factors across national boundaries, a tendency toward equalization of factor-prices will often result from the free movement of goods in international trade.*

It is clear, therefore, that although international trade increases national product in Europe, it may at the same time so reduce the share of particular groups that they are made worse off. Thus, the large British landowners who a century ago constituted the backbone of the Conservative party may have been selfish in opposing the famous repeal of the English corn-law tariffs in 1846, but they were not necessarily unintelligent in making their unsuccessful last-ditch fight to retain protective tariffs on imported grains.

The straight line represents the new consumption-possibility curve America can achieve as a result of trade. It is straight and not bent because the auctioneer offers to trade freely, giving America at the 10:6 ratio as much or little clothing for food as she wishes. The final levels of consumption, determined by supply and demand, are given by the point H'. As before, arrows indicate exports and imports.

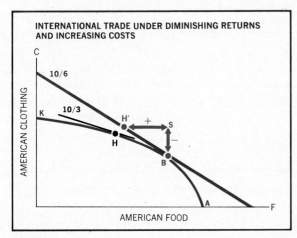

INTERNATIONAL TRADE UNDER DIMINISHING RETURNS AND INCREASING COSTS

FIG. 34-9.

There are still gains from trade; but because of diminishing returns and increasing costs, there is not so much specialization as before, and not quite such large gains. Note that at the equilibrium point, where no further trade is possible, relative (extra, or "marginal") production costs in the two countries are equal, each to the common price ratio 10:6.

[10] Bertil Ohlin, *Interregional and International Trade* (Harvard University Press, Cambridge, Mass., 1933).

35   The Economics of Tariff Protection and Free Trade

TO THE CHAMBER OF DEPUTIES: WE ARE SUBJECTED TO THE INTOLERABLE COMPETITION OF A FOREIGN RIVAL, WHO ENJOYS SUCH SUPERIOR FACILITIES FOR THE PRODUCTION OF LIGHT THAT HE CAN *INUNDATE* OUR *NATIONAL MARKET* AT REDUCED PRICE. THIS RIVAL IS NO OTHER THAN THE SUN. OUR PETITION IS TO PASS A LAW SHUTTING UP ALL WINDOWS, OPENINGS AND FISSURES THROUGH WHICH THE LIGHT OF THE SUN IS USED TO PENETRATE OUR DWELLINGS, TO THE PREJUDICE OF THE PROFITABLE MANUFACTURE WE HAVE BEEN ENABLED TO BESTOW ON THE COUNTRY. SIGNED: CANDLE MAKERS. F. BASTIAT

It would be absurd to try to decide whether God exists or not by counting on one hand all the arguments in the affirmative and on the other hand all the arguments in the negative, and then to award the decision to the side with the greater *number* of points. It is as absurd to evaluate the case for tariff protection by a mere count of unequally important pros and cons.

Indeed, as was shown in the previous chapter there is essentially only one argument for free or freer trade, but it is an exceedingly powerful one, namely:

■ Unhampered trade promotes a mutually profitable international division of labor, greatly enhances the potential real national product of all countries, and makes possible higher standards of living all over the globe.

Recall that putting on a tariff duty (i.e., tax) discourages imports and raises prices to the domestic consumer. By killing off the fruitful international division of labor, it "protects" the relatively inefficient domestic producer. Import quotas do the same.

The arguments for high tariff protection against the competition of foreign imports take many different forms. They may be divided into three categories:

1. Those that are definitely economically false, some so obviously and palpably as hardly to merit serious discussion, but some whose falsity can be detected only by subtle economic reasoning.

2. A few that are without validity in a perfectly competitive "classical" static full-employment world, but that do contain some kernels of truth for a sizable nation which produces much of a crop, or for a nation undergoing economic development and subject to underemployment and an overvalued currency.

3. Certain noneconomic arguments that may make it desirable national policy to sacrifice economic welfare in order to subsidize certain activities admittedly not economically efficient.

■ NONECONOMIC GOALS

Let us begin with the last category of arguments, for they are most simply disposed of. If you ever are on a debating team and are given the assignment to defend free trade, you will strengthen you case at the beginning by conceding that economic welfare is not the sole goal of life. Political considerations are also important. Thus, it may be necessary to become partially self-sufficient in certain lines of activity at great cost because of fear of future wars.

An example is the production of oil. If oil reserves and capacity are considered necessary for national defense and if the needed amount of capacity is not able to survive under free trade, the economist cannot assert that national policy should be against protection of this industry. But he can suggest that a *subsidy* to domestic production might be preferable to a tariff. This would bring the domestic price down to the international price instead of raising the price to the consumer up to the domestic cost; also, the subsidy would show clearly what the total costs of national defense are and would better enable the public to decide whether the flame is worth the candle.

The question of a national policy to foster the American merchant marine is a similar one. Doubtless the United States does *not* possess a comparative advantage in building or operating a merchant fleet. As soon as American seamen, through trade-unions or on their own, insist upon living conditions and wages remotely resembling those in Detroit factories, then we cannot compete with Dutch, Greek, Japanese, and Norwegian ships. If we give no weight to America's "glorious seafaring tradition"—a long way back!—and consider purely economic welfare, the correct policy is obvious. If America has a comparative advantage in factory production, let men go to factories where their real productivity is high. American international trade need not suffer by being carried in other countries' bottoms.

However, if national defense makes a large merchant marine necessary, that is another matter. Mail subsidies and subsidies for building ships with the extra speed to escape submarines may then be justified.

The problem of deciding how much to spend in peacetime on national defense is a perplexing one, especially since armament races are both *cause* and effect of international disunity. The economist can claim no special competence to advise on this problem. He can point out that selfish economic interests often wrap themselves in the flag and try to justify uneconomic projects in terms of national defense. He can ask suspiciously, "Would an increase in tariffs on Swiss watches be really justified by our defense needs for precision workers? Or is this merely a case of political pressure?" Finally, the economist can also point out that mutually profitable international trade may help to promote international understanding and unity, and that political interferences with trade have in the past provided some of the frictions that led to war.

In conclusion, it is well to point out other noneconomic goals that may deserve consideration. Society may feel that there is some special sanctity about farm life, something worth preserving in the way of life of the "stout agricultural yeoman or happy peasant." (It is to be doubted that people who rhapsodize in this fashion typically come from farms.) Or some may agree with the Soviet Union that rural living is worth fostering because the country has a higher birth rate than the cities.

In such cases, subsidies rather than tariffs seem called for. A tariff is simply a rather indirect and clumsy form of subsidy that draws attention away from the problem.

Do not be left with the impression that the political noneconomic arguments are generally favorable to tariffs. They are not. Every congressman knows that America has a tremendous diplomatic interest these days in winning friends and allies. And nothing is so disruptive to our popularity abroad as our reputation for being a high-tariff country. We do not deserve that reputation as much as we used to. So it is all the more to our political interest to resist many of the pressures that make for restrictions on international trade.

■ GROSSLY FALLACIOUS ARGUMENTS FOR TARIFFS

KEEPING MONEY IN THE COUNTRY   To Abraham Lincoln has been attributed the remark, "I don't know much about the tariff. But I do know that when I buy a coat from England, I have the coat and England has the money. But when I buy a coat in America, I have the coat and America has the money."

There is no evidence that he ever actually said this; but it does represent an age-old fallacy typical of the so-called "mercantilistic" writers of the seventeenth and eighteenth centuries who preceded Adam Smith. They considered a country lucky which *gave away* more goods than it received, because such a "favorable" (!) balance of trade meant that gold would flow into the country to pay for its export surplus.

In this day and age it should be unnecessary to labor the point that, while an increased amount of money in the hands of one person will make *him* better off, doubling the money in the hands of everybody in a full-employment economy will only serve to raise prices. Unless the single individual is a demented miser like King Midas, the money makes him better off, not for its own sake, but for what it will buy or bid away from other individuals. For society as a whole, once full employment is reached, new money cannot hope to buy any new goods.[1]

A TARIFF FOR HIGHER MONEY WAGES   Today it is agreed that extreme protection can raise prices and attract gold into one country, if all other countries do not retaliate with tariffs. The tariff may even increase *money* wages; but it will tend to increase the cost of living by more than the increase in money wages, so that *real* wages will fall as labor becomes less productive.[2]

One could go on endlessly giving examples of protectionist fallacies that every thoughtful person can explode in a minute by subjecting them to analysis. This does

---

[1] Of course, our gold might be spent abroad. But this perfectly sensible way of improving welfare by importing was precisely what the mercantilist "bullionists" were arguing against.
[2] See the last chapter's discussion of comparative advantage and effects of a tariff.

not mean that such crude fallacies can be dismissed as unimportant. Actually, they are most important of all in shaping legislation, the other fancier arguments simply being used as window dressing.

TARIFFS FOR SPECIAL-INTEREST GROUPS   The single most important motivation for protective tariff is obvious to anyone who has watched the "logrolling" in Congress when such legislation is on the floor. Powerful pressure groups and vested interests—both business and labor—know very well that a tariff on their products will help *them*, whatever its effect on total production and consumption. Outright bribery was used in the old days to get the necessary votes; today powerful lobbies exist in Washington to drum up enthusiasm for the good old crockery, watch, or buttonhook industry.

Economically the case for freer trade may be strong, but politically the case for protection tends to exert undue pressure. Why? Because *freer trade helps everybody a little*, while *protection helps a few people a lot*. Does it matter politically that the bad points of protection outweigh the good? Not if those few who benefit from protection (or who are kept by protection from suffering harm) are politically active in pressing for their cause. It is much harder to organize the masses of consumers and producers to agitate for the even larger gains that they get from an efficient pattern of national specialization and trade. If political votes were in exact proportion to *total* economic benefit, every country would selfishly legislate most of its tariffs out of existence.

■ SOME LESS OBVIOUS FALLACIES

A TARIFF FOR REVENUE   First, there is the claim that the tariff should be used to raise government tax revenue. Actually, a customs duty on imports is only one form of regressive sales tax, and a rather bad one. A customs duty or tariff is especially bad because it draws economic resources away from their best uses. If the people who advance the revenue argument were really sincere, they would advocate a sales tax which would *also* fall on domestic production. But this combination would provide no protection at all.

To clinch the case against the revenue argument, only remember that a prohibitively high tariff, which perfectly "protected" us from imports, would collect no revenue at all! Back in 1890, the so-called "billion-dollar Congress" found itself with a surplus of tax revenue over expenditure. Since there was no suitable debt to retire, Congress found the situation embarrassing. It finally met the problem of excessive tariff revenues, not by lowering tariff rates, but by *raising them high* enough to reduce the total of revenue collected.

TARIFFS AND THE HOME MARKET   A second argument, which by itself is on the whole false but whose fallacy is rather difficult to spot, goes as follows: "Farmers should support a tariff for industry because that will gain them a large home market for their products." Henry Clay, the perennial candidate who turned out to be neither "right" nor "President," used this argument.

Its falsity can be seen from different points of view. First, by cutting down industrial imports we are really at the same time indirectly tending to cut down our farm exports. Thus the farmer is hurt directly. "But," Clay might remonstrate, "what about the extra home market for farm produce?"

Well, what about it? Our detailed example of comparative cost showed that isolation from foreign trade decreases the total of national product or real income. The total domestic demand for farm products will certainly be less at a low level of real income than at a high level. So unless it can be buttressed by one of the quite different arguments for protection coming later, the slogan about "creating a home market" is seen once again to be fallacious.

COMPETITION FROM CHEAP FOREIGN LABOR   A third argument for protection has been the most popular of all in American history, because it appealed to the large number of labor votes. According to its usual version, "If we let in goods produced by cheap pauper foreign labor—by Chinese coolies who live on a few cents' worth of rice per day or by low-paid Japanese textile workers—then the higher standard of living of American workers cannot be maintained." So stated, the argument cannot stand up.

We have seen that trade is mutually profitable even if one country can produce every good more cheaply in terms of resources than the other. The important thing is comparative advantage, not absolute advantage. In the last analysis, trade boils down to two-sided barter. One country cannot indefinitely undersell the other in every line of merchandise.

Earlier we showed that full employment at home need not depend in the long run on foreign trade. If, then, everyone in this country remains fully employed at his most suitable occupation, is it not to *our selfish advantage* for the workers of other countries to be willing to work for very little? To put the matter another way:

The comparative-cost doctrine shows that we benefit most by trading with countries of the Far East or the tropics which are *very different* from ours, rather than with countries such as England or Germany which have an industrial economy like our own.[3] Against the pauper-labor argument, there is the clinching fact that the analysis of comparative advantage showed that absolute wage levels had nothing to do with the long-run increase in national income that resulted from trade.

So much from a theoretical point of view. If we turn to the real world, we find the arguments to be even more incorrect. In Europe and in Asia the workers beg for tariffs, saying, "Protect us from the 'unfair competition' of high-paid, efficient American workers who have skill and machinery far better than our own." The rest of the world lives in fear of competition from American mass-production industries. The English protectionist claims that the American worker in Bridgeport, Connecticut, who is paid $3 per hour is more than three times as efficient as the English worker who gets paid 95 cents an hour. This is perhaps an overstatement, but it is close to the

[3] This argument must be qualified and amplified. Backward countries, so poor that they have little real purchasing power with which to import, at best can export little to us. Most trade today is between industrialized countries. As a backward country advances industrially, it buys more from industrial countries, not less; but perhaps not proportionally more, and perhaps there is *less consumer's surplus from trade* accruing to both parties.

important truth: high American real wages come from high efficiency and do not handicap us in competing with foreign workers.

A TARIFF TO RAISE WAGE SHARE   Thus far we have had nothing but adverse criticism for the "cheap pauper foreign labor" tariff argument. To be objective—and without objectivity there can be no science—we must admit that it may have the following iota of possible truth. The Ohlin proposition in the Appendix to the last chapter suggested that free trade in goods may serve as a partial substitute for immigration of labor into the United States. This implies that labor scarcity in the United States could be alleviated by our international specialization in labor-economizing products and that real wages might actually fall under conditions of free trade. Real national product would go up, but the relative and absolute share of labor might go down.[4]

Although admitting this as a possibility, most economists believe its grain of truth for America is outweighed by more realistic considerations. No doubt immobile laborers such as textile workers might be hurt by removing a tariff. But with American labor such an important and flexible factor of production, it seems likely that other laborers would gain from expanded trade more than those hurt will lose. Labor as a whole would presumably share in the increased national product from trade.

A TARIFF FOR RETALIATION   Some people admit that a world of free trade would be preferable to a world of tariffs; but they say that as long as other countries are so foolish or so wicked as to pass restrictive tariff legislation, there is nothing that we can do but follow suit in self-defense.

Actually, however, a tariff is much like an increase in transportation costs. If other countries were foolish enough to let their roads go to ruin, would it pay us to chop holes in ours? The answer is, No. Analogously, if other countries hurt us and themselves by passing tariffs, we should not add to our own hurt by passing a tariff.

To make sure that you grasp the point that our tariff harms us as well as the foreigner, you should realize that there are four gains when a trade-agreements program succeeds in getting another country and ourselves to lower tariffs reciprocally. The other country's tariff reduction bestows gains (1) on us and (2) on them. Our tariff reduction adds two more gains: (3) for ourselves and (4) for them.

Therefore the only possible sense in the argument that we should retaliate when a foreign country raises tariffs is that our threat of retaliation may deter them from raising tariffs, and our promise to reduce tariffs may persuade them to reduce theirs. This would justify our passing an occasional tariff as a bluff, but if our bluffs do not work, we should give them up.

Most realistic students of political science infer from historical studies that retaliatory tariffs usually lead other nations to raise theirs still higher and are rarely an effective bargaining weapon for multilateral tariff reduction.

[4] A study by W. Leontief of Harvard suggests that in America capital rather than labor is the relatively scarce factor! If correct, this would be an argument for raising American real wages by *lowering* tariffs. (The presumed explanation for this Leontief Paradox of alleged capital scarcity is that each U.S. worker is technically like three foreign workers, but we lack triple the capital per head.)

THE "SCIENTIFIC" TARIFF   This is one of the most insidious arguments for a tariff; insidious because it often sounds plausible and moderate, but, if taken literally, would mean the end to all trade! According to its usual form, tariffs should be passed to "equalize the cost of production at home and abroad." The last chapter showed all the advantage from trade to rest on *differences* in cost or advantage. If tariffs were passed raising the costs of imports to that of the highest home producer, no goods would come in at all.[5]

There is nothing scientific about such a tariff. It is a grave reflection on the economic literacy of the American people that this least defensible of all protectionist arguments had tremendous political importance in our history, and was even written into law upon occasion.

PERIL-POINT TARIFF ARGUMENT   According to this congressional argument, America is to keep tariff duties low on an industry. However, if this results in so many imports that the very existence of that domestic industry is threatened, we have reached the so-called "peril point." When that point is reached, we are to increase duties or tighten quotas to keep our domestic industry from disappearing or becoming perilously small.

What about this argument? While it may sound moderate, note that its basic philosophy runs completely counter to the economic theory of comparative advantage. Our nation gains from trade by *specializing*, i.e., by giving up certain activities and moving their resources into other industries in which we have a greater comparative advantage. The industries in which we have strong comparative disadvantage should never have come into existence. And suppose an industry formerly had a comparative advantage but has lost it—because other industries have had greater technological improvements, because the domestic factors it uses have become more expensive through becoming more valuable elsewhere, because factors for that industry have become relatively cheaper abroad, or for any other reason. Then this industry *ought* to be imperiled. It ought to be killed off by the competition of our more productive industries. It ought to reach and pass the peril point.[6]

This sounds ruthless indeed. No industry willingly dies; no region gladly undergoes conversion to new factor uses. In truth, any field that is imperiled is probably already a sick industry with a past history of suffering. So the already weak industry and region feels it is being singled out to carry the burden of getting the country into a more productive configuration.

Perhaps the best policy, then, is to introduce tariff reductions gradually, so that vested factors will have time to move. And, as in the 1962 Trade Act, to give financial aid to retrain and relocate factors of production. This tends to speed the transition, share the burden among strong and weak, and perhaps lessen effective opposition to the needed reorganization of national production. Bicycles, glass, watch manufacture (as distinct

[5] With nonconstant costs the scientific-tariff formula is indeterminate. A zero tariff may equalize foreign costs with those of our few most efficient producers; an almost prohibitive tariff equalize with our high-cost producers. Where can one scientifically draw the line?

[6] Of course, national defense and other valid arguments for tariffs might apply; but if they do, it is *those* arguments, and not the peril-point argument, that have to be respected.

from domestic assembly of Swiss movements), oil, basic chemicals, wool growing, china, textiles, and generating equipment are some of the weak sisters that feel imperiled. Politics has forced protective concessions to some of these.

Fortunately, in a growing economy the ineffective industries gradually dwindle in importance relative to the dynamic effective ones. Fortunately, too, the strength of our export industries and the effective use of fiscal and monetary policies can keep over-all employment opportunities high, so that with good conscience the nation can strive for the increase in real income made possible by specialization according to the principles of comparative advantage.

■ THE "FOREIGNER WILL PAY," OR TERMS-OF-TRADE ARGUMENTS[7]

After dealing so long with fallacious tariff arguments, we find it refreshing to come now to a possibly valid one—which hopes to shift the terms of trade against the foreigner. Indeed, it is about the only argument that would be valid even under static competitive conditions, and it goes back 140 years to John Stuart Mill. Paradoxically, valid arguments for protection seem mostly to have come from free traders, not from protectionists!

If we put a tariff on rubber, Mill would argue, that will raise the price here over its price abroad. But with our demand now curtailed, and as we are an important demander of rubber, the price abroad will be bid down. So part of the tariff really falls on the foreigner. (Show that a very small country could not use this argument, since it cannot budge world prices.)

In summary, a judicious tariff might improve an important country's terms of trade (defined as the ratio of her export to her import prices).

But here is a warning. Prohibitive tariffs, which suit the protectionist who really is against all trade, could never be justified by this terms-of-trade argument. Why? Because killing off all trade would kill off all the advantage you get from shifting the terms of trade in your favor. Mill and modern economists therefore insist that the "optimal tariff" is one just large enough to improve your terms of trade and just small enough to keep your physical exchange of imports and exports at the level most favorable to your own country.

Most economists think that all this would imply rather small tariff rates for most countries. And they hasten to point out that when all nations pursue such terms-of-trade tariff policies, the world pattern of production and exchange becomes less efficient; most (if not all) tend to end worse off under such beggar-my-neighbor policies.

■ ARGUMENTS FOR PROTECTION UNDER DYNAMIC CONDITIONS

At last we are arriving at a point in the protection versus free-trade debate where those in favor of tariffs can begin to score some weighty points. Three important arguments fall in this category: (1) that a tariff may help to reduce unemployment, (2) that

---

[7] The argument is exactly like that of a domestic monopolist who raises his price above marginal cost but does not raise it sky-high, instead stopping where $MR = MC$.

tariffs may create diversified industries more immune to risk, and (3) that temporary tariff protection for an "infant industry" with growth potentialities may be desirable.

TARIFFS AND UNEMPLOYMENT   Historically, one of the strongest arguments for protection has been the desire to make or preserve jobs. Earlier we discussed the favorable multiplier effects of exports and foreign investment on jobs and domestic spending, and also the unfavorable "leakage" effects of imports. So beggar-my-neighbor high-tariff policy might increase employment in the short run before other nations retaliated.

But can we accept such measures as a valid part of our national full-employment program? Is not freer trade much like a scientific discovery of new machinery and methods? Both represent increases in our *potentially producible* level of real national output; but either *might* in the short run tend to lower our actual *attained* level of output and employment. And yet, there is no need, in either the short or the long run, to tolerate a gap between actual and potentially producible product, for that represents an unnecessary frittering away of the gains from progress.

How, then, do we meet the arguments relating unemployment to too low tariffs? We refute these arguments just as we refute arguments concerning "technological unemployment." We point out the existence of domestic monetary, foreign-exchange-rate, and fiscal policies that can successfully *and efficiently* solve the problem of economic slump. (Recall our hundreds of earlier pages on all this.[8]) If workers displaced by imports can find other jobs in a strong labor market, this protection plea loses its force.

Once again, we realize how vitally important it is to insist on a "neoclassical synthesis" that employs the tools of modern income analysis to create the favorable environment for stability and growth which is vitally necessary if the classical principles of economics are to be relevant and valid.

DIVERSIFICATION TO REDUCE TERMS-OF-TRADE RISK   Comparative advantage might tell a country to specialize completely on one good or a few goods. So she is to put all her eggs in one basket. But then what will happen if the prices of those goods drop? Or if her export prices oscillate? She will find such variations in her terms of trade very destabilizing to her real income; and she may be left with an industry become permanently unprofitable.

To avoid the perils of "monoculture," Latin American economists advise the introduction of tariffs. Just as an investor in securities will diversify to reduce risk rather than keeping all his eggs in one basket, so they believe a country should use tariffs to induce diversification.

This argument certainly deserves careful examination. Note that it assumes private citizens are neglecting to take account of the riskiness in future prices of the industries they put their money and labor skills into. This argument has to assume that the government is better informed than private investors, or at least that the government is more farseeing than private investors in taking account of the future perils of price drops

[8] If money wage rates are generally too high, the dollar may be "overvalued" (as defined in Chapter 33's Appendix). Chapter 36 shows this could call for a new exchange-rate parity.

and price gyrations. If the future risks are genuine and are foreseen by private investors, those investors will not be misled by temporarily high profits into investing in these few industries; in truth, such industries will not then have a genuine long-run comparative advantage, and there will be no effective tendency to specialize in them.[9]

At this point a related Latin American argument for tariffs should be mentioned. Dr. Raul Prebisch, long chief economic adviser to the United Nations' Economic Commission for Latin America, argued that the long-run terms of trade are always shifting against agricultural products. So nations that specialize in them are betting on the wrong horse. He argued their governments should instead impose tariffs aimed at building up manufacturing industries whose future terms of trade will be more favorable. (Against this argument is the following: If past and future reductions in food prices are matched by even greater drops in real food costs, as agriculture undergoes great technological progress, then long-run comparative advantage might still validly tell a nation to specialize in food to improve its real income or at least to minimize its losses.)

This argument is really an argument about what the *future* comparative advantage of the countries in question will be. To the degree that governments are smarter than private investors in discerning trends threatening to the terms of trade, a valid case can be made for their interfering with free-market forces. But if government is wrong in its comparative-advantage forecasts, the loss in real income to the nation can become very considerable, and the nation may find its rate of development slowed down rather than speeded up.

TARIFFS FOR "INFANT INDUSTRIES"   Alexander Hamilton, in his famous "Report on Manufactures," raised this argument. It is also associated with the name of a nineteenth-century German economist, Friedrich List, and it has received the cautious blessing of John Stuart Mill, Alfred Marshall, Frank Taussig, and other orthodox economists.

According to this doctrine, there are activities in which a country would really have a comparative advantage, *if only it could get them started.* If confronted with foreign competition, such infant industries are not able to weather the initial period of experimentation and financial stress; but given a breathing space, they can be expected to develop economies of mass production and the technological efficiency typical of many modern processes. Although protection will at first raise prices to the consumer, once the industry grows up it will be so efficient that cost and price will actually have fallen. If the benefit to consumers at that later date would be enough to more than make up for the higher prices during the period of protection, a tariff is justified.

There is certainly something to this, at least as a possibility. Historical studies have turned up some genuine cases of infant industries that grew up to stand on their own feet; and even more cases of the contrary—of perpetual infants! Unfortunately for the practical importance of this argument, even promising infant industries cannot

[9] Suppose private employers do foresee the risk, but think they can fire workers when export prices drop, thereby throwing the burden of the unemployed workers on the state. Then we face a genuine so-called "external diseconomy," which might justify government intervention in the form of tariffs, quotas, or other programs. Also, recall the limited conditions under which the "foreigner will pay" argument has terms-of-trade validity.

swing many votes. It is not they who get protection from Congress, but rather the old vested interests who have never shed their diapers for lo these many years.

THE "YOUNG-ECONOMY" ARGUMENT   Probably the infant-industry argument had more validity for America a century ago than it does today, and it has more validity for present-day undeveloped nations than for those which have already experienced the transition from an agricultural to an industrial way of life. In a sense, such nations are still asleep; they cannot be said to be truly in equilibrium. All over the world, farmers seem to earn less than industrial workers. Consequently, there is everywhere a relative growth of industry and a decline of agriculture. Populations migrate cityward, but this movement is not rapid enough to achieve an equilibrium of earnings and productivity. A strong case can be made for using moderate protection to accelerate these economically desirable long-run trends. Such a defense of protection might better be called a "young-economy" rather than an infant-industry argument.

One final word: Please note that the infant-industry or young-economy arguments are not contradictory to the principle of comparative advantage. On the contrary, their validity rests upon the presumption of an induced, dynamic shift of the production-possibility frontier outward and in the direction of a *new* comparative advantage in the lines needing temporary protection.

■ CONCLUSION

While this chapter has usually spoken of tariffs, almost everything it said would apply equally well to any other impediments to trade. Thus, quotas have all the bad effects of tariffs, and often quotas are even more restrictive.

Finally, we should mention the so-called "invisible tariff." In many countries— and the United States is no exception—the complicated administration of the customs can be as bad as the monetary duty that has to be paid. If an importer's shipments are unduly delayed or if a foreigner's exports to us are refused admittance for complicated reasons of health or of failure to comply with arbitrary regulations, then such red tape can be as harmful to trade as outright tariffs or quotas. Work toward simplification of customs administration still has a long way to go.

This completes our discussion of the tariff controversy. No fair-minded reader who takes the trouble to think the matter through can fail to see how shallow are most of the economic arguments for tariff protection. The only serious exception is the infant-industry or young-economy argument.

It is not surprising, therefore, that economists—who are supposed to agree on almost nothing—have been overwhelmingly in favor of the Hull Reciprocal Trade Agreements and GATT (General Agreement on Tariffs and Trade) aimed at lowering trade barriers. The Kennedy Trade Act (1962) gives hope for further multilateral progress, as does the "Kennedy Round" of international negotiations to reduce tariffs multilaterally as the 1970s come into view. See Fig. 35-1 for a dramatic illustration of the fact, too little appreciated at home and abroad, that America has at long last ceased to be a high-tariff nation.

Tariffs were long a political football:

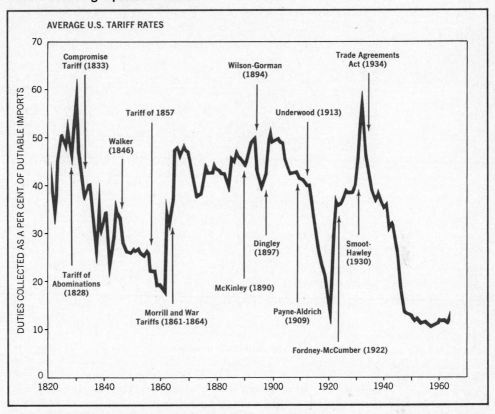

FIG. 35-1. America is no longer a high-tariff nation. Tariff rates have gone up and down in our history. Note how low they have become in the post–World War II era. If comparable figures were compiled for other countries, it would be seen that America no longer deserves her reputation as one of the most protectionist of all nations. Study of comparative quotas and exchange controls would confirm this vital change. (Source: U.S. Department of Commerce, *Statistical Abstract of the United States*, selected editions.)

SUMMARY

1 ■

The case for freer trade rests upon the increased productivity that international specialization, according to the law of comparative advantage, makes possible. Higher world production is made possible, and all countries can have higher standards of living. Trade between countries with different standards of living is likely to be especially mutually profitable.

2 ■

Most arguments for tariff protection are simply rationalizations for special benefits to particular pressure groups and do not stand up under analysis.

3 ■

An exception to the law of comparative advantage is provided by the need to favor certain uneconomical lines of activity for reasons of national defense. Perhaps outright government subsidies would be better in such cases.

4 ■

The only other exception of any practical importance in a full-employment economy[10] is provided by the case of infant industries or young economies that need temporary protection in order to realize their true long-run comparative advantages. To the degree that public planning for development can discern long-term trends better than the free market can, trade interventions might turn out to be beneficial.

QUESTIONS FOR DISCUSSION

1. What do you think is the single most favorable argument for a tariff or quota?

2. Make a list of fallacious tariff arguments. Weigh pros and cons.

3. Comment critically on the infant-industry and young-economy arguments. What is their relation to comparative advantage?

4. Mention some noneconomic considerations relevant to tariffs.

5. Relate the peril-point and "scientific-tariff" arguments to comparative-advantage theory.

6. Suppose labor productivity grows mightily abroad, and American goods start to be undersold in every line. Suppose that a mixed economy like ours has sticky wage rates. Suppose devaluation of the dollar is not feasible. Then can you show that new tariffs might be a stopgap measure?

7. Review your understanding of the following concepts:

tariff protection, quota	terms of trade
scientific tariff and peril point	specialization and risk
national-defense arguments	infant industry and young economy

---

[10]The "foreigner will pay" argument, for all its theoretical attractiveness, is probably of limited actual importance for most countries. Chapter 33's Appendix shows how overvaluation of a currency gives comfort to the enemies of fruitful international trade. And the next chapter will discuss, in the context of America's gold problem, what might be done about such an overvaluation of the dollar.

36 Current International Economic Problems

BEFORE I BUILT A WALL I'D ASK TO KNOW
WHAT I WAS WALLING IN OR WALLING OUT,
AND TO WHOM I WAS LIKE TO GIVE OFFENSE.

ROBERT FROST

We must now turn to the main international economic problems facing the United States and the rest of the world in the years ahead. How can we understand the important facts? Which economic policies must we avoid? Which policies must we follow?

Economists have achieved more unanimous agreement about the principles of international trade than about any other aspect of their subject. Yet the gulf between the plain man's beliefs about international finance and those of the experts is almost as wide as elsewhere in economics. Fortunately, that gulf has seemed to be narrowing in recent decades. A brief survey in Section A of the main historical and contemporary trends in foreign trade will pave the way for an examination in Section B of the chronic gold drain and other trade problems that America must solve in the years to come.

A. MODERN TRENDS AND INSTITUTIONS OF INTERNATIONAL FINANCE

■ TRENDS, 1914-1945

EXPORTS AND JOBS   When the war broke out in 1914, the belligerent nations—England, France, and Russia—increased their imports from the United States. The effect of this could not be analyzed by the tools known at that time to the highest experts; but the multiplier analysis of Part Two can, as the Appendix of Chapter 33 and common sense show, explain what actually happened.[1]

When the warring countries suddenly became avid customers for our exports, we sent them goods in return for barren gold and fancy gilt-edged certificates. The result

---

[1] Suppose (as on page 641) we each spend $8/12$ of each extra dollar on goods, but that $1/12$ represents expenditures on imports from abroad and only $7/12$ represents domestic respending. Then a 1-billion-dollar increase in exports will give rise to an ultimate multiplier chain of $[1 + 7/12 + (7/12)^2 + \cdots]$ = $1/(1 - 7/12) = 12/5 = 2\frac{2}{5}$-billion-dollar increase in NNP.

was a shift from a prewar depression to great prosperity in America. In the period after we entered World War I, when our shipments of shot and shell increased, again there resulted all the trappings of prosperity booms—high prices and job plenty.

During the 1920s, when we were making many foolish private loans to the rest of the world and whooping it up for tariffs, allegedly to "protect the American workers' standard of living," a contributing factor to our prosperity seemed to be heavy foreign lending. Like domestic investment or government deficit expenditure, the foreign-trade balance was adding to total money spending and jobs.

The hardboiled businessmen summed it up: "Of course, many of our foreign loans later turned sour, and investors lost their money, but while we were shipping goods abroad, jobs were created. It didn't matter, as far as *current* jobs and prices in the twenties were concerned, whether 10 years later the loans turned out good or bad or whether they represented public or private gifts." Or, as Leon Fraser, who used to be president of J. P. Morgan's First National Bank of New York, put it: "It is better to have lent and lost than never to have lent at all."

THE GREAT DEPRESSION   After 1929 the stock market crashed, foreign loans became worthless, new foreign lending ceased, and in every country there was much unemployment and unrest. With jobs scarce at home, the political forces of protectionism became rampant. Tariffs were raised, quotas imposed, and in many countries exchange controls were also imposed. Against the advice of almost 100 per cent of the economics profession (who signed a petition to Congress), the Hawley-Smoot (1930) high tariff was passed. Cynics were delighted at the spectacle of a country trying to collect debts from abroad and at the same time shutting out the import goods that could alone have provided the payment for those debts. H. L. Mencken, who never failed to call attention to the comedy of American life, rubbed his hands to see farmers—who were net exporters and not importers of goods—being given tariffs on their export(!) products in exchange for their voting for tariffs on manufactured imports.

The fallacy of composition was at work. Each country believed that, if it could develop a favorable balance of trade, its employment would increase at the expense of its neighbors; in effect, it would be succeeding in exporting some of its joblessness. But for everybody to run a favorable trade balance simultaneously is a self-contradiction—as impossible as for everybody to be taller than anybody else.

Of course, the attempt to be taller—I mean to generate a favorable surplus of exports over imports—could be predicted to cut down on the fruitful division of labor. And precisely that happened. As much as domestic and total world production declined, the volume of international trade declined still more. The situation reached its height of absurdity when countries would trade with each other only on a *bilateral* basis: A would buy from B only as much as B would buy from A; under Hitler's economic adviser Schacht, Latin American countries were sending staples in return for German aspirin, which was piling up in warehouses.

It was a non-Euclidean world, with triangles whose angles added up to anything or nothing and with intersecting parallel lines. Inefficiency was putting the world and each nation well inside its production-possibility frontier. But since contractionary

monetary and fiscal policies were being urged as the only penance for the sinful practices followed during the prosperity, destruction of goods seemed the order of the day.
Farmers were pouring milk into gutters, wheat was being burned to keep sharecroppers
warm, the government was paying people to plough under the unripened corn, and the
windows of empty factories were the targets for bored men who had been on relief
for years. Eliminating the efficiency of international trade was not out of line with the
idiocy of the day.

Today, even schoolboys ask why the people did not insist on deliberate programs
of fiscal and monetary expansion. It is only too easy to remake history *after* the fact.
But—and this is what concerns us here—one reason a single nation could not introduce
expansion at home was the genuine fear that if she increased her NNP while others
kept theirs depressed, her imports would grow in the face of languishing exports. Thus,
she would lose gold and, under the gold standard, she would either have to contract
again or be forced into devaluation or bankruptcy.

As it happened, by 1931 England was forced off the gold standard along with
Scandinavia and the Commonwealth. With the pound depreciated, these countries
could afford to push their *internal* expansion; and if you look at the records, you see
that Sweden and Britain were already recovering nicely from the Depression when the
United States, Germany, and France were experiencing the worst of it. Doubtless, some
of the gains to the depreciating countries were at the expense of those who stayed
orthodoxly on gold. But most authoritative studies suggest that the gain to the expanding
countries came primarily from the freedom it gave them to expand domestically.

Was old-fashioned virtue rewarded? Not in the 1930s. Belgium clung precariously
to the old gold mint parities, even after Roosevelt deliberately devalued the dollar.
Political unrest and depression were Belgium's reward—until 1936, when she gave up
the struggle and, instead of being smitten by thunderbolts for her apostasy, she immediately registered relief in her production and unemployment statistics. France, having
been the wayward inflationist in the 1920s, practically tore herself apart politically
by clinging to the old gold parity into the late 1930s. Only Switzerland seemed to be
able to afford Euclidean geometry in a world gone non-Euclidean.

WAR   The Depression, which hit Germany and the United States especially hard, contributed to Hitler's rise to power. When World War II came, the vast deficits in every
country financed vast increases in the G of $C + I + G$ and had the predictable effect
of, first, expanding production enough to get rid of unemployment, and second, swelling
total demand so much as to create inflationary gaps and outright inflation. As in World
War I, vast new shipments of exports for the warring nations again brought full employment and enhanced real product to the United States.

War meant scarcity, not superabundance. So again the world turned Euclidean.
Mercantilistic notions, that it is good to give away goods abroad in return for as few
imports as possible, went into discard. The emphasis again was on extending production-
possibility frontiers outward and on making sure to be on those frontiers, and not inside.
The classical theory of comparative advantage came into its own as the Allied powers
allocated to each nation the tasks it could perform *relatively* most efficiently.

THE PERIOD OF "DOLLAR SHORTAGE"   When the war was over, the scarcity remained. Only the United States had not been physically devastated by the war. Elsewhere there was a great need to rebuild, to develop, and to make up for wartime scarcities. At the prevailing exchange rates, the American dollar was a vastly "undervalued currency" in the following sense.

> ■ The total demand abroad for American dollars to finance needed imports from us was much greater than the total of dollars our private citizens would want to supply (to pay for trips to Paris and Rome, for goods imports, direct investments, etc.). If we had not introduced a governmental policy of providing relief and reconstruction aid, of making loans and gifts, no country would have had the needed amount of gold or credit worthiness to finance its international deficit with us. In a free-trade world, the price of the dollar would have been bid sky-high.

Under the conditions of 1945–1950, in the absence of vast American aid programs and tight regulation abroad of imports and capital movements, the dd and ss schedules of Chapter 33, Fig. 33-1, page 628, would have shown a tremendous "dollar gap" at existing foreign exchange rates; this could have been met only by dropping to an equilibrium intersection where the dollar was much, much dearer in terms of foreign currencies—perhaps at $2 per £1 rather than $4, which was then prevailing, and likewise for the mark, franc, and yen.

That is the technical meaning of the term that used to be heard so widely then, namely, the "dollar shortage," or "dollar gap." (Reread the above brown paragraph.)

How was the gap handled? Not by immediate postwar depreciations (although later in 1949 Britain and most nations did have to depreciate, the pound dropping from $4 to $2.80). Instead, the so-called dollar gap was handled primarily by comprehensive exchange and import controls on the part of the nations with "overvalued currencies" and, as we shall see, by vast American aid and loan programs.

■ MARSHALL PLAN, MILITARY AID, AND OTHER PROGRAMS

Table 36-1 shows how enormous the American aid programs have been. After the United Nations Relief and Rehabilitation Administration (UNRRA) had helped meet the immediate postwar emergency needs, we introduced our dramatic Marshall Plan for European recovery. Subsequently, our aid shifted toward grants to the North Atlantic Treaty Organization (NATO) and other military alliances. (Thus, the "Truman Doctrine" brought financial aid to Greece when that country was threatened by communism. Even Yugoslavia has received aid, as well as the Chinese Nationalists and the South Koreans.) Our aid to Asia, Africa, and Latin America, for economic development, has been on a scale without precedent in all history.

Undoubtedly, the motive for many of these programs was our fear of the spread of communism. Full stomachs may not save a democracy, but empty ones can seal its doom. Putting modern guns into the hands of our friends may both help their defense and save American soldiers' lives.

However, a close study of the events leading up to the Marshall Plan and other

For relief, recovery, development, and military security, we gave:

TYPE OF AID	1945–1950	1951–1956	1957–1962	1963–1965	TOTAL POSTWAR PERIOD
Net nonmilitary grants	**17.1**	**11.0**	**11.2**	**4.5**	**43.8**
Western Europe	10.9	5.4	1.0	0.0	17.3
Asia, Africa, and Near East	4.6	5.0	8.3	3.7	21.6
Rest of world	1.6	0.6	1.9	0.8	4.9
Net government loans	**9.4**	**1.5**	**2.5**	**5.0**	**18.4**
Western Europe	8.1	0.2	−2.1	−0.1	6.1
Asia, Africa, and Near East	0.7	0.8	2.8	4.2	8.5
Rest of world	0.6	0.5	1.8	0.9	3.8
Net military grants	**1.8**	**16.7**	**12.1**	**5.1**	**35.7**
Western Europe	0.3	11.0	4.2	0.7	16.2
Asia, Africa, and Near East	1.4	5.1	7.3	4.4	18.2
Rest of world	0.1	0.5	0.6	0.0	1.3
Net total, grants and loans	**28.3**	**29.2**	**25.8**	**14.6**	**97.9**

TABLE 36-1. UNITED STATES GOVERNMENT POST–WORLD WAR II FOREIGN AID—billions of dollars, fiscal years; excludes International Bank and Fund operations. (Source: U.S. Department of Commerce.)

foreign-aid plans will show that America in the postwar period has also had strong "do-good" motivations. Call this altruism if you wish, or call it long-run expediency. We recognize that the globe holds 15 non-Americans to every American, making our very future depend upon a stable international order that is not hostile to Western society. Close study of the facts will in any case discredit the hypothesis that we embraced aid programs because that was the only way to prevent a great depression at home. On the contrary, we gave most at times when domestic inflation problems were most pressing; and one of the gravest costs of aid was aggravation of our concurrent internal scarcities. (Other advanced nations, and the Soviet Union, have also been giving some foreign aid.)

THE POINT FOUR PROGRAM   Aside from providing substantial material aid, there is one important thing we do for foreign countries that costs us very little, namely, help them acquire the technical know-how to enable them to increase their levels of productivity and living standards. This is known as the "Point Four" program because it was first enunciated as the fourth point in the 1949 inaugural address of President Truman.

> Fourth, we must embark on a bold new program for making the benefits of our scientific advances and industrial progress available for the improvement and growth of undeveloped areas. . . . I believe that we should make available to peace-loving peoples the benefits of our store of technical knowledge in order to help them realize their aspirations for a better life. . . . We invite other countries to pool their technological resources in this . . . world-wide effort for the achievement of peace, plenty, and freedom.

Besides these government plans, we have been privately exporting our "know-how." Many of our largest companies are establishing branch factories abroad; often the capital is largely raised there, with Americans supplying the technical knowledge.

Some people throw up their hands in horror at the thought of our helping foreign nations to become our industrial competitors. Despite the statistical fact that international trade is largest between developed industrial nations and not between highly developed and backward countries, in terms of selfish long-run economic interest there is some factual basis for this gloomy view—as the post–Marshall Plan economic revival of Europe well illustrates. However, in terms of both long-run political interests and altruism, helping others to develop is definitely good policy for the United States.

■ FOREIGN LENDING AND THE INTERNATIONAL BANK

Since the United States is more developed industrially than the rest of the world, there is no doubt that South America, the Orient, Europe, and Africa could profitably use our capital for their industrial development. Such capital could be expected to increase their production by more than enough to pay generous interest and repay the principal.

But private American citizens were long loath to lend. Though American corporations will build branch plants abroad and will invest in oil or mineral resources, substantial private lending through Americans' buying risky foreign bonds or stocks disappeared sometime in 1929, seemingly forever. Yet American citizens have savings which they would be glad to lend if such capital transactions could be made safe; and the American nation would benefit by a higher future standard of living from such sound foreign lending.

Therefore the leading nations of the world (except Soviet Russia) came together in 1944 to form the International Bank for Reconstruction and Development and its sister institution, the International Monetary Fund. As its name implies, the International Bank is formed to provide sound long-term loans for reconstruction and development. (The International Monetary Fund is concerned, as we shall see shortly, with short-term credit and the cooperative stabilization of foreign exchange rates.)

The International Bank is easy to understand. The leading nations subscribe toward its 21 billion dollars of capital stock in proportion to their economic importance. (The United States quota is about one-third.) The bank can use its capital to make sound international loans, to people or countries whose projects seem economically sound but who cannot get private loans at reasonably low interest rates.

The International Bank's true importance arises from something greater than the loans that it can make out of its own capital. More important is the fact that it can float bonds and use the proceeds to make loans. (It has successfully floated bonds in the United States, in Switzerland, and elsewhere.) The bonds are safe because they are backed by the credit of all the nations (up to their 100 per cent of quotas). Also, the International Bank can *insure* loans in return for a $\frac{1}{2}$ or 1 per cent premium; private parties can then put up the money, knowing that the Bank's credit is behind the loan.

As a result of extending long-term credits, we can expect to see goods and services in the years ahead flowing out of the United States aimed at international development. If sound, these loans will be repaid in full. If some go sour, the loss will be paid out of the Bank's interest or premium earnings. If still more go sour, the loss will be spread over all the member nations—not on Uncle Sam alone. While the loans are being made, Uncle Sam will be getting jobs (and if spending is already too great, some increase in inflation problems). When the loans are being "serviced" or repaid, America should have an import surplus of useful goods. Production in the borrowing lands will rise by more than enough to pay interest on the loans, and domestic wage and other factor returns will be *greater*, not less, because of foreign capital.

Has the Bank been a financial success? Decidedly. If anything, the Bank may have been too conservative in its practice of lending to self-liquidating projects. By 1967 an embarrassing volume of profits had accumulated. An increasing proportion of these go to the International Development Agency, set up by the Bank to make "soft loans" to nations for education, roads, hospitals, etc.; and to its International Finance Corporation, set up to make loans to foreign development banks for financing private investment projects.[2]

■ THE INTERNATIONAL MONETARY FUND

The International Monetary Fund, like the International Bank, grew out of 1944 international conferences held in Bretton Woods, New Hampshire. It hopes to secure the advantages of the gold standard without its disadvantages; i.e., exchange rates are to be relatively stable, but international cooperation is to replace the previous automatic mechanism; also, countries are to be spared the need for making adjustments that involve deflating themselves into drastic unemployment. It hopes to lessen need for import controls.

Ordinarily, a country will go along paying for its imports by means of its exports or long-term borrowing. Suppose a country, say, England, is in need of short-term credit from the Fund. How does the Fund enable such a debtor country to get hold of dollars, for instance? It does this by extending "purchasing rights." It simply permits the British to buy with British currency some of the Fund's own holdings of dollars. After the British balance of payments has improved, they are expected to buy back with gold (or with dollars) the pounds they have sold to the Fund.

The Fund tries to set up rules and procedures to keep a country from going too deep into debt, year after year. After a country has been piling up debts for a considerable period, certain financial penalties are applied. More important, the Fund's directors consult with the country and make recommendations for remedying the disequilibrium. However, they do not advise a country to create a depression in order to cut its national income down to such a low level that its imports will finally fall to within its means. Instead, the country itself is permitted first to depreciate (or appreciate) its currency by 10 per cent. This tends to restore equilibrium in its trade by expanding its exports and contracting imports.

---

[2] Our own Export-Import Bank also makes foreign loans, e.g., enabling an American exporter to sell machine tools to Brazil on credit.

If this is still not enough to correct the so-called "overvaluation" of the debtor country's currency, the Fund authorities may, after proper consultation, permit still further depreciation of the debtor country's exchange rate. But note this: All changes in rates are to take place in an orderly way. Most of the time, there is to be international stability. There is also provision for flexibility when needed, which is better by far than waiting for a great smash.

At first the Fund was rather a disappointment. The postwar strains turned out to be much larger than people realized in 1944; and the Fund's resources were inadequate to cope with those disequilibria. Since 1955 and the end of the dollar gap, the Fund has become increasingly important. For example, the United States has reinforced its own international resources by drawing on the Fund.

> As an example of the renewed importance of the IMF, consider the sterling crisis faced by the United Kingdom Labor government in the years after November, 1964. This government borrowed several billion dollars from the IMF to support the pound, making the United Kingdom the greatest user of the Fund since its formation. In addition, the IMF helped coordinate the billions of dollars of support for the pound from the United States and continental European countries.
>
> In any future major reforms of international liquidity or any future dollar problems, the International Monetary Fund will undoubtedly play a pivotal role.

■ THE EUROPEAN COMMON MARKET AND THE FREE-TRADE AREA

The last few chapters analyzed the economic gains from freer trade. One way of getting trade impediments down is for several countries to form a customs union. Within such a union, tariffs and quotas might be reduced or banished; but they might still persist with respect to external trade. History provides us with many examples. The 50 states of the United States can be thought of as a large customs union. A century ago the many independent German states formed a *Zollverein*, or customs union.

One of the most exciting international developments of the century has been the formation of the six-nation European Common Market. In 1957 Belgium, France, Italy, Luxembourg, The Netherlands, and West Germany signed treaties to create a Common Market. Subject to exceptions, by 1970–1973 each nation is to eliminate tariffs and import quotas on nonfarm goods produced *within* the area; to set up a common tariff against goods from countries outside the Common Market; and to allow free movement of capital and labor. It looks to become the second-largest free-trade area in the world. If Great Britain is not again excluded by De Gaulle, the Common Market might become the largest area.

Anxious over the progress of the Common Market, seven other European nations have formed the "Outer Seven" free-trade area: this consists of Austria, Denmark, Norway, Portugal, Sweden, Switzerland, and the United Kingdom. This loose federation aims eventually at free trade, but its development thus far does not compare in importance with that of the Six and ultimately it may merge with the Common Market.

> Some economists have worried whether the lowering of tariffs between countries of a bloc is truly a movement toward a more efficient world pattern: "Won't there be a danger that the lower-than-average tariffs between the countries in the union will distort the 'normal' pattern of trade even more than it is already being distorted by separate nations'

tariffs? Won't the difference between the ins and the outs be magnified and represent as serious a distortion as the previous situation?"

Others have replied: "Two wrongs don't make a right. If you can't get rid of trade impediments everywhere, at least get rid of them where you can. Then maybe a few great customs unions can ultimately merge into a worldwide free-trade area."

No definitive answer will cover every case. Perhaps most economists would venture the guess that lowering of tariffs in Europe could have such good effects there on the division of labor as to lead to net benefit for these countries, and ultimately for others.

■ FREER MULTILATERAL TRADE

The Cordell Hull reciprocal-trade program for reducing American and other tariffs has now been with us for more than a quarter of a century. Contrary to common opinion, our high 1930 tariffs have been cut substantially (in some cases they have been halved and then halved again). As a result, careful measurement of the degree to which all the nations of the world restrict trade will show that in 1967 the United States is near the top of the list of "relatively free traders." To be sure, we ought (in our interest as well as in the interest of others) to go even further; and admittedly, foreigners never know when Congress will raise tariffs. Still, those who talk about American trade policy should study the true situation, and not become guilty of the informational lag that was already pointed out in Fig. 35-1 at the end of the last chapter.

All stand to gain if fruitful multilateral trade can be restored. As mentioned before, GATT (the General Agreement on Tariffs and Trade) is a most important development toward international cooperation. The Kennedy Trade Act (1962) looks to a new round of reciprocal tariff cuts, a fitting memorial to the man.

The so-called "Kennedy Round" for multilateral tariff reductions is a good example of the gradual progress being made toward trade liberalization. Actually the 1966–1967 effort was the sixth round of tariff reduction under the auspices of GATT, earlier efforts having taken place in 1947, 1949, 1951, 1956, and 1961. Agreement was made difficult by the wish of certain members of the Common Market, most notably France, to increase protective tariffs on agriculture. Thus, although most geographers and economists are impressed by America's comparative advantage in farm products, the French have always insisted that their higher-cost producers be protected, even if this would entail higher prices to German and other consumers. Indeed, the repeated difficulties placed in the way of Britain's entrance into the Common Market have been related to the strong French stand on this and other matters.

B. INTERNATIONAL TRADE PROBLEMS OF THE FUTURE

Now that we have surveyed the post–World War II institutions of international finance, we can face up to the burning issues that confront America and the world.

■ FROM DOLLAR SHORTAGE TO DOLLAR GLUT

The Marshall Plan and other aid programs soon began to have spectacularly favorable effects on the less-than-most-affluent countries—Japan, Germany, Holland, France, and Italy. Primarily on their own, by a process no one had predicted, they began a miraculous sprint of productivity growth in the 1950s.

This growth in the *competitiveness* of foreign economies, plus the expensiveness of our *cold-war programs* (the Korean conflict, the Viet Nam war, the Atlantic Alliance, etc.), plus our *civilian foreign-aid programs* (in Asia, Latin America, and elsewhere), plus the burgeoning outflow of *direct foreign investments by American corporations* facing juicy profitability opportunities abroad—all these factors led to a gradual cessation of the dollar shortage and an actual swing toward a shortage of foreign currencies.

■ The "dollar shortage" of the 1950s turned into the "dollar glut" (i.e., draining of gold from America) of the 1960s.

At first the drain on our gold supply went unnoticed. Just as the changed situation was beginning to be felt, the 1956–1957 crisis over the Suez Canal gave a temporary reversal to our ebbing trade surplus. But after 1958, everybody could see that a new trend was in the making.

Figure 36-1(a) shows how America has turned into a deficit nation in her balance of payments.[3] How was this international deficit financed? As Fig. 36-1(b) shows, in part it was financed by our shipping gold abroad. By 1967 our gold stock had dropped from its peak of 24 billion dollars in 1949 down to around 12 billion. But in larger part the international deficit was financed by foreigners accepting our short-term IOUs. Figure 36-1(b) shows how liquid claims on us have grown to exceed our gold holdings, even if all gold were released from the need to maintain minimum required ratios against FRB deposit and note liabilities.

Since America probably had a disproportionate share of the world's gold supply in 1950, American experts rather welcomed the first part of the gold drain. Even now, American economists would not be displeased with our present gold stock if they thought that an equilibrium was in clear sight. But Fig. 36-1 gives no assurance of this.

For the 25 years from 1933 to 1958, thanks in part to Hitler and the political uncertainties that sent gold to our shores for safekeeping, American economic policy was *emancipated completely* from any concern for our international balance of payments. Now the honeymoon is long-since over. America has rejoined the human race: we too have a balance-of-payments problem. We had to take it into account when, as in 1960–1965, we wished to lower interest rates in order to help achieve full-employment levels of investment and stimulate the capital formation that leads to faster growth rate of our producible NNP.

■ Every decision made about defense and civilian aid to underdeveloped countries has in the 1960s been limited by the constraint: What will it do to our balance of payments?

---

[3] The deficit shown here is not the "basic deficit" described in Chapter 33. It is the Official Settlements Balance of Payments that has been commonly used since 1965. Thus, for 1965 the United States "basic balance" was shown on page 633 to be −1.932 million dollars (= $ +4,281 surplus on current account minus $6,213 long-term investment outflow). The Official Settlements balance was only −1.3 billion dollars, the difference coming from short-term capital movements. The government also reports a "liquidity" balance, which differs slightly from the Official Settlements balance because some private foreign capital *inflows* into the United States are not included in it.

Chronic foreign deficits weaken the dollar, cause hemorrhage of gold:

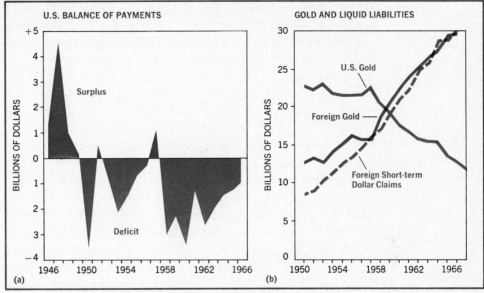

FIG. 36-1. The continued international deficit shows the swing from dollar shortage to over-valuation of the dollar. Although still the owner of the largest amount of gold, America's gold stock has dropped steadily. The rest of the world has increased its amount and share of total gold and has been accumulating short-term liquid claims on us. (Source: U.S. Department of Commerce. This deficit, on an official reserve transactions basis, differs from *basic* deficit of Chapter 33 in that it is affected by changes in short-term investments.)

■ REASONS FOR CHRONIC INTERNATIONAL DEFICIT, 1955–1967

Many reasons are given for America's chronic international deficit. Most have an element of truth in them, but we shall see that the crucial cause for the 1955–1967 period is probably to be found in the vast improvement of technical productivity abroad in recent years. Below are the causes commonly named for the deficit:

1. *Too much inflation here at home.* If a country has more rapid wage and price increases than its neighbor, and if these are not matched by compensating differentials in worker productivity gains, then it is indeed likely to find itself running into a deficit in the balance of international payments.[4]

If we turn from conjecture to fact, an examination of any of the usual over-all index numbers of money prices and wages will show that up to 1965, there had not been more inflation here than abroad. On the contrary, a list of the 20 principal countries of the world shows that the United States came almost at the bottom in terms of price-level increase in the last decade. The same is true of index numbers of money wage rates. Only after 1965 did our price indexes begin to soar.

There is this grain of truth, however, in the overpricing allegation. If one leaves over-all indices and turns to certain important sectoral price indices, it will indeed

[4] For further analysis, see Chapter 33's Appendix discussion on overvaluation of a currency.

be found that American steel prices long rose relative to those abroad. No wonder that Japanese steel invades the Pacific Coast; that foreign steel products such as *barbed wire* (and what could be more American than *that?*) have taken over many of our traditional home markets; that steel from England and Belgium, helped by lengthy domestic strikes and fears of strikes, has got a foothold in our markets. Similar occurrences are found in several of our machinery industries. There the great burst of demand in the equipment boom of 1956–1957 sent our prices soaring, whereas the price rise in steel was thought by the Joint Economic Committee of Congress to be more the result of "cost-push" by wages and maintained profit margins.[5]

We shall see that full employment has, in the last half of the 1960s, created a price-level problem that delays curing of America's basic balance-of-payments deficit.

2. *Overgenerosity in our aid and military programs.* It is natural when thinking of reducing our trade deficit by a billion dollars to think of simply cutting out that much foreign aid and military spending. However, it is somewhat misleading to think that such a cut will reduce the deficit by that same billion, since many of our export credit items are present in the balance of payments only because our government programs have given foreigners the funds to pay for them. Hence, cutting such programs by 1 billion dollars will thereby cut into our private exports and in turn reduce our deficit by something less than a billion, how much less being hard to estimate.

Until Viet Nam, our governmental foreign-aid and military programs had not grown much in relative size; rather, it was more the case that, with the growth in private long-term investment, our surplus on current *private* account was no longer large enough to let our aid programs be quite as generous as they had been previously.[6] After 1965, Viet Nam did become an important aggravator of our payments deficit.

3. *Lack of trust in the dollar.* From 1933 to 1955, the dollar was considered everywhere to be a holding even better than gold. It was *the* key international reserve currency. But what happens when people and governments begin to believe that America is in international disequilibrium? And when they become apprehensive that the dollar *might* be devalued relative to gold? And when, in depressed years like 1961–1963, the interest rates to be earned in the New York market are low relative to rates quoted in London, Amsterdam, or other foreign centers? It is natural enough, under these circumstances, that some governments and private persons should want to take out gold from the United States rather than continue to hold dollar currency or dollar

---

[5] If you plot (1) our declining share of world exports against (2) the post–World War II rise in the ratio of our export prices to those abroad, the result does look a little like a downward-sloping *dd* curve, with the rise in our relative *P* explaining the loss in our relative *Q*.

[6] Even some experts do not realize how high America's surplus on current private account must be if we are to stay in healthy equilibrium with free long-term investment and carry on desired government operations abroad. Equilibrium might then require us to expand our exports of goods and services, in comparison with our imports, by enough to create a current private surplus of as much as 8 to 10 billion dollars! It is quite wrong to think that developing such a sizable surplus would do harm to our trading partners. On the contrary, financial equilibrium and equilibrium of comparative advantage require that this be achieved; inasmuch as we are already supplying the rest of the world with the means to finance our enlarged surplus, they are in no genuine sense harmed. The private surplus must be large enough, however large that is, to fit in with over-all international equilibrium.

IOUs. This so-called "shift in international liquidity preference" can help explain some of the chronic gold drain from our shores.[7]

4. *Discriminations abroad against American goods.* While the dollar was in short supply abroad, it was understandable why barriers against our exports would have been common in other countries. With the Common Market lessening the impediments to intra-European trade, there is good reason to argue that remaining discriminations against American goods be removed or reduced, and some progress has taken place.

5. *The rapid growth of productivity abroad.* From a long-run viewpoint, the fundamental cause of the change in America's international position would seem to be the remarkable speeding up of productivity increase in Western Europe and Japan. Their production technology is still largely behind ours, but the gap, particularly in the goods which we customarily export and specialize in, has been narrowing. Even with real wages rising abroad more rapidly than here, foreigners can produce for themselves more cheaply than we have been producing for them; hence they can outsell us increasingly in third markets, and can even begin to outsell us in our own markets.

6. *High investment abroad by American firms.* The miraculous productivity spurt abroad created tremendous profit opportunities for American corporations. In the last decade, instead of wishing to invest in the underdeveloped world they hastened to build branch factories in Europe and Japan: when a market is growing by 10 per cent a year, how can you help but make high profits?

By 1965 the outflow of direct investments by American firms had become so large that the government introduced a *voluntary* capital control program. The Federal Reserve administered the voluntary program as applied to commercial bank loans; the Department of Commerce administered the voluntary program as applied to corporations. Like all voluntary programs, passage of time tends to decrease its effectiveness, as greater inequities develop and strains are put on public spirit and altruism.

■ EQUILIBRIUM IN THE 1970s?

Is the world moving toward international equilibrium as the 1960s come to a close? Here are the salient facts.

1. Certainly the decade of the 1960s began with the dollar and pound in fairly serious disequilibrium relative to the surplus countries of the Common Market.

> The patterns of comparative advantage were changing, and that is rarely a comfortable transition period. Moreover, it was not simply a question of our shifting factors from one industry to another. So long as our dollar costs tended to be high *all around*, the

---

[7]On the other hand, some experts—such as MIT's C. P. Kindleberger, Stanford's Emile Despres, and Princeton's Fritz Machlup—think the distrust of the dollar is a foolish state of mind that could be easily changed by a bold policy in which America makes the following kind of announcement: "Come exchange your dollars for gold right now at $35 per ounce—if you are foolish enough to want to do so. But don't think you can count on America to buy back that gold from you at a guaranteed price of $35 once again. Instead America may, at *its* pleasure, reduce its buying price of gold— perhaps abandoning gold altogether!" Given such an ultimatum, gold hoarders will realize the error of their ways and, so the argument goes, will swing over in liquidity preference to the dollar.

American currency could be called an "overvalued currency." A country with an over-valued currency tends to incur international deficits, to be undersold in most goods, to have capital outflow, and to be threatened with high unemployment and excess capac-ity. What may be needed is for her money prices and wages to fall relative to those abroad, either falling absolutely or rising less rapidly than theirs. Even if no *real wage* change were needed, we know that it is very far from easy in a modern democratic mixed society to have a deflation in money wage and other costs and in prices.[8]

2. For the first half of the decade there were definite signs of improvement for the dollar. Perhaps the principal reason for this was the over-full-employment on the Continent, which sent their wage and other money costs rising faster than costs in the more sluggish American economy.

3. After 1965, America too reached the goal of full employment. This, combined with the Viet Nam conflict, tended to increase our imports relative to our exports. No longer did our costs grow more slowly than those in many of the surplus countries. In 1967 the experts were no longer certain that the dollar disequilibrium was about to cure itself and enable dismantling of the *ad hoc* measures used to defend the dollar ("tying" of aid, interest-rate equalization tax, voluntary capital control program, etc.).

The important thing is not to try to outguess the murky future of a laissez-faire system left to seek its own equilibrium. Let us see what can be done by public policy to help solve a chronic deficit, or for that matter, a chronic international surplus.

■ THERAPY FOR A CHRONIC DEFICIT

Economists know what are the programs generally needed to reverse a chronic inter-national deficit. These are easy to preach but not so easy to follow.

1. American workers and industry can be urged to *increase domestic technical productivity.* Urging does not always accomplish much, but public pressure on unions and management may help. More important in the long run are supports for scientific research and investment.

2. American exporters can be urged to *improve selling practices* abroad. Since foreign salesmen are also constantly being similarly urged, mere exhortation may not lead to too much improvement in the over-all situation.

3. America can press for further *reductions in discriminations against the dollar.* There are still trade impediments, and the Common Market threatens more.

4. We can ask that the prospering nations of the free world take up a *larger share of the aid, development, and defense burdens.*

5. We could *keep our economy depressed* at home, eschewing low interest rates needed for expansion and growth, diminishing our demand for imports, and putting pressure on profit margins in export industries and making them hungry to drum up

---

[8] A rise in productivity abroad can often increase real wage here by cheapening imports. But (1) if it takes the form of improvement in productivity there in goods we have been specializing in and (2) if it reflects the discovery by American corporations that their know-how can be applied to non-American workers, then the whole process could actually slow up the rate of real wage growth here and could result in a *loss* of American consumer surplus from international trade. Cf. Chapter 33's Appendix.

export business. Such a solution lacks appeal for those concerned with high employment and growth, and they urge greater reliance on fiscal rather than monetary policy.[9] During the 1960s, the Kennedy-Johnson Administration rejected a policy of deliberate creation of unemployment and sluggish growth in order to lessen international deficits. But in 1966–1967, the British Labor Government had to introduce a deliberate slowdown in order to strengthen the weakening pound sterling.

6. There could be a *depreciation of the dollar* relative to other currencies, by a unilateral *devaluation* relative to gold or by some other move.

SECOND-BEST MEASURES   Any or all of the above measures are designed to get rid of any overvaluation of the dollar relative to other currencies. But suppose that they are not feasible in the needed amount, and that America will have to live with an overvalued dollar for some time. A host of new, and somewhat distasteful, measures can combat overvaluation.

7. We can *"tie" foreign-aid grants and loans,* requiring that their proceeds be spent directly in the United States even if our goods cost more. These are actions we join others in deploring; but without a solution of the international deficit, it may be better for the countries aided, for ourselves, and for the world to give tied aid than no aid at all. (Note that congressional cutting of tied aid will not help our payments deficit; and cutting of untied aid by a billion dollars will help our deficit by only a fraction of that sum, since much of our private surplus on current account comes from exports which take place only because of the aid grants and their repercussions.) Already we have tied our own military expenditures in the sense that an item must be bought at home even if it costs 50 per cent more than abroad. This is but one of many piecemeal devaluations or depreciations of the dollar that take place when outright devaluation is not feasible.

8. We can *limit tourism,* by cutting down on the amount of goods that travelers can bring home free of duty. (E.g., the New Frontier reduced the duty-free privilege from $500 per person to $100, a gesture of intention.) If matters got worse, free tourism could be interfered with, as is the case in so many other nations. Thus, in 1966 Wilson's Labor government cut down travel allowances for the British to $140 per year.

9. *Restrictions or tax penalties can be put on foreign investment.* Attracted by the high profits that growth and productivity improvements abroad make possible, as we have seen, there has been a vast outpouring of investment abroad by firms and individuals. Except for the obvious special case of oil discoveries in the Near East and Latin America, the bulk of this investment has not gone to the underdeveloped countries so much as to the developed nations. If one wanted to be simple-minded, one could blame this upsurge of long-term investment for most of the basic deficit.[10]

Reluctantly, Congress passed a so-called "interest equalization tax" of up to 15 per cent on any purchase by an American from a non-American of a foreign stock or

---

[9] To the degree that unemployment at home means low profit opportunities, it might worsen our balance by encouraging more foreign-investment (i.e. more debits)!

[10] In the long run, earnings from these investments would begin to help our deficit.

long-term bond. This was intended as a curb on foreign portfolio investments by Americans. And, as already mentioned, a voluntary program of foreign capital investment control was introduced in 1965 on commercial bank lending abroad and direct corporate foreign investment. Tax rebates on exports could also help our deficit.

10. We could revert to *protectionism* generally. Tariffs and quotas will not raise *real* wages, for the reasons seen in the previous chapters, but they can compensate a little for sticky money wages and an overvalued currency. Such a solution will be deplored by all who value the advantages that come from specialization according to comparative advantage and by all who think America's political advantage lies in our living down our old reputation as a bad neighbor.

11. *We can try to "twist" our interest-rate structure in depressed times.* If the Fed and Treasury force short-term government securities on the market and remove long-term bonds, that can do something toward keeping short-term rates high enough to attract, and keep, mobile international funds seeking highest yields; and at the same time the tight money need not lift the long-term interest rates so crucial for domestic capital formation and prosperity. We can also twist stabilization policy in the direction of expansionary fiscal policy rather than expansionary monetary policy, recognizing, though, that this may stimulate consumption more than investment—and in that sense fail to promote long-term growth. If Congress could institute an "incomes policy," which would keep down the rate of growth of wages and administered prices, that too would be a macroeconomic policy helpful to international equilibrium.

12. Finally, to bring the list to a close, we could hope that *the surplus countries of Europe and Japan would again experience an acceleration of inflation in their cost and price levels.* Money wages on the Continent did in 1960–1967 grow faster than productivity there, and this fact probably did more to promote an ultimate solution of America's basic balance than anything else. Alternatively, if surplus nations would undertake the politically unpopular task of *appreciating* their currencies (as West Germany and Holland did in 1961) and lowering remaining import restraints, the overvalued dollar could be cured without any depreciation on our part or inflation on theirs.

■ STRUCTURAL REFORM OF INTERNATIONAL FINANCE

Is the gold problem of the United States merely symptomatic of a more widespread *malaise?* Growing world production requires growing money supplies; but can gold mining keep up with this need? Growing international trade, and freer trade in a world more susceptible to political and economic irregularities, requires larger liquid reserves for countries to hold as protection against swings in their balance of payments—particularly in mixed economies that will not let the rules of the gold standard dictate internal inflation or depression to achieve Hume's classical equilibration. Will world gold supplies be adequate for this need, particularly in an environment where key currencies like the pound and dollar no longer command the respect that enabled them once to serve as a substitute for gold reserves?

Many economists, remembering the sobering experience of 1929, strongly believe that the whole world is in need of some basic structural reforms to provide needed elasticity in international reserves. They argue that the liquidity pinch has not yet been felt abroad *because the recovering economies have been living off the gold transfusions coincidentally supplied by the dollar problem.* When that problem gets solved, as it must one way or another, they warn that it may be too late to institute the needed structural reforms.

Many plans for structural reform have been propounded, each associated with the name of some illustrious expert (the Triffin Plan, the Bernstein Plan, the Keynes Plan, the Posthuma Plan, and still others). Here we need note only that they fall into three general groups:

Raising the price of gold more or less all around

Creating new international bank money, in much the way that a central bank is able to create new *M* internally

Abandoning stable exchange rates at unchanged parities in favor of "freely floating exchange rates equilibrated by supply and demand."

Of course, there are all kinds of blends and variants of these basic plans.

DEVALUATION WITH RESPECT TO GOLD   Since the long-term trend in gold mining has never kept up with the growth of total physical output, the history of capitalism (and feudalism) has been a history of debasement of the gold content of money everywhere. If liquidity now threatens to be scarce, think how scarce gold would be in the late 1960s if there had not been widespread devaluations in the Depression and post–World War II periods which permit the same number of ounces of gold to do more work. So goes the argument of those who favor raising the price of gold. (Their opponents point out wryly that maybe price levels would not be so high today if countries had not insisted on acting like mixed economies and had instead behaved according to classical principles that provide for long-term falling price levels.)

Suppose the United States were to double the price of gold, from $35 to $70 an ounce. Britain and Canada might do the same. But by multilateral agreement the surplus countries might choose to raise their price for gold by only 80 per cent. The result of such a 100 per cent devaluation of the dollar would be a more moderate depreciation of it relative to the surplus-country currencies. This, it is argued, might be just about the correct change needed to end the dollar's overvaluation and America's chronic deficit. Then freer trade could prevail to the advantage of all. Price levels need not rise much anywhere, the newly revalued reserves instead making it possible for healthy expansion of future output.

Would the surplus countries consent to an appreciation of their currencies, or would they competitively try to match or undercut our devaluation? If the surplus countries are suffering from inflation and overemployment, it might well be to their short- and long-run selfish interest to permit the adjustment that would help us *and* them. (Don't forget that this is not like the case of the Great Depression when each country tried to get more domestic employment.)

What are the arguments against such a change? First, the Soviet Union and South Africa would be the principal beneficiaries from a vast increase in the prices for their mined gold, and neither of these countries is particularly admired by the main Western countries. Second, hoarders of gold would be rewarded for their legal and illegal hoardings. Third, it is considered absurd and wasteful for men and machines to be used up in taking a barren metal out of the ground and storing it in vaults and caves just so that the world can have a stable medium of exchange; and raising gold's price would merely increase the absurdity. Fourth, there is the complicated question of how much America ought to give to her creditors of the "profit" on her gold stock created by the sudden rise in gold's price. Last, and most important, it is hard to get advance agreement in secrecy on such a basic change; yet if it were not all done secretly, rumors would lead to cataclysmic moves to hoard gold.

NEW LIQUIDITY ARRANGEMENTS   At Bretton Woods, Lord Keynes had proposed that a new kind of international currency be created, called "bancor," or anything else. It was to be issued by the International Monetary Fund or by some other international organization; it was to be accorded equivalent status with gold or any other convertible currency used for settling international balances; the rate at which its supply was to be increased, how it would be distributed geographically, and what projects it would help finance—all these were to be decided by responsible international agreement and not by the happenstance of gold discoveries.

Recent proposals have a family resemblance to this general plan. The criticisms they meet are various, some being like the criticisms that Esperanto or other new international languages meet: how can you get all to agree on this proposal rather than some other one? In addition, critics fear that such schemes will become engines for inflation and that it is better to trust random events like gold finds than the sure-to-be-blundering decisions of politics. Yet, under the aegis of the ten leading nations (with only France dragging her heels), some reforms seem bound to come.

FLOATING OR QUASI-FLOATING EXCHANGE RATES   In Chapter 33, we saw that an alternative to the gold standard and stable exchange rates could be a freely flexible exchange rate determined by the *changing balance of supply and demand.* Proponents argue:

> Since we think it optimal to let wheat and other goods adapt themselves to supply and demand rather than have fixed prices, why not apply the same logic to foreign exchange rates? If the demand for the dollar is relatively strong, as in 1945–1950, let the adjustment take place by having the dollar bid up in price until equilibrium is restored (as in Fig. 33-1, page 628). If, as was strongly the case in 1958–1967, the supply of dollars exceeds their demand at preexisting exchange rates, let the dollar be automatically depreciated by market bids. Fluctuation of the exchange rate will keep a currency from being either "overvalued" or "undervalued." Equilibrium will thus be constantly restored by the relative cheapening of exports relative to imports, brought about by variations in the exchange rate and without need of sizable reserves. The export and import industries can make the adjustments without having the whole domestic economy subjected to inflation and deflation. No committee need deliberate about international balances, and the government and people will be free to pursue policies they think optimal.

The usual criticism of these proposals goes thus: Fruitful international trade will be lessened if, to the ordinary risks of doing business, every importer, exporter, and lender must add the inevitable uncertainties involved in fluctuating exchange rates. Those favoring floating exchanges reply:

> Just as there is an organized futures market for wheat, in which speculators take on their own shoulders the risks of future crop and demand uncertainties, so will there grow up in free exchange markets future or forward price quotations, by means of which any trader in goods can hedge-shift onto the shoulders of speculators all the risks from the exchange-rate side. The cost of such hedging won't be exorbitant.

Critics reply:

> The analysis of hedging and speculation in a market for wheat (as described in the Appendix of Chapter 21) cannot be confidently applied to foreign exchange markets. Speculation in foreign exchange is likely to be destabilizing, since there is no natural par of supply and demand set by crop conditions and basic human demands for wheat. Instead, when the dollar is weak, all the speculators will pounce on it and make it weaker; they will force America into depreciation and into internal inflation, and thereby the new proper level for the dollar will be permanently lower, rewarding the speculators for their bear raid. If the authorities resist such raids by keeping a tight rein on the domestic money supply, price level, and NNP level, they are as much restrained by the balance of payments as under a stable exchange standard: so why give up advantages of stable exchange rates if you are going to have, in any case, their disadvantages?

Evidently, this is a thorny problem with many facets.[11] So drastic a change in practice does not seem now on the horizon for the chief large nations of the world. Yet this is not a settled question.

And many compromise procedures have been suggested, such as that the "gold points" described in Chapter 33 be artificially *widened,* so that the exchange rate can float freely within a sizable (but limited) range; and that countries with an overvalued currency, like the dollar, be permitted to depreciate by a *small* amount per year, thereby not attracting destabilizing speculators but still achieving a 10 or 15 per cent change in parity over a decade or more.[12] This "sliding-peg" scheme is gaining adherents.

We leave these issues unsettled. One does not have to be cynical, but merely realistic, to guess that if fundamental changes are to come, they will come in the wake of some international crisis rather than as a result of premeditated planning and agreement. What is clear is that the world must always steer a path between the rigidity that leads to ultimate breakdown, and the flexibility that invites disregard of all the discipline needed to prevent strong inflation. And it is also clear that a large country like the United States cannot go on indefinitely in international disequilibrium.

[11] A small country like Canada had a floating exchange rate for many years until 1962: in terms of the American dollar, the Canadian dollar fluctuated between $1.05 and $0.92. The experiment was not conclusive, in part because the government did not follow the advice of Canadian economists who argued that the slowdown in the Canadian economy in the late 1950s should have been met by expansionary domestic monetary policy, in full knowledge that this would cause the Canadian dollar to float downward.

[12] See Fig. 33-2 on page 644 for details of this "sliding peg" reform proposal.

■ CONCLUSION

While the new trade trend does create problems for America, it will be noted that it does imply a great improvement for the rest of the world. No mature nation expects things always to go its way; and to the degree that we are cosmopolitan in viewpoint, we shall welcome improvements in living standards elsewhere in the free world.

At the same time one realizes that there will be hard decisions to make at home. With the cost-push phenomena mentioned in the next chapters and a balance-of-payments problem, the challenge will be great for the American economy to make the neoclassical synthesis of old and new principles prevail. It would be a tragedy if, after learning so much about stability and growth, modern nations were now to fall back into the slough of stagnation where the classical precepts lose relevance.

SUMMARY

A. MODERN TRENDS AND INSTITUTIONS OF INTERNATIONAL FINANCE

1 ■

Expanded exports—as in World Wars I and II—will have multiplier expansionary effects on a country. If previously it had unemployment and excess capacity, the result will be more jobs and output. If previously it had inflationary pressures, the result will be an intensification of them.

2 ■

The beggar-my-neighbor policies of the depressed thirties, by which each nation vainly tries to export its unemployment abroad, are self-defeating.

3 ■

The International Bank, the International Monetary Fund, Marshall Plan and military-aid programs, Point Four, the reciprocal-trade program for tariff reduction, the European Common Market—all these are important factors in the postwar bid for more rational world trade.

4 ■

The first decade after World War II was the period of "dollar shortage." The dollar was "undervalued" in the sense that the other countries of the world, disrupted by war and with high cost structures, were avid to buy from us more than we wanted to buy from them. The sizable devaluations abroad in 1949—plus our Marshall Plan and other aid programs, America's cold-war spending, and finally, the miraculous spurt of productivity in the Common Market and Japan—all brought dollar shortage to an end.

B. INTERNATIONAL TRADE PROBLEMS OF THE FUTURE

5 ■

In the last decade, basic disequilibrium in America's balance of payments became evident: our substantial surplus on private current account simply was not large enough to offset (*a*) our substantial government defense and aid programs, and (*b*) the large volume of long-term foreign investment by American firms seeking the high profits offered in the miracle-growth countries abroad. The testimony of this "basic international deficit" was reinforced by the testimony of the more conventionally reported international deficit, shown in Fig. 36-1, which reveals some distrust of the dollar.

6 ■

No single factor can account for the reversal of dollar shortage. Certainly a basic cause seems to be the more rapid rate of growth in productivity in Western Europe and Japan than in America rather than any upswing in our generosity or domestic inflation. This "basic imbalance" in the annual international flows places important constraints on domestic growth and stabilization policies. However, continuing cost inflation abroad may lessen the dollar's "overvaluation."

No single remedy for a chronic payment disequilibrium can be prescribed. Steps to improve the situation would include sharing by others of the aid and military burdens, lessening of discriminations, programs designed to improve our productivity and selling efficiency, better control over the cost-push pressures at home, and various other measures. Resort to protectionism and controls on foreign investment and trade would involve a sacrifice of economic and political advantage, and devaluation of our seemingly overvalued currency would be a last desperate act of emergency. The recent increase in well-being abroad should be noted even if it means adjustments here (and even possibly a slight retardation in our growth in real wages and consumer's surplus from international trade). Perhaps the crucial question for the 1970s will be this:

Can America's full employment be maintained with price and wage drifts that are a bit more moderate than those which prevail in the over-full-employment economies of the surplus nations? If so, gradually basic equilibrium will be restored.

7 ■

America's gold drain, some fear, has been covering up a long-run problem of too little international liquidity, as gold mining fails to keep up with the need for international reserves. Raising the price of gold, creating new international means of payments and reserves, and adherence to freely floating rather than stable exchange rates have been alternative proposals for basic international reform. Perhaps the greatest probability favors an enhanced role of the IMF in providing new international liquidity for growing world trade.

Critics evaluate differently the pros and cons of these proposals and blends of them. They remain unsettled issues of great fascination.

QUESTIONS FOR DISCUSSION

1. Describe analytically post–World War II changes in the position of the dollar.

2. Contrast and compare the International Bank and Monetary Fund.

3. Draw up a list of what you consider our most important postwar economic problems. If you were in Congress, what would you do about them?

4. What effects can one expect from the European Common Market?

5. "Not a single American industry should be sacrificed in the name of the GATT program for realizing freer multilateral trade." Do you agree?

6. Describe the extent of our postwar aid to the rest of the world. Was this merely "generosity"? Did generosity play any important role?

7. Contrast "dollar shortage and glut." Diagnose and prescribe.

8. Apply to an overvalued pound the reasonings used earlier for the dollar.

9. Why would you expect an interest rate equalization tax of 15 per cent on all foreign long-term securities to help our capital accounts and international deficit. As "voluntary" control programs on bank and corporate investing abroad begin to spring leaks, how might explicit taxing of foreign investment help us buy the time needed to reattain equilibrium?

10. Review your understanding of the following concepts:

exports, foreign investment, and the
   multiplier
International Bank and Fund
Marshall Plan and other aid programs
Point Four
common market, customs union

dollar shortage, chronic deficit
productivity growth abroad
floating versus stable exchange rates
overvaluation, undervaluation
devaluation and gold's price
international liquidity plans

Part 6 Current Economic Problems

37 The Theory of Growth

The key word in most economic discussions these days is "growth." Why could Germany and Japan grow faster than the United States and the Soviet Union in the 1950s? Can a mixed enterprise system like those of the United States or Western Europe maintain rates of percentage growth as great as those of the U.S.S.R.? Or will Russia in the last part of this century surpass our standards of living? In a resource-poor country like India, can the desperate race between exploding population and improving technology of mechanized production have a happy outcome?

All the tools of economic analysis developed in this book are needed to throw light on such difficult and important social problems. This chapter will apply the *principles* of economic theory to the process of growth and development, in preparation for the next chapters' applications.[1]

■ STAGES OF HISTORY

Napoleon agreed with Voltaire that history is but "a fable agreed upon." It was long the fashion to regard economic development as proceeding according to a timetable. Dr. Spock can guess that a baby at so many weeks will begin to see things, and he can make predictions about when it will walk and talk. Often he may err, but *it is remarkable how predictable the stages of biological growth prove to be.* Scholars used to think economic history could be treated in the same way.

Friedrich List, in his 1841 *National System of Political Economy,* was one of the first to divide economic history into stages. Especially in Germany, this became a popular notion a century ago. A new group of scholars, called the Historical School, came near to saying: "Throw away fancy theories. Grub in the facts. Collect them. Sort and sift them. Let them tell their own story."

[1] For a short course, this chapter can be skipped. Or skip the theoretical discussion of pp. 710–716.

The first step for any scientist is indeed to maintain a respect for the facts. But alas, it is not the last. *The facts never tell their own story.* Truth, like beauty, is oft in the eye of the beholder. No two writers ever seem to be told the same fables of development by the accumulated almanacs of facts. Some, and they included Karl Marx (1818–1883), saw in history a one-way evolution:

PRIMITIVE CULTURE First, there were marauding hunters and self-sufficient tribal families cultivating crops. (Supposedly they still survive in some isolated jungles.)

FEUDALISM Gradually, as elbow room began to be scarce, the primitive economy was succeeded by feudalism. In the Middle Ages, a settled chain of command from nobility down to serf governed all economic and social life.

CAPITALISM Whether or not one thought the Middle Ages idyllic, feudalism in its turn was brought to an end when the periods of the Renaissance and Reformation ushered in the commercial and industrial revolutions. Peasants were alienated from the soil and forced into the cities as a proletariat. Rivers were dammed to harness water, and the invention of the steam engine enabled the energy of wood and coal to replace the energy of beast and man. The Calvinist ethic helped to create business-minded entrepreneurs. As if in a play, the curtain came down on feudalism and mankind was supposedly ushered onto the stage of bourgeois, middle-class capitalism. (Of course, isolated countries like Japan were not expected to move from feudalism to capitalism in exactly the same time periods; but when their time came, the process could be expected to be qualitatively similar even if more compressed in duration.)

Self-satisfied historians of the Victorian age, like Macaulay or Herbert Spencer, looked upon the evolution of society as an ascent of man toward higher forms. But now that the more or less perfect state of Victorian capitalism had been reached, they thought evolution could have its final rest. All that remained was further progress toward removing tariffs and the few other governmental fiats still interfering with the laissez-faire market place. Spencer could contemplate with mathematical certainty the withering away of the state and the supremacy of free markets. Invention by science, better education of the masses, and individual initiative could be expected to produce steady gains in living standards in this best of all possible worlds.

SOCIALISM AND COMMUNISM Having eaten of the fruit of the tree of evolution, why should men think that the play of history has to be written in only three acts? In a country like Germany, which had never been imbued with the tradition of individual and business freedom, philosophers thought that capitalism, too, was but a passing stage, to be succeeded in its turn by state socialism or communism, just as capitalism had succeeded dying feudalism. Marx and Engels wrote in *The Communist Manifesto:* "The modern bourgeois society has sprouted from the ruins of feudal society . . . The modern laborer . . . becomes a pauper . . . What the bourgeoisie therefore produces . . . are its own grave diggers. Its fall and the victory of the proletariat are equally inevitable."

■ FACT AND FICTION

Events rarely agree with fable.[2] Thus, the revolutions in France and Germany that Engels and Marx predicted to each other in their letters failed to materialize in the weeks, months, and years as they had confidently projected. And real wages, instead of falling or remaining constant in the decades since Marx's 1867 *Das Kapital*,[3] turn out on statistical examination to have been rising dramatically under industrial capitalism. Even the profit rate stubbornly refused to follow the law of decline predicted for it and instead oscillates and wanders without any strong trend.

It is true that *around the turn of the century there seemed to be a burgeoning of monopolies in advanced economies*. But it turned out that even the most capitalistic democracy, the United States, could and did produce antitrust legislation to curb this development; and study of the statistics of concentration of market shares among a few big oligopolists suggests that monopolistic concentration is less at mid-century than it was at the beginning. It is true that the Great Depression of the 1930s was one of the worst the capitalistic system has ever known; but it is also true that a mixed economic system subsequently replaced rugged individualism and *laissez faire*. The mixed economy introduced fiscal and monetary policies to moderate business cycles and control chronic slumps. We live in a world no prophet ever predicted!

We are thus warned to place limited confidence in the allegedly scientific proofs that one stage in history must inevitably be succeeded by a particular next stage. Nikita Khrushchev, when he said to an American audience, "We will bury you . . . your grandchildren will be communists," was repeating what he had learned in an elementary Russian economics textbook. Critics of Russia should not make a similar mistake about immutable timetables of development. It may involve wishful thinking to argue, as some scholars have done: "True, the U.S.S.R. is now showing a faster percentage rate of growth than the U.S. But wait until she becomes as mature as we; then she'll *have* to slow down!" Right-wing determinism is as poorly founded as left-wing.

This sketch of the development of the mixed economy is all too brief, but it represents a fair summary of the views of historians on this side of the Iron Curtain. Since it is completely rejected by communist scholars, Voltaire and Napoleon were wrong: apparently, "history is a fable *not* agreed upon." Let us turn now to various economic models which can help us to understand history rather than to compress it into neat explanations that pretend to predict the future with certainty. Our task is to understand the actual development of wages and profits, of labor and capital, and of national product.

[2]M. I. Rostovtzeff, *Social and Economic History of the Roman Empire* (New York, 1926), showed that an elaborate system of international markets and trade in nonluxury goods existed long before the Middle Ages. Compound interest appears on Babylonian cuneiform tablets, and some nations are repeating in the 1960s the worst errors of historic mercantilism. Neither progress nor perpetual oscillation correctly portrays the richness of economic history.

[3]Translated as *Capital,* and ultimately including posthumous Volume II (1885) and Volume III (1894).

■ THE "MAGNIFICENT DYNAMICS" OF SMITH AND MALTHUS

In *The Wealth of Nations* (1776), Adam Smith wrote a handbook of economic development. He preached the great efficiency that comes from specialization, division of labor, and exchange. He stressed the need to remove the blundering hand of mercantilistic governments; to cultivate attitudes of honesty, zeal, and thriftiness; to unleash the competitive profit motive, which would—as if led by an Invisible Hand—achieve the maximum well-being of all.

LABOR THEORY OF VALUE IN A GOLDEN AGE   Smith had also a theory of dynamic development. He and Malthus began with a hypothetical golden age—"that original state of things, which precedes both the appropriation of land and the accumulation of stock"—when labor alone counted, when land was freely available to all, and before the use of capital had begun. What determined pricing and distribution in this simple and timeless state? Answer: The labor theory of value.

To see this, recall from Chapter 2 Smith's famous case of deer and beaver (pages 28–29). Suppose 2 hours of hunting yields 1 deer; or 4 hours yields 1 beaver. Then the price ratio between deer and beaver will be set by comparative labor time alone: the price of 1 beaver will equal 2 deer. Why 2 deer per beaver? Because the price ratio can be computed in necessary labor time as 4 hours (of sweaty work)/2 hours (of sweaty work). This determination of price by labor cost alone would apply no matter how many goods there were; and it would be enforced in any primitive market by having hunters shift from one good to the other if ever that other good's price got out of line and offered a profit advantage. It is still true that supply and demand is operating in this golden age; but the situation is so simple that we do not need elaborate *dd* and *ss* curves. The long-run *ss* curves for the different goods are simple horizontal lines at the stated labor costs; so long as there is enough demand to have the goods produced at all, labor costs will be determining. (NOTE: Demand is still there in the background; thus, if it would cost 10 hours to hunt a skunk, and yet nobody received any utility from skunks, skunks would not be hunted and would not be bought and sold at a price of 10 hours, or of 5 deer.)

POPULATION GROWTH   Now consider Smith-Malthus dynamics. Life is pleasant in the golden age. Babies are born, and the population doubles about every 25 years. Since there is plenty of land, people move west and spill over onto more acres. National output exactly doubles as population doubles. Price ratios of deer and beaver remain exactly as before. What about real wages? Real wages still get all the national income, there being as yet no subtractions for land rent or interest on capital. What is the real wage per hour? So long as land can expand proportionally to the expansion of labor, the law of diminishing returns cannot come into operation. The wage rate per hour remains at one-half deer or at one-fourth beaver, as determined by labor productivity.

That would be the end of the story, unless some clever inventor found a new way of doing in 1 hour what used to take 2 hours. This would raise the national product per capita. Such a balanced improvement would leave the price ratio of beaver to deer unchanged; but it would double the real wage rate.[4]

SCARCE LAND AND DIMINISHING RETURNS   Even had golden ages ever existed, they could not have lasted once all land became fully populated. As we saw in Chapter 2, T. R. Malthus pointed to this flaw in the happily expanding economy. Once the frontier of virgin land disappears, new laborers begin to crowd onto existing cultivated soils. For the first time, private property in land springs up; now land is scarce, and a rent is charged to ration it.

Growth does take place in this classical world of Smith-Malthus following on the golden age. Population grows, and so does national product. But product cannot grow proportionally to labor. Why? *Because with new laborers added to fixed land, each worker now has less land to work with.* Naturally, therefore, the law of diminishing returns (of Chapters 2 and 27) comes into operation. The increasing labor-land and decreasing output-land ratios mean a declining contribution of each last (or marginal) worker to product, and hence declining real wage rates.

As David Ricardo, a later classical economist, pointed out:

■ A conflict of interests arises between classes. More babies mean lower per capita incomes and lower wage rates; lower wage rates mean higher rent rates per acre of land. Landlords gain as labor loses. This is why Thomas Carlyle criticized economics as the "dismal science."

PARADISE LOST AND REGAINED   How bad can things get? Gloomy Malthus thought, at least in his first edition of 1798, that the end of economic development could be only an equilibrium down at *the minimum level of subsistence.* Above this subsistence wage, population would continue to grow; below it, population would die off; only at this level could there be lasting equilibrium (as we saw in earlier discussion of Malthus).

[4]The graphical production-possibility frontier of Fig. 2-9(a), page 28, showed all this. For a society with 100 hours of labor, it was drawn as a straight line going from the intercept on the vertical axis of the 50 deer producible with that much labor to the intercept on the horizontal axis of 25 beaver. The absolute slope of this *p-p frontier* would give the 2/1 price ratio prevailing at any point where both goods were being produced and consumed. (The marginal-utility and indifference-curve analysis of Chapter 22 would still be needed to tell *where* society ends up on the *p-p frontier.*)

A doubling of labor productivity in all industries would move the *p-p frontier* out in a parallel position so as to depict an exact doubling of national product. The interested reader can show that an invention which tripled the productivity of beaver hunting, while only doubling that of deer hunting, would flatten the shifted-out curve, changing the price ratio from 2/1 (equals 4 hours per beaver ÷ 2 hours per deer) to 4/3 (equals 4/3 hours per beaver ÷ 1 hour per deer). Now the real wage rate has risen, but unequally when computed in terms of the different goods: the real wage has tripled in terms of beaver, but only doubled in terms of deer; lovers of fur coats have gained more than lovers of venison. (NOTE: Suppose laborers are not homogeneous. If men are *everywhere* twice as productive as women, Marx and Ricardo would redefine socially necessary labor units, treating 1 man as 2 basic labor units, etc. But if men are *unequally* superior to women in different jobs—being twice as productive in beaver, thrice as productive in deer, and half as productive in potatoes—the labor theory of value breaks down: now we must know the demand condition of non-Marxian economics to determine equilibrium prices.)

Biological fecundity was a fact of nature; diminishing returns was a fact of nature. Only sentimentalists could refuse to face the sad facts of life prevailing once man had left the golden Garden of Eden. It is for precisely these reasons that Adam Smith had earlier said: Lucky is a nation that is growing rapidly, for it has not yet made its sad rendezvous with its destined equilibrium at the minimum of subsistence. Sad is that nation which has reached the stationary equilibrium of the subsistence level, where deaths just cancel out births.

What did Malthus forget, or at least underestimate? He failed to realize how technical innovation could intervene—not to *repeal* the law of diminishing returns, but to *more than offset* it. He stood at the brink of a new century and failed to anticipate that the succeeding two centuries would show the greatest scientific gains history has ever recorded.

■ DETAILED ECONOMIC ANALYSIS OF SMITH-MALTHUS

To understand the world's population problem for the next centuries—and the problems of India, Indonesia, and China in the next two decades—we must master the above classical model, which may have more *future* relevance than it has had for us since Malthus' time. As a bonus, the same graphical tools will apply when we investigate the role of capital formation as a factor of growth for Germany, Japan, the United States, and the less developed countries of the world.

Table 37-1 and Fig. 37-1 show succinctly how the tendency of population to grow when the wage is above the level of minimum of subsistence will (1) end the golden age of abundant and free land, and (2) lead to an economic growth path that approaches a stationary equilibrium at the minimum of subsistence.

Table 37-1 shows the decline in wage rate when the fixity of land keeps output from growing as fast as labor. Column (1) shows unchanged land. Column (2) shows growing labor. Column (3) shows the resulting growth in output, which, because of the fixity of land, is *less* than proportional to labor growth. All the remaining information can be computed from these production-function data alone.

To get the declining wage rate of Column (4), we have to repeat Chapter 27's calculation of what the *last* worker *adds* to total product. (Recall that this is termed the marginal-physical-product of each of the identical workers.) Let us add one worker to 1,000 existing workers at A'. Note that output rises from $Q = 8,000$ to $Q = 8,008$ units. This gives extra product per extra worker of 8; so the marginal-product and real wage rate must then be 8 units of output per worker. Check that the extra product and wage does fall to 5.0 at B, to 4.2 at E, and finally to zero at Z, where land is so overcrowded as to be unable to produce any extra output regardless of added labor.

To get the relative share of labor in the net national product, we multiply the wage rate of each worker by the number of workers. Then we divide this total wage bill, wL, by total NNP, Q. Note that labor's share in Column (5) soon falls from 100 per cent of NNP to 75 per cent, and ultimately down to 0 per cent. Who gets the remaining share? By our assumption that there is no capital to clutter up the labor-and-land model, all other returns must go for land rent. With total acres unchanged,

Diminishing returns from population growth ends classical development:

	(1) ACRES OF LAND	(2) MAN-DAYS OF LABOR	(3) OUTPUT OF FOOD	(4) WAGE IN FOOD PER DAY	(5) LABOR'S SHARE OF NNP, %	(6) RENT IN FOOD PER ACRE
A	1,000	500 501	4,000 4,008	8	100	0
A'	1,000	1,000 1,001	8,000 8,008	8	100	0
B	1,000	3,000 3,001	20,000 20,005	5	75	5
E	1,000	6,000 6,001	33,600 33,604.2	4.2	75	8.4
Z	1,000	8,000 8,001	39,000 39,000	0	0	39

TABLE 37-1. RELATION OF OUTPUT TO LABOR AND LAND. Higher labor-land density reduces output per man, lowers the marginal-product wage, and hence raises rent per acre.

FIG. 37-1. Population growth moves us from the golden age of A, A', and a down the diminishing-returns marginal-product curve dd, until the Malthusian equilibrium at intersection with ss supply curve of subsistence wage. The fall in real wage rate from a to b to e implies rising rent rates along the "factor-price frontier" ff. Because inventions shift dd and ff upward and rightward, historically the real wage rose from B to B' to B'' levels, with rent rising from b to b' to b''.

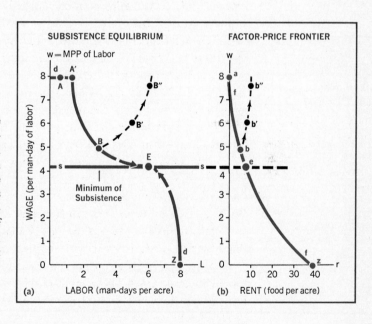

we simply divide up land's calculated share of total output by the fixed number of acres. Obviously, the rent per acre must therefore *rise* in Column (6) as the wage rate *falls* in Column (4), just as David Ricardo warned.

■ GRAPH OF MALTHUSIAN DEVELOPMENT

Figure 37-1 depicts all this. In Fig. 37-1(a), we see the wage rate declining as the law of diminishing returns pushes labor's marginal productivity downward. What keeps the wage from falling down to zero on this dd demand curve for labor? Actually, it stops falling where *dd* intersects the *ss* horizontal supply curve set by the minimum wage at which people can subsist and just barely reproduce their numbers. The Malthusian equilibrium at *E* is a gloomy one.

Gloomy or not, it does represent a *stable* equilibrium. Test it. Let a plague temporarily reduce numbers, moving us to the left of *E*. Real wages then become high (as they actually did after the Great Plague of 1665), standing at a point on the *dd* curve above *E*. But the system cannot stay there. With wages high enough to cause population to grow, we again move gradually back toward the equilibrium at *E*, as indicated by the converging brown arrows. (Show that a temporary growth of population beyond *E*, as used to result from an unusual run of good harvests, will mean a wage rate so much below subsistence as to kill people off until the arrow moves us up *dd* back to *E*.)

Figure 37-1(b) shows that the rent rate per acre rises as the wage rate per hour falls. On what may be called "the factor-price frontier" (shown as *ff*), landlords are seen to be better off at the high-rent Malthusian subsistence equilibrium *e* than they were in the earlier golden age at *a*. No wonder some landlords greeted with joy the introduction of the white potato, which enabled people to live on cheaper calories, and hence in effect lowered the old *ss* subsistence curve and raised equilibrium rents. And no wonder some few landlords regarded the spreading of birth-control information as a threat to their own standards of living. One man's slavery is another man's comfort.

The Ricardians actually exaggerated the conflict of class interest. While population growth might imply higher rent per acre, they were wrong to think it had to imply a larger *percentage share* of NNP going to land. Note in Column (5) of Table 37-1 that labor keeps getting 75 per cent of the total, even when the wage rate drops from *B* to *E* and the rent rises from *b* to *e*.[5]

■ END OF THE LABOR THEORY OF VALUE

The simple labor theory of value, which said that the price ratios of goods can be predicted from labor costs alone independently of the utilities which bring out a demand for the goods, has thus been refuted along the lines of Chapter 2's pages 28–29. Costs of production now include rent as well as wage payments. Two goods, like food and clothing, may now have equal labor costs per unit, but if food requires more land cost per unit than clothing does, they will no longer sell on a one-to-one basis.

[5] Historically, pure land rent has become a declining fraction of NNP. Edward Denison, in his study of American growth, estimates that land accounts for barely 3 per cent of product today as against 9 per cent before World War I. Colin Clark's estimates for various countries of the world also suggest that industrialized nations are able to substitute capital and labor for scarce land. E. Denison, *The Sources of Economic Growth in the United States* (Committee for Economic Development, New York, 1962); C. Clark, *Conditions of Economic Progress*, 3d ed. (Macmillan, London, 1957). Although modern science enables us to make nitrates and nylon out of air and of plentiful products like coal and oil rather than having to pay high rents to scarce natural nitrate resources in Chile or to silkworm-cultivation facilities in Japan, natural resources still command high scarcity rents; they represent a generalization of the simpler classical concept of nature's gift of fixed land. Land is not included in the later capital statistics.

Worse than that from the standpoint of an advocate hankering for a labor theory of value, suppose that people in a capitalistic or socialistic state shift their demand toward producing more food and less clothing. This must make the price of food *rise* relative to that of clothing. Why? Because food requires more land per worker than clothing does. Hence, the fixed land becomes more scarce when people want more of the product that is "land-intensive," thus bidding up rent at the expense of the wage.

   ■ Under neither socialism nor capitalism can we succeed in predicting commodity prices from labor requirements alone, taking no account of the pattern of tastes and demand and its effects on scarcity of nonlabor factors.[6]

What about labor's right to *all* the product? Labor is the only input that is human and can sweat, laugh, cry, and pray. True. Yet, even though dirt cannot sweat or cry, it does contribute toward the growing of potatoes.

One who wants to make a logical case for labor's being "exploited" should not handicap himself by a simple labor theory of value. If his philosophy or that of his state dictates it, he may challenge the *title* to land of those who call themselves landlords and their *right* to rents. He may claim that only the peasants have a valid title to the land and to rent, or that only the state does. Who receives rents is an ethical or legal problem. But whatever its solution, rational use of land does require that a rent cost be charged the consumers who buy its products and the factors that are best fitted to work with it. (Recall the Appendix to Chapter 32 on efficient socialist pricing.)

■ TECHNICAL ADVANCE AND CLASSICAL GROWTH THEORY

As mentioned, real wages have risen historically, not fallen. Population has not stabilized. Land rents per acre have risen surprisingly little and, relative to other factor-prices, have actually declined. It is evident that life has not consisted of a movement down an unchanged factor-price frontier or marginal-product curve. Inventions of science, of engineering, and of managerial practice have *shifted* the curves of Fig. 37-1 rightward and upward. The black lines of progress—$BB'B''$ and $bb'b''$—show the actual course of history; the reader is invited to draw on his copy of Fig. 37-1 the shifted *dd* and factor-price frontiers that correspond to B' or B'' and to b' or b''. Such shifts have more than won the race with diminishing returns, making the Malthusian equilibrium point of subsistence unrealistic in Western economies.

Not all inventions are *equally* favorable to labor and land. Thus, inventions which help to drain swamps or to grow more food on the same acres of land might help wages more than they help rents. Some economists would call these "land-saving inven-

[6] Footnote 4 has pointed out that, in the golden age of free land, society's production-possibility schedule was a straight line with slope determined by labor productivities alone. Now with land scarce and more important in food than in clothing production, the production-possibility schedule is bowed out for the reasons explained in page 29's discussion of the law of increasing (relative) cost. The slope of the *p-p frontier* which determines the competitive price ratio now depends on where people's demand leaves us. (It can be shown that Ricardians erred in thinking they could "get rid of land as a complicating factor" by going out to "the external margin" of poor, no-rent land upon which production was so low that all its costs would have to go to labor alone.)

tions." In contrast, any inventions that tended to raise rents more than wages, thereby tending to increase landlords' share of NNP, might be called "labor-saving" inventions. In between would be the case of inventions that raised both factor returns by the same percentage, leaving relative shares of NNP unchanged: these might be called "neutral inventions." In the history of the West, inventions have appeared to be land-saving on balance; but few inventions have been so land-saving as actually to lower rents *absolutely* along with lowering them relative to wages.

The ghost of Carlyle should be relieved to know that economics, after all, has not been a dismal science. It has been the cheerful, but impatient, science of growth.

■ RICARDO-MARX-SOLOW MODELS OF CAPITAL ACCUMULATION

So far we have stressed the classical preoccupation with scarce land. In the remainder of this chapter, we shall survey the more important model of capital and labor, pushing land to the side as being less important for the developed part of the world. We can now use exactly the same tools.

> ■ *Basic assumption of capital-labor model.* One factor grows relative to the other. Now population will be regarded primarily as a noneconomic variable, being stationary (or growing slowly for sociological reasons). Accumulation will make capital the varying factor. In an oversimplified model where output is produced by a relatively fixed and a relatively varying factor, the law of diminishing returns sets in. The return of the augmented factor falls; the return of the relatively scarce labor factor rises. In the absence of technical change, a stationary state of equilibrium will be reached.

NOTIONS OF CAPITAL   It is now capital,[7] written as K, that is the factor growing relative to labor, L. Capital goods consist of a great variety of things: machines of various kinds, plants and houses, tools, raw materials and goods in process (seed grain, growing wheat plants, harvested wheat, flour, dough, warm loaves, wrapped and delivered bread), and canned and frozen edibles. Society can sum the market values of these physical goods to get total wealth or total capital value; but it cannot command a million dollars of electric generators to transmute themselves into a million dollars of oil-refining equipment.

It is true, however, that as generators wear out, the resources which could have gone to replacing them can be shifted to turn out extra refining equipment; the financial counterpart of this physical alchemy is to have investors in the generator industry take the money funds accruing on account of depreciation there and transfer them over to finance extra investment in the equipment industry. Result: although the total balance sheet of money capital may show a practically unchanged total and although the national-income statistician shows only a cancellation of one kind of disinvestment against another kind of investment, still society has managed to change the physical composition of its capital stock without undergoing any change in current consumption of goods.

[7] Chapter 30 and Appendix discussed capital theory and problems of measuring it.

EFFECTS OF CAPITAL DEEPENING   What happens to per capita output when capital grows relative to labor? Recall what happened to output per acre when labor grew relative to land. Output there grew less than proportionally to the growth in labor, and the wage had to *fall*. A similar law of diminishing returns comes into operation in our oversimplified model whenever one factor (such as capital) grows faster than the other factor (such as labor) with all technical change absent:

1. Output will not grow in proportion to the growth in the capital stock.

2. The return to capital, the interest rate per annum—or what is the same thing if we rule out risk and technical change, the profit rate—will fall as capital deepens.

3. What happens to the wage rate now that each man works with more capital goods and with the more intricate capital goods the economy can now afford in the environment of a lower interest and profit rate? Just as the rent earned by relatively scarce land rose in Fig. 37-1, here the competitive wage return to relatively scarce labor will rise, as men become worth more to capitalists and meet with spirited bidding up of their market wage rates.

4. Higher wage rates and lower interest rates do *not* necessarily imply a higher percentage *share* for labor at the expense of the percentage share of capitalists. Why not? Because the increase in capital relative to labor might offset (or even more than offset) the decline in the interest rate and the rise in the real wage.[8]

5. Finally, since output (per capita or total) grew less than in proportion to the increase in capital (per capita or total), the capital-output ratio would rise in the absence of technical change (e.g., from capital value being 3 times annual NNP up to $3\frac{1}{2}$ times).

Here is a final summary:

Deepening of capital (unchanged technology)

Capital/labor up: interest or profit rate down: wage rate up: capital/output up

---

■ DEEPENING OF CAPITAL IN DIAGRAM FORM

Figure 37-2(a) and (b) needs no numerical table. It is like Fig. 37-1(a) and (b); but now capital is the relatively growing factor. Capital's amount per capita is given on the horizontal axis of (a), and its interest or profit return goes on the vertical axes. And now labor is the relatively fixed factor, and its wage goes on the horizontal axis of (b) just the way land rent did in Fig. 37-1(b).

In the absence of technical change, capital accumulation takes us down the *dd* curve from A to B and perhaps ultimately to the Ricardian equilibrium point E at which people feel it no longer pays them to save any per cent of their incomes for enhanced future consumption. On the factor-price frontier *ff* in Fig. 37-2(b), society

---

[8]EXAMPLE: Let capital double from 1 million dollars to 2 million dollars, while labor stays at 30 men; let interest drop from 5 to 4 per cent, and the wage rise from $5,000 per year to $8,000. Total wage's return then continues to be 3 times that of capital's, each having risen by 60 per cent from their initial respective values of $150,000 and $50,000 per year.

Accumulation of capital raises output and wage, tends to depress interest rate:

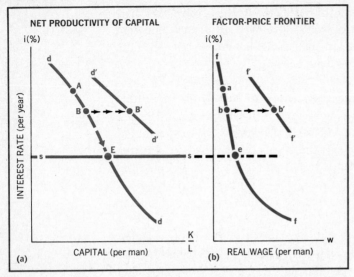

FIG. 37-2. Adding more and a greater variety of capital goods to fixed labor will, in the absence of technical change, add less and less to total product, causing interest rate earned to fall along *dd* from *B* to *E*, which is the Ricardian equilibrium point at which saving will cease. Along *ff*, fall in interest rate from *b* to *e* must raise the real wage earnable from labor's higher productivity.

Historically, technical innovation has shifted *dd* and *ff* rightward just about fast enough to offset diminishing returns and to keep the interest and profit rate almost unchanged, as shown by horizontal arrows from *B* to *B'* and *b* to *b'*.

can successively be at *a*; or at *b* with the higher wage rate and lower interest rate that are implied by an augmented capital stock (more machines available of every kind per man); or at *e* with a still higher capital-output and capital-labor ratio. The earlier literary summary of the effects of capital deepening is verified by these graphs.

■ TECHNICAL PROGRESS AND WAGES

Now let us reintroduce improving technology. This will shift the *dd* and *ff* curves outward, for example, to *d'd'* and *f'f'*. Instead of moving from *B* down to *E*, society may find that diminishing returns are offset; and the economy might in actual historical fact move from *B* to *B'*, negating or concealing the Ricardo-Marx law of the declining rate of profit. Note in Fig. 37-2(b) that the real wage rate must definitely rise, with or without technical improvements, so long as the profit rate stays the same or falls.[9]

An alternative theory would ascribe the rise of wages under capitalism to (1) trade-union pressure, (2) government regulation of monopoly, and (3) interventions of a welfare and regulatory kind by democratic governments reacting to militant political pressures from the masses. This cannot be rejected as without substance, for we have seen throughout this book that government actions do have consequences for both good and evil. But the magnitude and pattern of the rise in real wages in this last century have been such as to cast doubt on union or political action as an important element in its explanation. Thus, America in the 1920s was run on the basis of limited government intervention: trade-unions were weak; monopoly was certainly not shrinking in that decade; yet real wages rose strongly. Similarly, Japan and West Germany have shown sharp growth in real wages linked with sharp growth in labor productivity, and this at times when government seemed pro-business rather than pro-labor.

With the advance of technology and the piling up of a larger stock of capital goods, it would take a veritable miracle of the devil to keep real wages of men from being bid ever higher with each passing decade. Who fails to see that, fails to understand economic history as it actually happened. Economic theories that do not fit these facts have to be junked and replaced by others that do.

[9] Indeed, we shall see later in the chapter that, unless an invention is so "labor-saving" as to raise the profit rate enormously, it must definitely boost the real wage rate.

■ THE APPROXIMATE FACTS OF MODERN DEVELOPMENT

Let us summarize our theoretical researches.

> ■ So far we have studied the crucial role of limited land and growing labor in economic progress. Then we passed from the Smith-Malthus world to one that studied the role in economic growth of capital accumulation relative to labor. Last, but far from least, we stressed the factor of technological change and innovation. A look at the facts will now show why present-day economists think that scientific and engineering progress has been quantitatively the single most important factor for growth in the advanced countries.

Thanks to Professor Simon Kuznets and his coworkers at the National Bureau of Economic Research,[10] to Professor Robert Solow of MIT, and to Dr. Edward Denison of Brookings Institution (earlier, of the Committee for Economic Development), we can formulate certain general uniformities of economic development in the United States and the advanced nations of the world. The ratio chart of Fig. 37-3 shows the great trends of economic development for America in this century. Similar findings apply to the leading nations abroad. Figure 37-3 is crucially important. Linger over it.

[10]S. Kuznets, *Capital in the American Economy* (Princeton University Press, Princeton, N.J., 1961), gives reference to pioneering National Bureau researchers, such as A. F. Burns, D. Creamer, S. Fabricant, R. W. Goldsmith, and J. Schmookler. See also J. W. Kendrick, *Productivity Trends in the United States* (Princeton University Press, Princeton, N.J., 1961), a pioneering National Bureau study.

Economic growth has displayed long-run regularities:

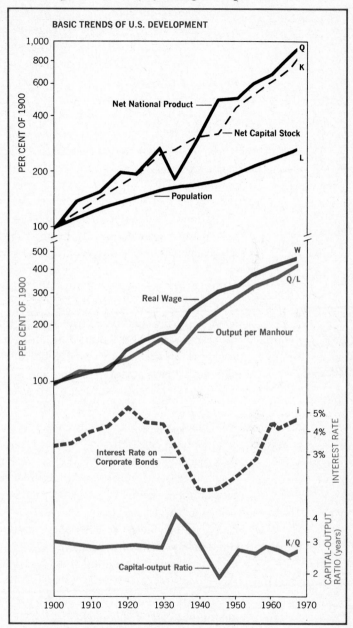

FIG. 37-3. The upper black curves show capital and output growth steadily outpacing labor growth. The middle curves show that the real wage and output per man-hour have risen together, leaving the relative shares of labor and capital about the same. The interest (or profit) rate displays no diminishing returns, and the capital-output ratio displays no steady rise. Hence, the statical curves of Fig. 37-2 must have been shifted by technological advance.

The top chart shows the growth since 1900 of labor, capital, and hence of output. Population has doubled in 65 years of steady growth. (Taking into account shortening of the working week and changes in age distribution and in labor-force participation, the growth in total number of man-hours has been even more modest.) While labor has about doubled, the stock of physical capital has increased about sixfold! Thus the substantial increase in capital per worker, the K/L ratio, does represent a significant amount of "capital deepening."

What about the growth in output? Has output grown less than in proportion to capital, as in the model that ignored technical change? No. The fact that the Q curve is not in between the two factor curves, but actually lies up near the capital curve itself, shows that there must have been technical change in actual history. The close proximity of the output and capital curves shows that the capital-output ratio has not risen as in the simple deepening model; instead, as the lowest curve in the bottom chart shows, the capital-output ratio has remained remarkably close to 3 years (i.e., a balance-sheet calculation of current value of all capital goods would show it to be approximately equal to 3 years of total product).[11]

RISING WAGES AND TRENDLESS PROFIT   The real wage has indeed risen steadily, in accordance with what one would expect from the growth in capital tools cooperating with labor and from favorable technological trends. The interest rate—or, if we could get complete statistics, the rate of profit actually earned on more risky investments—does *not* show the decline that would be predicted from simple deepening of capital and diminishing returns. Interest rates and profit rates fluctuate much in business cycle and war, but display no strong trend upward or downward for the whole period. Either by coincidence, or as the result of some economic mechanism that needs study, technological change has just about offset diminishing returns.[12]

Output per man-hour is the green curve shown in the middle chart. As could be expected from the deepening of capital and from technological advance, Q/L has risen steadily. Moreover—and this too represents a remarkable coincidence or the result of some economic mechanism needing study—the percentage growth in wage rates per hour has almost exactly matched the percentage growth in product per man-hour. This does not mean, as some Wall Street arithmetic has implied, that labor has captured *all* the fruits of productivity advance. It means, rather, that labor has kept about the *same* share of total product, with property also earning about the same relative share throughout the period. (A closer look at the middle chart suggests that there *might* have been a slow upward creep in the share of labor in NNP, with property's share dropping gently; but part of this might be the return to capital invested in education.)

---

[11] Many charts show a stronger tendency for the capital-output ratio to decline in the last part of the period. Much of such a decline in K/Q results from measuring the numerator so as to deflate out of it the relative rise that has taken place in capital-goods prices compared with other prices. Here in Fig. 37-3, the components of K/Q are each measured in current dollars, or in current dollars deflated by a *common* price index.

[12] Resist the temptation to think diminishing returns is not operating: if, instead of being merely hidden, it were actually not operating, the interest rate would have had to *rise* strongly as a result of technical change alone.

■ SIX BASIC TRENDS OF ECONOMIC DEVELOPMENT

These basic facts of economic history in the advanced nations can be summarized approximately by the following trends:

■ *Trend 1.* Population has grown, but at a much more modest rate than the capital stock, reflecting a "deepening of capital."

Trend 2. There has been a strong upward trend in real wage rates.

Trend 3. According to what is often called Bowley's Law, the share of wages and salaries relative to the total return to property has shown considerable constancy in the long run (but perhaps with slight signs of an edging upward of labor's share).

Trend 4. Instead of observing a fall in the rate of interest or profit, we actually observe their oscillation in the business cycle but no steady upward or downward trend in this century.

Trend 5. Instead of observing a steady rise in the capital-output ratio as the deepening of capital invokes the law of diminishing returns, we find that the capital-output ratio has been approximately constant in this century.

Trend 6. The ratio of saving to output has oscillated in the business cycle—reaching about the same level at various high-employment phases of the cycle. Or taking into account the approximate constancy of the capital-output ratio, we can convert this approximate constancy of the ratio of investment to income into the following: national product has generally been growing at a roughly constant percentage rate per year.[13]

■ ANALYZING THE BASIC TRENDS

While these are only approximate truths and not like the unrepealable laws of physics, they portray fundamental facts about economic growth. How can we explain them?

Trends 2 and 1—higher wage rates when capital deepens—fit nicely together with classical and neoclassical theories of production and distribution. Trend 3—Bowley's Law that the wage share is approximately constant—is an interesting coincidence that would be consistent with a *statical* neoclassical model only if it possessed a special kind of production function relating Q to L and K (what in advanced treatises is called the "Cobb-Douglas function," for which relative factor shares are constant).

Trends 4 and 5, however, warn us that neoclassical theory cannot hold in static form! A steady profit rate and a steady capital-output ratio are incompatible with the more basic law of diminishing returns under deepening of capital. We are forced, therefore, to introduce technical innovations into our statical neoclassical analysis to explain these dynamic facts. And a good thing it is that we are told to introduce technical change, since we have much independent evidence of the importance of science and engineering in the modern era.

In terms of the analysis back in Fig. 37-2, we are forced to introduce an outward shift in the *dd* and *ff* curves there to account for all five trends. Thus, the eastward move in

---

[13]EXAMPLE: Figure 37-3 shows K/Q about 3 and the percentage growth of capital per annum almost $3\frac{1}{3}$ per cent per year. Only if net capital formation is about 10 per cent (equals $3\frac{1}{3} \times 3$) of output is this possible, as footnote 14 and the Appendix make clear.

Fig. 37-2(a) from B on dd to B' on $d'd'$, which corresponds to the eastward move in Fig. 37-2(b) from b to b', will be consistent with trends 1 to 6. The tendency toward diminishing returns has just been offset by the technical shift, with interest remaining at the same horizontal level and the wage rate rising just as much as output per head. The capital-output ratio, which cannot easily be read in Fig. 37-2, must stay constant if the interest return on capital is to constitute the same relative share as before.[14]

Professor Solow, utilizing his own methods of analysis and corroborating the independent findings of numerous scholars at the National Bureau of Economic Research and elsewhere, has come up with the following remarkable conclusion:

■ Less than half of the increase in America's productivity per capita and in real wages can be accounted for by the increase in capital itself. Considerably more than half of the increase in productivity seems to be attributable to technical change—to scientific and engineering advance, to industrial improvements, and to "know-how" of management methods and educational training of labor.

This important finding needs careful interpretation.

First, although it is customary to measure and speak of the productivity of labor, there is no necessary implication that all of it (or most of it, or little of it) came from greater effort on the part of workers, or from more intensive conditions of sweat and strain; from more effort and education, or from more initiative and incentives of the human labor force.

Second, it is artificial to separate capital formation and technology completely. New techniques do tend to be embodied in new kinds of equipment. It is possible to imagine a stationary state—like the optimistic one of John Stuart Mill—in which there is no net saving and investment, but in which there is considerable technical progress as the depreciation charges of worn-out equipment finance their replacement by technically better equipment. Still, no one will deny that innovations can be introduced faster in a society which is performing *net* investment in addition to the gross investment corresponding to replacement. We all do learn from actually doing, and the society which gets to try out more new things will run that much ahead of the one which does little or no net saving.

■ ARE INVENTIONS LABOR-SAVING OR CAPITAL-SAVING?

Any invention that wins its way under competition must raise the real wage rate or the interest rate or both. [In terms of Fig. 37-2(b)'s factor-price frontier, ff must be shifted outward and upward or the invention will not succeed in the competitive market.[15]]

---

[14]As shown in the Appendix, trends 3, 4, and 5 cannot be independent, since arithmetically the constancy of any two of the three magnitudes $(iK/Q, i, K/Q)$ implies the constancy of the third.

[15]Karl Marx erred in overlooking this. He promulgated the "law of the declining rate of profit [or interest rate]" alongside the "law of the immiserization of the working class [falling real wage rate]." Unless one invokes diminishing returns to land in the Malthus fashion—and Marx, who hated Malthus as an apologist for the rich and a "plagiarist," paid insufficient attention to such phenomena—one has to give up at least one of the Marxian "laws."

However, some inventions will by their nature have a tendency to increase the relative share of labor; others to increase the relative share of capital and property generally; and others to affect both factors in about the same degree. This suggests the convenience of the following definition:

■ *Definition:* An invention is called "labor-saving," "capital-saving," or "neutral," depending upon whether it tends to lower the relative share of labor, lower the relative share of property, or leave relative shares unchanged.

An extreme example of a labor-saving invention would be one that enabled unmanned machines to turn out robots that could do any of the manual and intellectual tasks of human labor. This would no doubt reduce the competitive wage drastically and could conceivably drop labor's share of NNP from its present level of about 75 to 80 per cent to below 50 per cent. An example of a capital-saving invention would be the case of a cheap computer that enabled firms to get along with much less inventory; or the invention of Kleenex tissue to replace durable handkerchiefs; or the invention of easily launched Telstar wave-reflecting satellites that made ocean cables unnecessary.[16] It is easy to specify innumerable examples of capital-saving or labor-saving innovations and of neutral innovations in between.

The steady rise in wage rates is thought by many economists to *induce* employers to come up with labor-saving inventions. This tendency is often offered to help explain the failure of the profit-and-interest rate to fall as capital is accumulated. Marx a century ago had used such an explanation to account for the success of capitalists in resisting a rise in wages and in creating an industrial reserve army of the unemployed. Sir John Hicks of Oxford and Professor William Fellner of Yale have in our day advanced similar arguments of an inherent bias toward labor-saving innovation.

Whatever the ultimate merits of such arguments, we must recognize that *any* invention which lowers cost of production can benefit the first competitor who introduces it. Furthermore, since the relative share of wages in total costs has been approximately constant for a century, any employer who is planning his research expenditures over the coming years will reasonably take this into account and will do well to spend now the same number of pennies on experimentation designed to save a dollar of future cost, whatever its source.[17]

[16] A capital-saving invention tends to twist Fig. 37-2(a)'s productivity curve of capital down toward the vertical and greater inelasticity, thereby tending to reduce the fruits of sacrificing current consumption and accumulating capital. A neutral technical change would be one that shifts Fig. 37-2's curves generally outward and upward. Advanced treatises deal with various distinct definitions of what is meant by labor-saving; the discussion here is left general so as not to be inconsistent with either the definition associated with Hicks or that different one associated with R. F. Harrod.

[17] A theory of induced technical change can explain and unify all the six basic trends of economic development as follows: (1) Suppose any increase in capital relative to labor will raise labor's relative share. (2) Suppose that effort devoted to making each laborer the new equivalent of more than one laborer will go up when labor cost increases as the share of total costs (and like efforts to "augment" capital go down). (3) Finally, assume that a constant fraction of income is always saved and invested and that labor population grows at a constant slow rate. Then it will follow that the system will ultimately grow in "golden-age balance": (*a*) Capital and output will grow at the same high rate with

Growth theory is still at the frontier of economics, and the experts are not all agreed on the mechanisms of past and future paths of economic development. Some alternative theories are presented in the Appendix to this chapter. However, we are now armed to tackle in the next chapters the problems of growth in less developed economies, advanced economies, and collectivist economies like the Soviet Union.

SUMMARY

1 ■

Many writers have tried to read into economic history a linear progression through inevitable stages, such as primitive economy, feudalism, capitalism, and some form of communism. The actual facts have not agreeably stuck to such timetables; in particular, the mixed economies that dominate the Western world came into being without the permission of social prophets.

2 ■

The classical models of Smith and Malthus describe economic development in terms of fixed land and growing population. A simple labor theory of value prevails so long as land is superabundant; and output develops steadily with population in this golden age where labor gets all the national product.

3 ■

In the absence of technical change, increasing population ultimately exhausts the supply of free land. The resulting increase in population density invokes the law of diminishing returns: Fixity of land keeps output from growing proportionally to increased labor; with less and less of land to work with, each new man adds less and less extra product; the decline in labor's marginal-product means a decline in the competitively earned real wage. As each acre of land gets more and more labor to work with, its marginal-product and competitively earned rent go up. A fundamental factor-price frontier depicts how the rent rate must rise as the wage rate falls; but no one can predict what will happen to the relative shares of land and labor in national product.

4 ■

The Malthusian equilibrium comes when the wage has fallen to the subsistence level, below which the supply of labor will not reproduce itself. However, in realistic fact,

---

a constant K/Q ratio; (b) labor population will grow at a slower rate, but because of induced technological invention, "labor in effective or efficiency units" will grow at precisely the same rate as capital and output; (c) now with Q, K, and effective L growing in balance, there will be no diminishing returns to capital and hence there will be a constant interest rate and constant relative labor share; (d) finally, the real wage will grow because each worker is having his effectiveness raised by the induced technical change. Q.E.D.: Rigorous proof of this, proceeding from an induced-invention model of Professors Charles Kennedy of Canterbury and C. von Weizsäcker of Heidelberg, is presented by this author in a 1966 *Review of Economics and Statistics* paper.

technical change has kept economic development going by continually shifting the productivity curve of labor upward. How fast wages will rise must depend upon whether the technical changes are labor-saving or land-saving.

5 ∎

The Ricardo-Marx-Solow model stresses the deepening of capital, i.e., the process of accumulating capital goods of varied types faster than the growth in population and labor hours. In the absence of technical change, an increase in capital per capita will not be matched by a proportional increase in output per capita because of diminishing returns. Hence, capital deepening lowers the interest rate (which is the same as the "profit rate" if risk is ignored), raises the real wage along the factor-price frontier, and raises the capital-output ratio.

6 ∎

Historically, trends 1 and 2 on page 719—a rise in K/L and in w—are consistent with the *statical* model. Trend 3's approximate constancy of relative shares of labor and property—as measured by wL/Q and iK/Q, where $Q = wL + iK$—is not mandatory in the statical model, but is consistent with a special technical case of it (Cobb-Douglas). However, trends 4 and 5—the failure of the interest and profit rate to fall and of the capital-output ratio to rise—show clearly that technical change must be brought into the analysis. Trend 6—approximate constancy of the investment/income ratio—taken together with the constancy of the capital-output ratio, arithmetically implies a constant percentage growth of output per decade.

7 ∎

The facts suggest the hypothesis that capital accumulation is second to technical change in explaining rising productivity. But innovation and investment interact, as new techniques get embodied in new equipment and people learn by trying new investments. Increasing productivity can be expressed conveniently in terms of labor productivity— i.e., Q/L—but this does not necessarily imply anything about the reasons for the rise.

8 ∎

Inventions are defined as labor-saving, capital-saving, or neutral, depending upon whether they reduce labor's relative share of national product, reduce property's relative share, or leave shares unchanged. Experience with rising wage rates makes firms expect the trend to continue; whether or not they try for, and succeed in making, labor-saving inventions, firms will want to cut down on any cost items (labor, natural resources, capital costs).

Either by coincidence or by cancellation of offsetting trends or as the result of economic mechanisms needing study,[18] the pace of invention has turned out to be just about enough to offset the effect of diminishing returns to capital on the interest and profit rate; and innovations have not turned out to be so labor-saving or capital-saving as to cause much change in the relative shares of labor and property.

---

[18] Such as that described in footnote 17.

QUESTIONS FOR DISCUSSION

1. Does the mixed economy fit any of the timetables of history? Was it so hard to foresee?

2. Apply a labor theory of value to a golden age involving many goods. What will be the effects of technical innovation in such a model? Show that eventual land scarcity (and/or use of capital goods) invalidates the labor theory of value.

3. Draw the parallels between the models of Figs. 37-1 and 37-2: rising labor-output ratio and rising capital-output ratio; falling wage and falling interest rate; the two factor-price frontiers; technical shifts of dd and ff in both cases; land-saving or labor-saving and neutral innovations in both cases; relative factor shares; and other parallelisms.

4. "Saving helps capitalists today, workers tomorrow." Assess this filter-down view.

5. "Without technical change and unemployment, persistent capital accumulation would ultimately mean euthanasia (death) of the capitalists." Use Fig. 37-2 to explain this.

6. Since labor's share shows a slight uptrend and the capital-output ratio a slight downtrend, since the interest and profit rate fluctuate considerably, and since the ratio of private net investment to NNP shows fluctuation and in recent years signs of a downtrend—in view of these facts, would you be greatly surprised if the basic trends were to show future changes?

7. Give examples of labor-saving and capital-saving inventions.

8. "Had America saved less but spent more on experimentation, we'd be richer." Comment.

9. Review your understanding of the following concepts:

stages of history	capital deepening, K/L rise
Smithian golden age	capital-output ratio, K/Q
labor theory of value	interest rate and profit rate
Malthusian subsistence wage	technical progress
factor-price frontier ff	labor-saving
marginal-product dd	neutral
diminishing returns	capital-saving
relative factor shares	Q growth from inventions, from more K

APPENDIX: Modern Discussions of Development Theory

Economics, not being a settled subject, is itself still undergoing development. While the broad facts of historical development discussed in the chapter are not in dispute, different interpretations of them are given by different authors. Some of the ideas associated with the names of the late Joseph A. Schumpeter, Sir Roy Harrod of Oxford, W. W. Leontief of Harvard, Professors Joan Robinson and Nicholas Kaldor of Cambridge University, and various current American economists will be sketched briefly in this Appendix.

While an elementary textbook cannot pretend to resolve advanced topics, today one would consider an introduction to physics old-fashioned if it did not somewhere give the reader a glance at fundamental issues on the frontiers of knowledge: atomic theory, elementary particles, generalized relativity, and so forth.

Similarly many beginning students of economics will want to have a glimpse of the issues at the frontier of current economic analysis. Without mastering every intricacy of this Appendix, the interested reader can capture the flavor of developing economic thought from it. In particular, many readers who are not concerned with the rest of the theories discussed in this Appendix may still want to turn to its final discussion (pages 732 to 734) of the fascinating and useful subject of Leontief input-output analysis of interindustry flows.

SCHUMPETERIAN INNOVATION

Joseph Schumpeter (1883–1950) of Vienna and Harvard was author of two economic classics:[1] *The Theory of Economic Development* (English ed., Harvard University Press, Cambridge, 1934) and the posthumous *History of Economic Analysis* (Oxford University Press, Fair Lawn, N.J., 1954).

Schumpeter emphasized the role of the innovator—i.e., the inventor, the developer, the promoter, the man who initiates and recognizes technical improvements and who succeeds in getting them introduced. Like Carlyle's faith in the role of the great man in history, Schumpeter's theory regards the innovator as the dynamic actor of capitalism, who rules profitably for a day only to have his profits nibbled away by imitating competitors.

Figure 37-2(a) back on page 716 well represents Schumpeter's notion of what would happen if all innovations ceased. Competition and capital accumulation would quickly push society down the diminishing-returns curve *dd*; indeed, Schumpeter thought that the long-run *ss* horizontal line at which the supply of new saving will disappear would be at a zero rate of interest and profit, being properly drawn in Fig. 37-2(a) down on the horizontal axis itself. (His theory of a zero rate of interest in the innovationless stationary state can be replaced by a positive-interest-rate floor without appreciably altering his theory of cycles or development.)

But now Schumpeter plays his trump card. Innovation is periodically shifting the *dd* curve upward and outward. The violin string is plucked by innovation; without innovation it dies down to stationariness, but then along comes a new innovation to pluck it back into dynamic motion again. So it is with the profit rate in economic life.

The profits due to innovation, we have seen, will be competed away by imitators, with labor and consumers benefiting from price reductions. The innovation-induced rise in interest rates will soon coax out saving and capital formation, until the accumulation of the augmented capital stock leads to diminishing returns, a "profit squeeze," and minimal interest. But then along comes a new burst of innovations—railroads, electricity, automation—to pluck the system back into dynamic motion, and we are off on a new repetition of the process of development.

Ignoring Schumpeter's specific theories of the business cycle, we see that his theory of development is completely consistent with the first two trends of economic history: rising real wage rates, and capital increase outstripping population increase. Although his general theory does not specifically call for constant relative shares, a trendless profit rate, a constant capital-output ratio, or a trendless average propensity-to-consume-and-save, still all or any of these could be quite consistent with his general schema.

UNEMPLOYMENT IN THE STATIONARY STATE?

Ricardo, Alfred Marshall, and Schumpeter had one thing in common with Lord Keynes of *The General Theory of Employment, Interest, and Money.* They all thought that profit rates would be pushed to minimal levels in the absence of technical change. But Ricardo and company all thought that when this day of judgment came, the economy would be voluntarily consuming 100 per cent of its full-employment income; although positive investment would cease, people would then be spending enough on consumption to maintain full employment. (In terms of the diagrams of Part Two, in the Ricardian stationary state the $C + I + G$ curve would be intersecting the 45° line at the *ff* full-employment level, with $C + I + G$ actually equal

---

[1] As can be seen by readers of his stimulating *Capitalism, Socialism, and Democracy* (Harper & Brothers, New York, 1942), Schumpeter was more than an economist. Believing the economic system to be itself essentially stable, Schumpeter advanced sociological and political reasons for his predicted decay of capitalism: he held that the very efficiency of capitalism will be its ruin, as intellectuals and the masses come to despise the market ideology and contrive to introduce hampering government interferences in the name of welfare. Unlike Marx, who thought capitalism would die of its own cancers, Schumpeter thought it would eventually commit suicide for psychosomatic reasons. The tremendous resurgence of *mixed economies* in the 25 years since Schumpeter cheerfully gave his gloomy prediction is, apparently, a deviation from *his* timetable of history.

there to $C + zero + G$, because net investment ceases in the stationary state.)

Keynes, on the other hand, feared that such minimal rates of interest and of profit on risky ventures might create a stationary state of stagnation with chronic unemployment:

People might still want to save at full employment, but no matching real investment would be forthcoming when the promised profit rate is too low to coax out risk taking; and when the interest to be earned on short-term gilt-edge government bonds has become so low as to make people indifferent between hoarding much or little safe, idle money,[2] central bank policy cannot do much to prevent stagnation.

This notion of a troublesome stationary state did not die with the 1930s. Prominent followers of Keynes at Cambridge University, such as Professors Joan Robinson, Lord Kahn, and Nicholas Kaldor, have grave doubts concerning the possibility of a successful deepening of capital accompanied by full employment in a mixed economy. At the least they would stress that it will never happen by itself in a country that confines itself to orthodox fiscal and monetary policies. At the most they would harbor grave doubts that "managed capitalism" could, or would, pursue the unorthodox policies of monetary and fiscal expansion implied by a successful synthesis of neoclassical and post-Keynesian analysis.

Readers who go on to advanced economics can be referred to writings of these and other authors.[3] Here, briefly, will be presented some of the points that need to be considered in doing justice to both sides of the argument as it bears on long-term economic development: no attempt will be made to identify ideas and writers meticulously.

[2] This floor on the profit and interest rate could help account for the historical constancy of the profit rate named in trend 4 (page 719), particularly if someone could supply reasons for a profit ceiling. With the profit rate allegedly running between two channels, its constancy would be removed from the realm of coincidence. (Recall also the discussion of Say's Law on page 328; page 332's "liquidity trap" or "depression pole," when elevated by riskiness, might provide such a profit floor.
[3] J. Robinson, *Economic Philosophy*, Chap. 5 (Aldine, London, 1962); *Acccumulation of Capital* (Macmillan, London, 1956); N. Kaldor, *Essays on Value and Distribution; On Economic Stability and Growth; On Economic Policy* (Duckworth, London, 1960).

UNCHANGEABLE CAPITAL-OUTPUT RATIO?

The land-output and labor-output ratios were not constants in the first Smith-Malthus model of development. And the capital-output ratio in the Ricardo-Marx-Solow model of Fig. 37-2 was likewise not supposed to be a technical constant. In the absence of technical change, successful capital formation by society would enable output to grow; and the resulting phenomenon of diminishing returns would imply a *smoothly growing* capital-output ratio as capital deepening was taking place. On this view, dynamic technical change has seemed historically to provide about the extra productivity needed to offset statical diminishing returns, keeping the measured capital-output ratio constant.

Many modern economists—Professors Robert Eisner of Northwestern and Alvin Hansen of Harvard, Dr. Gerhard Colm of the National Planning Association, and others—are of the view that the capital-output ratio is very nearly a technical *constant*, and that any attempt to accumulate capital beyond the rate required by the annual growth in output will soon be unsuccessful. Profits or rents from equipment will fall off badly after any surge of capital investment like those of 1955–1957 and 1964–1967. Excess capacity will follow, and the resulting profit squeeze will kill off private investment, as it did in the sluggish years following 1957. Therefore, they argue, any long-term theory must utilize an *invariable* capital-output ratio like that shown in the historical data of Fig. 37-3.

HARROD-DOMAR GROWTH MODELS

These concepts can be illuminated by some interesting models of balanced compound-interest (or "exponential") growth developed by Sir Roy Harrod in England and Professor E. Domar in America.[4] This theory has two aspects: the long-term "natural rate of growth" and the so-called "warranted rate of growth."

THE NATURAL RATE OF GROWTH   The historical data of Fig. 37-3 can help explain Harrod's arithmetic; and,

[4] R. F. Harrod, *Towards a Dynamic Economics* (Macmillan, London, 1948); E. D. Domar, *Essays in the Theory of Economic Growth* (Oxford University Press, Fair Lawn, N.J., 1957). The discussion of interacting accelerator-multiplier models in Chapter 14 is here applied to the trend of economic development rather than to the business-cycle deviations from that trend.

in turn, a simple Harrod-Domar model can give an oversimplified "explanation" of those historical trends.

Suppose hours of labor L grow steadily at about 1 per cent per year.[5] And for extreme simplicity, assume that technical change is in effect making every man's efficiency as a laborer grow at another 2 per cent per year. Either because of more scientific methods of production or better education, it is as if 98 men can this year do what it took 100 to do last year; and this is repeated indefinitely. To coin a phrase, while *actual* L in its human man-hour units is growing at but 1 per cent per year, the number of "efficiency units of labor" L^* is growing at 3 per cent per year because of the annual 2 per cent efficiency improvement. This leads to the concept of the natural rate of growth.

■ *Definition:* The *natural rate of growth* of a simplified Harrod system is the percentage growth per year of its labor supply expressed in "efficiency units" (which means natural labor units as augmented by the presumed increase in technical effectiveness of each man-hour); as a condition of *balanced* growth, output and capital must also be growing at this same natural rate per year.

With NNP (or Q) and with L^* growing steadily at this natural rate of 3 per cent per year, the stock of capital K must also grow at the same natural rate of 3 per cent per year so as to keep in balanced pace. How much investment is required each year to keep K growing at this natural rate of 3 per cent? Or, in other words, how much must people be steadily saving and investing out of their annual full-employment product to keep growth nicely balanced?

Evidently the needed saving-income ratio must depend on the numerical value of the capital-output ratio K/Q times the natural growth rate.[6]

We are now in a position to write down the arithmetic formula relating three historical things: the Harrod natural rate of growth of 0.03 per year, or in the general case g per year; the historical capital-output ratio of 3 (to keep arithmetic simple, not $3\frac{1}{3}$ as in Fig. 37-3), or in the general case K/Q; the required saving-income ratio of 0.09, or in the general case s. We get

$$s = g \times \frac{K}{Q} \quad \text{or} \quad 0.09 = 0.03 \times 3$$

This relationship determines the amount of voluntary saving *and* investment that is needed if the Harrod natural rate of growth is to be an *equilibrium* situation.[7]

EXPLAINING THE TRENDS Can this simplified Harrod-Domar model of balanced natural rate of growth account for all six of the basic trends listed on page 719? Yes. Let us check them off.

The model certainly gives a deepening of capital relative to man-hours of actual L, since K grows at 3 per cent and L only at 1 per cent. (In this simplified model, an observer who concentrates only on L^*, labor in efficiency units, will see a constant K/L^* with no "deepening" going on but merely an apparent "widening of capital" to keep K and L^* balanced.)

Trend 2 is verified also. The wage rate rises—actually at 2 per cent per year. Why? Because each actual man (L, not L^*) collects the marginal product of the increasing efficiency units *in him,* and these units work with their full quota of capital goods.

Trend 3 is verified and is no longer a coincidence. Because technical change was so nicely neutral as to make each man take on "the strength of ten," the balanced growth in K and L^* means we are *dividing shares between the factors in precisely the same way as before.* (Recall that an observer of L^* alone merely sees balanced widening of capital, not deepening.)

Trend 4's constancy of the interest rate is now precisely verified, being neither an approximation nor a coincidence. Each unit of K, being matched exactly by the same amount of L^* as before, experiences no diminishing returns and has imputed to it the same competi-

---

[5] Expansion of an industrial sector through the utilization of an unlimited supply of rural labor is associated with the name of W. Arthur Lewis. Such diverse economists as the conservative Gustav Cassel of Sweden and the nonconservative Karl Marx had put forth similar Ricardian notions.

[6] Thus, suppose Q is 900 billion dollars per year, and that the capital stock is about $3\frac{1}{3}$ times as great, being 3,000 billion dollars. Then to add 3 per cent to K this year we must have net investment of 90 billion dollars (equals $0.03 \times 3,000$ billion dollars), which means that people must be saving and investing exactly 10 per cent (equals $3\% \times 3\frac{1}{3}$) of their incomes. [Check your understanding by showing that a 4 per cent natural growth rate would in this case require a $13\frac{1}{3}$

---

per cent (equals $4\% \times 3\frac{1}{3}$) saving ratio out of income; and that a 3 per cent natural growth rate with a K/Q ratio of only 2 would require only a 6 per cent saving-income ratio.]

[7] This is really the $I = S$ schedule equality of Part Two. For in the case of the natural growth rate, $g = I/K$ or $I = gK$; hence, $I/Q = S/Q = s = g(K/Q)$, the Harrod condition.

tive interest rate. (If degree of risk is the same, constancy of the interest rate means constancy of the somewhat higher profit rate.)[8]

Trend 5 is of course verified, since the Harrod natural rate of balanced growth assumes from the beginning an unchanged K/Q ratio. In terms of the Ricardo-Marx-Solow model, even if the capital-output ratio *could* smoothly change, it will not have to in a situation where widening of K to match L^* means no diminishing returns and entails Q growing in full proportion to K.

Trend 6's constancy of the saving-income ratio is verified from the basic Harrod formula for the natural rate of balanced growth at the same compound interest rate per year: $s = $ constant $g \times$ constant K/Q.

INTERDEPENDENCE OF TRENDS As mentioned in footnote 14, p. 720, the six trends are not all logically independent. We could have saved time by checking any two of the three trends 3, 4, and 5, knowing that their correctness would arithmetically guarantee the correctness of the remaining trend. Here is why. If property always gets the same fraction of output, say one-fourth, and if the profit rate stays constant, then the process of capitalization of an income stream discussed in Chapter 30 shows that the value of the capital stock must be a determinate multiple of output. [I.e., K's fractional share of Q divided by the interest rate is equal to the capital-output ratio: $i(K/Q) \div i = K/Q$. Thus, if capital gets one-fourth of 900-billion-dollar Q, and this property return of 225 billion is capitalized by dividing it through by $i = 0.08\frac{1}{3} = \frac{1}{12}$, then the value of capital is seen to be determinate at 2,700 billion dollars, or 3 (not $3\frac{1}{3}$ as in the main chapter's example) times the value of output.]

HARROD'S WARRANTED RATE OF GROWTH The natural rate of growth is designed to cope with long-term problems of economic development. A few words can be said about a related tool designed more to explain cyclical instability than trend.[8]

What if society's actual saving fraction differs from that needed to keep the natural growth rate in nice balance? That is, suppose actual desired S/Q at full employment is greater, or less, than s given by $g(K/Q)$. Too high a schedule of saving, we saw in Part Two, will tend to lead to unemployment. Too low a saving schedule, related to the investment schedule, was seen

to produce an inflationary gap and a tendency toward price inflation.

Very well. No longer is the natural growth rate g the one that the system will realize. Growth in balance has now become rather irrelevant. Still Harrod can ask this rather odd question:

■ Starting from enough unemployed resources so that the natural growth rate of labor and other resources provides no bottleneck or ceiling—starting from there, what rate of growth of output, W, if it could be achieved and maintained, would (through "the acceleration principle" of Chapter 14, page 249) lead to a large enough volume of investment to justify (via the multiplier analysis of Chapter 13) a continuance of its own growth rate W? The answering W is defined as the "warranted rate of growth."

In short, to get W, reinterpret the old Harrod relation $s = g(K/Q)$ and work it backward to solve for the growth rate of Q rather than for the needed saving ratio s. Follow these steps: (1) Replace s by the actual desired saving ratio S/Q. (2) Replace the g specified by labor force and technological growth by the unknown warranted rate of growth W. (3) Provided that the capital-output ratio K/Q is a hard constant, let it stand.[9] (4) Solve for W by removing K/Q to the denominator under S/Q.

We go from the natural rate to the warranted rate thus: $S/Q = W(K/Q)$ replaces $s = g(K/Q)$, and

$$W = \frac{S/Q}{K/Q}$$

An example will help. With $g = 0.03$ and $K/Q = 3$, Harrod needs $s = 0.09$ for his natural-growth process. But suppose people want to save $S/Q = 0.12 > 0.09$. This overthrift would lead to unemployment. If somehow Harrod could start an expansion of W per cent per year in Q, which can always get the labor it needs from the ranks of the unemployed, how fast must it expand to generate enough I/Q to match $S/Q = 0.12$? If every dollar of expanded Q always requires K to expand by 3 dollars, our answer is $W = 0.12/3 = 0.04$. Any Q growth higher than 0.04 per year will generate

[8] These next two sections can be skipped.

[9] If an extra amount of Q, written as ΔQ, calls for an amount of extra capital ΔK that gives a $\Delta K/\Delta Q$ *different* from K/Q, then we would have to replace the latter in the Harrod formula by the former, which is called the "*incremental* capital-output ratio" or the "accelerator coefficient." Those who like symbols should read the next footnote.

$I/Q > 0.12$, just as any Q growth less than $W = 0.04$ will generate $I/Q < 0.12$.[10]

The warranted rate is an odd concept. It does not tell you what will in fact happen, but only what would—if it came to happen by design or by luck—have certain self-warranting properties. Such a growth rate of output, W, if it could somehow be established and maintained, warrants a level of investment just big enough to match the voluntary saving that its own income growth entails.

CYCLES AND INSTABILITIES   Two observations should be made about cyclical instabilities involved in the warranted rate of growth.

1. Once all the unemployed are back at work, the natural rate of growth g must set a ceiling against which the faster warranted rate of growth must collide. Thus W of 4 or 5 per cent per year and g of only 3 per cent per year ultimately means the Harrod expansion will hit full employment. As was seen in Chapter 14 on business cycles, some writers[11] have constructed a theory of a collapse into recession based upon a bouncing back of the system from its collision with the natural-rate employment ceiling.

2. The warranted rate of growth, even if originally established, will not persist after being disturbed. In the Harrod model it is definitely unstable. To see this, note that if the actual growth rate temporarily exceeds $W = 4$ per cent, this new income will be generating in desired investment *more* than the 12 ($= 4\% \times 3$) per cent ratio of desired saving—thereby *accelerating* its own growth still faster above W. (Show that a *less* than 4 per cent initial growth rate will similarly create a deficiency of intended investment relative to the 12 per cent intended saving, thereby *decelerating* its own growth still further below W.)

Just as an unmanned bicycle, which is unstable if disturbed from the vertical, can be converted into a stable system by a steadying and compensating human hand, so can a Harrod-Domar growth path that would be unstable under *laissez faire* be made stable by compensating monetary and fiscal policies in a mixed economy.

NEOCLASSICAL DYNAMICS

The Ricardo-Marx-Solow model of smooth substitutability of labor for capital (i.e., of labor for a great variety of alternatively producible capital goods) has less need to work with Harrod-Domar concepts than those models which regard the capital-output ratio as a hard constant. However, it is useful to interpret the Harrod-Domar concepts for a neoclassical model like Fig. 37-2.

By a simple "neoclassical growth model" is meant one in which the state uses monetary and fiscal policies to make sure that thriftiness does not lead to unemployment and abortive thrift: by making equity and loan funds available at lower interest and profit rates (and possibly by unorthodox credit policies that provide guarantees against risks and uncertainties) such a managed system can contrive deepening of capital as described earlier.[12] Alternatively, this neoclassical model

---

[10]Suppose the capital-output ratio K/Q is not precisely equal to the incremental capital-output ratio $\Delta K/\Delta Q$ (where ΔQ means the annual change in Q or $Q_{t+1} - Q_t$, and $\Delta K = $ annual investment $= K_{t+1} - K_t$). Then we replace K/Q by $\Delta K/\Delta Q$ in the formula for the warranted rate. Economics aside, this can be seen from the obvious identity

$$\frac{\Delta K}{Q} \equiv \frac{\Delta Q}{Q} \frac{\Delta K}{\Delta Q}$$

which comes from multiplying the left-hand side by $1 \equiv \Delta Q/\Delta Q$ and rearranging terms. If investment matches voluntary saving, this is seen to be the same as $S/Q = W(\Delta K/\Delta Q)$.

The natural growth rate stems from the slightly different identity

$$\frac{\Delta K}{Q} \equiv \frac{\Delta K}{K} \frac{K}{Q}$$

where the left-hand side has merely been multiplied by $1 \equiv K/K$. Stipulating *balanced* natural growth, we require $g = \Delta K/K = \Delta Q/Q = \Delta L^*/L^*$. The last condition guarantees constancy of the K/Q ratio; and combining this last condition with the equilibrium requirement that maintained saving be equal to growth-induced investment, we convert the above identity into the already given natural-rate formula $s = g(K/Q)$.

[11]J. R. Hicks, *A Contribution to the Theory of the Trade Cycle* (Oxford University Press, Fair Lawn, N.J., 1950), gives a convenient summary of such nonlinear-cycle theories based on interacting accelerator-multiplier principles.

[12]This means that the variety of possible heterogeneous capital-goods processes is so great that any reduction of interest rate—even be it as little as from $i = 0.08$ to $i = 0.079$—will ultimately make it profitable to use some new pattern of known processes. E.g., at 0.079 the machine tools may be made a little more durable. In consequence, the factor-price frontier of Fig. 37-2(b) will look fairly smooth to the naked eye, even though a microscope will show that it contains little line segments that meet in corners. When we introduce realistic uncertainties into the model, one is first tempted to think that minute changes in interest rate will have negligible effects. Actually, however, replacing certainty by probabilities smooths the small steps in a demand function into a continuous curve:

can be interpreted as picturing the technology of an efficiently run collectivist society that never faces macroeconomic problems of unemployment or of inflation due to lack of proper effective demand.

In such a society, where whatever is withheld from consumption goes into capital formation, *any* rate of growth is essentially a "warranted rate of growth." This is because there is (1) no saving-investment problem, and (2) no hard constant for the capital-output ratio (or for the incremental capital-output ratio).

Here is an idealized example. Add a new supply of L to a system that has a certain K and has previously been producing a certain Q. This new L can be put to work with the given K *as rapidly* as we like. There will result a growth rate of Q that can be *as high* as the growth in L can produce. People can consume and can invest out of the new output *as much or little* as they like. Depending on *whatever* amount of capital formation they decide on, there will result a gradual accumulation of K with the K/L ratio being able to move *in any way* without causing trouble.

All the above is in sharp contrast to a model with fixed capital-output ratio, which calls for a specific W growth rate of Q. Contrast the Harrod case with the italicized words in the above paragraph!

THREE SOURCES OF GROWTH Neoclassical output growth can be decomposed into three separate sources: growth in labor or L, growth in capital or K, and technical innovation itself. Momentarily ignoring technical change, note that a 1 per cent per year growth rate in L together with a 1 per cent per year growth rate in K is assumed to cause output to grow also at a 1 per cent per year rate. (Resist the temptation to add 1 per cent to 1 per cent and come out with 2 per cent; L and K cooperate in production, each needing the other.)

Suppose L grows at 1 per cent per year and K at 5 per cent. It is tempting, but wrong, to guess that Q will then grow at 3 per cent, the simple average of 1 and 5. Why wrong? Because the two factors do not contribute equal shares to product: about three-fourths of all product goes to labor as wages and only one-fourth of Q goes to property as its interest-profit share.

a small change in i, long maintained, pushes some investment projects on the borderline of doubt into actual operation. See J. E. Meade, *A Neoclassical Growth Model* (Oxford University Press, Fair Lawn, N.J., 1961), for alternative interpretations in terms of a flexible aggregate of capital.

This means L's growth rate should get 3 times the weight of K's; hence, the correct answer is that Q will grow at 2 per cent per year ($= \frac{3}{4}$ of 1% $+ \frac{1}{4}$ of 5%).

Hence, output growth per year follows the law

$$\% \; Q \text{ growth} = \quad \frac{3}{4}(\% \; L \text{ growth})$$
$$+ \frac{1}{4}(\% \; K \text{ growth})$$
$$+ \text{T.C.}$$

where T.C. means technical changes that raise productivity by shifting the *dd* curve of Fig. 37-2; and where $\frac{3}{4}$ and $\frac{1}{4}$ would of course be replaced by new fractions if the relative shares of the factors had changed.

If we seek to explain *per capita* growth, matters are simpler still, since this enables us to get rid of L as a separate growth source. Now, using the fact that capital gets one-fourth share of output, we have simply

$$\% \; \frac{Q}{L} \text{ growth} = \frac{1}{4}\left(\% \; \frac{K}{L} \text{ growth}\right)$$
$$+ \text{t.c.}$$

This relation shows clearly how deepening of capital would raise the capital-output ratio if there were no technical improvements being made: output per capita grows only one-fourth as fast as capital per capita, reflecting one aspect of diminishing returns.

This relation now explains the meaning of Solow's conclusion—that more than half of the increased output recorded in historical statistics seems to be attributable to scientific advance rather than to thrift and capital formation. This means that the second term in the above relation—t.c. for per capita technical change—appears on statistical measurement to have been definitely bigger than the first term representing the investment contribution. When Solow tries to allow for the fact that new techniques get embodied in new capital goods, the relative importance of the first term rises; but apparently it still remains below 50 per cent. (While the primacy of technical change seems corroborated by German or Japanese statistics, the importance of the capital factor does seem greater in Britain, Canada, and Russia.)

ALTERNATIVE THEORIES

REPUDIATION OF AGGREGATE PRODUCTION FUNCTIONS Professors Joan Robinson and Nicholas Kaldor of Cambridge University are skeptical that "capital" can be usefully measured as an aggregate, which together with labor produces aggregate output. This is certainly a healthy skepticism. They are more skeptical that the marginal productivities calculated from such an alleged production function can be used to explain wage and profit rates and the relative shares in NNP of labor and property. They go even further and doubt that economists can work with a detailed breakdown of numerous heterogeneous capital goods—machines of type A, B, C, . . . —to get quantitative results at all like the neoclassical case, in an actual realistic mixed economy of uncertainty and uneven growth.[13]

DISSENTING VOICES Robinson and Kaldor by no means agree on what is to replace the aggregative analysis. Both incline, but in different degree, toward a macroeconomic theory of income distribution with the following property:

"Here is an economy with high property share and high growth. How wrong to think that it is the thrift of the rich (or anybody else) which *causes* that fast growth. The causation tends to run the other way: fast growth produces high profits, rather than vice versa."

This seems to say something more than does the familiar assertion that when a country like Japan or Western Germany experiences a miracle of productivity growth, people find it easiest to be thrifty out of the increase in income and to be slow in renegotiating real wage rates commensurate with the recent rises in marginal productivities. It is beyond controversy that such induced thrift does further speed up capital formation and (in neoclassical fashion) speeds up growth still further.

LIFETIME SAVING AND THE WEALTH-INCOME RATIO Professor Franco Modigliani of MIT has put forward an alternative theory that is quite at variance with those just above. Modigliani does not consider the constancy of the capital-output ratio a mere coinci-

dence. He tries to explain it, not in terms of technological production or by induced innovation as in page 721's footnote 17, but in terms of people's psychological decisions about wealth, consuming, saving, and dissaving. He puts the greatest stress on lifetime patterns of saving for old-age retirement.

Here is an example. An adult works for about 40 years and lives in retirement for 20. To keep his consumption standards somewhat equal all his life, he consumes less than his income during the working years; he gradually builds up his wealth to a maximum just before retirement; then he gradually uses up capital and pension rights by his retirement consumption; at death he leaves little wealth.

When population is growing at an even percentage rate, the age distribution remains constant over time. This steady increase in population, combined with confidently expected rising real income, causes the average level of wealth of the people as a whole to remain constant in ratio to total income. Except for the public-debt and land part of wealth, Modigliani has supplied a reason for K/Q to be constant!

A test of Modigliani's theory, as against that of someone like Kaldor who thinks that businessmen will somehow be led to make innovation and investment decisions in order to keep the K/Q ratio from changing much, would be to perform the hypothetical experiment of juggling the public debt up or down and seeing whether the K/Q ratio does change enough to keep the wealth-income ratio fairly constant. This experiment is not to be recommended, but it does remind us of the assertion of Chapter 19 that a public debt can make the present generation want to do more consuming and less saving for their old age.

COMPENSATING FISCAL POLICY

Suppose it were true that monetary policy—because of balance-of-payments constraints, Eisner-like capital-output fixity, or other impotency—could make no effective change in private investment spending I. Then compensating fiscal policy would lead to results quite different from those given by laissez-faire models of the simple Harrod and Kaldor type.

Whenever full-employment s was out of line with I/Q, the government would run a budgetary surplus or deficit just big enough to alter the effective s for society until it equaled I/Q. The effective "warranted rate of

[13]Their works cited earlier can be contrasted by the advanced student in economics with the general neo-neoclassical viewpoint exposited in an advanced work like R. Dorfman, P. A. Samuelson, R. M. Solow, *Linear Programming and Economic Analysis* (McGraw-Hill, New York, 1958). The latter makes the same supposition as was done here—that there are a great variety of alternative machines and processes known (or knowable) at any one time. If the interest rate changes even a little, say from 0.08 to 0.079 (as mentioned earlier), it will usually (but not inevitably!) pay to turn to a new blueprint that involves a slightly more durable machine. Hence, the *ff* curve of Fig. 37-2(b) will look almost smooth to the naked eye, even though a microscope reveals it to consist of many short line segments that meet in corners. The simplified K fable thus does give some useful insight into a more realistic model, be it the U.S.S.R., the United States, or India.

growth" could thereby be kept equal to any prescribed natural rate of full-employment growth.

Thus, in a year like 1966 when I/Q tended to exceed full-employment s, the rational thing for the government to do was to create a large budgetary surplus: to raise tax rates and lower people's disposable incomes and personal saving, to cut down on government use of resources and on transfers, or to do both. This surplus is, in effect, government saving: call it s_G and combine it with the private saving ratio s_{pr} to get $s =$ average (s_G, s_{pr}) as big as is needed to equal I/Q without inflation.

During the sluggish years of the early 1960s, the opposite fiscal policies would be designed to compensate: With $I/Q < s_{pr}$, a budget deficit creates government dissaving (or negative saving); then at full employment $I/Q = s$, the average of s_{pr} and the government dissaving ratio.

In summary, laissez-faire Harrodian discrepancies can lose their terror and relevance in a mixed economy.

THE EXPANDING UNIVERSE: A DIGRESSION

The late John von Neumann, a brilliant mathematician who helped build the hydrogen bomb and who founded the theory of games, described an economic model in which everything could be produced out of everything. If land and/or labor are no longer scarce limiting factors, then the law of diminishing returns no longer applies. All the fruits of production, above and beyond the costs of subsistence for horses, rabbits, looms, and comfortably living men, are plowed back into the system for growth of more horses, rabbits, looms, men.

In this system, which is like Smith's golden age except that it definitely involves capital goods, there is a maximal rate of balanced growth. And it turns out that such a growth rate—call it g because of its resemblance to the Harrod natural rate of growth—is exactly equal to the interest rate i.

Because development theory, for countries like India and the United States, is preoccupied with the concept of "balanced growth," the Neumann model is of considerable interest. It is particularly relevant to the case where an industrial sector in a poor country finds it can get an unlimited supply of laborers from the rural sector at the same wage cost in terms of subsistence; needing little land, the industrial sector can "take off" and grow at a constant Neumann-percentage rate per year, pro-

vided it can produce the capital goods needed to match the new labor or can be helped by imports from foreign lenders, aiders, or exporters.

If there is technical change, the system can advance at a rate even faster than the Neumann rate; indeed, if the system can, so to speak, manufacture new inventions that make labor grow in efficiency at a steady percentage rate, it will then appear to an observer to be capable of even faster Neumann growth.

A simplest example of an expanding system would be the case of rabbits (or men) who produce 1.05 rabbits of output for each rabbit of input. The interest rate and the growth rate will obviously then be 5 per cent per period. Other examples are not quite so simple.

LEONTIEF'S INTERINDUSTRY INPUT-OUTPUT

The important interindustry tableau of Wassily Leontief is a modern-day realization of the eighteenth-century dream of a physiocratic economist, Francois Quesnay, who first envisaged the *Tableau Économique* or circular flow of economic life. A score of nations—such as France, Norway, Egypt, the United States, the United Kingdom, and India—have computed input-output tables as an amplification of their national-income data and as a possible aid in development planning.[14]

Using agriculture and manufacturing as sample industries, Table 37-2 gives an oversimplified illustration of the table comprising several hundred industries that the government and Leontief have prepared for the American economy. Here is its general idea. Each industry is listed twice: in a *row* as an *ouput;* in a *column* as a needed *input.* In addition, the final consumption of households is treated as an extra column and their *labor* (or other primary factors of production supplied by households) as an extra row. These house-

[14] For additional discussion of theory and applications see Wassily Leontief, *The Structure of the American Economy, 1919–1929* (Harvard University Press, Cambridge, Mass., 1941) (2d ed.: *1919–1939*, Oxford University Press, Fair Lawn, N.J., 1951); or Wassily Leontief, *Input-Output Economics* (Oxford University Press, 1966). As part of the price that Leontief has to pay to make Walras's general equilibrium empirically measurable, he is forced to make the technical assumption that all factor proportions—to each other and to total output—are technologically *fixed* or constant. (Back in Chapter 27's Appendix, page 528, we found reason to doubt that such an engineering assumption can be strictly realistic; but Leontief's clever statistical use of the fixed-coefficient case deserves notice here.)

Leontief's input-output tableau x-rays the economy:

	AGRICULTURE	MANUFACTURING	HOUSEHOLD FINAL CONSUMPTIONS	GROSS TOTALS
AGRICULTURE		400	200	600
MANUFACTURING	200		600	800
HOUSEHOLD LABOR AND OTHER FACTORS	400	400	——	
GROSS TOTALS	600	800		1,400

TABLE 37-2. EXAMPLE OF INTERINDUSTRY MONEY FLOWS DURING HYPOTHETICAL COLD-WAR PERIOD (in billions of dollars). Each industry appears twice, in a row and column: its row lists allocation of its total gross output as inputs for other industries and for final consumption; its column shows inputs needed to produce it.

The green numbers show *gross* outputs, inclusive of amounts needed as intermediate inputs. To compute NNP without double counting, we add only the factor payments (or "value added") of the shaded row; or alternatively, only the final-consumption flows of the shaded column. (Fill in the proper NNP in the indicated blank, and check it two ways.)

hold figures are the numbers that enter into national income or net national product and are on the shaded part of the table. (Actually Leontief also includes government, foreign trade, investment, and other detail.)

The *gross* value of agricultural output is shown by the green $600 (billion) twice: at its row's right as the sum of all the places where farm output went—$400 as input to manufacturing plus $200 directly consumed by households as food—and at its column's bottom as the sum of the $200 cost it paid for manufacturing inputs (chemical fertilizers, etc) and the $400 cost it paid for labor input (and other household factors).

Give a similar interpretation of the $800 gross total for manufacturing.

The table also shows our old friend national income, or NNP. With no government or investment in the picture, NNP of 800 (billion, remember) equals the sum of the third shaded column's final products; or alternatively NNP equals the sum of all factor-cost or values added shown in the shaded third row's wages. (NNP definitely doesn't include the intermediate purchases of one sector from another; the total in green of $1,400 unquestionably involves double counting.)

This input-output table is more than a record of past history. How does Leontief or a planner hope to use it? *He hopes to use it to forecast the effects of changing consumption requirements.*

Thus, suppose Table 37-2 refers to a current cold-war situation where manufacturing employment and output has been swollen by military needs. (For dramatic effect we may think of peacetime goods or "butter" as coming largely from the agricultural sector

and military goods or "guns" as coming largely from the manufacturing sector.)

■ Now suppose "peace breaks out." What will have to be planned for the new deployment of labor and other inputs if full employment is still to be maintained? Suppose we now want to double agriculture's final consumption, from the old brown $200 to new $400, at the same time cutting the military manufacturing sector back from old brown $600 to new $400. On the basis of his assumption of fixed input-output coefficients, Leontief can solve linear equations for the new peacetime state and show that it *must* then be in the configuration given in Table 37-3. Ten per cent of the workers (i.e., $^{80}/_{800}$) must be shifted from war work to peace work. Similarly Leontief's tableau scheme can help plan for any development change in final-consumption goods.[15]

[15] All details aside, his key assumption is that $^{200}/_{600} = ^1/_3$ of agriculture receipts will always be spent on manufacturing input, with the remaining $^{400}/_{600} = ^2/_3$ always spent on labor input. Similarly, $^{400}/_{800} = ^1/_2$ is the fraction that manufacturing will always spend on its needed agricultural input, the remainder $^1/_2$ being spent on needed labor input.

0	400			0	$^1/_2$
200	0		→	$^1/_3$	0
400	400			$^2/_3$	$^1/_2$
600	800			1	1

Table 37-2 is repeated here in abbreviated form to show how one derives the green fixed input-output coefficients needed for the transition to Table 37-3 or to any other situation envisaged by the planner. Now, if we call *gross outputs* of the two sectors X_A and X_M and their *final-consumption*

Input-output tableau helps us plan:

	AGRICULTURE	MANUFACTURING	HOUSEHOLD FINAL CONSUMPTIONS	GROSS TOTALS
AGRICULTURE		320	400	720
MANUFACTURING	240		400	640
HOUSEHOLD LABOR AND OTHER FACTORS	480	320	800	
GROSS TOTALS	720	640		1,360

TABLE 37-3. NEW PEACETIME INPUT-OUTPUT FLOWS (in billions of dollars). End of cold war causes shift from guns to butter: agricultural final consumption goes up by 200 billion dollars, manufacturing down by same. Using fixed input-output coefficients from Table 36-2, Leontief calculates needed change in gross outputs shown here and resulting needed labor shifts and intermediate input changes. Same techniques help in development planning.

amounts C_A and C_M, Leontief must finally allocate the total X's thus:

$$X_A = C_A + \tfrac{1}{2} X_M \qquad X_M = C_M + \tfrac{1}{3} X_A$$

For the peacetime tableau of Table 37-3, this means

$$X_A = 400 + \tfrac{1}{2} X_M \qquad X_M = 400 + \tfrac{1}{3} X_A$$

These can be solved simultaneously by simple algebra to give $X_A = 720$, $X_M = 640$, from which all of Table 37-3 can be filled in using the green fractions.

REMARK: To avoid simultaneous equations, Leontief can use a "multiplier" method. Each manufacture requires $\tfrac{1}{2}$ of agriculture as input, and each of these in turn requires $\tfrac{1}{3}$ of manufacture as its input; so *indirectly* each manufacture requires $\tfrac{1}{2} \times \tfrac{1}{3} = \tfrac{1}{6}$ of extra manufactures to produce itself. So $[1 + \tfrac{1}{6} + (\tfrac{1}{6})^2 + \cdots]$ adds up to 1.2, which is the needed expansion of new *gross* manufacture for each 1.0 expansion of *consumption* manufacture. Similarly Leontief can calculate a multiplier for agriculture, showing how each billion-dollar

change in its final consumption requires its *own* gross output to go up (coincidentally!) by 1.2 billion dollars. To compute what the shift of 200 billion dollars from guns to butter entails, Leontief must know how much gross agriculture and how much labor is needed to accommodate the 1.2 of manufacture that its own consumption expansion generated. The answer is not hard: The second column's green manufacturing input requirements give the answers—$\tfrac{1}{2}$ of 1.2, or .6 in both cases. The reader should now be able to verify that when 1 new agriculture consumption entails 1.2 of its *own* gross output, the amounts needed for manufacturing and labor are $\tfrac{1}{3}(1.2) = .4$ and $\tfrac{2}{3}(1.2) = .8$. Given the knowledge of this paragraph's "own multipliers" and "cross multipliers"—the so-called "inverse matrix"—we perceive how Leontief is able to apply them to the $+200$ consumption shift to agriculture and -200 shift from manufacturing to get the changes needed to convert wartime Table 37-2 to peacetime Table 37-3.

SUMMARY TO APPENDIX

1 ■

Schumpeter's stress on innovation, followed by competitive erosion of profit, is an important version of neoclassical development.

2 ■

If the capital-output ratio is an inflexible constant, neoclassical deepening of capital cannot be engineered by expansionist monetary policy.

3 ■

The Harrod-Domar concept of the "natural rate of growth" g is determined by population growth and technical change. If K and Q are to grow at this balanced rate, the required fraction of income that has to be voluntarily saved is given by the Harrod condition,

$$s = g(K/Q).$$

4 ■

The warranted rate of growth W will be higher than the natural rate g if the actual desired saving ratio S/Q exceeds the s needed by Harrod's condition. In the case where K/Q is constant for previous and for new changes,

$$W = \frac{S/Q}{K/Q}$$

If this W rate persisted, it would be self-warranting in the sense of coaxing out investment just large enough to match desired saving.

It will not come of its own accord or be stable against upward or downward disturbances. When $W > g$, a self-warranting expansion from a low trough would ultimately bump into the ceiling set by population and other bottlenecks, possibly bouncing back into recession.

A stubborn divergence of S/Q from s, or of W from g, could be controlled by budget surpluses or deficits, which augmented (or subtracted from) private saving enough to keep $s = I/Q$ and $W = g$, and which by a steadying hand would overcome Harrodian instability of income growth.

5 ■

Where a neoclassical deepening of capital makes the K/Q ratio an accommodating variable, the Harrod conditions lose their terrors. Whatever people's thrift wants to make their private full-employment s be, a combination of monetary and fiscal policies can hope to induce the needed offsetting investment. Such fiscal and monetary policies can speed up capital formation and the technical changes embodied in, and stemming from, such new equipment. They can help the system grow faster than the natural growth of working population. They can stabilize the achievable rate of progress so that the system will be warranted in doing what comes naturally. But, even in a flexible neoclassical technology, *laissez faire* will not—in the absence of appropriate public monetary and fiscal policies—be led by an Invisible Hand to these ideal conditions.

6 ■

The neoclassical model can parcel out the sources of Q growth into growth from more L, from more K, and from technical change. The last factor interacts with L through education and training and with K through embodiment in new machines. Still, technical change seems to have been historically primary in advanced nations.

7 ■

Joan Robinson and Nicholas Kaldor agree in their suspicion of aggregates of so-called capital and in their doubts about smooth deepening of capital under capitalism; both look to factors of dynamic growth for determination of profit shares. (All this is still controversial.)

8 ■

It is intellectually unsatisfying to explain some constancy trends by appeal to "coincidence" or to fortuitous canceling out of diverse tendencies of diminishing returns and technical change. So one can applaud the attempts to find mechanisms (induced invention, lifetime saving, etc.) that bring the constancies about. However, if like the present writer, you would not be much surprised to see K/Q fall in the future or drift in any direction, the wage share gradually rise, or the rate of profit sag or soar, you must beware of "overexplanations." If a thing may actually be a coincidence, you are not saying much by calling it that. But to explain away a coincidence which truly is a coincidence, is worse than a banality; it is a scientific sin.

9 ■

Leontief's tableau of interindustry flows gives a useful picture of the relations lying behind aggregate NNP data. By positing fixed input-output coefficients, a planner can use the Leontief technique to program a shift from war pattern of consumption to peace, or any other developmental target goal.

QUESTIONS FOR DISCUSSION

1. Add acres of land, A, to the neoclassical discussion along with L, K, and T.C.

2. Contrast unemployment notions of Keynes and Eisner-Hansen with those of Schumpeter and Ricardo.

3. Why is g important for long trends? W for business cycles? Reread Chapter 14's acceleration principle.

4. Explain to yourself the basic idea of the two-way Leontief tableau.

5. Review your understanding of the following concepts:

innovation and deepening of capital

fixed versus variable K/Q ratio

natural versus warranted growth

$$s = g \frac{K}{Q} \quad \text{and} \quad W = \frac{S/Q}{K/Q}$$

% Q growth = % L growth + $\cdots$

von Neumann model

input-output tableau

38 Problems of Economic Growth and Development

I BELIEVE IN MATERIALISM. I BELIEVE IN ALL THE PROCEEDS OF A HEALTHY MATERIALISM,—GOOD COOKING, DRY HOUSES, DRY FEET, SEWERS, DRAIN PIPES, HOT WATER, BATHS, ELECTRIC LIGHTS, AUTOMOBILES, GOOD ROADS, BRIGHT STREETS, LONG VACATIONS AWAY FROM THE VILLAGE PUMP, NEW IDEAS, FAST HORSES, SWIFT CONVERSATION, THEATRES, OPERAS, ORCHESTRAS, BANDS,—I BELIEVE IN THEM ALL FOR EVERYBODY. THE MAN WHO DIES WITHOUT KNOWING THESE THINGS MAY BE AS EXQUISITE AS A SAINT, AND AS RICH AS A POET; BUT IT IS IN SPITE OF, NOT BECAUSE OF, HIS DEPRIVATION. FRANCIS HACKETT, IRELAND

All the economic principles we have learned can now be brought to bear on perhaps one of the most challenging problems of the next quarter century—the problem of underdeveloped economies.[1] There are about $3\frac{1}{2}$ billion people in the world, and at this moment half of them are hungry—literally hungry. Only someone who has been pursuing beauty or health on a temporary diet of less than 1,500 calories per day will know how food can fill one's dreams and every waking thought.

For conscience's sake, we are impelled to help. Besides, history teaches us that men do not always starve quietly.

■ DEFINING UNDERDEVELOPMENT

Writers used to speak of "backward" nations, which naturally irritated the people of those lands. To avoid offense the United Nations sometimes used the roundabout expression "less developed" nation. Today most people adopt the expression "underdeveloped" nation. What is meant by the term? Alternative definitions are given; most seem to involve the following:

■ An underdeveloped nation is simply one with real per capita income that is low relative to the present-day per capita incomes of such nations as Canada,

[1] Three useful anthologies on this subject are Theodore Morgan, George W. Betz, and N. K. Choudhry, *Readings in Economic Development* (Wadsworth Publishing Company, Belmont, Calif., 1963), A. N. Agarwala and S. P. Singh, *The Economics of Underdevelopment* (Oxford University Press, Fair Lawn, N.J., 1960), Bernard Okun and Richard W. Richardson, *Studies in Economic Development* (Holt, Rinehart and Winston, Inc., New York, 1961).

the United States, Great Britain, and Western Europe generally. Usually, an underdeveloped nation is one regarded as being capable of substantial improvement in its income level.

Of course, every country is underdeveloped in the sense that it is not yet perfect and hence is capable of being improved still further. Even the so-called "advanced" countries were once underdeveloped by our definition and had to go through the process of development. Table 38-1 gives a picture of the relative stages of development of different countries.

Less than one-seventh of the world's population live in the highly developed group A with more than $1,200 per capita; just over one-fifth live in the intermediate group B; about two-thirds live in the underdeveloped group C.

About one-third of the world's population lives behind the Iron Curtain. The Soviet Union now falls in the intermediate group B; but only barely, for soon it will push into the highly developed group A. As for the rest of the communist countries, how are their people divided among the groups? Recalling the vast population of China, we are not surprised to find two-thirds of the Iron Curtain peoples falling in the lowest group C and none in group A. Little wonder, then, that economic development is a lively subject everywhere.

■ CHARACTERISTICS OF UNDERDEVELOPED ECONOMIES

To bring out the contrasts between advanced and underdeveloped economies, imagine that you are a typical twenty-one-year-old in one of the underdeveloped countries, be it Haiti, India, or Nigeria.

You are poor: even after making generous allowance for the goods that you both produce and consume, your annual income averages barely $100 per head, as against $3,000 per head of your fellow man in North America; perhaps you can find cold comfort in the thought that only 1 in 10 of the human race averages more than $1,000 per year. To each of your people who can read, there are three like you who are illiterate. Your life expectancy is only two-thirds that of the average man in the advanced country: already one or two of your brothers and sisters have died before reaching adulthood; and though your mother has had fewer children than your grandmother did, more of your brothers and sisters have lived to maturity, thanks to imported medical techniques—and you must compete with them for subsistence.

Most of your countrymen work on rural farms; few can be spared from food production for factories or service trades. You work with but one-fiftieth the horsepower of your prosperous North American fellow man. You know little of science, but much of folklore. Your methods and tools are primitive. Neither the discipline of markets nor the deliberations of planning commissions mean much to you. As a citizen in Asia, Africa, or Latin America, you and your fellows together constitute 70 per cent of the world population, but you must divide among you only 20 per cent of world income. You brood over the fact that the United States, with 6 per cent of the people, enjoys about 30 per cent of world income; and that Western Europe, with 9 per cent of the people, enjoys 22 per cent of world income.

Most countries fall in the underdeveloped category:

A. Highly developed	C. Underdeveloped	
Australia	*Africa:*	*Americas* (continued):
Belgium	Algeria	El Salvador
Canada	Angola	Guatemala
Denmark	Cameroon	Haiti
Finland	Chad	Honduras
France	Congo	Nicaragua
Germany	Dahomey	Paraguay
Netherlands	Ethiopia	Peru
New Zealand	Ghana	
Norway	Guinea	
Sweden	Ivory Coast	*Asia:*
Switzerland	Kenya	Afghanistan
United Kingdom	Liberia	Burma
United States	Libya	Cambodia
	Malagasy Republic	Ceylon
B. Intermediate	Malawi	China
Argentina	Mali	Formosa
Austria	Morocco	India
Brazil	Mozambique	Indonesia
Chile	Niger	Iran
Costa Rica	Nigeria	Iraq
Czechoslovakia	Rwanda	Jordan
Greece	Senegal	Korea
Hungary	Sierra Leone	Laos
Ireland	Southern Rhodesia	Lebanon
Israel	Sudan	Nepal
Italy	Tanzania	Pakistan
Jamaica	Togo	Philippines
Japan	Tunisia	Saudi Arabia
Malaysia	Uganda	Syria
Mexico	United Arab Republic	Thailand
Panama	Upper Volta	Turkey
Poland	Zambia	Viet Nam
Portugal		Yemen
Puerto Rico		
Singapore	*Americas:*	
Spain	Bolivia	*Europe:*
Union of South Africa	British West Indies	Albania
U.S.S.R.	Colombia	Bulgaria
Uruguay	Cuba	Romania
Venezuela	Dominican Republic	Yugoslavia
	Ecuador	

TABLE 38-1. COUNTRIES GROUPED BY LEVEL OF ECONOMIC DEVELOPMENT. (Sources: Updated by author from E. Staley, *The Future of Underdeveloped Countries*, rev. ed., Harper, New York, 1961; United Nations Statistical Office; and Center for International Studies, MIT.)

■ URGENCY OF THE PROBLEM

There have always been differences between rich and poor. Why worry especially about the underdeveloped countries? Here are some reasons:

WIDENING DIFFERENTIALS   In contrast to the narrowing of income differentials within the advanced nations, the divergence between advanced and underdeveloped countries is probably now widening rather than narrowing. The United States and Western Europe have doubled their production per head since 1938. Many experts believe that living standards in India, Indonesia, and certain underdeveloped countries have improved little since then and may even have deteriorated in some regions.

IDEOLOGICAL STRUGGLE   In the modern ideological war between the free and the communist worlds, the communists regard the underdeveloped regions as our Achilles' heel. They ceaselessly agitate in such lands, never failing to point out the poverty there, never failing to contrast it with our wealth, never failing to remind the people there of real and fancied evils of "colonialism." Cuba is a nearby example. Africa and Asia are cases in point.

Alas, experience does not bear out the easy generalization, "Fill the stomachs of people and they will refrain from going communist." Not necessarily: men in utter misery often seem incapable of revolting; and the big revolutions of the past (such as the French and Russian) have often taken place at a time when some economic progress had already been achieved.

Nonetheless, to turn our backs on the problem of development is to court future disaster. Harvard's distinguished economic historian Alexander Gerschenkron has drawn the following important lesson from history:[2]

> The Soviet government can be properly described as a product of the country's economic backwardness. Had serfdom been abolished by Catherine the Great or . . . in 1825, the peasant discontent, the driving force and the earnest of success of the Russian Revolution, would never have assumed disastrous proportions, while the economic development of the country would have proceeded in a much more gradual fashion. . . . The delayed industrial revolution was responsible for a political revolution in the course of which the power fell in the hands of a dictatorial government to which in the long run the vast majority of the population was opposed. . . . The paramount lesson of the twentieth century is that the problems of backward nations are not exclusively their own. They are just as much problems of the advanced countries. It is not only Russia but the whole world that pays the price for the failure to emancipate the Russian peasants and to embark upon industrialization policies at an early time. Advanced countries cannot afford to ignore economic backwardness.

To reinforce this, tick off the advanced countries in Table 38-1. You cannot find a single one that has had a successful proletarian revolution.

---

[2] Alexander Gerschenkron, "Economic Backwardness in Historical Perspective," in Bert F. Hoselitz (ed.), *The Progress of Underdeveloped Areas* (University of Chicago Press, Chicago, 1952), pages 27–29.

GREAT EXPECTATIONS AND "DEMONSTRATION EFFECTS"   Within the underdeveloped countries, people are today acutely aware of their poverty and its contrasts with rich lands. They do not like it. What is more, they insist on doing something about it.

This was not always so: a century ago the Emperor of China sent a message to the Queen of England saying that his country neither needed nor desired economic improvement. Look at today's frantic efforts in China and mark the contrast. In the ancient formula,

$$\text{Happiness} = \frac{\text{material consumption}}{\text{desire}}$$

Thoreau's counsel to hold down the denominator now gives way to insistence on increasing the numerator of material real income.

So perfect are modern instruments of communication that people everywhere know about—and often envy—the comforts of modern Western life. No longer do they shrug their shoulders and accept their relative poverty as the divine will of Allah. Most important, this increased awareness comes at a time when the role of government is highly developed.

Today, when people want something done, they are likely to turn to government and to insist that programs be adopted toward the desired goal. They want to foreshorten history and get now what developed lands got late.

They want better health; land reform, the breaking up of landowners' holdings; better methods of land cultivation; industrialization; political rights as individuals. It is easy to see that men want these things for natural individualistic reasons. But economic welfare is not the only reason why men desire development. Modern peoples desire development also for reasons of *nationalism:* people want their country to be powerful, to be respected, and—let us face it—to be feared. Thus, the English and Dutch may have brought sanitation to their former colonies; they may have thereby increased people's life spans and material well-being. But they did at the same time set up exclusive clubs whose front doors were barred to the native citizenry. "Freedom from contempt" is one Asian's way of describing his goal.

■ SUPERFICIAL THEORIES OF DEVELOPMENT

GEOGRAPHY   A look at Table 38-1 shows that all the advanced countries are in the temperate zones. Every tropical country is a poor one. Hence, the argument used to go, it is all a matter of *climate.*

This sweeping explanation will not fit the facts. The first civilizations were in regions of the Mediterranean and Near East (or, if you will, in the Mayan regions of Central America). Greece was in her glory when Germans and Saxons were cowering over fireplaces in their caves.

Certainly, climate is an important factor, but it is not all-important. It does help not to have tropical heat and erosion from jungle floods. It does help not to have arctic snows. But one of the consequences of modern technology is that fevers can be checked by DDT. The bitter Oxford or Oslo cold can be offset by heating; and the humid heat of Texas need no longer inhibit the pace of body and mind.

■ The geographical distribution of *natural resources*—topsoil, rainfall, dammable water for irrigation and power, oil and ore deposits—all these are important. But in a world where trade is increasingly possible, grave deficiencies in this respect can be at least partially offset, as the examples of Denmark, Japan, and Israel have shown.

RACE   Throw a stone in the advanced countries and the skin you bruise is likely to be white. Ergo, the tale ran, prosperity is merely a matter of race.

No one has yet been able to find a causal link between a tendency toward albinism and productivity; the pioneers of Egyptian, Greek, Indian, and Roman cultures were generally not blond or tall. The most remarkable phenomenon of economic development in this last century and in this last decade has undoubtedly been the Japanese. Anthropologists cannot completely agree in classifying *homo sapiens* into the Mongolian, Caucasian, and other categories.

■ A glance at history—at the Ethiopian and Berber cultures, at ancient China, primitive northwestern Europe, and flowering Near Eastern cultures—reveals that many factors have been dominant, and that the factor of race itself cannot be isolated as a discernible determinant of economic development.

CUSTOM AND CULTURE   Victoria's England or Coolidge's America came as close as any culture ever has to being a business culture. In the 1920s a biography of Jesus in terms of accounting virtues could be a best-seller. Hence, some have leaped to the theory that people must behave like the *homo economicus* of the classical textbooks if a nation is to prosper.

This is a caricature. It provides a truth, and hides a more important truth.

■ Material progress does depend on replacement of a belief in magic and superstition by discernment of and belief in the cause-and-effect relations of engineering and science. If it is a nation's tradition to abhor manual work or work in general; if its people emphasize the hereafter as against this world; if they despise material prosperity; if they discourage ordinary honesty in contractual dealings with strangers; if their way of life puts a great premium on current consumption rather than provision for the future; if their government officials are corrupt and inefficient—all such cultural traits are not particularly conducive to economic development.

But putting stress on these noneconomic factors does not solve the problem of *explanation*. It poses new problems. Why did the brains that might have gone into business in many countries go into science? Why did the anthropologists who stressed the unchangeable inertia of custom in Mexico go wrong in their predictions that penetration of the money psychology would be slow there?

We must not throw away seminal explanations merely because they turn out to be superficial and even wrong. But we must not overlook their superficialities and errors. Max Weber's celebrated emphasis on the "Protestant ethic" as both cause and effect of capitalistic development is a case in point. It did fit some facts: many of the advanced nations are Protestant. John Calvin and *some* Protestant theologians did break away from the Catholic Church's ancient edicts against interest. John D. Rockefeller, Sr., was both an avaricious profit maximizer and an ardent Baptist, who referred to his gains as "God's Gold." Yet the "buts" that have to be applied to the Weber thesis are many and serious.

Northern Italy and Catholic Rhineland showed early development. You can find in eighteenth-century Japanese writings perfect passages of Weberian Protestantism. The Jews, Chinese, and Basques have in many places played the role of the alienated stranger who pioneers in economic entrepreneurship. And if Weber seriously regards Benjamin Franklin—who undoubtedly was a prototype of the scientist, innovator, and business go-getter—as an other-worldly Protestant, biographers of that cynical deist tell us the name has almost lost its meaning. Modern statistical research on the Protestant and Catholic neighborhoods in German cities, upon which Weber originally rested part of his case, has found that correct statistical tabulation even belies Weber's own findings.

Whether or not Weber in some subtle sense was right, think how badly a crude belief in his theory would have served for prediction 20 years ago: The economies that have shown the greatest miracles of growth since 1950 have been Japan, Catholic France and Italy, largely Catholic West Germany, and atheistical Russia. Such predominantly Protestant countries as Canada, Britain, and the United States have done poorly in comparison.

All this proves nothing, because there is almost nothing to prove.

■ RECENT CONCEPTS TO DESCRIBE DEVELOPMENT

For a quarter century economists have been intensely interested in economic development. While they have developed no unified theory that differs from the basic growth models introduced in the last chapter, they have added some special features to these models.

The following brief account represents a montage of the most important notions developed in the recent literature. It will pave the way for a systematic causal analysis in terms of the economic determinants of production: land and natural resources; labor (in quantity of man-hours and in quality of skills, training, and effort); capital formation; finally, technological knowledge and innovation. The chapter ends with a brief discussion of modern development planning.

PRECONDITIONS FOR GROWTH Human history is long and economic development is exceptional, being primarily the outcome of the last few centuries of Western history. During most of history, life was short, nasty, and brutish. A cruel Malthusian equilibrium prevailed in which deaths kept in balance with births.

In a few lucky places, warfare diminished. Superior production methods were applied to ample resources. A surplus over subsistence became possible. And usually wealth was so unequally divided among the aristocratic landowners and the bulk of the populace that the rich were able to abstain from consumption and to funnel savings into capital formation. Economic development could now take place.

THE TAKE-OFF The more historians study the facts, the more gradual and evolutionary seems the process of growth. But revolution is always better drama and journalism than evolution. So various economists like to use words such as "the take-off," "the spurt," and the "big push" to describe the period of accelerating growth. Thus, W. W. Rostow[3] develops stages of growth different from those of Marx and other writers described in the previous chapter. One of his stages is called the take-off, the obvious analogy being with an airplane, which can get off the ground only after it has attained a certain critical speed.

There is no purpose here in joining in the search to find out when each country had its take-off: England in the eighteenth century, Japan in the late nineteenth, the Congo in the 1980s. Nor shall we divide a country's development in stages the way Shakespeare divides a man's life into various ages. Instead, we abandon strict chronology to stress the important economic *principle* that the take-off serves to dramatize.

INCREASING RETURNS, SOCIAL OVERHEAD CAPITAL, AND EXTERNALITIES   The last chapter's models of production proceeded for the most part in terms of the conventional economic principle of diminishing returns—referring to statical variations in labor applied to relatively fixed land, or to variations in the stock of capital goods applied to less rapidly expanding labor supply. That conventional model of production assumed that doubling all the factors together would, typically, exactly double total product—a principle referred to as "constant returns to scale" and serving as a background to the law of diminishing returns to a varying factor.

In dynamic economic development, the phenomenon of "*increasing* returns" is to be expected. Smith's *Wealth of Nations* was in its day a manual of economic development: not for nothing did he encourage honesty and thrift. What Smith stressed was the advantage of *large-scale division of labor.* It is a case of the whole being bigger than the sum of its parts: if all factors together can be increased in size, product will grow *more* than proportionally. Each primitive region cannot develop the scale to achieve efficiency. A pile of enriched uranium suddenly goes active when it achieves a certain size. Similarly, the phenomenon of increasing returns can make it possible for dramatic spurts and accelerations to occur in economic development. (As we saw in Part Three, important areas of increasing returns cannot be left to the free play of competitive market forces; there is a case here for coordination, to prevent monopoly and to channel it into optimal patterns.)

Professor Paul Rosenstein-Rodan introduced, three decades ago, an important related phenomenon. He spoke of the crucial importance of "social overhead capital." To develop, a private economy must have public roads, a railroad, irrigation projects and dams, public health spraying against malarial mosquitoes. All these involve bulky *indivisibilities* of the increasing-returns type. No small firm or family can profitably undertake them; nor can pioneering private enterprise hope to make a profit from them before the markets have been developed. They spread their benefits *socially.* Hence, it is argued, public, as well as private, responsibility is intrinsically involved in economic development from the beginning.

[3] W. W. Rostow, *The Stages of Economic Growth: A Non-Communist Manifesto* (Cambridge University Press, Cambridge, Mass., 1960). See Paul A. Samuelson, J. R. Coleman, F. Skidmore, *Readings in Economics* (McGraw-Hill, New York, 1967, 5th ed.), for a strong critique of the Rostow theses by Harvard's Simon Kuznets.

Another way of putting this, as in Chapter 8 and the Appendix of Chapter 23, is thus:

> ■ Often there are strong *"external economies"* involved in development. A county agent adviser can simultaneously benefit all the farmers in his region. A railroad can benefit all industry. A multiple-purpose dam has similar externalities. It should be obvious that one can find examples of externalities that do not involve increasing returns, and examples of increasing returns that are unrelated to social overhead capital or externalities. But it should be evident that there is often a strong interrelationship between these three notions, which makes them worth being lumped together.

■ BALANCED GROWTH AND INDUSTRIALIZATION

In the development literature, there has often been a fascination with *balanced* growth. One would not want the skull to grow more rapidly than the head's skin. It is similarly argued that growth in a shoe factory should be accompanied by growth in a stocking factory and in a brewery, if what people want at a higher standard of living is shoes, socks, and beer.

For the world as a whole, the budgetary laws of Engel (which were reviewed on page 198) will impose some limited balance on consumption growth. Food will grow, but it will not keep pace with luxury items. Indeed, despite the emphasis on balanced growth, Colin Clark and other writers have long noted an apparent tendency for development to proceed in three stages: *agricultural* dominance first; then *manufacturing* dominance; and finally, as we all become affluent, a shift toward *services*. Supply and demand created these patterns in the old days of relatively free enterprise.

Is balanced growth inevitable or desirable for one region undergoing development? History suggests a negative answer:

> ■ America first developed by *specializing* in agricultural exports. Belgium early developed by specializing in glass and woolen production. The whole theory of comparative advantage, presented in Chapters 34 and 35, suggested that growth within a region does *not* best take place in balance.

This does remind us of an important issue discussed on page 677 as to whether there is not an "infant-industry" and "young-economy" argument that can validly be used to criticize extreme specialization of a country along a few vulnerable lines of comparative advantage. If coffee demand and supply are volatile, and if *future* comparative advantage may lie in certain nonagricultural industries, a country like Brazil may be well advised to interfere with the market tendency to specialize in coffee production. But diversification and truly balanced growth are by no means the same thing.

INDUSTRIALIZATION VERSUS AGRICULTURE   New Zealand, Denmark, Holland, Iowa, and Argentina are all regions where productivity in agriculture does not compare too unfavorably with productivity in industry. They are the exceptions. In most parts of the world, incomes in urban cities are almost double those in rural agriculture. And in the affluent nations large fractions of total resources are devoted to urban manufacture. Hence, many nations jump to the conclusion that industrialization is a *cause* rather than an *effect* of affluence.

One must be wary of making such an inference. As the saying goes, "Rich men smoke expensive cigars; but going out to buy an expensive cigar will not make you rich." Vanity seems to make each country want (1) an airline and (2) a steel mill. Analysis of present and future comparative advantage suggests that for most nations these are ornamental luxuries.

It simply is not true that the greatest productivity advances of the last century have been in industry rather than agriculture. (Recall Chapter 21's discussion of agriculture.) If India's five-year plan could increase the productivity of farming by 20 per cent, that would do more to release resources for production of comforts than would exclusive reliance on promoting industry.

The points made here are obvious. Yet they are often overlooked in political debate. But before leaving the subject, we should point to the germ of truth in the argument for pushing industrialization in order to speed development.

■ City and factory life tend to break up the cake of custom. People in close contact mutually stimulate each other. Hence, technical change is probably stimulated in the long run by subsidy to industrialization. Fortunately, there is often much "disguised unemployment" in rural areas, in the sense that several adult members of each family could move to the city or turn during off-harvest times to local industrial occupations without causing much loss of farm product.

■ CAPITAL NEEDS AND EFFICIENT RESOURCE ALLOCATION

To break out of a vicious circle of poverty and underdevelopment, capital formation is needed. But starving peasants cannot be expected to take much thought of the future. In past ages inequality of land ownership probably helped solve the problem of social thrift, but in a ruthless way. Collectivist economies like China and Russia can by fiat impose the same ruthless abstention from current consumption.

Why cannot free economies do the same? Why cannot they use the fiscal measures discussed throughout this book to curb consumption and stimulate investment? An important reason lies in the realm of political science. Some of the developed countries are able to impose progressive income taxes and find that the taxes do get paid. In most of the world, this is probably not possible. Tax administration is primitive and inefficient. People simply will not cooperate. The problem is made worse where poverty is so great that public officials become corrupt.

As a substitute for taxation and coercion, many writers (such as California's Professor Harvey Leibenstein) recommend that projects be favored which will produce incomes *for corporations and groups that can be counted on to do heavy investment.* They argue that this emphasis should be given even in some cases where there is an actual loss in current efficiency.

PLANNING, WITH OR WITHOUT RESOURCE PRICING   After 1930 Soviet Russia established a first, second, and third Five-Year Plan. Most nations today, including those neutral between East and West, have similar development plans. These set up quantitative goals. Alternative goals are scrutinized for their realism and compatibility. Compromises are made, and finally a compromise set of aggregate targets is worked out.

These targets may be specified in general terms or in quite detailed terms. Thus, India will take into account her growth in labor force; her growth in capital resources from internal sources; the amount of capital she can import from America or the Soviet Union. She will canvass her need for dams and electric power; for steel mills and machinery; etc. In the end a system of priorities will have to be worked out lest the demands on the system become so great as to produce galloping inflation, or as to produce so much expenditure on imports that the country will run out of foreign exchange and have to either devalue or ration severely by a system of import licensing.

Much of this planning will be in concrete physical terms. But much more has to be expressed in terms of rupees of *value*. More importantly, the planners will often find that the values quoted in the market place do not correspond to true national scarcities. Thus, in India people would starve if they were paid a zero wage; yet for many purposes labor is superabundant and ought to be regarded as almost a free factor of production. On the other hand, capital goods are truly scarce; charging fifty times as much for use of a tractor as use of a man may come nowhere near to doing justice to the tractor's scarcity and superior productivity. Hence, some sophisticated planners will actually apply corrected "shadow prices," or "accounting prices" to labor, capital, and imported goods for the purpose of getting a more rational valuation and allocation of scarce resources. That way growth can be maximized.

CAPITAL-OUTPUT RATIOS AND SCREENING OF INVESTMENT PROJECTS   Poor countries are long on labor, short on capital. They are advised, therefore, to economize on the use of heavily durable and intensely roundabout capital projects. Often they are advised to concentrate as much as they can on activities that have a low "capital-output ratio."

This advice is good. But it would be more accurate if expressed in terms of the investment concepts developed in Part Four. Each project should have calculated for it a percentage rate of return per annum: then a hydroelectric project that yields 20 per cent per annum ought to get done before a short-lived steam project that yields only 5 per cent per year—even if, to the superficial eye, the capital-output ratio of the steam plant seems smaller.[4]

We have described the general problem of underdevelopment, and provided tools supplementary to the last chapter's model of growth. Now we can turn to the constructive task of analyzing the four economic fundamentals: (1) population, (2) natural resources, (3) capital formation, and (4) technology.

[4] When experts shift from the capital-output ratio to the "marginal capital-output ratio" they can come out with the economists' correct yield procedures. Also, if capital will be less scarce 20 years from now—so that the correct interest rate society ought to use for its projects is 30 per cent this decade and 18 per cent next decade—a proper planning calculation will take this into account.

■ POPULATION PROBLEMS

Mere growth in numbers does not necessarily mean development. Indeed, as writers since Malthus have warned, unbridled increase in numbers is likely to invoke the law of diminishing returns and to work against increases in per capita living standards. This can create problems. Thus we find many underdeveloped countries repeating the pattern of the eighteenth- and nineteenth-century economies: improved medical technology (e.g., sanitation and in our day cheap DDT) first reduces the death rate; and with birth rates remaining high, population grows rapidly.

El Salvador, Java, and many other examples underline the twin lessons:

■ First, much of the increase in output made possible by technological advance may be spent on duplication of numbers. And second, modern science, conquering disease faster than it operates on food supply, may in the future keep people from dying from germs—only to threaten them with death from famine as they vie for insufficient food.

The big question being asked by demographers is this:

Will birth rates fall in developing countries as they did in older countries? And before living standards actually deteriorate?

IMPROVING HUMAN RESOURCES   Since labor is an important factor of production, there is much constructive programming to be done in this area. When planners draw up blueprints for hastening economic development, they write down the following specific manpower programs:

1. Control disease and increase health and nutrition programs—both to make people happier and to make them more productive workers. Accordingly, do not look on hospitals and sewerage projects as luxuries.

2. Educated people make more productive workers. Therefore budget for schools and other programs to reduce illiteracy. Beyond reading and writing, train people in new techniques of agriculture and industry. Send your best minds abroad to bring back knowledge of engineering and business. (But beware that they do not get drained off to the advanced nations!)

DISGUISED UNEMPLOYMENT   One important condition for promoting development is the better utilization of manpower. In poor countries, particularly rural ones, often a large part of the manpower pool does almost nothing because there is nothing for it to do. Such people may not be counted in the census of unemployment, but they can scarcely be called employed; they live with their kinfolk, and when a boom or a development plan comes along, sweeping them into productive city jobs, there is almost no reduction in the product back on the farm. The same phenomenon of disguised unemployment is met in advanced countries, both in the subsistence farming regions and in the city streets, where men eke out a bare existence doing door-to-door selling or begging whenever productive jobs are unavailable.

For a satisfactory solution to this underemployment and unemployment problem, governments sometimes find it desirable, along with manpower programs, to pursue expansionary fiscal and monetary policies—even though these methods raise problems of inflation and of deficit in the balance of international payments.

■ NATURAL RESOURCES

Poor countries typically have been poorly endowed by nature, and such land and minerals as they do possess must be divided among dense populations. The romantic notion of overlooked geographical areas rich in resources has largely been exploded by geographers. Generally, people have already settled in the most productive regions.

True, geologists are still seeking and finding new hidden resources; and there are authenticated cases where control of malaria by DDT has reclaimed from the jungle hundreds of square miles of fertile Indian land. Balanced against these cheerful considerations is the fact that many underdeveloped countries are rapidly depleting their mines, their topsoil, and their irreplaceable natural resources.

Moreover, as was noted, many of the present-day resources of tropical countries are becoming obsolete in competition with scientific creation of synthetic substitutes from cheap substances found in abundance within the advanced countries. Thus nylon harmed the silk industry and impoverished millions; if synthetic rubber were to replace natural rubber completely, Eastern Asia would find itself unable to maintain its standard of living, low as that is.

Economic geographers are agreed that further development now largely comes from discovery and better use of existing resources. Gone are the opportunities of a Columbus; and half-closing is the open door beckoning the poor of the older regions, begging them to migrate to the fertile prairies of North and South America or to the empty regions of Australia and New Zealand.

Of course, the quip still holds: "There's nothing wrong with any poor country that discovery of oil can't cure." Venezuela, Iraq, Saudi Arabia, Libya, Iran, and Kuwait are cases where oil could help finance development.

LAND REFORM Even without creating or finding new land, nations can make better use of the land they do have. The medieval village was divided into strips of land one could hardly turn around on, and each man might have to live off the produce of two or three such strips, frequently distant from each other. The same is still true in many parts of the world. It took from the thirteenth to the eighteenth century for the painful, and bitterly resented, *enclosure* movement in England to break up the common lands and to gather together into efficient larger-scale plots the land of the country. In the process many peasants were dispossessed and had to go to the city slums. The ruthless, and not altogether successful, "collectivization" of Russian agriculture in the 1920s provides an analogous case; whether China's collectivization is progressing more smoothly is an open question. The displacement of dust-bowl farmers during the 1930s by the tractor has, of course, been dramatically portrayed in John Steinbeck's bestseller *The Grapes of Wrath*. In many parts of the world, this same painful process of consolidating too-small holdings is yet to be carried out.

At the other extreme, we see in many underdeveloped countries landholding of huge estates too large for efficiency.[5] The tenant farmer has no incentive to improve the property, knowing that he can be dispossessed at any time and having learned from bitter experience that little of the fruit of his initiative will ever accrue to him. The landlord in turn has no incentive to improve the property, never knowing whether an irresponsible tenant will dissipate the costly resources placed at his disposal.

As the Communists well know, the situation is explosive, and agitation for land reform signifies a ground swell of public sentiment not long to be denied. As more than one eminent agricultural economist has aptly said:

> ■ Successful reform that puts land in the hands of owners who can count on the fruits of their own enterprise has again and again and in country after country literally "turned sand into gold."

The problems of natural-resource development merge with the problem of improved technology and with the problem of improved capital-goods capacity for utilizing and discovering natural resources.

■ CAPITAL FORMATION

The fingers and brains of men in the underdeveloped countries are much like the fingers and brains of their more prosperous brethren; but men in the advanced nations work with a plentiful supply of capital goods built up over the years. To pile up net capital formation requires, as we have earlier seen, a sacrifice of current consumption. But there's the rub: underdeveloped countries are already so poor as to be near the minimum of subsistence; they feel that they cannot—in fact, they do not—save a very large share of their current national incomes.

Thus, in the advanced nations, from 10 to 20 per cent of income may go into capital formation; but in the underdeveloped nations, the rate of saving and investment may be less than 5 per cent. According to some estimates, the current rate of net capital formation in countries like Nepal or Angola may be less than 5 per cent of total real income (inclusive of nonmonetary items).[6] Merely to provide for rapidly growing population, the primitive tools and housing now enjoyed can use up most of this saving. What is left, then, for development?

> ■ Until we learned how to prevent mass unemployment, many economists worried about *oversaving* in *advanced* countries. But for *underdeveloped* countries the problem is often the classical one of *undersaving:* more precisely, the problem is underinvestment in productive instruments capable of increasing the nation's rate of economic progress.

QUALITATIVE DISTORTION OF INVESTMENT. There is a further problem. Not only are saving and investment *quantitatively* low in these countries; equally serious is the fact

[5] We saw on page 539, Chapter 28, how inefficient systems of land tenancy can put society inside its production-possibility frontier.

[6] In countries going through civil disorders—like Indonesia or the Congo—net saving could be negative.

that the *qualitative composition of investment* is often bad from the standpoint of national development. Thus, too much of the limited saving of India goes into hoarding of gold and jewelry, imported legally or illegally into the country and using up its scarce foreign exchange.

Many underdeveloped countries, like Brazil or Chile, suffer from chronic inflation; hence, there is a natural tendency for people to invest in real estate and in hoarding of inventory. When you can make 20 per cent on your money by hoarding goods, why seek an additional and problematical few per cent from manufacturing? Thus, no less than 55 per cent of Brazil's 1947 investment was in the form of construction. Observers are also struck with the fact that, in many of the poorest regions of the world, *luxury* apartment dwellings seem to mushroom, at the same time that industry is languishing for lack of new equipment.

Still another qualitative dissipation of the limited saving in an underdeveloped country comes from the frequent tendency of the wealthy to pile up their savings *abroad*, legally and illegally, thereby making them unavailable to the nation for its internal development.

CAPITAL FROM ABROAD   If there are so many obstacles to domestic-financed capital formation, why not rely more heavily on foreign sources? After all, did not England in the nineteenth century invest heavily in the United States, Canada, Australia, and Latin America? Did not France before 1914 invest heavily in Czarist Russia and Egypt? And did not Germany invest heavily in Eastern Europe? Does not economic theory tell us that a rich country which has used up all its own high-interest investment projects can benefit itself and at the same time benefit a poor country if only it will shift investment to the high-interest projects not yet exploited abroad?

Actually, prior to 1914 economic development did proceed in this natural fashion. Britain in her heyday saved about 15 per cent of her national income and invested fully half this amount abroad! If the United States were to match these percentages today, *every year* we should have to lend and invest privately about 50 billion dollars, or many, many times the combined Marshall Plan and foreign-aid programs of the federal government, Export-Import Bank, International Bank, and all the rest.

For many reasons, we moderns cannot expect such great amounts of foreign investment. After all, was the pre–World War I pattern so natural, or was it perhaps the special result of fortuitous historical coincidences?

Thus, loans from Europe to the New World typically went together with migration of European peoples to those same new lands: Englishmen went along with their money, so to speak, to the American colonies, Canada, Australia, and other dominions; and notice that the same pattern of laws and customs prevailed in the capital-importing countries as in the capital-investing country.

Remember, too, that this antebellum world was an unbelievably cosmopolitan one. You could travel everywhere with no passport. You could migrate freely from country to country. You could expect low tariffs and no trade quotas. You knew the international gold standard would let you transfer capital from place to place at your slightest whim. You knew your property was safe abroad from government confiscation: back in those days few dreamed of questioning the sanctity of private property, and those nationalistic countries which did raise such questions could be easily intimidated by dispatching battleships for off-coast maneuvers. Finally, you could buy up—literally!—dictatorial governments in many backward countries and bribe them into giving you extremely favorable mining and other concessions.

If this sounds like an investor's paradise, be reminded that the historical facts were not really quite so rosy. Foreign investments often did go bankrupt, there being insufficient commercial demand for the railroads built across the plains of North America and elsewhere. Also, the people in the countries importing capital do not, from their historical utterances, seem to have been too happy over this investor's paradise. But the system did work. And it often did confer *mutual benefits* on both the advanced and backward areas.

Now all this is ancient history. This antebellum world is gone. Never was nationalism stronger than today. Never have borrower and lender been so in agreement: the underdeveloped countries are agreed not to sell to foreigners long-term rights in the development of their countries, no matter how advantageous the price; the developed countries are agreed it would be rash to buy bonds and stocks from backward countries in the old pattern.[7]

This does not mean we must rule out substantial foreign capital investment programs. But to be realistic, we must search out new instrumentalities for carrying them out. Often these will involve agreements between governments or various government guarantees of private ventures. Always foreign investment will have to take into account the rising tide of nationalism.

■ TECHNOLOGICAL CHANGE AND INNOVATIONS

In addition to the fundamental factors of population, natural resources, and capital formation, there is the vitally important fourth factor of technology. Here we can strike a cautiously optimistic note. Here the underdeveloped countries have one possible advantage. They can hope to benefit by copying the more advanced technology of the developed nations.

IMITATING TECHNOLOGY   The new lands do not have to develop still unborn Newtons to discover the law of gravity: they can read about it in any book. They do not have to go through the slow meandering climb of the Industrial Revolution: they can find in every machinery catalogue wonders undreamed of by the great inventors of the past.

Japan, Germany, and Russia clearly illustrate all this in their historical developments. Japan joined the industrial race late: at the end of the nineteenth century she sent her students abroad and began to copy Western technology. Her government took an active and creative role in stimulating the pace of development, building railroads and utilities, and taxing heavily the newly created increments of land value resulting

[7] Even in friendly Canada, citizens have resented the vast post–World War II investment by large United States corporations, and tax penalties were introduced in the 1960s.

from the improvements in agriculture. A few energetic, wealthy families were permitted to develop vast industrial empires, while at the same time the general population was made to work, and work hard, in order to earn its living. Without relying on net foreign capital imports, Japan in a few decades had moved into the front rank both as a military power and as an industrial nation.

Only after the Revolution of 1848 did Germany really accelerate her industrialization. Through government aid to her universities, German scientists soon became preeminent in mathematics, physics, chemistry, and engineering. Fifty years ago, most American professors of these subjects—and of history, economics, and philology, too—went to Germany for their postgraduate degrees. German prowess in organic chemistry, optics, glass manufacture, and electrical equipment was unsurpassed until the two world wars set her back. Russia, too, illustrates the possibility of fast development through technological imitation.

Finally, the case of the United States itself provides an optimistic example to the rest of the world. Until Hitler made us a present in the 1930s of many of the best Continental scientists of all faiths, we could not honestly boast of having quite reached the very front rank in the field of pure science. Yet for a century our applied technology had admittedly been outstanding. Examine one by one the key inventions involving the automobile. Where did they originate? Mostly abroad. Nevertheless, Henry Ford and General Motors long outproduced the rest of the world. "Yankee ingenuity" is a phrase that *explains* nothing; but it does refer to a real phenomenon.

INTERPLAY OF TECHNOLOGY AND CAPITAL   It is all very well to speak of underdeveloped countries copying advanced technology. But have we not overlooked something important? Is not advanced technology embodied in the form of complex capital goods? And have we not already seen that those countries are short of capital? So how can we expect them to copy superior technology?

Certainly there is much truth in these suggestions. Technological change and capital investment do go hand in hand; often they are inseparable. All the same, we are right to treat them as analytically distinct—albeit related—processes. Here is one of many examples to show why:

> Farming is inefficient in many backward countries. You see peasants breaking up the soil by the same primitive methods their ancestors were using back in the time of David and Solomon. Perhaps an ingenious light plow—something simple that would cost no more than a dollar and would pay for itself in the first month—can be found that will both lessen the total amount of capital needed and greatly increase output. This shows how technological innovation can often be capital-*saving* rather than capital-*using*.

Moreover, even in the poorest countries, some gross capital formation is always going on as things are wearing out and are being replaced. Why replace them with the same thing? Why let much of the economy's capital go into mere *duplicative projects*? Surely, it is much better to embody the newly available investment funds in the form of more efficient technological implements. Thus we see how the interrelated factors of capital formation and technology can be mutually reinforcing.

ENTREPRENEURSHIP AND INNOVATION   Does it sound like an easy task for an under-developed economy? All that it must do to telescope into a few years the scores of years it took us to develop is this: Go abroad and copy more efficient methods; bring them back and put them into effect at home; then sit back and wait for the extra product to roll in.

Of course, it does not work quite this way. People in the underdeveloped countries know this from bitter experience. Yet the same illusion keeps cropping up among the people in the so-called "advanced" countries. Too often we think we can send a few technical experts on a short junket to a poor country; after surveying the field for a month or so, they can write up their recommendations for improvement, and then the neatly typed report they leave behind can be "implemented." In this way development will be solved.

Occasionally, in connection with particular technological processes, experts have indeed been able to work wonders in this facile way; thus, an American expert on tanning was sent out to Libya to advise on some of its difficulties, and in a short time he did diagnose the chemical troubles and come up with an effective cure.

■ Technologists soon discover, however, that this sort of quick miracle is exactly what cannot be accomplished in connection with the *development of a whole economy*. Indeed, the typical pattern is one of complete disillusionment: after spending several months surveying an underdeveloped country, the expert is thoroughly impressed with the thousands of cultural and economic barriers to progress, so much so that he comes back with a hopeless feeling of defeat. This thoroughly pessimistic conclusion is probably just as wrong in its way as was the opposite optimistic illusion.

Experience shows development is truly a hard and slow process—but not an impossible one. To hasten its evolution, spontaneous entrepreneurship and innovation must develop among the peoples directly involved. Remember, many cultures begin with a contempt for dirty, hard work—a contempt they often inherit from the colonial elite who used to rule over them. Often, too, they have a contempt for business—for money-grubbing and production. Gradually, they must develop for themselves, *within their own mixed cultural pattern*, a creative group of producers alert to trying out new ways.

Why place the emphasis on creative innovation? Because it is by no means a cut and dried task to adapt advanced foreign technology to an underdeveloped country's own use. Remember, the advanced technology was itself developed to meet the special conditions of the advanced countries. What are these conditions? High money wage rates; laborers scarce in number but replete with industrial skills; plentiful capital inherited from the past; mass production; and so forth. These conditions do not prevail in underdeveloped lands.

Time and time again, experience has shown us how easy it is to obtain a foreign loan to put up a model factory in Turkey or Burma. Often it is imported piece by piece from abroad and embodies the latest wrinkles of Western technology. Yet, with what result? With high production and sales exceeding costs, so as to yield a comfortable profit which can be plowed back into further industrialization? Only too rarely. Often such grandiose imported projects turn out to be extremely unprofitable. The factory that is an optimal investment for New York may in Ankara or Rangoon be a fiasco.

This task of creative innovation is not one for rugged individualism alone. The government can do much to set up extension services in every agricultural province for consulting with farmers on the best seeds, methods of cultivation, and implements. By sponsoring vocational schools and training courses in machine methods—and in bookkeeping, too—the government itself can innovate creatively. Somewhere between complete *laissez faire* and totalitarianism a developing nation must work out its destiny.

■ FIVE-YEAR PLANS

The advanced nations did not develop by means of a formal plan. Historically, England and the United States grew primarily in a spontaneous and unselfconscious fashion. And the same holds for the nations late to become industrialized, such as Japan at the end of the nineteenth century. As we have seen, though, the Soviet Union introduced successive five-year plans from the 1920s onward.

Today all over the underdeveloped world, planning is a fashionable word. No country is too small or backward to have its five- or ten-year plan. Sometimes these are merely fancily worded documents that have little relationship to actual reality and performance. But sometimes they are carefully executed analyses which spell out in considerable detail programs for macroeconomic and microeconomic development. Here are some of the elements involved in a good plan.

1. The plan is based upon the *initial resources* of the country, presupposing a careful inventory of present and future availability of manpower and domestic resources.

2. The plan sets up feasible *targets* or *goals* for the terminal date.

3. The plan sets out the *feasible policies* that will permit achievement of the terminal goals from the initial resources, taking into account the intermediate economic resources that can be imported from abroad (through loans or gifts) and that can be produced at home out of the initial resources through the mechanism of investment or capital formation.

At the least, a plan will involve careful computation of the macroaggregates of gross national product: balance of saving and investment; allocation of resources between public and private sectors, between one region or another, between city and countryside. A good plan will not be so ambitious as to lead to inefficient galloping inflation, or so unambitious as to lead to stagnation and underemployment. Along with macroeconomic fiscal and monetary policies, it will take care that the resulting import demand does not exceed the available supply of foreign exchange, whether this is accomplished by the pricing system or by some method of central rationing. An ideal plan will provide for social overhead capital projects and be alert to the problems of externalities and indivisibilities.

Some plans will involve no more than "indicative planning" at the microeconomic levels, merely keeping diverse industries acquainted with what is going to happen to the aggregates and to their own share of the total, but leaving to their pursuit of profit the resulting net response. Other plans will involve detailed allocation of inputs among different output uses, taking care to check the balance between inputs and outputs. They may or may not use the input-output techniques of general equilibrium developed by Harvard's W. W. Leontief, which (as the last Appendix showed) gives a detailed view of interindustry dollar and resource flows. The plan may or may not use the modern techniques of linear and nonlinear programming, in a form suitable for the giant electronic computer.

Often the plan will make mistakes. A crop failure due to bad weather may throw it out of kilter. Overambitious targets may produce foreign exchange shortages and rampant inflation. Sometimes the subsequent five-year plan will learn from the mistakes of its predecessors. Sometimes a situation goes from bad to worse.

As we shall see in subsequent chapters, a great variety of development programs are possible within the framework of the modern mixed economy. A totalitarian state has certain advantages but also certain disadvantages for a backward country impatient to make progress. Socialism may or may not be desired for its own sake, but there is nothing in the historical experience of development which makes its choice mandatory or necessarily desirable for a nation eager to develop.

SUMMARY

1 ■

Most of the world consists of underdeveloped countries: countries with low per capita incomes relative to the most advanced economies; countries capable of improvement but now lagging behind the growth rates of the advanced nations. The increasing political self-consciousness of such countries, plus the eagerness of the communist ideology to help them "skip the capitalistic stage of development," reinforces our own self-interest in finding new sources of mutually advantageous trade—not, mind you, new objects for imperialistic make-work programs. All this, and altruism too, make the development problem of major interest to us.

2 ■

Geography and climate, race and custom, religion and business attitudes—each factor conditions economic development, but none does so in a simple and invariable way.

3 ■

The phenomena of increasing returns, externalities, and social overhead capital provide some substance to notions of take-offs, spurts, and big pushes. They suggest a scope for supplementation of competitive market forces. But they do not lead at all necessarily to any simple concept of "balanced growth."

4 ■

The key to development lies in four fundamental factors: population, natural resources, capital formation, and technology. Population causes sociological problems of explosive growth in numbers as death rates fall before birth rates fall; the Malthusian devil of diminishing returns stalks the underdeveloped realms. On the constructive economic agenda, improving the population's health, education, and technical training has high priority. The pool of "disguised unemployment" in country and city provides an important manpower source for extra product.

5 ∎

Even in densely populated areas, discovery and better utilization of natural resources can help offset the law of diminishing returns. Land reform raises tremendous problems of transition. The process of capital formation—of investing in soil conservation, irrigation, drainage, and improvement—interacts with the natural-resource category, just as it does with population—through investing in people.

6 ∎

Rates of productive capital formation in underdeveloped countries are low because of (*a*) poverty, (*b*) lack of a bourgeois ethic stressing frugality and acquisitiveness, (*c*) qualitative distortion of saving outlets toward unproductive hoarding of precious objects and idle inventory and toward luxurious real estate or money markets abroad, (*d*) emulation of consumption standards of advanced nations, and (*e*) nationalistic barriers to importing capital on terms acceptable to investors in the advanced countries.

7 ∎

Technological change interacts with, and is embodied in, new capital goods. Nevertheless, it is a distinct process, and one which offers much hope to underdeveloped nations inasmuch as they can copy from advanced nations. The experience of Japan, Russia, Germany, and the United States shows that the process of adapting to one's own fruitful uses the methods developed elsewhere is not easy. It takes a degree of entrepreneurship and creative innovation. One of development's most pressing tasks is to hasten internal growth of the scarce entrepreneurial and commercial spirit.

8 ∎

Five-year plans, involving feasible *targets* to be achieved out of *initial conditions* by suitable macroeconomic or microeconomic *intermediate programs*, occur widely.

QUESTIONS FOR DISCUSSION

1. Would you expect everyone to agree with the praise of material well-being expressed in the quotation at this chapter's beginning?

2. Bertrand Russell is one of the greatest contemporary philosophers, logicians, and writers, yet the following words of his are agreed by all competent historians to be absolutely wrong in asserting that the Industrial Revolution worsened living standards: "The industrial revolution caused unspeakable misery both in England and in America. I do not think any student of economic history can doubt that the average happiness in England in the early nineteenth century was lower than it had been a hundred years earlier; and this was due almost entirely to scientific technique." Actually, real per capita incomes increased. Why the widespread contrary notions?

3. Formulate your views on geography, race, culture, and development.

4. Briefly list the principal contrasts between life in America and in a typical underdeveloped country. Explain historically.

5. Delineate factors important in development; fit each into the outline involving the four main factors: population, ...

6. Suggest some constructive policies to improve net capital formation and entrepreneurship in backward lands. Evaluate each.

7. Review your understanding of the following concepts:

characteristics of underdevelopment

take-off, spurt, etc.

increasing returns, externalities

social overhead capital

balanced growth, diversification

disguised unemployment

planning, accounting "shadow prices"

population and natural resources

medical improvements without food

capital and technology

inequality, poverty, emulation, for-
    eign lending, and capital formation

entrepreneurship and planning

inflation and development

land reform

public and private responsibility

plans: goals, programs,
    initial states

39 Problems of Growth and Price Stability in an Advanced Economy

LET THE WORD GO FORTH FROM THIS TIME AND PLACE, TO FRIEND AND FOE ALIKE, THAT THE TORCH HAS BEEN PASSED TO A NEW GENERATION OF AMERICANS—BORN IN THIS CENTURY, TEMPERED BY WAR, DISCIPLINED BY A HARD AND BITTER PEACE, PROUD OF OUR ANCIENT HERITAGE. . . .   JOHN F. KENNEDY, INAUGURAL ADDRESS

Economic development of backward countries has great popular interest. And so does the problem of how an advanced mixed economy can improve its growth performance without sacrificing stability and equity.

These are issues of intense public debate everywhere. Although any intelligent person might seem equipped to form opinions, in fact all the economic tools of our previous chapters are genuinely needed. In certain ways the problems of prospering nations are more difficult to analyze than those of a poor nation. Not even advanced treatises on economics are able to provide confident, conclusive answers to all the problems in this truly complex area.

■ Survey of contemporary history shows the predominant importance of four related problems: economic growth; economic sluggishness and unemployment; inflationary price creeps, possibly of a new type, different from familiar demand-pull inflation; and international balance-of-payments equilibrium.

These dominate the scene in North America, Europe, and Japan. Under their headings would fall a problem like automation, already discussed in Chapter 18. And as will be seen here, the question of the degree to which post–World War II prosperity depends upon cold-war armaments can be tackled only in terms of the above larger categories; the same is also true of an issue like "structural unemployment." To understand the economics of the future, you must deploy the tools shaped out of the past.

This chapter tries to provide the economic analysis helpful in studying these current policy questions. The final chapter will discuss the variety of alternative economic systems, the gap between the United States and the Soviet Union, and how it may change in future years.

■ MEASURING ECONOMIC GROWTH

Growth is obviously a many-sided process. Although no single number can portray the varied dimensions of over-all growth, the real national product (net or gross) is perhaps the best single indicator. Because GNP and NNP tell largely the same story and GNP data are more commonly met with, this chapter will concentrate on GNP. But certain cautions are in order.

1. For some purposes, possibly such as war, the *absolute* magnitude of real GNP may count; but generally, in thinking about welfare, one would want to deflate GNP for population changes and concentrate on GNP *per capita*.

2. *Leisure* is one of the finest goods of life, but it is not registered in the GNP. Thus separate allowance is to be made for shortening of the work week and year and for degree of lifetime participation in the labor force.

3. A mere increase in the aggregate of GNP, if it were to be accompanied by a serious deterioration in its *distribution among people,* most people would deem no improvement at all. Many observers feel that the problem of WHAT should never be divorced from the problem of FOR WHOM, i.e., from the problem of "equity."

4. *Quality improvements* in goods and services may not be registered accurately in GNP and price-level data, thereby tending to give them an overly pessimistic bias. Some rough allowance for this should be made. (The problem is peculiarly important if one compares a GNP made up of goods that people really want as compared with shoddy and undesired goods allocated to them in some kind of inefficiently run totalitarian society or advertising-dominated mobocracy.)

5. The measuring rod of money cannot gauge many of the important spiritual and *noneconomic aspects of human welfare.* (Some will even argue that the money value of large-finned cars and other material items in an "affluent society" may be indicators of nothing but money value; and that the denizen of smog-ridden cities is to be pitied.)

Subject to these and other qualifications, we shall proceed to use real GNP (i.e., GNP that has been deflated for price-level changes) as the principal quantitative indicator of economic growth.

■ BRIEF HISTORY OF GROWTH

Economic growth has characterized the modern world. Nations have grown in population; in total production and employment; in real national product; in the standard of living that the typical family enjoys today, by comparison with what its grandparents enjoyed; in leisure hours off the job; in relief from the sweat and tedium that used to be man's lot in earning his subsistence. Any and all of these are aspects of economic growth. Each of these economic aspects can be loosely associated with the biological fact that people today live longer and enjoy more years free of sickness and pain.[1]

---

[1] Along with economic growth, a movement has taken place in much of the Western world toward greater political democracy. As the next chapter will discuss, no one is in a position to state what the causal relationships between these economic and political trends might be. Does economic growth induce a widening of political rights, or make such a widening of the suffrage possible? Does causa-

The front flyleaf charts show the steady advancement in real GNP per capita of leading nations. While all such absolute comparisons are difficult, it will be noted that a century ago, Great Britain dropped from her position as the most opulent nation in the world because the United States rate of growth permitted us to surpass her. When one considers how different France and Germany have been in many of their governmental institutions, the similarity of their development is striking. The similar growth patterns of socialistic Sweden and individualistic Switzerland present the same paradox. (Space does not permit showing these countries and France on the flyleaf.)

Although the institutions of capitalism seem to have given citizens an advancing standard of living, the chart shows that the pace of growth has not been perfectly regular. World Wars I and II have left their mark. Moreover, just prior to World War I, in the veritable heyday of *laissez faire,* so to speak, a number of historians thought they could detect a leveling off in growth rates generally for the advanced countries. The Great Depression of the thirties also left its mark, particularly in the American case.

■ Post–World War II growth in the mixed economies does outstrip the best performances of historic capitalism. When people speak nostalgically of the good old days, they should be reminded of this fact.

■ GROWTHMANSHIP

In the 1960s, preoccupation with development of poor regions and the challenge of Soviet growth rates has led to great concern over the questions: Is our growth rate satisfactory? How can it be improved? Many answers are given. Here are a few important viewpoints:

LAISSEZ FAIRE   When Abraham Lincoln was asked how tall a man's legs should be, he replied, "Tall enough to reach the ground." Some firm believers in classical economics are definitely of the following belief:

> However fast the citizenry want their economy to grow, as determined by their day-to-day decisions with respect to spending on present consumption and saving for the future, that is precisely how fast the economy ought to grow.
>
> Thus, if in the last half of the 1950s the annual rate of growth of the real GNP fell from a 4 per cent to a $2\frac{1}{2}$ per cent rate, then that primarily indicates the desire of the citizenry to live well now and not to grow so fast.[2] It would be a mistake to do what America did in the 1960s—to adopt a deliberate faster-growth policy.

---

tion run the other way, with economic growth the result of political emancipation? If this is indeed the case, how can one explain the acceleration of economic growth that has come about in recent decades, accompanied by greater and greater group controls over individual economic behavior? It is not within the province of economics to decide whether all this has been a coincidence or what the likely patterns of causation are. At best, the economist can try to provide some material for the political scientist and philosopher to work with in studying such matters.

[2] Classicists would have a ready answer to the gibe, "I suppose our loss of GNP from 1929 to 1935 was evidence that the American people did not want then to grow at all." They would perhaps aver that, had the proper environment been provided for individualism by proper monetary and other policies, there would have been no Great Depression, and growth would *then* truly have reflected basic desires.

This is not a popular view today, but there is no reason why its adherents should not be given a fair and scientifically objective hearing.

NO NEED FOR FURTHER GROWTH   Ideologically removed from the above view, but somewhat allied in terms of complacency and alarm about growth, would be the belief of some that we are already so affluent a society as to have no great need for further growth. "Why have a third and fourth monstrous car in each garage?" would represent a caricature of this position. Intellectual observers abroad, who regard America as way out in front and as too materialistic anyway, are especially attracted to this view.

FULL SPEED AHEAD   At the opposite extreme is the view of those who feel that the threat of the Soviet Union and our concern to keep neutrals from going communistic make GROWTH the No. 1 problem of the age.

While some would be prepared to grant the government extraordinary powers in order to force the pace of economic growth, others of this persuasion would merely insist that government keep growth in mind in all its actions. Those of the latter group shade into the following numerous camp.

STEPPING UP GROWTH BY PUBLIC AND PRIVATE MEASURES   Most people think a mixed economy like ours should not be satisfied with its spontaneous post–World War II growth rate, but should take positive measures to increase it.

■ WHY GROW?

Advocacy of more growth has attracted odd bedfellows. Here is a summary of the varied reasons given for additional growth:

> The Soviet challenge, military and/or economic
> The struggle to impress the neutral nations, anxious for their own development, that a mixed economy provides the better choice
> The belief that governmental goods and services are most needed by the people in the years ahead but that it will be politically easier for them to bring themselves to meet these needs out of extra growth of GNP rather than by taxing themselves more heavily within the existing GNP
> The belief that, even if more material goods are not themselves most important, nevertheless, a society is happier when it is moving forward and is unhappy when it is stagnating and beset by protectionist and other movements that thrive in such an environment
> A glorification of group participation as against quiet individual pleasures

If the urge to speed up growth is not merely to reflect a desire of a minority to coerce the great majority into doing what they are not really keen about doing, its defense would presumably have to follow a line of reasoning something like this:

> ■ **People exercise two kinds of choices, and each is a good thing.** Every day in the market place they exercise buying and selling choices with their dollars, which in the context of growth means they make various saving and consuming decisions. But also, every year or at other intervals, the people in a democracy exercise their free choices by means of the political ballot.

In making the latter choices, they reveal that they are not really satisfied to let their own day-to-day market choices be decisive with respect to the growth rate. They deliberately, as a sizable majority, impose upon themselves the public policies designed to lead to a higher GNP and higher future consumption of the private and public type.

It will perhaps be realized that, valid as such an argument undoubtedly is, eternal vigilance is needed to ensure that it does not become a subterfuge for dominance by government, or by a minority, over individuals' desires.

■ HOW TO GROW

Let us assume that, from sources outside economics, faster growth is set as a major goal for America or any advanced nation. How does a mixed economy go about increasing its own rate of growth? The answers are by no means obvious. It is clear that a totalitarian society can by ruthless methods of coercion simply channel goods away from current consumption and into capital formation. But can a free society increase its own growth rate and still remain free?

Earlier chapters in Parts Two and Four show how, if at all, a mixed society can, in a democracy, hope to speed up the rate at which its real GNP rises. First, however, some ineffectual solutions ought to be noted.

Why not simply set up the target of 5 per cent growth rate per year? This is indeed easy to do, and as the next chapter indicates, many have done so. But just as one cannot increase his own stature merely by thinking about it, mere exhortation is not likely to accelerate growth. Only if a promotion campaign were really to change people's *fundamental propensities* to consume could much be hoped for here, and a careful scrutiny of exhortation campaigns suggests that they are more effective at selling one brand of soap than at making significant changes in people's *fundamental propensities.*

As we saw in our studies of production in Part Two and in the discussion of development of poorer countries in the last chapters,

> ■ There are certain factors that have to be changed if the rate of growth is to be improved:
> The quantity and quality of population and natural resources
> The stock of capital goods of all kinds
> Finally, the technological efficiency with which the different factor inputs combine to produce a larger output (i.e., scientific and technical knowledge must be improved)

These provide the clues for a sensible program to stimulate growth.

■ EXPANDED PRIVATE AND PUBLIC RESEARCH

We can begin with the least controversial measure aimed at enhancing growth. All agree that expanded research—in pure science, applied science, development and engineering, administration and management—can pay high social dividends in terms of productivity. As was discussed on page 720, it has not been increased capital and labor so much as increased technical productivity that has been responsible for the historically achieved rates of growth. Having more people and more machines of the seventeenth-century variety would not be likely to take us far beyond the standards of living the Mayflower Pilgrims enjoyed once they became adjusted to the new continent. Better machines, not simply new machines, are needed for progress.

Business firms do much research and can be urged to do more. However, there is no reason to think that management is so stupid as not to see for itself how much research is likely to be profitable *to it;* so unless some new public policies on research are added, we are unlikely to achieve greater progress here than is already the case.

This is where the government comes in. Since 1940 the government has been directly and indirectly supporting much of the scientific research done in this country. It could expand the level of its support. But how can this be justified as a legitimate function of government?

Recall from Chapter 8 that there is a prima facie case for public intervention whenever there are such economic "externalities" present as to make it unlikely that each entrepreneur, as he reckons *his private benefit and costs* in money, will thereby be truly reflecting the nonmoney and money benefits and costs *to society* as a whole. Smoke nuisance was an example of an external diseconomy calling for public action. Similarly, research is an example of an "external economy" calling for public action, as the following soliloquy shows:

> When I, as a prudent businessman, balance the dollar cost to me of an extra unit of research with the benefit that it can bring me, I shall realize that most of the results of my research will soon—or in the case of patents, eventually—serve to benefit all other producers in my industry and in society generally. The benefit to society as a whole, then, is likely to be much greater than to me; so I shall not be motivated to do all the research that society needs. Because of this externality, the government has a reason to subsidize research—by direct grants to universities, firms, and its own laboratories and by favorable tax treatment of research.

We can therefore deduce this corollary.

■ The single least controversial measure for inducing greater growth is promotion and subsidy of more research and development.

■ EXPANDED EDUCATION AND TRAINING

We saw earlier that just as machinery is capital to society, so too are people. Investing in equipment might yield society an interest return of, say, 10 or 15 per cent per annum. If investing in people, by providing more in the way of education, can step up their economic productivity greatly—and the record suggests that this is indeed true—then society ought likewise to spend more for education to promote growth. (All this is in addition to the various noneconomic civic and humanistic reasons for devoting resources to education.)

It may be asked: "If education is such a good investment for society, why don't private individuals make such investments on their own?" The answer is that many of them do. A lawyer with $30,000 a year income and assets of $100,000 will make sure that his son gets the best education, knowing that this is a better family investment than buying IBM stock.

But what about an able boy in a poor family? His father just does not have the money to invest in his education, even if that promised to yield 25 per cent per annum in return. Moreover, a capitalist with spare funds cannot conveniently invest money in the boy and hope to get the lion's share of the fruits of such an investment. Slavery is forbidden under our laws, and the legal obstacles to owning an equity interest in a prizefighter, baseball player, or crooner are many—to say nothing of benefiting from helping to produce a junior executive, or a potential Nobel-prize winner.

Enlarged public funds for *scholarships* are clearly called for. The case is also strong for enlarged funds to *lend* to students for training in lucrative callings, to be paid back by them out of the extra earnings their education makes possible. If the people still feel that, after all this has been done, the nation can benefit from more resources spent on education, it is the manifest duty of the government to increase its support of schools, colleges, universities, and vocational retraining institutes.

■ APPRAISING AND REDUCING STRUCTURAL UNEMPLOYMENT

In stressing the role of technical change and improved quality of the trained labor force, we are applying Chapter 37's analysis of the forces that make the *potential product* of a nation grow: Output growth depends on factor inputs such as natural resources, labor, capital, and technical progress. Along with research stimulus to technical progress and an increase in the *quality* of labor, an increase in labor's *quantity* would also enhance real growth. But where quantity of labor is concerned, one must proceed with caution.

Few would want to emulate Dictator Mussolini's attempt to increase the birth rate merely for the purpose of enlarging the country's economic and military size. Nor would many want us to regress to a 45- or 50-hour week merely to increase our growth rate. Leisure is a correlative goal with tangible goods.[3] If fiscal and monetary policy do their work well, so that people have a genuine choice between full employment at 40 hours a week or at 35 hours a week, and they opt for the latter, then the resulting sacrifice in rate of potential growth will be a good thing and not to be regretted.

On the other hand, it was an unmitigated advantage in the mid-1960s to be able to increase our quantity of labor by being able to define full employment as a condition where 96 per cent of the labor force are employed, rather than where only 94 or 95 per cent are employed. This is an important point, because the upward drift of average unemployment rates in the 1950s was attributed by some to an increase in "structural unemployment." What does this term (already discussed on p. 563) mean?

Structural unemployment is used in a sense which allegedly contrasts with ordi-

[3] In an age where Saturday work has become rare and where summer and winter vacations are becoming more common, it is somewhat anomalous that youth from age 6 to 24 is being now urged to study and work harder than was ever before the case. Is one supposed to sprint while young in order to become rich enough to idle ever after?

nary unemployment. The latter can be created by having too little $C + I + G$ aggregate dollar spending and can be reduced by expansionary fiscal and monetary policies that swell total spending. Unlike ordinary unemployment, structural unemployment is supposed to consist of people who are stranded in the wrong regions—in distressed areas like the mining country of West Virginia, Pennsylvania, or Wales. It includes youths who have dropped out of school; the uneducated and the illiterate; the unskilled, semiskilled, or the highly skilled in obsolete arts like glass blowing or cigar rolling. It includes the neurotic and rebellious (and possibly the radical malcontents), who demand unrealistically high wages and contribute little net marginal-product to the employer. It includes the congenitally low-IQ and poorly coordinated populace, who used to be capable of getting menial jobs at low pay in a rural society, but who increasingly are thrown out of employment by minimum union-, legislative-, and company-promulgated wage fiats.

Structural unemployment is supposed to include those who belong to various minority groups: females, the relatively aged, immigrants, nonwhites, and so forth. It even includes those who have quit one job and are taking their time in moving to a new one. The mother with children over ten—who is almost indifferent between staying home or working outside the home at pay that does not leave much over after she has paid her carfare, lunch money, needed clothes, and possible babysitters and home help—is hard to classify as being in or out of the labor force; if classified in, she has to be considered as a potential member of the structural-unemployment pool.

DEFINING STRUCTURAL UNEMPLOYMENT   No one has been able to agree on the exact meaning of structural unemployment, but all are clear as to what it means in extreme instances. Thus, if brisk over-all spending results in only 2 per cent unemployment and prices are not being pushed upward by wage increases induced in a tight labor market, all would agree that so-called structural unemployment is low.

On the other hand, if unemployment is at 6 per cent, and every increase in aggregate dollar spending (whether brought about by a private-investment boom, or by expansionary fiscal policy, or by monetary policy) seems merely to result in a fast bidding up of wages of those already employed, with little effect on job opportunities for those who apparently have the wrong skills and talents in terms of what employers demand, then all will agree that structural unemployment appears to be high. This diagnosis will be confirmed if, with no concomitant change in aggregate demand, a vigorous program of reeducation and transportation subsidy leads to a marked reduction in unemployment.

A case that is less clear is the following: Suppose aggregate demand has been sluggish year after year; the percentage unemployed rises; skills decay; employers prefer to get extra output by working their existing employees longer hours. Then suppose private industry or the government engineers a great increase in aggregate demand in a short time period. This is followed in the short run by a wage-price upward spiral. But in the longer run people get sucked out of the distressed areas into high-employment regions. They switch gradually from blue-collar to supervisory work. Their limited skills become valuable to an employer who now finds high-IQ workers hard to attract.

Unemployment over a period of several years works its way down to below 4 per cent, and gradually down even to 3 per cent.

Which was originally present then? Structural unemployment or nonstructural? This is not an idle question: it deals with the actual history of our times, as surveying the 1920s, 1930s, 1940s, and 1950s will confirm. Experience here and abroad during the 1960s suggests this eclectic summary:

> ■ There is no hard and fast line between structural and nonstructural unemployment. The alleged hard core of the structurally unemployed is in fact a core made of ice and not of iron. The core of ice can be melted over a period of time by adequate effective demand, or it can become solidified from inadequate over-all demand. Specific measures for enhancing labor mobility, for retraining and relocating people, for improving employment exchanges and the organization of the labor market will by themselves help to melt the core of structural unemployment, but they are most needed and work most effectively when aggregate demand measures are being vigorously promulgated.
>
> All in all, as experience abroad so forcefully reminds us, there is no real opposition between the programs needed for structural and for nonstructural unemployment. Each is better than nothing. The two together will add up to more than the sum of each separately.[4]

The upshot for growth of the discussion of structural unemployment seems this: Increasing the fraction employed at what is defined as feasible full employment would be a powerful way of increasing the quantity of labor and would be conducive to growth. (Its social benefits would, of course, overshadow its mere growth benefits.)

■ FULL EMPLOYMENT AND REDUCING THE UNDERUTILIZATION GAP

In concentrating on the policies that can increase the rate of growth of our potential full-employment full-capacity GNP, we must not forget the less subtle contribution to growth that can come merely from *achieving a better approximation to full employment.* Which decade showed by far the worst record of growth in American history? It was the 1930s, when the Great Depression prevailed and there was no growth at all!

---

[4]The above formulation permits one to sidestep a notable 1961 debate between Chairman W. M. Martin of the Federal Reserve Board and Chairman W. W. Heller of President Kennedy's Council of Economic Advisers. Martin argued that much of the rising trend in unemployment had been due to an increase in structural unemployment. Heller argued that structural unemployment existed in 1953 or 1957, but that most of the subsequent *increase* in unemployment above 1957's 4 per cent level could not be attributed to a *genuine growth* in structural unemployment. He based this on study of statistical facts such as the following: High unemployment rates among, say, women, youths, or blue-collar workers have behaved in the years since 1957 almost exactly as they *had behaved in earlier years when over-all unemployment rates changed the way they have been changing since 1957.* Although many have been tempted in refuting these statistics to use new interpretations or statistics, no one seems to have presented a successful refutation up to press time for this new edition except in one troublesome respect: Negro unemployment, particularly among youths, went up in 1966 when other unemployment was going down. Why? Research is much needed here.

Those who speak most optimistically about 6 per cent targets for annual growth generally have in mind the improvements that would be possible if we could reduce unemployment down to minimal levels. This is a needed emphasis. It affirms the crucial importance—for the profit receivers as well as workers—of expansionary private and public policies that raise the $C + I + G$ equilibrium level of real NNP.

But a return to high employment is, in a sense, a once-and-for-all thing. From 1962 to 1966 our economy did sprint and achieve real growth of nearly 6 per cent per year! How? By getting rid of excess capacity and unemployment. While our *potential* GNP cannot grow at 6 per cent per year, our actual performance can temporarily do so, as it narrows the "gap" between our potential and actual performance. After we have succeeded in getting rid of this *gap*, our actual real GNP growth rate must revert to that of the potential GNP, which can be lifted above a 4 per cent rate only if the measures discussed in this chapter are successfully applied.

Fortunately, our potential GNP grows like compound interest. If we realize it, the generous profits and labor incomes that it will make available for reinvestment will reinforce its own rate of growth. (I put 96 cents in the bank and you put in only 93. Even if our sums compound at the same 4 per cent interest rate, if our heirs live long enough, mine will have thousands of dollars more than yours. And if my 96 cents, which corresponds to full—rather than partial—employment, should generate a rate of $4\frac{1}{2}$ per cent whereas your 93 cents generates only 3 per cent,[5] my heirs will eventually end up thousands of times as rich as yours. These are the elementary facts of compound interest applied to long-run growth.)

■ DEFENSE EXPENDITURE AND PROSPERITY: AN IMPORTANT DIGRESSION

Before leaving the problem of achieving and keeping full employment, we should examine what would happen if the cold war were to give way to relaxed international tension. If America could cut down drastically on her defense expenditures, would that confront her with a depression problem that has merely been suppressed by reliance on armament production?

The answer here is much like that given in Chapter 18 to the problem of some future acceleration of automation.

■ If there is a political will, our mixed economy can rather easily keep $C + I + G$ spending up to the level needed for full employment without armament spending.

There is nothing special about G spending on jet bomber and intercontinental missiles that leads to a larger multiplier support of the economy than would other kinds

[5] At high employment, attitudes of businessmen and labor toward increasing productivity may be better than in a soft-pressure economy with considerable idle manpower and capacity. If so, such attitudes enhance the growth contribution of full-employment policies. But, if the whip of fear that results from unemployment in a slack economy makes workers and management more efficient, then there is the possibility that the low-pressure economy *might* after a lag overtake the high-employment one. Yale's W. Fellner and H. Wallich hold the last view; Yale's J. Tobin, the first.

of G expenditure.[6] And the temporary increase in unemployment that would result from massive cutbacks in military expenditures could be offset by substantial tax reduction that would increase disposable incomes and lead to enhanced C to meet family demands. With cold-war expenditure no longer needed, our gigantic government expenditures abroad could be reduced and our international deficit would probably disappear almost overnight. With the dollar no longer overvalued, militant expansion of monetary and credit policy could stimulate capital formation (i.e. I) to utilize the resources released from armament production.

■ America's potential and actual growth rate, far from depending upon war preparations, would be markedly increased by an end to the cold war.

Is the story fully as optimistic as this? Yes. A laissez-faire economy might face a crisis of some duration; but a mixed economy that has been using the tools of macroeconomics developed in the last thirty years need fear no such debacle.

There is but one possible flaw in the story. It lies inside the realm of politics, and not economics. If the cutback in military use of resources were not matched by an equivalent expansion in government programs for urban renewal, conservation, education, and medical care, the alternative pattern to full employment might (for reasons discussed on page 234) require a larger budgetary deficit (or a smaller surplus) than now prevails. Such a deficit would *not* be inflationary, since it comes into being only to offset the deflationary impact of the military cutback. But it might provide an ideological problem to those congressmen and citizens who simply do not believe in any of the macroeconomic mechanisms that economic science has expounded.

Any citizenry, any time and any place, that cannot ideologically stomach the political moves necessary to maintain healthy growth and high-capacity economic activity can create for itself a problem of mass unemployment. But the Marxian critics of the capitalistic predecessors of the modern world should not blame such a depression eventuality on armament cuts or on the functioning of the mixed economy. Ideology on the left can be as distorting as ideology on the right.

■ THE NEOCLASSICAL SYNTHESIS AT WORK

Now there remains capital formation as the final factor of significant importance for growth. While the unemployment gap is being narrowed, capital investment and consumption expenditures may be mutually reinforcing in expanding growth. But once full employment were assured, a determination to accelerate growth at any cost would involve trying to change the full-employment mix of resource use away from current private and public consumption and toward net capital formation.

There is a most important way that a mixed economy can hope to increase its

[6] Actually, expenditures on aerospace probably lead to fewer valuable research findings applicable to industry in general than did earlier military expenditure. It may cost 10 million dollars to find a reliable control device that can be put into a match box; but to produce ordinary civilian products, there is no need to keep parts as light, small, and dependable as in traveling to the moon. Recent defense programs may have used up as much high-powered scientific and engineering resources as they have contributed to fruitful civilian uses.

own rate of growth. This is the mechanism referred to earlier in several places, chiefly in Chapter 18 of Part Two and Chapter 30 of Part Four.

■ By properly blending its reliance on fiscal and monetary policy, the citizenry of a mixed economy can hope to shift the composition of its high-employment NNP more toward capital formation and away from current consumption.

By this device, it can hope to change its own growth rate. If this neoclassical device should turn out to be ineffective, then simple honesty would require the observer to admit that a mixed economy is very limited in its ability to change the growth rate. It would then most definitely not be "captain of its soul, master of its fate."

What exactly is the control mechanism involved? First, recall from Part Two that Federal Reserve monetary policy can help to choke off investment spending and capital formation by making credit tight and very dear; alternatively, expansive monetary policy can hope to stimulate the rate of capital formation by making credit more easily available and interest rates lower. This whole process, by which a society undertakes more and more capital formation as interest rates become less and less and as credit becomes more widely available, was described in Chapters 30 and 37 as "deepening of capital." As we saw, the process of deepening capital may not always be a smooth one under *laissez faire;* but let us review its operations in an optimistic neoclassical model.

■ AUSTERE FISCAL POLICY COMBINED WITH EXPANSIONARY MONETARY POLICY

Assume that high employment is going to be maintained. (This could mean 97 per cent of all workers employed to allow for temporary switchings of jobs, or it could be any other agreed-upon percentage.) A fraction of such a high-employment output can be shifted away from consumption and toward capital formation by the following:

■ On the one hand, *monetary policy is to be expansionary,* making for a deepening of capital and much capital formation.

On the other hand, the tendency of such an increase in investment spending to create an inflationary gap is to be offset by an *austere fiscal policy* calling for high enough tax rates (and low enough government expenditure) to reduce people's disposable (after-tax) incomes enough to cause them to reduce their consumption enough to release resources for investment without inflation.

While the quantitative weight of taxes must be large in order to cut down on consumption, certain *qualitative* changes in taxes could stimulate investment directly. The 1962 Kennedy-Dillon investment tax credit provided a bribe to capital formation. Allowing faster depreciation also increases cash funds available for investment and increases the profit incentive for such investment; such measures have been liberalized here and abroad in the last decade.[7] Lightening the

---

[7] A problem with all such subsidies to investment is that they often confer benefits on those who would have invested anyway and even on those who can gain tax advantages without making new investment. Such devices can come to be regarded as "tax loopholes," meaning by this not something illegal, but rather regulations created to confer benefits on special groups. (Recall the saying, "Capitalism breathes through those loopholes.") Whether or not qualitative tax changes to promote investment directly are made, the neoclassical program would rely heavily on the healthy expansion in investment across the board that a lower social rate of interest would make economical.

tax burden on the rich and thrifty, and increasing it on the poor and relatively less thrifty, can increase capital formation at the sacrifice of egalitarianism. Reducing penalties for riskiness, by governmental insurance or unorthodox banking methods, can also stimulate net investment.

By this combination of policies—and, essentially, no others—a free society can hope to alter its own effective rate of capital formation and growth in potential.

President Eisenhower's last Economic Report and those of subsequent Presidents all stressed this possibility of stimulating the share of investment in full-employment product.[8] This optimistic doctrine does need two objective qualifications.

First, Chapter 36 showed that America's international payments deficit will make it impossible for her to push easy money militantly until she has solved the problem of possible overvaluation of the dollar. Hence the postulated process of investment stimulus may not get off the ground until this international problem is overcome.

Incidentally, this fact that America's balance of payments makes it difficult for her to realize domestic goals of high employment with high capital formation underlines the basic error in the Leninist thesis that prosperity of the advanced nations depends upon imperialistic exploitation of the backward countries. If the cold war ended and made foreign military spending unnecessary and if America turned her back on foreign aid to the underdeveloped countries, our international payments deficit would be cured over night and we would no longer fear drain of gold. The Federal Reserve would be given back its freedom to employ monetary policy vigorously to keep employment full and domestic investment high. Whatever was the truth back in 1900 when Lenin was forming his theories, students and statesmen in the underdeveloped countries should be able to spot the error in his view that a modern mixed economy like America needs colonies in order to avoid great depressions; if anything, the reverse is true today.

A second qualification was mentioned in the Appendix to Chapter 37. Some economists think that deepening of capital cannot be successfully achieved because the capital-output ratio is a stubborn constant. Here are their arguments.

If you stimulate investment as was done in the plant-and-equipment booms of 1956–1957 and 1965–1967, you will simply drive down to minimal levels the yield on further investment; and you will pay for it by reduced private capital formation in subsequent years. In the long run, investment will have to be held down to the requirements set by labor-force and technological growth. Be thankful for high consumption at full employment, because that is the only way you can maintain full employment.

A rebuttal might go along the following lines.

In examining a planned economy like that of the Soviet Union, one certainly feels that their product could be enhanced by faster accumulation of capital goods. If that is a

[8] To forestall the criticisms of the trade-unions that have long fought to increase rather than decrease the community's final propensity to consume, one may add this reminder. The resulting increase in thriftiness is not permitted to abort itself in accordance with the "paradox of thrift" discussed in Chapter 13. The shift away from consumption is not allowed to jeopardize the maintenance of full employment or any agreed-upon target level of high employment, for the tight budgetary surpluses will come into being only on condition that the credit-induced expansion in investment spending has indeed succeeded in taking place.

fact of technology, why does not the same hold for us? Current capital goods have a yield before taxes as high as 15 per cent; therefore, goes this rebuttal, it is hard to believe that yields would drop to zero or below a minimal profit level (needed to offset risk) just because net capital formation is speeded up for a decade. Moreover, the advocates of enhanced investment for growth are willing, if it should prove necessary, to recommend nonconventional methods of credit expansion—guarantees and insurances against loss from risks, etc.—to engineer a deepening of capital.

There remains a final difficulty with an optimistic neoclassical synthesis that keeps the economic system at full employment and keeps it there with the desired mix of investment and consumption. This is the problem of possible "cost-push (or sellers') inflation."

■ A NEW SELLERS' INFLATION?

No country in the world has been simultaneously enjoying (1) full employment, (2) free markets, and (3) stable price levels. Thus, from 1955 to 1958 our prices were generally rising: wholesale prices, farm prices, cost-of-living prices—in fact, all but staple prices. Everyone was disturbed about the month-after-month announcement of higher prices. But what was it due to? To excessive demand, like that of 1966's conventional $C + I + G$ inflationary gap?

Turning to look at each industry, one found it hard to perceive excessive demand in 1957–1958. Autos were not selling well; and farm-equipment salesmen sang the blues. TV manufacturers took out the red ink as sales slumped and as people began to buy the low-profit cheap models. The steel industry operated often far below 80 per cent of capacity. And so it went in industry after industry.

Still, the price index continued to advance. Therefore some experts began to wonder whether this was not the case of "wage-push" rather than "demand-pull." Money wages were raised each year, and often by more than the growth of productivity. Nor did it seem to take many strikes to accomplish this. The wage-push happened outside the unionized industries, too. In the unionized sectors some observers said: "In pushing for higher wages, labor is pushing against an open door. The employers do not fight the increases the way they used to. They act as if they think that the Treasury and the Fed will keep aggregate demand high enough to buy the higher-cost output; so they grant the wage increases, and this sends up costs of production, which sends up the prices that firms charge for their goods. The result is a new kind of inflation. When the Fed and Treasury try to handle it by the usual weapons that affect demand, they create unemployment and a recession as in 1957–1958. From 1958 to 1963, wholesale prices were stable, but it seemed to require unemployment of more than 5 per cent to make this so."

Explanatory emphasis has shifted away from exclusive reliance on wage-push to more general cost-push. Thus, in 1959 the Joint Economic Committee of Congress published research reports suggesting that the increase in the price of steel during the 1950s was by itself responsible for a significant fraction of the increase in the wholesale price index. But the committee also found that profit margins went up in this administered-price industry, along with wage increases, and concluded that the pressure of nonlabor as well as labor costs was responsible. A. P. Lerner broadened the whole concept to that of *sellers' inflation:*

■ If all sellers, whether of labor or of property services or of goods, negotiate and determine their prices to try to get among them all more than 100 per cent of the total national product, then the result cannot help but be a frustrating upward push of the price level—a case of sellers' inflation.[9]

■ ARE GROWTH AND PRICE STABILITY OPPOSING GOALS?

If the American economy behaved like a frictionless classical economy, wage rates would never rise while significant unemployment persisted. The authorities could blissfully pursue expansionary policies whenever there was unemployment, knowing that growth can be more rapid when more resources are being put to work. Similarly, any rise in prices could be attributed to inflationary gaps of the demand-pull type, and these could be successfully prevented by contractionary policies that were just strong enough to wipe out the price rise but that would not have to be so strong as to create any appreciable amount of unemployment.

If, however, consumer, wholesale, and general GNP prices all tend to creep upward when there is 4, 5, and even 6 per cent unemployment, what should the monetary and fiscal authorities do? Should they cut down on over-all demand (i.e., on $C + I + G$ or MV total spending), even though that means a further lowering of production and employment? Or should they increase total spending, even though that means some further increase in prices?

There is no easy answer. Nevertheless, here are four different viewpoints:

PRICE STABILITY AT ALL COSTS   Adherents of this view feel that a stable price level is itself so vital a social goal as to transcend other goals such as high employment and growth. Zealots would thus hold out for price stability if it were a question of having to choose among such goals.

Most adherents of this view, however, are not such zealots. They take the more hopeful view that *in the long run* there is really no clash between price stability and growth or high employment. They claim that inflation today means depression tomorrow. They claim that only in an environment of stable prices will efficient business decisions be made. They claim that countenancing a little inflation will result in the *creep* of inflation inevitably becoming a *trot,* the trot inevitably becoming a *gallop,* and the gallop inevitably becoming a *runaway.* Why, then, let the whole process begin? Why not, so to speak, sacrifice a little of current output and employment as an investment in higher *future* growth and employment? So they argue.

---

[9]Experience with modern mixed economies suggests there may be a current cost-push problem in this sense: our price level seems likely to creep up even when there is higher-than-desirable unemployment, e.g., even when more than 1 out of 30 men are without jobs. For more discussion of this and the "Phillips curve," refer to the Appendix of Chapter 18, page 333.

GROWTH AT ALL COSTS   Former President Truman's economic adviser Leon Keyserling (and many in England's Labor Party) represents a view which is at first glance far removed from that outlined above. Keyserling believes in full employment and growth as primary goals and would give them great emphasis in any case; but he, and members of this camp generally, do have the optimistic hope that, by insisting on achieving growth, society will in fact end up with better-behaved prices.

The argument that growth brings price stability, which is a kind of cousin to the earlier argument that price stability brings growth, runs thus:

> Higher output means downward pressure on prices, other things being equal.
> Since workers tend to get *money* wages that increase at a fixed rate, by achieving a faster rate of growth of productivity society can make this yield less price increases.
> At high levels of capacity, the unit costs of businessmen get lower; therefore they can charge lower prices and still make good profits.
> High employment and production make people efficient and venturesome.

Exponents of this view would, if necessary, make a short-run sacrifice of price stability as an investment in future growth and price stability.

COMPROMISING BETWEEN PRICE STABILITY AND GROWTH   According to testimony before Congress, articles in learned journals, deliberations of the Commission on Money and Credit, and reports for the President's Commission on National Goals, there is a considerable body of professional opinion which rejects both of the above positions.

Many economists feel that absolute price stability may detract from high employment and growth in a modern mixed economy like that of America today. They believe that it would be necessary to engineer slackness into the economic structure if the gentle price creep were to be stopped entirely. They believe that a slow price creep, if matched by a similar creep in the mixed economies abroad, need not cause any balance-of-payments difficulties. (Some of them argue that the failure of the official indices to take proper account of quality improvements in goods means that the true rate of increase in prices is less than the apparent one. Some would go so far as to argue that truly calculated price levels have been essentially stable.)

What follows from such a diagnosis? Two realizations: first, that pushing full employment and maximal growth *to their absolute limits* would create such strains on prices as to make some compromising of goals necessary; second, that it will probably be necessary during some periods in the years ahead to tolerate *some degree of price creep* rather than sacrifice economic progress and reasonably high employment.

If acquiescence to price rises may be necessary at some times,[10] this fact raises one of the most vital and difficult queries of the modern age:

---

[10]Charles L. Schultze, in research done for the Joint Economic Committee and for the nonprofit Committee for Economic Development (CED), has pointed out that an economy which has sticky prices as far as downward movements are concerned may end up with a more efficient configuration of relative microeconomic pricings, if the average price level is permitted to *rise* a little rather than being held constant.

Will tolerance of a price creep and insistence on reasonably high employment and growth most of the time inevitably snowball into a runaway inflation? Considerable evidence of a somewhat optimistic type was recently gathered for the Commission on Money and Credit, and it suggested that the transition from a creep, to a trot, to a gallop, . . . was by no means inevitable. Nevertheless, it would be idle to deny that economic analysis and historical experience here and abroad are insufficient to permit one to make a definitive finding in the matter.

AN "INCOMES POLICY"?   Extensive study is needed to learn what changes can be made in the workings of our modern institutions to minimize the amount of price creep that has to be tolerated in the most feasible compromise: for example, more vigorous antitrust activity in the administered-price area; changed legislation and attitudes toward trade-union attempts for higher money wage; presidential or congressional pressures in collective bargaining to uphold the consumer and national interest; and other policies yet to be explored.

Britain, looking longingly at what it thought were the successful mechanisms whereby The Netherlands and Sweden brought united employers and unions together and determined a satisfactory rate of advance of wage rates and other income items, tried in the 1960s to develop an "incomes policy" that would make full employment and price stability compatible. But in 1966, Harold Wilson's Labor Government felt it had to impose a legal wage and price freeze.

■ WANTED, AN "INCOMES POLICY": WAGE-PRICE GUIDEPOSTS?

In the United States there are no united unions and employers who could possibly come together and agree on permissible wage-rate increases. Presidents Kennedy and Johnson did suggest the wage guideposts already introduced in Chapter 29:

> ■ *Wage-price guideposts.* The average money-wage increase is to be no higher than the average national increase in physical productivity; but the increase in each industry is to be divorced from the increase in physical productivity in that industry itself, the difference to be taken up by price reductions to consumers of items with unusually high productivity growth (wheat? autos?) and by price increases to industries with unusually slow productivity growth (teaching?). Departures from the common wage increase are to be permitted primarily where an industry needs to raise wage rates to attract new labor entrants and where a declining industry needs to lower wages in order to expedite labor exit.

These guideposts cannot be validly criticized as giving to labor all the fruits of technical progress; such a conclusion reflects merely bad arithmetic, which fails to recognize that an increase in wage rates in the same percentage as product means an increase of profits in that same percentage, not a zero increase in profits! These guideposts, however, do not have the force of law; and scowls by the President, when an industry like steel raises its prices before excess capacity has been reduced to a low level, cannot solve the dilemmas of full employment and price stability.

How did these guideposts work out? As seen earlier, employers grumbled that they were slanted only against price increases. Unions grumbled that they were slanted only against wage increases. Many observers said they had no effect at all; or that if they had any effect, it was to make the suggested guidepost wage increase the minimum that the unions asked for.

What about the actual facts? From 1961 to 1964, wages and prices were remarkably well behaved in the face of an unprecedented economic expansion. By 1965, 1966, and 1967, prices began to be pulled up by Viet Nam spending, the Kennedy-Johnson tax cut, and a plant-and-equipment boom. Wages began to rise by more than the guidepost numbers; many statistical studies, however, found that wages were rising *less than could have been expected* from so high a profit environment and so tight a labor market.[11]

Even if history decides that the guideposts have had some restraining influence, by 1967 enough experience had been acquired to confirm the expectations of modern economic analysis:

> ■ Wage-price guideposts, or other forms of an "incomes policy," cannot be an adequate *substitute* for proper macroeconomic fiscal and monetary policies. They can moderate somewhat the resulting inflation, or temporarily suppress its symptoms. But they cannot themselves take the place of *stabilizing policies of aggregate demand.* This is not to belittle their importance. Rather it is to call attention to that important part of the job which they can truly do.

It would be nice if we could insist upon having complete price stability and maximal employment and growth, ruling out all compromises. But in an age of cold war and distressing conflicts of economic mechanisms, it may be that citizens of a modern mixed economy can find no shelters within which they can live with full security and without compromise.

■ CONCLUSION

Although growth presents challenges, the subject is really a cheerful one. Without doing much about it specifically, we can expect advanced economies to show a considerable measure of growth in the future, as they have in the past. The United States, for example, can hardly help but grow at the rate of $3\frac{1}{2}$ per cent or more, even if we do not rouse ourselves but merely keep our system working reasonably well.

If we do rouse ourselves and do the things which can speed up growth, a $4+$ per cent rate ought to be well within our grasp. Admittedly, this is not the 6 per cent rate which some proclaim, but that is no cause for despair.

Truly, it is a tremendous accomplishment if an economy can lift its annual growth rate by even $\frac{1}{2}$ per cent. That sounds small, but in terms of cumulative trends and absolute magnitudes, it would represent an important achievement. After carefully

[11] E.g., Minnesota's George Perry, on the basis of multiple-correlation analysis of pre–1962 patterns of wage change in relation to unemployment and profit trends, found that America's "Phillips curve" had apparently been shifted downward in 1962–1966 by the guidepost philosophy.

studying economics, one gradually perceives the importance of quantitative differences of degree, as opposed to journalistic alleged differences of kind.

The quantitative problem of growth in the Soviet Union and the United States will be discussed in the final chapter, after alternative economic systems and ideologies have been surveyed.

SUMMARY

1 ■

The best measure of growth is real GNP, qualified by data on leisure, population size, relative distribution, quality, and noneconomic factors.

2 ■

Advanced nations have historically shown rather steady growth, and recent trends have been generally favorable. Attitudes toward the desirability of expediting growth vary, and in most places the citizenry in their *periodic political decision making* seem to want to step up the rate of growth beyond that implied by their *daily market decisions* on private saving and consuming.

3 ■

Expanded *research and education* can accelerate growth. Attaining and maintaining *high employment levels* can also help. But to increase the rate of a nation's *capital formation* when there has been no change in individual and corporate propensities to consume and save requires, according to the neoclassical synthesis, the following:

(1) Low interest rates and *expansive* monetary policy designed to increase the net-capital-formation component of a high-employment national product; coupled with (2) a *restrictive fiscal policy* designed to eliminate the resulting inflationary tendencies by cutting down on disposable incomes and consumption (and also, possibly involving qualitative tax changes, such as accelerated depreciation, that grant subsidies and loopholes to investment spenders).

By this paired program of easy monetary and tight fiscal policy, a mixed economy can hope to lift the fraction of its high-employment income that goes to net investment for the future rather than to current consumption. (Possible qualifications to such an extremely optimistic program are these: Our international deficit and gold problem may limit our freedom to pursue expansionary credit policies designed to raise investment; making interest rates low and credit more available by orthodox central-banking means may not always succeed in inducing extra investment of the deepening-of-capital type, thereby raising the problem of supplementing orthodox programs by insurance or subsidy arrangements; finally, the presence of cost-push tendencies toward sellers' inflation, while it still permits us to get the proper mixture of consumption and investment for any degree of high employment we aim at, does limit our ability to aim for very high employment levels that are consistent with price-level stability.)

4 ■

The essence of a cost-push mechanism is this: Is there a tendency for price levels to rise even when a sizable and undesirable level of unemployment persists? If there is such a modern tendency, then policy decision becomes hard and compromises may be necessary. "Price stability is a prerequisite for growth." "Growth is a prerequisite for reasonable price stability." "New mechanisms for an incomes policy must coordinate free collective bargaining." "Some price creep may at times be the necessary compromise that must be made in the interest of growth and tolerably high employment." These are varying views, among which citizens and statesmen must today choose.

5 ■

Though growth presents problems, it is essentially a cheerful subject.

QUESTIONS FOR DISCUSSION

1. Evaluate the arguments that GNP growth is or is not a major goal.

2. "Cut down on consumption to promote growth? Are you mad? Only high C can give high I. I don't grasp this 'deepening of capital.'" Explain.

3. Why are education, research, and high employment conducive to growth?

4. What tax changes favor growth? Do they clash with "equity" notions? How?

5. "High $C + I + G$, even to the point of over-full-employment, will do more for the technically displaced, the aged, the illiterates, the geographically stranded, and the nonwhite workers than will any retraining programs or hour-shortening devices. How then can one speak of a clash between 'structural' and 'aggregate-demand' unemployment?" Appraise this.

6. Size up the creeping-inflation problem. What is to be done?

7. Review your understanding of the following concepts:

real NNP or GNP, per capita

neoclassical tight-fiscal and
    easy-monetary policies

structural unemployment

cost-push, or sellers' inflation

creep, trot, and gallop

"incomes policy"

dilemmas of goals

40 Alternative Economic Systems

YOUR OLD MEN SHALL DREAM DREAMS, YOUR YOUNG MEN SHALL SEE VISIONS. OLD TESTAMENT

■ THE CRISIS OF CAPITALISM?

After World War I, new governments were set up all over Europe. By 1925 an impartial observer might have said that the future of the capitalistic way of life appeared serene and assured. Yet within a half dozen years, country after country succumbed to dictatorship; totalitarian fascist governments covered the map of Europe. The depression decade of the 1930s finally ended in a great world war.

At the end of World War II, what was the outlook? The world was divided into great blocks: Soviet Russia and her satellites of Eastern Europe stood within the Iron Curtain in an uneasy alliance with mainland China, and outside was the rest of the world. But the nations outside the Iron Curtain were far from homogeneous. Labor-Socialist governments were ruling, or had recently been ruling, in Britain, in Australia and New Zealand, and in all of Scandinavia. Various forms of dictatorship still lingered on in Spain, Portugal, Egypt, and Latin America. France, Japan, and Italy had within them noisy and articulate left-wing political parties. The awakening nations of Asia and Africa did not view the world with laissez-faire-tinted glasses.

Only the United States and a few other countries remained as islands of declared capitalism in an increasingly collectivized world. Even here, the scene was drastically changed: ours had become a mixed economy with both private and public initiative and control and, in those disturbed days, a mixed system of a peace and a war economy.

Every news dispatch reminded us that the mixed-economy way of life was on trial. Not only did it have to perform adequately, but more than that, it was required to perform superlatively. Mass unemployment at home would have had disastrous repercussions upon our prestige abroad, to say nothing of the internal political unrest that a slump might involve. A faltering rate of our development and growth would have counted seriously against us.

■ THE NEW LOOK

Little wonder then that profound social philosophers, like Harvard's Joseph Schumpeter, thought they could foretell the end of capitalism in the years after 1945. Even profound philosophers can turn out to be quite wrong. Following World War II, gradually the "New Economics" of the modern mixed economy began to take over. And it actually worked!

In West Germany there was a miracle of recovery and development. The same thing happened in The Netherlands, France, Italy, and the Common Market countries of Europe generally. Japan, by a mixture of private initiative and state planning, embarked on a sprint hardly ever before equaled in history. Israel—helped, to be sure, by gifts and loans from abroad—had her miracle decades. Even ancient problem economies, like Greece and Austria, were able to find in the mixed economy a path to rapid and sustained economic growth. Taiwan and Thailand both sprinted forward.

Something new has been born under the sun. The prophesied timetable of inevitability—savagery to feudalism, feudalism to capitalism, capitalism to socialism, socialism to communism, and finally communism to more communism—has for the moment begun to take on the appearance of a fairy tale and fable.

But fables and legends have a hold on the minds of men. It is therefore worth reviewing, if only in a brief way, the traditional forms of alternative economic systems. These are of interest for their own sakes. They are also of interest as part of the intellectual history of the human race. But most of all, they are of interest in disabusing our minds of the tyranny of certain facile generalizations which, like most facile generalizations, simply will not stand up to the hard facts of actual experience.

Thus, is it true that without free markets for goods and services, democratic freedoms and political civil rights cannot prevail? Many economic libertarians argue this. But are they right?

At the other extreme, many advocates of socialism argue that "political democracy" is but a sham if the state does not get rid of "production for profit" and replace it by "production for use" and guarantee "fair shares" all around. But are they right?

And in particular, is the argument correct in the learned and persuasive book, *The Road to Serfdom* (1945), by Friedrich Hayek (of Austria, England, the United States, and Germany), that each step away from the market system and toward the social reforms of the welfare state, is *inevitably* a journey that must end in a totalitarian state with neither efficiency nor liberty? The opposing view, held by such evolutionists as Winston Churchill, is that gradual reforms are the only way to prevent a cataclysmic descent through revolution into a communist dictatorship. If the evolutionists are right, Hayek is quite wrong. Let us review the troops.

■ A BOUQUET OF ISMS

Men have always had visions of a more perfect society: Plato's Republic, Sir Thomas More's Utopia, Marx's Dictatorship of the Proletariat, and so on without number. It is only too easy to look at concrete present-day imperfections and then to contrast them with the ideal features of a vaguely defined utopia. Beyond agreeing that the present order has faults, different schools of reform have little in common.

At the one extreme are the anarchists, who believe in no government at all; at the other, the apologists for an all-powerful collectivized, totalitarian, communistic social order, where the first person singular is all but replaced by the first person plural. Within the field of socialism itself, we find subdivisions: Christian socialism, state and Marxian socialism, guild socialism, Fabian (evolutionary) socialism, and many others.

In the popular mind, socialists are characters who meet in a cellar lit by a candle thrust in an empty wine bottle to plot a bloody revolution, or at least to brew bombs sent in laundry parcels to government officials and capitalists. Or the term "socialist" is frequently used as a disparaging stereotype to discredit anyone who believes in social security, progressive taxation, bank-deposit insurance, or free love.

Whatever the strength of radical parties abroad, in America no third party has ever been able to develop in any strength.[1] The American Socialist party runs a candidate for the presidency—along with the Prohibition party—but gains only a negligible fraction of the vote. The Communist party never could gain any sizable vote, either under its own name or in disguise.

If we look at the picture in Europe, we find the names of almost all the parties have the word "socialism" in them. But this does not mean much: a party such as France's Radical Socialists turns out to be anything but radical, being one of the conservative parties. Even Hitler's fascistic party took the name of "National Socialism."

Often, however, the leading European reform parties can be characterized as "social democrats." For example, the Labor party in Britain, the German Social Democratic party, the ruling parties in much of Scandinavia—all these claim to be in favor of gradual, nonrevolutionary extension of socialism by peaceful and democratic methods.

It is clear, therefore, that we do not have to master all the thousand and one different "isms" in order to understand the world today. It is enough to understand something of (1) relative *laissez faire*, or mixed-economy private enterprise, (2) socialism, (3) communism, and (4) fascism. There is no hard and fast boundary between these; it is a matter of degree. Moreover, we cannot even range these along a line, with fascism at the extreme right wing and communism at the extreme left wing. In some ways— although neither would admit it—communism and fascism have much in common.

Capitalism, in the sense of undiluted *laissez faire*, died before Queen Victoria did. And most of this book has been concerned with describing the mixed-economy capitalistic system. So we may turn briefly to the others.

■ FASCISM

This is easier to characterize politically than economically. Be it in Hitler's Germany, Mussolini's Italy, Franco's Spain, Salazar's Portugal, or Perón's Argentina, fascism is usually characterized by a one-man dictatorship, by one political party with all others abolished, by the disappearance of civil liberties of the type granted in our Bill of Rights. Fascistic movements are always highly nationalistic, often with emphasis placed on a vaguely defined "master race" which exploits minority groups. In the

---

[1] Theodore Roosevelt's 1912 Bull Moose party was primarily an offshoot of the Republican party. Old Bob La Follette's 1924 Progressive party was the most successful third-party, yet was able to carry only his state, Wisconsin. Henry Wallace's 1948 Progressive party was an utter failure.

words of Mussolini, fascists are urged to "live dangerously"—to value war and national power as ends in themselves. The individual is to be secondary to the state.

On the economic side, Mussolini's fascism happened to toy with the notion of a "syndicalist," or "corporate," state; each industry and group of workers was organized in a syndicate, and these were to meet and bargain and plan how the economy should be run. However, this syndicalism has never come to much and has not been especially characteristic of other fascist regimes. Almost all of them are against free and militant trade-unionism; almost all give the central government great regulatory power over every sphere of economic life. Some work hand in glove with religious authorities; others are antichurch. Often capitalists and the lower middle classes contribute to the initial strength of fascist movements; but later, when the fascist movement begins to take on—as they sometimes do—revolutionary aspects, the capitalists may regret the Frankenstein's monster that they helped to create.

Their only consolation lies in the fact that one of the earmarks of a fascist regime is opposition to communism; often it sails into power by exaggerating the immediate likelihood of a Bolshevik revolution, and after it has come into power, the threat of communism is used as an excuse for the suppression of democratic processes.

■ SOCIALISM

In defining fascism, we were able to point to Nazi Germany or fascist Italy. Socialism cannot be so easily described. Of course, we can describe the Swedish socialist government or the British Labor party's program, but these do not present such dramatic contrasts with our system. They represent a middle way between our own "mixed system" and that of Soviet Russia or China.

There are a few common elements that seem to characterize socialist philosophy:

1. *Government ownership of productive resources.* The role of private property is gradually to be lessened as key industries such as railroads, coal, and even steel are gradually nationalized. Unearned profits from increases in land value are also limited. (In West Germany and the U.K., enthusiasm for nationalization seems to be ebbing.)

2. *Planning.* Instead of permitting the free play of profit motives in a laissez-faire market economy, coordinated planning is to be introduced. Sometimes the program of "production for use rather than profit" is advocated; advertising expenditure on gadgets is to be reduced; workers and professional people are to develop instincts of craftsmanship and social service so that they will be guided by other motives than those of our "acquisitive society."

3. *Redistribution of income.* Through government taxing powers, inherited wealth and swollen incomes are to be reduced. Social security benefits and cradle-to-grave welfare services provided by the collective purse are to increase the well-being of the less privileged classes.

4. *Peaceful and democratic revolution.* As distinct from communism, socialism often advocates the peaceful and gradual extension of government ownership—revolution by ballot rather than by bullet. This aim is often more than a tactical move; rather, it is a deep philosophical tenet of faith.

BRITISH SOCIALISM   A brief look at British socialism will point up the modern issues. Just when Adam Smith's classical economics had won the day from its mercantilistic and feudal predecessors, English intellectual opinion began to move beyond *laissez faire* and toward socialism. A key example is John Stuart Mill, who was brought up by an eighteenth-century exponent of utilitarian individualism, but who had by the last half of the nineteenth century turned to a kind of socialism. And in the twentieth century, university and night-school intellectuals were won to the Fabian doctrines of the inevitability of gradual socialism; and the socialist views of Bernard Shaw and Beatrice and Sidney Webb had also become the views of the trade-union movement.

All this was hidden until World War I. After that war, the Liberal party was ground away between the millstones of the Conservative and Labor parties. And after World War II, Labor really came into power. Its early goals included (1) vast extension of welfare services by the state—in which Conservative governments in large degree have acquiesced; (2) heavy redistributive income and estates taxation—in which to a degree the Conservatives also acquiesce; (3) extensive centralized planning, including stringent regulation of land use and zoning; and finally (4) initially a fairly sweeping program of nationalization, beginning with coal, power, and railroads and, in the doctrines of the left wing of the party, reaching beyond steel to many branches of wholesaling and distribution, engineering, and ordnance.

Today, the Labor party finds itself quite divided on how far to carry traditional socialism. This shows itself in debates over the extent to which nationalization should be pressed and the degree to which reliance should be placed on market mechanisms. At the intellectual level, now that so many of the goals set up years ago in *Fabian Essays* have been realized, there is much soul searching going on; and challenging new Fabian essays are hard to write. Is "mere New Dealism designed to make capitalism work well" adequate? And can the mixed economy command the idealistic enthusiasms that more sweeping reforms are able to fire? Has the improvement of living standards pushed the militant poor up into the contented middle classes? Has making society more fluid tended to drain off the bright son of poor parents to Oxford and the Establishment, alienating him from the radical trade-union tradition?

Nor is this quandary unique to Britain. In Sweden, Norway, Denmark, Australia, and New Zealand, the so-called "middle way" of moderate labor socialism has now been in or near power for a quarter century.[2] Yet every one of these economies begins to look more and more like what the United States itself has become after three decades of administration by Roosevelt, Truman, Eisenhower, Kennedy, and Johnson.

[2] Degree of public economic direction is a trait that ranges from a laissez-faire society through a collectivist communist regime. But a survey of history shows that this classification must not be confused with the degree of political freedom and democratic civil liberties. Fascist regimes have often passed socialistic measures, and communist bureaus have suppressed personal freedom. On the other hand, Britain, Scandinavia, and other socialist countries have retained all the familiar civil liberties and individual political freedoms that are guaranteed by our own Constitution.

It is one thing to tell a corporation what it may charge for electric power and quite another thing to tell a man what he can say, what he can believe, or how he must worship. But some will ask, "Can political freedoms be held when the state limits economic freedoms?" History and anthropology have not yet given a conclusive answer to this question.

FRENCH "INDICATIVE PLANNING" Ideologically rather removed from traditional socialism is the remarkable development in France of planning by the state. Even before De Gaulle, many important industries were owned and run by the French government: railroads, electricity, and mines, for example. The tools of economics—marginal-cost pricing of power, benefit-cost analysis of the worthwhile program of investments in these state industries—deserve much of the credit for the remarkable rate of real growth in France during the last two decades. But that is not all.

Even private industry is brought into a comprehensive national plan. There is, however, one important difference from the traditional planning of socialist societies. In the French mixed economy, participation in *Le Plan* is mostly voluntary. (But, as everywhere these days, what business firm dares get the authorities too angry at them— particularly when permission to go to the capital markets is controlled by government?)

Representatives of different industries sit down together in committees, presided over by the civil servants who serve the plan. Businessmen are given quantitative information on national goals for the years just ahead; and they respond with information on what these goals will mean for their own industries. In turn, these replies are made the basis for a recalculation of the aggregates and the details of the plan.

■ In the end, each industry learns that it can count on an expanding market. And as business firms in those industries proceed to meet these indicated goals, they do generate the production, income, and demand called for by the plan.

How has it all worked out? Apparently, remarkably well if we can judge by results. Almost too well to be credible, when one considers the informality of the arrangements and their quasi-voluntary nature. In the late 1960s, many an English reformer would trade some of the "pie in the sky" of traditional socialism for some pragmatic fruits of indicative planning. A National Economic Development Council ("NEDDY") was set up to imitate the French methods; and Harold Wilson's Labor government has set up a Ministry of Economic Affairs to promote such programs.

Similarity must not conceal diversity. In Egypt and many countries recently released from colonialism, there has been widespread nationalization of industry; in the repeated examples of this process during the last decades, there have as yet been few cases where the result has been a rapid rate of real economic growth. Similarly, economies like Argentina stagnated under state controls introduced by Dictator Perón; despite resources and technology that many a poor country would envy, Argentina continued to stagnate. Under Castro, Cuba's GNP has sharply declined.

■ MARXIAN COMMUNISM AND SOVIET RUSSIA: HISTORY

Marxian communism represents a departure both from earlier utopian socialist movements and also from evolutionistic socialist movements of the last century. Karl Marx (1818–1883), who began as a student of Hegelian philosophy but ended up as the messiah of a new doctrine of "scientific socialism," worked in exile with his friend and financial sponsor Friedrich Engels to establish a whole new theory of economics and history. For three-quarters of a century after Karl Marx and Friedrich Engels issued their 1848 Communist Manifesto, numerous international socialist conferences were held; yet outside the British Museum, not much seemed to be accomplished.

In 1917, the big moment came. Czarist Russia was knocked out of the war by the Germans. Lenin, a follower of Marx, was transported in a sealed railroad car across Germany and into Russia. Aided by Trotsky, a one-time New Yorker, Lenin's Bolsheviks snatched power from the moderate regime that had overthrown the monarchy. Preaching peace and promising land for the peasants and a dictatorship of the proletariat, the followers of the Red hammer and sickle gained adherents in the navy and army and forcibly took power.

There followed what John Reed (later buried in the Kremlin) called "ten days that shook the world." The meeting of the democratic Constituent Assembly, only few of whose elected representatives were procommunist, was forbidden. An army was organized and trained by Trotsky, and successive towns were won over to the revolutionary forces—often by strategic capture of the water and power supply alone. Then followed a great civil war between the Red and White armies, the latter aided by Poland and Western powers. In the end, the officers of the White army ended up chiefly in Paris, driving taxicabs and drinking vodka to the memory of Czar Nicholas.

THE REVOLUTION ACHIEVED   The world expected a Russian collapse; but the communist regime persisted—not without experiencing horrible famines, in which literally millions perished. Aristocrats and bourgeoisie were ruthlessly "purged" and "liquidated"—new words for age-old processes brought to a new perfection. The Communist party was the only political party permitted; only a few per cent of the population could belong to this elite group; it elected the members of local "soviets" of factories and farms. These elected representatives to still higher soviets, until, at the very top, over all the federated Union Republics, stood the Council of People's Commissars of the Supreme Soviet of the U.S.S.R. (Union of Soviet Socialist Republics).

The Soviet leaders had no blueprint to guide them. Marx had confined himself largely to the faults of capitalism and had revealed very little about what the promised land was to be like. It was not even on the timetable that backward Russia, which had hardly emerged from feudalism into capitalism, should experience its revolution before the downfall of the top-heavy industrialized nations. During the 1920s, Lenin compromised with capitalistic enterprise in the NEP (New Economic Policy). But in 1928–1929, the first Five-Year Plan for industrialization of manufacturing and collectivization of agriculture was introduced. This was followed by a second Five-Year Plan.

Because of the rapid pace of capital formation, war preparedness, and the state of Russian technology, consumption was severely rationed throughout these years. Workers had ration cards that were honored at specific stores, but money continued to be used. Excess money income could be spent only upon special goods at higher prices than the basic ration. Real and money wages differed among occupations, with piece rates and incentive pay for high productivity becoming ever more dominant.

Stalin, one of Lenin's many lieutenants, finally won out in the struggle for power after Lenin's death in the early 1920s. Trotsky and other old-line revolutionaries were accused of plotting with foreign powers against the Soviet Union, and in the middle 1930s a tremendous purge of generals and officials culminated in the sensational Moscow trials—sensational because all the defendants vied with each other in avowing their own guilt. After the Chamberlain-Hitler appeasement pact, Nazi Germany and Soviet Russia in 1939 signed a nonaggression pact, which lasted until Hitler—flushed with his victory over Poland and France—attacked Russia.

With fanatical patriotism and aided by United States lend-lease, the Russians traded their blood for the Germans' until few Germans were left in the Russian homeland. After the defeat of the Axis, the short-lived comradeship with the West flickered out, and the world stood in the shadow of the hydrogen bomb, with Russia trying to spread her influence over Europe and Asia and with the Atlantic nations and ourselves bent on stopping her on the one hand, and China threatening her on the other.

In the postwar period, Stalin's one-man rule became more and more paranoid, and his death in 1953 brought in the inevitable revulsion toward his regime. What seemed to be a thaw set in under the committee rule of Khrushchev, and sprigs of criticism began to push up their sprouts. But the Poles, Hungarians, and Leningrad students learned the hard way that winter was not quite over. Peaceful coexistence became the new official line, and was continued after Khrushchev's downfall.

■ THE SOVIET ECONOMY

So much for history. How does the Soviet Union get the three basic problems decided: WHAT shall be produced, HOW, and FOR WHOM?

In broad outline,[3] the picture is this: The state owns almost all factors of production: factories, mines, and land. Workers generally earn their living by wages; they do have considerable choice of occupation, but a Soviet citizen does not have unlimited right to seek employment in any region and industry that happens to capture his fancy.

WHAT   A political decision is made that defense and capital formation are to be pushed hard; what is left over is permitted to go to consumers' goods. While a Russian can indicate his preferences among different goods by the way he spends his income, any resulting shortages or gluts have only recently been permitted to result in the bidding up or down of consumer-goods prices, thereby automatically producing the positive or negative returns that serve to rechannel resources. So long as goods were very scarce, central planners could decide that people would want so much of food, so much of shoes, and so much of various other necessities of life. Any and all of these were eagerly bought as they became available: if the local store or commissary had shoes not exactly your size, you were glad to take them a little large rather than do without.

Now that some of the comforts—and even luxuries—of life are beginning to become available, it is no longer enough to think of giving people what they need, and centralized planning has become a little more difficult. These days certain goods will

[3]F. D. Holzman, *Readings in the Soviet Economy* (Rand McNally, Chicago, 1962), is a useful reference.

not get bought at all, and the planners have come to learn that they must cut back on them. Even advertising and selling have reared their heads in Russia! It is harder to learn what people do want than what they do not want, and marketing surveys are still in their infancy. The Soviet commissars are not so skilled in determining what people would want most if they had the choice; but they do find it useful to watch what Americans and others abroad like to consume and then belatedly introduce such products: thus that rare comrade who gets a car will find it resembling our cars of the past; and experts tell us this imitative pattern, which is not at all irrational since it assumes that what one human being will like will also be sought by another, is becoming more common.

With respect to capital goods and military expenditure, direct state decisions are made. Industrialization is pushed hard: electrification, transportation, mining development, a big push in chemicals and fertilizers, collectivization of agriculture and crop patterns—such matters are broadly determined by conscious political decision.

How   Private enterprise is negligible in importance. Instead, the typical Soviet factory will be a state-owned *enterprise:* just as the president of General Motors owns little of its total stock, the manager or head of this state-owned enterprise has no ownership of its capital; but he does get better-than-average pay for his work, plus various travel expenses, auto transport, and other special privileges. He may even get bonuses, and his chance of promotion to a bigger enterprise will depend upon how well his enterprise meets its quota. He gives orders much like any boss and expects his subordinates to obey them, just as he obeys orders from above. (To avoid penalties for failing to meet his quota, he may hoard steel and other materials rather than give them to some other enterprise; and many cases have been observed where bureaucrats will contrive to make it appear that their plant has been very productive, even if that means they must conceal its true potential efficiency. EXAMPLES: Enterprises may malinger so as to get a low quota that can be easily achieved or surpassed. Stories have been well told of a transportation enterprise which moved carloads of water back and forth in order to be able to say it had accomplished the target of so many ton-miles.)

In the late 1960s, such meaningless physical quotas are beginning to be replaced by "profitability" criteria of performance that do involve economic valuation of diverse goods—a step in the direction of Western pricing methods.

The decision of how to combine various productive factors—land and labor, degree of mechanization—appears to depend on a mixture of purely technical considerations and adaptations to the scarcities of various economic resources. A continual process of trial and error goes on. The observer finds operations curiously uneven: on the one hand, he may see a military ballistic plant which has achieved a precision of ball bearings and gyroscopes rivaling the best in the world; on the other hand, he may find things being done in an almost unbelievably primitive way, with the quality of output practically worthless. (EXAMPLE: A Soviet farmwoman may be assigned one cow to take care of; on a Wisconsin dairy farm, a man and wife may take care of 30 cows, in addition to performing countless other daily chores.)

All Soviet economic life is a pyramid tapering upward. Above the individual enterprises in an industry and region will be a regional economic council. Above the regional councils will be a council of ministers; alongside the ministries will be the planners of the Gosplan. Experts tell us it is quite misleading to concentrate on the organizational charts of the process, for there is a constantly changing mixture of centralization and decentralization; fiat, delegated responsibility, and initiative; carrots of reward and kicks or imprisonments as penalties.

Some things are very much the same everywhere. The head of an enterprise will, almost certainly, be a member of the Communist party. A successful bureaucrat there is something like a successful "organization man" here: he must be obedient but resourceful, both obsequious and arrogant, energetic and nonsentimental. The point is not that the worst types get ahead. The point is that ability does count on the average; but mere technical ability without the skill of getting along with people will not usually be enough.

Experts also tell us that it is quite naïve to think that there is an elaborate formalized structure of planning, so that one could write a treatise on pure communistic economics that would equal in length a treatise on the general equilibrium of purely competitive market systems.

For Whom To a considerable degree the Russian economy works for the security of the state and for the future. How much the present generation of Russians consume of private goods is not primarily determined by their day-to-day spending and working decisions. True, they do earn wages (and a small amount of interest or lottery winnings on government bonds is also permitted). Moreover, wages are by no means equal, and certainly not higher for the needy and handicapped than for the energetic and skilled. Skilled workers get much more than unskilled. Free trade-unions as we know them do not exist, but woe to the manager who gets all the workers against him. Piece rates and incentive systems are frequently used, and there is much exhortation toward working hard for the fatherland and for the "brotherhood of man." (Soviet novels often had for their plots the tale of how a good boy and girl foil the malingering of antisocial culprits and by use of a virtuous tractor overcome the recalcitrance of the stubborn soil. Boy meets girl here as everywhere, but the durable goods are much in evidence.)

Social classes as Marx and Engels knew them in 1848 may not exist in the Soviet Union, but there is a definite pattern of social and political stratification. A poor boy who is bright may become a physicist and live well. It is important for him to rank high in the exams that select the few who can go to college. (His way at the university is completely paid for, just as the comrade who puts the shot in the Olympics is paid to pursue that occupation.) After graduation he hopes to score well enough to be able to pursue the study of physics in Moscow, rather than be sent out as a technician and engineer to the Ural Mountains or some other distant post. As a well-paid professor he can look down on all but the top bureaucrats: he may have a car, a cottage in the country, and finely equipped laboratories. Of course, he cannot take it with him, but he can at least hope to give his son a good start in the stiff educational competition.

There are various economic devices by which the system ensures that it gets the FOR WHOM it desires—heavy emphasis on industrialization and military security.

For one thing, goods at every stage of production are subject to heavy taxation (the so-called "turnover tax," which contrasts with a tax on true value added). The resulting elevation of prices in relation to wages paid out ensures that the public will be able to consume only a part of all that they can produce, in quite the same way as our economy uses taxes to siphon resources away from private and into public channels. Macroeconomic equilibrium is needed there as here!

Another device is to set a much higher mark-up over costs for consumers' goods ensuring that they generally are priced much higher in relation to some set of true economic costs than are military and capital goods. As a third device, certain consumers' goods, such as comfortable housing, are just not purchasable at any price for any but the few lucky persons of peculiar economic and political advantage.

By all such methods the Soviet authorities fight the battle against the price inflation that would burst out as workers try to spend their incomes on the limited supply of consumers' goods. To one who has studied modern economics, it is evident that these are devices by which their society determines FOR WHOM goods will be produced in accordance with *social* decision making.

■ NEW TRENDS IN IRON CURTAIN ECONOMICS?

Soviet economics is in a state of flux. In recent years intense debates have broken out concerning the use of some kind of pricing and profitability criteria that begin to approach a little the analytical tools of Western economics. Marxian concepts seem to be reserved for training of the young and for alleged explanation and denouncement of capitalistic economies. Among the high-level planners themselves, few words are squandered on such subjects. Instead, as in the much-debated writings of E. Liberman, there are attempts to get away from setting of crude quantitative goals expressed in physical units. There is to be emphasis on quality and on weighting items by their importance, setting for the plant manager the goal of maximizing something like a profitability magnitude. The hope is to get him to try new products and methods and economize on input requirements, rather than concentrate on establishing a low quota for his plant. After 1967, pilot experiments with markets are planned.

Mathematical methods, such as the input-output analysis associated with W. W. Leontief of Harvard, have been released from Stalin's ban, and are debated as a possible tool for helping the planners allocate their available resources. More advanced methods, known in the West as linear and more general mathematical programming, have been developed by eminent Soviet mathematicians (Kantorowich, Pontryagin, . .); rates of discount, rather like the interest rates used in mixed economies to screen out less important capital projects, have been proposed in considerable variety. Although it cannot be said that they rely on the socialist game of a pricing system as described in Chapter 32's Appendix, there seems increasingly to be a pragmatic mixture of physical, accounting, and economic planning. And the pendulum oscillates between epochs of decentralization and of centralization.[4] Moreover, in the Satellite countries—Poland, Hungary, Czechoslovakia, . . .—the issues of pricing and planning are hotly debated.

This is not the place to describe the differences between Marxian and Western economics, nor the developments of either. But the back flyleaf of this book does give a sketch of the family tree of economic doctrines and ideas. Perhaps the widening gulf between the ideology of the Russians and the Chinese, despite the fact that both claim legitimate descent from Marx via Lenin, suggests that the Soviet is moving a small step toward reconciliation with the economic tools of modern analysis. This is not meant to suggest in the least that the Russians are turning to capitalistic enterprise systems or that mixed economies are veering down the road to serfdom and totalitarianism. Rather, the notions of scarcity, production, costs, substitution, and resource allocation have to be objectively regarded as fundamental in almost any economic system.

All in all, it is a mistake to think that most people are miserable there. While it is undoubtedly true that few citizens of the West would trade their degree of economic comfort and political freedom for life in the Soviet, it is also true that a Soviet citizen thinks that he is living in a paradise in comparison with life in Communist China, where family rights are much more restricted, industry is very much more primitive, comfort and living standards much lower, and the pressure on the individual to serve society infinitely greater. Remember, too, that life under the czars was no bed of roses for most classes; and to the eye of the traveler from impoverished Asia and Africa, the rising degree of Russian affluence must seem impressive.

As already mentioned, the family tree of Marxian economics shows a branching out in the middle 1960s. China and Russia cannot agree on the true apostolic succession to Lenin and Marx. The Chinese bitterly attack the Russians for their policy of peaceful coexistence. These ideological splits would be merely ironical, were it not that the future existence of the whole human race is at stake in this age of the nuclear bomb.

■ COMPARATIVE ECONOMIC GROWTH

Today we know many facts about the Russian system. Teams of our economic experts pore over U.S.S.R. statistics, and while they often find the data incomplete and occasionally deliberately misleading, the experts are largely in agreement that it is possible to make an objective appraisal of the approximate dimensions of the Russian economy. No longer is there any excuse for the extreme views that the Soviets are so hopelessly

---

[4] Agricultural performance, as in the case of China, still seems to be remarkably bad on the Russian collective and state farms. These appear to be much too large for efficiency, averaging 7,000 and 22,000 acres of sown land, in contrast to the 400-acre average of our efficient commercial farms. Private farming is permitted in only minute degree, but the product of these private efforts seems to be many times higher per unit of input than on the collective and state farms. Uniform rules, ill informed and subject to swings of fad and fashion, get imposed on everybody in a region. Supplies of tractor equipment, spare parts, fertilizers, and fungicides are quite limited, and optimal use is not made of them by the rural populace, who have little incentive to be efficient. Despite unfavorable weather, much improved efficiency would seem technically feasible.

inefficient that they cannot keep even one Model T Ford in good repair or that they are giants seven feet tall who will soon outstrip everyone else in productivity.

The basic facts, as audited by numerous independent scholars here and abroad, seem to be these: In 1967 the Soviet gross national product was between two-thirds and one-third of ours in size, depending on whether one makes this difficult comparison by using dollar price weights or ruble price weights.[5] By splitting the difference for the purpose of a rough approximate calculation, one can give a reasonable estimate:

■ In the 1960s, U.S.S.R. real GNP is about one-half U.S. real GNP.

Since the Soviet population is larger than the American and since she devotes a smaller fraction of her GNP to consumption, it follows that her real consumption per capita is an even smaller fraction of ours. This conclusion of the expert is well confirmed by casual observation of visitors to Russia.

But the issue that now dominates discussion and debate is not the comparative strengths of the two economies in the 1960s, but rather whether one is growing so much faster than the other as to be able to narrow or close the gap in the decades ahead. This has led to the great game of what has been called "growthmanship." While it would be idle to deny that a great deal of nonsense has been talked about this subject and while the experts are the first to admit that their estimates are only approximations, there is a nucleus of objective economic fact that deserves impartial analysis.

Depending upon what years have been selected for comparison, one can say that America's real GNP has been growing at a long-term rate of between $3\frac{1}{2}$ and $4\frac{1}{2}$ per cent per year. Although there is often talk of a 6 per cent growth rate as a goal for the United States, a careful canvass of economic experts of all shades of political opinion will suggest that most do not really think this likely in the decades ahead. Figure 40-1 therefore extrapolated from 1960 a range of growth rates, varying from the reasonably optimistic to the reasonably pessimistic.

Estimates for the Soviet Union are more difficult. All seem to agree that her post–World War II growth rates have been considerably greater than ours as a percentage per year,[6] even though they have not surpassed the performance of such mixed economies as West Germany, Japan, Italy, and France in the last decade. Furthermore, many experts believe that it is easier for an economy that starts out from a lower level of productivity to show high initial percentage improvement. (After all, to go from

---

[5] There is a technical index-number problem involved that need only be indicated. Here luxuries are fairly plentiful compared with necessities; the opposite is the case there, as can be illustrated by the fact that the ratio of auto prices to rye-bread price will there be many times the price ratio here. Result: If we calculate real GNPs for both places using their ruble price ratios, our numerous autos will show up with terrific weight and their GNP will be not much more than one-third ours. (They deny all this publicly; but their experts are probably in fairly close agreement privately.)

[6] In the 1960s we have been the better performer. And it should be pointed out that, if our GNP is twice that of Russia, then to equal our *absolute* rate of growth her percentage rate would now have to be twice ours. Expert testimony before Congress and elsewhere estimates the following percentage annual growth rates for the Soviet Union: 1950–1958, 6.8; 1955–1960, $6\frac{1}{2}$; 1958–1963, 4.2; 1963–1964, 3; 1964–1967, a bit better than this, particularly in view of the good 1966 wheat harvest.

America leads Russia, but will the gap narrow?

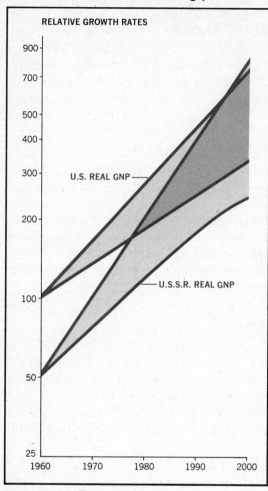

RELATIVE GROWTH RATES

U.S. REAL GNP

U.S.S.R. REAL GNP

FIG. 40-1. The range of estimates shown here can make no claim to accuracy, but they do portray the nature of the Soviet challenge. (NOTE: All indexes are based upon United States real GNP for 1960 = 100 and U.S.S.R. real GNP for 1960 = 50.) From 1960 to 1967 it would appear that the United States has moved at the very top of its projected range. But the U.S.S.R., because of bad weather and crops and shortening of the work week, may have moved at the bottom of her projected range.

zero to any positive level is an infinite jump.) They think that, as the Soviet Union reaches stages of development more comparable with ours and places greater emphasis on services, she is likely to show a retardation in her rate of growth and is also likely to lose the advantage of imitation of more advanced technologies. So they caution against blindly extrapolating the data of the recent past into the future.

While there is much that is persuasive in such arguments, there is also the fact that they may provide temptingly optimistic rationalizations to those who are wishful that America can stay ahead without effort. Moreover, the cases of Germany and other nations that are ahead of the Soviet Union in productivity, and yet seem to have hit a new rate of advance, warn us that such arguments can, at least for a while, go into reverse. And although Marxians have in the past argued as if society were like a child, sure to go through certain inevitable stages of development, modern scholars know better than to be dogmatic about pronouncing on the *necessary* time-shape of industrial development. Consequently, in Fig. 40-1 the extrapolation for the Soviet Union shows a spread that can encompass both optimistic and pessimistic views.

It will be evident that the Soviet Union is unlikely to overtake our real GNP for a long time to come, and our per capita welfare level for a still longer time to come. There will be found an element of reassurance in this; but in concluding any comparison of the growth patterns of the two systems, the economist ought to state two cautions:

■ First, war strength today cannot be measured by real GNP alone. Military analysts estimate that the U.S.S.R. now mounts about the same military effort as does the United States. Her real GNP may be half ours, but she devotes twice our fraction of the total to security purposes. Furthermore, once both parties have innumerable nuclear bombs and during the time period for which the U.S.S.R. may have a technical advantage in the rocket and missile area, it is not necessarily the case that the United States, even by considerably increasing the fraction of her GNP spent on defense, could thereby gain decisive military advantage. Hence, for those concerned by the power struggle, any retained superiority in real GNP is not a sufficient condition for complacency.

Second, there is the fact that our two systems are on trial in the eyes of many uncommitted underdeveloped nations. Even if the United States stays well ahead of the U.S.S.R., were we to stagnate and she to show a vastly more rapid percentage rate of growth, it might tempt neutrals to imitate in the years ahead the totalitarian pattern of "full speed ahead"—suppression of democratic and personal freedom, and collectivist decision to cut down ruthlessly on current consumption in order to enlarge capital formation and development.

Economics never did deserve the name of the "dismal science"; but it must never spurn the title of the "realistic science."

■ AN OPTIMISTIC LAST WORD

In earlier chapters we have seen how our modern economy operates. Throughout, we have subjected the economy to a searching examination, pulling no punches when it came to taking note of friendly and unfriendly criticisms of the working of the economic system. In this chapter we have glanced briefly at a variety of alternative systems such as communism, fascism, and socialism.

Our own mixed economic system is not perfect. No system is. But its imperfections can certainly be ameliorated within our existing framework of ideology and institutions.

It is too easy to compare the obvious imperfections of our known system with the ideal perfections of a nonexistent planned order. And it is only too easy to gloss over the tremendous dynamic vitality of our mixed free enterprise system, which, with all its faults, has given the world a century of progress such as an actual socialized order might find it impossible to equal.

■ We may conclude on a note of optimism. The American economy now has greater potential than it ever had in the past. At the present time, possessing only 6 per cent of the world's population, it accounts for some 30 per cent of the world's income. With all its defects, it has behind it a long-term record of the most rapid advance of productivity and living standards ever achieved anywhere. If our people really want faster growth, it is capable of giving this to them.

Our mixed economy—wars aside—has a great future before it.

Writing a textbook a third of a century ago, one could not have said all this: looking around at the shrinking international network of trade, at the collapsing banking structure, at the grim specter of poverty amidst plenty, some might then have despaired over the future of free societies. Careful, dispassionate study of the economic statistics and annals of the years since then enables one to take quite a different and much more optimistic view.

Especially important for a textbook writer is this development:

■ Modern economic analysis does provide us with a "neoclassical synthesis" that combines the essentials of the newer theories of aggregative income determination with the older classical theories of relative prices and of microeconomics. In a well-running system, with monetary and fiscal policies operating to validate the high-employment assumption postulated by the classical theory, that classical theory comes back into its own, and the economist feels he can state with renewed conviction the classic truths and principles of social economy.

The reader who has persisted this far now has a general knowledge of the economic analysis that is used all over the world—in the United States, Britain, Western Europe, Latin America, Africa, and Asia. The tools of economic analysis, developed and tested over more than a century, are turning out to have an applicability beyond the range of economics narrowly defined. In the hands of scholars like Michigan's Kenneth Boulding, they are applied to the pressing problem of conflict resolution and struggle; in countless departments of operations research, and in the Pentagon military establishment itself, they are being used to increase the efficiency of executive decision making. Like a gun, which can be used to defend a home or bully a harmless stranger, these tools have an efficiency whose final contribution to welfare must depend on how they are used and by whom. They also have a certain austere aesthetic grace.

QUESTIONS FOR DISCUSSION

1. Make a list of a number of "isms," describing each and its history.

2. Describe your own vision of Utopia. Does it differ from the present?

3. Compare and contrast fascism and communism. What is the relation of socialism and capitalism to each? To *laissez faire* and the mixed economy?

4. "The Russians claim that they have 'industrial democracy.' This is clearly a different commodity from political democracy as we know it. Even defenders of the Soviet Union will admit that expressions of opinion against the government or the Communist party will not be tolerated. Free press—in our sense—is forbidden. Even if a majority of the Russian people were to prefer their form of government, no one should blind himself to its great differences from our own concepts of democracy and freedom." Discuss this as objectively as you can.

5. Outline WHAT, HOW, FOR WHOM in Russia.

6. What economic policies in the free world might predispose developing countries, like Ghana, Egypt, and Indonesia, to eschew the closed-society totalitarian path to development?

7. Describe the problems of comparing growth rates in the United States and the U.S.S.R., in India and China, North and South Korea, East and West Germany.

8. Review your understanding of the following concepts:

laissez faire, mixed economy   centralized planning, Soviet style
anarchism, fascism, socialism, communism   new U.S.S.R. pricing and profitability trends
nationalization of industry   economic freedoms, democracy
indicative planning, French style   comparative growth rates

Index

1/2 lb
oz